The Neuropsychology of Psychopathology

Chad A. Noggle, PhD, is an Assistant Professor of Clinical Psychiatry and Chief of the Division of Behavioral and Psychosocial Oncology at Southern Illinois University–School of Medicine. He previously served as an Assistant Professor at both Ball State University and Middle Tennessee State University. Dr. Noggle holds a BA in Psychology from the University of Illinois at Springfield and completed his MA and PhD at Ball State University with specialization in Clinical Neuropsychology. He completed a two-year postdoctoral residency at the Indiana Neuroscience Institute at St. Vincent's Hospital with specialization in Pediatric and Adult/Geriatric Neuropsychology. To date, Dr. Noggle has published more than 300 articles, book chapters, encyclopedia entries, and research abstracts and has made over 100 presentations at national and international conferences in neuropsychology. He served as the lead editor of *The Encyclopedia of Neuropsychological Disorders*. He currently serves as a reviewer for a number of neuropsychology journals and is a member of the Editorial Board for Applied Neuropsychology-Adult and Applied Neuropsychology-Child. Dr. Noggle is a member of the American Psychological Association (APA; Divisions 5, 22, 38, 40), the National Academy of Neuropsychology, and the International Neuropsychological Society. He is a licensed psychologist in both Illinois and Indiana. His research interests focus on both adult and pediatric populations, spanning psychiatric illnesses, dementia, PDDs, and neuromedical disorders.

Raymond S. Dean, PhD, ABPP, ABN, holds a BA degree in Psychology (magna cum laude) and an MS degree in Research and Psychometrics from the State University of New York at Albany. As a Parachek-Frazier Research Fellow, he completed a PhD in School/Child Clinical Psychology at Arizona State University in 1978. Dr. Dean completed an internship focused on neuropsychology at the Arizona Neurophychiatric Hospital and postdoctoral work at the University of Wisconsin at Madison. Since his doctoral degree, he has served in a number of positions and has been recognized for his work. From 1978–1980, Dr. Dean was an Assistant Professor and Director of the Child Clinic at the University of Wisconsin at Madison. During this time, he was awarded the Lightner Witmer Award by the School Psychology Division of the American Psychological Association. From 1980–1981, he served as Assistant Professor of Psychological Services at the University of North Carolina at Chapel Hill. From 1981–1984, Dr. Dean served as Assistant Professor of Medical Psychology and Director of the Neuropsychology Internship at Washington University School of Medicine in St. Louis. During this same time, Dr. Dean received both the Outstanding Contribution Award from the National Academy of Neuropsychology and the Early Contribution Award by Division 15 of the APA. He was named the George and Frances Ball Distinguished Professor of Neuropsychology and Director of the Neuropsychology Laboratory at Ball State University and has served in this position since 1984. In addition, Dr. Dean served as Distinguished Visiting Faculty at the Staff College of the NIMH. Dr. Dean is a Diplomate of the American Board of Professional Psychology, the American Board of Professional Neuropsychology, and the American Board of Pediatric Neuropsychology. He is a Fellow of the APA (Divisions: Clinical, Educational, School and Clinical Neuropsychology), the National Academy of Neuropsychology, and the American Psychopathological Association. Dr. Dean is a past president of the Clinical Neuropsychology Division of the APA and the National Academy of Neuropsychology. He also served as editor of the *Archives of Clinical Neuropsychology, Journal of School Psychology,* and the *Bulletin of the National Academy of Neuropsychology*. Dr. Dean has published some 600 research articles, books, chapters, and tests. For his work, he has been recognized by awards from the National Academy of Neuropsychology, the *Journal of School Psychology,* and the Clinical Neuropsychology Division of the APA.

CONTEMPORARY NEUROPSYCHOLOGY SERIES

The Neuropsychology of Psychopathology

EDITORS

Chad A. Noggle, PhD

Raymond S. Dean, PhD, ABPP, ABN

Springer Publishing Company, LLC
11 West 42nd Street
New York, NY 10036
www.springerpub.com

Acquisitions Editor: Nancy S. Hale
Production Editor: Joseph Stubenrauch
Composition: Absolute Service, Inc.

ISBN: 978-0-8261-0700-8
E-book ISBN: 978-0-8261-0701-5

12 13 14 15 / 5 4 3 2 1

Library of Congress Cataloging-in-Publication Data

The neuropsychology of psychopathology / editors Chad A. Noggle, Raymond S. Dean.
p. cm.
Includes bibliographical references and index.
ISBN 978-0-8261-0700-8 -- ISBN 978-0-8261-0701-5 1. Clinical psychology. 2. Psychology, Pathological. 3. Neuropsychology. I. Noggle, Chad A. II. Dean, Raymond S.
RC467.N48 2012
616.89--dc23
2012035525

Printed in the United States of America by Bang Printing.

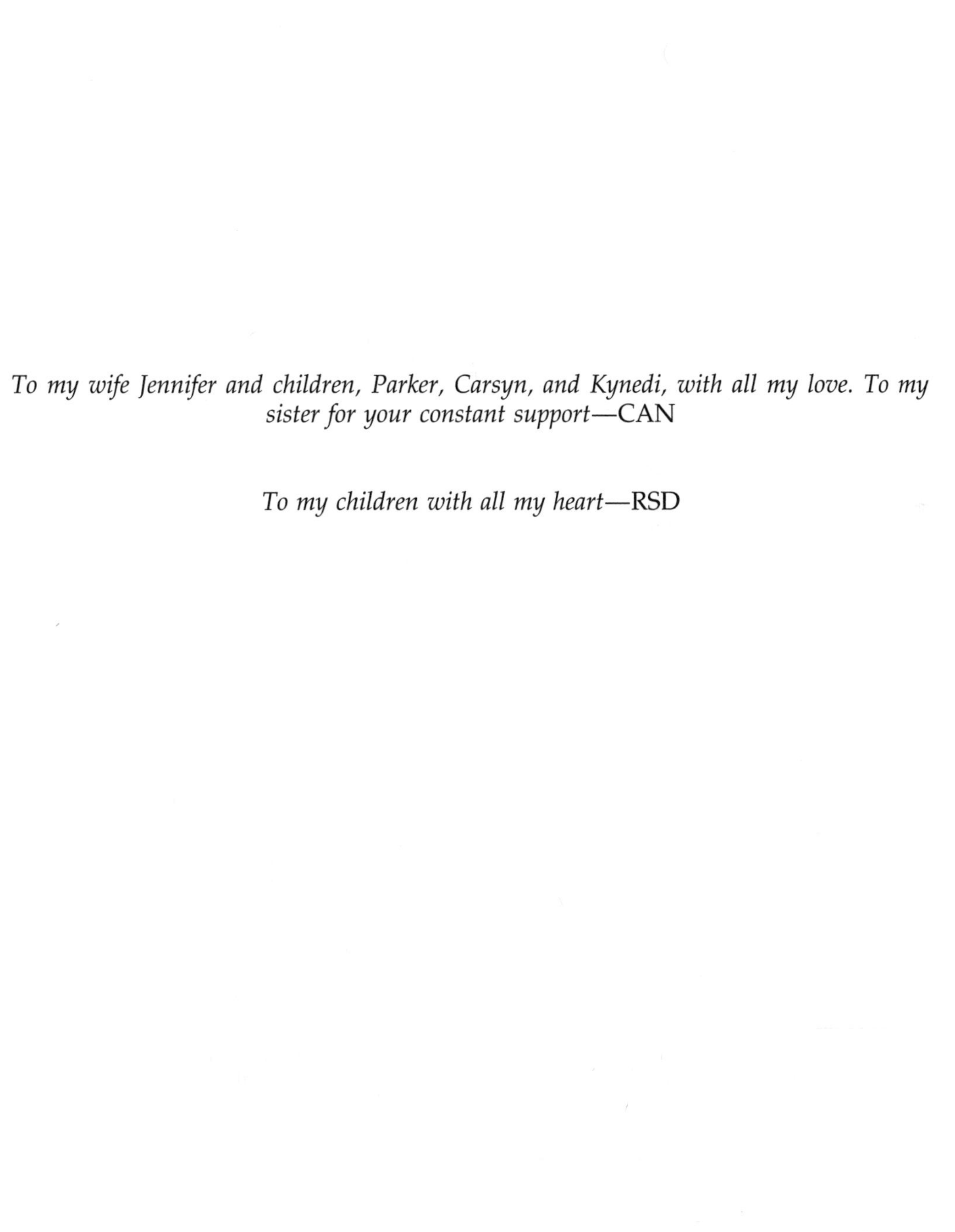

To my wife Jennifer and children, Parker, Carsyn, and Kynedi, with all my love. To my sister for your constant support—CAN

To my children with all my heart—RSD

Contents

Contributors

Daniel N. Allen, PhD
Lincy Professor of Psychology
Department of Psychology
University of Nevada, Las Vegas
Las Vegas, NV

Anjuli R. Amin, PhD
Psychologist
Home Based Primary Care (HBPC) Program
Edward Hines, Jr. VA Medical Center
Hines, IL

James R. Batterson, MD
Child & Adolescent Psychiatrist
Associate Professor of Pediatrics
Children's Mercy Hospitals and Clinics
University of Missouri–Kansas City SOM
Kansas City, MO

Desiree L. Bindus
Howard University
Washington, DC

Leslie H. Brown
Postdoctoral Fellow
Department of Psychiatry
University of Pittsburgh
Pittsburgh, PA

Deborah Ely Budding, PhD
Clinical Neuropsychologist
Private Practice
Manhattan Beach, CA

Gina Cancelliere
Philadelphia College of Osteopathic Medicine
Philadelphia, PA

Catherine Cook-Cottone, PhD
Associate Professor
Department of Counseling, School, and Educational Psychology
The University at Buffalo, SUNY
Buffalo, NY

Jeremy J. Davis, PsyD
Clinical Neuropsychologist
Assistant Professor (Clinical)
Division of Physical Medicine & Rehabilitation
University of Utah School of Medicine
Salt Lake City, UT

Raymond S. Dean, PhD, ABPP, ABN
George & Frances Ball Distinguished Professor of Neuropsychology
Director, BSU Neuropsychology Laboratory
Professor of Psychology
Director of Educational Psychology
Department of Educational Psychology
Ball State University
Muncie, IN

Esther Direnfeld
Graduate Student
Department of Psychology
University of Victoria
Victoria, British Columbia, Canada

Jeff Frazer
Graduate Student
Department of Psychology
University of Victoria
Victoria, British Columbia, Canada

Mauricio A. Garcia-Barrera, PhD
Assistant Professor
Department of Psychology
University of Victoria
Victoria, British Columbia, Canada

Emily Gilmore, PsyD
Department of Extended Care and Rehabilitation
VA Northern Indiana Health Care System
Marion, IN

Jodene Goldenring Fine, PhD
Assistant Professor
Department of Counseling, Educational Psychology, and Special Education
Michigan State University
East Lansing, MI

Gerald Goldstein, PhD
Senior Research Career Scientist
Mental Illness Research, Educational and Clinical Center
VA Pittsburgh Healthcare System
Pittsburgh, PA
and
Clinical Professor of Psychiatry
Department of Psychiatry
University of Pittsburgh
Pittsburgh, PA

Stéphane Guay, PhD
Associate Professor
School of Criminology
University of Montréal
Montréal, Québec, Canada

Gretchen L. Haas, PhD
Director
VA Mental Illness Research, Educational and Clinical Center
VA Pittsburgh Healthcare System
Pittsburgh, PA

Lisa A. Hain, PsyD, ABSNP
Assistant Professor
Department of Psychology
Philadelphia College of Osteopathic Medicine
Philadelphia, PA

Mary E. Haines, PhD, ABPP
Clinical Neuropsychologist
Clinical Associate Professor
Departments of Physical Medicine and Rehabilitation and Psychiatry
University of Toledo Medical Center
Toledo, OH

James B. Hale, PhD
Professor, Faculties of Education and Pediatrics
Department of School and Applied Child Psychology
University of Calgary
Calgary, Alberta, Canada

John Joshua Hall, PhD
Clinical Neuropsychologist
Assistant Professor
Department of Pediatrics
Children's Mercy Hospitals and Clinics
University of Missouri–Kansas City SOM
Kansas City, MO

Margie Hernandez
Graduate Student
Department of Psychology
University of North Carolina–Wilmington
Wilmington, NC

Javan Horwitz, PsyD
Clinical Neuropsychologist
Department of Extended Care and Rehabilitation
VA Northern Indiana Health Care System
Marion, IN

Natalie Horwitz, MA
Carmel Neuropsychology Services, P.C.
Carmel, IN

Rhonda Johnson, PhD
Associate Professor
Department of Psychiatry & Behavioral Sciences
Department of Medical Oncology
The University of Kansas School of Medicine
Westwood, KS

Leonard F. Koziol, PhD
Clinical Neuropsychologist
Private Practice
Arlington Heights, IL

Morten L. Kringelbach, PhD
Senior Research Fellow
Department of Psychiatry
University of Oxford, Oxford, UK
and
Professor of Neuroscience
Centre for Functionally Integrative Neuroscience (CFIN)
University of Aarhus, Aarhus, Denmark

Hanna A. Kubas
BrainGain Laboratory Director
Department of School and Applied Child Psychology
University of Calgary
Calgary, Alberta, Canada

Marc E. Lavoie, PhD
Director, Cognitive & Social Psychophysiology Laboratory
Associate Research Professor
Fernand-Seguin Research Center of the Louis-H Lafontaine Psychiatric Hospital
Department of Psychiatry
University of Montréal
Montréal, Québec, Canada

Jennifer Mariner, PsyD
Clinical Psychologist
Department of Geriatrics and Extended Care
Richard Roudebush VA Medical Center
Indianapolis, IN
and
Assistant Professor of Clinical Psychology
Department of Clinical Psychiatry
Indiana University–School of Medicine
Indianapolis, IN

Emily A. Mason
Research Assistant
Neuropsychology Program and Brain Imaging Laboratory
Department of Psychiatry
Dartmouth Medical School
Lebanon, NH

John McConnell, MA
Doctoral Student
Bell State University
Muncie, IN

William R. Moore
Graduate Student
Department of Psychology
University of Victoria
Victoria, British Columbia, Canada

Ryan Murphy, EdS
Philadelphia College of Osteopathic Medicine
Philadelphia, PA

Chad A. Noggle, PhD
Clinical Neuropsychologist
Assistant Professor of Psychiatry
Chief, Division of Behavioral & Psychosocial Oncology
Department of Psychiatry
Southern Illinois University–School of Medicine
Springfield, IL

Kieron P. O'Connor, PhD
Professor
Director, Center for Research on OCD and Tics
Fernand-Seguin Research Center of the Louis-H Lafontaine Psychiatric Hospital
Department of Psychiatry
University of Montréal
Montréal, Québec, Canada

Carlos Ojeda, MA
Graduate Student
Department of Psychology
University of Arkansas
Fayatteville, AR

C. E. Parsons
Department of Psychiatry
Warneford Hospital
University of Oxford, Oxford, UK
and
Centre for Functionally Integrative Neuroscience (CFIN)
University of Aarhus, Aarhus, Denmark

Antonio E. Puente, PhD
Clinical Neuropsychologist
Professor
Department of Psychology
University of North Carolina–Wilmington
Wilmington, NC

Robert M. Roth, PhD
Associate Professor of Psychiatry
Brain Imaging Laboratory
Director, DHMC Adult Neuropsychological Services
Department of Psychiatry
Dartmouth Medical School
Lebanon, NH

Melanie Rylander, MD
Clinical Instructor
Department of Psychiatry
University of Colorado
Denver, CO

Margaret Semrud-Clikeman, PhD
Professor of Pediatrics
Division Director of Clinical Behavioral Neuroscience
University of Minnesota Medical School
Minneapolis, MN

Amanda Smith, MS
Associate Professor
Department of Counseling, School, and Educational Psychology
The University at Buffalo, SUNY
Buffalo, NY

Jeffrey H. Snow, PhD
Associate Professor
University of Arkansas for Medical Sciences
Little Rock, AR

Stephen Soltys, MD
Professor and Chariman
Department of Psychiatry
Southern Illinois University–School of Medicine
Springfield, IL

Gerry A. Stefanatos, DPhil
Chairman, Department of Communication Science and Disorders
Temple University
Philadelphia, PA

Melissa M. Swanson, PhD
Neuropsychology Fellow
Department of Physical Medicine and Rehabilitation
University of Toledo Medical Center
Toledo, OH

Anthony Swentosky, PhD
School Psychologist
Harrison School District 2
Colorado Springs, CO

Nicholas S. Thaler
Graduate Student
Department of Psychology
University of Nevada, Las Vegas
Las Vegas, NV

Chriscelyn Tussey, PsyD
Director of Psychological Assessment
Bellevue Hospital Center
New York, NY
and
Clinical Assistant Professor
Department of Psychiatry
New York University School of Medicine
New York, NY

Jacqueline Remondet Wall, PhD, CRC
Associate Professor
School of Psychological Sciences
University of Indianapolis
Indianapolis, IN

Douglas Watt, PhD
Clinical Neuropsychologist
Cambridge Health Alliance
Harvard Medical School
Boston, MA
and
Clinic for Cognitive Disorders
Quincy Medical Center
Boston University School of Medicine
Boston, MA

Lisa L. Weyandt, PhD
Department of Psychology
University of Rhode Island
Kingston, RI

John M. Wryobeck, PhD, ABPP
Associate Professor
Department of Psychiatry
University of Toledo College of Medicine
Toledo, OH

Timothy F. Wynkoop, PhD
Clinical/Forensic Neuropsychologist
Private Practice
Maumee, OH
and
Clinical Assistant Professor of Psychiatry
Faculty, UTMC Clinical Neuropsychology Fellowship Program
University of Toledo College of Medicine
Toledo, OH

K. S. Young
Department of Psychiatry
Warneford Hospital
University of Oxford, Oxford, UK
and
Centre for Functionally Integrative Neuroscience (CFIN)
University of Aarhus, Aarhus, Denmark

Davor N. Zink, MA
Graduate Student
Department of Psychology
University of North Carolina–Wilmington
Wilmington, NC

Preface

Motivation, behavior, and emotions are by-products of brain activity. This serves as the foundation upon which modern shifts in the clinical neurosciences have been built. However, the centrality of neurobiology in human behavior is not intended to diminish the role the environment plays in such features. Rather, it serves to emphasize that the individual's neurological makeup mediates his or her interaction with the environment and the effect environmental experiences have on neurobehavioral outcomes. The clinical neurosciences, including neuropsychology, neuropsychiatry, and behavioral neurology, are disciplines focused on understanding the neurobiological correlates of behavior. In addition, these specialties are focused on the assessment, identification, and treatment of dysfunctional behavior and disorders.

With advances across the neurosciences, our understanding of behavior and neuropsychiatric disorders has grown by leaps and bounds. Since the earliest of times, humankind has been interested in behavior and its roots. Psychiatric presentations have received particular attention historically. Proposals as to the origin of these manifestations has shifted from beliefs in the role of evil spirits to our current understanding of the role neurophysiology plays in the development of these various disorders. Sizeable shifts have been seen even in the field of neuropsychology. In the past, neuropsychologists in the psychiatric setting were asked to differentiate "organic" and "functional" mental disorders because the two were viewed as mutually exclusive. This conceptualization is now recognized as flawed.

The integration of neuroscience, neuropsychology, and traditional psychiatric practices has refined our understanding of those presentations outlined by the *DSM-IV-TR* and the proposed *DSM-5*—presentations that have historically been termed psychopathologies. Studies in structural and functional imaging, genetic analysis, and molecular biology have expanded our knowledge of the biological basis of such behavior and disorders. The emergence of this literature has shifted not only our knowledge base, but also the nomenclature we utilize. Those behaviors and disorders traditionally falling under the *psychopathology* heading are now better defined as neuropsychiatric disorders.

Neuropsychology is a unique discipline within the clinical neurosciences because it integrates neuroscience and clinical and cognitive psychologies. When it comes to neuropsychiatric disorders, looking through a neuropsychological lens allows us to conceptualize such manifestations not simply by their behavioral features, but also their cognitive and neurobehavioral traits. In the current book, *The Neuropsychology of Psychopathology*, neuropsychiatric features and disorders are discussed from both a neuroscientific and neuropsychological perspective. Chapters cover both the neurobiological and neurocognitive correlates of common psychiatric presentations such as major depression, bipolar disorder, posttraumatic stress disorder (PTSD), and schizophrenia, among others. Additional presentations included within the *DSM-IV-TR* are discussed including Alzheimer's disease, pervasive developmental disorders, learning disabilities, and delirium, as well as others. Foundational concepts are also discussed, including discussion of the neuroanatomy of pleasure and emotion as well as neurological differences between children and adults that lead to discrepancies in the appearance of clinical manifestations. Clinical-based applications are also discussed, including the role of neuropsychology within the psychiatric setting, the utility of psychological assessment, and the neurobiological basis of psychotherapy.

Acknowledgments

We would like to acknowledge the work put forth by the assistant editors for this book, including Dr. John Joshua Hall, who served as Lead Assistant Editor, Dr. Michelle Pagoria, Dr. Amy R. Steiner, and Dr. Javan Horwitz.

Needless to say, seeing this project through to publication has only been made possible by the many authors who have volunteered their time and expertise to the chapters within this volume. We must also acknowledge the support of our colleagues and associated institutions, SIU School of Medicine, and Ball State University. Finally, we would like to express our sincerest gratitude to our publisher and those with whom we have worked very closely to complete this book, especially Nancy S. Hale and Joseph Stubenrauch.

CONTEMPORARY NEUROPSYCHOLOGY SERIES

SERIES EDITORS
Chad A. Noggle, PhD
Raymond S. Dean, PhD, ABPP, ABN

The Neuropsychology of Psychopathology

The Neuropsychology of Cancer and Oncology

Neuropsychological Rehabilitation

The Neuropsychology of Cortical Dementias

The Neuropsychology of Pervasive Developmental Disorders

The Neuropsychology of Psychopharmacology

SECTION I

Principles of Psychopathology

CHAPTER 1

The Neuropsychology of Psychopathology: Historical Shifts

Anjuli R. Amin & Chad A. Noggle

INTRODUCTION

The field of psychology has emerged from a mix of social, political, scientific, and philosophical sources. Throughout time, individuals from a variety of disciplines and across the world's cultures have made attempts to understand our diverse mental and behavioral processes. From mere speculation to actual hands-on experimentation, efforts to learn more about what motivates certain behaviors, the causes of psychopathology, and the methods of treating psychological illnesses have emerged from a wide range of sources.

At the very core of psychology as a discipline lie efforts to explain those behaviors that have been perceived as abnormal. The conceptualization of what behavior is considered out of the norm has changed over time, including how we define and explain such behavior. Over time there has been a movement from supernatural and religious considerations of psychopathology to a paradigm that has integrated biological and environmental variables. The most recent developments in the area of psychopathology, beginning in the 19th century, have consisted of an integration of various psychological theories and models with consistent advances in scientific thought and inquiry. Such changes in the field have led us to a contemporary approach to psychopathology that combines multiple elements.

HISTORICAL VIEWS OF PSYCHOPATHOLOGY

Ancient Times

Evidence of psychological thought, beyond the musings of Plato and Aristotle, have been found within many ancient cultures. Even though psychopathology did not emerge as a significant area of scientific interest until the late 19th century, speculation about the origin, causes, and functions of abnormal behavior has been traced as far back as the 16th century B.C. to the ancient Egyptians. Among the ancient Egyptians, concepts related to health emerged from a mix of scientific and religious perspectives. A commonly held belief was that most mental functions emanated from the heart (Viney & King, 2003). The brain, although noted to play a role in speech and memory disorders, was thought to be subservient to this vital organ and unimportant in comparison (Rains, 2002). The heart was perceived to embody an array of cognitive processes that included memory, wisdom, emotion, and intelligence. The importance of the heart was further emphasized in Egyptian spiritual beliefs, wherein one's heart was considered the key to being granted access to the afterlife. The Egyptians carried these beliefs, which they incorporated with empirical observation, into developing an integrated approach to medicine. They emphasized the importance of maintaining a balance in the soul and built special temples for the mentally ill, incorporating spiritual aspects into the treatment of emotional disorders. Factors such as insects, filth, and the devil were often viewed as causes of psychopathology, and these illnesses were often treated using a broad range of therapies (e.g., rituals, surgery, enemas, incantations, and medications; Viney & King, 2003).

Spirituality and religion were also integrated into discourses on psychology and human behavior within the region now known as India and Pakistan around 800 B.C. Many of these thoughts were found within the *Upanishads* (Brennan, 2002). Considered one of the oldest sacred scriptures of the Hindu religion, the *Upanishads* consisted of over 1,000 lectures given by various scholars. Included within these discourses were philosophical and spiritual notions about a person's relationship to the universe. In contrast to contemporary Western ideas of what constituted healthy psychological development (i.e., an emphasis on autonomy and independence), the views expressed in the *Upanishads* portrayed acts of individualism as wayward. Importance was placed on an individual's place within and connection to a larger, more valued entity—the universe. An emphasis on communalism and maintaining harmony within society was thus reflected in psychological thought at the time. For example, it was thought that mental disorders could result from an unwarranted amount of emotional expression and that one's personality traits could be traced back to characteristics displayed by the mother during pregnancy (Viney & King, 2003). It was common to believe that having an ill temper during pregnancy would result in giving birth to a child with some type of disorder, such as epilepsy. Thus, the value of an individual's relationship to her or his environment was reflected in societal ideas of acceptable human behavior at the time. Actions that appeared to be individualistic in nature were thought to be of harm to or in disfavor of one's community.

A strong emphasis on religious explanations of psychological disorders remained prevalent in the area of Persia. Around the 6th century B.C., and during the time of the birth of the Zoroastrian religion, emotional disorders were often viewed as being caused by the devil (Viney & King, 2003). Treatment of psychological issues thus consisted of religious practices such as exorcism, incantations, and magical rites. The integration of philosophy and science was not openly welcomed within Persian society, and thus a strong focus on religion within the field of health was sustained (Viney & King, 2003).

Views integrating empirical-rational and magical-religious perspectives about psychopathology were observed around 200 B.C. in early Chinese culture. Psychological thought during this time was influenced by the principles of *yin* and *yang*—two opposing forces that represented all universal opposites (e.g., softness/hardness, cold/heat, or creation/completion; Liu, 2006). Both *yin* and *yang* were used to explain different phenomena, including human behavior. Specifically, it was believed that maintaining a balance between these two forces was essential to ensuring one's physical and psychological well-being. At this time, it was also perceived that all mental processes were fostered within the physical structures of the body, opening the door to a physiological psychology that placed equal importance on mind and body components (Viney & King, 2003).

Hippocrates's and Galen's Contributions

What is known thus far regarding conceptualizations of psychopathology from ancient perspectives is that often a supernatural explanation was attached to an observed mental disorder (Chamorro-Premuzic, 2007). Treatment of such disorders also consisted of similar methodologies, which included exorcisms, shamanism, and other spiritual interventions. A significant change in the trajectory of thought concerning human nature appeared during the period of 600–400 B.C. This shift in thought emerged from the early Greek philosophers, who began to view the world in terms of natural explanations, emphasizing that things in the universe were controlled by natural principles and not "the whims of the gods" (Hergenhahn, 2005, p. 28).

Although much focus was placed on the heart, brain–behavior relationships began to emerge around this time. Archeologists have discovered several thousand skulls from this time period that show evidence of humans having survived trephination (Zillmer & Spiers, 2001). Trephination is the ancient practice of removing pieces of the skull to relieve swelling of the brain. Some believe the procedure was intended to allow the evil spirits that were plaguing the individual, and contributing to his or her psychological dysfunction, to escape. The ancient Greeks produced the first written records of brain–behavior relationships, although they still regarded cognitive functioning as arising from a divine nature. The first recorded observation that proposed the brain as the center of human reasoning was produced by Pythagoras (580–500 B.C.). Pythagoras and other scholars developed the idea of the brain hypothesis, which stipulated that the brain is the source of all behavior (Zillmer & Spiers, 2001).

Hippocrates (460–377 B.C.), who is commonly regarded as the father of modern Western medicine, was among the first to suggest that psychological disorders could be treated no differently than other "physical" diseases. As scribed in the *Hippocratic Corpus* (Maher & Maher, 1994), Hippocrates went as far as to hypothesize that these psychological "diseases" arose from the brain, which he had long held to be the site of wisdom, consciousness, intelligence, and emotion. Over the next 600 years, although followers of Hippocrates's works maintained the belief of the brain being the origin of psychological disorders, spiritual/religious theory remained dominant. Truly, the extent of Hippocrates's brilliance when taking into consideration time, place, resources, and prior knowledge was not fully appreciated until modern times.

Around the same time of Hippocrates, Plato (420–347 B.C.) began to propose his theories of the mind and soul. Plato wrote that the soul, responsible for rational thought, was located in the brain and noted, secondary to case studies, that head trauma can result in impairment in reasoning (Robinson, 1970). Aristotle (384–322 B.C.), though a student of Plato, disagreed with Plato's localization of mental processes. He instead postulated that the heart was the seat of all mental processes and emotions. Plato felt the brain's involvement in cognition and emotion was to regulate the actions of the heart, a viewpoint that came to be known as the cardiac hypothesis (Zillmer & Spiers, 2001). Though he made numerous contributions to ethics, psychology, poetry, and politics, Plato's viewpoint of the location of the soul led to a regression in the understanding of brain–behavior relationships. The ideas of the Greek philosophers, although anatomically wrong in many counts, provided the foundation upon which the study of neuropsychology was built, and future philosophers and physiologists may not have made their contributions without the advances of the Greeks.

Galen (129–198 A.D.), a follower of Hippocrates's writings, expanded his theories of the mind and origin of psychological disorders. Most notably, Galen expanded Hippocrates's Humoral Theory of Disorders. This Hippocratic-Galenic theory suggested normal functioning along cognitive, emotional, behavioral, and spiritual lines was dependent on a homeostasis, or balance, of four influential body fluids (i.e., blood, black bile, yellow bile, and phlegm). Hippocrates initially proposed that significant elevations or depletions of any of these fluids disrupted the homeostasis of the system and led to an "imbalance" of the person, thereby bringing about disordered behavior. He further proposed that the nature of the fluid imbalance corresponded with the specific behavioral constellation, and that by observing the dysfunctional behavior one may determine which fluids were elevated or depleted. Although we do not discuss "bile" in our modern day conceptualization of psychiatric disorders or functional domains, if one were to replace "humors" with neurotransmitters, it is easy to see the prominent overlap of Hippocrates's and Galen's theories with modern-day knowledge and thus appreciate their insight. Consequently, therapies were developed to "restore" balance of these fluid levels. Bloodletting, induced vomiting, and even manipulation of body temperature were methods employed to rebalance the different humors.

Beyond expansion of Hippocrates's work, Galen's unique contributions came in his description of the anatomy of the nervous system. Through combining his anatomical findings with behavioral observations, Galen proposed that causes of psychological disorders could be divided into physical and mental categories including head injuries, shock, fear, alcoholism, menstrual changes, economic trouble, and heartbreak (Butcher, Mineka, & Hooley, 2008, p.

12). His observations of the human body came from his work as a surgeon who was appointed to the care of gladiators (Finger, 1994a). Little elaboration was made over the next thousand years because Galen's view of humors became so ingrained. His expansions of Hippocrates's theories remained prominent until the 16th century, when his anatomic mistakes began to be corrected.

The Middle Ages

The Middle Ages saw a growth in the science of medicine within the Middle East. Baghdad became home to the first mental hospital in 792 A.D., with two more established soon after, in Damascus and Aleppo, (Polvan, 1969). It was at this time that Avicenna (980–1037 A.D.), a physician from Arabia, was recognized as the most highly touted physician. He often wrote of hysteria, epilepsy, manic reactions, and melancholia and discussed the benefit of humane treatment of patients. Still, rituals and superstition remained the most prominent treatment pursuits, particularly in Europe, where the treatment of patients was even far less humane. Scientific investigations were not readily undertaken as conceptualizations of psychiatric disorders reverted back to spiritual explanations and demonology. Consequently, clergy served as the primary care providers for mentally ill individuals. Treatment involved prayer, holy water, sanctified ointments, the breath or spittle of the priests, the touching of relics, visits to holy places, and mild forms of exorcism (Butcher et al., 2008, p. 13). Although many have long discussed the thought or concept of witchcraft in the Middle Ages as being a case of misdiagnosed mental illness, some have called this into question (Maher & Maher, 1985). In reality, those accused of witchcraft tended to be disheveled-looking, single women with a bad temper who tended to talk back to others or exhibit a "sharp tongue" (Schoeneman, 1984).

Challenges to the Church

Paracelsus (1490–1541) was recognized as a key opponent to the superstitious belief of mental illness. He suggested that various psychiatric presentations were not manifestations of possessions but by-products of physical disease. Paracelsus did, however, believe in the effects of astrology, the moon in particular. He felt the brain was directly affected by the moon and its phases (Mora, 1967).

Johann Weyer (1515–1588) was a German physician who shared the belief during this time period that mental illness was physically based. Weyer was particularly troubled by the way in which people with mental illnesses were treated, largely because of the spiritual beliefs of those around them. At this time, however, his views were seen as contradicting the Church itself. Consequently, Weyer was persecuted by those around him for his hypotheses.

St. Vincent de Paul (1576–1660) was another individual who stood against the suggestion of mental illness being a manifestation of possession or witchcraft. His stance was particularly important because he represented the first individual within the Church itself to take such a stance. St. Vincent de Paul proposed that psychiatric disorders were no different from bodily diseases and the Church should protect these individuals and aid in relieving their symptoms as opposed to persecuting them.

MODERN SHIFTS IN THE NEUROBIOLOGY OF PSYCHOPATHOLOGY

Although the theories of Hippocrates and Galen persisted on, historical review demonstrates they fell in and out of favor as different thoughts and concepts emerged throughout the centuries. It was not until the 19th century that interest in the biological basis of psychological disorders was again sparked. Interestingly, this was not brought about by an influential scientist or emerging scientific findings from controlled research studies; rather, it was stirred by the discovery of syphilis and its treatment. Practitioners charged with the care of those with psychosis noted over time that a subgroup of patients demonstrated a fairly steady deterioration in physical status, eventually leading to paralysis and death within approximately 5 years of symptom onset. This contrasted the pattern exhibited by other psychotic patients. The etiology of this subgroup was eventually termed general paresis. Through the work of Louis Pasteur and others, the bacterial organism that caused syphilis and syphilis's link with general paresis was eventually discovered. Autopsies demonstrated the invasion of brain tissue as the potential basis for the behavioral changes. Consequently, science and medicine had a clear example of how invasion of the brain by the bacteria involved in syphilis brought about psychological change, thereby suggesting other psychological disorders may also arise from the brain itself. When penicillin was eventually developed and demonstrated the capacity to ward off the neuropsychiatric sequelae of syphilis, it led many to question if other psychiatric features may also respond to biologically based treatments.

It was also during the 19th century that John Grey came into prominence as a leading figure in the biological movement. Much of his influence was seen through his work in the state hospital of New York. Grey firmly believed that psychiatric disorders were always of a physical origin. As such, patients were treated within the hospital as though they were physically ill, with patients getting rest, having a properly managed diet, having access to natural light, having clear and ventilated air, and having regulated room temperature. Just by making these environmental changes, improvements were seen. As patients did better physically, they also did better mentally. Consequently, these anecdotal findings reinforced for Grey that these disorders were physically based while also demonstrating the relative contribution of environmental factors. Around this same time, Emil Kraepelin (1856–1926) was instrumental in the refinement of the diagnosis and classification of psychiatric disorders. He described the concept of different psychiatric disorders, with different origins and times of onset, which he likened to different biological factors.

The revitalization of the neurobiological basis of psychiatric disorders came at the same time that our understanding of the brain's role in other functional domains was increasing through case studies and scientific investigation. Emanual Swedenborg (1688–1772) was one of the first to generate a theory of cortical localization of behavioral functions. Swedenborg wrote that separate areas of the brain were necessary to prevent psychological chaos, and charted his ideas of discrete areas for vision and hearing based on his studies of pathology and anatomy (Finger, 1994b).

Paul Broca (1824–1880) is one of the most recognized figures of the localization movement, identifying specific functional areas within the cerebrum. He is best remembered for identifying an area of the brain that we now call Broca's area that is related to expressive speech.

Carl Wernicke (1848–1904), another 19th century researcher, postulated that the ability to understand spoken language had a specific localization site in the brain, in the posterior half of the left superior temporal gyrus. Wernicke was also responsible for casting light on a disorder that may have been previously referred to as madness in earlier centuries, which was actually a problem of the left hemisphere (Harris, 1999). Wernicke's findings are important in brain localization theory because, along with Broca, he was able to demonstrate that language is located in at least two different cortical areas. Wernicke's findings cast a realistic shadow on 19th century proponents of brain localization theory who hypothesized functions had one specific location. At the same time, it provided a general support for the movement toward the brain being the center of functioning.

When it comes to personality, emotions, and behaviors specifically, the case of Phineas Gage, a railroad worker who suffered a traumatic brain injury when an explosion forced a large piece of metal into the front of his brain, serves as the most common case example. Although he recovered with his lower order functions (respiration, heart rate) intact, he suffered a noticeable change in personality and behavior. This and other cases of people surviving injuries led to speculation that elements of personality could be localized in the frontal lobes.

Biological Interventions

Renewed focus on the biological basis of psychiatric disorders brought about increased use of biologically focused interventions. In 1927, Manfred Sakel stumbled across what would come to be known as insulin shock therapy. Sakel, in trying to stimulate eating in psychotic patients, began to administer increasing amounts of insulin. He observed that once patients were given a certain amount, they would actually begin to convulse and eventually go comatose for a period of time (Sakel , 1958). As patients regained their faculties, Sakel and his colleagues noticed that some of the patients actually exhibited improvement in their mood and psychiatric status. Sakel suggested the convulsion was the source of the psychiatric improvement. However, insulin shock therapy never became widely used because there was significant risk for prolonged coma or even death. Still, insulin shock therapy led the way for electroconvulsive therapy (ECT) to be considered.

In fact, the potential benefits of ECT were proposed over 150 years earlier when Benjamin Franklin and a friend of his not only noted that a moderate electrical shock to the brain was safe, even though it caused a convulsion and brief amnesia, but that it also was accompanied by an improvement in mood, which Franklin's friend described as a "strange elation" (Finger & Zaromb , 2006, p. 245). In 1938, a depressed patient was successfully treated with ECT based on the suggestions of Ugo Cerletti and Lucio Bini, two Italian surgeons (Hunt , 1980). The methods used have been modified, but ECT remains a treatment used today.

The 1950s saw the development of psychotropic agents for severe psychotic disorders. Developers sought to offer chemical control of the psychiatric features while maintaining the greatest degree of functionality on the part of the patient. Prior to these newer agents, the chemicals used were primarily sedating. They offered a chemical restraint of individuals as opposed to physical restraint. Although this made patients easier to handle by staff in psychiatric institutions, patients had no real life or time for social interaction because of the sedating effects. Neuroleptics and benzodiazepines initially came into favor at this time, but they too were eventually linked with negative side effects. Their use continued to grow well into the 1970s.

CURRENT TRENDS AND MOVEMENTS

Contemporary technologies have offered great insight into the biological correlates of the various psychological disorders. Convergence of advances in neuroimaging, molecular genetics, and endocrinology has elucidated the nature of psychopathology. The combination of these scientific pursuits has provided valuable information attesting to the dependence of mental functioning on brain processes and to the mechanisms underlying various forms of psychopathology (Meissner, 2006). The end result is that the neurophysiology of many mental disorders is being increasingly and rapidly clarified and specified. As such, specific psychological-behavioral deficits can be directly or indirectly connected to brain dysfunction, yet there is a range of individual variation in the details of psychological impairment associated with otherwise identical lesions (Meissner, 2006).

The incorporation of neuropsychology within the scientific evaluation of psychiatric disorders emerged over the past few decades as a need emerged to use the theoretical models from normal cognitive psychology to understand psychiatric symptoms in a principled and testable manner (Halligan & David, 2001). As a result, psychiatric features are slowly coming to be understood in terms of disturbances to recognized information-processing systems (Halligan & David, 2001).

SUMMARY

The etiology of psychopathologies has seen many proposals over the centuries. Records show our concepts on the subject have shifted from a religious/spiritual mindset to a multidimensional model where biological and environmental factors interact to form the basis of the various psychiatric presentations. With advances in neuroimaging, genetics, and functional assessment, we find ourselves at a point when our understanding of the psychopathologies is growing by leaps and bounds. The following chapters will discuss what we now know of the neurobiology and genetics of the various recognized psychiatric disorders, how this corresponds with their psychiatric features and neuropsychological traits, and how this knowledge allows for refined diagnostics and treatment. In other words, the chapters to come will discuss *The Neuropsychology of Psychopathology*. This knowledge can be used to expand one's clinical skills and knowledge to better serve the patient populations discussed within this text because a neuropsychological formulation offers the most comprehensive view of the impact of these disorders on everyday functioning. Not to know this information is to attempt to treat those manifestations without a grasp of all the contributing factors.

REFERENCES

Brennan, J. F. (2002). *History and systems of psychology*. Upper Saddle River, NJ: Prentice Hall.

Butcher, J. N., Mineka, S., & Hooley, J. M. (2008). *Abnormal psychology: Core concepts*. New York: Pearson.

Chamorro-Premuzic, T. (2007). *Personality and individual differences*. Malden, MA: Blackwell.

Finger, S. (1994a). *Origins of neuroscience: A history of explorations into brain function*. New York: Oxford University Press.

Finger, S. (1994b). History of neuropsychology. In D. Zaidel (Ed.), *History of Neuropsychology* (pp. 1–25). San Diego: Academic Press.

Finger, S., & Zaromb, F. (2006). Benjamin Franklin and chock-induced amnesia. *American Psychologist, 61*, 240–248.

Halligan, P. W., & David, A. S. (2001). Cognitive neuropsychiatry: towards a scientific psychopathology. *Neuroscience, 2*, 209–215.

Harris, L. (1999). Early theory and research on hemispheric specialization. *Schizophrenia Bulletin, 35*, 11–39.

Hergenhahn, B. R. (2005). *An introduction to the history of psychology*. Belmont, CA: Thomson Wadsworth.

Hunt, W. A. (1980). History and classification. In A.E. Kazdin, A.S. Bellack, & M. Henson (Eds.), *New perspectives in abnormal psychology* (pp. 20–45). New York: Oxford University Press.

Liu, J. L. (2006). *An introduction to Chinese philosophy: From ancient philosophy to Chinese Buddhism*. Malden, MA: Blackwell.

Maher, B. A., & Maher, W. R. (1985). Psychopathology: 1. From ancient times to the eighteenth century. In G. A. Kimble & K. Schlesinger (Eds.), *Topics in the history of psychology* (pp. 251–294). Hillsdale, NJ: Erlbaum.

Maher, B. A., & Maher, W. R. (1994). Personality and psychopathology: A historical perspective. *Journal of Abnormal Psychology, 103*, 72–77.

Meissner, W. W. (2006). The mind-brain relation and neuroscientific foundations: III. Brain and psychopathology, the split brain, and dreaming. *Bulletin of the Menninger Clinic, 70*(3), 179–201.

Mora, G. (1967). Paracelsus' psychiatry. *American Journal of Psychiatry, 124*, 803–814.

Plomin, R., & McGuffin, P. (2003). Psychopathology in the postgenomic era. *Annual Review of Psychology, 54*, 205–228.

Polvan, N. (1969). Historical aspects of mental ills in Middle East discussed. *Roche Reports, 6*(12), 3.

Rains, G. D. (2002). *Principles of human neuropsychology*. Boston, MA: McGraw-Hill.

Robinson, T. M. (1970). *Plato's psychology*. Toronto, Canada: University of Toronto Press.

Sakel, M. (1958). *Schizophrenia*. New York: Philosophical Library.

Schoenmen, T. J. (1984). The mentally ill witch in text books of abnormal psychology: Current status and implications of fallacy. *Professional Psychiatry, 15*, 299–314.

Viney, W., & King, D. B. (2003). *A History of psychology: Ideas and context*. Boston, MA: Allyn and Bacon.

Zillmer, E., & Spiers, M. (2001). *Principles of neuropsychology*. Belmont, CA: Wadsworth/Thomson Learning.

CHAPTER 2

Pediatric Versus Adult Psychopathology: Differences in Neurological and Clinical Presentations

Margaret Semrud-Clikeman & Jodene Goldenring Fine

Psychological and psychiatric disorders in children and adults have historically been viewed as similar without considering developmental issues that are present both psychologically and neurologically (Semrud-Clikeman, Fine, & Butcher, 2007). Previously, most attention was paid to adult disorders, with child disorders viewed as the same disorder but in a smaller body. Research and clinical practice have now established that psychopathology in children and adults differs and is related to differences in neurological development as well as in expression of psychopathology.

Psychopathology has been related to brain dysfunction for several types of disorders in children and adults, but the contribution of direct and indirect effects of brain dysfunction have not been examined empirically (Tramontana & Hooper, 1989). Direct effects are those that are related to specific behaviors like disinhibition, attention deficits, memory deficits, and the like. Indirect effects are those that produce an emotional or behavioral disturbance as the person attempts to deal with difficulties, such as frustration and failure, as a result of the specific behaviors. At times, the caretakers in the child's life may view him or her as unmotivated, difficult, slow, or many other negative attributions, thus serving to exacerbate the problems at hand (Semrud-Clikeman & Ellison, 2009).

In many cases, there is an overlap in disorders such that symptoms that may indicate an attention deficit hyperactivity disorder (ADHD) may also be common to anxiety or depression or a metabolic disorder. An approach to evaluation that has been helpful and applicable for neuropsychologists is the use of hypothesis testing. When using this approach, a good history of the disorder is paramount, particularly to determine possible alternative diagnoses. The use of a hypothesis testing approach requires a familiarity with diagnostic nomenclature and disorders that are frequently comorbid or overlapping. This approach provides an opportunity to intertwine information from several sources, including medical personnel, school personnel, and family data. A well-trained clinical psychologist or neuropsychologist can combine medical, academic, and family data to determine appropriate interventions (Hartlage & Long, 1997).

The following sections of this chapter are designed to explore the developmental and neurological differences that may be present in children and adults with externalizing or internalizing disorders. We are limiting our chapter to these disorders as they are the most common presentations seen across the life span. Externalizing disorders include ADHD and intermittent explosive disorder in adults and children as well as oppositional defiant disorder

(ODD)/conduct disorder (CD) in children and antisocial personality disorder (APD) in adults. For the purposes of this chapter, internalizing disorders include depression, anxiety, and bipolar disorder.

EXTERNALIZING DISORDERS

Externalizing disorders generally involve difficulties in controlling behaviors due to impulsive responding and acting out. Such disorders may also be classified as disruptive behavior disorders as seen in the *Diagnostic and Statistical Manual of Mental Disorders, 4th edition, Text Revision* (*DSM-IV-TR*; American Psychiatric Association [APA], 2000). Many of the externalizing disorders co-occur at rates that are at greater-than-chance levels. For example, ADHD has been found to co-occur with ODD and conduct disorder (CD) between 29% and 71% of the time in large epidemiological studies as well as in clinical studies (Burt, Krueger, McGue, & Iacono, 2001).

ADHD

ADHD is a highly prevalent neurodevelopmental disorder that appears in early childhood and for many patients continues throughout adulthood. There are two main subtypes of ADHD: combined (ADHD-C) and inattentive (ADHD-PI). Children and adults with ADHD-C have significant difficulties with inattention, hyperactivity, and impulsivity, whereas those with ADHD-PI experience difficulties mainly with inattention. The expression of ADHD also changes with age. In childhood, the primary symptoms may be reflected in hyperactivity and impulsivity, whereas for adults, inattentive symptoms become more paramount (Semrud-Clikeman & Fine, 2010). Adults with ADHD-C report feelings of restlessness and a need to move, whereas those with ADHD-PI report significant problems with inattention. For children, ADHD-C is frequently found to be comorbid with ODD and CD, as discussed earlier. In adulthood, however, personality disorders such as borderline personality disorder, APD, and histrionic disorders have been found to frequently co-occur with a more severe form of the disorder (Miller, Nigg, & Faraone, 2007). In contrast, ADHD-PI has been found to be comorbid with dysthymia, substance abuse, and learning disabilities for both children and adults (Millstein, Wilens, Biederman, & Spencer, 1997).

Differences are also present in gender incidences. In childhood, the ratio of males to females is approximately 2:1 to 9:1, with the majority being diagnosed with ADHD-C (Biederman, Faraone, Keenan, Knee, & Tsuang, 1990). In contrast, for adults a more balanced ratio has been found with more women diagnosed with ADHD-PI than ADHD-C (Biederman et al., 2002). Additional studies find that men with ADHD are more likely to have a comorbid diagnosis of APD or substance abuse with equal incidence of bipolar disorder, social phobia, and anxiety disorders (Biederman et al., 2002). Women were also found to be diagnosed much later than men and were more likely to be diagnosed with ADHD in adulthood.

Neuropsychological differences are not as pronounced between adults and children. Whereas symptoms of hyperactivity decrease with age, signs of motoric disinhibition continue to be present into adulthood as do problems with inattention. Verbal memory difficulties continue from childhood, particularly when tasks become more complex and intricate. Cognitive flexibility difficulties also continue into adulthood and likely cause additional problems occupationally as requirements increase with responsibility. Executive functioning continues to be problematic for adults and has been found to negatively influence occupational functioning (Barkley & Murphy, 2010).

Neuroimaging findings are consistent across adults and children. Smaller volumes in the prefrontal cortex as well as in the anterior cingulate have been found in adults and children with ADHD (Castellanos et al., 1996; Hesslinger et al., 2002; Nakris et al., 2007; Semrud-Clikeman et al., 2000). Less brain activation has also been found in adults with ADHD, particularly in the right frontal regions of the brain (Valera, Faraone, Biederman, Poldrack, & Seidman, 2005) as well as for children (Pliszka, Liotti, & Woldorff, 2000) and for children in the dorsolateral regions of the frontal lobe (Pliszka et al., 2006).

Psychopathy

Our knowledge of psychopathy in childhood is less well-studied that than for adults. The rubric of psychopathy may include CD or Antisocial Personality Disorder (APD). A diagnosis of ODD or CD involves heterogeneous symptoms that generally involve inappropriate social behavior that is either physically or verbally aggressive. Most of the research has been conducted with adolescents, and if patients with a comorbid diagnosis of ADHD are excluded, very little is known about the neurological underpinnings of the disorder (Tramontana & Hooper, 1997). It has been strongly suggested that antisocial behavior can arise from many different causes and appear differently over development (Hinshaw & Lee, 2003).

ODD has been characterized by a persistent and age-inappropriate display of angry, noncompliant, and oppositional behavior, whereas CD involves aggressive and antisocial actions that hurt animals and/or other people as well as stealing, burglary, and running away from home (APA, 2000). ODD generally appears on the average by 6 years of age, whereas CD appears around 9 years (Loeber & Farrington, 2000). Key risk factors for CD but not ODD have been found to include poverty, family discord, and a family history of APD (Hinshaw & Lee, 2003).

Delinquents may or may not be diagnosed with CD depending on the nature of their symptoms. It has been found that delinquency may be transient and not involve the infliction of pain on others that is a hallmark of CD (Moffitt & Caspi, 2001). Socialized delinquency such as gang involvement has not been linked to CD and later APD. In contrast, in undersocialized persons, CD has been linked to APD, and these children are generally identified at an early age (Hinshaw & Lee, 2003). Under-socialized CD involves assaultive, aggressive behaviors that are generally committed alone (Quay, 1987). These children are at the highest risk for developing APD in adulthood (Semrud-Clikeman & Ellison, 2009). Moreover, in a large epidemiological study, 90% of youths diagnosed with CD were found to have previously met criteria for ODD while the vast majority of children with ODD (90%) did not progress to CD or APD (Hinshaw, 2002).

The transition from CD in adolescence to APD in adulthood has also been studied. The basic findings indicate that adults with APD almost always met CD criteria early in development, but only a small minority of youth with CD go on to meet criteria for APD (Zoccolillo, 1992). The most important indicators as to whether a diagnosis of CD leads to APD appear to be early onset and persistence of aggressive and antisocial behaviors, particularly for boys (Robins, 1986). For girls, CD is a strong predictor for internalizing disorders and antisocial behaviors.

Genetic Influences

One question that is frequently raised is the heritability of APD. Heritability refers to genetic influences on the individual that can be modified and influenced significantly by the environment of the individual (Hinshaw, 1999). Findings have indicated that heritability is strongest for ADHD symptomatology, moderate for APD, and small for less severe forms of APD (Edelbrock, Rende, Plomin, & Thompson, 1995), with the strongest heritability for childhood onset of CD and APD (Taylor, Iacono, & McGue, 2000). Moreover, the heritability of APD seems to increase with age, with adolescents showing stronger genetic contributions to aggression, whereas for children such contributions are small (Jacobson, Prescott, & Kendler, 2002). It has also been strongly suggested that for persistent CD and APD, the heritable effects are transactional with the environment such that dysfunctional families, aberrant parenting and socialization practices, peer rejection, and academic failure contribute to more severe APD (Lahey, Waldman, & McBurnett, 1999). The influences most affected by genes are temperamental irritability, disinhibition, and sensation seeking, which are also mediated by the environment (Maccoby, 2000).

Psychobiological Influences

Research utilizing neuroimaging is just beginning, and the findings should be viewed with caution. In summary, findings indicate that adolescents diagnosed with early-onset CD with aggression and under-socialized behavior patterns have been found to show low cortical arousal and autonomic reactivity, which has also been found with adults with APD (Quay, 1993). In contrast, adolescents with late onset CD and who are nonaggressive show arousal and reactivity indices that are elevated compared to normal controls (Lahey, McBurnett, Loeber, & Hart, 1995). These findings suggest that the system that involves behavioral activation and reward is stronger than the behavioral inhibition system in youths with CD who are under-socialized and aggressive (Lahey et al., 1995; Quay, 1993). It has also been suggested that genetic abnormalities found in persons with psychopathy may be related to a deficient neural system where the amygdala does not form the connections between punishment and behavior (Blair, 2006). This dissociation would result in people with CD or APD not learning to avoid actions that harm others and not responding to punishment when such acts are committed. Further study is needed to more fully understand what neural networks may be involved or aberrant in these patients.

Comorbidity of CD/ODD/APD and ADHD

Studies have found that similar risk factors are present in the history of children and adults with externalizing disorders that include high sensation-seeking behaviors, low avoidance of dangerous situations, and a history of chaotic and disruptive family environments including parental alcoholism, marital conflict, and child abuse/neglect (Kuperman, Schlosser, Lidral, & Reich, 1999). Similarly, conduct problems present in childhood have been found to relate to later problems with aggressive behavior, delinquency, and substance abuse in adolescence and young adulthood (Barkley & Murphy, 2010; Biederman, Faraone, & Spencer, 1993). It has been suggested that ADHD can be best represented on a continuum with ADHD plus CD being the most severe form of the disorder, ADHD with ODD an intermediate form, and ADHD without comorbidity the least severe form (Biederman, Newcorn, & Sprich, 1991).

Subsequent studies have suggested that a common vulnerability is present between hyperactive and antisocial behaviors. Using structural equation modeling with 206 families, Patterson, DeGarmo, and Knutson (2000) concluded that disruptive parental discipline resulted in hyperactivity and antisocial behaviors. They also concluded that multiple disorders are more severe than single disorders and that genetic and environmental aspects contribute to such comorbidity.

Twin studies have sought to further understand the variance present in ADHD, CD, and ODD. Structural equation modeling using monozygotic and dizygotic twin pairs has found significant genetic contributions to disruptive behaviors with each disorder due to unique genetic factors (Nadder, Silberg, Eaves, & Maes, 1998; Silberg et al., 1996). To more fully explore the relation between genetic and environmental factors, Burt and colleagues (2001) examined the correlations among genetic, shared environment, and non-shared environmental components in CD, ADHD, and ODD in dizygotic and monozygotic twin pairs. Findings indicated that CD is primarily influenced by genetic factors, whereas ADHD and ODD are strongly influenced by genetic and shared environmental factors. The shared environmental factor that appeared to be most influential was the presence of psychosocial adversity within the family system. More specifically, parental discipline was found to influence the child's behavior as well as to be influenced, in turn, by the child/adolescent. In this bidirectional schema, the parent influences the child/adolescent but is also influenced by the child/adolescent, thus, shared influences are important to understand for these three disorders. ADHD and conduct problems do continue into adulthood for some patients. These findings may shed light as to the relation of these disorders between childhood and adulthood.

Intermittent Explosive Disorder (IED)

Intermittent explosive disorder (IED) is a diagnosis applied to individuals who are repeatedly and impulsively aggressive and overreact to the situation at hand (APA, 2000). Although IED was initially thought to be a relatively rare disorder, more recent studies have found the incidence to range around 6% of the population (Coccaro, Posternak, & Zimmerman, 2005).

This disorder has been found to result in significant social and occupational impairment, and there is beginning evidence that there may be a generational transmission of this type of aggressive behavior (McCloskey, Berman, Nobelett, & Coccaro, 2006).

One of the issues for IED is the lack of specificity of the symptoms. *DSM IV-TR* excludes disorders that may be similar to IED (i.e., bipolar disorder, APD, ADHD, CD). There is no guideline as to how frequent the aggressive behaviors must be or how severe (Coccaro, 2003). A diagnosis of IED requires several discrete episodes of aggressiveness that result in assault on a person or property destruction, that the aggression be out of proportion to the triggering situation, and that another diagnosis would account for the symptoms such as APD, borderline personality disorder, CD, or ADHD. *DSM-IV-TR* does not require the aggression to be impulsive or explosive. Some have suggested that the criteria should include verbal aggression as well as specifying that the aggressive frequency occurs two or more times a week for at least a month and be impulsive in nature (Coccaro, Kavoussi, Berman, & Lish, 1998; McCloskey et al., 2006). These criteria, referred to as research criteria, found that participants identified by the research criteria showed more behavioral aggression than those diagnosed solely by *DSM IV-TR*.

Biological Basis for IED

Findings have implicated the serotonin system for IED with selective serotonin reuptake inhibitors (SSRI) being found to reduce aggression in adults with IED (Coccaro & Kavoussi, 1997). There have been few studies of children with IED and no published clinical trials on adults as to the efficacy of SSRIs. Whereas cognitive behavioral treatments (CBT) have been found to be helpful for people with anger issues (DiGuisseppe & Tafrate, 2003), the intensity of the anger seen in IED has been suggested to be similar to that of abusive spouses whose response to CBT has been less efficacious (Babcock, Green, & Robie, 2004). The use of manualized and multi-component cognitive–behavioral therapy was found to improve anger control for patients with IED compared to wait-list subjects using both small group and individual treatment settings (McCloskey, Noblett, Deffenbacher, Gollan, & Coccaro, 2008). Although a reduction in anger as well as aggressive behavior was found in these patients, the participants reported that they continued to be highly reactive and to respond quickly to provocation. Thus, the CBT did help to improve the control, but the tendencies continued to be strong and difficult to manage. One might wonder if CBT in conjunction with medication may be more successful in working with these patients.

Some studies have evaluated the similarity of bipolar disorder in adolescents and IED. A number of symptoms overlap between the two disorders, particularly in disinhibition and aggression. To study whether there are biological similarities between these two disorders, Davanzo and colleagues (2003) used magnetic resonance spectroscopy with adolescents with bipolar disorder or IED. The patients with bipolar disorder showed differences in the anterior cingulate cortex compared to those with IED or controls. These findings were interpreted to suggest that medication for mood may assist children and adolescents with bipolar disorder more effectively than those with IED and that these disorders, while symptomatically similar, are biologically different.

Electroencephalogram (EEG) and evoked response potential (ERP) findings suggest an abnormality in the positive wave seen at 100 milliseconds (P100). Children and adolescents with a history of strong aggressive and explosive behaviors were found to show a very pronounced P100 compared to controls (Bars, Hegrend, Simpson, & Munger, 2001). This marker for aggressive and explosive behavior may be related to a deficit in the descending inhibitory pathway that allows one to modulate responsivity to sensory input. If this inhibitory system is faulty, it may explain the hair-trigger responses frequently seen in children and adults with IED.

Summary

The empirical evidence for the lifespan of a specific disorder is inconsistent across diagnoses. For example, no studies were located that discussed differences that may be present between adults and children/adolescents in the expression of IED. Studies of IED have been focused on the impulsive aggressiveness seen as well as defining this disorder. Empirical support for IED is present, but the overlap of IED with bipolar disorder in childhood as well as CD makes it difficult to determine what separates these disorders. Larger epidemiological studies that evaluate the background of IED, risk factors, and how the disorder may evolve with development would be very helpful. Neuroimaging as well as ERP studies targeting adolescents and adults with IED and comparing to people diagnosed with bipolar or borderline personality disorder may also serve to elucidate what differences, if any, exist neurologically between these frequently confused disorders.

For ADHD, there are fewer differences between children and adults with ADHD than would be expected. Neuropsychological and neuroimaging findings do not suggest major differences between the ages. Executive functioning may more negatively impact occupational functioning for adults with ADHD. Women appear to be more likely to be identified in adolescence or adulthood compared to men. Comorbidity issues also appear to differ for the genders, with men showing more externalizing behaviors and women showing more problems with dysthymia and borderline personality disorder. Studies using neuroimaging of adult women with ADHD have not been completed at this time, and most of the neuroimaging findings across the ages concentrate on boys and men. This area of research is relatively unexplored, and further study is certainly strongly recommended.

Finally, CD and ODD in early childhood paired with aggression and solo acts of cruelty appear to be the strongest predictors of later APD. Heritability of APD is strong for those children who show early difficulties with irritable temperament, lack of rhythmicity, and aggression, and who also live in families where there is a great deal of marital discord and parental psychopathy, particularly in the fathers. The presence of CD or ODD in childhood has not been found to be predisposing for the majority of adolescents for APD. However, adolescents with CD who also have violent tendencies that appeared very early and involved cruelty to others and disregard for people's rights are highly likely to show significant problems in adulthood and qualify for a diagnosis of APD. Moreover, the causal pathway for APD in adulthood is likely complex and involves interplay among biology, psychology, sociology, and culture and complicates our ability to develop interventions as well as to identify these children at the earliest ages when interventions may be most helpful.

The change in psychiatric and psychological functioning from childhood to adulthood is inextricably linked to changes in brain maturation and function. It may well be that myelination and gray matter development over time changes how the disorder is manifested. Early studies are beginning to demonstrate, at least for ADHD, that brain maturation may be delayed for children and adolescents with ADHD (Shaw et al., 2007). For some of these patients, this delayed maturation of white matter may be related to improvement in functioning when the white matter development approaches that of clients without ADHD. For other patients, this delayed maturation may continue throughout adulthood, thus explaining why some clients require medication until adolescence whereas others require medication throughout the lifespan. Similar studies have not been conducted with patients with APD or with IED and such avenues should be further explored.

INTERNALIZING DISORDERS

Among the most common forms of mental illness, the internalizing disorders comprise mood and anxiety psychopathologies. In the adult population, anxiety has been estimated to be present in nearly 20% of the population, with mood disorders such as depression at about 9.5% (2005). Many children experience an episode of mood-related symptoms at some time, but these are often transient and may not necessarily persist into adulthood. However, because the adult symptoms of depression and anxiety can be so debilitating, identifying and understanding the risks and protective factors in childhood internalizing disorders is an area of considerable research attention.

One of the most difficult aspects of diagnosis and treatment is the overlap and co-occurrence of the various internalizing disorders across the lifespan. A developmental trend with certain diagnoses tending to be observed at different ages within the population has been observed. Anxiety is usually the earliest diagnosis observed, followed by externalizing disorders, dysthymic disorder, major depressive disorder (MDD), and substance abuse (Kovacs & Devlin, 1998). Longitudinal studies have shown the strong relationship between internalizing disorders in childhood and subsequent adult internalizing pathologies (Keenan, Feng, Hipwell, & Klostermann, 2009; Reef, Diamantopoulou, Meurs, Verhulst, & Ende, 2009), although some studies have found that disruptive disorders in childhood also predict mood disorders in adults (Kosterman et al., 2010). However, when coexisting internalizing symptoms are considered, it appears that externalizing behaviors alone, without early emergence of comorbid internalizing symptoms, are unlikely to lead to an adult mood disorder (Reef et al., 2009). Thus, internalizing disorders in childhood appear to be a good predictor of internalizing disorders in adulthood. However, the nature of the disorders may shift across the lifespan both epidemiologically within the community and along a heterotypic trajectory within each individual.

Anxiety Disorders

Nine *DSM-IV-TR* disorders sharing core symptoms related to anxiety are diagnosed in children. One of these, separation anxiety disorder (SAD), is regarded as specific to childhood onset, whereas panic disorder, agoraphobia, generalized anxiety disorder (GAD), social phobia, specific phobia, obsessive-compulsive disorder (OCD), posttraumatic stress disorder (PTSD) and acute stress disorder, are considered to be diagnosable throughout the lifespan (Albano, Chorpita, & Barlow, 2003; APA, 2000). Even though SAD is the one specific childhood-onset diagnosis, it has been found to be present in about 6% of adults, with about 20% of these cases having onset in adulthood (Shear, Jin, Ruscio, Walters, & Kessler, 2006). Thus, anxiety disorders of all types appear to be present across ages.

Although fears and worries are naturally a part of childhood, anxiety is the most prevalent form of childhood psychopathology. It moves from normative childhood fear to a disorder when the daily functioning of the child is disturbed by a response that is consistently out of proportion to a presumed threat. Normative development includes an escalation of anxiety, particularly to strangers, and fear of separation that usually begins to resolve at about 2 years of age, clearing for most by about age 6. Such transient symptoms of anxiety may also be experienced due to life events without progressing to functional impairment, and in the majority of cases, this is so. But for some, anxiety persists to the level of dysfunction and precedes poor adult functioning. For the 15% of children for whom fears persist, physiological symptoms including high heart rate, elevated startle responses, and high levels of cortisol may foreshadow a progression toward an anxiety disorder later in childhood (Kagan, Reznick, & Snidman, 1987).

Prevalence estimates of all types of anxiety in school-aged children and adolescents vary with age. In a longitudinal study of a community population comprising 6,674 persons aged 10–16 (Costello, Mustillo, Erkanli, Keeler, & Angold, 2003), the 3-month prevalence rate for any anxiety disorder was found to be highest in 10-year-olds (4.6%). As expected, SAD was generally diagnosed early and was largely extinguished by age 16. Simple phobia followed a similar pattern, with greater numbers at younger ages and tapering off with age. Thus, it may be expected that anxious symptoms involving difficulty going to school and fears regarding specific stimuli, such as thunder, recede as children mature. In contrast, difficulty with social situations and more generalized worry as seen in unspecified social phobia and GAD seem to be more consistent across school ages and into young adulthood. There appears, as well, to be a general progression involving a decrease of anxiety symptoms from later childhood to early adolescence followed by a slight increase in symptoms from middle to late adolescence (Costello et al., 2003; Van Oort, Greaves-Lord, Verhulst, Ormel, & Huizink, 2009).

In adults, anxiety disorders may take the same or different form if child anxiety preceded the adult diagnosis. For example, panic disorder is rarely seen in children (Merikangas, 2005) but is usually preceded by other types of anxiety earlier in life (Eaton et al., 1998), especially separation anxiety (Costello, Egger, & Angold, 2005; Klein, 1995). GAD in childhood is a more stable predictor of anxiety in adults, but it is also a predictor of depression (Keenan et al., 2009). In adulthood, anxiety has been found to be related to having a disability (Brenes et al., 2005), lower levels of education (Dahl & Dahl, 2010), and lower levels of cognitive performance (Gerstorf, Siedlecki, Tucker-Drob, & Salthouse, 2009).

In young and middle adulthood, GAD is the most likely diagnosis, but in a large epidemiological study, panic disorder was more common in those 65 years and older (King-Kallimanis, Gum, & Kohn, 2009). In general, anxiety disorders are less common late in life and onset late in life is not frequent (Wolitzky-Taylor, Castriotta, Lenze, Stanley, & Craske, 2009). In other words, anxiety is not likely in late adulthood if it was not present earlier in life. However, despite risk factors such as living alone and ill physical health, anxiety in elder persons is often overlooked as a mental health condition (Brenes et al., 2005; Wolitzky-Taylor et al., 2009).

Gender

Females are twice as likely as males to be diagnosed with anxiety disorders (Leach, Christensen, Mackinnon, Windsor, & Butterworth, 2008), although this influence across the lifespan is variable. Gender has been found to be a predictor of subsequent anxiety diagnoses in childhood (Ferdinand & Verhulst, 1995), but it appears to have less influence in predicting anxiety in adolescence (Essau, Conradt, & Petermann, 2002) and adulthood (Leach et al., 2008). Likewise, the prevalence rates for girls in early childhood are much higher, but this difference narrows approaching adolescence (Howell, Brawman-Mintzer, Monnier, & Yonkers, 2002). For children and adults, the rates of recovery are not similar for males and females (Howell et al., 2002). One study found that men and women have different responses to SSRIs. Women showed a poorer response to SSRIs when baseline severity and age of onset are accounted for (Simon et al., 2006).

Neuropsychological Presentation

Results of neuropsychological functioning in children and adults are not consistent. Some of these differences might be attributed to changes in the way anxiety disorders have been diagnosed over the years, specifically the transition from *DSM-III* to *DSM-IV-TR*. Additionally, the subtype of anxiety disorder may be important to consider along with severity, comorbidity, and age of onset. Unlike the more robust literature on depression, anxiety has been studied less. OCD is the most studied disorder (Airaksinen, Larsson, & Forsell, 2005), with findings centering on deficits in executive functioning, visual memory, attention, and processing speed in young adults. Episodic (neutral word) memory and Trails B deficits have been observed in a small study of adults with OCD and panic disorder with and without agoraphobia, whereas verbal fluency and perceptual-motor speed were intact (Airaksinen et al., 2005). Panic disorder has been associated with cognitive deficits (Lucas, Telch, & Bigler, 1991), but such deficits have been found to be associated with comorbid depression (Kaplan et al., 2006). GAD in adults has not been associated with cognitive impairment (Airaksinen et al., 2005), but this finding is based on only 7 subjects. In children, overanxious anxiety disorder, a *DSM-III* diagnosis related to the *DSM-IV-TR* GAD, was found to be associated with poorer performance on a word-learning task, but no differences were found on a visual-motor reproduction and memory task (Toren et al., 2000).

Neural Correlates

Evidence has mounted suggesting that anxiety is related to an attentional bias toward stimuli that are perceived to be threatening (Eysenck, Derakshan, Santos, & Calvo, 2007). The amygdalar–prefrontal circuitry is hypothesized as central to such difficulties, including managing attention to threat and the interpretation of ambiguous stimuli (Bishop, 2007). Bishop (2009) demonstrated that higher anxiety was associated with poor functioning in the dorso-lateral-prefrontal-cortex (DLPFC) circuitry associated with controlling one's attention in response to conflict. Notably, this finding was related to trait rather than state anxiety, suggesting a relation to a stable vulnerability rather than to transient moods. Dysregulation in activation of the anterior cingulate cortex and DLPFC have been associated with sentences that illicit worry in participants with GAD compared to normal controls. The GAD participants showed persistent activation of these areas during resting states *after* the stimuli were removed (Paulesu et al., 2010). In social anxiety disorder, the amygdala has been consistently implicated as dysregulated, and decreased activation has been observed following treatment (Freitas-Ferrari et al., 2010). No imaging studies in children were found, but one EEG study did suggest differences in frontal activation in children with anxiety disorders (Baving, Laucht, & Schmidt, 2002).

Comorbidity of Anxiety and Depression

Young children who are diagnosed with an anxiety disorder are most likely to have a co-occurring externalizing disorder, whereas older children and adults with anxiety are more likely to have co-occurring mood disorders. There has been the suggestion that anxiety and depression may be two phases of the same underlying pathology (Kessler et al., 2008; Williamson, Forbes, Dahl, & Ryan, 2005). Evidence for this comes from studies indicating that depression occurring in childhood is most often preceded by anxiety, whereas adults with a first depressive episode are less likely to have a comorbid anxiety disorder (Kovacs, Gatsonia, Paulauskas, & Richards, 1980; Parker et al., 1999). Data from the National Comorbidity Survey indicate that onset of GAD is a predictor for depression, but the reverse is not true (Kessler et al., 2008). Twin studies have suggested that there is a genetic overlap (Silberg et al., 1996) and the risk association between anxiety and depression appears to be greater for girls (Hammen & Rudolph, 2003). Although the genetic and neural mechanisms of both anxiety and depression have not been fully determined, there is reason to believe that the presence of one may include a high likelihood of the other. Moreover, those with both disorders are expected to have more severe symptoms resulting in greater functional impairment and a longer course of illness.

Mood Disorders

Twenty years ago, depression was just beginning to be recognized as a disorder that could occur in children. Since then, considerable research has been focused on the onset and trajectory of depression from early childhood into late adulthood. Depression and its many diagnostic subtypes do occur both in children and adults, although the presentation varies across the lifespan. The diagnosis of depressive disorders in children is particularly difficult because downward extension of the adult *DSM-IV-TR* diagnoses do not adequately capture symptoms occurring early in life (Hammen & Rudolph, 2003).

The *DSM-IV-TR* recognizes that the presentation of depressive symptoms in children differs from adults only in that children may appear irritable rather than dysthymic (APA, 2000). In children, comorbidity with externalizing disorders is frequent. Because the children may appear disruptive and behaviorally challenged, the presence of depression may be overlooked. Younger children are less likely than adolescents to report subjective dysphoria, but may show a depressed appearance and have more somatic symptoms (Hammen & Rudolph, 2003). Depressed adolescents are likely to sleep more than depressed children, whereas adults are more likely to have difficulty sleeping. Comorbid anxiety and behavioral disorders are common in both children and adolescents, but young children are more likely to have separation anxiety, whereas adolescents are more likely to have an eating or substance abuse problem (Hammen & Rudolph, 2003).

The lifetime rate of depression disorders in young children is very low, with dysthymia more common than MDD. The most commonly occurring diagnosis in young children is Depression Not Otherwise Specified (NOS; Costello et al., 2003). Depression rates rise approaching adolescence, but are still lower than those for adults. Results from the National Comorbidity Study indicated a lifetime prevalence of MDD at 14% for adolescents aged 15–18 years (Kessler, Avenevoli, & Ries Merikangas, 2001). Major depression appears to peak in early adulthood and lessen with age. Rates for respondents to the National Comorbidity Study-Replication who were aged ≥ 65 years had the lowest rate of MDD at 9.8 for lifetime and 2.6 for 12-month occurrences (Kessler et al., 2010). Similar results were observed in a large European epidemiological study (Angst et al., 2002).

The majority of young children who have experienced depression do not progress to having adult depressive disorders (Hammen & Rudolph, 2003). Recurring episodes along with a family history of depression increase the chances of continuity, and the progression toward a depressive disorder in adulthood may begin with behavioral problems (Mason et al., 2004) or anxiety as well (Beesdo, Pine, Lieb, & Wittchen, 2010). Retrospectively, having a major depressive episode by the age of 21 in young adults has been predicted by depressive and anxiety symptoms in early childhood (Reinherz, Giaconia, Hauf, Wasserman, & Paradis, 2000).

Depression in pre-pubescence does not seem to predict depression in adulthood very well, although it may predict a variety of other disorders, such as behavioral and conduct problems (Hammen & Rudolph, 2003). In contrast, depression occurring in adolescence does seem to have consistent continuity toward adult recurrence. One large clinical study found that nearly two-thirds of adolescents with symptoms of depression experienced an episode of major depression in early adulthood (Hammen & Rudolph, 2003). Depression in childhood and adolescence is also related to other adult disorders, including substance abuse, personality disorders, social problems (McClintock, Husain, Greer, & Cullum, 2010), and poor occupational and economic outcomes (Hammen & Rudolph, 2003). In older adults, depression appears to be less influenced by physical disability than for younger ages. Although many physical problems increase with age, the incidence of MMD significantly decreases with age across adulthood (Kessler et al., 2010). It has been hypothesized that some elderly depression may be related to vascular changes in the frontal and limbic systems that regulate norepinephrine and serotonin (McClintock et al., 2010).

The developmental trajectory of the manic and bipolar depressive diagnoses in children is less well understood (Kessler et al., 2001). Most of the prevalence data on child and adolescent mania has been with clinical samples. Estimates of childhood bipolar I, bipolar II and cyclothymia have typically been at 1% or lower (Kessler et al., 2001). In a large community sample, the 3-month estimate of any type of bipolar disorder among children aged 9–16 years of age was less than 0.1% (Costello et al., 2003). However, much higher numbers of children and adolescents, 5–11%, report manic-like symptoms lasting for only a few hours or days, which is below the threshold for bipolar I (Carlson & Kelly, 1988). An additional confusion is that symptoms of mania in pre-pubescent children may be difficult to differentiate from symptoms of ADHD (Carlson, 1998; Kessler et al., 2001). Thus, this is an area for which more research is needed.

Gender

Before the age of 10, large differences in the occurrence of depression between males and females is not observed (Mazza, Fleming, Abbott, Haggerty, & Catalano, 2010; Whiffen & Demidenko, 2006). In adolescence gender becomes a strong predictor of depression, with girls more likely to experience depression than boys. Two studies of gender influence on the trajectory of depression found differences between genders on the type of depression seen. Heath and Camarena (2002) observed that more than twice as many boys as girls were more likely to have a single experience of a high level of depression and a subsequent decrease in symptoms. In contrast, nearly three times as many girls as boys experienced increasing depressive symptoms over the 3 years of the study. In a community sample following more than 900 children from the second grade to the eighth grade, Mazza and colleagues (2010) found similar results, with depressive symptoms arising relatively equally between girls and boys in early childhood, but dropping below baseline for boys in adolescence and dropping slightly for girls in early adolescence and then persisting.

It is commonly reported that, post-adolescence, females are twice as likely to experience depression as males (McClintock et al., 2010). The reasons for this difference are not well understood, but some suggest that, rather than a difference in the incidence of depressive symptoms, there is a significant difference in the way that depression is displayed. Men are more likely to engage in aggression and drinking compared to women, and men report fewer symptoms of depression (Brownhill, Wilhelm, Barclay, & Schmied, 2005). Moreover, in communities where drinking alcohol is less tolerated (Egeland & Hostetter, 1983; Loewenthal, MacLeod, Cook, Lee, & Goldblatt, 2003), the gender gap closes. Thus, it may be that in adulthood, depression in men and women looks quite different.

Neuropsychological Presentation

Depression, particularly MDD, has been associated with reduced functioning in attention, concentration, memory, and processing speed. Chronic depression has been associated with higher levels of anxiety, substance abuse, personality disorders, somatic complaints, and poorer social functioning. The severity of a depressive episode has been found to be also related to higher levels of disability, which leaves open the question of whether severity or duration is more important to consider (McClintock et al., 2010).

Decreases in cognitive functioning, including mental flexibility, attention, working memory, and inhibition control, have been found to be associated with the recurring depression. However, there is evidence that after an episode of depression resolves, cognitive functioning does return to premorbid levels (McClintock et al., 2010). In children, depression has been associated with difficulty learning new material, which may in turn be related to attentional deficits (Semrud-Clikeman & Ellison, 2007). Like adults, children may present with slower reaction speed on timed tests and difficulty with work completion and memory in both verbal and visual tasks (McClintock et al., 2010), highlighting the importance of looking for depression when children present with a variety of school-based and behavioral problems (Baron, 2004; Semrud-Clikeman & Ellison, 2007).

Cognitive impairments among depressed patients with psychotic features are more severe than for unipolar depressed patients without psychosis, but less severe than is found in schizophrenia (Hill, Keshavan, Thase, & Sweeney, 2004). Thus, studies that did not differentiate between those with psychosis and those without may overestimate the degree of neuropsychological impairment associated with unipolar depression (Hill et al., 2009). Bipolar depression may also infer more severe neuropsychological deficits (McClintock et al., 2010), though less research has been completed with this group.

Neural Correlates

In a meta-analysis of brain volume differences in MDD, reductions were seen in areas of the brain that are involved in emotional processing and regulation of stress (Koolschijn, van Haren, Lensvelt-Mulders, Pol, & Kahn, 2009). The largest differences were seen in the anterior cingulate and the orbitofrontal cortex. Smaller but significant differences in the prefrontal cortex, hippocampus, putamen, and caudate were additionally seen in the preponderance of studies. Positron emission tomography (PET) studies and functional magnetic resonance imaging (fMRI) studies have also found differences in the anterior cingulate and frontal cortex (McClintock et al., 2010), suggesting that the volumetric differences in persons with MDD may be related to differences in functioning as well.

The areas implicated in these findings are related to the regulation of stress. The anterior cingulate and the pre- and orbitofrontal cortices are involved in providing a cognitive override to the body's initial limbic system response to negative stimuli. The hypothalamic-pituitary-adrenal (HPA) axis is also involved in MDD. Increased levels of cortisol are present in patients during presentation of MDD, in remission, and even in 2-week-old infants born to parents with bipolar disorder (Ellenbogen, Santo, Linnen, Walker, & Hodgins, 2010). Genetic susceptibility to depression has been suggested by the association of genes known to regulate the availability of serotonin in the brain (Koolschijn et al., 2009; McClintock et al., 2010). In one study involving geriatric patients, frontal volumes of depressed patients medicated with antidepressants had greater frontal volumes than those who were medication-naïve (Laveretsky et al., 2005), suggesting that medications may confer some protection against frontal lobe loss in this population.

SUMMARY

The internalizing disorders present in a variety of ways across the lifespan. Most importantly, research has shown that having an episode of anxiety or depression in early childhood doesn't necessarily predict mental illness later in life. However, most adults with the most recurring internalizing disorders do have onset in childhood. At this time, there is no reliable indication of which children are likely to progress; thus, early intervention is important not only to relieve symptoms for children, but also to confer resilience on those for whom progression is likely. Adolescence appears to be an important time in the development of lasting internalizing disorders, especially depression, because presence of depression in adolescence is more indicative of a possible long-term problem. In adulthood, men may show different symptoms than women regarding depression; thus, it is important to look for underlying depression in men for whom externalizing behaviors and substance abuse are present. Our eldest population experiences anxiety, especially panic disorder, and depression, though their symptoms may be overlooked and erroneously blamed on failing health. Vascular depression may be a possibility for older persons presenting with symptoms.

REFERENCES

Airaksinen, E., Larsson, M., & Forsell, Y. (2005). Neuropsychological functions in anxiety disorders in population-based samples: Evidence of episodic memory dysfunction. *Journal of Psychiatric Research, 39*(2), 207–214.

Albano, A. M., Chorpita, B. F., & Barlow, D. H. (2003). Childhood anxiety disorders. In E. J. Mash & R. A. Barkley (Eds.), *Child psychopathology* (2nd ed., pp. 279–329). New York: Guilford Press.

American Psychiatric Association. (2000). *Diagnostic and statistical manual of mental disorders* (4th Text Revision ed.). Washington, D.C.: American Psychiatric Association.

Angst, J., Gamma, A., Gastpar, M., Lépine, J. P., Mendlewicz, J., & Tylee, A. (2002). Gender differences in depression. *European Archives of Psychiatry and Clinical Neuroscience, 252*(5), 201–209.

Babcock, J. C., Green, C. E., & Robie, C. (2004). Does batterers' treatment work? A meta-analytic review of domestic violence treatment. *Clinical Psychology Review, 23*, 1023–1053.

Barkley, R. A., & Murphy, K. R. (2010). Impairment in occupational functioning and adult ADHD: The predictive utility of executive function (EF) ratings versus EF tests. *Archives of Clinical Neuropsychology, 25*, 157–173.

Baron, I. S. (2004). *Neuropsychological evaluation of the child*. New York: Oxford University Press.

Bars, D. R., Hegrend, F. L., Simpson, G. D., & Munger, J. C. (2001). Use of visual evoked-potential studies and EEG data to classify aggressive, explosive behavior of youths. *Psychiatric Services, 52*, 81–86.

Baving, L., Laucht, M., & Schmidt, M. H. (2002). Frontal brain activation in anxious school children. *Journal of Child Psychology and Psychiatry, 43*(2), 265–274.

Beesdo, K., Pine, D. S., Lieb, R., & Wittchen, H.-U. (2010). Incidence and risk patterns of anxiety and depressive disorders and categorization of Generalized Anxiety Disorder. *Arch Gen Psychiatry, 67*(1), 47–57.

Biederman, J., Faraone, S. V., Keenan, K., Knee, D., & Tsuang, M. T. (1990). Family-genetic and psychosocial risk factors in DSM III attention deficit disorder. *Journal of the American Academy of Child & Adolescent Psychiatry, 29*, 526–533.

Biederman, J., Faraone, S. V., & Spencer, T. (1993). Patterns of psychiatric comorbidity, cognition, and psychosocial functioning in adults with attention deficit hyperactivity disorder. *American Journal of Psychiatry, 150*, 1792–1798.

Biederman, J., Mick, E., Faraone, S. V., Braaten, E., Doyle, A. E., Spencer, T., et al. (2002). Influence of gender on attention deficit hyperactivity disorder in children referred to a psychiatric clinic. *American Journal of Psychiatry, 159*, 36–42.

Biederman, J., Newcorn, J. H., & Sprich, S. (1991). Comorbidity of attention deficit hyperactivity disorder with conduct, depression, anxiety, and other disorders. *American Journal of Psychiatry, 148*, 564–577.

Bishop, S. J. (2007). Neurocognitive mechanisms of anxiety: An integrative account. *Trends in Cognitive Sciences, 11*(7), 307–316.

Bishop, S. J. (2009). Trait anxiety and impoverished prefrontal control of attention. *Nat Neurosci, 12*(1), 92–98.

Blair, R. J. R. (2006). The emergence of psychopathy: Implications for the neuropsychological approach to developmental disorders. *Cognition, 101*, 414–442.

Brenes, G. A., Penninx, B. W. J. H., Judd, P. H., Rockwell, E., Sewell, D. D., & Wetherell, J. L. (2005). Anxiety, depression and disability across the lifespan. *Aging and Mental Health, 12*(1), 158–163.

Brownhill, S., Wilhelm, K., Barclay, L., & Schmied, V. (2005). 'Big Build': Hidden depression in men. *Aust N Z J Psychiatry, 39*, 921–931.

Burt, S. A., Krueger, R. F., McGue, M., & Iacono, W. G. (2001). Sources of covariation among attention-deficit/hyperactivity disorder, oppositional defiant disorder, and conduct disorder. *Journal of Abnormal Psychology, 110*, 516–525.

Carlson, G. A. (1998). Mania and ADHD: Comorbidity or confusion. *Journal of Affective Disorders, 51*, 177–187.

Carlson, G. A., & Kelly, K. L. (1988). Manic symptoms in a non-referred adolescent population. *Journal of Affective Disorders, 15*, 219–226.

Castellanos, F. X., Giedd, J. N., Marsh, W. L., Hamburger, S. D., Vaiturzis, A. C., & Dickstein, D. P. (1996). Quantitative brain magnetic resonance imaging in attention-deficit hyperactivity disorder. *Archives of General Psychiatry, 53*(7), 607–616.

Coccaro, E. F. (2003). Intermittent explosive behavior. In E. F. Coccaro (Ed.), *Aggression: Psychiatric assessment and treatment* (pp. 149–199). New York: Marcel Dekker, Inc.

Coccaro, E. F., & Kavoussi, R. J. (1997). Fluoxetine and impulsive aggressive behavior in personality-disordered subjects. *Archives of General Psychiatry, 54*, 1081–1088.

Coccaro, E. F., Kavoussi, R. J., Berman, M. E., & Lish, J. D. (1998). Intermittent explosive disorder–revised: Development, reliability, and validity of research criteria. *Comprehensive Psychiatry, 39*, 368–376.

Coccaro, E. F., Posternak, M. A., & Zimmerman, M. (2005). Prevalence and features of intermittent explosive disorder in a clinical setting. *Journal of Clinical Psychiatry, 66*, 1221–1227.

Costello, E. J., Egger, H. L., & Angold, A. (2005). The developmental epidemiology of anxiety disorders: Phenomenology, prevalence, and comorbidity. *Child and Adolescent Psychiatric Clinics of North America, 14*(4), 631–648.

Costello, E. J., Mustillo, S., Erkanli, A., Keeler, G., & Angold, A. (2003). Prevalence and development of psychiatric disorders in childhood and adolescence. *Archives of General Psychiatry, 60*(8), 837–844.

Dahl, C., Falk, A., & Dahl, A. A. (2010). Lifestyle and social network in individuals with high level of social phobia/anxiety symptoms: A community based study. *Social Psychiatric Epidemiology, 45*, 309–317.

Davanzo, P., Yue, K., Thomas, M. A., Belin, T., Mintz, J., Venkatraman, V., et al. (2003). Proton magnetic resonance spectroscopy of bipolar disorder versus intermittent explosive disorder in children and adolescents. *The American Journal of Psychiatry, 160*, 1442–1452.

DiGuisseppe, R., & Tafrate, R. C. (2003). Anger treatment for adults: A meta-analytic review. *Clinical Psychology: Science and Practice, 10*, 70–84.

Eaton, W. W., Anthony, J. C., Romanoski, A., Tien, A., Gallo, J., Cai, G., et al. (1998). Onset and recovery from panic disorder in the Baltimore Epidemiologic Catchment Area follow-up. *British Journal of Psychiatry, 173*, 501–507.

Edelbrock, C., Rende, R., Plomin, R., & Thompson, L. A. (1995). A twin study of competence and problem behavior in childhood and early adolescence. *Journal of Child Psychology and Psychiatry, 36*, 775–785.

Egeland, J. A., & Hostetter, A. M. (1983). Amish study I: Affective disorders among the Amish 1976–1980. *American Journal of Psychiatry, 140*, 56–61.

Ellenbogen, J. B., Santo, J. B., Linnen, A.-M., Walker, C.-D., & Hodgins, S. (2010). High cortisol levels in the offspring of parents with bipolar disorder during two weeks of daily sampling. *Bipolar Disorders, 12*(1), 77–86.

Essau, C. A., Conradt, J., & Petermann, F. (2002). Course and outcome of anxiety disorders in adolescents. *Journal of Anxiety Disorders, 16*(1), 67–81.

Eysenck, M. W., Derakshan, N., Santos, R., & Calvo, M. G. (2007). Anxiety and cognitive performance: Attentional control theory. *Emotion, 7*(2), 336–353.

Ferdinand, R. F., & Verhulst, F. C. (1995). Psychopathology from adolescence into young adulthood: An 8-year follow-up study. *American Journal of Psychiatry, 34*, 336–347.

Freitas-Ferrari, M. C., Hallak, J. E. C., Trzesniak, C., Filho, A. S., Machado-de-Sousa, J. P., Chagas, M. H. N., et al. (2010). Neuroimaging in social anxiety disorder: A systematic review of the literature. *Progress in Neuro-Psychopharmacology and Biological Psychiatry, 34*(4), 565–580.

Gerstorf, D., Siedlecki, K. L., Tucker-Drob, E. M., & Salthouse, T. A. (2009). Within-person variability in state anxiety across adulthood: Magnitude and associations with between-person characteristics. *International Journal of Behavioral Development, 33*(1), 55–64.

Hammen, C., & Rudolph, K. D. (2003). Childhood mood disorders. In E. J. Mash & R. A. Barkley (Eds.), *Child psychopathology* (2nd ed., pp. 233–278). New York: Guilford Press.

Hartlage, L. C., & Long, C. J. (1997). Development of neuropsychology as a professional psychological specialty: History, training, and credentialing. In C. R. Reynolds & E. Fletcher-Janzen (Eds.), *Handbook of clinical child neuropsychology* (pp. 3–16). New York: Plenum Press.

Heath, P. A., & Camarena, P. M. (2002). Patterns of depressed affect during early adolescence. *Journal of Early Adolescence, 22*(3), 252–276.

Hesslinger, B., Tebartz van Elst, L., Thiel, T., Haegele, K., Henning, J., & Ebert, D. (2002). Frontoorbital volume reductions in adult patients with attention deficit hyperactivity disorder. *Neuroscience Letters, 328*, 319–321.

Hill, S. K., Keshavan, M. S., Thase, M. E., & Sweeney, J. A. (2004). Neuropsychological dysfunction in antipsychotic-naive first-episode unipolar psychotic depression. *The American Journal of Psychiatry, 161*(6), 996–1003.

Hill, S. K., Reilly, J. L., Harris, M. S. H., Rosen, C., Marvin, R. W., DeLeon, O., et al. (2009). A comparison of neuropsychological dysfunction in first-episode psychosis patients with unipolar depression, bipolar disorder, and schizophrenia. *Schizophrenia Research, 113*(2–3), 167–175.

Hinshaw, S. P. (1999). Psychosocial intervention for childhood ADHD: Etiologic and developmental themes, comorbidity, and integration with pharmacotherapy. In B. P. Cicchetti & S. L. Toth (Eds.), *Rochester symposium on developmental psychopathology: Developmental approaches to prevention and intervention* (*Vol. 9*, pp. 221–270). Rochester, NY: University of Rochester Press.

Hinshaw, S. P. (2002). Intervention research, theoretical mechanisms, and causal processes related to externalizing behavior patterns. *Development and Psychopathology, 14*, 789–818.

Hinshaw, S. P., & Lee, S. S. (2003). Conduct and oppositional defiant disorders. In E. J. Mash & R. A. Barkley (Eds.), *Child psychopathology* (2nd ed., pp. 144–198). New York: Guilford Press.

Howell, H. B., Brawman-Mintzer, O., Monnier, J., & Yonkers, K. A. (2002). Generalized anxiety disorder in women. *Psychiatric Clinics of North America, 24*(1), 1748–1760.

Jacobson, K. C., Prescott, C. A., & Kendler, K. S. (2002). Sex differences in the genetic and environmental influences on the development of antisocial behavior. *Development and Psychopathology, 14*, 395–416.

Kagan, J., Reznick, J. S., & Snidman, N. (1987). The physiology and psychology of behavioral inhibition in children. *Child Development, 58*(6), 1459–1473.

Kaplan, J. S., Erickson, K., Luckenbaugh, D. A., Weiland-Fiedler, P., Geraci, M., Sahakian, B. J., et al. (2006). Differential performance on tasks of affective processing and decision-making in patients with panic disorder and panic disorder with comorbid major depressive disorder. *Journal of Affective Disorders, 95*, 165–171.

Keenan, K., Feng, X., Hipwell, A. E., & Klostermann, S. (2009). Depression begets depression: Comparing the predictive utility of depression and anxiety symptoms to later depression. *The Journal of Child Psychology and Psychiatry, 50*(9), 1167–1175.

Kessler, R. C., Avenevoli, S., & Ries Merikangas, K. (2001). Mood disorders in children and adolescents: An epidemiologic perspective. *Biological Psychiatry, 49*(12), 1002–1014.

Kessler, R. C., Birnbaum, H., Bromet, E., Hwang, I., Sampson, N., & Shahly, V. (2010). Age differences in major depression: Results from the National Comorbidity Survey Replication (NCS-R). *Psychological Medicine, 40*(2), 225–237.

Kessler, R. C., Chiu, W. T., Demler, O., & Walters, E. E. (2005). Prevalence, severity, and comorbidity of 12-month DSM-IV disorders in the National Comorbidity Survey Replication. *Archives of General Psychiatry, 62*(6), 617–627.

Kessler, R. C., Gruber, M., Hettema, J. M., Hwiang, I., Sampson, N., & Yonkers, K. A. (2008). Co-morbid major depression and generalized anxiety disorders in the National Comorbidity Survey follow-up. *Psychological Medicine, 38*, 365–364.

King-Kallimanis, B., Gum, A. M., & Kohn, R. (2009). Comorbidity of depressive and anxiety disorders for older Americans in the national comorbidity survey-replication. *The American Journal of Geriatric Psychiatry, 17*(9), 782–792.

Klein, R. G. (1995). Is panic disorder associated with childhood separation anxiety disorder? *Clinical Neuropharmacology, 18*(S), 7–14.

Koolschijn, P. C. M. P., van Haren, N. E. M., Lensvelt-Mulders, G. J. L. M., Pol, H., E. Hulshoff, & Kahn, R. S. (2009). Brain volume abnormalities in major depressive disorder: A meta-analysis of magnetic resonance imaging studies. *Human Brain Mapping, 30*(11), 3719–3735.

Kosterman, R., Hawkins, J., Mason, W., Herrenkohl, T., Lengua, L., & McCauley, E. (2010). Assessment of behavior problems in childhood and adolescence as predictors of early adult depression. *Journal of Psychopathology and Behavioral Assessment, 32*(1), 118–127.

Kovacs, M., & Devlin, B. (1998). Internalizing disorders. *Journal of Child Psychology, Psychiatry and Allied Disciplines, 39*, 47–63.

Kovacs, M., Gatsonia, C., Paulauskas, S., & Richards, C. (1980). Depressive disorders in childhood: IV. A longitudinal study of comorbidity with and risk for anxiety disorders. *Arch Gen Psychiatry, 46*(9), 776–782.

Kuperman, S., Schlosser, S. S., Lidral, J., & Reich, W. (1999). Relationship of child psychopathology to parental alcoholism and antisocial personality disorder. *Journal of the American Academy of Child & Adolescent Psychiatry, 38*, 686–692.

Lahey, B. B., McBurnett, K., Loeber, R., & Hart, E. (1995). Psychobiology of conduct disorder. In G. P. Shoevar (Ed.), *Conduct disorders in children and adolescents: Assessments and interventions* (pp. 27–44). Washington, D.C.: APA.

Lahey, B. B., Waldman, I. D., & McBurnett, K. (1999). The development of antisocial behavior: An integrative causal model. *Journal of Child Psychology and Psychiatry, 40*, 669–682.

Laveretsky, H., Kurbanyan, K., Ballmaier, M., Mintz, J., Toga, A. W., & Kumar, A. (2005). Antidepressant exposure may protect against decrement in frontal gray matter volumes in geriatric depression. *Journal of Clinical Psychiatry, 66*(8), 964–967.

Leach, L. S., Christensen, H., Mackinnon, A. J., Windsor, T. D., & Butterworth, P. (2008). Gender differences in depression and anxiety across the adult lifespan: The role of psychosocial mediators. *Soc Psychiatry Psychiatr Epidemiol, 43*, 983–998.

Loeber, R., & Farrington, D. P. (2000). Young children who commit crime: Epidemiology, developmental origins, risk factors, early interventions, and policy implications. *Development and Psychopathology, 12*, 737–762.

Loewenthal, K. M., MacLeod, A. K., Cook, S., Lee, M., & Goldblatt, V. (2003). Beliefs about alcohol among UK Jews and Protestants: Do they fit the alcohol-depression hypothesis? *Social Psychiatry and Psychiatric Epidemiology, 38*(3), 122–127.

Lucas, J. A., Telch, M. J., & Bigler, E. D. (1991). Memory functioning in panic disorder: A neuropsychological perspective. *Journal of Anxiety Disorders, 5*(1), 1–20.

Maccoby, E. E. (2000). Parenting and its effects on children: On reading and misreading behavior genetics. *Annual Review of Psychology, 51*, 1–27.

Mason, W. A. P. H. D., Kosterman, R. P. H. D., Hawkins, J. D. P. H. D., Herrenkohl, T. I. P. H. D., Lengua, L. J. P. H. D., & McCauley, E. P. H. D. (2004). Predicting depression, social phobia, and violence in early adulthood from childhood behavior problems. *Journal of the American Academy of Child & Adolescent Psychiatry, 43*(3), 307–315.

Mazza, J. J., Fleming, C. B., Abbott, R. D., Haggerty, K. P., & Catalano, R. F. (2010). Identifying trajectories of adolescents' depressive phenomena: An examination of early risk factors. *Journal of Youth and Adolescence, 39*, 579–593.

McClintock, S. M., Hussain, M., Greer, T. L., & Cullum, C. M. (2010). Association between depressive severity and neurocognitive function in major depressive disorder: A review and synthesis. *Neuropsychology, 24*(1), 9–34.

McCloskey, M. S., Berman, M. E., Nobelett, K. L., & Coccaro, E. F. (2006). Intermittent explosive disorder-integrated research diagnostic criteria: Convergent and discriminant validity. *Journal of Psychiatric Research, 40*, 231–242.

McCloskey, M. S., Noblett, K. L., Deffenbacher, J. L., Gollan, J. K., & Coccaro, E. F. (2008). Cognitive-behavioral therapy for intermittent explosive disorder: A pilot randomized clinical trial. *Journal of Consulting and Clinical Psychology, 76*, 876–886.

Merikangas, K. R. (2005). Vulnerability factors for anxiety disorders in children and adolescents. *Child and Adolescent Psychiatric Clinics of North America, 14*(4), 649–679.

Miller, T. W., Nigg, J. T., & Faraone, S. V. (2007). Axis I and II comorbidity in adults with ADHD. *Journal of Abnormal Psychology, 116*, 519–528.

Millstein, R., Wilens, T., Biederman, J., & Spencer, T. (1997). Presenting ADHD symptoms and subtypes of clinically referred adults with ADHD. *Journal of Attention Disorders, 2*, 159–166.

Moffitt, T. E., & Caspi, A. (2001). Childhood predictors differentiate life-course persistent and adolescence-limited antisocial pathways among males and females. *Development and Psychopathology, 13*, 355–375.

Nadder, T. S., Silberg, J., Eaves, L., & Maes, H. H. (1998). Genetic effects on ADHD symptomatology in 7- to 13-year-old twins: Results from a telephone survey. *Behavior Genetics, 28*, 83–99.

Nakris, N., Buka, S. L., Biederman, J., Papadimitriou, G. M., Hodge, S. M., Valera, E. M., et al. (2007). Attention and executive systems abnormalities in adults with childhood ADHD: A DT-MRI study of connections. *Cerebral Cortex, 10*, 1093–1104.

Parker, G., Wilhelm, K., Mitchell, P., Austin, M.-P., Roussos, J., & Gladstone, G. (1999). The influence of anxiety as a risk to early onset major depression. *Journal of Affective Disorders, 52*(1–3), 11–17.

Patterson, G. R., DeGarmo, D. S., & Knutson, N. (2000). Hyperactive and antisocial behaviors: Comorbid or two points in the same process? *Development and Psychopathology, 12*, 91–106.

Paulesu, E., Sambugaro, E., Torti, T., Danelli, L., Ferri, F., Scialfa, G., et al. (2010). Neural correlates of worry in generalized anxiety disorder and in normal controls: A functional MRI study. *Psychological Medicine, 40*(1), 117–124.

Pliszka, S. R., Glahn, D. C., Semrud-Clikeman, M., Franklin, C., Perez, R., Xiong, J., et al. (2006). Neuroimaging of inhibitory control areas in children with attention deficit hyperactivity disorder who were treatment naive or in long-term treatment. *American Journal of Psychiatry, 163*(6), 1052–1060.

Pliszka, S. R., Liotti, M., & Woldorff, M. G. (2000). Inhibitory control in children with attention deficit/hyperactivity disorder: Event related potentials identify the processing component and timing of an impaired right-frontal response-inhibition mechanism. *Biological Psychiatry, 48*, 238–246.

Quay, H. C. (1987). Patterns of delinquent behavior. In H. C. Quay (Ed.), *Handbook of juvenile delinquency* (pp. 118–138). New York: Wiley.

Quay, H. C. (1993). The psychobiology of undersocialized aggressive conduct disorder: A theoretical perspective. *Development and Psychopathology, 5*, 165–180.

Reef, J., Diamantopoulou, S., Meurs, I. V., Verhulst, F., & Ende, J. V. D. (2009). Child to adult continuities of psychopathology: A 24-year follow-up. *Acta Psychiatrica Scandinavica, 120*(3), 230–238.

Reinherz, H., Giaconia, R., Hauf, A., Wasserman, M., & Paradis, A. (2000). General and specific childhood risk factors for depression and drug disorders by early adulthood. *Journal of the American Academy of Child & Adolescent Psychiatry, 39*(2), 223–231.

Robins, L. N. (1986). The consequences of conduct disorder in girls. In D. Olweus, J. Block, & M. Radke-Yarrow (Eds.), *The development of antisocial and prosocial behavior: Research, theories, and issues* (pp. 385–414). Orlando, FL: Academic Press.

Semrud-Clikeman, M., & Ellison, P. A. T. (2007). *Child neuropsychology: Assessment and intervention*. New York: Springer.

Semrud-Clikeman, M., & Ellison, P. A. T. (2009). *Child neuropsychology: Assessment and intervention, 2nd Edt*. New York: Springer.

Semrud-Clikeman, M., & Fine, J. G. (2010). Adult ADHD. In S. J. Hunter & J. Donders (Eds.), *Principles and practice of lifespan developmental neuropsychology* (pp. 96–112). New York: Cambridge University Press.

Semrud-Clikeman, M., Fine, J. G., & Butcher, B. (2007). The assessment of depression in children and adolescents. In S. Smith & L. Handler (Eds.), *The clinical assessment of children and adolescents: A practitioner's handbook* (pp. 485–503). Mahwah, NJ: Lawrence Erlbaum Assoc. Publishers.

Semrud-Clikeman, M., Steingard, R. J., Filipek, P., Biederman, J., Bekken, K., & Renshaw, P. F. (2000). Using MRI to examine brain-behavior relationships in males with attention deficit disorder with hyperactivity. *Journal of the American Academy of Child and Adolescent Psychiatry, 39*(4), 477–484.

Shaw, P., b. Eckstrand, K., Sharp, W., Blumenthal, J., Lerch, J. P., Greenstein, D., et al. (2007). Attention-deficit/hyperactivity disorder is characterized by a delay in cortical maturation. *Proceedings of the National Academy of Science USA, 104*, 19649–19654.

Shear, K., Jin, c. R., Ruscio, A. M., Walters, E. E., & Kessler, R. C. (2006). Prevalence and correlates of estimated DSM-IV child and adult separation anxiety disorder in the National Comorbidity Survey replication. *Am J Psychiatry, 163*(6), 1074–1083.

Silberg, J., Rutter, M., Meyer, J., Maes, H., Hewitt, J., Simonoff, E., et al. (1996). Genetic and environmental influences on the covariation between hyperactivity and conduct disturbance in juvenile twins. *Journal of Child Psychology and Psychiatry, 37*, 803–816.

Simon, N. M., Zalta, A. K., Worthington, J. J. III Hoge, E. A., Christian, K. M., Stevens, J. C., et al. (2006). Preliminary support for gender differences in response to fluoxetine for generalized anxiety disorder. *Depression and Anxiety, 23*(6), 373–376.

Taylor, J., Iacono, W. G., & McGue, M. (2000). Evidence for a genetic etiology of early-onset delinquency. *Journal of Abnormal Psychology, 109*, 634–643.

Toren, P., Sadeh, M., Wolmer, L., Eldar, S., Koren, S., Weizman, R., et al. (2000). Neurocognitive correlates of anxiety disorders in children: A preliminary report. *Journal of Anxiety Disorders, 14*(3), 239–247.

Tramontana, M., & Hooper, S. (1989). Neuropsychology of child psychopathology. In C. R. Reynolds & E. Fletcher-Janzen (Eds.), *Handbook of clinical child neuropsychology* (pp. 87–106). New York: Plenum Press.

Tramontana, M., & Hooper, S. (1997). Neuropsychology of child psychopathology. In C. R. Reynolds & E. Fletcher-Janzen (Eds.), *Handbook of clinical child neuropsychology* (pp. 120–139). New York: Plenum Press.

Valera, E. M., Faraone, S. V., Biederman, J., Poldrack, R. A., & Seidman, L. (2005). Functional neuroanatomy of working memory in adults with attention-deficit/hyperactivity disorder. *Biological Psychiatry, 57*, 439–447.

Van Oort, F. V. A., Greaves-Lord, K., Verhulst, F. C., Ormel, J., & Huizink, A. C. (2009). The developmental course of anxiety symptoms during adolescence: The TRAILS study. *Journal of Child Psychology and Psychiatry, 50*(10), 1209–1217.

Whiffen, V. E., & Demidenko, N. (2006). Mood disturbance across the life span. In J. Worell & C. D. Goodheard (Eds.), *Handbook of girl's and women's psychological health* (pp. 51–59). Oxford: Oxford University Press.

Williamson, D. E., Forbes, E. E., Dahl, R. E., & Ryan, N. D. (2005). A genetic epidemiologic perspective on comorbidity of depression and anxiety. *Child and Adolescent Psychiatric Clinics of North America, 14*(4), 707–726.

Wolitzky-Taylor, K. B., Castriotta, N., Lenze, E. J., Stanley, M. A., & Craske, M. G. (2009). Anxiety disorders in older adults: A comprehensive review. *Depression and Anxiety, 27,* 190–211.

Zoccolillo, M. (1992). Co-occurrence of conduct disorder and its adult outcomes with depressive and anxiety disorders: A review. *Journal of the American Academy of Child & Adolescent Psychiatry, 31,* 547–556.

CHAPTER 3

Neuroanatomy of Pleasure and Emotion

C. E. Parsons, K. S. Young, & Morten L. Kringelbach

INTRODUCTION

For better, and sometimes for worse, our behavior is governed by pleasure and emotion (Kringelbach, 2005). The underlying hedonic processing is arguably at the heart of what makes us human, but at the same time it can also be one of the most important factors keeping us from staying healthy (Kringelbach, 2004a; Saper, Chou, & Elmquist, 2002). A better understanding of the underlying brain mechanisms and their development, therefore, can help us understand and potentially treat the major public health issue of affective disorders, including unipolar depression, bipolar disorder, chronic pain, and eating disorders.

This review is centered on the functional neuroanatomy of pleasure and hedonic processing in general. Pleasure here is defined as one of the positive dimensions of the broader category of hedonic processing, which also includes other negative and unpleasant dimensions, such as pain (Berridge & Kringelbach, 2008; Kringelbach, 2009; Kringelbach & Berridge, 2010). The fields of affective and social neuroscience have made substantial progress in identifying the brain mechanisms underlying aspects of pleasure reactions. Although a considerable volume of evidence has served to elucidate the intricacies of the social pleasure experience in the adult brain (Kringelbach, 2004a), less is known about its development in the early years. In this review, we focus on synthesizing current knowledge about the neuroanatomical underpinnings of emotional and behavior control, with specific reference to hedonic processing. We summarize what is known about the developing infant brain in terms of structure and function and how this may relate to aspects of hedonic processing.

EMOTION AND MOTIVATION

For many years, emotion and motivation were considered elusive topics for scientific enquiry and were generally defined in opposition to cognition as that which move us in some way, as implied by the Latin root *movere,* to move. Owing primarily to its perceived subjective nature, the science of emotion was stunted despite ideas put forward by pioneering individuals such as Charles Darwin (1872). Darwin examined the evolution of emotional responses and facial expressions, and suggested that emotions allow an organism to make adaptive responses to salient stimuli in the environment, thus enhancing its chances of survival.

A highly successful scientific strategy has been to divide the concept of emotion into two parts: the affective state, which has objective aspects in behavioral, physiological, and neural reactions; and conscious affective feelings, seen as the subjective experience of emotion. Such a definition allows conscious feelings to play a central role in hedonic experiences, but holds that the affective essence of a pleasure reaction encompasses more than a conscious feeling. This definition allows emotional states to be measured in animals and humans alike using, for example, conditioning. Much of the recent research has regarded emotions as states elicited by rewards and punishments (which is a circular definition; Weiskrantz, 1968). Reinforcers are defined such that positive reinforcers (rewards) increase the frequency of behavior leading to their acquisition, whereas negative reinforcers (punishers) decrease the frequency of behavior leading to their encounter and increase the frequency of behavior leading to their avoidance. The subsequent emotional processing of these reinforcers is a multistage process mediated by networks of brain structures. The results of this processing influence which autonomic responses are elicited, which behavior is selected, and which conscious feelings are produced, in humans at least.

HEDONIC PROCESSING: BASIC AND HIGHER-ORDER PLEASURES

The pleasure we derive through experiences such as food, sex, and social interaction are driving forces necessary to maintain life. Taking an evolutionary perspective, reward, pleasure, and hedonic processing have important roles in fulfilling the Darwinian imperatives of survival and procreation. The neural mechanisms for generating affective reactions are present and similar in most mammalian brains and therefore appear to have been selected for, and conserved, across species (see Figure 3.1).

It has proven useful to divide hedonic processing into at least two categories: basic and higher-order pleasures (Kringelbach & Berridge, 2008). The basic pleasures are linked to survival and procreation, including sensory pleasures such as food and sex (Berridge, 1996; Kringelbach, 2004a). As social interactions with conspecifics may potentially lead to the propagation of genes, social pleasures are also likely to be part of our repertoire of basic pleasures (Kringelbach & Rolls, 2003). Furthermore, in social animals, social interactions with conspecifics are also fundamental to enhancing the experience of other pleasures, such as the consumption of food. The second category, higher-order pleasures, includes the enjoyment of monetary, artistic, musical, altruistic, and transcendent experiences.

Humans are intensely social, and it may well be that interactions with other people are among the most pleasurable experiences available to us. Social pleasures include vital sensory visual and auditory cues such as smiling faces and laughter, aspects of touch such as grooming and caress, as well as more abstract and cognitive features of social reward and relationship evaluation (Adolphs, 2003). Almost immediately after birth, infants seek contact with a caregiver, and are equipped with reflexes such as the hand grasp reflex (palmar grasp) and reaching out of the arms (Moro reflex), to this end (Eliot, 1999). From a developmental perspective, early interactions between parents and infants are formative (Parsons, Young, Murray, Stein, & Kringelbach, 2010; Stein et al., 1991), and are likely to impact on subsequent hedonic processing generally.

It is also likely that social pleasures and related traits of positive hedonic mood all draw upon the same neurobiological roots that evolved for sensory pleasures (Diener, Lucas, & Scollon, 2006; Ryan & Deci, 2001; Seligman, 2005). To date, the available evidence suggests that brain mechanisms involved in fundamental pleasures overlap with those for higher-order pleasures (Kringelbach, 2005; Peciña, Smith, & Berridge, 2006; Small, Zatorre, Dagher, Evans, & Jones-Gotman, 2001). This neural overlap might offer a way to generalize from fundamental pleasures that are best understood to larger hedonic brain principles.

Both positive and negative affects are recognized as having adaptive functions (Nesse, 2004). Positive affect in particular has important roles in behavioral control in daily life, and in planning and building cognitive and emotional resources (Fredrikson et al., 2008). Such functional perspectives suggest that affective reactions may have objective features beyond the obvious subjective ones (Kringelbach, 2004a).

Pleasure encompasses more than just a sensation (Frijda, 2007; Kringelbach & Berridge, 2008; Ryle, 1954). The experience of pleasure requires a subsequent positive valuation, such

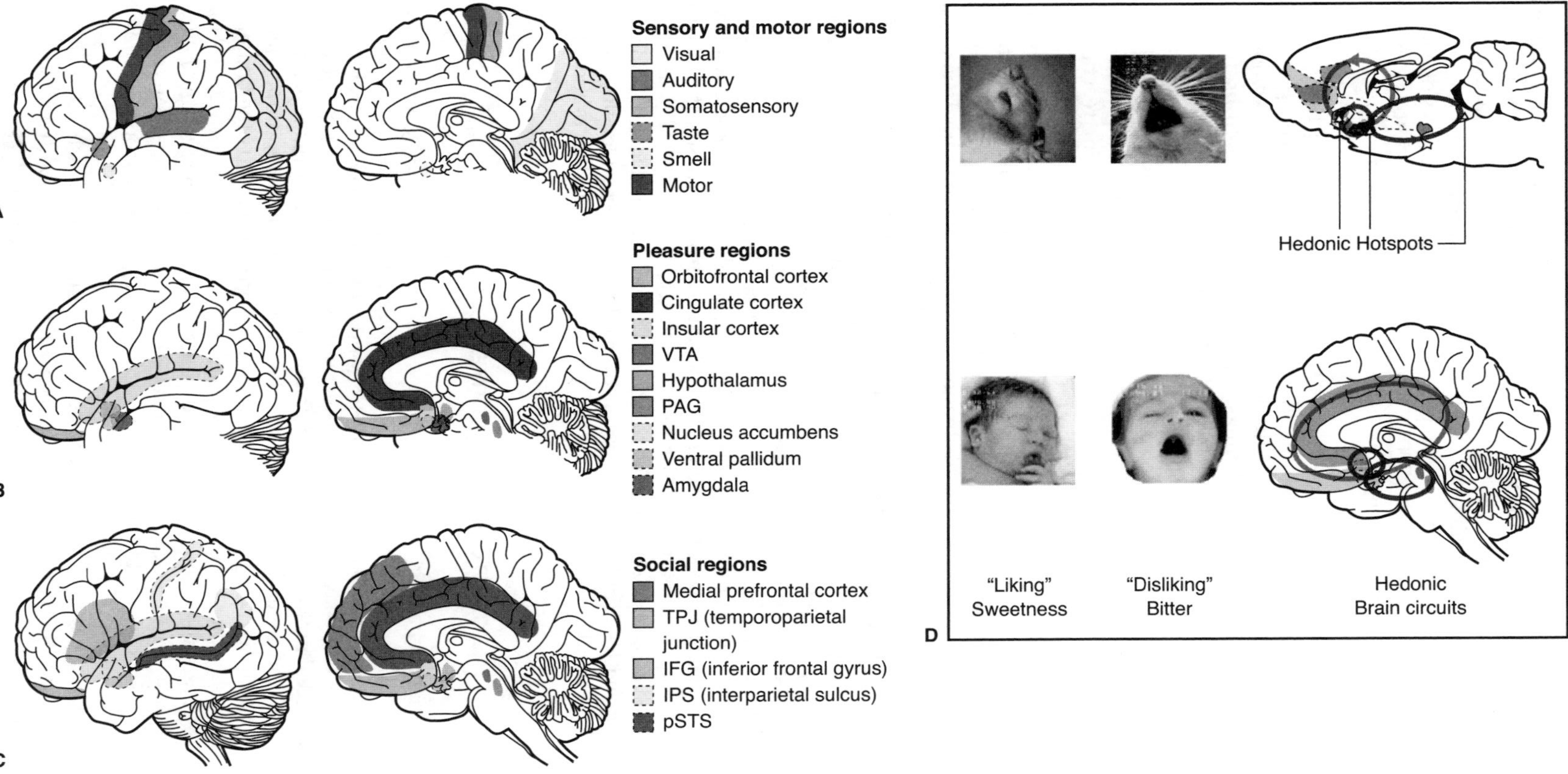

FIGURE 3.1 Brain systems from sensation to basic pleasures and higher-order social processing. (*See color insert.*) The schematic figure shows the approximate sensorimotor, pleasure, and social brain regions in the adult brain. **(A)** Processing linked to the identification of and interaction with stimuli is carried out in the sensorimotor regions of the brain, **(B)** which are separate from the valence processing in the pleasure regions of the brain. **(C)** In addition to this pleasure processing, there is further higher-order processing of social situations (such as theory-of-mind) in widespread cortical regions. **(D)** The hedonic mammalian brain circuitry can be revealed using behavioral and subjective measures of pleasures in rodents and humans (Berridge & Kringelbach, 2008, reprinted with permission from Springer-Verlag).

that it is "liked." Although the pleasure—or hedonic impact—of a reward such as sweetness can be measured by verbal reports in conscious humans, it is not dependent on the presence of language. In most nonlinguistic mammals, pleasure will elicit "acceptance wriggles." Pleasure-elicited behaviors (such as protruding tongue movements to sweet foods) are present in other animals, including rodents, and have been proposed as objective measures of elicited pleasure (Steiner, Glaser, Hawilo, & Berridge, 2001). Although human infants initially exhibit similar licking of their lips for sweet foods, these stereotyped behaviors disappear after a while.

Humans do, however, exhibit many pleasure-elicited behaviors, such as genuine smiles and laughter, but not all experiences of pleasure will be marked by these overt behaviors. In the same way that it has proven useful to divide emotion into the non-conscious and conscious subcomponents of emotions and feelings, we suggest that it is both useful and meaningful to divide pleasure into both non-conscious (core liking) and conscious (subjective liking) subcomponents of evaluative hedonic processing. Such a definition would hold that although pleasure plays a central role for emotions and conscious feelings, it is not itself a conscious feeling. This definition also paves the way for affective neuroscience studies of animals to help provide insights into neural mechanisms underlying core liking reactions by avoiding obstructions arising from uncertainty about criteria for consciousness.

A useful distinction has been proposed between two aspects of reward: hedonic impact and incentive salience, where the former refers to the "liking" or pleasure related to the reward, and the latter to the "wanting" or desire for the reward (Berridge, 1996; Berridge & Robinson, 1998). In order to provide hedonic evaluation of stimuli, the brain regions implicated in hedonic assessment must receive salient information about stimulus identity from the primary and secondary sensory cortices. We typically want what we like, and like what we want, but these findings suggest that wanting and liking are processed by distinct brain circuits and may not always go hand-in-hand. The wanting and liking components of pleasure also have conscious and non-conscious elements that can be studied in humans—and at least the latter can also be probed in other animals (see Figure 3.2).

Neuroimaging offers a powerful way to investigate both the liking and wanting components of pleasure in the human brain. One way to investigate liking is to take subjective hedonic ratings during a neuroimaging experiment and then correlate these ratings with changes in activity in the human brain (De Araujo, Kringelbach, Rolls, & McGlone, 2003b; De Araujo, Rolls, Kringelbach, McGlone, & Phillips, 2003c; Kringelbach, O'Doherty, Rolls, & Andrews, 2003). This provides a unique window on the hedonic processes evaluating the pleasantness of salient stimuli and has pointed to the central role of the orbitofrontal cortex.

THE ORBITOFRONTAL CORTEX (OFC)

A substantial body of neuroimaging, neuropsychology, and neurophysiology studies has indicated that the human OFC is a nexus for: (i) sensory integration, (ii) the modulation of autonomic reactions, and (iii) participation in learning, prediction, and decision making for emotional and reward-related behaviors. The OFC functions as part of various networks that include regions of the medial prefrontal cortex, hypothalamus, amygdala, insula/operculum, dopaminergic midbrain, and areas in the basal ganglia, including the ventral and dorsal striatum. These additional areas have been investigated in detail in rodents and other animals, and have been described in other reviews (Cardinal, Parkinson, Hall, & Everitt, 2002; Holland & Gallagher, 2004). Here, the focus is on evidence from human neuroimaging and neuropsychology studies because the phylogenetic expansion and resultant heterogeneous nature of this brain region across species limit the extent to which we can generalize from nonhuman studies.

Neuroimaging studies have found that the reward value (Kringelbach, O'Doherty, Rolls, & Andrews, 2000; O'Doherty et al., 2000), expected reward value (Gottfried, O'Doherty, & Dolan, 2003), and even the subjective pleasantness of other reinforcers, such as food (Kringelbach et al., 2003) are represented in the OFC. Such findings provide a basis for further

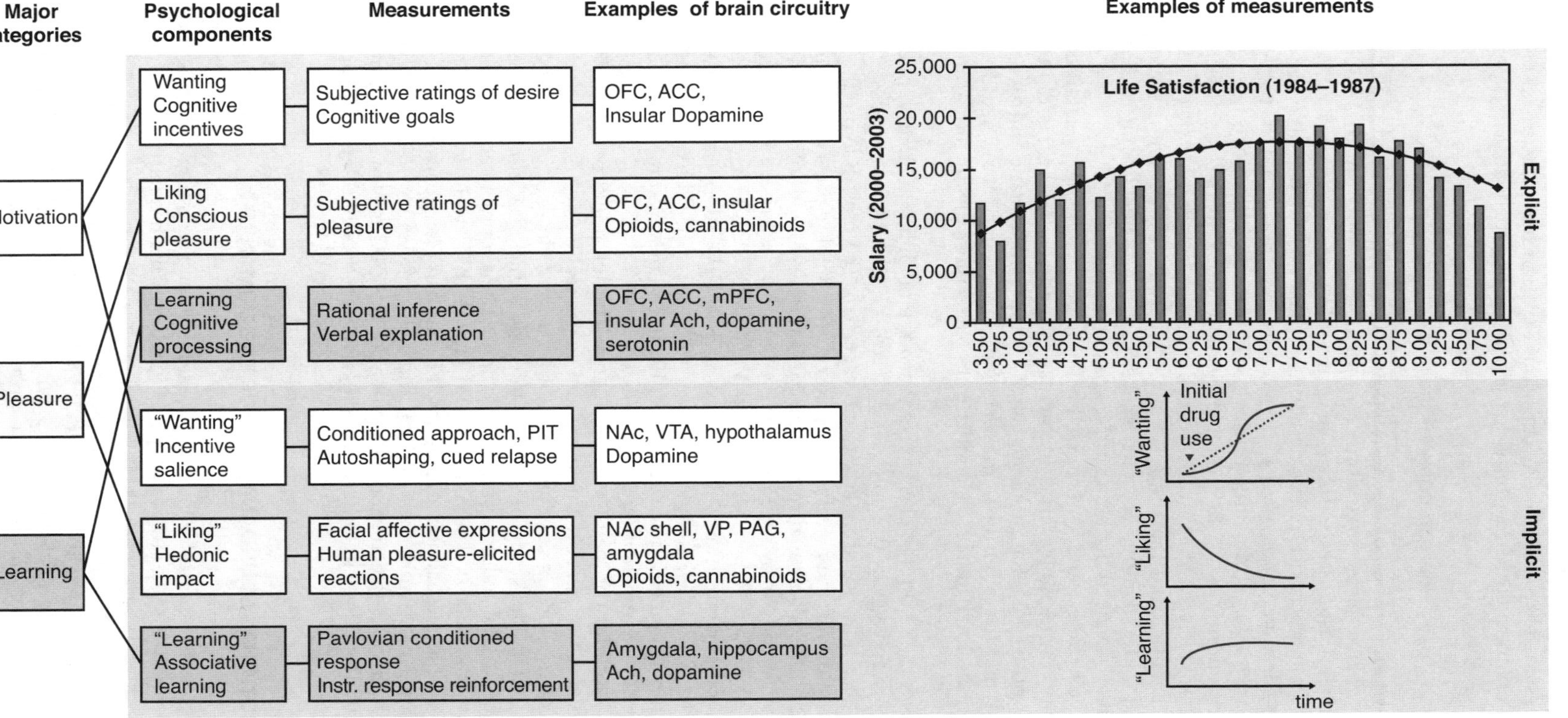

FIGURE 3.2 A scientific program for the study of pleasure. (*See color insert.*) Pleasure is a complex psychological concept with at least three major subcomponents of motivation or wanting, (white), pleasure liking or affect (light blue), and learning (blue). Each of these contains explicit (top rows, light yellow) and implicit (bottom rows, yellow) psychological components (second column) that constantly interact and require careful scientific experimentation to tease apart. Explicit processes are consciously experienced (e.g. explicit pleasure and happiness, desire, or expectation), whereas implicit psychological processes are potentially unconscious in the sense that they can operate at a level not always directly accessible to conscious experience (implicit incentive salience, habits, and "liking" reactions), and must be further translated by other mechanisms into subjective feelings. Measurements or behavioral procedures that are especially sensitive markers of the each of the processes are listed (third column). Examples of some of the brain regions and neurotransmitters are listed (fourth column), as well as specific examples of measurements (fifth column), such as an example of how highest subjective life satisfaction does not lead to the highest salaries (top) (Haisken-DeNew & Frick, 2005, reprinted with permission from GEI). Another example (bottom right) shows the incentive-sensitization model of addiction and how "wanting" to take drugs may grow over time independently of "liking" and "learning" drug pleasure as an individual becomes an addict (bottom) (Robinson & Berridge, 1993, reprinted with permission from Elsevier).

exploration of the brain systems involved in the conscious experience of pleasure and reward and, as such, provide a unique method for studying the hedonic quality of human experience.

Neuroanatomy of the OFC

The OFC occupies the ventral surface of the frontal part of the brain. It is defined as the part of the prefrontal cortex that receives projections from the magnocellular, medial nucleus of the mediodorsal thalamus (Fuster, 1997). This is in contrast to areas of the prefrontal cortex that receive projections from other parts of the mediodorsal thalamus. For example, the dorsolateral prefrontal cortex (Brodmann area [BA] 46/9) receives projections from the parvocellular, lateral part of the mediodorsal thalamic nucleus, whereas the frontal eye fields in the anterior bank of the arcuate sulcus (BA 8) receive projections from the paralamellar part of the mediodorsal thalamic nucleus. This is a broad connectional topography, in which each specific portion of the mediodorsal thalamus is connected to more than one architectonic region of the prefrontal cortex (Pandya & Yeterian, 1996), and a better definition therefore includes the cortical area's connectivity and morphological features.

Two important cytoarchitectonic features of the OFCs are the phylogenetic differences between species and the considerable variability across individuals (Chiavaras & Petrides, 2000, 2001). The former poses potential problems when trying to understand functional relationships across species, and the latter poses interesting methodological challenges for those who hope to normalize individual brains to a template brain to explore the functional anatomy of the human OFC.

The OFC receives inputs from the classic five sensory modalities: gustatory, olfactory, somatosensory, auditory, and visual (Carmichael & Price, 1995b). It also receives visceral sensory information, and all this input makes the OFC perhaps the most polymodal region in the entire cortical mantle, with the possible exception of the rhinal regions of the temporal lobes (Barbas, 1988). The OFC also has direct reciprocal connections with other brain structures, including the amygdala (Amaral & Price, 1984; Carmichael & Price, 1995a), cingulate cortex (Öngür & Price, 2000; Van Hoesen, Morecraft, & Vogt, 1993), insula/operculum (Mesulam & Mufson, 1982), hypothalamus (Rempel-Clower & Barbas, 1998), hippocampus (Cavada, Company, Tejedor, Cruz Rizzolo, & Reinoso Suarez, 2000), striatum (Eblen and Graybiel, 1995), periaqueductal grey (Rempel-Clower & Barbas, 1998), and dorsolateral prefrontal cortex (Barbas & Pandya, 1989; Carmichael & Price, 1995b).

Although the development of the OFC from infancy through adulthood has not been well characterized, measures of cortical thickness and neuronal density demonstrate that physical development of the OFC is not complete until the third decade of life (Gogtay et al., 2004; Sowell et al., 2004). One study of changes in cortical thickness demonstrated that the majority of regions of the OFC follow a nonlinear pattern of development across childhood and adolescence (Shaw et al., 2009). The anterior and lateral OFCs were found to have a cubic trajectory, whereas the medial and posterior OFC had simpler quadratic and linear trajectories. Such findings underscore the complex and heterochronous maturation of the human OFC. Understanding the structural development of the OFC is also complicated by the considerable cytoarchitectonic variability in the region across individuals (Chiavaras & Petrides, 2000, 2001).

FUNCTIONAL NEUROANATOMY OF THE HUMAN OFC

In terms of its neuroanatomical connectivity, the OFC is uniquely placed to integrate sensory and visceral motor information to modulate ongoing behavior. This has led to the proposal that the OFC is an important part of networks involved in emotional and hedonic processing (Nauta, 1971; Rolls, 1999).

The OFC has direct connections to the basolateral amygdala, and these two brain areas probably have an important role in goal-directed behavior (Rolls, 1999). The OFC is a comparatively large brain area in humans and nonhuman primates and is heterogeneous in terms of its connectivity and morphological features, so its constituent parts are likely to have different functional roles. One proposal based on neuroanatomical and neurophysiological evidence from nonhuman primates is that the OFC should be viewed as part of a functional network known as the orbital and medial prefrontal cortex (OMPFC; Öngür & Price, 2000).

This network includes both the OFC and parts of the anterior cingulate cortex, and it has distinct connections to other parts of the brain. The *orbital* network includes areas 11, 13, and 47/12 of the OFC; receives input from all the sensory modalities, including visceral afferent; and is proposed to be important for the regulation of food intake. The *medial* network (which includes medial areas 11, 13, 14, and lateral area 47/12s of the OFC as well as areas 25, 32, and 10 on the medial wall) has extensive visceromotor outputs. The two networks might therefore serve as a crucial sensory-visceromotor link for consummatory behaviors. It should be noted that the definition of the medial network partly overlaps with the *ventromedial prefrontal cortex* as used by Bechara, Damasio, Damasio, and Anderson (1994), but the latter does not include lateral regions of the OFC.

Another proposal extends the OMPFC network based on evidence from human neuroimaging and neuropsychology studies. This proposal suggests that there are medial-lateral and posterior-anterior distinctions within the human OFC (Kringelbach & Rolls, 2004). A large meta-analysis of the existing neuroimaging data showed that activity in the medial OFC is related to the monitoring, learning, and memory of the reward value of positive reinforcers, whereas lateral OFC activity is related to the evaluation of negative reinforcers, which can lead to a change in ongoing behavior. There was also a posterior-anterior distinction, with more complex or abstract reinforcers (such as monetary gain and loss) represented more anteriorly in the OFC than less complex reinforcers (such as taste).

Other proposed functions of the OFC include a role for the lateral parts in response inhibition (Elliott, Dolan, & Frith, 2000). This proposal is based on the observation that humans and nonhuman primates with lesions to the OFC will perseverate in choosing a previously but no-longer rewarded stimulus in object-reversal learning tasks (Dias, Robbins, & Roberts, 1996; Rolls, Hornak, Wade, & McGrath, 1994). There is now strong evidence that this inhibition cannot be a simple form of response inhibition. OFC lesion studies in monkeys have shown that errors on reversal-learning tasks might not be caused by perseverative responses but can be caused by failure to learn to respond to the currently rewarded stimulus (Iversen & Mishkin, 1970). Similarly, simple response inhibition cannot account for the severe impairment on the reversal part of an object-reversal learning task shown by patients with discrete bilateral surgical lesions to the lateral OFC (Hornak et al., 2004). It is possible that the OFC has a role in more complex behavioral changes that could be interpreted as being inhibitory to behavior, and that this behavior arises in conjunction with activity in other brain structures such as the anterior cingulate cortex, as discussed later.

Less is known about the functional development of the OFC region for a number of reasons. First, there are considerable individual differences in the physical development of this region and also differences in trajectories of maturation in different parts of this region within the same individual. Second, studies to date assessing functional activity of this region have used a variety of different experimental paradigms. For example, in prior studies, rewards were dependent upon participants' task performance and the requirements for obtaining rewards varied. Rewards could depend on reaction times (Bjork et al., 2004) or on response accuracy/probability matching (Eshel, Nelson, Blair, Pine, & Ernst, 2007; Galvan et al., 2006; van Leijenhorst, Crone, & Bunge, 2006). In addition, reward magnitude (Galvan et al., 2006), reward probability (May et al., 2004; van Leijenhorst et al., 2006), or both magnitude and probability (Eshel et al., 2007) have been manipulated. It therefore remains difficult to relate developmental differences in OFC activity to reward processing more generally.

However, there do appear to be reasonably robust differences in reward-related orbitofrontal activity from childhood and adolescence into adulthood. In one study, OFC activity in adolescents (13–17 years) more closely resembled that of children (7–11 years) than adults (23–29 years), with less focal patterns of activity in response to monetary rewards (Galvan et al., 2006). In another study, increased activity in left lateral OFC following the omission of monetary rewards was found only in the group of young adults, and not in the early and middle adolescent groups (van Leijenhorst et al., 2011). A further study reported that adolescents exhibited less activity in the OFC than adults when making risky economic choices

(Eshel et al., 2007). Taken together, these findings suggest that the OFC has a relatively protracted time-course of functional development.

The majority of cortical regions undergo a rise and fall in synaptic density, with density becoming stable at adult levels at different points during later childhood and adolescence (Bourgeois, 2005; Goldman-Rakic, Bourgeois, & Rakic, 1997; Huttenlocher, 1990). The rise and fall developmental sequence is also evidenced by other measures of brain physiology and anatomy. Findings from nonhuman primates and humans suggest protracted development of the prefrontal cortex relative to subcortical regions (Giedd et al., 1999; Huttenlocher & Dabholkar, 1997; Sowell et al., 2004).

The precise functions and underlying mechanisms of the various parts of the OFC have yet to be described. Here, new evidence from neuroimaging and neuropsychology studies is considered in order to illuminate the functions of the OFC in sensory integration, reward processing, decision making, reward prediction, and subjective hedonic processing. It is important to remember that studies using fMRI are prone to signal dropout, geometric distortion, and susceptibility artifacts in the OFC due to its close proximity to the air-filled sinuses (Deichmann, Josephs, Hutton, Corfield, & Turner, 2002; Wilson et al., 2002), so negative findings should be treated with caution.

SENSORY PLEASURES

Neurophysiological recordings have found that the nonhuman primate OFC receives input from all of the five senses (Rolls, 1999), and neuroimaging has confirmed that the human OFC is activated by auditory (Frey, Kostopoulos, & Petrides, 2000), gustatory (Small et al., 1999), olfactory (Zatorre, Jones-Gotman, Evans, & Meyer, 1992), somatosensory (Rolls et al., 2003b), and visual (Aharon et al., 2001) inputs. This cortical region also receives information from the visceral sensory system (Critchley, Mathias, & Dolan, 2002), and even abstract reinforcers such as money can activate the human OFC (O'Doherty, Kringelbach, Rolls, Hornak, & Andrews, 2001; Thut et al., 1997).

There is good evidence that the primary sensory cortices are the first to mature in the infant brain, helping the infant to process and filter sensory cues, particularly those relating to the caregiver. Within the first few days and weeks of life, infants demonstrate clear preferences for their caregiver above other individuals. They preferentially orient to view the mother's face rather than the face of an unknown woman (Bushnell, 2001), show preference for the mother's voice (DeCasper & Fifer, 1980) and even preference for the smell of the mother's breast milk (Macfarlane, 1975). Activity across a wide range of cortical areas including occipital, olfactory, and temporal cortices of the newborn brain has been demonstrated in response to basic sensory stimuli using near-infrared spectroscopy (NIRS; e.g., Bartocci et al., 2000; Hoshi et al., 2000; Kotilahti et al., 2005; Pena et al., 2003; Taga, Asakawa, Maki, Konishi, & Koizumi, 2003). Activity in frontal regions in response to more complex social stimuli, such as speech sounds, has also been reported (Gervain, Macagno, Cogoi, Pena & Mehler, 2008; Saito et al., 2007a, 2007b; Sakatani, Chen, Lichty, Zuo, & Wang, 1999).

Sensory inputs enter the OFC mostly through its posterior parts (see the next section). Here they are available for multisensory integration (De Araujo et al., 2003c; Kringelbach & Rolls, 2003; Small, Jones-Gotman, Zatorre, Petrides, & Evans, 1997) and subsequent encoding of the reward value of the stimulus. One approach to demonstrate the encoding of the reward value of a stimulus is by a manipulation called selective or sensory-specific satiety (Rolls, Rolls, Rowe, & Sweeney, 1981), which is a form of reinforcer devaluation. This approach has been used in neuroimaging experiments on hungry human participants who were scanned while being presented with two food-related stimuli. Participants were then fed to satiety on one of the corresponding food stimuli, which led to a selective decrease in reward value of the food eaten, and scanned again in their satiated state using exactly the same procedure.

Neuroimaging experiments using olfactory (O'Doherty et al., 2000) and whole-food (Kringelbach et al., 2000, 2003) stimuli have shown that the activity in more anterior parts of the OFC tracks the changes in reward value of the two stimuli, such that the activity selectively decreases for the food eaten but not for the other food. This is compatible with studies in nonhuman primates where monkeys with lesions to the OFC respond normally to associations between food and conditioners but fail to modify their behavior to the cues when the incentive value of the food was reduced (Butter, Mishkin, & Rosvold, 1963), and where lesions to the OFC alter food preferences in monkeys (Baylis & Gaffan, 1991). Similarly, unilateral crossed lesions between the OFC and the basolateral part of the amygdala in monkeys disrupts devaluation effects in a procedure in which the incentive value of a food was reduced by satiation on that specific food (Baxter, Parker, Lindner, Izquierdo, & Murray, 2000).

A malfunction of these satiation mechanisms could explain the profound changes in eating habits (escalating desire for sweet food coupled with reduced satiety) that are often followed by substantial weight gain in patients with frontotemporal dementia. Frontotemporal dementia is a progressive neurodegenerative disorder associated with major and pervasive behavioral changes in personality and social conduct resembling those produced by orbitofrontal lesions (Rahman, Sahakian, Hodges, Rogers, & Robbins, 1999); although it should be noted that more focal lesions to the OFC have not been associated with obesity to date.

SOCIAL PLEASURES: FACE PROCESSING

Humans are intensely social, and experiments have shown time and again that our preferred route to pleasure, and perhaps even happiness, is through social relationships with other people (Layard, 2005). The complexity inherent in human social relationships means that we are only beginning to describe the underlying brain processes (Adolphs, 2003). In humans and other primates, faces and facial expressions act as important social cues to regulate behavior (Darwin, 1872; Ekman & Friesen, 1971). In adults, the fusiform gyrus and superior temporal sulcus subserve face processing (Allison, Puce, & McCarthy, 2000; Chao, Martin, & Haxby, 1999; de Haan, Humphreys, & Johnson, 2002a; de Haan, Pascalis, & Johnson, 2002b). In young infants, there is evidence to suggest that face processing is guided by both subcortical (De Schonen & Mathivet, 1989; Johnson, 2005; Morton & Johnson, 1991) and cortical regions (Grossmann & Johnson, 2007; Tzourio-Mazoyer et al., 2002). There is good evidence for cortical involvement in face processing in infants aged between 6 and 9 months from a NIRS study demonstrating increased activity in the right frontotemporal cortex in response to a mother's face, but not to an unknown face (Carlsson, Lagercrantz, Olson, Printz, & Bartocci, 2008). At this age, infants demonstrate strong preferences for familiar caregivers, as evidenced by infant anxiety when separated from a caregiver or when approached by a stranger. A related ERP finding in infants is an increased negative central (Nc) component in response to the mother's face compared to a stranger's face (de Haan & Nelson, 1997, 1999), which may also be associated with the increased salience of the primary caregiver around this age.

It is clear that infant faces serve an important role in the early interaction between parents and children. From early after the birth of a child, parents intuitively attempt to stay in the center of the infant's visual field at exactly the infant's focal distance, maintain eye contact, and mimic infant facial expressions (Papousek & Papousek, 1977, 1987). The scientific interest in infant faces started with Charles Darwin (1872) who pointed out that in order for infants to survive, adults need to respond to and nurture their young. Later, Lorenz (1971) proposed that it is the specific structure of the infant face that serves to elicit these parental responses, but the biological basis for this has remained elusive. Lorenz argued that infantile features serve as "innate releasing mechanisms" for affection and nurturing in adult humans and that most of these features are evident in the face, including a relatively large head, predominance of the brain capsule, large and low-lying eyes and bulging cheek region. Thus, it is argued that these "babyish" features increase the infant's chance of survival by evoking parental responses (Bowlby, 1957; Bowlby, 1969), and the parents' ability to respond is important for the survival of their infant (Darwin, 1872).

Both infant and adult faces elicit activity in the primary and dedicated higher visual areas such as the fusiform face area, but infant faces also appear to elicit activity in additional brain areas. One of the most consistent findings across neuroimaging studies is increased activity in the OFC in response to images of infants compared with a variety of control stimuli

(Bartels & Zeki, 2004; Nitschke et al., 2004; Noriuchi, Kikuchi, & Senoo, 2008; Ranote et al., 2004b). It has been found that there is stronger activity in response to one's own children compared to other infants in striate and extrastriate visual areas and in reward-related areas such as the nucleus accumbens, anterior cingulate, and amygdala (Ranote et al., 2004a; Swain, Lorberbaum, Kose, & Strathearn, 2007). Increased activity in the OFC has also been found to correlate with mothers' self-reported increases in positive mood when viewing a picture of their own infant, compared with an unfamiliar infant using both fMRI (Nitschke et al., 2004) and NIRS (Minagawa-Kawai et al., 2009).

Although these studies have substantially increased our general knowledge of parental neural responses to children's faces, a substantial test of Lorenz's theory of the specificity of infant faces requires a direct comparison between adult faces and infant faces from the first year of life, preferably where the faces are unfamiliar and by using neuroimaging techniques that permit the temporal progression of brain activity to be studied. We used magnetoencephalography (MEG) to investigate the temporal and spatial distribution of the underlying neural systems for these facial responses in 12 adult human participants (Kringelbach et al., 2008). Consistent with previous findings, we found that processing of both adult and infant faces elicits a wave of activity starting in the striate cortices and spreading along ventral and dorsal pathways (Blair, 2003). In addition, however, we found that at around 130 ms after presentation of the infant faces, activity occurred in the medial OFC, identifying for the first time a neural basis for this vital evolutionary process (see Figure 3.3). This was not evident in response to the adult faces. Because the infant and adult faces used in this study were carefully matched by an independent panel of participants for emotional valence, arousal, and attractiveness, the findings provide evidence that it is the distinct features of the infant faces compared to adult faces that are important, rather than evaluative subjective processing such as attractiveness or emotional valence.

These specific responses to unfamiliar infant faces occur so fast that they are almost certainly quicker than anything under conscious control. The findings suggest a temporally earlier role than previously thought for the medial OFC in guiding affective reactions, which may even be preconscious. The medial OFC may thus provide the necessary attentional and perhaps hedonic tagging of infant faces that predisposes humans to treat infant faces as special, and to elicit caregiving behavior, as suggested by Lorenz (1971). It would be of considerable interest to investigate the brain responses to infants of other species to see whether a similar effect is present. Overall, these neuroimaging studies demonstrate that faces are important stimuli to help understand how social pleasures might govern behavior. In particular, they show that the sensory and social pleasures share a similar network of interacting brain regions.

Decision Making and Prediction

In making decisions, the predicted reward value of various behaviors must be compared and evaluated. This processing can be complex because reward estimations will vary in quality depending on the sampling rate of the behavior and the variance of reward distributions. For example, it is hard to provide a reliable estimate of the reward value of a food that appears to be highly desirable and is high in nutritional value but is only rarely available and varies significantly in quality. This raises the classic problem in animal learning of how to optimize behavior such that the amount of exploration is balanced with the amount of exploitation, where exploration is the time spent sampling the outcome of different behaviors and exploitation is the time spent using existing behaviors with known reward values. Food-related behaviors have to be precisely controlled because the decision to swallow toxins, microorganisms, or nonfood objects on the basis of erroneously determining the sensory properties of the food can be fatal. Humans and other animals have therefore developed elaborate food-related behaviors to balance conservative risk-minimizing and life-preserving strategies (exploitation) with occasional novelty seeking (exploration) in the hope of discovering new, valuable sources of nutrients (Rozin, 2001).

The orbitofrontal and anterior cingulate cortices were implicated in decision making by the early classic case of Phineas Gage, whose frontal lobes were penetrated by a metal rod

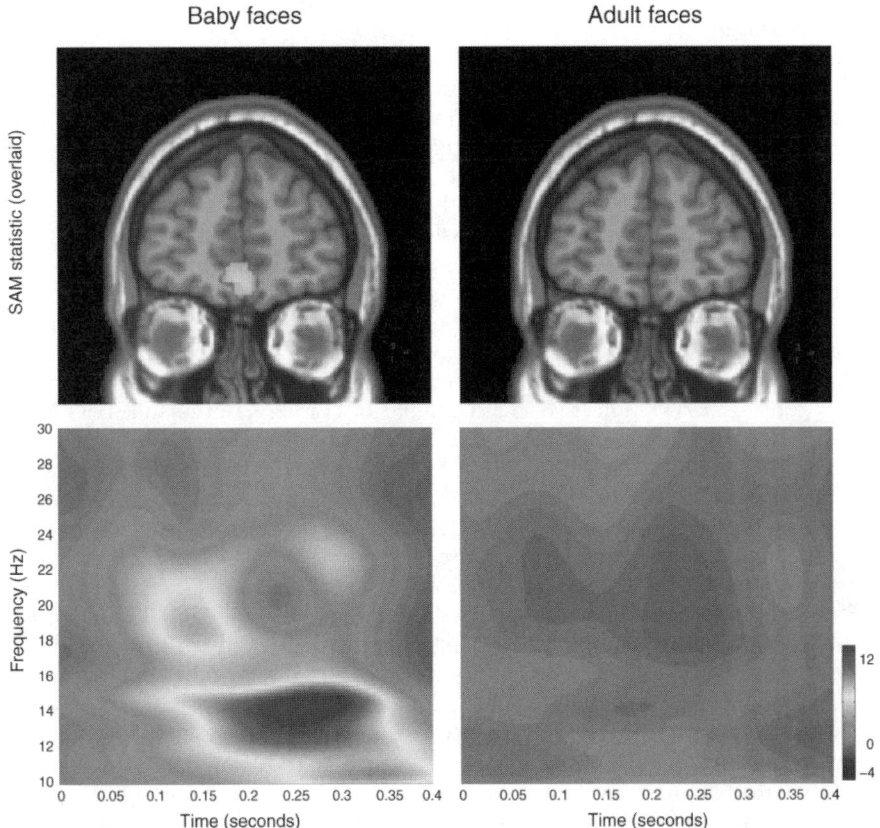

FIGURE 3.3 Infant faces elicit an early neural signature. (*See color insert.*) Top row: Significant activity was present from around 130 ms in the medial OFC when viewing infant faces but not when viewing adult faces. Bottom row: Time-frequency representations of the normalized evoked average group responses to baby and adult faces from the virtual electrodes show that the initial response to infant faces is present in the 12–20 Hz band from around 130 ms—and not present to adult faces (Kringelbach et al., 2008, reprinted with permission).

(Harlow, 1848). Gage survived, but his personality and emotional processing were changed completely (although the case should be viewed with caution because the available information is limited; Macmillan, 2000). In more recent cases of OFC damage, patients have often shown problems with decision making, a lack of affect, social inappropriateness, and irresponsibility (Anderson, Bechara, Damasio, Tranel, & Damasio, 1999; Blair & Cipolotti, 2000; Hornak et al., 2003; Rolls et al., 1994). Such patients are impaired in identifying social signals that are important for decision making, including, for example, facial and vocal expressions (Hornak et al., 2003; Hornak, Rolls, & Wade, 1996).

Reliable prediction underlies decision making (Schultz & Dickinson, 2000), and neuroimaging has been used to investigate the predicted reward value of various rewarding and punishing stimuli. Often this is done using classical conditioning paradigms, in which an arbitrary neutral stimulus is paired with a reward or punishment. After learning, the arbitrary stimulus takes on the predictive value of the specific reward of the unconditioned stimulus, but it can also code for various aspects of the sensory or general affective properties of the unconditioned stimulus. In an fMRI study using selective satiation, participants were presented with predictive cues associated with one of two food-related odors (Gottfried et al., 2003). By comparing the brain activity in response to the cues before and after devaluation (by feeding to satiety) of the associated food, it was found that relative changes in the specific predictive reward value of the odors were tracked in neural responses in the OFC, amygdala, and ventral striatum.

When the specific predictive reward values of different behaviors are in place, comparison and evaluation mechanisms must choose between them to optimize behavior. Bechara and colleagues developed a gambling task in which participants were asked to select cards from four decks and maximize their winnings (Bechara et al., 1994). After each selection of a card, facsimile money is lost or won. Two of the four packs produce large payouts with larger penalties (and can thus be considered high risk), whereas the other two packs produce small payouts but smaller penalties (low risk). The most profitable strategy is therefore to select cards from the two low risk decks; this strategy is adopted by normal control participants. During the task, electrodermal activity (skin conductance responses [SCR]) of the participant is measured as an index of visceral sensory arousal. Patients with damage to the ventromedial prefrontal cortex (including parts of the medial OFC) but not the dorsolateral prefrontal cortex persistently draw cards from the high risk packs and lack anticipatory SCRs while they consider risky choices (Bechara, Damasio, Tranel, & Anderson, 1998; but see also a recent critique of this experiment, Maia & McLelland, 2004).

Another informative decision-making task, the visual discrimination reversal task, requires participants to associate an arbitrary stimulus with monetary wins or losses, and then rapidly reverse these associations when the reinforcement contingencies are altered. Probabilistic reward and punishment schedules are used such that selecting either the currently rewarded stimulus or the unrewarded stimulus can lead to a monetary gain or loss, but only consistent selection of the currently rewarded stimulus results in overall monetary gain. An fMRI study of this task in healthy participants found a dissociation of activity in the medial and lateral parts of the OFC: Activity in the medial OFC correlated with how much money was won on single trials, and activity of the lateral OFC correlated with how much money was lost on single trials (O'Doherty et al., 2001). Another PET study also found that predominantly lateral parts of the OFC were significantly activated during decision making (Rogers et al., 1999). Other studies have since confirmed the role of the medial OFC in monitoring and learning about the reward value of stimuli that have no immediate behavioral consequences (see Figure 3.4). Neuroimaging experiments have found activity in the medial OFC that monitors the affective properties of olfaction (Anderson et al., 2003; Rolls et al., 2003a), gustation (Small et al., 2003), somatosensory (Rolls et al., 2003b), and multimodal (De Araujo et al., 2003c) stimuli. A PET study has found that the medial OFC monitors outcomes even when no reward is at stake (Schnider, Treyer, & Buck, 2005).

In contrast, the lateral OFC is often coactive with the anterior cingulate cortex when participants evaluate punishers, which, when detected, can lead to a change in behavior. A related PET study investigating analgesia and placebo found that the lateral orbitofrontal and anterior cingulate cortices were coactive in participants who responded to the placebo, suggesting that the pain relief effect of the placebo might be related to the co-activation of these two brain areas (Petrovic & Ingvar, 2002; Petrovic, Kalso, Petersson, & Ingvar, 2002). A neuroimaging study found evidence that the lateral OFC is related to changing behavior, in this case when there were unexpected breaches in expectation in a visual attention task (Nobre, Coull, Frith, & Mesulam, 1999).

A direct investigation of the role of the lateral OFC was carried out using a face reversal-learning task, addressing the problem inherent in the monetary reversal-learning task (mentioned previously; O'Doherty et al., 2001). The probabilistic nature of monetary task meant that the magnitude of negative reinforcers (money loss) was slightly confounded by the reversal event per se. This new face reversal-learning study showed that the lateral OFC and a region of the anterior cingulate cortex are together responsible for supporting general reversal learning in the human brain (Kringelbach, 2004b; Kringelbach & Rolls, 2003). This is consistent with the finding that passively presenting angry facial expressions—a signal that ongoing social behavior should be changed—results in activity in the orbitofrontal and anterior cingulate cortices (Blair et al., 1999). Further strong, causal evidence has come from a similar reversal-learning experiment in patients with discrete, surgical lesions to the OFC. Patients who had bilateral lesions to the lateral OFC—but not unilateral lesions to medial parts of the OFC—showed significant impairments in reversal learning (Hornak et al., 2004). A recent

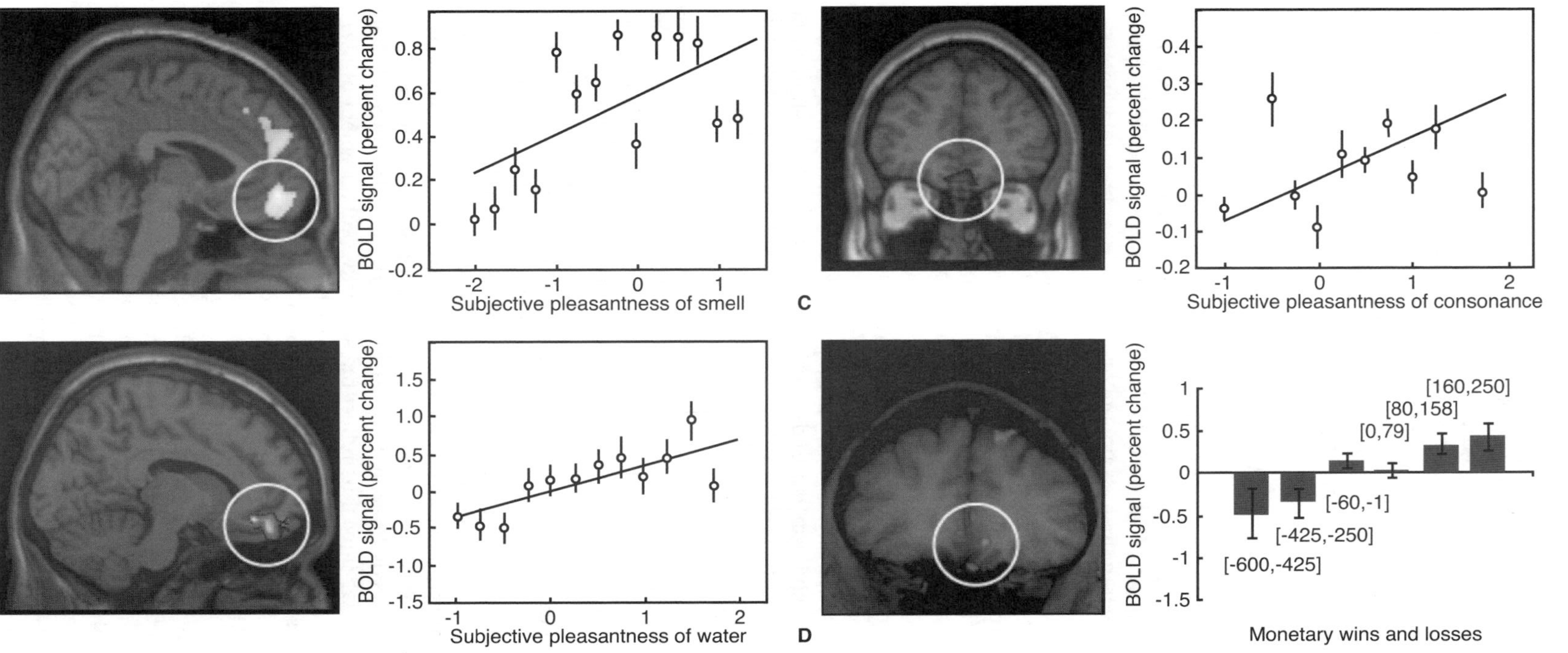

FIGURE 3.4 Valence coding in medial orbitofrontal cortex (OFC). (*See color insert.*) **(A)** The activity in medial OFC correlates with the subjective ratings of pleasantness in an experiment with three pleasant and three unpleasant odors (Rolls et al., 2003a, reprinted with permission from Blackwell Publishing Ltd.). **(B)** Similarly, the activity in medial OFC was also correlated with the subjective pleasantness ratings of water in a thirst experiment (De Araujo et al., 2003b, reprinted with permission from The American Physiological Society). A correlation in a very similar part of medial OFC was found with the pleasantness of other pure tastants used in the experiment (not shown). **(C)** This corresponded to the findings in an experiment investigating taste and smell convergence and consonance, which found that activity in the medial OFC was correlated to subjective consonance ratings (De Araujo et al., 2003c, reprinted with permission from Blackwell Publishing Ltd.). **(D)** Even higher-order rewards such as monetary reward was found to correlate with activity in the medial OFC (O'Doherty et al., 2001, reprinted with permission from Macmillan Publishers Ltd.).

fMRI study investigated the interaction between internal decision making and external performance monitoring (Walton, Devlin, & Rushworth, 2004). The OFC was more active during outcome monitoring for the externally instructed condition than in the internally generated volition condition. In contrast, the anterior cingulate cortex was more active when the selected response was internally generated than when it was externally instructed by the experimenter.

In summary, decision making, performance, and outcome monitoring require complex processing that relies strongly on frontal cortical areas and in particular on interactions between the orbitofrontal and anterior cingulate cortices.

SUBJECTIVE PLEASANTNESS

Using food as stimuli in neuroimaging has proved to be a fruitful avenue for studying sensory hedonic experience, perhaps unsurprisingly given that the essential energy to sustain life is obtained from food intake, as is much of the pleasure of life (especially on an empty stomach; Kringelbach, 2004a). Food intake in humans is not only regulated by homeostatic processes, as illustrated by our easy overindulgence on sweet foods and by rising obesity levels, but relies on the interactions between homeostatic regulation and hedonic experience (Saper et al., 2002). This complex subcortical and cortical processing involves higher-order processes such as learning, memory, planning, and prediction and gives rise to conscious experience of not only the sensory properties of the food (such as the identity, intensity, temperature, fat content, and viscosity) but also the valence elicited by the food (including, most importantly, the hedonic experience).

In humans and higher primates, the OFC receives multimodal information about the sensory properties of food and is therefore a candidate region for representing the incentive salience, the hedonic impact, and the subjective hedonic experience of food. A sensory-specific satiety neuroimaging study of activity in the mid-anterior region of the OFC showed not only a sensory-specific decrease in the reward value of the whole food eaten to satiety (and *not* of the whole food not eaten), but also a correlation between brain activity and pleasantness ratings (see Figure 3.5A; Kringelbach et al., 2003).

This indicates that the reward value of the taste, olfactory, and somatosensory components of whole food are represented in the OFC, and that the subjective pleasantness of food might also be represented there. A related fMRI study found that activity in adjacent mid-anterior parts of the OFC differentially decreased in a selective satiation paradigm. Activity decreased in response to an arbitrary visual cue that was linked to an odor that had been devalued by feeding participants to satiety on the associated food (Gottfried et al., 2003). Another recent PET study found that the extrinsic incentive value of foods was located in a similar part of the OFC (Hinton et al., 2004). Further evidence of neural correlates of subjective experience was found in an fMRI experiment investigating true taste synergism (De Araujo et al., 2003a). The results of this study showed that the strong subjective enhancement of *umami* taste was correlated with increased activity in a mid-anterior part of the OFC (see Figure 3.5B). The perceived synergy is unlikely to be expressed in the taste receptors themselves and the activity in the OFC might thus reflect the subjective enhancement of *umami* taste. Similarly, a neuroimaging study showed that the synergistic enhancement of a matched taste and retronasal smell (where the multimodal combination was significantly more pleasant than the sum of the unimodal stimuli) correlated with activity in a mid-anterior region of the OFC (see Figure 3.5C; De Araujo et al., 2003a).

Other neuroimaging studies have directly correlated brain activity with the subjective ratings of the pleasantness and intensity of different positive and negative reinforcers, but crucially without devaluing or otherwise manipulating the reinforcers to change their valence during the course of the experiment. The results of these correlations are therefore perhaps better thought of in terms of the monitoring processing in the OFC. Consistent with this suggestion, correlations with pleasantness have been found almost exclusively in the medial OFC. Pleasantness but not intensity ratings were correlated with activity in the medial orbitofrontal and anterior cingulate cortices for taste (De Araujo et al., 2003b), odor (Anderson et al., 2003; Rolls et al., 2003b), stimulus fat content (independent of viscosity; De Araujo &

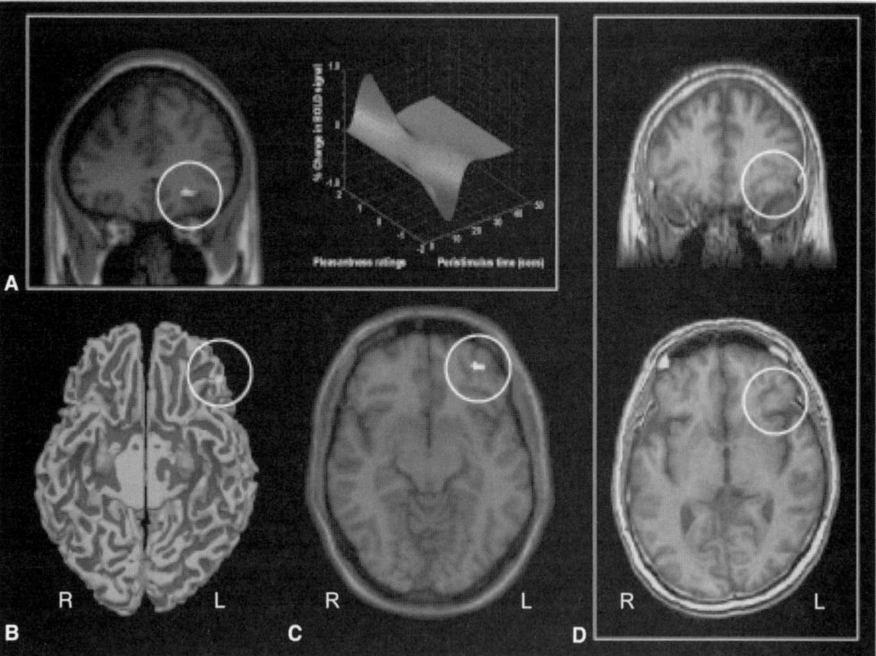

FIGURE 3.5 Hedonic experience. (*See color insert.*) **(A)** A neuroimaging study using selective satiation found that mid-anterior parts of the orbitofrontal cortex (OFC) are correlated with the subjects' subjective pleasantness ratings of the foods throughout the experiment (Kringelbach et al., 2003, part A reprinted with permission from Oxford University Press). On the right is shown a plot of the magnitude of the fitted hemodynamic response from a representative single subject against the subjective pleasantness ratings (on a scale from −2 to +2) and peri-stimulus time in seconds. **(B)** Additional evidence for the role of the OFC in subjective experience comes from another neuroimaging experiment investigating the supra-additive effects of combining the umami tastants monosodium glutamate and inosine monophosphate (De Araujo et al., 2003a, part B reprinted with permission from The American Physiological Society). The figure shows the region of mid-anterior OFC showing synergistic effects (rendered on the ventral surface of human cortical areas with the cerebellum removed). The perceived synergy is unlikely to be expressed in the taste receptors themselves and the activity in the OFC may thus reflect the subjective enhancement of umami taste, which must be closely linked to subjective experience. **(C)** Adding strawberry odor to a sucrose taste solution makes the combination significantly more pleasant than the sum of each of the individual components. The supra-linear effects reflecting the subjective enhancement were found to significantly correlate with the activity in a lateral region of the left anterior OFC, which is remarkably similar to that found in the other experiments (De Araujo et al., 2003c, part C reprinted with permission from Blackwell Publishing Ltd.). **(D)** These findings were strengthened by findings using deep brain stimulation (DBS) and magnetoencephalography (MEG; Kringelbach et al., 2007a, part D reprinted with permission from Wolters Kluwer). Pleasurable subjective pain relief for chronic pain in a phantom limb in a patient was causally induced by effective deep brain stimulation in the PVG/PAG part of the brainstem. When using MEG to directly measure the concomitant changes in the rest of the brain, a significant change in power was found in the mid-anterior OFC.

Rolls, 2004), and chocolate (Small et al., 2001). In addition, a study of thermal stimulation showed that the perceived thermal intensity was correlated with activity in the insula and OFCs, (Craig, Chen, Bandy, & Reiman, 2000). A correlation was also recently found between a reliable index of the rush of intravenous methamphetamine in drug-naïve participants and activity in the medial OFC (Völlm et al., 2004). Furthermore, activity in the OFC correlates with the negative dissonance (pleasantness) of musical chords (Blood, Zatorre, Bermudez, &

Evans, 1999), and intensely pleasurable responses, or chills, that can be elicited by music are correlated with activity in the OFC, ventral striatum, cingulate, and insula cortex (Blood & Zatorre, 2001).

Further evidence for the representation of the reward value of more abstract reinforcers comes from neuroimaging studies of, for example, social judgments (Farrow et al., 2001) and music (Blood et al., 1999). Supporting evidence for the interpretation that the medial OFC implements monitoring processing of the incentive salience comes from the study of patients with ventromedial prefrontal cortex damage, shown to have relatively intact skin conduction responses when receiving monetary rewards and punishments (Bechara et al., 1994). This monitoring process is distinct from activity in mid-anterior parts of the OFC, which was found to correlate directly with the subjective hedonic impact. It would thus appear that dissociable regions of the human OFC represent both the wanting and the liking aspect of reward. These exciting findings from neuroimaging extend previous findings in nonhuman primates of reinforcer representations to representations of the *subjective affective value* of these reinforcers. Although such findings provide windows into the understanding of subjective experience of pleasure, it is unlikely that hedonic processing depends on only one cortical region. Even so, it would be interesting to obtain more evidence on this issue by investigating patients with selective lesions to these areas to investigate whether their subjective affective experiences have changed. Some evidence has already been obtained to suggest that this is the case (Hornak et al., 2003). The field awaits the development of innovative neuroimaging paradigms to investigate how subjective hedonic experience develops throughout childhood and adolescence.

DEEP BRAIN PLEASURES

In the absence of sensory and social stimuli, positive hedonic experience can be elicited by direct stimulation of the brain (Kringelbach, Jenkinson, Owen, & Aziz, 2007b). Deep brain stimulation (DBS) has shown remarkable therapeutic benefits for patients with otherwise treatment-resistant movement disorders and chronic pain. Such disorders clearly have a substantial affective component, and are often accompanied by anhedonia, or an inability to experience pleasure. What is particularly exciting about DBS is that it offers the potential for *causally* changing brain activity and thus can potentially inform us about the fundamental mechanisms of the brain (Kringelbach et al., 2007b). This is particularly true when combined with a noninvasive whole-brain neuroimaging technique such as MEG (Kringelbach et al., 2007a). In some select patients, chronic pain can be significantly changed over a short period of time with DBS. This subjective change can be measured with MEG when changing DBS from effective to noneffective settings, while acquiring repeated subjective measurements on a visual scale. This can then be used in the data analysis to reveal the brain regions that mediate the change in subjective hedonic experience.

Current DBS targets for pain are in the brainstem (periventricular gray [PVG] and periaqueductal gray [PAG]) and thalamus (Nandi, Liu, Joint, Stein, & Aziz, 2002). Targets for Parkinson's disease (PD) are in the subthalamic nucleus (STN; Bittar et al., 2005a), internal segment of the globus pallidus (GPi; Bittar et al., 2005a; Krack et al., 2003), and pedunculopontine nucleus in the brain stem (Jenkinson, Nandi, Aziz, & Stein, 2005; Mazzone et al., 2005; Plaha & Gill, 2005). The current target for cluster headache is in the hypothalamus (Leone, Franzini, Broggi, May, & Bussone, 2004). Some promising targets for depression have been found in the inferior thalamic peduncle (Andy & Jurko, 1987), the nucleus accumbens (Schlaepfer et al., 2007), and the subgenual cingulate cortex (Mayberg et al., 2005). Programmable stimulators are implanted subcutaneously and thousands of patients have been restored to near-normal lives (Perlmutter & Mink, 2006).

Substantial mood changes linked to changes in reward and hedonic processing, such as unipolar depression, are found in up to 40% of PD patients, often starting before the onset of PD symptoms (Cummings, 1992). This is perhaps not surprising given the important role of the basal ganglia not only in movement but also in affect. The technique of stereotactic DBS thus has wide-reaching therapeutic applications clinically and in the neurosciences generally.

Patients with chronic pain who have DBS of the PVG/PAG report experiencing much less pain (Bittar et al., 2005a; Bittar et al., 2005b). The PVG/PAG receives noxious input from ascending spinothalamic pathways and descending regulatory input from higher brain structures such as the OFC. Electrical stimulation of the PAG induces stimulation-produced analgesia in animals and humans (Boivie & Meyerson, 1982; Reynolds, 1969). This effect is ascribed to a release of endogenous opioids because the effects are reversible with the administration of the opioid antagonist naloxone (Akil, Mayer, & Liebeskind, 1976; Hosobuchi, Adams, & Linchitz, 1977), and also to the activation of descending inhibitory systems that depress spinal noxious transmission (Fields & Basbaum, 1999).

We were the first group to use MEG to directly measure changes in whole-brain activity elicited by DBS. When DBS was turned off, the participant reported significant increases in subjective pain. During pain relief, we found corresponding significant changes in brain activity in a network that comprises the regions of the hedonic brain and includes the mid-anterior orbitofrontal and subgenual cingulate cortices (see Figure 3.5D; Kringelbach et al., 2007a). We found similar changes in brain activity in a patient with depression and in a patient with intractable cluster headache (Ray et al., 2007). This finding is strong evidence linking the OFC to pain relief. These findings raise some pertinent questions about the nature of DBS. Although stimulation of the PVG/PAG brings about pain relief, which is clearly pleasurable, it is not clear if this would also be the case in humans without chronic pain. It is well known that, although low-frequency stimulation has the opposite effect and actually makes the pain worse (Kringelbach et al., 2007a). Anecdotally, after successful surgery some of the DBS patients report that the pain remains, but is less salient to them (Aziz, personal communication). A PET study investigating analgesia and placebo found that the opioid-rich brain structures, lateral orbitofrontal, and anterior cingulate cortices are coactive in placebo responders, suggesting that the pain relief effect of the placebo might be related to co-activity in these two brain areas (Petrovic & Ingvar, 2002; Petrovic et al., 2002). It is also potentially of interest to note that lesions to an output structure of the OFC, the ventral pallidum (Öngür & Price, 2000), can lead to anhedonia (Miller et al., 2006). Similar evidence of anhedonia linked to lesions of some parts of the pallidum was also found in a large case series of 117 patients undergoing pallidotomies for movement disorders (Aziz, personal communication). This is of particular importance because lesions of the posterior ventral pallidum in rats abolish and replace liking reactions to sweetness with bitter-type disliking instead (e.g., gapes; Cromwell & Berridge, 1993).

Similarly, DBS of the nucleus accumbens, which is another output structure of the OFC, can alleviate anhedonia in patients with treatment-resistant depression (Schlaepfer et al., 2007). These results are not surprising given the animal literature on lesions and brain stimulation effects, where studies of rodents have indicated that pleasure (liking) reactions are generated by a network of hedonic hotspots distributed across the brain (Peciña & Berridge, 2005). Hotspot sites include cubic-millimeter localizations in nucleus accumbens, ventral pallidum, and possibly other forebrain and limbic cortical sites, and also deep brainstem sites, including the parabrachial nucleus in the pons (Peciña et al., 2006). Each hotspot is capable of supporting opioid-mediated, endocannabinoid-mediated, or other neurochemical enhancements of liking reactions to a sensory pleasure such as sweetness (Smith & Berridge, 2005). Only one hedonic hotspot so far appears to be necessary for normal pleasure, in the sense that damage to it abolishes and replaces liking reactions to sweetness with bitter-type disliking instead (e.g., gapes). This essential hotspot appears to be in the posterior ventral pallidum and perhaps adjacent areas in substantia innominata, extended amygdala, and lateral hypothalamus (Cromwell & Berridge, 1993).

These findings open up a number of interesting avenues for human research. It would be of considerable interest to investigate the effects of DBS on the mid-anterior OFC as well as on the ventral pallidum. But does DBS actually produce pleasure? It could plausibly be argued that DBS may help to modulate otherwise malignant oscillatory activity in the brain, based on current understanding of the neural mechanisms of DBS (Kringelbach et al., 2007b). The evidence suggests that although DBS may help to restore the brain's normal equilibrium in pathological states, DBS might have little effect on pleasure experience in the longer term in the normal brain. It might be possible for DBS to perturb the brain's equilibrium in the normal state, but such perturbations are likely to be short-lived, similar to those induced by various drugs. For now, DBS remains a useful technique for alleviating the acute symptoms of anhedonia, in order that patients might again experience normal sensory and social pleasures.

A Developmental Perspective on Deep Brain Structures

A number of studies have used functional MRI to examine differences in brain activity across children, adolescents, and young adults during the experience of gains or losses of various rewards. The hedonic hotspot, the nucleus accumbens (or the ventral striatum), has been the focus of much of this work. A consistent pattern of age-related changes in activity has yet to emerge from functional studies of the region. Some studies have found heightened activity in this structure during reward-seeking tasks in adolescents compared with other age groups (Ernst et al., 2005; Galvan et al., 2006) but others have not (Bjork et al., 2004). Different experimental paradigms and heterogeneity in the participant age groups are likely to account for some of the variance in findings.

Another subcortical region heavily emphasized in developmental studies of reward and emotional processing is the amygdala. Much of the work on functional activity in this region has explored responsivity to facial expressions, in particular fear, but findings to date on age-related differences in activity have been inconsistent. One study found greater left amygdala activity in adults to fearful faces versus neutral faces, and the opposite pattern in children (Thomas et al., 2001). Another study found greater right amygdala activity in response to the same stimuli categories in both adults and children (Monk et al., 2003). A third study found greater amygdala activity in adolescents compared to both adults and children in response to emotional faces (both fearful and happy; Hare et al., 2008). More recently, a meta-analysis of 105 fMRI studies of emotional face processing found no age-related changes in amygdala activity (Fusar-Poli et al., 2009).

The anatomical development of these subcortical structures is somewhat clearer than the functional development. At birth, subcortical structures can be clearly defined and are similar to their adult forms. Compared to the extensive changes in gray matter in cortical areas that occurs during adolescence, the volumes of subcortical regions remain relatively stable (Sowell et al., 2004). The amygdala and nucleus accumbens do show anatomical changes during adolescence, but to a far lesser degree than prefrontal regions (Somerville et al., 2010). Taking into account differences in overall brain size, the amygdala is typically larger in males than in females, both in adulthood and throughout development (Caviness et al., 1996; Giedd et al., 1996; Lenroot & Giedd, 2010). In males, significant age-dependent increases in bilateral amygdala volume with age have been consistently reported (Giedd et al., 2006; Schumann et al., 2004). The relation of these changes in physical volume to functional neural activity remains unclear.

SUMMARY

The scientific study of emotion, motivation, pleasure, and hedonic processing has made substantial progress in recent years. In particular, progress has been made in establishing a number of the putative brain structures involved in emotion and pleasure, largely based on animal models, but also, to some extent, on human neuroimaging studies. Animal models primarily using rodents have convincingly shown that the hypothalamus, nucleus accumbens, ventral pallidum, and various brainstem nuclei such as the PAG are important for hedonic processing (Berridge, 1996; Peciña et al., 2006). Human neuroimaging research has implicated primarily the orbitofrontal and cingulate cortices as well as the amygdala and the insular cortices. The subcortical brain regions identified with animal models (such as the nucleus accumbens and the ventral pallidum) provide some of the necessary input and output systems for multimodal association regions, such as the OFC, that are involved in representing and learning about the reinforcers that elicit emotions and conscious feelings (Kringelbach, 2005). The developmental studies to date indicate a differential relative maturity of subcortical regions, including the nucleus accumbens and amygdala, as compared to frontal regions.

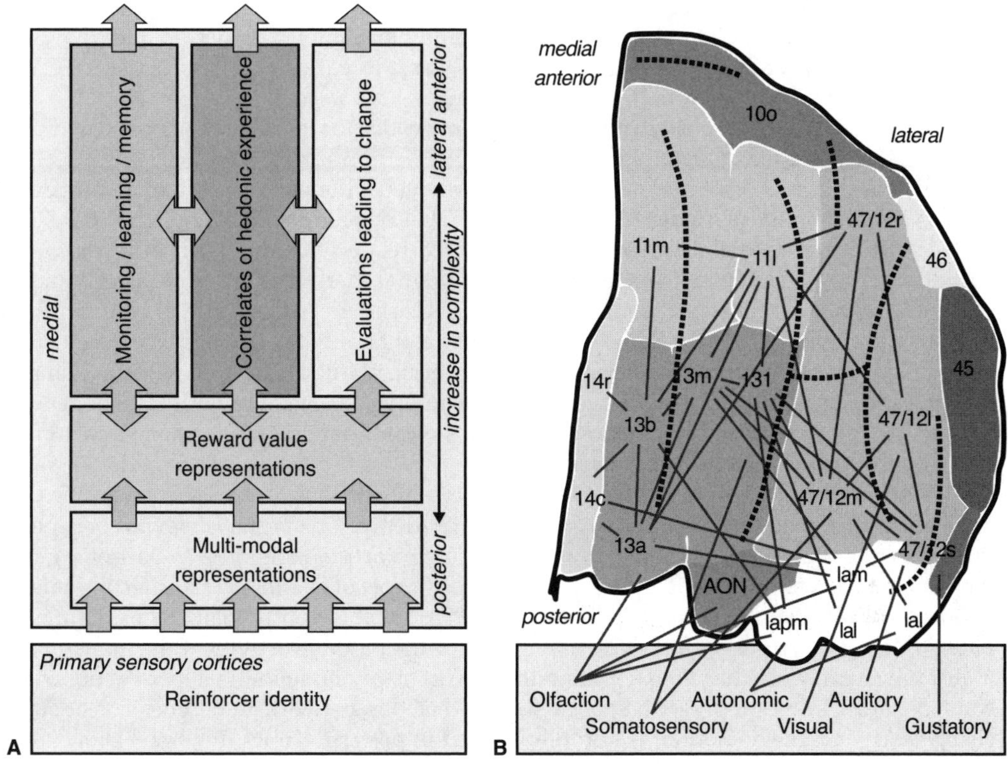

FIGURE 3.6 Model of the functions of the orbitofrontal cortex (OFC). (*See color insert.*) (Kringelbach, 2004a, reprinted with permission from Elsevier.)

The recent convergence of findings from neuroimaging, neuropsychology, neurophysiology, and neurosurgery has demonstrated that the human OFC is best thought of as an important nexus for sensory integration, emotional processing, and hedonic experience (see Figure 3.6). A model of the wide range of functions of the OFC might specify different functions for different regions. The posterior parts process sensory information for further multimodal integration, and the reward value of the reinforcer is assigned in more anterior parts of the OFC. From here, it can be modulated by hunger and other internal states, and can be used to influence subsequent behavior (in lateral parts of the anterior OFC with connections to the anterior cingulate cortex); stored for monitoring, learning, and memory (in medial parts of the anterior OFC); and made available for subjective hedonic experience (in mid-anterior OFC). At all times, there is important reciprocal information flowing between the various regions of the OFC and other brain regions subserving hedonic processing, including the anterior cingulate cortex, the amygdala, the nucleus accumbens, and the ventral pallidum. Lateralization does not appear to play a major role for the functions of the human OFC as shown by the largest meta-analysis of neuroimaging studies of this region (Kringelbach & Rolls, 2004).

The proposed model shows the interactions between sensory and hedonic systems in the OFC using as an example one hemisphere of the OFC (Kringelbach, 2004a). Information is flowing from bottom to top on the figure. Sensory information arrives from the periphery to the primary sensory cortices, where the stimulus identity is decoded into stable cortical representations. This information is then conveyed for further multimodal integration in brain structures in the posterior parts of the OFC. The reward value of the reinforcer is assigned in more anterior parts of the OFC, from where it can then be used to influence subsequent behavior (in lateral parts of the anterior OFC with connections to anterior cingulate cortex), stored for learning/memory (in medial parts of the anterior OFC), and made available for subjective hedonic experience (in mid-anterior OFC). The reward value and the subjective hedonic experience can be modulated by hunger and other internal states. In addition, there is important reciprocal information flowing between the various regions of the OFC and other brain regions involved in hedonic processing.

This model does not posit that medial OFC only codes for the valence of positive reinforcers and vice versa for the lateral parts. Instead, the neuroimaging evidence would seem to suggest that the valence of pleasures can be represented differently in different subparts of the OFC. The activity (as indexed by the blood level dependent [BOLD] signal measured with fMRI) in the medial OFC would appear to correlate with the valence of reinforcers such that positive reinforcers elicit a higher BOLD signal than negative reinforcers, which is consistent with a monitoring role for the medial OFC. The inverse appears to be true for the lateral parts of the OFC, but with the important caveat that only the lateral parts are generally concerned with those negative reinforcers that can bring about a change in behavior. Finally, the mid-anterior region of the OFC would appear to integrate valence with state-dependent mechanisms such as selective satiation and is thus a candidate region for taking part in the mediation of subjective hedonic experience.

The proposed link between the OFC and subjective hedonic processing places the OFC as an important gateway to subjective conscious experience. One possible way to conceptualize the role of the orbitofrontal and anterior cingulate cortices would be as part of a global workspace for access to consciousness, with the specific role of evaluating the affective valence of stimuli (Dehaene, Kerszberg, & Changeux, 1998). In this conceptualization, the medial parts of the OFC are part of a proposed network for the baseline activity of the human brain at rest (Gusnard & Raichle, 2001), placing the OFC as a key node in the network subserving consciousness. Interestingly, it has been shown that this network undergoes considerable change early in development. It is not fully formed in preterm babies (Fransson et al., 2007), or even at birth (Gao et al., 2009), but at about 2 years of age, activity begins to resemble the adult default network (Gao et al., 2009) and further refinements continue later in childhood (Fair et al., 2008).

A number of questions on the brain basis of hedonic experience have yet to be answered. We have still to understand the exact interactions and oscillations of the network of brain regions subserving hedonic processing. In particular, it is presently unclear which brain regions are necessary and/or sufficient for hedonic experience. Although pleasure typically refers to conscious, positive appraisal of an experience, many emotional stimuli can be processed on a non-conscious level as demonstrated by studies of subliminal priming (Naccache et al., 2005; Winkielman, Berridge, & Wilbarger, 2005).

Although functional imaging studies are beginning to illuminate functional maturation of neural circuits involved in hedonic experience, future studies need to substantially increase sample size and enhance the behavioral characterization of performance in order to learn more about brain-behavior relationships across development. Notwithstanding such difficulties, understanding the development of mature reward-related brain circuitry will remain of central importance, given the dramatic behavioral changes in reward processing that occur from childhood to adolescence and adulthood.

The most difficult question facing pleasure research remains the nature of its subjective experience. Although some progress has been made, it is important to interpret with caution correlations from neuroimaging studies with the complexities of subjective experience. A major challenge will be to map the developmental changes in reward processing over the life span. In summary, pleasure, motivations, and emotions are evolutionarily important for animals (including humans) in evaluating and preparing for appropriate actions. The evolution of conscious pleasure and emotion in humans could be adaptive because they allow us to consciously appraise our emotions and actions, and subsequently to learn to manipulate these appropriately. Pleasure is essential to a normal sense of well-being. Understanding the putative neural requisites of pleasure will continue to be a central goal of social and affective neuroscience, given that the pathological inability to experience pleasure is a hallmark of psychiatric disorder.

REFERENCES

Adolphs, R. (2003). Cognitive neuroscience of human social behaviour. *Nat Rev Neurosci, 4,* 165–178.

Aharon, I., Etcoff, N., Ariely, D., Chabris, C. F., O'Connor, E. & Breiter, H. C. (2001). Beautiful faces have variable reward value: fMRI and behavioral evidence. *Neuron, 32,* 537–551.

Akil, H., Mayer, D. J., & Liebeskind, J. C. (1976). Antagonism of stimulation-produced analgesia by naloxone, a narcotic antagonist. *Science, 191,* 961–962.

Allison, T., Puce, A., & McCarthy, G. (2000). Social perception from visual cues: Role of the STS region. *Trends Cogn Sci, 4,* 267–278.

Amaral, D. G., & Price, J. L. (1984). Amygdalo-cortical projections in the monkey (Macaca fascicularis). *J. Comp. Neurol., 230,* 465–496.

Anderson, A. K., Christoff, K., Stappen, I., Panitz, D., Ghahremani, D. G., Glover, G., et al. (2003). Dissociated neural representations of intensity and valence in human olfaction. *Nat. Neurosci., 6,* 196–202.

Anderson, S. W., Bechara, A., Damasio, H., Tranel, D., & Damasio, A. R. (1999). Impairment of social and moral behavior related to early damage in human prefrontal cortex. *Nat. Neurosci., 2,* 1032–1037.

Andy, O. J., & Jurko, F. (1987). Thalamic stimulation effects on reactive depression. *Appl Neurophysiol, 50,* 324–329.

Barbas, H. (1988). Anatomic organization of basoventral and mediodorsal visual recipient prefrontal regions in the rhesus monkey. *J. Comp. Neurol., 276,* 313–342.

Barbas, H., & Pandya, D. N. (1989). Architecture and intrinsic connections of the prefrontal cortex in the rhesus monkey. *J. Comp. Neurol., 286,* 353–375.

Bartels, A., & Zeki, S. (2004). The neural correlates of maternal and romantic love. *Neuroimage, 21,* 1155–1166.

Bartocci, M., Winberg, J., Ruggiero, C., Bergqvist, L. L., Serra, G., & Lagercrantz, H. (2000). Activation of olfactory cortex in newborn infants after odor stimulation: A functional near-infrared spectroscopy study. *Pediatric Research, 48,* 18–23.

Baxter, M. G., Parker, A., Lindner, C. C., Izquierdo, A. D., & Murray, E. A. (2000). Control of response selection by reinforcer value requires interaction of amygdala and orbital prefrontal cortex. *J. Neurosci., 20,* 4311–4319.

Baylis, L. L., & Gaffan, D. (1991). Amygdalectomy and ventromedial prefrontal ablation produce similar deficits in food choice and in simple object discrimination learning for an unseen reward. *Exp. Brain Res., 86,* 617–622.

Bechara, A., Damasio, A. R., Damasio, H., & Anderson, S. W. (1994). Insensitivity to future consequences following damage to human prefrontal cortex. *Cognition, 50,* 7–15.

Bechara, A., Damasio, H., Tranel, D,.& Anderson, S. W. (1998). Dissociation of working memory from decision making within the human prefrontal cortex. *J. Neurosci., 18,* 428–437.

Berridge, K. C. (1996). Food reward: Brain substrates of wanting and liking. *Neurosci. Biobehav. Rev., 20,* 1–25.

Berridge, K. C., & Kringelbach, M. L. (2008). Affective neuroscience of pleasure: Reward in humans and animals. *Psychopharmacology, 199,* 457–480.

Berridge, K. C., & Robinson, T. E. (1998). What is the role of dopamine in reward: Hedonic impact, reward learning, or incentive salience? *Brain Research Reviews, 28,* 309–369.

Bittar, R. G., Burn, S. C., Bain, P. G., Owen, S. L., Joint, C., Shlugman, D., et al. (2005a). Deep brain stimulation for movement disorders and pain. *J Clin Neurosci, 12,* 457–463.

Bittar, R. G., Kar-Purkayastha, I., Owen, S. L., Bear, R. E., Green, A., Wang, S., et al. (2005b). Deep brain stimulation for pain relief: A meta-analysis. *J Clin Neurosci, 12,* 515–519.

Bjork, J. M., Knutson, B., Fong, G. W., Caggiano, D. M., Bennett, S. M., & Hommer, D. W. (2004). Incentive-elicited brain activation in adolescents: Similarities and differences from young adults. *J. Neurosci., 24,* 1793–1802.

Blair, R. J. (2003). Facial expressions, their communicatory functions and neuro-cognitive substrates. *Philos Trans R Soc Lond B Biol Sci, 358,* 561–572.

Blair, R. J., & Cipolotti, L. (2000). Impaired social response reversal. A case of 'acquired sociopathy.' *Brain, 123* (6), 1122–1141.

Blair, R. J., Morris, J. S., Frith, C. D., Perrett, D. I., & Dolan, R. J. (1999). Dissociable neural responses to facial expressions of sadness and anger. *Brain, 122,* 883–893.

Blood, A. J., & Zatorre, R. J. (2001). Intensely pleasurable responses to music correlate with activity in brain regions implicated in reward and emotion. *Proc. Natl. Acad.* Sci. USA, *98,* 11818–11823.

Blood, A. J., Zatorre, R. J., Bermudez, P., & Evans, A. C. (1999). Emotional responses to pleasant and unpleasant music correlate with activity in paralimbic brain regions. *Nat. Neurosci., 2,* 382–387.

Boivie, J., & Meyerson, B. A. (1982). A correlative anatomical and clinical study of pain suppression by deep brain stimulation. *Pain, 13,* 113–126.

Bourgeois, J. P. (2005). Brain synaptogenesis and epigenesis. *Synaptogenéses et Pigenèses Cérébrales, 21,* 428–433.

Bowlby, J. (1957). An ethological approach to research in child development. *Br. J. Med. Psychot., 30,* 230–240.

Bowlby, J. (1969). *Attachment and loss, vol 1: Attachment.* London, England: Hogarth Press.

Bushnell, I. W. R. (2001). Mother's face recognition in newborn infants: Learning and memory. *Infant and Child Development, 10,* 67–74.

Butter, C. M., Mishkin, M., & Rosvold, H. E. (1963). Conditioning and extinction of a food-rewarded response after selective ablations of frontal cortex in rhesus monkeys. *Exp Neurol, 7,* 65–75.

Cardinal, R. N., Parkinson, J. A., Hall, J., & Everitt, B. J. (2002). Emotion and motivation: The role of the amygdala, ventral striatum, and prefrontal cortex. *Neuroscience and Biobehavioural Reviews, 26,* 321–352.

Carlsson, J., Lagercrantz, H., Olson, L., Printz, G., & Bartocci, M. (2008). Activation of the right fronto-temporal cortex during maternal facial recognition in young infants. *Acta Paediatrica, International Journal of Paediatrics, 97,* 1221–1225.

Carmichael, S. T., & Price, J. L. (1995a). Limbic connections of the orbital and medial prefrontal cortex in macaque monkeys. *J. Comp. Neurol., 363,* 615–641.

Carmichael, S. T., & Price, J. L. (1995b). Sensory and premotor connections of the orbital and medial prefrontal cortex of macaque monkeys. *J. Comp. Neurol., 363,* 642–664.

Cavada, C., Company, T., Tejedor, J., Cruz Rizzolo, R. J., & Reinoso Suarez, F. (2000). The anatomical connections of the macaque monkey orbitofrontal cortex. A review. *Cerebral Cortex, 10,* 220–242.

Caviness Jr, V. S., Kennedy, D. N., Richelme, C., Rademacher, J., & Filipek, P. A. (1996). The human brain age 7–11 years: A volumetric analysis based on magnetic resonance images. *Cerebral Cortex, 6,* 726–736.

Chao, L. L., Martin, A., & Haxby, J. V. (1999). Are face-responsive regions selective only for faces? *Neuroreport, 10,* 2945–2950.

Chiavaras, M. M., & Petrides, M. (2000). Orbitofrontal sulci of the human and macaque monkey brain. *J. Comp. Neurol., 422,* 35–54.

Chiavaras, M. M., & Petrides, M. (2001). Three-dimensional probabilistic atlas of the human orbitofrontal sulci in standardized stereotaxic space. *Neuroimage, 13,* 479–496.

Craig, A. D., Chen, K., Bandy, D., & Reiman, E. M. (2000). Thermosensory activation of insular cortex. *Nat. Neurosci., 3,* 184–190.

Critchley, H. D., Mathias, C. J., & Dolan, R. J. (2002). Fear conditioning in humans: The influence of awareness and autonomic arousal on functional neuroanatomy. *Neuron, 33,* 653–663.

Cromwell, H. C., & Berridge, K. C. (1993). Where does damage lead to enhanced food aversion: The ventral pallidum/substantia innominata or lateral hypothalamus? *Brain Res,* 624, 1–10.

Cummings, J. L. (1992). Depression and Parkinson's disease: A review. *Am J Psychiatry, 149,* 443–454.

Darwin, C. (1872). *The expression of the emotions in man and animals.* Chicago: University of Chicago Press.

De Araujo, I. E., & Rolls, E. T. (2004). Representation in the human brain of food texture and oral fat. *J. Neurosci., 24,* 3086–3093.

De Araujo, I. E. T., Kringelbach, M. L., Rolls, E. T., & Hobden, P. (2003a). The representation of umami taste in the human brain. *J Neurophysiol, 90,* 313–319.

De Araujo, I. E. T., Kringelbach, M. L., Rolls, E. T., & McGlone, (2003b). Human cortical responses to water in the mouth, and the effects of thirst. *J Neurophysiol, 90,* 1865–1876.

De Araujo, I. E. T., Rolls, E. T., Kringelbach, M. L., McGlone, F., & Phillips, N. (2003c). Taste-olfactory convergence, and the representation of the pleasantness of flavour, in the human brain. *European Journal of Neuroscience, 18,* 2059–2068.

de Haan, M., Humphreys, K., & Johnson, M. H. (2002a). Developing a brain specialized for face perception: A converging methods approach. *Dev Psychobiol, 40,* 200–212.

de Haan, M., & Nelson, C. A. (1997). Recognition of the mother's face by six-month-old infants: A neurobehavioral study. *Child Development, 68,* 187–210.

de Haan, M., & Nelson, C. A. (1999). Brain activity differentiates face and object processing in 6-month-old infants. *Developmental Psychology, 35,* 1113–1121.

de Haan, M., Pascalis, O., & Johnson, M. H. (2002b). Specialization of neural mechanisms underlying face recognition in human infants. *J Cogn Neurosci, 14,* 199–209.

De Schonen, S., & Mathivet, E. (1989). First come, first served: A scenario about the development of hemispheric specialization in face recognition during infancy. *European Bulletin of Cognitive Psychology, 9,* 3–44.

DeCasper, A. J., & Fifer, W. P. (1980). Of human bonding: Newborns prefer their mothers' voices. *Science, 208,* 1174–1176.

Dehaene, S., Kerszberg, M., & Changeux, J. P. (1998). A neuronal model of a global workspace in effortful cognitive tasks. *Proc. Natl. Acad. Sci. USA, 95*, 14529–14534.

Deichmann, R., Josephs, O., Hutton, C., Corfield, D. R., & Turner, R. (2002). Compensation of susceptibility-induced BOLD sensitivity losses in echo-planar fMRI imaging. *Neuroimage, 15*, 120–135.

Dias, R., Robbins, T., & Roberts, A. (1996). Dissociation in prefrontal cortex of affective and attentional shifts. *Nature, 380*, 69–72.

Diener, E., Lucas, R. E., & Scollon, C. N. (2006). Beyond the hedonic treadmill: Revising the adaptation theory of well-being. *American Psychologist, 61*, 305–314.

Eblen, F., & Graybiel, A. M. (1995). Highly restricted origin of prefrontal cortical inputs to striosomes in the macaque monkey. *J. Neurosci., 15*, 5999–6013.

Ekman, P., & Friesen, W.-V. (1971). Constants across cultures in the face and emotion. *Journal of Personality and Social Psychology, 17*(2), 124–129.

Eliot, L. (1999). *What's Going on in There? How the Brain and Mind Develop in the First Five Years of Life.* New York: Bantam.

Elliott, R., Dolan, R. J., & Frith, C. D. (2000). Dissociable functions in the medial and lateral orbitofrontal cortex: Evidence from human neuroimaging studies. *Cerebral Cortex, 10*, 308–317.

Ernst, M., Nelson, E. E., Jazbec, S., McClure, E. B., Monk, C. S., Leibenluft, E., et al. (2005). Amygdala and nucleus accumbens in responses to receipt and omission of gains in adults and adolescents. *Neuroimage, 25*, 1279–1291.

Eshel, N., Nelson, E. E., Blair, R. J., Pine, D. S., & Ernst, M. (2007). Neural substrates of choice selection in adults and adolescents: Development of the ventrolateral prefrontal and anterior cingulate cortices. *Neuropsychologia, 45*, 1270–1279.

Fair, D. A., Cohen, A. L., Dosenbach, N. U., Church, J. A., Miezin, F. M., Barch, D. M., et al. (2008). The maturing architecture of the brain's default network. *Proc Natl Acad Sci USA, 105*, 4028–4032.

Farrow, T. F., Zheng, Y., Wilkinson, I. D., Spence, S. A., Deakin, J. F., Tarrier, N., et al. (2001). Investigating the functional anatomy of empathy and forgiveness. *Neuroreport, 12*, 2433–2438.

Fields, H. L., & Basbaum, A. (1999). Central nervous system mechanisms of pain modulation. In P. D. Wall & R. Melzack (Eds), *Textbook of pain* (pp. 309–329). Edinburgh, Scotland: Churchill Livingstone.

Fransson, P., Skiöld, B., Horsch, S., Nordell, A., Blennow, M., Lagercrantz, H., et al. (2007). Resting-state networks in the infant brain. *Proceedings of the National Academy of Sciences of the United States of America, 104*, 15531–15536.

Fredrickson, B. L., Cohn, M. A., Coffey, K. A., Pek, J., & Finkel, S. M. (2008). Open hearts build lives: Positive emotions, induced through loving-kindness meditation, build consequential personal resources. *Journal of Personality and Social Psychology, 95*(5), 1045–1062.

Frey, S., Kostopoulos, P., & Petrides, M. (2000). Orbitofrontal involvement in the processing of unpleasant auditory information. *European Journal of Neuroscience, 12*, 3709–3712.

Frijda, N. H. (2007). The Laws of Emotion. *Mahwah, NJ: Lawrence Erlbaum Associates.*

Fusar-Poli, P., Placentino, A., Carletti, F., Landi, P., Allen, P., Surguladze, S., et al. (2009). Functional atlas of emotional faces processing: A voxel-based meta-analysis of 105 functional magnetic resonance imaging studies. *Journal of Psychiatry and Neuroscience, 34*, 418–432.

Fuster, J. M. (1997). *The Prefrontal Cortex.* New York: Raven Press.

Galvan, A., Hare, T. A., Parra, C. E., Penn, J., Voss, H., Glover, G., et al. (2006). Earlier development of the accumbens relative to orbitofrontal cortex might underlie risk-taking behavior in adolescents. *J. Neurosci., 26*, 6885–6892.

Gao, W., Zhu, H., Giovanello, K. S., Smith, J. K., Shen, D., Gilmore, J. H., et al. (2009). Evidence on the emergence of the brain's default network from 2-week-old to 2-year-old healthy pediatric subjects. *Proc Natl Acad Sci USA, 106*, 6790–6795.

Gervain, J., Macagno, F., Cogoi, S., Pena, M., & Mehler, J. (2008). The neonate brain detects speech structure. *Proc. Natl. Acad. Sci. USA, 105*, 14222–14227.

Giedd, J. N., Blumenthal, J., Jeffries, N. O., Castellanos, F. X., Liu, H., Zijdenbos, A., et al. (1999). Brain development during childhood and adolescence: A longitudinal MRI study [2]. *Nat. Neurosci., 2*, 861–863.

Giedd, J. N., Clasen, L. S., Lenroot, R., Greenstein, D., Wallace, G. L., Ordaz, S., et al. (2006). Puberty-related influences on brain development. *Molecular and Cellular Endocrinology, 254–255*, 154–162.

Giedd, J. N., Vaituzis, A. C., Hamburger, S. D., Lange, N., Rajapakse, J. C., Kaysen, D., et al. (1996). Quantitative MRI of the temporal lobe, amygdala, and hippocampus in normal human development: Ages 4–18 years. *J. Comp. Neurol., 366*, 223–230.

Gogtay, N., Giedd, J. N., Lusk, L., Hayashi, K. M., Greenstein, D., Vaituzis, A. C., et al. (2004). Dynamic mapping of human cortical development during childhood through early adulthood. *Proc. Natl. Acad. Sci. USA, 101*, 8174–8179.

Goldman-Rakic, P. S., Bourgeois, J. P., & Rakic, P. (1997). Synaptic development of the prefrontal cortex and the emergence of cognitive function. *Baltimore: Paul Brookes Publishing.*

Gottfried, J. A., O'Doherty, J., & Dolan, R. J. (2003). Encoding predictive reward value in human amygdala and orbitofrontal cortex. *Science, 22,*1104–1107.

Grossmann, T., & Johnson, M. H. (2007). The development of the social brain in human infancy. *Eur J Neurosci, 25,* 909–919.

Gusnard, D. A., & Raichle, M. E. (2001). Searching for a baseline: Functional imaging and the resting human brain. *Nature Reviews Neuroscience, 2,* 685–694.

Haisken-DeNew, J. P., & Frick, R. (2005). *Desktop companion to the German Socio-Economic Panel Study* (GSOEP). Berlin, Germany: German Institute for Economic Research (DIW).

Hare, T. A., Tottenham, N., Galvan, A., Voss, H. U., Glover, G. H., & Casey, B. J. (2008). Biological substrates of emotional reactivity and regulation in adolescence during an emotional go-nogo task. *Biological Psychiatry, 63,* 927–934.

Harlow, J. M. (1848). Passage of an iron rod through the head. *Boston Medical and Surgical Journal, 39,* 389–393.

Hinton, E. C., Parkinson, J. A., Holland, A. J., Arana, F. S., Roberts, A. C., & Owen, A. M. (2004). Neural contributions to the motivational control of appetite in humans. *Eur J Neurosci. 20,* 1411–1418.

Holland, P. C., & Gallagher, M. (2004). Amygdala-frontal interactions and reward expectancy. *Current Opinion in Neurobiology, 14,* 148–155.

Hornak, J., Bramham, J., Rolls, E. T., Morris, R. G., O'Doherty, J., Bullock, P. R., et al. (2003). Changes in emotion after circumscribed surgical lesions of the orbitofrontal and cingulate cortices. *Brain 126 (Pt 7),* 1671–1712.

Hornak, J., O'Doherty, J., Bramham, J., Rolls, E. T., Morris, R. G., Bullock, P. R., et al. (2004). Reward-related reversal learning after surgical excisions in orbitofrontal and dorsolateral prefrontal cortex in humans. *J. Cogn. Neurosci., 16,* 463–478.

Hornak, J., Rolls, E. T., & Wade, D. (1996). Face and voice expression identification in patients with emotional and behavioural changes following ventral frontal lobe damage. *Neuropsychologia, 34,* 247–261.

Hoshi, Y., Oda, I., Wada, Y., Ito, Y., Yutaka, Y., Oda, M., et al. (2000). Visuospatial imagery is a fruitful strategy for the digit span backward task: A study with near-infrared optical tomography. *Cognitive Brain Research, 9,* 339–342.

Hosobuchi, Y., Adams, J. E., & Linchitz, R. (1977). Pain relief by electrical stimulation of the central gray matter in humans and its reversal by naloxone. *Science, 197,* 183–186.

Huttenlocher, P. R. (1990). Morphometric study of human cerebral cortex development. *Neuropsychologia, 28,* 517–527.

Huttenlocher, P. R., & Dabholkar, A. S. (1997). Regional differences in synaptogenesis in human cerebral cortex. *J. Comp. Neurol., 387,* 167–178.

Iversen, S. D., & Mishkin, M. (1970). Perseverative interference in monkeys following selective lesions of the inferior prefrontal convexity. *Exp. Brain Res., 11,* 376–386.

Jenkinson, N., Nandi, D., Aziz, T. Z., & Stein, J. F. (2005). Pedunculopontine nucleus: A new target for deep brain stimulation for akinesia. *Neuroreport, 16,* 1875–1876.

Johnson, M. H. (2005). Subcortical face processing. *Nature Reviews Neuroscience, 6,* 766–774.

Kotilahti, K., Nissila, I., Huotilainen, M., Makela, R., Gavrielides, N., Noponen, T., et al. (2005). Bilateral hemodynamic responses to auditory stimulation in newborn infants. *Neuroreport, 16,* 1373–1377.

Krack, P., Batir, A., Van Blercom, N., Chabardes, S., Fraix, V., Ardouin, C., et al. (2003). Five-year follow-up of bilateral stimulation of the subthalamic nucleus in advanced Parkinson's disease. *N Engl J Med, 349,* 1925–1934.

Kringelbach, M. L. (2004a). Food for thought: Hedonic experience beyond homeostasis in the human brain. *Neuroscience, 126,* 807–819.

Kringelbach, M. L. (2004b). Learning to change. *PLoS Biol, 2,* E140.

Kringelbach, M. L. (2005). The orbitofrontal cortex: Linking reward to hedonic experience. *Nature Reviews Neuroscience, 6,* 691–702.

Kringelbach, M. L. (2009). *The pleasure center: Trust your animal instincts.* New York: Oxford University Press.

Kringelbach, M. L., & Berridge, K. C. (2008). *Pleasures of the brain.* New York: Oxford University Press.

Kringelbach, M. L., & Berridge, K. C. (2010). *Pleasures of the brain.* New York: Oxford University Press.

Kringelbach, M. L., Jenkinson, N., Green, A. L., Owen, S. L. F., Hansen, P. C., Cornelissen, P. L., et al. (2007a). Deep brain stimulation for chronic pain investigated with magnetoencephalography. *Neuroreport, 18,* 223–228.

Kringelbach, M. L., Jenkinson, N., Owen, S. L. F., & Aziz, T. Z. (2007b). Translational principles of deep brain stimulation. *Nature Reviews Neuroscience, 8,* 623–635.

Kringelbach, M. L., Lehtonen, A., Squire, S., Harvey, A. G., Craske, M. G., Holliday, I. E., et al. (2008). A specific and rapid neural signature for parental instinct. *PLoS ONE, 3*, e1664. doi:1610.1371/journal.pone.0001664.

Kringelbach, M. L., O'Doherty, J., Rolls, E. T., & Andrews, C. (2000). Sensory-specific satiety for the flavour of food is represented in the orbitofrontal cortex. *Neuroimage, 11*, S767.

Kringelbach, M. L., O'Doherty, J., Rolls, E. T., & Andrews, C. (2003). Activation of the human orbitofrontal cortex to a liquid food stimulus is correlated with its subjective pleasantness. *Cerebral Cortex, 13*, 1064–1071.

Kringelbach, M. L., & Rolls, E. T. (2003). Neural correlates of rapid context-dependent reversal learning in a simple model of human social interaction. *Neuroimage, 20*, 1371–1383.

Kringelbach, M. L., & Rolls, E. T. (2004). The functional neuroanatomy of the human orbitofrontal cortex: Evidence from neuroimaging and neuropsychology. *Progress in Neurobiology, 72*, 341–372.

Layard, R. (2005). *Happiness: Lessons from a new science.* London, England: Penguin Press.

Lenroot, R. K., & Giedd, J. N. (2010). Sex differences in the adolescent brain. *Brain and Cognition 72* 46–55.

Leone, M., Franzini, A., Broggi, G., May, A., & Bussone, G. (2004). *Long-term follow-up of bilateral hypothalamic stimulation for intractable cluster headache. Brain, 127*, 2259–2264.

Lorenz, K. (1971). *Studies in animal and human behavior, vol. II.* London, England: Methuen.

Macfarlane, A. (1975). Olfaction in the development of social preferences in the human neonate. In R. Porter & M. O'Connor (Eds.), *Parent-infant interactions(Ciba Found. Symp. 33)* (pp. 103–113). New York: Elsevier.

Macmillan, M. (2000). *An odd kind of fame: Stories of Phineas Gage*. Cambridge: MIT Press.

Maia, T. V., & McLelland, J. L. (2004). A reexamination of the evidence for the somatic marker hypothesis: What participants really know in the Iowa gambling task. *Proc Natl Acad Sci USA, 101*, 16075–16080.

May, J. C., Delgado, M. R., Dahl, R. E., Stenger, V. A., Ryan, N. D., Fiez, J. A., et al. (2004). Event-related functional magnetic resonance imaging of reward-related brain circuitry in children and adolescents. *Biological Psychiatry, 55*, 359–366.

Mayberg, H. S., Lozano, A. M., Voon, V., McNeely, H. E., Seminowicz, D., Hamani, C., et al. (2005). Deep brain stimulation for treatment-resistant depression. *Neuron, 45*, 651–660.

Mazzone, P., Lozano, A. M., Stanzione, P., Galati, S., Scanati, E., Peppe, A., et al. (2005). Implantation of human pedunculopontine nucleus: A safe and clinically relevant target in Parkinson's disease. *Neuroreport, 16*, 1877–1881.

Mesulam, M.-M., & Mufson, E. J. (1982). Insula of the old world monkey. III Efferent cortical output and comments on function. *J. Comp. Neurol., 212*, 38–52.

Miller, J. M., Vorel, S. R., Tranguch, A. J., Kenny, E. T., Mazzoni, P., van Gorp, W. G., et al. (2006). Anhedonia after a selective bilateral lesion of the globus pallidus. *Am J Psychiatry, 163*, 786–788.

Minagawa-Kawai, Y., Matsuoka, S., Dan, I., Naoi, N., Nakamura, K., & Kojima, S. (2009). Prefrontal activation associated with social attachment: Facial-emotion recognition in mothers and infants. *Cerebral Cortex, 19*, 284–292.

Monk, C. S., McClure, E. B., Nelson, E. E., Zarahn, E., Bilder, R. M., Leibenluft, E., et al. (2003). Adolescent immaturity in attention-related brain engagement to emotional facial expressions. *Neuroimage, 20*, 420–428.

Morton, J., & Johnson, M. H. (1991). CONSPEC and CONLERN: A two-process theory of infant face recognition. *Psychological Review, 98*, 164–181.

Naccache, L., Gaillard, R., Adam, C., Hasboun, D., Clemenceau, S., Baulac, M., et al. (2005). A direct intracranial record of emotions evoked by subliminal words. *Proc. Natl. Acad. Sci. USA, 102*, 7713–7717.

Nandi, D., Liu, X., Joint, C., Stein, J., & Aziz, T. (2002). Thalamic field potentials during deep brain stimulation of periventricular gray in chronic pain. *Pain, 97*, 47–51.

Nauta, W. J. (1971). The problem of the frontal lobe: A reinterpretation. *J Psychiatr Res, 8*, 167–187.

Nesse, R. M. (2004). Natural selection and the elusiveness of happiness. *Philos Trans R Soc Lond B Biol Sci, 359*, 1333–1347.

Nitschke, J. B., Nelson, E. E., Rusch, B. D., Fox, A. S., Oakes, T. R., & Davidson, R. J. (2004). Orbitofrontal cortex tracks positive mood in mothers viewing pictures of their newborn infants. *Neuroimage, 21*, 583–592.

Nobre, A. C., Coull, J. T., Frith, C. D., & Mesulam, M. M. (1999). Orbitofrontal cortex is activated during breaches of expectation in tasks of visual attention. *Nat. Neurosci., 2*, 11–12.

Noriuchi, M., Kikuchi, Y., & Senoo, A. (2008). The functional neuroanatomy of maternal love: Mother's response to infant's attachment behaviors. *Biol Psychiatry, 63*, 415–423.

O'Doherty, J., Kringelbach, M. L., Rolls, E. T., Hornak, J., & Andrews, C. (2001). Abstract reward and punishment representations in the human orbitofrontal cortex. *Nat. Neurosci., 4*, 95–102.

O'Doherty, J., Rolls, E. T., Francis, S., Bowtell, R., McGlone, F., Kobal, G., et al. (2000). Sensory-specific satiety-related olfactory activation of the human orbitofrontal cortex. *Neuroreport, 11*, 893–897.

Öngür, D., & Price, J. L. (2000). The organization of networks within the orbital and medial prefrontal cortex of rats, monkeys and humans. *Cerebral Cortex, 10*, 206–219.

Pandya, D. N., & Yeterian, E. H. (1996). Comparison of prefrontal architecture and connections. *Philos Trans R Soc Lond B Biol Sci, 351*, 1423–1432.

Papousek, H., & Papousek, M. (1977). Mothering and the cognitive headstart: Psychobiological considerations. In H. R. Shaffer (Ed.), *Studies in mother-infant interaction* (pp. 63–85). London, England: Academic Press.

Papousek, H., & Papousek, M. (1987). Intuitive parenting: A dialectic counterpart to the infant's integrative competence. In J. D. Osofsky (Ed.), *Handbook of infant development* (pp. 669–720). New York: Wiley.

Parsons, C. L., Young, K. S., Murray, L., Stein, A., & Kringelbach, M. L. (2010). The functional neuroanatomy of the evolving parent-infant relationship. *Progress in Neurobiology, 91*, 220–240.

Peciña, S., & Berridge, K. C. (2005). *Hedonic hot spot in nucleus accumbens shell: Where do mu-opioids cause increased hedonic impact of sweetness? J Neurosci, 25*, 11777–11786.

Peciña, S., Smith, K. S., & Berridge, K. C. (2006). Hedonic hot spots in the brain. *Neuroscientist, 12*, 500–511.

Pena, M., Maki, A., Kovacic, D., Dehaene-Lambertz, G., Koizumit, H., Bouquet, F., et al. (2003). Sounds and silence: An optical topography study of language recognition at birth. *Proc Natl Acad Sci USA, 100*, 11702–11705.

Perlmutter, J. S., & Mink, J. W. (2006). Deep brain stimulation. *Annu Rev Neurosci, 29*, 229–257.

Petrovic, P., & Ingvar, M. (2002). Imaging cognitive modulation of pain processing. *Pain, 95*, 1–5.

Petrovic, P., Kalso, E., Petersson, K. M., & Ingvar, M. (2002). Placebo and opioid analgesia— imaging a shared neuronal network. *Science, 295*, 1737–1740.

Plaha, P., & Gill, S. G. (2005). Bilateral deep brain stimulation of the pedunculopontine nucleus for idiopathic Parkinson's disease. *Neuroreport, 16*, 1883–1887.

Rahman, S., Sahakian, B. J., Hodges, J. R., Rogers, R. D., & Robbins, T. W. (1999). Specific cognitive deficits in mild frontal variant frontotemporal dementia. *Brain, 122*, 1469–1493.

Ranote, S., Elliott, R., Abel, K. M., Mitchell, R., Deakin, J. F., & Appleby, L. (2004a). The neural basis of maternal responsiveness to infants: An fMRI study. *Neuroreport, 15*, 1825–1829.

Ranote, S., Elliott, R., Abel, K. M., Mitchell, R., Deakin, J. F. W., & Appleby, L. (2004b). The neural basis of maternal responsiveness to infants: An fMRI study. *Neuroreport, 15*, 1825–1829.

Ray, N. J., Kringelbach, M. L., Jenkinson, N., Owen, S. L. F., Davies, P., Wang, S., et al. (2007). Using magnetoencephalography to investigate deep brain stimulation for cluster headache. *Biomedical Imaging and Intervention Journal, 3*, e25.

Rempel-Clower, N. L., & Barbas, H. (1998). Topographic organization of connections between the hypothalamus and prefrontal cortex in the rhesus monkey. *J. Comp. Neurol., 398*, 393–419.

Reynolds, D. V. (1969). Surgery in the rat during electrical analgesia induced by focal brain stimulation. *Science, 164*, 444–445.

Robinson, T. E., & Berridge, K. C. (1993). The neural basis of drug craving: An incentive-sensitization theory of addiction. *Brain Res Brain Res Rev, 18*, 247–291.

Rogers, R. D., Owen, A. M., Middleton, H. C., Williams, E. J., Pickard, J. D., Sahakian, B. J., et al. (1999). Choosing between small, likely rewards and large, unlikely rewards activates inferior and orbital prefrontal cortex. *J. Neurosci., 19*, 9029–9038.

Rolls, B. J., Rolls, E. T., Rowe, E. A., & Sweeney, K. (1981). Sensory specific satiety in man. *Physiology and Behavior, 27*, 137–142.

Rolls, E. T. (1999). *The Brain and Emotion*. Oxford, England: Oxford University Press.

Rolls, E. T., Hornak, J., Wade, D., & McGrath, J. (1994). Emotion-related learning in patients with social and emotional changes associated with frontal lobe damage. *J Neurol Neurosurg Psychiatry, 57*, 1518–1524.

Rolls, E. T., Kringelbach, M. L., & de Araujo, I. E. T. (2003a). Different representations of pleasant and unpleasant odors in the human brain. *European Journal of Neuroscience, 18*, 695–703.

Rolls, E. T., O'Doherty, J., Kringelbach, M. L., Francis, S., Bowtell, R., & McGlone, F. (2003b). Representations of pleasant and painful touch in the human orbitofrontal and cingulate cortices. *Cerebral Cortex, 13*, 308–317.

Rozin, P. (2001). Food preference. In N. J. Smelser, P. B. Baltes (Eds.), *International Encyclopedia of the Social & Behavioral Sciences* (pp.). Amsterdam, The Netherlands: Elsevier.

Ryan, R. M., & Deci, E. L. (2001). On happiness and human potantials: A review of research on hedonic and eudaimonic well-being. *Annual Review of Psychology, 52*, 141.

Ryle, G. (1954). Pleasure. *Proceedings of the Aristotelian Society, 28*, 135–146.

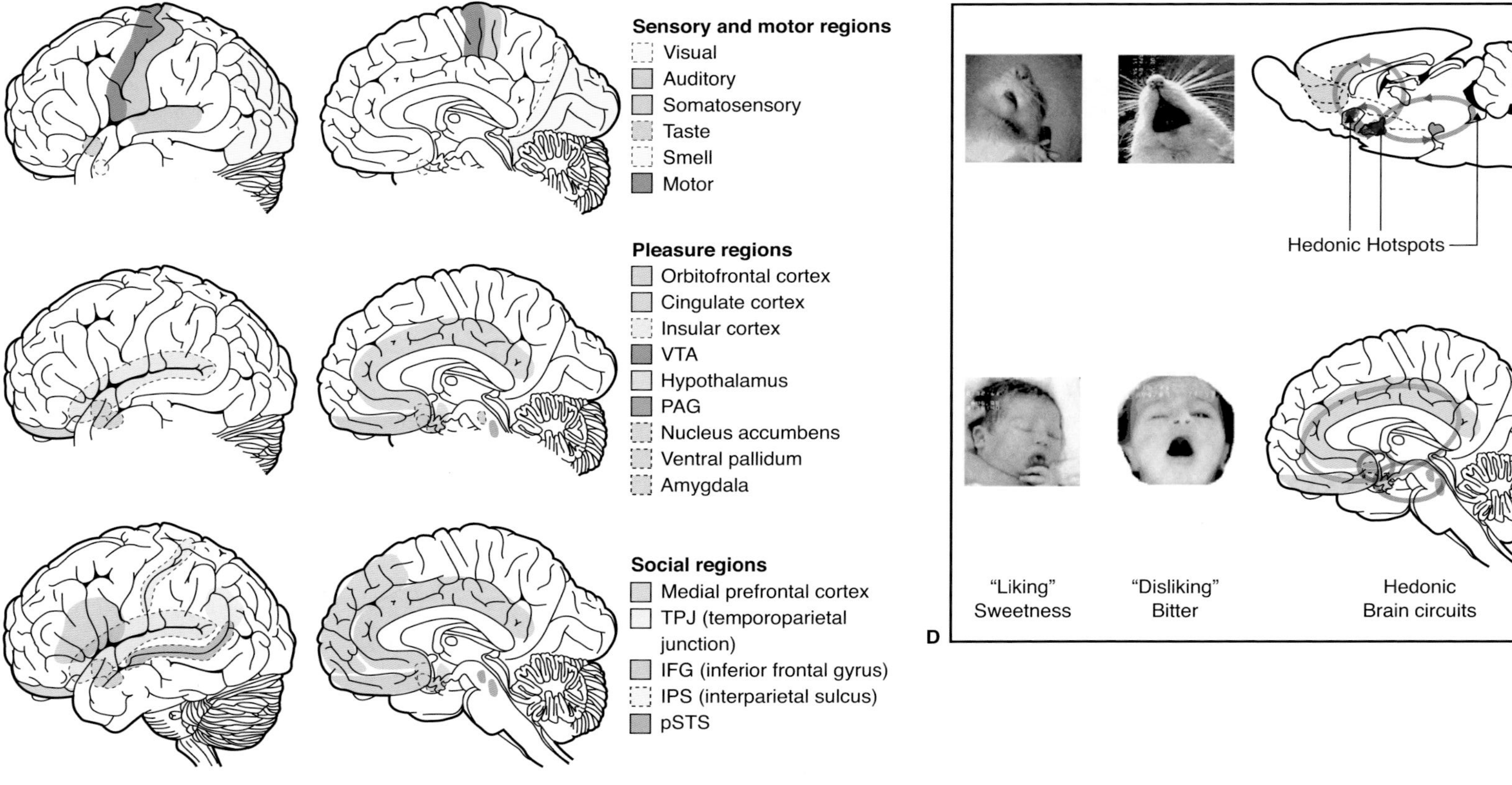

FIGURE 3.1 Brain systems from sensation to basic pleasures and higher-order social processing. The schematic figure shows the approximate sensorimotor, pleasure, and social brain regions in the adult brain. **(A)** Processing linked to the identification of and interaction with stimuli is carried out in the sensorimotor regions of the brain, **(B)** which are separate from the valence processing in the pleasure regions of the brain. **(C)** In addition to this pleasure processing, there is further higher-order processing of social situations (such as theory-of-mind) in widespread cortical regions. **(D)** The hedonic mammalian brain circuitry can be revealed using behavioral and subjective measures of pleasures in rodents and humans (Berridge & Kringelbach, 2008, reprinted with permission from Springer-Verlag).

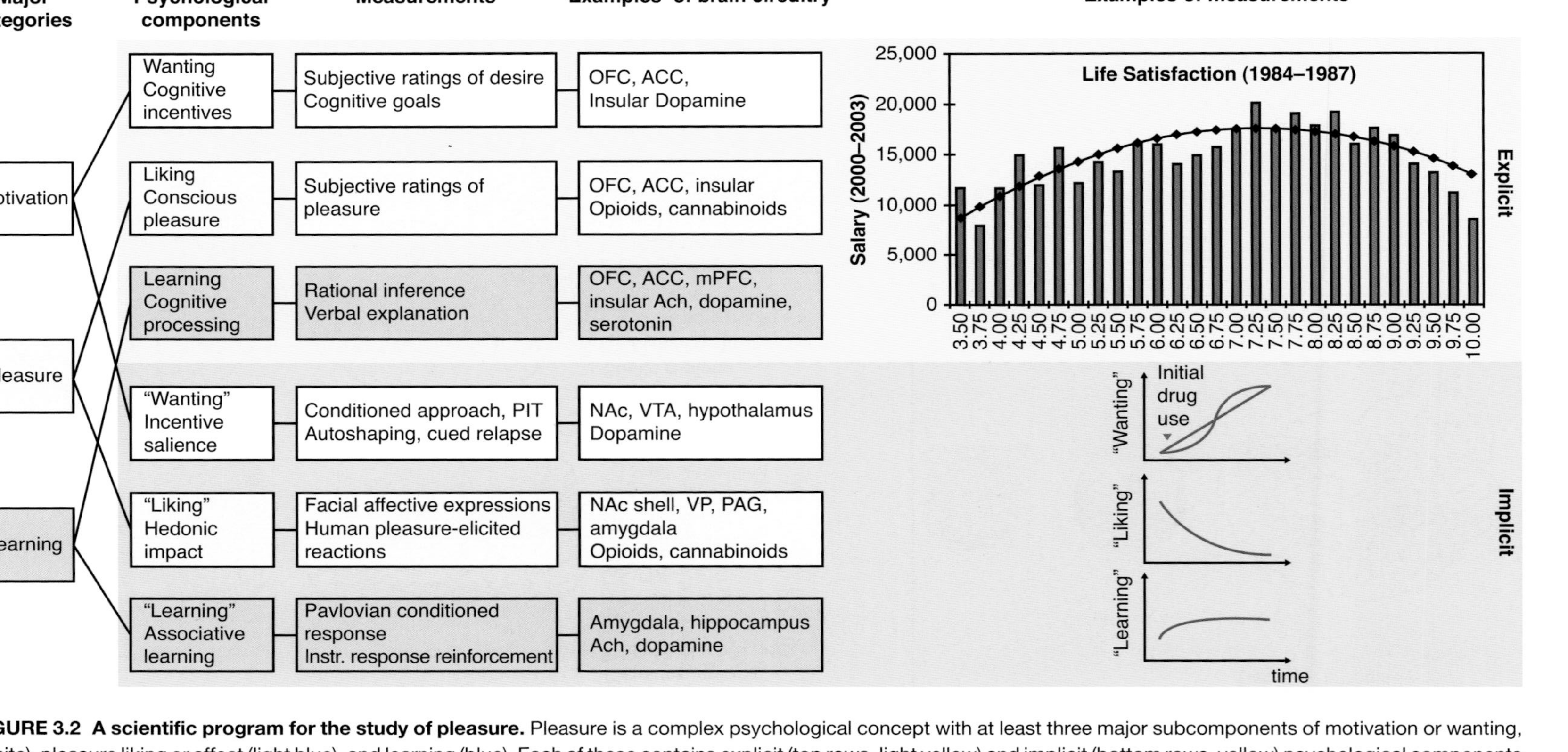

FIGURE 3.2 A scientific program for the study of pleasure. Pleasure is a complex psychological concept with at least three major subcomponents of motivation or wanting, (white), pleasure liking or affect (light blue), and learning (blue). Each of these contains explicit (top rows, light yellow) and implicit (bottom rows, yellow) psychological components (second column) that constantly interact and require careful scientific experimentation to tease apart. Explicit processes are consciously experienced (e.g. explicit pleasure and happiness, desire, or expectation), whereas implicit psychological processes are potentially unconscious in the sense that they can operate at a level not always directly accessible to conscious experience (implicit incentive salience, habits, and ''liking'' reactions), and must be further translated by other mechanisms into subjective feelings. Measurements or behavioral procedures that are especially sensitive markers of each of the processes are listed (third column). Examples of some of the brain regions and neurotransmitters are listed (fourth column), as well as specific examples of measurements (fifth column), such as an example of how highest subjective life satisfaction does not lead to the highest salaries (top) (Haisken-DeNew & Frick, 2005, reprinted with permission from GEI). Another example (bottom right) shows the incentive-sensitization model of addiction and how ''wanting'' to take drugs may grow over time independently of ''liking'' and ''learning'' drug pleasure as an individual becomes an addict (bottom) (Robinson & Berridge, 1993, reprinted with permission from Elsevier).

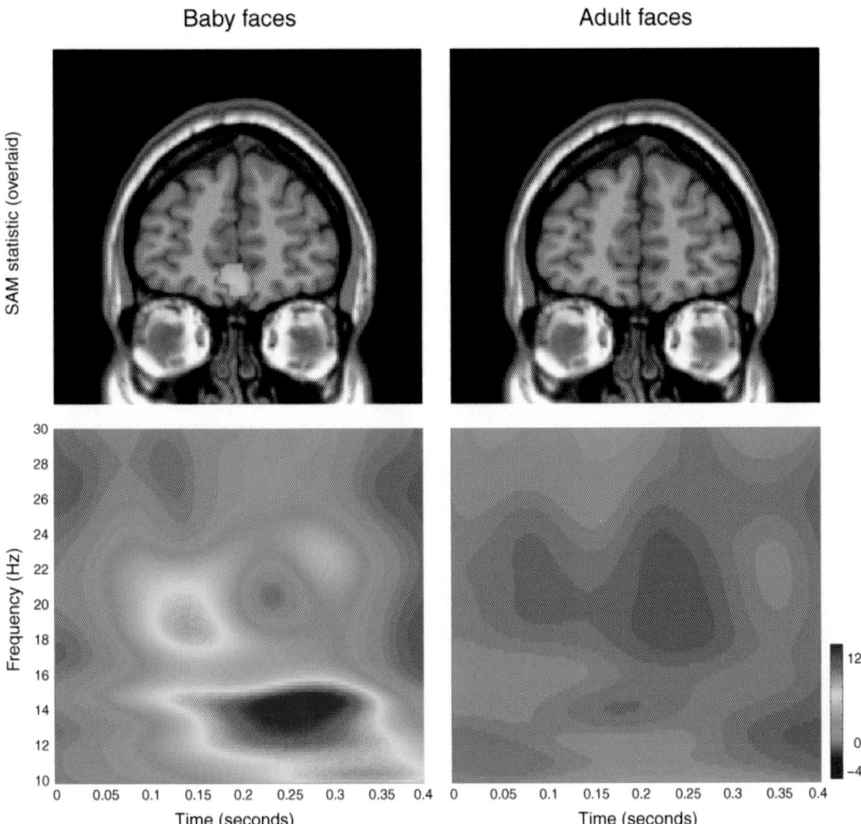

FIGURE 3.3 Infant faces elicit an early neural signature. Top row: Significant activity was present from around 130 ms in the medial OFC when viewing infant faces but not when viewing adult faces. Bottom row: Time-frequency representations of the normalized evoked average group responses to baby and adult faces from the virtual electrodes show that the initial response to infant faces is present in the 12–20 Hz band from around 130 ms—and not present to adult faces (Kringelbach et al., 2008, reprinted with permission).

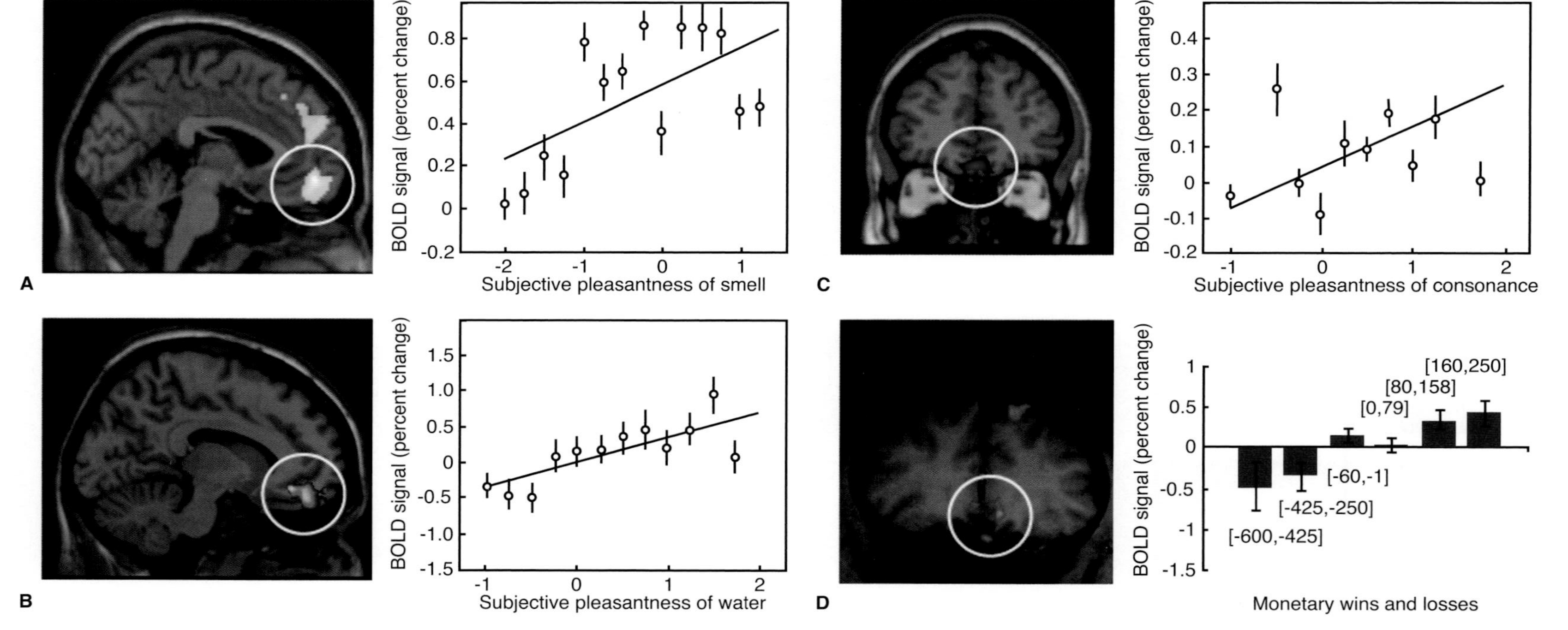

FIGURE 3.4 Valence coding in medial orbitofrontal cortex (OFC). (A) The activity in medial OFC correlates with the subjective ratings of pleasantness in an experiment with three pleasant and three unpleasant odors (Rolls et al., 2003a, reprinted with permission from Blackwell Publishing Ltd.). **(B)** Similarly, the activity in medial OFC was also correlated with the subjective pleasantness ratings of water in a thirst experiment (De Araujo et al., 2003b, reprinted with permission from The American Physiological Society). A correlation in a very similar part of medial OFC was found with the pleasantness of other pure tastants used in the experiment (not shown). **(C)** This corresponded to the findings in an experiment investigating taste and smell convergence and consonance, which found that activity in the medial OFC was correlated to subjective consonance ratings (De Araujo et al., 2003c, reprinted with permission from Blackwell Publishing Ltd.). **(D)** Even higher-order rewards such as monetary reward was found to correlate with activity in the medial OFC (O'Doherty et al., 2001, reprinted with permission from Macmillan Publishers Ltd.).

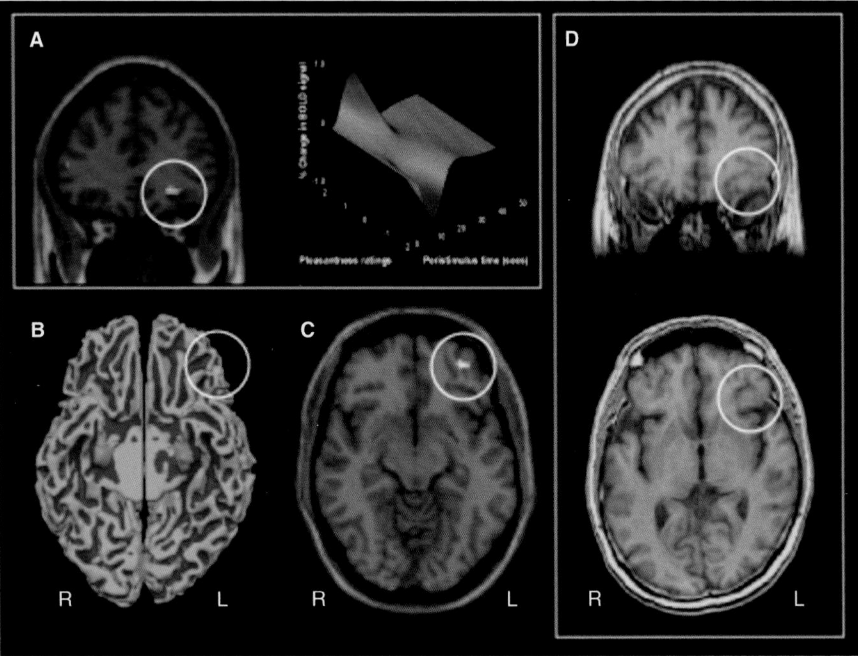

FIGURE 3.5 Hedonic experience. (A) A neuroimaging study using selective satiation found that mid-anterior parts of the orbitofrontal cortex (OFC) are correlated with the subjects' subjective pleasantness ratings of the foods throughout the experiment (Kringelbach et al., 2003, part A reprinted with permission from Oxford University Press). On the right is shown a plot of the magnitude of the fitted hemodynamic response from a representative single subject against the subjective pleasantness ratings (on a scale from -2 to $+2$) and peri-stimulus time in seconds. **(B)** Additional evidence for the role of the OFC in subjective experience comes from another neuroimaging experiment investigating the supra-additive effects of combining the umami tastants monosodium glutamate and inosine monophosphate (De Araujo et al., 2003a, part B reprinted with permission from The American Physiological Society). The figure shows the region of mid-anterior OFC showing synergistic effects (rendered on the ventral surface of human cortical areas with the cerebellum removed). The perceived synergy is unlikely to be expressed in the taste receptors themselves and the activity in the OFC may thus reflect the subjective enhancement of umami taste, which must be closely linked to subjective experience. **(C)** Adding strawberry odor to a sucrose taste solution makes the combination significantly more pleasant than the sum of each of the individual components. The supra-linear effects reflecting the subjective enhancement were found to significantly correlate with the activity in a lateral region of the left anterior OFC, which is remarkably similar to that found in the other experiments (De Araujo et al., 2003c, part C reprinted with permission from Blackwell Publishing Ltd.). **(D)** These findings were strengthened by findings using deep brain stimulation (DBS) and magnetoencephalography (MEG; Kringelbach et al., 2007a, part D reprinted with permission from Wolters Kluwer). Pleasurable subjective pain relief for chronic pain in a phantom limb in a patient was causally induced by effective deep brain stimulation in the PVG/PAG part of the brainstem. When using MEG to directly measure the concomitant changes in the rest of the brain, a significant change in power was found in the mid-anterior OFC.

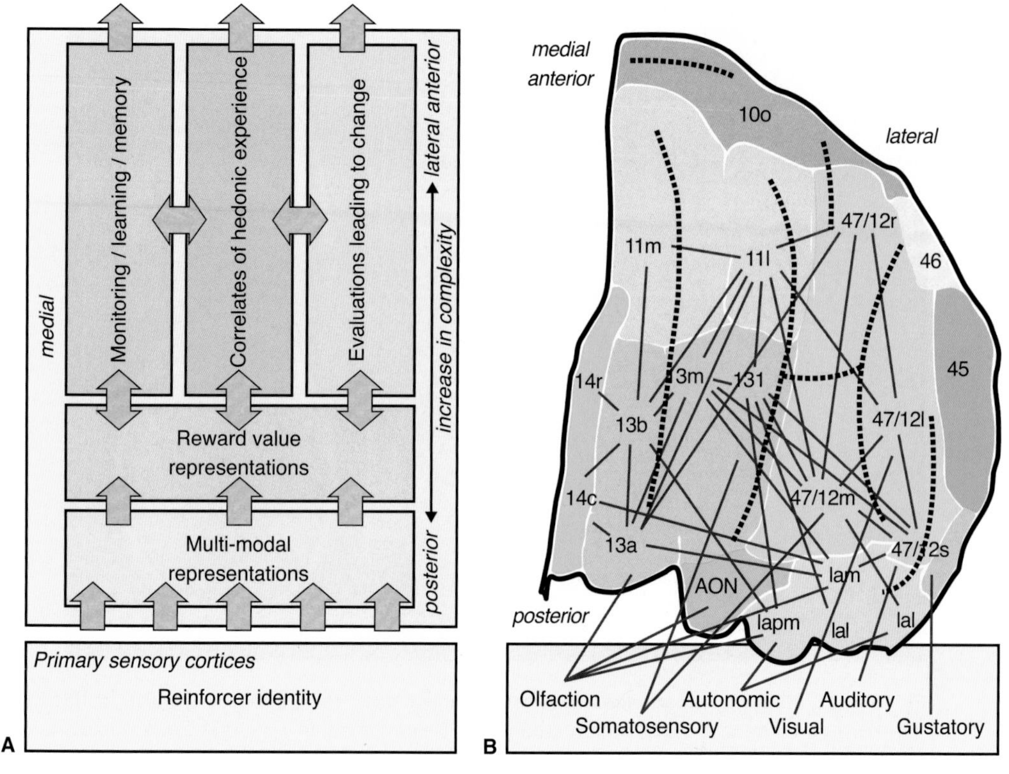

FIGURE 3.6 Model of the functions of the orbitofrontal cortex (OFC). (Kringelbach, 2004a, reprinted with permission from Elsevier.)

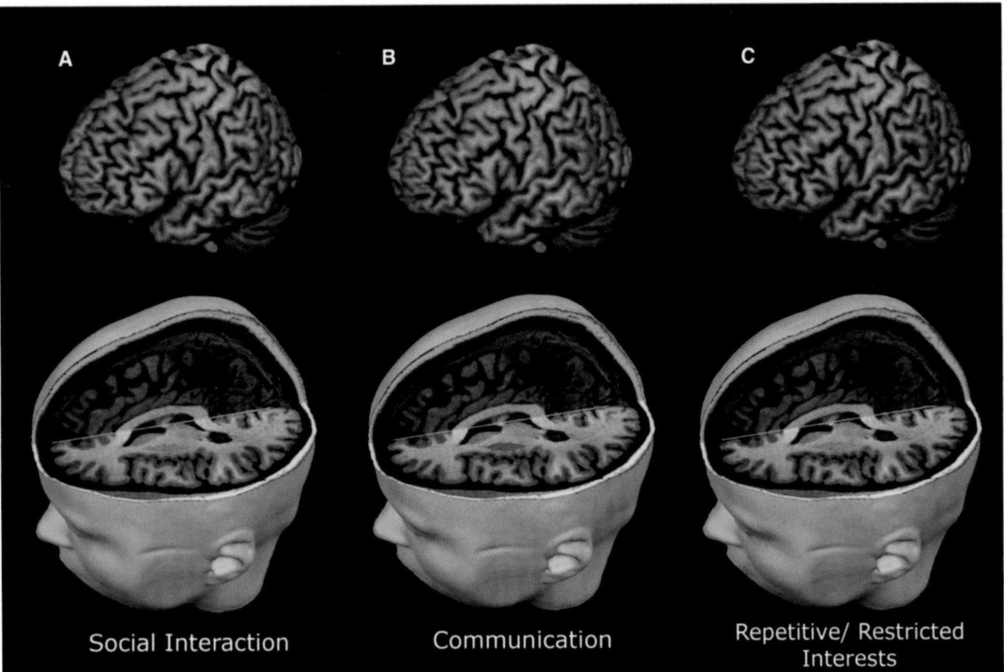

FIGURE 6.1 Areas of dysfunction implicated by neuropsychological and functional neuroimaging studies of AD. Color-shaded areas indicate brain regions implicated as areas of dysfunction in individuals with AD. Some structures are not visible given the plane of the image. Problems with social interaction (*green*) have been related to dysfunction of a complex distributed network involving the following areas and connecting pathways: orbitofrontal cortex, inferior frontal cortex, cingulate cortex, superior temporal sulcus, fusiform gyrus, and amygdala. Problems with communication (*red*) have been related to dysfunction of a complex distributed neural network involving the following areas and connecting pathways: inferior frontal cortex, superior temporal gyrus, superior temporal sulcus, supramarginal gyrus, insula, basal ganglia, thalamus, and cerebellum. Problems with repetitive and stereotyped behaviors (*blue*) have been related to dysfunction of a complex distributed neural network involving the following areas and connecting pathways: orbitofrontal cortex, posterior parietal cortex, supplementary motor cortex, cingulate gyrus, basal ganglia, thalamus, and cerebellum.

Saito, Y., Aoyama, S., Kondo, T., Fukumoto, R., Konishi, N., Nakamura, K., et al. (2007a). Frontal cerebral blood flow change associated with infant-directed speech. *Archives of disease in childhood: Fetal and neonatal edition, 92,* 113–116.

Saito, Y., Kondo, T., Aoyama, S., Fukumoto, R., Konishi, N., Nakamura, K., et al. (2007b). The function of the frontal lobe in neonates for response to a prosodic voice. *Early Human Development, 83,* 225–230.

Sakatani, K., Chen, S., Lichty, W., Zuo, H., & Wang, Y. P. (1999). Cerebral blood oxygenation changes induced by auditory stimulation in newborn infants measured by near infrared spectroscopy. *Early Human Development, 55,* 229–236.

Saper, C. B., Chou, T. C., & Elmquist, J. K. (2002). The need to feed: Homeostatic and hedonic control of eating. *Neuron, 36,* 199–211.

Schlaepfer, T. E., Cohen, M. X., Frick, C., Kosel, M., Brodesser, D., Axmacher, N., et al. (2007). Deep brain stimulation to reward circuitry alleviates anhedonia in refractory major depression. *Neuropsychopharmacology, 33,* 368–377.

Schnider, A., Treyer, V., & Buck, A. (2005). The human orbitofrontal cortex monitors outcomes even when no reward is at stake. *Neuropsychologia, 43,* 316–323.

Schultz, W., & Dickinson, A. (2000). Neuronal coding of prediction errors. *Annu. Rev. Neurosci., 23,* 473–500.

Schumann, C. M., Hamstra, J., Goodlin-Jones, B. L., Lotspeich, L. J., Kwon, H., Buonocore, M. H., et al. (2004). The amygdala is enlarged in children but not adolescents with autism; the hippocampus is enlarged at all ages. *J. Neurosci., 24,* 6392–6401.

Seligman, M. E. P. (2005). Positive psychology progress: Empirical validation of interventions. *American Psychologist, 60,* 410.

Shaw, P., Lalonde, F., Lepage, C., Rabin, C., Eckstrand, K., Sharp, W., et al. (2009). Development of cortical asymmetry in typically developing children and its disruption in attention-deficit/hyperactivity disorder. *Archives of General Psychiatry, 66,* 888–896.

Small, D. M., Gregory, M. D., Mak, Y. E., Gitelman, D., Mesulam, M. M., & Parrish, T. (2003). Dissociation of neural representation of intensity and affective valuation in human gustation. *Neuron, 39,* 701–711.

Small, D. M., Jones-Gotman, M., Zatorre, R. J., Petrides, M., & Evans, A. C. (1997). Flavor processing: More than the sum of its parts. *Neuroreport, 8,* 3913–3917.

Small, D. M., Zald, D. H., Jones-Gotman, M., Zatorre, R. J., Pardo, J. V., Frey, S., et al. (1999). Human cortical gustatory areas: A review of functional neuroimaging data. *Neuroreport, 10,* 7–14.

Small, D. M., Zatorre, R. J., Dagher, A., Evans, A. C., & Jones-Gotman, M. (2001). Changes in brain activity related to eating chocolate: From pleasure to aversion. *Brain, 124,* 1720–1733.

Smith, K. S., & Berridge, K. C. (2005). The ventral pallidum and hedonic reward:Neurochemical maps of sucrose "liking" and food intake. *J Neurosci, 25,* 8637–8649.

Somerville, L. H., Jones, R. M., & Casey, B. J. (2010) A time of change: Behavioral and neural correlates of adolescent sensitivity to appetitive and aversive environmental cues. *Brain and Cognition, 72,* 124–133.

Sowell, E. R., Thompson, P. M., Leonard, C. M., Welcome, S. E., Kan, E., & Toga, A. W. (2004). *Longitudinal mapping of cortical thickness and brain growth in normal children. J.* Neurosci., *24,* 8223–8231.

Stein, A., Gath, D. H., Bucher, J., Bond, A., Day, A., & Cooper, P. J. (1991). The relationship between post-natal depression and mother-child interaction. *Br J Psychiatry, 158,* 46–52.

Steiner, J. E., Glaser, D., Hawilo, M. E., & Berridge, K. C. (2001). Comparative expression of hedonic impact: Affective reactions to taste by human infants and other primates. *Neurosci Biobehav Rev, 25,* 53–74.

Swain, J. E., Lorberbaum, J. P., Kose, S., & Strathearn, L. (2007). Brain basis of early parent-infant interactions: Psychology, physiology, and in vivo functional neuroimaging studies. *J Child Psychol Psychiatry, 48,* 262–287.

Taga, G., Asakawa, K., Maki, A., Konishi, Y., & Koizumi, H. (2003). Brain imaging in awake infants by near-infrared optical topography. *Proc. Natl. Acad. Sci. USA, 100,* 10722–10727.

Thomas, K. M., Drevets, W. C., Whalen, P. J., Eccard, C. H., Dahl, R. E., Ryan, N. D., et al. (2001). Amygdala response to facial expressions in children and adults. *Biological Psychiatry, 49,* 309–316.

Thut, G., Schultz, W., Roelcke, U., Nienhusmeier, M., Missimer, J., Maguire, R. P., et al. (1997). Activation of the human brain by monetary reward. *Neuroreport, 8,* 1225–1228.

Tzourio-Mazoyer, N., De Schonen, S., Crivello, F., Reutter, B., Aujard, Y., & Mazoyer, B. (2002). Neural correlates of woman face processing by 2-month-old infants. *Neuroimage, 15,* 454–461.

Van Hoesen, G. W., Morecraft, R. J., & Vogt, B. A. (1993). Connections of the monkey cingulate cortex. In B. A. Vogt, M. Gabriel (Eds.), *The neurobiology of the cingulate cortex and limbic thalamus: A comprehensive handbook* (pp. 249–284). Boston: Birkhäuser.

van Leijenhorst, L., Crone, E. A., & Bunge, S. A. (2006). Neural correlates of developmental differences in risk estimation and feedback processing. *Neuropsychologia, 44*, 2158–2170.

van Leijenhorst, L., Zanolie, K., Van Meel, C. S., Westenberg, P. M., Rombouts, S. A. R. B., & Crone, E. A. (2011). What motivates the adolescent? brain regions mediating reward sensitivity across adolescence. *Cerebral Cortex, 20*, 61–69.

Völlm, B. A., de Araujo, I. E. T., Cowen, P. J., Rolls, E. T., Kringelbach, M. L., Smith, K. A., et al. (2004). Methamphetamine activates reward circuitry in drug naïve human subjects. *Neuropsychopharmacology, 29*, 1715–1722.

Walton, M. E., Devlin, J. T., & Rushworth, M. F. (2004). Interactions between decision making and performance monitoring within prefrontal cortex. *Nat Neurosci., 7*, 1259–1265.

Weiskrantz, L. (1968). Emotion. In L. Weiskrantz (Ed.), *Analysis of behavioural change* (pp. 50–90). New York and London: Harper and Row.

Wilson, J., Jenkinson, M., de Araujo, I. E. T., Kringelbach, M. L., Rolls, E. T., & Jezzard, P. (2002). Fast, fully automated global and local magnetic field optimization for fMRI of the human brain. *Neuroimage, 17*, 967–976.

Winkielman, P., Berridge, K. C., & Wilbarger, J. L. (2005). Unconscious affective reactions to masked happy versus angry faces influence consumption behavior and judgments of value. *Pers Soc Psychol Bull, 31*, 121–135.

Zatorre, R. J., Jones-Gotman, M., Evans, A. C., & Meyer, E. (1992). Functional localization and lateralization of human olfactory cortex. *Nature, 360*, 339–340.

SECTION II

Forms of Psychopathology

CHAPTER 4

Attention Deficit Hyperactivity Disorder

Lisa L. Weyandt & Anthony Swentosky

DEVELOPMENTAL AND BEHAVIORAL SEQUELAE

Attention deficit hyperactivity disorder (ADHD) is characterized by pervasive and developmentally inappropriate levels of attention, impulsivity, and hyperactivity (American Psychiatric Association [APA], 2000). Three subtypes of ADHD are currently recognized by the APA and include ADHD combined type (ADHD-C), ADHD predominately inattentive type (ADHD-I), and ADHD predominantly hyperactive-impulsive type. The disorder affects approximately 3%–7% of the child population and 4%–5% of the adult population (Kessler et al., 2006). ADHD is diagnosed more often in males than females with ratios ranging from 3:1 in the general population to 6:1 in children referred to clinical settings (Gaub & Carlson, 1997; Rucklidge, 2008).

Developmentally, maternal alcohol use, smoking, stress, premature delivery, and low birth weight are associated with increased risk of ADHD (Cornelius & Day, 2009; Hartsough & Lambert, 1985; Kim et al., 2009; Millichap, 2008; Pringsheim, Sandor, Lang, Shah, & O'Connor, 2009). During toddlerhood and preschool years, children with ADHD are more likely to have a difficult temperament and to display more inappropriate, defiant, and noncompliant behaviors than children without the disorder (Pierce, Ewing, & Campbell, 1999; Riley et al., 2008). Research also suggests that parents of children with ADHD are more likely to display negative behaviors toward their children and to experience greater stress and poorer adaptive skills than parents of children without ADHD (DuPaul, McGoey, Eckert, & VanBrakle, 2001).

During childhood, children with ADHD are likely to experience academic achievement problems and many have coexisting learning disabilities, most commonly reading disability (Willcutt, Pennington, Olson, & DeFries, 2007). In general, these children are more likely to have poorer grades, lower scores on standardized tests, higher retention rates, and an increased use of school-based services (Loe & Feldman, 2007). Approximately 40%–70% of children diagnosed with ADHD also have comorbid conduct and oppositional disorders (Barkley, 2006). Given these comorbidity rates, it is not surprising that studies have found that children with ADHD are more likely to be rejected socially and to have greater difficulties with their peers than children without the disorder (Barbaresi, Katusic, Colligan, Weaver, & Jacobsen, 2007; Hinshaw, 2002). To compound the problem, teachers are more likely to perceive a child with an ADHD label less favorably with respect to intelligence, personality, and behavior (Batzle, Weyandt, Janusis, & Devietti, 2009).

Research concerning adolescents with ADHD has revealed that these students continue to struggle with academic, attention, and impulsivity problems. Hyperactivity symptoms tend to decrease during adolescence; however, feelings of mental or internal restlessness tend to increase (APA, 2000; Weyandt et al., 2003). Studies have also revealed that adolescents with ADHD are more likely to have a higher absenteeism rate and are at greater risk for dropping out of high school than their peers without the disorder (Barbaresi et al., 2007). Students with ADHD who do graduate from high school are less likely than their peers to pursue a post-secondary education (DuPaul & Weyandt, 2009). With regard to driving, adolescents with ADHD are more likely to receive traffic citations for speeding, be involved in motor vehicle accidents and accidents for which the driver is at fault, and have more severe crashes as determined from dollar damage and likelihood of bodily injuries from the accident (Thompson, Molina, Pelham, & Gnagy, 2007). Adolescents with ADHD are also more likely to have their licenses suspended or fully revoked (Barkley, 2004). Socially, adolescents with ADHD are at greater risk for antisocial behavior, criminal activity, and substance use problems (Barkley, Fischer, Smallish, & Fletcher, 2004; Langley et al., 2010). Longitudinal findings suggest that those with comorbid conduct disorder are at even greater risk for criminality in adolescence and adulthood compared to those without comorbid conduct disorder (Satterfield et al., 2007).

Empirical information concerning ADHD in adulthood is less abundant than information concerning ADHD in childhood; however, a growing body of literature is emerging concerning this population. Preliminary findings, for example, suggest that most young adults with ADHD do not pursue a college education, but those who do appear to be at risk for academic, social, and psychological difficulties (Weyandt & DuPaul, 2006; Weyandt & DuPaul, 2008). Studies have also reported that students with ADHD perform more poorly on a variety of inhibition tasks (Ossmann & Mulligan, 2003) and are more likely to experience unwanted intrusive and worrisome thoughts (Abramovitch & Schweiger, 2009). Interestingly, parents of college students with ADHD have been found to provide more support than students without ADHD, who reportedly receive greater support from friends rather than parents (Wilmhurst, Peele, & Wilmhurst, 2011). DuPaul, Weyandt, O'Dell, and Varejao (2009) aptly noted, however, that studies with college students with ADHD are often characterized by lack of controlled investigations, use of small samples, and lack of confirmation of diagnostic status. Methodologically sound investigations are needed in the areas of assessment and intervention to better understand this population of individuals with ADHD and to help promote the success of students with ADHD in higher education.

On a related note, stimulant medication is often the first line of treatment for students with ADHD; however, recent studies have revealed that non-prescribed use (i.e., diversion) of stimulant medication is a growing problem among middle and high school students as well as on college campuses. McCabe, Teter, and Boyd (2004), for example, found that 23% of middle and high school students with a valid prescription reported being approached to sell, give, or trade their stimulant medication. Poulin (2007) reported that 6% of a large sample (n = 12,990) of adolescents reported non-medical use of prescription stimulants. A number of studies have reported that approximately 7% of college students report that they misuse prescription stimulant medication (Weyandt et al., 2009; Wilens et al., 2008). What remains unclear is whether students with documented ADHD are also likely to misuse prescription stimulant medication.

Research with adults with ADHD in the general population has found that they continue to experience ADHD symptoms and are at an increased risk for social, psychological, and occupational impairments. For example, adults with ADHD are at greater risk for substance use and abuse, comorbid psychiatric conditions, criminality, and lower educational attainment (de Graaf et al., 2008; Lie, 1992; Sobanski et al., 2007; Wilens et al. 2009). Over a decade ago, Mannuzza, Klein, Bessler, Malloy, and LaPadula (1998) found that very few adults with ADHD held professional positions and, instead, the most common occupations of adults with ADHD were skilled and physical labor (Mannuzza, Klein, Bessler, Malloy, & Hynes, 1997). Recently, Barkley and Murphy (2010) reported that executive function impairments (i.e., deficits in planning, organization, inhibition) contribute to occupational impairments frequently found in adults with ADHD. Research has also found that adults with ADHD are also more likely to experience marital and interpersonal difficulties (Wymbs et al., 2008).

Summary

In summary, ADHD is estimated to affect 3%–7% of the school age population and 4%–5% of the adult population. Developmentally, prenatal factors such as maternal smoking and alcohol use increase the risk of ADHD in children. During the preschool years, children with ADHD are more likely to engage in inappropriate social behaviors, including aggression and noncompliance. Academic problems emerge during the elementary school years and many children with ADHD are diagnosed with coexisting learning or behavior problems. Adolescents with ADHD are at risk for peer rejection, substance use and abuse, and high school dropout. College students with the disorder are also at risk for academic, social, and psychological problems. Adults with ADHD continue to experience ADHD symptoms as well as impairments in social, interpersonal, psychological, and occupational functioning.

The underlying pathophysiology of ADHD is complex and the precise etiology remains unknown. Neuropsychological theories involving abnormalities of the dopaminergic and frontal–striatal brain systems have received substantial support, however, and will be discussed in the following sections (Sharp, McQuillin, & Gurling, 2009; Weyandt, 2006).

NEUROPSYCHOLOGICAL SEQUELAE

An abundance of studies have documented neuropsychological deficits in children and adolescents with ADHD (Barkley, 2003; Pennington & Ozonoff, 1996; Weyandt, 2005). These studies are based on several competing theories that view ADHD symptomatology as resulting from core neuropsychological deficits. For example, some authors suggest that primary deficits in executive functioning lead directly or indirectly to behavioral symptoms of impulsivity, inattention, and hyperactivity (Willcutt, Doyle, Nigg, Faraone, & Pennington, 2005a). In contrast, Barkley's (1997) unifying theory of ADHD purports that behavioral inhibition leads to secondary executive functioning deficits, including working memory, self-regulation, and goal-directed behavior. Other neuropsychological theories of ADHD, usually referred to as dual-pathway models, suggest that in addition to executive functioning deficits, neuropsychological impairments in arousal, effort, and attention (Sergeant, 2005) and/or motivational processes (Sonuga-Barke, 2005) lead to the manifestation of ADHD. A discussion of the empirical evidence supporting these as well as other neuropsychological findings regarding ADHD follows.

Childhood

The neuropsychological functioning of children with ADHD has been studied extensively. Executive functioning is a construct that refers to a specific type of neuropsychological functioning, involving cognitive abilities such as strategic planning, impulse control, cognitive flexibility, and goal-directed behavior. Several definitions of executive functioning exist (e.g., Anderson, Anderson, Northam, Jacobs, & Mikiewicz, 2002; Mikaye et al., 2000; Welsh & Pennington, 1988), although the processes of response inhibition and goal-directed behavior are central components across most definitions (Weyandt, 2009). Executive function deficits have been found to be predictive of academic and social outcomes in adolescence (Miller & Hinshaw, 2009) and studies have suggested that children as young as 3 years old with ADHD may demonstrate executive functioning deficits (Byrne, DeWolfe, & Bawden, 1998). For example, Mahone, Pillion, Hoffman, Hiemenz, and Denckla (2005) found that children with ADHD ages 3–6.5 years were significantly impaired compared to controls on measures of errors of omission, mean response times, and variability in response times while performing an auditory continuous performance task, supporting executive functioning impairments in inhibitory control and response preparation. Using a behavioral measure of executive functioning (BRIEF-P), Mahone and Hoffman (2007) found significant impairments in preschool and kindergarten-age children on a wider range of executive functions, including working memory, set shifting, inhibition, and planning.

Executive function impairments appear to persist into childhood and possibly become more pronounced in young school-aged children (Berlin, Bohlin, & Rydell, 2003; Fugetta,

2006). For example, Nigg, Blaskey, Huang-Pollock, and Rappley (2002) found that compared to controls, 7–12-year-old children with ADHD-C made significantly more errors on measures of behavioral inhibition, inhibitory control (Stop Task), and interference control (Stroop Task). Children with ADHD-C and children with ADHD-I were both significantly impaired on measures of planning and working memory (Tower of London). Furthermore, in addition to the executive functioning measures, both ADHD groups demonstrated significantly slower motor output speeds. This is a critical finding because multiple studies have reported neuropsychological deficits in both executive and nonexecutive functioning tasks, which strongly implies that *neuropsychological impairments in ADHD are not specific to executive functions* (Geurts, Verte, Oosterlaan, Roeyers, & Sergeant, 2005; Solanto, et al., 2007; Wu, Anderson, & Castiello, 2002). Similarly, response time variability across tasks is sometimes classified as an executive functioning measure, whereas others suggest that it represents deficits in regulation of affect, motivation, and arousal (Sergeant, 2005). Multiple studies of children with ADHD have demonstrated increased response time variability on a number of different tasks (Johnson et al., 2007; Wahlstedt, Thorell, & Bohlin, 2009; Klein, Wendling, Huettner, Ruder, & Peper, 2006), suggesting this may be a core neuropsychological impairment in ADHD. It should be noted that response time variability has also been reported in other populations, including individuals with reading disabilities (Willcutt, Pennington, Olson, Chhabildas, & Hulslander, 2005b). Therefore, just as neuropsychological impairments in ADHD are not specific to executive functions, response time variability may not be specific to ADHD. Recently, Weyandt (2009) noted that ADHD is *not* associated with *global* executive functioning deficits but instead with specific impairments on some executive function tasks. Together, these findings strongly suggest that individuals with ADHD demonstrate impairments on some but not all neuropsychological and/or executive function tasks. Additional research is needed to better understand the specific types of executive function tasks that may be uniquely associated with ADHD.

In an effort to tease apart the contribution of neuropsychological deficits to ADHD symptomology, Sonuga-Barke (2005) proposed a dual-pathway model of ADHD in which executive functions and delay aversion deficits represent distinct neuropsychological impairments that each contribute to ADHD symptomatology. Supporting empirical evidence demonstrating unique contributions of executive functioning and delay aversion to ADHD symptoms exists for both preschoolers (Sonuga-Barke, Dalen, & Remington, 2003) and older children (Solanto et al., 2001). For example, Solanto and colleagues (2001) found that the Stop Signal task, which served as a measure of executive functioning (i.e., inhibitory control), and the Choice-Delay Task, which was purported to measure delay aversion, exhibited significantly better discriminant validity when used in combination as opposed to being used independently. In a community sample of 3–5-year-old children, Sonuga-Barke and colleagues (2003) found that measures of executive functioning and delay aversion made significant independent contributions to parental ratings of ADHD symptoms.

Adolescence

Various types of executive function and other neuropsychological deficits have been documented in adolescents with ADHD (Rhodes, Coghill, & Matthews, 2005; Rommelse et al., 2007; Seidman et al., 1997; Seidman et al., 2005). For example, Seidman, Biederman, Monuteaux, Doyle, and Faraone (2001) assessed the neuropsychological performance of adolescent boys with ADHD and comorbid learning disabilities compared to boys with pure ADHD and controls. Boys with ADHD and a comorbid learning disability tended to perform significantly worse than ADHD boys and controls on measures of planning and organization, vigilance, response inhibition, set shifting and categorization, selective attention and visual scanning, verbal and visual learning, and memory. Although the "pure" ADHD group also showed a few neuropsychological impairments compared to controls, overall these findings suggest that adolescents with ADHD and a comorbid reading disorder are likely to have increased neuropsychological impairments compared to non-comorbid ADHD. Similar findings from a study by Willcutt and colleagues (2005b) showed that adolescents with ADHD were significantly impaired compared to controls on response inhibition and processing speed tasks, but adolescents with ADHD and comorbid reading disability tended to show a much wider range of neuropsychological impairments on a larger number of tasks. Adolescents with ADHD also tend to display increased response time variability on a number of neuropsychological measures (Johnson et al., 2007; Willcutt et al., 2005a) suggesting that for many individuals with ADHD this is a neuropsychological impairment that persists throughout development.

College Students

The neuropsychological functioning of college students with ADHD has not been studied to the degree it has in younger age groups (DuPaul et al., 2009). Based on the handful of studies that have examined this population, results have been mixed. For example, Gropper and Tannock (2009) found that college students with ADHD had significant impairments in auditory working memory and visual-spatial working memory compared to controls. In a large sample ($n = 770$) of college students, Weyandt, Linterman, and Rice (1995) found significant impairments on the Wisconsin Card Sorting Task in students who demonstrated elevated levels (above the 93rd percentile) of ADHD symptoms, although impairments on several other neuropsychological tasks were not found. Similar findings were found in a related study by Weyandt and colleagues (2002) in which college students with ADHD, compared to controls, committed an increased level of omission errors on the Test of Variables of Attention, but had comparable performances on measures of commission errors, mean response time, and variability in response time. Based on these and other findings (Linterman & Weyandt, 2001), it appears that neuropsychological impairments may not be as evident in college students with ADHD. Further investigations using reliable and valid measures of a larger number of neuropsychological abilities, however, are needed before definitive conclusions can be made regarding this population.

Adulthood

Studies examining the neuropsychological functioning in adults with ADHD suggest impairments across both executive functioning and nonexecutive functioning tasks (Boonstra, Oosterlaan, Sergeant, & Buitelaar, 2005; Bramham, et al., 2009; Nigg et al., 2005a; Seidman, Biederman, Weber, Hatch, & Faraone, 1998), although these findings are not as consistent as they are in the child and adolescent literature. For instance, Fischer, Barkley, Smallish, and Fletcher (2005) found that young adults with ADHD were significantly impaired compared to controls on several measures of attention and inhibition. Nigg and colleagues (2005a) found that adults with ADHD ages 18–37 were significantly impaired on measures of executive functioning and processing speed. Furthermore, while controlling for symptoms of hyperactivity and impulsivity, symptoms of inattention were significantly related to executive functioning. Also, as expected, hyperactivity was associated with faster output speed and inattention was associated with slower output speeds. These findings indicate that different ADHD subtypes in adulthood may be related to specific neuropsychological profiles.

In a meta-analysis by Boonstra and colleagues (2005), impairments in executive and nonexecutive neuropsychological measures were found in adults with ADHD compared to controls. Across the 13 studies that were used, executive functioning effect sizes (Cohen's *d*) ranged from 0.62–0.89, while effect sizes for nonexecutive functioning neuropsychological tasks ranged from 0.57–0.62. Although all effect sizes were in the medium-to-large range, the authors explain that due to a lack of published studies, several specific executive functions (e.g., working memory, planning) were not able to be analyzed. Based on these findings, it appears that at least some adults with ADHD demonstrate neuropsychological impairments, although additional studies within this age group are needed to determine the level of impairment across a wider range of neuropsychological measures. Further studies are also needed to examine the effects that possible moderating variables such as intelligence, education level, and symptom severity may have on executive functioning impairment.

Summary

As discussed previously, a number of studies have indicated that children, adolescents, and, to a lesser degree, adults with ADHD demonstrate impairments in neuropsychological functioning, especially executive functions. It should be noted, however, that not all individuals with ADHD demonstrate executive function impairments (Nigg et al., 2005b; Weyandt, 2009) and executive function impairments are not unique to ADHD; rather, they have been found in a number of disorders (Dickstein et al., 2004; Roth, Milovan, Baribeau, & O'Conner, 2005; Toren et al., 2000). Methodological problems characterize many of the existing studies, and statistical controls are not typically used for the presence of comorbid disorders. Most of the studies use small sample sizes that often result in low statistical power, particularly when the effect sizes are small. Also, it is important to note that although many studies find executive function impairments in children, adolescents, and adults with ADHD on some neuropsychological tasks, they often fail to find impairments on other tasks. This may be due in part to the variety of definitions and interpretations of the construct of "executive functions" that exist, hence the level of executive functioning impairments in ADHD may depend on the specific definition used (Barkley, 1997; Miyake et al., 2000; Pennington & Ozonoff, 1996). Lastly, the psychometric properties of many of the neuropsychological instruments used in the literature are questionable. Obviously, consistent use of psychometrically sound measures is necessary in order to arrive at more precise and accurate conclusions. Future studies are sorely needed to explore differences in executive functioning performance across ADHD subtypes, gender, and level of symptom severity (Weyandt, 2009). In addition, the literature base concerning childhood and adolescent neuropsychology needs to be supplemented by more studies focusing on adult populations in order to better understand the homotypic and heterotypic continuity of neuropsychological impairments in ADHD.

NEUROPATHOLOGY AND PATHOPHYSIOLOGY

Main Theories

A specific and definitive cause of ADHD is unknown; however, findings across genetic, neuroanatomical, neuroimaging, and neuropsychological disciplines implicate frontal–striatal systems (Barkley, 1997; Castellanos et al., 2002; Weyandt, 2006, 2009; Willcutt et al., 2005b). Arguably the most common pathophysiological explanation for ADHD involves dopaminergic transmission throughout frontal–striatal and frontal–parietal pathways. Dopaminergic pyramidal neurons located in the ventral tegmental area of the midbrain and the substantia nigra project to regions in the prefrontal and parietal cortices. These pathways play a critical role in the regulation of attention, inhibition, and planned motor behavior (Arnsten, Berridge, & McCracken, 2009; Bush, Valera, & Seidman, 2005; Dickstein, Bannon, Castellanos, & Milham, 2006). Additional types of neurotransmitters are found in this region as well; however, research supports that dopamine plays a critical role in ADHD-related behavior (Middleton & Strick, 2000; Mink, 1996; Silk, Vance, Rinehart, Bradshaw, & Cunnington, 2008). In addition, increasing evidence suggests that a wider number of networks, structures, and neurotransmitters likely contribute to the disorder (Halperin & Schulz, 2006; Kieling, Goncalves, Tannock, & Castellanos, 2008; Weyandt, 2006). Neuroimaging and neuropharmacological evidence supporting the influence of dopaminergic frontal–striatal networks, as well as other neurotransmitters and neuronal networks implicated in ADHD, are subsequently discussed.

Neuroimaging Studies

Neuroimaging studies have become more plentiful during the last decade, and the findings across studies have been equivocal. For example, using magnetic resonance imaging (MRI) techniques, children and adolescents with ADHD have been compared to controls and have been found to have reduced total brain volumes (Castellanos et al., 1994; Castellanos et al., 2002). In a more recent study, Narr, Woods, and Lin (2009) also found significant reductions in overall brain volume, gray matter volume, and mean cortical thickness in children and adolescents with ADHD compared to age- and sex-matched controls. In the same study, white matter volumes were significantly larger in the ADHD group. Yang and colleagues (2008) used a sample of Chinese youth and found that both boys and girls with ADHD had significant reductions in total brain volumes compared to controls. Contrary to these findings, however, Seidman and colleagues (2006) did not find significant total brain volume reductions in adults with ADHD, although they did report that adults with ADHD had significantly smaller amounts of cortical gray matter and significantly greater amounts of cortical white matter compared to controls. Similarly, McAlonan et al. (2007) did not find differences in global brain volume between children with and without ADHD.

Valera, Faraone, Murray, and Seidman (2007) conducted a meta-analysis that included 11 MRI studies comparing total cerebral volumes of ADHD individuals (n = 353) to controls (n = 356) and reported significant reductions for individuals with ADHD. Kates and colleagues (2002) found that school-aged boys with ADHD had significant reductions in mean cerebral, total frontal lobe, total prefrontal lobe, left prefrontal, and right prefrontal volumes compared to boys with Tourette's syndrome and controls. In a related study using MRI, Mostofsky, Cooper, Kates, Denckla, and Kaufmann (2002) found that the average total cerebral volumes of boys with ADHD were 8.3% smaller compared to age- and sex-matched controls. However, when the four individual lobes were analyzed, only the frontal lobes were significantly smaller in volume in ADHD boys compared to controls. Similarly, the ratio of the frontal lobe tissue volume in the boys with ADHD tended to be smaller than that of the control group. Together, these findings suggest that total cerebral volumes, and more specifically, frontal lobe volumes, tend to be smaller in individuals with ADHD compared to controls; however, it is crucial to note that this finding is not true of all studies, and more importantly, these anatomical differences are not unique to ADHD and have been found in other clinical disorders, such as autistic disorder (Bloss & Courchesn, 2007).

In addition to gross measures of brain structures (e.g., total brain volume, cerebral volume, frontal lobes), neuroimaging studies have also provided more precise analyses of individual brain structures in individuals with ADHD. For example, boys with ADHD have been found to have significant differences in basal ganglia volume and shape compared to controls (Qiu et al., 2009). More specifically, using MRI and Large Deformation Diffeomorphic Metric Surface Mapping (LDDMM-surface), Qiu and colleagues found significant reductions in left caudate, left and right putamen, and left and right globus pallidus in children with ADHD. Although volume reductions for basal ganglia structures are sometimes found in individuals with ADHD, findings regarding hemispheric specificity of the reductions have been inconsistent. For example, decreased volume of the left globus pallidus has been reported by some authors (Aylward et al., 1996), whereas others have reported decreased volume in the right globus pallidus (Castellanos et al., 1996). Some studies have found males with ADHD to have significant reductions in left total caudate and caudate head volumes compared to controls (Filipek, Semrud-Clikeman, & Steingard, 1997), whereas others have found decreased right caudate volumes (Castellanos et al., 1996). Pliszka, Lancaster, Liotti, and Semrud-Clikeman (2006) found significant bilateral reductions in caudate volumes for children with ADHD compared to controls. This study also showed that a stimulant treatment–naïve ADHD group had significantly smaller right anterior cingulate cortex volumes compared to ADHD children who have taken stimulants and the control group. Interestingly, there were no significant differences between ADHD children who have taken stimulants and the control group, possibly suggesting that stimulant medication may help regulate the development of certain brain structures.

Reductions in cerebellar volumes have also been reported in children and adolescents with ADHD (Berquin et al., 1998), and this finding has been associated with deficits in fronto-striatal–cerebellar neurocircuitry. For example, girls with ADHD have been found to have significant reductions in cerbellar vermis volumes compared to controls (Castellanos et al., 2001). Bledsoe, Semrud-Clikeman, and Pliszka (2009) found that children with ADHD who had no history of stimulation medication treatment had significant reductions in cerebellar vermis volumes compared to chronically treated (via stimulant medication) children with ADHD and controls. Consistent with these findings, Mackie and colleagues (2007) found superior cerebellar vermis volumes to be significantly smaller in ADHD individuals compared to controls. These authors also found that right and left inferior posterior cerebellar lobes of ADHD children who had worse clinical outcomes exhibited significant reductions in volume compared to ADHD children with more favorable outcomes. What remains unclear, however, is whether these anatomical differences are indeed related to ADHD symptomology. As discussed by Weyandt (2006), brain anatomy is not necessarily directly related to brain function and additional studies are needed to demonstrate a relationship between brain morphology and the cognitive and behavioral symptoms associated with ADHD.

It is also important to note that individuals with ADHD have been found to have volume reductions in brain regions other than the frontal–striatal regions. For example, Frodl and colleagues (2010) recently found significant bilateral reductions in amygdala volumes but not hippocampal volumes in adults with ADHD compared to adults with major depression and controls. Furthermore, increased hyperactivity symptoms were associated with smaller right amygdala volumes. The corpus callosum, which is the brain's primary commissure connecting the right and left hemispheres, has also been found to have reduced volumes in children with ADHD (Hill et al., 2003). These findings raise serious questions about the significance of anatomical differences and how they pertain to theoretical models concerning the pathophysiology of ADHD.

Perhaps what is more meaningful than anatomical differences is whether there is evidence that brain functioning is compromised in individuals with ADHD. Indeed, a growing body of evidence suggests catecholamines (i.e., neuroepinephrine and dopamine) play an important role in prefrontal functioning, and given that the prefrontal cortex is believed to exert top-down control over attention, impulsivity, and other cognitions and behaviors, it has been hypothesized that dysfunctional dopaminergic and noradrenergic frontal–striatal pathways are implicated in ADHD symptomatology (Arnsten, 2009). For example, studies using fMRI and positron emission tomography (PET) have found reduced activation (i.e., blood flow or glucose metabolism) in frontal-striatal-parietal and frontal-temporal networks in individuals with ADHD (Rubia et al., 2009; Silk et al., 2008). Specifically, Durston, Mulder, Casey, Ziermans, and van Engeland (2006) found that when performing a cognitive inhibition task, children and adolescents with ADHD, as well as their unaffected siblings, showed decreased activation in the ventral prefrontal and inferior parietal cortices based on fMRI scanning.

PET studies have also revealed reduced levels of dopamine transporters and receptors (D_2 and D_3) in the caudate, nucleus accumbens, and midbrain in adults with ADHD (Volkow et al., 2009). Reduced activation in the ventral striatum during a reward anticipation task has been found in adolescents with ADHD compared to controls (Scheres, Milhan, Knutson, & Castellanos, 2007). Importantly, this decreased activation has been found to be negatively correlated with parent ratings of hyperactivity and impulsivity symptoms. Similarly, during an immediate and delayed reward task, hyporesponsiveness of the ventral–striatum pathway was found in adults with ADHD compared to controls (Plichta et al., 2009). In the same study, increased activation of the caudate nucleus and amygdala was found for ADHD adults during the delayed reward task only. However, not all studies have found reduced activation in the frontal–striatal regions. In fact, Teicher and colleagues (2000) actually found *increased* rCBF in the striatum of 6–12-year-old boys with ADHD compared to controls. Similarly, Zametkin and colleagues (1993) did not find reductions in global glucose metabolism in adolescents with and without ADHD.

Based on these structural and functional findings, it appears that multiple neuronal networks are likely involved in ADHD symptomatology. Nigg and Casey (2005) explain that ADHD is likely the result of a dysfunctional interaction between frontal–striatal loops involved in response output control, suppression, and selection; frontal–cerebellar loops involved in temporal information processing; and frontal–limbic loops involved in reinforcement learning and avoidance conditioning. Increasing, decreasing, or stabilizing neurotransmitter availability throughout these implicated networks is believed to reduce ADHD symptomatology. The following section discusses some of the empirical support for this hypothesis.

Medication Studies

Whereas some authors have suggested dopamine deficit hypotheses for ADHD (Levy, 1991; Tripp & Wickens, 2009), others have suggested a dopamine excess hypothesis (Solanto, 1998). However, given the complexity of the brain's neurotransmitter systems, both of these hypotheses appear overly simplistic and subtle alterations in dopaminergic or other neurotransmitter systems can likely impair prefrontal systems that help to regulate thought and behavior (Arnsten, 2009).

The most common pharmacological treatment for ADHD is psychostimulant medication, especially methylphenidate (MPH; Dodson, 2005; Findling, 2008). Meta-analyses have consistently found significant effects of MPH in reducing ADHD symptomatology, and effect sizes have ranged from medium (d = 0.42) to large (d = 0.90; Faraone, Spencer, Aleardi, Pagano, & Biederman, 2004; Koesters, Becker, Kilian, Fegert, & Weinmann, 2009). Unfortunately, despite the demonstrated effectiveness of MPH, it is not completely clear how the stimulant reduces symptomatology. It is theorized that methylphenidate inhibits presynaptic dopamine and neuroepinephrine transporters, ultimately leading to increased dopamine availability in extracellular synapses (Patrick, Straugh, Perkins, & Gonzalez, 2009). Volkow and colleagues (1998) found that MPH administered to normal subjects was effective in blocking dopamine transporters in the striatum. Atomoxetine, a nonstimulant medication that has demonstrated effectiveness in treating ADHD, is also believed to achieve its therapeutic effects by inhibiting presynaptic neuroepinephrine transporters (Bymaster, Katner, & Nelson, 2002; Findling, 2008).

Using single photon emission computed tomography (SPECT), Lee and colleagues (2005) found that after MPH treatment ADHD children showed increased regional cerebral blood flow (rCBF) in the superior prefrontal area and decreased rCBF in the right striatum and somatosensory areas. In this same study, ADHD symptomatology also improved after MPH treatment. The authors suggest MPH may have regulated activity in these cortical and subcortical areas. Schweitzer and colleagues (2003) found that MPH administration was associated with increased rCBF in the cerebellar vermis, which was correlated with an improvement in ADHD symptoms. Vles and colleagues (2003) used SPECT to examine the effects of methylphenidate on dopamine transporter and receptor activity in boys with ADHD. Along with improvements in neuropsychological performance, a down-regulation was found in the postsynaptic dopamine receptors of the striatum, suggesting increased levels of dopamine transmission. Barry and colleagues (2009) found that after 2 weeks of atomoxetine administration, children with ADHD had more normalized electroencephalograph (EEG) patterns than they did before treatment. These normalized EEG patterns were accompanied by a reduction in omission errors on the CPT. Collectively, these medication studies lend support to the hypothesis implicating frontal–striatal pathways in the underlying pathophysiology of ADHD because stimulant medication targets this region, affects the dopaminergic system, and is associated with symptom improvement.

It is important to note that studies suggest that neuroepinephrine and dopamine transporter genes may mediate the relationship between MPH administration and treatment outcomes. For example, Yang, Yu-Feng Li, and Faraone (2004) found that polymorphisms of a neuroepinephrine transporter gene (G1287A) were associated with differential MPH responses in youth with ADHD. Similarly, Bellgrove and colleagues (2005) found that a polymorphism of a dopamine transporter gene (DAT1) was linked to improved response to methylphenidate. These genetic factors may help to explain the differential responses among ADHD individuals who receive psychostimulant treatment (Becker et al., 2010).

Summary

Empirical evidence suggests that the pathophysiology of ADHD may be characterized by widespread impairments in frontal–striatal, frontal–parietal, and frontal–striatal-cerebellar networks. Despite the growing literature suggesting impairments in neural structures, functions, and circuitry, this body of research should be interpreted cautiously and as preliminary for a number of reasons. First, neuroimaging studies rely primarily on correlational data and do not address causation. Therefore, although a relationship may be found between brain functioning and ADHD symptomology, the cause of the aberrant brain functioning remains unclear. For example, do genetic factors influence the brain functioning patterns observed or do the behavioral symptoms result in the differences found in brain function? Furthermore, similar abnormalities in neuroanatomical structures and neuronal functioning have been found in disorders other than ADHD and indicate that these irregularities are not specific to ADHD (Weyandt, 2006). Methodologically, neuroimaging studies are often characterized by serious weaknesses: small samples that often include individuals with comorbid disorders; low statistical power; lack of or inappropriate control or clinical comparison groups; multiple statistical comparisons without controls for type I error; and lack of control for intelligence, ethnicity, sex, or prior treatment history. In a nutshell, current neuroimaging techniques often lack sensitivity and specificity for clinical disorders and additional studies are needed to substantiate the validity and reliability of the findings before definitive conclusions can be drawn concerning the pathophysiology of ADHD.

CONCLUSION

ADHD, characterized by pervasive and developmentally inappropriate levels of attention, impulsivity, and hyperactivity, affects 3%–7% of the school-age population and approximately 4% of the adult population. For most individuals, ADHD is a chronic condition that emerges early in childhood and is often characterized by a difficult temperament, academic underachievement, interpersonal difficulties, and peer rejection during the school-age years. Many children with ADHD have coexisting learning problems and/or behavior disorders; the core symptoms typically continue into adolescence; and these students are at greater risk for dropping out of school, substance use and abuse, and driving accidents. Few students with ADHD attend college, but those that do are at increased risk for academic, social, and psychological difficulties. During adulthood, individuals with ADHD are at greater risk for interpersonal, substance use, and occupational difficulties. Neuropsychological deficits, particularly executive function deficits, are often found in individuals with ADHD. It should be emphasized, however, that executive function deficits are not characteristic of all individuals with ADHD nor are they unique to ADHD. The etiology of ADHD is unclear, although genetic factors play a role, as do prenatal and perinatal factors. Similarly, the pathophysiology of ADHD is not well understood, but converging lines of research across genetic, anatomical, and neurochemical disciplines strongly implicate frontal–striatal pathways. Various forms of treatment exist for ADHD, including non-pharmacological and pharmacological interventions. Stimulant medications are most commonly used in the treatment of ADHD and are often effective for children, adolescents, and adults. Additional, methodologically sound studies are needed to elucidate and differentiate the role of various brain systems in the pathophysiology of ADHD.

REFERENCES

Abramovitch, A., & Schweiger, A. (2009). Unwanted intrusive and worrisome thoughts in adults with attention deficit/hyperactivity disorder. *Psychiatry Research, 168*(3), 230–233.

American Psychiatric Association. (2000). *Diagnostic and statistical manual of mental disorders* (4th ed.), text revision. Washington, DC: American Psychiatric Association.

Anderson, V. A., Anderson, P., Northam, E., Jacobs, R., & Mikiewicz, O. (2002). Relationships between cognitive and behavioral measures of executive functioning in children with brain disease. *Child Neuropsychology, 8*, 231–240.

Arnsten, A. F. T. (2009). Toward new understanding of attention-deficit hyperactivity disorder pathophysiology: An important role for prefrontal cortex dysfunction. *CNS Drugs, 23*(1), 33–41.

Arnsten, A. F. T., Berridge, C. W., & McCracken, J. T. (2009). The neurobiological basis of attention-deficit/hyperactivity disorder. *Primary Psychiatry, 16*(7), 47–54.

Aylward, E. H., Reiss, A. L., Reader, M. J., Singer, H. S., Brown, J. E., & Denckla, M. B. (1996). Basal ganglia volumes in children with attention-deficit hyperactivity disorder. *Journal of Child Neurology, 11*, 112–115.

Barbaresi, W. J., Katusic, S. K., Colligan, R. C., Weaver, A. L., & Jacobsen, S. J. (2007). Long-term school outcomes for children with attention deficit/hyperactivity disorder: A population-based perspective. *Journal of Developmental and Behavioral Pediatrics, 28*, 265–273.

Barkley, R. A. (1997). Behavioral inhibition, sustained attention, and executive functions: Constructing a unifying theory of ADHD. *Psychological Bulletin,121*(1), 650–694.

Barkley, R. A. (2003). Issues in the diagnosis of attention-deficit/hyperactivity disorder in children. *Brain Development, 25*(2), 77–83.

Barkley, R. A. (2004). Driving impairments in teens and adults with attention-deficit/hyperactivity disorder. *Psychiatric Clinics of North America, 27*(2), 233–260.

Barkley, R. A. (2006). *Attention-deficit hyperactivity disorder: A handbook for diagnosis and treatmen*t (3rd ed.). New York: Guilford Press.

Barkley, R. A., Fischer, M., Smallish, L., & Fletcher, K. (2004). Young adult follow-up of hyperactive children: Antisocial activities and drug use. *Journal of Child Psychology and Psychiatry, 45*(2), 195–211.

Barkley, R. A., & Murphy, K. R. (2010). Impairment in occupational functioning and adult ADHD: The predictive utility of executive function (EF) ratings versus EF tests. *Archives of Clinical Neuropsychology.*

Barry, R. J., Clarke, A. R., Hajos, M., McCarthy, R., Selikowitz, M., & Bruggemann, J. M. (2009). Acute atomoxetine effects on the EEG of children with Attention-Deficit/Hyperactivity Disorder. *Neuropharmacology, 57*, 702–707.

Batzle, C., Weyandt, L. L., Janusis, G. M., & DeVietti, T. (2009). Potential impact of ADHD with stimulant medication label on teacher expectations. *Journal of Attention Disorders. Prepublished September 22, 2009.*

Becker, K., Blomeyer, D., El-Faddagh, M., Esser, G., Schmidt, M. H., Banaschewski, T., et al. (2010). From regulatory problems in infancy to attention deficit/hyperactivity disorder in childhood: A moderating role for the dopamine D4 receptor gene? *Journal of Pediatrics, 156*, 798–803.

Bellgrove, M. A., Hawi, Z., Kirley, A., Fitzgerald, M., Gill, M., & Robertson, I. H. (2005). Association between dopamine transporter (DAT1) genotype, left-sided inattention, and an enhanced response to methylphenidate in attention-deficit hyperactivity disorder. *Neuropsychopharmacology, 30*(12), 2290–2297.

Berlin, L., Bohlin, G., & Rydell, A. M. (2003). Relations between inhibition, executive functioning, and ADHD symptoms: A longitudinal study from age 5 to 8 1\2 years. *Child Neuropsychology, 9*, 255–266.

Berquin, P. C., Giedd, J. N., Jacobsen, L. K., Hamburger, S. D., Krain, A. L., Rapaport, J. L., et al. (1998). Cerebellum in attention-deficit hyperactivity disorder: A morphometric MRI study. *Neurology, 50*, 1087–1093.

Bledsoe, J., Semrud-Clikeman, M., & Pliszka, S. R. (2009). A magnetic resonance imaging study of the cerebellar vermis in chronically treated and treatment-naive children with attention-deficit/hyperactivity disorder combined type. *Biological Psychiatry, 65*, 620– 624.

Boonstra, A. M., Oosterlann, J., Sergeant, J. A., & Buitelaar, J. K. (2005). Executive functioning in adult ADHD: A meta-analytic review. *Psychol Med., 35*, 1097–1108.

Bramham, J., Ambery, F., Young, S., Morris, R., Russell, A., & Xenitidis, K. (2009). Executive functioning differences between adults with attention deficit hyperactivity disorder and autistic spectrum disorder in initiation, planning and strategy formation. *Autism, 13*(3), 245–264.

Bush, G., Valera, E. M., & Seidman, L. J. (2005). Functional neuroimaging of attention-deficit/hyperactivity disorder: a review and suggested future directions. *Biological Psychiatry, 57*(11), 1273–1284.

Bymaster, F. P., Katner, J. S., & Nelson, D. L. (2002). Atomoxetine increases extracellular levels of norepinephrine and dopamine in prefrontal cortex of rat: A potential mechanism for efficacy in attention deficit/hyperactivity disorder. *Neuropsychopharmacology, 27*, 699–711.

Byrne, J. M., DeWolfe, N. A., & Bawden, H. N. (1998). Assessment of attention-deficit/hyperactivity disorder in pre-schoolers. *Child Neuropsychology, 4*, 49–66.

Castellanos, F. X., Giedd, J. N., & Berquin, P. C. (2001). Quantitative brain magnetic resonance imaging in girls with attention-deficit/hyperactivity disorder. *Archives of General Psychiatry, 58*, 289–295.

Castellanos, F. X., Giedd, J. N., Eckburg, P., Marsh, W. L., Vaituzis, A. C., Kaysen, D., et al. (1994). Quantitative morphology of the caudate nucleus in attention deficit hyperactivity disorder. *American Journal of Psychiatry, 151*, 1791–1796.

Castellanos, F. X., Giedd, J. N., Marsh, W. L., Hamburger, S. D., Vaituzis, A. C., Dickstein, D. P., et al. (1996). Quantitative brain magnetic resonance imaging in attention-deficit hyperactivity disorder. *Archives of General Psychiatry, 53*, 607–616.

Castellanos, F. X., Lee, P. P., Sharp, W., Jeffries, N. O., Greenstein, D. K., Clasen, L. S., et al. (2002). Developmental trajectories of brain volume abnormalities in children and adolescents with attention-deficit/hyperactivity disorder. *Journal of American Medical Association, 288*, 1740–1748.

Cornelius, M. D., & Day, N. L. (2009). Developmental consequences of prenatal tobacco exposure. *Current Opinion in Neurology, 22*(2), 121–125.

de Graaf, R., Kessler, R. C., Fayyad, J., ten Have, M., Alonso, J., Angermeyer, M., et al. (2008). The prevalence and effects of adult attention-deficit/hyperactivity disorder (ADHD) on the performance of workers: Results from the WHO World Mental Health Survey Initiative. *Occupation and Environmental Medicine, 65*(12), 835–842.

Dickstein, D. P., Treland, J. E., Snow, J., McClure, E. B., Mehta, M. S., Towbin, K. E., et al. (2004). Neuropsychological performance in pediatric bipolar disorder. *Biological Psychiatry, 55*, 32–39.

Dickstein, S. G., Bannon, K., Castellanos, F. X., & Milham, M. P. (2006). The neural correlates of attention deficit hyperactivity disorder: An ALE meta-analysis. *Journal of Child Psychology and Psychiatry, 47*(10), 1051–1062.

Dodson, W. W. (2005). Pharmacotherapy of adult ADHD. *Journal of Clinical Psychology, 61*, 589–606.

DuPaul, G. J., McGoey, K. E., Eckert, T. L., & VanBrakle, J. (2001). Preschool children with attention-deficit/hyperactivity disorder: Impairments in behavioral, social, and school functioning. *Journal of the American Academy of Child and Adolescent Psychiatry, 40*(5), 508–515.

DuPaul, G. J., & Weyandt, L. L. (2009). Introduction to special series on college students with ADHD. *Journal of Attention Disorders, 13*(3), 232–233.

DuPaul, G. J., Weyandt, L. L., O'Dell, S. M., & Varejao, M. (2009). College students with ADHD: Current status and future directions. *Journal of Attention Disorders, 13*(3), 234–250.

Durston, S., Mulder, M., Casey, B. J., Ziermans, T., & van Engeland, H. (2006). Activation in ventral prefrontal cortex is sensitive to genetic vulnerability for attention-deficit hyperactivity disorder. *Biological Psychiatry, 60*, 1062–1070.

Faraone, S. V., Spencer, T., Aleardi, M., Pagano, C., & Biederman, J. (2004). Meta-analysis of the efficacy of methylphenidate for treating adult attention-deficit/hyperactivity disorder. *Journal of Clinical Psychopharmacology, 24*, 24–29.

Filipek, P. A., Semrud-Clikeman, M., & Steingard, R. J. (1997). Volumetric MRI analysis comparing subjects having attention-deficit hyperactivity disorder with normal controls. *Neurology, 48*, 589–601.

Findling, R. L. (2008). Evolution of the treatment of attention-deficit/hyperactivity disorder in children: A review. *Clinical Therapeutics, 30*(5), 942–957.

Fischer, M., Barkley, R. A., Smallish, L., & Fletcher, K. (2005). Executive functioning in hyperactive children as young adults: Attention, inhibition, response perseveration, and the impact of comorbidity. *Developmental Neuropsychology, 27*, 107–133.

Frodl, T., Stauber, J., Schaaff, N., Koutsouleris, N., Scheuereeker, J., Ewers, M., et al . (2010). Amygdala reduction in patients with ADHD compared with major depression and healthy volunteers. *Acta Psychiatrica Scandinavica, 121*, 111–118.

Fugetta, G. P. (2006). Impairment of executive functions in boys with attention deficit/hyperactivity disorder. *Child Neuropsychology, 12*, 1–21.

Gaub, M., & Carlson, C. L. (1997). Gender differences in ADHD: A meta-analysis and critical review. *Journal of the American Academy of Child and Adolescent Psychiatry, 36*(8), 1036–1045.

Gropper, R. J., & Tannock, R. (2009). A pilot study of working memory and academic achievement in college students with ADHD. *Journal of Attention Disorders, 12*(6), 574–581.

Geurts, H. M., Verte, S., Oosterlaan, J., Roeyers, H., & Sergeant, J.A. (2005). ADHD subtypes: Do they differ in their executive functioning profile? *Archives of Clinical Neuropsychology, 20*, 457–477.

Halperin, J. M., & Schulz, K. P. (2006). Revisiting the role of the prefrontal cortex in the pathophysiology of attention-deficit hyperactivity disorder. *Psychological Bulletin, 132*(4), 560–581.

Hartsough, C. S., & Lambert, N. M. (1985). Medical factors in hyperactive and normal children: Prenatal, developmental, and health history findings. *American Journal of Orthopsychiatry, 55*(2), 190–201.

Hill, D. E., Yeo, R. A., Campbell, R. A., Hart, B., Vigil, J., & Brooks, W. (2003). Magnetic resonance imaging correlates of attention-deficit/hyperactivity disorder in children. *Neuropsychology, 17*, 496–506.

Hinshaw, S. P. (2002). Is ADHD an impairing condition in childhood and adolescence? In P. S. Jensen & J. R. Cooper (Eds.), *Attention deficit hyperactivity disorder: State of the science, best practices*. Kingston, NJ: Civic Research Institute.

Johnson, K. A., Kelly, S. P., Bellgrove, M. A., Barry, E., Cox, M., Gill, M., et al . (2007). Response variability in attention deficit hyperactivity disorder: Evidence for neuropsychological heterogeneity. *Neuropsychologia, 45*, 630–638.

Kates, W. R., Frederikse, M., Mostofsky, S. H., Folley, B. S., Cooper, K., Mazur-Hopkins, P., et al. (2002). MRI parcellation of the frontal lobe in boys with attention deficit hyperactivity disorder or Tourette syndrome. *Psychiatry Research Neuroimaging, 116*, 63–81.

Kessler, R. C., Adler, L., Barkley, R., Biederman, J., Conners, C. K., Demier, O. et al. (2006). The prevalence and correlates of adult ADHD in the United States: Results from the National Comorbidity Survey Replication. *American Journal of Psychiatry, 163*(4), 716– 723.

Kieling, C., Goncalves, R. R., Tannock, R., & Castellanos, F. X. (2008). Neurobiology of attention deficit hyperactivity disorder. *Child and Adolescent Psychiatric Clinics in North America, 17*(2), 285–307.

Kim, H. W., Cho, S. C., Kim, B. N., Kim, J. W., Shin, M. S., & Kim, Y. (2009). Perinatal and familial risk factors are associated with full syndrome and subthreshold attention-deficit hyperactivity disorder in a Korean community sample. *Psychiatry Investigation, 6*(4), 278–285.

Klein, C., Wendling, K., Huettner, P., Ruder, H., & Peper, M. (2006). Intra-subject variability in attention-deficit hyperactivity disorder. *Biological Psychiatry, 60*, 1088–1097.

Koesters, M., Becker, T., Kilian, R., Fegert, J. M., & Weinmann, S. (2009). Limits of meta-analysis: Methylphenidate in the treatment of adult attention-deficit hyperactivity disorder. *Journal of Psychopharacology, 23*(7), 733–744.

Langley, K., Fowler, T., Ford, T., Thapar, A. K., van den Bree, M., Harold, G., et al . (2010). Adolescent clinical outcomes for young people with attention-deficit hyperactivity disorder. *British Journal of Psychiatry, 196*, 235–240.

Lee, J. S., Kim, B. N., Kang, E., Lee, D. S., Kim, Y. K., Chung, J. K., et al . (2005). Regional cerebral blood flow in children with attention deficit hyper-activity disorder: comparison before and after methylphenidate treatment. *Human Brain Mapping, 24*, 157–164.

Levy, F. (1991). The dopamine theory of attention deficit hyperactivity disorder. *Australian and New Zealand Journal of Psychiatry, 25*, 277–283.

Lie, N. (1992). Follow-ups of children with attention deficit hyperactivity disorder (ADHD). Review of literature. *Acta Psychiatrica Scandinavica. Supplementum., 368*, 1–40.

Linterman, I., & Weyandt, L. (2001). Divided attention skills in college students with ADHD: Is it advantageous to have ADHD? *ADHD Report, 9*, 1–10.

Loe, I. M., & Feldman, H. M. (2007). Academic and educational outcomes of children with ADHD. *Journal of Pediatric Psychology, 32*(6), 643–654.

Mackie, S., Shaw, P., Lenroot, R., Pierson, R., Greenstein, D. K., Nugent III, T. F., et al . (2007). Cerebellar development and clinical outcome in attention deficit hyperactivity disorder. *American Journal of Psychiatry, 164*, 647–655.

Mahone, E. M., & Hoffman, J. (2007). Behavior ratings of executive function among preschoolers with ADHD. *Clinical Neuropsychology, 21*, 569–586.

Mahone, E. M., Pillion, J. P., Hoffman, J., Hiemenz, J. R., & Denckla, M. B. (2005). Construct validity of the auditory continuous performance test for preschoolers. *Developmental Neuropsychology, 27*, 11–33.

Mannuzza, S., Klein, R. G., Bessler, A., Malloy, P., & Hynes, M. E. (1997). Educational and occupational outcome of hyperactive boys grown up. *Journal of the American Academy of Child and Adolescent Psychiatry, 36*(9), 1222–1227.

Mannuzza, S., Klein, R. G., Bessler, A., Malloy, P., & LaPadula, M. (1998). Adult psychiatric status of hyperactive boys grown up. *American Journal of Psychiatry, 155*(4), 493–498.

McAlonan, G. M., Cheung, V., Cheung, C., Chua, S. E., Murphy, D. G., Suckling, J., et al . (2007). Mapping brain structure in attention deficit-hyperactivity disorder: A voxel-based MRI study of regional grey and white matter volume. *Psychiatry Research Neuroimaging, 154*, 171–180.

McCabe, S. E., Teter, C. J., & Boyd, C. J. (2004). The use, misuse, and diversion of prescription stimulants among middle and high school students. *Substance Use and Misuse, 39*(7), 1095–1116.

Middleton, F. A., & Strick, P. L. (2000). Basal ganglia and cerebellar loops: Motor and cognitive circuits. *Brain Research Reviews, 31*, 236–250.

Miller, M., & Hinshaw, S. P. (2009). Does childhood executive functioning predict adolescent functional outcomes in girls with ADHD? *Journal of Abnormal Child Psychology, 38*, 315–326.

Millichap, J. G. (2008). Etiologic classification of attention-deficit/hyperactivity disorder. *Pediatrics, 121*(2), 358–365.

Mink, J. W. (1996). The basal ganglia: Focused selection and inhibition of competing motor programs. *Progress in Neurobiology, 50*, 381–425.

Mostofsky, S. H., Cooper, K. L., Kates, W. R., Denckla, M. B. & Kaufmann, W. E. (2002). Smaller prefrontal and premotor volumes in boys with attention-deficit/hyperactivity disorder. *Biological Psychiatry, 52*, 785–794.

Miyake, A., Friedman, N. P., Emerson, M. J., Witzki, A. H., Howerter, A., & Wager, T. D. (2000). The unity and diversity of executive functions and their contributions to complex "frontal lobe" tasks: A latent variable analysis. *Cognitive Psychology, 41*, 49–100.

Narr, K. L., Woods, R. P. & Lin, J. (2009). Widespread cortical thinning is a robust anatomical marker for attention deficit/hyperactivity disorder (ADHD). *Journal of the American Academy of Child and Adolescent Psychiatry, 48*, 1014–1022.

Nigg, J. T., Blaskey, L. G., Huang-Pollock, C., & Rappley, M. D. (2002). Neuropsychological executive functions and DSM-IV ADHD subtypes. *Journal of the American Academy of Child and Adolescent Psychiatry, 41*, 59–66.

Nigg, J., & Casey, B. (2005). An integrative theory of attention-deficit/hyperactivity disorder based on the cognitive and affective neurosciences. *Developmental Psychopathology, 17*, 785–806.

Nigg, J. T., Stavro, G., Ettenhofer, M., Hambrick, D. Z., Miller, T., & Henderson, J. M. (2005a). Executive functions and ADHD in adults: Evidence for selective effects on ADHD symptom domains. *Journal of Abnormal Psychology, 114*(4), 706–717.

Nigg, J. T., Willcutt, E. G. & Doyle, A. E. (2005b). Causal heterogeneity in attention-deficit hyperactivity disorder: Do we need neuropsychologically impaired subtypes. *Biological Psychiatry, 57*, 1224–1230.

Ossmann, J. M., & Mulligan, N. W. (2003). Inhibition and attention deficit hyperactivity disorder in adults. *American Journal of Psychology, 116*(1), 35–50.

Patrick, K. S., Straugh, A. B., Perkins, J. S., & Gonzalez, M. A. (2009). Evolution of stimulants to treat ADHD: Transdermal methylphenidate. *Human Psychopharmacology, 24*, 1–17.

Pennington, B. F., & Ozonoff, S. (1996). Executive functions and developmental psychopathology. *Journal of Child Psychology and Psychiatry, 37*, 51–87.

Pierce, E. W., Ewing, L. J., & Campbell, S. B. (1999). Diagnostic status and symptomatic behavior of hard-to-manage preschool children in middle childhood and early adolescence. *Journal of Clinical Child Psychology, 28*(1), 44–57.

Plichta, M. M., Vasic, N., Wolf, R. C., Lesch, K. P., Brummer, D., Jacob, C., et al. (2009). Neural hyporesponsiveness and hyperresponsiveness during immediate and delayed reward processing in adult attention-deficit/hyperactivity disorder. *Biological Psychiatry, 65*, 7–14.

Pliszka, S. R., Lancaster, J., Liotti, M., & Semrud-Clikeman, M. (2006). Volumetric MRI differences in treatment-naive vs chronically treated children with ADHD. *Neurology, 67*, 1023–1027.

Poulin, C. (2007). From attention-deficit/hyperactivity disorder to medical stimulant use to the diversion of prescribed stimulants to non-medical use: Connecting the dots. *Addiction, 102*(5), 740–751.

Pringsheim, T., Sandor, P., Lang, A., Shah, P., & O'Connor, P. (2009). Prenatal and perinatal morbidity in children with Tourette syndrome and attention-deficit hyperactivity disorder. *Journal of Developmental and Behavioral Pediatrics, 30*(2), 115–121.

Rhodes, S. M., Coghill, D. R., & Matthews, K. (2005). Neuropsychological functioning in stimulant-naïve boys with hyperkinetic disorder. *Psychological Medicine, 35*, 1109–1120.

Riley, C., DuPaul, G. J., Pipan, M., Kern, L., VanBrakle, J., & Blum, N. J. (2008). Combined type versus ADHD predominantly hyperactive impulsive type: Is there a difference in functional impairment? *Journal of Developmental and Behavioral Pediatrics, 29*(4), 270–275.

Rommelse, N. N., Altink, M. E., de Sonneville, L. M., Buschgens, C. J., Buitelaar, J., Oosterlaan, J., et al. (2007). Are motor inhibition and cognitive flexibility dead ends in ADHD? *Journal of Abnormal Child Psychology, 35*, 957–967.

Roth, R. M., Milovan, D., Baribeau, J., & O'Connor, K. (2005). Neuropsychological functioning in early- and late-onset obsessive-compulsive disorder. *Journal of Neuropsychiatry and Clinical Neurosciences, 17*, 208–213.

Rubia, K., Halari, R., Smith, A. B., Mohammad, M., Scott, S., Brammer, M. J. (2009). Shared and disorder-specific prefrontal abnormalities in boys with pure attention-deficit/hyperactivity disorder compared to boys with pure CD during interference inhibition and attention allocation. *Journal of Child Psychology and Psychiatry, 50*(6), 669–678.

Rucklidge, J. J. (2008). Gender differences in ADHD: Implications for psychological treatments. *Expert Review of Neurotherapeutics, 8*(4), 643–655.

Qiu, A., Crocetti, D., Adler, M., Mahone, E. M., Denckla, M. B., Miller, M. I., et al. (2009). Basal ganglia volume and shape in children with attention deficit hyperactivity disorder. *American Journal of Psychiatry, 166*(1), 74–82.

Satterfield, J. H., Faller, K. J., Crinella, F. M., Schell, A. M., Swanson, J. M., & Homer, L. D. (2007). A 30-year prospective follow-up study of hyperactive boys with conduct problems: Adult criminality. *Journal of the American Academy of Child and Adolescent Psychiatry, 46*(5), 601–610.

Scheres, A., Milham, M. P., Knutson, B., & Castellanos, F. X. (2007). Ventral striatal hyporesponsiveness during reward anticipation in Attention Deficit/Hyperactivity Disorder. *Biological Psychiatry, 61*, 720–724

Schweitzer, J. B., Lee, D. O., Hanford, R. B., Tagamets, M. A., Hoffman, J. M. & Grafton, S. T. (2003). A positron emission tomography study of methylphenidate in adults with ADHD: Alterations in resting blood flow and predicting treatment response. *Neuropsychopharmacology, 28*, 967–973.

Sergeant, J.A. (2005). Modeling attention-deficit/hyperactivity disorder: A critical appraisal of the cognitive-energetic model. *Biological Psychiatry, 57*, 1248–1255.

Seidman, L. J., Biederman, J., Faraone, S. V., Weber, W., Mennin, D., & Jones, J. (1997). A pilot study of neuropsychological function in ADHD girls. *Journal of the American Academy of Child and Adolescent Psychiatry, 36*, 366–373.

Seidman, L. J., Biederman, J., Weber, W., Hatch, M., & Faraone, S. V. (1998). Neuropsychological functioning in adults with attention-deficit hyperactivity disorder. *Biological Psychiatry, 44*, 260–268.

Seidman, L. J., Biederman, J., Monuteaux, M. C., Doyle, A. E., & Faraone, S. V. (2001). Learning disabilities and executive dysfunction in boys with attention-deficit/hyperactivity disorder. *Neuropsychology, 15*, 544–556.

Seidman, L. J., Biederman, J., Monuteaux, M. C., Valera, E., Doyle, A. E., & Faraone, S. V. (2005). Impact of gender and age on executive functioning: Do girls and boys with and without attention deficit hyperactivity disorder differ neuropsychologically in preteen and teenage years? *Developmental Neuropsychology, 27*, 79–105.

Seidman, L., Valera, E., & Makris, N. (2005). Structural brain imaging of attention-deficit/hyperactivity disorder. *Biological Psychiatry, 57*, 1263–1272.

Seidman, L. J., Valera, E. M., Makris, N., Monuteaux, M. C., Boriel, D. L., & Kelkar, K. (2006). Dorsolateral prefrontal and anterior cingulate cortex volumetric abnormalities in adults with attention-deficit/ hyperactivity disorder identified by magnetic resonance imaging. *Biological Psychiatry, 60*, 1071–1080.

Sharp, S. I., McQuillin, A., & Gurling, H. M. D. (2009). Genetics of attention-deficit hyperactivity disorder. *Neuropharmacology.*

Silk, T. J., Vance, A., Rinehart, N., Bradshaw, J. L., & Cunnington, R. (2008). Dysfunction in the fronto-parietal network in attention deficit hyperactivity disorder (ADHD): An fMRI study. *Brain Imaging and Behavior, 2*, 123–131.

Sobanski, E., Bruggemann, D., Aim, B., Kern, S., Deschner, M., Schubert, T., et al. (2007). Psychiatric comorbidity and functional impairment in a clinically referred sample of adults with attention-deficit/hyperactivity disorder (ADHD). *European Archives of Psychiatry and Clinical Neuroscience, 257*(7), 371–377.

Solanto, M. V. (1998). Neuropsychopharmacological mechanisms of stimulant drug action in attention-deficit hyperactivity disorder: a review and integration. *Behavioural Brain Research, 94*, 127–152.

Solanto, M. V., Abikoff, H., Sonuga-Barke, E., Schachar, R., Logan, G. D., Wigal, T., et al. (2001). The ecological validity of delay aversion and response inhibition as measures of impulsivity in ADHD: A supplement to the NIMH multimodal treatment study of ADHD. *Journal of Abnormal Child Psychology, 29*, 215–228.

Solanto, M. V., Gilbert, S. N., Raj, A., Zhu, J., Pope-Boyd, S., Stepak, B., et al. (2007). Neurocognitive functioning in AD/HD, predominantly inattentive and combined subtypes. *Journal of Abnormal Child Psychology, 35*, 729–744.

Sonuga-Barke, E. J., Dalen, L., & Remington, B. (2003). Do executive deficits and delay aversion make independent contributions to preschool attention-deficit/hyperactivity disorder symptoms. *Journal of the American Academy of Child and Adolescent Psychiatry, 42*, 1335–1342.

Sonuga-Barke, E. J. S. (2005) Causal models of attention-deficity/hyperactivity disorder: From common simple deficits to multiple developmental pathways. *Biological Psychiatry, 57*, 1231–1238.

Teicher, M. H., Anderson, C. M., Polcari, A., Glod, C. A., Maas, L. C., & Renshaw, P. F. (2000). Functional deficits in basal ganglia of children with attention-deficit/hyperactivity disorder shown with functional magnetic resonance imaging relaxometry. *Nature Medicine, 6*(4), 470–473.

Thompson, A. L., Molina, B. S. G., Pelham, W., & Gnagy, E. M. (2007). Risky driving in adolescents and young adults with childhood ADHD. *Journal of Pediatric Psychology, 32*, 745–759.

Toren, P., Sadeh, M., Wolmer, L., Eldar, S., Koren, S., Weizman, R., et al. (2000). Neurocognitive correlates of anxiety disorders in children: A preliminary report. *Journal of Anxiety Disorders, 14*, 239–247.

Tripp, G., & Wickens, J. R. (2009). Neurobiology of ADHD. *Neuropharmacology, 57*, 579–589.

Valera, E. M., Faraone, S. V., Murray, K. E., & Seidman, L. J. (2007). Meta-analysis of structural imaging findings in attention-deficit/hyperactivity disorder. *Biological Psychiatry, 61*, 1361–1368.

Vles, J. S., Feron, F. J., Hendriksen, J. G., Jolles, J., van Kroonenburgh, M. J., & Weber, W. E. (2003). Methylphenidate down-regulates the dopamine receptor and transporter system in children with attention deficit hyperkinetic disorder (ADHD). *Neuropediatrics, 34*(2), 77–80.

Volkow, N. D., Wang, G. J., Fowler, J. S., Gatley, S. J., Logan, J., Ding, Y. S., et al. (1998). Dopamine transporter occupancies in the human brain induced by therapeutic doses of oral methylphenidate. *American Journal of Psychiatry, 155*, 1325–1331.

Volkow, N. D., Wang, G. J., Kollins, S. H., Wigal, T. L., Newcorn, J. H., Telang, F., et al. (2009). Evaluating dopamine reward pathway in ADHD: Clinical implications. *JAMA, 302*(10), 1084–1091.

Wahlstedt, C., Thorell, L. B., & Bohlin, G. (2009). Heterogeneity in ADHD: Neuropsychological pathways, comorbidity, and symptom domains. *Journal of Abnormal Child Psychology, 37*, 551–564.

Welsh, M. C., & Pennington, B. F. (1988). Assessing frontal lobe functioning in children: Views from developmental psychology. *Developmental Neuropsychology, 4*, 199–230.

Weyandt, L. L. (2005). Executive function in children, adolescents, and adults with attention deficit hyperactivity disorder: Introduction into the special issue. *Developmental Neuropsychology, 27*(1), 1–10.

Weyandt, L. L. (2006). *The physiological basis of cognitive and behavioral disorders*. Mahwah, New Jersey: Lawrence Erlbaum and Associates.

Weyandt, L. L. (2009). Executive functions and attention deficit hyperactivity disorder. *The ADHD Report, 17*(6), 1–7.

Weyandt, L. L., & DuPaul, G. (2006). ADHD in college students. *Journal of Attention Disorders, 10*(1), 9–19.

Weyandt, L. L., & DuPaul, G. J. (2008). ADHD in college students: Developmental findings. *Developmental Disabilities Research Reviews, 14*(4), 311–319.

Weyandt, L. L., Iwaszuk, W., Fulton, K., Oilerton, M., Beatty, N., Fouts, H., et al. (2003). The internal restlessness scale: Performance of college students with and without ADHD. *Journal of Learning Disabilities, 36*(4), 382–389.

Weyandt, L. L., Janusis, G., Wilson, K. G., Verdi, G., Paquin, G., Lopes, J., et al. (2009). Nonmedical prescription stimulant use among a sample of college students: Relationship with psychological variables. *Journal of Attention Disorders, 13*(3), 284–296.

Weyandt, L. L., Linterman, I., & Rice, J. A. (1995). Reported prevalence of attentional difficulties in a general sample of college students. *Journal of Psychopathology and Behavioral Assessment, 17*, 293–304.

Weyandt, L. L., Mitzlaff, L., & Thomas, L. (2002). The relationship between intelligence and performance on the test of variables of attention (TOVA). *Journal of Learning Disabilities, 35*, 114–120.

Wilens, T. E., Adler, L. A., Adams, J., Sgambati, S., Rotrosen, J., Sawtelle, R., et al. (2008). Misuse and diversion of stimulants prescribed for ADHD: A systematic review of the literature. *Journal of the American Academy of Child and Adolescent Psychiatry, 47*(1), 21–31.

Wilens, T. E., Beiderman, J., Faraone, S. V., Martelon, M., Westerberg, D., & Spencer, T. J. (2009). Presenting ADHD symptoms, subtypes, and comorbid disorders in clinically referred adults with ADHD. *Journal of Clinical Psychiatry, 70*(11), 1557–1562.

Wilmhurst, L., Peele, M., & Wilmhurst, L. (2011). Resilience and well-being in college students with and without a diagnosis of ADHD. *Journal of Attention Disorders.*

Willcutt, E. G., Doyle, A. E., Nigg, J. T., Faraone, S. V. & Pennington, B. F. (2005a). Validity of the executive function theory of ADHD: Meta-analytic review. *Biological Psychiatry, 57*, 1336–1346.

Willcutt, E. G., Pennington, B. F., Olson, R. K., & DeFries, J. C. (2007). Understanding comorbidity: A twin study of reading disability and attention-deficit/hyperactivity disorder. *American Journal of Medical Genetics Part B: Neuropsychiatric Genetics, 144B*(6), 709–714.

Willcutt, E. G., Pennington, B. F., Olson, R. K., Chhabildas, N., & Hulslander, J. (2005b). Neuropsychological analyses of comorbidity between reading disability and attention deficit hyperactivity disorder: In search of the common deficit. *Developmental Neuropsychology, 21*, 35–78.

Wu, K. K., Anderson, V., & Castiello, U. (2002). Neuropsychological evaluation of deficits in executive functioning for ADHD children with or without learning disabilities. *Developmental Neuropsychology, 22*, 501–531.

Wymbs, B. T., Pelham, W. E., Molina, B. S., Gnagy, E. M., Wilson, T. K., & Greenhouse, J. B. (2008). Rate and predictors of divorce among parents of youths with ADHD. *Journal of Consulting and Clinical Psychology, 76*(5), 735–744.

Yang, P., Wang, P.-N., Chuang, K.-H., Jong, Y.-J., Chao, T.-C., & Wu, M. T. (2008). Absence of gender effect on children with attention deficit/hyperactivity disorder as assessed by optimized voxel based morphometry. *Psychiatry Research Neuroimaging, 164*(3), 245– 253.

Yang, L. W., Yu-Feng Li, J., & Faraone, S. V. (2004). Association of norepinephrine transporter gene with methylphenidate response. *Journal of the American Academy of Child and Adolescent Psychiatry, 43*, 1154–1158.

Zametkin, A. J., Liebenauer, L. L., Fitzgerald, G. A., King, A. C., Minkunas, D. V., Herscovitch, P., et al. (1993). Brain metabolism in teenagers with attention-deficit hyperactivity disorder. *Archives of General Psychiatry, 50*, 333–340.

CHAPTER 5

The Enigma of Learning Disabilities: Examination via a Neuropsychological Framework

James B. Hale, Lisa A. Hain, Ryan Murphy, Gina Cancelliere, Desiree L. Bindus, & Hanna A. Kubas

THE ENIGMA OF SPECIFIC LEARNING DISABILITIES: A NEUROPSYCHOLOGICAL FRAMEWORK

Defining and Identifying Specific Learning Disabilities

As scientific evidence supporting brain-behavior relationships emerges in modern times (Hale, Fiorello, & Thompson, 2010b), it has become increasingly clear that early arguments for seeing behavior and neurology as interconnected and inseparable (Hynd & Willis, 1988) have staying power. Although once focused on physical brain damage, the field of neuropsychology has benefited from this understanding of brain–behavior reciprocity to become increasingly focused on understanding what has traditionally been the provenance of cognitive, educational, and behavioral psychologists: high incidence learning and psychiatric disorders in children (Fiorello, Hale, Decker, & Coleman, 2009; Hale et al., 2010b; Hynd & Reynolds, 2005). When the special education laws were first passed in the 1970s (e.g., Education for All Handicapped Children Act of 1975), questions regarding the biological bases of specific learning disabilities (SLD) first emerged, and this remains an important issue today. Is SLD a learning disorder where achievement scores are most relevant for identifying these children (Reschly, 2005), or is it a neurobiological disorder where a neuropsychological framework is most relevant for understanding and serving children with SLD (Berninger & May, 2011)? The answer to this question provides a lens through which practitioners and researchers alike can evaluate the relationship between SLD and psychopathology, so we begin this chapter with an examination of this critical issue.

SLD affects how children with average or above-average intelligence learn, retain, and/or convey information (Mash & Wolfe, 2010); therefore, SLD is different from low achievement in that specific neuropsychological deficits cause interference with learning (Fiorello et al., 2009; Hale et al. 2008a). Empirical evidence has emerged to support this contention, demonstrating clear neurobiological differences between children with SLD and children with typical academic achievement (Berninger & Richards, 2002; D'Amato, Fletcher-Janzen, & Reynolds, 2005; Hale et al., 2010a; Hynd & Reynolds, 2005; Miller & Hale, 2008), confirming that SLD is a central nervous system disorder affecting learning (Semrund-Clikeman, Goldenring Fine, & Harder, 2005) and behavior (Hain, Hale, & Glass-Kendorski, 2008).

For children with SLD, it is clear that brain–behavior relationships are in part related to, and determined by, environmental influences in a reciprocal manner (Hale & Fiorello, 2004). However, adept clinicians must attempt to differentiate children with neuropsychologically determined SLD from children who can be considered to have delayed learning, or as some have suggested, "instructional casualties" (Lyon, Shaywitz, & Shaywitz, 2003), or from those children who are experiencing learning difficulties due to other neurobiological causes, such as ADHD (e.g., Hale et al., 2010a; Hale, Wycoff, & Fiorello, 2010c). Hampering this diagnostic differentiation, especially if overt behavior or achievement outcomes are the focus of evaluation (Hale et al., 2009), is the high prevalence of comorbidity in SLD and other disorders (Angold, Costello, & Erkanli, 1999; Landerl & Moll, 2010). Comorbidity underscores the importance of examining brain–behavior relationships in children with learning and behavior disorders (Semrund-Clikeman et al., 2005) and highlights why one-size-fits-all approaches to diagnosis and intervention are so problematic, as they limit diagnostic accuracy and attenuate treatment effects when large heterogeneous populations are identified (Hale & Fiorello, 2004; Hale et al., 2009).

Finally, both federal law (e.g., IDEA, 2004; Hale et al., 2010a) and recent United States Supreme Court litigation (Dixon, Eusebio, Turton, Wright, & Hale, 2011) stress the importance of uncovering all areas of suspected disability for proper identification and intervention of children with SLD and other disorders. The *child find* IDEA (2004) statute requires that children receiving comprehensive evaluations are evaluated in *all* areas of suspected disability, including attention, memory, and executive function (Dixon et al., 2011), not just academic achievement. Despite this legislative and legal mandate, the comprehensive evaluative approach we advocate in this chapter is rarely completed for individuals with SLD, primarily because the diagnostic focus has been on whether affected children display an ability–achievement discrepancy, even though it is a poor method for determining the presence of a SLD (Fletcher, Lyon, Fuchs, & Barnes, 2007; Hale et al., 2010c; Kavale, Holdnack, & Mostert, 2005; Siegel, 2003). Additionally, there has been little consistency in SLD identification practices across schools, districts, states, and regions, leading to substantial SLD group heterogeneity and tenuous diagnostic practices that seldom lead to effective interventions (Reschly & Hosp, 2004). Clearly, more effective approaches for SLD diagnosis are needed, not only for identification purposes, but also to help tailor interventions to individual needs (Berninger, 2006; Fuchs, Hale, & Kearns, 2011; Hale et al., 2010c). Moreover, effective intervention models are also needed to inform and guide scientifically based instruction techniques that provide all children with appropriate learning experiences, so as not to mistake inadequate instruction and education with SLD (Ofiesh, 2006).

For SLD identification, school teams have largely focused on whether children meet regulatory requirements for an ability–achievement discrepancy, and as a consequence, the statutory SLD definition has typically been minimized or ignored (Hale et al., 2010c; Kavale et al., 2005; Mather & Gregg, 2006). The current IDEA (2004) SLD statutory definition continues to recognize that these children have a disorder *in one or more of the basic psychological processes* involved in understanding or in using language, spoken or written, which may manifest itself in the imperfect ability to listen, think, speak, read, write, spell, or perform mathematical calculations (Title 20 United States Code Section 1401(30) [cited as 20 USC 1401(30)]). Most practitioners would abhor the thought of making diagnoses without first examining the disorder's definition, yet this is often the case for children with SLD identified in school systems. This curious practice of ignoring or avoiding the SLD definition when determining whether a child has SLD is quite perplexing to many seasoned practitioners and, in our eyes, an anathema for effective practice.

Discrepancy, Response-to-Intervention, or a Third Method Approach?

According to Title 20 of Section 1414, subsection b(6) (cited as 20 USC 1414(b)(6)), in determining whether a child has SLD, IDEA (2004) does not require a severe discrepancy between intellectual ability and achievement, and allows a process that determines if a child responds to scientific, research-based intervention. Although the response-to-intervention (RTI) approach was initially seen as a viable alternative to ineffectual ability–achievement discrepancy approaches for identifying SLD (Brown-Chidsey & Steege, 2005; Reschly, 2005), both methods have been heavily criticized on empirical grounds (see Hale et al., 2010c). One criticism they both share is that these methods ignore the basic psychological processing deficits that lead to SLD (Fiorello, Hale, & Snyder, 2006; Fiorello et al., 2009; Hale, 2006; Hale, Kaufman, Naglieri, & Kavale, 2006; Hale et al., 2010c; Mather & Gregg, 2006; Ofiesh, 2006; Schrank, Miller, Catering, & Desrochers, 2006; Willis & Dumont, 2006; Wodrich, Spencer, & Daley, 2006).

In response to initial criticisms of using RTI for diagnostic practice (Hale, Naglieri, Kaufman, & Kavale, 2004; Kavale et al., 2005), the final federal regulations (34 C.F.R. Parts 300 and 301; 2006) also permitted the use of alternative research-based procedures for identifying SLD. Often labeled the "third method" for SLD identification (§ 300.8(c)(10); Hale et al., 2008b), these approaches have typically focused on identifying the cognitive and neuropsychological processing strengths and weaknesses inherent in SLD (Hale et al., 2010b), and are growing in popularity as alternatives to traditional discrepancy and RTI methods among practitioners (Machek & Nelson, 2010), state regulators (Zirkel & Krohn, 2008), and test publishers (Wechsler, 2009). Most advocates of third method approaches also advocate using RTI and value its use in early intervention for children with learning problems (Fuchs et al., 2011). As a result, third method approaches can be considered balanced practice approaches that typically include RTI and comprehensive evaluation for nonresponders, therefore ensuring that both the IDEA (2004) SLD statutory and regulatory requirements are met (Fiorello et al., 2009; Hale et al., 2010c) before children are identified as having the disorder.

For example, in Hale's (2006) Balanced Practice Model (see Figure 5.1), children receive standard protocol RTI and curriculum-based progress monitoring during Tier 1, and a more individualized problem-solving RTI approach at Tier 2, both of which can be accomplished in the general education setting (Fiorello et al., 2009; Hale, 2006; Hale et al., 2006). Prior to SLD determination and Tier 3 intervention, which Hale (2006) suggests should be systematic,

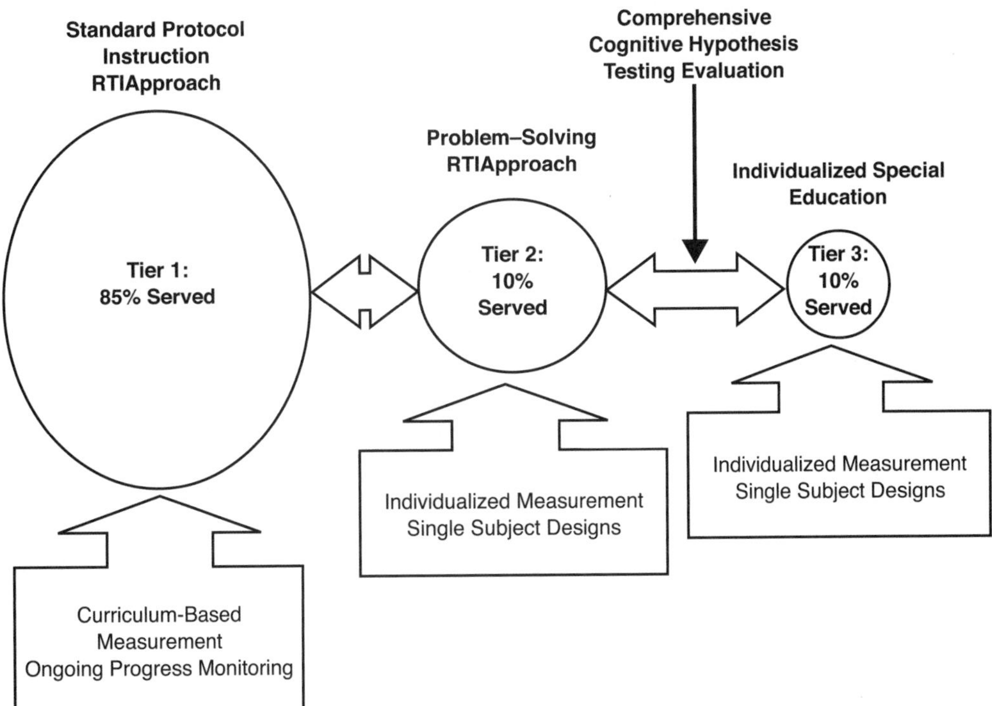

FIGURE 5.1 Hale Balance Practice Model. Source: Hale, J.B. (2006). Copyright 2006 by the National Association of School Psychologists, Bethesda, MD. Reprinted with permission of the publisher, www.nasponline.org.

individualized special education instruction, children receive a comprehensive evaluation in all areas of suspected disability, as is required by law (e.g., Dixon et al., 2011). Hale (2006) argues that many children will be effectively served in RTI, but no study to date has resulted in all children showing a RTI, so nonresponders continue to exist no matter what RTI approach is used. Because RTI methods are not sufficient for diagnosis since they are unreliable in differentiating responders from nonresponders (e.g., Barth et al., 2008; Fuchs, Fuchs, & Compton, 2004; Speece, 2005; Waesche, Schatschneider, Maner, Ahmed, & Wagner, in press), comprehensive evaluations using multiple data sources are needed to assess individuals in all areas of suspected disability for differential diagnosis (Dixon et al., 2011; Fiorello et al., 2009; Hale et al., 2010a). These comprehensive evaluations are necessarily thorough and complex, especially when one considers the importance of establishing concurrent, discriminant, ecological, and treatment validity of the decisions derived from them (Hale & Fiorello, 2004).

For those not responding to standard interventions in RTI, a comprehensive evaluation including cognitive and neuropsychological processing assessment is necessary, not only for accurate identification of SLD (Fuchs et al., 2011) but targeted and individualized intervention as well (Hale et al., 2010a). For an accurate comprehensive evaluation, the Hale and Fiorello Cognitive Hypothesis Testing model (CHT; Hale & Fiorello, 2004; see Figure 5.2) approach can be used to ensure accurate diagnosis (i.e., increasing likelihood of determining true positives or negatives while reducing false positives or negatives) of SLD and/or other disorders, and provide assessment data to guide empirically supported interventions (Fiorello et al., 2009; Hale et al., 2008a; Reddy & Hale, 2007). This model and those similar are aligned with current thinking about brain–behavior relationships, one that combines knowledge gained from the latest cognitive (e.g., Cattell-Horn-Carroll; CHC) and neuropsychological (e.g., Lurian process approach) theories of individual differences (e.g., Fiorello, Hale, Snyder, Forrest, & Teodori, 2008).

The integration of brain, behavior, and environment is critical in the determination of SLD, as highlighted in a recent 58-scholar white paper addressing the need for neuropsychological principles and practices in SLD identification and service delivery (Hale et al., 2010a). In this paper, a consensus position on SLD policy and practice was developed by leaders in neuropsychology, education, and SLD in concert with the Learning Disabilities Association of America. The paper provided five summative conclusions derived from the empirical literature:

1. The SLD definition should be maintained and statutory requirements should be strengthened
2. Neither ability–achievement discrepancy analysis nor failure to respond to intervention alone were sufficient for SLD identification
3. A "third method" approach that identifies a pattern of psychological processing strengths and weaknesses, and achievement deficits consistent with this pattern should be used for SLD identification

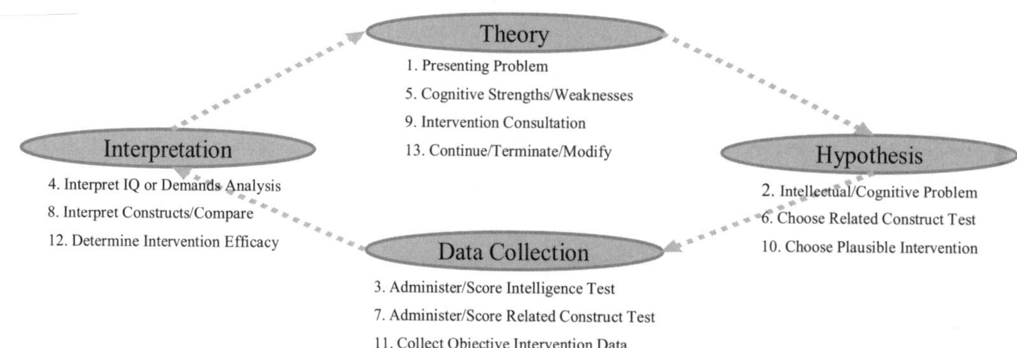

FIGURE 5.2 Cognitive Hypothesis Testing Model. Source: Hale, J. B., & Fiorello, C. A. (2004). Reprinted with permission of The Guilford Press.

4. An empirically validated RTI model could be used to prevent learning problems, but comprehensive evaluations were necessary for SLD identification purposes
5. Comprehensive evaluations were not only relevant for diagnosis, but should also lead to targeted, individualized interventions, rather than more intense interventions as prescribed by RTI proponents (Hale et al., 2010a)

The pattern of strengths and weaknesses approach to identifying SLD is also supported by the 14 professional organizations that composed the Learning Disabilities Roundtable Advisory Panel (2002, 2004), representative samples of school psychology practitioners (Caterino et al., 2008; Machek & Nelson, 2010), and national organizations, including the National Association of School Psychologists (2007), the American Academy of School Psychology (Schrank et al., 2006), and the Learning Disabilities Association of America (Hale et al., 2010d). This growing consensus suggests that considerable empirical efforts must be undertaken to identify processing strengths and weaknesses, and how these processes are related to achievement (McGrew & Wendling, 2010). It is efforts like these that can lead to effective SLD diagnostic practices not only for recognizing the processing patterns associated with learning deficits, but psychosocial and behavioral deficits as well.

Operationalizing SLD Third Method Approaches: The Concordance-Discordance Model

Although the available processing strengths and weaknesses models share similar characteristics (Hale et al., 2008b), we will focus our attention on the Concordance-Discordance Model (C-DM; Hale & Fiorello, 2004). The C-DM provides a statistically sound methodology that can be used across standardized tests (Fiorello et al., 2009; Hale et al., 2008a), has been used in previous research to identify children with SLD (Elliott, Hale, Fiorello, Dorvil, & Moldovan, 2010; Hain et al., 2008; Hale et al., 2008a) and, when combined with CHT, has been recognized as a viable model for disability determination in neuropsychological practice (Burns, 2010; Clements, Christner, McLaughlin, & Bolton, 2011; Della Toffalo, 2010; Feifer & Della Toffalo, 2007; Flanagan, Alfonso, Mascolo, & Hale, 2010; Hale et al., 2010b; Fletcher-Janzen, 2005; Miller, Getz, & Leffard, 2006; Miller & Hale, 2008).

Using the standard error of the difference for statistical comparisons of standard scores (Anastasi & Urbina, 1997), the C-DM was developed as an empirically valid method for identifying basic psychological processing weakness(es) that result in the academic deficit(s) (concordance), and these cognitive and academic deficits must be different from the cognitive asset(s) (discordance), as seen in Figure 5.3. This model notes that there can be multiple cognitive and/or neuropsychological causes for the academic deficits seen in SLD; thus, pinpointing these cognitive-achievement relationships can lead to more targeted interventions (Hale & Fiorello, 2004). Recent reviews and papers highlight these important cognitive-achievement associations for typical children and children with disabilities (Elliott et al., 2010; Hale et al., 2008a; McGrew & Wendling, 2010), and these reviews are critical for practitioner use of the C-DM model. Hale and Fiorello (2004) admonish practitioners to avoid a cookbook approach to using C-DM, but if done correctly, it has the potential to reduce false positives and negatives during comprehensive evaluation. A step-by-step approach for the process can be found in Hale and colleagues (2010c), and the appendix to this chapter provides a worksheet for these steps.

Need for Subtyping of SLD and Psychopathology

Previous research on the relationship between SLD and psychopathology must be considered within the context of previous problematic ability–achievement discrepancy identification practices, and our call for more effective third method approaches such as the C-DM model. Once children have been accurately identified as having SLD or another disorder using CHT and C-DM methods, clinicians can then focus their attention on the types of interventions that might ameliorate the learning and psychosocial difficulties these children experience.

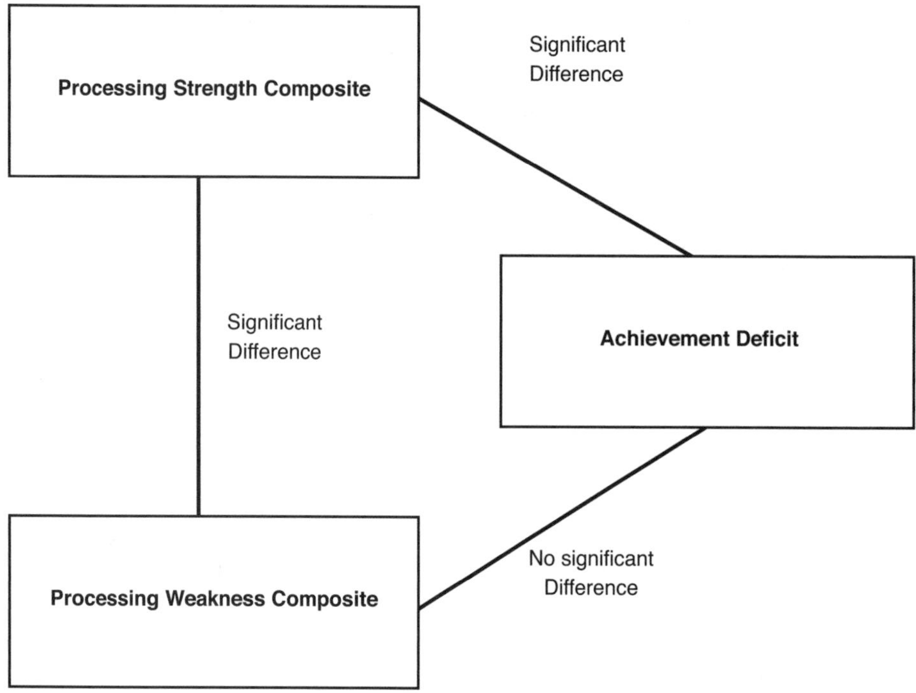

FIGURE 5.3 Concordance-Discordance Model of SLD Identification. Source: Hale, J. B., & Fiorello, C. A. (2004). Reprinted with permission of The Guilford Press.

Children with SLD frequently have comorbid behavior problems or psychopathology, and numerous empirical efforts have been undertaken to decipher this interrelationship (Rourke, 2008; Wong & Donahue, 2002). Prevalence estimates of comorbid emotional/behavioral disorders may exceed 40% of the SLD population (Taggart, Cousins, & Milner, 2007). Comorbid SLD has been identified in children with mood disorder, ADHD and other externalizing disorders, and autism spectrum disorders (Mayes & Calhoun, 2006, 2008). However, an important question remains to be addressed: Are these true comorbidities, or are there different neuropsychological patterns of performance that cause the SLD and the psychopathology? An attempt to answer this critical question will serve as the focus for the remainder of this chapter.

Obviously, the impact of SLD heterogeneity and comorbidity is significant, especially if the educational and mental health systems are not designed to provide needed individualized services for children who display significant learning and psychosocial problems. Comprehensive evaluations are necessary to uncover the cognitive, neuropsychological, academic, behavioral, and psychosocial determinants of behavior because children with SLD are clearly too heterogeneous in etiology and presentation to suggest that a single approach will address their different needs (Berninger & Richards, 2002; Fiorello et al., 2009; Hale et al., 2010b; Kavale et al., 2005; Semrud-Clikeman, 2005). Despite this consensus regarding SLD heterogeneity in etiology and presentation, what is not clear is how learning problems affect behavior, or how behavior problems affect learning. Perhaps it is important to recognize that cognitive, behavioral, and environmental factors all play an important role in influencing a child's overt behavior, and it is virtually impossible to separate these dynamic and reciprocal influences (Bandura, 1986). Thus, as is the case with localization of brain function, the question of causation is not merely an "either-or" one, but rather a "how much" one (Goldberg, 2001). We can surely recognize that various factors influence behavior in a reciprocal fashion and that providing interventions that enhance one area of functioning will likely benefit the other (Hale & Fiorello, 2004).

Empirical Forays Into SLD Subtyping of Psychopathology

Children with reading SLD and/or math SLD have higher rates of school and clinical maladjustment, emotion regulation problems, poorer school attitudes, atypical thoughts and behaviors, and mood disturbance than their typically functioning peers (Martinez & Semrud-Clikeman, 2004). Meta-analyses suggest that as many as 75% of children with SLD experience some type of social skills deficits (Kavale & Forness, 1996). In an effort to reveal individual differences in learning and psychopathology in SLD, researchers have used various methods to subtype SLD based on cognitive, neuropsychological, academic, and/or psychosocial profiles. Early studies postulated the existence of at least seven SLD subtypes that could be differentiated by emotional/behavioral variables (e.g., task orientation, independence, attention, distractibility, hostility, social skills, introversion-extroversion, and considerateness), with a 3-year longitudinal examination revealing SLD behavioral subtype stability over time (McKinney & Speece, 1986; Speece, McKinney, & Appelbaum, 1985). SLD subtype differences have also been found on measures of depression, social withdrawal, hyperactivity, adjustment, and anxiety (Nussbaum & Bigler, 1986; Nussbaum, Bigler, & Koch, 1986) using both neuropsychological and behavioral data. When cognitive and neuropsychological data are included in these early studies, results were often inconsistent, so that no clear pattern emerged (Hain et al., 2008).

Of these early studies, probably the most significant contribution has come from Rourke and colleagues (Rourke, 2000). Rourke has identified SLD subtypes based on intellectual, neuropsychological, academic, and behavior ratings of psychosocial functioning. Studies have generally found normal psychosocial adjustment, internalized psychopathology, and externalized psychosocial subtypes (Fuerst, Fisk, & Rourke, 1989). Fuerst, Fisk, and Rourke (1990) delineated six SLD psychopathology subtypes associated with specific patterns of neurocognitive processing, including normal, mild anxious, mild hyperactive, somatic, internalizing, and externalizing subtypes. Children with stronger psycholinguistic and reading/spelling skills and weaker visual/spatial skills and math disability tend to demonstrate the most significant psychopathology (Rourke & Fuerst, 1991). This "nonverbal" SLD (NVLD) is presumed to be due to difficulty with processing complex social information because of white matter dysfunction affecting intermodal integration (Fuerst et al., 1989; Fuerst et al., 1990; Rourke, 2000).

Disorders thought to be related to right hemisphere/white matter dysfunction, such as Williams syndrome (Leyfer, Woodruff-Borden, & Mervis, 2009; Marenco et al., 2007), Turner syndrome (Holzapfel et al., 2006; Lasker, Mazzocco, & Zee, 2007), and Asperger's disorder (Hale et al., 2006; McAlonan et al., 2009) also present with significant math disability and psychopathology consistent with Rourke's NVLD theory. The right hemisphere has more white matter relative to gray matter, so it is specialized for integrating complex stimuli and novel problem-solving (Goldberg, 2001; Hale & Fiorello, 2004; Rourke, 2008), both of which are important during social exchange. Relying on primarily automatized, ritualized behavior in social relationships, children with NVLD are likely to have difficulty adapting flexibly to novel, dynamic, social exchanges, which in turn leads to psychopathology.

Although Rourke's findings are indeed convincing, they have been challenged because not all NVLD and math SLD subtypes display NVLD profiles (e.g., Forrest, 2004; Hain et al., 2008; Hale et al., 2008a). Moreover, some children with SLD and psychopathology do not display the visual/perceptual, mathematics, and social relationship difficulties found in Rourke's studies, with some children with auditory-verbal-routinized processing and reading deficits also experiencing significant psychopathology (Forrest, 2004; Hain et al., 2008; Hale, Rosenberg, Hoeppner, & Gaither, 1997). In addition, right hemisphere/white matter dysfunction not only leads to "nonverbal" problems as most clinicians think, but also difficulty with implicit, higher-order language (e.g., metaphor, idiom, sarcasm, indirect messages, humor, prosody; Bryan & Hale, 2001), a point that Rourke (2008) actually acknowledges, suggesting the "nonverbal" label may be a misnomer.

Our recent study (Hain et al., 2008) used the C-DM model to classify children with SLD and subsequently found six subtypes with different neurocognitive, academic, and psychosocial/behavioral profiles. Two subtypes appeared to display patterns consistent with right hemisphere/white matter dysfunction and mathematics SLD, similar to the two mathematics SLD subtypes found in a separate sample (Hale et al., 2008a), and further refining differences among Rourke's (2000) suggested unitary NVLD profile. Interestingly, those thought to display more right frontal dysfunction and fluid reasoning/attention problems had clinically significant psychopathology, whereas those presumed to have right posterior visual-spatial-holistic processing deficits showed only mild attention problems, with some depression and anxiety symptoms. In addition, externalizing disorders were not evident in this subtype, consistent with another study showing lower rates of psychopathology in children with NVLD as compared to controls and children with verbal SLD (Forrest, 2004).

Two of Hain and colleagues' (2008) SLD subtypes with the greatest level of psychosocial impairment did not show any signs of right hemisphere dysfunction. Instead, one SLD subtype appeared to have left hemisphere deficits affecting receptive and expressive language; crystallized knowledge; concordant/convergent thought; and clinically significant levels of aggression, conduct problems, and hyperactivity. This subtype may likely be emergent in conduct-disordered children, possibly due to neuropsychological deficits and repeated school and social failures (Hale & Fiorello, 2004; Hale et al., 1997). In combination with the executive deficits and working memory problems experienced by this group, it was not surprising that this subtype had the lowest levels of achievement and increased psychopathology, similar to Forrest's (2004) findings.

The most severely impaired group demonstrated a plethora of executive/working memory and severe emotional and behavioral deficits, with clinically significant levels found for hyperactivity, conduct problems, anxiety, depression, attention problems, learning problems, atypicality, and withdrawal. The seat of psychopathology is thought to lie in the prefrontal–subcortical circuits (Lichter & Cummings, 2001; Hale et al., 2009; Miller & Hale, 2008; Powell & Voeller, 2004), so this subtype pattern results in both global executive dysfunction and the most disabling emotional and behavioral deficits. Finally, one subtype appeared to display mild attention/hyperactivity and executive deficits consistent with an ADHD profile, whereas the other displayed executive deficits (e.g., processing speed) associated with depressive symptomology (Hain et al., 2008).

Externalizing Disorders and SLD

Children who display significant hemispheric processing differences on standardized tests have higher rates of delinquency than children whose scores are consistent (Walsh, Petee, & Beyer, 1987). This higher rate of delinquency among individuals with significant processing differences leads to overrepresentation in the juvenile justice system (Quinn, Rutherford, Leone, Osher, & Poirer, 2005), so it is not surprising that delinquents are likely to demonstrate a pattern of neuropsychological deficits that lead to specific learning problems (Teichner & Golden, 2000). Early studies have shown that children exhibiting antisocial and delinquent behavior experience a higher incidence of traumatic brain injuries (Hux, Bond, Skinner, Belau, & Sanger, 1998), frontal lobe dysfunction (Deckel, Hesselbrook, & Bauer, 1998), and auditory-verbal-linguistic deficits (Moffitt, Lynam, & Silva, 1994).

Children with conduct disorder (CD) have difficulty keeping social values or future rewards in mind and seldom think about how their inappropriate behavior may affect others, which may be in part due to poor response inhibition (Mash & Wolfe, 2010). Although the executive deficits seen in CD resemble those seen in ADHD because response inhibition problems are associated with both disorders (Toupin, Déry, Pauzé, Mercier, & Fortin, 2000), controlling for the effects of ADHD may limit the utility of executive measures in differential diagnosis (Pennington & Ozonoff, 1996) because ADHD deficits appear to be distinct from CD (Clark, Prior, & Kinsella, 2000; Klorman et al., 1999; Schachar & Tannock, 1995). More recent evidence suggests that emotion regulation problems due to orbital dysfunction may be more characteristic of CD, whereas attention problems and ventrolateral dysfunction may be more indicative of ADHD (Rubia et al., 2008). This would suggest that the executive deficits that frequently lead to comorbid ADHD and SLD, because this is a common comorbidity (Mattison & Mayes, 2010; Mayes & Calhoun, 2006), would not lead to comorbid CD. This, then, begs the question: How do so many children with SLD end up with comorbid CD?

Despite Rourke's (2000) contention that children with left hemisphere dysfunction have auditory-verbal-linguistic SLD in reading and spelling but adequate psychosocial functioning, other research suggests these children appear to have high rates of externalizing psychopathology that increases with age (Forrest, 2004; Sundheim & Voeller, 2004). Consistent with this finding, Baker and Cantwell (1987) found that 50% of their large sample (n = 300) of children with language disorders also had comorbid psychiatric problems. Given that several studies have suggested that executive and language problems lead to conduct problems, it should not be surprising that these children have considerable difficulty with academic achievement, solving social problems, and verbally mediating social conflict (Teichner & Golden, 2000). The apparent discrepancy between Rourke's (2000) position and findings that many children with SLD and auditory-verbal-linguistic deficits have CD (Sundheim & Voeller, 2004) makes one wonder how children who have few problems in early childhood (Rourke, 2000) become so behaviorally impaired later in life.

Hale and Fiorello (2004) argue that part of the explanation may be related to what is considered socialized versus undersocialized delinquency (Quay, 2008). It may be that children with right hemisphere or frontal dysfunction have undersocialized delinquency—their processing and executive deficits lead to difficulty with social information processing, the ability to take the perspectives of others (i.e., theory of mind), and self-regulation during social exchanges (Hain et al., 2008; Hale & Fiorello, 2004; Hale et al., 2009), which would be consistent with Rourke's (2000) position. Conversely, socialized delinquents might have left hemisphere and/or left frontal dysfunction but relatively good initial psychosocial functioning. They may be socially adept because of their good right hemisphere function, but because of their continued academic failure and SLD, they may experience exogenous depression and alienation. As a result, these children find satisfaction in socializing with others who have struggled academically and gain recognition and acceptance for complying with antisocial norms (Hale & Fiorello, 2004). Clearly, more research exploring the relationship between the neuropsychology of SLD and externalizing psychopathology is needed, especially in the areas of prevention and intervention for these disorders.

Internalizing Disorders and SLD

Although deleterious both academically and socio-emotionally, internalizing disorders such as depression and anxiety are often unintentionally disregarded and undertreated (Hazler & Mellin, 2004). Unfortunately, parents may underestimate the impact of internalizing disorders in their children with SLD because the focus is on their academic difficulties (Koulopoulou, 2010). Meta-analyses have revealed that children with SLD are more likely to experience stress, anxiety, depression, and poor self-concept than peers without SLD (Maag & Reid, 2006). They are more likely to experience loneliness, victimization, and reduced social satisfaction as a result (Sabornie, 1994).

Sundheim and Voeller (2004) found that children with language problems were more likely to experience externalizing and internalizing problems. They found that children with depression and social withdrawal often experienced language/reading disabilities, yet mood disorders were more commonly found in children with math SLD. Although some research has suggested that internalizing problems may be specifically associated with language-based SLD and reading disorder (Forrest, 2004; Sundheim & Voeller, 2004; Willcutt & Pennington, 2000), there is a paucity of literature regarding reading disability subtypes and this association, and high rates of anxiety and depression have been reported in several studies of children with NVLD and math disability (see Rourke, 2000). Martinez and Semrud-Clikeman (2004) found math SLD was commonly associated with DE symptomology, consistent with the Rourke and Fuerst (1991) findings. In addition, disorders associated with right hemisphere/white matter dysfunction, such as Turner syndrome, Williams syndrome, and Asperger's disorder, are known to have high rates of internalizing psychopathology (Dodd & Porter, 2009; Keysor & Mazzocco, 2002; Pfeiffer, Kinnealey, Reed, & Herzberg, 2005).

Anxiety occurs in 2%–27% of children and adolescents, making it one of the most common psychiatric problems experienced by youth (Mychailyszyn, Mendez, & Kendall,

2010; Wood, McLeod, Piacentini, & Sigman, 2009). Although not all children with SLD experience significant anxiety, 70% experience more anxiety symptoms than is typical (Nelson & Harwood, 2010). Symptoms such as rumination, catastrophic thought patterns, and elevated physiological arousal interfere with learning efficiency, so it is easy to see why children experiencing anxiety have greater impairment in school performance (Nelson & Harwood, 2010; Wood, 2006). Children with SLD and AD may have difficulty with long-term memory retrieval, mental inflexibility, language formulation, and difficulty with adaptive decision making, which could affect oral and written expression and accuracy of performance (see Hale & Fiorello, 2004).

Of the executive deficits commonly found in depression, those most likely to lead to academic impairments are lack of motivation affecting persistence on difficult tasks, difficulty with decision making, limited working memory, and poor processing speed, which in turn affects new learning and academic performance in reading comprehension as well as work completion and test-taking skills (Fossati, Ergis, & Allilaire, 2002; Hale & Fiorello, 2004; Rogers et al., 2004). These deficits have been related to dysfunction in the dorsolateral prefrontal cortex and dorsal anterior cingulate (Mayberg, 2001; Rogers et al., 2004), with hypoactivity in the left and hyperactivity in the right frontal areas leading to depressive symptoms (Shenal, Harrison, & Demaree, 2003).

Prefrontal cortical and subcortical limbic (e.g., amygdala) structures influence each other in reciprocal fashion (Hale et al., 2009), so deciphering the frontal–subcortical relationships among these internalizing disorders may be useful in understanding internalizing comorbidity in SLD. Unlike depression, which appears to be more related to hypoactive dorsal (dorsolateral–dorsal cingulate) systems, children with anxiety likely have overactive orbital functioning (Baxter, Clark, Iqbal, & Ackerman, 2001; Milad & Rauch, 2007). Because orbital hyperactivity is overwhelming for children with AD, these children may mentally retreat from interacting with the world, withdrawing from the overarousal experienced from environmental contact and interaction. As a result, these children are more likely to experience attention deficits because of internal distractibility and may be labeled ADHD-Inattentive Type, whereas children with hypoactivity may experience external distractibility and be labeled ADHD-Combined Type (Hale et al., 2009). According to Hale's Balance Theory of Frontal-Subcortical Function (Hale et al., 2009), one possible reason why anxiety and depression are often comorbid is that overactivity in the ventral system leads to underactivity in the dorsal system, which is consistent with the neurobiological literature on these related disorders (e.g., Baxter et al., 2001; Koenigs et al., 2008).

Because children with both depression (an internalizing disorder) and ADHD (an externalizing disorder) may experience attention problems that result in similar behavior ratings, neuropsychological testing is needed to differentiate the two disorders (Hale et al., 2009). Although both causes of inattention may lead to significant academic concerns for affected children, differences in neuropsychological patterns of performance may reveal the relationship between SLD and psychosocial adjustment for individual children (Hain et al., 2008).

For instance, does a child with external distractibility have poor work completion because of difficulty staying on task and poor sustained attention, whereas a child with internal distractibility has difficulty initiating a task or thinking flexibly about the task's demands? Is written expression hampered in externalizers because of poor planning, organization, and error monitoring, whereas internalizers may not write well because of inflexible thoughts and perseverative responding? These are questions that practitioners must explore when conducting comprehensive CHT evaluations for children with SLD and psychopathology, patterns that are best revealed through careful idiographic analysis of data, not nomothetic approaches to understanding SLD and psychopathology (Hale & Fiorello, 2004).

Disentangling the Comorbidity of SLD and Psychopathology

As noted earlier, many psychosocial problems and psychopathologies can be traced to executive dysfunction and the prefrontal–subcortical circuits, with different circuit patterns leading to different forms of psychopathology (Hale et al., 2009). Although reading and math SLD can both happen following frontal dysfunction, written expression SLD may be the most common (see Berninger et al., 2009; Hale & Fiorello, 2004). When determining the type of psychosocial problems that might result from frontal dysfunction, it is important to consider these systems in addition to left and right hemisphere function in the development of psychopathology. Of relevance here is what Gray (1987) described as the behavioral activation system (BAS) and behavioral inhibition system (BIS). Children who have externalizing disorders such as CD or ADHD (Combined Type) appear to have an overactive BAS and an underactive BIS, whereas the opposite appears to be true for those with internalizing disorders, such as anxiety disorder and obsessive-compulsive disorder, a position supported by numerous neuroimaging studies (Hale et al., 2009). In addition, there may be hemispheric differences in frontal involvement associated with psychopathology, as the right hemisphere appears to be activated during processing of negative emotional stimuli, whereas the left hemisphere is activated for positive stimuli in typical individuals (Davidson, 2000), with dysfunction in these systems leading to psychosocial dysfunction (Hale et al., 2009).

Given these neuropsychological findings regarding circuit and hemispheric differences influencing socio-emotional functioning, it can be reasoned that a hyperactive right hemisphere combined with hypoactivity in the left hemisphere would likely lead to depression symptoms like anhedonia, lethargy, and withdrawal, whereas left hemisphere hyperactivity and right hemisphere hypoactivity could lead to hypomania and indifference, which is consistent with lesion and hemispheric anesthetization studies (Sackheim et al., 1982). As a result, Hale and colleagues (2009) argue that the key to adaptive executive functioning and psychosocial adjustment is a *balance* between these regulatory frontal–subcortical circuits, with imbalance leading to different forms of psychopathology. Because children with SLD, by definition, have an *imbalance* between processing assets and deficits, it seems clear they are at greater risk for psychopathology as a result, with the pattern of performance leading to certain types of psychopathology (Hale et al., 2009).

The profile variability observed for children with SLD would seemingly produce a straightforward pattern of psychopathology, given what we know about cortical–subcortical and left/right hemisphere imbalance. A child with SLD and strong fluid reasoning/novel problem-solving/memory/memory retrieval skills (e.g., right frontal), but poor expressive language/routinized motor/memory-encoding skills (e.g., left frontal) would be more likely to experience depression, whereas a child with the opposite pattern may be more ADHD or hypomanic. However, when balance is considered along left-right (hemisphere), top-down (e.g., dorsolateral–orbital circuits), and anterior-posterior (frontal/temporal–parietal–occipital) axes of interpretation, relationships are less definitive.

For instance, right parietal lobe dysfunction has been related to primary attention deficits (Tamm, Menon, & Reiss, 2002), whereas strong right parietal lobe function has been related to the hypervigilance characteristic of anxiety disorder (Heller et al., 1997). Relationships among anterior and posterior regions have been found in several psychopathologies, including depression, anxiety, schizophrenia, ADHD, and CD (Blair, 2006; Cleghorn et al., 1989; Heller & Nitschke, 1998; Silk et al., 2005), so balance theory must extend beyond the prefrontal cortex and frontal–subcortical circuits. In addition, cognitive affective syndrome can happen following damage to the cerebellar vermis (Koziol & Budding, 2009), and research has shown many children with SLD experience cerebellar dysfunction (Nicholson & Fawcett, 2001). Clearly, there are more complex relationships among processing strengths and weaknesses inherent in SLD that will need elucidation in future research, especially for SLD subtypes.

Relevance for Intervention: The Ultimate Purpose of SLD Differential Diagnosis

Despite the interdependence of the cognitive, neuropsychological, academic, behavioral, and environmental determinants of learning and psychosocial functioning, many parents and educators may focus solely on the academic challenges experienced by a child with SLD and ignore or minimize the psychosocial aspects of the disorder. In order to effectively treat the underlying difficulties experienced by a child with SLD, various facets of the child's life should be taken into consideration when developing an individualized treatment plan and educational program. Because children with SLD approach learning in different ways using different cognitive processes, the individual learning and behavioral characteristics should be recognized and valued during CHT evaluations. Intervention methods should then be tailored to the child's individual strengths and weaknesses, with a focus on providing remedial or compensatory services that foster cognitive and academic development and psychosocial adjustment.

Collaboration among parents, educators, and specialized professionals is pivotal in attaining intervention efficacy, so regular contact and communication among these individuals is critical for success. After interventions are implemented, it is important for parents and teachers alike to regularly monitor the child's academic and behavioral progress and discuss this information with other practitioners to ensure individualized treatment plans are executed with integrity. Lastly, parents and teachers themselves need to be educated as to the various psychological processes that may be contributing to the academic and behavioral struggles a child with SLD experiences. This will not only help them better serve the child with SLD, but also sensitize them to challenges the child faces so they can provide a warm and caring support system that will in turn foster intervention efficacy.

The CHT evaluation we advocate here does not stop with differential diagnosis of SLD and related psychopathological conditions. The first half of the CHT model is about differential diagnosis, but the second half is about how practitioners can develop, monitor, and evaluate targeted interventions to achieve treatment efficacy. One major purpose of this chapter is to highlight the need to examine the cognitive, neuropsychological, academic, and psychosocial characteristics of children with SLD to help readers develop a holistic understanding of these children so that their individual needs can be met. Comprehensive evaluations that address the neuropsychological characteristics of individuals might help delineate the SLD subtype, and in the case of those individuals with frontal–subcortical circuit dysfunction, lead to differential diagnosis of various psychopathologies (Hale et al., 2010d), which can in turn lead to targeted treatment strategies specific to the individual child's academic and behavioral needs.

Diagnosis does not occur in an environmental vacuum but instead is intimately related to the child's natural environment and the people who have the greatest influence on the child's life. As a result, effective interventions must occur within the context of a collaborative and flexible problem-solving approach, with ongoing data collected over time to evaluate treatment efficacy, if the true utility of comprehensive evaluation is to be realized (Fiorello et al., 2009; Hale et al., 2010c). Although an in-depth discussion is beyond the scope of this chapter, multimethod, multimodal intervention approaches that target learning and behavior may include psychotropic medication treatment (e.g., methylphenidate for SLD and ADHD, selective serotonin reuptake inhibitors for SLD and depression) as well, so collaboration among medical professionals is often an essential practice for psychologists (Feifer & Rattan, 2010).

The CHT model is designed to link cognitive and neuropsychological assessment data to intervention on an individual level to ensure that instruction can be truly individualized to meet the child's needs (Hale & Fiorello, 2004). Much empirical work is needed to establish the utility of the CHT approach in clinical practice, and to identify intervention approaches that are most effective for different SLD processing patterns. Once practitioners move beyond simple discrepancy or RTI approaches to SLD identification, and instead understand the dynamic interplay between processing strengths, processing weaknesses, and associated achievement and psychosocial deficits, they may begin the important task of linking these assessment data to intervention. Some have argued that these types of data are not relevant for intervention (Reschly, 2005), but a growing body of literature shows how cognitive and neuropsychological assessment can inform intervention, as evidenced by a recent special issue of the *Journal of Learning Disabilities* edited by Hale and Fuchs (March/April, 2011). Neuropsychological data can provide insight into individual differences not revealed during traditional assessments that focus on summative behavior rating scores or RTI assessments that examine overt behavior, thereby helping determine treatment choice, course, and efficacy (e.g., Hale et al. 2011).

Evidence is emerging that cognitive and neuropsychological processes are relevant for both academic and behavioral intervention; however, considerable empirical work is needed to establish the concurrent, ecological, and treatment validity of these relationships (Fiorello et al., 2009; Fuchs et al., 2011; Hale et al., 2010c). Recent empirical work shows that interventions tailored to individual needs not only lead to amelioration of learning and psychosocial deficits, but they also result in changes in brain structure and function as well (Pliszka, Lancaster, Liotti, & Semrud-Clikeman, 2006; Richards et al., 2007; Simos et al., 2007). This testament to the brain's amazing plasticity and responsiveness to intervention should serve as an impetus for researchers and practitioners alike to use neuropsychological data to identify disability subtypes so that targeted interventions can be developed to meet individual needs. Although empirical validation of subtype–intervention relationships is greatly needed before widespread adoption of such methodologies is warranted (Fuchs et al., 2011), this fact does not preclude the use of single-subject designs to document treatment efficacy for each individual with learning and psychosocial difficulties. In this way, special education services provided to individuals who fail to respond to intervention can be individualized (Hale et al., 2010c), and the spirit of special education can be realized in clinical practice.

REFERENCES

Anastasi, A. & Urbina, S. (1997). *Psychological testing* (7th ed.). Upper Saddle River, NJ: Prentice Hall.

Angold, A., Costello, E. J., & Erkanli, A. (1999). Comorbidity. *Journal of Child Psychology and Psychiatry, and Allied Disciplines, 40*, 57–87.

Baker, L., & Cantwell, D. P. (1987). A prospective psychiatric follow-up of children with speech and language disorders. *Journal of the American Academy of Child and Adolescent Psychiatry, 26*, 546–553.

Bandura, A. (1986). *Social foundations of thought and action: A social cognitive theory*. Englewood Cliffs, NJ: Prentice-Hall.

Barth, A., Stuebing, K. K., Anthony, J. L Denton, C. A., Mathes, P. G., Flethcher, J. M., et al. (2008). Agreement among response to intervention criteria for identifying responder status. *Learning and Individual Differences, 18*, 196–307.

Baxter, L. R., Clark, E. C., Iqbal, M., & Ackerman, R. F. (2001). Cortical-subcortical systems in the mediation of obsessive-compulsive disorder. In D. G. Lichter & J. L. Cummings (Eds.), *Frontal-subcortical circuits in psychiatric and neurological disorders* (pp. 207–230). New York, NY: Guilford Press.

Berninger, V. W. (2006). Research supported ideas for implementing reauthorized IDEA with intelligent professional psychological services. *Psychology in the Schools, 43*, 781–796.

Berninger, V. W., & May, M. O. (2011). Evidence-based diagnosis and treatment for specific learning disabilities involving impairments in oral and/or written language. *Journal of Learning Disabilities, 44*, 167–183.

Berninger, V. W., & Richards, T. L. (2002). *Brain literacy for educators and psychologists*. San Diego, CA: Academic Press/Elsevier Science.

Berninger, V. W., Richards, T. L., Stock, P. S., Abbott, R. D., Trivedi, P. A., Altemeier, L., et al. (2009). fMRI activation related to nature of ideas generated and differences between good and poor writers during idea generation. *BJEP Monograph Series II, Number 6 – Teaching and Learning Writing, 1*, 77–93.

Blair, R. J. R. (2006). The emergence of psychopathy: Implications for the neuropsychological approach to developmental disorders. *Cognition, 101*, 414–442.

Brown-Chidsey, R., & Steege, M. (2005). *Response to intervention: Principles and strategies for effective practice*. NY: Guilford Press.

Bryan, K. L., & Hale, J. B. (2001). Differential effects of left and right hemisphere accidents on language competency. *Journal of the International Neuropsychology Society, 7*, 655–664.

Burns, T. J. (2010). Wechsler Individual Achievement Test – III: What is the 'gold standard' for measuring academic achievement? *Applied Neuropsychology, 17*, 234–236.

Caterino, L. C., Sullivan, A., Long, L., Bacal, E., Kaprolet, C. M Beard, R., et al. (2008). Assessing school psychologists' perspectives on independent educational evaluations. *APA Division 16 School Psychology, 62*, 6–12.

Clark, C., Prior, M., & Kinsella, G. J. (2000). Do executive function deficits differentiate between adolescents with ADHD and oppositional defiant/conduct disorder? A neuropsychological study using the Six Elements Test and Hayling Sentence Completion Test. *Journal of Abnormal Child Psychology, 28*, 403–424.

Cleghorn, J. M., Garnett, E. S., Nahmias, C., Firnau, G., Brown, G. M., Kaplan, R., et al. (1989). Increased frontal and reduced parietal glucose metabolism in acute untreated schizophrenia. *Psychiatry Research, 28,* 119–133.

Clements, S., Christner, R. W., McLaughlin, A. L., & Bolton, J. B. (2011). Assessing student skills using process-oriented approaches. In T. M. Lionetti, E. P. Snyder, & R. W. Christner (Eds.), *Practical guide to building professional competencies in school psychology* (pp. 101–119). New York, NY: Springer.

D'Amato, R. C., Fletcher-Janzen, E., & Reynolds, C. R. (2005). *Handbook of school neuropsychology.* Hoboken, NJ: John Wiley & Sons.

Davidson, R. J. (2000). Affective style, psychopathology, and resilience: Brain mechanisms and plasticity. *American Psychologist, 55*(11), 1196–1214.

Deckel, A. W., Hesselbrook, V., & Bauer, L. (1996). Antisocial personality disorder, childhood delinquency, and frontal brain functioning: EEG and neuropsychological findings. *Journal of Clinical Psychology, 52,* 639–650.

Della Toffalo, D. A. (2010). Linking school neuropsychology with response to intervention models. In D. Miller (Ed.), *Best practices in school neuropsychology* (pp. 159–175). Hoboken, NJ: John Wiley & Sons.

Dixon, S. G., Eusebio, E. C., Turton, W. J., Wright, P. W. D., & Hale, J. B. (2011). Forest Grove v. T.A. Supreme Court decision: Implications for school psychologists. *Journal of Psychoeducational Assessment, 29,* 103–113.

Dodd, H. F., & Porter, M. A. (2009). Psychopathology in Williams syndrome: The effect of individual differences across the lifespan. *Journal of Mental Health Research in Intellectual Disabilities, 2,* 89–109.

Elliott, C., Hale, J. B., Fiorello, C. A., Dorvil, C., & Moldovan, J. (2010). Differential Ability Scales-II prediction of reading performance: Global scores are not enough. *Psychology in the Schools, 47,* 698–720.

Feifer, S. G., & Della Toffalo, D. A. (2007). *Integrating RTI with cognitive neuropsychology: An scientific approach to reading.* Middletown, MD: School Neuropsych Press.

Feifer, S. G., & Rattan, G. (2010). *Emotional disorders: A neuropsychological, psychopharmacological, and educational perspective* (pp. 199–225). New York, NY: W.W. Norton & Company.

Fiorello, C. A., Hale, J. B., Decker, S. L., & Coleman, S. (2009). Neuropsychology in school psychology. In E. Garcia Vazquez, T. D. Crespi, & C. A. Riccio (Eds). *Handbook of education, training, and supervision of school psychologists in school and community* (pp. 213–233). New York: Routledge.

Fiorello, C. A., Hale, J. B., & Snyder, L. E. (2006). Cognitive hypothesis testing and response to intervention for children with reading disabilities. *Psychology in the Schools, 43,* 835–854.

Fiorello, C. A., Hale, J. B., Snyder, L. E., Forrest, E., & Teodori, A. (2008). Validating individual differences through examination of converging psychometric and neuropsychological models of cognitive functioning. In S. K. Thurman & C. A. Fiorello (Eds.), *Applied cognitive research in K–3 classrooms* (pp. 151–186). New York: Routledge.

Flanagan, D. P., Alfonso, V. C., Mascolo, J., & Hale, J. B. (2010). The WISC-IV in neuropsychological assessment and intervention. In A. S. Davis (Ed.), *Handbook of pediatric neuropsychology.* New York, NY: Springer Publishing.

Flanagan, D. P., Ortiz, S. O., Alfonso, V. C., & Dynda, A. M. (2006). Integration of response to intervention and norm-referenced tests in learning disability identification: Learning from the Tower of Babel. *Psychology in the Schools, 43,* 807–825.

Flanagan, P. P., Ergis, A. M., & Allilaire, J. F. (2002). Executive functioning in unipolar depression: A review. *L'Encephale, 28,* 97–107.

Fletcher, J. M., Lyon, G. R., Fuchs, L. S., & Barnes, M. A. (2007). *Learning disabilities: From identification to intervention.* New York, NY: Guilford Press.

Fletcher-Janzen, E. (2005). The school neuropsychological evaluation. *Handbook of school neuropsychology.* (pp. 172–212). Hoboken, NJ: John Wiley & Sons.

Forrest, B. J. (2004). The utility of math difficulties, internalized psychopathology, and visual-spatial deficits to identify children with the nonverbal learning disability syndrome: Evidence for a visuospatial disability. *Child Neuropsychology, 10,* 129–146.

Fossati, P. P., Ergis, A. M., & Allilaire, J. F. (2002). Executive functioning in unipolar depression: A review. *L'Encephale, 28,* 97–107.

Fuchs, D., Fuchs, L. S., & Compton, D. L. (2004). Identifying reading disabilities by responsiveness-to-instruction: Specifying measures and criteria. *Learning Disability Quarterly, 27,* 216–227.

Fuchs, D., Hale, J. B., & Kearns, D. M. (2011). On the importance of a cognitive processing perspective: An introduction. *Journal of Learning Disabilities, 44,* 99–104.

Fuerst, D. R., Fisk, J. L., & Rourke, B. P. (1989). Psychosocial functioning of learning disabled children: Replicability of statistically derived subtypes. *Journal ofConsulting and Clinical Psychology, 57,* 275–280.

Fuerst, D. R., Fisk, J. L., & Rourke, B. P. (1990). Psychosocial functioning of learning-disabled children: Relations between WISC Verbal IQ-Performance-IQ discrepancies and personality subtypes. *Journal of Consulting and Clinical Psychology, 58*, 657–660.

Goldberg, E. (2001). *The executive brain: Frontal lobes and the civilized mind*. New York: Oxford University Press.

Gray, J. A. (1987). *The psychology of fear and stress* (2nd ed.). New York, NY: Cambridge University Press.

Hain, L. A., Hale, J. B., & Glass-Kendorski, J. (2008). The comorbidity of psychopathology in cognitive and academic SLD subtypes. In S. Feifer & G. Rattan (Eds.), *Emotional disorders: A neuropsychological, psychopharmacological, and educational perspective* (pp. 199–225). Middletown, MD: School Neuropsych Press.

Hale, J. B. (2006). Implementing IDEA with a three-tier model that includes response to intervention and cognitive assessment methods. *School Psychology Forum: Research and Practice, 1*, 16–27.

Hale, J. B., Alfonso, V., Berninger, V., Bracken, B., Christo, C., Clark, E., et al. (2010a). Critical issues in response-to-intervention, comprehensive evaluation, and specific learning disabilities identification and intervention: An expert white paper consensus. *Learning Disability Quarterly, 33*, 223–236.

Hale, J. B., Alfonso, V., Berninger, V., Bracken, B., Christo, C., Clark, E., et al. (2010d). Critical issues in response-to-intervention, comprehensive evaluation, and specific learning disabilities identification and intervention: An expert white paper consensus. Retrieved from http://www.ldanatl.org/pdf/LDA%20White%20Paper%20on%20IDEA%20Evaluation%20Criteria%20for%20SLD.pdf

Hale, J. B., & Fiorello, C. A. (2004). *School neuropsychology: A practitioner's handbook*. New York, NY: Guilford Press.

Hale, J. B., Fiorello, C. A., Miller, J. A., Wenrich, K., Teodori, A. M., & Henzel, J. (2008a). WISC-IV assessment and intervention strategies for children with specific learning disabilities. In A. Prifitera, D. H. Saklofske, & L. G. Weiss (Eds.), *WISC-IV clinical assessment and intervention* (2nd ed.) (pp. 109–171). New York, NY: Elsevier Science.

Hale, J. B., Fiorello, C. A., & Thompson, R. (2010b). Integrating neuropsychological principles with response-to-intervention for comprehensive school-based practice. In E. Arzubi & E., Mambrino (Eds.), *A guide to neuropsychological testing for health care professionals* (pp. 229–262). New York, NY: Springer Publishing Company.

Hale, J. B., Flanagan, D. P., & Naglieri, J. A. (2008b). Alternative research-based methods for IDEA (2004) identification of children with specific learning disabilities. *Communiqué, 36*(8), 1, 14–17.

Hale, J. B., Kaufman, A., Naglieri, J. A., & Kavale, K. A. (2006). Implementation of IDEA: Integrating response to intervention and cognitive assessment methods. *Psychology in the Schools, 43*, 753–770.

Hale, J. B., Naglieri, J. A., Kaufman, A. S., & Kavale, K. A. (2004). Specific learning disability classification in the new Individuals with Disabilities Education Act: The Danger of Good Ideas. *The School Psychologist, 58*(1), 6–14.

Hale, J. B., Reddy, L. A., Decker, S. L., Thompson, R., Henzel, J., Teodori, A., et al. (2009). Development and validation of an executive function and behavior rating screening battery sensitive to ADHD. *Journal of Clinical and Experimental Neuropsychology, 31*, 897–912.

Hale, J. B., Reddy, L. A., Wilcox, G., McLaughlin, A., Hain, L., Stern, A., et al. (2009). Assessment and intervention for children with ADHD and other frontal-striatal circuit disorders. In D. C. Miller (Ed.), *Best practices in school neuropsychology: Guidelines for effective practice, assessment and evidence-based interventions* (pp. 225–279). Hoboken, NJ: John Wiley & Sons.

Hale, J. B., Rosenberg, D., Hoeppner, J. B., & Gaither, R. (1997, April). Cognitive predictors of behavior disorders in children with learning disabilities. *Paper presented at the Annual Convention of the National Association of School Psychologists*, Anaheim, CA.

Hale, J. B., Wycoff, K. L., & Fiorello, C. A. (2010c). RTI and cognitive hypothesis testing for specific learning disabilities identification and intervention: The best of both worlds. In D. P. Flanagan & V. C. Alfonso (Eds.), *Essentials of Specific Learning Disability Identification* (pp. 173–202). Hoboken, NJ: John Wiley & Sons.

Hazler, R. J., & Mellin, E. A. (2004). The developmental origins and treatment needs of female adolescents with depression. *Journal of Counseling and Development, 82*, 18–24.

Heller, W., & Nitschke, J. B. (1998). The puzzle of regional brain activity in depression and anxiety: The importance of subtypes and comorbidity. *Cognition and Emotion, 12*, 421–447.

Heller, W., Nitschke, J. B. Etienne, M. A., & Miller, G. A. (1997). Patterns of regional brain activity differentiate types of anxiety. *Journal of Abnormal Psychology, 106*(3), 376–385.

Holzapfel, M., Barnea-Goraly, N., Eckert, M. A., Kesler, S. R., Reiss, A. L. (2006). Selective alterations of white matter associated with visuospatial and sensorimotor dysfunction in Turner Syndrome. *Journal of Neuroscience, 26*, 7007–7013.

Hux, K., Bond, V., Skinner, S., Belau, D., & Sanger, D. (1998). Parental report of occurrences and consequences of traumatic brain injury among delinquent and non delinquent youth. *Brain Injury, 12*, 667–681.

Hynd, G. W., & Reynolds, C. R. (2005). School neuropsychology: The evolution of a specialty in school psychology. In R. C. D'Amato, E. Fletcher-Janzen, & C. R. Reynolds (Eds.), *Handbook of School Neuropsychology* (pp. 3–14). Hoboken, NJ: John Wiley & Sons.

Hynd, G. W., & Willis, W. G. (1988). *Pediatric Neuropsychology*. New York: Grune & Stratton. Individuals with Disabilities Education Improvement Act of 2004 (IDEA), Pub. L. No. 108–446, 118 Stat. 2647 (2004). [Amending 20 U.S.C. §§ 1400 et seq.].

Kavale, K. A., & Forness, S. R. (1996). Social skills deficits and learning disabilities: A meta-analysis. *Journal of Learning Disabilities, 29*, 226–237.

Kavale, K. A., Holdnack, J. A., & Mostert, M. P. (2005). Responsiveness to intervention and the identification of specific learning disability: A critique and alternative proposal. *Learning Disability Quarterly, 28*, 2–16.

Keysor, C. S., & Mazzocco, M. M. M. (2002). Physiological arousal in females with Fragile X or Turner syndrome. *Developmental Psychobiology, 41*, 133–146.

Klorman, R., Hazel-Fernandez, L. A., Shaywitz, S. E., Fletcher, J. M., Marchione, K. E., Holohan, J., et al. (1999). Executive functioning deficits in attention-deficit/hyperactivity disorder are independent of oppositional defiant or reading disorder. *Journal of the American Academy of Child and Adolescent Psychiatry, 38*, 1148–1155.

Koenigs, M., Huey, E. D., Calamia, M., Raymont, V., Tranel, D., & Grafman, J. (2008). Distinct regions of the prefrontal cortex mediate resistance and vulnerability to depression. *The Journal of Neuroscience, 28*, 12341–12348.

Koulopoulou, A. (2010). Anxiety and depression symptoms in children-comorbidity with learning disabilities. *European Psychiatry, 25*, 432–432.

Koziol, L. F., & Budding, D. E. (2009). *Subcortical structures and cognition. Implications for neuropsychological assessment*. New York, NY: Springer.

Landerl, K., & Moll, K. (2010). Comorbidity of learning disorders: Prevalence and familial transmission. *The Journal of Child Psychiatry and Psychology, 51*, 287–294.

Lasker, A. G., Mazzocco, M. M. M., & Zee, D. S. (2007). Ocular motor indicators of executive dysfunction in Fragile X and Turner syndromes. *Brain and Cognition, 63*, 203–220.

Learning Disabilities Roundtable (2002). *Specific learning disabilities: Finding common ground*. Washington, D.C.: U.S. Department of Education Office of Special Education Programs, Office of Innovation and Development.

Learning Disabilities Roundtable (2005). *Comments and recommendations on regulatory issue under the Individuals with Disabilities Education Improvement Act of 2004 P.L.* 108–446.Washington, D.C.: U.S. Department of Education Office of Special Education Programs.

Leyfer, O., Woodruff-Borden, J., & Mervis, C.B. (2009). Anxiety disorders in children with Williams syndrome, their mothers, and their siblings: Implications for the etiology of anxiety disorders. *Journal of Neurodevelopmental Disorders, 1*, 4–14.

Lichter, D. G., & Cummings, J. L. (Eds.) (2001). *Frontal–subcortical circuits in psychiatric and neurological disorders*. New York, NY: Guilford Press.

Lyon, G. R., Shaywitz, S. E., & Shaywitz, B. A. (2003). Defining dyslexia, comorbidity, teachers' knowledge of language and reading: A definition of dyslexia. *Annals of Dyslexia, 53*, 1–14.

Maag, J. W., & Reid, R. (2006). Depression among students with learning disabilities: Assessing the risk. *Journal of Learning Disabilities, 39*, 3–10.

Machek, G. R., & Nelson, J. M. (2010). School psychologists' perceptions regarding the practice of identifying reading disabilities: Cognitive assessment and response to intervention considerations. *Psychology in the Schools, 47*, 230–245.

Marenco, S., Siuta, M. A., Kippenhan, J. S., Grodofsky, S., Chang, W. L., Kohn, P., et al. (2007). Genetic contributions to white matter architecture revealed by diffusion tensor imaging in Williams syndrome. *Proceedings of the National Academy of Sciences, 104*, 15177–15222.

Martinez, R. S., & Semrud-Clikeman, M. (2004). Emotional adjustment and school functioning of young adolescents with multiple versus single learning disabilities. *Journal of Learning Disabilities, 37*(5), 411–420.

Mash, A. J., & Wolfe, D. A. (2010). *Abnormal child psychology* (4th ed.). Belmont, CA: Wadsworth Cengage Learning.

Mather, N., & Gregg, N. (2006). Specific learning disabilities: Clarifying, not eliminating a construct. *Professional Psychology: Research and Practice, 37*, 99–106.

Mattison, R. E., & Mayes, S. D. (2010). Relationships between learning disability, executive function, and psychopathology in children with ADHD. *Journal of Attention Disorders, 16*, 138–146.

Mayberg, H. (2001). Depression and frontal-subcortical circuits: Focus on prefrontal-limbic interactions. In D.G. Lichter & J.L. Cummings (Eds.), *Frontal-subcortical circuits in psychiatric and neurological disorders* (pp. 177–206). New York: Guilford Press.

Mayes, S. D., & Calhoun, S. (2006). WISC-IV and WISC-III profiles in children with ADHD. *Journal of Attention Disorders, 9*, 486–493.

Mayes, S. D., & Calhoun, S. (2008). WISC-IV and WIAT-II profiles in children with high functioning autism. *Journal of Autism and Developmental Disorders, 38*, 428–439.

McAlonan, G. M., Cheung, C., Cheung, V., Wong, N., Suckling, J., & Chau, S. E. (2009). Differential effects on white matter systems in high functioning autism and Asperger's syndrome. *Psychological Medicine, 39*, 1885–1893.

McGrew, K. S., & Wendling, B. L. (2010). CHC cognitive-achievement relations: What we have learned from the past 20 years of research. *Psychology in the Schools*, 651–675.

McKinney, J. D., & Speece, D. L. (1986). Academic consequences and longitudinal stability of behavioral subtypes of learning disabled children. *Journal of Educational Psychology, 78*, 365–372.

Milad, M. R., & Rauch, S. L. (2007). The role of the orbitofrontal cortex in anxiety disorders. *Annals of the New York Academy of Sciences, 1121*, 546–561.

Miller, D. C., & Hale, J. B. (2008). Neuropsychological applications of the WISC-IV and WISC-IV Integrated. In A. Prifitera, D. Saklofske, & L. Weiss (Eds.), *WISC-IV clinical use and interpretation: Scientist–practitioner perspectives* (2nd ed.). New York, NY: Elsevier.

Miller, J. A., Getz, G., & Leffard, S. A. (2006, February). Neuropsychology and the diagnosis of learning disabilities under IDEA 2004. *Poster presented at the 34th* annual meeting of the International Neuropsychological Society, Boston, MA.

Moffitt, T. E., Lynam, D. R., & Silva, P. A. (1994). Neuropsychological tests predicting persistent male delinquency. *Criminology, 32*, 277–300.

Mychailyszyn, M. P., Mendez, J. L., & Kendall, P. C. (2010). School functioning in youth with and without anxiety disorders: Comparisons by diagnosis and comorbidity. *School Psychology Review, 39*, 106–121.

National Association of School Psychologists. (2007). *Identification of students with specific learning disabilities* (Position Statement).Bethesda, MD: National Association of School Psychologists .

Nelson, J. M., & Harwood, H. (2010). Learning disabilities and anxiety: A meta-analysis. *Journal of Learning Disabilities, 44*(1), 3–17. DOI: 10.1177/00222|9409359939.

Nicholson, R. I., & Fawcett, A. J. (2001). Dyslexia, learning, and the cerebellum. In M. Wolf (Ed.), *Dyslexia, fluency, and the brain* (pp. 159–188). Timonium, MD: York Press.

Nussbaum, N. L., & Bigler, E. D. (1986). Neuropsychological and behavioral profiles of empirically derived subtypes of learning disabled children. *The International Journal of Clinical Neuropsychology, 18*, 82–89.

Nussbaum, N. L., Bigler, E. D., & Koch, W. R. (1986). Neuropsychologically derived subgroups of learning disabled children. *Journal of Research and Development in Education, 19*, 57–67.

Ofiesh, N. (2006). Response to intervention and the identification of specific learning disabilities: Why we need comprehensive evaluations as part of the process. *Psychology in the Schools, 43*, 883–888.

Pennington, B. F., & Ozonoff, S. (1996). Executive functions and developmental psychopathology. *Journal of Child Psychology and Psychiatry, 37*, 51–87.

Pfeiffer, B., Kinnealey, M., Reed, C., & Herzberg, G. (2005). Sensory modulation and affective disorders in children and adolescents with Asperger's disorder. *American Journal of Occupational Therapy, 59*, 335–345.

Pliszka, S. R., Lancaster, J., Liotti, M., & Semrud-Clikeman, M. (2006). Volumetric MRI differences in treatment-naïve vs. chronically-treated children with ADHD. *Neurology, 67*, 1023–1027,

Powell, K. B., & Voeller, K. K. S. (2004). Prefrontal executive function syndromes in children. *Journal of Child Neurology, 19*, 785–797.

Quay, H. C. (1993). The psychobiology of undersocialized aggressive conduct disorder: A theoretical perspective. *Development and Psychopathology, 5*, 165–180.

Quinn, M. M., Rutherford, R. B., Leone, P. E., Osher, D. M., & Poirer, J. M. (2005). Youth with disabilities in juvenile corrections: A national survey. *Exceptional Children, 71*, 339–345.

Reddy, L. A., & Hale, J. B. (2007). Inattentiveness. In A. R. Eisen (Ed). *Treating childhood behavioral and emotional problems: A step-by-step evidence-based approach* (pp. 156–211). New York, NY: Guilford Press.

Reschly, D. J. (2005). Learning disabilities identification: Primary intervention, secondary intervention, and then what? *Journal of Learning Disabilities, 38*, 510–515.

Reschly, D. J., & Hosp, J. L. (2004). State SLD policies and practices. *Learning Disability Quarterly, 27*, 197–213.

Richards, T., Berninger, V., Winn, W., Stock, P., Wagner, R., Muse, A., et al. (2007). fMRI activation in children with dyslexia during pseudoword aural repeat and visual decode: Before and after instruction. *Neuropsychology, 21*, 732–747.

Rogers, M. A., Kasai, K., Koji, M., Fukeda, R., Iwanami, A., Nakagome, K., et al. (2004). Executive and prefrontal dysfunction in unipolar depression: A review of neuropsychological and imaging research. *Neuroscience Research, 50*, 1–11.

Rourke, B. P. (2000). Neuropsychological and psychosocial subtyping: A review of investigations within the University of Windsor Laboratory. *Canadian Psychology, 41*, 34–51.

Rourke, B. P. (2008). Neuropsychology as a (psycho) social science: Implications for research and clinical practice. *Canadian Psychology/Psychologie Canadienne, 49*, 35–41.

Rourke, B. P., & Fuerst, D. E. (1991). *Learning disabilities and psychosocial functioning: A neuropsychological perspective*. New York, NY: Guilford Press.

Rubia, K., Smith, A. B., Halari, R., Matsukura, F., Mohammed, M., Taylor, E., et al. (2008). Disorder-specific dissociation of orbitofrontal dysfunction in boys with pure conduct disorder during reward and ventrolateral prefrontal dysfunction in boys with pure ADHD during sustained attention. *American Journal of Psychiatry, 166*, 83–94.

Sabornie, E. J. (1994). Social-affective characteristics in early adolescents identified as learning disabled and nondisabled. *Learning Disability Quarterly, 17*, 268–279.

Sackheim, H. A., Greenberg, M. S., Weiman, A. L., Gur, R. C., Hungerbuhler, J. P., Geschwind, N. (1982). Hemispheric asymmetry in the expression of positive and negative emotions: Neurological evidence. *Archives of Neurology, 39*, 210–218.

Schachar, R., & Tannock, R. (1995). Test of four hypotheses for the comorbidity of attention-deficit hyperactivity disorder and conduct disorder. *Journal of the American Academy of Child and Adolescent Psychiatry, 34*, 639–648.

Schrank, F. A., Miller, J. A., Catering, L., & Desrochers, J. (2006). American Academy of School Psychology survey on the independent educational evaluation for a specific learning disability: Results and discussion. *Psychology in the Schools, 43*, 771–780.

Semrud-Clikeman, M. (2005). Neuropsychological aspects for evaluating learning disabilities. *Journal of Learning Disabilities, 38*, 563–568.

Semrund-Clikeman, M., Goldenring Fine, J., & Harder, L. (2005). Providing neuropsychological services to students with learning disabilities. In R. C. D'Amato, E. Fletcher-Janzen, & C. R. Reynolds (Eds.), *Handbook of school neuropsychology* (pp. 403–424). Hoboken, NJ: John Wiley & Sons.

Shenal, B. V., Harrison, D. W., & Demaree, H. A. (2003). The neuropsychology of depression: A literature review and preliminary model. *Neuropsychology Review, 13*, 33–42.

Siegel, L. S. (2003). IQ-discrepancy definitions and the diagnosis of LD: Introduction to the special issue. *Journal of Learning Disabilities, 36*, 2–3.

Silk, T., Vance, A., Rinehart, N., Egan, G., O'Boyle, M., Bradshaw, J. L., et al. (2005). Decreased fronto-parietal activation in attention deficit hyperactivity disorder combined type (ADHD-CT): An fMRI study. *British Journal of Psychiatry, 187*, 282–283.

Simos, P. G., Fletcher, J. M., Sarkari, S., Billingsley, R. L., Denton, C., & Papanicolaou, A. C. (2007). Altering the brain circuits for reading through intervention: A magnetic source imaging study. *Neuropsychology, 21*, 485–496.

Speece, D. L. (2005). Hitting the moving target known as reading development: Some thoughts on screening children for secondary interventions. *Journal of Learning Disabilities, 38*, 487–493.

Speece, D., McKinney, J. D., & Appelbaum, M. (1985). Classification and validation of behavioral subtypes of learning-disabled children. *Journal of Educational Psychology, 77*, 67–77.

Sundheim, S. T. P. V., & Voeller, K. K. S. (2004). Psychiatric implications of language disorders and learning disabilities: Risks and management. *Journal of Child Neurology, 19*, 814–826.

Taggart, L., Cousins, W., & Milner, S. (2007). Young people with learning disabilities living in state care: Their emotional, behavioural and mental health status. *Child Care in Practice, 13*, 401–416.

Tamm, L., Menon, V., & Reiss, A. L. (2002). Maturation of brain function associated with response inhibition. *Journal of the American Academy of Child & Adolescent Psychiatry, 41*, 1231–1238.

Teichner, G., & Golden, C. J. (2000). The relationship of neuropsychological impairment to conduct disorder in adolescence: A conceptual review. *Aggression and Violent Behavior, 5*, 509–528.

Toupin, J., Déry, M., Pauzé, R., Mercier, H., & Fortin, L. (2000). Cognitive and familial contributions to conduct disorder in children. *Journal of Child Psychology and Psychiatry, 41*, 333–344.

Waesche, J. S. B., Schatschneider, C., Maner, J., Ahmed, Y., & Wagner, R. (in press). Examining agreement and longitudinal stability among traditional and RTI-based definitions of reading disability using the affected-status agreement statistic. *Journal of Learning Disabilities.*

Walsh, A., Petee, T. A., & Beyer, J. A. (1987). Intellectual imbalance and delinquency. Comparing high verbal and high performance IQ delinquents. *Criminal Justice and Behavior, 14*, 370–379.

Wechsler, D. (2009). *Wechsler individual achievement test – Third edition*. San Antonio, TX: Pearson.

Willcutt, E., & Pennington, B. (2000). Psychiatric comorbidity in children and adolescents with reading disability. *Journal of Child Psychology & Psychiatry & Allied Disciplines, 41*(8), 1039 .

Willis, J. O., & Dumont, R. (2006). And never the twain shall meet: Can response to intervention and cognitive assessment be reconciled? *Psychology in the Schools, 43*, 901–908.

Wodrich, D. L., Spencer, M. L. S., & Daley, K. B. (2006). Combining RTI and psychoeducational assessment: What we must assume to do otherwise. *Psychology in the Schools, 43*, 797–806.

Wong, B. Y. L., & Donahue, M. L. (2002). *The social dimensions of learning disabilities: Essays in the honor of Tanis Bryan*. Mahwah, NJ: Lawrence Erlbaum Associates.

Wood, J. J. (2006). The effect of anxiety on reduction on children's school performance and social adjustment. *Developmental Psychology, 42*, 345–349.

Wood, J. J., McLeod, B. D., Piacentini, J. C., & Sigman, M. (2009). One-year follow up of family versus child CBT for anxiety disorders: Exploring the roles of child age and parental intrusiveness. *Child Psychiatry and Human Development, 40*, 301–217

Zirkel, P. A., & Thomas, L. B. (2009). State laws for RTI: An updated snapshot. *TEACHING Exceptional Children, 42*, 56–63.

Zirkel, P. A., & Krohn, N. (2008). RTI after IDEA: A survey of state laws. *Teaching Exceptional Children, 40*(3), 71–73.

APPENDIX A: CONCORDANCE–DISCORDANCE MODEL (C-DM) OF SLD IDENTIFICATION

Step-by-Step Approach

Step 1
Score standard cognitive test and determine whether global composite score (e.g., IQ), factor scores, or subtest scores should be interpreted.

a) Are all subtest and factor scores consistent enough to interpret global composite score?
- □ Yes C-DM unlikely
- □ No C-DM possible (go to Step 1b)

b) Are the subtest scores consistent enough within the factors to interpret factor scores?
- □ Yes C-DM possible (go to Step 2)
- □ No Consider subtest combinations to form new factor score (go to Step 1c)

c) If no subtest combinations appear to represent a new factor, can other standardized measures be added to cognitive measure to create new factor score?
- □ Yes New subtest combination appropriate for use in C-DM (go to Step 2)
- □ No Consider combining subsets from an additional measure of at least two subtests to create new factor score for use in C-DM (go to Step 2)

Step 2
Score standard achievement test and examine to see if composites or subtests indicate achievement deficit.

a) Do standardized achievement scores indicate an academic deficit that is consistent with prior evaluation, classroom permanent products, and teacher-reported achievement deficits?
- □ Yes C-DM possible (go to Step 3)
- □ No Explore other possible causes for poor test performance, or explanations for poor performance in the classroom; consider achievement re-testing to verify or refute achievement deficit (return to Step 2 or discontinue)

Step 3
Review cognitive (e.g., CHC) and/or neuropsychological literature to ensure obtained cognitive deficit(s) is associated with achievement deficit(s).

a) Could obtained cognitive deficits interfere with deficient academic achievement area?
- □ Yes Cognitive and/or neuropsychological deficits have been found to be related to deficient achievement area as reported in the clinical or empirical literature (go to Step 4)
- □ No C-DM unlikely unless research not conducted, check for ecological validity of cognitive and achievement deficits (return to Step 2 or discontinue)

Step 4
Obtain reliability coefficients for cognitive strength(s), cognitive deficit(s), and achievement deficit(s).

a) Are factor/subtest reliability coefficients (e.g., coefficient alpha) available in the cognitive and achievement technical manuals?

- □ Yes Get factor strengths and deficits and achievement score reliabilities in the instrument technical manuals (go to Step 5)
- □ No New factor scores and reliability coefficients must be computed; average factor scores and reliability coefficients for new factors (use Fisher's z-transformation, see Hale et al., 2008; go to Step 5)

Step 5

Calculate SED formula to establish discordance between cognitive strength and achievement deficit.

a) Enter reliability coefficients for cognitive strength(s) and academic deficit(s) into SED formula and solve for SED.

b) Multiply obtained SED value by 1.96 for $p < .05$, or 2.58 for $p < .01$

c) Is obtained difference between cognitive strength and deficit greater than SED critical value?

- □ Yes There is a significant difference between cognitive strength and cognitive deficit, child likely has a deficit in the basic psychological processes that is interfering with academic achievement (go to Step 6)
- □ No Consider other possible cognitive deficits responsible for achievement deficit (go to Step 1), or the child may have another disability interfering with achievement; consider further evaluation using cognitive and/or neuropsychological measures

---

Step 6

Calculate SED formula to establish discordance between cognitive strength and achievement deficit.

a) Enter reliability coefficients for cognitive strength and academic deficit into SED formula and solve for SED.

b) Multiplyobtained SED value by 1.96 for $p < .05$, or 2.58 for $p < .01$

c) Is obtained difference between cognitive strength and academic deficit greater than SED critical value?

- □ Yes There is a significant difference between cognitive strength and academic deficit; child likely has unexpected underachievement consistent with a SLD (go to Step 7)
- □ No Consider other possible cognitive deficits and/or achievement deficit (go to Step 1), or the child may have another disability interfering with achievement; consider further evaluation; discontinue as child does not have SLD

Step 7
Calculate SED formula to establish concordance between cognitive deficit and achievement deficit.

a) Enter reliability coefficients for cognitive deficit and academic deficit into SED formula and solve for SED.

b) Multiply obtained SED value by 1.96 for $p < .05$, or 2.58 for $p < .01$

c) Is obtained difference between cognitive strength and academic deficit less than SED critical value?

- □ Yes There is no significant difference between cognitive deficit and the achievement deficit, consider SLD classification (go to Step 8)
- □ No Is the achievement deficit significantly below the cognitive deficit? If so, this could mean other factors are causing additional impairment; consider SLD classification or conduct further evaluation to determine why achievement deficit is substantial (go to Step 8)

Step 8
Determine if C-DM findings have ecological validity and achieve team consensus for SLD or other disorder determination. Re-examine empirical literature, RTI data, teacher and classroom permanent products, classroom observations, and other evaluation data to determine if child meets IDEA SLD statutory and regulatory requirements or other disorder warranting special education services.

If another disorder is evident but the child does not meet IDEA criteria for a disability, consider ADA/Section 504 identification and service delivery.

If another disorder is evident in addition to SLD, consider whether SLD is primary, secondary, or comorbid with condition, and reflect finding in classification and intervention decision making.

Source: Copyright 2010 James B. Hale and Lisa A. Hain, used with permission.

CHAPTER 6

Autism Spectrum Disorders

Gerry A. Stefanatos

INTRODUCTION

Pervasive developmental disorder (PDD) is a collective term currently used in both the *Diagnostic and Statistical Manual of Mental Disorders* (*DSM-IV-TR*; American Psychiatric Association [APA], 2000) and International Classification of Diseases (ICD-10; WHO, 1992) to refer to a category of childhood disorders characterized by significant impairment spanning three key behavioral domains: (1) reciprocal social interaction, (2) communication, and (3) repetitive and restricted behavior and interests (RRBI). The category was conceived over 30 years ago (*DSM-III*; APA, 1980) in an effort to devise a diagnostic framework to parse autism and related forms of pervasive developmental psychopathology into distinguishable disorders based on differences in patterns of behavioral symptoms, their severity, and age of presentation. Conceptions of PDD have since undergone substantial remodeling, necessitating major changes to the composition of the category and the associated diagnostic criteria. The disorders presently classified under PDD in *DSM-IV-TR* include autistic disorder (AD), Asperger's disorder (AspD), childhood disintegrative disorder (CDD), Rett's disorder (RD), and a nonspecific category designated as pervasive developmental disorder–not otherwise specified (PDD-NOS).

AD is the prototype for the category and is the most well-established and intensively studied of the disorders. Delineated as a distinct syndrome by Leo Kanner in 1943, AD is recognized as a lifelong condition that emerges in infancy and early childhood. Disturbances of social relatedness and reciprocity are considered foundational and are reflected in markedly diminished social interest and responsiveness, limitations of emotional reciprocity (empathy), difficulties forming appropriate interpersonal relationships, and an impoverished understanding of shared interests and experiences (Dawson & Bernier, 2007; Frith, 2001; Sigman, Dijamco, Gratier, & Rozga, 2004). Coexisting communication impairments vary greatly, ranging from a near absence of speech to generally intact basic language (phonology, morphology, grammar), but poor pragmatics and difficulty understanding implicit or gestural referencing (Rapin, Dunn, Allen, Stevens, & Fein, 2009; Tager-Flusberg, 2006). Manifestations of problems with RRBI are also diverse and can include stereotyped body movements (e.g., hand flapping), preoccupation with parts of objects or their sensory qualities, inflexible adherence to nonfunctional routines, restricted patterns of play or interests, and limited imagination and generativity (Bodfish, Symons, Parker, & Lewis, 2000; Szatmari et al., 2006; Wing, Gould, & Gillberg, 2011). The presentation of these difficulties can vary greatly depending on the severity of the disorder and the child's developmental level. As a result of substantial individual differences in the pattern, severity, and developmental course of impairments in each of these psychological domains, the AD behavioral phenotype is remarkably heterogeneous. It is not considered a singular entity per se, but many different conditions that share a common constellation of symptoms in their behavioral expression (Wing, 1997).

The fundamental basis of AD and its pathogenesis remain unclear. Kanner originally contended that the syndrome was based in an "innate inability to form the usual, biologically provided affective contact with people" (1943, p. 250), yet his early discussions of potential causal factors focused on the role of cold and emotionally unavailable parents (Kanner, 1949). The latter notion was eventually dispelled by compelling evidence implicating neurobiological origins for the disorder (Rimland, 1964). It is now widely accepted that the brain in AD is both functionally and structurally atypical, although no unitary "signature" anomaly has been identified. Abnormalities have been discovered at multiple levels, including brain cytoarchitecture, neurochemistry, gross neuroanatomy, electrophysiology, and regional cerebral metabolism (Courchesne, Campbell, & Solso, 2010; Neuhaus, Beauchaine, & Bernier, 2010; Rudie, Shehzad, Hernandez, Colich, Bookheimer, Iacoboni, & Dapretto, 2012). The etiological basis for these alterations are multifactorial, entailing complex interactions between genetic susceptibility (Folstein & Rosen-Sheidley, 2001; Liu, Paterson, & Szatmari, 2008; Weiss, Arking, Daly, & Chakravarti, 2009), epigenetic effects (Grafodatskaya, Chung, Szatmari, & Weksberg, 2010; Kinney, Barch, Chayka, Napoleon, & Munir, 2010), and environmental risk factors (Herbert, 2010; Landrigan, 2010).

These influences ultimately result in perturbations of neurodevelopment that compromise the normal elaboration of distributed neural networks required for social communication and an appropriately diverse and flexible repertoire of behaviors and interests. Brain regions that have been particularly implicated include frontal and temporal neocortex, limbic structures, and the cerebellum. Given the widespread distribution of the underlying pathophysiology and its developmental context, the disorder is associated with a complex array of primary, secondary, and tertiary residuals spanning multiple domains of function. This chapter examines current conceptions of AD from a developmental neuropsychological perspective. The primary behavioral characteristics currently considered diagnostic of AD are presented along with a description of antecedent developmental disturbances that are now being identified in some children as early as the first year of life. Neuropathological and pathophysiological correlates of the disorder are then reviewed, followed by a discussion of associated neuropsychological disturbances. The chapter closes with a brief overview of mainstream treatment approaches.

EMERGENCE OF THE CONCEPT OF AUTISM

The term *autism* (from Greek *autos* + *ismos* → self + action or state) was coined by the renowned Swiss psychiatrist Eugen Bleuler (1911) to refer to a state of "detachment from the outside world" and the "preponderance of introversion" that he considered to be cardinal features of adult schizophrenia (also a term he originated). Although the concept was periodically adopted to describe behavioral disturbances in children (Asperger, 1938; Ssucharewa, 1926), its tremendous significance to developmental psychopathology went largely unappreciated until Leo Kanner (1943) published his seminal paper, "Autistic Disturbances of Affective Contact", in which he lucidly described 11 children (average age 5.3 years) who had in common an "inability to relate themselves in the ordinary way to people and situations from the very beginning of life" (p. 248). Their profound lack of social relatedness and emotional disconnection from the people around them appeared to form part of a broader symptom complex that included "an obsessive desire for the preservation of sameness" (p. 245), impaired use of language for interpersonal communication, and unusual relations with objects. Kanner proposed that this constellation of behaviors represented a distinct syndrome – *early infantile autism* – that was similar to childhood schizophrenia in many ways but had an earlier onset.

Diagnostic criteria for early infantile autism remained ill-defined for many years. Guidelines eventually proposed by Kanner and Eisenberg (1956) failed to define a unique or homogeneous population and questions regarding its definition and validity as a distinct clinical entity persisted. AD was first included in the American Psychiatric Association's *Diagnostic and Statistical Manual of the Mental Disorders* in its third edition (*DSM-III*, APA, 1980), published 37 years after Kanner's original report. The diagnostic criteria outlined in the *DSM-III* were associated with high sensitivity but low specificity, whereas revisions incorporated in *DSM-III-R* (APA, 1987) produced the converse pattern. Substantial modifications were again implemented in *DSM-IV* (APA, 1994), resulting in reasonable sensitivity and specificity for the diagnosis of AD. These were carried forward in a text revision (*DSM-IV-TR*; APA, 2000) without modification. However, substantial changes have been proposed for the PDD category in the forthcoming fifth edition (*DSM-5*, due for release in 2013) because of perceived problems with the current framework. The proposed revisions can be previewed at www.dsm5.org.

CURRENT DIAGNOSTIC CRITERIA

The *DSM-IV-TR* diagnostic criteria for AD are presented in Table 6.1. In order to be diagnosed with AD, a child must demonstrate a minimum of six symptoms of impaired function across the three domains of behavior constituting the so-called autistic triad—social interaction, communication, and RRBI (Wing & Gould, 1979). A minimum of two symptoms must involve qualitative impairments in social interaction, and these must be accompanied by at least one symptom of impaired communication and no less than one symptom related to RRBI. Problems in at least one of these domains must be evident before 3 years of age.

Some clinicians have criticized the *DSM-IV* criteria for AD as being poorly conceived, gender-biased, difficult to apply to infants and adults, and of questionable help in clinical practice (Leekam, Libby, Wing, Gould, & Gillberg, 2000; Wing et al., 2011). It has been argued, more generally, that medically-oriented categorical approaches to diagnosis are inherently flawed when applied to behavioral conditions such as AD, in which symptoms vary along a severity continuum and blend seamlessly into behaviors seen in other less severe disorders (Brown, Hobson, Lee, & Stevenson, 1997; Mulligan et al., 2009; Reiersen, Constantino, Volk, & Todd, 2007) or indeed the general population (Brown et al., 2003; Kennedy, 2009). In view of the sometimes arbitrary boundaries associated with categorical diagnostic approaches, the term *autism spectrum disorder* (ASD; Allen, 1988) has come into increasingly common usage to refer collectively to AD and the closely related disorders such as AspD and PDD-NOS.

ONTOGENY OF AD: EARLY SIGNS

Kanner's conceptualization of AD as a congenital disorder was based on his interpretation of retrospective accounts by parents who recalled that during infancy, their children failed to demonstrate developmentally appropriate social behaviors such as raising their arms in anticipation of being picked up or conforming their posture to being held. It is now appreciated that most parents (~80%) recognize developmental anomalies or delays in their children with AD by 2 years of age (De Giacomo & Fombonne, 1998), and 30%–50% harbor concerns as early as the first year (Harrington, Rosen, & Garnecho, 2006; Young, Brewer, & Pattison, 2003). Despite this, a definitive diagnosis of AD is often not made until children are 3–4 years of age (Howlin & Moore, 1997; Mandell, Novak, & Zubritsky, 2005; Yeargin-Allsopp et al., 2003).

In recent years, numerous studies have sought to identify reliable early manifestations of risk for AD (Zwaigenbaum et al., 2009). More precise specification of the initial signs of the disorder and the subsequent evolution of the symptom complex could potentially allow for earlier and better-targeted interventions (Dawson, 2008). In addition, this information may possibly facilitate a better understanding of the diverse pathogenic mechanisms underlying the disorder, inform the identification of endophenotypes, or guide subtyping based on early developmental trajectory (e.g., early vs. late onset vs. regressive) of the disorder (Shumway et al., 2011; Stefanatos, Kinsbourne, & Wasserstein, 2002). Given evidence that the risk of having a second child with autism is considerably increased (≥19 times) over that of the

TABLE 6.1 *DSM-IV-TR* Criteria for Autistic Disorder Compared to Antecedent Behaviors in Infancy

***DSM-IV-TR* criteria**	***Behaviors at 2 years or earlier***
1. Qualitative Abnormalities in Social Interaction (Minimum 2 Symptoms)	
• Marked impairment in the use of multiple nonverbal behaviors, e.g., eye-to-eye gaze • Failure to develop peer relationships appropriate to developmental level • Lack of spontaneous seeking to share enjoyment with other people • Lack of social or emotional reciprocity	• Poor eye contact, failure to follow gaze • Failure to produce or understand gestures (e.g., head nodding, waving, pointing, showing) and facial expressions • Limited social smiling • Limited imitation of others (also seen in play; e.g., pretending to mow lawn) • Failure to show an interest in others and in sharing enjoyment (e.g., tickling) • Lack of social overtures (e.g., showing things of interest, bringing toys) • Atypical response to others' emotions, facial affect, unusual reactivity • Limited social play (e.g., peekaboo, pat-a-cake)
2. Qualitative Abnormalities in Communication (Minimum 1 Symptom)	
• Delay in, or total lack of, the development of spoken language that is not accompanied by an attempt to compensate through the use of gesture or mime • In individuals with adequate speech, marked impairment in initiating or sustaining a conversation with others • Stereotyped and repetitive use of language or idiosyncratic language • Lack of varied, spontaneous make-believe or imitative play	• Delay or lack of development of spoken language • A lack of directed vocalizations (e.g., social babbling) • A lack of pointing to express interest or a lack of spontaneous pointing • Lack of communicative gestures (e.g. waving, clapping, nodding, shaking hands)
3. Restricted and Repetitive Interests and Behaviors (Minimum 1 Symptom)	
Preoccupation with one or more stereotyped or restricted pattern of interest • Adherence to nonfunctional routines or rituals • Stereotyped and repetitive motor mannerisms • Persistent preoccupation with parts of objects • Sensory hypo/hypersensitivity	• Repetitive play (e.g., lining up cars) • Limited pretend and imaginative play • Excessive adverse reaction to change in routine • Motor mannerisms or stereotyped behavior (e.g., hand flapping) • Unusual interests, interest in nonfunctional elements of play material • Oversensitivity to household noises

The left column presents the *DSM-IV-TR* criteria for AD. The diagnosis requires that a child demonstrates a minimum of six symptoms of impaired function across the three domains. The right column lists some of the early behavioral markers of high risk for the development of AD that have been identified in infancy and toddlerhood.

general population (Abrahams & Geschwind, 2008; Ozonoff et al., 2011), early detection can also have a substantial impact on family planning.

Building on some groundbreaking efforts (Adrien et al., 1991), several of these studies have combined retrospective parental recall of the child's early history with careful examination of the child's behavior as captured on home videos at several time points over the first 2 years of life (Baranek, 1999; Clifford & Dissanayake, 2008; Goldberg, Thorsen, Osann, & Spence, 2008). Despite inherent methodological issues (Saint Georges et al., 2010), notably the potential for bias in recall from memory (Zwaigenbaum et al., 2007) and the sometimes idiosyncratic contextual constraints surrounding the video recordings (e.g., birthday parties, family holidays), these studies have yielded valuable information that has facilitated the operationalization of new tools for screening and identifying at-risk children as early as the first 12 months (Bryson, Zwaigenbaum, McDermott, Rombough, & Brian, 2008; Feldman et al., 2012; Reznick, Baranek, Reavis, Watson, & Crais, 2007; Wetherby, Brosnan-Maddox, Peace, & Newton, 2008). In addition, these studies have guided the design of prospective studies of early development in AD (Barbaro & Dissanayake, 2010b; Chawarska, Klin, Paul, Macari, & Volkmar, 2009; Ozonoff et al., 2010). The following sections provide an overview of current developments in this area. For consistency, the discussion is partitioned according to the key behavioral domains currently used to define AD. However, interdependencies in the development of social interaction and communicative capacities make it difficult to categorically segregate behaviors along these lines, particularly at early stages of development. These domains will likely be merged in *DSM-5*.

Anomalies of Social and Emotional Engagement

Human infants possess a number of biologically determined proclivities that promote early attachment and support the development of neural networks that mediate social interaction (Johnson, Grossman, & Farroni, 2010; Parsons, Young, Murray, Stein, & Kringelbach, 2010). Despite limitations of visual acuity (20/400 to 20/800) and spatial frequency sensitivity (<1 cycle per degree sensitivity), human infants demonstrate attentional and perceptual biases for orienting to and processing socially relevant visual patterns such as faces (Leo & Simion, 2009) and biological motion (Bardi, Regolin, & Simion, 2011) that are important for establishing the identity, actions, and intentions of significant people in their environment. Early in development, infants will look at and track faces more than non-face-like stimuli (Johnson, Dziurawiec, Ellis, & Morton, 1991), and although they are unable to resolve subtle facial expressions, their vision is typically sufficient to recognize highly salient facial features such as when the mouth or eyes are opened or closed (Leppanen & Nelson, 2009). These gross features provide a preliminary basis for learning to recognize certain emotions in the first few months, such as discerning happy from surprised or angry expressions (Grossmann, 2010). These early "orienting" biases subserve the evolving parent-child relationship and shape the experience-dependent development of cortical circuitry specialized for processing faces and other types of socially important visual information.

Mothers often optimize dyadic communications by intuitively positioning themselves centrally in the child's visual field and using exaggerated facial expressions that are easier for the child to recognize (Papousek & Papousek, 1983). Within a few days to weeks of birth, an infant learns to recognize significant others and will preferentially orient to its mother's face rather than toward an unknown woman (Bushnell, 2001). Visual capacities increase in the first 6 months such that by 5 to 7 months, infants can recognize most static facial expressions and their variations across individuals (Bornstein & Arteberry, 2003; Hainline & Abramov, 1992; Nelson, Morse, & Leavitt, 1979). As development progresses, the infant's behavioral repertoire grows more sophisticated and by the end of the first year, infants can recognize a variety of common emotional states from information present in the face and voice.

Eye contact and eye gaze play a particularly vital role in early social interaction and communication. The configuration of the eyes (e.g., size, shape, spacing, color) provide salient visual cues for establishing the identity of another person, as well as the direction of gaze, which is critical to establishing social contact (mutual gaze) and for conveying emotional information and intentions (Schyns, Petro, & Smith, 2007). In the course of normal development, newborns show a preference for direct over averted eye gaze (Farroni, Menon, Rigato, & Johnson, 2007) and automatically orient their attention according to the direction of motion of another person's eyes (Farroni, Johnson, & Csibra, 2004). Monitoring the direction of eye gaze also provides a window as to what is capturing another person's interest, and by directing gaze to the same object (joint attention), infants have the opportunity to share in those interests and experiences. Additionally, eye gaze can be used in a directive manner to compel another person to allocate attention to a particular object or event. Thus, monitoring eye gaze yields important information that is fundamental to promoting social cognition as well as aspects of learning.

Newborns are also sensitive to a variety of nonfacial visual cues and are capable, for example, of discriminating between goal-directed or non-goal-directed actions in others (Craighero, Leo, Ultima, & Simion, 2011). The increasing skill in visual analysis of behavior that unfolds in the early course of development is used to engender intersubjectivity, that is, the attunement and sharing of subjective states between individuals (e.g., attention, intentions, and emotions; Trevarthen & Aitken, 2001). By 6 weeks, infants demonstrate remarkable sensitivity to qualitative features of adult communications and actively pursue specific kinds of social interaction. When a mother's facial expressions fail to adhere to the infant's expectations, the infant may respond negatively, becoming distressed and eventually withdrawn (Legerstee & Markova, 2007). Noting a case where neonatal damage to inferior temporal and occipital cortex resulted in lifelong face recognition deficits with relatively intact object recognition, Farah, Rabinowitz, Quinn, and Liu (2000) suggested that the neural mechanisms mediating the processing of faces at this early stage of development are likely genetically specified and can be distinguished from processes associated with object recognition. In keeping with this, a form of developmental prosopagnosia has been identified that has a genetic contribution (Gruter, Gruter, & Carbon, 2008).

Early in the postnatal period, visual recognition of facial features is largely mediated by subcortical pathways, including the amygdala, superior colliculus, and pulvinar. These pathways, which are involved in the rapid processing of low spatial frequency information, modulate the activity of cortical areas such as the fusiform gyrus, which is concerned with processing higher spatial frequencies (Johnson, 2005). By 2 months, infants begin to recognize faces by the configuration of internal features, and cortical activation during face processing begins to resemble patterns observed in adults. Areas stimulated by face processing at 2 months include the right fusiform "face area" and inferior occipital cortex bilaterally (Tzourio-Mazoyer et al., 2002). The superior temporal sulcus (STS), an area involved in encoding biological motion, does not become activated during face processing until about 4 months of age, at which time the medial prefrontal cortex (mPFC) also becomes engaged. The involvement of the STS may facilitate recognition of changeable aspects of face perception, such as eye gaze shifts and lip expression (Pelphrey, Morris, & McCarthy, 2005), whereas the mPFC may be involved in detecting and allocating attention to communicative signals such as mutual gaze (Hoehl et al., 2009). Around this time, an infant's visually mediated behavioral repertoire begins to diversify significantly to incorporate play with objects and action games, and as a result the infant may spend less time in direct eye contact (Trevarthen, Murray, & Hubley, 1981).

A fundamental question then arises whether the earliest signs of AD involve a breakdown of some of the early emerging capacities, as Kanner (1943) had implied, or whether manifestations of the disorder entail faulty development of higher-order processes that gradually unfold over the course of development over the first or second year. To address the question, studies have examined the development of social behaviors and their precursors during this critical period of development. Most of these investigations have focused on deficiencies of "eye-to-eye gaze" because this is a key symptom of impaired use of nonverbal behaviors to regulate social interaction and communication in AD (*DSM-IV-TR*; APA, 2000). Kanner had noted that children with infantile autism were often avoidant of direct eye contact, and more recent reports have suggested that poor eye-to-eye gaze may underlie some of their difficulties in recognizing faces and deriving important social information from facial expressions (Itier & Batty, 2009; Wallace, Coleman, Pascalis, & Bailey, 2006). In social contexts, the failure to make direct eye-to-eye contact limits access to a rich source of social information conveyed by the eye region of the face. Children with AD who are unsuccessful in social perception often fail to spontaneously scan the socially informative eye region of faces and instead spend more time scanning less important areas such as around the mouth (Falck-Ytter, Fernell, Gillberg, & von Hofsten, 2010; Pelphrey et al., 2002). Problems in processing faces may contribute to later difficulties in remembering faces (Hauck, Fein, Maltby, Waterhouse, & Feinstein, 1998) and recognizing emotional facial expressions (Hobson, Ouston, & Lee, 1988c; Wright et al., 2008).

A variety of anomalies of gaze have been observed in the first 2 years, including "empty gaze" (Dahlgren & Gillberg, 1989), abnormal intensity of eye contact (Wimpory, Hobson,

Williams, & Nash, 2000), or unpredictable eye gaze such as inconsistently following another person's eye gaze or making use of eye gaze to share experiences or accomplishments (Zwaigenbaum et al., 2005). Several reports have suggested that these anomalies are evident as early as the first 12 months in some children (Mars, Mauk, & Dowrick, 1998; Osterling & Dawson, 1994). Clifford and Dissanayake (2008) examined the onset and time course of the emergence of problems with eye gaze in children with AD by retrospectively examining video material recorded during consecutive 6-month periods in the first 2 years of life. In addition, they conducted retrospective parental interviews referenced to the same time frames (0–5, 6–11, 12–17, and 18–24 months). Consistent with previous findings, subtle signs of anomalies of eye gaze emerged in the first year, although these early differences did not appear to be predictive of later social behavior. Interestingly, problems with eye gaze seemed to progressively worsen in the 12–17 and 18–24 months periods, with gaze aversion—the tendency to avoid eye contact—emerging in the latter part of this progression. The quality of eye contact (and not its frequency) during the second year was predictive of later social responsiveness (Clifford & Dissanayake, 2009). Interestingly, infants also tended to show disproportionate visual fixation to nonsocial aspects of their visual environment (e.g., objects) and had difficulties disengaging their visual attention.

Anomalies of eye contact form part of a broader constellation of abnormalities involving the deployment of visual attention to mediate social interactions. This includes poor visual tracking behavior, diminished orienting to faces, reduced reciprocal smiling and imitation, lack of social interest, and difficulties coordinating eye gaze with actions during play (Baranek, 1999; Barbaro & Dissanayake, 2009; Clifford & Dissanayake, 2008; Maestro et al., 2005; Werner, Dawson, Munson, & Osterling, 2005; Zwaigenbaum et al., 2005). The factors underlying these difficulties remain speculative, but together they implicate functional impairment of frontal and parietal neural networks that mediate the control of visual attention (Bryson, Wainwright-Sharp, & Smith, 1990; Townsend et al., 2001). In addition, involvement of specialized higher-order perceptual processes mediating the analysis of faces and biological motion suggests functional compromise of fusiform gyrus and STS.

Impairment of visual orienting behavior in early development is closely tied to problems with joint attention—the ability to share an attentional focus with that of another person toward some common object or event. Joint attention normally begins to emerge at about 4-months of age (Mundy, Sullivan, & Mastergeorge, 2009). By around 10 months, typically developing children can use eye gaze to direct their parent's attention to an object of interest (Striano & Rochat, 1999), and by the end of their first year, infants engage in joint attention to negotiate fairly sophisticated object-related actions, such as pointing to or picking up a designated object and showing or offering it to another person (Baldwin, 1993; Woodward & Hoyne, 1999). This capacity to coordinate self–other attention is critical to the development of social and communicative functioning, imitation skills, and symbolic thought (Dawson et al., 2004; Mundy et al., 2009; Yoder, Stone, Walden, & Malesa, 2009).

Impaired joint attention is arguably one of the most salient behavioral characteristics of AD (Charman, 2003; Colombi et al., 2009; Mundy, Sigman, & Kasari, 1990). Young children with AD often demonstrate a relative lack of responsiveness to others who attempt to engage them or direct their attention to an object of potential interest (Charman, 2003; Clifford & Dissanayake, 2008; Mundy & Newell, 2007; Mundy, Sigman, & Kasari, 1994). Additionally, children with AD initiate fewer attempts to engage others in joint attention. Diminished responsiveness may be evident in a failure to follow another person's eye gaze or their pointing to an object, whereas poor initiation of joint attention may be reflected in the relative absence of behaviors such as offering objects to others, pointing to objects, and protodeclarative showing (e.g., check this out). It has been suggested that deficits in initiating joint attention may be associated with impaired function of the dorsal mPFC and anterior cingulate gyrus (Mundy, 2003).

Poor joint attention indicates that children with AD are less likely to engage in shared experience and this appears to differentiate infants with AD from typically developing infants or those with language delay (Clifford, Young, & Williamson, 2007). The paucity of joint attention may interfere with the child's learning the reward value of social interaction, with consequent negative implications for the development of social understanding (Dawson et al., 2004; Mundy, 2003), the appreciation of emotional cues (Baron-Cohen, Golan, & Ashwin, 2009; Rieffe, Meerum Terwogt, & Kotronopoulou, 2007; Silani et al., 2008), and the understanding of the mental states and intentions of others (Charman, 2005; Frith, 2001; Hill & Frith, 2003). The ability to respond to and initiate joint attention, particularly between 18 and 24 months, is predictive of social responsiveness later in development (Clifford & Dissanayake, 2009).

A recent prospective study by Ozonoff and colleagues (2010) has shed light on some of the complications encountered when investigating early manifestations of problems in joint attention to predict later difficulties in social responsiveness. They examined the frequency of gaze to faces, shared smiles, and vocalizations directed to others at 6, 12, 18, 24, and 36 months in children who were at low or high risk for developing AD. No group differences were evident at 6 months, but by 12 months, deficiencies were evident in the high-risk group. Subsequent evaluations revealed progressive declines in performance in some of these areas, suggesting a regressive course. These findings parallel those of Clifford and Dissanayake (2008) and others in illustrating that a subtle but quantifiable deterioration of social function may occur in infants with AD between 12 and 24 months of age.

Other manifestations of AD that can emerge as early as the first year include reduced social interest and reciprocity (e.g., social smiles, response to joint attention overtures, imitation) as well as anomalies of behavioral reactivity and play (Barbaro & Dissanayake, 2009; Bryson et al., 2007; Maestro et al., 2005; Ozonoff et al., 2010). In addition, children with incipient AD often demonstrate variability of emotional expression early in life with fewer expressions of positive affect (Zwaigenbaum et al., 2005). Overall, anomalies of behaviors that entail some aspect of social interaction are among the earliest and best predictors of a later diagnosis of AD (Dawson & Bernier, 2007; Wimpory et al., 2000). However, the narrow and relatively undifferentiated behavioral repertoires of infants pose significant obstacles for using a specific behavioral sign to distinguish AD from other developmental disorders at this age (Bryson et al., 2007). Specific markers may not be reliably observed in a single visit in an individual infant but may require repeated evaluations to establish their presence or absence (Barbaro & Dissanayake, 2010a). Indeed, the reliable identification of children at risk may require the integration of information across *several* behaviors obtained at more than one time point. Overall, it appears that observations in the first year are not as predictive of later social outcome as are the anomalies identified between the first and second year (Barbaro & Dissanayake, 2010b).

Anomalies of Verbal and Nonverbal Communication

Early in infant development, communication is intertwined with social interaction and dependent to a significant degree on visual processing. However, from birth, normally developing infants exhibit attentional and perceptual biases suggesting special sensitivity to speech (Grossmann, Oberecker, Koch, & Friederici, 2011). Neonates show a preference for listening to voices over nonsocial sounds (Ecklund-Flores & Turkewitz, 1996), can recognize their mother's voice (Fifer & Moon, 2003; Kisilevsky et al., 2009), and, although they are able to discriminate a broad range of phonemes (Diehl, 2004; McMurray & Aslin, 2005), they favor the sounds of speech comprising their native language (Krentz & Corina, 2008; Kuhl, 2004). Within a few months, the sound of their mother's voice is able to exert powerful influences in alleviating distress or otherwise modulating an infant's affective state. By around the midpoint of their first year, infants recognize their own name being called and orient their eyes toward the person calling them (Bates, 1999). Shortly thereafter, they are able recognize that other spoken words (e.g., Mommy, Daddy) refer to specific individuals and can demonstrate this by shifting their eye gaze to the specified individual or the named object (e.g., "binkie").

Infants and toddlers with incipient AD often demonstrate anomalies in their sensitivity or responsiveness to speech. One of the frequently observed early manifestations of this is an inconsistency in directing their attention to vocalizations or verbal communications. At a time when typically developing infants orient fairly dependably to their name being called, infants at risk for AD often fail to consistently exhibit this orienting behavior (Baranek, 1999; Osterling & Dawson, 1994; Osterling, Dawson, & Munson, 2002; Saint Georges et al., 2010; Zwaigenbaum et al., 2005). This irregularity is commonly evident by the time of their first birthday and may persist into toddlerhood (Maestro et al., 2001; Nadig et al., 2007; Wetherby et al., 2004).

The factors underlying this failure remain to be fully specified. In order to show a selective orienting response, the infant must have intact auditory skills to detect and differentiate the human voice from other sounds. In addition, they must be able to identify the sequence of phonemes comprising their own name and to distinguish this sequence through statistical learning from the many other recurring strings of speech sounds produced in their language environment (Saffran, Aslin, & Newport, 1996). The infant must therefore be able to learn associations and map phonetic forms of spoken words onto concepts (Werker & Yeung, 2005). In addition to auditory-linguistic factors, cognitive variables such as intelligence and the integrity of representational processes may also play a role. Responsiveness to this type of communicative overture is also contingent upon social awareness and interest. Interestingly, infants with AD orient less frequently to their name than do infants with mental retardation (Osterling et al., 2002). Irrespective of the specific mechanisms involved, this failure may signal dysfunction that can also potentially impede receptive vocabulary development more generally. As a group, children with AD commonly understand significantly fewer phrases by 12 months than normal controls, a disparity that continues to be evident at 18 months (Mitchell et al., 2006).

Efficient word learning also requires adequate levels of joint attention. Learning word-object associations, for example, often entails a parent or caregiver producing a spoken word as the child's attention is directed to the referenced object (Baron-Cohen, Baldwin, & Crowson, 1997). Without joint attention, the conditions for pairing words and their associated objects are compromised. Correspondingly, children who demonstrate good joint attention at 20 months of age tend to have better language and social outcomes at 42 months (Charman, 2003; Toth, Munson, Meltzoff, & Dawson, 2006). Conversely, children with AD who fail to develop language by the age of 5 years commonly demonstrate poor joint attention as well as severely impaired vocal and motor imitative skills at 2 years (Thurm, Lord, Lee, & Newschaffer, 2007).

It has been suggested that expressive language problems in some children with AD may be related to more general difficulties with aspects of motor development and imitation. Minimally fluent children with AD, for example, may demonstrate oromotor-programming difficulties early in development, reflected in delayed onset of babbling (Iverson & Wozniak, 2007) and decreased vocalizations (Ozonoff et al., 2010). These children are more likely to produce vowels than consonants (Wetherby, Yonclas, & Bryan, 1989) and voiced rather than voiceless consonants (e.g., /d/ vs /t/), because of the relative ease of orchestrating the necessary articulatory movements (McCleery, Tully, Slevc, & Schreibman, 2006). Gernsbacher, Sauer, Geye, Schweigert, and Goldsmith (2008) observed that abilities such as blowing raspberries and grabbing dangling toys were correlated with verbal fluency later in development, suggesting that motor programming difficulties may not be specific to speech production. Phonological development can interact with lexical and grammatical development at early stages of acquisition such that a failure to produce a particular speech sound will seemingly postpone the production of words that contain that sound (Vihman & Croft, 2007). These and other findings have prompted a renewed look at the relationship between poor motor imitation, use of gesture, and difficulties with language acquisition in AD.

Infants with AD also appear to have problems using gestures to communicate in the first 2 years (Gernsbacher et al., 2008). At 12 months, infants who eventually receive the diagnosis of AD produce fewer gestures than low-risk controls and have difficulty understanding common communicative gestures (e.g., nodding, waving, clapping, extending arms to be picked up or hugged; Mitchell et al., 2006). They also show substantial reductions in the diversity and frequency of various forms of gesture. Between 18 and 24 months, they use fewer deictic gestures (e.g., this, that, here, there, these, those) than children with developmental delays (Shumway & Wetherby, 2009) and rely on more primitive forms of gesture in isolation (Wetherby, Watt, Morgan, & Shumway, 2007).

Problems remain evident throughout the second year of life (Mitchell et al., 2006; Shumway & Wetherby, 2009). Interestingly, nonsocial communicative acts such as imperative requesting are not as impaired as social communications (e.g., showing, initiating joint attention), which intrinsically require greater integration of attention and social skills with communication (Mundy et al., 2009; Wetherby, Prizant, & Hutchinson, 1998q). Deficiencies in gestural communication, imitation, and nonverbal cognitive ability at this age are predictive of later levels of expressive language development (Stone & Yoder, 2001). A child's ability to participate in games and routines also appears to be predictive of expressive language abilities over time (Bopp & Mirenda, 2010).

Serious concerns regarding communication in AD typically emerge around 18–21 months, secondary to delays in key language milestones such as producing first words or expanding their expressive language vocabulary (Goldberg et al., 2008; Landa, 2007). By 2 years of age, children with AD often demonstrate striking delays in language development that span both comprehension and production (Charman, Drew, Baird, & Baird, 2003). First words typically emerge around the end of the first year or a few months thereafter in normally developing infants, whereas in children with AD, this milestone is often significantly delayed, occurring at an average age of 38 months (Howlin, 2003).

As a general rule, an inability to communicatively use single words by 2 years or to produce meaningful phrases by 3 years are "red flags" for the possible diagnosis of AD. Several studies have indicated that the advantage of receptive ability over expressive ability that is normally evident in children is substantially reduced in children with AD. This becomes evident in the first 2 years (Ellis Weismer, Lord, & Esler, 2010) and persists into childhood. Indeed, preschool- and school-aged children with AD demonstrate greater impairments in receptive language development than is typically seen in most other developmental disorders including specific language impairment (SLI) (Hudry et al., 2010; Rapin et al., 2009). Better language outcomes at 4 or 5 years not only appear to be associated with greater responsiveness to joint attention bids but also higher nonverbal cognitive abilities and more symbolic schemes during play (Bopp & Mirenda, 2010; Charman et al., 2005; Luyster, Qiu, Lopez, & Lord, 2007).

Repetitive and Restricted Behavior and Interests

Discerning the manifestations of clinically meaningful repetitive or restricted patterns of activity is difficult at this early stage of development. Consequently, relatively few differences in RRBI have been observed in the first year among children with AD. Infants with AD reportedly engage in more repetitive sensory self-stimulation such as excessive mouthing of objects (Baranek, 1999) and rubbing furniture surfaces or dangling beads in front of their eyes (Zwaigenbaum et al., 2005). They also exhibit more rotating, spinning, and unusual visual inspection of objects (Ozonoff et al., 2008a). Repetitive motor behaviors may distinguish children with AD from typically developing children at 1 year of age but not from children with mental retardation (Osterling et al., 2002). Repetitive behaviors become more characteristic of AD than of developmentally delayed children by about 2 years of age (Militerni, Bravaccio, Falco, Fico, & Palermo, 2002; Mooney, Gray, & Tonge, 2006), although signs may be sufficiently variable that their utility in differentiating children with AD from other populations at this age remains to be adequately established (Charman et al., 2005; Stone et al., 1999).

Stereotyped motor mannerisms (e.g., hand flapping) tend to become more salient at around age 3 years (Gray & Tonge, 2001). Younger children with AD tend to exhibit these "lower order" sensory motor behaviors, whereas older children demonstrate higher-order disturbances such as cognitive rigidity, overreliance on routinized activities, and a propensity for *sameness* (Richler, Bishop, Kleinke, & Lord, 2007; Richler, Huerta, Bishop, & Lord, 2010; Szatmari et al., 2006). The lower-order and higher-order disturbances not only appear to have different developmental trajectories but are also correlated with different factors. Lower-order disturbances tend to be associated with lower nonverbal cognitive abilities and therefore are more likely to be seen early in more severely impaired children (Bishop, Richler, & Lord, 2006).

Anomalies of pretend play have also been observed during infancy in children who receive the AD diagnosis (Barbaro & Dissanayake, 2010a). To some extent, this reflects their diminished social interest or problems with interaction. However, their preference for playing alone may also reflect their cognitive rigidity and reluctance to deal with the challenges of negotiating novel situations and exchanges with individuals whose behavior they have difficulty understanding or predicting. As development progresses, imaginative deficits become increasingly evident in a paucity of pretend play and in restricted or repetitive patterns of play, which may include an inordinate fascination for nonfunctional components of toys (e.g., spinning tires on a toy truck rather than pretending to drive the truck).

AD is commonly associated with unusual sensory reactivity, evident in either hypersensitivity or hyposensitivity to sensory stimulation (DeGangi, Breinbauer, Roosevelt, Porges, & Greenspan, 2000). Relatively few studies have specifically and systematically studied these problems in infancy. Although such problems may be more salient later in development (Baranek, 2002; Bryson et al., 2007), it is clear that sensory anomalies can emerge as early as the first year (Baranek, 1999; Zwaigenbaum et al., 2005). Somatosensory anomalies include a realm of tactile hypersensitivities sometimes subsumed by the term "tactile defensiveness." In AD, these behaviors may be evident in a pronounced intolerance of certain skin sensations related to touch, temperature, and pain (Pernon, Pry, & Baghdadli, 2007) that may be manifested in an aversion of social touch (Baranek, 1999). Children with AD may be avoidant of physical contact, certain articles of clothing or fabrics (e.g., tags), or even certain foods because of their texture (e.g., creamy liquids). They tend to play with hard objects and demonstrate unusual attachments to particular objects (Rogers & Ozonoff, 2005).

Hypersensitivity in the auditory modality, often referred to as hyperacusis, is frequently encountered in preschool- and school-aged children with AD. Hyperacusis is a symptom complex associated with "consistently exaggerated or inappropriate responses to sounds that are neither threatening nor uncomfortably loud to a typical person" (Klein, Armstrong, Greer, & Brown, 1990). It is commonly reflected in noxious responses to everyday loud broadband noises such as vacuum cleaners or food blenders (Moller, Kern, & Grannemann, 2005).

Unusual reactivity to visual stimulation is also common in AD. Children may alternatively be fascinated with reflections and brightly colored objects or demonstrate aversive responses to these stimuli (Bogdashina, 2003; Simmons et al., 2009). Hypersensitivity can also be evident to particular smells, tastes, or somatosensory experiences (Wiggins, Robins, Bakeman, & Adamson, 2009). Although most commonly described in children with AD and correlated with severity of social symptoms (Kern et al., 2007), these symptoms appear somewhat less effective in differentiating AD from other developmental disorders in infancy than the disturbances related to social communication.

From 30%–50% of parents report that initial concerns included issues of temperament reflected in either extreme irritability or disconcerting passivity (Bryson et al., 2007; Gillberg et al., 1990; Zwaigenbaum et al., 2005). These behaviors have received less attention because they are not specific to AD, but remain important to recognize because temperament can be a good marker of genetic influences on behavior early in development. Infants at high risk for AD manifest temperament profiles characterized by lower positive affect, high negative affect, and difficulty controlling attention and behavior (Garon et al., 2009).

Self-regulatory issues such as sleep disturbances and feeding problems are also common in children with AD (Cortesi, Giannotti, Ivanenko, & Johnson, 2010; Goldman et al., 2009; Mayes & Calhoun, 2009). These difficulties can become evident in infants and toddlers, contributing to reports of irritable and difficult-to-console children, and persist into childhood and adolescence. They pose enormous difficulties for parents and may have functional implications for the affected child by their influence on psychological function. Sleep problems, for example, are thought to have negative effects on memory and learning and may possibly influence mood (Hollway & Aman, 2011; Mayes & Calhoun, 2009). In addition, these difficulties may disclose the presence of comorbid conditions (e.g., epilepsy, gastrointestinal problems) that will require diagnosis and treatment.

Problems with mobility, motor coordination, and imitation are sometimes observed in AD infants in the first year and can become increasingly evident in the second or third year (Charman et al., 2011). Retrospective analysis of home videos of children with AD have revealed a variety of movement disturbances evident while lying down, righting, sitting, crawling, walking, and in anticipatory posturing (Baranek, 1999; Esposito, Venuti, Maestro, &

Muratori, 2009; Loesche, 1990; Teitelbaum, Teitelbaum, Nye, Fryman, & Maurer, 1998), although some studies have failed to replicate these findings (Ozonoff et al., 2008b). Motor problems may also include hypotonia (muscle weakness), hyporeflexia (diminished reflexes), instability in mobility, unusual postural control, and dyspraxia (Adrien et al., 1992; Akshoomoff, Farid, Courchesne, & Haas, 2007; Ming, Brimacombe, & Wagner, 2007). Patterns of motor imitation in 1-year-olds at risk for AD appear to have value in predicting future diagnosis (Vanvuchelen, Roeyers, & De Weerdt, 2011). These problems appear to be partially predicted by deficits in basic motor skill (e.g., time to complete repetitive motor movements) and may be markers of the neurological abnormalities associated with the disorder. The assessment of motor imitation in 2- to 5-year olds suspected of AD appears to have value in predicting future diagnosis (Dziuk et al., 2007; Fournier, Hass, Naik, Lodha, & Cauraugh, 2010). The dimensions of temperament, self-regulation, and motor control appear to have added value in the screening of infants and toddlers and for assessing risk related to the later emergence of AD (Brian et al., 2008).

Summary

Overall, development in the first few months of life for infants who later develop AD is not substantially different from typically developing infants (Zwaigenbaum et al., 2005). Problems become increasingly salient in the latter half of the first year such that signs of risk for AD can be identified in a proportion of children at 12 months of age (Feldman et al., 2012; Reznick et al., 2007; Zwaigenbaum et al., 2009). Although there is no single reliable marker, an aggregate of risk markers can potentially be used to identify the presence of developmental delays or deviations that merit continued developmental surveillance. These risk markers include anomalies of sensory-oriented behaviors such as atypicalities in eye contact, problems with visual tracking and disengaging visual attention, inconsistencies in orienting to their name being called, and poor imitative skills. In the social domain, manifestations include diminished social smiling, social interest, and affect (decreased expression of positive affect) as well as atypical reactivity, anomalies of temperament (marked passivity), and extreme distress reactions. Finally, children at risk may demonstrate delayed expressive and receptive language. Overall, behaviors related to social interaction and communication may be more likely to disclose early developmental anomalies than signs of repetitive behaviors and restricted interest, although repetitive behaviors can be present at this time (Ozonoff et al., 2008a).

Signs of increased risk for AD become clearer between 12 and 24 months, in part because developmental disparities between neurotypical infants and those with AD widen during this period, and in part because a proportion of at-risk children demonstrate a deterioration of behavior. Wetherby and colleagues (2004) examined children in the second year of life and identified 13 behaviors that classified children with AD, developmental delay, and typical development with 94.4% accuracy. This included lack of eye contact, social smiles, imitation, responses to name being called, interest and pleasure in others, emotional expression, directed vocalizations, joint attention skills (e.g., pointing to show, monitoring others' gaze, and referencing objects by pointing), requesting behaviors, and use of communicative gestures (e.g., waving, clapping, nodding, shaking hands). Zwaigenbaum and colleagues (2009) compiled a similar list that also incorporated a number of sensory-motor and self-regulatory behaviors. These signs included atypical under- and/or overreaction to sensory stimulation, anomalies of fine and gross motor skills, repetitive motor behaviors, problems with visual tracking, and unusual inspection of objects. In addition, they included atypical regulatory functions such as problems with eating, sleeping, and attending.

The compilation of behaviors listed in the right column of Table 6.1 represents many of the more frequently observed early markers of risk for the development of AD at the time of this writing. This enumeration is based on a rather small number of research studies and will likely undergo modification as further prospective studies refine our understanding of AD during this critical period. The items are paired with potentially related behaviors designated in the *DSM-IV-TR* diagnostic criteria. These correspondences remain speculative because the association between early behaviors and the later development of symptoms is only now being systematically examined.

EARLY DEVELOPMENTAL TRAJECTORY

Kanner conceptualized AD as a "congenital" disorder based on observations that the behavioral manifestations of AD emerged in the first year or two. However, the description of at least one of Kanner's cases was suggestive of a second pattern of onset, one involving a developmental regression of sufficient severity to prompt parental comment (Stefanatos, 2008). Subsequent clinical observations of larger samples also alluded to a loss of previously acquired milestones in a proportion of children (Creak, 1963). Regression was again noted in an epidemiological study (Lotter, 1966), which further suggested a third pattern of onset involving a developmental plateau or stagnation described as a "failure to progress after a satisfactory beginning." Lotter observed that a history of regression or stagnation was present in nearly one-third (31.3%) of children diagnosed with AD.

Subsequent studies have suggested that regression usually emerges between 14 and 24 months (Fombonne & Chakrabarti, 2001; Kurita, 1985) as a loss of previously acquired abilities that often, but not invariably, involves a conspicuous deterioration of the ability to produce and understand language (Kurita, 1985; Lord, Shulman, & DiLavore, 2004; Rogers & DiLalla, 1990; Stefanatos et al., 2002). The loss of language is generally accompanied by some decline of social behavior, typically involving reductions in eye contact, reciprocal smiling, spontaneous imitation, and social interest/interaction (Bernabei, Cerquiglini, Cortesi, & D'Ardia, 2007; Goldberg et al., 2003; Ozonoff, Williams, & Landa, 2005b). Fairly selective deterioration of social function with *relative* preservation of language has more recently been described (Goldberg et al., 2003; Hansen et al., 2008; Luyster et al., 2005).

The change in behavior often emerges gradually, becoming increasingly apparent over the course of weeks to months, although in some, fairly abrupt changes become evident over the course of days. In less than a quarter of these cases, regression occurs after a period of a seemingly normal language and social development, whereas most demonstrate evidence of prior social difficulties or developmental delays (Kurita, 1985; Ozonoff et al., 2005b). Recent estimates of the prevalence of regression in AD have ranged from 15% (Fombonne & Chakrabarti, 2001) to 47% (Davidovitch, Glick, Holtzman, Tirosh, & Safir, 2000), depending on whether regression is narrowly or broadly defined (Kurita, 1985; Rogers & DiLalla, 1990; Stefanatos et al., 2002). However, available evidence suggests that the frequency of regression is substantially higher in children on the autistic spectrum than in children with developmental delays (3%), suggesting it may have a special association with AD (Pickles et al., 2009). A picture of developmental stagnation is also generally observed in the second year of life (Landa & Garrett-Mayer, 2006; Landa, Holman, & Garrett-Mayer, 2007) and may account for approximately 9% of children who receive an AD diagnosis (Siperstein & Volkmar, 2004).

Recent prospective investigations of early symptoms of AD suggest that developmental regression may occur more often than previously considered and can be sufficiently subtle that it escapes parental recognition. Ozonoff and colleagues (2010) performed serial evaluations of children at high and low risk for subsequently developing AD. They observed subtle decrements in social behavior between 12 and 24 months, seemingly restricted to the social domain. These psychometrically defined changes were often not evident to parents or at least did not raise sufficient concern to warrant mention. Questions remain whether these changes reflect a true loss of ability or simply changes in the infant's repertoire of behavior as the disorder is expressed. The same criticism has been levied on parent-reported regression, although retrospective studies using videotaped material have validated the phenomena (Goldberg et al., 2008; Werner & Dawson, 2005). Whether or not parents recognize regression may depend on the age of onset, temporal course, severity, and the specific domain(s) of function that are involved. To some extent, different viewpoints on regression stem from inconsistencies in the definition and operationalization (Rogers, 2004; Stefanatos, 2008). Unfortunately, documentation of regression is rarely accomplished at the time it is occurring, so that descriptions of the premorbid developmental course are typically based mainly on vague memories, limited videotape material, and incomplete records pulled together months or even years later.

Several studies have suggested that the history of late regression paradoxically carries a worse prognosis than children with congenital onset (Baird et al., 2008; Meilleur & Fombonne, 2009, Stefanatos et al., 2002). However, outcomes may potentially vary depending on features of the regression itself. Zappella (2010) described good outcome whereas Parr and colleagues (2011) observed that the loss of language, with or without concurrent declines in other domains, was associated with relatively poor outcome. These issues are theoretically highly important because the phenomenon of regression has provided reasonable grounds for suspecting that distinctive underlying etiological mechanisms may be operative in association with late language loss (Baird et al., 2008; Meilleur & Fombonne, 2009; Stefanatos et al., 2002).

NEUROPATHOLOGY AND PATHOPHYSIOLOGY OF AD

Early studies directed to understanding the neural basis of the behavioral difficulties in AD failed to reveal any consistent morphological anomalies. AD seemed to emerge in the absence of gross lesions or abnormalities in gyral configuration, obvious abnormalities of myelination, or evidence of cell loss and gliosis. However, with advances in systematic computer-assisted histopathological analyses, subtle yet widespread anomalies of neural microstructure and organization have been noted in postmortem brain tissue samples derived from affected individuals (Palmen, van Engeland, Hof, & Schmitz, 2004; Schmitz & Rezaie, 2008). Although cell loss in the hippocampus had been alluded to in an early report (Schain & Yannet, 1960), Bauman and Kemper (1985) were among the first to systematically identify microarchitectural anomalies in limbic structures. Through rigorous comparison with the brain of a normal control, Bauman and Kemper noted that neurons in the hippocampus and amygdala of a 29-year-old autistic man were reduced in size and had increased cell-packing density (higher number of neurons-per-unit volume). Similar anomalies were evident in the subiculum, entorhinal cortex, mammillary bodies, and medial septal nucleus. In addition, hippocampal neurons in layers CA1 and CA4 showed decreased complexity and extent of dendritic arbors, indicative of diminished intercellular connectivity and capacity for communication. These observations attracted considerable attention because the amygdala and hippocampus had previously been implicated in AD based on similarities in patterns of behavioral deficits with patients with acquired damage to these structures (Boucher & Warrington, 1976; Damasio & Maurer, 1978). The overall pattern was characteristic of neural architecture at an earlier stage of maturation. Like the previous report by Schain and Yannet (1960), the results from this case were confounded by the presence of epilepsy (Amaral, Bauman, & Schumann, 2003). However, similar findings were observed in two subjects by Raymond, Bauman, and Kemper (1996), although only one of five subjects studied by Bailey and colleagues (1998) revealed this pattern. More recently, Schuman and Amaral (2006) observed significantly reduced neuron counts overall but found no structural anomalies related to neuron size in the amygdala.

Recent structural neuroimaging studies have revealed an abnormal trajectory of amygdala volume in children with AD. The amygdala becomes relatively enlarged in the first 2 years of development of children with AD, and this excess growth appears to be correlated with the severity of social impairment (Schumann, Barnes, Lord, & Courchesne, 2009) as well as the ability to engage in joint attention (Mosconi et al., 2009). Because isolated lesions of the amygdala do not result in autistic behavior, it has been suggested that these symptoms may result from abnormal connectivity between the amygdala and other structures that comprise a network that mediates social behaviors (Paul, Corsello, Tranel, & Adolphs, 2010). The amygdala may be involved in modulating social attention and in evaluating the saliency or relevance of sensory input and contextual cues during the processing of social information and reward learning (Adolphs, 2010).

Neuropathological abnormalities have fairly consistently been found in the cerebellum and the inferior olive of the brainstem. The most frequent finding is decreased number and size of Purkinje cells (PCs; Bailey et al., 1998; Fatemi et al., 2002; Kemper & Bauman, 1993; Palmen et al., 2004; Ritvo, Freeman, & Scheibel, 1986). PCs are GABAergic neurons that represent the major neural output of the cerebellum. They receive inhibitory GABAergic input from interneurons (basket and stellate cells) in the underlying molecular layer of the cerebellum. The cell packing density of these interneurons is apparently normal in individuals in AD, suggesting that PCs successfully migrated to their proper location in cerebellar cortex and subsequently died for as yet unknown reasons at some point late in the gestational period (after 30 weeks; Whitney, Kemper, Rosene, Bauman, & Blatt, 2009). Consistent with this viewpoint, cerebellar gliosis, which is indicative of damage, often accompanies PC loss (Bailey et al., 1998). PCs have an exceptionally high metabolic demand during development and are susceptible to multiple influences, including ischemia (Welsh et al., 2002), hypoxia (Cervos-Navarro & Diemer, 1991), excitotoxicity (Brorson, Manzolillo, Gibbons, & Miller, 1995), viral infections (Hornig, Mervis, Hoffman, & Lipkin, 2002), thiamine deficiency (Butterworth, 1993), and exposure to heavy metals (Sorensen, Larsen, Eide, & Schionning, 2000) and toxins (Ingram, Peckham, Tisdale, & Rodier, 2000; MacDonald & Stoodley, 1998). The differences in neuropathological findings may relate to variability in the underlying etiology. Kemper and Bauman (1998), for example, observed PC disturbances in the absence of gliosis, suggesting that the underlying problem emerged early in the prenatal period (prior to 30 weeks gestation).

Although some studies have reported diffuse or widespread distribution of these anomalies, the findings are most prominent in the posterolateral neocerebellar cortex, with lesser involvement of more medial structures, such as the vermis. The precise significance of these findings to the symptoms of autism remains somewhat speculative. Current theoretical accounts suggest that functional compromise of a fronto-cerebellar pathway extending from the right lateral cerebellar hemisphere to left frontal lobe may be related to impaired expressive language, working memory, attention, and aspects of gross motor function (Hodge et al., 2010; Rogers et al., 2011; Townsend et al., 2001). Reductions of vermis volume (Stanfield et al., 2008) seem to be associated with more global impairments of development, including behavioral disturbances associated with AD (Bolduc et al., 2011). However, the findings are inconsistent (Scott, Schumann, Goodlin-Jones, & Amaral, 2009).

Anomalies have also been observed in several brainstem structures, including the inferior (Bailey et al., 1998; Bauman & Kemper, 2005; Rodier, 2002) and superior olive (Kulesza, Lukose, & Stevens, 2010), and the nucleus of the diagonal band of Broca (NDB) in the septum (Kemper & Bauman, 1998). There appear to be some age-related trends associated with these findings insofar as hypertrophy of neurons in the inferior olive and NDB has been noted in young brains (ages 5–13 years) but not older ones. The significance of this pattern in AD is not unclear, but in other conditions, hypertrophy has been associated with abnormalities of connectivity of circuits involving cerebellum and nearby brainstem nuclei. Because of a special relationship between the development of the cerebellum and the inferior olivary nucleus that emerges at about 28–30 weeks of gestation, the loss of PCs in the absence of loss of inferior olivary neurons suggests that the loss of PCs occurred at an earlier stage of neurodevelopment (Bauman & Kemper, 2005).

Several studies have reported anomalies in the cellular organization of neocortical areas in the brains of autistic individuals. Casanova and colleagues (Casanova, 2007; Casanova, Buxhoeveden, & Brown, 2002) reported that cortical minicolumns were unusually configured in autistic brains in at least three areas of cortex: (1) prefrontal cortex (BA 9), (2) middle temporal gyrus (BA 21), and (3) superior temporal gyrus (BA 22). Cortical minicolumns are modular units formed during neurodevelopment as cells migrate from the periventricular proliferative zone to locations in the multiple layers of the cerebral cortex. They are thought to represent complex processing units that link inputs (e.g., thalamic afferents) and outputs of multiple layers of cortex via overlapping processing chains. In AD, minicolumns were smaller and showed more dispersion between cells, with less neuropil space in their periphery that normally contains dendrites axons and synapses. It has been suggested that these anomalies reflect aberrant patterns of connectivity with adjacent columns as well as with thalamic afferent terminals. The resulting circuitry may lack sufficient inhibitory influences and thus affects the ability to discriminate between competing types of sensory information. Minicolumns may also be susceptible to neural noise generated by uninhibited adjacent cell clusters, which could possibly relate to observations of hypersensitivity seen in many children with AD.

A recently published study by Courchesne and colleagues (2011) reported that areas of frontal cortex have excess numbers of neurons in AD compared to controls. The results are most dramatic in dorsolateral PFC, where individuals with AD had 79% more neurons, whereas in mesial PFC, the increase was in the range of 29%. Because cortical neurons are generated during embryogenesis, the excess counts observed in this study could potentially implicate a problem of neurogenesis. Alternatively, the findings may reflect a failure of pruning processes that normally follow exuberant growth and that are necessary to fine-tune the system and optimize the efficiency and effectiveness of the surviving neural networks.

Van Kooten and colleagues (2008) recently reported significant reductions of neuron density in the fusiform gyrus (FG). Given that FG is thought to play a special role in face recognition, they suggested that this anomaly might relate to problems observed in AD in reading facial expressions. Another study reported no abnormalities in FG but found irregularly organized neurons in posterior areas of the cingulate gyrus (CG; Oblak, Rosene, Kemper, Bauman, & Blatt, 2011). This report extends the observations by Kemper and Bauman (1993), who reported that five of six cases studied demonstrated poorly laminated and unusually coarse cortical organization in the anterior cingulate cortex. These findings have yet to be replicated in neuropathological studies by other investigators, although it is noteworthy that several functional neuroimaging studies have implicated cingulate involvement (Agam, Joseph, Barton, & Manoach, 2010; Chiu et al., 2008; Minshew & Keller, 2010; Shafritz, Dichter, Baranek, & Belger, 2008). Disturbances in the cingulate cortex has been implicated in anomalies of cognitive control and increased severity of restricted or repetitive behaviors in AD.

In summary, pathophysiological studies have pointed to atypical brain microstructure and organization involving the cerebellum, brainstem, amygdala, hippocampus, cingulate cortex, and in cortical samples obtained from temporal and frontal lobes. The results of these studies must be interpreted cautiously given their very small sample sizes (typically less than seven) and selection bias. Often, information regarding the use of medications and presence of seizures and mental retardation in many of the cases is lacking. It remains unclear to what extent these anomalies are causal or reflect secondary or tertiary consequences of AD. However, these findings provide some clues to understanding potential mechanisms underlying perturbations that have been observed at the macrostructural level in gross morphological features of the brains of autistic individuals. Although the inconsistency and diversity of these findings is, at first glance, both puzzling and confusing, it may not be unexpected given emerging notions of the etiologic heterogeneity of the disorder. Different pathological mechanisms may affect brain growth and connectivity at different periods of development.

BRAIN STRUCTURE AND DEVELOPMENT

Kanner (1943) noted that despite the absence of gross dysmorphic features, 5 of the 11 children he described had large heads. Subsequently, numerous reports have noted increased head circumference or "macrocephaly" (> 97th percentile) in 10%–20% of children with AD (Fidler, Bailey, & Smalley, 2000; Lainhart et al., 1997; Miles, Hadden, Takahashi, & Hillman, 2000; Stevenson, Schroer, Skinner, Fender, & Simensen, 1997; Woodhouse et al., 1996), whereas the prevalence in an unselected population of neonates is less than 1% (Petersson, Pedersen, Schalling, & Lavebratt, 1999). Corresponding to larger head size, young children with AD (2–4 years) demonstrate larger brain volume on structural neuroimaging (Aylward, Minshew, Field, Sparks, & Singh, 2002; Courchesne et al., 2001; Piven, Arndt, Bailey, & Andreasen, 1996; Sparks et al., 2002).

Cross-sectional studies that have subsequently examined the developmental trajectory of whole brain volume in children with AD have suggested that the brain undergoes accelerated growth starting sometime in the first 6 months after birth (Courchesne, Carper, & Akshoomoff, 2003). This continues for approximately 2 years such that by 2–4 years of age, brain volumes are approximately 10% larger than neurotypical controls (Hazlett et al., 2005; Redcay & Courchesne, 2005). This growth spurt eventually subsides between 2–4 years, with some studies reporting normalization of total brain volume by mid-childhood (Courchesne et al., 2001; Stanfield et al., 2008), whereas others suggest that increased brain volume persists into adolescence and adulthood (Freitag et al., 2009a; Hazlett, Poe, Gerig, Smith, & Piven, 2006). The changes appear to follow an anterior-to-posterior gradient, with greatest enlargement in frontal and temporal lobes (Courchesne et al., 2007), followed by parietal areas

(Amaral, Schumann, & Nordahl, 2008), and is least evident in the occipital lobes (Brun et al., 2009; Carper, Moses, Tigue, & Courchesne, 2002; Hazlett et al., 2006).

Significantly thinner cortex has been noted in AD, predominantly in left temporal and parietal regions (e.g., the superior temporal sulcus, inferior temporal, postcentral/superior parietal, and supramarginal gyrus; Hadjikhani, Joseph, Snyder, & Tager-Flusberg, 2006; Hardan, Muddasani, Vemulapalli, Keshavan, & Minshew, 2006; Wallace, Dankner, Kenworthy, Giedd, & Martin, 2010). By contrast, increases in cortical thickness have been noted in primary and associative auditory and visual cortex. Relatively few studies have directly correlated whether patterns of cortical thinning or thickening are related to specific patterns of neuropsychological deficit at the individual level. However, Hyde, Samson, Evans and Mottron (2010) suggest that the pattern of variation in cortical thickness may provide a structural correlate to observations of enhanced auditory and visual processing skills commonly observed in AD.

Although some of these findings implicate overly exuberant proliferation, others are suggestive of a failure of the normal subtractive processes, such as programmed cell death (apoptosis) and the pruning of axons dendrites and synapses. A number of the findings in AD point to disturbances of neuronal migration (Piven et al., 1995). These include observations of cortical malformations such as polymicrogyria, schizencephaly, and macrogyria. Additional indications of cortical dysgenesis include ectopias, poor gray-white matter differentiation, and a number of the cytoarchitectonic anomalies noted in the neuropathological studies discussed in the previous sections such as higher neuronal density, irregular laminar patterns, and minicolumn alterations (Bailey et al., 1998; Casanova et al., 2006).

Volumetric differences in white matter have implicated disturbances of neural connectivity (Herbert et al., 2003; McAlonan et al., 2005; Stigler, McDonald, Anand, Saykin, & McDougle, 2011). Diffusion tensor imaging (DTI) studies have identified anomalies of white matter in both long and short fiber tracts (Sundaram et al., 2008), including but not limited to corpus callosum, arcuate fasciculus (Fletcher et al., 2010; Knaus et al., 2010; Radua, Via, Catani, & Mataix-Cols, 2010), uncinate fasciculus (Kumar et al., 2009; Radua et al., 2010), as well as pathways in the cingulum (Cg; Weinstein et al., 2011), superior temporal gyrus (STG), and the temporal stem (TS; Lange et al., 2010). These pathways include some of the most critical communication links for neural networks subserving language, social communication, and regulatory behavior (see Stefanatos & Baron, 2011 for a review). Alterations in anisotropy and diffusivity of white matter tracts such as the arcuate fasciculus suggest some decrements in functional integrity of this pathway, potentially accompanied by delays in myelination. Several recent studies have explored the functional significance of some of these white matter anomalies. Von dem Hagen et al. (2011), for example, reported that decreased white matter volume in posterior superior temporal sulcus, an area critical for both communication and social information processing, was associated with higher scores on a measure of the severity of AD.

Overall, it appears that approximately 20% of individuals with AD demonstrate atypical neurodevelopment associated with accelerated growth of neocortex in the first year or two of life, resulting in enlargement of brain volume and macrocephaly in early childhood. Rather than a marker of the neurodevelopmental anomalies associated with the symptom complex of AD, the finding more likely reflects a potential risk factor because macrocephaly occurs in the same proportion of unaffected family members (Bolton, Roobol, Allsopp, & Pickles, 2001). In addition, the phenotype is associated with other morphological features such as polymicrogyria, macrogyria, and schizencephaly. On balance, the findings are suggestive of significant alterations of embryonic corticogenesis resulting in anomalies of neural migration and overgrowth that begin in the prenatal period and then persist in early postnatal development. Overgrowth combined with perturbations of regulatory subtractive processes (pruning) likely results in an overabundance of inefficient neurons and synapses. Theoretically, the deviant growth trajectory seen in AD can lead to anomalous patterns of functional connectivity and atypical psychological development (Lewis & Elman, 2008). Concentrations of metabolites of neural activity measured with magnetic resonance spectroscopy (MRS) suggest widespread reductions of neuronal activity and gray matter integrity in the cortex, amygdala, hippocampus, and cerebellum (DeVito et al., 2007; Endo et al., 2007; Hardan et al., 2008;

Suzuki et al., 2009). Anomalies are evident in a number of the major white matter tracts connecting these areas.

Etiological Factors

Environmental Factors

Estimates of the prevalence of AD have risen from approximately 4:10,000 to 20:10,000 in the last 40 years (Fombonne, 2009). Some have suggested that this increase is an epiphenomenon of such factors as greater public and professional awareness of the disorder, increased developmental surveillance, and enhanced sensitivity of more recent diagnostic criteria. However, the rise has also prompted concerns that environmental factors are potentially contributory (Herbert, 2010). Environmental risk factors include pre- and perinatal risk events such as stressful life events (Kinney, Munir, Crowley, & Miller, 2008); complications during pregnancy, delivery, and the neonatal phase (Juul-Dam, Townsend, & Courchesne, 2001; Larsson et al., 2005); advanced parental age (Saha et al., 2009); exposure to exogenous stressors such as pollutants (e.g., heavy metals, lead, ethyl alcohol and methyl mercury, insecticides; Kalia, 2008; McDonald & Paul, 2010); and teratogenic influences (thimerosal, thalidomide, valproic acid, ultrasound; Landrigan, 2010; Williams & Casanova, 2010; Young, Geier, & Geier, 2008).

Several lines of evidence have implicated neuroimmune abnormalities in AD (Ashwood et al., 2010; Comi, Zimmerman, Frye, Law, & Peeden, 1999; Stefanatos et al., 2002; Stigler, Sweeten, Posey, & McDougle, 2009; Warren et al., 1996). This involves the upregulation of cytokines, which are secreted by immune cells (including microglia and astroglia in the brain) that have detected a pathogen. This can occur in response to direct infection of the central nervous system (CNS) or through infection that occurs elsewhere in the body but acts as a trigger for changes in the CNS. Animal models have suggested that abnormal immune responses can also reflect alterations in the immune system sensitivity passed on by mothers to their offspring (Fatemi, Pearce, Brooks, & Sidwell, 2005; Libbey, Sweeten, McMahon, & Fujinami, 2005).

Microglial and astroglial activation has been noted in the anterior cingulate and both middle and dorsolateral frontal gyri in individuals with AD (Morgan et al., 2010; Vargas, Nascimbene, Krishnan, Zimmerman, & Pardo, 2005). This activation of the immune system can result in inflammation and in some instances the production of antibodies that target particular populations of neurons in the brain. For example, antibodies have been identified in the plasma of individuals with AD that demonstrate intense reactions to GABAergic Golgi neurons of the cerebellum (Rossi, Van de Water, Rogers, & Amaral, 2011). Some children demonstrate evidence of autoantibodies in their blood that target brain proteins and are associated with lower adaptive and cognitive functions (Goines et al., 2011). The factors prompting these immune responses remain to be fully specified. In some cases, an autoimmune reaction may occur as a pathological response to normal childhood diseases, whereas in other instances it may reflect an innate response to synaptic or neural network disturbances (Morgan et al., 2010).

Genetic Contributions

More than 60 medical conditions have been associated with AD, accounting for approximately 10%–15% of cases of autism (Coleman & Betancur, 2005). These medical conditions include congenital infections, metabolic disorders, toxic embryopathies, epilepsy syndromes (Barton & Volkmar, 1998; Bauman, 2010), as well as a host of neurogenetic conditions (e.g., tuberous sclerosis, fragile X, phenylketonuria). Many of the neurogenetic disorders are single-gene conditions and are often excluded from genetic studies that focus on *idiopathic* forms of autism.

Since the seminal studies by Folstein & Rutter (1977) and Ritvo and colleagues (1985), numerous reports have revealed substantially higher concordance of AD in monozygotic (36%–91%) compared to dizygotic (0%–10%) twins (Bailey, Le Couteur, Gottesman, & Bolton, 1995; Steffenburg et al., 1989; Thomas et al., 2001). AD currently ranks among the most heritable of child psychiatric disorders (>90% heritability; Szatmari et al., 2007). Children born into families with an autistic child have a 10- to 25-fold higher risk than the general population of also receiving a diagnosis of AD (Abrahams & Geschwind, 2008; Constantino, Zhang,

Frazier, Abbacchi, & Law, 2010; Ozonoff et al., 2011). This may be an underestimate of the true recurrence risk as a result of reproductive stoppage rules whereby parents of a child with a severe disability choose not to have additional children. Despite the evidently substantial genetic contribution, the search for the specific genes that contribute to the disorder has resulted in many candidates but few consistent findings. A recent review of the literature identified 103 disease genes and 44 genomic loci that have been associated with AD or autistic behavior, underscoring the substantial heterogeneity of the genetic determinants of the disorder (Betancur, 2010).

The mode of transmission in the vast majority of cases is thought to be polygenic, possibly involving as few as two or as many as 15 genes in various combinations (Folstein & Rosen-Sheidley, 2001; Rutter, 2005). An X-linked genetic or epigenetic contribution has been suggested, given that boys are four times more likely than girls to be diagnosed with the disorder (Loat, Haworth, Plomin, & Craig, 2008; Piton et al., 2010). The results of linkage, association, and cytogenetic studies have pointed to multiple candidates, involving mutations (e.g., single nucleotide polymorphisms [SNP]) or common variants in genes that code for gene products that influence some aspect of neural development and function. Genome-wide scans have provided suggestive evidence for linkage to AD on several chromosomes, although the results vary considerably among studies. A number of suspect genes code for products that influence cell-to-cell interactions in synaptic functions (e.g., the development of dendritic spines) or are involved in neural migration and neurotransmission (for a review, see Freitag, Staal, Klauck, Duketis, & Waltes, 2009b). For example, animal models have implicated anomalies involving a gene on chromosome 22 (*SHANK3*) that plays a role in synaptic formation and in the proliferation of dendritic spines (Peca et al., 2011). Mutations of genes that encode neuroligands 3 and 4 (*NLGN3* and *NLGN4*, respectively) have been implicated in AD (Jamain et al., 2003). Neuroligands are molecules that are critically involved in synaptic formation and remodeling (Gutierrez et al., 2009; Yamakawa et al., 2007). Genes that code for neurexins and neuroligands have captured significant interest because of their potential role in mediating the properties of neural networks (Szatmari et al., 2007; Vorstman et al., 2006). A recent genome-wide association study implicated SNPs in genes that code for cell adhesion molecules (Wang et al., 2009). Because cell adhesion molecules play an essential role in shaping the cytoarchitecture and functional connectivity of the brain, these findings are of considerable interest, particularly in light of growing concern that cortical under-connectivity may play a major role in determining the processing disturbances that appear to underlie AD (Reichelt, Rodgers, & Clapcote, 2011). Another candidate is *FMR1*, a gene located on the X chromosome that encodes a protein (FMR1) involved in regulating synaptic plasticity (Bailey, Hatton, Skinner, & Mesibov, 2001). Finally, *NLG4Y*, a Y-linked gene involved in dendritic development, has been implicated in AD (Joober & El-Hussein, 2006; Laumonnier et al., 2004).

Evidence that 10%–20% of the siblings of autistic children demonstrate similar but subtler abnormalities in the development of social and communication skills suggests the existence of a "broader autism phenotype" with shared vulnerability (Bishop, Maybery, Wong, Maley, & Hallmayer, 2006; Stone, McMahon, Yoder, & Walden, 2007). As infants, siblings of affected children may demonstrate problems with visual orienting (Elsabbagh et al., 2009) and selective attention (Holmboe et al., 2010) and later exhibit mild deficits of social communicative function (Whitehouse, Coon, Miller, Salisbury, & Bishop, 2010). Similarly, parents of autistic children have elevated rates of particular personality traits such as anxiety, rigidity, and aloof or withdrawn behavior (Murphy et al., 2000; Piven, 2001) and can demonstrate intense preoccupations (Smith et al., 2009). Some studies have suggested that, as a group, parents may also display deficits on measures of executive function (Hughes, Plumet, & Leboyer, 1999; Piven, 2001), have relatively depressed performance IQs (Piven, 2001), perform poorly on measures of face recognition (Wilson, Freeman, Brock, Burton, & Palermo, 2010), and demonstrate anomalies of communication (Ruser et al., 2007), particularly in pragmatic aspects of language (Landa et al., 1992).

The expression of the disorder involves complex interactions between environmental factors, genetic predispositions, epigenetic mechanisms, and other biological variables (Abrahams & Geschwind, 2008; Grafodatskaya et al., 2010; Herbert, 2010). As discussed previously, some genetic mutations have rather direct effects on gene products (e.g., proteins) that influence some aspect of neurodevelopment. Other genes may influence risk for AD, not through a direct route on neurodevelopment per se, but rather through their role in increasing risk for disease states that can have neurodevelopmental implications. For example, some studies have suggested a strong association with an allele that appears to play a role in immune function (Ashwood, Wills, & Van de Water, 2006; Odell et al., 2005).

The genetic influences on the three key behavioral domains associated with AD appear to be largely nonoverlapping, suggesting that the symptom complex is fractionable (Happé & Ronald, 2008). Current models acknowledge at least three possible dimensions of critical importance: genes, environment, and developmental time. Developmental time is a factor that appears to influence interactions between genes and environmental factors whereby there are critical periods or windows of development when genetic susceptibility interacts with environmental stressors in a manner that can have particularly crucial impact. For example, particular polymorphisms have been shown to interact with perinatal factors such as maternal smoking during pregnancy to increase problems with social interaction and rigid behavior (Nijmeijer et al., 2010). Similarly, during fetal development, exposure to maternal infections may expose the fetus to immunologic responses or to the use of potentially teratogenic agents that, in turn, can raise the risk of developing AD.

Neurotransmitter Anomalies

Several of the genetic anomalies associated with AD appear to have a direct or indirect influence on the activity of specific neurotransmitter systems. One of the more consistent biological markers of AD is elevated whole blood (platelet) level of serotonin (5-HT). Approximately 25%–30% of individuals with the diagnosis demonstrate whole blood serotonin levels that are 25% higher than average. Serotonin is a monoamine neurotransmitter involved in modulation of sleep and blood pressure, which has significant influences on several behaviors including mood, anxiety, and a form of behavioral inhibition. Neuroimaging data from positron emission tomography (PET) studies have suggested that individuals with AD may have diminished serotonin metabolism in the frontal cortex, thalamus, and dentate nucleus (Chugani, 2004; Kolevzon, Mathewson, & Hollander, 2006). Serotonergic neurons are present in the human brain as early as the fifth gestational week (Sundstrom et al., 1993), and recent studies have suggested that serotonin has important neurotrophic properties during brain development (Whitaker-Azmitia, 2001). Serotonin influences aspects of neurogenesis; neuronal differentiation; the formation of neuropil, axonal myelination, and synaptogenesis; and modulation of brain-derived neurotrophic factor levels (Dooley, Pappas, & Parnavelas, 1997; Vaidya, Marek, Aghajanian, & Duman, 1997). Given cytoarchitectonic evidence of anomalous dendritic development in AD, it is noteworthy that serotonin influences overall dendritic length, spine formation, and arborization in the hippocampus and cortex (Sikich, Hickok, & Todd, 1990).

Discovery of common polymorphisms of the serotonin transporter gene (on chromosome 17) in AD (Anderson et al., 2009; Yirmiya et al., 2001; Zafeiriou, Ververi, & Vargiami, 2009) has generated considerable interest, in part because of evidence that pharmacologic modulation of serotonin metabolism can mitigate anxiety, aggression, and repetitive thoughts in AD and can improve some cognitive symptoms such as language functioning and aspects of social behavior (Kolevzon et al., 2006; McDougle, Kresch, & Posey, 2000). However, anomalies of the serotonin transporter gene neither account for hyperserotonemia (Persico et al., 2002), nor do they strongly determine the likely emergence of autistic symptoms. Indeed, these anomalies are common in individuals without autism. However, particular forms of the polymorphism seem to be associated with differences in attentional biases when processing emotional information that may predispose carriers to anxiety and neuroticism (Beevers, Ellis, Wells, & McGeary, 2009a). It has therefore been suggested that particular genotypic variations may interact with other genetic anomalies as well as environmental factors (e.g., stress) to influence the severity of particular behaviors in AD (Tordjman et al., 2001). Individuals with AD who have a short allele variant of the polymorphism have been rated as more severe on symptoms such as "failure to use nonverbal communication to regulate social interaction," whereas those with the long allele variant were rated as more aggressive and showed more stereotyped and repetitive motor mannerisms (Brune et al., 2006). The short allele variant has been related to significantly lower levels of N-acetylaspartate/creatine in the right medial prefrontal cortex (Endo et al., 2010) and morphological differences in the lateral prefrontal cortex that correlate with attentional biases in processing emotional information (Beevers, Pacheco, Clasen, McGeary, & Schnyer, 2009b).

Genes regulating GABA metabolism have also been implicated in AD (Collins et al., 2006; Harada et al., 2010; Shao et al., 2003). GABA is the most common inhibitory neurotransmitter in the brain. However, during neurodevelopment it is thought to have excitatory influences, modulating the activity of brain microcircuitry and ultimately inducing lasting alterations in cerebral cortical structure and function. Anomalies of GABA metabolism have been identified in the cingulate cortex, fusiform gyrus (Oblak, Gibbs, & Blatt, 2010), and frontal lobe (Harada et al., 2010) in AD. Animal models have linked genetic influences on GABAergic circuitry to striatal development (Martins, Shahrokh, & Powell, 2011) and to the emergence of stereotyped behaviors (Chao et al., 2010).

The involvement of the mesial frontal and temporal cortex implicated by neuropsychological, neuropathological, and neuroimaging studies has led to speculation that disturbances in dopamine transmission may also contribute to the AD behavioral phenotype. Dopamine antagonists (e.g., haloperidol) have been beneficial in treatment of stereotypies and overactivity but not social relatedness and communication problems (Buitelaar & Willemsen-Swinkels, 2000). One PET study demonstrated that dopaminergic activity was diminished by 39% in the anterior medial prefrontal cortex in a group of autistic individuals compared to controls (Ernst, Zametkin, Matochik, Pascualvaca, & Cohen, 1997). However, Nakamura et al. (2010) found increased dopaminergic metabolism in medial orbitofrontal cortex. More recently, it has been suggested that aberrant dopaminergic activity in the prefrontal cortex may be causally related to the influence of neuropathological changes in the cerebellum on the function of cerebellar–medial prefrontal cortex pathways (Rogers et al., 2011).

Finally, the noradrenergic system has long been implicated in autism, although specific associations have been elusive (Minderaa, Anderson, Volkmar, Akkerhuis, & Cohen, 1994). The noradrenergic system is intimately involved in aspects of arousal and attention, but it is also associated with behavioral flexibility (Aston-Jones, Rajkowski, & Cohen, 2000). Recently, it has also been implicated in a curious phenomenon often reported by parents of autistic children that fever frequently results in transient improvements in the behavior of their children. Mehler and Purpura (2009) recently postulated that the autism behavioral phenotype is, in part, related to dysregulation of the locus coeruleus noradrenergic system. They suggested that fever transiently restores modulatory function of the system and consequently ameliorates autistic behaviors.

ASSESSMENT

Practice parameters for the assessment of AD have been issued by several professional agencies, including the American Academy of Neurology (Filipek et al., 2000), the American Academy of Child and Adolescent Psychiatry (Volkmar, Cook, Pomeroy, Realmuto, & Tanguay, 1999), the Interdisciplinary Council on Developmental and Learning Disorders (ICDL; Greenspan, 2000) and the Cure Autism Now Foundation (Geschwind et al., 1998). There is broad agreement on the critical importance of early detection and diagnosis.

The American Academy of Pediatrics, for example, has recommended "universal" screening for ASD at both 18 months and 2 years (Johnson & Myers, 2007). The suggested protocol is divided into two stages. The first, Level 1 screening, involves monitoring for signs of AD by clinicians, such as pediatricians, who provide general services for infants, toddlers, and young children. The identification of problems should result in prompt referral for an appropriate Level 2 assessment. Level 2 evaluations involve comprehensive diagnostic assessments by knowledgeable clinicians experienced in the examination of children with AD. The goal of this two-tiered system is to foster early identification so that interventions targeting areas of concern can be initiated as soon as possible to take advantage of neural plasticity of the developing nervous system (Dawson, 2008).

Level 1 Evaluations

As discussed in previous sections, signs of AD may or may not be readily apparent in the first 6 months. Given considerable individual differences in normal development, the challenge in infancy is to reliably discriminate those behavioral patterns indicative of high risk for AD and establish their predictive validity. As development proceeds and the infant's behavioral repertoire becomes more diversified and elaborate, developmental delays, qualitative behavioral differences, or manifestations of deviant behaviors become more readily apparent. By the end of the first year, these differences may be sufficient in magnitude and nature to be detected in a proportion of children. However, as a general guideline, the milder the disorder, the more difficult it is to identify reliably at a very young age.

The age at identification is heavily influenced by the child's developmental course and trajectory. Children who display slow development from an early age may be more readily identified between 12 to 18 months due to the increasing divergence from a normal developmental progress. Children who demonstrate a history of regression, on the other hand, may show normal or near normal development in the first year and then demonstrate a change in their development in the months preceding their second birthday. The timing of regression with respect to an 18-month pediatric checkup has positive and negative aspects. Although these evaluations are well-positioned for detecting problems that may have emerged up to that time, they may be too early to detect problems associated with late regression, which tend to occur in a critical temporal window between 18 and 24 months.

The 18-month pediatric checkup provides a timely opportunity both for Level 1 screening and to advise parents to seek immediate attention should signs of developmental loss emerge. Until recently, there were regrettably few diagnostic tools to assist in the screening and assessment of infants and toddlers suspected of an ASD. However, in the last few years, several instruments have become available to assist in the process. Many of the Level 1 screening instruments are questionnaires completed by parents or caregivers. Several of these measures are briefly described in Table 6.2 (e.g., M-CHAT, PDDST-II, ITC, POEMS, FYI). In addition, Table 6.2 contains some descriptions of screening tools that require the administration of specific interactive tasks by trained professionals (e.g., STAT, AOSI).

Level 2 Evaluations

As previously mentioned, Level 2 evaluations are undertaken when a child fails the Level 1 screening and therefore has been identified as potentially at risk. Its purpose is to differentiate children with AD from those with other types of disorders. Level 2 evaluations are often multidisciplinary in nature, involving professionals from psychology or neuropsychology, psychiatry, developmental pediatrics, and other medical and allied health specialties (e.g., neurology, speech-language pathology, audiology). Pediatric neuropsychologists are among the professionals who assess the cognitive and behavioral functioning of children with a known or suspected ASD, both to assist in diagnostic assessment and to contribute to the development of treatment recommendations.

The evaluation of an infant or toddler differs in important ways from assessments in preschoolers and school-aged children. The focus of these early evaluations is on identifying impairments or behaviors that may be early manifestations or precursors to deficits typically associated with AD. This includes problems with social orienting, joint attention, responding to verbal communications, language development, imitation or the use of gesture, repetitive behavior, imaginative activity, play, and reciprocal affective behaviors. In addition, it is important to examine for sensory or motor problems, or regulatory issues such as sleep and feeding.

The structure of an evaluation is tailored to address the referral issues, the presentation of the child, and the goal of the assessment. Goals can include diagnostic assessment, treatment planning, monitoring of treatment, early intervention and school placement issues,

TABLE 6.2 Early Diagnostic Screening Measures for AD During Infancy

Measure	Format	Comments
Modified Checklist for Autism in Toddlers (M-CHAT; Robins, Fein, Barton, & Green, 2001)	Completed by parents, telephone follow-up by clinicians	A 23-item parent questionnaire completed at 18 months. Good estimates of specificity and sensitivity when follow-up interview is added to review failed items. Positive predictive value reported as 0.68–0.74 after interview (Kleinman et al., 2008). Does not allow good differentiation of ASD, language delays, and global delays.
Pervasive Developmental Disorders Screening Test-II (PDDST-II - Siegel, 2004)	Completed by parents	A screening questionnaire completed by parent. Stage 1 completed for pediatricians has high sensitivity (0.92) and specificity (0.91). Useful as a Stage 2 screener for children in developmental clinics (McQuistin & Zieren, 2006).
Infant-Toddler Checklist (ITC; Wetherby et al., 2008)	Completed by parents	Comprises 25 questions from the Communication and Symbolic Behavior Scales and Developmental Profile (Wetherby & Prizant, 2002). Can be used as a broadband screener for ASD. Positive predictive values above 70% for children age 9–24 months for communication delays, and 93.3% sensitivity for ASD in particular, but does not discriminate ASD from other communication delays unless social competence score is less than the 10th percentile.
Parent Observation of Early Markers Scale (POEMS; Feldman et al., 2012)	Completed by parents	Developed to monitor the behavioral development of infants considered at risk for ASD. Preliminary data indicate acceptable psychometric properties.
First Year Inventory (FYI; Reznick et al., 2007)	Completed by parents	Developed to assess behaviors in 12-month-olds suggestive of an eventual diagnosis of AD. Large-scale longitudinal study has not yet been reported to evaluate predictive validity.
Screening Tool for Autism in Two-Year-Olds (STAT; Stone, Coonrod, & Ousley, 2000)	Administered by trained clinicians	A 12-item, 20-minute interactive test administered by trained professionals measuring play, requesting behavior, directing attention, and motor imitation. Good sensitivity (0.93) and specificity (0.83). Designed to differentiate toddlers with autism from those with other developmental disabilities.
Autism Observation Scale for Infants (AOSI; Bryson et al., 2008)	Administered by trained clinicians	Developed to detect and monitor early signs of autism as they emerge in high-risk infants at 6, 12, and 18 months. Uses structured activities to elicit 18 behaviors including visual tracking and disengaging attention, orienting to name, reciprocal smiling, differential response to facial emotion, imitation, and social anticipation. Excellent inter-rater reliability (0.94 at 18 months) and fair to good test–retest reliability at 12 months. Early data suggested potential to distinguish high- from low-risk infants as early as 12 months.
Early Screening of Autistic Traits (ESAT; Swinkels et al., 2006)	Completed by parents	A 14-item screening instrument used to detect autistic traits. Items assess the diverse behaviors of the child such as his or her interest in toys, enjoyment of social play, emotional understandability, and production of stereotypical movement. Questions are answered with a "yes" for typical behavior and "no" for atypical behavior. Three or more negative answers on the ESAT are considered to be screen positive and at high risk of developing ASD.

Instruments used to screen for signs of AD in the first 2 years of life. These are broadly aimed at identifying atypical development of verbal and nonverbal social communication, social orienting, imitation, use of gesture, joint attention, repetitive behavior, imaginative activity, play, and reciprocal affective behaviors.

TABLE 6.3 Diagnostic Assessment Measures for Autistic Disorder*

Measure	Comments
Parent Interview for Autism-Clinical Version (PIA-CV; Stone, Coonrod, Pozdol, & Turner, 2003)	A 118-item, semi-structured interview that provides information about the presence and severity of autistic symptomology across several behavioral domains. Good psychometric properties and sensitive to symptomology present in younger samples. Good sensitivity to behavioral change in 2-year-olds.
Autism Diagnostic Interview-Revised (ADI-R; Lord, Rutter, & Le Couteur, 1994; Rutter, Le Couteur, & Lord, 2003)	Semi-structured interview that elicits information from a parent or caregiver regarding and behaviors required to make an ICD-10 or *DSM-IV-TR* diagnosis of autism (social interaction, communication skills, repetitive activities, stereotyped interests). Designed to distinguish developmental delays, qualitative impairments, and behaviors that would be regarded deviant at any age. Inter-rater reliability is excellent. Gold standard measure for research because of high inter-rater reliability. Not advised for use for children with IQs below 20 or mental age below 20 months.
Social Communication Questionnaire (SCQ; Rutter, Bailey, & Lord, 2003)	Uses 40 critical questions from the ADI-R and the same diagnostic algorithm. Items are arranged in four subscales: Social Interaction, Communication, Abnormal Language, and Stereotyped Behaviors. Applicable in children from 4 years (or mental age of 2 years) to adulthood. Also not advised for use with profound intellectual disability.
Autism Diagnostic Observation Schedule (ADOS; Lord, Rutter, DiLavore, & Risi, 2002)	A semi-structured, interactive observation widely accepted as a gold standard diagnostic instrument developed for children from 2–9 years of age. Children should preferably have a nonverbal mental age of 15 months. A revision added two new domains (Social Affect and Restricted, Repetitive Behaviors) and improved predictive value. A toddler module (Module T) was recently developed for use in children from 12 to 30 months (Luyster et al., 2009). No presses are available to examine the presence or absence of repetitive and stereotyped behaviors.
PDD Behavior Inventory (PDDBI; Cohen, Schmidt-Lackner, Romanczyk, & Sudhalter, 2003)	Composed of rating scales completed by caregivers or teachers assessing both adaptive and nonadaptive behaviors. Sensitive to change in maladaptive behaviors. Assesses joint attention skills, pretend play, and referential gesture. Good internal consistency and test–retest reliability.
Child Autism Rating Scale (CARS; Schopler, Reichler, & Renner, 1998)	The single most widely used standardized instrument specifically designed for the diagnosis of autism. A considerable amount of research supports its utility, but limited evidence is available on its usefulness in children under 3 years. For use mainly by experienced clinicians.
Social Responsiveness Scale (SRS; Constantino et al., 2003)	Composed of 65 items using a four-point Likert response scale, this measure assesses reciprocal social behavior and yields a single score that indexes the severity of impairment in reciprocal social behaviors. It has acceptable psychometric properties (sensitivity of 0.78 and a specificity of 0.77) but is highly focused on measurement of social impairment. Not advised for children with moderate to profound intellectual disability.
Autism Spectrum Screening Questionnaire (ASSQ; Ehlers, Gillberg, & Wing, 1999)	Unlike the previous instruments, this questionnaire was designed for older children (6–17 years of age) with mild to no intellectual impairment. Consists of 27 yes/no questions assessing social interaction (11 items), communication (6 items), and restricted behavior and interest (5 items) and associated symptoms (5 items). Psychometric properties vary depending on the characteristics of the sample and the respondents (parents, teachers). A cutoff score of 19 for parent respondents in a clinical setting yielded a sensitivity of 0.62 and specificity of 0.91. Has been used to differentiate AD from other behavior and learning disorders.

*This table provides a selection of instruments developed for use in diagnostic assessments of children suspected of having AD.

program admission or discharge, or assessing eligibility for special services. Initial steps involve a detailed characterization of the presenting symptoms and behaviors through a discussion of parents' current and past concerns, a thorough review of the child's developmental/medical history, interaction with the child, and observation of the child in different settings. Primary efforts are directed to gathering information relevant to behaviors included in the *DSM-IV-TR* diagnostic criteria or the associated antecedent behaviors discussed in previous sections. A thorough and comprehensive interview is a key aspect of these evaluations. They provide the examiner with an opportunity to obtain a detailed account of the parent's full range of experience because observations made by the examiner in the clinic setting may not disclose problems that are readily evident in other settings and contexts.

A summary of selected measures designed for the assessment of young children with ASD are briefly described in Table 6.3 . Behavioral inventories assessing problems associated with AD are generally better suited for assessing children on the autism spectrum than general-purpose child behavior checklists because the latter tend to have remarkably few items directly pertinent to this diagnosis. Unfortunately, at present, there are relatively few unbiased sources to guide clinicians in the choice of these instruments (Norris & Lecavalier, 2010).

Symptoms of AD vary across the lifespan and are commonly most difficult to manage in the preschool years. Behavior and compliance often improve over time, allowing later evaluations to examine a broader range of behavioral domains and in a more formal manner than is often possible with infants and young children. In addition, the developmental profile of children with AD varies with increasing age. Correspondingly, children and adults with AD present with a distinctly different and more diversified symptom complex than do infants and toddlers.

In many respects, neuropsychologists are particularly well-suited to the assessment of children with AD due to their expertise in assessing and integrating information across a wide range of cognitive and behavioral domains relevant to ASD. By delineating areas of strength or weakness, neuropsychological evaluations can provide useful information to guide the provision of services to the child and facilitate the task of educators and therapists in designing and implementing appropriate interventions. For more extensive discussions concerning the neuropsychological evaluation of children with ASD, the reader is referred to Black and Stefanatos (2000), Ozonoff, Goodlin-Jones, and Solomon (2005a), and Losh, Adolphs, Poe, Couture, Penn, Baranek, & Piven (2009). Tager-Flusberg and colleagues (2009) offer guidelines for assessment of expressive language. In addition, the reader is referred to Kanne, Randolph, and Farmer (2008) for discussion of the role of evaluations in educational and behavioral treatment planning.

Follow-Up Evaluations and the Cognitive Phenotype

In recent years, there's been considerable interest in using information derived from neuropsychological evaluations as a means of potentially subtyping children. This approach may be particularly useful in understanding the genetic determinants of the disorder, insofar as it exploits the probability that the genetic liability for AD is mediated by the influence of genes on the development and function of neural systems affected in the disorder. Given that performance on neuropsychological measures can serve as an index of brain dysfunction involving specific neural systems, neuropsychological measures can potentially be exploited as markers of the effects of genetic anomalies on these systems. In this way, patterns of neuropsychological performance may be used to define endophenotypes for the disorder—that is, intermediary causal links between genetic anomalies and the overt expression of the disorder. As stated by Gottesman and Hanson (2005, p. 264), endophenotypes provide the "road markers that bring us closer to the biological origins of the developmental journey."

Although a general consensus is currently lacking, several potential cognitive phenotypes have been proposed (Charman et al., 2011a; Hughes et al., 1999; Tager-Flusberg & Joseph, 2003). In addition, neuropsychological profiles associated with the broader autism phenotype have been examined (Hughes et al., 1999; Lindgren, Folstein, Tomblin, & Tager-Flusberg, 2009; Losh et al., 2009). In the following sections, neuropsychological findings observed in school-aged children, adolescents, and adults with AD are outlined. This is followed by a section entitled "Advanced Diagnostic Considerations and Practices," which discusses the implications of these findings to current conceptualizations of AD.

Neuropsychological Domains of Assessment

Intelligence

Intelligence estimates in AD span an enormous range, from severe intellectual disability to the very superior range of intelligence (Szatmari & Jones, 1991). A couple of decades ago, studies established that approximately 75% of children with AD have IQs below 70, corresponding to the cognitively deficient range (Rapin, 1991). The remaining 25% score 70 or above and on this basis are classified as having "high-functioning autism" (HFA; Rutter & Schopler, 1987). These proportions are somewhat outdated given changes to the diagnostic criteria over the years (Charman et al., 2011a). More recent studies have suggested that intellectual disability may be present in only half of children with ASD (Chakrabarti & Fombonne, 2005; Charman et al., 2011b).

IQ test results do not reveal diagnostically relevant traits in individuals with AD (Zander & Dahlgren, 2010). Although there is a strong genetic contribution to IQ, it is not a sensitive marker of genetic risk factors for the disorder (LeCouteur et al., 1996). Autistic traits appear to be genetically independent of intellectual functioning (Hoekstra, Happé, Baron-Cohen, & Ronald, 2010). However, IQ is reasonably stable in AD and is considered a good predictor of long-term outcome (Gillberg & Steffenburg, 1987; Howlin, Goode, Hutton, & Rutter, 2004) and academic achievement (Mayes & Calhoun, 2008).

Some investigators have proposed that patterns of performance on subtests of the Wechsler Intelligence Scales for Children may be useful in indexing the neurological heterogeneity of AD and provide a basis for subtyping (Bolton et al., 1994; Fein et al., 1999; Zwaigenbaum et al., 2000). Performance on the Comprehension and Vocabulary subtests are often relatively weak, reflecting difficulties with language and a poor appreciation of social norms and expectations. In addition, low scores are often evident on Symbol Search and Coding, in part because of relative deficiencies in visual motor skills (Green et al., 2009). By contrast, numerous reports have shown that children with AD characteristically show relative strengths in performance on the Block Design (BD) subtest (Mayes & Calhoun, 2003b). A peak on BD is seen in the subtest profile of almost half (47%) of individuals with AD compared to only 2% of the typical population (Caron, Mottron, Berthiaume, & Dawson, 2006). Strong performance may also be evident on Matrix Reasoning and Picture Concepts (Mayes & Calhoun, 2008), in part because of relatively preserved or even enhanced visual perceptual functioning (Mottron, Dawson, Soulieres, Hubert, & Burack, 2006; Simmons et al., 2009) and visual imagery (Soulieres, Zeffiro, Girard, & Mottron, 2011) that has been observed in AD.

Family studies have shown that nonverbal IQ decreases with birth order. The significance of this finding is unclear, but some have speculated that the effect may be associated with increasing maternal immunosensitivity and reaction to fetal brain tissue (Singer et al., 2008). A performance IQ of less than 70 appears to be associated with much poorer prognosis in adulthood (Howlin et al., 2004). Overall, independent living is a possibility for individuals with AD who have an IQ in the normal range (≥80), although outcome can still be variable at this level (Howlin et al., 2004).

Although IQ is as steady and predictable in AD as in non-autistic clinical populations, the temporal stability of specific patterns of subtest or index scores is generally poor (Borsuk, Watkins, & Canivez, 2006). Measures of intelligence requiring verbal information processing tend to produce lower estimates of intelligence than those dependent on spatial reasoning, and this may be especially true early in development. Mayes and Calhoun (2003a), for example, found that early in development, 67% of a cohort of children with AD had relatively depressed verbal IQ estimates (compared to performance IQ) throughout their preschool years. This disparity was considered a reflection of delayed language development. As their language improved with increasing age, this gap diminished, resulting in higher overall IQ estimates.

Given the inter-subtest variability associated with AD, the use of "short form" IQ tests or "abridged administration" of standard tests is associated with some reductions in the predictive validity. However, according to Minshew, Turner, and Goldstein (2005), these declines do not seem disproportionate to those seen in neurotypical individuals. Nevertheless, it is important to bear in mind that the specific content of the form used can have a significant impact on an individual's score.

Motor Abilities

In his original description of autism, Kanner (1943) noted that 7 of the 11 school-aged children in his original cohort were "somewhat clumsy in gait and gross motor performances" (p. 248) while all were skillful in fine motor coordination. Anomalies of balance (Jansiewicz et al., 2006) and upright postural stability and control have been described in preschool and school-aged children as well as young adults (Kohen-Raz, Volkmar, & Cohen, 1992; Minshew, Sung, Jones, & Furman, 2004; Molloy, Dietrich, & Bhattacharya, 2003). Gepner and colleagues (Gepner & Mestre, 2002; Gepner, Mestre, Masson, & de Schonen, 1995) have suggested that hypoactive postural correction is correlated with the severity of later overall impairment and may differentiate between children with AD and those with AspD.

Contrary to Kanner's impression that fine motor coordination was preserved in AD, deficits have been noted in performance on speeded graphomotor tasks such as Coding on the Wechsler scales (Mayes & Calhoun, 2003a), and on motor impersistence measures such as the Statues subtest on the NEPSY (Mahone et al., 2006). Children with AD also tend to perform poorly on a variety of measures of repetitive and timed movements as assessed on neurological soft signs batteries, such as Denckla's Physical and Neurological Examination for Soft Signs (Jansiewicz et al., 2006; Mandelbaum et al., 2006). Overall, motor deficits in AD are highly variable, and it is sometimes difficult to discern the underlying significance of positive findings. For example, measures of impersistence require the ability to sustain attention to a task, often with the implicit expectation that children will be as compliant and persistent as possible. In some if not many instances, children with AD may not fully appreciate or accede to these expectations.

Fournier and colleagues (2010) recently performed a meta-analysis of 51 studies reporting the performance of individuals with AD on measures requiring motor coordination. A large and significant effect clearly indicated the presence of motor impairments in AD compared to neurologically normal controls on tasks requiring movement preparation and planning and on measures of upper extremity function as well as gait and balance. The neural basis for these findings remains unclear, although poor activation of the cerebellum during performance of motor tasks (Allen, Muller, & Courchesne, 2004) and evidence of frontostriatal dysfunction (McAlonan et al., 2008; Rinehart et al., 2006) have implicated both cortical and subcortical structures and the pathways that connect them.

Imitation and the production of gesture are often conspicuously compromised in children with AD from a very early age (Charman et al., 2000; Watson, Baranek, & DiLavore, 2003). In order to explore the relationship between problems with basic motor function and higher-order motor programming difficulties, Mostofsky and colleagues (2006) examined the performance of individuals with HFA on a variety of measures of motor ability and praxis. The findings revealed poor performance on measures requiring gestured imitation, gesture to command, and tool use. They concluded that a generalized praxis deficit is present in HFA and is not entirely attributable to simple motor deficits. These problems may reflect anomalies of frontal/parietal/subcortical circuitry involved in learning the sensory representations of movements and in the production of sequential motor programs necessary for complex actions.

It has been suggested that the difficulties with imitation observed in AD may be related to dysfunction of the so-called "mirror neurons" system distributed in the inferior frontal and temporoparietal cortex (Perkins, Stokes, McGillivray, & Bittar, 2010; Rizzolatti, Fabbri-Destro, & Cattaneo, 2009). The mirror neuron system is thought to mediate the understanding of actions performed by others with reference to motor representations for those actions when performed by the observer. Thus far, evidence for mirror neuron system involvement in AD is mixed. A key finding in support of the "broken mirror" hypothesis pertains to the absence of *mu rhythm* suppression in the EEG of autistic individuals when observing another person performing a movement. In neurotypical individuals, the mu rhythm is normally suppressed over motor cortex during the performance of a voluntary movement and also when another person performs the movement. Initial reports had indicated that children with ASD failed to demonstrate mu rhythm suppression during performance of movements by others (Martineau, Cochin, Magne, & Barthelemy, 2008; Oberman et al., 2005), seemingly supporting the "broken mirror" hypothesis. However, more recent investigations have shown that mu suppression does occur when children with AD are observing familiar adults (Oberman, Ramachandran, & Pineda, 2008) as well as during self-executed and observed movement (Raymaekers, Wiersema, & Roeyers, 2009). Moreover, individuals with AD who demonstrate normal mu rhythm suppression may nevertheless fail to imitate observed actions. Further evidence against a primary role of mirror neuron system involvement in AD stems from a recent functional magnetic resonance imaging (fMRI) study, which reported normal activation of mirror systems in individuals with AD during observation and execution of hand movements (Dinstein et al., 2010).

Attention

Attentional deficits are common in AD. Early in development, children with AD frequently demonstrate poor alerting and orienting responses to salient events, stimulus properties, or to other people (Anderson & Colombo, 2009; Dawson & Lewy, 1989; Maestro et al., 2002; Ornitz, 1988; Osterling et al., 2002; Renner, Grofer Klinger, & Klinger, 2006). These problems, which appear to reflect underreactivity, are apparent whether information is social (e.g., speech) or nonsocial in nature (Dawson, Meltzoff, Osterling, Rinaldi, & Brown, 1998; Lepisto et al., 2005). Children may, for example, ignore the appearance of significant others in their environment but also show a disregard for painful bumps and bruises or lack responsiveness to loud and sudden noises in their environment (Ornitz, 1988).

In addition, children with AD often exhibit decreased novelty-seeking (Dawson, Finley, Phillips, & Lewy, 1989) and exploratory behavior (Pierce & Courchesne, 2001). However, if given a task of sufficient intrinsic interest, they can demonstrate adequate sustained attention. Indeed, they can attend for extended periods of time to particular tasks, often to the exclusion of other salient occurrences in their environment (Casey, Gordon, Mannheim, & Rumsey, 1993; Gersten, 1983; Lovaas, Koegel, & Schreibman, 1979; Matthews, Shute, & Rees, 2001; Waterhouse, Fein, & Modahl, 1996). This overselectivity is not present in all individuals with AD and indeed may not be specific to ASD (Ploog, 2010). However, when it occurs in AD, it is often accompanied by over-reactivity, perservative behavior and interests, and exceptional memory (Liss, Saulnier, Fein, & Kinsbourne, 2006).

In children with AD, attention is often captured by or directed to irrelevant or extraneous stimuli or details and remains focused on this information at the expense of missing important, meaningful information that is co-occurring elsewhere. Devoting attention to important but perceptually nonsalient information in the presence of more perceptually salient but irrelevant information appears to involve inhibition of early visual processing areas by mechanisms distributed in the region of the left intraparietal sulcus responsible for directing attention and coordinating perceptuomotor movements. It has been speculated that the dynamic interaction between these areas may break down in AD (Mevorach, Hodsoll, Allen, Shalev, & Humphreys, 2010). Orienting to a new stimulus requires disengagement from the currently attended-to stimulus, shifting of attentional resources to the new stimulus, and then reengagement of attention. Several studies have indicated that individuals with AD have difficulty disengaging from currently attended stimuli (Casey et al., 1993; Townsend, Harris, & Courchesne, 1996; Wainwright-Sharp & Bryson, 1993), taking several hundred milliseconds longer than controls to redirect or shift covert attention and overt attention to a new target (Townsend et al., 1999, 1996; Wainwright-Sharp & Bryson, 1993). Extending these results, Landry and Bryson (2004) found that 82% of autistic children had difficulties in disengaging but not shifting overt attention. Overall, these deficits in ignoring irrelevant information and in redirecting the focus of attention to relevant targets implicate dysfunction of a distributed attentional network involving the frontal and parietal lobes and connections to the cerebellum.

Individuals with AD also demonstrate a relatively narrow dispersion of attention, which can cause preferential analysis to one aspect of a stimulus or one portion of the visual field over another (Bryson et al., 1990; Koegel & Wilhelm, 1973). This may relate to evidence that individuals with AD can demonstrate abnormally narrowed regions of sensory enhancement to visual information at attended spatial locations (Townsend & Courchesne, 1994) and have problems in distributing or dispersing visual attentional resources at both attended and unattended locations. For example, when attending to information presented in central vision, they demonstrate delayed or absent event related potentials (ERP) when required to orient attention to targets presented in peripheral portions of their visual fields (Townsend et al., 2001). Problems with attention also exist in other modalities and may be as or more pronounced in the auditory domain (Casey et al., 1993; Ciesielski, Courchesne, & Elmasian, 1990; Rutter, 1983). These problems will be discussed in the section on auditory processing that follows. These attentional problems may contribute to a more general inclination to focus on details rather than the "bigger picture" that is often referred to as a problem of "central coherence" and affects information processing at multiple levels. It has been characterized more as a cognitive style than a specific problem with attention (Frith & Happé, 1994; Happé & Frith, 2006).

AD is also associated with difficulties segregating and dividing attentional resources between modalities (Ciesielski et al., 1995; Courchesne et al., 1994) or between visual attributes (Casey et al., 1993). Overall, it appears that perceptual filtering mechanisms respond in a dysregulated manner in AD. From a clinical perspective, there is recognition that a proportion of children with AD have a comorbid attention deficit hyperactivity disorder (ADHD), demonstrating attentional problems, impulsivity, distractibility, and hyperactivity (Noterdaeme, Amorosa, Mildenberger, Sitter, & Minow, 2001). Like children with ADHD, children with AD display problems with vigilance, impulse control, and working memory (Corbett, Constantine, Hendren, Rocke, & Ozonoff, 2009). Pharmacologic treatments appropriate for ADHD, such as psychostimulants, have been used with some degree of success in AD, although results are generally variable (Aman, Farmer, Hollway, & Arnold, 2008; Birmaher, Quintana, & Greenhill, 1988). Children with AD and comorbid ADHD have more neuropsychological difficulties that those with AD or ADHD alone (Nyden et al., 2010).

Memory

Performance on memory tasks is highly variable, moderated by numerous factors, including cognitive level and the specific task requirements. Basic memory processes involved in encoding, storing, and recognizing simple information are broadly commensurate with expectations based on general cognitive abilities (Hermelin & O'Connor, 1975; Rumsey & Hamburger, 1988). Children with AD generally perform as well as ability-matched controls on simple short-term memory tasks such as Digit Span (Bennetto, Pennington, & Rogers, 1996; Mayes & Calhoun, 2003b), recognition memory tasks (Bennetto et al., 1996; Williams, Goldstein, & Minshew, 2006a), and on tasks where recall is cued or supported (e.g., paired-associates learning; Boucher & Warrington, 1976; Williams et al., 2006a). They benefit from some forms of contextual cuing and priming (Lopez & Leekam, 2003). However, problems become apparent with more complex or open-ended task requirements, such as free recall of words, sentences, and stories (Bennetto et al., 1996; Gaigg, Gardiner, & Bowler, 2008; Minshew & Goldstein, 2001; Williams et al., 2006a) or when memory performance is influenced by other psychological processes, such as executive function, emotional processing, or perspective-taking. They have greater difficulties remembering faces than nonsocial visual stimuli (Hauck et al., 1998) and in recalling the temporal order of information or the particular situation in which it was learned (source memory; Bennetto et al., 1996). On list-learning tasks, individuals with AD demonstrate higher intrusion rates and poor strategy application, reflected in depressed semantic and global clustering scores on the California Verbal Learning Test (Minshew & Goldstein, 1993; Minshew, Goldstein, & Siegel, 1996). The overall pattern suggests an executive contribution to their difficulties with memory.

Children with AD commonly have difficulty remembering information important to everyday functioning. They appear to exhibit particular difficulties when information must be recalled from long-term memory and entails their personal involvement (Jones et al., 2010). Problems have been noted, for example, in consciously recollecting contextual information regarding everyday events (Boucher, 1981), self-performed activities, and personal experiences (Klein, Chan, & Loftus, 1999). They do not demonstrate an advantage in recalling their personal involvement in events (Hare, Mellor, & Azmi, 2007; Millward, Powell, Messer, & Jordan, 2000) and indeed have relative difficulty remembering whether they themselves or another person engaged in a given activity (Russell & Jarrold, 1999). They are more likely to take a third-person perspective (observer) in recalling past events rather than re-experiencing past events from their own viewpoint (Lind & Bowler, 2010; Williams et al., 2006a). Memory performance may therefore falter when recall is dependent on aspects of self-awareness, awareness of others, or an understanding of social implications surrounding an event.

Overall, individuals with AD have significant limitations of episodic memory in encoding "contextually rich" information, including the temporal, spatial, and other situational contexts. This kind of information can influence the affective tone of memories and may interact with their capacity to prospectively remember to perform certain activities. For example, remembering to perform some future activity not only depends on executive/organizational skills but also entails some intrinsic social motivational factors, such as concern not to let someone down by failing to remember to perform a particular activity (Jones et al., 2010). They are better at tasks that require "knowing" (semantic memory) than "remembering" (episodic memory; Ben Shalom, 2003). Compromise of the hippocampus can result in relative preservation of semantic memory in the face of greater deficits in episodic memory.

There is also growing evidence that non-limbic subcortical structures may play a role in the memory problems evident in individuals with AD. Mostofsky and colleagues (2000) have suggested that individuals with HFA demonstrate significant impairments in procedural learning compared with typically developing controls. On the Serial Reaction Time Test (Nissen & Bullemer, 1987), HFA subjects did not demonstrate a decrease in response time to repeated sequences, nor did they show the expected increase in response time or "rebound" effect when sequences returned to random presentation. The absence of these effects suggested that they did not implicitly process stimulus patterns. This was interpreted as a reflection of cerebellar pathology, although frontostriatal circuitry is also involved in performance on procedural and other forms of implicit learning (Poldrack & Gabrieli, 1997; Vakil & Herishanu-Naaman, 1998). Consequently, these findings could not rule out an explanation in terms of a frontostriatal dysfunction rather than anomalies of fronto-cerebellar circuits.

Visual Perceptual Abilities and Spatial Abilities

Experimental analyses of visual processing skills in AD have yielded contradictory or inconsistent results (Dakin & Frith, 2005; Simmons et al., 2009). One of the more consistent findings suggests that individuals with AD have particular difficulty in reading emotional information conveyed in facial expressions. Some studies suggest that these deficits are mainly evident with negative emotions (Humphreys, Minshew, Leonard, & Behrmann, 2007) such as fear (de Jong, van Engeland, & Kemner, 2008) or sadness (Boraston, Blakemore, Chilvers, & Skuse, 2007) and are attributable, at least in part, to lower sensitivity to information present in the eyes compared to the mouth (Baron-Cohen, Wheelwright, Hill, Raste, & Plumb, 2001; Langdell, 1978; Riby, Doherty-Sneddon, & Bruce, 2009) or a failure to spontaneously scan (Spezio, Adolphs, Hurley, & Piven, 2007b) or attend to the eyes (Pelphrey et al., 2002). These deficits do not appear to be equally present in all individuals with AD (Barton, Hefter, Cherkasova, & Manoach, 2007), but reliable predictors of this pattern of performance have not been specified.

A prime factor motivating the intense interest in face recognition is its central role in interpersonal interaction and communication from an early point in human development. Some of the problems observed in AD resemble difficulties associated with bilateral lesions of the amygdala (Adolphs, Baron-Cohen, & Tranel, 2002). Consistent with this, widespread hypoactivation has been described in several structures comprising a distributed face-processing network that includes the right amygdala, inferior frontal cortex, superior temporal sulcus, and face-related areas of somatosensory and motor cortex (Hadjikhani, Joseph, Snyder, & Tager-Flusberg, 2007). Kleinhans and colleagues (2011) have suggested that basic face processing may be functional in individuals with AD, but they fail to engage subcortical brain regions such as the amygdala, pulvinar, and superior colliculus, which are involved in automatic emotional face processing. These abnormalities, it was suggested, may contribute to deficits in social orienting and attention seen early in development and impede the subsequent development of neural networks involved in social cognition and cortical face processing.

By contrast, individuals with AD outperform neurotypical peers on tasks requiring the discrimination of visual figure-ground relationships (Jarrold, Gilchrist, & Bender, 2005; Mottron, Burack, Iarocci, Belleville, & Enns, 2003; Shah & Frith, 1993) and on other measures requiring disembedding of visual information (Brenner, Turner, & Muller, 2007; Joseph, Keehn, Connolly, Wolfe, & Horowitz, 2009; O'Riordan, Plaisted, Driver, & Baron-Cohen, 2001). This perceptual endowment may underlie their relatively strong performance on the Block Design subtest of the Wechsler Scales of Intelligence (Rumsey & Hamburger, 1988; Shah & Frith, 1993). Caron and colleagues (2006) have suggested that this superiority is based on well-developed processes underlying the detection, discrimination, and binding of local features, possibly related to enhanced functioning of areas of the primary visual cortex devoted to extraction of stimulus dimensions in small areas of the visual field. A similar explanation was also advanced to account for apparently higher-than-average levels of performance in individuals with AD on tasks requiring visual search. Consistent with this, an fMRI study by Keehn, Brenner, Palmer, Lincoln, and Müller (2008) observed greater activation in occipital and frontal regions in an AD group compared to neurotypical controls during performance of a visual search task. The occipital activation results were interpreted as consistent with their enhanced discrimination, whereas the frontoparietal activation reflected processes involved in top-down modulation of visual attention.

Children with AD commonly respond to nonsocial physical aspects of visual stimulation that occur by chance and are normally ignored as irrelevant (Klin, Lin, Gorrindo, Ramsay, & Jones, 2009). However, they appear to be relatively insensitive to global or complex visual features that have social significance, such as biological motion coherence (Atkinson, 2009; Parron et al., 2008; Pellicano, Gibson, Maybery, & Durkin, 2003). These issues may explain their difficulties recognizing emotions expressed in body movements. Some reports have suggested that the insensitivity to biological motion may implicate dysfunction of the dorsal magnocellular visual processing stream, which projects to motion-sensitive areas in the inferior and superior parietal lobule (Milne et al., 2002; Spencer et al., 2000). However, biological motion also normally elicits activation in the lingual gyrus (LG) and FG as well as portions of the temporal pole and STS.

Auditory Processing

Children with AD commonly manifest unusual sensory responses to auditory stimulation, which can range from distress to inordinate fascination (Dahlgren & Gillberg, 1989). As previously discussed, an early manifestation of anomalies in this domain is the failure of an infant to orient to his or her name being called in the latter half of the first year of life (Nadig et al., 2007). Up to 80% of children with AD are thought to be deaf at some point in their development (Bartak & Rutter, 1976). Several studies have underscored the presence of peripheral hearing impairment in a non-negligible number of autistic subjects (Ho, Keller, Berg, Cargan, & Haddad, 1999; Rosenhall, Nordin, Sandstrom, Ahlsen, & Gillberg, 1999). However, for a greater proportion of children, problems emerge as information is being conveyed from ear to cortex. Abnormalities in both the timing and frequency coding of auditory stimulation have been identified in brainstem auditory evoked responses to spectrotemporally complex stimuli, such as speech (Khalfa et al., 2001; Russo, Nicol, Trommer, Zecker, & Kraus, 2009a; Russo, Zecker, Trommer, Chen, & Kraus, 2009b). Consistent with this, structural neuroimaging studies have shown that the brainstem of individuals with AD are significantly smaller with less gray matter than typically developing peers (Hashimoto et al., 1993; Jou, Minshew, Melhem, Keshavan, & Hardan, 2009), and this appears to be correlated with sensory anomalies (Toal et al., 2009). Positron emission tomography (PET) studies have also revealed reductions of activation of auditory cortex and cerebellum during the processing of both nonverbal and verbal stimuli (Muller et al., 1999). The presence of brainstem pathology may vary considerably from individual to individual and, consequently, many cases present with normal auditory brainstem-evoked responses to simple stimuli such as clicks and tones (Tharpe et al., 2006). However, responses to simple stimuli may not disclose problems that may otherwise be apparent in the processing of spectrally and temporally complex stimuli such as speech (Russo et al., 2009a).

Other difficulties with auditory processing in AD include deficits in processing auditory duration (Lepisto et al., 2005), temporal complexity (Samson et al., 2011), and prosody in the human voice (Boucher, Lewis, & Collis, 2000; Hobson, Ouston, & Lee, 1988a; Hubbard & Trauner, 2007; Loveland, Steinberg, Pearson, Mansour, & Reddoch, 2008). A recent magnetoencephalographic (MEG) study revealed latency delays in cortical neural responses from the superior temporal gyrus in response to speech and nonspeech stimuli (Roberts et al., 2011, 2010). Despite such findings, some individuals with AD demonstrate enhanced pitch discrimination, labeling, and memory (Bonnel et al., 2003; Heaton, 2003).

Several studies have suggested that the cortical processing of speech stimuli is more difficult than processing nonverbal (e.g., musical) auditory stimuli. Ceponiene and colleagues (2003), for example, found normal cortical auditory–evoked responses to simple and complex tone changes but abnormal responses to vowels. This suggests that auditory orienting deficits in autism may be particularly evident in response to speech sounds. Consistent with this, some children with AD fail to preferentially orient to intelligible speech over a jumble of voices (Klin, 1992). Using fMRI, Gervais and colleagues (2004) reported that individuals with AD failed to activate regions of the STS that selectively respond to vocal sounds, whereas they demonstrated normal activation in response to nonvocal sounds. This may parallel their difficulties with processing socially important visual cues, such as facial expressions and gestures (see previous section). These findings highlight the abnormalities of cortical processing for socially relevant auditory information in this population. Auditory inattention and difficulties processing speech can often appear similar to those seen in children with a verbal auditory agnosia (Stefanatos et al., 2002; Tuchman & Rapin, 2002).

Hypersensitivity to sound (hyperacusis) has been described in 18%–81% of children with AD, a significantly higher percentage than other developmentally delayed populations (Tharpe et al., 2006). Hypersensitivity in this context does not imply lower sensory thresholds but instead refers to low tolerance for suprathreshold levels or forms of stimulation (e.g., air conditioner, hair dryer, police sirens) that are easily tolerated by typically developing individuals. It is typically manifested in acute distress reactions (e.g., crying, anxious avoidant behavior), stereotypic responses (e.g., covering the ears), or both.

Hyperacusis is not specific to AD and can result from a variety of causes, including serotonin dysfunction, peripheral hearing damage, or dysfunction of the auditory central nervous system (Baguley, 2003; Stefanatos & DeMarco, 2011). One possible mechanism is a disruption of efferent influences from the superior olivary complex (SOC) to the cochlea (via the olivocochlear bundle) with consequent loss of regulatory control over input to cortex (Khalfa et al., 2001). As previously discussed, neuropathology of SOC has been described in some cytoarchitectonic studies in association with anomalies of the brain stem and cerebellum (Kulesza et al., 2010). Alternatively, hyperacusis may occur due to abnormal patterns of connectivity in the auditory brainstem whereby nonclassical auditory pathways (extralemniscal pathways) may be recruited in the processing of auditory information (Moller et al., 2005). This pathway diverges from the traditional auditory pathway and projects to dorsal and medial thalamus and then directly to the amygdala and auditory association cortex, bypassing primary auditory cortex. It is possible that this re-routed, fairly raw, auditory information induces atypical responses due to its influence on the amygdala.

Language

Impairments of communication are arguably the most varied of the symptoms of AD, considering both the diversity of deficits and the range of severity (Boucher, 2003; Stefanatos & Baron, 2011; Tager-Flusberg, 2006). Kanner's (1943) initial description of autism outlined profound and unusual disturbances in language and communication. Three of the original cohort of 11 children were seemingly mute but on rare occasions elicited a full sentence. The majority were able to speak, but their verbal productions were strikingly lacking in communicative value and marked by flat or exaggerated intonation and inconsistent rates of articulation (unusually fast or slow). Noteworthy characteristics of their expressive language disturbance included the presence of pronoun reversal errors (e.g., "you" for "I"), immediate and delayed echolalia, and the production of irrelevant speech, neologisms, and metaphoric utterances. A variety of problems with language comprehension were also evident, including marked unresponsiveness to verbal overtures or questions and a propensity for literal interpretation stemming from difficulties in processing synonyms or different connotations of the same word (Kanner, 1946). Indeed, problems with language comprehension form a major component of their communicative difficulties, more so than is typically seen in intellectually impaired (Bartak & Rutter, 1976) or developmentally language-disordered children (Allen & Rapin, 1992) matched for nonverbal intelligence.

Views of language impairment in AD have changed as conceptions of the disorder have evolved. When the diagnostic criteria were highly specific and somewhat restrictive, approximately 50%–75% of children who received the diagnosis were considered to be nonverbal, producing five or fewer words used daily (Rapin, 1991). Changes in diagnostic criteria have broadened the scope of the diagnosis and, as a consequence, estimates of the prevalence of nonverbal children with AD are in the 14%–20% range.

As discussed in a previous section, children with AD, on average, do not produce their first words until the second or third year of life (Howlin, 2003). Attainment of language milestones and the subsequent development of language abilities has a substantial impact on long-term prognosis (Szatmari, Bryson, Boyle, Streiner, & Duku, 2003). This is in part related to the fact that the severity of language disturbance is closely tied to overall level of cognitive function, so that most children considered mute or nonverbal have severe mental retardation (Bryson, Clark, & Smith, 1988; Lord & Paul, 1997b). Whereas children who are mute at age 5 are likely to continue to be so several years later, those children with normal intelligence often exhibit fluent speech (Minshew, Goldstein, Muenz, & Payton, 1992). In the latter group, basic aspects of language acquisition such as phonological and morphological development and the reception of grammar appear broadly commensurate with expectations based on their general cognitive development (Tager-Flusberg & Caronna, 2007). Overall, approximately half of individuals with AD eventually develop functional speech, reflected in some ability to communicate basic needs and engage in social communication (Lord & Paul, 1997b).

Although articulatory or phonological problems have long been noted in AD (Bartak, Rutter, & Cox, 1975; Bartolucci, Pierce, Streiner, & Eppel, 1976), Kjelgaard and Tager-Flusberg (2001) contended that speech was relatively spared in AD. However, closer analysis of this question in more recent studies has suggested that one-quarter (Rapin et al., 2009) to one-third (Shriberg et al., 2001) of school-aged children with AD demonstrate problems with speech production that cannot be explained by cognitive limitations or lack of communicative intent. Recently, Rapin et al. (2009) reported that approximately three out of every four children with impaired phonology also demonstrated poor comprehension. These children resembled the Allen-Rapin SLI subtype called *phonologic-syntactic disorder* and *verbal auditory agnosia* (Allen & Rapin, 1992). In their review and extension of this literature, Shriberg et al. (2010) concluded that, as a group, individuals with AD demonstrate substantially higher rates of speech errors (e.g., dentalized sibilants and derhotacized rhotic consonants) relative to population estimates, although the nature of the errors did not conform to features of an apraxia of speech.

About three-quarters of children with AD engage in the production of echolalia at some point in their development. Echolalia refers to utterances elicited in a rote fashion comprised of spoken words or phrases that were previously produced by other individuals (Fay, 1973; Philips & Dyer, 1977; Ricks & Wing, 1975; Schuler, 1979). This often entails the recitation of narratives that children have picked up from movies, cartoons, or television programs. Delayed echolalia can be elicited hours, days, or even months after the initial utterance was heard, whereas immediate echolalia reflects repetition of an utterance produced in the preceding exchange. For example, in response to being asked, "What are you eating?" a child with AD might reply, "Are you eating." Typically developing children may transiently produce echolalia in the course of vocabulary development up to 2–2 ½ years of age (Turkeltaub et al., 2004), but it abates with increasing expressive language proficiency. Echolalia forms a larger percentage of verbal productions in children with AD compared to other language-disordered groups (Baker, Cantwell, Rutter, & Bartak, 1976). Prizant and Duchan (1981) concluded that immediate echolalia may serve a variety of communicative and cognitive functions. For example, when in conversation and unsure of how they should respond, they may engage in echolalia as a processing aid or an overt rehearsal strategy. Alternatively, echolalia may serve as a turn-filler, a self-regulatory function, or an expression of communicative intent.

It has been argued that echolalia and pronoun reversal do not represent symbolic deficits but rather are indicative of poor referential abilities in communicative contexts. Essentially, in deictic exchanges, they hear other speakers refer to them as "you" and to themselves as "I." A person with AD may then carry over the same personal pronouns to their own productions and elicits a pronoun reversal. In doing so, they fail to make the necessary transformation when the anchor point of a statement shifts from a "referred-to listener" to an "utterance-generating speaker." Somewhat related difficulties may underlie the tendency of autistic children to produce overly formal and pedantic or inappropriate utterances (Lord & Pickles, 1996; Rutter, Mawhood, & Howlin, 1992), use idiosyncratic labels, or invent nonsense terms that appear to have consistent meanings (Lord & Paul, 1997a). Their occurrence may reflect the child's failure to correct, update, or adaptively modify and expand relevant mental representations in the course of semantic development (Nation, 1999; Ungerer & Sigman, 1987). Consequently, they may interpret statements in an excessively literal fashion and fail to grasp the meaning of idioms or metaphors or the use of irony or sarcasm (Kerbel & Grunwell, 1998; Wang, Lee, Sigman, & Dapretto, 2006). More generally, they appear to have difficulties processing words in context (Brock, Norbury, Einav, & Nation, 2008).

As in SLI, children with AD have difficulties with grammatical morphemes, particularly verb tenses and articles (Bartolucci, 1982; Bartolucci, Pierce, & Streiner, 1980). Several recent studies have suggested that grammatical development in AD may be more problematic than previously considered (Condouris, Meyer, & Tager-Flusberg, 2003). Delays in syntactic development have been identified in children with AD who are well matched for level of lexical development and nonverbal mental age with developmentally delayed children and children with typical development (Eigsti, Bennetto, & Dadlani, 2007). Children with AD perform poorly on grammaticality judgment tasks, showing low sensitivity to anomalies with third person singular and "present progressive" markings (Eigsti & Bennetto, 2009). Contrary to previous contentions, it has been suggested that AD may be associated with some consistent morphosyntactic deficits (Eigsti et al., 2007; Jarrold, Boucays, & Russel, 1997).

The most widespread anomaly in AD, one common to both low- and high-functioning individuals, is a disorder of pragmatics (Burke, 1994; Mundy & Markus, 1997; Ramberg, Ehlers, Nyden, Johansson, & Gillberg, 1996). Specifically, individuals with AD demonstrate an inability to use existing verbal and nonverbal communication skills to mediate the give-and-take of social discourse. In conversation, they are less likely to contribute new information and are more likely to insert irrelevant remarks, exhibit poor turn-taking, persist in perseverative questioning, and have difficulty structuring and managing their narratives (Capps, Losh, & Thurber, 2000; Diehl, Bennetto, & Young, 2006; Wetherby, 1986). These characteristics increase with the complexity of the social context. This impairment is inordinate to, and cannot be accounted for, by generalized impairment of their verbal abilities (Eales, 1993). As evidence of this disassociation, high-functioning children with autism show severe deficits in pragmatics in the context of relatively preserved articulation, vocabulary, and grammatical skills (Tager-Flusberg & Caronna, 2007).

In addition, children with AD demonstrate higher rates of inappropriate or unusual prosody and voice pitch, including loud or high-pitched words and phrases, hypernasality, misplaced sentential stress, and increased repetitions and revisions (Bonneh, Levanon, Dean-Pardo, Lossos, & Adini, 2011; Hubbard & Trauner, 2007; McCann & Peppe, 2003; Paul et al., 2005). As a consequence, their verbal productions may be inappropriately loud or soft, fast or slow, and sound flat or have a singsong quality. In addition to problems with linguistic prosody (intonation, rhythm, and emphasis), the ability to use prosody to convey emotion also seems to be affected. Problems with productive prosody may be accompanied by comparable problems with perception of prosody, at least for some prosodic components such as rhythm, emphasis, and affect (Hesling et al., 2010; Peppe, McCann, Gibbon, O'Hare, & Rutherford, 2007). However, expressive linguistic prosody (e.g., production of lexical stress) may be impaired in the context of adequate receptive emotional prosody (Grossman, Bemis, Plesa Skwerer, & Tager-Flusberg, 2010), suggesting that different aspects of prosody can be dissociated.

Executive Function

Behavioral disturbances considered to reflect impairments of executive function pervade the behavior of children with AD (Hill, 2004). This includes difficulties with impulse control;

distractibility; repetitive, stereotypic behavior; poor self-monitoring; perseveration; mental inflexibility; and problems adapting to change. In addition, poor problem solving, lack of foresight, and organizational problems are also commonplace. The cognitive operations involved in executive function are highly integrative and dynamic, requiring constant monitoring, re-evaluation, and modification as necessary in an "online" manner.

Specific aspects of executive function that have been extensively studied in AD include vigilance (Garretson, Fein, & Waterhouse, 1990), the executive component of working memory (Ozonoff et al., 2004; Steele, Minshew, Luna, & Sweeney, 2007), inhibitory control (Happé, Booth, Charlton, & Hughes, 2006; Raymaekers, Antrop, van der Meere, Wiersema, & Roeyers, 2007), planning and problem solving (Hughes, Russell, & Robbins, 1994; Robinson, Goddard, Dritschel, Wisley, & Howlin, 2009), mental flexibility (Minshew, Meyer, & Goldstein, 2002; Ozonoff, 1995; Pascualvaca, Fantie, Papageorgiou, & Mirsky, 1998), and generativity (Dichter, Lam, Turner-Brown, Holtzclaw, & Bodfish, 2009; Jarrold, Boucher, & Smith, 1996). Drawing clear conclusions from these studies is difficult because they have varied both in terms of the characteristics of the AD subjects studied and the measures used to assess each of these aspects of executive function. Many of these tasks may appear somewhat artificial and of questionable relevance to the problems of AD. However, a recent study suggested positive correlations between laboratory measures of cognitive rigidity (perseverative errors on the Wisconsin Card Sorting Test [WCST]) and the frequency and intensity of repetitive behavior, as indexed by general stereotyped behavior scores from AD diagnostic instruments (South, Ozonoff, & McMahon, 2007).

Based on comparisons across numerous studies, it appears that not all aspects of executive function are equally involved. In particular, a number of reports have suggested that attention and working memory function was not as severely impaired in AD as performance on measures of inhibition of responses (Stroop effect, Go/No-Go, Junior Hayling Test; Ozonoff & Strayer, 2001). Moreover, performance on measures of planning and cognitive flexibility were highly variable, with some studies showing deficits in these areas (Ozonoff & McEvoy, 1994; Shu, Lung, Tien, & Chen, 2001; Tsuchiya, Oki, Yahara, & Fujieda, 2005), whereas others have failed to uncover significant problems (Liss et al., 2001; Ozonoff, 1995). Similarly, individuals with AD seemed to perform poorly on some aspects of inhibitory control and not others (Brian, Tipper, Weaver, & Bryson, 2003; Christ, Holt, White, & Green, 2007).

Recent studies have attempted to resolve these inconsistencies by using multiple measures of executive function in the same group of children with ASD. However, inconsistencies remain apparent comparing studies using this approach. Corbett, Constantine, Hendren, Rocke, and Ozonoff (2009), for example, used a number of executive function measures to compare children with ASD to a group with ADHD and to normal controls. They found that working memory was impaired in ASD, both when compared to neurotypical controls and the ADHD group. In addition, the children with ASD demonstrated significant problems with vigilance, response inhibition and cognitive flexibility relative to normal controls. Robinson and colleagues (2009) also observed significant impairments in the inhibition of prepotent responses (Stroop), but found preserved performance on measures of mental flexibility (WCST) and generativity (Verbal Fluency). However, contrary to Corbett and colleagues (2009), planning was also impaired. Goldberg and colleagues (2005) reported significant differences from controls on a measure of spatial working memory and not on response inhibition, planning, or set-shifting tasks.

Given the continuing variability in findings across studies, a consensus of opinion is currently lacking regarding the extent to which different aspects of executive function may be fundamentally related to AD. Zinke and colleagues (2010), for example, have recently argued that deficits on Tower tasks may be explained by problems with visual spatial short-term memory. Robinson and colleagues (2009) have proposed a multidimensional model of executive function and suggest that difficulties with planning, inhibition of pre-potent responses, and self-monitoring are particularly related to ASD. The links between problems with executive function and poor theory of mind (TOM) have also been long debated (Ozonoff, Pennington, & Rogers, 1991; Pellicano, 2010). Establishing this relationship is difficult given that intelligence, language ability, and several other key abilities appear to be moderating factors in the development of TOM. Pellicano (2010) has recently suggested that domain-general cognitive processes such as executive function and central coherence play a significant role in the emergence of later problems with TOM, whereas TOM does not appear to be predictive of later development of executive function in central coherence.

ADVANCED DIAGNOSTIC CONSIDERATIONS AND PRACTICES

Neuropsychological Conceptualizations of AD

The early onset of symptoms, as well as their nature and chronicity, have long argued for a neurobiological basis to AD. Postmortem histopathological studies of the brains of individuals with AD have revealed subtle but widespread anomalies of neural microstructure and organization, but the scope and functional impact of these perturbations remains speculative. For many years, the behavioral domains comprising the autism triad have been regarded as largely inseparable, in part because the diagnosis requires that impairment must be observed across all three domains. However, the strength of association among these domains varies from high (e.g., social interaction and communication) to low (e.g., social interaction and repetitive/restricted behavior). Based on this, Happé and Ronald (2008) have cogently argued that the symptom complex that defines AD is fractionable and that deficits in each domain are likely related to largely independent genetic influences.

From a neuropsychological perspective, the acquisition of complex abilities comprising each domain is contingent upon the coordinated interaction and integration of information from different brain regions. Problems in each behavioral domain can thereby be understood in terms of a breakdown in the function of these widely distributed networks, which are composed of components (e.g., modules, buffers) and connections with distinct computational responsibilities. The function of each network can be influenced by the quality of input, the functional integrity of its components, the timely and effective control of information flow, and the integration of information. The pattern and severity of impairment in each of the behavioral domains defined by the autistic triad—social interaction, communication, and repetitive and restricted behaviors—will presumably vary according to which neural networks are compromised, the severity of the dysfunction, and the extent to which alternative processes, resources, and strategies can make up for the loss of processing capacity. Accordingly, impairments of neuropsychological processing can be viewed as intermediary causal links between brain dysfunction and the diverse overt behaviors that comprise the manifest disorder.

The maps depicted in Figure 6.1 provide a schematic representation of the brain areas that have been implicated in AD for each behavioral domain (green for social interaction, red for communication, and blue for repetitive/restricted behavior). This graphic is not intended to reflect a comprehensive representation of our current state of knowledge but is included here mainly for heuristic purposes. As can be appreciated by visually comparing the three separate panels, there is considerable overlap in neural systems mediating behaviors relevant to social interaction and communication. This may account for the closer association that exists between these two domains. Indeed, these two domains are likely to be collapsed in the forthcoming revision of *DSM-5* into a single domain that is likely to be entitled "social communication." A brief summary of current conceptualizations is outlined in the following sections.

Neural Networks for Social Interaction

Because AD is fundamentally a disorder of social interaction, considerable interest has been devoted to delineating the locus and nature of neural dysfunction that could result in the pattern of social impairment characteristic of the disorder. Early psychological theories sought to attribute the social difficulties of AD to general failures in nonsocial aspects of processing, such as an inability to generalize (Rimland, 1964) or difficulties handling semantic information (Hermelin & O'Connor, 1970). However, through the work of Baron-Cohen (2001), Happé and Frith (2006), and others, it has become apparent that the deficits central to AD are based in dysfunction of psychological processes specifically devoted to social cognition and commu-

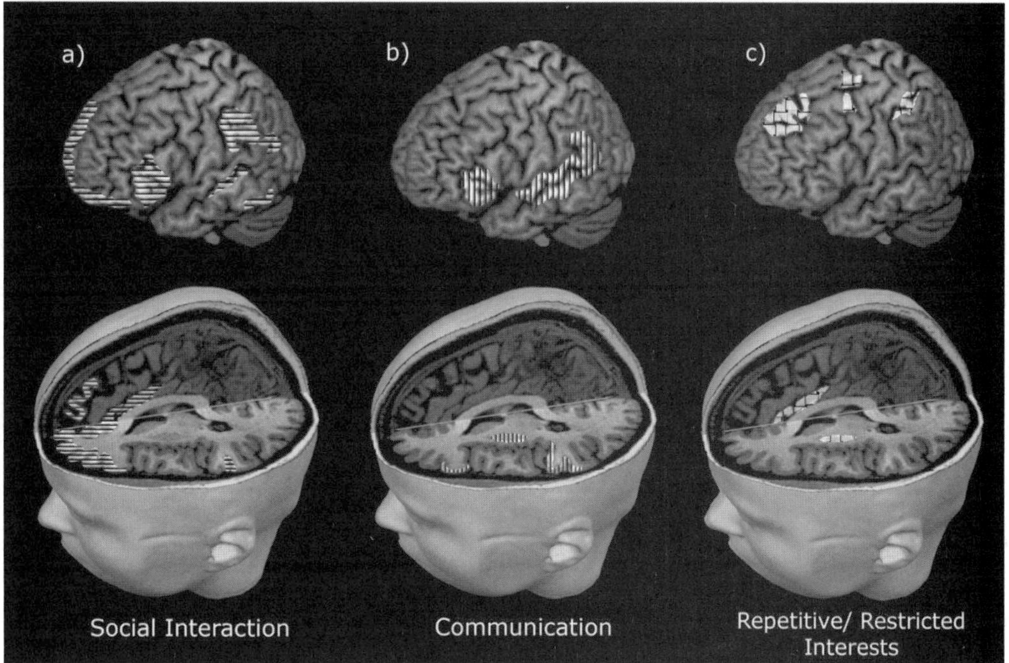

FIGURE 6.1 Areas of dysfunction implicated by neuropsychological and functional neuroimaging studies of AD. (*See color insert.*) Color-shaded areas indicate brain regions implicated as areas of dysfunction in individuals with AD. Some structures are not visible given the plane of the image. Problems with social interaction (*green*) have been related to dysfunction of a complex distributed network involving the following areas and connecting pathways: orbitofrontal cortex, inferior frontal cortex, cingulate cortex, superior temporal sulcus, fusiform gyrus, and amygdala. Problems with communication (*red*) have been related to dysfunction of a complex distributed neural network involving the following areas and connecting pathways: inferior frontal cortex, superior temporal gyrus, superior temporal sulcus, supramarginal gyrus, insula, basal ganglia, thalamus, and cerebellum. Problems with repetitive and stereotyped behaviors (*blue*) have been related to dysfunction of a complex distributed neural network involving the following areas and connecting pathways: orbitofrontal cortex, posterior parietal cortex, supplementary motor cortex, cingulate gyrus, basal ganglia, thalamus, and cerebellum.

nication. This reconceptualization was heavily influenced by the notion that our "social brain" is in some ways uniquely adapted to mediate our ability to understand, communicate, and interact with one another (Adolphs, 2009; Brothers, 1997; Dunbar, 2009; Tomasello, 2008). AD is a model syndrome to understand the breakdown in the ontogeny of the social brain (Stefanatos & Baron, 2011).

Numerous studies suggest that deficits in gaze (Materna, Dicke, & Thier, 2008; Pelphrey et al., 2005) and face processing may be especially relevant to the social communication problems of children with AD (Hobson, Ouston, & Lee, 1988b; Lahaie et al., 2006; Schultz, 2005). Functional neuroimaging studies of face processing in older children and adults with AD have pointed to anomalies of amygdala and the FG, which has received wide attention for its seemingly special role in processing faces (Corbett et al., 2009a; Critchley et al., 2000; Schultz, 2005). However, these disturbances are interwoven with other early signs of difficulties related to social orienting and the allocation/disengagement of attention. Deficiencies of face processing in children and adults with AD include reduced attention to the eyes (Dalton et al., 2005; Spezio, Adolphs, Hurley, & Piven, 2007a; Sterling et al., 2008). This can have a significant impact on face processing because information in the eye region of the face provides critical cues for the recognition of the age, gender, identity, and expression of a face. As a consequence, direct eye gaze improves recognition of another individual (Itier & Batty,

2009) and modulates activation of neural structures comprising the social brain network (Senju & Johnson, 2009). In early infancy, however, looking preferences during face processing appear to be determined by subcortical components of this network (Johnson, Grossmann, & Farroni, 2008).

Whether anomalous activations of the FG disclose a potential causal link to the social impairments that characterize AD or merely reflect the lack of expertise that individuals with AD have in processing faces is unclear (Gauthier, Curran, Curby, & Collins, 2003). Accordingly, some have suggested that poor activation of the FG is secondary to primary impairments in social motivation (Dawson, Webb, & McPartland, 2005) or the allocation of visual attention, because normal patterns of activation occurred when participants were explicitly directed to fixate on the eye region (Hadjikhani et al., 2004; Hadjikhani et al., 2007) or when pictures of personally familiar individuals were presented (Pierce, Haist, Sedaghat, & Courchesne, 2004; Pierce & Redcay, 2008). It appears that evaluative and interpretive processes mediated by the amygdala (e.g., emotional significance, unfamiliarity) may determine the deployment of visual attention to stimuli and this, in turn, influences the likelihood of anomalous patterns of activation in the FG (Kim et al., 2010; Monk et al., 2010; Schultz, 2005). The amygdala also seems to be implicated in later-emerging problems of social interaction in AD, particularly in deficits in the development of empathy (Baron-Cohen, 2009).

The temporoparietal junction (TPJ) and STS also play a critical role in several aspects of social cognition (Lombardo, Chakrabarti, Bullmore, & Baron-Cohen, 2011; Zilbovicius et al., 2006). These areas are involved in the attribution of intentions to others (Vollm et al., 2006) and the perception of complex biological motion (Pelphrey & Carter, 2008). Involvement of the STS in processing biologically based motion (Castelli, Happé, Frith, & Frith, 2000; Freitag et al., 2008) may relate to its broader participation in the perception of action and the analysis of gesture. This area often fails to show normal patterns of activation during performance of tasks in which individuals with AD must process and interpret the significance of biological motion, such as emotional significance as conveyed by gestures and facial expressions (Grezes, Wicker, Berthoz, & de Gelder, 2009; Hirai & Hiraki, 2005; Klin & Jones, 2008; Klin et al., 2009; Pelphrey, Morris, McCarthy, & Labar, 2007). The STS and TPJ are also implicated in the development of TOM and empathy, along with precuneus and mPFC (Dodell-Feder, Koster-Hale, Bedny, & Saxe, 2011). Both the mPFC and precuneus may be involved in detecting and allocating attention to communicative signals such as mutual gaze (Hoehl et al., 2009), while the precuneus seems to play a role in shifting attention between people, locations, or different points in time (Whitney, Huber, Klann, Weis, Krach, & Kircher, 2009). Both the STS and mPFC fail to demonstrate typical patterns of activation in individuals with AD during tasks requiring mentalizing and TOM (Kana, Keller, Cherkassky, Minshew, & Just, 2009; Schulte-Ruther et al., 2010; Williams et al., 2006b). These areas overlap with regions implicated in human mirror neuron systems (STS/TPJ, ventral prefrontal cortex), and it has been suggested that dysfunctional mirror neuron systems may contribute to the problems with TOM and empathy as well as some other social deficits experienced by individuals with AD (Dapretto et al., 2006; Greimel et al., 2010). However, a very recent study has suggested differential involvement of brain areas involved in mirroring and mentalizing functions in AD (Marsh & Hamilton, 2011).

Neural Networks for Communication

Neural networks mediating communication overlap substantially with those implicated in social impairment. This is perhaps not surprising, given the interdependency of these abilities in the course of human evolution (discussed in Stefanatos & Baron, 2011). Conceptualizations of the neurophysiological mechanisms that mediate different aspects of linguistic function have undergone substantial revision in recent years. Neural networks mediating language are conceptualized as multiple overlapping large-scale networks comprised of collections of specialized areas or processing nodes with complex patterns of inter-connectivity via extensive white fiber tracts (Hickok & Poeppel, 2007). A dorsal network is involved in mapping sound to articulation. This pathway originates in the caudal portion of the superior temporal cortex (Wernicke's area) concerned with the auditory analysis of speech. Fibers from this area form the arcuate fasciculus and blend with the fibers of the superior longitudinal fasciculus as they course anteriorly to connect with Broca's region in the frontal lobe (BA 44 and 45), and to adjacent premotor areas (BA 6) and dorsolateral prefrontal cortex involved in executive function (BA 9/46). A ventral language processing stream is involved in mapping sound to meaning. This pathway originates in superior, middle, and inferior temporal areas (BA 22, 41, 42) and connects with the frontal lobe (BA 45, 47, and to some extent 44; Petrides, Tomaiuolo, Yeterian, & Pandya, 2012; Weiller, Bormann, Saur, Musso, & Rijntjes, 2011) via a band of fibers known as the extreme capsule. This processing pathway mediates considerable interaction between the temporal and frontal cortex in the processing of verbal information. It appears to be involved in the strategic retrieval and selection of information from verbal memory and the mental lexicon as well as in semantic processing of conceptual information.

Both of these processing streams may be affected in AD. Functional neuroimaging studies have revealed that individuals with AD fail to demonstrate the expected activation of the STS that normally occurs during voice recognition, while having normal activation and response to nonvocal sounds (Gervais et al., 2004). Several evoked-potentials studies have indicated that problems may not be specific to language but may affect the processing of temporally and spectrally complex aspects of both speech and nonspeech sounds (Ceponiene et al., 2003; Kuhl, Coffey-Corina, Padden, & Dawson, 2005; Samson, Mottron, Jemel, Belin, & Ciocca, 2006). The STS appears to play a broader role in analyzing changing sequences of input, whether auditory or visual, and interpreting the significance of those inputs for social communication (Redcay, 2008). Both the STS and supra-marginal gyrus (SMG) demonstrate atypical activation patterns in AD during performance of prosody perception (Hesling et al., 2010) and sentence comprehension. Sentence processing in AD has further revealed anomalous activation in the inferior temporal gyrus (left and right; Groen et al., 2010b), STG (Just, Cherkassky, Keller, & Minshew, 2004; Pierce, 2010), posterior insula (Anderson et al., 2010), SMG (Hesling et al., 2010), and IFG (Tesink et al., 2011).

Like social perception, the processing of speech entails the efficient and rapid transmission of information between components of a highly distributed neural network (Just et al., 2004; Stefanatos & Baron, 2011). As a consequence, language function may be highly susceptible to disturbances of connectivity that have been identified in recent imaging studies of white matter tracts. Recent findings suggest increased short-range functional connectivity and decreased long-range functional connectivity in AD. Examining the microstructure of white matter in postmortem human brain tissue of individuals with AD, Zikopoulos and Barbas (2010) reported considerable regional variations in these findings. White matter in the region of the anterior cingulate gyrus was distinguished by large numbers of thin axons connecting the neighboring cortex but decreased numbers of large axons that provide connectivity over long distances. In the orbital frontal cortex, axons had decreased myelin thickness whereas the lateral prefrontal cortex appeared relatively unaffected.

Diffusion tensor imaging studies have observed white matter anomalies in the parieto-temporal junction segment of the arcuate fasciculus as well as the extreme capsule (Radua et al., 2010). In addition, differences have been observed in the uncinate fasciculus, which connects limbic structures such as the hippocampus and amygdala to frontal orbital areas (Fletcher et al., 2010; Groen, Buitelaar, van der Gaag, & Zwiers, 2010a; Weinstein et al., 2011). It has been suggested that these disturbances may constrain integrative processes because of limited bandwidth for transmitting necessary information between frontal and posterior cortical areas as well as components of the limbic system (Schipul, Keller, & Just, 2011).

Interhemispheric pathways such as the corpus callosum are also affected (Kumar et al., 2009). Indeed, anomalies of the corpus callosum are one of the most consistent structural neuroimaging findings in AD and may possibly be related to disturbances in minicolumn formation (Casanova et al., 2009). A recent neuroimaging study has suggested that language laterality may be atypical in individuals with AD (Knaus et al., 2010), supporting and further refining results from a neuropsychological study conducted nearly 30 years ago (Dawson, 1983). As can be appreciated by visually comparing Figures 6.1a and 6.1b , there is considerable colocalization of the cortical areas that have been implicated as underlying problems in social behavior and communication.

Neural Networks for Flexible Behavior

One of the more long-standing neuropsychological theories of autism proposes that key aspects of the disorder are based in disturbances of executive function. Damasio and Maurer

(1978) likened certain symptoms of AD to those of frontal patients, specifically the characteristic disturbances of motility, communication, and attention and the presence of repetitive, stereotyped behaviors; cognitive inflexibility; and restricted range of interests. The theory holds that these behaviors can be understood in terms of dysfunction of fronto–striatal and fronto–parietal circuits that result in difficulties with higher-order cognitive functions, such as sustained attention, response inhibition and monitoring, cognitive flexibility, and generative capacity (Turner, 1999a; Turner, 1999b; Verte, Geurts, Roeyers, Oosterlaan, & Sergeant, 2005).

In recent years, impairments in restrictive interests and repetitive behavior have been incorporated into this conceptualization. In support of this approach, a recent study of high-functioning individuals with AD revealed reduced activation in frontal, striatal, and parietal regions during performance of a task that required shifting behavioral response sets (Shafritz et al., 2008). The severity of repetitive or restricted behaviors in the AD group was associated with decreased activation of the anterior cingulate and posterior parietal regions. Involvement of the cingulate cortex was also suggested by a study of response inhibition (Agam et al., 2010).

Summary

Overall, studies using functional neuroimaging in AD must be interpreted cautiously because they often provide a mixed and frequently difficult to interpret picture regarding anomalies of neurodevelopment in AD (Frith, 2003). Because functional studies require the active and ongoing cooperation of participants, they have mainly been conducted on older and high-functioning individuals with AD. In addition, many of these studies have serious methodological shortcomings, such as small sample sizes, sample heterogeneity, or lack of standardized diagnostic criteria. Nevertheless, with these caveats in mind and against the background of some support from clinical neuropsychological studies, they add heuristic value to a rapidly evolving conceptualization of the neural basis of AD. As it stands, functional neuroimaging studies provide a glimpse of brain function mainly in mildly affected individuals with AD who are at a point in their lives where genetic, epigenetic, and environmental factors have all exerted an influence on brain development. A major area for future expansion of the field, both from a neuropsychological and neuroimaging viewpoint, will be to understand factors influencing brain development in the first 2 years of life. Moving closer to this end, Redcay, Haist, and Courchesne (2008) have pioneered methods that yield activations to speech presented during sleep. In addition, event-related potentials studies and infrared neuroimaging techniques are becoming increasingly adept at modeling intracranial activity from sensors placed on the scalp in very young individuals.

CONTEMPORARY MODES OF TREATMENT

Historically, AD has posed remarkable challenges for the selection and implementation of treatment strategies. Children and adults with AD present with a great diversity of issues and, as a consequence, require involvement of a broad range of disciplines. Given the substantial heterogeneity of the behavioral phenotype, comprehensive treatment approaches must be individualized to incorporate the results of recent multidisciplinary evaluations. The success of behavioral treatment is optimized by early initiation of intensive intervention (Aman, 2005; Howlin, Magiati, & Charman, 2009; Ospina et al., 2008; Simpson, 2005). Parent training (Baharav & Reiser, 2010; Coolican, Smith, & Bryson, 2010) and parental implementation of therapeutic activities has become an increasingly critical component to many treatment approaches (Glascoe, 1999; Green et al., 2010; Ozonoff & Cathcart, 1998; Rinehart, Brereton, Tonge, & King, 2003; Sheinkopf & Siegel, 1998; Smith, Buch, & Gamby, 2000). Assessments of the efficacy of behavioral treatments in AD have often suffered from inconsistencies in methodology, flawed designs, and inadequate description. However, with growing emphasis on evidence-based practice, greater attention is being paid to assessing treatment efficacy in a more rigorous fashion.

One of the earliest and extensively used programs is Applied Behavioral Analysis (ABA; Lovaas, Schreibman, & Koegel, 1974). The approach is firmly based in the scientific principles of learning theory and provides a clearly defined and systematic approach to target undesirable behaviors for extinction using operant reinforcement techniques and replace them with more socially acceptable behaviors. In practice, therapy entails the highly systematic implementation of a three-step process whereby a stimulus is presented to the child, the child responds, and a consequence is administered based on the child's response (Jensen & Sinclair, 2002). Numerous trials of this type are administered in each session in a graded hierarchical fashion so that the level of difficulty is only increased once the child has demonstrated adequate performance. The therapy is therefore highly labor-intensive; intervention takes place in the home, school, and community, often for an average of 40 hours per week. Parents are also trained in therapy techniques for intervention so that the treatment regime continues outside the prescribed time blocks. The approach is designed as a two-phase process over 2–3 years. The first phase of therapy is intensive, one-on-one direct modeling and training for specific behaviors and communication. Children are explicitly taught communicative and social behaviors that would be naturally acquired by a typically developing child. The second phase works on the application of expressive and receptive language in educational and social settings (Lovaas, 1987). The ultimate goal of this approach is to allow a child to participate in a typical classroom setting and develop into an independent adult.

A meta-analysis of three controlled clinical trials suggested that ABA was superior to special education on numerous indices assessing communication, social interaction, daily living skills, and overall intellectual function (Ospina et al., 2008). After reviewing over 20 studies examining the effectiveness of ABA for AD, Eikeseth (2009) considered that six studies lacked scientific value. Based on the remaining studies, he concluded that the effectiveness of ABA was well established. A more recent meta-analysis again demonstrated a positive treatment outcome with ABA, reflected in medium to large treatment effects in the areas of intellectual functioning, language development, acquisition of daily living skills, and aspects of social functioning (Virues-Ortega, 2010). Gains in nonverbal IQ, daily living skills, and social functioning lagged behind outcomes in language-related areas and communication. A pronounced dose-dependent effect was apparent with better outcome with more hours of treatment (Virues-Ortega, 2010). One of the criticisms that have repeatedly been levied on this method of treatment is its rigidity and artificiality. Children may make gains in therapy that do not readily generalize to typical social situations and environments.

A contrasting method employs a more naturalistic treatment model. The TEACCH model developed by Schopler (1986) is exemplary of this approach. This intervention, which draws upon behavioral, environmental, and developmental theories, uses a child-centered approach to ABA therapy where opportunities for behavioral modification are incorporated into daily activities and play (Mesibov & Shea, 2010). This involves: (1) using physical structure and scheduling to make the learning environment understandable to the individual; (2) supplementing relative weaknesses in concepts of time, transition, and proprioception with strengths in visual detail; 3) employing an individual's interests and strengths to engage in opportunities for intervention; and 4) encouraging self-initiated communication (Mesibov & Shea, 2010). TEACCH is fundamentally a multi-disciplinary approach, requiring family involvement in addition to the work of speech-language pathologists, physical therapists, occupational therapists, and special education professionals. Evidence supporting the efficacy of the approach has been slow to appear. Early studies (Lord & Schopler, 1989) showed positive results but lacked adequate controls and specification of parameters. TEACCH was classified as a "promising practice" based on its apparent efficacy but somewhat limited empirical evidence (Ospina et al., 2008; Wieder & Greenspan, 2003). Scattered recent reports have shown positive results (Probst & Leppert, 2008), particularly relative to nonspecific special-education approaches (Panerai et al., 2009).

Pivotal response therapy (PRT), developed by Koegel and Koegel (Koegel, Koegel, Harrower, & Carter, 1999), applies a classical behavioral approach to family-based therapy that focuses on specific pivotal areas. Three central objectives of the PRT method are to increase the child's: (1) responsiveness to a variety of naturally occurring stimuli; (2) safety awareness, self-care, and independence; and (3) behavioral and education progress. Four specific pivotal behaviors that emphasize the development of executive functions are targeted for intervention. Self-reported results for PRT have shown improved initiation and expression in communication (Koegel, Koegel, Shoshan, & McNerney, 1999). One systematic review of the evidence base for PRT concluded that studies of PRT therapy have revealed sufficient reliability and validity of testing measures and efficacy of treatment (Ospina et al., 2008).

The Developmental, Individual-Difference, Relationship-Based model (DIR) developed by Wieder and Greenspan (2003) focuses on using play as a vehicle for building key cognitive functions, such as communication, complex thought, and a sense of self. During play, often referred to as "Floor Time," children learn to find meaning in social interaction by use of the salient features of communication, such as affect, tone of voice, and movement. A key aspect of the model requires that the therapist follow the child through play activities, continuously creating connection and communicating using affect cues. Continuous, back-and-forth communication provides the child with practice in fundamental communicative skills. There is evidence to support DIR therapy as an effective therapy in improving symbolic and emotional understanding and problem-solving skills (Wieder & Greenspan, 2003). One systematic review of the limited research on DIR therapy found little evidence to support the effectiveness of DIR therapy for aggression, self-stimulation behaviors, or social skills, but did not provide analysis for other aspects of ASD behavior (Ospina et al., 2008).

The Learning Experiences and Alternative Programs for Preschoolers and their Parents (LEAP) was developed by Strain and colleagues (Hoyson, Jamieson, & Strain, 1984). The LEAP method incorporates the principles of ABA in a social–developmental model for learning. The program encourages interaction and learning between children with AD and typically developing peers in a naturalistic therapy context that also requires intervention by both teachers and families across environments including home, school, and community. The classroom setting provides an opportunity to address individual goals within a broader context of skills such as group interaction and peer imitation (Erba, 2000). One systemic review of research methods judged LEAP research scientifically based on the merits of cognitive benefits to children with ASD (Simpson, 2005). An evaluation of efficacy claimed 50% of ASD children transitioned from a LEAP preschool classroom to a mainstream public school classroom successfully (Dawson & Osterling, 1997).

Studies examining interventions for children with AD younger than 2 years of age are largely restricted to case studies, descriptive reports, or quasi-experimental designs (Green, Brennan, & Fein, 2002; McGee, Morrier, & Daly, 1999; Wetherby & Woods, 2006). Several early intervention treatment approaches for children with PDD are available and are currently being evaluated in clinical trials. These include the Hanen More Than Words Program (Sussman, 1999), the Early Start Denver Model (Smith, Rogers, & Dawson, 2006), the Responsive Teaching approach (Mahoney, Perales, Wiggers, & Herman, 2006), the Social Communication, Emotional Regulation, and Transactional Support Model (Prizant, Wetherby, Rubin, Laurent, & Rydell, 2006) and the Early Achievements Model (Landa, 2008). At present, several of these programs are not widely available.

Summary

Each of these approaches can be said to have their own respective advantages and disadvantages. Lovaas's (1987) approach consists of intensive early intervention using discrete trial teaching. Although the method is considered reasonably effective in improving behavior and social skills within a structured environment of therapy, issues exist about generalization to other contexts. Pivotal response therapy focuses on teaching specific skills thought to increase overall behavior and social interaction. Although scientifically sound, strong evidence for efficacy can only be applied to improved cognitive functioning and not social interaction. TEACCH, DIR, and LEAP can be considered naturalistic treatment approaches where a structured learning environment is crucial to improving cognition and communication. These interventions use play and other structured or semi-structured activities to foster communication and complex thought, rather than the strictly controlled and incremental approach advocated by Lovaas and related therapies. This seems to make considerable sense given the dynamic nature of social interactions, but it provides less opportunity for repetition and practice than might be needed for some children. Direct comparisons of these methods are few and far between.

Several legitimate and important concerns have historically stemmed the flow of more thorough reliability and validity to support the efficacy of behavioral AD treatments and to directly compare treatments. Ethical issues and logistical concerns make it difficult and very expensive to construct highly reliable and valid evaluation studies. Overall, systematic reviews of the efficacy of these widely practiced models lament a distinct lack of reliable and valid evidence surrounding these practices (Bassett & Green, 2000; Ospina et al., 2008; Simpson, 2005).

The information presented earlier in this chapter outlining widespread perturbations of neural architecture and cognitive structure provides a compelling argument that early intervention holds an important key to unlocking the seeming intransigence of AD to substantial resolution using behavioral treatments. The increased emphasis on evidence-based treatment approaches has enhanced efforts to conduct randomized controlled clinical trials of various treatment approaches, and this has recently included various early intervention programs (Dawson et al., 2010; Karanth, Shaista, & Srikanth, 2010; Wong & Kwan, 2010). However, these efforts are in their early stages, so it is premature to make strong statements regarding the relative merits of each approach. It seems that as more is learned about differences between the manifestations of impairment early in life compared to those that emerge later, the more work will be required to refine and optimize early intervention approaches.

CONCLUSION

Although the *DSM-IV-TR* criteria represent an important consensus on how to identify AD, issues discussed in this review underscore and amplify a number of the shortcomings of the application of this type of schema to a condition such as AD. Firstly, the current criteria are based largely on observations of school-aged children with the disorder. The static nature of these criteria makes it difficult to accommodate for variations in the manifestations of the disorder that occur across the lifespan. In particular, the review of current knowledge regarding early manifestations of the disorder make very clear the point that these manifestations have a notably different nature and flavor from the problems that emerge in later childhood and adolescence. Schemas like the *DSM* need to accommodate methods to account for changes that occur over the lifespan.

Secondly, descriptive categorical nosological schemas such as the *DSM* sidestep several issues important for a complete explanatory framework of AD. This includes: (1) etiological factors, (2) brain structures and processes involved, (3) neuropsychological patterns of impairment, and (4) preserved functions or enhanced cognitive abilities. Consequently, there has been growing interest in recent years to move beyond the preoccupation with identifying cross-sectional differences between PDD subtypes and to develop a better understanding of the broader repertoire of symptoms or behaviors associated with AD, the neural networks involved, and the patterns of neuropsychological impairment that may link the underlying neuropathology with the behavioral manifestations of the disorder.

Fractionating behavior into component neuropsychological processes has proven remarkably productive in the study of other developmental disorders, and when applied to AD, this approach has the potential to reframe and integrate seemingly diverse symptoms that would otherwise appear unrelated. Furthermore, this approach can help elucidate the neural basis of autism and shed light on how deficits associated with faulty neural circuitry may be compounded by their influence on transactions with the social environment and experience. Emerging evidence suggests that analyses of neurocognitive profiles may be an effective approach to delineate phenotypic subgroups within the spectrum of AD, and this may facilitate the identification of genetic contributions to the disorder. It may be time to begin to incorporate this kind of information into formal diagnostic schemas.

The neuropsychological approach endeavors to understand the complex behavioral symptoms of AD in terms of alterations in the development of a number of fundamental neuropsychological processes and the neural architecture that supports the function of these processes. Implicit in this approach is recognition that the atypical development that characterizes AD cannot be adequately conceptualized simply in terms of the juxtaposition of intact and damaged sets of *modules* (Karmiloff-Smith, 1998). Rather, an explanation must incorporate an appreciation of the influence of complex dynamic interactions between neurobiological constraints and experience. Accordingly, anomalies of a given function early in development can have implications for neural networking and transactions with the environment that may prompt other, potentially more widespread, perturbations in cognitive structure or neural architecture. Although tremendous strides have been made in understanding the nature and some of the determinants of the disorder in the past 15 years, much more work needs to be done before a comprehensive understanding of this enigmatic condition can be reached. Lessons from recent studies suggest that a better understanding of its early evolution is critical to unlocking key features of the disorder.

ACKNOWLEDGMENTS

I would like to thank Laurie Sherman, Kate O'Connor, and Jillian Hendricks for their assistance in reviewing the literature, tracking down references, and editing previous drafts. Arianna Stefanatos proofread the manuscript and Alexandra Stefanatos and Jessica Weinstein created the tables and drawings. In addition, I am grateful to Temple University for their support during its preparation. Finally, I would like to thank Chad Noggle for his patience and forbearance.

REFERENCES

Abrahams, B. S., & Geschwind, D. H. (2008). Advances in autism genetics: On the threshold of a new neurobiology. *Nature Review Genetics*, *9*(5), 341–355.

Adolphs, R. (2009). The social brain: Neural basis of social knowledge. *Annual Review of Psychology*, *60*, 693–716.

Adolphs, R. (2010). What does the amygdala contribute to social cognition? *Annals of the New York Academy of Sciences*, *1191*, 42–61.

Adolphs, R., Baron-Cohen, S., & Tranel, D. (2002). Impaired recognition of social emotions following amygdala damage. *Journal of Cognitive Neuroscience*, *14*(8), 1264–1274.

Adrien, J., Perrot, A., Hameury, L., Martineau, J., & et al . (1991). Family home movies: Identification of early autistic signs in infants later diagnosed as autistics. *Brain Dysfunction*, *4*(6), 355–362.

Adrien, J. L., Perrot, A., Sauvage, D., Leddet, I., Larmande, C., Hameury, L., et al. (1992). Early symptoms in autism from family home movies. Evaluation and comparison between 1st and 2nd year of life using I.B.S.E. scale. *Acta Paedopsychiatrica*, *55*(2), 71–75.

Agam, Y., Joseph, R. M., Barton, J. J., & Manoach, D. S. (2010). Reduced cognitive control of response inhibition by the anterior cingulate cortex in autism spectrum disorders. *Neuroimage*, *52*(1), 336–347.

Akshoomoff, N., Farid, N., Courchesne, E., & Haas, R. (2007). Abnormalities on the neurological examination and EEG in young children with pervasive developmental disorders. *Journal of Autism and Developmental Disorders*, *37*(5), 887–893.

Allen, D., & Rapin, I. (1992). Autistic children are also dysphasic. In H. Naruse & E. M. Ornitz (Eds.), *Neurobiology of infantile autism.* (pp 72–80). Amsterdam, The Netherlands: Excerpta Medica.

Allen, D. A. (1988). Autistic spectrum disorders: Clinical presentation in preschool children. *Journal of Child Neurology*, *3*(Suppl), S48–S56.

Allen, G., Muller, R. A., & Courchesne, E. (2004). Cerebellar function in autism: Functional magnetic resonance image activation during a simple motor task. *Biological Psychiatry*, *56*(4), 269–278.

Aman, M. G. (2005). Treatment planning for patients with autism spectrum disorders. *Journal of Clinical Psychiatry*, *66*(Suppl 10), 38–45.

Aman, M. G., Farmer, C. A., Hollway, J., & Arnold, L. E. (2008). Treatment of inattention, overactivity, and impulsiveness in autism spectrum disorders. *Child and Adolescent Psychiatric Clinics of North America*, *17*(4), 713–738.

Amaral, D. G., Bauman, M. D., & Schumann, C. M. (2003). The amygdala and autism: Implications from non-human primate studies. *Genes Brain and Behavior*, *2*(5), 295–302.

Amaral, D. G., Schumann, C. M., & Nordahl, C. W. (2008). Neuroanatomy of autism. *Trends in Neuroscience, 31*(3), 137–145.

American Psychiatric Association. (1980). *Diagnostic and statistical manual of mental disorders* (3rd Edition). Washington, D.C.

American Psychiatric Association. (1987). *Diagnostic and statistical manual of mental disorders* (3rd Edition-Revised). Washington, D.C.

American Psychiatric Association. (1994). *Diagnostic and statistical manual of mental disorders* (4th Edition). Washington, D.C.

American Psychiatric Association. (2000). *Diagnostic and statistical manual of mental disorders* (4th Edition-Text Revision). Washington, D.C.

Anderson, B. M., Schnetz-Boutaud, N. C., Bartlett, J., Wotawa, A. M., Wright, H. H., Abramson, R. K., et al. (2009). Examination of association of genes in the serotonin system to autism. *Neurogenetics, 10*(3), 209–216.

Anderson, C. J., & Colombo, J. (2009). Larger tonic pupil size in young children with autism spectrum disorder. *Developmental Psychobiology, 51*(2), 207–211.

Anderson, J. S., Lange, N., Froehlich, A., DuBray, M. B., Druzgal, T. J., Froimowitz, M. P., et al. (2010). Decreased left posterior insular activity during auditory language in autism. *American Journal of Neuroradiology, 31*(1), 131–139.

Ashwood, P., Krakowiak, P., Hertz-Picciotto, I., Hansen, R., Pessah, I., & Van de Water, J. (2010). Elevated plasma cytokines in autism spectrum disorders provide evidence of immune dysfunction and are associated with impaired behavioral outcome. *Brain, Behavior, and Immunity, 25*(1), 40–45.

Ashwood, P., Wills, S., & Van de Water, J. (2006). The immune response in autism: A new frontier for autism research. *Journal of Leukocyte Biology, 80*(1), 1–15.

Asperger, H. (1938). Das psychisch abnormale Kind. *Wiener Klinische Wochenschrift, 51*, 1314–1317 .

Aston-Jones, G., Rajkowski, J., & Cohen, J. (2000). Locus coeruleus and regulation of behavioral flexibility and attention. *Progress in Brain Research, 126*, 165–182.

Atkinson, A. P. (2009). Impaired recognition of emotions from body movements is associated with elevated motion coherence thresholds in autism spectrum disorders. *Neuropsychologia, 47*(13), 3023–3029.

Aylward, E. H., Minshew, N. J., Field, K., Sparks, B. F., & Singh, N. (2002). Effects of age on brain volume and head circumference in autism. *Neurology, 59*(2), 175–183.

Baguley, D. M. (2003). Hyperacusis. *Journal of the Royal Society of Medicine, 96*(12), 582–585.

Baharav, E., & Reiser, C. (2010). Using telepractice in parent training in early autism. *Telemedicine Journal and E-Health, 16*(6), 727–731.

Bailey, A., Le Couteur, A., Gottesman, I., & Bolton, P. (1995). Autism as a strongly genetic disorder: Evidence from a British twin study. *Psychological Medicine, 25*(1), 63–77.

Bailey, A., Luthert, P., Dean, A., Harding, B., Janota, I., Montgomery, M., et al. (1998). A clinicopathological study of autism. *Brain, 121*, 889–905.

Bailey, D. B., Hatton, D. D., Skinner, M., & Mesibov, G. (2001). Autistic behavior, FMR1 protein, and developmental trajectories in young males with fragile X syndrome. *Journal of Autism and Developmental Disorders, 31*(2), 165–174.

Baird, G., Charman, T., Pickles, A., Chandler, S., Loucas, T., Meldrum, D., et al. (2008). Regression, developmental trajectory and associated problems in disorders in the autism spectrum: The SNAP study. *Journal of Autism and Developmental Disorders, 38*(10), 1827–1836.

Baker, L., Cantwell, D., Rutter, M., & Bartak, L. (1976). *Language and autism*. New York: Spectrum.

Baldwin, D. A. (1993). Early referential understanding: Infants' ability to recognize referential acts for what they are. *Developmental Psychology, 29*, 832–843.

Baranek, G. T. (1999). Autism during infancy: A retrospective video analysis of sensory-motor and social behaviors at 9–12 months of age. *Journal of Autism and Developmental Disorders, 29*(3), 213–224.

Baranek, G. T. (2002). Efficacy of sensory and motor interventions for children with autism. *Journal of Autism and Developmental Disorders, 32*(5), 397–422.

Barbaro, J., & Dissanayake, C. (2009). Autism spectrum disorders in infancy and toddlerhood: A review of the evidence on early signs, early identification tools, and early diagnosis. *Journal of Developmental and Behavioral Pediatrics, 30*(5), 447–459.

Barbaro, J., & Dissanayake, C. (2010a). Infancy and toddlerhood using developmental surveillance: The social attention and communication study. *Developmental Pediatrics, 31*(5), 376–385.

Barbaro, J., & Dissanayake, C. (2010b). Prospective identification of autism spectrum disorders in infancy and toddlerhood using developmental surveillance: The social attention and communication study. *Journal of Developmental and Behavioral Pediatrics, 31*(5), 376–385.

Bardi, L., Regolin, L., & Simion, F. (2011). Biological motion preference in humans at birth: Role of dynamic and configural properties. *Developmental Science, 14*(2), 353–359.

Baron-Cohen, S. (2001). Theory of mind and autism: A review. *International Review of Research in Mental Retardation, 23,* 169–184.

Baron-Cohen, S. (2009). Autism: The empathizing-systemizing (E-S) theory. *Annals of the New York Academy of Sciences, 1156,* 68–80.

Baron-Cohen, S., Baldwin, D. A., & Crowson, M. (1997). Do children with autism use the speaker's direction of gaze strategy to crack the code of language? *Child Development, 68*(1), 48–57.

Baron-Cohen, S., Golan, O., & Ashwin, E. (2009). Can emotion recognition be taught to children with autism spectrum conditions? *Philosophical Transactions of the Royal Society B-Biological Sciences, 364*(1535), 3567–3574.

Baron-Cohen, S., Wheelwright, S., Hill, J., Raste, Y., & Plumb, I. (2001). The "Reading the Mind in the Eyes" Test revised version: A study with normal adults, and adults with Asperger syndrome or high-functioning autism. *Journal of Child Psychology and Psychiatry, 42*(2), 241–251.

Bartak, L., & Rutter, M. (1976). Differences between mentally retarded and normal intelligence autistic children. *Journal of Autism and Childhood Schizophrenia, 6*(2), 109–120.

Bartak, L., Rutter, M., & Cox, A. (1975). A comparative study of infantile autism and specific developmental receptive language disorder: I. The children. *British Journal of Psychiatry, 126,* 127–145.

Bartolucci, G. (1982). Formal aspects of language in childhood autism. *Advances in Child Behavioral Analysis & Therapy, 2,* 159–185.

Bartolucci, G., Pierce, S., Streiner, D., & Eppel, P. (1976). Phonological investigation of verbal autistic and mentally retarded subjects. *Journal of Autism & Childhood Schizophrenia, 6,* 303–316.

Bartolucci, G., Pierce, S. J., & Streiner, D. (1980). Cross-sectional studies of grammatical morphemes in autistic and mentally retarded children. *Journal of Autism and Developmental Disorders, 10*(1), 39–50.

Barton, J. J., Hefter, R. L., Cherkasova, M. V., & Manoach, D. S. (2007). Investigations of face expertise in the social developmental disorders. *Neurology, 69*(9), 860–870.

Barton, M., & Volkmar, F. (1998). How commonly are known medical conditions associated with autism? *Journal of Autism and Developmental Disorders, 28*(4), 273–278.

Bassett, K., & Green, C. J. (2000). *Autism and Lovaas treatment: A systematic review of effectiveness evidence.* Vancouver, B.C.: University of British Columbia.

Bates, E. (1999). Language and the infant brain. *Journal of Communication Disorders, 32*(4), 195–205.

Bauman, M. L. (2010). Medical comorbidities in autism: Challenges to diagnosis and treatment. *Neurotherapeutics, 7*(3), 320–327.

Bauman, M. L., & Kemper, T. L. (1985). Histoanatomic observations of the brain in early infantile autism. *Neurology, 35,* 866–874.

Bauman, M. L., & Kemper, T. L. (2005). Neuroanatomic observations of the brain in autism: A review and future directions. *International Journal of Developmental Neuroscience, 23*(2–3), 183–187.

Beevers, C. G., Ellis, A. J., Wells, T. T., & McGeary, J. E. (2009a). Serotonin transporter gene promoter region polymorphism and selective processing of emotional images. *Biological Psychology, 83*(3), 260–265.

Beevers, C. G., Pacheco, J., Clasen, P., McGeary, J. E., & Schnyer, D. (2009b). Prefrontal morphology, 5-HTTLPR polymorphism and biased attention for emotional stimuli. *Genes, Brain and Behavior, 9*(2), 224–233.

Ben Shalom, D. (2003). Memory in autism: Review and synthesis. *Cortex, 39*(4–5), 1129–1138.

Bennetto, L., Pennington, B. F., & Rogers, S. J. (1996). Intact and impaired memory functions in autism. *Child Development, 67*(4), 1816–1835.

Bernabei, P., Cerquiglini, A., Cortesi, F., & D'Ardia, C. (2007). Regression versus no regression in the autistic disorder: Developmental trajectories. *Journal of Autism and Developmental Disorders, 37*(3), 580–588.

Betancur, C. (2010). Etiological heterogeneity in autism spectrum disorders: More than 100 genetic and genomic disorders and still counting. *Brain Research Bulletin, 1380,* 42–77.

Birmaher, B., Quintana, H., & Greenhill, L. L. (1988). Methylphenidate treatment of hyperactive autistic children. *Journal of the American Academy of Child & Adolescent Psychiatry, 27*(2), 248–251.

Bishop, D. V., Maybery, M., Wong, D., Maley, A., & Hallmayer, J. (2006). Characteristics of the broader phenotype in autism: A study of siblings using the children's communication checklist-2. *American Journal of Medical Genetics Part B: Neuropsychiatric Genetics, 141B*(2), 117–122.

Bishop, S. L., Richler, J., & Lord, C. (2006). Association between restricted and repetitive behaviors and nonverbal IQ in children with autism spectrum disorders. *Child Neuropsychology, 12*(4–5), 247–267.

Black, L., & Stefanatos, G. A. (2000). Neuropsychological assessment of developmental and learning disorders. In S. I. Greenspan & S. Weider (Eds.), *Interdisciplinary Council on Developmental and Learning Disorders: Clinical Practice Guidelines* (pp. 425–488). Bethesda, MD: ICDL Press.

Bleuler, E. (1911). *Dementia Praecox or the Group of Schizophrenias* (J. Zinkin, Trans.). New York: International University Press.

Bodfish, J. W., Symons, F. J., Parker, D. E., & Lewis, M. H. (2000). Varieties of repetitive behavior in autism: Comparisons to mental retardation. *Journal of Autism and Developmental Disorders, 30*(3), 237–243.

Bogdashina, O. (2003) *Sensory perceptual issues in autism: Different sensory experiences – different perceptual worlds*. London: Jessica Kingsley.

Bolduc, M. E., Du Plessis, A. J., Sullivan, N., Khwaja, O. S., Zhang, X., Barnes, K., et al. (2011). Spectrum of neurodevelopmental disabilities in children with cerebellar malformations. *Developmental Medicine and Child Neurology, 53*(5), 409–416.

Bolton, P., Macdonald, H., Pickles, A., Rios, P., Goode, S., Crowson, M., et al. (1994). A case-control family history study of autism. *Journal of Child Psychology and Psychiatry and Allied Disciplines, 35*(5), 877–900.

Bolton, P. F., Roobol, M., Allsopp, L., & Pickles, A. (2001). Association between idiopathic infantile macrocephaly and autism spectrum disorders. *Lancet, 358*(9283), 726–727.

Bonneh, Y. S., Levanon, Y., Dean-Pardo, O., Lossos, L., & Adini, Y. (2011). Abnormal speech spectrum and increased pitch variability in young autistic children. *Frontiers in Human Neuroscience, 4*, 237.

Bonnel, A., Mottron, L., Peretz, I., Trudel, M., Gallun, E., & Bonnel, A. M. (2003). Enhanced pitch sensitivity in individuals with autism: A signal detection analysis. *Journal of Cognitive Neuroscience, 15*(2), 226–235.

Bopp, K. D., & Mirenda, P. (2010). Prelinguistic predictors of language development in children with autism spectrum disorders over four–five years. *Journal of Child Language, 1–19*.

Boraston, Z., Blakemore, S. J., Chilvers, R., & Skuse, D. (2007). Impaired sadness recognition is linked to social interaction deficit in autism. *Neuropsychologia, 45*(7), 1501–1510.

Bornstein, M. H., & Arteberry, M. E. (2003). Recognition, discrimination and categorization of smiling by five-month-old infants. *Developmental Science, 6*, 585–599.

Borsuk, E. R., Watkins, M. W., & Canivez, G. L. (2006). Long-term stability of membership in a Weschler Intelligence Scale for Children–Third Edition (WISC-III) subtest core profile taxonomy. *Journal of Psychoeducational Assessment, 24*, 52–68.

Boucher, J. (1981). Memory for recent events in autistic children. *Journal of Autism and Developmental Disorders, 11*(3), 293–301.

Boucher, J. (2003). Language development in autism. *International Journal of Pediatric Otorhinolaryngology, 67*(Suppl 1), S159–S163.

Boucher, J., Lewis, V., & Collis, G. M. (2000). Voice processing abilities in children with autism, children with specific language impairments, and young typically developing children. *Journal of Child Psychology and Psychiatry, 41*(7), 847–857.

Boucher, J., & Warrington, E. K. (1976). Memory deficits in early infantile autism: Some similarities to the amnesic syndrome. *British Journal of Psychology, 67*(1), 73–87.

Brenner, L. A., Turner, K. C., & Muller, R. A. (2007). Eye movement and visual search: Are there elementary abnormalities in autism? *Journal of Autism and Developmental Disorders, 37*(7), 1289–1309.

Brian, J., Bryson, S. E., Garon, N., Roberts, W., Smith, I. M., Szatmari, P., et al. (2008). Clinical assessment of autism in high-risk 18-month-olds. *Autism, 12*(5), 433–456.

Brian, J. A., Tipper, S. P., Weaver, B., & Bryson, S. E. (2003). Inhibitory mechanisms in autism spectrum disorders: Typical selective inhibition of location versus facilitated perceptual processing. *Journal of Child Psychology and Psychiatry, 44*(4), 552–560.

Brock, J., Norbury, C., Einav, S., & Nation, K. (2008). Do individuals with autism process words in context? Evidence from language-mediated eye-movements. *Cognition, 108*(3), 896–904.

Brorson, J. R., Manzolillo, P. A., Gibbons, S. J., & Miller, R. J. (1995). AMPA receptor desensitization predicts the selective vulnerability of cerebellar Purkinje cells to excitotoxicity. *Journal of Neuroscience, 15*(6), 4515–4524.

Brothers, L. (1997). *Friday's footprint: How society shapes the human mind*. New York: Oxford University Press.

Brown, R., Hobson, R. P., Lee, A., & Stevenson, J. (1997). Are there "autistic-like" features in congenitally blind children? *Journal of Child Psychology and Psychiatry and Allied Disciplines, 38*(6), 693–703.

Brown, W. A., Cammuso, K., Sachs, H., Winklosky, B., Mullane, J., Bernier, R., et al. (2003). Autism-related language, personality, and cognition in people with absolute pitch: Results of a preliminary study. *Journal of Autism and Developmental Disorders, 33*(2), 163–167; discussion 169.

Brun, C. C., Nicolson, R., Lepore, N., Chou, Y. Y., Vidal, C. N., DeVito, T. J., et al. (2009). Mapping brain abnormalities in boys with autism. *Human Brain Mapping, 30*(12), 3887–3900.

Brune, C. W., Kim, S. J., Salt, J., Leventhal, B. L., Lord, C., & Cook, E. H. Jr. (2006). 5-HTTLPR genotype-specific phenotype in children and adolescents with autism. *American Journal of Psychiatry, 163*(12), 2148–2156.

Bryson, S. E., Clark, B. S., & Smith, I. M. (1988). First report of a Canadian epidemiological study of autistic syndromes. *Journal of Child Psychology and Psychiatry, 29*(4), 433–445.

Bryson, S. E., Wainwright-Sharp, J., & Smith, I. M. (1990). Autism: A developmental spatial neglect syndrome? In J. T. Enns (Ed.), *The Development of Attention: Research and Theory* (*Vol. 69*, pp. 405–427). New York: Elsevier.

Bryson, S. E., Zwaigenbaum, L., Brian, J., Roberts, W., Szatmari, P., Rombough, V., et al. (2007). A prospective case series of high-risk infants who developed autism. *Journal of Autism and Developmental Disorders, 37*(1), 12–24.

Bryson, S. E., Zwaigenbaum, L., McDermott, C., Rombough, V., & Brian, J. (2008). The autism observation scale for infants: Scale development and reliability data. *Journal of Autism and Developmental Disorders, 38*(4), 731–738.

Buitelaar, J. K., & Willemsen-Swinkels, S. H. (2000). Medication treatment in subjects with autistic spectrum disorders. *European Child and Adolescent Psychiatry, 9(Suppl* 1), I85–I97.

Burke, L. J. (1994). Pragmatic analysis of communicative behavior in three groups of mentally retarded adults. Ontario, Canada: York University.

Bushnell, I. W. R. (2001). Mothers face recognition in newborn infants: Learning and memory. *Infant and Child Development, 10*, 67–74.

Butterworth, R. F. (1993). Maternal thiamine-deficiency – A factor in intrauterine growth-retardation. *Annals of the New York Academy of Sciences, 678*, 325–329.

Capps, L., Losh, M., & Thurber, C. (2000). "The frog ate the bug and made his mouth sad: Narrative competence in children with autism. *Journal of Abnormal Child Psychology, 28*(2), 193–204.

Caron, M. J., Mottron, L., Berthiaume, C., & Dawson, M. (2006). Cognitive mechanisms, specificity and neural underpinnings of visuospatial peaks in autism. *Brain, 129*(Pt 7), 1789–1802.

Carper, R. A., Moses, P., Tigue, Z. D., & Courchesne, E. (2002). Cerebral lobes in autism: Early hyperplasia and abnormal age effects. *Neuroimage, 16*(4), 1038–1051.

Casanova, M. F. (2007). The neuropathology of autism. *Brain Pathology, 17*(4), 422–433.

Casanova, M. F., Buxhoeveden, D. P., & Brown, C. (2002). Clinical and macroscopic correlates of minicolumnar pathology in autism. *Journal of Child Neurology, 17*(9), 692–695.

Casanova, M. F., El-Baz, A., Mott, M., Mannheim, G., Hassan, H., Fahmi, R., et al. (2009). Reduced gyral window and corpus callosum size in autism: Possible macroscopic correlates of a minicolumnopathy. *Journal of Autism and Developmental Disorders, 39*(5), 751–764.

Casanova, M. F., van Kooten, I. A., Switala, A. E., van Engeland, H., Heinsen, H., Steinbusch, H. W., et al. (2006). Minicolumnar abnormalities in autism. *Acta Neuropathologica, 112*(3), 287–303.

Casey, B. J., Gordon, C. T., Mannheim, G. B., & Rumsey, J. M. (1993). Dysfunctional attention in autistic savants. *Journal of Clinical and Experimental Neuropsychology, 15*(6), 933–946.

Castelli, F., Happé, F., Frith, U., & Frith, C. (2000). Movement and mind: A functional imaging study of perception and interpretation of complex intentional movement patterns. *Neuroimage, 12*(3), 314–325.

Ceponiene, R., Lepisto, T., Shestakova, A., Vanhala, R., Alku, P., Naatanen, R., et al. (2003). Speech-sound-selective auditory impairment in children with autism: They can perceive but do not attend. *Proceedings of the National Academy of Sciences, 100*(9), 5567–5572.

Cervos-Navarro, J., & Diemer, N. H. (1991). Selective vulnerability in brain hypoxia. *Critical Reviews in Neurobiology, 6*(3), 149–182.

Chakrabarti, S., & Fombonne, E. (2005). Pervasive developmental disorders in preschool children: Confirmation of high prevalence. *The American Journal of Psychiatry, 162*(6), 1133–1141.

Chao, H. T., Chen, H., Samaco, R. C., Xue, M., Chahrour, M., Yoo, J., et al. (2010). Dysfunction in GABA signalling mediates autism-like stereotypies and Rett syndrome phenotypes. *Nature, 468*(7321), 263–269.

Charman, T. (2003). Why is joint attention a pivotal skill in autism? *Philosophical Transactions of the Royal Society Biological Sciences, 358*(1430), 315–324.

Charman, T. (2005). Why do individuals with autism lack the motivation or capacity to share intentions? *Behavioral & Brain Sciences, 28*(5), 695–696.

Charman, T., Baron-Cohen, S., Swettenham, J., Baird, G., Cox, A., & Drew, A. (2000). Testing joint attention, imitation, and play as infancy precursors to language and theory of mind. *Cognitive Development, 15*(4), 481–498.

Charman, T., Drew, A., Baird, C., & Baird, G. (2003). Measuring early language development in preschool children with autism spectrum disorder using the MacArthur Communicative Development Inventory (Infant Form). *Journal of Child Language, 30*(1), 213–236.

Charman, T., Jones, C. R., Pickles, A., Simonoff, E., Baird, G., & Happé, F. (2011a). Defining the cognitive phenotype of autism. *Brain Research, 1380*, 10–21.

Charman, T., Pickles, A., Simonoff, E., Chandler, S., Loucas, T., & Baird, G. (2011b). IQ in children with autism spectrum disorders: Data from the special needs and autism project (SNAP). *Psychologial Medicine, 41*, 619–627.

Charman, T., Taylor, E., Drew, A., Cockerill, H., Brown, J. A., & Baird, G. (2005). Outcome at 7 years of children diagnosed with autism at age 2: Predictive validity of assessments conducted at 2 and 3 years of age and pattern of symptom change over time. *Journal of Child Psychology and Psychiatry, 46*(5), 500–513.

Chawarska, K., Klin, A., Paul, R., Macari, S., & Volkmar, F. (2009). A prospective study of toddlers with ASD: Short-term diagnostic and cognitive outcomes. *Journal of Child Psychology and Psychiatry, 50*(10), 1235–1245.

Chiu, P. H., Kayali, M. A., Kishida, K. T., Tomlin, D., Klinger, L. G., Klinger, M. R., & Montague, P. R. (2008). Self responses along cingulate cortex reveal quantitative neural phenotype for high-functioning autism. *Neuron, 57*(3), 463–473.

Christ, S. E., Holt, D. D., White, D. A., & Green, L. (2007). Inhibitory control in children with autism spectrum disorder. *Journal of Autism and Developmental Disorders, 37*(6), 1155–1165.

Chugani, D. C. (2004). Serotonin in autism and pediatric epilepsies. *Mental Retardation and Developmental Disabilities Research Reviews, 10*(2), 112–116.

Ciesielski, K. T., Courchesne, E., & Elmasian, R. (1990). Effects of focused selective attention tasks on event-related potentials in autistic and normal individuals. *Electroencephalography and Clinical Neurophysiology, 75*(3), 207–220.

Ciesielski, K. T., Knight, J. E., Prince, R. J., Harris, R. J., & Handmaker, S. D. (1995). Event-related potentials in cross-modal divided attention in autism. *Neuropsychologia, 33*(2), 225–246.

Clifford, S., & Dissanayake, C. (2009). Dyadic and triadic behaviours in infancy as precursors to later social responsiveness in young children with autistic disorder. *Journal of Autism and Developmental Disorders, 39*(10), 1369–1380.

Clifford, S. M., & Dissanayake, C. (2008). The early development of joint attention in infants with autistic disorder using home video observations and parental interview. *Journal of Autism and Developmental Disorders, 38*(5), 791–805.

Clifford, S., Young, R., & Williamson, P. (2007). Assessing the early characteristics of autistic disorder using video analysis. *Journal of Autism and Developmental Disorders, 37*(2), 301–313.

Cohen, I. L., Schmidt-Lackner, S., Romanczyk, R., & Sudhalter, V. (2003). The PDD Behavior Inventory: A rating scale for assessing response to intervention in children with pervasive developmental disorder. *Journal of Autism and Developmental Disorders, 33*(1), 31–45.

Coleman, M., & Betancur, C. (2005). *The neurology of autism*. New York: Oxford University Press.

Collins, A. L., Ma, D., Whitehead, P. L., Martin, E. R., Wright, H. H., Abramson, R. K., et al. (2006). Investigation of autism and GABA receptor subunit genes in multiple ethnic groups. *Neurogenetics, 7*(3), 167–174.

Colombi, C., Liebal, K., Tomasello, M., Young, G., Warneken, F., & Rogers, S. J. (2009). Examining correlates of cooperation in autism: Imitation, joint attention, and understanding intentions. *Autism, 13*(2), 143–163.

Comi, A. M., Zimmerman, A. W., Frye, V. H., Law, P. A., & Peeden, J. N. (1999). Familial clustering of autoimmune disorders and evaluation of medical risk factors in autism. *Journal of Child Neurology, 14*(6), 388–394.

Condouris, K., Meyer, E., & Tager-Flusberg, H. (2003). The relationship between standardized measures of language and measures of spontaneous speech in children with autism. *American Journal of Speech-Language Pathology, 12*(3), 349–358.

Constantino, J. N., Davis, S. A., Todd, R. D., Schindler, M. K., Gross, M. M., Brophy, S. L., et al. (2003). Validation of a brief quantitative measure of autistic traits: Comparison of the social responsiveness scale with the autism diagnostic interview-revised. *Journal of Autism and Developmental Disorders, 33*(4), 427–433.

Constantino, J. N., Zhang, Y., Frazier, T., Abbacchi, A. M., & Law, P. (2010). Sibling recurrence and the genetic epidemiology of autism. *American Journal of Psychiatry, 167*(11), 1349–1356.

Coolican, J., Smith, I. M., & Bryson, S. E. (2010). Brief parent training in pivotal response treatment for preschoolers with autism. *Journal of Child Psychology and Psychiatry, 51*(12), 1321–1330.

Corbett, B. A., Carmean, V., Ravizza, S., Wendelken, C., Henry, M. L., Carter, C., et al. (2009a). A functional and structural study of emotion and face processing in children with autism. *Psychiatry Research, 173*(3), 196–205.

Corbett, B. A., Constantine, L. J., Hendren, R., Rocke, D., & Ozonoff, S. (2009b). Examining executive functioning in children with autism spectrum disorder, attention deficit hyperactivity disorder and typical development. *Psychiatry Research, 166*(2–3), 210–222.

Cortesi, F., Giannotti, F., Ivanenko, A., & Johnson, K. (2010). Sleep in children with autistic spectrum disorder. *Sleep Medicine, 11*(7), 659–664.

Courchesne, E., Campbell, K., & Solso, S. (2010). Brain growth across the life span in autism: Age-specific changes in anatomical pathology. *Brain Research, 1380*, 138–145.

Courchesne, E., Carper, R., & Akshoomoff, N. (2003). Evidence of brain overgrowth in the first year of life in autism. *Journal of the American Medical Association, 290*(3), 337–344.

Courchesne, E., Karns, C. M., Davis, H. R., Ziccardi, R., Carper, R. A., Tigue, Z. D., et al. (2001). Unusual brain growth patterns in early life in patients with autistic disorder – An MRI study. *Neurology, 57*(2), 245–254.

Courchesne, E., Mouton, P. R., Calhoun, M. E., Semendeferi, K., Ahrens-Barbeau, C., Hallet, M. J., et al. (2011). Neuron number and size in prefrontal cortex of children with autism. *Journal of the American Medical Association, 306*(18), 2001–2010.

Courchesne, E., Pierce, K., Schumann, C. M., Redcay, E., Buckwalter, J. A., Kennedy, D. P., et al. (2007). Mapping early brain development in autism. *Neuron, 56*(2), 399–413.

Courchesne, E., Townsend, J., Akshoomoff, N. A., Saitoh, O., Yeung-Courchesne, R., Lincoln, A. J., et al. (1994). Impairment in shifting attention in autistic and cerebellar patients. *Behavioral Neuroscience, 108*(5), 848–865.

Cox, A., Klein, K., Charman, T., Baird, G., Baron-Cohen, S., Swettenham, J., et al. (1999). Autism spectrum disorders at 20 and 42 months of age: Stability of clinical and ADI-R diagnosis. *Journal of Child Psychology and Psychiatry, 40*(5), 719–732.

Craighero, L., Leo, I., Ultima, C., & Simion, F. (2011). Newborns preference for goal oriented actions. *Cognition, 120*, 26–32.

Creak, E. M. (1963). Childhood psychosis: A review of 100 cases. *British Journal of Psychiatry, 109*, 84–89.

Critchley, H. D., Daly, E. M., Bullmore, E. T., Williams, S. C., Van Amelsvoort, T., Robertson, D. M., et al. (2000). The functional neuroanatomy of social behaviour: Changes in cerebral blood flow when people with autistic disorder process facial expressions. *Brain, 123*(Pt 11), 2203–2212.

Dahlgren, S. O., & Gillberg, C. (1989). Symptoms in the first two years of life: A preliminary population study of infantile autism. *European Archives of Psychiatry & Neurological Sciences, 238*(3), 169–174.

Dakin, S., & Frith, U. (2005). Vagaries of visual perception in autism. *Neuron, 48*(3), 497–507.

Dalton, K. M., Nacewicz, B. M., Johnstone, T., Schaefer, H. S., Gernsbacher, M. A., Goldsmith, H. H., et al. (2005). Gaze fixation and the neural circuitry of face processing in autism. *Nature Neuroscience, 8*(4), 519–526.

Damasio, A. R., & Maurer, R. G. (1978). A neurological model for childhood autism. *Archives of Neurology, 35*(12), 777–786.

Dapretto, M., Davies, M. S., Pfeifer, J. H., Scott, A. A., Sigman, M., Bookheimer, S. Y., et al. (2006). Understanding emotions in others: Mirror neuron dysfunction in children with autism spectrum disorders. *Nature Neuroscience, 9*(1), 28–30.

Davidovitch, M., Glick, L., Holtzman, G., Tirosh, E., & Safir, M. P. (2000). Developmental regression in autism: Maternal perception. *Journal of Autism and Developmental Disorders, 30*(2), 113–119.

Dawson, G. (1983). Lateralized brain dysfunction in autism: Evidence from the Halstead-Reitan neuropsychological battery. *Journal of Autism and Developmental Disorders, 13*(3), 269–286.

Dawson, G. (2008). Early behavioral intervention, brain plasticity, and the prevention of autism spectrum disorder. *Developmental Psychopathology, 20*(3), 775–803.

Dawson, G., & Bernier, R. (2007). Social brain circuitry in autism. In D. Coch, G. Dawson & K. Fischer (Eds.), *Human Behavior and the Developing Brain: Atypical Development* (*Vol. 2*). New York: Guilford Press.

Dawson, G., Finley, C., Phillips, S., & Lewy, A. (1989). A comparison of hemispheric asymmetries in speech-related brain potentials of autistic and dysphasic children. *Brain & Language, 37*(1), 26–41.

Dawson, G., & Lewy, A. (1989). Reciprocal subcortical-cortical influences in autism: The role of attentional mechanisms. In Dawson, G. (Ed) *Autism: Nature, diagnosis, and treatment* (pp. 144–173). New York: Guilford Press.

Dawson, G., Meltzoff, A. N., Osterling, J., Rinaldi, J., & Brown, E. (1998). Children with autism fail to orient to naturally occurring social stimuli. *Journal of Autism and Developmental Disorders, 28*(6), 479–485.

Dawson, G., & Osterling, J. (1997). Early intervention in autism: Effectiveness and common elements of current approaches. In M. J. Guralnick (Ed.), *The effectiveness of early intervention: Second generation research* (pp. 307–326). Baltimore: Brookes.

Dawson, G., Rogers, S., Munson, J., Smith, M., Winter, J., Greenson, J., et al. (2010). Randomized, controlled trial of an intervention for toddlers with autism: The Early Start Denver Model. *Pediatrics, 125*(1), e17–e23.

Dawson, G., Toth, K., Abbott, R., Osterling, J., Munson, J., Estes, A., et al. (2004). Early social attention impairments in autism: Social orienting, joint attention, and attention to distress. *Developmental Psychology, 40*(2), 271–283.

Dawson, G., Webb, S. J., & McPartland, J. (2005). Understanding the nature of face processing impairment in autism: Insights from behavioral and electrophysiological studies. *Developmental Neuropsychology, 27*(3), 403–424.

De Giacomo, A., & Fombonne, E. (1998). Parental recognition of developmental abnormalities in autism. *European Child & Adolescent Psychiatry, 7*(3), 131–136.

de Jong, M. C., van Engeland, H., & Kemner, C. (2008). Attentional effects of gaze shifts are influenced by emotion and spatial frequency, but not in autism. *Journal of the American Academy of Child and Adolescent Psychiatry, 47*(4), 443–454.

DeGangi, G. A., Breinbauer, C., Roosevelt, J. D., Porges, S., & Greenspan, S. (2000). Prediction of childhood problems at three years in children experiencing disorders of regulation during infancy. *Infant Mental Health Journal, 21*(3), 156–175.

DeVito, T. J., Drost, D. J., Neufeld, R. W., Rajakumar, N., Pavlosky, W., Williamson, P., et al. (2007). Evidence for cortical dysfunction in autism: A proton magnetic resonance spectroscopic imaging study. *Biological Psychiatry, 61*(4), 465–473.

Dichter, G. S., Lam, K. S., Turner-Brown, L. M., Holtzclaw, T. N., & Bodfish, J. W. (2009). Generativity abilities predict communication deficits but not repetitive behaviors in autism spectrum disorders. *Journal of Autism and Developmental Disorders, 39*(9), 1298–1304.

Diehl, J. J., Bennetto, L., & Young, E. C. (2006). Story recall and narrative coherence of high-functioning children with autism spectrum disorders. *Journal of Abnormal Child Psychology, 34*(1), 87–102.

Diehl, R. L. (2004). Speech perception. *Annual Review of Psychology, 55*, 149–179.

Dinstein, I., Thomas, C., Humphreys, K., Minshew, N., Behrmann, M., & Heeger, D. J. (2010). Normal movement selectivity in autism. *Neuron, 66*(3), 461–469.

Dodell-Feder, D., Koster-Hale, J., Bedny, M., & Saxe, R. (2011). fMRI item analysis in a theory of mind task. *Neuroimage, 55*(2), 705–712.

Dooley, A. E., Pappas, I. S., & Parnavelas, J. G. (1997). Serotonin promotes the survival of cortical glutamatergic neurons in vitro. *Experimental Neurology, 148*, 205–214.

Dunbar, R. I. (2009). The social brain hypothesis and its implications for social evolution. *Annals of Human Biology, 36*(5), 562–572.

Dziuk, M. A., Larson, J. C. G., Apostu, A., Mahone, E. M., Denckla, M. B., & Mostofsky, S. H. (2007). Dyspraxia in autism: Association with motor, social, and communicative deficits. *Developmental Medicine and Child Neurology, 49*(10), 734–739.

Eales, M. J. (1993). Pragmatic impairments in adults with childhood diagnoses of autism or developmental receptive language disorder. *Journal of Autism and Developmental Disorders, 23*(4), 593–617.

Ecklund-Flores, L., & Turkewitz, G. (1996). Asymmetric headturning to speech and nonspeech in human newborns. *Developmental Psychobiology, 29*(3), 205–217.

Ehlers, S., Gillberg, C., & Wing, L. (1999). A screening questionnaire for Asperger syndrome and other high-functioning autism spectrum disorders in school age children. *Journal of Autism and Developmental Disorders, 29*(2), 129–141.

Eigsti, I. M., & Bennetto, L. (2009). Grammaticality judgments in autism: Deviance or delay. *Journal of Child Language, 36*(5), 999–1021.

Eigsti, I. M., Bennetto, L., & Dadlani, M. B. (2007). Beyond pragmatics: Morphosyntactic development in autism. *Journal of Autism and Developmental Disorders, 37*(6), 1007–1023.

Eikeseth, S. (2009). Outcome of comprehensive psycho-educational interventions for young children with autism. *Research in Developmental Disabilities, 30*(1), 158–178.

Ellis Weismer, S., Lord, C., & Esler, A. (2010). Early language patterns of toddlers on the autism spectrum compared to toddlers with developmental delay. *Journal of Autism and Developmental Disorders, 40*(10), 1259–1273.

Elsabbagh, M., Volein, A., Holmboe, K., Tucker, L., Csibra, G., Baron-Cohen, S., et al. (2009). Visual orienting in the early broader autism phenotype: Disengagement and facilitation. *Journal of Child Psychology and Psychiatry, 50*(5), 637–642.

Endo, T., Kitamura, H., Tamura, R., Egawa, J., Sugai, T., Fukui, N., et al. (2010). 5-HTTLPR polymorphism influences prefrontal neurochemical metabolites in autism spectrum disorder. *Psychiatry Research, 183*(2), 170–173.

Endo, T., Shioiri, T., Kitamura, H., Kimura, T., Endo, S., Masuzawa, N., et al. (2007). Altered chemical metabolites in the amygdala-hippocampus region contribute to autistic symptoms of autism spectrum disorders. *Biological Psychiatry, 62*(9), 1030–1037.

Erba, H. W. (2000). Early intervention programs for children with autism: Conceptual frameworks for implementation. *American Journal of Orthopsychiatry, 70*(1), 82–94.

Ernst, M., Zametkin, A. J., Matochik, J. A., Pascualvaca, D., & Cohen, R. M. (1997). Low medial prefrontal dopaminergic activity in autistic children. *Lancet, 350*(9078), 638.

Esposito, G., Venuti, P., Maestro, S., & Muratori, F. (2009). An exploration of symmetry in early autism spectrum disorders: Analysis of lying. *Brain and Development, 31*(2), 131–138.

Falck-Ytter, T., Fernell, E., Gillberg, C., & von Hofsten, C. (2010). Face scanning distinguishes social from communication impairments in autism. *Developmental Science, 13*(6), 864–875.

Farah, M. J., Rabinowitz, C., Quinn, G. E., & Liu, G. T. (2000). Early commitment of neural substrates for face recognition. *Cognitive Neuropsychology, 17*(1), 117–123.

Farroni, T., Johnson, M. H., & Csibra, G. (2004). Mechanisms of eye gaze perception during infancy. *Journal of Cognitive Neuroscience, 16*(8), 1320–1326.

Farroni, T., Menon, E., Rigato, S., & Johnson, M. H. (2007). The perception of facial expressions in newborns. *European Journal of Developmental Psychology, 4*(1), 2–13.

Fatemi, S. H., Halt, A. R., Realmuto, G., Earle, J., Kist, D. A., Thuras, P., et al. (2002). Purkinje cell size is reduced in cerebellum of patients with autism. *Cellular and Molecular Neurobiology, 22*(2), 171–175.

Fatemi, S. H., Pearce, D. A., Brooks, A. I., & Sidwell, R. W. (2005). Prenatal viral infection in mouse causes differential expression of genes in brains of mouse progeny: A potential animal model for schizophrenia and autism. *Synapse, 57*(2), 91–99.

Fay, W. H. (1973). On the echolalia of the blind and of the autistic child. *Journal of Speech and Hearing Disorders, 38*(4), 478–489.

Fein, D., Stevens, M., Dunn, M., Waterhouse, L., Allen, D., Rapin, I., et al. (1999). Subtypes of pervasive developmental disorder: Clinical characteristics. *Child Neuropsychology, 5*(1), 1–23.

Feldman, M. A., Ward, R. A., Savona, D., Regehr, K., Parker, K., Hudson, M., et al. (2012). Development and initial validation of a parent report measure of the behavioral development of infants at risk for autism spectrum disorders. *Journal of Autism and Developmental Disorders, 42*, 13–22

Fidler, D. J., Bailey, J. N., & Smalley, S. L. (2000). Macrocephaly in autism and other pervasive developmental disorders. *Developmental Medicine and Child Neurology, 42*(11), 737–740.

Fifer, W. P., & Moon, C. (2003). Prenatal development. In A. Slater & G. Bremner (Eds.), *An Introduction to Developmental Psychology* (pp. 95–114). Oxford: Blackwell.

Filipek, P. A., Accardo, P. J., Ashwal, S., Baranek, G. T., Cook, E. H. Jr., Dawson, G., et al. (2000). Practice parameter: screening and diagnosis of autism: Report of the Quality Standards Subcommittee of the American Academy of Neurology and the Child Neurology Society. *Neurology, 55*(4), 468–479.

Fletcher, P. T., Whitaker, R. T., Tao, R., DuBray, M. B., Froehlich, A., Ravichandran, C., et al. (2010). Microstructural connectivity of the arcuate fasciculus in adolescents with high-functioning autism. *Neuroimage, 51*(3), 1117–1125.

Folstein, S., & Rutter, M. (1977). Infantile autism: A genetic study of 21 twin pairs. *Journal of Child Psychology & Psychiatry & Allied Disciplines, 18*(4), 297–321.

Folstein, S. E., & Rosen-Sheidley, B. (2001). Genetics of autism: Complex aetiology for a heterogeneous disorder. *Nature Reviews Genetics, 2*(12), 943–955.

Fombonne, E. (2009). Epidemiology of pervasive developmental disorders. *Pediatric Research, 65*(6), 591–598.

Fombonne, E., & Chakrabarti, S. (2001). No evidence for a new variant of measles-mumps-rubella-induced autism. *Pediatrics, 108*(4), E58.

Fournier, K. A., Hass, C. J., Naik, S. K., Lodha, N., & Cauraugh, J. H. (2010). Motor coordination in autism spectrum disorders: A synthesis and meta-analysis. *Journal of Autism and Developmental Disorders, 40*(10), 1227–1240.

Freitag, C. M., Konrad, C., Haberlen, M., Kleser, C., von Gontard, A., Reith, W., et al. (2008). Perception of biological motion in autism spectrum disorders. *Neuropsychologia, 46*(5), 1480–1494.

Freitag, C. M., Luders, E., Hulst, H. E., Narr, K. L., Thompson, P. M., Toga, A. W., et al. (2009a). Total brain volume and corpus callosum size in medication-naive adolescents and young adults with autism spectrum disorder. *Biological Psychiatry, 66*(4), 316–319.

Freitag, C. M., Staal, W., Klauck, S. M., Duketis, E., & Waltes, R. (2009b). Genetics of autistic disorders: Review and clinical implications. *European Journal of Child and Adolescent Psychiatry, 19*(3), 169–178.

Frith, C. D. (2003). What do imaging studies tell us about the neural basis of autism? *Novartis Found Symp, 251*, 149–166; discussion 166–176, 281–197.

Frith, U. (2001). Mind blindness and the brain in autism. *Neuron, 32*(6), 969–979.

Frith, U., & Happé, F. (1994). Autism: Beyond "theory of mind." *Cognition, 50*(1–3), 115–132.

Gaigg, S. B., Gardiner, J. M., & Bowler, D. M. (2008). Free recall in autism spectrum disorder: The role of relational and item-specific encoding. *Neuropsychologia, 46*(4), 983–992.

Garon, N., Bryson, S. E., Zwaigenbaum, L., Smith, I. M., Brian, J., Roberts, W., et al. (2009). Temperament and its relationship to autistic symptoms in a high-risk infant sib cohort. *Journal of Abnormal Child Psychology, 37*(1), 59–78.

Garretson, H. B., Fein, D., & Waterhouse, L. (1990). Sustained attention in children with autism. *Journal of Autism & Developmental Disorders, 20*(1), 101–114.

Gauthier, I., Curran, T., Curby, K. M., & Collins, D. (2003). Perceptual interference supports a non-modular account of face processing. *Nature Neuroscience, 6*(4), 428–432.

Gepner, B., & Mestre, D. (2002). Rapid visual-motion integration deficit in autism. *Trends in Cognitive Science, 6*(11), 455.

Gepner, B., Mestre, D., Masson, G., & de Schonen, S. (1995). Postural effects of motion vision in young autistic children. *Neuroreport: An International Journal for the Rapid Communication of Research in Neuroscience, 6*(8), 1211–1214.
Gernsbacher, M. A., Sauer, E. A., Geye, H. M., Schweigert, E. K., & Hill Goldsmith, H. (2008). Infant and toddler oral- and manual-motor skills predict later speech fluency in autism. *Journal of Child Psychology and Psychiatry, 49*(1), 43–50.
Gersten, R. (1983). Stimulus overselectivity in autistic, trainable mentally retarded, and non-handicapped children: Comparative research controlling chronological (rather than mental) age. *Journal of Abnormal Child Psychology, 11*(1), 61–75.
Gervais, H., Belin, P., Boddaert, N., Leboyer, M., Coez, A., Sfaello, I., et al. (2004). Abnormal cortical voice processing in autism. *Natural Neuroscience, 7*(8), 801–802.
Geschwind, D., Cummings, J. L., Hollander, E., Di Mauro, S., Cook, E. H., Lombard, J., et al. (1998). Autism screening and diagnostic evaluation: CAN consensus statement. *CNS Spectrums, 3*(3).
Gillberg, C., Ehlers, S., Schaumann, H., Jakobsson, G., Dahlgren, S. O., Lindblom, R., Bågenholm, A., Tjuus, T. Blidner, E. (1990). Autism under age 3 years: A clinical study of 28 cases referred for autistic symptoms in infancy. *Journal of Child Psychology & Psychiatry & Allied Disciplines, 31*(6), 921–934.
Gillberg, C., & Steffenburg, S. (1987). Outcome and prognostic factors in infantile autism and similar conditions: A population-based study of 46 cases followed through puberty. *Journal of Autism & Developmental Disorders, 17*(2), 273–287.
Glascoe, F. P. (1999). Using parents' concerns to detect and address developmental and behavioral problems. *Journal of Social Pediatric Nursing, 4*(1), 24–35.
Goines, P., Haapanen, L., Boyce, R., Duncanson, P., Braunschweig, D., Delwiche, L., et al. (2011). Autoantibodies to cerebellum in children with autism associate with behavior. *Brain Behavior and Immunology, 25*(3), 514–523.
Goldberg, M. C., Mostofsky, S. H., Cutting, L. E., Mahone, E. M., Astor, B. C., Denckla, M. B., et al. (2005). Subtle executive impairment in children with autism and children with ADHD. *Journal of Autism and Developmental Disorders, 35*(3), 279–293.
Goldberg, W. A., Osann, K., Filipek, P. A., Laulhere, T., Jarvis, K., Modahl, C., et al. (2003). Language and other regression: Assessment and timing. *Journal of Autism and Developmental Disorders, 33*(6), 607–616.
Goldberg, W. A., Thorsen, K. L., Osann, K., & Spence, M. A. (2008). Use of home videotapes to confirm parental reports of regression in autism. *Journal of Autism and Developmental Disorders, 38*(6), 1136–1146.
Goldman, S. E., Surdyka, K., Cuevas, R., Adkins, K., Wang, L., & Malow, B. A. (2009). Defining the sleep phenotype in children with autism. *Developmental Neuropsychology, 34*(5), 560–573.
Gottesman, II & Hanson, D. R. (2005). Human development: Biological and genetic processes. *Annual Review of Psychology, 56*, 263–286.
Grafodatskaya, D., Chung, B., Szatmari, P., & Weksberg, R. (2010). Autism spectrum disorders and epigenetics. *Journal of the American Academy of Child and Adolescent Psychiatry, 49*(8), 794–809.
Gray, K. M., & Tonge, B. J. (2001). Are there early features of autism in infants and preschool children? *Journal of Pediatrics and Child Health, 37*(3), 221–226.
Green, D., Charman, T., Pickles, A., Chandler, S., Loucas, T., Simonoff, E., et al. (2009). Impairment in movement skills of children with autistic spectrum disorders. *Developmental Medicine and Child Neurology, 51*(4), 311–316.
Green, G., Brennan, L. C., & Fein, D. (2002). Intensive behavioral treatment for a toddler at high risk for autism. *Behavior Modification, 26*, 69–102.
Green, J., Charman, T., McConachie, H., Aldred, C., Slonims, V., Howlin, P., et al. (2010). Parent-mediated communication-focused treatment in children with autism (PACT): A randomized controlled trial. *Lancet, 375*(9732), 2152–2160.
Greenspan, S. I. (2000). *Clinical practice guidelines: Refining the Standards of Care for Infants, Children and Families with Special Needs.* Bethesda, MD: ICDL Press.
Greimel, E., Schulte-Ruther, M., Fink, G. R., Piefke, M., Herpertz-Dahlmann, B., & Konrad, K. (2010). Development of neural correlates of empathy from childhood to early adulthood: An fMRI study in boys and adult men. *Journal of Neural Transmission, 117*(6), 781–791.
Grezes, J., Wicker, B., Berthoz, S., & de Gelder, B. (2009). A failure to grasp the affective meaning of actions in autism spectrum disorder subjects. *Neuropsychologia, 47*(8–9), 1816–1825.
Groen, W. B., Buitelaar, J. K., van der Gaag, R. J., & Zwiers, M. P. (2010a). Pervasive microstructural abnormalities in autism: A DTI study. *Journal of Psychiatry & Neuroscience, 36*(1), 32–40.
Groen, W. B., Tesink, C., Petersson, K. M., van Berkum, J., van der Gaag, R. J., Hagoort, P., et al. (2010b). Semantic, factual, and social language comprehension in adolescents with autism: An FMRI study. *Cerebral Cortex, 20*(8), 1937–1945.

Grossman, R. B., Bemis, R. H., Plesa Skwerer, D., & Tager-Flusberg, H. (2010). Lexical and affective prosody in children with high-functioning autism. *Journal of Speech Language and Hearing Research, 53*(3), 778–793.

Grossmann, T. (2010). The development of emotion perception in face and voice during infancy. *Restorative Neurology and Neuroscience, 28,* 219–236.

Grossmann, T., Oberecker, R., Koch, S. P., & Friederici, A. D. (2011). The developmental origins of voice processing in the human brain. *Neuron, 65*(6), 852–858.

Gruter, T., Gruter, M., & Carbon, C. C. (2008). Neural and genetic foundations of face recognition and prosopagnosia. *Journal of Neuropsychology, 2*(Pt 1), 79–97.

Gutierrez, R. C., Hung, J., Zhang, Y., Kertesz, A. C., Espina, F. J., & Colicos, M. A. (2009). Altered synchrony and connectivity in neuronal networks expressing an autism-related mutation of neuroligin 3. *Neuroscience, 162*(1), 208–221.

Hadjikhani, N., Joseph, R. M., Snyder, J., Chabris, C. F., Clark, J., Steele, S., et al. (2004). Activation of the fusiform gyrus when individuals with autism spectrum disorder view faces. *Neuroimage, 22*(3), 1141–1150.

Hadjikhani, N., Joseph, R. M., Snyder, J., & Tager-Flusberg, H. (2006). Anatomical differences in the mirror neuron system and social cognition network in autism. *Cerebral Cortex, 16*(9), 1276–1282.

Hadjikhani, N., Joseph, R. M., Snyder, J., & Tager-Flusberg, H. (2007). Abnormal activation of the social brain during face perception in autism. *Human Brain Mapping, 28*(5), 441–449.

Hainline, L., & Abramov, I. (1992). Assessing visual development: Is infant vision good enough? In C. Rovee-Collier & L. P. Lipsett (Eds.), *Advances in Infant Research* (pp. 30–102). Norwood, NJ.: Ablex.

Hansen, R. L., Ozonoff, S., Krakowiak, P., Angkustsiri, K., Jones, C., Deprey, L. J., et al. (2008). Regression in autism: Prevalence and associated factors in the CHARGE Study. *Ambulatory Pediatrics, 8*(1), 25–31.

Happé, F., Booth, R., Charlton, R., & Hughes, C. (2006). Executive function deficits in autism spectrum disorders and attention-deficit/hyperactivity disorder: Examining profiles across domains and ages. *Brain and Cognition, 61*(1), 25–39.

Happé, F., & Frith, U. (2006). The weak coherence account: Detail-focused cognitive style in autism spectrum disorders. *Journal of Autism and Developmental Disorders, 36*(1), 5–25.

Happé, F., & Ronald, A. (2008). The 'fractionable autism triad': A review of evidence from behavioural, genetic, cognitive and neural research. *Neuropsychology Review, 18*(4), 287–304.

Harada, M., Taki, M. M., Nose, A., Kubo, H., Mori, K., Nishitani, H., et al. (2010). Non-invasive evaluation of the GABAergic/glutamatergic system in autistic patients observed by MEGA-editing proton MR spectroscopy using a clinical 3 tesla instrument. *Journal of Autism and Developmental Disorders, 41*(4), 447–454.

Hardan, A. Y., Minshew, N. J., Melhem, N. M., Srihari, S., Jo, B., Bansal, R., et al. (2008). An MRI and proton spectroscopy study of the thalamus in children with autism. *Psychiatry Research: Neuroimaging Section, 163*(2), 97–105.

Hardan, A. Y., Muddasani, S., Vemulapalli, M., Keshavan, M. S., & Minshew, N. J. (2006). An MRI study of increased cortical thickness in autism. *American Journal of Psychiatry, 163*(7), 1290–1292.

Hare, D. J., Mellor, C., & Azmi, S. (2007). Episodic memory in adults with autistic spectrum disorders: Recall for self- versus other-experienced events. *Research in Developmental Disabilities, 28*(3), 317–329.

Harrington, J. W., Rosen, L., & Garnecho, A. (2006). Parental perceptions and use of complementary and alternative medicine practices for children with autistic spectrum disorders in private practice. *Journal of Developmental and Behavioral Pediatrics, 27*(2), S156–S161.

Hashimoto, T., Tayama, M., Miyazaki, M., Murakawa, K., Shimakawa, S., Yoneda, Y., et al. (1993). Brainstem involvement in high functioning autistic children. *Acta Neurologica Scandinavica, 88*(2), 123–128.

Hauck, M., Fein, D., Maltby, N., Waterhouse, L., & Feinstein, C. (1998). Memory for faces in children with autism. *Child Neuropsychology, 4*(3), 187–198.

Hazlett, H. C., Poe, M., Gerig, G., Smith, R. G., Provenzale, J., Ross, A., et al. (2005). Magnetic resonance imaging and head circumference study of brain size in autism – Birth through age 2 years. *Archives of General Psychiatry, 62*(12), 1366–1376.

Hazlett, H. C., Poe, M. D., Gerig, G., Smith, R. G., & Piven, J. (2006). Cortical gray and white brain tissue volume in adolescents and adults with autism. *Biological Psychiatry, 59*(1), 1–6.

Heaton, P. (2003). Pitch memory, labelling and disembedding in autism. *Journal of Child Psychology and Psychiatry, 44*(4), 543–551.

Herbert, M. R. (2010). Contributions of the environment and environmentally vulnerable physiology to autism spectrum disorders. *Current Opinion in Neurology, 23*(2), 103–110.

Herbert, M. R., Ziegler, D. A., Makris, N., Bakardjiev, A., Hodgson, J., Adrien, K. T., et al. (2003). Larger brain and white matter volumes in children with developmental language disorder. *Developmental Science, 6*(4), F11–F22.

Hermelin, B., & O'Connor, N. (1970). *Psychological experiments with autistic children*. London: Pergamon Press.

Hermelin, B., & O'Connor, N. (1975). The recall of digits by normal, deaf and autistic children. *British Journal of Psychology, 66*(2), 203–209.

Hesling, I., Dilharreguy, B., Peppe, S., Amirault, M., Bouvard, M., & Allard, M. (2010). The integration of prosodic speech in high functioning autism: A preliminary FMRI study. *Plos One, 5*(7), e11571.

Hickok, G., & Poeppel, D. (2007). The cortical organization of speech processing. *Nature Reviews Neuroscience, 8*(5), 393–402.

Hill, E. L. (2004). Evaluating the theory of executive dysfunction in autism. *Developmental Review, 24*(2), 189–233.

Hill, E. L., & Frith, U. (2003). Understanding autism: Insights from mind and brain. *Philosophical Transactions of the Royal Society of London Series B-Biological Sciences, 358*(1430), 281–289.

Hirai, M., & Hiraki, K. (2005). An event-related potentials study of biological motion perception in human infants. *Cognitive Brain Research, 22*, 301–304.

Ho, P. T., Keller, J. L., Berg, A. L., Cargan, A. L., & Haddad, J. Jr. (1999). Pervasive developmental delay in children presenting as possible hearing loss. *Laryngoscope, 109*(1), 129–135.

Hobson, R., Ouston, J., & Lee, A. (1988a). Emotion recognition in autism: Coordinating faces and voices. *Psychological Medicine, 18*(4), 911–923.

Hobson, R., Ouston, J., & Lee, A. (1988b). What's in a face? The case of autism. *British Journal of Psychology, 79*(4), 441–453.

Hobson, R. P., Ouston, J., & Lee, A. (1988c). What's in a face? The case of autism. *British Journal of Psychology, 79*(Pt 4), 441–453.

Hodge, S. M., Makris, N., Kennedy, D. N., Caviness, V. S. Jr., Howard, J., McGrath, L., et al. (2010). Cerebellum, language, and cognition in autism and specific language impairment. *Journal of Autism and Developmental Disorders, 40*(3), 300–316.

Hoehl, S., Reid, V. M., Parise, E., Handl, A., Palumbo, L., & Striano, T. (2009). Looking at eye gaze processing and its neural correlates in infancy-implications for social development and autism spectrum disorder. *Child Development, 80*(4), 968–985.

Hoekstra, R. A., Happé, F., Baron-Cohen, S., & Ronald, A. (2010). Limited genetic covariance between autistic traits and intelligence: Findings from a longitudinal twin study. *American Journal of Medical Genetics Part B-Neuropsychiatric Genetics, 153B*(5), 994–1007.

Hollway, J. A., & Aman, M. G. (2011). Sleep correlates of pervasive developmental disorders: A review of the literature. *Research in Developmental Disabilities, 32*(5), 1399–1421.

Holmboe, K., Elsabbagh, M., Volein, A., Tucker, L. A., Baron-Cohen, S., Bolton, P., et al. (2010). Frontal cortex functioning in the infant broader autism phenotype. *Infant Behavior and Development, 33*(4), 482–491.

Hornig, M., Mervis, R., Hoffman, K., & Lipkin, W. I. (2002). Infectious and immune factors in neurodevelopmental damage. *Molecular Psychiatry, 7*, S34–S35.

Howlin, P. (2003). Outcome in high-functioning adults with autism with and without early language delays: Implications for the differentiation between autism and Asperger syndrome. *Journal of Autism and Developmental Disorders, 33*(1), 3–13.

Howlin, P., Goode, S., Hutton, J., & Rutter, M. (2004). Adult outcome for children with autism. *Journal of Child Psychology and Psychiatry, 45*(2), 212–229.

Howlin, P., Magiati, I., & Charman, T. (2009). Systematic review of early intensive behavioral interventions for children with autism. *American Journal of Intellectual and Developmental Disabilities, 114*(1), 23–41.

Howlin, P., & Moore, A. (1997). Diagnosis in autism: A survey of over 12,000 patients in the UK. *Autism, 1* , 135–162.

Hoyson, M., Jamieson, B., & Strain, P. S. (1984). Individualized group instruction of normally developing and autistic-like children: The LEAP curriculum model. *Journal of the Division for Early Childhood, 8*, 157–172.

Hubbard, K., & Trauner, D. A. (2007). Intonation and emotion in autistic spectrum disorders. *Journal of Psycholinguistic Research, 36*(2), 159–173.

Hudry, K., Leadbitter, K., Temple, K., Slonims, V., McConachie, H., Aldred, C., et al. (2010). Preschoolers with autism show greater impairment in receptive compared with expressive language abilities. *International Journal of Language & Communication Disorders, 45*(6), 681–690.

Hughes, C., Plumet, M. H., & Leboyer, M. (1999). Towards a cognitive phenotype for autism: Increased prevalence of executive dysfunction and superior spatial span amongst siblings of children with autism. *Journal of Child Psychology and Psychiatry, 40*(5), 705–718.

Hughes, C., Russell, J., & Robbins, T. W. (1994). Evidence for executive dysfunction in autism. *Neuropsychologia, 32*(4), 477–492.
Humphreys, K., Minshew, N., Leonard, G. L., & Behrmann, M. (2007). A fine-grained analysis of facial expression processing in high-functioning adults with autism. *Neuropsychologia, 45*(4), 685–695.
Hyde, K. L., Samson, F., Evans, A. C., & Mottron, L. (2010). Neuroanatomical differences in brain areas implicated in perceptual and other core features of autism revealed by cortical thickness analysis and voxel-based morphometry. *Human Brain Mapping, 31*(4), 556–566.
Ingram, J. L., Peckham, S. M., Tisdale, B., & Rodier, P. M. (2000). Prenatal exposure of rats to valproic acid reproduces the cerebellar anomalies associated with autism. *Neurotoxicol Teratol, 22*(3), 319–324.
Itier, R. J., & Batty, M. (2009). Neural bases of eye and gaze processing: The core of social cognition. *Neuroscience & Biobehavioral Reviews, 33*(6), 843–863.
Iverson, J. M., & Wozniak, R. H. (2007). Variation in vocal-motor development in infant siblings of children with autism. *Journal of Autism and Developmental Disorders, 37*(1), 158–170.
Jamain, S., Quach, H., Betancur, C., Rastam, M., Colineaux, C., Gillberg, I. C., et al. (2003). Mutations of the X-linked genes encoding neuroligins NLGN3 and NLGN4 are associated with autism. *Nature Genetics, 34*(1), 27–29.
Jansiewicz, E. M., Goldberg, M. C., Newschaffer, C. J., Denckla, M. B., Landa, R., & Mostofsky, S. H. (2006). Motor signs distinguish children with high functioning autism and Asperger's syndrome from controls. *Journal of Autism & Developmental Disorders, 36*(5), 613–621.
Jarrold, C., Boucays, A., & Russel, J. (1997). Language profiles in children with autism: Theoretical and methodological implications. *Autism, 1*, 57–76.
Jarrold, C., Boucher, J., & Smith, P. K. (1996). Generativity deficits in pretend play in autism. *British Journal of Developmental Psychology, 14*, 275–300.
Jarrold, C., Gilchrist, I. D., & Bender, A. (2005). Embedded figures detection in autism and typical development: Preliminary evidence of a double dissociation in relationships with visual search. *Developmental Science, 8*(4), 344–351.
Jensen, V. K., & Sinclair, L. V. (2002). Treatment of autism in young children: Behavioral intervention and applied behavior analysis. *Infants and Young Children, 14*(4), 42–52.
Johnson, C. P., & Myers, S. M. (2007). Identification and evaluation of children with autism spectrum disorders. *Pediatrics, 120*(5), 1183–1215.
Johnson, M. H. (2005). Subcortical face processing. *Nature Reviews Neuroscience, 6*(10), 766–774.
Johnson, M. H., Dziurawiec, S., Ellis, H., & Morton, J. (1991). Newborns' preferential tracking of face-like stimuli and its subsequent decline. *Cognition, 40*(1–2), 1–19.
Johnson, M. H., Grossman, T., & Farroni, T. (2010). The social cognitive neuroscience of infancy: Illuminating the early development of social brain functions. In R. Kail (Ed.), *Advances in Child Development and Behavior:* (*Vol. Vol. 36.*, pp. 331–372). New York: Academic Press.
Jones, C. R., Happé, F., Pickles, A., Marsden, A. J., Tregay, J., Baird, G., et al. (2010). 'Everyday memory' impairments in autism spectrum disorders. *Journal of Autism and Developmental Disorders, 41*(4), 455–464.
Joober, R., & El-Hussein, A. (2006). Synaptic abnormalities and candidate genes in autism. In A. Dityatev & A. El-Hussein (Eds.), *Molecular mechanisms of synaptic genesis* (pp. 409–418). New York: Springer.
Joseph, R. M., Keehn, B., Connolly, C., Wolfe, J. M., & Horowitz, T. S. (2009). Why is visual search superior in autism spectrum disorder? *Developmental Science, 12*(6), 1083–1096.
Jou, R. J., Minshew, N. J., Melhem, N. M., Keshavan, M. S., & Hardan, A. Y. (2009). Brainstem volumetric alterations in children with autism. *Psychological Medicine, 39*(8), 1347–1354.
Just, M. A., Cherkassky, V. L., Keller, T. A., & Minshew, N. J. (2004). Cortical activation and synchronization during sentence comprehension in high-functioning autism: Evidence of underconnectivity. *Brain, 127*(Pt 8), 1811–1821.
Juul-Dam, N., Townsend, J., & Courchesne, E. (2001). Prenatal, perinatal, and neonatal factors in autism, pervasive developmental disorder-not otherwise specified, and the general population. *Pediatrics, 107*(4), E63.
Kalia, M. (2008). Brain development: Anatomy, connectivity, adaptive plasticity, and toxicity. *Metabolism, 57* Supplement 2, S2–S5.
Kana, R. K., Keller, T. A., Cherkassky, V. L., Minshew, N. J., & Just, M. A. (2009). Atypical frontal-posterior synchronization of Theory of Mind regions in autism during mental state attribution. *Social Neuroscience, 4*(2), 135–152.
Kanne, S. M., Randolph, J. K., & Farmer, J. E. (2008). Diagnostic and assessment findings: A bridge to academic planning for children with autism spectrum disorders. *Neuropsychology Review, 18*(4), 367–384.

Kanner, L. (1943). Autistic disturbances of affective contact. *Nervous Child, 2*, 217–250.

Kanner, L. (1946). Irrelevant and metaphorical language early infantile autism. *American Journal of Psychiatry, 103*, 242–246.

Kanner, L. (1949). Problems of nosology and psychodynamics of early infantile autism. *American Journal of Orthopsychiatry, 19*(3), 416–426.

Kanner, L., & Eisenberg, L. (1956). Early infantile autism, 1943–1955. *American Journal of Orthopsychiatry, 26*, 55–65.

Karanth, P., Shaista, S., & Srikanth, N. (2010). Efficacy of communication DEALL–An indigenous early intervention program for children with autism spectrum disorders. *Indian Journal of Pediatrics, 77* 957–962.

Karmiloff-Smith, A. (1998). Development itself is the key to understanding developmental disorders. *Trends in Cognitive Sciences, 2*, 389–398.

Keehn, B., Brenner, L., Palmer, E., Lincoln, A. J., & Müller, R. A. (2008). Functional brain organization for visual search in ASD. *Journal of the International Neuropsychological Society, 14*:(6), 990–1003.

Kemper, T. L., & Bauman, M. L. (1993). The contribution of neuropathologic studies to the understanding of autism. *Neurologic Clinics, 11*(1), 175–187.

Kennedy, D. P. (2009). Neural correlates of autistic traits in the general population: Insights into autism. *American Journal of Psychiatry, 166*(8), 849–851.

Kerbel, D., & Grunwell, P. (1998). A study of idiom comprehension in children with semantic-pragmatic difficulties. Part II: Between-groups results and discussion. *International Journal of Language & Communication Disorders, 33*(1), 23–44.

Kern, J. K., Trivedi, M. H., Grannemann, B. D., Garver, C. R., Johnson, D. G., Andrews, A. A., et al. (2007). Sensory correlations in autism. *Autism, 11*(2), 123–134.

Khalfa, S., Bruneau, N., Roge, B., Georgieff, N., Veuillet, E., Adrien, J. L., et al. (2001). Peripheral auditory asymmetry in infantile autism. *European Journal of Neuroscience, 13*(3), 628–632.

Kim, J. E., Lyoo, I. K., Estes, A. M., Renshaw, P. F., Shaw, D. W., Friedman, S. D., et al. (2010). Laterobasal amygdalar enlargement in 6- to 7-year-old children with autism spectrum disorder. *Archives of General Psychiatry, 67*(11), 1187–1197.

Kinney, D. K., Barch, D. H., Chayka, B., Napoleon, S., & Munir, K. M. (2010). Environmental risk factors for autism: Do they help cause de novo genetic mutations that contribute to the disorder? *Medical Hypotheses, 74*(1), 102–106.

Kinney, D. K., Munir, K. M., Crowley, D. J., & Miller, A. M. (2008). Prenatal stress and risk for autism. *Neuroscience & Biobehavioral Reviews, 32*(8), 1519–1532.

Kisilevsky, B. S., Hains, S. M., Brown, C. A., Lee, C. T., Cowperthwaite, B., Stutzman, S. S., et al. (2009). Fetal sensitivity to properties of maternal speech and language. *Infant Behavior and Development, 32*(1), 59–71.

Kjelgaard, M. M., & Tager-Flusberg, H. (2001). An investigation of language impairment in autism: Implications for genetic subgroups. *Language and Cognitive Processes, 16*(2–3), 287–308.

Klein, A. J., Armstrong, B. L., Greer, M. K., & Brown, F. R. (1990). Hyperacusis and otitis media in individuals with Williams syndrome. *Journal of Speech and Hearing Disorders, 55*, 339–334.

Klein, S. B., Chan, R. L., & Loftus, J. (1999). Independence of episodic and semantic self-knowledge: The case from autism. *Social Cognition, 17*(4), 413–436.

Kleinhans, N. M., Richards, T., Johnson, L. C., Weaver, K. E., Greenson, J., Dawson, G., et al. (2011). fMRI evidence of neural abnormalities in the subcortical face processing system in ASD. *Neuroimage, 54*(1), 697–704.

Kleinman, J. M., Robins, D. L., Ventola, P. E., Pandey, J., Boorstein, H. C., Esser, E. L., et al. (2008). The modified checklist for autism in toddlers: A follow-up study investigating the early detection of autism spectrum disorders. *Journal of Autism and Developmental Disorders, 38*(5), 827–839.

Klin, A. (1992). Listening preferences in regard to speech in four children with developmental disabilities. *Journal of Child Psychology & Psychiatry & Allied Disciplines, 33*(4), 763–769.

Klin, A., & Jones, W. (2008). Altered face scanning and impaired recognition of biological motion in a 15-month-old infant with autism. *Developmental Science, 11*(1), 40–46.

Klin, A., Lin, D. J., Gorrindo, P., Ramsay, G., & Jones, W. (2009). Two-year-olds with autism orient to non-social contingencies rather than biological motion. *Nature, 459*(7244), 257–261.

Knaus, T. A., Silver, A. M., Kennedy, M., Lindgren, K. A., Dominick, K. C., Siegel, J., et al. (2010). Language laterality in autism spectrum disorder and typical controls: A functional, volumetric, and diffusion tensor MRI study. *Brain and Language, 112*(2), 113–120.

Koegel, L. K., Koegel, R. L., Harrower, J. K., & Carter, C. M. (1999). Pivotal response intervention I: Overview of approach. *Journal of the Association for Persons with Severe Handicaps, 24*(3), 174–185.

Koegel, L. K., Koegel, R. L., Shoshan, Y., & McNerney, E. (1999). Pivotal response intervention II: Preliminary long-term outcome data. *Journal of the Association for Persons with Severe Handicaps, 24*(3), 186–198.

Koegel, R. L., & Wilhelm, H. (1973). Selective responding to the components of multiple visual cues by autistic children. *Journal of Experimental Child Psychology, 15*(3), 442–453.

Kohen-Raz, R., Volkmar, F. R., & Cohen, D. J. (1992). Postural control in children with autism. *Journal of Autism & Developmental Disorders, 22*(3), 419–432.

Kolevzon, A., Mathewson, K. A., & Hollander, E. (2006). Selective serotonin reuptake inhibitors in autism: A review of efficacy and tolerability. *Journal of Clinical Psychiatry, 67*(3), 407–414.

Krentz, U. C., & Corina, D. P. (2008). Preference for language in early infancy: The human language bias is not speech specific. *Developmental Science, 11*(1), 1–9.

Kuhl, P. K. (2004). Early language acquisition: Cracking the speech code. *Nature Reviews Neuroscience, 5*(11), 831–843.

Kuhl, P. K., Coffey-Corina, S., Padden, D., & Dawson, G. (2005). Links between social and linguistic processing of speech in preschool children with autism: Behavioral and electrophysiological measures. *Developmental Science, 8*(1), F1–F12.

Kulesza, R. J. Jr., Lukose, R., & Stevens, L. V. (2010). Malformation of the human superior olive in autistic spectrum disorders. *Brain Research, 1367*, 360–371.

Kumar, A., Sundaram, S. K., Sivaswamy, L., Behen, M. E., Makki, M. I., Ager, J., et al. (2009). Alterations in frontal lobe tracts and corpus callosum in young children with autism spectrum disorder. *Cerebral Cortex, 20*(9), 2103–2113.

Kurita, H. (1985). Infantile autism with speech loss before the age of thirty months. *Journal of the American Academy of Child Psychiatry, 24*(2), 191–196.

Lahaie, A., Mottron, L., Arguin, M., Berthiaume, C., Jemel, B., & Saumier, D. (2006). Face perception in high-functioning autistic adults: evidence for superior processing of face parts, not for a configural face-processing deficit. *Neuropsychology, 20*(1), 30–41.

Lainhart, J. E., Piven, J., Wzorek, M., Landa, R., Santangelo, S. L., Coon, H., et al. (1997). Macrocephaly in children and adults with autism. *Journal of the American Academy of Child and Adolescent Psychiatry, 36*(2), 282–290.

Landa, R. J. (2008). Diagnosis of autism spectrum disorders in the first 3 years of life. *Nature Clinical Practice Neurology, 4*, 138–147.

Landa, R., & Garrett-Mayer, E. (2006). Development in infants with autism spectrum disorders: A prospective study. *Journal of Child Psychology and Psychiatry, 47*(6), 629–638.

Landa, R., Piven, J., Wzorek, M., Gayle, J., Chase, G. A., & Folstein, F. A. (1992). Social language use in parents of autistic individuals. *Psychological Medicine, 22*, 1245–1254.

Landa, R. J. (2007). Early communication development and intervention for children with autism. *Mental Retardation and Developmental Disabilities Research Reviews, 13*(1), 16–25.

Landa, R. J., Holman, K. C., & Garrett-Mayer, E. (2007). Social and communication development in toddlers with early and later diagnosis of autism spectrum disorders. *Archives of General Psychiatry, 64*(7), 853–864.

Landrigan, P. J. (2010). What causes autism? Exploring the environmental contribution. *Current Opinion in Pediatrics, 22*(2), 219–225.

Landry, R., & Bryson, S. E. (2004). Impaired disengagement of attention in young children with autism. *Journal of Child Psychology and Psychiatry and Allied Disciplines, 45*(6), 1115–1122.

Langdell, T. (1978). Recognition of faces: An approach to the study of autism. *Journal of Child Psychology and Psychiatry, 19*, 255–268.

Lange, N., Dubray, M. B., Lee, J. E., Froimowitz, M. P., Froehlich, A., Adluru, N., et al. (2010). Atypical diffusion tensor hemispheric asymmetry in autism. *Autism Research, 3*(6), 350–358.

Larsson, H. J., Eaton, W. W., Madsen, K. M., Vestergaard, M., Olesen, A. V., Agerbo, E., et al. (2005). Risk factors for autism: Perinatal factors, parental psychiatric history, and socioeconomic status. *American Journal of Epidemiology, 161*(10), 916–925; discussion 926–918.

Laumonnier, F., Bonnet-Brilhault, F., Gomot, M., Blanc, R., David, A., Moizard, M. P., et al. (2004). X-linked mental retardation and autism are associated with a mutation in the NLGN4 gene, a member of the neuroligin family. *American Journal of Human Genetics, 74*(3), 552–557.

LeCouteur, A., Bailey, A., Goode, S., Pickles, A., Robertson, S., Gottesman, I., et al. (1996). A broader phenotype of autism: The clinical spectrum in twins. *Journal of Child Psychology and Psychiatry and Allied Disciplines, 37*(7), 785–801.

Leekam, S., Libby, S., Wing, L., Gould, J., & Gillberg, C. (2000). Comparison of ICD-10 and Gillberg's criteria for Asperger syndrome. *Autism, 1 4*, 11–28.

Legerstee, M., & Markova, G. (2007). Intentions make a difference: Infant responses to still-face and modified still-face conditions. *Infant Behavior and Development, 30*, 232–250.

Leo, I., & Simion, F. (2009). Face processing at birth: A Thatcher illusion study. *Developmental Science, 12*(3), 492–498.

Lepisto, T., Kujala, T., Vanhala, R., Alku, P., Huotilainen, M., & Naatanen, R. (2005). The discrimination of and orienting to speech and non-speech sounds in children with autism. *Brain Research, 1066*(1–2), 147–157.

Leppanen, J. M., & Nelson, C. A. (2009). Tuning the developing brain to social signals of emotions. *Nature Reviews Neuroscience, 10*(1), 37–47.

Lewis, J. D., & Elman, J. L. (2008). Growth-related neural reorganization and the autism phenotype: A test of the hypothesis that altered brain growth leads to altered connectivity. *Developmental Science, 11*(1), 135–155.

Libbey, J. E., Sweeten, T. L., McMahon, W. M., & Fujinami, R. S. (2005). Autistic disorder and viral infections. *Journal of Neurovirology, 11*(1), 1–10.

Lind, S. E., & Bowler, D. M. (2010). Episodic memory and episodic future thinking in adults with autism. *Journal of Abnormal Psychology, 119*(4), 896–905.

Lindgren, K. A., Folstein, S. E., Tomblin, J. B., & Tager-Flusberg, H. (2009). Language and reading abilities of children with autism spectrum disorders and specific language impairment and their first-degree relatives. *Autism Research, 2*(1), 22–38.

Liss, M., Fein, D., Allen, D., Dunn, M., Feinstein, C., Morris, R., et al. (2001). Executive functioning in high-functioning children with autism. *Journal of Child Psychology and Psychiatry and Allied Disciplines, 42*(2), 261–270.

Liss, M., Saulnier, C., Fein, D., & Kinsbourne, M. (2006). Sensory and attention abnormalities in autistic spectrum disorders. *Autism: The International Journal of Research & Practice, 10*(2), 155–172.

Liu, X. Q., Paterson, A. D., & Szatmari, P. (2008). Genome-wide linkage analyses of quantitative and categorical autism subphenotypes. *Biological Psychiatry, 64*(7), 561–570.

Loat, C. S., Haworth, C. M., Plomin, R., & Craig, I. W. (2008). A model incorporating potential skewed X-inactivation in MZ girls suggests that X-linked QTLs exist for several social behaviours including autism spectrum disorder. *Annals of Human Genetics, 72*(Pt 6), 742–751.

Loesche, G. (1990). Sensorimotor and action development in autistic children from infancy to early childhood. *Journal of Child Psychology and Psychiatry and Allied Disciplines, 31*(5), 749–761.

Lombardo, M. V., Chakrabarti, B., Bullmore, E. T., & Baron-Cohen, S. (2011). Specialization of right temporo-parietal junction for mentalizing and its relation to social impairments in autism. *Neuroimage, 56*(3), 1832–1838.

Lopez, B., & Leekam, S. R. (2003). Do children with autism fail to process information in context? *Journal of Child Psychology and Psychiatry, 44*(2), 285–300.

Lord, C., & Paul, R. (1997a). Language and communication and autism. In D. J. Cohen & F. R. Volkmar (Eds.), *Handbook of Autism and Pervasive Developmental Disorders* (pp. 195–225). New York: John Wiley & Sons.

Lord, C., & Paul, R. (1997b). Language and communication in autism. In D. J. Cohen & F. R. Volkmar (Eds.), *Handbook of Autism and Pervasive Developmental Disorders* (pp. 195–225). New York: John Wiley & Sons.

Lord, C., & Pickles, A. (1996). Language level and nonverbal social-communicative behaviors in autistic and language-delayed children. *Journal of the American Academy of Child and Adolescent Psychiatry, 35*(11), 1542–1550.

Lord, C., Rutter, M., DiLavore, P. C., & Risi, S. (2002). *Autism Diagnostic Observation Schedule Manual.* Los Angeles: Western Psychological Services.

Lord, C., Rutter, M., & Le Couteur, A. (1994). Autism diagnostic interview–revised: A revised version of a diagnostic interview for caregivers of individuals with possible pervasive developmental disorders. *Journal of Autism & Developmental Disorders, 24*(5), 659–685.

Lord, C., & Schopler, E. (1989). The role of age at assessment, developmental level, and test in the stability of intelligence scores in young autistic children. *Journal of Autism & Developmental Disorders, 19*(4), 483–499.

Lord, C., Shulman, C., & DiLavore, P. (2004). Regression and word loss in autistic spectrum disorders. *Journal of Child Psychology and Psychiatry, 45*(5), 936–955.

Losh, M., Adolphs, R., Poe, M. D., Couture, S., Penn, D., Baranek, G. T., et al. (2009). Neuropsychological profile of autism and the broad autism phenotype. *Archives of General Psychiatry, 66*(5), 518–526.

Lotter, V. (1966). Epidemiology of autistic conditions in young children. *Psychiatry, 1*, 124–137.

Lovaas, O. I. (1987). Behavioral treatment and normal educational and intellectual functioning in young autistic children. *Journal of Consulting and Clinical Psychology, 55*(1), 3–9.

Lovaas, O. I., Koegel, R. L., & Schreibman, L. (1979). Stimulus overselectivity in autism: A review of research. *Psychological Bulletin, 86*, 1236–1254.

Lovaas, O. I., Schreibman, L., & Koegel, R. L. (1974). A behavior modification approach to the treatment of autistic children. *Journal of Autism and Childhood Schizophrenia, 4*(2), 111–129.

Loveland, K. A., Steinberg, J. L., Pearson, D. A., Mansour, R., & Reddoch, S. (2008). Judgments of auditory-visual affective congruence in adolescents with and without autism: A pilot study of a new task using fMRI. *Perceptual and Motor Skills, 107*(2), 557–575.

Luyster, R., Gotham, K., Guthrie, W., Coffing, M., Petrak, R., Pierce, K., et al. (2009). The autism diagnostic observation schedule–toddler module: A new module of a standardized diagnostic measure for autism spectrum disorders. *Journal of Autism and Developmental Disorders, 39*(9), 1305–1320.

Luyster, R., Qiu, S., Lopez, K., & Lord, C. (2007). Predicting outcomes of children referred for autism using the MacArthur-Bates Communicative Development Inventory. *Journal of Speech Language and Hearing Research, 50*(3), 667–681.

Luyster, R., Richler, J., Risi, S., Hsu, W. L., Dawson, G., Bernier, R., et al. (2005). Early regression in social communication in autism spectrum disorders: A CPEA Study. *Developmental Neuropsychology, 27*(3), 311–336.

MacDonald, R. L., & Stoodley, M. (1998). Pathophysiology of cerebral ischemia. *Neurologia Medico-Chirurfica (Tokyo), 38*(1), 1–11.

Maestro, S., Muratori, F., Barbieri, F., Casella, C., Cattaneo, V., Cavallaro, M. C., et al. (2001). Early behavioral development in autistic children: The first 2 years of life through home movies. *Psychopathology, 34*(3), 147–152.

Maestro, S., Muratori, F., Cavallaro, M. C., Pei, F., Stern, D., Golse, B., et al. (2002). Attentional skills during the first 6 months of age in autism spectrum disorder. *Journal of the American Academy of Child and Adolescent Psychiatry, 41*(10), 1239–1245.

Maestro, S., Muratori, F., Cesari, A., Cavallaro, M. C., Paziente, A., Pecini, C., et al. (2005). Course of autism signs in the first year of life. *Psychopathology, 38*(1), 26–31.

Mahone, E. M., Powell, S. K., Loftis, C. W., Goldberg, M. C., Denckla, M. B., & Mostofsky, S. H. (2006). Motor persistence and inhibition in autism and ADHD. *Journal of the International Neuropsychological Society, 12*(5), 622–631.

Mahoney, G., Perales, F., Wiggers, B., & Herman, B. (2006). Responsive teaching: Early intervention for children with Down syndrome and other disabilities. *Downs Syndrome Research Practices, 11*, 18–28.

Mandelbaum, D. E., Stevens, M., Rosenberg, E., Wiznitzer, M., Steinschneider, M., Filipek, P., et al. (2006). Sensorimotor performance in school-age children with autism, developmental language disorder, or low IQ. *Developmental Medicine and Child Neurology, 48*(1), 33–39.

Mandell, D. S., Novak, M. M., & Zubritsky, C. D. (2005). Factors associated with age of diagnosis among children with autism spectrum disorders. *Pediatrics, 116*(6), 1480–1486.

Mars, A. E., Mauk, J. E., & Dowrick, P. W. (1998). Symptoms of pervasive developmental disorders as observed in prediagnostic home videos of infants and toddlers. *Journal of Pediatrics, 132*(3), 500–504.

Marsh, L. E., & Hamilton, A. F. (2011). Dissociation of mirroring and mentalising systems in autism. *Neuroimage, 56*, 1511–1519.

Martineau, J., Cochin, S., Magne, R., & Barthelemy, C. (2008). Impaired cortical activation in autistic children: Is the mirror neuron system involved? *International Journal of Psychophysiology, 68*(1), 35–40.

Martins, G. J., Shahrokh, M., & Powell, E. M. (2011). Genetic disruption of Met signaling impairs GABAergic striatal development and cognition. *Neuroscience, 176*, 199–209.

Materna, S., Dicke, P. W., & Thier, P. (2008). The posterior superior temporal sulcus is involved in social communication not specific for the eyes. *Neuropsychologia, 46*, 2759–2765.

Matthews, B., Shute, R., & Rees, R. (2001). An analysis of stimulus overselectivity in adults with autism. *Journal of Intellectual & Developmental Disability, 26*(2), 161–176.

Mayes, S. D., & Calhoun, S. L. (2003a). Ability profiles in children with autism: Influence of age and IQ. *Autism, 7*(1), 65–80.

Mayes, S. D., & Calhoun, S. L. (2003b). Analysis of WISC-III, Stanford-Binet-IV, and academic achievement test scores in children with autism. *Journal of Autism and Developmental Disorders, 33*(3), 329–341.

Mayes, S. D., & Calhoun, S. L. (2008). WISC-IV and WIAT-II profiles in children with high-functioning autism. *Journal of Autism and Developmental Disorders, 38*(3), 428–439.

Mayes, S. D., & Calhoun, S. L. (2009). Variables related to sleep problems in children with autism. *Research in Autism Spectrum Disorders, 3*(4), 931–941.

McAlonan, G. M., Cheung, V., Cheung, C., Suckling, J., Lam, G. Y., Tai, K. S., et al. (2005). Mapping the brain in autism. A voxel-based MRI study of volumetric differences and intercorrelations in autism. *Brain, 128*(Pt 2), 268–276.

McAlonan, G. M., Suckling, J., Wong, N., Cheung, V., Lienenkaemper, N., Cheung, C., et al. (2008). Distinct patterns of grey matter abnormality in high-functioning autism and Asperger's syndrome. *Journal of Child Psychology and Psychiatry, 49*(12), 1287–1295.

McCann, J., & Peppe, S. (2003). Prosody in autism spectrum disorders: A critical review. *International Journal of Language & Communication Disorders, 38*(4), 325–350.

McCleery, J. P., Tully, L., Slevc, L. R., & Schreibman, L. (2006). Consonant production patterns of young severely language-delayed children with autism. *Journal of Communication Disorders, 39*(3), 217–231.

McDonald, M. E., & Paul, J. F. (2010). Timing of increased autistic disorder cumulative incidence. *Environmental Science & Technology, 44*(6), 2112–2118.

McDougle, C. J., Kresch, L. E., & Posey, D. J. (2000). Repetitive thoughts and behavior in pervasive developmental disorders: Treatment with serotonin reuptake inhibitors. *Journal of Autism and Developmental Disorders, 30*(5), 427–435.

McGee, G. G., Morrier, M. J., & Daly, T. (1999). An incidental teaching approach to early intervention for toddlers with autism. *Journal of the Association for Persons with Severe Handicaps, 24*, 133–146.

McMurray, B., & Aslin, R. N. (2005). Infants are sensitive to within category variation in speech perception. *Cognition, 95*, B15–B26.

McQuistin, A., & Zieren, C. (2006). Clinical experiences with the PDDST-II. *Journal of Autism and Developmental Disorders, 36*(4), 577–578.

Mehler, M. F., & Purpura, D. P. (2009). Autism, fever, epigenetics and the locus coeruleus. *Brain Research Reviews, 59*(2), 388–392.

Meilleur, A. A., & Fombonne, E. (2009). Regression of language and non-language skills in pervasive developmental disorders. *Journal of Intellectual Disability Research, 53*(2), 115–124.

Mesibov, G. B., & Shea, V. (2010). The TEACCH program in the era of evidence-based practice. *Journal of Autism and Developmental Disorders, 40*(5), 570–579.

Mevorach, C., Hodsoll, J., Allen, H., Shalev, L., & Humphreys, G. (2010). Ignoring the elephant in the room: A neural circuit to downregulate salience. *Journal of Neuroscience, 30*(17), 6072–6079.

Miles, J. H., Hadden, L. L., Takahashi, T. N., & Hillman, R. E. (2000). Head circumference is an independent clinical finding associated with autism. *American Journal of Medical Genetics, 95*(4), 339–350.

Militerni, R., Bravaccio, C., Falco, C., Fico, C., & Palermo, M. T. (2002). Repetitive behaviors in autistic disorder. *European Child and Adolescent Psychiatry, 11*(5), 210–218.

Millward, C., Powell, S., Messer, D., & Jordan, R. (2000). Recall for self and other in autism: Children's memory for events experienced by themselves and their peers. *Journal of Autism and Developmental Disorders, 30*(1), 15–28.

Milne, E., Swettenham, J., Hansen, P., Campbell, R., Jeffries, H., & Plaisted, K. (2002). High motion coherence thresholds in children with autism. *Journal of Child Psychology and Psychiatry, 43*(2), 255–263.

Minderaa, R. B., Anderson, G. M., Volkmar, F. R., Akkerhuis, G. W., & Cohen, D. J. (1994). Noradrenergic and adrenergic functioning in autism. *Biological Psychiatry, 36*(4), 237–241.

Ming, X., Brimacombe, M., & Wagner, G. C. (2007). Prevalence of motor impairment in autism spectrum disorders. *Brain & Development, 29*(9), 565–570.

Minshew, N. J., & Goldstein, G. (1993). Is autism an amnesic disorder? Evidence from the California Verbal Learning Test. *Neuropsychology, 7*(2), 209–216.

Minshew, N. J., & Goldstein, G. (2001). The pattern of intact and impaired memory functions in autism. *Journal of Child Psychology and Psychiatry, 42*(8), 1095–1101.

Minshew, N. J., Goldstein, G., Muenz, L. R., & Payton, J. B. (1992). Neuropsychological functioning in nonmentally retarded autistic individuals. *Journal of Clinical and Experimental Neuropsychology, 14*(5), 749–761.

Minshew, N. J., Goldstein, G., & Siegel, D. J. (1996). Neuropsychological functioning in autism: Evidence for a generalized complex information processing deficit. *International Journal of Psychology, 31*(3–4), 1362–1362.

Minshew, N. J., & Keller, T. A. (2010). The nature of brain dysfunction in autism: Functional brain imaging studies. *Current Opinion in Neurology, 23*(2), 124–130.

Minshew, N. J., Meyer, J., & Goldstein, G. (2002). Abstract reasoning in autism: A dissociation between concept formation and concept identification. *Neuropsychology, 16*(3), 327–334.

Minshew, N. J., Sung, K., Jones, B. L., & Furman, J. M. (2004). Underdevelopment of the postural control system in autism. *Neurology, 63*(11), 2056–2061.

Minshew, N. J., Turner, C. A., & Goldstein, G. (2005). The application of short forms of the Wechsler Intelligence scales in adults and children with high functioning autism. *Journal of Autism and Developmental Disorders, 35*(1), 45–52.

Mitchell, S., Brian, J., Zwaigenbaum, L., Roberts, W., Szatmari, P., Smith, I., et al. (2006). Early language and communication development of infants later diagnosed with autism spectrum disorder. *Journal of Developmental & Behavioral Pediatrics, 27*(2 Suppl), S69–S78.

Moller, A. R., Kern, J. K., & Grannemann, B. (2005). Are the non-classical auditory pathways involved in autism and PDD? *Neurological Research, 27*(6), 625–629.

Molloy, C. A., Dietrich, K. N., & Bhattacharya, A. (2003). Postural stability in children with autism spectrum disorder. *Journal of Autism and Developmental Disorders, 33*(6), 643–652.

Monk, C. S., Weng, S. J., Wiggins, J. L., Kurapati, N., Louro, H. M., Carrasco, M., et al. (2010). Neural circuitry of emotional face processing in autism spectrum disorders. *Journal of Psychiatry & Neuroscience, 35*(2), 105–114.

Mooney, E. L., Gray, K. M., & Tonge, B. J. (2006). Early features of autism: Repetitive behaviours in young children. *European Journal of Child and Adolescent Psychiatry, 15*(1), 12–18.

Morgan, J. T., Chana, G., Pardo, C. A., Achim, C., Semendeferi, K., Buckwalter, J., et al. (2010). Microglial activation and increased microglial density observed in the dorsolateral prefrontal cortex in autism. *Biological Psychiatry, 68*(4), 368–376.

Mosconi, M. W., Cody-Hazlett, H., Poe, M. D., Gerig, G., Gimpel-Smith, R., & Piven, J. (2009). Longitudinal study of amygdala volume and joint attention in 2- to 4-year-old children with autism. *Archives of General Psychiatry, 66*(5), 509–516.

Mostofsky, S. H., Dubey, P., Jerath, V. K., Jansiewicz, E. M., Goldberg, M. C., & Denckla, M. B. (2006). Developmental dyspraxia is not limited to imitation in children with autism spectrum disorders. *Journal of the International Neuropsychological Society, 12*(3), 314–326.

Mostofsky, S. H., Goldberg, M. C., Landa, R. J., & Denckla, M. B. (2000). Evidence for a deficit in procedural learning in children and adolescents with autism: Implications for cerebellar contribution. *Journal of the International Neuropsychological Society, 6*(7), 752–759.

Mottron, L., Burack, J. A., Iarocci, G., Belleville, S., & Enns, J. T. (2003). Locally oriented perception with intact global processing among adolescents with high-functioning autism: Evidence from multiple paradigms. *Journal of Child Psychology and Psychiatry and Allied Disciplines, 44*(6), 904–913.

Mottron, L., Dawson, M., Soulieres, I., Hubert, B., & Burack, J. (2006). Enhanced perceptual functioning in autism: An update, and eight principles of autistic perception. *Journal of Autism and Developmental Disorders, 36*(1), 27–43.

Muller, R. A., Behen, M. E., Rothermel, R. D., Chugani, D. C., Muzik, O., Mangner, T. J., et al. (1999). Brain mapping of language and auditory perception in high-functioning autistic adults: A PET study. *Journal of Autism and Developmental Disorders, 29*(1), 19–31.

Mulligan, A., Anney, R. J., O'Regan, M., Chen, W., Butler, L., Fitzgerald, M., et al. (2009). Autism symptoms in attention-deficit/hyperactivity disorder: A familial trait which correlates with conduct, oppositional defiant, language and motor disorders. *Journal of Autism and Developmental Disorders, 39*(2), 197–209.

Mundy, P. (2003). Annotation: The neural basis of social impairments in autism: The role of the dorsal medial-frontal cortex and anterior cingulate system. *Journal of Child Psychology and Psychiatry and Allied Disciplines, 44*(6), 793–809.

Mundy, P., & Markus, J. (1997). On the nature of communication and language impairment in autism. *Mental Retardation and Developmental Disabilities Research Reviews, 3*(4), 343–349.

Mundy, P., & Newell, L. (2007). Attention, joint attention, and social cognition. *Current Directions in Psychological Science, 16*(5), 269–274.

Mundy, P., Sigman, M., & Kasari, C. (1990). A longitudinal study of joint attention and language development in autistic children. *Journal of Autism and Developmental Disorders, 20*(1), 115–128.

Mundy, P., Sigman, M., & Kasari, C. (1994). Joint attention, developmental level, and symptom presentation in autism. *Development & Psychopathology, 6*(3), 389–401.

Mundy, P., Sullivan, L., & Mastergeorge, A. M. (2009). A parallel and distributed-processing model of joint attention, social cognition and autism. *Autism Research, 2*(1), 2–21.

Murphy, M., Bolton, P. F., Pickles, A., Fombonne, E., Piven, J., & Rutter, M. (2000). Personality traits of the relatives of autistic probands. *Psychological Medicine, 30*(6), 1411–1424.

Nadig, A. S., Ozonoff, S., Young, G. S., Rozga, A., Sigman, M., & Rogers, S. J. (2007). A prospective study of response to name in infants at risk for autism. *Archives of Pediatric and Adolescent Medicine, 161*(4), 378–383.

Nakamura, K., Sekine, Y., Ouchi, Y., Tsujii, M., Yoshikawa, E., Futatsubashi, N., et al. (2010). Brain serotonin and dopamine transporter bindings in adults with high-functioning autism. *Archives of General Psychiatry, 67*(1), 59–68.

Nation, K. (1999). Reading skills in hyperlexia: A developmental perspective. *Psychological Bulletin, 125*(3), 338–355.

Nelson, C. A., Morse, P. A., & Leavitt, L. A. (1979). Recognition of facial expressions by seven-month-old infants. *Child Development, 50*(4), 1239–1242.

Neuhaus, E., Beauchaine, T. P., & Bernier, R. (2010). Neurobiological correlates of social functioning in autism. *Clinical Psychology Review, 30*, 733–748.

Nijmeijer, J. S., Hartman, C. A., Rommelse, N. N., Altink, M. E., Buschgens, C. J., Fliers, E. A., et al. (2010). Perinatal risk factors interacting with catechol O-methyltransferase and the serotonin transporter gene predict ASD symptoms in children with ADHD. *Journal of Child Psychology and Psychiatry, 51*, 1242–1250.

Nissen, M. J., & Bullemer, P. (1987). Attentional requirements of learning: Evidence from performance measures. *Cognitive Psychology, 19*(1), 1–32.

Norris, M., & Lecavalier, L. (2010). Screening accuracy of Level 2 autism spectrum disorder rating scales. A review of selected instruments. *Autism, 14*(4), 263–284.

Noterdaeme, M., Amorosa, H., Mildenberger, K., Sitter, S., & Minow, F. (2001). Evaluation of attention problems in children with autism and children with a specific language disorder. *European Child and Adolescent Psychiatry, 10*(1), 58–66.

Nyden, A., Niklasson, L., Stahlberg, O., Anckarsater, H., Wentz, E., Rastam, M., et al. (2010). Adults with autism spectrum disorders and ADHD neuropsychological aspects. *Research in Developmental Disabilities, 31*(6), 1659–1668.

O'Riordan, M. A., Plaisted, K. C., Driver, J., & Baron-Cohen, S. (2001). Superior visual search in autism. *Journal of Experimental Psychology-Human Perception and Performance*, *27*(3), 719–730.

Oberman, L. M., Hubbard, E. M., McCleery, J. P., Altschuler, E. L., Ramachandran, V. S., & Pineda, J. A. (2005). EEG evidence for mirror neuron dysfunction in autism spectrum disorders. *Brain Research Cognitve Brain Research*, *24*(2), 190–198.

Oberman, L. M., Ramachandran, V. S., & Pineda, J. A. (2008). Modulation of mu suppression in children with autism spectrum disorders in response to familiar or unfamiliar stimuli: The mirror neuron hypothesis. *Neuropsychologia*, *46*(5), 1558–1565.

Oblak, A. L., Gibbs, T. T., & Blatt, G. J. (2010). Decreased GABA(B) receptors in the cingulate cortex and fusiform gyrus in autism. *Journal of Neurochemistry*, *114*(5), 1414–1423.

Oblak, A. L., Rosene, D. L., Kemper, T. L., Bauman, M. L., & Blatt, G. J. (2011). Altered posterior cingulate cortical cyctoarchitecture, but normal density of neurons and interneurons in the posterior cingulate cortex and fusiform gyrus in autism. *Autism Research*, *4*, 200–211.

Odell, D., Maciulis, A., Cutler, A., Warren, L., McMahon, W. H. C., Coon, H., Stubbs, G., Henley, K., & Torres, A. (2005). Confirmation of the association of the C4B null allele in autism. *Human Immunology*, *66*, 140–145.

Ornitz, E. M. (1988). Autism: A disorder of directed attention. *Brain Dysfunction*, *1*(5–6), 309–322.

Ospina, M. B., Krebs Seida, J., Clark, B., Karkhaneh, M., Hartling, L., Tjosvold, L., et al. (2008). Behavioural and developmental interventions for autism spectrum disorder: A clinical systematic review. *Plos One*, *3*(11), e3755.

Osterling, J., & Dawson, G. (1994). Early recognition of children with autism: A study of first birthday home videotapes. *Journal of Autism & Developmental Disorders*, *24*(3), 247–257.

Osterling, J. A., Dawson, G., & Munson, J. A. (2002). Early recognition of 1-year-old infants with autism spectrum disorder versus mental retardation. *Development and Psychopathology*, *14*(2), 239–251.

Ozonoff, S. (1995). Reliability and validity of the Wisconsin Card Sorting Test in studies of autism. *Neuropsychology*, *9*(4), 491–500.

Ozonoff, S., & Cathcart, K. (1998). Effectiveness of a home program intervention for young children with autism. *Journal of Autism and Developmental Disorders*, *28*(1), 25–32.

Ozonoff, S., Cook, I., Coon, H., Dawson, G., Joseph, R. M., Klin, A., et al. (2004). Performance on Cambridge Neuropsychological Test Automated Battery subtests sensitive to frontal lobe function in people with autistic disorder: Evidence from the Collaborative Programs of Excellence in Autism network. *Journal of Autism and Developmental Disorders*, *34*(2), 139–150.

Ozonoff, S., Goodlin-Jones, B. L., & Solomon, M. (2005a). Evidence-based assessment of autism spectrum disorders in children and adolescents. *Journal of Clinical Child and Adolescent Psychology*, *34*(3), 523–540.

Ozonoff, S., Iosif, A. M., Baguio, F., Cook, I. C., Hill, M. M., Hutman, T., et al. (2010). A prospective study of the emergence of early behavioral signs of autism. *Journal of the American Academy of Child & Adolescent Psychiatry*, *49*(3), 256–266.

Ozonoff, S., Macari, S., Young, G. S., Goldring, S., Thompson, M., & Rogers, S. J. (2008a). Atypical object exploration at 12 months of age is associated with autism in a prospective sample. *Autism*, *12*(5), 457–472.

Ozonoff, S., & McEvoy, R. E. (1994). A longitudinal study of executive function and theory of mind development in autism. *Development & Psychopathology*, *6*(3), 415–431.

Ozonoff, S., Pennington, B. F., & Rogers, S. J. (1991). Executive function deficits in high-functioning autistic individuals: Relationship to theory of mind. *Journal of Child Psychology and Psychiatry*, *32*(7), 1081–1105.

Ozonoff, S., & Strayer, D. L. (2001). Further evidence of intact working memory in autism. *Journal of Autism and Developmental Disorders*, *31*(3), 257–263.

Ozonoff, S., Williams, B. J., & Landa, R. (2005b). Parental report of the early development of children with regressive autism: The delays-plus-regression phenotype. *Autism*, *9*(5), 461–486.

Ozonoff, S., Young, G. S., Carter, A., Messinger, D., Yirmiya, N., Zwaigenbaum, L., et al. (2011). Recurrence risk for autism spectrum disorders: A baby siblings research consortium study. *Pediatrics*, *128*, e488–e495.

Ozonoff, S., Young, G. S., Goldring, S., Greiss-Hess, L., Herrera, A. M., Steele, J., et al. (2008b). Gross motor development, movement abnormalities, and early identification of autism. *Journal of Autism and Developmental Disorders*, *38*(4), 644–656.

Palmen, S. J., van Engeland, H., Hof, P. R., & Schmitz, C. (2004). Neuropathological findings in autism. *Brain*, *127*, 2572–2583.

Panerai, S., Zingale, M., Trubia, G., Finocchiaro, M., Zuccarello, R., Ferri, R., et al. (2009). Special education versus inclusive education: The role of the TEACCH program. *Journal of Autism and Developmental Disorders*, *39*(6), 874–882.

Papousek, H., & Papousek, M. (1983). Biological basis of social interactions: Implications of research for an understanding of behavioral deviance. *Journal of Child Psychology and Psychiatry and Allied Disciplines, 24*, 117–129.

Parr, J. R., Le Couteur, A., Baird, G., Rutter, M., Pickles, A., Fombonne, E., et al. (2011). Early developmental regression in autism spectrum disorder: Evidence from an international multiplex sample. *Journal of Autism and Developmental Disorders, 41*(3), 332–340.

Parron, C., Da Fonseca, D., Santos, A., Moore, D. G., Monfardini, E., & Deruelle, C. (2008). Recognition of biological motion in children with autistic spectrum disorders. *Autism, 12*(3), 261–274.

Parsons, C. E., Young, K. S., Murray, L., Stein, A., & Kringelbach, M. L. (2010). The functional neuroanatomy of the evolving parent-infant relationship. *Progress in Neurobiology, 91*(3), 220–241.

Pascualvaca, D. M., Fantie, B. D., Papageorgiou, M., & Mirsky, A. F. (1998). Attentional capacities in children with autism: Is there a general deficit in shifting focus? *Journal of Autism and Developmental Disorders, 28*(6), 467–478.

Paul, L. K., Corsello, C., Tranel, D., & Adolphs, R. (2010). Does bilateral damage to the human amygdala produce autistic symptoms? *Journal of Neurodevelopmental Disorders, 2*(3), 165–173.

Paul, R., Shriberg, L. D., McSweeny, J., Cicchetti, D., Klin, A., & Volkmar, F. (2005). Brief report: Relations between prosodic performance and communication and socialization ratings in high functioning speakers with autism spectrum disorders. *Journal of Autism and Developmental Disorders, 35*(6), 861–869.

Peca, J., Feliciano, C., Ting, J. T., Wang, W., Wells, M. F., Venkatraman, T. N., et al. (2011). Shank3 mutant mice display autistic-like behaviours and striatal dysfunction. *Nature, 472*, 437–442.

Pellicano, E. (2010). Individual differences in executive function and central coherence predict developmental changes in theory of mind in autism. *Developmental Psychology, 46*(2), 530–544.

Pellicano, E., Gibson, L., Maybery, M., & Durkin, K. (2003). Elevated motion coherence thresholds in autism: Further evidence of 'weak' central coherence. *Australian Journal of Psychology, 55*, 202.

Pelphrey, K. A., & Carter, E. J. (2008). Brain mechanisms for social perception: lessons from autism and typical development. *Annals of the New York Academy of Science, 1145*, 283–299.

Pelphrey, K. A., Morris, J. P., & McCarthy, G. (2005). Neural basis of eye gaze processing deficits in autism. *Brain, 128*(Pt 5), 1038–1048.

Pelphrey, K. A., Morris, J. P., McCarthy, G., & Labar, K. S. (2007). Perception of dynamic changes in facial affect and identity in autism. *Social Cognitive and Affective Neuroscience, 2*(2), 140–149.

Pelphrey, K. A., Sasson, N. J., Reznick, J. S., Paul, G., Goldman, B. D., & Piven, J. (2002). Visual scanning of faces in autism. *Journal of Autism and Developmental Disorders, 32*(4), 249–261.

Peppe, S., McCann, J., Gibbon, F., O'Hare, A., & Rutherford, M. (2007). Receptive and expressive prosodic ability in children with high-functioning autism. *Journal of Speech Language and Hearing Research, 50*(4), 1015–1028.

Perkins, T., Stokes, M., McGillivray, J., & Bittar, R. (2010). Mirror neuron dysfunction in autism spectrum disorders. *Journal of Clinical Neuroscience, 17*(10), 1239–1243.

Pernon, E., Pry, R., & Baghdadli, A. (2007). Autism: Tactile perception and emotion. *Journal of Intellectual Disability Research, 51*(Pt 8), 580–587.

Persico, A. M., Pascucci, T., Puglisi-Allegra, S., Militerni, R., Bravaccio, C., Schneider, C., et al. (2002). Serotonin transporter gene promoter variants do not explain the hyperserotoninemia in autistic children. *Molecular Psychiatry, 7*(7), 795–800.

Petersson, S., Pedersen, N. L., Schalling, M., & Lavebratt, C. (1999). Primary megalencephaly at birth and low intelligence level. *Neurology, 53*(6), 1254–1259.

Petrides, M., Tomaiuolo, F., Yeterian, E. H., & Pandya, D. N. (2012). The prefrontal cortex: Comparative architectonic organization in the human and the macaque monkey brains. *Cortex, 48*(1), 46–57.

Philips, G. M., & Dyer, C. (1977). Late onset echolalia in autism and allied disorders. *British Journal of Disorders of Communication, 12*(1), 47–59.

Pickles, A., Simonoff, E., Conti-Ramsden, G., Falcaro, M., Simkin, Z., Charman, T., et al. (2009). Loss of language in early development of autism and specific language impairment. *Journal of Child Psychology and Psychiatry, 50*(7), 843–852.

Pierce, K. (2010). Early functional brain development in autism and the promise of sleep fMRI. *Brain Research Bulletin, 1380*, 162–174.

Pierce, K., & Courchesne, E. (2001). Evidence for a cerebellar role in reduced exploration and stereotyped behavior in autism. *Biological Psychiatry, 49*(8), 655–664.

Pierce, K., Haist, F., Sedaghat, F., & Courchesne, E. (2004). The brain response to personally familiar faces in autism: Findings of fusiform activity and beyond. *Brain, 127*(Pt 12), 2703–2716.

Pierce, K., & Redcay, E. (2008). Fusiform function in children with an autism spectrum disorder is a matter of "who." *Biological Psychiatry, 64*(7), 552–560.

Piton, A., Gauthier, J., Hamdan, F. F., Lafreniere, R. G., Yang, Y., Henrion, E., et al. (2010). Systematic resequencing of X-chromosome synaptic genes in autism spectrum disorder and schizophrenia. *Molecular Psychiatry, 16*, 867–880.

Piven, J. (2001). The broad autism phenotype: A complementary strategy for molecular genetic studies of autism. *American Journal of Medical Genetics, 105*(1), 34–35.

Piven, J., Arndt, S., Bailey, J., & Andreasen, N. (1996). Regional brain enlargement in autism: A magnetic resonance imaging study. *Journal of the American Academy of Child and Adolescent Psychiatry, 35*(4), 530–536.

Piven, J., Arndt, S., Bailey, J., Havercamp, S., Andreasen, N. C., & Palmer, P. (1995). An MRI study of brain size in autism. *American Journal of Psychiatry, 152*(8), 1145–1149.

Ploog, B. O. (2010). Stimulus overselectivity four decades later: A review of the literature and its implications for current research in autism spectrum disorder. *Journal of Autism and Developmental Disorders, 40*, 1332–1349.

Poldrack, R. A., & Gabrieli, J. D. (1997). Functional anatomy of long-term memory. *Journal of Clinical Neurophysiology, 14*(4), 294–310.

Prizant, B. M., & Duchan, J. F. (1981). The functions of immediate echolalia in autistic children. *Journal of Speech and Hearing Disorders, 46*(3), 241–249.

Prizant, B. M., Wetherby, A. M., Rubin, E., Laurent, A. C., & Rydell, P. J. (2006). *The SCERTS Model: A Comprehensive Educational Approach for Children With Autism Spectrum Disorders*. Baltimore, MD: Paul H. Brookes.

Probst, P., & Leppert, T. (2008). Brief report: Outcomes of a teacher training program for autism spectrum disorders. *Journal of Autism and Developmental Disorders, 38*(9), 1791–1796.

Radua, J., Via, E., Catani, M., & Mataix-Cols, D. (2010). Voxel-based meta-analysis of regional white-matter volume differences in autism spectrum disorder versus healthy controls. *Psychological Medicine*, 1–12.

Ramberg, C., Ehlers, S., Nyden, A., Johansson, M., & Gillberg, C. (1996). Language and pragmatic functions in school-age children on the autism spectrum. *European Journal of Disorders of Communication, 31*(4), 387–413.

Rapin, I. (1991). Autistic children: Diagnosis and clinical features. *Pediatrics, 87*(5 Pt 2), 751–760.

Rapin, I., Dunn, M. A., Allen, D. A., Stevens, M. C., & Fein, D. (2009). Subtypes of language disorders in school-age children with autism. *Developmental Neuropsychology, 34*(1), 66–84.

Raymaekers, R., Antrop, I., van der Meere, J. J., Wiersema, J. R., & Roeyers, H. (2007). HFA and ADHD: A direct comparison on state regulation and response inhibition. *Journal of Clinical & Experimental Neuropsychology, 29*(4), 418–427.

Raymaekers, R., Wiersema, J. R., & Roeyers, H. (2009). EEG study of the mirror neuron system in children with high functioning autism. *Brain Research, 1304*, 113–121.

Raymond, G. V., Bauman, M. L., & Kemper, T. L. (1996). Hippocampus in autism: A Golgi analysis. *Acta Neuropathologica, 91*(1), 117–119.

Redcay, E. (2008). The superior temporal sulcus performs a common function for social and speech perception: Implications for the emergence of autism. *Neuroscience and Biobehavioral Review, 32*(1), 123–142.

Redcay, E., & Courchesne, E. (2005). When is the brain enlarged in autism? A meta-analysis of all brain size reports. *Biological Psychiatry 58*, 1–9.

Redcay, E., Haist, F., & Courchesne, E. (2008). Functional neuroimaging of speech perception during a pivotal period in language acquisition. *Developmental Science, 11*(2), 237–252.

Reichelt, A. C., Rodgers, R. J., & Clapcote, S. J. (2011). The role of neurexins in schizophrenia and autistic spectrum disorder. *Neuropharmacology, 62*, 1519–1526.

Reiersen, A. M., Constantino, J. N., Volk, H. E., & Todd, R. D. (2007). Autistic traits in a population-based ADHD twin sample. *Journal of Child Psychology and Psychiatry, 48*(5), 464–472.

Renner, P., Grofer Klinger, L., & Klinger, M. R. (2006). Exogenous and endogenous attention orienting in autism spectrum disorders. *Child Neuropsychology, 12*(4–5), 361–382.

Reznick, J. S., Baranek, G. T., Reavis, S., Watson, L. R., & Crais, E. R. (2007). A parent-report instrument for identifying one-year-olds at risk for an eventual diagnosis of autism: The first year inventory. *Journal of Autism and Developmental Disorders, 37*(9), 1691–1710.

Riby, D. M., Doherty-Sneddon, G., & Bruce, V. (2009). The eyes or the mouth? Feature salience and unfamiliar face processing in Williams syndrome and autism. *Quarterly Journal of Experimental Psychology, 62*(1), 189–203.

Richler, J., Bishop, S. L., Kleinke, J. R., & Lord, C. (2007). Restricted and repetitive behaviors in young children with autism spectrum disorders. *Journal of Autism and Developmental Disorders, 37*(1), 73–85.

Richler, J., Huerta, M., Bishop, S. L., & Lord, C. (2010). Developmental trajectories of restricted and repetitive behaviors and interests in children with autism spectrum disorders. *Developmental Psychopathology, 22*(1), 55–69.

Ricks, D. M., & Wing, L. (1975). Language, communication, and the use of symbols in normal and autistic children. *Journal of Autism & Childhood Schizophrenia, 5*(3), 191–221.

Rieffe, C., Meerum Terwogt, M., & Kotronopoulou, K. (2007). Awareness of single and multiple emotions in high-functioning children with autism. *Journal of Autism and Developmental Disorders, 37*(3), 455–465.

Rimland, B. (1964). *Infantile autism: The syndrome and its implications for a neural theory of behavior.* New York: Appleton-Century-Crofts.

Rinehart, N. J., Brereton, A. V., Tonge, B. J., & King, N. (2003). Autism: A parent-based early intervention. *Australian Journal of Psychology, 55,* 208.

Rinehart, N. J., Tonge, B. J., Iansek, R., McGinley, J., Brereton, A. V., & Enticott, P. G. (2006). Gait function in newly diagnosed children with autism: Cerebellar and basal ganglia related motor disorder. *Developmental Medicine and Child Neurology, 48,* 819–824.

Ritvo, E. R. Freeman, B. J., Mason-Brother, A., Mo, A., & Ritvo, A. M. (1985). Concordance for the syndrome of autism in 40 pairs of afflicted twins. *American Journal of Psychiatry, 142*(1), 74–77.

Ritvo, E. R., Freeman, B. J., & Scheibel, A. B. (1986). Lower Purkinje cell counts in the cerebella of four autistic subjects: Initial findings of the UCLA-NSAC research report. *American Journal of Psychiatry, 143*(7), 862–866.

Rizzolatti, G., Fabbri-Destro, M., & Cattaneo, L. (2009). Mirror neurons and their clinical relevance. *Nature Clinical Practice Neurology, 5*(1), 24–34.

Roberts, T. P., Cannon, K. M., Tavabi, K., Blaskey, L., Khan, S. Y., Monroe, J. F., et al. (2011). Auditory magnetic mismatch field latency: A biomarker for language impairment in autism. *Biological Psychiatry, 70,* 263–269.

Roberts, T. P., Khan, S. Y., Rey, M., Monroe, J. F., Cannon, K., Blaskey, L., et al. (2010). MEG detection of delayed auditory evoked responses in autism spectrum disorders: Towards an imaging biomarker for autism. *Autism Research, 3*(1), 8–18.

Robins, D. L., Fein, D., Barton, M. L., & Green, J. A. (2001). The modified checklist for autism in toddlers: An initial study investigating the early detection of autism and pervasive developmental disorders. *Journal of Autism and Developmental Disorders, 31*(2), 131–144.

Robinson, S., Goddard, L., Dritschel, B., Wisley, M., & Howlin, P. (2009). Executive functions in children with autism spectrum disorders. *Brain and Cognition, 71*(3), 362–368.

Rodier, P. M. (2002). Converging evidence for brain stem injury in autism. *Developmental Psychopathology, 14*(3), 537–557.

Rogers, S. J. (2004). Developmental regression in autism spectrum disorders. *Mental Retardation and Developmental Disabilities Research Reviews, 10*(2), 139–143.

Rogers, S. J., & DiLalla, D. L. (1990). Age of symptom onset in young children with pervasive developmental disorders. *Journal of the American Academy of Child & Adolescent Psychiatry, 29*(6), 863–872.

Rogers, S. J., & Ozonoff, S. (2005). Annotation: What do we know about sensory dysfunction in autism? A critical review of the empirical evidence. *Journal of Child Psychology and Psychiatry, 46*(12), 1255–1268.

Rogers, T. D., Dickson, P. E., Heck, D. H., Goldowitz, D., Mittleman, G., & Blaha, C. D. (2011). Connecting the dots of the cerebro-cerebellar role in cognitive function: Neuronal pathways for cerebellar modulation of dopamine release in the prefrontal cortex. *Synapse, 65*(11), 1204–1212.

Rosenhall, U., Nordin, V., Sandstrom, M., Ahlsen, G., & Gillberg, C. (1999). Autism and hearing loss. *Journal of Autism and Developmental Disorders, 29*(5), 349–357.

Rossi, C. C., Van de Water, J., Rogers, S. J., & Amaral, D. G. (2011). Detection of plasma autoantibodies to brain tissue in young children with and without autism spectrum disorders. *Brain, Behavior and Immunology, 25*(6), 1123–1135.

Rudie, J. D., Shehzad, Z., Hernandez, L. M., Colich, N. L., Bookheimer, S. Y., Iacoboni, M., & Dapretto, M. (2012). Reduced functional integration and segregation of distributed neural systems underlying social and emotional information processing in autism spectrum disorders. *Cerebral Cortex, 22*(5), 1025–1037.

Rumsey, J. M., & Ernst, M. (2000). Functional neuroimaging of autistic disorders. *Mental Retardation and Developmental Disabilities Research Reviews, 6*(3), 171–179.

Rumsey, J. M., & Hamburger, S. D. (1988). Neuropsychological findings in high-functioning men with infantile autism, residual state. *Journal of Clinical & Experimental Neuropsychology, 10*(2), 201–221.

Ruser, T. F., Arin, D., Dowd, M., Putnam, S., Winklosky, B., Rosen-Sheidley, B., et al. (2007). Communicative competence in parents of children with autism and parents of children with specific language impairment. *Journal of Autism and Developmental Disorders, 37*(7), 1323–1336.

Russell, J., & Jarrold, C. (1999). Memory for actions in children with autism: Self versus other. *Cognitive Neuropsychiatry, 4*(4), 303–331.

Russo, N., Nicol, T., Trommer, B., Zecker, S., & Kraus, N. (2009a). Brainstem transcription of speech is disrupted in children with autism spectrum disorders. *Developmental Science, 12*(4), 557–567.

Russo, N., Zecker, S., Trommer, B., Chen, J., & Kraus, N. (2009b). Effects of background noise on cortical encoding of speech in autism spectrum disorders. *Journal of Autism and Developmental Disorders, 39*(8), 1185–1196.

Rutter, M. (1983). Cognitive deficits in the pathogenesis of autism. *Journal of Child Psychology & Psychiatry & Allied Disciplines, 24*(4), 513–531.

Rutter, M. (2005). Aetiology of autism: Findings and questions. *Journal of Intellectual Disability Research, 49*(Pt 4), 231–238.

Rutter, M., Bailey, A., & Lord, C. (2003). Social Communication Questionnaire (SCQ) manual. *Los Angeles: Western Psychological Services.*

Rutter, M., LeCouteur, A., & Lord, C. (2003). Autism Diagnostic Interview–Revised. Torrance, CA: Western Psychological Services.

Rutter, M., Mawhood, L., & Howlin, P. (1992). Language delay and social development. In P. Fletcher & D. Hall (Eds.), *Specific speech and language disorders in children: Correlates, characteristics, and outcomes* (pp. 63–78). London: Whurr.

Rutter, M., & Schopler, E. (1987). Autism and pervasive developmental disorders: Concepts and diagnostic issues. *Journal of Autism & Developmental Disorders, 17*(2), 159–186.

Saffran, J. R., Aslin, R. N., & Newport, E. L. (1996). Statistical learning by 8-month old infants. *Science, 274*, 1926–1928.

Saha, S., Barnett, A. G., Foldi, C., Burne, T. H., Eyles, D. W., Buka, S. L., et al. (2009). Advanced paternal age is associated with impaired neurocognitive outcomes during infancy and childhood. *PLoS Medicine, 6*(3), e40.

Saint Georges, C., Cassel, R. S., Cohen, D., Chetouani, M., Laznik, M. C., Maestro, S., et al. (2010). What studies of family home movies can teach us about autistic infants: A literature review. *Research in Autism Spectrum Disorders, 4*, 355–366.

Samson, F., Hyde, K. L., Bertone, A., Soulieres, I., Mendrek, A., Ahad, P., et al. (2011). Atypical processing of auditory temporal complexity in autistics. *Neuropsychologia, 49*(3), 546–555.

Samson, F., Mottron, L., Jemel, B., Belin, P., & Ciocca, V. (2006). Can spectro-temporal complexity explain the autistic pattern of performance on auditory tasks? *Journal of Autism and Developmental Disorders, 36*(1), 65–76.

Schain, R. J., & Yannet, H. (1960). Infantile autism: An analysis of 50 cases and a consideration of certain neurophysiologic concepts. *Journal of Pediatrics, 57*, 560–567.

Schipul, S. E., Keller, T. A., & Just, M. A. (2011). Inter-regional brain communication and its disturbance in autism. *Frontiers in Systems Neuroscience, 5*, 10.

Schmitz, C., & Rezaie, P. (2008). The neuropathology of autism: Where do we stand? *Neuropathology and Applied Neurobiology, 34*(1), 4–11.

Schopler, E. (1986). A new approach to autism. *Social Science, 71*(2–3), 183–185.

Schopler, E., Reichler, J., & Renner, B. (1998). *The Childhood Autism Rating Scale* (CARS). Modesto, CA: Western Psychological Services.

Schuler, A. L. (1979). Echolalia: Issues and clinical applications. *Journal of Speech and Hearing Disorders, 44*(4), 411–434.

Schulte-Ruther, M., Greimel, E., Markowitsch, H. J., Kamp-Becker, I., Remschmidt, H., Fink, G. R., et al. (2010). Dysfunctions in brain networks supporting empathy: An fMRI study in adults with autism spectrum disorders. *Social Neuroscience, 6*(1), 1–21.

Schultz, R. T. (2005). Developmental deficits in social perception in autism: The role of the amygdala and fusiform face area. *International Journal of Developmental Neuroscience, 23*(2/3), 125–141.

Schumann, C. M., & Amaral, D. G. (2006). Stereological analysis of amygdala neuron number in autism. *Journal of Neuroscience, 26*(29), 7674–7679.

Schumann, C. M., Barnes, C. C., Lord, C., & Courchesne, E. (2009). Amygdala enlargement in toddlers with autism related to severity of social and communication impairments. *Biological Psychiatry, 66*(10), 942–949.

Schyns, P. G., Petro, L. S., & Smith, M. L. (2007). Dynamics of visual information integration in the brain for categorizing facial expressions. *Current Biology, 17*(18), 1580–1585.

Scott, J. A., Schumann, C. M., Goodlin-Jones, B. L., & Amaral, D. G. (2009). A comprehensive volumetric analysis of the cerebellum in children and adolescents with autism spectrum disorder. *Autism Research, 2*(5), 246–257.

Senju, A., & Johnson, M. H. (2009). Atypical eye contact in autism: Models, mechanisms and development. *Neuroscience and Biobehavioral Reviews, 33*, 1204–1214.

Shafritz, K. M., Dichter, G. S., Baranek, G. T., & Belger, A. (2008). The neural circuitry mediating shifts in behavioral response and cognitive set in autism. *Biological Psychiatry, 63*(10), 974–980.

Shah, A., & Frith, U. (1993). Why do autistic individuals show superior performance on the block design task? *Journal of Child Psychology & Psychiatry & Allied Disciplines, 34*(8), 1351–1364.

Shao, Y., Cuccaro, M. L., Hauser, E. R., Raiford, K. L., Menold, M. M., Wolpert, C. M., et al. (2003). Fine mapping of autistic disorder to chromosome 15q11–q13 by use of phenotypic subtypes. *American Journal of Human Genetics, 72*(3), 539–548.

Sheinkopf, S. J., & Siegel, B. (1998). Home-based behavioral treatment of young children with autism. *Journal of Autism and Developmental Disorders, 28*(1), 15–23.

Shriberg, L. D., Paul, R., Black, L. M., & van Santen, J. P. (2010). The hypothesis of apraxia of speech in children with autism spectrum disorder. *Journal of Autism and Developmental Disorders, 41*(4), 405–426.

Shriberg, L. D., Paul, R., McSweeny, J. L., Klin, A. M., Cohen, D. J., & Volkmar, F. R. (2001). Speech and prosody characteristics of adolescents and adults with high-functioning autism and Asperger syndrome. *Journal of Speech Language and Hearing Research, 44*(5), 1097–1115.

Shu, B. C., Lung, F. W., Tien, A. Y., & Chen, B. C. (2001). Executive function deficits in non-retarded autistic children. *Autism, 5*(2), 165–174.

Shumway, S., Thurm, A., Swedo, S. E., Deprey, L., Barnett, L. A., Amaral, D. G., et al. (2011). Brief report: Symptom onset patterns and functional outcomes in young children with autism spectrum disorders. *Journal of Autism and Developmental Disorders, 41*, 1727–1732.

Shumway, S., & Wetherby, A. M. (2009). Communicative acts of children with autism spectrum disorders in the second year of life. *Journal of Speech Language and Hearing Research, 52*(5), 1139–1156.

Siegel, B. (2004). *Pervasive developmental disorders screening test – II*. San Antonio, TX: Harcourt.

Sigman, M., Dijamco, A., Gratier, M., & Rozga, A. (2004). Early detection of core deficits in autism. *Mental Retardation and Developmental Disabilities Research Reviews, 10*(4), 221–233.

Sikich, L., Hickok, J. M., & Todd, R. D. (1990). 5-HT1A receptors control neurite branching during development. *Brain Research*. Developmental Brain Research, *56*(269–274).

Silani, G., Bird, G., Brindley, R., Singer, T., Frith, C., & Frith, U. (2008). Levels of emotional awareness and autism: An fMRI study. *Social Neuroscience, 3*(2), 97–112.

Simmons, D. R., Robertson, A. E., McKay, L. S., Toal, E., McAleer, P., & Pollick, F. E. (2009). Vision in autism spectrum disorders. *Vision Research, 49*(22), 2705–2739.

Simpson, R. L. (2005). Evidence-based practices and students with autism spectrum disorders. *ProQuest Educational Journals, 20*(3), 140–149.

Singer, H. S., Morris, C. M., Gause, C. D., Gillin, P. K., Crawford, S., & Zimmerman, A. W. (2008). Antibodies against fetal brain in sera of mothers with autistic children. *Journal of Neuroimmunology, 194*(1–2), 165–172.

Siperstein, R., & Volkmar, F. (2004). Brief report: Parental reporting of regression in children with pervasive developmental disorders. *Journal of Autism and Developmental Disorders, 34*(6), 731–734.

Smith, C. J., Lang, C. M., Kryzak, L., Reichenberg, A., Hollander, E., & Silverman, J. M. (2009). Familial associations of intense preoccupations, an empirical factor of the restricted, repetitive behaviors and interests domain of autism. *Journal of Child Psychology and Psychiatry, 50*(8), 982–990.

Smith, T., Buch, G. A., & Gamby, T. E. (2000). Parent-directed, intensive early intervention for children with pervasive developmental disorder. *Research in Developmental Disabilities, 21*(4), 297–309.

Smith, C. M., Rogers, S. J., & Dawson, G. (2006). The Early Start Denver Model: A comprehensive early intervention approach for toddlers with autism. In Handleman, J. S. & Harris, S. L. (Eds.), *Preschool Education Programs for Children with Autism*. 3rd ed., pp. 65–101. Austin, TX: Pro-Ed.

Sorensen, F. W., Larsen, J. O., Eide, R., & Schionning, J. D. (2000). Neuron loss in cerebellar cortex of rats exposed to mercury vapor: A stereological study. *Acta Neuropathologica, 100*(1), 95–100.

Soulieres, I., Zeffiro, T. A., Girard, M. L., & Mottron, L. (2011). Enhanced mental image mapping in autism. *Neuropsychologia, 49*, 848–857.

South, M., Ozonoff, S., & McMahon, W. M. (2007). The relationship between executive functioning, central coherence, and repetitive behaviors in the high-functioning autism spectrum. *Autism: The International Journal of Research & Practice, 11*(5), 437–451.

Sparks, B. F., Friedman, S. D., Shaw, D. W., Aylward, E. H., Echelard, D., Artru, A. A., et al. (2002). Brain structural abnormalities in young children with autism spectrum disorder. *Neurology, 59*(2), 184–192.

Spencer, J., O'Brien, J., Riggs, K., Braddick, O., Atkinson, J., & Wattam-Bell, J. (2000). Motion processing in autism: Evidence for a dorsal stream deficiency. *Neuroreport, 11*(12), 2765–2767.

Spezio, M. L., Adolphs, R., Hurley, R. S., & Piven, J. (2007a). Abnormal use of facial information in high-functioning autism. *Journal of Autism and Developmental Disorders, 37*(5), 929–939.

Spezio, M. L., Adolphs, R., Hurley, R. S., & Piven, J. (2007b). Analysis of face gaze in autism using "Bubbles." *Neuropsychologia, 45*(1), 144–151.

Ssucharewa, G. E. (1926). The first account of the syndrome Asperger described? Translation by S. Wolff of a paper entitled "Die schizoiden Psychopathien im Kindesalter" by Dr. G.E. Ssucharewa; scientific assistant, which appeared in 1926 in the Monatsschrift fur Psychiatrie und Neurologie 60:235–261. *Eur Child Adolesc Psychiatry, 5*(3), 119–132.

Stanfield, A. C., McIntosh, A. M., Spencer, M. D., Philip, R., Gaur, S., & Lawrie, S. M. (2008). Towards a neuroanatomy of autism: A systematic review and meta-analysis of structural magnetic resonance imaging studies. *European Psychiatry, 23*(4), 289–299.

Steele, S. D., Minshew, N. J., Luna, B., & Sweeney, J. A. (2007). Spatial working memory deficits in autism. *Journal of Autism and Developmental Disorders, 37*(4), 605–612.

Stefanatos, G., Kinsbourne, M., & Wasserstein, J. (2002). Acquired epileptiform aphasia: A dimensional view of Landau-Kleffner Syndrome and the relation to regressive autistic spectrum disorders. *Child Neuropsychology, 8*(3), 195–228.

Stefanatos, G. A. (2008). Regression in autistic spectrum disorders. *Neuropsychology Review, 18*(4), 305–319.

Stefanatos, G. A., & Baron, I. S. (2011). The ontogenesis of language impairment in autism: a neuropsychological perspective. *Neuropsychology Review, 21*(3), 252–270.

Stefanatos, G. A., & DeMarco, A. T. (2011). Central auditory processing disorders. In V. S. Ramachandran (Ed.), *Encyclopedia of Human Behavior*. Oxford: Elsevier.

Steffenburg, S., Gillberg, C., Hellgren, L., Andersson, L., Gillberg, I. C., Jakobssen, G., et al. (1989). A twin study of autism in Denmark, Finland, Iceland, Norway and Sweden. *Journal of Child Psychology & Psychiatry & Allied Disciplines, 30*(3), 405–416.

Sterling, L., Dawson, G., Webb, S., Murias, M., Munson, J., Panagiotides, H., et al. (2008). The role of face familiarity in eye tracking of faces by individuals with autism spectrum disorders. *Journal of Autism and Developmental Disorders, 38*(9), 1666–1675.

Stevenson, R. E., Schroer, R. J., Skinner, C., Fender, D., & Simensen, R. J. (1997). Autism and macrocephaly. *Lancet, 349*(9067), 1744–1745.

Stigler, K. A., McDonald, B. C., Anand, A., Saykin, A. J., & McDougle, C. J. (2011). Structural and functional magnetic resonance imaging of autism spectrum disorders. *Brain Research, 1380*, 146–161.

Stigler, K. A., Sweeten, T. L., Posey, D. J., & McDougle, C. J. (2009). Autism and immune factors: A comprehensive review. *Research in Autism Spectrum Disorders, 3*(4), 840–860.

Stone, W. L., Coonrod, E. E., & Ousley, O. Y. (2000). Brief report: Screening tool for autism in two-year-olds (STAT): Development and preliminary data. *Journal of Autism and Developmental Disorders, 30*(6), 607–612.

Stone, W. L., Coonrod, E. E., Pozdol, S. L., & Turner, L. M. (2003). The Parent Interview for Autism-Clinical Version (PIA-CV): A measure of behavioral change for young children with autism. *Autism, 7*(1), 9–30.

Stone, W. L., Lee, E. B., Ashford, L., Brissie, J., Hepburn, S. L., Coonrod, E. E., et al. (1999). Can autism be diagnosed accurately in children under 3 years? *Journal of Child Psychology and Psychiatry and Allied Disciplines, 40*(2), 219–226.

Stone, W. L., McMahon, C. R., Yoder, P. J., & Walden, T. A. (2007). Early social-communicative and cognitive development of younger siblings of children with autism spectrum disorders. *Archives of Pediatric and Adolescent Medicine, 161*(4), 384–390.

Stone, W. L., & Yoder, P. J. (2001). Predicting spoken language level in children with autism spectrum disorders. *Autism, 5*(4), 341–361.

Striano, T., & Rochat, P. (1999). Developmental link between dyadic and triadic social competence in infancy. *British Journal of Developmental Psychology, 17*(4), 551–562.

Sundaram, S. K., Kumar, A., Makki, M. I., Behen, M. E., Chugani, H. T., & Chugani, D. C. (2008). Diffusion tensor imaging of frontal lobe in autism spectrum disorder. *Cerebral Cortex, 18*(11), 2659–2665.

Sundstrom, E., Kolare, S., Souverbie, F., Samuelsson, E. B., Pschera, H., Lunell, N. O., et al. (1993). Neurochemical differentiation of human bulbospinal monoaminergic neurons during the first trimester. *Developmental Brain Research, 75*, 1–12.

Sussman, F. (1999). *More Than Words: Helping Parents Promote Communication and Social Skills in Children With Autism Spectrum Disorder*. Toronto, Ontario: The Hanen Centre.

Suzuki, K., Nishimura, K., Sugihara, G., Nakamura, K., Tsuchiya, K. J., Matsumoto, K., et al. (2009). Metabolite alterations in the hippocampus of high-functioning adult subjects with autism. *International Journal of Neuropsychopharmacology, 13*(4), 529–534.

Swinkels, S. H., Dietz, C., van Daalen, E., Kerkhof, I. H., van Engeland, H., & Buitelaar, J. K. (2006). Screening for autistic spectrum in children aged 14 to 15 months. I: the development of the Early Screening of Autistic Traits Questionnaire (ESAT). *Journal of Autism and Developmental Disorders, 36*(6), 723–732.

Szatmari, P., Bryson, S. E., Boyle, M. H., Streiner, D. L., & Duku, E. (2003). Predictors of outcome among high functioning children with autism and Asperger syndrome. *Journal of Child Psychology and Psychiatry, 44*(4), 520–528.

Szatmari, P., Georgiades, S., Bryson, S., Zwaigenbaum, L., Roberts, W., Mahoney, W., et al. (2006). Investigating the structure of the restricted, repetitive behaviours and interests domain of autism. *Journal of Child Psychology and Psychiatry, 47*(6), 582–590.

Szatmari, P., & Jones, M. B. (1991). IQ and the genetics of autism. *Journal of Child Psychology & Psychiatry & Allied Disciplines, 32*(6), 897–908.

Szatmari, P., Paterson, A. D., Zwaigenbaum, L., Roberts, W., Brian, J., Liu, X. Q., et al. (2007). Mapping autism risk loci using genetic linkage and chromosomal rearrangements. *Nature Genetics, 39*(3), 319–328.

Tager-Flusberg, H. (2006). Defining language phenotypes in autism. *Clinical Neuroscience Research, 6*(3/4), 219–224.

Tager-Flusberg, H., & Caronna, E. (2007). Language disorders: Autism and other pervasive developmental disorders. *Pediatric Clinics of North America, 54*(3), 469–481, vi.

Tager-Flusberg, H., & Joseph, R. M. (2003). Identifying neurocognitive phenotypes in autism. *Philosophical Transactions of the Royal Society B-Biological Sciences, 358*(1430), 303–314.

Tager-Flusberg, H., Rogers, S., Cooper, J., Landa, R., Lord, C., Paul, R., et al. (2009). Defining spoken language benchmarks and selecting measures of expressive language development for young children with autism spectrum disorders. *Journal of Speech Language and Hearing Research, 52*(3), 643–652.

Teitelbaum, P., Teitelbaum, O., Nye, J., Fryman, J., & Maurer, R. G. (1998). Movement analysis in infancy may be useful for early diagnosis of autism. *Proceedings of the National Academy of Sciences of the United States of America, 95*(23), 13982–13987.

Tesink, C. M., Buitelaar, J. K., Petersson, K. M., van der Gaag, R. J., Teunisse, J. P., & Hagoort, P. (2011). Neural correlates of language comprehension in autism spectrum disorders: when language conflicts with world knowledge. *Neuropsychologia, 49*(5), 1095–1104.

Tharpe, A. M., Bess, F. H., Sladen, D. P., Schissel, H., Couch, S., & Schery, T. (2006). Auditory characteristics of children with autism. *Ear and Hearing, 27*(4), 430–441.

Thomas, A. C., Osann, K., Modahl, C., Laulhere, T., Smith, M., Escamilla, J., et al. (2001). Twin zygosity and concordance for the autism phenotype. *American Journal of Human Genetics, 69*(4), 389.

Thurm, A., Lord, C., Lee, L. C., & Newschaffer, C. (2007). Predictors of language acquisition in preschool children with autism spectrum disorders. *Journal of Autism and Developmental Disorders, 37*(9), 1721–1734.

Toal, F., Daly, E. M., Page, L., Deeley, Q., Hallahan, B., Bloemen, O., et al. (2009). Clinical and anatomical heterogeneity in autistic spectrum disorder: A structural MRI study. *Psychological Medicine, 40*(7), 1171–1181.

Tomasello, M. (2008). *Origins of human communication*. Cambridge, MA: MIT Press.

Tordjman, S., Gutknecht, L., Carlier, M., Spitz, E., Antoine, C., Slama, F., et al. (2001). Role of the serotonin transporter gene in the behavioral expression of autism. *Molecular Psychiatry, 6*(4), 434–439.

Toth, K., Munson, J., Meltzoff, A. N., & Dawson, G. (2006). Early predictors of communication development in young children with autism spectrum disorder: Joint attention, imitation, and toy play. *Journal of Autism and Developmental Disorders, 36*(8), 993–1005.

Townsend, J., & Courchesne, E. (1994). Parietal damage and narrow "spotlight" spatial attention. *Journal of Cognitive Neuroscience, 6*(3), 220–232.

Townsend, J., Courchesne, E., Covington, J., Westerfield, M., Harris, N. S., Lyden, P., et al. (1999). Spatial attention deficits in patients with acquired or developmental cerebellar abnormality. *Journal of Neuroscience, 19*(13), 5632–5643.

Townsend, J., Harris, N. S., & Courchesne, E. (1996). Visual attention abnormalities in autism: Delayed orienting to location. *Journal of the International Neuropsychological Society, 2*(6), 541–550.

Townsend, J., Westerfield, M., Leaver, E., Makeig, S., Jung, T., Pierce, K., et al. (2001). Event-related brain response abnormalities in autism: Evidence for impaired cerebello-frontal spatial attention networks. *Cognitive Brain Research, 11*(1), 127–145.

Trevarthen, C., & Aitken, K. J. (2001). Infant intersubjectivity: Research, theory, and clinical applications. *Journal of Child Psychology and Psychiatry, 42*(1), 3–48.

Trevarthen, C., Murray, L., & Hubley, P. (1981). Psychology of infants. *Scientific Foundations of Clinical Paediatrics*, 211–274.

Tsuchiya, E., Oki, J., Yahara, N., & Fujieda, K. (2005). Computerized version of the Wisconsin Card Sorting Test in children with high-functioning autistic disorder or attention-deficit/hyperactivity disorder. *Brain & Development, 27*(3), 233–236.

Tuchman, R., & Rapin, I. (2002). Epilepsy in autism. *Lancet Neurology, 1*(6), 352–358.

Turkeltaub, P. E., Flowers, D. L., Verbalis, A., Miranda, M., Gareau, L., & Eden, G. F. (2004). The neural basis of hyperlexic reading: An fMRI case study. *Neuron, 41*(1), 11–25.

Turner, M. (1999a). Annotation: Repetitive behaviour in autism: A review of psychological research. *Journal of Child Psychology and Psychiatry and Allied Disciplines, 40*(6), 839–849.

Turner, M. A. (1999b). Generating novel ideas: Fluency performance in high-functioning and learning disabled individuals with autism. *Journal of Child Psychology and Psychiatry, 40*(2), 189–201.

Tzourio-Mazoyer, N., De Schonen, S., Crivello, F., Reutter, B., Aujard, Y., & Mazoyer, B. (2002). Neural correlates of woman face processing by 2-month-old infants. *Neuroimage, 15*(2), 454–461.

Ungerer, J. A., & Sigman, M. (1987). Categorization skills and receptive language development in autistic children. *Journal of Autism and Developmental Disorders, 17*(1), 3–16.

Vaidya, V. A., Marek, G. J., Aghajanian, G. K., & Duman, R. S. (1997). 5-HT2A receptor-mediated regulation of brain-derived neurotrophic factor mRNA in the hippocampus and the neocortex. *Journal of Neuroscience Methods, 17*, 2785–2795.

Vakil, E., & Herishanu-Naaman, S. (1998). Declarative and procedural learning in Parkinson's disease patients having tremor or bradykinesia as the predominant symptom. *Cortex, 34*(4), 611–620.

van Kooten, I. A., Palmen, S. J., von Cappeln, P., Steinbusch, H. W., Korr, H., Heinsen, H., et al. (2008). Neurons in the fusiform gyrus are fewer and smaller in autism. *Brain, 131*(Pt 4), 987–999.

Vanvuchelen, M., Roeyers, H., & De Weerdt, W. (2011). Imitation assessment and its utility to the diagnosis of autism: Evidence from consecutive clinical preschool referrals for suspected autism. *Journal of Autism and Developmental Disorders, 41*(4), 484–496.

Vargas, D. L., Nascimbene, C., Krishnan, C., Zimmerman, A. W., & Pardo, C. A. (2005). Neuroglial activation and neuroinflammation in the brain of patients with autism. *Annals of Neurology, 57*(1), 67–81.

Verte, S., Geurts, H. M., Roeyers, H., Oosterlaan, J., & Sergeant, J. A. (2005). Executive functioning in children with autism and Tourette syndrome. *Developmental Psychopathology, 17*(2), 415–445.

Vihman, M., & Croft, W. (2007). Phonological development: Toward a "radical" templatic phonology. *Linguistics, 45*(4), 683–725.

Virues-Ortega, J. (2010). Applied behavior analytic intervention for autism in early childhood: Meta-analysis, meta-regression and dose-response meta-analysis of multiple outcomes. *Clinical Psychology Review, 30*(4), 387–399.

Volkmar, F., Cook, E., Pomeroy, J., Realmuto, G., & Tanguay, P. (1999). Summary of the practice parameters for the assessment and treatment of children, adolescents, and adults with autism and other pervasive developmental disorders. *Journal of the American Academy of Child and Adolescent Psychiatry, 38*(12), 1611–1615.

Vollm, B. A, Taylor, A. N., Richardson, P., Corcoran, R., Stirling, J., McKie, S., et al. (2006). Neuronal correlates of theory of mind and empathy: a functional magnetic resonance imaging study in a nonverbal task. *Neuroimage*, 29: 90–98.

von dem Hagen, E. A., Nummenmaa, L., Yu, R., Engell, A. D., Ewbank, M. P., & Calder, A. J. (2011). Autism spectrum traits in the typical population predict structure and function in the posterior superior temporal sulcus. *Cerebral Cortex, 21*(3), 493–500.

Vorstman, J. A., Staal, W. G., van Daalen, E., van Engeland, H., Hochstenbach, P. F., & Franke, L. (2006). Identification of novel autism candidate regions through analysis of reported cytogenetic abnormalities associated with autism. *Molecular Psychiatry, 11*(1), 18–28.

Wainwright-Sharp, J., & Bryson, S. E. (1993). Visual orienting deficits in high-functioning people with autism. *Journal of Autism & Developmental Disorders, 23*(1), 1–13.

Wallace, G. L., Dankner, N., Kenworthy, L., Giedd, J. N., & Martin, A. (2010). Age-related temporal and parietal cortical thinning in autism spectrum disorders. *Brain, 133*(Pt 12), 3745–3754.

Wallace, S., Coleman, M., Pascalis, O., & Bailey, A. (2006). A study of impaired judgment of eye-gaze direction and related face-processing deficits in autism spectrum disorders. *Perception, 35*(12), 1651–1664.

Wang, A. T., Lee, S. S., Sigman, M., & Dapretto, M. (2006). Neural basis of irony comprehension in children with autism: The role of prosody and context. *Brain, 129*(Pt 4), 932–943.

Wang, K., Zhang, H., Ma, D., Bucan, M., Glessner, J. T., Abrahams, B. S., et al. (2009). Common genetic variants on 5p14.1 associate with autism spectrum disorders. *Nature, 459*(7246), 528–533.

Warren, R. P., Singh, V. K., Averett, R. E., Odell, J. D., Maciulis, A., Burger, R. A., et al. (1996). Immunogenetic studies in autism and related disorders. *Molecular and Chemical Neuropathology, 28*(1–3), 77–81.

Waterhouse, L., Fein, D., & Modahl, C. (1996). Neurofunctional mechanisms in autism. *Psychological Review, 103*(3), 457–489.

Watson, L. R., Baranek, G. T., & DiLavore, P. C. (2003). Toddlers with autism – Developmental perspectives. *Infants and Young Children, 16*(3), 201–214.

Weiller, C., Bormann, T., Saur, D., Musso, M., & Rijntjes, M. (2011). How the ventral pathway got lost—And what its recovery might mean. *Brain & Language*, 118, 29–39.

Weinstein, M., Ben-Sira, L., Levy, Y., Zachor, D. A., Ben Itzhak, E., Artzi, M., et al. (2011). Abnormal white matter integrity in young children with autism. *Human Brain Mapping, 32*(4), 534–543.

Weiss, L. A., Arking, D. E., Daly, M. J., & Chakravarti, A. (2009). A genome-wide linkage and association scan reveals novel loci for autism. *Nature, 461*(7265), 802–808.

Welsh, J. P., Yuen, G., Placantonakis, D. G., Vu, T. Q., Haiss, F., O'Hearn, E., et al. (2002). Why do Purkinje cells die so easily after global brain ischemia? Aldolase C, EAAT4, and the cerebellar contribution to posthypoxic myoclonus. *Advances in Neurology, 89*, 331–359.

Werker, J. F., & Yeung, H. H. (2005). Infant speech perception bootstraps word learning. *Trends in Cognitive Science, 9*(11), 519–527.

Werner, E., & Dawson, G. (2005). Validation of the phenomenon of autistic regression using home videotapes. *Archives of General Psychiatry, 62*(8), 889–895.

Werner, E., Dawson, G., Munson, J., & Osterling, J. (2005). Variation in early developmental course in autism and its relation with behavioral outcome at 3–4 years of age. *Journal of Autism and Developmental Disorders, 35*(3), 337–350.

Wetherby, A., Brosnan-Maddox, S., Peace, V., & Newton, L. (2008). Validadtion of the Infant-Toddler Checklist as a broadband screener for autism spectrum disorders from 9 to 24 months of age. *Autism, 12*(5), 487–511.

Wetherby, A. M., & Woods, J. (2006). Early social interaction project for children with autism spectrum disorders beginning in the second year of life: A preliminary study. *Topics in Early Childhood Special Education, 2*, 67–82.

Wetherby, A., Watt, N., Morgan, L., & Shumway, S. (2007). Social communication profiles of children with autism spectrum disorders in the second year of life. *Journal of Autism and Developmental Disorders, 37*, 960–975.

Wetherby, A. M. (1986). Ontogeny of communicative functions in autism. *Journal of Autism and Developmental Disorders, 16*(3), 295–316.

Wetherby, A. M., & Prizant, B. M. (2002). *Communication and symbolic behavior scales and developmental profile*. Baltimore, MD: Brookes.

Wetherby, A. M., Prizant, B. M., & Hutchinson, T. A. (1998). Communicative, social/affective, and symbolic profiles of young children with autism and pervasive developmental disorders. *American Journal of Speech-Language Pathology, 7*(2), 79–91.

Wetherby, A. M., & Woods, J. (2006). *Early social interaction project for children with autism spectrum disorders beginning in the second year of life: A preliminary study. Topics in Early Childhood Special Education, 2*, 67–82.

Wetherby, A. M., Woods, J., Allen, L., Cleary, J., Dickinson, H., & Lord, C. (2004). Early indicators of autism spectrum disorders in the second year of life. *Journal of Autism and Developmental Disorders, 34*(5), 473–493.

Wetherby, A. M., Yonclas, D. G., & Bryan, A. A. (1989). Communicative profiles of preschool children with handicaps: Implications for early identification. *Journal of Speech & Hearing Disorders, 54*(2), 148–158.

Whitaker-Azmitia, P. M. (2001). Serotonin and brain development: Role in human developmental diseases. *Brain Research Bulletin, 56*(5), 479–485.

Whitehouse, A. J., Coon, H., Miller, J., Salisbury, B., & Bishop, D. V. (2010). Narrowing the broader autism phenotype: A study using the Communication Checklist-Adult Version (CC-A). *Autism, 14*(6), 559–574.

Whitney, C., Huber, W., Klann, J., Weis, S., Krach, S., & Kircher, T. (2009). Neural correlates of narrative shifts during auditory story comprehension. *Neuroimage*, 47, 360–366.

Whitney, E. R., Kemper, T. L., Rosene, D. L., Bauman, M. L., & Blatt, G. J. (2009). Density of cerebellar basket and stellate cells in autism: Evidence for a late developmental loss of Purkinje cells. *Journal of Neuroscience Research, 87*(10), 2245–2254.

World Health Organization. (1992). *Tenth Revision of the Internaional Classification of Diseases and Related Health Problems* (ICD-10). Geneva: World Health Organization.

Wieder, S., & Greenspan, S. I. (2003). Climbing the symbolic ladder in the DIR model through floor time/interactive play. *Autism, 7*(4), 425–435.

Wiggins, L. D., Robins, D. L., Bakeman, R., & Adamson, L. B. (2009). Brief report: Sensory abnormalities as distinguishing symptoms of autism spectrum disorders in young children. *Journal of Autism and Developmental Disorders, 39*(7), 1087–1091.

Williams, D. L., Goldstein, G., & Minshew, N. J. (2006a). The profile of memory function in children with autism. *Neuropsychology, 20*(1), 21–29.

Williams, E. L., & Casanova, M. F. (2010). Potential teratogenic effects of ultrasound on corticogenesis: Implications for autism. *Medical Hypotheses, 75*(1), 53–58.

Williams, J. H., Waiter, G. D., Gilchrist, A., Perrett, D. I., Murray, A. D., & Whiten, A. (2006b). Neural mechanisms of imitation and 'mirror neuron' functioning in autistic spectrum disorder. *Neuropsychologia, 44*(4), 610–621.

Wilson, C. E., Freeman, P., Brock, J., Burton, A. M., & Palermo, R. (2010). Facial identity recognition in the broader autism phenotype. *Plos One, 5*(9), e12876.

Wimpory, D. C., Hobson, R. P., Williams, J. M., & Nash, S. (2000). Are infants with autism socially engaged? A study of recent retrospective parental reports. *Journal of Autism and Developmental Disorders, 30*(6), 525–536.

Wing, L. (1997). The autistic spectrum. *Lancet, 350*(9093), 1761–1766.

Wing, L., & Gould, J. (1979). Severe impairments of social interaction and associated abnormalities in children: Epidemiology and classification. *Journal of Autism and Developmental Disorders, 9*(1), 11–29.

Wing, L., Gould, J., & Gillberg, C. (2011). Autism spectrum disorders in the DSM-V: Better or worse than the DSM-IV? *Research in Developmental Disabilities, 32*(2), 768–773.

Wong, V. C., & Kwan, Q. K. (2010). Randomized controlled trial for early intervention for autism: A pilot study of the Autism 1-2-3 Project. *Journal of Autism and Developmental Disorders, 40*(6), 677–688.

Woodhouse, W., Bailey, A., Rutter, M., Bolton, P., Baird, G., & LeCouteur, A. (1996). Head circumference in autism and other pervasive developmental disorders. *Journal of Child Psychology and Psychiatry and Allied Disciplines, 37*(6), 665–671.

Woodward, A. L., & Hoyne, K. L. (1999). Infants' learning about words and sounds in relation to objects. *Child Development, 80*, 65–77.

Wright, B., Clarke, N., Jordan, J., Young, A. W., Clarke, P., Miles, J., et al. (2008). Emotion recognition in faces and the use of visual context in young people with high-functioning autism spectrum disorders. *Autism, 12*(6), 607–626.

Yamakawa, H., Oyama, S., Mitsuhashi, H., Sasagawa, N., Uchino, S., Kohsaka, S., et al. (2007). Neuroligins 3 and 4X interact with syntrophin-gamma2, and the interactions are affected by autism-related mutations. *Biochemical and Biophysical Research Communications, 355*(1), 41–46.

Yeargin-Allsopp, M., Rice, C., Karapurkar, T., Doernberg, N., Boyle, C., & Murphy, C. (2003). Prevalence of autism in a US metropolitan area. *Journal of the American Medical Association, 289*(1), 49–55.

Yirmiya, N., Pilowsky, T., Nemanov, L., Arbelle, S., Feinsilver, T., Fried, I., & Ebstein, R. P. (2001). Evidence for an association with the serotonin transporter promoter region polymorphism and autism. *American Journal of Medical Genetics, 105*(4), 381–386.

Yoder, P., Stone, W. L., Walden, T., & Malesa, E. (2009). Predicting social impairment and ASD diagnosis in younger siblings of children with autism spectrum disorder. *Journal of Autism and Developmental Disorders, 39*(10), 1381–1391.

Young, H. A., Geier, D. A., & Geier, M. R. (2008). Thimerosal exposure in infants and neurodevelopmental disorders: An assessment of computerized medical records in the Vaccine Safety Datalink. *Journal of the Neurological Sciences, 271*(1/2), 110–118.

Young, R. L., Brewer, N., & Pattison, C. (2003). Parental identification of early behavioural abnormalities in children with autistic disorder. *Autism, 7*(2), 125–143.

Zafeiriou, D. I., Ververi, A., & Vargiami, E. (2009). The serotonergic system: Its role in pathogenesis and early developmental treatment of autism. *Current Neuropharmacology, 7*(2), 150–157.

Zander, E., & Dahlgren, S. O. (2010). WISC-III index score profiles of 520 Swedish children with pervasive developmental disorders. *Psychological Assessment, 22*(2), 213–222.

Zappella, M. (2010). Autistic regression with and without EEG abnormalities followed by favourable outcome. *Brain & Development, 32*(9), 739–745.

Zikopoulos, B., & Barbas, H. (2010). Changes in prefrontal axons may disrupt the network in autism. *Journal of Neuroscience, 30*(44), 14595–14609.

Zilbovicius, M., Meresse, I., Chabane, N., Brunelle, F., Samson, Y., & Boddaert, N. (2006). Autism, the superior temporal sulcus and social perception. *Trends in Neurosciences, 29*(7), 359–366.

Zinke, K., Fries, E., Altgassen, M., Kirschbaum, C., Dettenborn, L., & Kliegel, M. (2010). Visuospatial short-term memory explains deficits in tower task planning in high-functioning children with autism spectrum disorder. *Child Neuropsychology, 16*(3), 229–241.

Zwaigenbaum, L., Bryson, S., Lord, C., Rogers, S., Carter, A., Carver, L., et al. (2009). Clinical assessment and management of toddlers with suspected autism spectrum disorder: Insights from studies of high-risk infants. *Pediatrics, 123*(5), 1383–1391.

Zwaigenbaum, L., Bryson, S., Rogers, T., Roberts, W., Brian, J., & Szatmari, P. (2005). Behavioral manifestations of autism in the first year of life. *International Journal of Developmental Neuroscience, 23*(2–3), 143–152.

Zwaigenbaum, L., Szatmari, P., Goldberg, J., Bryson, S., Mahoney, W., & Bartolucci, G. (2000). The broader autism phenotype: Defining genetically informative dimensions. *American Journal of Human Genetics, 67*(4), 213.

Zwaigenbaum, L., Thurm, A., Stone, W., Baranek, G., Bryson, S., Iverson, J., et al. (2007). Studying the emergence of autism spectrum disorders in high-risk infants: Methodological and practical issues. *Journal of Autism and Developmental Disorders, 37*(3), 466–480.

CHAPTER 7

Conduct and Oppositional Defiant Disorders

Chriscelyn Tussey

INTRODUCTION

Oppositional defiant disorder (ODD) and conduct disorder (CD) are two diagnoses subsumed under the category of Disruptive Behavior Disorders (DBD). ODD and CD have a relatively high prevalence (ODD, 3.2% and CD, 2%; Lahey et al., 1999) and are two of the predominant reasons that children are referred for mental health services (Loeber, Burke, Lahey, Winterns, & Zera, 2000). ODD is marked by a pattern of persistently negativistic, hostile, defiant, and disruptive behavior. This behavior is atypical in comparison to the behavior of same-aged children from within the same sociocultural context. CD is often diagnosed whenever a child's behavior persistently violates the basic rights of others or age-appropriate societal norms. ODD is usually diagnosed before the age of 9–10 years, and CD is usually diagnosed after the age of 9 years. CD is characterized according to the time it emerges in childhood (i.e., early onset or adolescent onset). If such symptoms persist into adulthood, a diagnosis of antisocial personality disorder (APD) should be considered.

Childhood conduct problems are particularly disturbing because they can be precursors of adult antisocial behavior (Fombonne, Wostear, Cooper, Harrington, & Rutter, 2001), substance abuse and dependence (Kazdin, 1995), persistent health problems (Odgers et al., 2007), and other psychiatric illnesses (Van Goozen & Fairchild, 2008). In addition to the difficulties these children face throughout adulthood, society suffers consequences of childhood behavioral disturbances. Indeed, the cumulative cost of public services and associated mental and physical health services devoted to children with antisocial behavior through adulthood is 10 times or more higher than their counterparts (Scott, Knapp, Henderson, & Maughan, 2001; Odgers et al., 2007)

NEUROPATHOLOGY AND PATHOPHYSIOLOGY OF ODD AND CD

Currently, our understanding of the neurobiological causes of ODD and CD remains limited, and contradictory theories have been proposed in the research. Many, though not all, researchers consider the pathology of CD and ODD to be heterogeneous (Blair, Mitchell, & Blair, 2005; Frick & White, 2008; Steiner & Remsing, 2007). As evidence of heterogenous causality, these authors cite the extent to which CD and ODD are comorbid with other disorders, such as posttraumatic stress disorder (PTSD), bipolar disorder, attention deficit hyperactivity disorder (ADHD), and psychopathic tendencies. Researchers agree that these disorders have differing pathophysiologies. In fact, some are seemingly mutually exclusive from a biological perspective. For instance, psychopathic tendencies are associated with reduced amygdala responsiveness as opposed to PTSD, which is associated with increased amygdala responsiveness. As such, it is hypothesized that CD and ODD may be the result of differing developmental trajectories and neurobiological bases (Crowe & Blair, 2008).

Although contemporary imaging techniques such as functional magnetic resonance imaging (fMRI) have increased our ability to investigate the underlying psychopathology of disorders such as ODD and CD, there are limited neuroimaging studies of children or adolescents meeting the criteria for these conditions. Nevertheless, several hypotheses can be gleaned from the slightly larger body of literature examining related comorbidities in children and antisocial behavior in the adult populations. However, before proceeding to a summary of the key neuropathological and pathophysiological considerations for ODD and CD, a distinction must be made between two differing forms of aggression—reactive and instrumental.

Reactive aggression is triggered by a frustrating or threatening event, and involves unplanned, furious attacks on the object perceived to be the source of the threat/frustration. This aggression type is initiated without regard for any potential goal, is often accompanied by anger, and may be referred to as "hot." In contrast, instrumental aggression is purposeful and goal-directed. Instrumental aggression is not always accompanied by an emotional state (e.g., anger or frustration), and is often perceived as "cold" (Steiner et al., 2003).

Articulating the distinction between reactive and instrumental aggression is relevant for at least three reasons. First, a large amount of data supports the existence of two relatively separable populations of aggressive individuals: individuals who present with predominately reactive aggression and individuals who present with high levels of mostly proactive and some reactive aggression (Connor, 2002; Crick & Dodge, 1996). Second, reactive and instrumental aggression rely on partially separable neural systems, and thus a distinction can be made among individuals who display the different forms of antisocial behavior. Lastly, there are notable differences in the pathophysiologies implicated in the psychiatric conditions associated with an increased risk for only reactive aggression (e.g., PTSD, childhood bipolar disorder, and intermittent explosive disorder [IED]) as opposed to the pathophysiology associated with psychopathy, where there is an increased risk for instrumental and reactive aggression (Cornell et al., 1996; Frick, Stickle, Dandreaux, Farrell, & Kimonis, 2005).

The Neuropathology of Reactive Aggression

Years of animal research has demonstrated that when a threat is minimal and distant, an animal tends to freeze. However, when a threat is very close and escape is impossible, higher levels of danger are perceived and reactive aggression is initiated (Blanchard et al., 1977). According to animal research, this progressive response to threat is mediated by a basic threat system that runs from medial amygdaloidal areas downward, largely via the stria terminalis to the medial hypothalamus and from there to the dorsal half of the periaqueductal gray (Gregg & Siegel, 2001; Panksepp, 1998). This system operates in a hierarchical manner. Therefore, aggression evoked by stimulation of the amygdala is dependent on the functional integrity of the medial hypothalamus and periaqueductal gray, but aggression evoked by stimulation of the periaqueductal gray is not dependent on the functional integrity of the amygdala (Gregg & Siegel, 2001; Panksepp, 1998). This amygdala–hypothalamus–periaqueductal gray neural system is thought to mediate reactive aggression in humans as well and is further regulated by higher order structures such as the orbital, medial, and inferior frontal cortices (Blair, 2004a).

According to Crowe and Blair (2008), reactive aggression in CD and ODD may be linked to two pathologies that are not necessarily mutually exclusive. First, the responsiveness of the basic threat system may be exogenously or endogenously elevated. Second, frontal cortex regulatory regions may be disrupted.

As previously noted, CD and ODD are comorbid with a variety of mood and anxiety disorders, including PTSD and bipolar disorder (Steiner & Remsing, 2007). Both PTSD (Silva,

Derecho, Leong, Weinstock, & Ferrori, 2001) and childhood bipolar disorder (Danielyan, Pathak, Kowatch, Arszman, & Johns, 2007) are associated with an increased risk for reactive aggression. Furthermore, exposure to trauma, including violence in the home and neighborhood, has long been linked with an increased probability of reactive aggression (Neller, Denney, Pietz, & Thomlinson, 2006). Exposure to trauma has been shown to increase responsiveness of basic threat circuitry and PTSD has been associated with decreased responding within regions of the middle prefrontal cortex (e.g., Shin et al., 2004; Williams et al., 2006). It follows that an increased risk for reactive aggression in patients with PTSD reflects a reduction of frontal regulation. Also, there is neuroimaging and behavioral support for the notion that IED, which is characterized by reactive aggression, compromises the amygdala–prefrontal cortical regions (van Elst, Woermann, Lemieux, Thompson, & Trimble, 2000; Best, Williams, & Coccaro, 2002). IED has been linked to bipolar disorder (McElroy, 1999), and the two disorders share many overlapping symptoms. Thus, it is not surprising that amygdala dysfunction and prefrontal cortex (PFC) differences are noted in structural, behavioral, and imaging data among children and adolescents with bipolar disorder (e.g., Blumberg et al., 2003, 2005; Chen et al., 2004; Pavuluri et al., 2007).

The Neuropathology of Instrumental Aggression

In the case of instrumental aggression, an individual uses forceful and/or violent methods with the expectation that this will help him/her achieve a set goal. Individuals might choose an antisocial behavior because they are under social or situational pressures to do so, and in turn, the antisocial acts are simply the most viable options available. In some cases, although instrumental aggression/antisocial behavior may be socially undesirable, it may not be maladaptive. Consider, for instance, a young child who steals food because he or she has not eaten in days. Although stealing is inappropriate, given the circumstances, one can more readily understand how stealing may, in the child's perception, be his or her only option for survival. Instrumental aggression/antisocial behavior is ultimately considered maladaptive if the decision making that leads to the choice of the action is dysfunctional. For example, an individual may choose antisocial behavior because his or her calculation of the costs related to the actions, empathic responding, or use of this information is deficient.

Based on the definition of instrumental aggression, it is reasonable to conclude that socialization plays a role in this behavior. A fundamental component of socialization is the ability to form appropriate stimulus-reinforcement associations. Research suggests that the amygdala plays a vital role in the formation of these associations (Baxter & Murray, 2002). Blair (2003) points out that the aversive unconditioned stimulus perhaps most important for moral socialization is seeing the distress of others via expressions of fear and sadness. The amygdala is implicated in responses to fearful and sad expressions (Blair, 2003) and shows greater activity when presented with a stimulus (e.g., sad expression) versus no stimulus (Hooker, Germain, Knight, & d'Esposito, 2006). Indeed, fearfulness has been deemed an indicator of the functional integrity of the amygdala (Crowe and Blaire, 2008).

It is reasonable to conclude that pathology that impedes socialization is likely to increase the risk for instrumental aggression. This is hypothesized to explain, at least in part, the construct of psychopathy. This construct and its neural circuitry have been studied extensively, and fMRI studies have implicated the amygdala and ventromedial PFC in individuals with psychopathic traits (Crowe & Blaire, 2008). To highlight a difference in the dysfunction of psychopathy and PTSD (most often linked with reactive aggression), recall that the psychopathology of each is incompatible. That is, psychopathy is associated with decreased amygdala responsiveness, whereas PTSD is associated with increased amygdala responsiveness.

Furthermore, it has been suggested that psychopathy is protective against the emergence of mood and anxiety disorders (Verona, Patrick, & Joiner, 2001). The deficits found in psychopathy may relate to the atypical stimulus-reinforcement learning and representation of outcome information that interferes with moral socialization and results in increased risk of instrumental aggression. In fact, individuals with psychopathic tendencies are at increased risk for both reactive and instrumental aggression. It is important to emphasize that psychopathy is not synonymous with ODD and CD. In fact, fewer than 25% of individuals meeting the criteria for CD or APD meet cutoffs for psychopathy (Hare, Glass, & Newman, 2006). However, there are several overlapping symptoms, particularly with regard to antisocial behavior, and it is understandable why the aforementioned deficits may also be associated with ODD and CD and are worthy of mention.

The Role of Neurotransmitters

In addition to understanding the neural circuitry related to reactive and instrumental aggression, and thus ODD and CD, it is essential to be aware of the impact of neurotransmitters on aggressive behavior. Although between 50 and 100 molecules have been identified as neurotransmitters in the central nervous system, only the monoamines [i.e., 5-HT, (5-hydroxytryptamine) norepinephrine (NE), and dopamine (DA)] have been systematically studied with respect to human aggression. For example, it has been suggested that the NE system affects both arousal and the degree of sensitivity an organism displays toward the environment, which may prepare an organism to respond aggressively to novel or threatening environmental stimuli (Siever et al., 1991). Animal research (Higley et al., 1992) provides evidence of a positive correlation between NE activity and aggressive behavior. In humans, increased NE activity has been associated with measures of sensation-seeking, extraversion, and risk-taking behaviors (Roy, Adinoff, & Linnoila, 1988). Furthermore, Brown, Goodwin, Ballenger, Goyer, and Major (1979) have found a positive relationship between cerebrospinal fluid (CSF) 3-methoxy-4-hydroxyphenylglycol (MHPG), a central NE metabolite, and a history of aggression in males. In CD or aggressive ADHD children, higher levels of MHPG or a positive correlation between MHPG and aggression have also been found (Castellanos et al., 1994; Gabel, Stadler, Bjorn, Shindledecker, & Bowden, 1993). Although it is outside the scope of this chapter to discuss the role of all pertinent neurotransmitters, it is prudent for anyone working with this disorder to have at least a general understanding of the influence of these chemicals on behavior.

NEUROPSYCHOLOGICAL AND BEHAVIORAL SEQUELAE

Neuropsychological research of antisocial behavior, conducted predominantly on male adolescents, has found some evidence of verbal/language weaknesses, memory difficulties, deficits in intellectual functioning, and executive cognitive dysfunction (Raine et al., 2005; Teichner & Golden, 2000). Moffitt (1993) identified a negative developmental trajectory of boys that was thought to be consistent throughout the course of one's life. Moffitt claimed that this path is characterized by early and persistent neuropsychological dysfunction and aggression. This trajectory has been replicated by others, even after alternative explanations for the neuropsychological deficits were ruled out (Raine, Moffitt, Caspi, Loeber, Stouthamer-Loeber, & Lynam, 2005; Moffitt & Silva, 1988). Similarly, more recent research by Pajer and colleagues (2008) found that females with CD demonstrated worse neuropsychological functioning in general intelligence, visuospatial and executive function and academic achievement.

Interesting differences have emerged with regard to the neuropsychological sequelae of early-onset versus adolescent-onset CD. Specifically, early-onset CD is thought to have a neurodevelopmental basis, whereas adolescent-onset is considered secondary to social mimicry of deviant peers. This hypothesis is argued in the presence of neuropsychological deficits in both CD subtypes. Passamonti and colleagues (2010) recently found that neuropsychological abnormalities were observed in both CD subtypes, findings that did not support the aforementioned developmental taxonomic theory. However, Passamonti and colleagues (2010) noted that additional amygdala hypofunction was found in response to sad expressions, and this may explain why early-onset CD is considered more problematic and persistent than that which begins in adolescence.

Given that executive function (EF) deficits are thought to have such a prominent role in antisocial behavior, it is important to briefly review the literature in this area. Despite the hypothesized role of EF in antisocial behavior, in contrast to the extensive literature on EF deficits in ADHD, there is a dearth of research specifically addressing EF deficits in ODD/CD. Given that ODD/CD is viewed as a possible precursor for antisocial behavior in adulthood (Lynam, 1998), indirect support for EF deficits in ODD/CD is derived from studies of antisocial behavior in adults (Morgan & Lilienfeld, 2000; Moffitt, Lynam, & Silva, 1994). ADHD and ODD/CD have been found frequently to co-occur (e.g., Angold, Costello, & Erkanli, 1999) and are thought to be associated with EF deficits. This has prompted the question of how these two different disorders can share the same deficits. Per Oosterlann, Scheres, & Sergeant (2005), if impairments in EF are only present in ADHD, the association between EF deficits and ODD/CD may be an artifact of the presence of comorbid (subthreshold) ADHD in the ODD/CD samples examined. Likewise, if only ODD/CD revealed EF dysfunction, the reported EF deficits in children with ADHD may be due to the high comorbidity of ODD/CD in these children. Lastly, impaired EF may underlie both disorders. Unfortunately the majority of previous studies have not controlled for comorbidity (e.g., Pennington & Ozonoff, 1996).

Multiple studies support the hypothesis of Pennington and Ozonoff (1996) that ADHD, but not ODD/CD, is affiliated with deficits in EF. For instance, Klorman and colleagues (1999) examined almost 400 children and is the largest study to date that has reported on the specificity of EF deficits in ADHD. That study found planning deficits as measured with the Tower of Hanoi (ToH) in children with ADHD-Combined type, but not in children with ADHD-Inattentive type. Interestingly, ODD was associated with superior performance on the ToH. Furthermore, set-shifting, measured by the Wisconsin Card Sorting Test (WCST), did not discriminate between groups. Similarly, Clark, Prior, and Kinsella (2000) compared adolescents with ADHD, ODD/CD, and comorbid ADHD+ODD/CD with normal controls on two EF measures. Adolescents with ADHD performed worse than adolescents without ADHD, whether or not they also had ODD/CD. Kalff and colleagues (2002) used the same diagnostic groups of children and found similar results when examining three different measures of working memory. That is, deficient performance on these measures was only evident in children with a diagnosis of ADHD, regardless of whether or not they also had ODD/CD.

Some research supports the hypothesis that ODD/CD, but not ADHD, is associated with deficits in EF. For example, after statistically controlling for ADHD, some studies found evidence for EF deficits in ODD/CD (e.g., Séguin et al., 1999; Toupin, Déry, Pauzé, Mercier, & Fortin, 2000). Yet other studies have found that both ADHD and ODD/CD are associated with EF deficits. For example, in a study of adolescents, MacLeod and Prior (1996) found that ADHD and CD were associated with poor performance on the Stroop Task, a measure of attention and interference control. Also, Aronowitz and colleagues (1994) studied a sample of adolescents with ODD, CD, and ADHD, most of whom exhibited a combination of these diagnoses. Adolescents with a diagnosis of CD had poor performance on the WCST, a measure of cognitive flexibility and planning, and the Rey-Osterreith Complex Figure Test, a task associated with planning and organization. ADHD was associated with poor performance on the WCST only.

Oosterlaan, Scheres, and Sergeant (2005) sought to further investigate the overlap between ADHD and ODD/CD. The authors examined: (1) whether ADHD was associated with EF deficits while controlling for ODD/CD, (2) whether ODD/CD is associated with EF deficits while controlling for ADHD, and (3) whether a combination of ADHD and ODD/CD is associated with EF deficits (and the possibility that there is no association between EF deficits and ADHD or ODD/CD in isolation). Taken together, the results from the regression analyses and ANCOVAs confirm the hypothesis that ADHD, but not ODD/CD, is related to EF deficits. Also of note, Oosterlaan, Scheres, and Sergeant (2005) found little evidence for verbal fluency deficits in children with ODD/CD.

In addition to the aforementioned neuropsychological considerations of ODD and CD, these disorders are associated with a variety of behavioral sequelae. It is important to consider risk factors for children who develop these disorders. Indeed, environmental factors impact neurobiological and developmental functioning and can contribute to both neuropsychological and behavioral sequelae. For example, pre- and postnatal factors (e.g., exposure to smoking in utero and maltreatment, respectively) are likely to have an impact on biological systems. Stress responsiveness, variation in quality of parental care, parental and child psychopathology, poverty, child abuse, and neglect can have significant negative impacts on children (Moffitt, 2005) and can exacerbate behavior dyscontrol and emotional regulation. As previously mentioned, ODD and CD are associated with significant negative outcomes in adulthood (e.g., future antisocial behavior, Fombonne, Wostear, Cooper, Harrington, & Rutter, 2001; substance abuse and dependence, Kazdin, 1995; early pregnancy in antisocial girls, Bardone et al., 1998, etc.).

ADVANCED DIAGNOSTIC CONSIDERATIONS AND PRACTICES

The fundamental conceptualization of ODD and CD has remained consistent over several decades (American Psychiatric Association [APA], 1980), but the criteria for diagnosing these disorders has evolved over time with each new iteration of the *Diagnostic and Statistical Manual of Mental Disorders (DSM)*. See *DSM-IV-TR* (2000) for the most recent criteria.

Differential Diagnoses

Given the many comorbidities with ODD and CD, careful differential diagnosis is paramount. For instance, in children with ADHD, ODD is present in 35%–40% and CD in 20%–25% (Halperin, Marks, & Schultz, 2008). ODD symptoms are typically evident before age 8, and usually do not emerge later than early adolescence. Typical differential diagnoses that warrant consideration with regard to ODD include CD (currently ODD is not diagnosed if criteria are met for CD), mood and psychotic disorders (it is not uncommon for a child to express sadness via behavioral disruption), ADHD, intellectual disability, and impaired language comprehension. Also, when evaluating symptoms, it is important that typical features of developmental stages are not overpathologized. For example, most young children engage in defiant behavior from time to time.

Possible differential diagnoses for CD include ODD, ADHD, mood disorder, and adjustment disorder. Again, evaluators should be cautious not to overinterpret isolated conduct problems that may be reflective of developmentally typical child or adolescent behavior. See Table 7.1 for distinguishing features of ODD, CD, and several of the aforementioned disorders.

It is important to use caution and complete a comprehensive assessment of a child's circumstances prior to providing a diagnosis. At times, clinicians may falsely believe that antisocial behavior and genuine psychopathology are mutually exclusive. For example, it is essential to consider that a child with CD may also have low self-esteem, despite his or her projected "toughness." Furthermore, ODD or CD should only be diagnosed when problematic behavior is the *underlying dysfunction*, not a reaction to an immediate social context. For instance, immigrants from war-ravaged countries may not warrant a diagnosis of ODD or CD, even though some of their behaviors may be antisocial in nature.

Assessing ODD/CD

When assessing for ODD/CD, it is essential to conduct a thorough clinical interview of the child and his or her caregivers. Collateral information from teachers and any other family members who have regular contact with the child is also crucial. During the interviews, it is essential to consider factors that may predispose a child to ODD/CD, such as parental rejection and neglect, difficult infant temperament, inconsistent child-rearing practices with harsh discipline, physical or sexual abuse, lack of supervision, institutional living, frequent changes in caregivers, large family size, history of maternal smoking during pregnancy, peer rejection, association with deviant peer group, neighborhood exposure to violence, and familial psychopathology (Caspi et al., 2002; Silberg et al., 2003; Foley et al., 2004; Moffitt, 2005).

Various parent and teacher questionnaires may be useful in helping to diagnose ODD/CD. For instance, the disruptive behavior disorder (DBD) Rating Scale (Oosterlaan, Scheres,

Antrop, Roeyers, & Sergeant, 2000; Pelham, Gnaggy, Greenslade, & Milich, 1992) is a symptom severity rating scale comprising four scales with the behavioral descriptions of ADHD inattentive subtype, ADHD hyperactive-impulsive subtype, ODD, and CD. Also, the Child Behavior Checklist (CBCL; Achenback, 1991; Verhulst, Van der Ende, & Koot, 1996a) and the Conners' Parent Rating Scale (CPRS-CP; Connors, Parker, Sitarenios, & Epstein, 1998) can be useful. Although there are no specific neuropsychological tests for ODD or CD specifically, as has been mentioned, neuropsychological measures can be useful for assessing domains of cognitive functioning, which are thought to potentially be associated with these disorders. For instance, measures of executive functioning such as the Stroop Color and Word Test: Children's Version (Golden, Freshwater, & Golden, 2003) and the Wisconsin Card Sorting Test (WCST; Berg, 1948) can provide insight into a child's cognitive flexibility and planning. Also, a global measure of intelligence, such as the Wechsler Intelligence Scale for Children-Fourth Edition (WISC-IV; Wechsler, 2003), can provide useful information about a child's aptitude and clinical presentation.

The Future of ODD/CD Diagnosis

According to Pardini, Frick, and Moffitt (2010), there are several debates about how to incorporate ODD and CD into the *DSM-5*. Reportedly, the *DSM-5* ADHD and DBD work group have focused on several primary issues: (1) The research investigating CD and ODD in females has been limited; (2) controversy remains regarding the appropriateness of retaining the hierarchical rule that precludes a diagnosis of ODD when the criteria for CD are met, and, therefore, further clarifying the developmental progression from ODD to CD; (3) it remains a question about how to recognize the developmental associations between CD in children and antisocial personality disorder in adults and relatedly, how best to incorporate the affective and interpersonal features of psychopathy into these definitions (Hare & Neumann, 2008); and (4) there are continued debates regarding the relative benefits of a dimensional versus categorical conceptualization of mental disorder in general and with regard to ODD and CD specifically.

TABLE 7.1 Differential Diagnoses of Oppositional Defiant Disorder, Conduct Disorder, and Related Conditions

Diagnosis	*Distinctive Features*
Oppositional defiant disorder	Chronic argumentativeness; refusal to comply with adult requests
Conduct disorder	Persistent pattern of violating others' rights; aggression and illegal acts; more severe symptoms than seen in oppositional defiant disorder
Attention deficit hyperactivity disorder	Hyperactivity; behavior disinhibition; inattention and distractibility; symptoms were present before 7 years of age
Substance abuse/ dependence	Pattern of substance use associated with adverse social/personal consequences or physiologic tolerance or withdrawal
Major depressive disorder (MDD)	Dysphoric, irritable mood (in children irritability may only be observed); sleep and appetite disturbance (in children, watch for failure to make expected weight gains); anhedonia; suicidal ideation
Bipolar disorder	Depressive symptoms coexist or alternate with periods of excess energy and/or thought racing; mania or hypomania may include hallucinations, delusions
Intermittent explosive disorder	Sudden, unpredictable, physically/verbally aggressive outbursts that result in assaultive acts toward others and/or property
Adjustment disorder	Development of emotional or behavioral symptoms in response to an identifiable stressor occurring within 3 months of the onset of the stressor

Several studies have been conducted to examine these issues (Keenan, Wroblewski, Hipwell, Looeber, & Stouthhamer-Loeber, 2010; Kolko & Pardini, 2010; Burke, Waldman, & Lahey, 2010). It is hoped that the results of these and subsequent studies will provide an evidence base to guide development of the new *DSM-5* criteria for ODD and CD. Challenges remain regarding how to define symptom thresholds and address subclinical symptoms, particularly in light of ongoing managed care changes. Nevertheless, it is promising that a larger evidence base will be available for the evolution of these diagnoses than has ever been available in prior *DSM* iterations.

CONTEMPORARY MODES OF TREATMENT

Children with disruptive behavior disorders left untreated have a poorer prognosis. Oppositional defiant disorder (ODD) and CD can lead to harm to the child as well as the victims, and can have long-lasting detrimental effects. Historically, prognosis for these disorders has been grim because such behaviors are typically consistent and perceived as very difficult to alter. Although behavioral interventions have demonstrated some efficacy in mild forms of these disorders, the effectiveness in more severely impacted children has been limited. Intervention is often impeded by the frequent finding that parents coping with children with ODD and CD are often frustrated, may feel helpless, and may be struggling with their own stressors, such as financial and/or mental health concerns. Given that the etiology of conduct disorder involves an interaction of genetic, familial, and social factors, comprehensive and multifaceted intervention may be most effective. For example, treatment may include medication, psychological, psychoeducational, family interventions, and consultation with a child's school.

Pharmacological and Medical Interventions

Thus far, no medications have been designed to specifically treat ODD/CD. Nevertheless, the use of medication for these behavioral disorders is rising (Steiner et al., 2003; Turgay, 2004). The majority of published studies examining the utility of pharmacological treatment for DBDs involve patients with CD and comorbid conditions, such as ADHD or major depression. Notably, because of the high degree of overlap between ODD/CD and ADHD and the importance of treating comorbid disorders, when considering pharmacological intervention, clinicians should perform an evaluation of ADHD symptoms.

In the short term, stimulant medicine has proven effective in controlling the specific symptoms of inattention, impulsivity, and hyperactivity. By improving attention and increasing inhibitory activity, medication may improve a child's capacity to benefit from other psychosocial intervention (Frick, 1998). Of the stimulants, dextroamphetamine (Dexedrine) and methylphenidate (Ritalin) are the most promising agents used in the treatment of CD (Searright, Rottnek, & Abby, 2001). However, it is important to emphasize that by itself, stimulant medication typically does not result in improved parent–child, teacher–child, or peer relationships. As with the approach to ODD/CD, a multidisciplinary and multimodal approach to ADHD is necessary. Also, it is necessary to note that substance abuse occurs in a high number of children with CD, independent of whether they are treated with psychoactive medication. In recent years, psychoactive medication abuse and illegal selling of such medications have been on the rise. Consequently, physicians should use caution when prescribing these medications and take extra care to ensure they are necessary for treatment.

In addition to stimulant medications, antidepressants, lithium, anticonvulsants, clonidine (Catapres), and antipsychotics have all been used in the treatment of CD (Campbell, Gonzalez, & Silva, 1992; Scott, 2008). With regard to antidepressants, one small, open-label trial by Simeon, Ferguson, Van Wyck, and Fleet (1986) evaluated the efficacy and toxicity of bupropion in ADHD and CD. Results indicated parental-rated and self-rated improvement in conduct. This study suggested that bupropion was safe and effective for use in this population. However, controlled double-blind studies are needed for further evaluation. Fluoxetine (Prozac) has also been associated with a significant reduction in impulsive-aggressive behavior in adults with a personality disorder (Coccaro & Kavoussi, 1997). The selective serotonin reuptake inhibitors (SSRIs) may be particularly helpful in treating children with CD and comorbid major depression. Lithium is a psychoactive agent with calming properties. Some studies have demonstrated a reduction of aggression with this medication (e.g., Campbell et al., 1995; Rifkin et al., 1997). Also, anticonvulsants have also been used to reduce aggression (Cueva, et al., 1996). However, both lithium and anticonvulsants require regular monitoring to assess for possible toxicity and have a potentially serious side effect profile. Therefore, these medications are often prescribed conservatively for conduct problems.

Recently, there has been increased use of medications such as clonidine and antipsychotics to treat conduct problems. Clonidine has demonstrated significant reduction in impulsivity and aggressive outbursts in some studies (Kemph, DeVane, Levin, Jarecke, & Miller, 1993). However, significant side effects such as somnolence, hypotension, bradycardia, and depression can occur. Thus, close monitoring is also necessary with this medication. A study conducted by Connor, McLaughlin, and Jeffers-Terry (2008) found that quetiapine, an antipsychotic medication, was superior to placebo in the treatment of a small sample of adolescents with conduct disorder. The authors concluded that the methodologically controlled pilot study provided data that quetiapine may have efficacy in the treatment of adolescents with conduct disorder. However, future research with larger samples and replicated findings is necessary to further examine the efficacy of this medication in treating ODD and CD.

Some researchers have argued that understanding the neurobiological causes of children's behavioral difficulties can help tailor treatment accordingly (van Goozen & Fairchild, 2008). For example, an examination of cortisol reactivity to stress could be used to assess the probability of successful treatment outcome, and in the selection of more targeted interventions. Van deWiel and colleagues (2004) found that cortisol reactivity to stress predicted response to a standard psychotherapeutic intervention (i.e., a combination of cognitive behavioral therapy and parent management training). It was found that the problem behavior of ODD/CD children who showed cortisol hyporeactivity was not altered, whereas the behavior of children exhibiting normal cortisol reactivity improved significantly. Thus, if the individual's hypothalamic–pituitary–adrenal (HPA) axis is normally reactive, traditional interventions such as those involving cognitive and emotional processing and using negative feedback could be predicted to have an increased chance of success. However, in the absence of a normal cortisol stress response, psychotherapy is unlikely to be effective and pharmacological interventions, for example, influencing levels of HPA axis steroids, should be considered.

van Goozen and Fairchild (2008) acknowledged that their research was the first to examine the effect of a specific neurobiological risk factor (i.e., cortisol stress hyporeactivity) on prognosis and outcome of a therapeutic intervention. Thus, more research is certainly needed before conclusions can be drawn. However, if the findings are replicated, it may be possible in the future to select the best possible treatment option for an individual based on the outcomes of a biological screening procedure.

A second clinical implication follows directly from the animal research conducted by Haller and colleagues (2004). They showed that restoration of the stress hormonal response via injections of corticosterone prevented abnormal aggressive behavior and proposed that an increase in stress hormones is important in the appraisal of conflict situations. One prediction arising from the model is that reinstatement of normal HPA axis functioning should ameliorate some forms of therapeutic interventions. By restoring stress response systems to a relatively normal state of activity, it may be possible to repair the disconnect between strong, often inappropriate emotional reactions and weak or nonexistent stress responses to situations that normally elicit affective responses (e.g., anger, fear, etc.). This connection between the cognitive/affective components of an experience and the accompanying physiological reaction may be crucial for some aspects of emotional regulation and development.

There are two possible methods that have shown promise for future use in improving some of the functional deficits observed in antisocial behavior. Transcranial magnetic stimulation (TMS) involves the use of a magnetic coil to induce electric fields in the brain. It is a noninvasive and well-tolerated method of altering cortical physiology. TMS disrupts the normal pattern of cortical processing by adding "neural noise" (Walsh & Rushworth, 1999). High-frequency TMS excites neural activity and low-frequency TMS inhibits neural activity in a localized fashion (George, 2006). In psychiatry, TMS has mostly been used in the treatment of depression, and the available evidence supports the antidepressant effect of TMS when applied to the dorsolateral prefrontal cortex. van Goozen and Fairchild (2008) hypothesize that such an increase, applied to selected areas of the PFC, would enhance inhibitory function and result in more controlled, less impulsive behavior. However, currently the ventral areas in the brain that are important in emotional processing (e.g., orbitofrontal and anterior cingulate cortices) are not easily or directly accessible to transcranial stimulation. Thus, the clinical efficacy of TMS is currently limited (Wasserman & Lisanby, 2001), although this may change with ongoing technological advancement (Schutter & van Honk, 2006).

A second method that involves changing brain activity is neurofeedback (NF). NF is a form of biofeedback training in which an individual learns, through a process of immediate feedback and positive reinforcement, to modulate electrical activity in his or her brain as a way of improving symptoms (Heinrich, Gevensleben, & Strehl, 2007). NF training has mostly been used in treatment of ADHD and epilepsy. As is the case for other neuropsychiatric disorders characterized by self-regulation deficits, children and teenagers with severe antisocial behavior could profit from NF, given their difficulties with impulse control and emotional regulation. This method of treatment is noninvasive, although it is a technical and time-consuming procedure. NF may be considered after a thorough assessment of underlying pathophysiology and, if possible, administered in conjunction with other available treatment options (e.g., parent management training [PMT], cognitive behavioral therapy [CBT]).

Psychological Interventions

Parent Management Training

Of the psychological therapies, PMT is the method demonstrated to have the most impact on the child's coercive pattern of behavior (Feldman & Kazdin, 1995). In PMT, parents are trained to alter their child's behavior in the home. PMT was developed in light of research that found that conduct problems are inadvertently developed and sustained by maladaptive parent-child interactions. Although such conflict is frequently triggered by the irritable temperament of the child, a prominent component of this pattern of relating is ineffective parenting (e.g., the parent inadvertently reinforces negative behavior, fails to provide consistent punishment, has a tendency not to notice or reinforce positive bahaviors, etc.). The goal of PMT is to modify the parent's ineffective techniques by encouraging the parent to practice prosocial behavior (positive, specific feedback for desirable behavior), employ the use of natural and logical consequences, and use effective, brief, nonaversive punishments on a limited basis when specific encouragement and consequences are not applicable.

Cognitive-Behavioral Interventions and Problem-Solving Training

These forms of intervention are used to teach both parent and child how to deal with a problem in a healthy, productive way. This training can be empowering to a child because it teaches him or her to approach problems from a new perspective. Simultaneously, adults learn to capitalize on their parenting skills rather than using anger or frustration to solve problems. Parent-child interaction therapy (Eyberg, 1988) is an example of these types of intervention with particular success in addressing conduct problems (Nixon et al., 2003; Hood & Eyberg, 2003).

Group Therapy

Group treatment has had both benefits and disadvantages for children with ODD and CD. Although some evidence exists that group social skills or problem-solving treatment has some benefit in children aged 12 years and younger, concerns exist about group treatment of adolescents diagnosed with CD. With younger children, combined treatment in which parents attend a PMT group while the children attend a social skills group has consistently exhibited good effects. However, research demonstrates that treatment of adolescents with CD conducted in groups of individuals with CD tends to worsen the behavior, particularly if the group participants engage in discussions of oppositional and illegal behaviors (Kazdin, 1997).

Thus, group treatment should be initiated only after careful consideration of group goals and the potential negative effects. More radical solutions (e.g., boot camps) have consistently demonstrated initial good outcome but worsening outcome in the long term, with higher rates of arrests and serious crimes found in boot camp graduates. Poor long-term outcome following this treatment is believed to be due in part to group mutual reinforcement and discussion of criminal activity and to the lack of family or community change in many of these programs. Thus, the adolescents are released back into the same environment, in which little support for the newly acquired skills and behavior is present (Tyler et al., 2001; Benda, 2005; Cullen et al., 2005; Stinchcomb, 2005).

Individual Therapy

In general, individual psychotherapy as a single treatment has not proven effective for conduct problems. However, individual therapy sessions can facilitate compliance with a larger-scale intervention that emphasizes changes in the family, the school, and in social settings. Thus, individual counseling may actually increase the likelihood that a child will adhere to a more comprehensive treatment program, and may be considered in the context of a larger intervention plan.

Multisystemic Therapy

The multisystemic approach (Henggeler, Melton, & Smith, 1992), to treatment is comprehensive and includes behavioral PMT, social skills training, academic support, pharmacological treatment of comorbid disorders (if present), and individual counseling as needed. Outcome data for this type of comprehensive approach have been encouraging (Ogden & Hagen, 2009).

SUMMARY

Research on ODD and CD is still in its early years; however, there is a strong impetus for learning more about risk assessment, accurate diagnosis, and intervention of these disorders. Ongoing education about warning signs of ODD and CD may lead to early intervention, which could decrease the prevalence of severe forms of these disorders, which are particularly treatment-resistant. As we learn more about the pathophysiologies and developmental trajectories of these conditions, it is hoped that specific neural systems can be targeted, interventions can occur at the most pivotal point in development, and prognoses can be positively impacted.

REFERENCES

American Psychiatric Association. (1980). *Diagnostic and statistical manual of mental disorders* (3rd ed.). Washington, DC: Author.

American Psychiatric Association. (2000). *Diagnostic and statistical manual of mental disorders* (4th ed., text rev.). Washington, DC: Author.

Angold, A., Costello, E. J., & Erkanli, A. (1999). Comorbidity. *Journal of Child Psychology and Psychiatry, 40*, 57–87.

Aronowitz, B., LIebowitz, M., Hollander, E., Fazzini, E., Durlach-Misteli, C., Frenkel, M. et al. (1994). Neuropsychiatric and neuropsychological findings in conduct disorder and attention-deficit hyperactive disorder. *Journal of Neuropsychiatry, 3*, 245–249.

Bardone, A. M., Moffitt, T. E., Caspi, A., Dickson, N., Stanton, W. R., & Silva, P.A. (1998). Adult physical health outcomes of adolescent girls with conduct disorder, depression, and anxiety. *Journal of the American Academy of Child & Adolescent Psychiatry, 37*, 594–601.

Baxter, M. G., & Murray, E. A. (2002). The amygdala and reward. *Nature Reviews: Neuroscience, 3*, 563–573.

Benda, B. B. (2005). *Introduction. Boot camp revisited: Issues, problems, prospects*. In *Rehabilitation Issues, Problems, and Prospects in Boot Camp*. Eds. B. B. Benda and N.J. Pallone, pp. 1–25. Hawthorne Press.

Berg, E. A. (1948). A simple objective test for measuring flexibility in thinking. *Journal of General Psychology, 39*, 15–22.

Best, M., Williams, J. M., & Coccaro, E.F. (2002). Evidence for a dysfunctional prefrontal circuit in patients with an impulsive aggressive disorder. *Proceedings of the National Academy of Sciences of the United States of America, 99*, 8448–8453.

Blair, R. J. (2004). The roles of orbital frontal cortex in the modulation of antisocial behavior. *Bran and Cognition, 55,* 198–208.

Blair, R. J. (2003). Facial expressions, their communicatory functions, and neuro-cognitive substrates. *Philosophical Transactions of the Royal Society B: Biological Sciences, 358,* 561–572.

Blair, R. J., Mitchell, D., & Blair, K. (2005). *The psychopath. Emotion and the brain.* New York: Blackwell.

Blanchard, R. J., Blanchard, D. C. Takahashi, T., & Kelley, M. J. (1977). Attack and defensive behavior in the albino rat. *Animal Behavior, 25,* 622–634.

Blumberg, H. P., Kaufman, J., Martin, A., Whiteman, R., Zhang, J. H., Gore, J. C., et al. (2003). Amygdala and hippocampal volumes in adolescents and adults with bipolar disorder. *Archives of General Psychiatry, 60,* 1201–1208.

Blumberg, H. P., Fredericks, C., Wang, F., Kalmar, J. H., Spencer, L., Papademetris, X., et al. (2005). Preliminary evidence for persistent abnormalities in amygdala volumes in adolescents and young adults with bipolar disorder. *Bipolar Disorder, 7,* 570–576.

Brown, G. L., Goodwin, F. K., Ballenger, J. C., Goyer, P. F., & Major, L. F. (1979). Aggression in human correlates with cerebrospinal fluid amine metabolites. *Psychiatry Research, 1,* 131–139.

Burke, J. D., Waldman, I., & Lahey, B. B. (2010). Predictive validity of childhood oppositional defiant disorder and conduct disorder: Implications for the DSM-V. *Journal of Abnormal Psychology, 119,* 739–751.

Campbell, M., Gonzalez, N. M., & Silva, R. R. (1992). The pharmacologic treatment of conduct disorders and rage outbursts. *The Psychiatric Clinics of North America, 15,* 69–85.

Campbell, M., Adams, P. B., Small, A. M., Kafantaris, V., Silva, R. R., Shell, J., Perry, R. & Overall, J. E. (1995). Lithium in hospitalized aggressive children with conduct disorder: A double-blind and placebo-controlled study. *Journal of the American Academy of Child and Adolescent Psychiatry, 34,* 445–453.

Caspi, A., McClay, J., Moffit, T. E., Mill, J., Martin, J., Craig, I. W., et al. (2002). Role of the genotype in the circle of violence in maltreated children. *Science, 297,* 851–854.

Castellanos, F. X., Elia, J., Kruesi, M. J., Gulotta, C. S., Mefford, I. N., Potter, W. Z., et al. (1994). Cerebrospinal fluid monoamine metabolites in boys with attention-deficit hyperactive disorder. *Psychiatric Research, 52,* 305–316.

Clark, C., Prior, M., & Kinsella, G. J. (2000). Do executive function deficits differentiate between adolescents with AD/HD and oppositional defiant disorder/conduct disorder/ A neuropsychological study using the six elements test and the Hayling sentence completion test. *Journal of Abnormal Child Psychology, 28,* 403–414.

Coccaro, E. F., & Kavoussi, R. J. (1997). Fluoxetine and impulsive aggressive behavior in personality-disordered subjects. *Archives of General Psychiatry, 54,* 1081–1088.

Conners, C. K., Parker, J. D. A., Sitarenios, G., & Epstein, J. N. (1998). The Revised Conners' Parent Rating Scale (CPRS-R): Factor structure, reliability, and criterion validity. *Journal of Abnormal Child Psychology, 26,* 257–268.

Connor, D. F. (2002). *Aggression and anti-social behavior in children and adolescents: Research and treatment.* New York: Guilford Press.

Connor, D. F., McLaughlin, T. J., & Jeffers-Terry, M. (2008). Randomized controlled pilot study of quetiapine in the treatment of adolescent conduct disorder. *Journal of Child and Adolescent Psychopharmacology, 18,* 140–56.

Cornell, D. G., Warren, J., Hawk, G., Stafford, E., Oram, G., & Pine, D. (1996). Psychopathy in instrumental and reactive violent offenders. *Journal of Consulting and Clinical Psychology, 64,* 783–790.

Crick, N. R., & Dodge, K. A. (1996). Social information-processing mechanisms on reactive and proactive aggression. *Child Development, 67,* 993–1002.

Crowe, S. L., & Blair, R. (2008). The development of antisocial behavior: What can we learn from functional neuroimaging studies? *Developmental Psychopathology, 20,* 1145–1159.

Cueva, J. E., Overall, J. E., Small, A. M., Armenteros, J. L., Perry, R., & Campbell, M. (1996). Carbamazepine in aggressive children with conduct disorder: A double-blind and placebo-controlled study. *Journal of the American Academy of Child and Adolescent Psychiatry, 35*:480–490.

Cullen, F. T., Blevins, K. R., Trager, J. S. (2005). The rise and fall of boot camps: A case study in common-sense corrections. *Journal of Offender Rehabilitation, 40,* 53–70.

Danielyan, A., Pathak, S., Kowatch, R. A., Arszman, S. P., & Johns, E. S. (2007). Clinical characteristics of bipolar disorders in very young children. *Journal of Affective Disorders, 97,* 51–59.

Eyberg, S. M. (1988). Parent-child interaction therapy: Integration of traditional and behavioral concerns. *Child and Family Behavior Therapy, 10,* 33–48.

Fombonne, E., Wostear, G., Cooper, V., Harrington, R., & Rutter, M. (2001). The Maudsley long-term follow-up of child and adolescent depression. I. Psychiatric outcomes in adulthood. *British Journal of Psychiatry, 179,* 210–217.

Feldman, J., & Kazdin, A. E. (1995). Parent management training for oppositional and conduct problem children. *The Clinical Psychologist, 48*(4), 3–5.

Frick, P. J. (1998). *Conduct Disorders and Severe Antisocial Behavior*. New York: Plenum Press.

Frick, P. J., & White, S. F. (2008). Research review: The importance of callous-unemotional traits for developmental models of aggressive and antisocial behavior. *Journal of Child Psychology and Psychiatry, 49*, 359–375.

Frick, P. J., Stickle, T. R., Dandreaux, D. M., Farrell, J. M., & Kimonis, E.R. (2005). Callous-unemotional traits in predicting the severity and stability of conduct problems and delinquency. *Journal of Abnormal Child Psychology, 33*, 471–484.

Gabel, S., Stadler, J., Bjorn, J., Shindledecker, R., & Bowden, C.L. (1993). Biodevelopmental aspects of conduct disorder in boys. *Child Psychiatry and Human Development, 24*, 125–141.

George, M. S. (2006). Transcranial magnetic stimulation: A stimulating new method for treating depression, but saddled with the same old problems. *International Journal of Neuropsychopharmacology. 9*, 637–40.

Golden, C. J., Freshwater, S. M., & Golden, Z. (2003). *Stroop color and word test children's version for ages 5–14; A manual for clinical and experimental uses*. Wood Dale, Ill: Stoelting.

Gregg, T. R., & Siegel, A. (2001). Brain structures and neurotransmitters regulating aggression in cats: Implications for human aggression. *Progress in Neuro-Psychopharmacology and Biological Psychiatry, 25*, 91–140.

Haller, J., Halasz, J., Mikics, E., & Kruk, M. R. (2004). Chronic glucocorticoid deficiency-induced abnormal aggression, autonomic hypoarousal, and social deficits in rats. *Journal of Neuroendocrinology, 16*, 550–557.

Halperin, J. M., Marks, D. J., & Schulz, K. P. (2008). Neuropsychological perspectives of ADHD. In: Morgan, J.E., Ricker, J.H., Eds. *Handbook of Clinical Neuropsychology*. Swets and Zeitlinger; 2008. pp. 333–345.

Hare, R., Glass, S. J., & Newman, J. P. (2006). Current perspectives on psychopathy. *Annual Review of Clinical Psychology, 4*, 217–246.

Hare, R. D., & Neumann, C. S. (2008). Psychopathy as a clinical and empirical construct. *Annaul Review of Clinical Psychology, 4*, 217–246. 10.1146/annurev.clinpsy.3.022806.091452

Heinrich, H., & Gevensleben, H., & Strehl, U. (2007). Annotation: Neurofeedback- Train your brain to train behavior. *Journal of Clinical Psychology and Psychiatry, 48*, 3–16.

Henggeler, S. W., Melton, G. B., & Smith, L. A. (1992). Family preservation using multisystemic therapy: An effective alternative to incarcerating serious juvenile offenders. *Journal of Consulting and Clinical Psychology, 60*, 953–961.

Higley, J. D., Mehlman, P. T., Taub, D. M., Higley, S. B., Suomi, S. J., Vickers, J. H., ET AL (1992). Cerebrospinal fluid monoamine and adrenal correlates of aggression in free-ranging rhesus monkeys. *Archives of General Psychiatry, 49*, 436–441.

Hood, K., & Eyberg, S. M. (2003). Outcomes of parent-child interaction therapy. Mothers' reports on maintenance three to six years after treatment. *Journal of Clinical Child and Adolescent Psychology, 32*, 419–429.

Hooker, C. I., Germaine, L. T., Knight, R. T., & D'Esposito, M. (2006). Amygdala response to facial expressions reflects emotional learning. *Journal of Neuroscience, 26*, 8915–8922.

Kalff, A. C., Hendriksen, J. G., Kroes, M., Vles, J. S., Steyaert, J., Feron, F. J., et al. (2002). Neurocognitive performance of 5-and-6-year old children who met criteria for attention-deficit/hyperactive disorder at 18-months follow-up. Results from a prospective population study. *Journal of Child Psychology and Psychiatry, 30*, 589–598.

Kazdin, A. E. (1995). Scope of child and adolescent psychotherapy research: Limited sampling of dysfunctions. *Journal of Clinical Child Psychology, 24*(2), 125. Retrieved from

Kazdin, A. E. (1997). Practitioner review: Psychosocial treatments for conduct disorder in children. *Journal of Child Psychology and Psychiatry, 38*, 161–178.

Keenan, K., Wroblewski, K., Hipwell, A., Loeber, R., & Stouthamer-Loeber, M. (2010). Age of onset, symptom threshold, and expansion of the nosology of conduct disorder for girls. *Journal of Abnormal Psychology, 119*, 689–698.

Kemph, J. P., DeVane, C. L., Levin, G. M., Jarecke, R., & Miller, R. L. (1993). Treatment of aggressive children with clonidine: Results of an open pilot study. *Journal of the American Academy of Child and Adolescent Psychiatry, 32*, 577–581.

Klorman, R., Hazel-Fernandez, L. A., Shaywitz, S. E., Fletcher, J. M., Marchione, K. E., Holahan, J. M. et al. (1999). Executive functioning deficits in attention deficit/hyperactivity disorder are independent of oppositional defiant or reading disorder. *Journal of the American Academy of Child and Adolescent Psychiatry, 38*,1148–1155.

Kolko, D. J., & Pardini, D. A. (2010). ODD dimensions, ADHD, and callous-unemotional traits as preceptors of treatment response in children with disruptive behavior disorders. *Journal of Abnormal Psychology, 119*, 713–725.

Lahey, B. B., Waldman, I. D., & McBurnett, K. (1999). Annotation: The development of antisocial behavior: An integrative causal model. *Journal of Child Psychology and Psychiatry, 40*, 669–682.

Loeber, R., Burke, J. D., Lahey, B. B., Winters, A., & Zera, M. (2000). Oppositional defiant and conduct disorder: A review of the past 10 years, part 1. *Journal of the American Academy of Child & Adolescent Psychiatry, 39*, 1468–1484.

Lynam, D. R. (1998). Early identification of the fledging psychopathy: Locating the psychopathic child in the current nomenclature. *Journal of Abnormal Psychology, 107*, 566–575.

McElroy, S. L. (1999). Recognition and treatment of DSM-IV intermittent explosive disorder. *Journal of Clinical Psychiatry, 60*(Suppl. 15), 12–16.

MacLeod, D., & Prior, M. (1996). Attention deficits in adolescents with AD/HD and other clinical groups. *Clinical Neuropsychology, 2*, 1–10.

Moffitt, T. E. (1993). Adolescence-limited and life-course-persistent antisocial behavior: A developmental taxonomy. *Psychological Review, 100*, 674–701. 10.1037/0033–295X.100.4.674

Moffitt, T. E. (2005). The new look of behavioral genetics in developmental psychopathology: Gene-environment interplay in antisocial behaviors. *Psychological Bulletin, 131*, 533–554.

Moffitt, T. E. (1988). Self-reported delinquency, neuropsychological deficit, and history of attention deficit disorder. *Journal of Abnormal Child Psychology, 16*, 553–569.

Moffitt, T. E., Lynam, D. R., & Silva, P. A. (1994). Neuropsychological tests predicting persistent male delinquency. *Criminology, 32*, 277–300.

Morgan, A. B., & Lilienfeld, S. O. (2000). A meta-analytic review of the relation between antisocial behavioral and neuropsychological measures of executive function. *Clinical Psychology Review, 20*, 113–136.

Neller, D. J., Denney, R. L., Pietz, C. A., & Thomlinson, R.P. (2006). The relationship between trauma and violence in a jail inmate sample. *Journal of Interpersonal Violence, 21*, 1234–1241.

Nixon, R. D., Sweeney, L., Erickson, D. B. & Touyz, S. W. (2003). Parent-child interaction therapy: A comparison of standard and abbreviated treatments for oppositional defiant preschoolers. *Journal of Consulting and Clinical Psychology, 71*, 251–260.

Odgers, C. L., Caspi, A., Broadbent, J. M., Dickson, N., Hancox, R. J., Harrington, H., Poulton, R., Sears, M. R., Thomsom, W. M., & Moffitt, T. E. (2007). Prediction of differential adult health burden by conduct problem subtypes in males. *Archives of General Psychiatry, 64*, 476–484.

Ogden, T., & Hagen, K. A. (2009). What works for whom? Gender differences in intake characteristics and treatment outcomes following multisystemic therapy. *Journal of Adolescence*, 1–11.

Oosterlaan, J., Scheres, A., Antrop, I., Roeyes, H., & Sergeant, J.A. (2000). *Vrgaenlijst voor gedragsproblemen bij kinderen: Handleiding* [Manual for the disruptive behaviors rating scale]. Lisse: Swets & Zeitlinger.

Oosterlann, J., Schreres, A., & Sergeant, J. A. (2005). Which executive functioning deficits are associated with AD/HD, ODD/CD, and comorbid AD/HD+ODD/CD? *Journal of Abnormal Child Psychology, 33*, 69–85.

Pajer, K., Chung, J., Leininger, L., Wang, W., Gardner, W., & Yeates, K. (2008). Neuropsychological function in adolescent girls with conduct disorder. *Journal of the Academy of Child and Adolescent Psychiatry, 47*, 416–425.

Panksepp, J. (1998). Attention deficit hyperactivity disorders, psychostimulants, and intolerance of childhood playfulness: A tragedy in the making? *Current Directions In Psychological Science (Wiley-Blackwell), 7*(3), 91–98. 10.1111/1467–8721.ep10774709

Pardini, D. A., Frick, P. J., & Moffitt, T. E. (2010). Building an evidence base for DSM-5 conceptualizations of oppositional defiant disorder and conduct disorder: Introduction to the special section. *Journal of Abnormal Psychology, 119*, 683–688. 10.1037/a0021441

Passamonti, L., Fairchild, G., Goodyer, I. M., Hurford, G., Hagan, C. C., Rowe, J. B., & Calder, A. J. (2010). Neural abnormalities in early-onset and adolescence-onset conduct disorder. *Archives of General Psychiatry, 67*, 729–738.

Pavuluri, M. N., O'Connor, M. M., Harral, E., & Sweeney, J.A. (2007). Affective neural circuitry during facial emotion processing in pediatric bipolar disorder. *Biological Psychiatry, 62*, 158–167.

Pelham, W. E., Gnagy, E. M., Greenslade, K. E., & Milich, R. (1992). Teacher ratings of DSM-III-R symptoms for disruptive behavior disorders. *Journal of the American Academy of Child and Adolescent Psychiatry, 21*, 210–218.

Pennington, B. F., & Ozonoff, S. (1996). Executive functions and developmental psychopathology. *Journal of Child Psychology and Psychiatry, 37*, 51–87.

Raine, A., Moffitt, T. E., Caspi, A., Loeber, R., Stouthamer-Loeber, M., & Lynam, D. (2005). Neurocognitive impairments in boys on the life-course persistent antisocial path. *Journal of Abnormal Psychology, 114*, 38–49.

Rifkin, A., Karajgi, B., Dicker, R., et al. (1997). Lithium treatment of conduct disorders in adolescents. *American Journal of Psychiatry, 154*, 554–555.

Scott, S. (2008). An update on interventions for conduct disorder. *Advances in Psychiatric Treatment, 14,* 61–70. doi: 10.1192/apt.bp.106.002626

Scott, S., Knapp, M., Henderson, J., & Maughan, B. (2001). Financial cost of social exclusion: Follow up study of antisocial children into adulthood. *British Medical Journal, 323,* 1–5.

Schutter, D. J. L. G., & van Honk, J. (2006). Increased positive emotional memory after receptive transcranial magnetic stimulation over the orbitofrontal cortex. *Journal of Psychiatry and Neuroscience, 31,* 101–104.

Searright, H. R., Rottnek, F., & Abby, S. L. (2001). Conduct disorder: Diagnosis and treatment in primary care. *American Family Physician, 63,* 1579–1588.

Seguin, J. R., Boulerice, B., Harden, P. W., Tremblay, R. E., & Pihl, R. O. (1999). Executive functions and physically aggression after controlling for attention deficit hyperactivity disorder, general memory, and IQ. *Journal of Child Psychology and Psychiatry, 40,* 1197–1208.

Shin, L. M., Orr, S. P., Carson, M. A., Rauch, S. L., Macklin, M. L., Lasko, N. B., et al. (2004). Regional cerebral blood flow in the amygdala and medial prefrontal cortex during training imagery in male and female Vietnam veterans with PTSD. *Archives of General Psychiatry, 61,* 168–176.

Siever, L. J., Kahn, R. S., Lawlor, B. A., Trestman, R. L., Lawrence, T. L., & Coccaro, E. F. (1991). Critical issues in defining the role of serotonin in psychiatric disorders. *Pharmacological Reviews, 43,* 509–525.

Silberg, J. L., Parr, T., Neale, M. C., Rutter, M., Angold, A., & Eaves, L. J. (2003). Maternal smoking during pregnancy and risks to boys' conduct disturbance: An examination of the causal hypothesis. *Biological Psychiatry, 53,* 130–135.

Silva, J. A., Derecho, D. V., Leong, G. B., Weinstock, R., & Ferrari, M. M. (2001). A classification of psychological factors leading to violent behavior in posttraumatic stress disorder. *Journal of Forensic Science, 46,* 309–316.

Simeon, J. G., Ferguson, H. B., Van Wyck, & Fleet, J. (1986). Bupropion effects in attention deficit and conduct disorders. *Canadian Journal of Psychiatry, 31,* 581–585.

Steiner, P., & Remsing, L. (2007). Practice parameter for the assessment and treatment of children and adolescents with oppositional defiant disorder. *Journal of the American Academy of Child and Adolescent Psychiatry, 46,* 126–141.

Steiner, H., Saxena, K., & Chang, K. (2003). Psychopharmacological strategies for the treatment of aggression in juveniles. *CNS Spectrums, 8,* 298–308.

Stinchcomb, J. B. (2005). From optimistic policies to pessimistic outcomes: Why won't boot camps either succeed pragmatically or succumb politically? In *Rehabilitation Issues, Problems, and Prospects* (Eds. B. B. Brenda & N. J. Pallone), pp. 27–52. Haworth Press.

Teichner, G., & Golden, C. J. (2000). The relationship of neuropsychological impairment to conduct disorder in adolescence: A conceptual review. *Aggressive Violent Behavior, 5,* 509–528.

Toupin, J., Dery, M. Pauze, R., Mercier, H., & Fortin, L. (2000). Cognitive and family constrictions to conduct disorder in children. *Journal of Child Psychology and Psychiatry, 41,* 333–344.

Turgay, A. (2004). Aggression and disruptive behavior disorders in children and adolescents. *Expert Review of Neurotherapeutics, 4,* 623–632.

Tyler, J., Darville, R., & Stalnaker, K. (2001). Juvenile boot camps. A descriptive analysis of program diversity and effectiveness. *Social Science Journal, 38,* 445–460.

Van Elst, L. T., Woermann, F. G., Lemieux, L., Thompson, P. J., & Trimble, M.R. (2000). Affective aggression in patients with temporal lobe epilepsy: A quantitative MRI study of the amygdala. *Brain, 123,* 234–243.

van Goozen, S. M., & Fairchild, G. (2008). How can the study of biological processes help deisgn new interventions for children with severe antisocial behavior? *Development and Psychopathology, 20,* 941–973. 10.1017/S095457940800045X

van Goozen, S. M., Fairchild, G., & Harold, G. T. (2008). The role of neurobiological deficits in childhood antisocial behavior. *Current Directions In Psychological Science, 17,* 224–228. 10.1111/j.1467-8721.2008.00579.x

Van de Wiel, N. M. H., Van Goozen, S. H.M., Matthys, W., Snoek, H., & Van Engeland, H. (2004). Cortisol and treatment effects in children with disruptive behavior disorders: A preliminary study. *Journal of the American Academy of Child & Adolescent Psychiatry, 43,* 1011–1018.

Verhulst, F. C., Van den Ende, J., & Koot, H. M. (1996). *Handeiding voor de CBCL (4–18)* [Manual for the CBCL (4–18)]. Rotterdam, The Netherlands: Afdeling kinder-en-jeugdpsychiatrie, Sophie kinderziekenhuis/Academisch Ziekenhuis Rotterdam/Erasmus Universiteit.

Verona, E., Patrick, C. J., & Joiner, T. E. (2001). Psychopathy, antisocial personality, and suicide risk. *Journal of Abnormal Psychology, 110,* 462–470.

Walsh, V. & Rushworth, M. (1999). A primer of magnetic stimulation as a tool for neuropsychology. *Neuropsychologia, 37,* 125–135.

Wasserman, E. M., & Lisanby, S. H. (2001). Therapeutic application of repetitive transcranial magnetic stimulation: A review. *Clinical Neurophysiology, 112,* 1367–1377.

Wechsler, D. (2003). *Wechsler Intelligence Scale for Children—4th Edition (WISC-IV).* San Antonio, TX: Harcourt Assessment.

Williams, L. M., Kemp, A. H., Felmingham, K., Barton, M., Olivieri, G., Peduto, A., et al. (2006). Trauma modulates amygdala and medial prefrontal responses to consciously attended fear. *NeuroImage, 29,* 347–357.

CHAPTER 8

Tic Disorders

John Joshua Hall, James R. Batterson, & Jeffrey H. Snow

INTRODUCTION: ADVANCED DIAGNOSTIC CONSIDERATIONS AND PRACTICES

Tic disorders are a group of neurodevelopmental disorders with childhood onset (Spencer, Biederman, Harding, Wilens, & Faraone, 1995). Tic disorders have been described throughout history. Most notably, in 1482, there was a detailed description of a young priest with vocal and motor tics who was saved from persecution and death by a successful treatment with exorcism. French 17th century historical accounts described Prince de Conde, a nobleman in the court of Louis XIV, who frequently stuffed objects in his mouth to prevent vocal tics, in this case, barking in the presence of the King (Bloch & Leckman, 2007). The phenomenology of tic disorders was most famously described by Gilles de la Tourette over a century ago, initially while a student under Charcot (Towbin, 2010).

Despite our growing understanding of epidemiology, genetics, neurophysiology, and the significant changes in technology, the phenomenology of tic disorders as described by Gilles de la Tourette has remained essentially unchanged (Walkup, Ferrao, Leckman, Stein, & Singer, 2010). Tic disorders are described as acute or chronic conditions characterized by quick, sudden, repetitive, nonrhythmic, stereotyped gestures or vocal utterances that can vary in intensity (American Psychiatric Association [APA], 2000). Tics can occur in any voluntary muscle and can affect the same muscles over days and hours; however, they can spread to different parts of the body over months and years (Popper & West, 1999). Towbin (2010) indicates that a good measure of tic severity is to assess how much effort a person must exert in order to suppress and successfully inhibit a tic.

Tic disorders are divided into motor, vocal, or phonic tics. Motor and vocal tics can vary in nature from more simple movements or utterances to more complex, purposeful actions or vocalizations. Simple motor tics may present as a jerk of the arm, nose twitching, or shrug whereas simple vocal tics may consist of throat clearing, coughing, or grunting. Complex motor tics seem more purposeful in nature, with more complex facial or body movements; complex vocal tics are also more meaningful, such as palilalia (repeating one's own words), echolalia (repeating others' words), or, in rare cases, coprolalia (uttering obscenities; Bloch & Leckman, 2007).

Tic disorders were first included in the *DSM-III* (APA, 1980). Three significant changes have been made since its initial entry. The age of onset was changed from 21 to 18 in the *DSM-IV* (APA, 1994) and impairment criteria were included; however, the impairment criteria were removed in the *DSM-IV-TR* (APA, 2000) due to concerns regarding those individuals diagnosed with Tourette's disorder (TD) who did not experience significant impairment (Walkup et al., 2010).

There are four categories of tic disorders in the *DSM-IV-TR*: transient tic disorder, chronic motor or vocal tic disorder, Tourette's disorder (TD), and tic disorder, not otherwise specified. Age of onset for tic disorders can vary widely; however, in order to meet diagnostic criteria for transient tic disorder, chronic motor or vocal tic disorder, or TD, the age of onset must occur before the age of 18. In general, children between the ages of 7 and 11 appear to have the highest rates of tic behaviors (Popper & West, 1999). For individuals who demonstrate tic behaviors after the age of 18, a diagnosis of tic disorder, not otherwise specified is most appropriate. The *DSM-IV-TR* also specifies that the disturbance is not related to physiological effects of substances, such as stimulants, or a general medical condition, such as postviral encephalitis.

The prevalence of tic disorders is estimated to be 1%–2% but is likely higher in children and adolescents, with males being three times more likely than females to have the disorder (Popper & West, 1999). However, few rigorous population-based studies have been performed, making the 1%–2% prevalence rate a preliminary estimate at best (Leckman, 2002). Some authors have argued that socioeconomic factors and race do not seem to influence the prevalence of tic disorders, whereas others have suggested that tic symptoms may be more common in White and Asian groups, especially when discussing TD (Leckman, 2002; Mathews et al., 2007).

Tics often increase in response to emotionally stimulating events, such as being excited or distressed. Tics often decrease during periods of concentration, focused activity, and when being suddenly alerted to stimuli, but are generally worse immediately prior to and following the activity (Popper & West, 1999; Towbin, 2010). Individuals with tic disorders, especially those diagnosed with chronic motor or vocal tic and TD, often report two types of mental events: premonitory urges and obsessions and/or compulsions. Premonitory urges have been reported by 75%–80% of people diagnosed with chronic tic disorders and TD, and they commonly occur prior to tic behavior (Banaschewski, Neale, Rothenberger, & Roessner, 2007; Kwak, Dat, & Jankovic, 2003). These premonitory urges may have physical qualities such as tingling, itching, and tension in the muscles or have a mental quality such as uncomfortable thoughts or unpleasant sensations prior to tics (Leckman, Walker, & Cohen, 1993). Obsessions and/or compulsions may arise with or precede tics and are reported in 50%–90% of people with TD (Gaze, Kepley, & Walkup, 2006). Obsessions and compulsions can manifest in varying ways in different individuals; however, a few common trends have been identified. Specifically, when comparing individuals diagnosed solely with obsessive compulsive disorder (OCD) versus individuals with TD and OCD, individuals with TD and OCD are more likely to have aggressive, sexual, and religious obsessions (Zohar et al., 1997).

Transient tic disorder is often diagnosed when single or multiple motor and/or vocal tics occur. Age of onset of the disorder is typically 2–8 years with boys being of greater risk; however, some cases have been reported as early as 2 years of age (Leckman, 2002; Rapoport & Ismond, 1996). Tics involving the face are most common, but the limbs or torso may be involved. Vocal tics may also occur in transient tic disorder, but this is rare (Rapoport & Ismond, 1996). Transient tics are common and may occur in 10%–20% of school-aged children. The diagnosis is often confounded by the fact that tics tend to wax and wane, and by the time they are evaluated by the appropriate medical professional, the symptoms may have completely disappeared (Leckman, 2002).

Chronic motor or vocal tic disorder differs from transient tic disorder in several ways. Specifically, single or multiple motor or vocal tics, but not both, have been present. For one to meet diagnostic criteria for chronic motor or vocal tic disorder, tics must occur frequently throughout the day on a relatively consistent basis for more than 1 year with the tics not having subsided for more than 3 months (APA, 2000). Being a chronic condition, tics can wax and wane similarly to transient tic disorder, and there is a broad range of symptom severity. However, chronic simple and complex tics are most common and typically involve the head, neck, and upper extremities (Leckman, 2002). Chronic vocal tics are unusual in this disorder. If both motor and vocal tics are occurring and have occurred for more than 1 year, a diagnosis of TD may be more appropriate (Popper & West, 1999).

The third, and most debilitating, type of tic disorder is TD. TD is different from the other conditions in that multiple motor and one or more vocal tics have occurred simultaneously or at different periods. The typical age of onset is early childhood and tics often present as bouts of simple motor tics that fluctuate initially. As the child ages, the tics become more persistent and often progress to a more severe complex motor tic (Leckman, 2002). On average, vocal tics begin 1–2 years after the onset of motor symptoms. Vocal tics initially present as simple motor tic behavior, such as throat clearing or grunting, and can progress to more complex vocal symptoms such as dramatic changes in the volume and rhythm of speech to the rarer conditions of echolalia, palilalia, and coprolalia (Leckman, 2002). As with the other tic disorders, individuals with TD often experience a waxing and waning of symptoms over time. The severity of tic behavior varies from mild cases that often go unnoticed to more disabling conditions (Rapoport & Ismond, 1996).

TD is a lifelong disease, and although tics can be suppressed, the individual is likely to experience significant stress until the tics are relieved (Popper & West, 1999). The pattern of tic behavior in TD can vary from individual to individual. Tic behaviors tend to remit in late adolescence; however, adulthood can be a period when the most severe and debilitating forms of tic disorders can be seen (Leckman, 2002; Leckman et al., 1998). TD is three times more common in boys than girls (Rapoport & Ismond, 1996).

Genetics appear to play a significant role in tic disorders, especially TD. The role of genetics in tic disorders is best illustrated by twin studies. Specifically, there are higher concordance rates of TD in monozygotic versus dizygotic twins (Hyde, Aaronson, Randolph, Rickler, & Weinberger, 1992). In fact, it has been reported that the twin concordance rates for TD is 53%–56% for monozygotic pairs and 8% for dizygotic (Hyde et al., 1992; Price, Kidd, Cohen, Pauls, & Leckman, 1985). When criteria are broadened to include chronic motor or vocal tic disorder, the concordance rates jump to 77%–94% for monozygotic and 23% for dizygotic, further supporting that tic disorders likely have a strong genetic component (Towbin, 2010). Cross-cultural studies have shown that individuals with TD display similar symptomology, treatment outcomes, comorbidity, and family history, further illustrating the role of genetics in the disorder (Staley, Wand, & Shady, 1997).

Although concordance rates are significantly elevated, it cannot be assumed that genetic factors only play a role in the acquisition of the disorder because concordance rates are not 100%. Some children without a past family history of tic disorders of any kind have been diagnosed, suggesting that tic disorders can also be an acquired phenomenon. In fact, one-third of individuals with TD have a past history of autoimmune disorder from early streptococcal infection, which is thought to attack the basal ganglia (Pennington, 2002; Popper & West, 1999). In these affected individuals, TD is thought to result from an autoimmune reaction to the streptococcal infection, with the resulting condition being termed pediatric autoimmune neuropsychiatric disorder associated with streptococcal infections, or PANDAS. Swedo and Grant (1998) reported that in children who met PANDAS criteria, streptococcal infection, specifically group A beta-hemolytic streptococci (GABHS), was likely to have preceded the manifestation of tic disorder in 44% of children, versus 28% of children with no history of infection. It is well known that GABHS can trigger autoimmune-mediated disease in certain genetically predisposed individuals (Bisno, 1991).

Acute rheumatic fever is a delayed manifestation of GABHS and can affect the central nervous system. Individuals with a history of rheumatic fever can exhibit choreiform movements termed Sydenham's chorea (SC; Leckman, 2002). Individuals with SC often display motor and vocal tics, obsessive-compulsive symptoms, and ADHD symptoms. In fact, symptoms related to SC, TD, ADHD, and OCD are likely related to basal ganglia, cortical, and thalamic sites (Husby, van de Rijn, Zabriskie, Abdin, & Williams, 1976). Furthermore, choreiform "piano-playing movements" are quite commonly associated with PANDAS. Comorbid diagnoses of ADHD and OCD are also quite common in PANDAS, with upward of 80% of individuals with PANDAS meeting criteria for OCD and 50% meeting criteria for ADHD (Popper & West, 1999). Other symptoms associated with PANDAS are emotional lability, oppositional behavior, separation anxiety, bedtime rituals, and deterioration of math skills (Swedo & Grant, 1998).

It has also been suggested that complications during pregnancy may play a role in the acquisition of TD. This was first suggested by Pasamanick and Kawi (1956), who found that mothers of children with tics were one and one-half times more likely to have experienced a complication during pregnancy than mothers with children without tics. Retrospective studies of mothers with a child diagnosed with TD showed that increased prenatal complications, lower birthrate (in affected monozygotic more than dizygotic twins), greater emotional stress during pregnancy, and more nausea/vomiting during the first trimester were reported (Leckman, Dolnansky, Hardin, Clubb, Walkup, et al., 1990). In sum, genetics certainly play a role in a majority of individuals with TD, but TD can also result from other environmental conditions, prenatal factors, and a host of other factors that need to be further addressed when diagnosing TD and other tic disorders.

Family members are much more prone to acquire the disorder than the general population, and family studies with TD reveal that tics are found in two-thirds of relatives (Rapoport & Ismond, 1996). First-degree family members of individuals with TD are at a substantially higher risk for developing not only TD, but also chronic tic disorder and OCD (Walkup et al., 1996). As previously mentioned, the incidence of TD and other tic disorders was higher among family members across different countries, ethnic groups, and socioeconomic conditions (Walkup et al., 1996; Eapen, Pauls, & Robertson, 1993; Hebebrand et al., 1997). In families of European origin, the prevalence of TD or comorbid TD (CTD) in first-degree relatives ranges from 15%–53%, but when these rates are compared to the general population, prevalence of these disorders is 10 to 50 times higher, further supporting the role of genetics in tic disorders (Tobin, 2010). Furthermore, rates of obsessive and compulsive symptoms and diagnosis of OCD are 10 to 20 times higher in first-degree relatives of an individual with TD when compared to those rates of the general population (Bloch et al., 2006). However, within these affected families of individuals with TD, boys are more likely to have tic disorders whereas girls are more likely to have symptoms of OCD (Pauls & Leckman, 1986).

Children with TD often report significant teasing, shame, guilt, social isolation and social withdrawal, and issues with self-esteem and self-confidence. Children with TD and CTD are also commonly referred to clinics for problems with aggression, oppositional behavior, rigidity in behavior, and problems with social skill development, particularly understanding others' perspectives and reciprocity in social interactions (Towbin, 2010). Furthermore, these children are at risk for more severe behavioral disorders, such as attention deficit hyperactivity disorder (ADHD), OCD, and learning disabilities (LD; Yeates & Bornstein, 1995). TD and tic disorders are also much more common among individuals with autism spectrum disorders and vice versa (Canitano & Vivanti, 2007). With adults, individuals diagnosed with TD have higher rates of unemployment than the normal populations, with some suggesting it may be as high as 50% (Popper & West, 1999).

NEUROANATOMY AND NEUROPHYSIOLOGY OF TIC DISORDERS

Investigation into tic disorders has led to a greater appreciation and understanding of how neurology and neuroanatomy can influence behavior, perception, and cognitive functions. Specifically, the study of tic disorders has illustrated the breadth of interaction between neural circuitry critical for sensory and motor function and how that same circuitry connects the frontal lobes, the striatum, and the thalamus (Towbin, 2010). Autopsy studies completed in individuals with TD reveal abnormalities of dopamine in the striatum, of serotonin in the basal ganglia, of dynorphin in the globus pallidus, and of glutamic acid in the subthalamic region (Leckman et al., 1998). Neurological symptoms are also commonly observed in individuals diagnosed with TD. For example, neurological soft signs, choreiform movements, and, in over half the cases, abnormal EEGs are seen; the most common abnormality on EEGs involves excess slow waves and posterior sharp waves (Popper & West, 1999).

The basal ganglia have long been recognized as being critical to motor control and sensorimotor integration via the cortico–striato–thalamo–cortical (CSTC) loop circuits (Parent & Hazrati, 1995). The basal ganglia are a collection of gray matter nuclei located within the deep white matter of the cerebral hemispheres and are composed of four structures: the striatum (which consists of the caudate and the putamen), the pallidum, the substantia nigra, and the subthalamic nucleus. Circuits within the CSTC originating in the motor and dorsolateral cortex are considered to be most important (Tobin, 2010). Therefore, an area of particular interest in the basal ganglia is the striatum.

The striatum is considered an input structure in that all sensory input into the basal ganglia is routed through the striatum (Kozoil & Budding, 2009). It can be broken down into two primary subdivisions, the dorsal striatum and the ventral striatum. The dorsal striatum consists of the caudate nucleus and the putamen, and the ventral striatum consists of the nucleus accumbens, the septum, and the olfactory tubercle. Being the input structure of the basal ganglia, the striatum receives input from all major cortical regions (Kozoil & Budding, 2009). The caudate nucleus receives input from the dorsolateral prefrontal cortex, the ventral striatum receives input from the orbitofrontal cortex (OFC), and the nucleus accumbens receives input from the anterior cingulated regions. The caudate also receives input from the temporal and parietal lobes. The putamen receives input from the motor cortex and somatosensory cortex. Given the rich interconnections between the striatum and other major structures, it can be assumed that it plays a major role in behavior and cognition.

The basal ganglia are often thought to be the area of movement; however, they have been linked to various motor, cognitive, and affective symptoms and are also involved in the pathology of a host of different psychiatric disturbances (Kozoil & Budding, 2009). Neurological disorders, such as Parkinson's disease, Huntington's disease, and dystonia are considered to result from abnormal functioning within the basal ganglia (Utter & Basso, 2008; Eddy, Rizzo, & Cavanna, 2009). The basal ganglia are also implicated in TD and other forms of tic disorder. Studies of individuals with TD have revealed structural changes within the basal ganglia, such as decreased volume of the left side of the caudate, putamen, and globus pallidus, and decreased striatal metabolism (Eddy, Rizzo, & Cavanna, 2009; Peterson, Leckman, & Cohen, 1995). Quantitative MRI studies of monozygotic twins with tics have found that the right caudate nucleus size is much smaller than is typically seen and normal asymmetry of the lateral ventricles was seen in the more severely affected twin (Hyde et al., 1995). Decreased cerebral blood flow in the left lenticular nucleus and decreased activity in the right basal ganglia activity has also been seen in SPECT studies (Riddle, Rasmusson, Woods, & Hoffer, 1992).

It seems clear that tics in TD originate from a primary subcortical disorder affecting the motor cortex and problems with inhibition related to the motor cortex and/or subcortical functions. Serrien, Orth, Evans, Lees, and Brown (2005) found that patients with TD exhibited increased activity in the fronto–mesial network when compared to controls. Given that the fronto–mesial network was also active during tic suppression, the authors concluded that decreased inhibitory control in TD can result in compensatory increases in brain activity. Others have argued that decreased activation of orbitofrontal, cingulated, and insular brain regions are also partly responsible for the symptoms of TD (Peterson, Leckman, & Cohen, 1995).

NEUROPSYCHOLOGICAL AND BEHAVIORAL SEQUELAE

Regardless of the cause of tics in TD, cognitive dysfunction is believed to relate to three frontal areas: the lateral orbitofrontal cortex, the dorsolateral prefrontal cortex, and the anterior cingulate cortex, collectively referred to as the prefrontal cortex (Eddy et al., 2009). The lateral orbitofrontal cortex is often associated with Phineas Gage, and primary deficits can be related to personality changes including disinhibition, impulsivity, irritability, and emotional lability (Koziol & Budding, 2009). Engaging in socially inappropriate behavior and social disinhibition are also thought to result from damage to this area. An affective tone characterized by euphoria or mania is also related to dysfunction within the lateral OFC (Miller & Cummings, 2007). The anterior cingulated cortex is often thought of as the "limbic striatum," and dysfunction within this area is often characterized by apathy (Heimer, Van Hoesen, Trimble, & Zahm, 2008). Similar to the lateral OFC, neuropsychological tests often fall short of identifying dysfunction within this area. Often, traits of apathy are attributed to emotional functions rather than an underlying brain dysfunction.

The dorsolateral prefrontal cortex is thought to be intimately related to executive functioning and attention. Lesions within the dorsolateral prefrontal area commonly result in deficits in attention (Kozoil & Budding, 2009). Neurological changes in TD involving the anterior cingulated pathways have been suggested to be related to mild impairments in crucial attention and inhibitory processes. However, attention is a broad concept and is frequently conceptualized as involving multiple components. Inhibition is one of these components and is often thought to be related to dysexecutive syndrome. Poor initiation, sustained, and selective attention, and poor maintenance have also been discussed in relation to executive dysfunction and can commonly result in problems with shifting attention between tasks and with multitasking (Kozoil & Budding, 2009). With regard to neuropsychological performance, problems with dorsolateral prefrontal cortex functioning often result in delays in working memory, planning, and organization (Lichter & Cummings, 2001). Problem solving can also be affected, specifically in that perseveration can interfere with mental flexibility.

Given the complexity of TD and the various areas affected, learning problems and other areas of cognitive delay are quite common. Children with TD are more vulnerable to poor school performance, academic deficits, and psychosocial problems that can have a deleterious effect if not properly addressed. Bornstein (1990) found that the degree of neuropsychological impairment can be more severe based upon age of onset, with earlier age of onset being more severe, and the prominence of complex tics. Bornstein (1991a) also found that the pattern of neuropsychological deficits in TD persists into adulthood. Therefore, neuropsychological assessment is invaluable to aid in improving their quality of educational performance and quality of life by identifying areas of cognitive strengths and weaknesses to assist in treatment planning across the lifespan. Specifically, neuropsychological evaluations may be helpful in identifying problems with speech and language, memory, learning, and executive functioning deficits (Semrud-Clikeman & Teeter-Ellison, 2009).

Given the fact that the prefrontal lobe is implicated, it is common for individuals with TD to experience delays with executive functions. The term "executive function" refers to higher-order functions that help to regulate and supervise cognitive functions, specifically planning, mental flexibility, attention allocation, working memory, and inhibition, functions that are believed to be related largely to the frontal lobes (Zillmer, Spiers, & Culbertson, 2008). Of particular interest with TD are the basal ganglia, which are thought to be most prominent of the interconnecting structures involved in executive functioning. Within the executive functioning domain, difficulties may emerge in any of the following areas: self-regulation, set-maintenance, selective inhibition of verbal and nonverbal response, cognitive flexibility, planning, prioritizing, organizing time and space, and output-efficiency, or preparedness-to-act (Harris et al., 1995). Individuals with TD have been found to experience problems with inhibition. Inhibition is a central issue in TD because of the nature of the individual's involuntary movements and utterances. Planning has also been described as a significant problem in children and adults with TD and ADHD. Problems with cognitive flexibility have also been reported in individuals with TD and OCD (Bornstein, 1991b). Working memory delays are also noted in individuals with TD and ADHD. Poor letter but not semantic fluency has been described. However, it is often the case that executive functioning delays seem to be more inherent to TD with comorbid ADHD or OCD rather than TD by itself.

The complexity of TD, with its frequently occurring comorbid disorders, has plagued research. ADHD and OCD, which are commonly comorbid with TD, can interfere with specifically identifying neuropsychological deficiencies that are solely caused by TD. Some have gone as far as saying that ADHD, OCD, and TD share common neurobiological substrates given that the cognitive dysfunction amongst these disorders is so similar (Lombroso & Leckman, 1999; McDougle, 1999). Recent neuroimaging studies support this statement in that brain regions implicated in OCD, TD, and anxiety disorder do in fact overlap (Pennington, 2002). ADHD and OCD themselves can have a negative effect upon academic functioning, and studies of TD and neuropsychological functioning have been criticized for not controlling the effects of comorbid ADHD and OCD when assessing TD. Studies have also been criticized for having small sample sizes and using a wide variety of measures to assess similar traits.

Others have found that specific attention deficits are still seen in individuals diagnosed with TD when the effects of ADHD and OCD are controlled. Chang, McCracken, and Piacentini (1990) found evidence of poor performance on tests of spatial attention in TD even after controlling for ADHD. Other findings indicate that tasks involving sustained attention, particularly CPTs, may be more sensitive to impairment in TD (Harris et al., 1995; Shucard, Benedict, TekokKilic, & Lichter, 1997). Therefore, it appears that more perceptual tasks, such as spatial attention and sustained attention during a visual task, better illustrate the deficits in frontal functions of TD rather than more traditional executive functioning tasks.

Although controversy exists with regard to the degree of impairment of executive functions within TD, neuropsychological studies have clearly shown that delays in TD appear to be more frequently seen in right hemisphere tasks and are likely related to subcortical or basal ganglia abnormalities implicated with TD. Perceptual, motor, and visual-motor integration delays have frequently been reported. Sutherland and colleagues found that children and adults with TD struggled at drawing and remembering complex geometric patterns regardless of level of IQ (Kolb & Whishaw, 2010). Many studies have found significant differences between verbal and performance IQ on the Wechsler Intelligence Tests. Shapiro, Shapiro, Young, and Feinberg (1978) reported statistically significant differences between performance IQ (PIQ) and verbal IQ (VIQ) with VIQ being significantly higher. However, when patients with TD and ADHD were excluded, the amount of individuals with TD alone who had a significant discrepancy between VIQ and PIQ dropped by 10% (Bornstein, 1990).

Nonverbal, visual memory impairment has also been found to be present in both patients with TD and patients with tic disorders. Specifically, Lavoie, Thibault, Stip, and O'Conner (2007) found that immediate and delayed recall of the RCFT in individuals with TD and tic disorders differed significantly from their performance on immediate and delayed recall of word lists on the California Verbal Learning Test (CVLT; Delis, Kramer, Kaplan, & Ober, 2000). Bornstein (1990) reported that nonverbal memory performance appears to decrease linearly with the intensity of tic severity in both children and adults. It is important to note that the use of the RCFT as a measure of memory may be confounded by the previously referenced research that suggests that global processing is a deficit found in individuals with TD. It may be difficult to differentiate whether the deficit, RCFT immediate and delayed recall is related to poor global processing and organization or whether it is a true visual memory deficit. Given that TD involves delays with motor planning, however, it is clear that the delay does relate to the right hemisphere in some manner.

It is possible that dysfunction within the frontal lobe and the interconnecting structures affect functioning in a more global manner in TD. Matsui and colleagues (2007) suggested that conventional "frontal" tasks correlate with both frontal and parietal lobe function such that posterior brain system involvement can contribute to executive dysfunction as well. The RCFT is particularly interesting because it assesses a variety of processes. Specifically, the RCFT has been found to assess planning, organizational skills, and problem-solving strategies as well as perceptual, motor, and episodic memory functions (Meyers & Meyers, 1995). Bradshaw and Sheppard (2000) proposed that children with Tourette's syndrome (TS), in particular, fail to show a normal pattern of processing at the global level. Based upon neuroimaging studies, other authors have suggested the right hemisphere specializes in processing information at a global level (Proverbio, Minniti, & Zani, 1998). Therefore, the authors concluded that dysfunction in the right hemisphere associated with TD could affect global processing; a key component in the ability to fully recall and reconstruct complex figures.

Given the subcortical structures involved, visual, motor, and perceptual delays, and problems with global processing, cognitive delays in TD are very similar to delays seen in individuals researched and described by Rourke (1988). Rourke has suggested that right hemisphere dysfunction is largely attributed to a white matter syndrome affecting the right hemisphere. He has provided convincing evidence in his numerous studies that these individuals display poor visual–spatial organization and psychomotor, tactile–perceptual, and concept formation skills while having intact rote, automatic verbal skills (Hale & Fiorello, 2004). Rourke also suggested that this combination often leads to pedantic speech, social isolation, low self-esteem, anxiety, and depression, problems often described in children with TD and other tic disorders.

Learning disorders are frequently associated with TD, but the lack of control for comorbid conditions again makes conclusions about specific learning disabilities related to TD alone unclear. It is clear that underlying learning issues do exist, especially if ADHD is a comorbid condition. Children with TD plus ADHD are up to four times as likely to have academic difficulty compared to children with TD alone (Schultz, Carter, Scahill, & Leckman, 1999). Reading disabilities have been found to be no more common in TD than in the general population and do not appear to be intrinsically related to TD (Yeates & Bornstein, 1994). The authors did find that arithmetic disabilities are much more common in TD than in the general population; however, they concluded that the deficits are more likely linked to deficits in executive functions rather than being attributed to a nonverbal learning disability or its presumed basis in the right hemisphere. However, based upon previous research studies that demonstrated that executive functioning delays were not necessarily present when the effects of comorbid ADHD were controlled, it seems more likely that the nonverbal learning disability description more closely resembles the cognitive delays in TD.

CONTEMPORARY MODES OF TREATMENT

Tobin (2010) indicates that the "cornerstone" of treatment of TD and other tic disorders is observation. Observations from parents, caregivers, clinicians, and teachers can all play a role in documenting how the symptoms present and how the individual copes with these symptoms, both positive and negative coping strategies. For children, completing behavioral observations in the school setting, whether it be by a school psychologist, teacher, or counselor, can be important in monitoring the number of tic behaviors, whether the behaviors coincide with the time of day (i.e., more during the morning hours versus the afternoon or vice versa), and if there are patterns in when the tics occur, such as being more frequent during lunchtime and more social settings or during math classes, for example. Observation can have the potential effect of reducing symptoms through raising awareness of the behaviors and intervening to provide more helpful coping strategies during stressful periods or times when tics are most commonly occurring. However, it is important to balance increasing awareness while not focusing too intensely on the tics themselves, which can increase anxiety and cause the tics to potentially worsen.

It is also important that parental anxiety not be significantly increased during the course of treatment. Cooper, Robertson, and Livingston (2003) found that parental stress associated with TD exceeded that of parents of children with asthma. These mothers also reported that the source of their stress was related to managing the child's daily activities and behavior whereas mothers of children with asthma reported illness-related stress. Therefore, it seems the study illustrated that parents have a higher propensity of attributing their stress to the child rather to the child's illness. It is very likely that this same dynamic occurs at school, where teachers may be more likely to attribute a child's behaviors as being willful defiance rather than being caused by TD. Therefore, bringing more attention to tics may further intensify scrutiny, leading the individual to feel greater pressure to monitor and contain his or her tic behaviors, increasing anxiety and further exacerbating tics. It is important to note that parental stress is significantly higher when children with TD have one or more comorbid disorders; with children with TD without comorbid disorders, parents indicated no significant increase in stress (Cooper et al., 2003).

With regard to specific treatment, behavioral interventions have been shown to greatly reduce the severity and frequency of tics. In adults, studies have shown that habit reversal training has been more successful at lessening tic behavior when compared to controls (Peterson & Azrin, 1992). Habit reversal is based upon a competing response procedure; an action is developed that can interfere with, or inhibit, the tic behavior (Towbin, 2010). It is important that the action does not draw attention to the individual and can be sustained for several minutes until the compulsion to engage in tic behavior has passed. For children and adults, relaxation training can act as a competing response procedure. In regard to relaxation training, the muscles are systematically tensed and relaxed, generally starting from the top of the body down. Certainly, individuals with a history of premonitory urges are perfect candidates for habit reversal; however, providing a coping strategy for a child who has recently developed more severe tics could act to lessen the stress of the behavior by providing methods to feel more in control. In general, intervening early when the condition arises to provide education to the family, providing short-term behavioral therapy to develop better coping strategies during periods of stress, and then providing ongoing family and/or individual therapy to address family concerns and potential individual symptoms of depression, anxiety, and social skill deficits that may arise as a result of tics is essential for good mental health in TD and other tic disorders.

Psychopharmacological treatment is a critical aspect in treating tic disorder and TD. It has been recommended that a prescribing physician should consider the tic severity; the effect of the tics upon the individual, the family, and the social environment; and the working relationship with the patient and/or the family if working with children (Towbin, 2010). The working relationship is of particular importance given that treatment for tic disorders is typically a long-term endeavor. An important aspect of psychopharmacological treatment of tics is that the goal is to reduce, not eliminate, tics. In this sense, the patient's quality of life and need is balanced against the risks of side effects of medications such that the best possible course of treatment is constructed with the patient being an active participant. Again, monitoring tic behavior is critically important whether medication has been prescribed or not so that decisions can be made regarding whether medication is warranted, and if so, to what degree the medication will be gradually increased to achieve optimal therapeutic levels. It is also necessary to have consistent and frequent reevaluations to determine if medication should be increased or decreased based upon severity.

If medications are used, two classes of medications are often prescribed. Dopamine antagonists, or medications that block dopamine, are common treatments for moderate to severe tics. These medications have a robust history of study in the use of treatment of tic disorders and have provided the most consistent and positive results (Towbin, 2010). The other class of medications is the alpha-2 adrenergic agonists. Medications such as clonidine and guanfacine are thought to regulate norepinephrine, leading to decreased serotonin production in the median raphe, which thereby decreases dopamine release in the substantia nigra (Bunney & DeRiemer, 1982). Given the relatively benign side effects, clonidine has led some authorities to consider it a first-line agent for treating mild to moderate tics (Gilbert, 2006; Swain, Scahill, Lombroso, King, & Leckman, 2007). However, cognitive functions may be inadvertently affected by clonidine given that it can cause sedation and requires multiple dosing throughout the day, and that depression has been reported by many patients taking the medication (Towbin, 2010).

Treatment of tics also includes treating potential comorbid conditions. As previously indicated, ADHD and OCD are commonly diagnosed with TD. Individuals diagnosed with OCD with a family history of tic disorders may not respond as well to treatment as those with no such family history (Towbin, 2010). Cognitive-behavioral therapy, use of selective serotonin reuptake inhibitors (SSRIs), or some combination of the two is often useful in treating the obsessive and compulsive symptoms. Goodman, Storch, Geffken, and Murphy (2006) suggest that adding a dopamine antagonist may be helpful if individuals do not respond to SSRIs initially.

Treatment of TD or complex tics with comorbid ADHD typically involves the usage of methylphenidate or dextroamphetamine; however, these medications may have the undesired effect of exacerbating tics (Towbin, 2010). Some have argued against prescribing these medications with TD or complex tics and encourage instead the use of alpha-adrenergic agonists in TD (Robertson, 2006). However, other longitudinal studies report that tics do not increase with the use of stimulants and appear to be more effective in treating the symptoms of ADHD as well as potentially lessening the amount of tics (Tourette's Syndrome Study Group, 2002). The group did report that tics are exacerbated in approximately 25% of individuals with TD whether they are given stimulants, clonidine, or some combination; however, other authors have noted that the increase in tics after starting stimulants often subsides after 3 months (Castellanos et al., 1997).

In general, treatment of TD is a complex endeavor. It is likely to include a combination of pharmacological and therapeutic treatments as well as the need for involvement of multiple individuals, including the patient, parents, family, teachers, or others, to help monitor the effectiveness of treatment and to assist professionals in making educated decisions regarding treatment. The complexity of the disorder itself complicates many aspects of academic, family, and social functioning, which can contribute to the increased rates of anxiety, depression, and oppositional behaviors often seen in more severe forms of tic disorders, particularly TD. Although the challenges are great, it is clear that neuropsychological testing can contribute greatly to the identification of cognitive strengths and weaknesses as well as to help identify potential treatment considerations and treatment planning recommendations.

SUMMARY

Tic disorders are classified into four categories based on the types of tics exhibited, the duration of symptoms, and whether or not both vocal and motor tics present together or singularly. Research has revealed correlations between the occurrence of tic disorders and neurochemical abnormalities in the striatum, basal ganglia, blobus pallidus, and subthalamic region. While such findings are most commonly tied with the manifestation of the tics themselves, cognitive deficits have been linked with abnormalities of the lateral orbitofrontal cortex, dorsolateral prefrontal cortex, and the anterior cingulated cortex. Consequently, tic disorders have been linked with deficits in attentional control, inhibition, executive functioning, working memory, nonverbal problem solving, and visual memory. The potential for such difficulties demonstrates the necessity for neuropsychological services being regularly included in the standard care of individuals with tic disorders.

REFERENCES

American Psychiatric Association. (2000). *Diagnostic and statistical manual of mental disorders* (4th Edition), Text Revision. Washington, D. C: American Psychiatric Association.

American Psychiatric Association. (1994). *Diagnostic and statistical manual of mental disorders* (4th Edition). Washington, DC: American Psychiatric Press, Inc.

American Psychiatric Association. (1980). *Diagnostic and statistical manual of mental disorders* (3rd Edition). Washington, DC: American Psychiatric Association.

Banaschewski, T., Neale, B. M., Rothenberger, A., & Roessner, V. (2007). Comorbidity of tic disorders and ADHD: Conceptual and methodological considerations. *European Child and Adolescent Psychiatry* (Supplement 1), *16*, 5–14.

Bisno, A. L. (1991). Group A streptococcal infections and rheumatic fever. *New England Journal of Medicine, 325*, 783–793.

Bloch, M. H., Peterson, B. S., Scahill, L., Otka, J., Katsovich, Zhang, H., et al . (2006). Adulthood outcome of tic and obsessive-compulsive symptom severity in children with Tourette syndrome. *Archives of Pediatrics and Adolescent Medicine, 160*, 65–69.

Bloch, M. H. & Leckman, J. F. (2007). Tic Disorders. In Lewis's Child and Adolescent Psychiatry: A Comprehensive Textbook, 4th Edition, (A. Martin & F. Volkmar, Eds), pp 569–581. Philadelphia, PA: Lippincott, Williams & Williams.

Bornstein, R. A. (1991a). Neuropsychological performance in adults with Tourette's syndrome. *Psychiatry Research, 37*, 229–236.

Bornstein, R. A. (1991b). Neuropsychological correlates of obsessive compulsive characteristics in Tourette's syndrome. *Journal of Neuropsychiatric and Clinical Neuroscience, 3*, 157–162.

Bornstein, R. A. (1990). Neuropsychological performance in children with Tourette's syndrome. *Psychiatry Research, 33*, 73–81.

Bradshaw, J. L., & Sheppard, D. M. (2000). The neurodevelopmental frontostriatal disorders: Evolutionary adaptiveness and anomalous lateralization. *Brain and Language, 73*, 297–320.

Bunney, B. S., & DeRiemer, S. (1982). Effect of clonidine on dopaminergic neuron activity in the substantia nigra: Possible indirect mediation by noradrenergic regulation of the serotonergic raphe system. *Advanced Neurology, 35*, 99–104.

Canitano, R., & Vivanti, G. (2007). Tic and Tourette syndrome in autism spectrum disorder. *Autism, 11*, 19–28.

Castellanos, F. X., Giedd, J. N., Elia, J., Marsh, W. L., Ritchie, G. F., Hamburger, S. D., et al. (1997). Controlled stimulant treatment of ADHD and comorbid Tourette's syndrome: Effects of stimulant and dose. *Journal of American Academy of Child and Adolescent Psychiatry, 39*, 589–596.

Chang, S. W., McCracken, J. T., & Piacentini, J. C. (1990). Neurocognitive correlates of child obsessive compulsive disorder and Tourette syndrome. *Journal of Clinical and Experimental Neuropsychology, 29*, 724–733.

Cohen, D. J., Riddle, M. A., & Leckman, J. F. (1992). Pharmacotherapy of Tourette's syndrome and associated disorders. *The Psychiatric Clinic of North America, 15*, 109–129.

Cooper, C. Robertson, M. M., & Livingston, G. (2003). Psychological morbidity and caregiver burdens in parents of children with Tourette's disorder and psychiatric comorbidity, *Journal of American Academy of Child and Adolescent Psychiatry, 42*, 1370–1375.

Delis, D. C., Kramer, J. H., Kaplan, E., & Ober, B. A. (2000). *California verbal learning test*. San Antonio, TX: Psychological Corporation.

Eapen, V., Pauls, D. L., & Robertson, M. M. (1993). Evidence for autosomal dominant transmission in Tourette's syndrome: United Kingdom cohort study. *British Journal of Psychiatry, 162*, 593–596.

Eddy, C. M., Rizzo, R., & Cavanna, A. E. (2009). Neuropsychological aspects of Tourette syndrome: A review. *Journal of Psychosomatic Research, 67*, 503–513.

Gaze, C., Kepley, H. O., & Walkup, J. T. (2006). Co-occuring psychiatric disorders in children and adolescents with Tourette syndrome. *Journal of Child Neurology, 21*, 690–700.

Gilbert, D. (2006). Treatment of children and adolescents with tic and Tourette syndrome. *Journal of Child Neurology, 21*, 690–700.

Goodman, W. K., Storch, E. A., Geffken, G. R., & Murphy, T. K. (2006). Obsessive-compulsive disorder in Tourette syndrome. *Journal of Child Neurology, 8*, 704–714.

Hale, J. B., & Fiorello, C. A. (2004). *School neuropsychology: A practitioner's handbook*. New York: Guilford Press.

Harris, E. L., Schuerholz, L. J., Singer, H. S., Reader, M. J., Brown, J. E., Cox, C., et al. (1995). Executive function in children with Tourette syndrome and/or attention deficit hyperactivity disorder. *Journal of the International Neuropsychological Society, 1*, 511–516.

Hebebrand, J., Klug, B., Fimmers, R., Seuchter, S. A., Wettke-Schafer, R., Deget, F., et al. (1997) Rates for tic disorders and obsessive compulsive symptomology in families of children and adolescents with Gilles de la Tourette syndrome. *Journal of Psychiatric Research, 31*, 519–530.

Heimer, L., Van Hoesen, G. W., Trimble, M. R., & Zahm, D. S. (2008). *Anatomy of Neuropsychiatry*. Amsterdam, Netherlands: Elsevier Press.

Husby, G., van de Rijn, I., Zabriskie, J., Abdin, Z. H., & Williams, R. C. (1976). Antibodies reacting with cytoplasm of subthalamic and caudate nuclei neurons in chorea and acute rheumatic fever. *Journal of Experimental Medicine, 144*, 1094–1110.

Hyde, T. M., Aaronson, B. A., Randolph, C., Rickler, K. C., & Weinberger, D. R. (1992). Relationship of birth weight to the phenotypic expression of Gilles de la Tourette's syndrome in monozygotic twins. *Neurology, 42*, 652–658.

Hyde, T. M., Stacey, M. E., Coppola, R., Handel, S. F., Rickler, K. C., & Weinberger, D. R. (1995). Cerebral morphometric abnormalities in Tourette's syndrome. *Neurology, 45*, 1176–1182.

Kolb, B., & Whishaw, I. Q. (2010). *Fundamentals of Human Neuropsychology* (6th Edition). New York: Worth Publishers.

Koziol, L. F., & Budding, D. E. (2009). *Subcortical Structures and Cognition: Implications for Neuropsychological Assessment*. New York: Springer Publishing.

Kwak, C., Dat, V. K., & Jankovic, J. (2003). Premonitory sensory phenomenon in Tourette's syndrome. *Movement Disorders, 18*, 1530–1533.

Lavoie, M. E., Thibault, G., Stip, E., & O'Conner, K. P. (2007). Memory and executive functions in adults with Gilles de la Tourette syndrome and chronic tic disorder. *Cognitive Neuropsychiatry, 12*, 165–181.

Leckman, J. F. (2002). Tourette's syndrome. *Lancet, 360*, 1577–1586.

Leckman, J. F., & Block, M. H. (2008). A developmental and evolutionary perspective on obsessive-compulsive disorder: Whence and whither compulsive hoarding? *American Journal of Psychiatry, 165*, 1229–1233.

Leckman, J. F., Dolnansky, E. S., Hardin, M. T., Clubb, M., Walkup, J. T., Stevenson, J., et al. (1990). Perinatal factors in the expression of Tourette's syndrome: An exploratory study. *Journal of the American Academy of Child and Adolescent Psychiatry, 29*, 220–226.

Leckman, J. F., Pauls, D. L., Zhang, H., Rosario-Campos, M. C., Katsovich, L., Kidd, K. K., et al. (2003). Obsessive-compulsive symptom dimensions in affected sibling pairs diagnosed with Gilles de la Tourette Syndrome. *American Journal of Medical Genetics: Neuropsychiatric Genetics, 116B*, 60–68.

Leckman, J. F., Walker, D. E., & Cohen, D. J. (1993). Premonitory urges in Tourette's syndrome. *American Journal of Psychiatry, 150*, 98–102.

Leckman, J. F., Zhang, H., Vitale, A., Lahnin, F., Lynch, K., Bondi, C., et al . (1998). Course of tic severity in Tourette syndrome: The first two decades. *Pediatrics, 102*, 14–19.

Lichter, D. G., & Cummings, J. L. (2001). Introduction and overview. In D. G. Lichter & J. L. Cummings (Eds.), *Fronto-subcortical circuits in psychiatric and neurological disorders* (pp. 1–43). New York: Guilford Press.

Lombroso, P., & Leckman, J. (1999). The neurobiology of Tourette's syndrome and tic-related disorders in children. In D. S. Charney, E. J. Nestler, & B. S. Bunney (Eds.), *Neurobiology of mental illness* . New York: Oxford University Press.

Matsui, H., Nishinaka, K., Oda, M., Niikawa, H., Komatsu, K., Kubori, T., et al. (2007). Wisconsin Card Sorting Test in Parkinson's disease: Diffusion tensor imaging. *Acta Neurologica Scandinavica, 116,* 108–112.

Mathews, C. A., Jang, K. L., Herrera, L. D., Lowe, T. L., Budman, C. L., Erenberg, G., et al. (2007). Tic symptom profiles in subjects with Tourette syndrome from two genetically isolated populations. *Biological Psychiatry, 61,* 292–300.

McDougle, C. J. (1999). The neurobiology and treatment of obsessive-compulsive disorders. In D. S. Charney, E. J. Nestler, & B. S. Bunney (Eds.), *Neurobiology of Mental Illness* (pp. 518–533). New York: Oxford University Press.

Meyers, J. E., & Meyers, K. R. (1995). *Rey Complex Figure Test and Recognition Trial.* Odessa, FL: Psychological Assessment Resources.

Miller, B. L., & Cummings, J. L. (2007). *The human frontal lobes.* (2nd Ed.) New York: Guilford Press.

Parent, A,. & Hazrati, L. N. (1995). Functional anatomy of the basal ganglia, I: The cortico-basal ganglia-thalamo-cortical loop. *Brain Research Reviews, 20,* 91–127.

Pasamanick, B., & Kawi, A. (1956). A study of the association of prenatal and perinate factors in the development of tics in children. *Journal of Pediatrics, 48,* 596–601.

Pauls, D. L., & Leckman, J. F. (1986). The inheritance of Gilles de la Tourette syndrome and associated behaviors: Evidence for autosomal dominant transmission. *New England Journal of Medicine, 315,* 993–997.

Pennington, B. F. (2002). *The development of psychopathology: Nature and nurture.* New York: Guilford Press.

Peterson, A. L., & Azrin, N. H. (1992). An evaluation of behavioral treatments for Tourette syndrome. *Behavioral Research and Therapy, 30,* 167–174.

Peterson, B. S., Leckman, J. F., & Cohen, D. J. (1995). Tourette's syndrome: A genetically predisposed and an environmentally specified developmental psychopathology. In D. Ciccetti & D. J. Cohen (Eds.), *Developmental Psychopathology* (pp. 213–242). New York: Wiley.

Peterson, B., Riddle, M. A., Cohen, J., Katz, L. D., Smith, J. C., Hardin, M. T., et al. (1993). Reduced basal ganglia volumes in Tourette's syndrome using three-dimensional reconstruction techniques from magnetic resonance images. *Neurology, 43,* 941–949.

Popper, C., & West, S. A. (1999). Disorders usually first diagnosed in infancy, childhood, or adolescence. In R. E. Hales, S. C. Yudofsky, & J. A. Talbott (Eds.), *The American Psychiatric Press textbook of psychiatry* (3rd ed., pp. 904–910). Washington, DC: American Psychiatric Press, Inc.

Price, R. A., Kidd, K. K., Cohen, D. J., Pauls, D. L., & Leckman, J. F. (1985). A twin study of Tourette syndrome. *Archives of General Psychiatry, 42,* 815–820.

Proverbio, A. M., Minniti, A., & Zani, A. (1998). Electrophysiological evidence of a perceptual precedent of global versus local visual information. *Brain Research: Cognitive Brain Research, 6,* 321–334.

Rapoport, J. L. & Ismond, D. R. (1996). *DSM-IV training guide for diagnosis of childhood disorders.* New York: Brunner/Mazel.

Riddle, M. A., Rasmusson, A. M., Woods, S. W., & Hoffer, P. B. (1992). SPECT imaging of cerebral blood flow in Tourette syndrome. *Advances in Neurology, 58,* 207–211.

Robertson, M. M. (2006). Attention deficit hyperactivity disorder, tics and Tourette syndrome: The relationship and treatment implications: A commentary. *European Child and Adolescent Psychiatry, 15,* 1–11.

Rourke, B. P. (1988). The syndrome of nonverbal learning disabilities: Developmental manifestations in neurological disease, disorder, and dysfunction. *The Clinical Neuropsychologist, 2,* 293–330.

Schultz, R. T., Carter, A. S., Scahill, L., & Leckman, J. F. (1999). Neuropsychological findings. In J. F. Leckman & D. J. Cohen (Eds.), *Tourette's syndrome–tics, obsessions, and compulsions: Developmental psychopathology and clinical care* (pp. 80–103). New York: John Wiley and Sons.

Semrud-Clikeman, M., & Teeter-Ellison, P. A. (2009). *Child neurology: Assessment and intervention for neurodevelopmental disorders* (2nd ed.). New York: Springer Publishing.

Serrien, D. J., Orth, M., Evans, A. H., Lees, A. J., & Brown, P. (2005). Motor inhibition in patients with Gilles de la Tourette syndrome: Functional activation patterns as revealed by EEG coherence. *Brain, 128,* 116–125.

Shapiro, A. K., Shapiro, E., Young, J. G., & Feinberg, T. E. (1978). *Gilles de la Tourette's Syndrome* (2nd ed.). New York: Raven Press.

Shucard, D. W., Benedict, R. H. B., TekokKilic, A., & Lichter, D. G. (1997). Slowed reaction time during a continuous performance test in children in Tourette's syndrome. *Neuropsychology, 11,* 147–155.

Spencer, T., Biederman, J., Harding, M., O'Donnel, D., Wilens, T., Faraone, S., et al . (1995). Disentangling the overlap between Tourette's disorder and ADHD. *Journal of Child Psychology and Psychiatry, 39,* 1037–1044.

Staley, D., Wand, R., & Shady, G. (1997). Tourette disorder: A cross-cultural review. *Comprehensive Psychiatry, 38,* 6–16.

Swain, J. E., Scahill, L., Lombroso, P. J., King, R. A., & Leckman, J. F. (2007). Tourette syndrome and tic disorders: A decade of progress. *Journal of the American Academy of Child and Adolescent Psychiatry, 46,* 947–968.

Swedo, S.E., & Grant, P. J. (1998). Annotation: PANDAS: A model for human autoimmune disease. *Journal of Child Psychology and Psychiatry, 46,* 227–234.

Tourette's Syndrome Study Group. (2002). Treatment of ADHD in children with tics: A randomized control trial. *Neurology, 58,* 527–536.

Towbin, K. E. (2010). Tic disorders. In M. K. Duncan (Ed), *Duncan's Textbook of Child and Adolescent Psychiatry* . Washington, DC: American Psychiatric Publishing, Inc.

Utter, A. A. & Basso, M. A. (2008). The basal ganglia: An overview of circuits and function. *Neuroscience and Biobehavioral Reviews, 32,* 333–342.

Walkup, J. T., Ferrao, Y., Leckman, J. F., Stein, D. J., & Singer, H. (2010). Tic disorders: Some key issues for DSM-V. *Depression and Anxiety, 27,* 600–610.

Walkup, J. T., LaBuda, M. C., Singer, H. S., Brown, J., Riddle, A., & Hurko, O. (1996). Family study and segregation analysis of Tourette syndrome: Evidence for a mixed model of inheritance. *American Journal of Human Genetics, 59,* 684–693.

Yeates, K. O., & Bornstein, R. A. (1995). Neuropsychological correlates of learning disability subtypes in children with Tourette's syndrome. *Journal of the International Neuropsychological Society, 2,* 375–382.

Yeates, K. O., & Bornstein, R. A. (1994). Attention-deficit disorder and neuropsychological functioning in children with Tourette's disorder. *Neuropsychology, 8,* 65–74.

Zillmer, E. A., Spiers, M. V., & Culbertson, W. C. (2008). *Principles of neuropsychology* (2nd ed.). Belmont, CA: Wadsworth Publishing.

Zohar, A. H., Pauls, D. L., Ratzoni, G., Apter, A., Dycian, A., Binder, M., et al. (1997). Obsessive-compulsive disorder with and without tics in an epidemiological sample of adolescents. *American Journal of Psychiatry, 154,* 274–276.

CHAPTER 9

Depressive Disorders

John M. Wryobeck, Mary E. Haines, Timothy F. Wynkoop, & Melissa M. Swanson

INTRODUCTION

Depression of various types is encountered frequently in both mental health and medical settings and can occur episodically or chronically. It affects 10%–25% of women and 5%–12% of men at some time in their lives (American Psychiatric Association [APA], 2000). It is often recurrent, with more than 75% of depressed patients experiencing more than one episode (Boland & Keller, 2009), and the lifetime risk of suicide stands at 15% (APA 2000). The prevalence and functional impairments of depression have garnered the attention of clinicians and researchers. Over the past 100 years, the conceptualization of depression as a strictly affective disorder has evolved to recognize its effects on cognition as well. The growing body of knowledge on depression from a variety of scientific domains such as clinical, genetic, biological, neurological, psychological, and cognitive makes a synthesis of this information important, albeit difficult. Although not an exhaustive review, we attempt to synthesize what is known about depression in terms of its clinical, biological, and neurological perspectives, and how these can shape the assessment and treatment of depressive disorders.

Depression is one of two categories of mood disorders listed in the *Diagnostic and Statistical Manual of Mental Disorders, 4th edition, Text Revision* (*DSM-IV-TR*; APA, 2000), the other being bipolar (with mania). Its subtypes include major depressive disorder (MDD; one or more discrete episodes of depression), dysthymia (chronic, non-remitting low-level depression), and depressive disorder not otherwise specified (when symptoms do not meet criteria for another depressive disorder). An important differential diagnosis is mood disorder due to a general medical condition, which is used when mood disturbance is thought to be the result of a specific medical disorder (e.g., hypo-/hyperthyroidism, stroke, Parkinson disease, multiple sclerosis).

Persons with MDD show notable changes in energy, mood, cognitive functioning, and social behavior. The difficulty individuals have in meeting their own and others' expectations contributes to reduced quality of life and even to disability (Papakostas, Peterson, Mahal, Mischoulon, Nierenberg, & Fava 2004). To meet *DSM-IV-TR* criteria for MDD, a person must experience ongoing low mood and/or anhedonia (inability to experience pleasure) for at least 2 weeks, along with four or more additional symptoms such as insomnia or hypersomnia; fatigue; attention and memory difficulties; marked changes in weight; psychomotor agitation; and having feelings of guilt, worthlessness, and/or thoughts of death. The *DSM-IV-TR* diagnostic criteria for depression are relatively straightforward, but often not easily applied in specific cases. For example, diagnosing depression in the medically ill or elderly requires close attention because symptoms related to memory, concentration, fatigue, and sleep disturbances may be related as much to medical condition or age as to depression. In addition, two depressed persons may describe strikingly different symptoms: one may report having no energy to get out of bed, crying easily, and eating sparingly, while the other may report restlessness, anger, and eating throughout the day.

To further complicate the picture, research from multiple disciplines into the mechanisms of depression has yielded information on the predispositional genetic factors, neurochemical mechanisms, and cerebral structural and functional abnormalities associated with MDD. This has resulted in a more comprehensive understanding of depression, but increases the challenge for neuropsychologists to assimilate this vast amount of research information in an effort to link neurocognitive profiles to underlying mood pathology. Given the complexity of depressive disorders, in this chapter we limit our focus to what may be termed clinical depression or those forms of depression that are substantial, often debilitating, or which at least interfere with efforts at neurorehabilitation. Consequently, we use the term depression as a phenomenological description of the experience of depressive symptoms without reference to specific *DSM-IV-TR* diagnoses unless otherwise stated.

GENETICS OF DEPRESSION

This chapter's focus is on the relationship of the clinical and neurobiological facets of depression to neurocognitive deficits and their impact on assessment and treatment, but a brief overview of the genetics of depression is needed because of its relationship to the preceding factors. There is an abundance of evidence suggesting that depression arises from the effects of multiple susceptibility genes, each contributing small effects, and that heritability for depression may be as high as 40% (Levinson, 2006; Sullivan, Neale, & Kendler, 2000). The goal of genetic research in depression is to determine what might make individuals vulnerable to depression in an effort to improve outcome. Two promising lines of genetic research include examining: (1) genes that influence the stress response (serotonin transporter gene, *5-HTTLPR*) and (2) gene variations that seem to influence an individual's response to treatment (the DNA sequence *G1463A* and the *TREK1* gene; Levinson, 2006; Beck, 2008; Zhang et al., 2005; Perlis et al., 2008).

The short variant of the 5-HTTLPR gene, associated with the transportation of serotonin, is found more frequently in individuals with depression (Anguelova, Benkelfat, & Turecki, 2003; Caspi et al., 2003). It is believed that a lack of serotonin may be responsible for depressive symptoms in some individuals. In a review of the genetics of depression, Levinson (2006) suggests that the 5-HTTLPR gene may affect mood negatively through its influence on stress reactivity. Aaron Beck (2008), who theorized that depressed individuals have a cognitive style that focuses on the negative (what is wrong), rather than on the positive (what is right) has synthesized data on the pathophysiology of depression and suggested that the *5-HTTLPR* activates the amygdala, thus increasing an individual's sensitivity to negative stimuli. Beck's model suggests that the 5-HTTLPR gene: (1) is associated with a reactive amygdala, which (2) produces a cognitive bias that exaggerates stressful events, which (3) activates the hypothalamic–pituitary–adrenal (HPA) axis, and (4) creates increased limbic activity over prefrontal function, which (5) causes deficient reappraisal of negative cognitions, resulting in (6) depressive symptoms. This model brings genetic, neurochemical, and neuroanatomical factors together to describe how cognitive vulnerability to depression may occur.

Persons with the *G1463A* nucleotide polymorphism appear to produce low levels of serotonin but are also relatively resistant to SSRI antidepressants (Zhang, et al., 2005). Those with a particular variation of the *TREK1* gene are also more likely to have treatment-resistant depression. Genetic research is likely to result in our better understanding of predisposing factors to depression as well as guiding us in its effective treatment.

PATHOPHYSIOLOGY AND NEUROPATHOLOGY OF DEPRESSIVE DISORDERS

Response to Chronic Stress and the HPA Axis

Risk for depression is associated with genetic and social factors as well as a dysregulated response to chronic stress (Ögren, Kuteeva, Hökfelt, & Keher, 2006). The HPA axis is the neuroendocrine circuit that manages stress in the body (Lee, Jeong, Kwak, & Park, 2010). With acutely stressful events, the HPA axis activates, leading to the release of epinephrine and glucocorticoids (Reagan, Grillo, & Piroli, 2008). These neurochemicals work in conjunction to provide a protective and adaptive response to the stress, including activation of the autonomic nervous system, which increases activation of the cardiac and pulmonary systems and decreases activation of the gastrointestinal and immune systems.

However, when the body is under constant stress because of a chronic situation, the response that is protective in the short-term may lead to long-term and wide-ranging deleterious effects (Reagan et al., 2008). Under chronic stress, the body continually releases glucocorticoids (steroid hormones), leading to hypercortisolemia (Girdler & Klatzkin, 2007), a state that increases excitotoxicity of neurons, particularly in the hippocampus (Lee at al., 2010). Because of the excitotoxic nature of this phenomenon, dendritic atrophy and apoptosis of neurons may occur (McEwen, 2007). Indeed, neuroimaging and postmortem studies indicate that depressed individuals exhibit reduced hippocampal volume (Drevets, 2001), which may lead to long-term potentiation, impairing a person's working memory ability so that anticipating a future reward or envisioning a positive future (correlates of depression) is more difficult or impossible (Savitz, Lucki, & Drevets, 2009).

Another hypothesis for the dysregulation of the HPA axis leading to the pathogenesis of depression comes from animal models of chronic stress in which lower concentrations of glucocorticoids are found. If these glucocorticoids are depleted, the body has no resource to combat stress, thus leading to the development of psychiatric disorders, including depression (Girdler & Klatzkin, 2007). See Tsigos and Chrousos (2002) for a discussion of the particular psychiatric disorders associated with hyper-activation or hypo-activation of the HPA axis.

Evidence has accumulated for the importance of specific neurotransmitter disturbances in the pathogenesis of depression, related to the experience of chronic stress (Nemeroff, 2008). Interest in central nervous system 5-HT and NE circuitry and their roles in depressive disorders has been significant over the past several decades. Current treatment of choice for depressive disorders is based on the ability of SSRI and serotonin-norepinephrine reuptake inhibitors (SNRI) to ameliorate depressive symptoms through enhancing neurotransmission by blocking the reuptake mechanism (Ögren et al., 2006). However, there are many individuals for whom SSRIs and SNRIs have only partial or no effects in ameliorating symptoms and, as mentioned earlier, genetic research may help us to understand why. However, research into the role of central nervous system dopamine (DA) circuitry in depressive disorders is just now burgeoning, and most recently efforts to explore the roles of the amino acid neurotransmitters glutamate and gamma-aminobutyric acid (GABA) and the neuropeptide galanin have begun.

Monoamine Hypothesis of Depression

The observed success of SSRIs and SNRIs in ameliorating depressive symptoms has fueled increased clinical and experimental interest in the monoamines. Monoamines include two classes of transmitters: catecholamines, which include norepinephrine (NE) and its precursor DA, and indolamines, which include serotonin (5-HT). NE is produced predominantly in the locus ceruleus, DA in the substantia nigra and ventral tegmental area, and 5-HT in the dorsal and median raphe nucleus (Joseph, 1996).

Monoamines are associated with the development and maintenance of depressive disorders. Evidence for their role was incidentally derived from in vivo studies of reserpine, an antipsychotic medication that depletes vesicular monoamines and reduces mood; amphetamines, which increase central nervous system monoamines and elevate mood; and monoamine oxidase inhibitor medications, which can be successful in treating depression (Dunlop & Nemeroff, 2007).

Serotonergic Function

Serotonergic (5-hydroxytryptamine or 5-HT) neurons mediate both excitatory and inhibitory neurotransmission. 5-HT receptors modulate the release of many other neurotransmitters and hormones, influencing brain areas responsible for modulating appetite, fear, pain, and mood (Joseph, 1996). 5-HT also acts to suppress attention for stimuli that are irrelevant and not rewarding (Benninger, 1989). It is known to be decreased in depressed patients, but what is not known is whether this is the *genesis* or the *result* of depression.

There are seven families of 5-HT receptors (5-HT 1 through 7) and multiple subtypes within those families (e.g., $5HT_{1A}$ through $5HT_{1F}$), each with various functions (Glennon & Dukat, 1991). The 5-HT receptor subtype $5\text{-}HT_{1A}R$ partially controls a wide range of phenomena and appears to be particularly important in mood regulation. Based on observed human responses to $5\text{-}HT_{1A}R$ agonists and postmortem studies of binding in brain tissue, $5\text{-}HT_{1A}R$ function is decreased in individuals with MDD (Drevets et al., 2007). Researchers have made a case based on a review of pharmacological, postmortem, functional neuroimaging and genetic evidence for $5\text{-}HT_{1A}R$ dysfunction playing a role in the development of MDD (Drevets et al., 2007; Savitz et al., 2009).

Interestingly, upward of 80% of persons with MDD experience pain (Gureje et al., 2008). For individuals with MDD who experience cognitive and somatic symptoms, $5\text{-}HT_{1A}R$ dysfunction likely plays a role, as this receptor is associated with cognitive function and pain perception (Savitz, et al., 2009). Patients with pain and/or cognitive symptoms treated with SSRIs may experience improvement in these symptoms, whereas patients whose depression is characterized by amotivation and anhedonia may experience little relief from SSRI therapy (McCabe, Mishor, Cowen, & Harmer, 2010).

Noradrenergic Function

The receptors for noradrenaline (also known as norepinephrine or NE) are grouped together with epinephrine (adrenaline) and are termed the adrenoreceptors. There are two main groups of adrenergic receptors (alpha and beta) with a variety of subtypes (alpha 1 and 2 and beta 1 through 3). The alpha-1 receptors appear to be critical in depression, based on the efficacy of tricyclic antidepressants (alpha-1 antagonists) in treatment of depression. Also, increased densities of beta-adrenergic receptors are found postmortem in the brains of depressed persons who commit suicide (Nemeroff, 2008).

As noted previously, NE is predominantly produced in the locus ceruleus (LC). Activation of the LC-NE system stimulates arousal and attention, the "fight-or-flight" response, and is responsible in part for subserving a variety of functions, including motivation and response to pleasure (Joseph, 1996). Low levels of NE may be associated with anhedonia, and as a result, patients may have a positive response to SNRI treatment (although there are individuals whose depression appears resistant to SNRIs or SSRIs).

Dopaminergic Function

Dopamine (DA) is involved in learning and reward-seeking behavior (Joseph, 1996). Therefore, as the major neurotransmitter that mediates the ability to experience pleasure, a DA hypothesis of depression (Nemeroff, 2008) was inevitable. DA is a catecholamine neurotransmitter that activates five families of DA receptors (D1 through D5), each with its irregularly named subtypes (e.g., D2Sh or D4.7).

In animal studies, DA transmission from thalamus to prefrontal cortex is necessary for the learning of associations between behaviors or stimuli and reward (Cannon et al., 2009). This has led to the hypothesis that DA dysfunction underlies the amotivation, psychomotor slowing, concentration difficulties, and anhedonia associated with severe forms of depression (e.g., melancholia; APA, 2000).

As with 5-HT and NE, data on the role of DA in depression have come obliquely from studies in which DA antagonists have been shown to increase depressive symptoms and DA agonists have been shown to decrease depressive symptoms. Because there is a dearth of highly selective agonists and antagonists, the specific DA receptor subtypes that mediate reward processing and depression have not been completely identified (Cannon et al., 2009), although animal studies suggest that the D1 receptor may be a good starting point. Anxiolytic effects of an experimental D1-receptor antagonist were found in rat studies in which they received an intra-amygdaloid injection (de la Mora et al., 2005). The D1 receptor has also proved important based on postmortem studies of persons experiencing MDD (Cannon et al., 2009); increased D1-receptor density was found in a study of medicated versus unmedicated persons who had committed suicide (Bowden et al., 1997).

With the advent of sophisticated neuroimaging techniques, a PET-ligand study with an experimental D1 agonist indicated that the mean D1-receptor binding was significantly lower in persons with MDD versus controls (Cannon et al., 2009). In addition, this study found that illness duration and self-ratings of anhedonia were inversely correlated with D1-receptor binding for the depressed individuals. Psychomotor speed was inversely correlated with D1-receptor binding in the controls. The disruption in DA function may be the result of reduced DA release from the presynaptic neuron or faulty transmission across the synapse, either of which could be due to changes in receptor number or function and/or to deficiencies in intracellular transmission (Dunlop & Nemeroff, 2007). Suggestions are that patients for whom depression does not resolve with SSRIs or SNRIs may benefit from interventions that promote efficiency of DA transmission (Dunlop & Nemeroff, 2007), particularly with regard to anhedonia. In addition to 5-HT, NE, and DA, the relation of other neurotransmitters and neuropeptides to depression are being explored.

Emerging Role of Central Amino Acids in Depression

Glutamate is a neurotransmitter that belongs to the class of central nervous system amino acids. Glutamate is the major excitatory neurotransmitter in the brain and has two primary postsynaptic receptors: alpha-amino-3-hydroxyl-5-methyl-4-isoxazole-proprionate (AMPA) and N-methyl-D-aspartate (NMDA), each of which has various subtypes (e.g., GluA2 is one subtype of AMPA receptor; NR1 is one subtype of NMDA receptor). Glutamate's role in depression was originally derived from evidence that NMDA antagonists have demonstrated antidepressant-like properties (Trullas & Skolnick, 1990). In support, Hashimoto (2009) presents evidence of alterations in glutamate levels in the blood, cerebrospinal fluid, and brain of people experiencing depression, including modified glutamate receptors observed postmortem.

Proton magnetic resonance spectroscopy has identified *reduced* glutamate levels in the anterior cingulate cortex (Mirza et al., 2004) and *increased* glutamate levels in the occipital cortex of individuals with depressive disorders (Sanacora et al., 2004). In the latter study, depressed individuals also exhibited decreased GABA (another amino acid neurotransmitter) levels, indicating that depressed individuals may have an imbalance between excitatory and inhibitory neurotransmitters.

Emerging Role of Galanin

Galanin is a neuropeptide that coexists with NE in the locus ceruleus and 5-HT in the dorsal raphe nucleus (Lu, Sharkey, & Barfai, 2007). The indication is that galanin has an inhibitory role as a regulator of central 5-HT as well as transmission to 5-HT_{1A}R (Ögren et al., 2006). Animal model data suggest that signaling in the galanin receptor subtypes 1, 2, and 3 (GalR1, GalR2, and GalR3) leads to antidepressant-like effects (Lu et al., 2007), and antidepressant efficacy may be associated with GalR1 and GalR3 *antagonists* and GalR2 *agonists* (Ögren et al., 2006).

NEUROPATHOLOGY OF DEPRESSION

Neuroanatomy of Depression

Neurochemical systems are clearly implicated in depression. These systems occur in the context of neuroanatomical functions, which when dysfunctional are known to contribute to depression. Three anatomic areas considered critical in the genesis of endogenous depression are the right frontal cerebrum, left frontal cerebrum, and right posterior cerebrum (Shenal, Harrison, & Demaree, 2003).

FRONTAL CEREBRUM

Prefrontal Cortex/Subcortical Connections

The generation of emotion is generally believed to take place in the subcortical regions (e.g., limbic system), precipitated by changes within the autonomic nervous system (Shenal et al., 2003). For example, emotional reactions are linked to increased cerebral blood flow and glucose metabolism in the amygdala (Drevets, 2000). Additionally, elderly depressed persons exhibit lower fractional anisotropy in the white matter of the right superior frontal gyrus than do nondepressed elderly persons, supporting the hypothesis that microstructural changes in white matter may result in disconnection of cortical and subcortical regions (Taylor et al., 2004).

Positron emission tomography (PET) demonstrates hypometabolism in the temporal lobes and at the basal ganglia level of depressed persons (Mayberg, 1994). However, the prefrontal cortex plays a vital role in modulating activity in the limbic regions, including the basal ganglia. Imaging and postmortem studies of depressed individuals have demonstrated reductions not only in the prefrontal cortex blood flow and glucose metabolism but also in the frontal cortex volume as well (Botteron, Raichle, Drevets, Heath, & Todd, 2002; Bremner et al., 2002; Drevets et al., 1997). A review by Ketter and Drevets (2002) on neuroimaging studies of depressive disorders found that decreased dorsomedial/dorsolateral prefrontal cortical activity is a common finding in depression.

The hypometabolism and reduced anatomic volume differences between depressed individuals and normal controls may be likely secondary to differences that are found at the cellular level in the prefrontal cortex. Miguel-Hidalgo and Rajikowska (2003) found reductions in all cortical layers in the prefrontal cortex in individuals with MDD. Further, reduced *glial* density has been demonstrated in this region in individuals with MDD (Knable, Barci, Bartko, Webster, & Torrey, 2002). Additionally, reduced glial density has been demonstrated in the subgenual prefrontal cortex in individuals with a diagnosis of, and family history of, MDD (Ongur, Drevets, & Price, 1998). Also, reduced *neuronal* density has been demonstrated in the dorsolateral prefrontal cortex, rostral orbitofrontal cortex, and in the caudal orbitofrontal cortex in individuals diagnosed with MDD (Rajikowska et al., 1999). There is also evidence for prominent reductions in the number of *oligodendroglial* cells in the prefrontal cortex (Uranova, Vostrikov, Orlovskaya, & Rachmanova, 2004).

However, other studies have not supported reductions in neuronal size in the prefrontal cortex in individuals with MDD. For instance, Van Otterloo and colleagues (2009) found no significant difference in neuronal size or density between older depressed individuals compared with age- and gender-matched non-psychiatric controls. Additionally, Janssem and colleagues (2004) found no significant differences in orbitofrontal cortex volume when comparing depressed individuals with healthy individuals. Problems with sample size, exclusion criteria, and measurement techniques likely contribute to the inconsistent findings.

Research has demonstrated correlations with dysfunction in the prefrontal cortex and severity of depression. Koenigs and colleagues (2008), using individuals with known neurological lesions, found that individuals with bilateral ventromedial prefrontal cortex (PFC) damage reported significantly lower depression severity than did individuals with damage involving other areas of the brain or matched controls. Conversely, individuals with bilateral dorsal PFC damage reported significantly greater depression severity and were more frequently diagnosed with MDD than those individuals with neurological lesions involving other areas of the brain or matched controls.

Right Versus Left Prefrontal Cortex

Evidence from studies of the effects of cerebral lesions on emotions (Heilman, Blonder, Bowers, & Valenstein, 2003) suggests that the right hemisphere processes negative emotions and the left hemisphere processes positive emotions (Shenal et al., 2003). Additional evidence supporting the disruption of cerebral laterality in depression are studies indicating lower activation of EEG-evoked responses in the left versus right frontal lobe (d'Elia & Perris, 1973; Henriques & Davidson, 1991). Such studies support a right hemisphere model of depression (Shenal et al., 2003) where emotionality and arousal are experienced but perhaps unchallenged by the "thinking" left hemisphere.

SUBCORTICAL REGIONS

Cingulate Cortex

Wang and colleagues (2008) posited that the anterior and posterior portions of the posterior cingulate appear to have distinct roles in geriatric depression. Acutely depressed older persons exhibit decreased activation in the right middle frontal gyrus during target detection (depressive state dependent), whereas remitted older persons demonstrate attenuated activation during target detection, suggesting disease-related alterations in these regions. Further, individuals with MDD demonstrated significant differences in glial density, neuronal size, and cortical activity in the cingulate cortex of individuals with depressive disorders compared to controls, including significantly reduced compound value of gray matter glial cells in the anterior cingulate gyrus compared to matched controls (Weis et al., 2007).

Hippocampus and Limbic System

Using MRI, Shah, Ebmeier, Glabus, and Goodwin (1998) found reduced hippocampal volume in persons with chronic depression, but not in those with remitted depression. Such findings are consistent with self-reported memory difficulties of many depressed patients. It appears that within the hippocampus, the intensity of CA2 interneurons and the compound value of gray matter glial cells and axon-dendrites of CA1 stratum radiatum neurons appear to be significantly reduced in persons with MDD versus those without (Weis et al., 2007).

In summary, whether neurochemical or anatomical changes contribute to the onset of depression or are the result of depression is not known. However, there is evidence to suggest that in at least some cases, lesions associated with neurological disorders (e.g., epilepsy, multiple sclerosis, Parkinson's disease, CVA) may produce neuroanatomical or neurochemical changes that are associated with the onset of depression.

NEUROPSYCHOLOGICAL SEQUELAE

Serious deleterious effects of depression on neurocognitive functioning have previously been termed *pseudodementia* (Kiloh, 1961), which has been the subject of many research studies. In fact, a MEDLINE search of the term results in over 2,300 citations. When *pseudodementia* and depression are entered together, nearly 300 citations result. Although the term is still encountered, it is falling out of favor for two reasons. First, the prefix *pseudo* implies that the cognitive dysfunction due to depression is not real. Cognitive dysfunction in depression, when it occurs, may be temporary, but it is very real (i.e., not *pseudo*). Additionally, instances of pseudodementia in late-onset depression are now believed to suggest the possibility of a prodromal dementia state (Ganguli, 2009; Reifler, 2000). Second, many clinicians prefer to reserve the term dementia for progressive, or at least static, substantial neurocognitive loss. This section of the chapter is concerned with any form of neurocognitive dysfunction caused by depression (specifically as measured by standardized observation), regardless of whether formal criteria for dementia are met (such as APA, 2000, which requires dysfunction of memory and at least one other area of neurocognition).

Many medical professionals assume that depression causes neurocognitive deficits. This assumption is not always supported by research findings. Our review of the literature found strikingly conflicting results between individual studies, even when considering potential confounding influences (e.g., sample size and composition, control group composition, medication effects, depression severity, definitional issues). The result is a lack of consistent and unequivocal research findings as to whether depression does and/or should affect neurocognition (Shenal et al., 2003).

Further, many patients who experience depression also experience other conditions that affect neurocognition, particularly patients referred for neuropsychological evaluation (e.g., TBI, CVA, progressive neurological disorders, various encephalopathies). Consequently, although it is necessary to study the effects of pure depression on neurocognitive functioning, what is equally and perhaps more important to study are the effects on neurocognition of the potentially synergistic interaction between depression and the various neurological conditions common to neuropsychological practice.

The relationship between depression and neurocognitive functioning is complex to say the least. Given that functional imaging studies implicate medial and orbital frontal cortices and the anterior cingulate in disorders of mood (Dolan, Bench, Brown, Scott, & Frackowiak, 1994; Elderkin-Thompson, Boone, Hwang, & Kumar, 2004), we should expect to observe disrupted frontal/frontal–subcortical type functions on neuropsychological tests. However, this is not always the case. For example, in a fairly thorough review of the literature exploring the possibility that conflicting research findings may be the result of depression severity, McClintock, Husain, Greer, and Cullum (2010) found conflicting results in the domains of attention, memory, and executive functions among young depressed patients and during periods of depression remission. In each instance, results ranged from nonsignificant to significant effects of depression on neurocognitive functioning. Even the apparent trend in the literature toward the common sense notion that neurocognitive difficulties are related to depression severity did not hold across all studies (Murphy, Michael, Robbins, & Sahakian, 2003).

In his review of the literature, Veiel (1997) noted the lack of consistency in findings across studies, which he attributed to varying study designs. In his estimation, studies generally did not control demographics between patients and control subjects (e.g., age and education, which can affect test scores), and many included patients with known CNS diseases in addition to depression, which could further complicate findings.

Veiel's (1997) solution was to conduct a meta-analysis using stringent inclusion criteria to circumvent these potential confounds, ultimately including 13 studies in his analysis (representing 374 MDD patients and 302 non-depressed controls, all young to middle-aged adults [1.5:1 female to male ratio] spanning the years 1976 through 1990). Primary patient inclusionary criteria included MDD diagnosed using accepted criteria (e.g., *DSM*, research diagnostic criteria [Spitzer, Endicott & Robbins, 1975]), while excluding participants from groups known to suffer organic brain disease or mainly bipolar disorder. In the context of general consistency across studies for most neurocognitive indices, there was a fair degree of variability among depressed patients on neurocognitive tests compared to controls. The results suggested that 50% of depressed patients may exhibit substantial neurocognitive deficit (defined as a score 2 standard deviations below the mean of controls) based on problems in at least one area of the mental flexibility/control domain (e.g., Trails B, Stroop Color-Word). Composite indices (such as the Luria-Nebraska Pathognomonic Scale) also suggested difficulties for depressed patients (38.8% impaired rate for MDD patients). While simple attention (e.g., digits forward) was relatively spared in MDD, being problematic in only 2.8% of patients, other neurocognitive tests/domains with depression-related impairments (i.e., ≤2nd percentile compared to controls) included verbal fluency (i.e., FAS; 11.0%), scanning/visuomotor-motor tracking (e.g., Trails A, WAIS-R Digit Symbol; 18.2%), visuospatial functions (e.g., Rey CFT, WAIS Block Design and Object Assembly; 15.2%), verbal learning: acquisition (immediate recall of paired associates [tests not specified], word lists [e.g., RAVLT, CVLT], short stories [e.g., WMS]; 14.5%), verbal learning: retention/retrieval (delayed recall and/or recognition; 15.5%), nonverbal learning: acquisition (design reproductions [no examples provided]; 15.1%), and nonverbal learning: retention/retrieval (15.7%). Veiel (1997) nicely summarizes these results in tabular form for ease in clinical reference (however, readers should be aware that the last column to the right of Veiel's table is offset in two places by carry-over from previous lines, making interpretation a little tricky).

Potential shortcomings of Veiel's (1997) study include the inclusion of medicated patients (which could have introduced medication effects into the data, particularly for studies antedating the use of SSRIs), limited number of tests per domain (only one in some instances), unknown sensitivity of the neuropsychological tests to depression, and no means of gauging the effects of depression severity on neurocognitive test findings.

Despite Veiel's (1997) attempt to promote coherence in research into the effects of depression on neuropsychological test performance, McClintock and colleagues' (2010) review (and that of several other reviewers) suggests that we have not progressed in an organized fashion. However, there are some studies that should probably be given extra weight. For example, when considering the relative effects of single-episode depression severity versus recurring episodes on adaptive functioning (or disability), a large-scale community study from the Netherlands suggests that episode severity is more influential than repeat depressive episodes (Kruijshaar, Hoeymans, Bijl, Spijker, & Essink-Bot, 2003). If the focus of attention is on comorbidities that often accompany recurrent depression and that also contribute to disability (e.g., substance abuse, maladaptive personality traits), then a study by Katon (2003) concludes that recurrent depression may be more influential. In other words, it falls to the consumer of research to determine which studies are most relevant and accurate for his or her patient population.

Neuropsychology seems to be somewhat unique among the behavioral sciences in its acceptance of studies with nonsignificant findings across groups, and then to interpret these nonsignificant findings as evidence for equivalence. However, before one accepts a particular researcher's null hypothesis that no differences in neurocognitive function truly exist between two groups (e.g., depressed and nondepressed patients), the study should be vetted rigorously by the consumer. For example, such studies should be prospective, not based on retrospective analysis of data. They should also be of sufficient statistical power to reject the null hypothesis if true differences exist (many nonsignificant studies reviewed for this chapter had small samples and cell sizes), and the usual potential confounds should be addressed: sex; race; the nature of participant recruitment (e.g., volunteer, referred by physicians, referred by attorneys or courts); known sensitivity to depression of the neuropsychological tests used in the study; effort (Rohling, Green, Allen, & Iverson, 2002); whether the research is atheoretical or is based on a theory of the neuropsychology of depression (Shenal et al., 2003); nature of statistical analysis (adequate for the question) and reporting of effect sizes; medications and supplements, including those incidental to the study (e.g., narcotic analgesics, antihypertensives, anticholinergics, gingko). In addition, the groups should be free of other conditions that could affect neurocognition (unless the focus is depression in a particular condition, in which case the control group should be matched on the condition), inpatient versus outpatient populations should be specified (i.e., hospitalization in and of itself has accounted for more variance in neuropsychological test performance than depression; Rohling & Scogin, 1993), and depression subtyping (e.g., melancholia, dysthymia, presence of psychotic symptoms) should not be overlooked (e.g., acute bipolar symptoms are known to be more deleterious to neurocognitive functioning than are unipolar depressive symptoms; Quraishi & Frangou, 2002).

Additionally, if follow-up testing is employed to determine the effectiveness of intervention for depression, the consumer should examine whether the interval was sufficient to limit test learning, whether alternate forms were used (although this may limit test learning, it may not eliminate it), the effects of attrition on sample matching (the longer the delay generally the higher the attrition, perhaps by participants who may experience more pathology), and how the results were interpreted (e.g., without a normal control group a legitimate statement cannot be made that the functioning of depressed patients returned to normal during the study).

Lastly, some authors recommend the use of standardized psychometric instruments to measure depression rather than rely on clinician subjective judgment (e.g., BDI, Hamilton, ref. Table 1; Rohling et al., 2002). Although they correctly state that such instruments are useful in measuring severity of the affective state and are helpful in statistical analysis, conceptually such instruments merely correlate with a diagnosis of depression and are inadequate to diagnose depression independently. Consequently, the clinician should be aware of the potential differences in depression between the patient diagnosed based on *DSM* criteria versus individuals in a study cohort deemed depressed based on a screening instrument score.

Based on the foregoing, the following recommendations are made: (1) test authors and publishers should research the effects of depression and anxiety on instruments with the populations for which the instrument is designed (e.g., dementia, TBI); (2) test consumers should research the literature for studies on depression and anxiety specific to the tests that are used and specific to the populations on which they are to be used (e.g., depression, TBI with or without substance abuse, depression, Alzheimer's disease), including medication effects.

ADVANCED DIAGNOSTIC CONSIDERATIONS AND PRACTICES

Although sadness is the most common subjective complaint in patients presenting with depression, some may report dominant feelings of anhedonia, irritability, anger, anxiety, and/or guilt, while others may report somatic symptoms such as pain, gastrointestinal and/or neurological difficulties (e.g., memory, attention, processing speed), as well as symptoms of fatigue or lethargy. Often it is a somatic complaint, not an affective complaint, that brings the patient to the doctor. Without a unifying theory to explain the pathologic process of depression, diagnosis is based on categorizing these symptoms into recognizable patterns within specific contexts (e.g., *DSM-IV-TR* [APA, 2000]). To this end, George Engel (1977) proposed a biopsychosocial model of assessment. This thinking integrates a patient's overall medical, mental, and behavioral functioning, as well as personality and social circumstances. The goal of the biopsychosocial assessment is to understand each patient as an individual and to analyze his or her symptoms within the context of his or her life (McHugh & Slavney, 1998). This approach can be particularly important for the neuropsychologist who frequently sees patients in the context of life-changing events such as injury or illness, and so requires expertise with the clinical interview.

The diagnostic interview is an essential tool in neuropsychological assessment, providing the contextual information for interpretation of standardized test results and generally following a sequence developed by the clinician based on his or her knowledge and skill. However, the unstructured nature of the clinical interview leaves it vulnerable to the pitfalls of clinical judgment (Dawes, Faust, & Meehl, 1989). One way to improve clinical accuracy is to use validated semi-structured interviews (see Table 9.1: SCID and MINI, although it is critical to recall that many neurocognitively compromised patients fail to provide accurate personal/symptom information due to reduced insight inherent in many neurological disorders). Semi-structured diagnostic interviews are known to increase diagnostic accuracy for *DSM* Axis I disorders, including depression, in general clinical settings (Zimmerman, 2003; Zimmerman & Mattia, 1999) and, being broad in scope, allow for clarification of differential diagnostic issues (e.g., mood, stream of thought, psychosis, personality). However, we found no evidence confirming that the addition of structured interviews in neuropsychological evaluation improves accuracy in identification of depression in patients where emotional, cognitive, and physical symptoms may be prevalent but related to the neurological event itself.

Another method for increasing diagnostic accuracy for depression in neurocognitively compromised patients is the use of validated self/other-report measures to screen specifically for the presence of depression. The more commonly used and cited measures are listed in Table 9.1. It is important to note that these instruments are widely used and validated in a number of settings, but that the HADS and the GDS emphasize psychological over somatic symptoms of depression to avoid false-positive indicators in environments where somatic symptoms abound (e.g., hospitals, nursing homes) for reasons other than depression (e.g., medical condition). Being narrowly focused, these instruments may miss other noncognitive disorders. Again, it is important to consider the patient's capacity to provide accurate symptom endorsement when deciding which instrument(s) to employ (self- versus informant re-

TABLE 9.1 Common Screening and Diagnostic Scales for Depression

Scale	Recall Period	Patient/Informant/ Clinician Rated	Time to Complete (min)	Screening/Structured
BDI-II[1]	2 weeks	Patient	5	Screening
CSDD[2]	1 week	Patient/Informant	10–15	Screening
CES-D[3]	1 week	Patient	5	Screening
HADS[4]	1 week	Patient	2–5	Screening
PHQ-9[5]	2 weeks	Patient	1–2	Screening
Zung[6]	Past several days	Patient	5–10	Screening
GDS[7]	1 week	Patient	2–3	Screening
SCID-CV[8]	2 weeks	Clinician	60–180	Structured
MINI[9]	2 weeks	Clinician	15	Structured

Abbreviations/References: (1) BDI-II = Beck Depression Inventory-II (Beck, Steer, & Brown, 1996); (2) CSDD = Cornel Scale for Depression in Dementia (Alexopoulos, et al., 1988); (3) CES-D = Center for Epidemiological Studies-Depression Scale (Radloff, 1977); (4) HADS = Hospital Anxiety and Depression Scale (Zigmond & Snaith, 1983); (5) PHQ-9 = Patient Health Questionaire-9 (Kroenke, Spitzer, & Williams, 2001); (6) Zung = Zung Self-Rating Depression Scale (Zung, 1965); (7) GDS = Geriatric Depression Scale (Yesavage et al., 1982); (8) SCID-CV = Structured Clinical Interview for *DSM-IV* Axis I Disorders, Clinician Version (First, Spitzer, Gibbon, & Williams, 1996); (9) MINI = Mini International Neuropsychiatric Interview (Sheehan et al., 1998).

port). Clinical experience has taught us that, for example, GDS scores may be attenuated in many individuals with Alzheimer disease (as a function of its self-report format), suggesting that the CSDD may be a better choice when lack of insight/recollection is suspected, as the CSDD can be completed using information from the individual, an observer, or both.

In addition, there are more involved personality/psychopathology inventories that can be used to help characterize mood in neuropsychological assessment. With perhaps the most research in neurological disorders among the personality inventories, the Minnesota Multiphasic Personality Inventory-2 (MMPI-2) is used widely among neuropsychologists (Lees-Haley, Smith, Williams, & Dunn, 1996; McCaffrey & Lynch 1996). The MMPI-2 Depression Scale (Scale 2) contains 57 items assessing common symptoms of depression including dysphoria, sadness, psychomotor retardation, hopelessness, change in appetite, fatigue, and insomnia, clustered into five descriptive subscales: (1) subjective depression, (2) psychomotor retardation, (3) physical malfunctioning, (4) mental dullness, and (5) brooding (Harris & Lingoes, 1968). The literature suggests that the MMPI-2 depression scale is often elevated in patients with mild head trauma, dementia, or stroke (Foley, Garcia, Harris, & Golden, 2006; Golden & Golden, 2003), and by itself Scale 2 does not provide enough information to rule depression out in a population with neuropsychological impairments. Consequently, the majority of neuropsychologists use clinical judgment to interpret MMPI-2 results in light of their specific patient's ailment(s) or other medical symptoms (e.g., physical injury or decline, pain, neurocognitive deficits; Cripe, Gass, Greene, Perry, & Zillmer, 1997). However, there are correction factors available to score and interpret the MMPI-2 for individuals with TBI, multiple sclerosis, and cerebrovascular accident (Nelson & Do, 1998; Alfano, Finlayson, Stearns, & Neilson, 1990; Gass, 1992), and Pearson offers a Personal Injury (Neurological) Interpretive Report to assist clinicians in interpretation with neurologically injured persons involved in litigation (Butcher, 2003). It is yet to be determined how the MMPI-2-Restructured Form will assist neuropsychologists. The Personality Assessment Inventory (PAI, a self-report inventory) and Revised NEO Personality Inventory (and the new NEO-PI-3, both with observer rating capacity) are other instruments worthy of consideration, but require significant clinician knowledge of the instrument for interpretation in neurological patient populations. Common shortcomings to the lengthy self-report personality assessments are the patient's stamina, ability to maintain a consistent mindset while responding to the instrument, willingness to provide accurate information, and a significant time investment.

Self/other-report scales, whether brief or comprehensive, should be used with thoughtful consideration of the possibility of underlying depression based on clinical suspicion, and the patient's capacity to accurately complete them, which should be based on the patient's history and presenting symptoms. A diagnosis of depression should not be based on the use of screening instruments alone. Although their scores may correlate with the presence of depression in clinical samples, they do not always provide the extent of symptomatic information required to render a *DSM* diagnostic impression. The semi-structured interview, conversely, explores and categorizes symptoms more broadly using a decision-tree approach and requires more detailed information about individual symptoms (duration, frequency, intensity) and symptom clusters, and so may be better suited to diagnostic impression. However, structured interviews require ample additional time, and so the neuropsychologist may base the decision of whether to use a structured interview on the referral source. For example, if the patient was referred by a psychologist or psychiatrist in whom the neuropsychologist has faith, there may be less need to invest time in the structured interview.

A common referral question for neuropsychologists is depression versus dementia. The outcome of such a referral is often depression overlaying dementia/mild cognitive impairment. There are several medical conditions that can mimic (e.g., apathy/avolition resulting from subcortical white/gray matter dysfunction or frontal TBI changes) or cause (e.g., hypothyroidism) depression and neurocognitive dysfunction. Other neurological conditions that are often accompanied by comorbid depression include Parkinson's and Huntington's disease and epilepsy (Starkstein, Mayberg, Leiguarda, Preziosi, & Robinson, 1992; Pirozzolo, Swihart, Rey, Mahurin, & Jankovic, 1993; Kanner, 2003). This is by no means a comprehensive list of depression in neuropsychology, but it demonstrates the importance of knowledge of these syndromes in determining the presence of depression and how it may interact with the neurological disease process.

Accurately diagnosing depression in the elderly can be particularly problematic. Three elements of aging often interfere with symptom recognition: comorbid medical conditions, cognitive impairment, and recent life events (Bellino, Bogetto, Vaschetto, Ziero, & Ravizza, 2000), to which we add the lack of trust that the elderly often exhibit toward mental health professionals. When neurocognitive complaints accompany depression, the history of symptom onset can be helpful in distinguishing the presence of progressive dementia along with depression. For example, an abrupt onset and/or an onset in the context of stress of neurocognitive deficits may suggest emotional causes. Late life onset depression, however, can be a harbinger of dementia to come, even if the depression and cognitive dysfunction remit with medical management (Jorm, 2001; Ganguli, 2009; Reifler, 2000).

CONTEMPORARY MODES OF TREATMENT

It seems clear that depression is a multi-factored illness with genetic, phenotypic, internal, and environmental influences, lacking a single satisfactory unifying theory to understand its origins and, hence, its treatment. For example, if one subscribes to a neurotransmitter hypothesis of depression, then treatment should focus on finding the right agonist/antagonist medication to alleviate symptoms. If one subscribes to the hypothesis that changes in neurochemistry and neuroanatomical functioning are the source of the problem, then electroconvulsive therapy, transcranial magnetic stimulation, and vagus nerve stimulation should play a role in treatment. If one subscribes to cognitive schemata and/or psychosocial influences as being paramount, then psychotherapy will be prescribed. Outcome studies clearly suggest that treatment decisions are not so simple, and, in reality, optimal treatments are often combinations of the foregoing.

The pharmacotherapy literature on depression is vast, and its discussion here will be limited. Pharmacotherapy is meant to affect the neurotransmitters believed to play a role in depression, and so antidepressants may affect 5HT, NE, DA, and glutamate.

Psychopharmacologically, first-line treatment is typically the use of an SSRI due to superior tolerability. Since their introduction in the 1980s, there has been no shortage of studies indicating the effectiveness of SSRIs. The other classes of antidepressants, tricyclics

(TCA) and monoamine oxidase inhibitors (MAOI), have significant problems associated with their use: TCAs with anticholinergic and antihistaminergic effects (Roose, 2003) and MAOIs with hypertensive crises brought about by not following dietary restrictions (Lecrubier, 1994). However, TCAs and MAOIs continue to be a treatment choice for severe or refractory depression (Krishnan, 2001; Quitkin, 2002). Other antidepressant medications do not fit neatly into these categories (e.g., tetracyclics such as mirtazapine, augmenters such as buspirone). We do not yet have widely accepted and available biological markers to assist in choosing the right medication for an individual, and the choice is based on clinical judgment of symptoms, history of depression (in the patient and family), response to previously prescribed antidepressant medications, age, medical condition, other medications taken (present and past), and the use of alcohol or drugs. For current treatment guidelines, see Davidson (2010).

The effectiveness of antidepressant medication has been questioned, particularly for mild to moderate depression. Turner, Matthews, Lindardatos, Tell, and Rosenthal (2008) conducted a meta-analysis examining both the proportion of positive outcome studies and the effect sizes of antidepressants from both published and unpublished FDA data, and found that when unpublished FDA data were used, only half of the studies showed positive results (versus about 92% in published studies) and the mean average effect size dropped by nearly one-third. As can be seen in Table 9.2, the effect sizes for antidepressant medications are small, with none reaching moderate to large effect sizes (Turner et al., 2008).

The STAR*D study (Sinyor, Schaffer, & Levitt, 2010), however, demonstrated the effectiveness of switching or augmenting antidepressant medications when ineffective. Roughly 70% of individuals who remained in the study experienced relief from their symptoms of depression in one of the four levels of treatment (initial medication; if no response, then switch to another medication; if no response, then add one or more medications). Up to 45% of participants had a response to an SSRI (citalopram), and of those who did not respond, by switching to another SSRI (sertraline, bupropion-SR, or venlafaxine-XR) or adding a second SSRI to the citalopram (bupropion-SR or buspirone), up to one-third of these participants became symptomfree.

As described earlier, genetic variations may be associated with depression through its role in synthesizing serotonin. Depression in patients with the nucleotide polymorphism G1463A is resistant to SSRIs, and preliminary studies suggest that the presence of enzyme TPH2 may account for why some depression shows resistance to SSRIs (Zhang et al., 2005). Another study has found an association between certain variations in the *TREK1* gene and

TABLE 9.2 Adjusted* Effect Sizes of Antidepressant Treatments

Antidepressant Medication	Effect Size
<u>SSRI</u>	
Citalopram	0.24
Sertraline	0.24
Fluoxetine	0.26
Paroxetine	0.42
<u>SNRI</u>	
Duloxetine	0.30
Mirtazapine	0.35
Venlafaxine	0.40
<u>DRI</u>	
Bupropion	0.17
Psychotherapy	**Effect Size**
All Therapies	0.42
Cognitive–Behavior	0.49

* = effect sizes adjusted due to non-published/publication bias; small effect size = 0.20–0.49; moderate = 0.50–0.79; large = 0.80 or greater (Cohen, 1988).

SSRI = selective serotonin reuptake inhibitor; SNRI = serotonin-norepinephrine reuptake inhibitor; DRI = dopaminergic reuptake inhibitor resistance to multiple classes of antidepressant medication (Perlis et al., 2008). A better understanding of why patients respond differently to antidepressant medications allows for the possibility of developing tests that can guide the clinician in choosing the right medication. This area of research is in its infancy but offers potential promise in making antidepressant medication use more effective for depressed patients.

Psychotherapy takes various forms (e.g., cognitive, interpersonal, psychodynamic), and meta-analyses support the efficacy of psychotherapy in depression (Gloaguen, Cottraux, Cucherat, & Blackburn, 1998; Dobson, 1989; Butler, Chapman, Forman, & Beck, 2006; Driessen & Hollon, 2010). However, just as with pharmacotherapy, when one takes into account publication bias in psychotherapy studies, effect sizes also drop. A meta-analytic study of publication bias in psychological treatments found the mean effect sizes for all interventions dropping from 0.67 to 0.42 and for cognitive behavioral therapy dropping from 0.69 to 0.49 (Cuijpers, Smit, Bohlmeijer, Hollon & Andersson, 2010). As seen in Table 9.2, psychotherapy may offer a slight advantage over some medications in the treatment of depression. Cognitive-behavioral therapy (CBT) and interpersonal therapy (IPT) for depression enjoy widespread use and are predicated on the fundamental assumption that thought and experience is mediated by changes in the brain and, conversely, brain changes affect thought and experience. They are uniquely suited to neuropsychological disorders that often disrupt both the patient's personal and interpersonal life.

CBT stems from Beck, Rush, Shaw, and Emery's cognitive theory of depression, which states that we all have core beliefs or schemas that allow us to process information and interpret the world around us (Beck et al., 1979). Depression can result when pathological beliefs or schemas are activated by stressful life events. Hence, as the pathological schemas are activated, a person's interpretation of current events become increasingly distorted and negative, which results in increasing levels of depression (Scher, Ingram, & Segal, 2005). It is thought that these cognitions play a mediator role in depression but do not of themselves cause depression. The purpose of psychotherapy, consequently, is for the therapist and patient to identify pathological or distorted core beliefs/schemas and to work to replace them with more realistic thoughts and beliefs. In IPT, the therapist helps the patient identify interpersonal needs, assesses if and how those needs are being met, and then helps guide the patient to devise healthy strategies to have his or her interpersonal needs met (Weissman, Markowitz, & Klerman, 2003).

PET scan studies examining changing brain function after various depression treatments (e.g., medication, psychotherapy) have found changes in cortical (i.e., prefrontal, parietal), limbic (i.e., cingulate cortex, amygdala), and subcortical (i.e., caudate, thalamus) regions. Neuroimaging studies demonstrate that antidepressant medications result in a bottom-up subcortical to cortical effect (Goldapple et al., 2004; Kennedy et al., 2001; Martin, Martin, Rai, Richardson, & Royal, 2001; Mayberg et al., 2000; Seminowicz et al., 2004), whereas psychotherapy results in a top-down cortical to subcortical effect (Brody et al., 2001; Goldapple et al., 2004; Martin et al., 2001). Imaging studies find IPT to be associated with increased blood flow in the basal ganglia and limbic systems (Martin et al., 2001), and metabolic changes in the prefrontal cortex, anterior cingulate gyrus, and temporal lobe (Brody et al., 2001). CBT interventions lead to reduced prefrontal and increased hippocampal activity (Goldapple et al., 2004). Researchers hypothesize that the cerebral changes consequent to psychotherapy observed on functional neuroimaging are likely the result of cognitive processing associated with problem identification and solving, Socratic questioning, active reframing, challenging self-perceptions, and consequent emotional activation (Frewen, Dozois, & Lanius, 2008).

When pharmacotherapy and psychotherapy fail, other approaches to treatment are available. Electroconvulsive therapy (ECT) has many negative connotations associated with it, but remains one of the most effective treatments for severe and/or treatment-resistant depression (McDonald, Thompson, McCall, Zorumxki, 2004; Sonawalla & Fava, 2001). The purpose of ECT is to induce a seizure as the therapeutic agent. Our understanding of the mechanisms by which the seizure works is limited and based on animal studies. It is thought that ECT may: (1) increase neurogenesis, reversing the degeneration and decreased proliferation of nerve cells on diencephalic limbic structures; (2) serve to regulate neurotransmitters such as 5HT, NE, DA, and GABA; and (3) correct dysregulation of neuropeptides (Grover, Mattoo, & Gupta, 2005).

Newer biological approaches without long track records of results are vagus nerve stimulation (VNS) and repetitive transcranial magnetic stimulation (rTMS). The vagus nerve extends from the brain (linked to amygdala and hypothalamus) to the abdomen and regulates the larynx, esophagus, heart, and most gastrointestinal organs. A vagus nerve stimulator is implanted in the chest with electrodes wrapped around the nerve where it passes through the neck. The mechanisms by which VNS manages depression are unclear but may work by alteration of norepinephrine release and elevating levels of inhibitory GABA (Groves, Duncan, Brown, & Verity, 2005; Nemeroff et al., 2006). rTMS generates and concentrates magnetic energy over areas of the brain modifying cerebral brain flow, and cortical excitability is either increased or decreased depending on stimulation frequency (Nemeroff et al., 2006). Stimulation of the right frontal lobe is known to reduce depressive symptoms (Ehud Klein, et al., 1999). Preliminary research findings suggest that stimulation of the inferior thalamic peduncle (Jimenez et al., 2005; Jimenez et al., 2007), cingulate gyrus (Mayberg et al., 2005; Lozano et al., 2008), and the ventral capsule/ventral striatum areas (Malone et al., 2009) may result in some relief of treatment-resistant depression (Lakhan & Callaway, 2010; Andrade et al., 2010).

SUMMARY

We conclude that depression has a multisystem etiology. Both genetic and environmental stressors are associated with depression vulnerability, with one or both predisposing an individual to heightened reactivity to later or ongoing stressors through several hypothesized mechanisms (HPA axis, monoamine, neuropeptide, and amino acid abnormalities), which might be the cause and/or the effect of structural brain changes, further affecting cognitive and behavioral functioning. Studies suggest that depression is associated with brain abnormalities and sometimes with neurocognitive changes, but the information available is insufficient to provide new biological/neurological diagnostic and/or treatment methods. In conclusion, this chapter highlights the complexity of depression and the need for ongoing prospective research to examine the many components involved in depression in the diverse but distinct populations that experience this disorder.

REFERENCES

Alexopoulos, G. S., Abrams, R. C., Young, R. C., & Shamoian, C. A. (1988). Cornell scale for depression in dementia. *Biological Psychiatry, 23*, 271–284.

Alfano, D. P., Finlayson, M. A., Stearns, G. M., & Neilson, P. M. (1990). The MMPI and neurological dysfunction: Profile configuration and analysis. *The Clinical Neuropsychologist, 4*, 69–79.

American Psychiatric Association (2000). Diagnostic and statistical manual of mental disorders (4th ed., Text Revision). Washington, DC: American Psychiatric Association.

Andrade, P., Lieke, H. M., Noblesse, H. M., Temel, Y. Ackermans, L., Lim, L.W., et al. (2010). Neurostimulatory and ablative treatment options in major depressive disorder: A systematic review. *Acta Neurochirurgica, 152*, 546–577.

Anguelova, M., Benkelfat, C., Turecki, G. (2003). A systematic review of association studies investigating genes coding for serotonin receptors and the serotonin transporter: I. Affective disorders. *Molecular Psychiatry, 8*, 574–591.

Beck, A. T. (2008). The evolution of the cognitive model of depression and its neurobiological correlates. *American Journal of Psychiatry, 165*, 969–977.

Beck, A. T., Rush, J. A., Shaw, B. F., & Emery, G. (1979). *Cognitive therapy for depression*. New York: Guilford Press.

Beck, A. T., Steer, R. A., & Brown, G. K. (1996). *Beck depression inventory manual* (2nd ed.). San Antonio, Texas: Psychological Corporation.

Bellino, S., Bogetto, F., Vaschetto, P., Ziero, S., & Ravizza, L. (2000). Recognition and treatment of dysthymia in elderly patients. *Drugs & Aging, 16*(2), 107–121.

Benninger, R. J. (1989). The role of serotonin and dopamine in learning to avoid aversive stimuli. In T. Archer, L-G. Nilsson (Eds.), *Aversion, avoidance and anxiety* (pp. 264–284). New Jersey: Erlbaum.

Boland, R. J. & Keller, M. B. (2009). Course and outcome of depression. In I. H. Gotlib C. L. Hammen (Eds.), *Handbook of depression* (2nd ed., pp. 23–43). New York: Guilford.

Botteron, K. N., Raichle, M. E., Drevets, W. C., Heath, A. C., & Todd, R. D. (2002). Volumetric reduction in left subgenual prefrontal cortex in early onset depression. *Biological Psychiatry, 51*, 342–344.

Bowden, C., Theodorou, A., Cheetham, S. C., Lowther, S., Katona, C. L., Crompton, M. R., et al. (1997). Dopamine D1 and D2 receptor binding sites in brain samples from depressed suicides and controls. *Brain Research, 752*, 227–233.

Bremner, J. D., Vythilingam, M., Vermetten, E., Nazeer, A., Adil, J., Khan, S., et al. (2002). Reduced volume of orbitofrontal cortex in major depression. *Biological Psychiatry, 51*, 273–279.

Brody, A. L., Saxena, S., Stoessel, P Gillies, L. A., Fairbanks, L. A., Alborzian, S., et al. (2001). Regional brain metabolic changes in patients with major depression treated with either paroxetine or interpersonal therapy: Preliminary findings. *Archives General Psychiatry, 58*, 631–640.

Butcher, J. N. (2003). *MMPI-2 personal injury (neurological) interpretive report: The Minnesota report: Reports for forensic settings*. Shokopee, MN: Pearson Assessments.

Butler, A. C., Chapman, J. E., Forman, E. M., &Beck, A. T. (2006). The empirical status of cognitive behavioral therapy: A review of meta-analyses. *Clinical Psychology Review, 26*, 17–31.

Caspi, A., Sugden, K., Moffitt, T. E., Taylor, A., Craig, I. W., Harrington, H., et al. (2003). Influence of life stress on depression moderation by a polymorphism in the 5-HTT gene. *Science, 301*, 386–389.

Cannon, D., Klaver, J., Peck, S., Rallis-Voak, D., Erickson, K., & Drevets, W. (2009). Dopamine type-1 receptor binding in major depressive disorder assessed using positron emission tomography and [11C]NNC-112. *Neuropsychopharmacology: Official Publication of the American College of Neuropsychopharmacology, 34*, 1277–1287.

Cripe, L. I., Gass, C. S., Greene, R., Perry, W., & Zillmer, E. (1997). Using the MMPI-2 in Neuropsychology. *Symposium conducted at the 17th annual National Academy of Neuropsychology Conference*, Las Vegas, NV.

Cohen, J. (1988). *Statistical power analysis for the behavioral sciences* (2nd ed.). New York: Lawrence Erlbaum Associates.

Cuijpers, P., Smit, F., Bohlmeijer, E., Hollon, S. D., Andersson, G. (2010). Efficacy of cognitive-behavioral therapy and other psychological treatments for adult depression: A meta-analytic study of publication bias. *The British Journal of Psychiatry, 196*, 173–178.

Davidson, J. (2010). Major depressive disorder treatment guidelines in America and Europe. *Journal of Clinical Psychiatry, 71* Suppl E1, e04.

D'Elia, G., & Perris, C. (1973). Cerebral functional dominance and depression, an analysis of EEG amplitude in depressed patients. *Acta Psychiatrica Scandinavia, 49*, 191–197.

Dawes, R. M., Faust, D., & Meehl, P. E. (1989). Clinical versus actuarial judgment. *Science, 243*, 1668–1674.

de la Mora, M. P., Cardenas-Cachon, L., Vasquez-Garcia, M., Crespo-Ramirez, M., Jacobsen, K., Hoistad, M., et al. (2005). Anxiolytic effects of intra-amygdaloid injection of the D1 antagonist SCH233390 in the rat. *Neuroscience Letters, 377*, 101–105.

Dobson, K. S. (1989). A meta-analysis of the efficacy of cognitive therapy for depression. *Journal of Consulting and Clinical Psychology, 57*, 414–419.

Dolan, R. J., Bench, C. J., Brown, R. G., Scott, L. C., & Frackowiak, R. S. J. (1994). Neuropsychological dysfunction in depression: The relationship to regional cerebral blood flow. *Psychological Medicine, 24*, 849–857.

Drevets, W. C. (2000). Neuroimaging studies of mood disorder. *Biological Psychiatry, 48*, 813–829.

Drevets, W. C. (2001). Neuroimaging and neuropathological studies of depression: Implication of the cognitive-emotional features of mood disorders. *Current Opinions in Neurobiology, 11*, 240–249.

Drevets, W. C., Price, J. L., Simpson, J. R Todd, R. D., Reich, T., Vannier, M., et al. (1997). Subgenual prefrontal cortex abnormalities in mood disorders. *Nature, 386*, 824–827.

Drevets, W., Thase, M., Moses-Kolko, E., Price, J., Frank, E., Kupfer, D., et al. (2007). Serotonin-1A receptor imaging in recurrent depression: Replication and literature review. *Nuclear Medicine and Biology, 34*, 865–877.

Driessen, E., & Hollon, S. D. (2010). Cognitive behavioral therapy for mood disorders: Efficacy, moderator and mediators. *Psychiatric Clinics of North America, 33*, 537–555.

Dunlop, B. D., & Nemeroff, C. B. (2007). The role of dopamine in the pathophysiology of depression. *Archives of General Psychiatry, 64*, 327–337.

Ehud Klein, M., Kreinin, I., Chistyakov, A., Koren, D., Mecz, L., Marmur, S., et al. (1999). Therapeutic efficacy of right prefrontal slow repetitive transcranial magnetic stimulation in major depression: A double-blind controlled study. *Archives of General Psychiatry, 56*, 315–320.

Elderkin-Thompson, V., Boone, K. B., Hwang, S., & Kumar, A. (2004). Neurocognitive profiles in elderly patients with frontotemporal degeneration or major depressive disorder. *Journal of the International Neuropsychological Society, 10*, 753–771.

Engel, G. (1977). The need for a new medical model: A challenge for biomedicine. *Science, 197*, 129–136.
First, M. B., Spitzer, R. L., Gibbon, M., & Williams, J. B. 1996). *Structured clinical interview for DSM-IV Axis I disorders, clinician version (SCID-CV)*. Washington, DC: American Psychiatric Press.
Foley, J., Garcia, J., Harris, K., & Golden, C. (2006). Can the MMPI-2 discriminate between mild-moderate TBI and other neurological conditions? *International Journal of Neuroscience, 116*, 1377–1389.
Frewen, P. A., Dozois, D. J., & Lanius, R. A. (2008). Neuroimaging studies of psychological interventions for mood and anxiety disorders: Empirical and methodological review. *Clinical Psychology Review, 28*, 228–246.
Ganguli, M. (2009). Depression, cognitive impairment and dementia: Why should clinicians care about the web of causation? *Indian Journal of Psychiatry, 51*, 29–34.
Gass, C. S. (1992). MMPI-2 interpretation of patients with cerebrovascular disease: A correction factor. *Archives of Clinical Neuropsychology, 7*, 17–27.
Girdler, S., & Klatzkin, R. (2007). Neurosteroids in the context of stress: Implications for depressive disorders. *Pharmacology & Therapeutics, 116*, 125–139.
Glennon, R., & Dukat, M. (1991). Serotonin receptors and their ligands: A lack of selective agents. *Pharmacology, Biochemistry & Behavior, 40*(4), 1009–1017.
Gloaguen, V., Cottraux, J., Cucherat, M., & Blackburn, I. M. (1998). A meta-analysis of the effects of cognitive therapy in depressed patients. *Journal of Affective Disorders, 49*, 59–72.
Goldapple, K., Segal, Z., Garson, C., Lau, M., Bieling, P., Kennedy, S., et al. (2004). Modulation of cortical limbic pathways in major depression: Treatment specific effects of cognitive behavior therapy. *Archives of General Psychiatry, 61*, 34–41.
Golden, Z., & Golden, C.J. (2003). The differential impacts of Alzheimer's dementia, head injury, and stroke on personality dysfunction. *International Journal of Neuroscience, 113*, 869–878.
Grover, S., Mattoo, S. K., & Gupta, N. (2005). Theories on mechanism of action of electroconvulsive therapy. *German Journal of Psychiatry, 8*, 70–84.
Groves, D. A., Brown , V. J. (2005). Vagus nerve stimulation: A review of its applications and potential mechanisms that mediate its clinical effects. *Neuroscience and Biobehavioral Reviews, 29*, 493–500.
Gureje, O., Von Korff, M., Kola, L., Demyttenaere, K., He, Y Posada-Villa, J., et al. (2008). The relation between multiple pains and mental disorders: Results from the World Mental Health Surveys. *Pain, 135*, 82–91.
Hashimoto, K. (2009). Emerging role of glutamate in the pathophysiology of major depressive disorder. *Brain Research Reviews, 61*, 105–122.
Harris, R., & Lingoes, J. (1968). *Subscales for the Minnesota Multiphasic Personality Inventory. Mimeographed materials*. Los Angeles, CA: The Langley Porter Clinic.
Heilman, K. M Blonder, L. X., Bowers, D., & Valenstein, E. (2003). Emotional disorders associated with neurological diseases. In K. M. Heilman & E. Valenstein (Eds.), *Clinical Neuropsychology* (4th ed.) (pp. 447–478). Oxford University Press: New York.
Henriques, J. B., & Davidson, R. J. (1991). Left frontal hypoactivation in depression. *Journal of Abnormal Psychology, 100*, 535–545.
Janssem, J., Pol, H. E. H., Lampe, I. K., Schnak, H.G ., de Leeuw, F., Kahn, R. S., et al. (2004). Hippocampal changes and white matter lesions in early-onset depression. *Biological Psychiatry, 56*, 825–831.
Jimenez, F., Velasco, F., Salin-Pascual, R., Hernandez, J. A., Velasco, M., Criales, J. L., et al. (2005). A patient with a resistant major depression disorder treated with deep brain stimulation in the inferior thalamic peduncle. *Neurosurgery, 57*, 585–593.
Jimenez, F., Velasco, F., Salin-Pascual, R., Velasco, M., Nicolini, H., Velasco, A. L., et al. (2007). Neuromodulation of the inferior thalamic peduncle for major depression and obsessive compulsive disorder. *Acta Neurochirurgica Supplement, 97*, 393–398.
Jorm, A. F. (2001). History of depression as a risk factor for dementia: An updated review. *The Australian and New Zealand Journal of Psychiatry, 35*, 776–781.
Joseph, R. (1996). *Neuropsychiatry, neuropsychology, and clinical neuroscience*. (2nd ed.). Media, PA: Lippincott Williams & Wilkins.
Kanner, A. M. (2003). Depression in epilepsy: Prevalence, clinical semiology, pathogenic mechanisms, and treatment. *Biological Psychiatry, 54*, 388–398.
Katon, W. J. (2003). Clinical and health services relationships between major depression, depressive symptoms, and general medical illness. *Biological Psychiatry, 54*, 216–226.
Kennedy, S., Evans, K., Krüger, S., Mayberg, H., Meyer, J., McCann, S., et al. (2001). Changes in regional brain glucose metabolism measured with positron emission tomography after paroxetine treatment of major depression. *American Journal of Psychiatry, 158*(6), 899–905.
Ketter, T. A. & Drevets, W. C. (2002). Neuroimaging studies of bipolar depression: Functional neuropathology, treatment effects, and predictors of clinical response. *Clinical Neuroscience Research, 2*, 182–192.

Kiloh, L. G. (1961). Pseudo-dementia. *Acta Psychiatrica Scandinavia, 37,* 336–351.

Knable, M. B., Barci, B. M., Bartko, J. J., Webster, M. J., & Torrey, E. F. (2002). Abnormalities of the cingulate gyrus in bipolar disorder and other severe psychiatric illness: Postmortem findings from the Stanley Foundation Neuropathology Consortium and literature review. *Clinical Neuroscience Research, 2,* 171–181.

Koenigs, M., Huey, E. D., Calamia, M., Raymont, V., Tranel, D., & Grafman, J. (2008). Distinct regions of prefrontal cortex mediate resistance and vulnerability to depression. *The Journal of Neuroscience, 28,* 12341–12348.

Krishnan, K. R. R. (2001). Monoamine oxidase inhibitors. In A. F. Schatzberg & C. B. Emeroff (Eds.), *Essentials of clinical psychopharmacology* (3rd ed., pp. 43–53). Washington DC: American Psychiatric Press.

Kroenke, K., Spitzer, R. L., & Williams, J. W. (2001). The PHQ-9. *Journal of General Internal Medicine, 16,* 606–613.

Kruijshaar, M. E., Hoeymans, N., Bijl, R. V., Spijker, J., & Essink-Bot, M. L. (2003). Levels of disability in major depression: Findings from the Netherlands Mental Health Survey and Incidence Study (NEMESIS). *Journal of Affective Disorders, 77,* 53–64.

Lakhan, S. E., & Callaway, E. (2010). Deep brain stimulation for obsessive-compulsive disorder and treatment-resistant depression: Systematic review. *BioMedCentral Research Notes, 3,* 60.

Lecrubier, Y. (1994). Risk benefit assessment of newer versus older monoamine oxidase (MAO) inhibitors. *Drugs and Safety, 10,* 292–300.

Lee, S., Jeong, J., Kwak, Y., & Park, S. (2010). Depression research: Where are we now? *Molecular Brain, 3,* 1–10.

Lees-Haley, P. R., Smith, H. H., Williams, C. W., & Dunn, J. T. (1996). Forensic neuropsychology test usage: An empirical survey. *Archives of Clinical Neuropsychology, 11,* 45–52.

Levinson, D. F. (2006). The genetics of depression: A review. *Biological Psychiatry, 60,* 84–92.

Lozano, A. M., Mayberg, H. S., Giacobbe, P., Hamani, C., Craddock, R. C., & Kennedy, S. H. (2008). Subcallosal cingulated gyrus deep brain stimulation for treatment-resistant depression. *Biological Psychiatry, 64,* 461–467.

Lu, X., Sharkey, L., & Bartfai, T. (2007). The brain galanin receptors: Targets for novel antidepressant drugs. *CNS & Neurological Disorders – Drug Targets, 6,* 183–192.

Malone, D. A., Dougherty, D. D., Rezai, A. R., Carpenter, L. L., Friehs, G. M., Eskander, E. N., et al. (2009). Deep brain stimulation of the ventral capsule/ventral striatum for treatment-resistant depression. *Biological Psychiatry, 65,* 267–275.

Martin, S. D., Martin, E., Rai, S. S., Richardson, M. A., & Royall, R. (2001). Brain blood flow changes in depressed patients treated with interpersonal psychotherapy or venlafaxine hydrochloride: Preliminary findings. *Archives of General Psychiatry, 58,* 641–648.

Mayberg, H. S. (1994). Frontal lobe dysfunction in secondary depression. *Journal of Neuropsychiatry and Clinical Neurosciences, 6,* 428–442.

Mayberg, H. S., Brannan, S., Tekell, J. L., Silva, J. A., Mahurin, R. K., McGinnis, S., et al. (2000). Regional metabolic effects of fluoxetine in major depression: Serial changes and relationship to clinical response. *Biological Psychiatry, 48,* 830–843.

Mayberg, H. S., Lozano, A. M., Voon, V., McNeely, H. E., Seminowicz, D., Hamani, C., et al. (2005). Deep brain stimulation for treatment-resistant depression. *Neuron 45,* 651–660.

McCabe, C., Mishor, Z., Cowen, P. J., & Harmer, C. J. (2010). Diminished neural processing of aversive and rewarding stimuli during selective serotonin reuptake inhibitor treatment. *Biological Psychiatry, 67,* 439–445.

McCaffrey, R. J., & Lynch, J. K. (1996). Survey of the educational backgrounds and specialty training of instructors of clinical neuropsychology in APA-approved graduate training programs: A 10-year follow-up. *Archives of Clinical Neuropsychology, 11,* 11–19.

McClintock, S. M., Husain, M. M., Greer, T. L., & Cullum, C. M. (2010). Association between depression severity and neurocognitive function in major depressive disorder: A review and synthesis. *Neuropsychology, 24,* 9–34.

McDonald, W. M., Thompson, T. R., McCall, W. V., & Zorumxki, C. F. (2004). *Electroconvulsive therapy.* In: A.F. Schatzberg & C.B. Nemeroff (eds.), *Textbook of psychopharmacology* (3rd ed., pp. 685–714). Washington DC: American Psychiatric Publishing.

McEwen, B. S. (2007). Physiology and neurobiology of stress and adaptation: Central role of the brain. *Physiological Reviews, 87,* 873–904.

McHugh, P. R., & Slavney, P. R. (1998). *The perspectives on psychiatry* (2nd ed.). Baltimore, MD: Johns Hopkins.

Miguel-Hidalgo, J. J. & Rajikowska, G. (2003). Comparison of prefrontal cell pathology between depression and alcohol dependence. *Journal of Psychiatric Research, 37,* 411–420.

Mirza, Y., Tang, J., Russell, A., Banerjee, S. P., Bhandari, R., Ivey, J., et al. (2004). Reduced anterior cingulate cortex glutamergic concentration in childhood major depression. *Journal of the American Academy of Child & Adolescent Psychiatry, 43,* 341–348.

Murphy, F. C., Michael, A., Robbins, T. W., & Sahakian, B. J. (2003). Neuropsychological impairment in patients with major depressive disorder: The effects of feedback on task performance. *Psychological Medicine, 33,* 455–467.

Nelson, L. D., & Do, T. (1998). Using the MMPI-2 in patients with multiple sclerosis. *Archives of Clinical Neuropsychology, 13,* 92.

Nemeroff, C. B. (2008). Recent findings in the pathophysiology of depression. *Focus, 6,* 3–14.

Nemeroff, C. B., Mayberg, H. S., Krahl, S. E., McNamara, J., Frazer, A., Henry, T. R., et al. (2006). VNS therapy in treatment-resistant depression: Clinical evidence and putative neurobiological mechanisms. *Neuropsychopharmacology, 31,* 1345–1355.

Ögren, S., Kuteeva, E. H., Hökfelt, T., & Kehr, J. (2006). Galanin receptor antagonists: A potential novel pharmacological treatment for mood disorders. *CNS Drugs, 20,* 633–654.

Ongur, D., Drevets, W. C., & Price, J. L. (1998). Glial reduction in the subgenual prefrontal cortex in mood disorders. *Proceedings of the National Academy of Sciences, 95,* 13290–13295.

Papakostas, G. I., Peterson, T., Mahal, Y., Mischoulon, D., Nierenberg, A. A., & Fava, M. (2004). Quality of life assessments in major depressive disorder: A review of the literature. *General Hospital Psychiatry, 26,* 13–17.

Perlis, R. H., Moorjani, P., Fagerness, J., Purcell, S., Trivedi, M. H., Fava, M., et al. (2008). Pharmacogenetic analysis of genes implicated in rodent models of antidepressant response: Association of TREK I and treatment resistance in the STAR*D study. *Neuropsychopharmacology, 33,* 2810–2819.

Pirozzolo, F. J., Swihart, A. A., Rey, G. J., Mahurin, R., & Jankovic, J. (1993). Cognitive impairment associated with Parkinson's disease and other movement disorders. In J. Jankovic & E. Tolosa (Eds.), *Parkinson's disease and movement disorders* (2nd ed., pp. 493–510). Baltimore, MD: Lippincott Williams & Wilkins.

Quitkin, F. M. (2002). Depression with atypical features: Diagnostic validity, prevalence, and treatment. *Primary Care Companion Journal of Clinical Psychiatry, 4,* 94–99.

Quraishi, S., & Frangou, S. (2002). Neuropsychology of bipolar disorder: A review. *Journal of Affective Disorders, 72,* 209–226.

Radloff, L. S. (1977). The CES-D scale: A self-report depression scale for research in the general population. *Applied Psychological Measurement, 1,* 385–401.

Rajikowska, G., Miguel-Hidalgo, J. J., Wei, J., Dilley, G., Pittman, S. D., Meltzer, H. Y., et al. (1999). Morphometric evidence for neuronal and glial prefrontal pathology in major depression. *Biological Psychiatry, 45,* 1085–1098.

Reagan, L., Grillo, C., & Piroli, G. (2008). The As and Ds of stress: Metabolic, morphological and behavioral consequences. *European Journal of Pharmacology, 585,* 64–75.

Reifler, B. (2000). A case of mistaken identity: Pseudodementia is really predementia. *Journal of the American Geriatrics Society, 48,* 593–594.

Rohling, M. L., & Scogin, F. (1993). Automatic and effortful cognitive processing in depressed persons. *The Journals of Gerontology: Psychological Sciences, 48,* 122–138.

Rohling, M. L., Green, P., Allen, L. M. III & Iverson, G. L. (2002). Depressive symptoms and neurocognitive test scores in patients passing symptom validity tests. *Archives of Clinical Neuropsychology, 17,* 205–222.

Roose, S. P. (2003). Treatment of depression in patients with heart disease. *Biological Psychiatry, 54,* 262–268.

Sanacora, G., Gueorguieva, R., Epperson, C. N., Wu, Y. T., Appel, M., Rothman, D. L., et al. (2004). Subtype-specific alterations of gamma-aminobutyric acid and glutamate in patients with major depression. *Archives of General Psychiatry, 61,* 705–713.

Savitz, J., Lucki, I., & Drevets, W. (2009). 5-HT(1A) receptor function in major depressive disorder. *Progress in Neurobiology, 88,* 17–31.

Seminowicz, D. A., Mayberg, H. S., McIntosh, A. R., Goldapple, K., Kennedy, S., Segal, Z., et al. (2004). Limbic-frontal circuitry in major depression: A path modeling meta-analysis. *Neuroimage, 22,* 409–418.

Scher, C. D., Ingram, R. E., & Segal, Z. V. (2005). Cognitive reactivity and vulnerability: Empirical evaluation of construct activation and cognitive diatheses in unipolar depression. *Clinical Psychology Review, 25,* 487–510.

Shah, P. J., Ebmeier, K. P., Glabus, M. F., & Goodwin, G. M. (1998). Cortical grey matter reductions associated with treatment-resistant chronic unipolar depression: Controlled magnetic resonance imaging study. *British Journal of Psychiatry, 172,* 527–532.

Sheehan, D. V., LeCrubier, Y., Sheehan, K. H., Amorim, P., Janavs, J., Weiller, E., et al. (1998). The Mini-international Neuropsychiatric Interview (M.I.N.I.): The development and validation of a structured diagnostic psychiatric interview for DSM-IV and ICD-10. *Journal of Clinical Psychiatry, 59*(Suppl. 20), 22–33.

Shenal, B. V., Harrison, D. W., & Demaree, H. A. (2003). The neuropsychology of depression: A literature review and preliminary model. *Neuropsychology Review, 13,* 33–42.

Sinyor, M. S., Schaffer, A., & Levitt, A. (2010). The sequenced treatment alternatives to relieve depression (STAR*D) trial: A review. *Canadian Journal of Psychiatry, 55,* 126–135.

Sonawalla, S. B., & Fava, M. (2001). Severe depression: Is there a best approach? *CNS Drugs, 15,* 765–776.

Spitzer, R., Endicott, J., & Robbins, E. (1975). Clinical criteria for psychiatric diagnoses and DSM-III. *American Journal of Psychiatry, 132,* 1187–1192.

Starkstein, S. E., Mayberg, H. S., Leiguarda, R., Preziosi, T. J., & Robinson, R. G. (1992). A prospective longitudinal study of depression, cognitive decline, and physical impairments in patients with Parkinson's disease. *Journal of Neurology, Neurosurgery and Psychiatry, 55,* 377–382.

Sullivan, P. F., Neale, M. C., & Kendler, K. S. (2000). Genetic epidemiology of major depression: Review and meta-analysis. *American Journal of Psychiatry, 157,* 1552–1562.

Taylor, W. D., MacFall, J. R., Payne, M. E., McQuoid, D. R., Provenzale, J. M., Stephens, D. C., et al. (2004). Late-life depression and microstructural abnormalities in dorsolateral prefrontal cortex white matter. *American Journal of Psychiatry, 161,* 1293–1296.

Tolin, D. F. (2010). Is cognitive-behavioral therapy more effective than other therapies? *Clinical Psychology Review, 30,* 710–720.

Trullas, R., & Skolnick, P. (1990). Functional antagonists at the NMDA receptor complex exhibit antidepressant actions. *European Journal of Pharmacology, 185,* 1–10.

Tsigos, C., & Chrousos, G. (2002). Hypothalamic-pituitary-adrenal axis, neuroendocrine factors and stress. *Journal of Psychosomatic Research, 53,* 865–871.

Turner, E. H., Matthews, A. M., Lindardatos, E., Tell, R. A., & Rosenthal, R. (2008). Selective publication of antidepressant trials and its influence on apparent efficacy. *New England Journal of Medicine, 358,* 252–260.

Uranova, N. A., Vostrikov, V. M., Orlovskaya, D. D., & Rachmanova, V. I. (2004). Oligodendroglial density in the prefrontal cortex in schizophrenia and mood disorders: A study from the Stanley Neuropathology Consortium. *Schizophrenia Research, 67,* 269–275.

Van Otterloo, E., O'Dwyer, G., Stockmeier, C. A., Steffens, D. C., Krishnan, R. R., & Rajikowska, G. (2009). Reductions in neuronal density in elderly depressed are region specific. *International Journal of Geriatric Psychiatry, 24,* 856–864.

Veiel, H. O. (1997). A preliminary profile of neuropsychological deficits associated with major depression. *Journal of Clinical and Experimental Neuropsychology, 19,* 587–603.

Wang, L., Krishna, K. R., Steffens, D. C., Potter, G. G., Dolcos, F., & McCarthy, G. (2008). Depressive state- and disease-related alterations in neural responses to affective and executive challenges in geriatric depression. *American Journal of Psychiatry, 165,* 863–871.

Weis, S., Llenos, I. C., Sabunciyan, S., Dulay, J. R., Isler, L., Yolken, R., et al. (2007). Reduced expression of human endogenous retrovirus (HERV)-W GAG protein in the cingulate gyrus and hippocampus in schizophrenia, bipolar disorder, and depression. *Journal of Neural Transmission, 114,* 645–655.

Weissman, M. M., Markowitz, J. C., & Klerman, G. L. (2003). Comprehensive guide to interpersonal psychotherapy. *American Journal of Psychiatry, 160,* 398–400.

Yesavage, J. A., Brink, T. L., Rose, T. L., Lum, O., Huand, V., Adey, M., et al. (1982). Development and validation of a geriatric depression screening scale: A preliminary report. *Journal of Psychiatry Research, 17,* 37–49.

Zhang, X., Gainetdinov, R. R., Beaulieu, J. M., Sotnikova, T. D., Burch, L. H., Williams, R. B., et al. (2005). Loss-of-function mutation in tryptophan hydroxylase-2 identified in unipolar major depression. *Neuron, 6,* 11–16.

Zigmond, A. S., & Snaith, R. P. (1983). The hospital anxiety and depression scale. *Acta Psychiatrica Scandinavica, 97,* 361–370.

Zimmerman, M. (2003). What should the standard of care for psychiatric diagnostic evaluations be? *Journal of Nervous and Mental Disease, 191,* 281–286.

Zimmerman, M., & Mattia, J. I. (1999). Psychiatric diagnosis in clinical practice: Is comorbidity being missed. *Comprehensive Psychiatry, 40,* 182–191.

Zung, W. W. K. (1965). A self-rating depression scale. *Archives of General Psychiatry, 12,* 63–70.

CHAPTER 10

Bipolar Disorders

Nicholas S. Thaler, Daniel N. Allen, & Gerald Goldstein

INTRODUCTION

Bipolar disorder (BD), or manic-depressive illness, is a mood disorder characterized by alternating and recurrent manic and depressive episodes as well as periods of euthymic mood. Mania or a manic episode is a state of increased activity, elevated or irritable mood, decreased sleep, distractibility, and racing thoughts. The depressive episodes that are common in BD have the same characteristics as found in unipolar depression, or major depressive disorder (MDD), and include depressed mood or anhedonia, neurovegetative symptoms including disrupted sleep and weight loss, and cognitive difficulties such as decreased attention. Mixed episodes, although less common, are also sometimes observed and have the essential features of both manic and depressed episodes that occur during the same time period. There are two main types of BD included in the *Diagnostic and Statistical Manual of Mental Disorders* (*DSM-IV-TR*; American Psychiatric Association [APA], 2000). In bipolar I disorder (BD I), a full manic or mixed episode is required for diagnosis, although depressed episodes are also often present. Bipolar II disorder (BD II) is characterized by hypomanic episodes accompanied by at least one major depressive episode and no history of manic or mixed episodes. The length of the cycle of the manic, mixed, and depressed episodes varies among individuals, but there is an identified rapid cycling subtype that has at least four separate episodes within a year. In addition to BD I and BD II, the *DSM-IV-TR* includes a diagnosis for cyclothymia, which is diagnosed when there is a history of hypomanic episodes as well as a period of depression that does not meet full criteria for a major depressive episode. Also, there is a diagnosis of bipolar disorder not otherwise specified (BD NOS). BD NOS is used to capture affective symptoms that are negatively impacting functioning but that do not meet full criteria for the other BDs. For example, individuals might be diagnosed with BD NOS if they had periods of depression and hypomania, but these periods were not severe enough to meet criteria for one of the other disorders.

An estimated 1.0%–1.6% of the general population have a lifetime prevalence of BD I, with initial symptoms often occurring during late adolescence (Keck, McElroy, & Arnold, 2001; Skjelstad, Malt, & Holte, 2010). Age of onset varies but appears to fall within one of three periods including adolescence, the mid twenties, and the late thirties/early-forties, depending upon environmental and genetic factors (Bellivier et al., 2003). Approximately 20% of individuals undergo a prodromal period in which symptoms of mood dysregulation emerge but are not severe enough to receive a formal diagnosis. Others are initially diagnosed with MDD until their first manic, mixed, or hypomanic episode (Bourgeois & Marneros, 2000). BD I is associated with significant functional impairment and mortality with an estimated 25%

of patients with BD I attempting suicide and between 4% and 19% succeeding in their attempts (Novick, Swartz, & Frank, 2010). In addition, the affective instability often associated with BD I may complicate existing medical conditions such as cardiovascular disease and diabetes (Chue & Cheung, 2006; Connerny et al., 2001; De Hert et al., 2009) as well as impair social and occupational functioning (Depp et al., 2010; O'Shea et al., 2010). This combined impact of medical and psychiatric complications substantially raises the cost of managing BD and it is estimated that treating BD costs 2.5 times more than treating unipolar depression (Harley, Li, Corey-Lisle, L'Italien, & Carson, 2007).

Although BD is diagnosed clinically using the *DSM-IV-TR*, recent advances in neuropsychology, neurology, and genetics have provided evidence for key genetic, neuroanatomical, biochemical, and neurocognitive differences that may distinguish between individuals with BD and unaffected individuals, including those with other mental disorders. However, findings remain heterogeneous and at times inconclusive in identifying BD geno- and phenotypes, although understanding of key biological and cognitive expressions related to the disease is steadily increasing. Aiding this increase in knowledge are findings of intermediate cognitive and biological phenotypes, or "endophenotypes," which can be objectively evaluated and may have clinical, behavioral, genetic, neuroimaging, and biochemical correlates that are central to the disorder (Ewald, 2000; Murphy & Sahakian, 2001) and are mediating processes between genotypes and phenotypes. Identification of endophenotypes is useful for a number of reasons, including that it may facilitate genetic linkage studies, assist in predicting those individuals who are at increased risk for developing BD, and serve to increase effectiveness of early diagnosis and intervention strategies. Criteria for establishing a neurocognitive or other variable as an endophenotype include that the marker must be associated with illness in the population, be state independent, be heritable, and that both the illness and marker must co-segregate within affected families (Gershon & Goldin, 1986; Gottesman & Gould, 2003; Gottesman & Shields, 1973; Leboyer et al., 1998).

This chapter outlines recent findings on the pathological mechanisms underlying BD, reviews current research on cognitive impairment and endophenotypic candidates relevant in neuropsychological assessment, and outlines current diagnostic and treatment practices and issues.

GENETIC FINDINGS

Although the causative genetic basis of BD has not been discovered, population genetics research has indicated that it is highly heritable, with an estimated 15%–20% of first-degree relatives of BD I individuals either having BD I or MDD (Ewald, 2000), and a 40%–60% concordance rate in monozygotic twin studies (Kieseppa, Partonen, Haukka, Kaprio, & Lonnqvist, 2004; Mathews, Reus, & Freimer, 2003). This heritability lends support for the importance of identifying genetic factors in the disease, although the fact that the concordance rates for identical twins implicates environmental factors as well. Despite the strong evidence for a genetic role in BD I, the actual mode of transportation from genes to the disease remains unclear. Indeed, Thaker (2008) stated that after an initial surge of interest, subsequent genetic studies in both schizophrenia (SZ) and BD I have been disappointing. Ideally, researchers may identify a genotypic definition that is clearly linked to the BD phenotype. Some genes have been implicated, but attempts to replicate findings have been inconsistent (Potash & DePaulo, 2000; Thaker, 2008). This may be due to the fact that BD is a polygenetic disorder that demonstrates imperfect penetrance (Lenox, Gould, & Manji, 2002; MacQueen, Hajek, & Alda, 2005).

Numerous candidate genes have been examined, typically via association studies (Mathews et al., 2003), which examine the frequency of alleles in the target population. In contrast, linkage studies identify genes by mapping genetic markers through a family tree. Both association and linkage studies have generally been inconsistent in BD research, although some findings have been replicated (Burmeister, McInnis, & Zollner, 2008). For example, chromosome 4p16 was implicated in a study of Scottish families with BD I and BD II (Lander & Kruglyak, 1995), which has been replicated in other studies (Ewald, 2000). Chromosomes 12,

18, and 21 have also been identified as candidate genes in linkage studies (Potash & DePaulo, 2000). Chromosome 18p11.3 in particular has been noted to have a high logarithm of odds (LOD) scores in families with BD I (Ewald, 2000). A more recent review has also identified several candidate genes for SZ that may also have associations with BD I with particular promise for chromosome 13q45 as well as the X chromosome (Kato, 2007).

Liu and colleagues (2010) conducted a meta-analysis of patients with BD I and patients with MDD and found variants on the *CACN1C* gene, which encodes an alpha-1 subunit on voltage-dependent calcium channels. In addition, the BD I group had significant aberrations on the *ANK3* gene not present in MDD. Although these candidate genes for disease risk show potential, they are limited in identifying key markers due to their sheer quantity and ultimately suggest that BD is genetically heterogeneous and dependent on the interaction of numerous genes and the environment.

Although not unique to BD I, recent attention has been given to the catechol-O-methyltransferase gene (*COMT*) in its role in psychosis. The *COMT* gene is located on chromosome 22 and is responsible for producing an enzyme that degrades dopamine and other neurotransmitters (Payton, 2006). The Val158Met variant on the *COMT* gene is thought to affect dopamine signaling in the frontal lobe, resulting in disorders of executive functioning, response inhibition, abstract thought, working memory, and task learning (Bruder et al., 2005), and has been linked to a number of psychiatric disorders with psychotic symptoms (Basterreche et al., 2009). One study compared the Val158Met variant among 48 patients with SZ and 31 patients with bipolar disorder and found that both groups had an association between the variant and lifetime symptomatology (as opposed to current symptomatology; Goghari & Sponheim, 2008). Further, the SZ group had associations between positive symptoms and the Val allele, whereas the BD group had greater associations between symptoms and the Met allele. Although implicated in both populations, variations of the *COMT* gene may serve as a valuable marker for disease phenotype. Thus, identifying key candidate genes specific to BD remains challenging and there is as of yet no conclusive evidence about genetic risk factors despite the clear genetic contribution to the disorder (Kato, 2007; Thaker, 2008). It may take several years before researchers can pick apart the basic biological effects of current candidate genes and how these effects may contribute to BD (Ewald, 2000), but one promising approach may be to continue to investigate genes that may be candidates for specific symptoms often expressed in BD I (e.g., mania), as well as identifying specific markers to the disease itself, such as the *COMT* gene.

NEUROPATHOLOGY AND PATHOPHYSIOLOGY: POSTMORTEM FINDINGS

Advances in molecular biology have enabled researchers to investigate the neuropathology of BD via postmortem brain studies. One such study examined 18 cases of BD I, assessing the neuronal and glial cells in Brodmann's area 24 and the ventral anterior cingulate cortex and comparing them to patients with MDD, SZ, and controls (Ongur, Drevets, & Price, 1998). Neuronal number and density was found to be unchanged, but glial cells were significantly reduced at 24% for the group with MDD and 41% for the group with BD I. Further, individuals who had a familial history of mood disorders accounted for most of the reduction. Of particular interest, the group with SZ did not have significantly reduced glial density, raising the possibility that reduced glial density in the ventral cortex is specifically related to mood disorders. However, the study is also criticized for not specifying whether the reduced glial cells were astrocytes, microglia, or oligodendroglia (Vawter, Freed, & Kleinman, 2000).

Another postmortem study examined Brodmann's area 9, the dorsolateral prefrontal area, using a three-dimensional morphometric method in 10 participants with BD I and 11 controls (Rajkowska, Halaris, & Selemon, 2001). Results found significant neuronal and glial density reduction in area 9, and the researchers concluded that this provides further evidence that BD I and SZ have distinct pathologies and by extension are distinct diseases. Further supporting this, research on SZ brains have shown increased neuronal and glial density in area 9 (Selemon, Rajkowska, & Goldman-Rakick, 1995) and reduced cortical thickness

(Harvey, Persaud, Ron, Baker, & Murray, 1994). Limitations of this study include a failure to control for medication effects as well as preexisting differences between the BD I group and controls, such as age, gender, and other potentially complicating factors.

Despite the potential confounds in these studies, the evidence indicates that individuals with BD I have significant reductions of glial density in the ventral anterior cingulate cortex and reductions of both glial and neuronal densities in the dorsolateral prefrontal cortex. These findings suggest that there is regional variation in cellular pathology associated with BD I, but also show promise of a prototypical profile of pathology in BD I that is distinct from SZ and from healthy individuals. Vawter and colleagues (2000) summarize prefrontal cortex findings by comparing the postmortem studies to that by Drevets and colleagues (1997), who observed gray matter volume, glucose metabolism, and blood flow of living patients with BD I. In their study, the researchers found decreases on all three variables in the left subgenual prefrontal cortex. However, postmortem studies find reduction in glial cell counts across both hemispheres in individuals with familial mood disorders, suggesting that individuals with BD I have gray matter reduction in the left subgenual prefrontal cortex, whereas glial reduction occurs in familial cases of BD I and MDD.

Studies of the limbic system have identified reduced nonpyramidal neuronal density and count in the CA2 sector of the hippocampus of both patients with BD I and SZ (Benes, Kwok, Vincent, & Todtenkopf, 1998). There were no such differences in the CA1, CA3, or CA4 sectors, pinpointing nonpyramidal cells in the CA2 sector as a signature area for both disorders. The subcortical regions may have further promise in differentiating BD I from MDD; a study by Soares and Mann (1997) found that patients with MDD had smaller basal ganglia volumes whereas patients with BD I did not. In addition, patients with BD I had more large pigmented neurons in the locus coeruleus compared to patients with MDD (Baumann et al., 1999). The increase of locus coeruleus neurons suggests that norepinephrine is altered in individuals with BD I, particularly in projections to the prefrontal cortex (Vawter et al., 2000), although further studies are needed to confirm this hypothesis.

Signal transduction studies observe the biochemical reactions within cells, which are then transmitted via enzymes and activated by secondary messengers. Secondary messenger guanine nucleotide-binding proteins, or G proteins, are a signal cascade for dopamine, adrenergic, and serotonin receptors, among others (Vawter et al., 2000), and alterations of the protein have been implicated in numerous disorders. The G protein G alpha subunit is of particular interest in BD I because it was found to be in greater concentrations within the occipital, prefrontal, and temporal cortexes of patients with BD I compared to controls (Young et al., 1993) whereas no such differences were noted in SZ or Alzheimer's disease patients. Although this finding has been replicated with some success by other researchers, the implications of G alpha subunit increase in BD I remain unknown. However, patients with MDD showed no such alterations, patients with alcohol dependence showed decreases, and lithium did not alter the protein levels, highlighting the potential of the G alpha subunit increases in BD I to be a unique trait to the disease (Colin et al., 1991; Ozawa et al., 1993a, 1993b).

Researchers have also found that the phosphoinositide signal transduction system's phosphatidylinositol (PI) pathway contains signals required for the synthesis of inositol, a key chemical compound in cell lipid production (Vawter et al., 2000). Cyclic adenosine monophosphate (cAMP) has also been indirectly measured in postmortem BD I studies, and significant reductions of cAMP have been found in many major regions of the brain (Rahman et al., 1997). The enzyme protein kinase C (PKC), which has been shown to be inhibited by lithium (Wang & Friedman, 1989), may have increased activity in neuronal membranes of individuals with BD I (Wang & Friedman, 1996).

Vawter and colleagues (2000) sum up these findings by suggesting that overactive cAMP and PI cascades lead to increased G protein and PKC concentrations, which may be related to the increase of neurons in the locus coeruleus, which project to the hypothalamus and cortex. The neuropathology of BD thus may be related to changes in neurotransmission, signal transduction, and glial production, with alterations in the subcortical regions impacting higher-order regions such as the prefrontal cortex. Although these preliminary findings begin to identify cortical and subcortical abnormalities in BD I, results are too tentative to draw any conclusive unified theory of BD's neuropathology. Furthermore, postmortem studies are difficult to conduct and often have small sample sizes due to a scarcity of appropriate brain tissue, comorbid complications, and heterogeneity in manner of the donor's death (Deep-Soboslay et al., 2008). Neuroimaging studies, by contrast, have the advantage of access to a greater number of subjects as well as the opportunity to study patients at various phases of illness (e.g., manic, euthymic, depressed) that may provide additional insights.

NEUROPATHOLOGY AND PATHOPHYSIOLOGY: NEUROIMAGING FINDINGS

Structural imaging studies have found evidence of gray volume loss in the anterior cingulate and the ventral striatum although studies on lateral differences between the left and right hemispheres have had inconsistent findings (e.g., Fornito et al., 2009; Sassi et al., 2004). Different results have also been found for other structures, including the lateral ventricles, third ventricle, left subgenual prefrontal cortex, amygdala, and thalamus, highlighting the heterogeneous nature of both methodology and clinical sample variation in neuroimaging studies (McDonald et al., 2004). Of interest, patients with BD I with psychotic features may account for some of this heterogeneity, as it has been suggested that BD I with psychosis may have genetic differences that are biologically closer to schizophrenia rather than BD I without psychotic features (Potash et al., 2001). However, the extent to which this translates to structural and functional differences between BD I with and without psychotic features is uncertain.

A recent meta-analysis by Kempton, Geddes, Ettinger, Williams, and Grasby (2008) examined 98 MRI studies while controlling for demographic and clinical variables and found that BD I patients exhibited increased size in bilateral ventricles and increased white matter hyperintensities compared to controls. The increased hyperintensities in white matter regions is perhaps the most replicated finding in BD I studies (Mathews et al., 2003). Hyperintensities are present throughout the brain although most commonly noted in the frontal and parietal/frontal regions of the brain. These hyperintensities occur in deep white matter structures that communicate between the fronto-temporal regions and may be a stable trait of pathology in BD I (Kujawa & Nemeroff, 2000). Other consistently replicated structural findings include abnormalities in the cerebellum and mild sulcal prominence (Stoli, Renshaw, Yurgelun-Todd, & Cohen, 2000). Another meta-analysis of MRI studies conducted by Vita, De Peri, and Sacchetti (2009) looked only at first-episode patients with BD I. The researchers found structural abnormalities that were not found in previous meta-analyses that examined chronic patients with BD I only. In contrast to other findings (Kempton et al., 2008), there was only significant reduction of intracranial volume and total white matter volume with first-episode patients with BD I. The authors suggest a number of possible explanations for these differences, including possible medication effects associated with patients with a chronic history, morphological changes associated with repeated mood episodes, differences in methodology among the meta-analyses, or diagnostic shifts that occur between first-episode patients and those who have chronic episodes (Vita et al., 2009). Nonetheless, the results present clear evidence that brain morphology in BD I exhibits clear changes over the course of the disease.

Researchers have posited that there is a neuronal network comprising the prefrontal cortex, striatum, thalamus, and the amygdala that is responsible for mood states, and thus the amygdala is a region of interest in BD I (Phillips, Drevets, Rauch, & Lane, 2003; Strakowski, Adler, Holland, Mills, & DelBello, 2004; Vawter et al., 2000). A meta-analysis of structural MRI studies of the amygdala by Usher, Leucht, Falkai, and Scherk (2010) examined both pediatric and adult patients. Findings suggested that amygdala volume was bilaterally reduced in the overall and pediatric sample but less pronounced in adult studies. The results also found a positive relationship between age and amygdala volume, suggesting that amygdala volume is smaller at onset of disease and may increase with age. The study's authors suggest three hypotheses for this finding: Chronic BD I may increase amygdala over time due to number of episodes, medication effects, and other clinical variables; increased amygdala volume represents a prototypical pattern of illness course; and subtypes of BD I may exist that may have different volumes contingent upon age of onset.

Functional neuroimaging studies suggest changes in glucose metabolism related to affective state in the frontal regions, whereas reduced cerebral blood flow may be more of a stable trait of the disease. A review by Haldane and Frangou (2006) noted that reduced prefrontal metabolism during depressive episodes in patients with BD I is indistinguishable from patients with MDD. They further noted that cerebral blood flow reduction is most consistently reported in frontal regions only and not so much in other regions during depressed episodes in both BD I and MDD. Other studies have reported reduced metabolism in the basal ganglia and temporal lobe in patients with BD I during depressed states (Post et al., 1989) and increased metabolism in the amygdala in both medicated and unmedicated groups (Drevets et al., 2002).

During manic states, studies have also found reduced blood flow in the frontal and temporal regions (Migliorelli et al., 1993; Rubin et al., 1995), although one study found increased blood flow in the temporal region only (O'Connell et al., 1995). Of interest, PET studies report an increase in blood flow in the left dorsal regions of the anterior cingulate cortex and the basal ganglia, suggesting that changes in cerebral blood flow are region specific (Blumberg et al., 2000; O'Connell et al., 1995). Further, although cortical perfusion is consistently reduced in the frontal region, frontal lobe glucose metabolism may be mood dependent, with significant decreases during depressed episodes and increases during manic episodes (Goodwin et al., 1997).

Studies have examined neural correlates to behavioral tasks within patient samples. Individuals with BD I exhibit reduced activation in the left prefrontal cortex and bilateral amygdala while completing response inhibition tasks (Kaladijan et al., 2009). While completing a working memory task, patients with BD I across manic, depressed, and euthymic mood states performed comparable to controls. However, they also evidenced significantly less activation in right frontal and parietal regions compared to normal controls with additional activation in temporal and other frontal lobe regions, suggesting a compensatory mechanism (Townsend, Bookheimer, Foland–Ross, Sugar, & Altshuler, 2010). There is further evidence that patients use compensatory activation of limbic and visual association cortical regions to maintain sustained attention at a rate comparable to controls (Strawkowski et al., 2004). These findings suggest that individuals with BD I exhibit abnormal functioning in both cortical and subcortical regions, and that although patients may perform comparably to controls on certain behavioral tasks, they also harness different regions of the brain to compensate for hypoactive activity in regions of the brain typically used to complete such tasks.

PET studies on dopamine have found that dopamine D1 receptor binding potentials are reduced in the frontal cortex but not in the caudate nucleus (Suhara et al., 1992; Wong et al., 1985), whereas D2 receptor density was found to be higher in patients with psychosis (Pearlson et al., 1995). Another study by Zubieta and colleagues (2000) found increased thalamic and brain stem concentrations of central vesicular monoamine transporter protein (VMAT2), which is a marker of monoaminergic activity. Although the implications of these studies are yet unclear, they do provide further evidence of the different functional processes involved in frontal and subcortical structures of patients with BD I.

In summary, neuroimaging findings remain heterogeneous, though some consistencies exist. Recent meta-analyses (Kempton et al., 2008; McDonald et al., 2004) have presented general findings that enlarged lateral ventricles and increased white matter hyperintensities are often exhibited in individuals with BD I, although another study suggests a distinction in structural abnormalities between first-episode and chronic patients (Vita et al., 2009), with first-episode patients actually exhibiting a loss of white matter volume. There is also evidence of increased amygdala volume associated with chronicity of the disease (Usher et al., 2010). The links between cortical and subcortical structures are in part modulated by a frontal-striatal-thalamic-limbic circuit. Dysfunction in the orbitofrontal cortex and subcortical structures such as the anterior cingulate gyrus and other structures within the circuit may disrupt the frontal-subcortical network, leading to aberrant activity in the frontal cortex. Of interest, acquired brain damage to the ventromedial caudate system has been linked to cycling states similar to those observed in individuals with BD I (Strakowski & Sax, 2000), which may support this hypothesis. Regardless, loss of activity due to this disruption then leads to loss of input to the prefrontal cortex. Studies also consistently show that glucose metabolism in the frontal cortex is hyperactive during manic states and hypoactive during depressed states, whereas cerebral blood flow in the region is generally hypoactive regardless of mood state.

As the literature shows, recent scientific advances have been promising in elucidating some of the pathophysiology of BD I. However, many questions remain, such as the implications of some of the mechanisms that are consistently associated with BD I (e.g., white matter hyperintensities and reduced frontal glial cell count). It is also yet unknown whether such mechanisms can differentiate BD subtype or predict course and outcome. With regard to genetic diatheses, research has implicated several candidate genes but has yet to form any definitive genetic contributors that can supersede the current classification schemas used to diagnose BD I. Ultimately, in endeavoring to better understand the underlying characteristics of BD I, researchers have investigated putative endophenotypes that may connect clinically observable phenotypes with their genes. Endophenotypes may be neurophysiological by nature, and indeed some of the morphological findings of BD have lead to proposals that these findings may be putative endophenotype candidates. For example, Hasler, Drevets, Gould, Gottesman, and Manji (2006) suggested that the white matter hyperintensities and reduced anterior cingulate cortex volume are viable endophenotypes in BD, although they also caution that such abnormalities may have an environmental rather than genetic origin. In contrast, neurocognitive endophenotypes may have an advantage because they have been shown to be highly heritable, often stable, and comparably easier to measure than neurophysiological abnormalities. As such, neuropsychological studies of BD have the additional benefit of identifying candidate endophenotypes as well as establish links between cognitive variables and behavioral/symptom correlates.

NEUROPSYCHOLOGICAL FEATURES

It is understood that the neuropsychological manifestations of BD are both state and trait features of the disorder. With regard to state considerations, medications and fluctuations in mood are associated with variability in neuropsychological functioning in a number of domains. Other influences, such as disease severity and chronicity, may influence neurocognitive abilities to increase overall level of deficit as length or severity of illness increases (Clark & Goodwin, 2008). However, because neurocognitive deficits persist during euthymic states in medicated and unmedicated patients, and some deficits are also apparent in unaffected family members of individuals with BD, there is also evidence supporting trait neurocognitive deficits that may represent core features of the disorder. As mentioned before, in some cases these trait deficits have been conceptualized as endophenotypic markers for the disorder, and so these deficits do appear to be more than the simple result of medication effects, mood fluctuations, or other transient influences. Therefore, the common neurocognitive deficits found in BD, which include attention, executive functioning, visuoperception, and verbal memory (Arts, Jabben, Krabbendam, & van Os, 2008; Clark & Goodwin, 2008; Elgamal, Sokolowska, & MacQueen, 2008), should be considered with regard to both trait and state features.

NEUROCOGNITIVE DEFICITS IN EUTHYMIA

Some of the strongest support for trait neurocognitive deficits in BD has come from studies of affected individuals who are in euthymic states. A challenge for the researcher is that when individuals with BD I are euthymic, they are often medicated, presenting a potential confound given that medication can influence neurocognitive functioning (Goldberg, 2008; Holmes et al., 2008; Roiser et al., 2009). Nonetheless, impairments in verbal memory are reliably present in euthymic patients (Krabbendam et al., 2000; Van Gorp, Altshuler, Theberge, Wilkins, & Dixon, 1998) and in monozygotic twins of patients with BD I (Gourovitch et al., 1999). Sustained attention has also received some interest in euthymic patients. For example, Clark and Goodwin (2008) argued that sustained attention may represent a state-trait deficit in BD I. They note that sustained attention, as measured by continuous performance tasks (CPT) was found to be impaired in euthymic patients (Clark, Iversen, & Goodwin, 2002) and even further impaired in manic patients (Clark, Iversen, & Goodwin, 2001). However, no mention was made of depressed patients, who have been found to have normal sustained attention after controlling for medication effects. Further, no indication was made whether or not medication was accounted for in the euthymic patients as well. A follow-up study found that sustained attention was not adversely affected in first-degree relatives of individuals with BD I, providing strong evidence that this neurocognitive construct may mostly be affected in medicated and manic states only and is not linked to an underlying genetic trait (Clark, Kempton, Scarnà, Grasby, & Goodwin, 2005).

Studies of unaffected first-degree relatives of patients with BD have also provided insight into trait deficits (Bora, Yucel, & Pantelis, 2010; Ferrier, Chowdhury, Thompson, Waston, & Young, 2004; Frantom, Allen, & Cross, 2008). For instance, Arts and colleagues (2008) followed up on a prior meta-analysis that implicated executive function and verbal memory as consistent deficits in euthymic patients (Robinson et al., 2006) and added first-degree relatives into their study. Verbal memory, attention, and executive functions all appear to be cognitive dysfunctions present in depressive or manic patients and were also deficient in the euthymic patients in this study. In summarizing studies, the authors found that euthymic patients universally performed poorly on all neurocognitive domains except for visuoconstruction and intelligence. The largest effect sizes were found in domains of working memory, executive control, concept shifting, fluency, immediate and delayed verbal recall, and processing speed. The variables that appeared the most sensitive included Digit Span backwards, Wisconsin Card Sorting Test (WCST) perseverative errors, Trails B, and fluency. In general, deficits in attention and executive functions may be linked to pathophysiological mechanisms found in the prefrontal cortex and anterior cingulate cortex (Strakowski, BelBello, Adler, & Sax, 2000). In addition, the basal ganglia has been identified as impaired in BD I (Strakowski et al., 2000), and such pathology may disrupt the connectivity between the frontal cortex and basal ganglia, further impeding attention and executive functions. When examining unaffected first-degree relatives of patients with BD I, the authors found small yet significant effect sizes in executive functioning and verbal memory only, providing support for considering these two neurocognitive variables as trait markers for genetic predisposition to BD I (Arts et al., 2008).

A second and more recent meta-analysis looked at 42 euthymic studies, 14 manic studies, and 9 depressed studies (Kurtz & Gerraty, 2009). Findings support the conclusion that verbal learning and memory had the largest effect sizes across all three mood states, with some additional impairment in nonverbal memory. Further, individuals in depressed states had reduced verbal fluency and both manic and depressed BD patients had exacerbated impairment in measures of verbal memory and learning. Most other neurocognitive domains had moderate to large effect sizes across all mood states, although visuospatial skills had the smallest effect size. These combined studies confirm that verbal learning and memory deficits remain the signature markers for BD I, with less consistent findings for other neurocognitive domains.

NEUROCOGNITIVE DEFICITS IN DEPRESSION AND MANIA

State-related deficits are characterized as transient and may change across mood episodes, whereas trait-related deficits are enduring and may reflect either underlying genetic components, making them potential endophenotypes for diagnosing BD, or acquired deficits that reflect length or severity of illness (Clark & Goodwin, 2008). Several studies have addressed this consideration by studying homogenous populations of depressed, manic, and euthymic patients with BD I.

It is well established that there is a wide range of neuropsychological abnormalities present in individuals with depression (Miller, 1975). Multiple subsequent studies have observed specific deficits in several neurocognitive domains during depressed episodes of BD I (Hermens, Naismith, Redoblado Hodge, Scott, & Hickie, 2010; Fossati et al., 2004). For instance, one early study compared normal controls with depressed patients with MDD and depressed patients with BD I. Although both the MDD and BD groups performed worse than the controls on the learning tasks, the BD I group performed at an even poorer level than the MDD group (Wolfe, Granholm, Butters, & Saunders, 1987). A more recent study compared depressed patients with BD with depressed patients with MDD (both first episode and recurrent episode) on a verbal learning test and found that both the BD I and recurrent MDD groups performed worse on the verbal learning tasks compared to the first episode MDD group. It may be, then, that deficits in verbal learning and memory may be worsened by repeated depressed episodes. Given that BD I is a more severe mood disorder than MDD with typically more depressed episodes (as well as manic or mixed episodes), verbal memory impairment may be an effect of recurring depression and less so a characteristic specific to BD I, which might be due to difficulties in encoding information in an organized manner and/or a lack of effort to retrieve memory, which is associated with increased dysfunction in the prefrontal cortex.

Nonverbal memory tasks are historically relevant, as it has been hypothesized in the past that right hemispheric impairment may be specific to BD whereas left hemispheric impairment may be more related to SZ (Flor-Henry, 1976, 1983). Although some subsequent studies have also identified lateralized differentiation in BD I (Frantom et al., 2008), overall the results have been negative in this regard. However, the fact remains that nonverbal tasks are often impaired in depressed patients with BD. For instance, a recent study examined depressed patients with matched controls and found selective impairment in visual and spatial recognition tasks (Rubinsztein, Michael, Underwood, Tempest, & Sahakian, 2006). However, a review of the extant literature prior to 2002 suggests that visuospatial tasks in general seem dependent on the tasks used and may not represent a global deficit in depressed patients as verbal learning and memory tasks appear to represent (Quraishi & Frangou, 2002).

Most controlled studies comparing IQ functioning in patients with BD I in depressed episodes and patients with MDD have found no differences between the two groups (Quraishi & Frangou, 2002). Although other cognitive deficits such as attention, executive functions, and affective processing have also been implicated in depressed patients with BD I, two recently published studies have challenged the notion that these deficits are inherently related to the depressed state, but rather related to the impact that medication plays in blunting cognitive processes in these areas (Holmes et al., 2008; Roiser et al., 2009). It may be difficult, then, to separate the neurocognitive deficits in depressed patients that are stable traits and those that may be side effects of medication. The one cognitive deficit that seems to be the exception to this is verbal learning and memory, as highlighted by the recent meta-analysis of five studies of patients with depressed function (Kurtz & Gerraty, 2009). However, such deficits may be a result of repeated mood episodes and not a preexisting characteristic of the disease itself. Recent studies also suggest that cognitive deficits requiring emotional processing may also be impaired independently of medication effects, providing support that such deficits may be enduring traits within BD I (Roiser et al., 2009). Murphy and Sahakian (2001) note that given the mood component of BD, tasks employing affective material may be fruitful in further examining the relationship between mood and cognition.

As might be expected, patients in acute manic phases have more impaired neurocognitive functioning than patients in depressed or euthymic phases. Two neurocognitive domains that appear impaired in patients in mania, while less affected in patients in depression, are executive functions and sustained attention (McGrath, Scheldt, Welham, & Clair, 1997; Quraishi & Frangou, 2002; Sweeney, Kmiec, & Kupfer, 2000). Patients with BD I in manic phases with acute psychosis also suffer significant impairment in verbal learning with levels approaching that of SZ patients (Albus et al., 1996). Another study found that patients in manic states perform worse than nonmanic patients, who in turn performed worse than controls (Fleck et al., 2003), suggesting an incremental decline in verbal memory that is further impeded by manic episodes. This further indicates that verbal memory and learning may not reflect preexisting characteristics of BD I but rather are cognitive "scars" that result from repeated mood episodes, particularly in the manic phase (Bebbington, 2004). Deficits have also been noted in nonverbal memory and learning performance for patients in mania both with and without a history of psychosis (Albus et al., 1996; Sweeney et al., 2000). Further, patients in manic episodes may have lower performance on measures of general intellectual functioning compared to controls (Quraishi & Frangou, 2002).

NEUROCOGNITIVE DEFICITS AND PSYCHOSIS IN BD

In addition to symptoms of mania and depression, some patients with BD I may express psychotic features during mood episodes, suggesting possible overlap between psychotic and affective disorder phenotypes. Further, the distinction between schizoaffective disorder and BD with psychotic features is not always clear, and it is possible that BD I and SZ represent two ends of a spectrum of disease with shared underlying genetic and cognitive traits, with BD I on the affective side and SZ on the psychotic side, and schizoaffective disorder and BD I with psychotic episodes in the intermediate zone (Ghaemi, Wingo, Fikowski, & Baldessarini, 2008; Jones et al., 2007). Given this possible overlap, there may be unique neurocognitive markers that distinguish BD I with psychosis (BD+) from BD I without psychosis (BD-) and indeed, there is a growing body of research that BD+ has been associated with greater neurocognitive impairment (Albus et al., 1996; Kravariti, Dixon, Frith, Murry, & McGuire, 2005).

More specifically, studies have implicated both spatial working memory and executive functions as markers that differentiate BD+ from BD− (Allen et al., 2010; Bora et al., 2007; Glahn et al., 2007; Tabarés-Seisdedos et al., 2003). A meta-analysis by Bora and colleagues (2010) examined 14 studies that compared patients with BD+ with patients with BD− on a number of cognitive variables. Results found that the BD+ group had greater impairment on global cognition, processing speed, working memory, and executive functions. The overall findings may suggest that the deficits related to working memory and executive functions represent an association between psychosis and frontal lobe abnormalities. However, the authors note that the effect sizes were in general small and psychosis alone could not explain neurocognitive deficits. Further research is needed because there have been similar neurocognitive deficits noted in BD+ and in SZ. As with other studies of neurocognition in BD I, the increased severity of deficits in BD+ have been identified in patients who are euthymic (Allen et al., 2010), suggesting that they may be useful as endophenotypes. Because patients in these studies are typically receiving psychotropic medications for management of mood symptoms, the influence of these medications cannot be ruled out. Additional support for overlap between the two disorders comes from the observation that the two most consistent neurocognitive deficits found in individuals with BD I, verbal memory and executive functions, are also typically impaired in individuals with SZ as well as their first-degree relatives (Heydebrand, 2006). When comparing neurocognitive functioning of patients with BD I with SZ, there are largest effect sizes in the differences between executive functions and verbal memory, with patients with BD I at an intermediate level between patients with SZ and controls (Krabbendam, Arts, van Os, & Aleman, 2005). This difference between the two disorders has been suggested by some to indicate that there are shared candidate genes (e.g., *COMT*) (Hill, Harris, Herbener, Pavuluri, & Sweeney, 2008; Murray, Sham, van Os, Zanelli, Cannon, 2004).

SOCIAL COGNITIVE DEFICITS IN BD

Social cognitive processes reflect unique cognitive operations that are dedicated to the processing of social information and allow for adaptive social interaction (Ostrum, 1984). Given that impairment in social functioning is often associated with psychiatric disorders, particularly SZ and more severe forms of BD I, this area has received increasing attention over the past decade. Support for distinguishing between nonsocial and social cognitive processes is provided by studies reporting only small to moderate correlations among social cognitive measures and standard neuropsychological tests, differential involvement of neural substrates when processing nonsocial and social information (Couture, Penn, & Roberts, 2006), and the view that development of the specialized information processing systems for social information is adaptive (Tooby & Cosmides, 2000). Like nonsocial cognitive processes, social cognitive processes encompass a variety of distinct yet related operations, with some common examples including facial affect perception and processing, social perception, and knowledge of social norms.

The available literature on social cognitive deficits associated with BD I is less comprehensive than it is for other cognitive deficits, although tentative conclusions can be made.

Studies on emotional recognition have suggested that patients with BD I have significant impairment in identifying primary emotions of faces (Getz, Shear, & Strakowski, 2003; Harmer, Grayson, & Goodwin, 2002; Lembke & Ketter, 2002; Yurgelun-Todd et al., 2000), although not all studies have found significant results (Addington & Addington, 1998), and it may be that such deficits are unique only in manic or possibly psychotic patients (Hill et al., 2008). Few studies have looked at recognition of emotional prosody, but some preliminary evidence suggests that this is impaired in patients in mania (Bozikas et al., 2007).

There is also support for theory of mind deficits in BD I, perhaps more so than with emotional recognition (Bora et al., 2005). These deficits may relate more to cognitive impairment with executive dysregulation associated with cognitive empathy deficits and less so with affective empathy (Montag et al., 2010; Shamay-Tsoory, Harari, Szepsenwol, & Levkovitz, 2009). Such impairments are further exacerbated by an inhibited neural network in key regions that process theory of mind tasks (Malhi et al., 2008). Further research may provide insight on how theory of mind relates to other domains of social cognition, as well as overall cognitive and functional outcome in individuals with BD I. Studies on emotional regulation suggest that individuals with BD I have deficits on signal-detection, decision-making, and reinforcement paradigm tasks (Murphy et al., 1999; 2001; Roiser et al., 2009). Other studies show deficits in patients in other areas thought to be related to social cognition including social perception (Shean, Murphy, & Meyer, 2005) and mirror neuron firings (Kim et al., 2009).

NEUROCOGNITIVE DEFICITS IN BD I AND BD II

There is some support for neurocognitive differences between BD I and BD II. Studies comparing the two groups generally find that patients with BD I exhibit impairment on tasks of sustained attention, verbal memory, and executive functions compared to patients with BD II and controls (Hsiao et al, 2009; Kung et al., 2010; Torrent et al., 2006). Hsiao and colleagues (2009) also found that patients with BD II had impairments only in processing speed and working memory compared to controls. Individuals with BD I may exhibit more impaired performance because of increased medication usage or psychotic features. Though these findings are promising, other studies have suggested that BD II is actually associated with worse cognitive outcome (Harkavy-Friedman et al., 2006), emphasizing the need for further research on BD II cognition. In addition, there still remains minimal research on the biological and genetic differences between BD I and BD II. This is an issue because BD II is often misdiagnosed as unipolar depression or a personality disorder, yet it may be more prevalent within the population than first thought (Vieta & Suppes, 2008).

DIAGNOSTIC PRACTICES

BD is clinically diagnosed via the *DSM-IV-TR*'s criteria, and there currently are no known neuropsychological profiles, neuroimaging studies, or laboratory findings that are accepted alternatives to the current behavioral diagnostic criteria (Mathews et al., 2003). As previously discussed, a manic or mixed episode meets criteria for a *DSM-IV-TR* diagnosis of BD I and is typically preceded or followed by a depressive episode, though this is not required. BD severity is usually determined by frequency of cyclic changes and presence of psychotic symptoms. The *DSM-IV-TR* lists several BD subtypes that are generally accepted within the mental health field. BD II is defined as having one or more hypomanic episodes, one or more major depressive episodes, and no manic or mixed episodes. Further, hypomania cannot cause significant impairment in the individual. The *DSM-IV-TR* also recognizes cyclothymic disorder, which is characterized by fluctuating hypomanic and depressive symptoms, though these depressive symptoms do not rise to the severity that characterizes a major depressive episode. These symptomatically distinct forms of BD have garnered interest in a spectrum model of BD, with extreme manic and unipolar depression representing one end and mild dysthymia with recurrent hypomanic episodes representing the middle area (Vieta & Suppes, 2008).

Vieta and Phillips (2007) review some of the current limitations in the diagnostic practice of BD including: (1) Psychotic symptoms are often present in BD but not part of the diagnostic criteria; (2) mood-congruent and mood-incongruent psychotic symptoms are not well defined; (3) depression in BD is indistinguishable from depression present in MDD; (4) previous depressive episodes are not recognized as a premorbid indicator of BD but rather may be diagnosed as MDD; (5) cognitive symptoms are not included; (6) substance-induced mood episodes are excluded; (7) family history, biological markers, and previous treatment response are not included; (8) duration criteria of manic and hypomanic episodes may be too long; (9) overactivity might be more common than euphoria during hypomanic episodes and (10) BD-NOS is often used as a "wastebasket" diagnosis, particularly in children and adolescents. Although supplemental tools such as the Bipolar Spectrum Diagnostic Scale (Ghaemi et al., 2005), the Hypomania Checklist (Angst et al., 2003), and the Young Mania Scale (Young, Biggs, Ziegler, & Meyer, 1978) may assist in identifying differences among BD subtypes, there remain clear challenges in accurate diagnoses. Mitchell, Goodwin, Johnson, and Hirschfeld (2008) attempted to resolve some of these challenges by identifying pathognomonic signs of bipolar depression that are qualitatively distinct from unipolar depression. They suggested that bipolar depression is more associated with hypersomnia, increased appetite, psychomotor retardation, psychotic symptoms, and mood lability with earlier age of onset, shorter depressive episodes, and family history of BD. In contrast, unipolar depression is associated with insomnia, decreased appetite, normal activity levels, and somatic complaints with later age of onset, longer episodes, and no family history of BD.

Recent forays into pediatric BD have demonstrated that it is difficult to accurately diagnose in youth and have caused some controversy (Danner et al., 2009). Indeed, the rate of diagnosing children with BD has increased an estimated 40-fold from 1987 to 2003 (Singh, 2008). One challenge in identifying pediatric BD is that *DSM-IV-TR* adult criteria are typically used to diagnose children and adolescents. However, BD has different symptom expression in youth. For instance, an estimated 70% of children with BD exhibit mood swings several times a day, rather than the sustained mood episodes typically expressed in adult cases (Biederman et al., 2000). Children with BD also appear to have longer symptomatic stages, fewer psychotic symptoms, and less diagnostic stability with diagnoses frequently changing between BD I and other subtypes such as BD-NOS. In addition, symptoms may be mistaken for attention deficit/hyperactivity disorder (ADHD) or, alternatively, ADHD might be misdiagnosed as BD. Longitudinal outcome studies largely confirm the validity of diagnosing children with BD, with many children identified as such continuing to meet criteria as they age (Birmaher et al., 2006; Geller, Tillman, Craney, & Bolhofner, 2004). Nevertheless, there remains a need for better diagnostic guidelines for identifying clinical cases, with many current assessment tools largely inadequate in correctly classifying pediatric BD (Diler et al., 2009).

Diagnosing BD in both adult and child populations might be assisted by identifying a reliable prodrome period. Unfortunately, no definitive prodrome stage has been identified at this time. Skjelstad and colleagues (2010) outlined common symptom clusters present in individuals before they are diagnosed with BD I including irritability, aggressiveness, sleep changes, depressive/manic signs, hyperactivity, anxiety, and mood swings with symptoms increasing in strength and frequency until criteria for a full mood episode are met. For individuals who are at risk of developing BD I, presence of these symptom clusters may signify the need for early intervention to prevent onset of the disorder or reduce its severity.

Vieta and Phillips (2007) present a dimensional model subsumed within the current categorical system of diagnosing BD, which may be considered in later iterations of the DSM. Certain symptoms prevalent in BD, such as psychosis, positive/negative symptoms, manic/depressive symptoms, cognitive impairment, anxiety, impulsivity, suicidality, among others might be rated across a four-point dimensional scale and factored into consideration when identifying subtype and severity. Vieta and Phillips also propose implementing a six-layered modular system that places the primary diagnosis on the first module but adds relevant dimensional features to the second module. The third module would include laboratory information such as genetic and neuroimaging findings, and the fourth module would factor current medical conditions (similar to the *DSM-IV-TR*'s Axis III). The fifth module would include personality factors and other variables derived through standard psychological assessment, and the sixth module would consider environmental factors. This system may provide further refinement and detail of the criteria needed to classify BD and other mental health disorders, as well as stimulate additional research derived from the information provided within each module. The forthcoming *DSM-5* does not include major changes in the diagnostic criteria for BD. The distinction between BD I and BD II will be continued, but a recommendation will be made to include a diagnosis of "Mixed Anxiety Depression."

TREATMENT

Pharmacotherapy remains the gold standard for treating BD, with supportive psychotherapy often provided concurrently. Recent meta-analyses consistently show the efficacy of mood stabilizers, particularly in treating the acute manic stages (Fountoulakis, Gonda, Vieta, & Schmidt, 2009; Tamayo, Zarate, Vieta, Vázquez, & Tohen, 2010). There is also evidence that mood stabilizers are safer and more effective than antidepressants in treating BD, highlighting the need for accurate diagnostic procedures differentiating BD from MDD (Ghaemi et al., 2008). Perhaps the most well-known mood stabilizer is lithium carbonate. The exact mechanism of action of lithium in stabilizing mood is still unclear, although it is thought to influence several neurotransmitters including catecholamine and acetylcholine (Wood & Goodwin, 1987), GABA (Volonte, Ciotti, & Merlo, 1994), and dopamine (Dunigan & Shamoo, 1995). Studies have also implicated glutamate as a key neurotransmitter and indicate that lithium facilitates glutamate uptake transporter capacity, hence reducing excitatory neurotransmission (Dixon, Los, & Hokin, 1994; Los, Artemenko, & Hokin, 1995). Lithium then may have neuroprotective qualities that block excitotoxicity due to excess glutamate and other metabolites, including ones linked to dementia (Kessing, Forman, & Andersen, 2010). Despite its effectiveness, lithium appears to have adverse effects on cognition with deficits in short-term memory, motor functioning, and verbal fluency typically observed (Goldberg, 2008). However, a recent meta-analysis of 12 studies led to the conclusion that lithium treatment has few and minor negative effects on cognition (Wingo, Wingo, Harvey, & Baldessarini, 2009).

Anticonvulsant drugs including carbamazepine, valproate, and lamotrigine have been shown to be effective in treating BD (Mathews et al., 2003) and may have less severe effects on cognitive abilities compared to lithium (Goldberg, 2008). There is some evidence that lamotrigine is as effective as lithium (Licht, Nielsen, Gram, Vestergaard, & Bendz, 2010). Further, second-generation antipsychotic drugs such as olanzapine have shown promise in treating manic symptoms (McElroy & Keck, 2000). Some researchers have looked for common mechanisms of action among lithium, anticonvulsant drugs, and atypical antipsychotics to better understand the biochemistry of BD. Although empirical data are still sparse and no clear hypothesis has emerged, general findings do suggest that all medications may have neuroprotective effects. For example, inositol, a chemical compound vital for the formation of cell membranes, is protected by lithium and anticonvulsants (Williams, Cheng, Mudge, & Harwood, 2002). However, these findings are equivocal in nature and so the potential neuroprotective effects remain uncertain.

The common cognitive deficits in executive functions, verbal memory, and attention may be a target of intervention in BD treatment planning. Treating cognitive dysfunction in BD has yet to receive the same attention as in SZ, where such initiatives as the Measurement of Treatment Effects on Cognition in Schizophrenia (MATRICS; Marder & Fenton, 2004) and the Cognitive Neuroscience-Based Approach to Measuring and Improving Treatment Effects on Cognition in Schizophrenia (CNTRICS; Carter & Barch, 2007) were formed to develop test batteries that may be used to evaluate changes in neurocognition in response to specific treatments designed to ameliorate neurocognitive deficits. However, targeting cognitive impairment in BD may also prove to be a fruitful endeavor, in part because such impairment is sometimes a side effect of medication. It remains unknown how to target the cognitive effects of medication in BD, which is an issue in managing the long-term outcomes of this disease (Goldberg & Chengappa, 2009). Although at least one recent study examined the effects of targeted cognitive rehabilitation on BD, with promising findings that such treatment can improve mood symptoms (Deckersbach et al., 2010), the extent to which cognitive rehabilitation may factor into treatment planning remains unclear.

Findings on the efficacy of psychotherapy have also been mixed. A recent meta-analysis found only a small effect size for cognitive-behavioral therapy (CBT) for reducing manic symptoms in BD patients (Gregory, 2010). Another meta-analysis of randomized controlled studies found that CBT may reduce depressive symptoms, but overall is ineffective for treating manic symptoms and has no effect on preventing relapse rates (Lynch, Laws, & McKenna, 2010). However, some of the conclusions of this meta-analysis have met with criticism (Lincoln, 2010), and there is also evidence that supportive psychotherapies used in tandem with medication can lead to reduction in relapse rates (Lam, Burbeck, Wright, & Pilling, 2009; Scott, Colom, & Vieta, 2007). Aside from standard CBT or general psychotherapy, there is some promise in the efficacy of integrative therapies such as dialectical behavior therapy or family-focused therapy in treating BD, given their emphasis on emotional regulation, psychoeducation, and systems support (Miklowitz & Goldstein, 2010).

SUMMARY

Bipolar disorder (BD) is characterized by alternating and recurrent shifts in mood. Recent advances have identified genetic, neuroanatomical, biochemical, and neurocognitive correlates of BD that have expanded our understanding of the presentations etiological roots and functional impact. A number of factors including mood state, measures administered, medication effects, and subject pool can influence the results of studies examining cognition in BD. Nonetheless, when the literature is reviewed, some consistent findings are evident. Most consistent are the deficits found in verbal learning and memory, which appear in all three mood states as well as in unmedicated patients (Arts et al., 2008; Kurtz & Gerraty, 2009; Quraishi & Frangou, 2002; Roiser et al., 2009; Sanchez-Morla et al., 2009). Impairments in verbal learning then may be trait deficits in BD I, although they may be linked to duration of illness and number and number of episodes, raising the possibility that they are "scars" rather than preexisting deficits (Bebbington, 2004). On the other hand degree relatives of patients with BD I also exhibit verbal memory deficits, providing some evidence that verbal impairment may be genetically linked and then further exacerbated by mood episodes. Executive dysfunction appears to be a core cognitive impairment as well (Krabbendam et al., 2005), although some findings suggest that executive function deficits are selective (Robinson et al., 2006) whereas other findings indicate that there is a more global dysfunction (Sanchez-Morla et al., 2009). Recent findings that have separated BD+ from BD- have further suggested that working memory may be a unique marker for psychosis in BD+ (Allen et al., 2010; Bora et al., 2007, 2010). Although visual memory and learning and sustained attention have also been found to be impaired in BD I (Clark & Goodwin, 2008; Sanchez-Morla et al., 2009), such findings are less consistent than those on verbal memory and executive functions and may be more influenced by mood state or medication status.

Executive functioning may serve as an endophenotype candidate, given its persistent impairment across mood state and remission status (Arts et al., 2008; Clark & Goodwin, 2008; Hasler et al., 2006). Deficits in verbal learning and memory are also viable candidates. A meta-analysis of familial studies of BD I specifically examined potential neurocognitive endophenotypes, and of these, verbal learning and memory most consistently showed significant differences between first-degree relatives and healthy controls with 54% of all studies finding differences (Balanza-Martinez et al., 2008). Working memory came in second at 33% of the studies. About 12%-25% of the studies found significant differences on other domains. The authors conclude from this that verbal learning and memory and possibly working memory are the most promising endophenotype candidates in BD, whereas verbal fluency, immediate memory, and general intelligence show less consistency. Given working memory's relationship with executive functions (Baddeley, 2000), we can possibly further infer that executive function is implicated from this meta-analysis, although executive functions were not directly evaluated in the study.

However, some studies have failed to find support for verbal learning and memory as a cognitive endophenotype (Ferrier et al., 2004; Frantom et al., 2008; Langenecker, Saunders, Kade, Ransom, & McInnis, 2010), highlighting the need to further evaluate the genetic risk that may be associated with this cognitive domain. Also, as previously suggested, deficits in verbal learning and memory may reflect a long history of mood and particularly manic episodes, rather than representing a genetically linked endophenotype (Bebbington, 2004). Verbal memory may also be influenced by external factors, such as education or socioeconomic status. Alternative endophenotypic candidates proposed in these studies include visual memory, processing speed, and fine motor speed (Frantom et al., 2008; Langenecker et al., 2010).

From both a diagnostic and treatment standpoint, practices remain rooted in tradition. Diagnostic practices continue to utilize the traditional behavioral diagnostic criteria as set forth by the *DSM-IV-TR* with limitations of this system being conveyed in the literature (e.g. Vieta & Phillips, 2007; Mitchell et al. 2008). Within the pediatric domain, accurate diagnosis becomes more vexing as there remains a need for refined diagnostic guidelines and better objective measures.

Pharmacotherapy remains the gold standard in the treatment of BD. Mood stabilizers and anticonvulsants represent the most commonly employed agents; both demonstrating efficacy within the literature. Psychotherapy remains a useful supplement to the treatment benefits of pharmacotherapy. Moving forward, the cognitive deficits associate with BD and its treatment may be increasingly targeted for intervention. Such a movement may prove beneficial in reducing the functional burden of the disorder and thereby improving the quality of life of patients.

REFERENCES

Addington, J., & Addington, D. (1998). Facial affect recognition and information processing in schizophrenia and bipolar disorder. *Schizophrenia Research, 32,* 171–181.

Albus, M., Hubmann, W., Wahlheim, C., Sobizack, N., Franz, U., et al. (1996). Contrasts in neuropsychological test profile between patients with first-episode schizophrenia and first-episode affective disorder. *Acta Psychiatrica Scandinavica, 94,* 87–93.

Allen, D. N., Randall, C., Bello, D., Armstrong, C., Frantom, L., et al. (2010). *Are working memory deficits in bipolar disorder markers for psychosis? Neuropsychology, 24*(2), 244–254.

American Psychiatric Association. (2000). *Diagnostic and statistical manual of mental disorders* (4th ed., text revision).Washington, DC: American Psychiatric Association.

Angst, J., Gamma, A., Benazzi, F., Ajdacic, V., Eich, D., et al. (2003). Toward a re-definition of subthreshold bipolarity: Epidemiology and proposed criteria for bipolar-II, minor bipolar disorders, and hypomania. *Journal of Affective Disorders, 73,* 133–146.

Arts, B., Jabben, N., Krabbendam, L., & van Os, J. (2008). Meta-analysis of cognitive functioning in euthymic bipolar patients and their first-degree relatives. *Psychological Medicine, 38,* 771–785.

Baddeley, A. (2000). Short-term and working memory. In E. Tulving & F. I. M. Craik (Eds.), *The Oxford handbook of memory.* Oxford: Oxford University Press.

Balanza-Martinez, V., Rubio, C., Selva-Vera, G., Martinez-Aran, A., Sanchez-Moreno, J., et al. (2008). Neurocognitive endophenotypes (Endophenocognitypes) from studies of relatives of bipolar disorder subjects. *Neuroscience and Biobehavioral Reviews, 32,* 1426–1438.

Basterreche, N., Dávila, R., Zumárraga, M., Arrúe, A., González-Torres, M., Zamalloa, M., et al. (2009). Biological correlates of the congruence and incongruence of psychotic symptoms in patients with type 1 bipolar disorder. *Neuropsychobiology, 58*(3), 111–117.

Baumann, B., Danos, P., Krell, D., Diekmann, S., Wurthmann, C., Bielau, H., et al. (1999). Unipolar-bipolar dichotomy of mood disorders is supported by noradrenergic brainstem system morphology. *Journal of Affective Disorders, 54,* 217–224.

Bebbington, P. (2004). Recent findings in bipolar affective disorder. *Psychological Medicine, 34*(5), 767–776.

Bellivier, F., Golmard, J., Rietschel, M., Schulze, T. G., Malafosse, A., et al. (2003). Age of onset in bipolar I affective disorder: Further evidence for three subgroups. *American Journal of Psychiatry, 160,* 999–1001.

Benes, F. M., Kwok, E. W., Vincent, S. L & Todtenkopf, M. S. (1998). A reduction of nonpyramidal cells in sector CA2 of schizophrenics and manic depressives. *Biological Psychiatry, 44,* 88–97.

Biederman, J., Mick, E., Faraone, S. V., Spencer, T., Wilens, T. E., et al. (2000). Pediatric mania: A developmental subtype of bipolar disorder? *Biological Psychiatry, 48,* 458–466.

Birmaher, B., Axelson, D., Strober, M., Gill, M. K., Valeri, S., et al. (2006). Clinical course of children and adolescents with bipolar spectrum disorders. *Archives of General Psychiatry, 63*(2), 175–183.

Blumberg, H. P., Stern, E., Martinez, D., et al. (2000). Increased anterior cingulate and caudate activity in bipolar mania. *Biological Psychiatry, 48,* 1045–1052.

Bora, E., Vahip, S., Akdeniz, F., Gonul, A. S., Eryavuz, A., Ogut, M., et al. (2007). The effect of previous psychotic mood episodes on cognitive impairment in euthymic bipolar patients. *Bipolar Disorders, 9,* 468–477.

Bora, E., Vahip, S., Gonul, A. S., Akdeniz, F., Alkan, M., et al. (2005). Evidence for theory of mind deficits in euthymic patients with bipolar disorder. *Acta Psychiatrica Scandinavica, 112,* 110–116.

Bora, E., Yucel, M., & Pantelis, C. (2010). Neurocognitive markers for psychosis in bipolar disorder: A meta-analytic study. *Journal of Affective Disorders, 127*(1–3), 1–9.

Bourgeois, M. L., & Marneros, A. (2000). The prognosis of bipolar disorders: Course and outcome. In A. Marneros & J. Angst (Eds.), *Bipolar disorders: 100 Years after manic-depressive insanity* (pp. 405–436). UK: Kluwer Academic Publishers.

Bozikas, V. P., Kosmidis, M. H., Tonia, T., Andreou, C., Focas, K., et al. (2007). Impaired perception of affective prosody in remitted patients with bipolar disorder. *The Journal of Neuropsychiatry and Clinical Neurosciences, 19,* 436–440.

Bruder, G. E., Keilp, J. G., Xu, H., Shikhman, M., Schori, E., et al. (2005). Catechol-O-methyltransferase (COMT) gentoypes and working memory: Associations with differing cognitive operations. *Biological Psychiatry, 58*(11), 901–907.

Burmeister, M., McInnis, M. G., & Zollner, S. (2008). Psychiatric genetics: Progress amid controversy. *Nature Reviews Genetics, 9,* 527–540.

Carter, C. S., & Barch, D. M. (2007). Cognitive neuroscience-based approaches to measuring and improving treatment effects on cognition in schizophrenia: the CNTRICS initiative. Schizophr Bulletin, *33*(5), 1131–1137.

Chue, P., & Cheung, R. (2006). Minimizing the risk of diabetes in patients with schizophrenia and bipolar disorder. *International Journal of Psychiatry in Clinical Practice, 10*(2), 105–116.

Clark, L., & Goodwin, G. (2008). Attentional and executive functioning in bipolar disorder. In J. F. Goldberg & K. E. Burdick (Eds.), *Cognitive dysfunction in bipolar disorder* (pp. 23–47). VA: American Psychiatric Publishing, Inc.

Clark, L., Iversen, S. D., & Goodwin, G. M. (2001). A neuropsychological investigation of prefrontal cortex involvement in acute mania. *American Journal of Psychiatry, 158,* 1605–1611.

Clark, L., Iversen, S. D., & Goodwin, G. M. (2002). Sustained attention deficit in bipolar disorder. *British Journal of Psychiatry, 180,* 313–319.

Clark, L., Kempton, M., Scarnà, A., Grasby, P., & Goodwin, G. (2005). Sustained attention-deficit confirmed in euthymic bipolar disorder but not in first-degree relatives of bipolar patients or euthymic unipolar depression. *Biological Psychiatry, 57*(2), 183–187.

Colin, S. F., Chang, H. C., Mollner, S., Pfeuffer, T., Reed, R. R., et al. (1991). Chronic lithium regulates the expression of adenylate cyclase and Gi-protein alpha subunit in rat cerebral cortex. *Proceedings of the National Academy of Science USA, 88,* 10634–10637.

Connerny, I., Shapiro, P. A., McLaughlin, J. S., et al. (2001). Relation between depression after coronary artery bypass surgery and 12-month outcome: A prospective study. *Lancet, 358,* 1766–1771.

Couture, S. M., Penn, D. L., & Roberts, D. L. (2006). The functional significance of social cognition in schizophrenia: A review. *Schizophrenia Bulletin, 32, S1,* 44–63.

Danner, S., Fristad, M. A., Arnold, L. E., Youngstrom, E. A., Birmaher, B., Horwitz, S. M., et al. (2009). Early-onset bipolar spectrum disorders: diagnostic issues. *Clinical Child Family Psychology Review, 12*(3), 271–293.

De Hert, M., Dekker, J., Wood, D., Kahl, K., Holt, R., & Möller, H. (2009). Cardiovascular disease and diabetes in people with severe mental illness position statement from the European Psychiatric Association (EPA), supported by the European Association for the Study of Diabetes (EASD) and the European Society of Cardiology (ESC). *European Psychiatry, 24*(6), 412–424.

Deckersbach, T., Nierenberg, A., Kessler, R., Lund, H., Ametrano, R., Sachs, G., et al. (2010). Cognitive rehabilitation for bipolar disorder: An open trial for employed patients with residual depressive symptoms. *CNS Neuroscience & Therapeutics, 16*(5), 298–307.

Deep-Soboslay, A., Iglesias, B., Hyde, T., Bigelow, L., Imamovic, V., Herman, M., et al. (2008). Evaluation of tissue collection for postmortem studies of bipolar disorder. *Bipolar Disorders, 10*(7), 822–828.

Depp, C. A., Mausbach, B. T., Harvey, P. D., Bowie, C. R., Wolyniec, P. S., Thornquist, M. H., et al. (2010). Social competence and observer-rated social functioning in bipolar disorder. *Bipolar Disorders, 12*(8), 843–850.

Diler, R., Birmaher, B., Axelson, D., Goldstein, B., Gill, M., Strober, M., et al. (2009). The Child Behavior Checklist (CBCL) and the CBCL-bipolar phenotype are not useful in diagnosing pediatric bipolar disorder. *Journal of Child and AdolescentPsychopharmacology, 19*(1), 23–30.

Dixon, J. F., Los, G. V., & Hokin, L. E. (1994) Lithium stimulates glutamate 'release' and inositol 1, 4, 5-trisphosphate accumulation via activation of the N-methyl-D-aspartate receptor in monkey and mouse cerebral cortex slices. *Proceedings of the National Academy of Sciences USA, 91*, 8358–8362.

Drevets, W. C., Price, J. L., Bardgett, M. E., Reich, T., Todd, R. D., et al. (2002). Glucose metabolism in the amygdala in depression: Relationship to diagnostic subtype and plasma cortical levels. *Pharmacology Biochemistry and Behavior, 71*, 431–447.

Drevets, W. C., Price, J. L., Simpson, J. R. Jr., Todd, R. D. Riech, T., et al. (1997). Subgenual prefrontal cortex abnormalities in mood disorders. *Nature, 386*, 824–827.

Dunigan, C. D., & Shamoo, A. E. (1995). LI+ stimulates ATP-regulated dopamine uptake in PC12 cells. *Neuroscience, 65*, 1–4.

Elgamal, S., Sokolowska, M., & MacQueen, G. (2008). Memory deficits associated with bipolar disorder. In J. F. Goldberg & K. E. Burdick (Eds.), *Cognitive dysfunction in bipolar disorder* (pp. 49–67). VA: American Psychiatric Publishing, Inc.

Ewald, H. (2000). Genetics of bipolar affective disorder. In A. Marneros & J. Angst (Eds.), *Bipolar disorders: 100 Years after manic-depressive insanity* (pp. 243–280). UK: Kluwer Academic Publishers.

Ferrier, I. N., Chowdhury, R., Thompson, J. M., Waston, S., & Young, A. H. (2004). Neurocognitive function in unaffected first-degree relatives of patients with bipolar disorder: A preliminary report. *Bipolar Disorders, 6*, 319–322.

Fleck, D. E., Shear, P. K., Zimmerman, M. E., Getz, G. E., Corey, K. B., Jak, A.,et al. (2003). Verbal memory in mania: Effects of clinical state and task requirements. *Bipolar Disorders, 5*, 375.

Flor-Henry, P. (1976). Lateralized temporal-limbic dysfunction and psychopathology. *Annals of the New York Academy of Science, 280*, 777–797.

Flor-Henry, P. (1983). Functional hemispheric asymmetry and psychopathology. *Integrative Psychiatry, 1*, 46–52.

Fornito, A., Yücel, M., Wood, S., Bechdolf, A., Carter, S., Adamson, C., et al. (2009). Anterior cingulate cortex abnormalities associated with a first psychotic episode in bipolar disorder. *British Journal of Psychiatry, 194*(5), 426–433.

Fossati, P., Harvey, P., Bastard, G., Ergis, A., Jouvent, R., & Allilaire, J. (2004). Verbal memory performance of patients with a first depressive episode and patients with unipolar and bipolar recurrent depression. *Journal of Psychiatric Research, 38*(2), 137–144.

Fountoulakis, K., Gonda, X., Vieta, E., & Schmidt, F. (2009). Treatment of psychotic symptoms in bipolar disorder with aripiprazole monotherapy: A meta-analysis. *Annals of General Psychiatry, 8*, 10.1186/1744-859X-8-27.

Frantom, L., Allen, D. N., & Cross, C. (2008). Neurocognitive endophenotypes for bipolar disorder. *Bipolar Disorders, 10*(3), 387–399.

Geller, B., Tillman, R., Craney, J. L., Bolhofner, K. (2004). Four-year prospective outcome and natural history of mania in children with a prepubertal and early adolescent bipolar disorder phenotype. *Archives of General Psychiatry, 61*, 459–467.

Gershon, E. S., & Goldin, L. R. (1986). Clinical methods in psychiatric genetics. I. Robustness of genetic marker investigative strategies. *Acta Psychiatrica Scandinavica, 74*, 113–118.

Getz, G. E., Shear, P. K., & Strakowski, S. M. (2003). Facial affect recognition deficits in bipolar disorder. *Journal of the International Neuropsychology Society, 9*(4), 623–632.

Ghaemi, N. S., Miller, C. J., Berv, D. A., Klugman, J., Rosenquist, K. J., et al. (2005). Sensitivity and specificity of a new bipolar spectrum diagnostic scale. *Journal of Affective Disorders, 84*, 273–277.

Ghaemi, S., Wingo, A., Filkowski, M., & Baldessarini, R. (2008). Long-term antidepressant treatment in bipolar disorder: Meta-analyses of benefits and risks. *Acta Psychiatrica Scandinavica, 118*(5), 347–356.

Glahn, D. C., Bearden, C. E., Barguil, M., Barrett, J., Reichenberg, A., Bowden, C. L., et al. (2007). The neurocognitive signature of psychotic bipolar disorder. *Biological Psychiatry, 62*, 910–916.

Goghari, V., & Sponheim, S. (2008). Differential association of the COMT Vall58Met polymorphism with clinical phenotypes in schizophrenia and bipolar disorder. *Schizophrenia Research, 103*(1), 186–191.

Goldberg, J. F. (2008). Adverse cognitive effects of psychotropic medications. In J. F. Goldberg & K. E. Burdick (Eds.), *Cognitive dysfunction in bipolar disorder: A guide for clinicians* (pp. 137–158). Washington, DC: American Psychiatric Press.

Goldberg, J. F., & Chengappa, K. N. (2009). Identifying and treating cognitive impairment in bipolar disorder. *Bipolar Disorders, 11*(2), 123–137.

Goodwin, G. M., Cavanagh, J. T., Glabus, M. T., et al. (1997). Uptake of 99mTc-exametazime shown by single photon emission single computed tomography before and after lithium withdrawal in bipolar patients: Association with mania. *The British Journal of Psychiatry, 170*, 426–430.

Gottesman, I. I., & Gould, T. J. (2003). The endophenotype concept in psychiatry: Etymology and strategic interventions. *American Journal of Psychiatry, 160,* 636–645.

Gottesman, I. I., & Shields, J. (1973). Genetic theorizing and schizophrenia. *The British Journal of Psychiatry, 122,* 15–30.

Gourovitch, M. L., Torrey, E. F., Gold, J. M., Randolph, C., Weinberger, D. R., et al. (1999). Neuropsychological performance of monozygotic twins discordant for bipolar disorder. *Biological Psychiatry, 45,* 639–646.

Gregory, V. (2010). Cognitive-behavioral therapy for mania: A meta-analysis of randomized controlled trials. *Social Work in Mental Health, 8*(6), 483–494.

Haldane, M., & Frangou, S. (2006). Functional neuroimaging studies in mood disorders. *Acta Neuropsychiatrica, 18,* 88–99.

Harkavy-Friedman, J. M., Keilp, J. G., Grunebaum, L. S., Sher, L., Printz, D., et al. (2006). Are BPI and BPII suicide attempters distinct neuropsychologically? *Journal of Affective Disorders, 94,* 255–259.

Harley, C., Li, H., Corey-Lisle, P., L'Italien, G., & Carson, W. (2007). Influence of medication choice and comorbid diabetes: The cost of bipolar disorder in a privately insured US population. *Social Psychiatry and Psychiatric Epidemiology, 42*(9), 690–697.

Harmer, C. J., Grayson, L., & Goodwin, G. M. (2002). Enhanced recognition of disgust in bipolar illness. *Biological Psychiatry, 51,* 298–304.

Harvey, I., Persaud, R., Ron, M. A., Baker, G., & Murray, R. M. (1994). Volumetric MRI measurements in bipolars compared with schizophrenics and healthy controls. *Psychological Medicine, 24,* 689–699.

Hasler, G., Drevets, W., Gould, T., Gottesman, I., & Manji, H. (2006). Toward constructing an endophenotype strategy for bipolar disorders. *Biological Psychiatry, 60*(2), 93–105.

Hermens, D., Naismith, S., Redoblado Hodge, M., Scott, E., & Hickie, I. (2010). Impaired verbal memory in young adults with unipolar and bipolar depression. *Early Intervention in Psychiatry, 4*(3), 227–233.

Heydebrand, G. (2006). Cognitive deficits in the families of patients with schizophrenia. *Current Opinion in Psychiatry, 19,* 277–281.

Hill, K. S., Harris, M. S. H., Herbener, E. S., Pavuluri, M., & Sweeney, J. A. (2008). Neurocognitive allied phenotypes for schizophrenia and bipolar disorder. *Schizophrenia Bulletin, 34*(4), 743–759.

Holmes, M. K., Erickson, K., Luckenbaugh, D. A., Drevets, W. C., Bain, E. E. Cannon, D. M., et al. (2008). A comparison of cognitive functioning in medicated and unmedicated subjects with bipolar depression. *Bipolar Disorders, 10,* 806–815.

Hsiao, Y., Wu, Y., Wu, J., Hsu, M., Chen, H., Lee, S., et al. (2009). Neuropsychological functions in patients with bipolar I and bipolar II disorder. *Bipolar Disorders, 11*(5), 547–554.

Jones, I., Hamshere, M., Nangle, J. M., Bennett, P., Green, E., Heron, J., et al. (2007). Bipolar affective puerperal psychosis: genome-wide significant evidence for linkage to chromosome 16. *American Journal of Psychiatry, 164*(7), 1099–1104.

Kaladjian, A., Jeanningros, R., Azorin, J., Nazarian, B., Roth, M., & Mazzola-Pomietto, P. (2009). Reduced brain activation in euthymic bipolar patients during response inhibition: An event-related fMRI Study. *Psychiatry Research: Neuroimaging, 173*(1), 45–51.

Kato, T. (2007). Molecular genetics of bipolar disorder and depression. *Psychiatry and Clinical Neurosciences, 61*(1), 3–19.

Keck, P. E., McElroy, S. L., & Arnold, L. M. (2001). Advances in the pathophysiology and treatment of psychiatric disorders: Implications of internal medicine. Bipolar disorder. *Medical Clinics of North America, 84,* 645–661.

Kempton, M. J., Geddes, J. R., Ettinger, U., Williams, S. C. R., & Grasby, P. M. (2008). Meta-analysis, database, and meta-regression of 98 structural imaging studies in bipolar disorder. *Archives of General Psychiatry, 65*(9), 1017–1032.

Kessing, L., Forman, J., & Andersen, P. (2010). Does lithium protect against dementia? *Bipolar Disorders, 12*(1), 87–94.

Kieseppa, T., Partonen, T., Haukka, J., Kaprio, J., & Lonnqvist, J. (2004). High concordance of bipolar I disorder in a nationwide sample of twins. *American Journal of Psychiatry, 10,* 1814–1821.

Kim, E., Jung, Y., Ku, J., Kim, J., Lee, H., Kim, S., et al. (2009). Reduced activation in the mirror neuron system during a virtual social cognition task in euthymic bipolar disorder. *Progress in Neuro-Psychopharmacology & Biological Psychiatry, 33*(8), 1409–1416

Krabbendam, L Arts, B., van Os, L., & Aleman, A. (2005). Cognitive functioning in patients with schizophrenia and bipolar disorder: A quantitative review. *Schizophrenia Research, 80,* 137–149.

Krabbendam, L., Honig, A., Weisman, J., Vuurman, E. F. P. M., Hofman, P. A. M., et al. (2000). Cognitive dysfunctions and white matter lesions in patients with bipolar disorder in remission. *Acta Psychatrica Scandinavica, 101,* 274–280.

Kravariti, E., Dixon, T., Frith, C., Murry, R., & McGuire, P. (2005). Association of symptoms and executive function in schizophrenia and bipolar disorder. *Schizophrenia Research, 74*(2–3), 221–231.

Kujawa, M. J., & Nemeroff, C. B. (2000). The biology of bipolar disorder. In A. Marneros & J. Angst (Eds.), *Bipolar disorders: 100 Years after manic-depressive insanity* (pp. 281–314). UK: Kluwer Academic Publishers.

Kung, C., Lee, S., Chang, Y., Wu, J., Chen, S., Chen, S., et al. (2010). Poorer sustained attention in bipolar I than bipolar II disorder. *Annals of General Psychiatry, 10.* Retrieved from PsycINFO database.

Kurtz, M., & Gerraty, R. (2009). A meta-analytic investigation of neurocognitive deficits in bipolar illness: Profile and effects of clinical state. *Neuropsychology, 23*(5), 551–562.

Lam, D., Burbeck, R., Wright, K., & Pilling, S. (2009). Psychological therapies in bipolar disorder: The effect of illness history on relapse prevention—A systematic review. *Bipolar Disorders, 11*(5), 474–482.

Lander, E. S., & Kruglyak, L. (1995). Genetic dissection of complex traits in humans: New methods using a complete RFLP linkage map. *Nature Genetics, 11,* 241–217.

Langenecker, S., Saunders, E., Kade, A., Ransom, M., & McInnis, M. (2010). Intermediate: Cognitive phenotypes in bipolar disorder. *Journal of Affective Disorders, 122*(3), 285–293.

Leboyer, M., Bellivier, F., Nosten-Bertrand, M., Jouvent, R., Pauls, D., et al. (1998). Psychiatric genetics: Search for phenotypes. *Trends in Neurosciences, 21,* 102–105.

Lembke, A., & Ketter, T. A. (2002). Impaired recognition of facial emotion in mania. *American Journal of Psychiatry, 159*(2), 302–304.

Lenox, H., Gould, T. D., & Manji, H. F. (2002). Endophenotypes in bipolar disorder. *American Journal of Medical Genetics, 114,* 391–406.

Licht, R. W., Nielsen, J. N., Gram, L. F., Vestergaard, P., & Bendz, H. (2010). Langrotine versus lithium as maintenance treatment in bipolar I disorder: an open randomized effectiveness study mimicking clinical practice: The 6th trial of the Danish University Antidepressant Group (DUAG06). *Bipolar Disorders, 12,* 483–493.

Lincoln, T. (2010). A comment on Lynch et al. (2009): Cognitive behavioural therapy for major psychiatric disorder: Does it really work? A meta-analytical review of well-controlled trials. *Psychological Medicine: A Journal of Research in Psychiatry and the Allied Sciences, 40*(5), 877–879.

Liu, Y., Blackwood, D. H., Caesar, S., de Geus, E. J., Farmer, A., et al. (2010). Meta-analysis of genome-wide association data of bipolar disorder and major depressive disorder. *Molecular Psychiatry.* Retrieved April 11, 2010 from http://www.tweelingenregister.org/nederlands/verslaggeving/NTR-publicaties_2010/Liu_MP_2010epub.pdf.

Los, G. V., Artemenko, I. P., & Hokin, L. E. (1995). Time-dependent effects of lithium on the agonist-stimulated accumulation of second messenger inositol 1, 4, 5-trisophosphate in SH-SY5Y human neuroblastoma cells. *Biochemical Journal, 311,* 225–232.

Lynch, D., Laws, K., & McKenna, P. (2010). Cognitive behavioural therapy for major psychiatric disorder: Does it really work? A meta-analytical review of well-controlled trials. *Psychological Medicine: A Journal of Research in Psychiatry and the Allied Sciences, 40*(1), 9–24.

McDonald, C., Zanelli, J., Rabe-Hesketh, S., Ellison-Wright, I., Sham, P., et al. (2004). Meta-analysis of magnetic resonance imaging brain morphometry studies in bipolar disorder. *Biological Psychiatry, 56,* 411–417.

McElroy, S. L., & Keck, P. E. (2000). Pharmacologic agents for the treatment of acute bipolar mania. *Biological Psychiatry, 48,* 539–557.

McGrath, J., Scheldt, S., Welham, J., & Clair, A. (1997). Performance on tests sensitive to impaired executive ability in schizophrenia, mania and well controls: Acute and subacute phases. *Schizophrenia Research, 26*(2), 127–137.

MacQueen, G. M., Hajek, T., & Alda, M. (2005). The phenotypes of bipolar disorder: Relevance for genetic investigations. *Molecular Psychiatry, 10,* 811–826.

Malhi, G. S., Lagopoulos, J., Das, P., Moss, K., Berk, M., et al. (2008). A functional MRI study of Theory of Mind in euthymic bipolar disorder patients. *Bipolar Disorders, 10,* 943–956.

Marder, S. R., & Fenton, W. (2004). Measurement and treatment research to improve cognition in schizophrenia: NIMH MATRICS initiative to support the development of agents for improving cognition in schizophrenia. *Schizophrenia Research, 72,* 5–9.

Mathews, C. A., Reus, V. I., & Freimer, N. B. (2003). Bipolar disorder. In R. N. Rosenberg, S. Prusiner, S. DiMauro, & R. Barchi (Eds.), *The molecular and genetic basis of neurologic and psychiatric disease, vol. 3* (pp. 741–753). UK: Butterworth-Heinemann.

Migliorelli, R., Starkstein, S. E., Teson, A. et al. (1993). SPECT findings in patients with primary mania. *The Journal of Neuropsychiatry and Clinical Neurosciences,* 379–383.

Miklowitz, D., & Goldstein, T. (2010). Family-based approaches to treating bipolar disorder in adolescence: Family-focused therapy and dialectical behavior therapy. *Understanding bipolar disorder: A developmental psychopathology perspective* (pp. 466–493). New York, NY: Guilford Press.

Miller, W. R. (1975). Psychological deficit in depression. *Psychological Bulletin, 82,* 238–260.

Mitchell, P. B., Goodwin, G. M., Johnson, G. F., & Hirschfeld, R. M. A. (2008). Diagnostic guidelines for bipolar depression: A probabilistic approach. *Bipolar Disorders, 10*, 144–152.

Montag, C., Ehrlich, A., Neuhaus, K., Dziobek, I., Heekeren, H., Heinz, A., et al. (2010). Theory of mind impairments in euthymic bipolar patients. *Journal of Affective Disorders, 123*(1–3), 264–269.

Murphy, F. C., & Sahakian, B. J. (2001). Neuropsychology of bipolar disorder. *British Journal of Psychiatry, 178*(41), s120–s127.

Murphy, F. C., Rubinsztein, J., Michael, A., Rogers, R., Robbins, T., Paykel, E., et al. (2001). Decision-making cognition in mania and depression. *Psychological Medicine, 31*(4), 679–693.

Murphy, F. C., Sahakian, B. J., Rubinsztein, J. S., Michale, A., Rogers, R. D., Robbins, T. W., et al. (1999). Emotional bias and inhibitory control processes in mania and depression. *Psychological Medicine, 29*, 1307–1321.

Murray, R. M., Sham, P., van Os, J., Zanelli, J., Cannon, M. (2004). A developmental model for similarities and dissimilarities between schizophrenia and bipolar disorder. *Schizophrenia Research, 71*, 405–416.

Novick, D. M., Swartz, H. A., & Frank, E. (2010). Suicide attempts in bipolar I and bipolar II disorder: A review and meta-analysis of the evidence. *Bipolar Disorders, 12*(1), 1–9.

O'Connell, R. A., Van Heertum, R. L., Luck, D. et al. (1995). Single-photon emission computed tomography of the brain in acute mania and schizophrenia. *Journal of Neuroimaging, 5*, 101–104.

O'Shea, R. R., Poz, R. R., Michael, A. A., Berrios, G. E., Evans, J. J., & Rubinsztein, J. S. (2010). Ecologically valid cognitive tests and everyday functioning in euthymic bipolar disorder patients. *Journal of Affective Disorders, 125*(1–3), 336–340.

Ongur, D., Drevets, W. C., & Price, J. L. (1998). Glial reduction in the subgenual prefrontal cortex in mood disorders. *Proceedings of the National Academy of Science USA, 95*, 13290–13295.

Ostrum, T. M. (1984). The sovereignty of social cognition. In R. S. Wyer & T. K. Skrull (Eds.), *Handbook of social cognition, vol. 1*, (pp. 1–37). Hillsdale, NJ: Laurence Erlbaum.

Ozawa, H., Gsell, W., Frolich, L., Zochling, R., Pantucek, F., et al. (1993a). Imbalance of the Gs and Gi/o function in post-mortem brain of depressed patients. *Journal of Neural Transmission, 94*, 63–69.

Ozawa, H., Katamura, Y., Hatta, S., Saito, T., Katada, T., et al. (1993b). Alterations of guanine nucleotide-binding proteins in post-mortem human brain in alcoholics. *Brain Research, 920*, 174–179.

Payton, A. (2006). Investigating cognitive genetics and its implications for the treatment of cognitive deficits. *Genes, Brain, & Behavior, 5*, 44–53.

Pearlson, G. D., Wong, D. F., Tune, L. E., Ross, C. A., Chase, G. A., et al. (1995). In vivo D2 dopamine receptor density in psychotic and nonpsychotic patients with bipolar disorder. *Archives of General Psychiatry, 52*, 471–477.

Phillips, M., Drevets, W., Rauch, S., & Lane, R. (2003). Neurobiology of emotion perception I: The neural basis of normal emotion perception. *Biological Psychiatry, 54*(5), 504–514.

Post, R. M., Rubinow, D. R., Uhde, T. W., et al. (1989). Dysphoric mania: Clinical and biological correlates. *Archives of General Psychiatry, 46*, 353–358.

Potash, J., & DePaulo, J. (2000). Searching high and low: A review of the genetics of bipolar disorder. *Bipolar Disorders, 2*(1), 8–26.

Potash, J. B., Willour, V. L., Chiu, Y. F., Simpson, S. G., MacKinnon, D. F., Pearlson, G. D., et al. (2001). The familial aggregation of psychotic symptoms in bipolar disorder pedigrees. *American Journal of Psychiatry, 158*(8), 1258–1264.

Quraishi, S., & Frangou, S. (2002). Neuropsychology of bipolar disorder: A review. *Journal of Affective Disorders, 72*(3), 209–226.

Rahman, S., Li, P. P., Young, L. T., Kofman, O., Kish, S. J., et al. (1997). Reduced [3H]cyclic AMP binding in postmortem brain from subjects with bipolar affective disorders. *Journal of Neurochemistry, 68*, 297–304.

Rajkowska, G., Halaris, A., & Selemon, L. D. (2001). Reductions in neuronal and glial density characterize the dorsolateral prefrontal cortex in bipolar disorder. *Biological Psychiatry, 49*, 741–752.

Robinson, L. J., Thompson, J. M., Gallagher, P., Goswami, U., Young, A. H., et al. (2006). A meta-analysis of cognitive deficits in euthymic patients with bipolar disorder. *Journal of Affective Disorders, 93*, 105–115.

Roiser, J., Cannon, D., Gandhi, S., Tavares, J., Erickson, K., Wood, S., et al. (2009). Hot and cold cognition in unmedicated depressed subjects with bipolar disorder. *Bipolar Disorders, 11*(2), 178–189.

Rubin, E., Sackeim, H. A., Prohovnik, I., Moeller, J. R., Schnur, D. B., et al. (1995). Regional cerebral blood flow in mood disorders. IV. Comparison of mania and depression. *Psychiatry Research, 61*, 1–10.

Rubinsztein, J., Michael, A., Underwood, B., Tempest, M., & Sahakian, B. (2006). Impaired cognition and decision-making in bipolar depression but no 'affective bias' evident. *Psychological Medicine, 36*(5), 629–639.

Sanchez-Morla, E. M., Barabash, A., Martinez-Vizcaino, V., Tabares-Seissdedos, R., Balanza-Martinez, V., et al. (2009). Comparative study of neurocognitive function in euthymic bipolar patients and stabilized schizophrenia patients. *Psychiatry Research, 169*, 220–228.

Sassi, R., Brambilla, P., Hatch, J., Nicoletti, M., Mallinger, A., Frank, E., et al. (2004). Reduced left anterior cingulate volumes in untreated bipolar patients. *Biological Psychiatry, 56*(7), 467–475.

Scott, J., Colom, F., & Vieta, E. (2007). A meta-analysis of relapse rates with adjunctive psychological therapies compared to usual psychiatric treatment for bipolar disorders. *International Journal of Neuropsychopharmacology, 10*(1), 123–129.

Selemon, L. D., Rajkowska, G., & Goldman-Rakick, P. S. (1995). Abnormally high neuronal density in the schizophrenic cortex: A morphometric analysis of prefrontal area 9 and occipital area 17. *Archives of General Psychiatry, 52*, 805–818.

Shamay-Tsoory, S., Harari, H., Szepsenwol, O., & Levkovitz, Y. (2009). Neuropsychological evidence of impaired cognitive empathy in euthymic bipolar disorder. *The Journal of Neuropsychiatry and Clinical Neurosciences, 21*(1), 59–67.

Shean, G., Murphy, A., & Meyer, J. (2005). Social cognition and symptom dimensions. *Journal of Nervous & Mental Disease, 193*(11), 751–755.

Singh, T. (2008). Pediatric bipolar disorder: Diagnostic challenges in identifying symptoms and course of illness. *Psychiatry, 5*(6), 34–41.

Skjelstad, D. V., Malt, U. F., & Holte, A. (2010). Symptoms and signs of the initial prodrome of bipolar disorder. A systematic review. *Journal of Affective Disorders, 126*, 1–13.

Soares, J. C., & Mann, J. J. (1997). The anatomy of mood disorders–Review of structural neuroimaging studies. *Biological Psychiatry, 41*, 86–106.

Stoli, A. L., Renshaw, P. F., Yurgelun-Todd, D. A., & Cohen, B. (2000). Neuroimaging in bipolar disorder: What have we learned? *Biological Psychiatry, 48*(6), 505–517.

Strakowski, S. M., Adler, C. M., Holland, S. K., Mills, N., & DelBello, M. P. (2004). A preliminary fMRI study of sustained attention in euthymic, unmedicated bipolar disorder. *Neuropsychopharmacology, 29*, 1734–1740.

Strakowski, S. M., BelBello, M. P., Adler, C., & Sax, K. W. (2000). Neuroimaging in bipolar disorder. *Bipolar Disorders, 2*, 148–164.

Strakowski, S. M., & Sax, K. W. (2000). Secondary mania: A model of the pathophysiology of bipolar disorder? In J. C. Soares & S. Gershon (Eds.). *Basic mechanisms and therapeutic implications of bipolar disorder*. NY: Mareel Dekker, Inc.

Suhara, T., Nakayama, K., Inoue, O., Fukuda, H., Shimizu, M., et al. (1992). D1 dopamine receptor binding in mood disorders measured by positron emission topography. *Psychopharmacology, 106*, 14–18.

Sweeney, J. A., Kmiec, J. A., & Kupfer, D. J. (2000). Neuropsychological impairments in bipolar and unipolar mood disorders on the CANTAB neurocognitive battery. *Biological Psychiatry, 48*, 674–685.

Tabarés-Seisdedos, Balanzá-Martinez, Salazar-Fraile, Selva-Vera, Lea-Cercós, et al. (2003). Specific executive/attentional deficits in patients with schizophrenia or bipolar disorder who have a positive family history of psychosis. *Journal of Psychiatric Research, 37*(6), 479–486.

Tamayo, J., Zarate, C., Vieta, E., Vázquez, G., & Tohen, M. (2010). Level of response and safety of pharmacological monotherapy in the treatment of acute bipolar I disorder phases: A systematic review and meta-analysis. *International Journal of Neuropsychopharmacology, 13*(6), 813–832.

Thaker, G. K. (2008). Neurophysiological endophenotypes across bipolar and schizophrenia psychosis. *Schizophrenia Bulletin, 34*(4), 760–773.

Tooby, J., & Cosmides, L. (2000). Toward mapping the evolved functional organization of mind and brain. In M. S. Gazzaniga (Ed.), *The new cognitive neurosciences* (pp. 1167–1178). Cambridge, MA: MIT Press.

Torrent, C., Martinez-Aran, A., Daban, C., Sanchez-Moreno, J., Comes, M., et al. (2006). Cognitive impairment in bipolar II disorder. *British Journal of Psychiatry, 189*, 254–259.

Townsend, J., Bookheimer, S., Foland–Ross, L., Sugar, C., & Altshuler, L. (2010). fMRI abnormalities in dorsolateral prefrontal cortex during a working memory task in manic, euthymic and depressed bipolar subjects. *Psychiatry Research: Neuroimaging, 182*(1), 22–29.

Usher, J., Leucht, S., Falkai, P., & Scherk, H. (2010). Correlation between amygdala volume and age in bipolar disorder–A systematic review and meta-analysis of structural MRI studies. *Psychiatry Research, 182*, 1–8.

Van Gorp, W., Altshuler, L., Theberge, D., Wilkins, J., & Dixon, W. (1998). Cognitive impairment in euthymic bipolar patients with and without prior alcohol dependence. *Archives of General Psychiatry, 55*, 41–46.

Vawter, M. P., Freed, W. J., & Kleinman, J. E. (2000). Neuropathology of bipolar disorder. *Biological Psychiatry, 48*, 486–504.

Vieta, E., & Phillips, M. (2007). Deconstructing bipolar disorder: A critical review of its diagnostic validity and a proposal for DSM-V and ICD-11. *Schizophrenia Bulletin, 33*, 886–892.

Vieta, E., & Suppes, T. (2008). Bipolar II disorder: Arguments for and against a distinct diagnostic entity. *Bipolar Disorders, 10*, 163–178.

Vita, A., De Peri, L., & Sacchetti, E. (2009). Gray matter, white matter, brain, and intracranial volumes in first-episode bipolar disorder: A meta-analysis of magnetic resonance imaging studies. *Bipolar Disorders, 11*, 807–814.

Volonte, C., Ciotti, M. T., & Merlo, D. (1994). LiCL promotes survival of GABAergic neurons from cerebellum and cerebral cortex: LiCL induces survival of GABAergfic neurons. *Neuroscience Letters, 162*, 6–10.

Wang, H. Y., & Friedman, E. (1989). Lithium inhibition of protein kinase C activation-induced serotonin release. *Psychopharmacology (Berl), 99*, 213–218.

Wang, H. Y., & Friedman, E. (1996). Enhanced protein kinase C activity and translocation in bipolar affective disorder brains. *Biological Psychiatry, 40*, 568–575.

Williams, R. S. B., Cheng, L., Mudge, A. W., & Harwood, A. J. (2002). A common mechanism of action for three mood stabilizing drugs. *Nature, 417*, 292–295.

Wingo, A. P Wingo, T. S., Harvey, P. D., Baldessarini, R. J. (2009). Effects of lithium on cognitive performance: A meta-analysis. *Journal of Clinical Psychiatry, 70*, 1588–1597).

Wolfe, J., Granholm, E., Butters, N., & Saunders, E. (1987). Verbal memory deficits associated with major affective disorders: A comparison of unipolar and bipolar patients. *Journal of Affective Disorders, 13*(1), 83–92.

Wong, D. F., Wagner, H. N. Jr., Pearlson, G., Dannals, R. F., Links, J. M., et al. (1985). Dopamine receptor binding of C-11-3-N-methylspiperone in the caudate in schizophrenia and bipolar disorder: A preliminary report. *Psychopharmacology Bulletin, 21*, 595–598.

Wood, A. J., & Goodwin, G. M. (1987). A review of the biochemical and neuropharmacological actions of lithium. *Psychological Medicine, 17*, 579–600.

Young, L. T., Li, P. P., Kish, S. J., SIu, K. P., Kamble, A., Hornykiewicz, O., et al. (1993). Cerebral cortex Gs alpha protein levels and forskolin-stimulated cyclic AMP formation are increased in bipolar affective disorder. *Journal of Neurochemistry, 61*, 890–898.

Young, R. C., Biggs, J. T., Ziegler, V. E., and Meyer, D. A. (1978). A rating scale for mania: Reliability, validity and sensitivity. *British Journal of Psychiatry, 133*, 429–435.

Yurgelun-Todd, D. A., Gruber, S. A., Kanayama, G., Killgore, W. D., Baird, A. A., & Young, A. D. (2000). fMRI during affect discrimination in bipolar affective disorder. *Bipolar Disorders, 2*, 237–248.

Zubieta, J. K., Huguelet, P., Ohl, L. E., et al. (2000). High vesicular monoamine transporter binding in asymptomatic bipolar I disorder: Sex differences and cognitive correlates. *American Journal of Psychiatry, 157*, 1619–1628.

CHAPTER 11

Generalized Anxiety Disorder and Panic Disorder

Davor N. Zink, Carlos Ojeda, Margie Hernandez, & Antonio E. Puente

INTRODUCTION

Anxiety—formally "discovered" in 1844 by Sören Kierkegaard in the book titled *Begrebet angest,* translated into English in 1944 as *The Concept of Dread*—has undergone a series of changes in conceptions (McReynolds, 1985). Anxiety was thought to be the result of having the freedom to choose as well as having an apprehension associated with seeking the unknown (Goodwin, 1986; McReynolds 1985). Since then, the awareness of and knowledge about anxiety, including definition, symptoms, treatments, and etiology, have significantly increased.

Concepts such as anxiety, apprehension, worry, nervousness, panic, fright, and fear have caused confusion and misunderstandings, and although some believe that these constructs interact with each other (Gray, 1991), others believe that these constructs are certainly separable (Craske, 1999; Perkins, Kemp, & Corr, 2007). Research has shown that there are basic emotions, those that are hardwired or innate, and emotions that are a product of cognitions and associations of the basic emotions (Craske, 1999). In a study conducted by Power and Tarsia (2007), results showed that five independent basic emotions that include sadness, anger, disgust, and happiness lead to more complex emotions such as irritation, annoyance, nostalgia, love, and anxiety. Precisely, fear was found to be the basic emotion of anxiety, nervousness, tension, and worry. Perkins and colleagues (2007) found that fear was not only distinguishable from anxiety, but also accounted for a significant amount of unique discrepancies in applied performance. Miceli and Castelfranchi (2005) stated that fear and anxiety are similar in that they both share concern for threat; however, anxiety involves an indefinite threat because there is no specific threat or cue producing the anxiety, whereas fear indicates a specific threat or injury. Craske (1999) classified fear as one of the basic emotions, a hardwired biological event, whereas anxiety characterized those cognitive emotions that represent cognitive processes that are less imbedded biologically and vary depending on life experiences. Craske et al. (2009) defined anxiety as a future-oriented mood state that prepares the individual for an impending adverse event, whereas fear is an alarm response to a present or an apparent event.

Considered a universal feeling, anxiety commonly suggests an experience of varying blends of uncertainties, agitation, and dread with the individual experiencing cardiovascular, gastrointestinal, muscular, and respiratory symptoms (Zal, 1990). Anxiety is a nervous and restless state of mind usually over a forthcoming or anticipated threat ("Anxiety," 2011). It is a feeling of pressure in the chest, of butterflies in the stomach, and of depersonalization or derealization (Stone, 2010). Unlike basic emotions that are thought to be relatively noncognitive, anxiety is a mood state that is believed to involve cognitive processing and differs from basic emotions in that the duration of the mood is considerably longer (Craske, 1999). It is an emotion that signifies the presence of a danger that is unidentifiable, or, if identified, is not sufficiently threatening to validate and explain the intensity of the emotion (Goodwin, 1986).

Anxiety is very often comorbid with other mood disorders including depression, personality disorders, and substance abuse. It is a diverse condition that affects individuals of different ages, genders, and cultures, and is affected by traumas, stressors, biological features, and cognitive processes (Craske, 1999). Overall, anxiety is a broad term used for several disorders that develop from a complex set of risk factors, including genetics, brain chemistry, personality, and life events.

Anxiety, often characterized by somatic, emotional, cognitive, and behavioral components, is a psychological and physiological state that is an inherent part of the human being (McReynolds, 1985). Considered to be a normal reaction to a stressor and a fundamental part of individuals, anxiety has been shown to help individuals in the following ways: safety, preparation of fight or flight, alertness of danger, motivation in resolving problems, along with building character and creativity (Goodwin, 1986; Zal, 1990). Although a healthy amount of anxiety grants some survival value, too much may lead to excessive worry and several clinical conditions. The *Diagnostic and Statistical Manual for Mental Disorders, 4th edition, Text Revision* (*DSM-IV-TR*; American Psychiatric Association [APA], 2000) describes several anxiety disorders including but not limited to the following: generalized anxiety disorder (GAD), panic disorder (PD), phobic disorder, obsessive-compulsive disorder (OCD), and posttraumatic stress disorder (PTSD).

Anxiety is a natural emotion that is experienced by everyone; statistics report that anxiety disorders affect 40 million adults in the United States, thus ranking it as the most common mental illness in the United States (ADAA, 2011; "Facts and Statistics"). The Anxiety Disorders Association of America (ADAA) reports that anxiety disorders are costing the United States more than $42 billion a year—one-third of the country's total mental health bill (ADAA, 2011; "Facts and Statistics"). Because individuals with high levels of anxiety experience symptoms associated with physical illnesses, more than $22.84 billion of the $42 billion are associated with repeated health care services. Hence, compared to individuals without excessive anxiety, individuals diagnosed with an anxiety disorder are three to five times more likely to go to a physician's office and six times more likely to be hospitalized for psychiatric disorders (ADAA, 2011; "Facts and Statistics").

Recent scientific knowledge about the brain and its functioning has shown that mental disorders, including anxiety disorders, are the result of a complex interaction between neurobiology and life experiences (i.e., behavior; Wehrenberg & Prinz, 2007). Advances in the study of brain–behavior relationships have led to a better understanding of psychopathologies in humans. In the case of anxiety disorders, knowledge about the neural structures and substrates involved in the symptoms and their neuropsychological and behavioral consequences have had a great impact in their diagnosis and treatment. This chapter provides a general overview of the different components involved in the neuropsychology of GAD and PD. We start with a general description of the disorders; then we go on to the neuropathology and pathophysiology, then neuropsychological and behavioral sequelae, diagnostic concerns, and finally contemporary treatment.

GENERALIZED ANXIETY DISORDER (GAD)

GAD, also defined as worrying without a reason, is a chronic condition that is characterized by excessive anxiety and worry, occurring with a number of events or activities, lasting for at least 6 months (APA, 2000; Wehrenberg & Prinz, 2007). Three out of six symptoms from the *DSM-IV-TR* diagnostic criteria are associated with anxiety and worry accounting for more days than not during 6 months. Symptoms include, but are not limited to, having muscle tension, trembling, feeling shaky, muscle aches and soreness, sweating, nausea, sleep disturbances, and exaggerated startle responses. Wehrenberg and Prinz (2007) stated that GAD manifests itself through the following three clusters of symptoms: (1) physiological, which include headaches, fibromyalgia, fatigue, muscle tensions, and sleep disturbances; (2) cognitive, which include ruminating fears about health, mental hypervigilance, perfectionist carefulness, and intolerance of ambiguity; and (3) behavioral, which include several types of avoidance such as working extra hours with great care, cognitive exertion, and checking things over. Because GAD's symptoms are present to some degree in other anxiety disorders, GAD is considered the most basic anxiety disorder (Craske, 1999; Lightfoot, Seay, & Goddard, 2010). Unlike other anxiety disorders such as PD and PTSD, increased heart rate, shortness of breath, dizziness, and any other autonomic hyperarousal symptoms are not as noticeable in GAD (APA, 2000; Ritter, Blackmore & Heimberg, 2010).

GAD is affected by biological factors along with psychosocial factors (Lightfoot et al., 2010). The genetics, neurochemistry, and neurophysiology together with behavioral inhibition in childhood, temperament, and social and learning situations appear to affect an individual with GAD. Neurobiological causes of GAD can be the product of an overactive anterior cingulate gyrus, elevated norepinephrine levels, overactive basil ganglia, serotonin deficits affecting the limbic system and the prefrontal cortex (PFC), an insufficiency of GABA receptors, and/or an overactive hypothalamic-pituitary-arsenal (HPA) axis (Wehrenberg & Prinz, 2007).

With children being affected as often as adults, GAD can occur at any age (Wehrenberg & Prinz, 2007). About 6.8 million adults or 3.1% of the U.S. population are affected by GAD, with women being twice more likely to be affected than men (ADAA, 2011; "Generalized Anxiety Disorder"). GAD is comorbid with depression about 50% of the time; therefore, it is important to determine whether depression or GAD existed first (Wehrenberg & Prinz, 2007). Aside from depression, GAD is also commonly comorbid with substance abuse, other mood disorders, and other anxiety disorders. Because of its high comorbidity rate and debilitating symptoms, GAD produces substantial changes in people's occupational and social lives (APA, 2000; Ritter et al., 2010.

PANIC DISORDER (PD)

Although individuals with PD often complain of anxiety and tension, the anxiety is so overwhelming and the autonomic nervous system becomes so highly aroused that a panic attack is reached (Zal, 1990). The *DSM-IV-TR* (APA, 2000) defines panic disorder as the presence of recurrent and unexpected panic attacks followed by at least 1 month of persistent concern or worrying about having another attack, its consequences, or behavioral changes related to the attacks. A panic attack is characterized by a discrete period, in the absence of real danger, that is described as a sudden onset of intense fear or discomfort, which is often associated with feelings of impending doom (APA, 2000; Pollack, Smoller, Otto, Hoge, & Simon, 2010). The *DSM-IV-TR* (APA, 2000), criteria entails that four out of 13 symptoms develop abruptly and reach a peak within 10 minutes.

Features of panic attacks include but are not limited to the following: chest pain or discomfort; feeling dizzy, unsteady, or faint; sensations of shortness of breath; sweating and accelerated heart rate; and paresthesias. More specifically, three clusters of symptoms were described by Wehrenberg and Prinz (2007). First, the physiological symptoms that include, but are not limited to, palpitations, sensations of choking, chest pains, and psychological sensations of derealization and depersonalization. Second, the cognitive symptoms, which develop once the physiological symptoms have started; these include cognitive thoughts such as the person feeling as if he or she is going to die, is going crazy, or is losing control. Lastly, behavioral symptoms develop, which include mental avoidance, avoiding activities, and avoidance of the feeling of fear. Agoraphobia, the anxiety or avoidance of places in which escape might be difficult or no help is available, also occurs in the context of panic disorders. PD can occur with or without agoraphobia. PD has been associated with major life transitions, high levels of stress, medical conditions, trauma experiences, early disturbances in the attachments to parents or caregivers, psychological conflicts, medical conditions, stimulant use, and medication withdrawal, as well as neurobiological causes including neurotransmitter imbalances.

Though 2% of the adult population in the United States will experience a panic attack in a year, the ADAA reports that 6 million, or 2.7% of the U.S. population, have panic disorders, with women being twice as likely to be affected as men (ADAA, 2011; "Facts and Statistics"). Although panic disorder is not frequently seen in children, symptoms are often noted throughout puberty; however, it is not impossible for PD to have its first onset early in life (Wehrenberg & Prinz, 2007). Because panic attacks are caused by triggers such as loss of family, friends, abilities, independence, and so forth, it is important to dismiss any other underlying causes of PD symptoms or any early symptoms of dementia in the elderly population (Wehrenberg & Prinz, 2007). Panic disorder, or for that matter panic attacks, should not be due to the direct physiological effects of substance use, a general medical condition, or another mental disorder (APA, 2000). Although panic disorder has a very high comorbidity rate with major depressive disorder, ranging from 10%–65%, comorbidity with other anxiety disorders and hypochondriasis is also common (APA, 2000; Pollack et al., 2010).

NEUROPATHOLOGY AND PATHOPHYSIOLOGY OF GAD AND PD

Whereas psychologists tend to understand the underlying psychological factors, the concomitant physiological variables are less understood. This section provides an introductory overview of the complexities surrounding the physiological underpinnings of the pathology for GAD and PD.

In the past two decades, a growing amount of neuroscientific investigations have provided further information regarding brain circuitry that plays a role in the etiology of GAD and PD (Pine & Grun, 1999). Findings indicated that a septo-hippocampal circuit is related in the development of GAD and that a brain stem periaqueductal gray-medial hypothalamic circuit is related in the development of PD (Pine & Grun, 1999). Moreover, Pine and Grun (1999) suggested that the comorbidity of several anxiety symptoms associated with different anxiety disorders (e.g., phobias, GAD, PD) might be produced by an interaction of these recursive limbic circuits. These findings are useful because they allow the identification of individuals who might be at risk of developing anxiety disorders by detecting abnormalities in the developing and functioning of these brain circuits.

NEUROPATHOLOGY AND PATHOPHYSIOLOGY OF GAD

Research has shown that anxiety symptoms are produced by disorders or abnormalities in the amygdala and related brain circuits (Beesdo et al., 2009; Damsa, Kosel, & Moussally, 2008; De Bellis et al., 2000; Krain et al., 2008, 2006). For instance, Besdo and colleagues (2009) found that individuals with anxiety symptoms have higher activation of the amygdala when compared to nonanxious individuals during a fear-inducing situation. Furthermore, Besdo and colleagues (2009) indicated that the hyperactivation of the amygdala during anxiety symptoms depends on the emotion specific to a situation. In other words, experiencing a specific emotion in a situation (e.g., fear) plays a role in the functioning of the amygdala, which is responsible for anxiety disorders, including GAD.

According to De Bellis and colleagues (2000), the size of the right section and total amygdala is significantly larger in individuals with GAD compared to controls. Furthermore, they hypothesized that the increased size of the amygdala could have one of the following implications: 1) might be attributed to genetic factors such as vulnerability to threatening stimuli, or 2) might be due to a continuous anticipatory response to anxiety during development. Thus, genetic and situational factors might play a role in the amygdala functioning, which produces the symptoms of GAD. Similarly, vulnerability to uncertain situations has been shown to be a characteristic of individuals with GAD; particularly individuals with high levels of intolerance to uncertainty tend to have higher activation of frontal and limbic regions of the brain compared to individuals with lower levels of intolerance to uncertainty (Krain et al. 2006, 2008). These findings suggest that external situational factors (e.g., uncertainty, fear) play a role in the development and manifestations of anxiety symptoms that are characteristic of GAD by affecting the brain regions associated with this condition.

Additional evidence regarding the neuropathology of GAD is related to abnormal functioning in neurochemical, neuroendocrine, neurophysiological, and neuroanatomical factors. For instance, Nieto-Escámez et al. (2007) indicated that the following neurotransmitters play a role in the occurrence of anxiety disorders: GABA/benzodiazepine (BZ) complex, norepinephrine, 5-HT, cholecystokinin (CCK), corticotrophin releasing factor (CRF), HPA axis, and neurosteroids. In addition, it has been shown that alterations in autonomic reactivity and systems might produce anxiety symptoms (Nieto-Escámez et al., 2007).

According to Wehrenberg and Prinz (2007), the neurobiological causes of GAD are the following: Anterior cingulated gyrus (ACG) overactivity produces ruminating worry. Elevated norepinephrine (NE) or overactivity in the basal ganglia (BG) results in hypervigilance. Serotonin (SE) deficits, which affect the limbic system and the PFC, may be responsible for rumination, despair, and a predisposition to feeling anxious. Low-level or ineffective GABA may result in heightened worry and feelings of dread, and an overreactive HPA axis may produce overreactivity to stress.

NEUROPATHOLOGY AND PATHOPHYSIOLOGY OF PD

According to Gorman et al. (2000), the physiology of panic disorder is explained by an irregular sensitive fear system, involving the amygdala, PFC, insula, thalamus, brain stem, and hypothalamus. Other researchers such as Yoo and colleagues (2005) have discovered that lower levels of putamen in gray matter volumes and lower GABA levels in the BG play a role in PD (Ham et al., 2007). Van den Heuvel and colleagues (2005) concluded that aberrant putamen activation is related to the neurophysiology of PD. Marchand and colleagues (2009) reportedly found that patients diagnosed with PD had lower levels of activation in the bilateral putamen when compared to subjects in the control group. The authors suggested that subcortical mediated fight-or-flight reactions may be aberrant for individuals diagnosed with PD. According to Marchand and colleagues (2009), an individual diagnosed with PD will exhibit increased putamen activity and increased cortical activity when encountering a threatening situation, whereas a similar subject exposed to a nonthreatening condition will show lower putamen activation levels (typical of normal cortical activation). Another study showed increased bilateral putamen and lower cortical activation to a fearful situation among healthy subjects (Butler et al., 2007). The researchers concluded that the motor cortex deactivation pattern and activation of the BG in a threatening situation may indicate processing may move from the cortical to the subcortical structures. This finding is commensurate with research on animal studies showing fight-or-flight responses are used mainly by subcortical rather than cortical structures (Butler et al., 2007). Individuals diagnosed with PD have demonstrated decreased resting partial pressure of end-tidal carbon dioxide (PCO_2) in comparison to control groups, indicating that subjects with PD at rest could hyperventilate (Blechert, Michael, Grossman, Lajtman, & Wilhelm, 2007; Giardino, Friedman, & Dager, 2007).

According to Wehrenberg and Prinz (2007) the neuroanatomical structures associated with PD are the following: Dysregulation occurs in BG function as many PD patients show increased activity in the BG. NE acts on the peripheral nervous system (PNS) and produces heightened arousal in muscles, heart rate, and vascular system. Lactate sensitivity produces an increase in respiration and triggers panic symptoms. Locus coeruleus dysfunction and dysregulation of NE projections to the hippocampus occur. Seizure-like activity may occur, with patients who have epilepsy in their temporal lobes more likely to develop symptoms of panic.

NEUROPSYCHOLOGICAL AND BEHAVIORAL SEQUELAE

An interactive model is proposed in which anxiety may affect neuropsychological functioning and vice versa, that is, neuropsychological deficits producing anxiety. Although the former is more frequently considered, both are critical in understanding the interactive aspects of both variables.

ANXIETY-PRODUCING NEUROPSYCHOLOGICAL DEFICITS

Increased anxiety levels produce impairment in the measurement of cognitive domains such as attention and executive function (Craig, Phil, & Chamberlain, 2010). Regarding attention across different tasks, moderate levels of anxiety allow for better performance because anxiety improves task goal-setting, feedback monitoring of task performance, and resource allocation. However, high levels of anxiety (arousal) lead to poorer task performance because the efficacy of attentional allocation is negatively affected. Cognitive resources such as attention are limited in their capacity; therefore, when stimuli are competing for attention, as in the case of an anxiety situation, less cognitive resources are available to perform the task correctly and attain goals (Koob, 1991; Yerkes & Dodson, 1908; Craig et al., 2010). Regarding the effect of anxiety on executive functions, Baddeley (1986, 2001) developed a model of working memory that is a good starting point to address this interface. He suggested three components: 1) the phonological loop, which is specialized in the processing and maintenance of verbal information; 2) the visuospatial sketchpad, which processes and maintains visual and spatial information; and 3) the central executive, which is a central control structure responsible for the control and regulation of executive functions (performance monitoring, planning, and strategy selection), which are usually linked to frontal lobe structures. The first two are automatic, whereas the third is not. Consequently, the third component is the most affected by anxiety (Eysenck, Derakshan, Santos, & Calvo, 2007). Further, Miyake et al. (2000) described three functions of the central executive: 1) shifting between tasks and mental sets, 2) updating and monitoring of working memory representations, and 3) inhibition of dominant or proponent responses. According to Eysenck and colleagues' (2007) attentional control theory, anxiety impairs the ability to inhibit incorrect proponent responses, increases the susceptibility to distraction, impairs performance on secondary tasks in dual task paradigms, and detriments task-switching performance. Moreover, distraction effects in high-anxiety individuals are greater when the task requires the functions of the central executive. Anxiety impairs the inhibiting function of the central executive because of resource allocation costs. External and internal task-irrelevant stimuli (e.g., worrying thoughts) tend to distract anxious individuals more than nonanxious individuals. In dual task studies, anxious participants tend to perform worse in the secondary task when the secondary stimuli are nonsalient or inconspicuous (Eysenck et al., 2007; Craig et al., 2010). Worrisome thoughts consume limited attentional resources in working memory, leaving fewer resources available to expend in secondary or concurrent tasks. Subsequently, anxiety reduces the processing and temporary storage capacity of working memory, producing cognitive interference (Craig et al., 2010). In studies using the Stroop Test, compared to controls, highly anxious individuals performed worse when they had to color-name a colored word because their ability to inhibit proponent responses is negatively affected (Hochman 1967; Pallak, Pittman, Heller, & Munson, 1975). Highly anxious individuals show greater distraction effects when the distraction stimulus is threat related. Anxiety results in placing more attention to threat-related stimuli, and this leads to impaired cognitive control. This phenomenon is referred to as attentional bias, which is the tendency to focus on threat-related stimuli or to show slow attentional disengagement from such stimuli when a neutral stimuli is presented at the same time (Eysenck, 1992; Eysenck et al., 2007; Craig et al., 2010). Corbetta and Shulman (2002) differentiated between a goal-directed attentional system and a stimulus-driven attentional system. The goal-directed system (top down) is influenced by current goals, knowledge, and expectations, whereas the stimulus-directed system (bottom up) responds to behaviorally relevant sensory events (e.g., threat related), specifically when they are salient and unattended, and it is linked to the temporoparietal and ventrofrontal cortex. Anxiety is related to elevated sensitivity to stimulus threat-related cues (Mathews & Mackintosh, 1998) and is also associated with reduced efficiency of goal-directed cognitive control in areas such as the anterior cingulated and PFC (less activation of these areas; Bishop, Duncan, Brett, & Lawrence, 2004). In the dot probe task, anxious people show an attentional bias by detecting dots that replace anxiety-related stimuli faster than dots that replace neutral stimuli (Mogg et al. 2000; Pishyar, Harris, & Menzies, 2004). In the emotional Stroop task, anxiety slows the rate of color naming when the words are threat related (emotional Stroop interference effect; Williams, Mathews, & MacLeod, 1996). Phaf and Kan (2007) did a meta-analysis that showed that the largest Stroop effect was found in clinically anxious patients, followed by highly anxious nonclinical participants.

NEUROPSYCHOLOGICAL DEFICITS ASSOCIATED TO CUED AND CONTEXT FEAR CONDITIONING

Anxiety in humans has been explained using classical and operant conditioning. Animal studies have shown that temporo-amygdala-limbic paths are responsible for fear conditioning, and human studies have suggested that similar neural structures are involved in fear conditioning in people (Blair, Schafe, Bauer, Rodrigues, & LeDoux, 2001; Schafe, Nader, Blair, & LeDoux, 2001; LaBar, Gatenby, Gore, LeDoux, & Phelps, 1998). Cued fear conditioning occurs when a neutral stimulus is paired with a conditioned stimulus (CS) that represents a threat to the individual. Once the association is learned, the CS alone produces fear. Context conditioning occurs when the testing environment is linked to the possibility of aversive events occurring in the future, therefore producing anxiety. The state of hypervigilance and stress that context conditioning produces leads to an increased baseline startle response to contextual cues in humans (Grillon & Ameli, 1998; Craig et al., 2010). When compared to control participants, patients with anxiety disorders show increased baseline startle responses when they are expecting an aversive stimulus, such as threat of shock. Baseline startle responses to nonthreatening stimuli were similar in the two groups (Grillon 2002; Grillon, Morgan, Davis, & Southwick, 1998). Anxious patients seem to be overly responsive to threatening contexts; however, they do not show an increased fear response in cued fear experiments like phobic patients do (de Jong, Peter, Visser, & Merckelbach, 1996; Vrana, Constantine, & Westman, 1992). Animal studies suggest that the nuclei of the amygdala are important in cued fear conditioning (Davis, 1998; LeDoux, 1998), and the dorsal hippocampus and the amygdala are important in context conditioning (Phillips & LeDoux, 1992). Selden and colleagues (1991) did a study that showed that lesions in the hippocampus impaired contextual conditioning, but did not affect cued fear conditioning, whereas lesions in the amygdala impaired cued fear conditioning without affecting contextual conditioning.

NEUROPSYCHOLOGICAL DEFICITS IN GAD

In a review of the literature on cognitive deficits in anxiety disorders, Craig and colleagues (2010) indicated that there is a strong effect of working memory deficits and attentional bias, and a moderate effect of increased baseline startle response in GAD patients. People diagnosed with GAD have an attention and interpretative bias. They tend to see ambiguous stimuli or information as threatening and they pay more attention to this information. Attentional bias could be a state marker for anxiety (Craig et al., 2010). In a study by Gualtieri and Morgan (2008), adult patients with GAD, major depressive disorder, bipolar disorder, and healthy controls were compared using a neurocognitive assessment that measured memory, psychomotor speed, reaction time, attention, and cognitive flexibility. Results showed 19% of participants with GAD were impaired in at least one of the aforementioned neuropsychological domains. Further, GAD patients showed the greatest impairment in complex attention (measured by the Stroop Test, Continuous Performance Test, and Shifting Attention Test). In another study, Bradley and colleagues (1998) investigated attentional biases in GAD. They compared the reactions of patients with GAD and healthy controls to photographs of threatening, neutral, and happy faces. Attentional bias was assessed using a dot probe task. Compared to controls, anxious participants showed greater vigilance for threatening faces, providing evidence for an attentional bias in GAD. Studies using the emotional Stroop task have shown that generally anxious participants are considerably slower at naming threat-related words, providing more evidence for an attentional bias (Mathews & MacLeod, 1985; Mogg, Mathews, & Weinman, 1989). More evidence was provided in another study with GAD patients in which the dot probe task was used. The authors concluded that anxious participants shifted their attention toward threatening stimuli in the environment, whereas normal participants did not (MacLeod et al., 1986). Mogg and Bradley (2005) reviewed the literature on attentional bias and GAD and they concluded that there is evidence to suggest that there is an automatic attentional bias in GAD for a wide range of negative external stimuli and that this bias can sometimes operate subconsciously.

Neuropsychological deficits produced by GAD have also been seen in children. Micco and colleagues (2009) investigated executive functioning in children with anxiety disorders (GAD, SOOC, SEP) and depression. Participants were 6–17 years old and were assessed using structured interviews and neuropsychological tests. Results indicated participants with GAD showed impairment in verbal working memory as measured by the California Verbal Learning Test Child Edition (CVLT-C), whereas participants with social phobia displayed deficits in sustained attention as measured by Seidman Continuous Performance Test (CPT-omissions). Children with anxiety disorders showed no impairment in set shifting (Micco et al., 2009). Waters and Valvoi (2009) used an emotional go/no go task to assess attentional bias in children from 8–12 years with GAD, social phobia, specific anxiety disorder, and separation anxiety disorder. Participants were presented with happy, angry, or neutral faces. Anxious girls and boys were slower at responding to angry faces on no go trials. In a similar study with children (7–12 years), GAD attention bias was assessed using an emotional dot probe task. The task consisted of pairs of visual face stimuli (happy, angry). Results showed that children with severe GAD displayed an attentional bias for angry and happy faces. Children with milder GAD and controls did not show attentional bias (Waters, Mogg, Bradley, & Pine, 2008). In another study which investigated differences in cognitive bias across emotional disorders, children and adolescents (ages 7–18 years) with GAD, PTSD, and clinical depression were tested using measures of attention, memory, and prospective cognition that had threat- and depression-related stimuli. Some of the specific measures included were the British Picture Vocabulary Scale, Wechsler Objective Reading Dimensions, the Attentional Dot Probe Task, the Modified Stroop Task, and a memory task. Significant results were found for the dot probe task, with GAD patients showing a selective attention bias for threat-related stimuli, relative to depression-related material, compared to the depressed group. No differences were found between groups in vocabulary and reading (Dalgleish et al., 2003). Vasa et al. (2007) found no deficits in memory in children with and without GAD.

There is some evidence for GAD producing neuropsychological problems in older adults. For instance, Mantella and colleagues (2007) examined cognitive functioning in elderly patients with GAD. Participants with GAD, major depression, and normal controls were compared using the Mattis Dementia Rating Scale. Naming, executive ability, and memory were also assessed. When compared to controls, GAD patients showed impairment in short-term and delayed memory and difficulties in set shifting (attention) as measured by the trail-making test. More research is needed in order to elucidate differences in neuropsychological deficits in adults, children, and older adults. Preliminary findings suggest that similar deficits are present across the age groups.

NEUROPSYCHOLOGICAL DEFICITS IN PANIC DISORDER (PD)

Airaksinen, Larsson, and Forsell (2005) conducted a study to assess the neuropsychological functioning of individuals diagnosed with anxiety disorders compared to healthy controls. The sample consisted of participants diagnosed with PD, social phobia, GAD, OCD, specific phobia, and healthy controls. Episodic memory (remembering neutral words), verbal fluency

(The Word Association Test), psychomotor speed, and executive function (Trail Making Test) were evaluated using a neuropsychological battery. Overall results indicated that anxiety disorders are related to impairments in episodic memory and executive function. Participants with PD and OCD showed impairment in executive functions and episodic memory; participants with social phobia exhibited episodic memory dysfunction; participants with specific phobia and GAD did not show neuropsychological impairment, and verbal fluency and psychomotor speed were not affected by anxiety. Concerning PD specifically, Lucas, Telch, and Bigler (1991) did a study to investigate the neuropsychological functioning in patients with PD. Results indicated that compared to volunteer controls, PD patients showed impairments in visual learning and memory and verbal memory. In a similar study, Asmundson, Stein, Larson, and Walker (1994) found impairment in PD patients in tests of verbal learning and verbal recall, but no impairment in immediate visual memory. In contrast with these findings, Gladsjo and colleagues (1998) found no neuropsychological dysfunction in patients with PD; however, the participants in this study had mild to moderate PD. The participants were assessed in various neuropsychological domains such as attention, learning, memory, visuospatial thinking, and psychomotor speed. Similar results were found by Purcell, Maruff, Kyrios, and Pantelis (1998). The researchers compared the performance of patients with OCD, PD, and unipolar depression in a neuropsychological battery. Results indicated that patients with OCD had impaired spatial working memory, speed of motor initiation and execution, and spatial recognition; however, patients with PD did not show any cognitive impairment in attention, memory, and planning. In another study, Basso and colleagues (2007) compared the performance of nonpsychotic depressed inpatients with and without comorbid anxiety disorders and healthy controls on a brief neuropsychological test battery. Results showed that participants with comorbid anxiety disorders (GAD, PTSD, and PD) were more neuropsychologically impaired than the other two groups. Both groups of depressed participants showed impairment in memory function, but the group with comorbid anxiety disorder also showed deficits in executive function and psychomotor speed. Another study evaluated decision strategies using a two choice prediction task. Results indicated that PD patients were more sensitive to errors showing high response sequence unpredictability (Ludewig, Paulusb, Ludewig, & Vollenweidera, 2003), suggesting an executive function deficit.

Impairment in attention has also been associated with PD. Lautenbacher, Spernal, and Krieg (2002) did a study on the attentional functioning of inpatients diagnosed with PD or with major depressive disorder (MDD). They used neuropsychological tests to assess selective attention (Signal Detection, Wiener Test System) and divided attention (Gesichtfeld-/Neglectprufung, TAP). Compared to healthy controls, PD and MDD inpatients showed significant impairment in divided attention, but not in selective attention. The authors suggested that the visual dual task paradigm of the divided attention test was responsible for the results because it is more demanding than the single task paradigm. They also suggested that the severity of the disorder might play a role in attention deficit because, in contrast with previous studies that assessed mild to moderate PD patients, they assessed inpatients with severe PD (Lautenbacher et al., 2002). Dupont, Mollard, and Cottraux (2000) assessed attentional processing in patients with PD compared to healthy controls using a visual discrimination task designed for the study. Even though an interaction effect was found, no significant between-group differences were found, and PD patients did not show impairment in attention. However, there is evidence that indicates PD patients have an attentional bias towards anxiety-related stimuli and are easily distracted and slower at processing threat-related information. Studies using the emotional Stroop Test showed that PD patients were slower at color-naming threat-related words; in other words, PD patients displayed a greater Stroop interference effect compared to healthy controls (Ehlers, Margraf, Davies, & Roth, 1988; McNally, Riemann, & Kim, 1990). In a review of the literature on cognitive deficits in anxiety disorders, Craig and colleagues (2010) indicated that there is a strong effect of increased baseline startle response and attention bias in PD patients.

Even though there are contradicting results in the literature, there is some evidence for memory and executive function deficits in PD, and there is clear evidence for attention deficits. These deficits seem to be present in children, too, but more research is needed in order to clearly understand and recognize the neuropsychological deficits in older adults with PD.

NEUROPSYCHOLOGICAL PROBLEMS PRODUCING ANXIETY

Anxiety is a variable that can be present in neuropsychological conditions. For instance, Higginson, Fields, and Troster (2001) examined whether anxiety symptoms decreased after patients had surgery for Parkinson's disease instead of experiencing a subtle amelioration of parkinsonian symptoms. They found that patients with Parkinson's disease had an improvement in anxiety symptoms after surgery, which suggests that anxiety symptoms are different from Parkinson's disease and also different from those symptoms of anxiety that overlap with Parkinson's disease (Higginson et al., 2001). Similarly, Tan, Thomas, and Chan (2007) found similar results in a case study in which a patient with Parkinson's disease presented reduction of anxiety symptoms.

Anxiety symptoms have also been associated with Alzheimer's disease. Furthermore, anxiety symptoms might be comorbid with other disorders during the course of Alzheimer's disease. For example, Teri and colleagues (1999) investigated the presence of anxiety symptoms as well as their relationship with depression, behavioral problems, age, and gender in Alzheimer's disease patients and found that anxiety symptoms were common and significantly associated with Alzheimer's disease. Furthermore, in order to better understand the relationship between anxiety symptoms and mild cognitive impairment, Rozzini and colleagues (2009) used the Geriatric Anxiety Inventory (GAI) to measure whether individuals with mild cognitive impairment and anxiety present differences in executive functioning when compared to individuals with mild cognitive impairment without anxiety symptoms. It was found that anxiety symptoms interact with executive functions in individuals with mild cognitive impairment; thus, anxiety symptoms in mild cognitive impairment might be an alarm of an upcoming cognitive decline (Rozzini et al., 2009).

There is some evidence available regarding how brain problems produce GAD and PD. For example, Hiott and Labbate (2002) indicated that there is an increased frequency of anxiety disorders after a traumatic brain injury, which suggests an overlap between brain regions vulnerable to traumatic brain injury and the neural circuits active during anxiety symptoms. Specifically, individuals who have had a traumatic brain injury are twice as likely as the general population to develop GAD, yet there is limited information regarding locations of brain lesions associated with GAD. Furthermore, neuroimaging procedures have been useful in demonstrating what brain regions are active during panic attacks, including the orbitofrontal, cingulate, and medial temporal cortical areas, which are common locations of traumatic brain injuries (Hiott & Labatte, 2002). Overall, Hiott and Labatte (2002) suggest that individuals with traumatic brain injuries are more likely to develop anxiety disorders, particularly GAD and PD. Other than traumatic brain injury, additional situational aspects might activate the brain circuits that play a role in the development of anxiety symptoms, such as PD or GAD. For example, as the possibility of a threat increases, it activates a reaction in the forebrain and midbrain, thus producing qualitative changes that lead to the experience of fear (Maren, 2007). Similarly, activation of the PFC by unexpected threat might produce anxiety. As a result, these findings (Maren, 2007) suggest that any abnormality present in the respective brain circuits might put an individual at risk of developing GAD or PD.

ADVANCED DIAGNOSTIC CONSIDERATIONS AND PRACTICES

Comorbidity

Malyszczak and Pawlowski (2006) investigated the functional characteristics and symptomatic characteristics present in individuals with mixed anxiety and depressive disorders. Results indicated that distress and decline in level of functioning are associated with mixed anxiety and depressive disorder; thus, symptoms of mixed anxiety and depressive disorder are related to distress and interference in personal functioning. Furthermore, the authors found that symptoms of anxiety, specifically GAD characteristics, are worsened by mild depression symptoms.

General anxiety symptoms have also been associated with PD. For instance, Overbeek, Schruers, Van Leeuwen, Klaassen, and Griez (2005) found that anxiety symptoms increased in individuals with PD as well as in individuals with MDD. However, it has been suggested that health-related workers (e.g., physicians, psychologists, neuropsychologists) should address other symptoms beyond anxiety, specifically, affective symptoms related to depression and aggression (Overbeek et al., 2005). Furthermore, general anxiety symptoms might also be comorbid with PD, which raises the risk of an erroneous diagnosis. For example, Sheehan (2004) investigated the case of a 37-year-old married Hispanic female who presented with a history of panic attacks, PD, and four attempts of suicide within 2 years. The challenge indicated by Sheenan (2004) is that anxiety symptoms tend to be comorbid with other Axis I disorders in which anxiety symptoms appear in a very prominent manner, including PD. Thus, distinguishing between PD and anxiety characteristics as either anxiety symptoms or anxiety disorders is a difficult task when making a diagnosis.

Anxiety symptoms have been reported as a result of brain surgery, although it has been challenging to determine whether the anxiety symptoms are a result of the surgery or whether they are comorbid with other disorders. Thus, learning which brain networks contribute to the potential anxiety symptoms can help to prevent and detect risky conditions. For instance, Silton and colleagues (2011) indicated that performance impairments in dACC activity of anxious individuals during conflict resolution suffer attention disruption due to worries or ruminations. Furthermore, another study indicated that children and adolescents with repaired arteriovenous malformations displayed adequate emotional functioning, which might be attributed to characteristics of defensiveness and worry (O'Toole, Borden, & Miller, 2006). These findings (O'Toole et al., 2006; Silton et al., 2011) are useful because they allow us to gain a better understanding of how surgical brain procedures can affect a displayed anxiety condition. In addition, anxiety symptoms have been detected after individuals suffered a traumatic brain injury, but anxiety symptoms before brain injury also exist (Meares et al., 2011). These findings can be used to prepare treatment strategies for anxiety symptoms with individuals who suffered from brain lesions.

Testing Anxiety

Performance/evaluation anxiety can influence neuropsychological test scores considerably, resulting in mistaken diagnoses (Straus, Sherman, & Spreen, 2006). There are studies that consistently show highly test-anxious participants perform worse than their nontest-anxious counterparts across a variety of outcome measures (Chapell et al., 2005; Everson , Millap, & Rodriguez, 1991). In neuropsychological tests used with both children and adults, highly anxious individuals tend to perform worse. There is evidence for poorer performance in the finger tapping test (Chavez, Trautt, Brandon, & Steyart, 1893), digit span (Firetto, 1971), block design, verbal fluency (Buckelew & Hannay, 1986), the Stroop Test (Batchelor, Harvey, & Bryant, 1995), the Wechsler Memory Scales (Cannon, 1999), and scales of intelligence (Oostdam & Meijer, 2003). Test anxiety did not affect performance on the trail-making test and digit symbol test (Chavez et al., 1893). Because test anxiety has a negative effect on the performance of neuropsychological tests, it can lead to incorrect diagnosis or irrelevant inferences from neuropsychological scores (Tramontana, Hooper, Watts-English, Ellison, & Bethea, 2009).

CONTEMPORARY MODES OF TREATMENT

The aim of treatments for anxiety disorder are to help an individual with his or her worriedness, anticipatory anxiety, and fear, as well as the physiological, behavioral, and cognitive symptoms that are associated with the anxiety (Craske, 1999). Although anxiety disorders are treatable and several forms of treatment are available, only one-third of the population receives some sort of treatment (ADAA, 2011; "Treatment"). With treatment being more complicated when the person has other conditions such as depression or substance abuse, attainment of treatment success ranges from a few weeks to more than a year (ADAA, 2011; "Treatment"). Thus, treatment for individuals with anxiety is often individualized. Current considerations for the treatment for anxiety disorders include, but are not limited to, behavioral treatments, systematic desensitization, exposure therapy, relaxation, mastery exposure therapy, response prevention, behavioral rehearsal, cognitive treatment methods, and pharmacological treatments (Craske, 1999). Nonetheless, certain treatments have proven to be more effective with certain types of anxiety disorder.

Knowledge and detection of abnormalities in the developing and functioning of the neuropathology and neuropsychology of anxiety can lead to the recognition of individuals who might be at risk of developing anxiety disorders and assist with treatment. Treatment methods can have a direct effect on brain structures and neurochemicals involved in GAD and PD, which in turn have an effect on behavior and improving the anxiety symptoms. Further, treatment can be focused on changing behavior or cognition, which in turn will have an effect on the neural substrates and neurochemicals involved in GAD and PD.

Treatment of GAD

Of the aforementioned treatment options for anxiety, empirical research has most prominently supported the use of cognitive-behavioral therapy (CBT; Rygh & Sanderson, 2004). CBT is a form of psychotherapy that emphasizes thinking about how one feels and what one does and focuses on symptom relief. It is a form of psychotherapy that helps individuals become more aware of inaccurate and negative thinking and allows them to view and respond to situations in a more effective way. With results attained between 12 and 16 weeks, the individual is actively involved in the recovery process through psychoeducation, maintaining a record log between appointments, completing homework, and practicing problem-solving skills. Craske (1999) states that CBT involves several steps, including cognitive restructuring (CR), relaxation training, imagery exposure, behavior modification, and problem-solving strategies. Others (Rygh & Sanderson, 2004) believe that psychoeducation, CR, positive imagery, worry exposure, improving problem orientation, cost-benefit analysis of coping, and cognitive response prevention are techniques that target the cognitive components of GAD, whereas behavioral response prevention, in vivo exposure, and pleasurable activity scheduling target the behavioral components of GAD. Among other techniques, CBT involves systematic desensitization, applied relaxation, and stimulus control.

CBT uses the executive functions of the PFC to reduce the generation of anxiety by way of its targeting of the ACG, the BG, and the limbic system. The PFC allows CBT to change ruminating worry at a neurochemical level. Conscious thoughts and concentration in the PFC affect the ACG where ruminating worry occurs (PFC can override ACG). By purposely changing thinking patterns, the left PFC can control the overactive limbic system that is producing negativity (Wehrenberg & Prinz, 2007).

Mogg et al. (1995) examined whether CBT could be useful in reducing cognitive bias in GAD. Participants were patients with GAD without comorbid depression and healthy controls. They were tested using a modified Stroop task that contained anxiety-related, depression-related, and neutral words in masked and unmasked exposure conditions. During the test–retest time interval, patients with GAD participated in CBT and then were retested again 20 months after the initial testing (follow-up). Results indicated that after the first testing session, GAD patients showed significantly more interference in color-naming negative words than controls. However, after treatment, there were no differences between groups, and the interference effect and anxious thoughts were reduced at post-treatment and follow-up.

Other treatment options for GAD include exposure therapy, acceptance and commitment therapy, dialectical behavioral therapy, interpersonal therapy, eye movement desensitization, and reprocessing therapy (ADAA, 2011; "Treatment").

Psychopharmacological treatment is also prescribed for individuals with GAD. Psychoactive medications include, among others, the benzodiazepines, azapirones, and the antidepressants. Providing immediate relief from anxiety, the benzodiazepines are the most commonly prescribed of the psychoactive drugs for clients with GAD (Gosselin, Ladouceur, Morin, Dugas, & Baillargeon, 2006). Although their effectiveness for short-term treatment has been noted, the use of benzodiazepines has also been proven to create dependence within weeks for regular users, and, with abrupt withdrawal, symptoms of increased anxiety, insomnia, agitation and irritability, headaches, and difficulty concentrating are often reported (Rygh & Sanderson, 2004; Gosselin et al., 2006). Other side effects of the azapirones and the antidepressants include, but are not limited to, headaches, nausea, dizziness, tension, somnolence and insomnia, hypertension, decreased libido, dry mouth, constipation, urinary hesitance, and weight gain.

Benzodiazepines work mainly by modulating the effects of GABA. These medications increase GABA's inhibitory effects, resulting in an overall decrease in physiological and psychological arousal (Costa & Guidotti, 1979). Azapirones (buspirone), SSRIs, SSNRIs , tricyclics, and MAOIs increase the levels of serotonin in the brain, regulating and restoring the normal levels of the neurotransmitter and how it acts on different neural structures (Wehrenberg & Prinz, 2007; Van Ameringen, 2010). To decrease the release of norepinephrine, beta blockers and alpha 2 autoreceptor agonists are used (Wehrenberg & Prinz, 2007).

Treatment of PD

To treat PD, the individual has to have an understanding of the fears, the consequences, and the anxiety or impending doom associated with the fears (Rosenbaum & Pollack, 1998). In order for treatment to be effective, it has to target fears of bodily sensations (Craske, 1999; Rosenbaum & Pollack, 1998). Because CBT helps the individual become aware and develop effective problem-solving skills, it has become increasingly effective in treating PD. Rosenbaum and Pollack (1998) stated that to achieve wanted results, CBT needs to include informing the individual about the disorder, interoceptive and in vivo exposure, cognitive restructuring, and anxiety management skills. With the aforesaid method and the use of self-help books and patient manuals, panic-free outcome findings of 74%–85% have been reported in short-term treatment, whereas good maintenance of CBT has produced 1–2 years of panic-free symptoms (Rosenbaum & Pollack, 1998).

CBT activates the PFC executive functions (decision-making, inhibition of behavior, making meaning of experience) in order to control or modulate the limbic system arousal. Using the executive functions, the patient can engage in calming techniques (e.g., relaxation, breathing) to change the meaning of the symptoms eradicating irrational beliefs and superstitions about them. The result is a desensitizing of the emotional limbic system reducing the frequency of panic attacks (Wehrenberg & Prinz, 2007). For example, a patient can decide to engage in diaphragmatic breathing; this changes the rate or respiration, which turns the parasympathetic nervous system; this lowers heart rate and blood pressure and raises blood flow, which makes the patient feel calm and relaxed (Wehrenberg & Prinz, 2007). According to Gorman and colleagues (2000), CBT may enhance the ability to handle phobic avoidance and catastrophic thinking (cortical processes), which decreases panic attacks. Psychotherapy can be responsible for improving the ability of the PFC to better regulate the autonomic behavior and response of the amygdala (LeDoux, 1996).

Like GAD, PD is treated with medications. In addition to antidepressants, tricyclic antidepressants, and benzodiazepines, monoamine oxidase inhibitors (MAOIs) are also prescribed to individuals affected by PD (Craske, 1999; Rosenbaum & Pollack, 1998). The antidepressants have proven to be effective for comorbid disorders and, as well, have demonstrated a low potential for abuse and safety in overdose. The benzodiazepines have the highest potential for abuse among abuse-prone individuals, but they also have a rapid onset of action and are the most efficacious psychoactive drug when treating PD (Rosenbaum & Pollack, 1998). SSRIs, SNRIs, atypical SSRIs, tricyclics, and MAOIs are used in order to raise serotonin levels and create balance with norepinephrine. Beta blockers and alpha 2 autoreceptor agonists decrease the release of norepinephrine (Wehrenberg & Prinz, 2007). Benzodiazepines raise the levels of GABA in the PFC, which reduces panic symptoms. Specifically, the benzodiazepines' improvement of the inhibitory effects of the PFC serves to correct the imbalance between GABA and glutamate (Shrestha, Natarajan, & Coplan, 2010). Additionally, the PFC can have an inhibitory effect on the amygdala and whole fear network (Grace & Rosenkranz, 2002).

SUMMARY

Anxiety disorders are among the most common mental disorders. Knowledge of the neuropsychology and neuropathology of anxiety disorders allows for a better understanding of the symptoms, development, and treatment of these disorders. In the past two decades, a growing amount of neuroscientific investigations have provided large amounts of information regarding brain circuitry that plays a role in the etiology of GAD and PD. Anxiety symptoms in GAD are produced by disorders or abnormalities in the amygdala and related brain circuits. A septo-hippocampal circuit is related to the development of GAD. The following neurotransmitters play a role in the occurrence of anxiety disorders: GABA/benzodiazepine complex, NE, 5-HT, cholecystokinin (CCK), CRF, HPA axis, and neurosteroids.

The physiology of PD is explained by an irregular, sensitive fear system, involving the amygdala, PFC, insula, thalamus, brainstem, and hypothalamus. A brainstem periaqueductal gray–medial hypothalamic circuit is related to the development of PD. Levels of putamen in gray matter volumes and lower GABA levels in the BG also play a role in PD.

Increased anxiety levels produce impairment in the measurement of cognitive domains such as attention, memory, and executive function. There is evidence for attention bias in GAD and PD. Attention deficits are the most prevalent in GAD, but there is also evidence for memory and executive function deficits. In PD, there is some evidence for deficits in memory and executive function, and there is clear evidence for attention deficits in PD as well.

Anxiety is often a secondary symptom in neuropsychological problems and brain surgery. Some neuropsychological deficits can produce anxiety symptoms. GAD and PD have a high rate of comorbidity, especially with depression, which makes appropriate diagnosis difficult. Another factor to be considered is test anxiety, which can negatively affect the scores in neuropsychological tests. As our understanding of these various mechanisms of anxiety increases, the role of neuropsychology in multidimensional assessment and treatment will likely also increase.

REFERENCES

Airaksinen, E., Larsson, M., & Forsell, Y. (2005). Neuropsychological functions in anxiety disorders in population-based samples: Evidence of episodic memory dysfunction. *Journal of Psychiatric Research, 39*, 207–214.

American Psychiatric Association. (2000). *Diagnostic and statistical manual of mental disorders, 4th edition, text revision*. Washington, DC: American Psychiatric Association.

Anxiety Disorders Association of America (2011). Generalized anxiety disorder. Retrieved June 30, 2011, from http://www.adaa.org/understanding-anxiety/generalized-anxiety-disorder-gad.

Anxiety Disorders Association of America (2011). Facts and statistics. Retrieved June 30, 2011, from http://www.adaa.org/about-adaa/press-room/facts-statistics.

Anxiety Disorders Association of America. (2011). Treatment. Retrieved July 1, 2011, from http://www.adaa.org/about-adaa/press-room/facts-statistics.

Anxiety. (2011). Retrieved June 28, 2011, from http://www.merriamwebster.com/dictionary/anxiety?show=0&t=1310007078.

Asmundson, G. S. G., Stein, M. B., Larson, D. C., & Walker, J. R. (1994). Neurocognitive function in panic disorder and social phobia patients. *Anxiety 1*, 201–207.

Baddeley, A. (1986). *Working memory*. New York, NY: Clarendon Press/Oxford University Press.

Baddeley, A. D. (2001). Is working memory still working? *American Psychologist, 56*(11), 851–864.

Basso, M. R., Lowery, N., Ghormley, C., Combs, D., Purdie, R., Neel, J., et al. (2007). Comorbid anxiety corresponds with neuropsychological dysfunction in unipolar depression. *Cognitive Neuropsychiatry, 12*(5), 437–456.

Batchelor, J., Harvey, A. G., & Bryant, R. A. (1995). Stroop color word test as a measure of attentional déficit following mild head injury. *The Clinical Neuropsychologist, 9*, 180–186.

Beesdo, K., Lau, J., Guyer, A., McClure-Tone, E., Monk, C., Nelson, E., et al. (2009). Common and distinct amygdala-function perturbations in depressed vs. anxious adolescents. *Archives of General Psychiatry, 66*, 275–285.

Bishop, S., Duncan, J., Brett, M., & Lawrence, A. D. (2004). Prefrontal cortical function and anxiety: Controlling attention to threat-related stimuli. *Nature Neuroscience*, *7*(2), 184–188.

Blair, H. T., Schafe, G. E., Bauer, E. P., Rodrigues, S. M., & LeDoux, J. E. (2001). Synaptic plasticity in the lateral amygdala: A cellular hypothesis of fear conditioning. *Learning & Memory*, *8*(5), 229–242.

Blechert, J., Michael, T., Grossman, P., Lajtman, M., & Wilhelm, F. H. (2007). Autonomic and respiratory characteristics of posttraumatic stress disorder and panic disorder. *Psychosomatic Medicine 69*, 935–943.

Bradley, B. P., Mogg, K., Falla, S. J., & Hamilton, L. R. (1998). Attentional bias for threatening facial expressions in anxiety: Manipulation of stimulus duration. *Cognition and Emotion*, *12*(6), 737–753.

Buckelew, S. P., & Hannay, H. J. (1986). Relationships among anxiety, defensiveness, sex, task difficulty, and performance on various neuropsychological tasks. *Perceptual and Motor Skills*, *63*, 711–718.

Butler, T., Pan., H., Tuescher, O. Engelien, A., Goldstein, M., Epstein, J., et al. (2007). Human fear-related motor neurocircuitry. *Neuroscience 150*, 1–7.

Cannon, B. J. (1999). Relative interference on Logical Memory I Story A versus Story B of the Wechsler Memory Scale-Revised in a clinical sample. *Applied Neuropsychology*, *6*(3), 178–180.

Chapell, M. S., Blanding, Z. B., Silverstein, M. E., Takahashi, M., Newman, B., Gubi, A., et al. (2005). Test anxiety and academic performance in undergraduate and graduate students. *Journal of Educational Psychology*, *97*(2), 268–274.

Chavez, E. L., Trautt, G. M., Brandon, A., & Steyart, J. (1893). Effect of test anxiety and sex of subject on neuropsychological test performance: Finger tapping, trail making, digit span and digit symbol test. *Perceptual and Motor Skills*, *56*, 923–929.

Corbetta, M. & Shulman, G. L. (2002). Control of goal directed and stimulus driven attention in the brain. *Natures Review Neuroscience*, *3*, 201–215.

Costa, E. & Guidotti, A. (1979). Molecular mechanisms in the receptor action of benzodiazepines. *Annual Review in Pharmacology and Toxicology*, *19*, 531–545.

Craske, M. G. (1999). *Anxiety disorders*. Boulder, CO: Westview Press.

Craske, M. G., Rauch, S. L., Ursano, R., Prenoveau, J., Pine, D. S., & Zinbarg, R. E. (2009). What is anxiety disorder? *Depression and Anxiety*, *26*(12), 1066–1085.

Craig, K. J., Phil, M., & Chamberlain, S. R. (2010). The neuropsychology of anxiety disorders. In D. J. Stein E. Hollander & B. O. Rothbaum (Eds.), *Textbook of anxiety disorders* (2nd ed, pp. 87–102). Arlington, VA: American Psychiatric Publishing.

Dalgleish, T., Neshat-Doost, H., Moradi, A., Canterbury, R., & Yule, W. (2003). Patterns of processing bias for emotional information across clinical disorders: A comparison of attention, memory, and prospective cognition in children and adolescents with depression, generalized anxiety, and post-traumatic stress disorder. *Journal of Clinical Child and Adolescent Psychology*, *32*(1), 10–21.

Damsa, C., Kosel, M., & Moussally, J. (2008). Current status of brain imaging on anxiety disorders. *Current Opinion in Psychiatry*, *22*, 96–110.

Davis, Michael (1998). Are different parts of the extended amygdala involved in fear versus anxiety? *Biological Psychiatry*, *44*(12), 1239–1247.

De Bellis, M., Casey, B., Dahl, R., Birmaher, B., Williamson, D., Thomas, K., et al. (2000). A pilot study of amygdala volumes in pediatric generalized anxiety disorder. *Biological Psychiatry*, *48*, 51–57.

De Jong, Peter, J., Visser, S., & Merckelbach, H. (1996). Startle and spider phobia: Unilateral probes and the prediction of treatment effects. *Journal of Psychophysiology*, *10*(2), 150–160.

Dupont, H., Mollard, E., & Cottraux, J. (2000). Visuo-spatial attention processes in panic disorder with agoraphobia: A pilot study using a visual target discrimination task. *European Psychiatry*, *15*, 254–260.

Ehlers, A., Margraf, J., Davies, S., & Roth, W. T. (1988). Information processing and the emotional disorders. *Cognition and Emotion*, *2*(3), 201–219.

Everson, H. T., Millsap, R. E., & Rodriguez, C. M. (1991). Isolating gender differences in test anxiety: A confirmatory factor analysis of the Test Anxiety Inventory. *Educational and Psychological Measurement*, *51*(1), 243–251.

Eysenck, M. W. (1992). *Anxiety: The cognitive perspective*. Hillsdale, NJ: Lawrence Erlbaum Associates.

Eysenck, M. W., Derakshan, N., Santos, R., Calvo, M. G. (2007). Anxiety and cognitive performance: Attentional control theory. *Emotion*, *7*(2), 336–353.

Firetto, A. C. (1971). Subjectively reported anxiety as a discriminator of digit span performance. *Psychological Reports*, *28*, 98.

Giardino, N., Friedman, S. D., & Dager, S. R. (2007). Anxiety, respiration, and cerebral blood flow: Implications for functional brain imaging. *Comprehensive Psychiatry 48*, 103–112.

Gladsjo, J. A., Rapaport, M. H., McKinney, R., Lucas, J. A., Rabin, A., Oliver, T., et al. (1998) A neuropsychological study of panic disorder: Negative findings. *Journal of Affective Disorders 49*, 123–131.

Goodwin, D. W. (1986). *Anxiety*. New York, NY: Oxford University Press.

Gray, J. A. (1991). Fear, panic, and anxiety: What's in a name? *Psychological Inquiry, 2*(1), 77–78.

Gorman, J. M., Kent, J. M., Sullivan, G. M., & Coplan, J. D. (2000). Neuroanatomical hypothesis of panic disorder, revised. *The American Journal of Psychiatry, 157*(4), 493–505.

Gosselin, P., Ladouceur, R., Morin, C. M., Dugas, M. J., & Baillargeon, L. (2006). Benzodiazepine discontinuation among adults with GAD: A randomized trial of cognitive-behavioral therapy. *Journal of Consulting and Clinical Psychology, 74*(5), 908–919.

Grace, A. A., & Rosenkranz, J., Amiel, A. (2002). Regulation of conditioned responses of basolateral amygdala neurons. *Physiology & Behavior, 77*(4–5), 489–493.

Grillon, C. (2002). Startle reactivity and anxiety disorders: Aversive conditioning, context, and neurobiology. *Biological Psychiatry, 52*(10), 958–975.

Grillon, C., & Ameli, R. (1998). Effects of threat of shock, shock electrode placement and darkness on startle. *International Journal of Psychophysiology, 28*(3), 223–231.

Grillon, C., Morgan, C. A. 3rd Davis, M., Southwick, S. M. (1998). Effects of experimental context and explicit threat cues on acoustic startle in Vietnam veterans with posttraumatic stress disorders. *Biological Psychiatry, 44*(10), 1027–1036.

Gualtieri, C. T., & Morgan, D. W. (2008). The frequency of cognitive impairment in patients with anxiety, depression, and bipolar disorder: An unaccounted source of variance in clinical trials. *Journal of Clinical Psychiatry, 69*(7), 1122–1130.

Ham, B. J., Sung, Y., Kim, N., Kim, S. J., Jim, J. E., Kim, D. J., et al. (2007). Decreased GABA levels in anterior cingulated and basal ganglia in medicated subjects with panic disorder: A proton magnetic resonance spectroscopy (1H-MRS) study. *Progressive Neuropsychopharmacology Biology Psychiatry 31*, 403–411.

Higginson, C., Fields, J., & Troster, A. (2001). Which symptoms of anxiety diminish after surgical interventions for Parkinson disease? *Neuropsychiatry, Neuropsychology, and Behavioral Neurology, 11*, 117–123.

Hiott, D., & Labbate, L. (2002). Anxiety disorders associated with traumatic brain injuries. *NeuroRehabilitation, 17*, 345–355.

Hochman, S. H. (1967). The effects of stress on Stroop color-word performance. *Psychonomic Science, 9*(8), 475–476.

Koob, G. F. (1991). Arousal, stress, and inverted U-shaped curves: Implications for cognitive function. In R. G. Lister & H. J. Weingartner (Eds.). *Perspectives on cognitive neuroscience* (pp. 300–313). New York, NY: Oxford University Press.

Krain, A., Gotimer, K., Hefton, S., Ernst, M., Castellanos, F., Pine, M., et al. (2008). A functional magnetic resonance imaging investigation of uncertainty in adolescents with anxiety disorders. *Biological Psychiatry, 63*, 563–568.

Krain, A., Hefton, S., Pine, D., Ernst, M., Castellanos, F., Klein, R., et al. (2006). An fMRI examination of developmental differences in the neural correlates of uncertainty and decision-making. *Journal of Child Psychology and Psychiatry, 47*, 1023–1030.

LaBar, K. S., Gatenby, J. C., Gore, J. C., LeDoux, J. E., & Phelps, E. A. (1998). Human amygdala activation during conditioned fear acquisition and extinction: A mixed-trial fMRI study. *Neuron, 20*, 937–945.

Lautenbacher, S., Spernal, J., & Krieg, J. (2002). Divided and selective attention in panic disorder: A comparative study of patients with panic disorder, major depression and healthy controls. *European Archive of Psychiatry and Clinical Neuroscience, 252*, 210–213.

LeDoux, J. (1998). Fear and the brain: Where have we been, and where are we going? *Biological Psychiatry, 44*(12), 1229–1238.

LeDoux, J. E. (1996). *The emotional brain: The mysterious underpinnings of emotional life*. New York, NY: Simon & Schuster.

Lightfoot, J. D., Seay, S. R., & Goddard, A. W. (2010). Pathogenesis of generalized anxiety disorder. In D. J. Stein, E. Hollander, & B. O. Rothbaum, (Eds.). *Textbook of anxiety disorders* (2nd ed.) (pp. 173–192).Arlington, VA: American Psychiatric Publishing.

Lucas, J. A., Telch, M. J., & Bigler, E. D. (1991) Memory functioning in panic disorder: A neuropsychological perspective. *Journal of Anxiety Disorders, 5*(1), 1–20.

Ludewig, S., Paulusb, M. P., Ludewig, K., & Vollenweidera, F. X. (2003). Decision-making strategies by panic disorder subjects are more sensitive to errors. *Journal of Affective Disorders, 76*, 183–189.

MacLeod, C., Mathews, A., & Tata, P. (1986). Attentional bias in emotional disorders. *Journal of Abnormal Psychology, 95*(1), 15–20.

Malyszczak, K., & Pawlowski, T. (2006). Distress and functioning in mixed anxiety and depressive disorder. *Psychiatry and Clinical Neurosciences, 60*, 168–173.

Mantella, R. C., Butters, M. A., Dew, M. A., Mulsant, B. H., Begley, A. E., Tracey, B., et al. (2007). Cognitive impairment in late-life generalized anxiety disorder. *The American Journal of Geriatric Psychiatry, 15*(8), 673–679.

Marchand, W. R., Lee, J. N., Healy, L., Thatcher, J. W., Rashkin, E., Starr, J., et al. (2009). An fMRI motor activation paradigm demonstrates abnormalities of putamen activation in females with panic disorder. *Journal of Affective Disorders 116*, 121–125.

Maren, S. (2007). The threatened brain. *Science, 317*, 1043–1044.

Mathews, A., & MacLeod, C. (1985). Selective processing of threat cues in anxiety states. *Behaviour Research and Therapy, 23*(5), 563–569.

Mathews, A., & Mackintosh, B. (1998) A cognitive model of selective processing in anxiety. *Cognitive Therapy and Research, 22*(6), 539–560.

McNally, R. J., Riemann, B. C., & Kim, E. (1990) Selective processing of threat cues in panic disorder. *Behaviour Research and Therapy, 28*(5), 407–412.

McReynolds, P. (1985). Changing conceptions of anxiety: A historical review and a proposed integration. *Issues in Mental Health Nursing, 7*(1–4), 131–158.

Meares, S., Shores, E., Taylor, A., Batchelor, J., Bryant, R., Baguley, I., et al. (2011). The prospective course of post concussion syndrome: The role of mild traumatic brain injury. *Neuropsychology, 25*(4), 454–465.

Micco, J. A., Henin, A., Biederman, J., Rosenbaum, J. F., Petty, C., Rindlaub, L. A., et al. (2009). Executive functioning in offspring at risk for depression and anxiety. *Depression and Anxiety, 26*, 780–790.

Miceli, M., & Castelfranchi, C. (2005). Anxiety as an 'epistemic' emotion: An uncertainty theory of anxiety. *Anxiety, Stress & Coping: An International Journal, 18*(4), 291–319.

Miyake, A., Friedman, N. P., Emerson, M. J., Witzki, A. H., & Howerter, A. (2000). The unity and diversity of executive functions and their contributions to complex frontal lobe tasks: A latent variable analysis. *Cognitive Psychology, 41*(1), 49–100.

Mogg, K., & Bradley, B. P. (2005). Attentional bias in generalized anxiety disorder versus depressive disorder. *Cognitive Therapy and Research, 29*(1), 29–45.

Mogg, K., Bradley, B. P., Millar, N., & White, J. (1995). A follow-up study of cognitive bias in generalized anxiety disorder. *Behavior Research and Therapy, 33*(8), 927–935.

Mogg, K., Bradley, B. P., Dixon, C., Fisher, S., Twelftree, H., & McWilliams, A. (2000). Trait anxiety, defensiveness and selective processing of threat: An investigation using two measures of attentional bias. *Personality and Individual Differences, 28*(6), 1063–1077.

Mogg, K., Mathews, A., & Weinman, J. (1989). Selective processing of threat cues in anxiety states: A replication. *Behaviour Research and Therapy, 27*(4), 317–323.

Nieto-Escámez, F., López-Crespo, G., Roldan-Tapia, L., & Cañadas- Pérez, F. (2007). Neurobiology of anxiety (II): Childhood anxiety, generalized anxiety disorder and mixed anxiety-depressive disorder. In H. Buschmann, J. Díaz, J. Holenz, A. Párraga, A. Torrens, J. Vela, et al. (Eds.) *Antidepressants, antipsychotics, anxiolytics from chemistry and pharmacology to clinical application (Vol 1 & 2)* (pp. 761–801). Weinheim, Germany: Wiley-VCH Veriag GmbH & Co KGaA.

O'Toole, K., Borden, K., & Miller, C. (2006). Long-term psychosocial and adaptive outcomes in children with arteriovenous malformations. *Rehabilitation Psychology, 51*, 60–68.

Oostdam, R., & Meijer, J. (2003). Influence of test anxiety on measurement of intelligence. *Psychological Reports, 92*, 3–20.

Overbeek, T., Schruers, K., Van Leeuwen, I., Klaassen, T., & Griez, E. (2005). Experimental affective symptoms in panic disorder patients. *The Canadian Journal of Psychiatry, 50*, 175–178.

Pallak, M. S., Pittman, T. S., Heller, J. F., & Munson, P. (1975). The effect of arousal on Stroop color-word task performance. *Bulletin of the Psychonomic Society, 6*(3), 248–250.

Perkins, A. M., Kemp, S. E., & Corr, P. J. (2007). Fear and anxiety as separable emotions: An investigation of the revised reinforcement sensitivity theory of personality. *Emotion, 7*(2), 252–261.

Phaf, R. H., & Kan, K. J. (2007). The automaticity of emotional Stroop: A meta-analysis. *Journal of Behavior Therapy and Experimental Psychiatry, 38*(2), 184–199.

Phillips, R. G., & LeDoux, J. E. (1992). Differential contribution of amygdala and hippocampus to cued and contextual fear conditioning. *Behavioral Neuroscience, 106*(2), 274–285.

Pine, D., & Grun, J. (1999). Childhood anxiety: Integrating developmental psychopathology and affective neuroscience. *Journal of Child and Adolescent Psychopharmacology, 9*, 1–12.

Pishyar, R., Harris, L. M., & Menzies, R. G. (2004). Attentional bias for words and faces in social anxiety. *Anxiety, Stress & Coping: An International Journal, 17*(1), 23–36.

Pollack, M. H., Smoller, J. W., Otto, M. W., Hoge, E., & Simon, N. (2010). Phenomenology of panic disorder. In D. J. Stein, E. Hollander, & B. O. Rothbaum (Eds.). *Textbook of anxiety disorders* (2nd ed.) (pp. 367–377). Arlington, VA: American Psychiatric Publishing.

Power, M. J., & Tarsia, M. M. (2007). Basic and complex emotions in depression and anxiety. *Clinical Psychology & Psychotherapy, 14*(1), 19–31.

Purcell, R., Maruff, P., Kyrios, M., & Pantelis, C. (1998). Neuropsychological deficits in obsessive-compulsive disorder: A comparison with unipolar depression, panic disorder, and normal controls. *Archives of General Psychiatry, 55*, 415–423.

Ritter, M. R., Blackmore, M. A., & Heimberg, R. G. (2010). Generalized anxiety disorder. In D. McKay, J. S. Abramowitz, S. Taylor, D. McKay, J. S. Abramowitz, S. Taylor (Eds.). *Cognitive-behavioral therapy for refractory cases: Turning failure into success* (pp. 111–137). Washington, DC: American Psychological Association.

Rosenbaum, J. F., & Pollack, M. H. (1998). *Panic disorder and its treatment*. New York, NY: Marcel Dekker.

Rozzini, L., Chilovi, B., Peli, M., Conti, M., Rozzini, R., Trabucchi, M., et al. (2009). Anxiety symptoms in mild cognitive impairment. *International Journal of Geriatric Psychiatry, 24,* 300–305.

Rygh, J. L., & Sanderson, W. C. (2004).*Treating generalized anxiety disorder*. New York, NY: Guilford Press.

Schafe, G. E., Nader, K., Blair, H. T., & LeDoux, J. E. (2001). Memory consolidation of Pavlovian fear conditioning: A cellular and molecular perspective. *Trends in Neurosciences, 24*(9), 540–546.

Sheehan, D. (2004). A 37 year old woman with treatment resistant panic disorder. Or is it bipolar anxiety? *Psychiatric Annals, 34,* 904–910.

Shrestha, R., Natarajan, N., & Coplan, J. D. (2010). Pathogenesis of panic disorder. In D. J. Stein, E. Hollander, & B. O. Rothbaum (Eds.). *Textbook of anxiety disorders* (2nd ed.) (pp. 381–398). Arlington, VA: American Psychiatric Publishing.

Silton, R., Heller, W., Engels, A., Towers, D., Spielberg, J., Edgar, J., et al. (2011). Depression and anxious apprehension distinguish frontocingulate cortical activity during top-down attentional control. *Journal of Abnormal Psychology, 120,* 272–285.

Stone, M. H. (2010). History of anxiety disorders. In D. J. Stein, E. Hollander, B. O. Rothbaum, D. J. Stein, E. Hollander, B. O. Rothbaum (Eds.). *Textbook of anxiety disorders* (2nd ed.) (pp. 3–15). Arlington, VA: American Psychiatric Publishing.

Straus, E., Sherman, E. M. S., & Spreen, O. (2006). *A compendium of neuropsychological tests: Administration, norms, and commentary*. New York, NY: Oxford University Press.

Tan, E., Thomas, J., & Chan, L. (2007). Unexpected cause of anxiety and Parkinsonism. *The American Journal of Psychiatry, 164,* 347–348.

Teri, L., Ferretti, L., Gibbons, L., Logsdon, R., McCurry, S., Kukull, W., et al. (1999). Anxiety in Alzheimer's disease: Prevalence and comorbidity. *The Journals of Gerontology: Series A: Biological Sciences and Medical Sciences, 54,* 348–352.

Tramontana, M. G., Hooper, S. R., Watts-English, T., Ellison, T., & Bethea, T. C. (2009). Neuropsychology of child psychopathology. In C. R. Reynolds, & E. Fletcher-Janzen (Eds.). *Handbook of clinical child neuropsychology* (pp. 117–146). New York, NY: Springer Science + Business Media.

Van Ameringen, M. V., Mancini, C., Patterson, B., Simpson, W., & Truong, C. (2010). Pharmacotherapy for generalized anxiety disorder. In D. J. Stein, E. Hollander, & B. O. Rothbaum (Eds.) *Textbook of anxiety disorders* (2nd ed.) (pp. 193–218). Arlington, VA:American Psychiatric Publishing.

Van den Heuvel, O. A., Veltman, D. J., Groenewegen, H. J., Witter, M. P., Merkelbach, J., Cath, D.C., et al. (2005). Disorder-specific neuroanatomical correlates of attentional bias in obsessive-compulsive disorder, panic disorder, and hypochondriasis. *Archives of General Psychiatry 62,* 922–933.

Vasa, R. A., Roberson-Nay, R., Klein, R. G., Mannuzza, S., Moulton, J. L., Guardino, M., Merikangas, A., Carlino, A. R., Pine, D. S. (2007). Memory deficits in children with and at risk for anxiety disorders. *Depression and Anxiety, 24*(2), 85–94.

Vrana, S. R., Constantine, J. A., & Westman, J. S. (1992). Startle reflex modification as an outcome measure in the treatment of phobia: Two case studies. *Behavioral Assessment, 14*(3–4), 279–291.

Waters, A. M., & Valvoi, J. S. (2009). Attentional bias for emotional faces in pediatric anxiety disorders: An investigation using the emotional go/no go task. *Journal of Behavior Therapy and Experimental Psychiatry, 40,* 306–316.

Waters, A. M., Mogg, K., Bradley, B. P., & Pine, D. S. (2008). Attentional bias for emotional faces in children with generalized anxiety disorder. *Journal of the American Academy of Child & Adolescent Psychiatry, 47*(4), 435–442.

Wehrenberg, M., & Prinz, S. (2007). *The anxious brain*. New York, NY: W.W. Norton & Company.

Williams, J. M. G., Mathews, A., & MacLeod, C. (1996). The emotional Stroop task and psychopathology. *Psychological Bulletin, 120*(1) 3–24.

Yerkes, R. M., & Dodson, J. D. (1908). The relation of strength of stimulus to rapidity of habit formation. *Journal of Comparative Neurology & Psychology, 18,* 459–482.

Yoo, H. K., Kim, M. J., Kim, S. J., Sung, Y. H., Sim, M. E., Lee, Y. S., et al.. (2005). Putamenal gray matter volume decrease in panic disorder: An optimized voxel-based morphometry study. *Europe Journal of Neuroscience 22,* 2089–2094.

Zal, H. M. (1990). *Panic disorder*. New York, NY: Plenum Press.

CHAPTER 12

Obsessive-Compulsive Disorder

Robert M. Roth, Marc E. Lavoie, Emily A. Mason, & Kieron P. O'Connor

INTRODUCTION

Obsessive-compulsive disorder (OCD) is characterized by intrusive, repetitive, and distressing thoughts, images, and impulses (obsessions), as well as repetitive behaviors or mental acts (compulsions) that the person feels compelled to perform, typically in response to obsessions and aimed at preventing an unwanted event or situation and/or reducing distress (American Psychiatric Association [APA], 2000). The symptoms are typically recognized as being excessive or unrealistic, although insight may be limited in some adults and especially in children with the disorder (De Berardis et al., 2005; Storch et al., 2008).

The symptom presentation of OCD is heterogeneous. Factor and cluster analytical studies of symptom measures, such as the Yale Brown Obsessive Compulsive Scale (YBOCS; Goodman et al., 1989), have identified a number of symptom dimensions that tend to be relatively stable over time within individuals (Fullana et al., 2009; Mataix-Cols et al., 2002b). These include repeatedly washing hands or other parts of the body to free oneself from imagined contamination, repeated checking behaviors to ensure that nothing has been forgotten or missed that may result in harm to oneself or others, excessive concern with order or symmetry, and hoarding (Bloch, Landeros-Weisenberger, Rosario, Pittenger, & Leckman, 2008; McKay et al., 2004). Obsessions pertaining to religious, sexual, or aggressive themes or health concerns are also reported. Obsessional doubt may manifest itself as slowness, indecisiveness, or rumination without any overt compulsion. It should be noted that although compulsive hoarding is currently listed as a symptom of OCD, there is evidence suggesting that it may represent a distinct subgroup or syndrome (Mataix-Cols et al., 2010; Pertusa et al., 2008; Samuels et al., 2007).

OCD is associated with significant disruption of psychosocial functioning (Moritz, 2008; Steketee, 1997), reduced quality of life in patients (Eisen et al., 2006; Huppert, Simpson, Nissenson, Liebowitz, & Foa, 2009; Moritz, 2008) and their relatives (Stengler-Wenzke, Kroll, Matschinger, & Angermeyer, 2006), as well as considerable economic cost to the individual and society (DuPont, Rice, Shiraki, & Rowland, 1995). This is particularly concerning given the typically lengthy period of time taken by people with OCD to seek treatment (Belloch, Del Valle, Morillo, Carrio, & Cabedo, 2009).

In this chapter, we first provide a brief overview of the epidemiology of OCD. We then review the neuropsychological correlates of the disorder, including variables that may contribute to the heterogeneity of findings. Treatments for OCD are briefly discussed along with evidence for their impact on neuropsychological functioning in the disorder. This is followed by a discussion of the neural substrates of OCD and its associated cognitive limitations, highlighting contributions from neuroimaging and neurophysiology.

EPIDEMIOLOGY

OCD is reported to be the fourth most prevalent mental illness after major depression, drug abuse, and panic disorder (Robins, Helzer, Weissman, & Orvaschel, 1984). Epidemiological studies of community samples have reported prevalence rates of approximately 1%–3% in adults (Fullana et al., 2009; Kolada, Bland, & Newman, 1994; Weissman et al., 1994) and 1%–4% in children and adolescents (Rapoport et al., 2000; Valleni-Basile et al., 1994; Zohar, 1999), rates being relatively consistent cross-nationally (Mohammadi et al., 2004; Weissman et al., 1994). OCD is more common in males in pediatric samples (Geller, 2006), whereas adult samples have revealed either equivalent or somewhat higher rates for women (Rasmussen & Eisen, 1992; Weissman et al., 1994). First-degree relatives of people with OCD are at considerably greater risk for developing the disorder than the general population (Hanna, Himle, Curtis, & Gillespie, 2005; Nestadt et al., 2000).

The onset of idiopathic OCD is typically insidious, although precipitating events or stressors such as childbirth (Abramowitz, Moore, Carmin, Wiegartz, & Purdon, 2001; Uguz, Akman, Kaya, & Cilli, 2007) have been reported. Age of onset has been reported to be bimodal, with one peak between 10 and 12 years of age and a second peak in the early to mid 20s (Delorme et al., 2005). Age of onset may be especially relevant to the etiology and treatment of OCD because early onset has been associated with male gender predominance, greater symptom severity, a higher rate of tic disorders, poorer response to treatment, and a greater likelihood of having a family history of OCD (Fontenelle, Mendlowicz, Marques, & Versiani, 2003; Rosario-Campos et al., 2001).

OCD is chronic in most individuals. A meta-analysis of 22 longitudinal studies involving a total of 521 children with OCD, with follow-up periods ranging from 1–15.6 years, reported a persistence rate of 41% for full OCD and 60% for full or subthreshold OCD (Stewart et al., 2004). A longitudinal study of mostly untreated persons with OCD revealed that the disorder persisted in 48% after 30 years, 44% after 40 years, and 37% after 50 years (Skoog & Skoog, 1999). Furthermore, a substantial percentage of those who do not meet full criteria for OCD at follow-up continue to report only partial remission (Skoog & Skoog, 1999; Steketee, Eisen, Dyck, Warshaw, & Rasmussen, 1999).

NEUROPSYCHOLOGICAL FUNCTIONING

OCD has been the subject of numerous neuropsychological investigations since the late 1980s. These have been prompted by the observation of OCD symptoms in patients with neurological disorders (see following), clinical characteristics of OCD such as difficulty suppressing intrusive thoughts, and neuroimaging studies of OCD implicating brain circuitry involved in a variety of cognitive processes. Here, we discuss research on the performance of patients with OCD in major domains of neuropsychological functioning.

Intellectual Functioning

Many studies of neuropsychological functioning matched groups of patients with OCD and healthy controls either on a single measure estimating intellectual functioning, a composite of Wechsler Adult Intelligence Scale (WAIS) subtests (Wechsler, 1981), or least commonly on the full WAIS or other similar measures. Lower performance IQ has been observed on the WAIS-R in adults with OCD (Boone, Ananth, Philpott, & Kaur, 1991; Bucci et al., 2007), with picture completion and object assembly subtests being notably impaired (Bucci, et al., 2007). A study of children with OCD showed poor performance on arithmetic, block design, and object assembly subtests (M.-S. Shin et al., 2008). Studies that provided a group comparison have otherwise typically not observed significant difference between adults with OCD and healthy controls (Boldrini et al., 2005; Boone, et al., 1991; Hwang et al., 2007; Mataix-Cols et al., 2006; Purcell, Maruff, Kyrios, & Pantelis, 1998b). Together, findings suggest that intellectual functioning in OCD is generally comparable to healthy controls, but when differences do emerge, they are most likely to be seen on tests involving visuoperceptual and visuoconstruction skills.

Attention

Although abnormal sustained attention in persons with subclinical OCD (Mataix-Cols et al., 1997) and impaired selective attention in adults with OCD on the Tests of Everyday Attention (Clayton, Richards, & Edwards, 1999) have been reported, the majority of studies have found little evidence of dysfunction in auditory attention span (Boldrini et al., 2005; Sawamura, Nakashima, Inoue, & Kurita, 2005; Zielinski, Taylor, & Juzwin, 1991) or selective attention (Boone et al., 1991; Schmidtke, Schorb, Winkelmann, & Hohagen, 1998). Furthermore, patients with OCD have been observed to have intact speed and accuracy during sustained attention on the continuous performance test, irrespective of modality (auditory or visual), task difficulty (undegraded or degraded) or medication status (Lee, Chiu, Chiu, Chang, & Tang, 2009; Milliery, Bouvard, Aupetit, & Cottraux, 2000; Nordahl et al., 1989).

Executive Functions

Several theoretical models have emphasized the potential role of executive dysfunction in OCD (Chamberlain, Blackwell, Fineberg, Robbins, & Sahakian, 2005; Rosenberg & Keshavan, 1998; Stein & Ludik, 2000). The ability to inhibit thoughts and behaviors, in particular, has been the focus of considerable theoretical and empirical attention. Deficient response inhibition has been observed in several studies of OCD using measures such as the stop-signal, go/no-go, and Stroop tasks (Bannon, Gonsalvez, Croft, & Boyce, 2002; Chamberlain et al., 2007b; Morein-Zamir, Fineberg, Robbins, & Sahakian, 2010; Penadés et al., 2007; Van der Linden, Ceschi, Zermatten, Dunker, & Pearlson, 2005), albeit with some contradictory findings (Krikorian, Zimmerman, & Fleck, 2004; Schmidtke et al., 1998).

Watkins and colleagues (2005) reported impaired response inhibition during a go/no-go task in OCD after the response contingencies of the stimuli designated as "go" and "no-go" were switched. This finding appears consistent with several studies that have observed impaired cognitive flexibility in the disorder (Chamberlain, Fineberg, Blackwell, Robbins, & Sahakian, 2006), including perseveration on alternation learning tasks (Abbruzzese, Ferri, & Scarone, 1997; Gross-Isseroff et al., 1996; Moritz et al., 2009a). A meta-analysis of Wisconsin Card Sorting Task (WCST) performance in OCD reported small to moderate effect sizes for categories completed, perseverative errors, and total errors, but concluded that the deficit likely reflects more generalized cognitive impairment, possibly secondary to cognitive slowing (Henry, 2006). Several studies have also failed to observe a deficit on the WCST in the disorder (Abbruzzese, Ferri, & Scarone, 1995; Nakao et al., 2009; Simpson et al., 2006).

Evidence for impairment in other aspects of executive function is more limited. Planning and problem-solving ability, as measured by such tasks as the Tower of London and Tower of Hanoi, has generally not been observed to be impaired with respect to accuracy in OCD (Purcell et al., 1998b; Veale, Sahakian, Owen, & Marks, 1996; Watkins et al., 2005; Rampacher et al., 2010). Patients have been observed, however, to require longer times to generate alternate strategies following errors (Veale et al., 1996) and take longer to make initial and subsequent movements (Purcell et al., 1998b).

Performance on spatial working memory tasks from the Cambridge Neuropsychological Test Automated Battery (Robbins et al., 1994) has been reported to be impaired in OCD (Chamberlain et al., 2007a; Purcell, Maruff, Kyrios, & Pantelis, 1998a; Purcell et al., 1998b). Spatial working memory was reported to be intact on an N-back task (Nakao et al., 2009), and normal working memory has been noted on a visual delayed matching-to sample task (Ciesielski et al., 2007) and paper-pencil versions of the self-ordered pointing task (Martin, Wiggs, Altemus, Rubenstein, & Murphy, 1995; Roth, Milovan, Baribeau, O'Connor, &

Todorov, 2004), although slowness in completing the latter was observed in one study (Martin et al., 1995). Reverse Digit Span has been reported to be intact (Aronowitz, Hollander, DeCaria, & Cohen, 1994), but otherwise auditory working memory has received little attention.

It has been suggested that OCD may involve difficulties with decision making (Cavedini, Gorini, & Bellodi, 2006). Most studies of decision-making in OCD have employed the Iowa Gambling Task (IGT; Bechara, Damasio, Damasio, & Anderson, 1994), many observing impairment on the task (Cavallaro et al., 2003; Cavedini et al., 2002; Starcke, Tuschen-Caffier, Markowitsch, & Brand, 2010). Other studies have observed intact performance on the IGT (Lawrence et al., 2006; Nielen, Veltman, de Jong, Mulder, & den Boer, 2002) or other decision-making tasks (Chamberlain et al., 2007b). Of note, a recent study reported that IGT performance in OCD varied based on the presence of certain polymorphisms of a serotonin transporter gene (da Rocha et al., 2008). This raises the possibility that heterogeneity in decision-making ability, and likely other executive functions in OCD, may at least partially have a genetic basis.

A number of investigations have also examined reasoning ability in OCD. Specifically, studies using experimental methods and questionnaires have suggested that patients with OCD have difficulty with inferential (Aardema, O'Connor, Emmelkamp, Marchand, & Todorov, 2005; Wu, Aardema, & O'Connor, 2009), inductive (Pélissier, O'Connor, & Dupuis, 2009; Pélissier & O'Connor, 2002; Simpson, Cove, Fineberg, Msefti, & Ball, 2007), and probabilistic (Fear & Healy, 1997) reasoning. Such reasoning deficits have been argued to be central to the development of the disorder (O'Connor, Aardema, & Pélissier, 2005).

Overall, the current state of the literature provides some support for the involvement of executive dysfunction in OCD. Nevertheless, inconsistencies across investigations and the failure of some studies to find any evidence of executive dysfunction across several measures (Roth, Baribeau, Milovan, & O'Connor, 2004b; Simpson et al., 2006) suggest heterogeneity in this cognitive domain in patients with the disorder.

Memory

Several studies have employed the California Verbal Learning Test (CVLT; Delis, Kramer, Kaplan, & Ober, 2000) to assess verbal memory in OCD, but findings have been mixed. For example, some have observed poorer encoding across Trials 1–5 but intact delayed recall (Burdick, Robinson, Malhotra, & Szeszko, 2008), impaired encoding and long but not short delay free recall (Deckersbach et al., 2004; Savage et al., 2000), or completely intact encoding, recall, and recognition memory (Bohne et al., 2005; de Geus, Denys, Sitskoorn, & Westenberg, 2007). Comparable scores to healthy controls have also been observed on other verbal memory measures (Boldrini et al., 2005; Boone et al., 1991; Burdick et al., 2008; Cha et al., 2008), albeit with some dissenting findings (Exner et al., 2009; Zitterl et al., 2001). There is also evidence of an elevated number of intrusion errors in the context of otherwise intact recall (Boldrini et al., 2005; Zielinski, Taylor, & Juzwin, 1990). Thus, at present there is little evidence for a consistent verbal memory deficit in OCD.

In contrast, there is stronger support for the presence of a visual memory deficit in OCD. Several studies have reported impaired recall on the Rey Complex Figure Test (RCFT; Boldrini et al., 2005; Penadés, Catalán, Andrés, Salamero, & Gastó, 2005; Savage et al., 1999), as well as recall on other tests of visual memory (Burdick, et al., 2008; Simpson et al., 2006). Intact performance on visual memory tests has, however, also been observed (Bohne et al., 2005; Exner et al., 2009; Simpson et al., 2006). Recognition memory has generally been reported to be intact (Bohne et al., 2005; Savage et al., 1996). At least one study observed a trend toward worse visual memory in patients with OCD having a family history of the disorder but not in those without such a background (Boone et al., 1991).

Other aspects of memory have also been examined in OCD. Intact performance was observed across a variety of tasks tapping into memory for everyday situations (Jelinek, Moritz, Heeren, & Naber, 2006). Prospective memory has been reported to be intact (Jelinek et al., 2006), although other work found impairment that appeared to be due to over-monitoring of the memory cues in the task employed (Racsmany, Demeter, Csigo, Harsanyi, & Nemeth, 2010), suggesting that the finding may have been related to executive dysfunction. Executive dysfunction may also have contributed to impairment on other memory tests. Several investigations have reported that OCD is associated with deficient use of organizational strategies during encoding on the CVLT and RCFT that contributed to impaired recall (Deckersbach, Otto, Savage, Baer, & Jenike, 2000; Penadés et al., 2005; Savage et al., 1999, 2000; Shin et al., 2004). This has not been consistently replicated (Bohne et al., 2005; Shin et al., 2010; Simpson et al., 2006), however, and other work suggests that impaired strategy use does not generalize across measures (Roth et al., 2004c). When deficient organizational strategy use is present, it appears to be due to a failure to spontaneously generate strategies such as semantic clustering (Deckersbach et al., 2005) or slowness in analyzing semantic features of material to be encoded (Sawamura et al., 2005), rather than difficulty implementing strategies.

Confidence in one's memory, or metamemory, has been considered by some as important in OCD, especially with respect to compulsive checking (MacDonald, Antony, Macleod, & Richter, 1997; Rachman, 2002). Numerous studies have reported poorer metamemory in OCD relative to healthy controls (Tolin et al., 2001; Tuna, Tekcan, & Topcuoglu, 2005; Zitterl et al., 2001), although some have reported no association with either OCD in general or checking in particular (Moritz, Ruhe, Jelinek, & Naber, 2009b). Interestingly, there is evidence to suggest that diminished memory confidence in OCD is more likely to be elicited in situations where perceived responsibility for one's actions is high (Boschen & Vuksanovic, 2007; Moritz et al., 2007). Thus, methodological differences between studies with respect to perceived responsibility may have contributed to the heterogeneity of metamemory findings.

Implicit Learning

Theoretical models have implicated implicit learning in OCD (Rauch & Savage, 2000; Saint-Cyr, Taylor, & Nicholson, 1995), a cognitive function associated with frontostriatal circuitry (Rauch et al., 1997). Implicit learning, as measured using serial reaction time tasks (SRT), has been reported to be reduced in both children (Vloet et al., 2010) and adults (Deckersbach et al., 2002; Goldman et al., 2008; Kathmann, Rupertseder, Hauke, & Zaudig, 2005) with OCD, and negatively impacted by concurrent demands for explicit memory (Deckersbach et al., 2002). In contrast, a study employing the Pursuit Rotor Task, which places greater demand on motor ability, showed abnormally enhanced procedural learning during the early, but not later course of learning (Roth, Baribeau, Milovan, O'Connor, & Todorov, 2004a). It is likely that the discrepant findings are due at least partly to the cognitive (SRT) versus motor (Rotor) nature of the tasks, but direct comparison in the same sample would be informative.

Language

Multiple studies have reported deficits in verbal fluency in OCD (Head, Bolton, & Hymas, 1989; Schmidtke et al., 1998). A recent meta-analysis found reduced phonemic and semantic fluency in the disorder, based on 20 and 9 studies respectively, that were of equivalent magnitude (Henry, 2006). That nonverbal fluency has also been reported to be impaired in the disorder (Schmidtke et al., 1998) suggests that diminished verbal fluency may be at least partly the result of psychomotor slowing.

The performance of patients with OCD on other tests of language has received little empirical attention. Ludlow, Bassaich, Connor, & Rapoport (1989) reported that adolescents with OCD were intact on tests of verbal fluency, sentence construction, sentence and digit repetition, and writing the names of objects or writing to dictation. In contrast, response latency was slow on the Boston Naming Test and when naming objects presented to either hand, but items that could be named on the latter task had normal response speed, suggesting that the deficit was not due to impaired tactile perception.

Visuospatial and Visuoconstruction Skills

Abnormalities in visuospatial and visuoconstruction skills have been observed in OCD, particularly on measures such as the RCFT copy trial (Boone et al., 1991; Flessner et al., 2010;

Lacerda et al., 2003) and Block Design (Head et al., 1989; Hollander et al., 1993; Moritz et al., 2005b), although contradictory findings have also been reported (Savage et al., 1999; Simpson et al., 2006). A more detailed examination of these skills was conducted by Moritz and colleagues (2005b) in a large sample of 71 patients with OCD, 33 psychiatric controls, and 30 healthy controls. Results revealed poorer performance in the OCD relative to healthy group on some of the more complex visuospatial measures such as Block Design, visuospatial transformation, and figure completion. Notably, the OCD and healthy group did not differ in their RCFT copy or Corsi Block Tapping scores, and differed on only two out of 96 scores reported for more elementary visuospatial measures such as line orientation and bisection, distance estimation, and form discrimination. Overall, these findings suggest a possible subtle difficulty with more complex visuospatial and visuoconstruction skills in OCD, although it remains unclear whether this may be due to deficits in other domains such as processing speed or executive functions.

Psychomotor Speed

Several studies have reported slower psychomotor speed on measures such as Trail Making Test A and Symbol Digits Modalities Test in OCD (Burdick et al., 2008; Hashimoto et al., 2008; Schmidtke et al., 1998). Slowed speed has also been noted during performance on tasks designed primarily as measures of other skills such as visuoconstruction and executive function (Galderisi, Mucci, Catapano, D'Amato, & Maj, 1995; Roth et al., 2004). Contradictory evidence has also been observed (Aronowitz et al., 1994; Roth et al., 2004), and some studies have suggested that when impairment is observed it is related to comorbid symptoms of depression (Basso, Bornstein, Carona, & Morton, 2001) or medication (Kuelz, Hohagen, & Voderholzer, 2004).

Sensory and Motor Skills

Sensory and motor skills have received little attention in studies of OCD. Sensory deficits have been reported on tests of olfactory perception (Barnett et al., 1999, Gross-Isseroff et al., 1994, Hermesh, Zohar, Weizman, Voet, & Gross-Isseroff, 1999), Tactile Forms Recognition time to respond (Basso et al., 2001), and Finger Tip Number Writing (Basso et al., 2001). Adults with OCD have also been reported to show deficits on tests of motor skills such as the Purdue Pegboard (Bedard, Joyal, Godbout, & Chantal, 2009) and Grooved Pegboard (Basso et al., 2001; Burdick et al., 2008), but not Finger Tapping (Burdick et al., 2008). Unfortunately, whether deficits are lateralized has not been reported. In contrast, normal motor skill and tactile perception has been reported in pediatric OCD (Beers et al., 1999; Cox, Fedio, & Rapoport, 1989). Interestingly, a recent study observed that poorer Grooved Pegboard performance at age 13, among other tests, was associated with the presence of OCD in adulthood (Grisham, Andersen, Poulton, Moffit, & Andrews, 2009).

CONTRIBUTORS TO NEUROPSYCHOLOGICAL PERFORMANCE

Age and Gender

The impact of age on neuropsychological functioning in OCD is difficult to ascertain because cognition has not been examined longitudinally over an extended period in the disorder. The small number of studies involving children with OCD has yielded variable results. The first such study by Beers and colleagues (1999) observed no deficits in 21 children with OCD on tests of fine motor coordination, processing speed, visuoconstruction, auditory attention, verbal fluency, verbal memory, planning, response inhibition, and cognitive flexibility. Other studies have also observed largely intact auditory attention, sustained visual attention, verbal and visual memory, executive functions, verbal fluency, visuospatial skills, or psychomotor speed (Ornstein, Arnold, Manassis, Mendlowitz, & Schacher, 2010; M.-S. Shin et al., 2008), although one noted impaired WCST performance (M.-S. Shin et al., 2008) and another found poorer spatial attention (Chang, McCracken, & Piacentini, 2007). Ornstein and colleagues (2010) reported relatively small differences between 14 children with OCD and a healthy control group on some aspects of measures of design fluency, sequencing, motor speed, and planning, as well as more intrusions during verbal memory recall. Other studies have observed poorer visual memory, as well as speed of information processing and executive functions (Andres et al., 2007; Andres et al., 2008). Overall, these findings suggest that at least some children with OCD may present with problems in the areas of executive function, memory, and attention consistent with that seen in some of the adult OCD literature.

As with age, few studies have examined whether gender impacts neuropsychological functioning in OCD. A study of 32 patients reported that males and females with OCD were equivalent on the WCST and a test of object alternation (Zohar, Hermesh, Weizman, Voet, & Gross-Isseroff, 1999). The study also noted that object alternation showed opposite patterns of correlation with symptom severity depending on gender. A larger study of 55 patients that also included a healthy control sample revealed poorer performance in women with OCD relative to healthy women on measures of verbal fluency, category alternation, the Stroop test word reading trial, and auditory attention (Mataix-Cols et al., 2006). In addition, a significant negative correlation was noted between OCD symptom severity and performance on Stroop word reading and category alternation in women but not men with the disorder. The authors interpreted their findings as suggesting cross-sex shifts on some tasks, but that overall, gender is not a major contributor to cognitive functioning in the disorder.

Age of Onset

A small number of studies have examined the relationship between age of onset and cognition in OCD. Although the age ranges used to define early and late onset subgroups have varied, older age of onset in adults with OCD has been found to be associated with poorer memory (Hwang et al., 2007; Roth, Milovan, Baribeau, & O'Connor, 2005; Segalas et al., 2008), verbal fluency (Hwang, et al., 2007), as well as auditory attention and executive function (Roth et al., 2005). Failures to observe differences in memory (Henin et al., 2001), intellect, or executive function (Hwang et al., 2007) have also been reported. Those with early onset have been consistently found not to differ from healthy controls in these studies.

Severity of Illness

Neuropsychological studies of OCD have most often reported minimal or no significant correlations between OCD symptom severity and cognitive functioning (Andres et al., 2007; Burdick et al., 2008; Moritz, Kloss, Schick, & Hand, 2003; Simpson et al., 2006), although some have observed relationships with only certain memory or executive function tests (de Geus et al., 2007; Mataix-Cols et al., 2006). Furthermore, one study reported no differences on executive function measures between remitted and symptomatic patients with OCD (Bannon, Gonsalvez, Croft, & Boyce, 2006). Another found deficits in cognitive flexibility, alternation, response inhibition, and nonverbal memory in recovered patients (Rao, Reddy, Kumar, Kandavel, & Chandrashekar, 2008). Deficits were not seen for planning, visuoconstruction, auditory attention, sustained visual attention, verbal fluency, or verbal memory. Together, these findings suggest that symptom severity of OCD symptoms is unlikely to account for cognitive dysfunction in the disorder.

Symptom Subtypes

Several subtyping schemes have been proposed for OCD, including those based on symptom clusters, presence or absence of a tic disorder, and a schizo-obsessive subtype (Geller et al., 1998; Leckman, Bloch, & King, 2009; Zohar, 1997). The earliest studies examining cognitive functioning in relation to subtypes suggested that compulsive checking in clinical and subclinical samples is associated with memory deficits (Cha et al., 2008; Sher, Frost, Kushner, Crews, & Alexander, 1989; Sher, Frost, & Otto, 1983), including memory for actions, as well as executive functions (Nedeljkovic et al., 2009; Roth & Baribeau, 1996). More recent work has observed an association between checking and prospective memory (Cuttler & Graf, 2007). Although failure to find a relationship between compulsive checking and memory has also been reported (Jelinek, Moritz, Heeren, & Naber, 2006), a meta-analysis of 22 studies indicated that checkers are impaired in their memory for verbal and visual information as well as their actions, and are less confident in their memory than non-checkers (Woods, Vevea, Chambless, & Bayen, 2002).

Other symptom subtypes may also contribute to variability in cognitive findings in OCD. A study of 39 patients with OCD revealed impaired decision-making on the Iowa Gambling Task only in patients with prominent hoarding symptoms, whereas symmetry/ordering symptoms were associated with poorer cognitive flexibility (Lawrence et al., 2006). Another study reported normal decision-making in compulsive hoarders relative to a mixed clinical sample and healthy controls (Grisham, Brown, Savage, Steketee, & Barlow, 2007). The latter study did, however, observe slower reaction time and greater impulsivity in hoarders that could not be accounted for by depression, schizotypal traits, or the severity of other OCD symptoms.

The presence of schizotypal personality traits in patients with OCD has itself been associated with deficient verbal fluency and WCST performance (N. Y. Shin et al., 2008) and a more diffuse pattern of executive dysfunction than in OCD patients without such traits (Harris & Dinn, 2003). Furthermore, schizotypal traits, along with depression, were reported to account for deficits in executive function and verbal fluency in OCD (Aycicegi, Dinn, Harris, & Erkmen, 2003). Interestingly, the severity of overvalued ideation in patients with OCD has also been found to be associated with poorer cognitive functioning (Kitis et al., 2007).

Co-occurring Psychiatric Disorders

Research on the impact of comorbid psychiatric problems on neuropsychological functioning in OCD has focused almost exclusively on depression, typically examining correlations between performance on continuous measures such as the Beck Depression Inventory (Beck, 1987) or Hamilton Depression rating Scale (Williams, 1988). Several such studies have reported that depression contributes to deficits in OCD on measures such as those tapping executive functions, memory, and verbal fluency (Basso et al., 2001; Moritz et al., 2001; Moritz et al., 2003). However, the specific tests implicated have been inconsistent across studies, the association with depression has not been observed consistently (Burdick et al., 2008; Rampacher et al., 2010), and deficits have also been noted in non-depressed patients (Boone et al., 1991; Christensen, Kim, Dysken, & Hoover, 1992). A few studies have directly compared patients with OCD to those with major depressive disorder (MDD). Patients with OCD have been reported to be more perseverative on an object alternation test than those with MDD (Cavedini, Ferri, Scarone, & Bellodi, 1998), and OCD but not MDD was associated with executive function and memory deficits in other work (Purcell et al., 1998b; Rampacher et al., 2010). One study reported no differences between OCD-only and OCD with comorbid Axis I disorder (mostly depressive and anxiety disorders) groups, although neither of these groups differed from healthy controls (Simpson et al., 2006). Although these findings certainly raise the issue of the impact of comorbid psychiatric disorders (either DSM Axis I or Axis II) on neuropsychological functioning in OCD, there are too few studies to date addressing the issue to draw any firm conclusions.

Medication Status

The majority of studies examining the role of medication status on neuropsychological functioning in OCD have compared unmedicated and medicated subgroups. Most of these have involved selective serotonin reuptake inhibitors (SSRI) and have shown no significant impact of medication status in a variety of domains including intelligence, attention, memory, visuoconstruction, or executive functions (Mataix-Cols, Alonso, Pifarre, Menchon, & Vallejo, 2002a;

Shin et al., 2010; Simpson et al., 2006). In one study, benzodiazepine use was associated with better semantic fluency, and the combination of SSRI and benzodiazepines was related to fewer perseverative errors on the WCST and faster reaction times (Mataix-Cols et al., 2002a). Importantly, cognitive deficits have also been observed in unmedicated patients with OCD (Savage et al., 1999; Schmidtke et al., 1998). Overall, these findings indicate that medication status cannot readily account for cognitive deficits in the disorder.

Cause or Consequence

Recent research has begun to examine whether cognitive deficits are present in the unaffected first-degree relatives of patients with OCD. As compared to those without such a family history, relatives of patients with OCD have been reported to show poorer planning (Delorme et al., 2007), cognitive flexibility, and response inhibition (Chamberlain et al., 2007b; Menzies et al., 2007), as well as decision-making and delayed alternation (Viswanath, Janardhan Reddy, Kumar, Kandavel, & Chandrashekar, 2009). Although attention, memory, and verbal and design fluency have been reported to be intact in relatives (Viswanath et al., 2009), there is a dearth of research on nonexecutive processes in this population. Although additional research is required, these findings suggest that executive dysfunction may contribute to the vulnerability to OCD.

TREATMENT AND NEUROPSYCHOLOGICAL FUNCTIONING

The current state of evidence supports the use of SSRIs (Geller et al., 2003; Soomro, Altman, Rajagopal, & Oakley-Browne, 2008) and cognitive-behavioral psychotherapies (Abramowitz, Franklin, & Foa, 2002; Gava et al., 2007) as first-line treatments for OCD. Among psychotherapies, exposure with response prevention, cognitive restructuring, and the combination of these appear to be effective for many patients (Rosa-Alcazar, Sanchez-Meca, Gomez-Conesa, & Marin-Martinez, 2008). A variety of other medications, medication combinations, psychotherapeutic approaches, or combined pharmacotherapy and psychotherapy can also be effective (Foa et al., 2005; Matsunaga et al., 2009; O'Connor et al., 2006). For those for whom these are not effective, psychosurgery may afford significant symptom relief (Greenberg, Rauch, & Haber, 2010). In particular, recent research has supported the use of deep brain stimulation for OCD in at least some otherwise treatment-refractory patients (Greenberg et al., 2010).

Unfortunately, few studies have directly examined the effects of treatment on neuropsychological functioning in OCD. Treatment with SSRIs has been associated with improved focused attention and strategic ability (Nielen & Den Boer, 2003) as well as visual memory (Kang et al., 2003) in adults with OCD. Andres and colleagues (2008) examined 29 children and adolescents with OCD before and after 6 months of pharmacological intervention (90% received an SSRI, 10% clomipramine), a subset of whom also participated in a structured cognitive-behavioral therapy (CBT). Results revealed a more pronounced improvement overall in cognition in the OCD relative to a healthy control group, especially on measures of immediate visual memory and information processing speed.

A small number of studies have examined the effects of behavioral therapy on cognitive functioning in OCD, although some of these did not include a control group (Bolton, Raven, Madronal-Luque, & Marks, 2000). Significantly greater improvement in visual memory was observed in patients showing a "major" versus "minor" response to 12 weeks of CBT in one study (Kuelz et al., 2006). Interestingly, a recent study reported that worse pretreatment visual memory was associated with worse outcome following CBT alone than for a sertraline alone or combined CBT-sertraline group (Flessner et al., 2010). In contrast, other studies have reported that neuropsychological functioning is not predictive of outcome following CBT (Bolton et al., 2000; Moritz et al., 2005a) or treatment with SSRIs (Thienemann & Koran, 1995).

Two studies have examined the effects of a cognitive remediation on organization strategy use and memory in OCD. Buhlmann and colleagues (2006) evaluated RCFT performance before and after either training on how to organize the copy of the Taylor Figure (an alternate form of the Rey Figure) or a non-training condition that involved simply looking at the Taylor Figure for 1 minute. As expected, training was associated with better organization and recall, but the patient group improved more in their organizational strategy use than controls irrespective of whether they were trained or not. These findings were interpreted as suggesting that OCD is associated with impairment in the ability to spontaneously generate, but not ability to implement, organizational strategies. In another study, patients completed nine 60-minute sessions over 5 weeks focused on improving organizational strategy use using a variant of the Block Design test as well as guidance for ameliorating organization in everyday life (Park et al., 2006). Results revealed a significant effect of treatment, relative to a control group, for copy, recall, and organizational strategy use on the RCFT, as well as a reduction of symptom severity. Together, these findings suggest that at least some of the cognitive difficulties reported in OCD may be amenable to cognitive remediation.

NEUROBIOLOGICAL BASIS OF OCD

The idea that OCD symptoms may originate from the brain goes back over 100 years (Berrios, 1989). In the early 20th century, such symptoms were observed in post-encephalis lethargica patients (Cheyette & Cummings, 1995), a condition associated with antibodies reactive against the basal ganglia (Dale et al., 2004). Since that time, elevated rates of OCD or subclinical obsessive-compulsive (OC) symptoms have been reported in a variety of neurological conditions. The association between OCD and tic disorders is particularly well established (Grados et al., 2001; Pauls, Towbin, Leckman, Zahner, & Cohen, 1986), but other movement disorders have also been associated with OCD symptoms, including Parkinson disease (Alegret et al., 2001; Hardie, Lees, & Stern, 1984), Huntington disease (Cummings & Cunningham, 1992), primary dystonia (Bugalho, Correa, Guimaraes, & Xavier, 2006), and Sydenham chorea (Asbahr, Ramos, Negrao, & Gentil, 1999), although some studies have failed to show a relationship (Harbishettar, Pal, Janardhan Reddy, & Thennarasu, 2005; Maia, Pinto, Barbosa, Menezes, & Miguel, 2003). Elevated rates of OC symptoms have also been reported in patients with epilepsy, particularly those with temporal lobe involvement (Ertekin et al., 2009; Isaacs, Philbeck, Barr, Devinsky, & Alper, 2004; Monaco et al., 2005), as well as new onset of OCD following resection of medial temporal lobe (Kulaksizoglu et al., 2004; Roth, Jobst, Thadani, Gilbert, & Roberts, 2009) or after "modified" right temporal lobectomy (Chemali & Bromfield, 2003). These reports, along with a variety of other case reports or case series, have most commonly involved the basal ganglia or more broadly frontal–striatal circuitry, and less commonly temporal lobe regions, in OCD.

Not surprisingly, for over two decades, neurobiological models of OCD have emphasized the role of frontal-striatal-thalamic-cortical circuitry dysfunction (Chamberlain et al., 2005; Modell, Mountz, Curtis, & Greden, 1989; Rosenberg & Keshavan, 1998). This circuitry plays an important role in a variety of cognitive processes, especially those falling under the rubric of executive functions (Roth, Randolph, Koven, & Isquith, 2006). This section will provide a brief review of the contributions of modern structural and functional neuroimaging research, as well as event-related potentials, to our understanding of the cognitive characteristics and pathophysiology of OCD.

Structural Neuroimaging

Numerous studies have employed magnetic resonance imaging (MRI) scans to investigate brain structure in OCD. Studies investigating the volume of regions of interest (ROIs) have most commonly focused on the frontal lobe, striatum, and thalamus. Findings have been inconsistent, however, and some studies have reported both abnormally increased volume in some regions such as the anterior cingulate gyrus and reduced volume in other regions (Szeszko et al., 2004; Roth & Pendergrass, 2006). Furthermore, while the hippocampus has been infrequently implicated in neurobiological models of OCD, there is evidence of volume loss and shape abnormalities in this region (Atmaca et al., 2008; Hong et al., 2007).

A recent meta-analysis examined regional brain volumes on MRI scans in 371 patients with OCD and 407 healthy control subjects (Rotge et al., 2009). OCD was associated with reduced volume of the left anterior cingulate cortex (ACC) and the left and right orbitofrontal cortex (OFC), and increased volume of the thalamus bilaterally. Furthermore, greater left thalamic effect size was correlated with the severity of obsessions. No difference in volume was found for the whole brain, intracranial region, gray matter, prefrontal cortex, or striatum. Interestingly, despite evidence for reduced caudate nucleus volume in at least some studies of pediatric OCD (Rosenberg et al., 1997), when data for children with OCD was excluded from the meta-analysis results showed significantly smaller caudate volume in adults with the disorder.

Apart from volumetric analysis of ROIs, other studies have employed analytic tools such as voxel-based morphometry (VBM) and cortical thickness mapping to investigate brain morphology without being restricted to a small number of ROIs. For example, a VBM study by Valente et al. (Valente et al., 2005) observed that patients with OCD have increased gray matter volume in the posterior orbitofrontal and parahippocampal gyrus, as well as decreased gray matter in the anterior cingulate cortex. A study of cortical thickness mapping revealed thicker right inferior frontal cortex and posterior middle temporal gyrus in patients with OCD compared with healthy controls (Narayan et al., 2008).

Diffusion tensor imaging (DTI) studies have provided evidence of abnormality of white matter pathways in OCD (Menzies et al., 2008; Szeszko et al., 2005). Of particular importance is a recent study that observed reduced white matter integrity in the parietal lobe but abnormally enhanced integrity in the medial frontal lobe in OCD and unaffected first-degree relatives, suggesting that it may reflect a vulnerability marker (Menzies et al., 2008). Interestingly, there is evidence that the pattern of white matter abnormality observed may be different depending on symptom subtypes (Ha et al., 2009) and may be normalized following effective treatment for the disorder (Yoo et al., 2007).

Overall, structural neuroimaging studies have provided additional evidence for abnormality of frontal-striatal-thalamic-cortical circuitry in OCD. There are numerous potential contributors to the heterogeneity of the findings, including sample and methodological characteristics. Particularly intriguing is the possibility that variability may be related to genetic variation. A recent study of a pediatric OCD sample reported that smaller volume of the orbitofrontal cortex and anterior cingulate cortex, and larger thalamic volume, was associated with polymorphisms of specific glutamate system genes previously implicated in OCD (Arnold et al., 2009a).

Magnetic Resonance Spectroscopy (MRS)

Several investigations have used MRS to examine brain chemistry and metabolism in OCD. These have the most consistently observed abnormality of glutamate and N-acetylaspartate (NAA) concentrations. Glutamate abnormality has been seen in brain regions such as the caudate (Rosenberg et al., 2000) and anterior cingulate gyrus (Rosenberg et al., 2004; Yucel et al., 2008), and reduced glutamate in the anterior cingulate gyrus has been linked to a polymorphism of a glutamate receptor gene (Arnold et al., 2009b). Lower NAA, a marker of neuronal health, has been observed in regions such as the striatum (Bartha et al., 1998; Ebert et al., 1997) and anterior cingulate gyrus (Ebert et al., 1997; Jang et al., 2006), although it was noted to be increased in the dorsolateral prefrontal cortex of a pediatric OCD sample (Russell et al., 2003). Pharmacotherapy has been reported to improve the regional concentration of both glutamate (Rosenberg et al., 2000) and NAA (Jang et al., 2006) in OCD.

Functional Neuroimaging

Functional neuroimaging studies of OCD have relied heavily on positron emission tomography (PET) and functional MRI (fMRI). Investigations of the disorder using these technologies may be classified in three broad domains: Studies conducted while patients are instructed to rest (i.e., no task to perform); symptom provocation studies where anxiety- or obsession-related stimuli are presented (e.g., pictures of dirty toilets); and cognitive challenges designed to examine the integrity of neural circuitry subserving a particular cognitive process.

Resting State

Studies using ^{18}Fluorodeoxyglucose-PET have commonly reported abnormally increased glucose metabolism in the orbitofrontal cortex, caudate nucleus, thalamus, and anterior cingulate cortex, as well as other regions of the prefrontal cortex in patients with OCD relative to healthy controls (Baxter et al., 1987; Nordahl et al., 1989; Swedo et al., 1989). A meta-analysis of PET and single photon emission computed tomography (SPECT) studies of OCD yielded the largest effect sizes for abnormality of the left orbitofrontal cortex and head of the caudate nucleus bilaterally (Whiteside, Port, & Abramowitz, 2004). Furthermore, an fMRI resting state study observed abnormally heightened connectivity of vental corticostriatal regions in OCD (Harrison et al., 2009). This indicates that the interrelationships between several brain regions are functionally abnormal, consistent with a circuitry dysfunction model of the disorder. The pattern of abnormalities has been reported, however, to depend partly on the presence of comorbid major depression (Saxena et al., 2001) and symptom subtype (Jang et al., 2010; Saxena et al., 2004). Significantly improved metabolism has been reported following both pharmacotherapy (Saxena et al., 1999) and behavior therapy (Schwartz, Stoessel, Baxter, Martin, & Phelps, 1996).

Symptom Provocation

Symptom provocation studies of OCD have revealed a similar pattern of abnormalities as that observed during the rested state, including most prominently over-activation of orbitofrontal cortex, anterior cingulate gyrus, and caudate nucleus (Adler et al., 2000; Rauch et al., 1994). Interestingly, it has been reported that greater orbitofrontal cortex activation or metabolism during symptom provocation is associated with less increase of OCD severity ratings during symptom provocation (Adler et al., 2000; Rauch et al., 1994). This may suggest that engagement of the orbitofrontal cortex reflects attempts to suppress obsessions and/or anxiety when faced with disorder-related cues (Roth et al., 2007). Furthermore, abnormal amygdala activation has not commonly been seen in such studies of OCD, which contrasts with studies of anxiety disorders such as PTSD, social anxiety disorder, and specific phobia (Etkin & Wager, 2007). As in resting state studies, the pattern of abnormal brain activation or metabolism during symptom provocation varies depending on symptom subtype (Mataix-Cols et al., 2004; Tolin, Kiehl, Worhunsky, Book, & Maltby, 2009), interpreted as suggesting that subtypes are mediated by relatively distinct neural circuitry involved in cognitive and emotional processing (Mataix-Cols et al., 2004).

Cognitive Challenges

The majority of cognitive challenge investigations of OCD have focused on activation of brain circuitry during the performance of tasks that place demands on executive functions. Several fMRI studies have revealed abnormal frontostriatal activation during response inhibition in children (Rubia et al., 2010; Woolley et al., 2008) and adults (Page et al., 2009; Roth et al., 2007) with the disorder. Other work has implicated exaggerated performance monitoring, as reflected by over-activation of the anterior cingulate cortex, among other regions, subsequent to behavioral errors (Maltby, Tolin, Worhunsky, O'Keefe, & Kiehl, 2005; Ursu, Stenger, Shear, Jones, & Carter, 2003). There is also evidence of abnormal recruitment of the hippocampus during implicit learning in OCD (Rauch et al., 1997; Rauch et al., 2007), interpreted as suggesting reliance on declarative memory circuitry secondary to dysfunction of frontostriatal circuitry subserving implicit learning (Rauch & Savage, 2000). Recent research has also revealed reduced activation of frontostriatal circuitry when patients were required to think flexibly (Chamberlain et al., 2008; Gu et al., 2008). Furthermore, under-activation of the orbitofrontal cortex was observed during a reversal learning task in both patients with OCD and unaffected first-degree relatives (Chamberlain et al., 2008).

Overall, neuroimaging findings are generally consistent with other evidence for frontal-striatal-thalamic cortical dysfunction in OCD. It appears, however, that placing demands on executive functions through cognitive challenges is more commonly associated with under-activation of this circuitry, with the exception of performance monitoring, whereas the circuitry during the resting state and symptom provocation is typically over-activated.

Event-Related Potentials (ERPs)

ERP studies of OCD have mainly focused on three cognitive functions: attention, response inhibition, and performance monitoring. The findings have provided valuable information about brain and cognitive function in the disorder at a more temporally refined level than available with current fMRI technology.

Misallocation of Cognitive Resources

Several ERP studies have implicated over-focused attention in OCD as manifested by shorter latency P300 (Beech, Ciesielski, & Gordon, 1983; Towey et al., 1990; Towey et al., 1994), particularly when task difficulty was increased (Towey et al., 1990; Towey et al., 1993). OCD has also been reported to be associated with larger processing negativity over the frontal area and a smaller P300 to attended target stimuli, while the N200 is intact, during attention tasks (Towey et al., 1994). Similar finding with a visual oddball task showed reduced P300 amplitude to rare/target stimuli specific to OCD patients, particularly in the anterior region (Thibault et al., 2008). Furthermore, while latency of P300 is faster, that of the N100 and P200 have been observed to be delayed in OCD (Morault, Bourgeois, Laville, Bensch, & Paty, 1997). Together, these findings suggest misallocation of cognitive resources during stimulus evaluation in OCD.

Response Inhibition

The ability to inhibit motor responses has been investigated in a number of ERPs studies of OCD using several versions of the go/no-go task. Smaller orbitofrontal P300 amplitude during no-go trials requiring response inhibition (Malloy, Rasmussen, Braden, & Haier, 1989) or larger frontal P300 to go trials only (Di Russo, Zaccara, Ragazzoni, & Pallanti, 2000) have been observed. Frontal N200 amplitude has also been reported to be larger (Johannes et al., 2001) or smaller (Kim, Kim, Yoo, & Kwon, 2007) to both go and no-go stimuli or only to no-go stimuli (Herrmann, Jacob, Unterecker, & Fallgatter, 2003) in the disorder. Despite these seemingly contradictory findings, the results have been generally interpreted as reflecting abnormal response inhibition in OCD. Furthermore, they also suggest that cognitive dysfunction in OCD may fluctuate due to a problem of cognitive flexibility mediated by specific impairment in frontal circuitry inhibitory capacity.

Performance Monitoring

It has been argued that OCD is the result of abnormal activity within a system involved in the detection and correction of errors (Pitman, 1987a, 1987b). This is consistent with evidence from neuroimaging studies indicating the presence of a frontal–striatal network that monitors events and generates error signals when the events conflict with an individual's internal goals (Taylor, Stern, & Gehring, 2007). It has been suggested that an ERP component, the error-related negativity (ERN), which appears to be generated by the anterior cingulate cortex, reflects performance monitoring or, more specifically, the detection and correction of errors (Gehring, Coles, Meyer, & Donchin, 1995; Gehring & Knight, 2000; Scheffers & Coles, 2000). Several studies have reported abnormally enhanced frontal ERN amplitude to errors in both children (Hajcak, Franklin, Foa, & Simons, 2008; Santesso, Segalowitz, & Schmidt, 2006) and adults (Endrass, Klawohn, Schuster, & Kathmann, 2008; Gehring, Himle, & Nisenson, 2000; Hajcak & Simons, 2002) with OCD, a finding that is unrelated to medication status (Stern et al., 2010). A recent study showed differential ERN amplitude in neutral versus punishment conditions in healthy adults but not in those with OCD, who showed no such variation, suggesting that OCD is associated with difficulty in down-regulating monitoring activity according to context (Endrass et al., 2010). Another study showed, however, that trial-by-trial feedback significantly reduced the ERN in patients with OCD, suggesting that they may be reassured by a verification of their performance, potentially relieving some of the burden placed on the performance monitoring system (Nieuwenhuis, Nielen, Mol, Hajcak, & Veltman, 2005). These results further support the view of an impaired capacity to modulate the conflict monitoring system and suggest exaggerated perception of error-likelihood in the disorder. Such a disturbance could contribute to the psychological characteristics present in many patients with OCD, such as perfectionism and inflated responsibility.

SUMMARY

Neuropsychological studies have contributed significantly to our understanding of OCD. Although findings have been somewhat inconsistent across investigations, the weight of the evidence suggests that at least some patients with OCD exhibit problems with executive functions, most commonly involving reduced response inhibition, cognitive flexibility, and organizational strategy use. Although the evidence for a declarative memory deficit is variable, it appears that when this is present, it may occur at least partly secondary to deficient organizational strategy use. Subtle deficits in other cognitive processes have also been occasionally observed, in particular complex visuospatial/visuoconstruction skills. Furthermore, potential contributors to the heterogeneity of the neuropsychological impairment in OCD have only relatively recently begun to be a significant focus of empirical investigation. Nonetheless, several variables have been reported to be of salience, including age of OCD onset, symptom subtypes, comorbid depression, and the presence of schizotypal traits.

Structural and functional neuroimaging studies have most commonly implicated frontal-striatal-thalamic cortical dysfunction in OCD, whereas ERPs have pinpointed impairments in attention, inhibition, and performance monitoring. This is generally consistent with the neuropsychological literature and has begun to inform the development of novel interventions such as deep brain stimulation for treatment-refractory OCD (Greenberg et al., 2010).

Finally, there is a small body of research indicating that neuropsychological deficits in OCD may be improved following pharmacological or behavioral treatment for the disorder. In addition, recent work has raised the possibility that cognitive remediation may be beneficial, although it remains unclear which patients would most likely benefit from this intervention. Despite these promising findings, considerably more research is needed before any conclusions may be drawn with respect to the role of neuropsychological assessment in treatment monitoring or the prediction of treatment response in OCD.

REFERENCES

Aardema, F., O'Connor, K. P., Emmelkamp, P. M., Marchand, A., & Todorov, C. (2005). Inferential confusion in obsessive-compulsive disorder: The inferential confusion questionnaire. *Behaviour Research & Therapy, 43*(3), 293–308.

Abbruzzese, M., Ferri, S., & Scarone, S. (1995). Wisconsin Card Sorting Test performance in obsessive-compulsive disorder: No evidence for involvement of dorsolateral prefrontal cortex. *Psychiatry Research, 58*(1), 37–43.

Abbruzzese, M., Ferri, S., & Scarone, S. (1997). The selective breakdown of frontal functions in patients with obsessive-compulsive disorder and in patients with schizophrenia: A double dissociation experimental finding. *Neuropsychologia, 35*(6), 907–912.

Abramowitz, J., Moore, K., Carmin, C., Wiegartz, P. S., & Purdon, C. (2001). Acute onset of obsessive-compulsive disorder in males following childbirth. *Psychosomatics, 42*(5), 429–431.

Abramowitz, J. S., Franklin, M. E., & Foa, E. B. (2002). Empirical status of cognitive-behavioral therapy for obsessive-compulsive disorder: A meta-analytic review. *Romanian Journal of Cognitive & Behavioral Psychotherapies, 2*(2), 89–104.

Adler, C. M., McDonough-Ryan, P., Sax, K. W., Holland, S. K., Arndt, S., & Strakowski, S. M. (2000). fMRI of neuronal activation with symptom provocation in unmedicated patients with obsessive compulsive disorder. *Journal of Psychiatric Research, 34*(4–5), 317–324.

Alegret, M., Junque, C., Valldeoriola, F., Vendrell, P., Marti, M. J., & Tolosa, E. (2001). Obsessive-compulsive symptoms in Parkinson's disease. *Journal of Neurology, Neurosurgery & Psychiatry, 70*(3), 394–396.

American Psychiatric Association (2000). *Diagnostic and statistical manual of mental disorders* (revised, 4th ed.). Washington, DC: American Psychiatric Press.

Andres, S., Boget, T., Lazaro, L., Penades, R., Morer, A., Salamero, M., et al. (2007). Neuropsychological performance in children and adolescents with obsessive-compulsive disorder and influence of clinical variables. *Biological Psychiatry, 61*(8), 946–951.

Andres, S., Lazaro, L., Salamero, M., Boget, T., Penadés, R., & Castro-Fornieles, J. (2008). Changes in cognitive dysfunction in children and adolescents with obsessive-compulsive disorder after treatment. *Journal of Psychiatric Research, 42*(6), 507–514.

Arnold, P. D., MacMaster, F. P., Hanna, G. L., Richter, M. A., Sicard, T., Burroughs, E., et al. (2009a). Glutamate system genes associated with ventral prefrontal and thalamic volume in pediatric obsessive-compulsive disorder. *Brain Imaging and Behavior, 3*, 64–76.

Arnold, P. D. MacMaster, F. P., Richter, M. A., Hanna, G. L., Sicard, T., Burroughs, E., et al. (2009b). Glutamate receptor gene (GRIN2B) associated with reduced anterior cingulate glutamatergic concentration in pediatric obsessive-compulsive disorder. *Psychiatry Research, 172*(2), 136–139.

Aronowitz, B. R., Hollander, E., DeCaria, C., & Cohen, L. (1994). Neuropsychology of obsessive compulsive disorder: Preliminary findings. *Neuropsychiatry, Neuropsychology, & Behavioral Neurology, 7*(2), 81–86.

Asbahr, F. R., Ramos, R. T., Negrao, A. B., & Gentil, V. (1999). Case series: Increased vulnerability to obsessive-compulsive symptoms with repeated episodes of Sydenham chorea. *Journal of the American Academy of Child & Adolescent Psychiatry, 38*(12), 1522–1525.

Atmaca, M., Yildirim, H., Ozdemir, H., Ozler, S., Kara, B., Ozler, Z., et al. (2008). Hippocampus and amygdalar volumes in patients with refractory obsessive-compulsive disorder. *Progress in Neuro-Psychopharmacology & Biological Psychiatry, 32*(5), 1283–1286.

Aycicegi, A., Dinn, W. M., Harris, C. L., & Erkmen, H. (2003). Neuropsychological function in obsessive-compulsive disorder: Effects of comorbid conditions on task performance. *European Psychiatry, 18*(5), 241–248.

Bannon, S., Gonsalvez, C. J., Croft, R. J., & Boyce, P. M. (2002). Response inhibition deficits in obsessive-compulsive disorder. *Psychiatry Research, 110*(2), 165–174.

Bannon, S., Gonsalvez, C. J., Croft, R. J., & Boyce, P. M. (2006). Executive functions in obsessive-compulsive disorder: State or trait deficits? *Australian & New Zealand Journal of Psychiatry, 40*(11–12), 1031–1038.

Barnett, R., Maruff, P., Purcell, R., Wainwright, K., Kyrios, M., Brewer, W., et al. (1999). Impairment of olfactory identification in obsessive-compulsive disorder. *Psychological Medicine, 29*(5), 1227–1233.

Bartha, R., Stein, M. B., Williamson, P. C., Drost, D. J., Neufeld, R. W., Carr, T. J., et al. (1998). A short echo 1H spectroscopy and volumetric MRI study of the corpus striatum in patients with obsessive-compulsive disorder and comparison subjects. *American Journal of Psychiatry, 155*(11), 1584–1591.

Basso, M. R., Bornstein, R. A., Carona, F., & Morton, R. (2001). Depression accounts for executive function deficits in obsessive-compulsive disorder. *Neuropsychiatry, Neuropsychology, & Behavioral Neurology, 14*(4), 241–245.

Baxter, L. R. Jr., Phelps, M. E., Mazziotta, J. C., Guze, B. H., Schwartz, J. M., & Selin, C. E. (1987). Local cerebral glucose metabolic rates in obsessive-compulsive disorder: A comparison with rates in unipolar depression and in normal controls. *Archives of General Psychiatry, 44*(3), 211–218.

Bechara, A., Damasio, A. R., Damasio, H., & Anderson, S. W. (1994). Insensitivity to future consequences following damage to human prefrontal cortex. *Cognition, 50*(1), 7–15.

Beck, A. T. (1987). *Beck depression inventory.* San Antonio, TX: The Psychological Corporation.

Bedard, M.-J., Joyal, C. C., Godbout, L., & Chantal, S. (2009). Executive functions and the obsessive-compulsive disorder: On the importance of subclinical symptoms and other concomitant factors. *Archives of Clinical Neuropsychology, 24*(6), 585–598.

Beech, H. R., Ciesielski, K. T., & Gordon, P. K. (1983). Further observations of evoked potentials in obsessional patients. *British Journal of Psychiatry, 142*, 605–609.

Beers, S. R., Rosenberg, D. R., Dick, E. L., Williams, T., O'Hearn, K. M., Birmaher, B., et al. (1999). Neuropsychological study of frontal lobe function in psychotropic-naive children with obsessive-compulsive disorder. *American Journal of Psychiatry, 156*(5), 777–779.

Belloch, A., Del Valle, G., Morillo, C., Carrio, C., & Cabedo, E. (2009). To seek advice or not to seek advice about the problem: The help-seeking dilemma for obsessive-compulsive disorder. *Social Psychiatry & Psychiatric Epidemiology, 44*(4), 257–264.

Berrios, G. E. (1989). Obsessive-compulsive disorder: Its conceptual history in France during the 19th century. *Comprehensive Psychiatry, 30*(4), 283–295.

Bloch, M. H., Landeros-Weisenberger, A., Rosario, M. C., Pittenger, C., & Leckman, J. F. (2008). Meta-analysis of the symptom structure of obsessive-compulsive disorder. *American Journal of Psychiatry, 165*(12), 1532–1542.

Bohne, A., Savage, C. R., Deckersbach, T., Keuthen, N. J., Jenike, M. A., Tuschen-Caffier, B., et al. (2005). Visuospatial abilities, memory, and executive functioning in trichotillomania and obsessive-compulsive disorder. *Journal of Clinical & Experimental Neuropsychology, 27*(4), 385–399.

Boldrini, M., Del Pace, L., Placidi, G. P. A., Keilp, J., Ellis, S. P., Signori, S., et al. (2005). Selective cognitive deficits in obsessive-compulsive disorder compared to panic disorder with agoraphobia. *Acta Psychiatrica Scandinavica, 111*(2), 150–158.

Bolton, D., Raven, P., Madronal-Luque, R., & Marks, I. M. (2000). Neurological and neuropsychological signs in obsessive compulsive disorder: Interaction with behavioural treatment. *Behaviour Research & Therapy, 38*(7), 695–708.

Boone, K. B., Ananth, J., Philpott, L., & Kaur, A. (1991). Neuropsychological characteristics of nondepressed adults with obsessive-compulsive disorder. *Neuropsychiatry, Neuropsychology, & Behavioral Neurology, 4*(2), 96–109.

Boschen, M. J., & Vuksanovic, D. (2007). Deteriorating memory confidence, responsibility perceptions and repeated checking: Comparisons in OCD and control samples. *Behaviour Research & Therapy, 45*(9), 2098–2109.

Bucci, P., Galderisi, S., Catapano, F., Di Benedetto, R., Piegari, G., Mucci, A., et al. (2007). Neurocognitive indices of executive hypercontrol in obsessive-compulsive disorder. *Acta Psychiatrica Scandinavica, 115*, 380–387.

Bugalho, P., Correa, B., Guimaraes, J., & Xavier, M. (2006). Obsessive-compulsive disorder and executive deficits in two patients with primary dystonia. *Parkinsonism & Related Disorders, 12*(6), 388–391.

Buhlmann, U., Deckersbach, T., Engelhard, I., Cook, L. M., Rauch, S. L., Kathmann, N., et al. (2006). Cognitive retraining for organizational impairment in obsessive-compulsive disorder. *Psychiatry Research, 144*(2–3), 109–116.

Burdick, K. E., Robinson, D. G., Malhotra, A. K., & Szeszko, P. R. (2008). Neurocognitive profile analysis in obsessive-compulsive disorder. *Journal of the International Neuropsychological Society, 14*(4), 640–645.

Cavallaro, R., Cavedini, P., Mistretta, P., Bassi, T., Angelone, S. M., Ubbiali, A., et al. (2003). Basal-corticofrontal circuits in schizophrenia and obsessive-compulsive disorder: A controlled, double dissociation study. *Biological Psychiatry, 54*(4), 437–443.

Cavedini, P., Ferri, S., Scarone, S., & Bellodi, L. (1998). Frontal lobe dysfunction in obsessive-compulsive disorder and major depression: A clinical-neuropsychological study. *Psychiatry Research, 78*(1–2), 21–28.

Cavedini, P., Gorini, A., & Bellodi, L. (2006). Understanding obsessive-compulsive disorder: Focus on decision making. *Neuropsychology Review, 16*(1), 3–15.

Cavedini, P., Riboldi, G., D'Annucci, A., Belotti, P., Cisima, M., & Bellodi, L. (2002). Decision-making heterogeneity in obsessive-compulsive disorder: Ventromedial prefrontal cortex function predicts different treatment outcomes. *Neuropsychologia, 40*(2), 205–211.

Cha, K. R., Koo, M.-S., Kim, C.-H., Kim, J. W., Oh, W.-J., Suh, H. S., et al. (2008). Nonverbal memory dysfunction in obsessive-compulsive disorder patients with checking compulsions. *Depression & Anxiety, 25*(11), E115–E120.

Chamberlain, S. R., Blackwell, A. D., Fineberg, N. A., Robbins, T. W., & Sahakian, B. J. (2005). The neuropsychology of obsessive compulsive disorder: The importance of failures in cognitive and behavioural inhibition as candidate endophenotypic markers. *Neuroscience and Biobehavioral Reviews, 29*(3), 399–419.

Chamberlain, S. R., Fineberg, N. A., Blackwell, A. D., Clark, L., Robbins, T. W., & Sahakian, B. J. (2007a). A neuropsychological comparison of obsessive-compulsive disorder and trichotillomania. *Neuropsychologia, 45*(4), 654–662.

Chamberlain, S. R., Fineberg, N. A., Blackwell, A. D., Robbins, T. W., & Sahakian, B. J. (2006). Motor inhibition and cognitive flexibility in obsessive-compulsive disorder and trichotillomania. *American Journal of Psychiatry, 163*, 1282–1284.

Chamberlain, S. R., Fineberg, N. A., Menzies, L. A., Blackwell, A. D., Bullmore, E. T., Robbins, T. W. et al. (2007b). Impaired cognitive flexibility and motor inhibition in unaffected first-degree relatives of patients with obsessive-compulsive disorder. *American Journal of Psychiatry, 164*(2), 335–338.

Chamberlain, S. R., Menzies, L., Hampshire, A., Suckling, J., Fineberg, N. A., del Campo, N., et al. (2008). Orbitofrontal dysfunction in patients with obsessive-compulsive disorder and their unaffected relatives. *Science, 321*(5887), 421–422.

Chang, S. W., McCracken, J. T., & Piacentini, J. C. (2007). Neurocognitive correlates of child obsessive compulsive disorder and Tourette syndrome. *Journal of Clinical & Experimental Neuropsychology, 29*(7), 724–733.

Chemali, Z., & Bromfield, E. (2003). Tourette's syndrome following temporal lobectomy for seizure control. *Epilepsy & Behavior, 4*(5), 564–566.

Cheyette, S. R., & Cummings, J. L. (1995). Encephalitis lethargica: Lessons for contemporary neuropsychiatry. *Journal of Neuropsychiatry & Clinical Neuroscience, 7*(2), 125–134.

Christensen, K. J., Kim, S. W., Dysken, M. W., & Hoover, K. M. (1992). Neuropsychological performance in obsessive-compulsive disorder. *Biological Psychiatry, 31*(1), 4–18.

Ciesielski, K. T., Hamalainen, M. S., Geller, D. A., Wilhelm, S., Goldsmith, T. E., & Ahlfors, S. P. (2007). Dissociation between MEG alpha modulation and performance accuracy on visual working memory task in obsessive compulsive disorder. *Human Brain Mapping, 28*(12), 1401–1414.

Clayton, I. C., Richards, J. C., & Edwards, C. J. (1999). Selective attention in obsessive-compulsive disorder. *Journal of Abnormal Psychology, 108*(1), 171–175.

Cox, C. S., Fedio, P., & Rapoport, J. L. (1989). Neuropsychological testing of obsessive-compulsive adolescents. In J. L. Rapoport (Ed.), *Obsessive-compulsive disorder in children and adolescents* (pp. 73–85). Washington, D.C.: American Psychiatric Press.

Cummings, J. L., & Cunningham, K. (1992). Obsessive-compulsive disorder in Huntington's disease. *Biological Psychiatry, 31*(3), 263–270.

Cuttler, C., & Graf, P. (2007). Sub-clinical compulsive checkers' prospective memory is impaired. *Journal of Anxiety Disorders, 21*(3), 338–352.

da Rocha, F. F., Malloy-Diniz, L., Lage, N. V., Romano-Silva, M. A., de Marco, L. A., & Correa, H. (2008). Decision-making impairment is related to serotonin transporter promoter polymorphism in a sample of patients with obsessive-compulsive disorder. *Behavioural Brain Research, 195*(1), 159–163.

Dale, R. C., Church, A. J., Surtees, R. A. H., Lees, A. J., Adock, J. E., Harding, B., et al.(2004). Encephalitis lethargica syndrome: 20 new cases and evidence of basal ganglia autoimmunity. *Brain, 127*, 21–33.

De Berardis, D., Campanella, D., Gambi, F., Sepede, G., Salini, G., Carano, A., et al. (2005). Insight and alexithymia in adult outpatients with obsessive-compulsive disorder. *European Archives of Psychiatry & Clinical Neuroscience, 255*(5), 350–358.

de Geus, F., Denys, D. A. J. P., Sitskoorn, M. M., & Westenberg, H. G. M. (2007). Attention and cognition in patients with obsessive-compulsive disorder. *Psychiatry & Clinical Neurosciences, 61*(1), 45–53.

Deckersbach, T., Otto, M. W., Savage, C. R., Baer, L., & Jenike, M. A. (2000). The relationship between semantic organization and memory in obsessive-compulsive disorder. *Psychotherapy & Psychosomatics, 69*(2), 101–107.

Deckersbach, T., Savage, C. R., Curran, T., Bohne, A., Wilhelm, S., Baer, L., et al. (2002). A study of parallel implicit and explicit information processing in patients with obsessive-compulsive disorder. *American Journal of Psychiatry, 159*(10), 1780–1782.

Deckersbach, T., Savage, C. R., Dougherty, D. D., Bohne, A., Loh, R., Nierenberg, A., et al. (2005). Spontaneous and directed application of verbal learning strategies in bipolar disorder and obsessive-compulsive disorder. *Bipolar Disorders, 7*(2), 166–175.

Deckersbach, T., Savage, C. R., Reilly-Harrington, N., Clark, L., Sachs, G., & Rauch, S. L. (2004). Episodic memory impairment in bipolar disorder and obsessive-compulsive disorder: The role of memory strategies. *Bipolar Disorders, 6*(3), 233–244.

Delis, D. C., Kramer, J. H., Kaplan, E., & Ober, B. A. (2000). *California Verbal Learning Test* (2nd ed.). San Antonio, TX: The Psychological Corporation.

Delorme, R., Golmard, J. L., Chabane, N., Millet, B., Krebs, M. O., Mouren-Simeoni, M. C., et al. (2005). Admixture analysis of age at onset in obsessive-compulsive disorder. *Psychological Medicine, 35*(2), 237–243.

Delorme, R., Gousse, V., Roy, I., Trandafir, A., Mathieu, F., Mouren-Simeoni, M.-C., et al. (2007). Shared executive dysfunctions in unaffected relatives of patients with autism and obsessive-compulsive disorder. *European Psychiatry, 22*(1), 32–38.

Di Russo, F., Zaccara, G., Ragazzoni, A., & Pallanti, S. (2000). Abnormal visual event-related potentials in obsessive-compulsive disorder without panic disorder or depression comorbidity. *Journal of Psychiatric Research, 34*, 75–82.

DuPont, R. L., Rice, D. P., Shiraki, S., & Rowland, C. R. (1995). Economic costs of obsessive-compulsive disorder. *Medical Interface, 8*(4), 102–109.

Ebert, D., Speck, O., Konig, A., Berger, M., Hennig, J., & Hohagen, F. (1997). 1H-magnetic resonance spectroscopy in obsessive-compulsive disorder: Evidence for neuronal loss in the cingulate gyrus and the right striatum. *Psychiatry Research, 74*(3), 173–176.

Eisen, J. L., Mancebo, M. A., Pinto, A., Coles, M. E., Pagano, M. E., Stout, R. (2006). Impact of obsessive-compulsive disorder on quality of life. *Comprehensive Psychiatry, 47*, 270–275.

Endrass, T., Klawohn, J., Schuster, F., & Kathmann, N. (2008). Overactive performance monitoring in obsessive-compulsive disorder: ERP evidence from correct and erroneous reactions. *Neuropsychologia, 46*(7), 1877–1887.

Endrass, T., Schuermann, B., Kaufmann, C., Spiedlberg, R., Kniesche, R., & Kathmann, N. (2010). Performance monitoring and error significance in patients with obsessive-compulsive disorder. *Biological Psychology, 84*, 257–263.

Ertekin, B. A., Kulaksizoglu, I. B., Ertekin, E., Gurses, C., Bebek, N., Gokyigit, A., et al. (2009). A comparative study of obsessive-compulsive disorder and other psychiatric comorbidities in patients with temporal lobe epilepsy and idiopathic generalized epilepsy. *Epilepsy & Behavior, 14*(4), 634–639.

Etkin, A., & Wager, T. D. (2007). Functional neuroimaging of anxiety: A meta-analysis of emotional processing in PTSD, social anxiety disorder, and specific phobia. *American Journal of Psychiatry, 164*, 1476–1488.

Exner, C., Kohl, A., Zaudig, M., Langs, G., Lincoln, T. M., & Rief, W. (2009). Metacognition and episodic memory in obsessive-compulsive disorder. *Journal of Anxiety Disorders, 23*(5), 624–631.

Fear, C. F., & Healy, D. (1997). Probabilistic reasoning in obsessive-compulsive and delusional disorders. *Psychological Medicine, 27*(1), 199–208.

Flessner, C. A., Allgair, A., Garcia, A., Freeman, J., Sapyta, J., Franklin, M. E. (2010). The impact of neuropsychological functioning on treatment outcome in pediatric obsessive-compulsive disorder. *Depression & Anxiety, 27*, 365–371.

Foa, E. B., Liebowitz, M. R., Kozak, M. J., Davies, S., Campeas, R., Franklin, M. E. (2005). Randomized, placebo-controlled trial of exposure and ritual prevention, clomipramine, and their combination in the treatment of obsessive-compulsive disorder. *American Journal of Psychiatry, 162*(1), 151–161.

Fontenelle, L. F., Mendlowicz, M. V., Marques, C., & Versiani, M. (2003). Early- and late-onset obsessive-compulsive disorder in adult patients: An exploratory clinical and therapeutic study. *Journal of Psychiatric Research., 37*(2), 127–133.

Fullana, M. A., Mataix-Cols, D., Caspi, A., Harrington, H., Grisham, J. R., Moffitt, T. E., et al. (2009). Obsessions and compulsions in the community: Prevalence, interference, help-seeking, developmental stability, and co-occurring psychiatric conditions. *American Journal of Psychiatry, 166*(3), 329–336.

Galderisi, S., Mucci, A., Catapano, F., D'Amato, A. C., & Maj, M. (1995). Neuropsychological slowness in obsessive-compulsive patients: Is it confined to tests involving the fronto-subcortical systems? *British Journal of Psychiatry, 167*, 394–398.

Gava, I., Barbui, C., Aguglia, E., Carlino, D., Churchill, R., De Vanna, M., et al. (2007). Psychological treatments versus treatment as usual for obsessive compulsive disorder (OCD). *Cochrane Database of Systematic Reviews* (2), CD005333.

Gehring, W. J., Coles, M. G., Meyer, D. E., & Donchin, E. (1995). A brain potential manifestation of error-related processing. *Electroencephalography & Clinical Neurophysiology - Supplement, 44*, 261–272.

Gehring, W. J., Himle, J., & Nisenson, L. G. (2000). Action-monitoring dysfunction in obsessive-compulsive disorder. *Psychological Science, 11*(1), 1–6.

Gehring, W. J., & Knight, R. T. (2000). Prefrontal-cingulate interactions in action monitoring. *Nature Neuroscience, 3*(5), 516–520.

Geller, D. A. (2006). Obsessive-compulsive and spectrum disorders in children and adolescents. *Psychiatric Clinics of North America, 29*(2), 353–370.

Geller, D., Biederman, J., Jones, J., Park, K., Schwartz, S., Shapiro, S., et al. (1998). Is juvenile obsessive-compulsive disorder a developmental subtype of the disorder? A review of the pediatric literature. *Journal of the American Academy of Child & Adolescent Psychiatry, 37*(4), 420–427.

Geller, D. A., Biederman, J., Stewart, S. E., Mullin, B., Martin, A., Spencer, T., (2003). Which SSRI? A meta-analysis of pharmacotherapy trials in pediatric obsessive-compulsive disorder. *American Journal of Psychiatry, 160*(11), 1919–1928.

Goldman, B. L., Martin, E. D., Calamari, J. E., Woodard, J. L., Chik, H. M., Messina, M. G., et al. (2008). Implicit learning, thought-focused attention and obsessive-compulsive disorder: A replication and extension. *Behaviour Research & Therapy, 46*(1), 48–61.

Goodman, W. K., Price, L. H., Rasmussen, S. A., Mazure, C., Delgado, P., Heninger, G. R., et al. (1989). The Yale-Brown Obsessive-Compulsive Scale: I. Development, use, and reliability. *Archives of General Psychiatry, 46*, 1012–1016.

Grados, M. A., Riddle, M. A., Samuels, J. F., Liang, K. Y., Hoehn-Saric, R., Bienvenu, O. J., et al. (2001). The familial phenotype of obsessive-compulsive disorder in relation to tic disorders: The Hopkins OCD family study. *Biological Psychiatry, 50*(8), 559–565.

Greenberg, B. D., Rauch, S. L., & Haber, S. H. (2010). Invasive circuitry-based neurotherapeutics: Stereotactic ablation and deep brain stimulation for OCD invasive circuitry-based neurotherapeutics. *Neuropsychopharmacology, 35*, 317–336.

Grisham, J. R., Andersen, T. M., Poulton, R., Moffit, T. E., & Andrews, G. (2009). Childhood neuropsychological deficits associated with adult obsessive-compulsive disorder. *British Journal of Psychiatry, 195*, 138–141.

Grisham, J. R., Brown, T. A., Savage, C. R., Steketee, G., & Barlow, D. H. (2007). Neuropsychological impairment associated with compulsive hoarding. *Behaviour Research & Therapy, 45*(7), 1471–1483.

Gross-Isseroff, R., Luca-Haimovici, K., Sasson, Y., Kindler, S., Kotler, M., & Zohar, J. (1994). Olfactory sensitivity in major depressive disorder and obsessive compulsive disorder. *Biological Psychiatry, 35*(10), 798–802.

Gross-Isseroff, R., Sasson, Y., Voet, H., Hendler, T., Luca-Haimovici, K., Kandel-Sussman, H., et al. (1996). Alternation learning in obsessive-compulsive disorder. *Biological Psychiatry, 39*(8), 733–738.

Gu, B.-M., Park, J.-Y., Kang, D.-H., Lee, S. J., Yoo, S. Y., Jo, H. J., et al. (2008). Neural correlates of cognitive inflexibility during task-switching in obsessive-compulsive disorder. *Brain, 131*(1), 155–164.

Ha, T. H., Kang, D.-H., Park, J. S., Jang, J. H., Jung, W. H., Choi, J.-S., et al. (2009). White matter alterations in male patients with obsessive-compulsive disorder. *NeuroReport, 20*, 735–739.

Hajcak, G., Franklin, M. E., Foa, E. B., & Simons, R. F. (2008). Increased error-related brain activity in pediatric obsessive-compulsive disorder before and after treatment. *American Journal of Psychiatry, 165*, 116–123.

Hajcak, G., & Simons, R. F. (2002). Error-related brain activity in obsessive-compulsive undergraduates. *Psychiatry Research, 110*(1), 63–72.

Hanna, G. L., Himle, J. A., Curtis, G. C., & Gillespie, B. W. (2005). A family study of obsessive-compulsive disorder with pediatric probands. *American Journal of Medical Genetics Part B, Neuropsychiatric Genetics, 134*(1), 13–19.

Harbishettar, V., Pal, P. K., Janardhan Reddy, Y. C., & Thennarasu, K. (2005). Is there a relationship between Parkinson's disease and obsessive-compulsive disorder? *Parkinsonism & Related Disorders, 11*(2), 85–88.

Hardie, R. J., Lees, A. J., & Stern, G. M. (1984). On-off fluctuations in Parkinson's disease. *Brain, 107*, 487–506.

Harris, C. L., & Dinn, W. M. (2003). Subtyping obsessive-compulsive disorder: Neuropsychological correlates. *Behavioural Neurology, 14*(3–4), 75–87.

Harrison, B. J., Soriano-Mas, C., Pujol, J., Ortiz, H., Lopez-Sola, M., Hernandez-Ribas, R., et al. (2009). Altered corticostriatal functional connectivity in obsessive-compulsive disorder. *Archives of General Psychiatry, 66*(11), 1189–1200.

Hashimoto, T., Shimizu, E., Koike, K., Orita, Y., Suzuki, T., Kanahara, N., et al. (2008). Deficits in auditory P50 inhibition in obsessive-compulsive disorder. *Progress in Neuro-Psychopharmacology & Biological Psychiatry, 32*(1), 288–296.

Head, D., Bolton, D., & Hymas, N. (1989). Deficit in cognitive shifting ability in patients with obsessive-compulsive disorder. *Biological Psychiatry, 25*, 929–937.

Henin, A., Savage, C. R., Rauch, S. L., Deckersbach, T., Wilhelm, S., Baer, L., et al. (2001). Is age at symptom onset associated with severity of memory impairment in adults with obsessive-compulsive disorder? *American Journal of Psychiatry, 158*(1), 137–139.

Henry, J. D. (2006). A meta-analytic review of Wisconsin Card Sorting Test and verbal fluency performance in obsessive-compulsive disorder. *Cognitive Neuropsychiatry, 11*(2), 156–176.

Hermesh, H., Zohar, J., Weizman, A., Voet, H., & Gross-Isseroff, R. (1999). Orbitofrontal cortex dysfunction in obsessive-compulsive disorder? II. Olfactory quality discrimination in obsessive-compulsive disorder. *European Neuropsychopharmacology, 9*(5), 415–420.

Herrmann, M. J., Jacob, C., Unterecker, S., & Fallgatter, A. J. (2003). Reduced response-inhibition in obsessive-compulsive disorder measured with topographic evoked potential mapping. *Psychiatry Research, 120*, 265–271.

Hollander, E., Cohen, L., Richards, M., Mullen, L., DeCaria, C., & Stern, Y. (1993). A pilot study of the neuropsychology of obsessive-compulsive disorder and Parkinson's disease: basal ganglia disorders. *Journal of Neuropsychiatry & Clinical Neurosciences, 5*(1), 104–107.

Hong, S. B., Shin, Y.-W., Kim, S. H., Yoo, S. Y., Lee, J.-M., Kim, I. Y., et al. (2007). Hippocampal shape deformity analysis in obsessive-compulsive disorder. *European Archives of Psychiatry & Clinical Neuroscience, 257*, 185–190.

Huppert, J. D., Simpson, H. B., Nissenson, K. J., Liebowitz, M. R., & Foa, E. B. (2009). Quality of life and functional impairment in obsessive-compulsive disorder: A comparison of patients with and without comorbidity, patients in remission, and healthy controls. *Depression & Anxiety, 26*(1), 39–45.

Hwang, S. H., Kwon, J. S., Shin, Y.-W., Lee, K. J., Kim, Y. Y., & Kim, M.-S. (2007). Neuropsychological profiles of patients with obsessive-compulsive disorder: Early onset versus late onset. *Journal of the International Neuropsychological Society, 13*(1), 30–37.

Isaacs, K. L., Philbeck, J. W., Barr, W. B., Devinsky, O., & Alper, K. (2004). Obsessive-compulsive symptoms in patients with temporal lobe epilepsy. *Epilepsy and Behavior, 5*, 569–574.

Jang, J. H., Kim, J.-H., Jung, W. H., Choi, J.-S., Jung, M. H., Lee, J.-M., et al. (2010). Functional connectivity in fronto-subcortical circuitry during the resting state in obsessive-compulsive disorder. *Neuroscience Letters, 474*, 158–162.

Jang, J. H., Kwon, J. S., Jang, D. P., Moon, W. J., Lee, J. M., Ha, T. H., et al. (2006). A proton MRSI study of brain N-acetylaspartate level after 12 weeks of citalopram treatment in drug-naive patients with obsessive-compulsive disorder. *American Journal of Psychiatry, 163*(7), 1202–1207.

Jelinek, L., Moritz, S., Heeren, D., & Naber, D. (2006). Everyday memory functioning in obsessive-compulsive disorder. *Journal of the International Neuropsychological Society, 12*(5), 746–749.

Johannes, S., Wieringa, B. M., Mantey, M., Nager, W., Rada, D., Muller-Vahl, K. R., et al. (2001). Altered inhibition of motor responses in Tourette syndrome and obsessive-compulsive disorder. *Acta Neurologica Scandinavica, 104*(1), 36–43.

Kang, D.-H., Kwon, J. S., Kim, J.-J., Youn, T., Park, H.-J., Kim, M. S., et al. (2003). Brain glucose metabolic changes associated with neuropsychological improvements after 4 months of treatment in patients with obsessive-compulsive disorder. *Acta Psychiatrica Scandinavica, 107*, 291–297.

Kathmann, N., Rupertseder, C., Hauke, W., & Zaudig, M. (2005). Implicit sequence learning in obsessive-compulsive disorder: Further support for the fronto-striatal dysfunction model *Biological Psychiatry, 58*(3), 233–238.

Kim, M.-S., Kim, Y. Y., Yoo, S. Y., & Kwon, J. S. (2007). Electrophysiological correlates of behavioral response inhibition in patients with obsessive-compulsive disorder. *Depression & Anxiety, 24*, 22–31.

Kitis, A., Akdede, B. B. K., Alptekin, K., Akvardar, Y., Arkar, H., Erol, A., et al. (2007). Cognitive dysfunctions in patients with obsessive-compulsive disorder compared to the patients with schizophrenia patients: Relation to overvalued ideas. *Progress in Neuro-Psychopharmacology & Biological Psychiatry, 31*(1), 254–261.

Kolada, J. L., Bland, R. C., & Newman, S. C. (1994). Epidemiology of psychiatric disorders in Edmonton: Obsessive-compulsive disorder. *Acta Psychiatrica Scandinavica, Supplementum, 376*, 24–35.

Krikorian, R., Zimmerman, M. E., & Fleck, D. E. (2004). Inhibitory control in obsessive-compulsive disorder. *Brain & Cognition, 54*(3), 257–259.

Kuelz, A. K., Hohagen, F., & Voderholzer, U. (2004). Neuropsychological performance in obsessive-compulsive disorder: A critical review. *Biological Psychology, 65*(3), 185–236.

Kuelz, A. K., Riemann, D., Halsband, U., Vielhaber, K., Unterrainer, J., Kordon, A., et al. (2006). Neuropsychological impairment in obsessive-compulsive disorder: Improvement over the course of cognitive behavioral treatment. *Journal of Clinical & Experimental Neuropsychology, 28*, 1273–1287.

Kulaksizoglu, I. B., Bebek, N., Baykan, B., Imer, M., Gurses, C., Sencer, S., et al. (2004). Obsessive-compulsive disorder after epilepsy surgery. *Epilepsy & Behavior, 5*(1), 113–118.

Lacerda, A. L., Dalgalarrondo, P., Caetano, D., Haas, G. L., Camargo, E. E., & Keshavan, M. S. (2003). Neuropsychological performance and regional cerebral blood flow in obsessive-compulsive disorder. *Progress in Neuro-Psychopharmacology & Biological Psychiatry, 27*(4), 657–665.

Lawrence, N. S., Wooderson, S., Mataix-Cols, D., David, R., Speckens, A., & Phillips, M. L. (2006). Decision making and set shifting impairments are associated with distinct symptom dimensions in obsessive-compulsive disorder. *Neuropsychology, 20*, 409–419.

Leckman, J. F., Bloch, M. H., & King, R. A. (2009). Symptom dimensions and subtypes of obsessive-compulsive disorder: A developmental perspective. *Dialogues in Clinical Neuroscience, 11*(1), 21–33.

Lee, C.-H., Chiu, C.-C., Chiu, C.-H., Chang, C.-J., & Tang, H.-S. (2009). Continuous performance test in drug-naive patients with obsessive-compulsive disorder: A case-controlled study. *Psychiatry Research, 169*(2), 183–185.

Ludlow, C. L., Bassaich, C. J., Connor, N. P., & Rapoport, J. L. (1989). Psycholinguistic testing in obsessive-compulsive adolescents. In J. L. Rapoport (Ed.), *Obsessive-compulsive disorder in children and adolescents* (pp. 87–106). Washington, D.C.:American Psychiatric Press.

MacDonald, P. A., Antony, M. M., Macleod, C. M., & Richter, M. A. (1997). Memory and confidence in memory judgments among individuals with obsessive compulsive disorder and non-clinical controls. *Behaviour Research & Therapy, 35*(6), 497–505.

Maia, A. F., Pinto, A. S., Barbosa, E. R., Menezes, P. R., & Miguel, E. C. (2003). Obsessive-compulsive symptoms, obsessive-compulsive disorder, and related disorders in Parkinson's disease. *Journal of Neuropsychiatry & Clinical Neurosciences, 15*, 371–374.

Malloy, P., Rasmussen, S., Braden, W., & Haier, R. J. (1989). Topographic evoked potential mapping in obsessive-compulsive disorder: Evidence of frontal lobe dysfunction. *Psychiatry Research, 28*(1), 63–71.

Maltby, N., Tolin, D. F., Worhunsky, P., O'Keefe, T. M., & Kiehl, K. A. (2005). Dysfunctional action monitoring hyperactivates frontal-striatal circuitry in obsessive-compulsive disorder: An event-related fMRI study. *NeuroImage, 24*, 495–503.

Martin, A., Wiggs, C. L., Altemus, M., Rubenstein, C., & Murphy, D. L. (1995). Working memory as assessed by subject-ordered tasks in patients with obsessive-compulsive disorder. *Journal of Clinical & Experimental Neuropsychology, 17*(5), 786–792.

Mataix-Cols, D., Alonso, P., Pifarre, J., Menchon, J. M., & Vallejo, J. (2002a). Neuropsychological performance in medicated vs. unmedicated patients with obsessive-compulsive disorder. *Psychiatry Research, 109*(3), 255–264.

Mataix-Cols, D., Frost, R. O., Pertusa, A., Clark, L. A., Saxena, S., Leckman, J. F., et al. (2010). Hoarding disorder: A new diagnosis for DSM-V. *Depression & Anxiety, 27*, 556–572.

Mataix-Cols, D., Junque, C., Vallejo, J., Sanchez-Turet, M., Verger, K., & Barrios, M. (1997). Hemispheric functional imbalance in a sub-clinical obsessive-compulsive sample assessed by the Continuous Performance Test, Identical Pairs version. *Psychiatry Research, 72*(2), 115–126.

Mataix-Cols, D., Rahman, Q., Spiller, M., Alonso, M. P., Pifarre, J., Menchon, J. M., et al. (2006). Are there sex differences in neuropsychological functions among patients with obsessive-compulsive disorder? *Applied Neuropsychology, 13*, 42–50.

Mataix-Cols, D., Rauch, S. L., Baer, L., Eisen, J. L., Shera, D. M., Goodman, W. K., et al. (2002b). Symptom stability in adult obsessive-compulsive disorder: Data from a naturalistic two-year follow-up study. *American Journal of Psychiatry, 159*(2), 263–268.

Mataix-Cols, D., Wooderson, S., Lawrence, N., Brammer, M. J., Speckens, A., & Phillips, M. L. (2004). Distinct neural correlates of washing, checking, and hoarding symptom dimensions in obsessive-compulsive disorder. *Archives of General Psychiatry, 61*(6), 564–576.

Matsunaga, H., Nagata, T., Hayashida, K., Ohya, K., Kiriike, N., & Stein, D. J. (2009). A long-term trial of the effectiveness and safety of atypical antipsychotic agents in augmenting SSRI-refractory obsessive-compulsive disorder. *Journal of Clinical Psychiatry, 70*(6), 863–868.

McKay, D., Abramowitz, J. S., Calamari, J. E., Kyrios, M., Radomsky, A., Sookman, D., et al. (2004). A critical evaluation of obsessive-compulsive disorder subtypes: Symptoms versus mechanisms. *Clinical Psychology Review, 24*(3), 283–313.

Menzies, L., Achard, S., Chamberlain, S. R., Fineberg, N., Chen, C.-H., del Campo, N., et al. (2007). Neurocognitive endophenotypes of obsessive-compulsive disorder. *Brain, 130*(12), 3223–3236.

Menzies, L., Williams, G. B., Chamberlain, S. R., Ooi, C., Fineberg, N., Suckling, J., et al. (2008). White matter abnormalities in patients with obsessive-compulsive disorder and their first-degree relatives. *American Journal of Psychiatry, 165*(10), 1308–1315.

Milliery, M., Bouvard, M., Aupetit, J., & Cottraux, J. (2000). Sustained attention in patients with obsessive-compulsive disorder: A controlled study. *Psychiatry Research, 96*, 199–209.

Modell, J. G., Mountz, J. M., Curtis, G. C., & Greden, J. F. (1989). Neurophysiologic dysfunction in basal ganglia/limbic striatal and thalamocortical circuits as a pathogenetic mechanism of obsessive-compulsive disorder. *Journal of Neuropsychiatry & Clinical Neurosciences, 1*(1), 27–36.

Mohammadi, M. R., Ghanizadeh, A., Rahgozar, M., Noorbala, A. A., Davidian, H., Afzali, H.M., et al. (2004). Prevalence of obsessive-compulsive disorder in Iran. *BMC Psychiatry, 4*(1), 2.

Monaco, F., Cavanna, A., Magli, E., Barbagli, D., Collimedaglia, L., Cantello, R., at al. (2005). Obsessionality, obsessive-compulsive disorder, and temporal lobe epilepsy. *Epilepsy & Behavior, 7*(3), 491–496.

Morault, P. M., Bourgeois, M., Laville, J., Bensch, C., & Paty, J. (1997). Psychophysiological and clinical value of event-related potentials in obsessive-compulsive disorder. *Biological Psychiatry, 42*(1), 46–56.

Morein-Zamir, S., Fineberg, N. A., Robbins, T. W., & Sahakian, B. J. (2010). Inhibition of thoughts and actions in obsessive-compulsive disorder: Extending the endophenotype? *Psychological Medicine, 40*, 263–272.

Moritz, S. (2008). A review on quality of life and depression in obsessive-compulsive disorder. *CNS Spectrums, 13*(9 Suppl 14), 16–22.

Moritz, S., Birkner, C., Kloss, M., Jacobsen, D., Fricke, S., Bothern, A., et al. (2001). Impact of comorbid depressive symptoms on neuropsychological performance in obsessive-compulsive disorder. *Journal of Abnormal Psychology, 110*(4), 653–657.

Moritz, S., Hottenrott, B., Randjbar, S., Klinge, R., Von Eckstaedt, F. V., Lincoln, T. M., et al. (2009a). Perseveration and not strategic deficits underlie delayed alternation impairment in obsessive-compulsive disorder (OCD). *Psychiatry Research, 170*(1), 66–69.

Moritz, S., Kloss, M., Jacobsen, D., Fricke, S., Cuttler, C., Brassen, S., et al. (2005a). Neurocognitive impairment does not predict treatment outcome in obsessive-compulsive disorder. *Behaviour Research & Therapy, 43*, 811–819.

Moritz, S., Kloss, M., Jacobsen, D., Kellner, M., Andresen, B., Fricke, S., et al. (2005b). Extent, profile and specificity of visuospatial impairment in obsessive-compulsive disorder (OCD). *Journal of Clinical & Experimental Neuropsychology, 27*(7), 795–814.

Moritz, S., Kloss, M., Schick, M., & Hand, I. (2003). Impact of comorbid depressive symptoms on nonverbal memory and visuospatial performance in obsessive-compulsive disorder. *Cognitive Neuropsychiatry, 8*(4), 261–272.

Moritz, S., Ruhe, C., Jelinek, L., & Naber, D. (2009b). No deficits in nonverbal memory, metamemory and internal as well as external source memory in obsessive-compulsive disorder (OCD). *Behaviour Research & Therapy, 47*, 308–315.

Moritz, S., Wahl, K., Zurowski, B., Jelinek, L., Hand, I., & Fricke, S. (2007). Enhanced perceived responsibility decreases metamemory but not memory accuracy in obsessive-compulsive disorder (OCD). *Behaviour Research & Therapy, 45*(9), 2044–2052.

Nakao, T., Nakagawa, A., Nakatani, E., Nabeyama, M., Sanematsu, H., Yoshiura, T., et al. (2009). Working memory dysfunction in obsessive-compulsive disorder: A neuropsychological and functional MRI study. *Journal of Psychiatric Research, 43*(8), 784–791.

Narayan, V. M., Narr, K. L., Phillips, O. R., Thompson, P. M., Toga, A. W., & Szeszko, P. R. (2008). Greater regional cortical gray matter thickness in obsessive-compulsive disorder. *Neuroreport, 19*(15), 1551–1555.

Nedeljkovic, M., Kyrios, M., Moulding, R., Doron, G., Wainwright, K., Pantelis, C., et al. (2009). Differences in neuropsychological performance between subtypes of obsessive-compulsive disorder. *Australian & New Zealand Journal of Psychiatry, 43*(3), 216–226.

Nestadt, G., Samuels, J., Riddle, M., Bienvenu, O. J., Liang, K. Y., LaBuda, M., et al. (2000). A family study of obsessive-compulsive disorder. *Archives of General Psychiatry, 57*(4), 358–363.

Nielen, M. M., & Den Boer, J. A. (2003). Neuropsychological performance of OCD patients before and after treatment with fluoxetine: Evidence for persistent cognitive deficits. *Psychological Medicine, 33*(5), 917–925.

Nielen, M. M. A., Veltman, D. J., de Jong, R., Mulder, G., & den Boer, J. A. (2002). Decision making performance in obsessive compulsive disorder. *Journal of Affective Disorders, 69*(1–3), 257–260.

Nieuwenhuis, S., Nielen, M. M., Mol, N., Hajcak, G., & Veltman, D. J. (2005). Performance monitoring in obsessive-compulsive disorder. *Psychiatry Research, 134*(2), 111–122.

Nordahl, T. E., Benkelfat, C., Semple, W. E., Gross, M., King, A. C., & Cohen, R. M. (1989). Cerebral glucose metabolic rates in obsessive compulsive disorder. *Neuropsychopharmacology, 2*(1), 23–28.

O'Connor, K. P., Aardema, F., & Pélissier, M.-C. (2005). *Beyond reasonable doubt: Reasoning processes in obsessive-compulsive disorder and related conditions.* West Sussex, England: John Wiley & Sons Ltd.

O'Connor, K. P., Aardema, F., Robillard, S., Guay, S., Pelissier, M. C., Todorov, C., et al. (2006). Cognitive behaviour therapy and medication in the treatment of obsessive-compulsive disorder. *Acta Psychiatrica Scandinavica, 113*(5), 408–419.

Ornstein, T. J., Arnold, P., Manassis, K., Mendlowitz, S., & Schacher, R. (2010). Neuropsychological performance in childhood OCD: Preliminary study. *Depression & Anxiety, 27*, 372–380.

Page, L. A., Rubia, K., Deeley, Q., Daly, E., Toal, F., Mataix-Cols, D., et al. (2009). A functional magnetic resonance imaging study of inhibitory control in obsessive-compulsive disorder. *Psychiatry Research: Neuroimaging, 174*, 202–209.

Park, H. S., Shin, Y.-W., Ha, T. H., Shin, M. S., Kim, Y. Y., Lee, Y. H., et al. (2006). Effect of cognitive training focusing on organizational strategies in patients with obsessive-compulsive disorder. *Psychiatry & Clinical Neurosciences, 60*(6), 718–726.

Pauls, D. L., Towbin, K. E., Leckman, J. F., Zahner, G. E., & Cohen, D. J. (1986). Gilles de la Tourette's syndrome and obsessive-compulsive disorder: Evidence supporting a genetic relationship. *Archives of General Psychiatry, 43*(12), 1180–1182.

Pélissier, M.-C., O'Connor, K. P., & Dupuis, G. (2009). When doubting begins: Exploring inductive reasoning in obsessive-compulsive disorder. *Journal of Behavior Therapy & Experimental Psychiatry, 40*(1), 39–49.

Pélissier, M. C., & O'Connor, K. P. (2002). Deductive and inductive reasoning in obsessive-compulsive disorder. *British Journal of Clinical Psychology, 41*, 15–27.

Penadés, R., Catalan, R., Andres, S., Salamero, M., & Gasto, C. (2005). Executive function and nonverbal memory in obsessive-compulsive disorder. *Psychiatry Research, 133*(1), 81–90.

Penadés, R., Catalán, R., Rubia, K., Andrés, S., Salamero, M., & Gastó, C. (2007). Impaired response inhibition in obsessive compulsive disorder. *European Psychiatry, 22*, 404–410.

Pertusa, A., Fullana, M. A., Singh, S., Alonso, P., Menchon, J. M., & Mataix-Cols, D. (2008). Compulsive hoarding: OCD symptom, distinct clinical syndrome, or both? *American Journal of Psychiatry, 165*(10), 1289–1298.

Pitman, R. K. (1987a). A cybernetic model of obsessive-compulsive psychopathology. *Comprehensive Psychiatry, 28*(4), 334–343.

Pitman, R. K. (1987b). Pierre Janet on obsessive-compulsive disorder (1903): Review and commentary. *Archives of General Psychiatry, 44*, 226–232.

Purcell, R., Maruff, P., Kyrios, M., & Pantelis, C. (1998a). Cognitive deficits in obsessive-compulsive disorder on tests of frontal-striatal function. *Biological Psychiatry, 43*(5), 348–357.

Purcell, R., Maruff, P., Kyrios, M., & Pantelis, C. (1998b). Neuropsychological deficits in obsessive-compulsive disorder: A comparison with unipolar depression, panic disorder, and normal controls. *Archives of General Psychiatry, 55*(5), 415–423.

Rachman, S. (2002). A cognitive theory of compulsive checking. *Behaviour Research & Therapy, 40*(6), 625–639.

Racsmany, M., Demeter, G., Csigo, K., Harsanyi, A., & Nemeth, A. (2010). An experimental study of prospective memory in obsessive-compulsive disorder. *Journal of Clinical & Experimental Neuropsychology, 6*, 1–7.

Rampacher, F., Lennertz, L., Vogeley, A., Schulze-Rauschenbach, S., Kathmann, N., Falkai, P., et al. (2010). Evidence for specific cognitive deficits in visual information processing in patients with OCD compared to patients with unipolar depression. *Progress in Neuro-Psychopharmacology & Biological Psychiatry, 34*, 984–991.

Rao, N. P., Reddy, Y. C. J., Kumar, K. J., Kandavel, T., & Chandrashekar, C. R. (2008). Are neuropsychological deficits trait markers in OCD? *Progress in Neuro-Psychopharmacology & Biological Psychiatry, 32*(6), 1574–1579.

Rapoport, J. L., Inoff-Germain, G., Weissman, M. M., Greenwald, S., Narrow, W. E., Jensen, P. S., et al. (2000). Childhood obsessive-compulsive disorder in the NIMH MECA study: Parent versus child identification of cases. *Journal of Anxiety Disorders., 14*(6), 535–548.

Rasmussen, S. A., & Eisen, J. L. (1992). The epidemiology and clinical features of obsessive compulsive disorder. *Psychiatric Clinics of North America, 15*(4), 743–758.

Rauch, S. L., Jenike, M. A., Alpert, N. M., Baer, L., Breiter, H. C., Savage, C. R., et al. (1994). Regional cerebral blood flow measured during symptom provocation in obsessive-compulsive disorder using oxygen 15-labeled carbon dioxide and positron emission tomography. *Archives of General Psychiatry, 51*(1), 62–70.

Rauch, S. L., & Savage, C. R. (2000). Investigating cortico-striatal pathophysiology in obsessive-compulsive disorders: Procedural learning and imaging probes. In W. K. Goodman, M. V. Rudorfer & J. D. Maser (Eds.), *Obsessive-compulsive disorder: Contemporary issues in treatment* (pp. 133–154). Mahwah, New Jersey: Lawrence Erlbaum Associates, Inc.

Rauch, S. L., Savage, C. R., Alpert, N. M., Dougherty, D., Kendrick, A., Curran, T., et al. (1997). Probing striatal function in obsessive-compulsive disorder: A PET study of implicit sequence learning. *Journal of Neuropsychiatry and Clinical Neurosciences, 9*(4), 568–573.

Rauch, S. L., Wedig, M. M., Wright, C. I., Martis, B., McMullin, K. G., Shin, L. M., et al. (2007). Functional magnetic resonance imaging study of regional brain activation during implicit sequence learning in obsessive-compulsive disorder. *Biological Psychiatry, 61*(3), 330–336.

Robins, L. N., Helzer, J. E., Weissman, M. M., & Orvaschel, H. (1984). Lifetime prevalence of specific psychiatric disorders in three sites. *Archives of General Psychiatry, 41*, 949–958.

Robbins, T. W., James, M., Owen, A. M., Sahakian, B. J., McInnes, L., & Rabbitt, P. (1994). Cambridge Neuropsychological Test Automated Battery (CANTAB): A factor analytic study of a large sample of normal elderly volunteers. *Dementia, 5*, 266–281.

Rosa-Alcazar, A. I., Sanchez-Meca, J., Gomez-Conesa, A., & Marin-Martinez, F. (2008). Psychological treatment of obsessive-compulsive disorder: A meta-analysis. *Clinical Psychology Review, 28*(8), 1310–1325.

Rosario-Campos, M. C., Leckman, J. F., Mercadante, M. T., Shavitt, R. G., Prado, H. S., Sada, P., et al. (2001). Adults with early-onset obsessive-compulsive disorder. *American Journal of Psychiatry, 158*(11), 1899–1903.

Rosenberg, D. R., & Keshavan, M. S. (1998). Toward a neurodevelopmental model of obsessive-compulsive disorder. *Biological Psychiatry, 43*(9), 623–640.

Rosenberg, D. R., Keshavan, M. S., O'Hearn, K. M., Dick, E. L., Bagwell, W. W., Seymour, A. B. (1997). Frontostriatal measurement in treatment-naive children with obsessive-compulsive disorder. *Archives of General Psychiatry, 54*(9), 824–830.

Rosenberg, D. R., MacMaster, F. P., Keshavan, M. S., Fitzgerald, K. D., Stewart, C. M., & Moore, G. J. (2000). Decrease in caudate glutamatergic concentrations in pediatric obsessive-compulsive disorder patients taking paroxetine. *Journal of the American Academy of Child & Adolescent Psychiatry, 39*(9), 1096–1103.

Rosenberg, D. R., Mirza, Y., Russell, A., Tang, J., Smith, J. M., Banerjee, S. P., et al. (2004). Reduced anterior cingulate glutamatergic concentrations in childhood OCD and major depression versus healthy controls. *Journal of the American Academy of Child & Adolescent Psychiatry, 43*(9), 1146–1153.

Rotge, J.-Y., Guehl, D., Dilharreguy, B., Tignol, J., Bioulac, B., Allard, M., et al. (2009). Meta-analysis of brain volume changes in obsessive-compulsive disorder. *Biological Psychiatry, 65*(1), 75–83.

Roth, R. M., & Baribeau, J. (1996). Performance of subclinical compulsive checkers on putative tests of frontal and temporal lobe memory functions. *Journal of Nervous & Mental Disease, 184*(7), 411–416.

Roth, R. M., Baribeau, J., Milovan, D., O'Connor, K., & Todorov, C. (2004a). Procedural and declarative memory in obsessive-compulsive disorder. *Journal of the International Neuropsychological Society, 10*(5), 647–654.

Roth, R. M., Baribeau, J., Milovan, D. L., & O'Connor, K. (2004b). Speed and accuracy on tests of executive function in obsessive-compulsive disorder. *Brain and Cognition, 54*, 263–265.

Roth, R. M., Jobst, B. C., Thadani, V. M., Gilbert, K. L., & Roberts, D. W. (2009). New-onset obsessive-compulsive disorder following neurosurgery for medication-refractory seizure disorder. *Epilepsy & Behavior, 14*(4), 677–680.

Roth, R. M., Milovan, D., Baribeau, J., & O'Connor, K. (2005). Neuropsychological functioning in early- and late-onset obsessive-compulsive disorder. *Journal of Neuropsychiatry & Clinical Neurosciences, 17*(2), 208–213.

Roth, R. M., Milovan, D. L., Baribeau, J., O'Connor, K., & Todorov, C. (2004c). Organizational strategy use in obsessive-compulsive disorder. *Psychiatry Research, 128*, 267–272.

Roth, R. M., & Pendergrass, J. C. (2006). Advances in the neurobiology of pediatric obsessive-compulsive disorder. *Current Medical Literature - Psychiatry, 17*(2), 33–39.

Roth, R. M., Randolph, J. J., Koven, N. S., & Isquith, P. K. (2006). Neural substrates of executive functions: Insights from functional neuroimaging. In J. R. Dupri (Ed.), *Focus on Neuropsychology Research* (pp. 1–36). New York: Nova Science Publishers.

Roth, R. M., Saykin, A. J., Flashman, L. A., Pixley, H. S., West, J. D., & Mamourian, A. C. (2007). Event-related fMRI of response inhibition in obsessive-compulsive disorder. *Biological Psychiatry, 62*, 901–909.

Rubia, K., Cubillo, A., Smith, A. B., Woolley, J., Heyman, I., & Brammer, M. J. (2010). Disorder-specific dysfunction in right inferior prefrontal cortex during two inhibition tasks in boys with attention-deficit hyperactivity disorder compared to boys with obsessive-compulsive disorder. *Human Brain Mapping, 31*(2), 287299.

Russell, A., Cortese, B., Lorch, E., Ivey, J., Banerjee, S. P., Moore, G. J., et al. (2003). Localized functional neurochemical marker abnormalities in dorsolateral prefrontal cortex in pediatric obsessive-compulsive disorder. *Journal of Child & Adolescent Psychopharmacology, 13* Suppl 1, S31–38.

Saint-Cyr, J. A., Taylor, A. E., & Nicholson, K. (1995). Behavior and the basal ganglia. *Advances in Neurology, 65*, 1–28.

Samuels, J. F., Bienvenu, O. J., Pinto, A., Fyer, A. J., McCracken, J. T., Rauch, S. L., et al. (2007). Hoarding in obsessive-compulsive disorder: Results from the OCD Collaborative Genetics Study. *Behaviour Research & Therapy, 45*(4), 673–686.

Santesso, D. L., Segalowitz, S. J., & Schmidt, L. A. (2006). Error-related electrocortical responses are enhanced in children with obsessive-compulsive behaviors. *Developmental Neuropsychology, 29*(3), 431–445.

Savage, C. R., Baer, L., Keuthen, N. J., Brown, H. D., Rauch, S. L., & Jenike, M. A. (1999). Organizational strategies mediate nonverbal memory impairment in obsessive-compulsive disorder. *Biological Psychiatry, 45*(7), 905–916.

Savage, C. R., Deckersbach, T., Wilhelm, S., Rauch, S. L., Baer, L., Reid, T., et al. (2000). Strategic processing and episodic memory impairment in obsessive compulsive disorder. *Neuropsychology, 14*(1), 141–151.

Savage, C. R., Keuthen, N. J., Jenike, M. A., Brown, H. D., Baer, L., Kendrick, A. D., et al. (1996). Recall and recognition memory in obsessive-compulsive disorder. *Journal of Neuropsychiatry & Clinical Neurosciences, 8*(1), 99–103.

Sawamura, K., Nakashima, Y., Inoue, M., & Kurita, H. (2005). Short-term verbal memory deficits in patients with obsessive-compulsive disorder. *Psychiatry and Clinical Neurosciences, 59*(5), 527–532.

Saxena, S., Brody, A. L., Ho, M. L., Alborzian, S., Ho, M. K., Maidment, K. M., et al. (2001). Cerebral metabolism in major depression and obsessive-compulsive disorder occurring separately and concurrently. *Biological Psychiatry, 50*(3), 159–170.

Saxena, S., Brody, A. L., Maidment, K. M., Dunkin, J. J., Colgan, M., Alborzian, S., et al. (1999). Localized orbitofrontal and subcortical metabolic changes and predictors of response to paroxetine treatment in obsessive-compulsive disorder. *Neuropsychopharmacology, 21*(6), 683–693.

Saxena, S., Brody, A. L., Maidment, K. M., Smith, E. C., Zohrabi, N., Katz, E., et al. (2004). Cerebral glucose metabolism in obsessive-compulsive hoarding. *American Journal of Psychiatry, 161*(6), 1038–1048.

Scheffers, M. K., & Coles, M. G. (2000). Performance monitoring in a confusing world: Error-related brain activity, judgments of response accuracy, and types of errors. *Journal of Experimental Psychology: Human Perception & Performance, 26*(1), 141–151.

Schmidtke, K., Schorb, A., Winkelmann, G., & Hohagen, F. (1998). Cognitive frontal lobe dysfunction in obsessive-compulsive disorder. *Biological Psychiatry, 43*(9), 666–673.

Schwartz, J. M., Stoessel, P. W., Baxter, L. R., Martin, K. M., & Phelps, M. E. (1996). Systemic changes in cerebral glucose metabolic rate after successful behavior modification treatment of obsessive-compulsive disorder. *Archives of General Psychiatry, 53*(2), 109–113.

Segalas, C., Alonso, P., Labad, J., Jaurrieta, N., Real, E., Jimenez, S., et al. (2008). Verbal and nonverbal memory processing in patients with obsessive-compulsive disorder: Its relationship to clinical variables. *Neuropsychology, 22*(2), 262–272.

Sher, K. J., Frost, R. O., Kushner, M., Crews, T. M., & Alexander, J. E. (1989). Memory deficits in compulsive checkers: Replication and extension in a clinical sample. *Behaviour Research & Therapy, 27*(1), 65–69.

Sher, K. J., Frost, R. O., & Otto, R. (1983). Cognitive deficits in compulsive checkers: An exploratory study. *Behaviour Research & Therapy, 21*(4), 357–363.

Shin, M.- S., Choi, H., Kim, H., Hwang, J.-W., Kim, B.-N., & Cho, S.-C. (2008). A study of neuropsychological deficit in children with obsessive-compulsive disorder. *European Psychiatry, 23*(7), 512–520.

Shin, M.- S., Park, S. J., Kim, M. S., Lee, Y. H., Ha, T. H., & Kwon, J. S. (2004). Deficits of organizational strategy and visual memory in obsessive-compulsive disorder. *Neuropsychology, 18*(4), 665–672.

Shin, N. Y., Kang, D.-H., Choi, J.-K., Jung, M. H., Jang, J. H., & Kwon, J. S. (2010). Do organizational strategies mediate nonverbal memory impairment in drug-naïve patients with obsessive-compulsive disorder? *Neuropsychology, 24*(4), 527–533.

Shin, N. Y., Lee, A. R., Park, H. Y., Yoo, S. Y., Kang, D.-H., Shin, M. S., et al. (2008). Impact of coexistent schizotypal personality traits on frontal lobe function in obsessive-compulsive disorder. *Progress in Neuro-Psychopharmacology & Biological Psychiatry, 32*(2), 472–478.

Simpson, H. B., Rosen, W., Huppert, J. D., Lin, S. H., Foa, E. B., & Liebowitz, M. R. (2006). Are there reliable neuropsychological deficits in obsessive-compulsive disorder? *Journal of Psychiatric Research, 40*(3), 247–257.

Simpson, J., Cove, J., Fineberg, N. A., Msefti, R. M., & Ball, L. J. (2007). Reasoning in people with obsessive-compulsive disorder. *British Journal of Clinical Psychology, 46*, 397–411.

Skoog, G., & Skoog, I. (1999). A 40-year follow-up of patients with obsessive-compulsive disorder. *Archives of General Psychiatry, 56*, 121–127.

Soomro, G. M., Altman, D., Rajagopal, S., & Oakley-Browne, M. (2008). Selective serotonin re-uptake inhibitors (SSRIs) versus placebo for obsessive compulsive disorder (OCD). *Cochrane Database of Systematic Reviews, 1*, CD001765.

Starcke, K., Tuschen-Caffier, B., Markowitsch, H. J., & Brand, M. (2010). Dissociation of decisions in ambiguous and risky situations in obsessive-compulsive disorder. *Psychiatry Research, 175*(1–2), 114–120.

Stein, D. J., & Ludik, J. (2000). A neural network of obsessive- compulsive disorder: Modelling cognitive disinhibition and neurotransmitter dysfunction. *Medical Hypotheses, 55*(2), 168–176.

Steketee, G. (1997). Disability and family burden in obsessive-compulsive disorder. *Canadian Journal of Psychiatry, 42*(9), 919–928.

Steketee, G., Eisen, J., Dyck, I., Warshaw, M., & Rasmussen, S. (1999). Predictors of course in obsessive-compulsive disorder. *Psychiatry Research, 89*(3), 229–238.

Stengler-Wenzke, K., Kroll, M., Matschinger, H., & Angermeyer, M. C. (2006). Quality of life of relatives of patients with obsessive-compulsive disorder. *Comprehensive Psychiatry, 47*, 523–527.

Stern, E. R., Liu, Y., Gehring, W. J., Lister, J. J., Yin, G., Zhang, J., et al. (2010). Chronic medication does not affect hyperactive error responses in obsessive-compulsive disorder. *Psychophysiology, 47*, 913–920.

Stewart, S. E., Geller, D. A., Jenike, M., Pauls, D., Shaw, D., Mullin, B., et al. (2004). Long-term outcome of pediatric obsessive-compulsive disorder: A meta-analysis and qualitative review of the literature. *Acta Psychiatrica Scandinavica, 110*(1), 4–13.

Storch, E. A., Milsom, V. A., Merlo, L. J., Larson, M., Geffken, G. R., Jacob, M. L., et al. (2008). Insight in pediatric obsessive-compulsive disorder: Associations with clinical presentation. *Psychiatry Research, 160*(2), 212–220.

Swedo, S. E., Schapiro, M. B., Grady, C. L., Cheslow, D. L., Leonard, H. L., Kumar, A., et al. (1989). Cerebral glucose metabolism in childhood-onset obsessive-compulsive disorder. *Archives of General Psychiatry, 46*(6), 518–523.

Szeszko, P. R., Ardekani, B. A., Ashtari, M., Malhotra, A. K., Robinson, D. G., Bilder, R. M., et al. (2005). White matter abnormalities in obsessive-compulsive disorder: A diffusion tensor imaging study. *Archives of General Psychiatry, 62*(7), 782–790.

Szeszko, P. R., MacMillan, S., McMeniman, M., Chen, S., Baribault, K., Lim, K. O., et al. (2004). Brain structural abnormalities in psychotropic drug-naive pediatric patients with obsessive-compulsive disorder. *American Journal of Psychiatry, 161*(6), 1049–1056.

Taylor, S. F., Stern, E. R., & Gehring, W. J. (2007). Neural systems for error monitoring: Recent findings and theoretical perspectives. *Neuroscientist, 13*(2), 160–172.

Thibault, G., Felezeu, M., O'Connor, K. P., Todorov, C., Stip, E., & Lavoie, M. E. (2008). Influence of comorbid obsessive-compulsive symptoms on brain event-related potentials in Gilles de la Tourette syndrome. *Progress in Neuro-Psychopharmacology & Biological Psychiatry, 32*(3), 803–815.

Thienemann, M., & Koran, L. M. (1995). Do soft signs predict treatment outcome in obsessive-compulsive disorder? *Journal of Neuropsychiatry & Clinical Neuroscience, 7*, 218–222.

Tolin, D. F., Abramowitz, J. S., Brigidi, B. D., Amir, N., Street, G. P., & Foa, E. B. (2001). Memory and memory confidence in obsessive-compulsive disorder. *Behaviour Research & Therapy, 39*(8), 913–927.

Tolin, D. F., Kiehl, K. A., Worhunsky, P., Book, G. A., & Maltby, N. (2009). An exploratory study of the neural mechanisms of decision making in compulsive hoarding. *Psychological Medicine, 39*(2), 325–336.

Towey, J., Bruder, G., Hollander, E., Friedman, D., Erhan, H., Liebowitz, M., et al. (1990). Endogenous event-related potentials in obsessive-compulsive disorder. *Biological Psychiatry, 28*(2), 92–98.

Towey, J., Bruder, G., Tenke, C., Leite, P., DeCaria, C., Friedman, D., et al. (1993). Event-related potential and clinical correlates of neurodysfunction in obsessive-compulsive disorder. *Psychiatry Research, 49*(2), 167–181.

Towey, J. P., Tenke, C. E., Bruder, G. E., Leite, P., Friedman, D., Liebowitz, M., et al. (1994). Brain event-related potential correlates of overfocused attention in obsessive-compulsive disorder. *Psychophysiology, 31*(6), 535–543.

Tuna, S., Tekcan, A. I., & Topcuoglu, V. (2005). Memory and metamemory in obsessive-compulsive disorder. *Behaviour Research & Therapy, 43*(1), 15–27.

Uguz, F., Akman, C., Kaya, N., & Cilli, A. S. (2007). Postpartum-onset obsessive-compulsive disorder: Incidence, clinical features, and related factors. *Journal of Clinical Psychiatry, 68*(1), 132–138.

Ursu, S., Stenger, V. A., Shear, M. K., Jones, M. R., & Carter, C. S. (2003). Overactive action monitoring in obsessive-compulsive disorder: Evidence from functional magnetic resonance imaging. *Psychological Science, 14*(4), 347–353.

Valente, A. A. Jr., Miguel, E. C., Castro, C. C., Amaro, E. Jr., Duran, F. L., Buchpiguel, C. A., et al. (2005). Regional gray matter abnormalities in obsessive-compulsive disorder: a voxel-based morphometry study. *Biological Psychiatry, 58*(6), 479–487.

Valleni-Basile, L. A., Garrison, C. Z., Jackson, K. L., Waller, J. L., McKeown, R. E., Addy, C., et al. (1994). Frequency of obsessive-compulsive disorder in a community sample of young adolescents. *Journal of the American Academy of Child & Adolescent Psychiatry, 33*(6), 782–791.

Van der Linden, M., Ceschi, G., Zermatten, A., Dunker, D., & Pearlson, G. D. (2005). Investigation of response inhibition in obsessive-compulsive disorder using the Hayling task. *Journal of the International Neuropsychological Society, 11*(6), 776–783.

Veale, D. M., Sahakian, B. J., Owen, A. M., & Marks, I. M. (1996). Specific cognitive deficits in tests sensitive to frontal lobe dysfunction in obsessive-compulsive disorder. *Psychological Medicine, 26*(6), 1261–1269.

Viswanath, B., Janardhan Reddy, Y. C., Kumar, K. J., Kandavel, T., & Chandrashekar, C. R. (2009). Cognitive endophenotypes in OCD: A study of unaffected siblings of probands with familial OCD. *Progress in Neuro-Psychopharmacology & Biological Psychiatry, 33*(4), 610–615.

Vloet, T. D., Marx, I., Kahraman-Lanzerath, B., Zepf, F. D., Herpertz-Dahlman, B., & Konrad, K. (2010). Neurocognitive performance in children with ADHD and OCD. *Journal of Abnormal Child Psychology, 38*, 961–969.

Watkins, L. H., Sahakian, B. J., Robertson, M. M., Veale, D. M., Rogers, R. D., Pickard, K. M., et al. (2005). Executive function in Tourette's syndrome and obsessive-compulsive disorder. *Psychological Medicine, 35*(4), 571–582.

Wechsler, D. (1981). *Wechsler Adult Intelligence Scale - Revised*. Cleveland, OH: The Psychological Corporation.

Weissman, M. M., Bland, R. C., Canino, G. J., Greenwald, S., Hwu, H. G., Lee, C. K., et al. (1994). The cross national epidemiology of obsessive compulsive disorder. *Journal of Clinical Psychiatry, 55*(Suppl), 5–10.

Whiteside, S. P., Port, J. D., & Abramowitz, J. S. (2004). A meta-analysis of functional neuroimaging in obsessive-compulsive disorder. *Psychiatry Research, 132*(1), 69–79.

Williams, J. B. (1988). A structured interview guide for the Hamilton Depression Rating Scale. *Archives of General Psychiatry, 45*(8), 742–747.

Woods, C. M., Vevea, J. L., Chambless, D. L., & Bayen, U. J. (2002). Are compulsive checkers impaired in memory? A meta-analytic review. *Clinical Psychology: Science & Practice, 9*(4), 353–366.

Woolley, J., Heyman, I., Brammer, M., Frampton, M., McGuire, P. K., & Rubia, K. (2008). Brain activation in paediatric obsessive-compulsive disorder during tasks of inhibitory control. *British Journal of Psychiatry, 192*, 25–31.

Wu, K. D., Aardema, F., & O'Connor, K. P. (2009). Inferential confusion, obsessive beliefs, and obsessive-compulsive symptoms: A replication and extension. *Journal of Anxiety Disorders, 23*(6), 746–752.

Yoo, S. Y., Jang, J. H., Shin, Y. W., Kim, D. J., Park, H. J., Moon, W. J., et al. (2007). White matter abnormalities in drug-naive patients with obsessive-compulsive disorder: A diffusion tensor study before and after citalopram treatment. *Acta Psychiatrica Scandinavica, 116*(3), 211–219.

Yucel, M., Wood, S. J., Wellard, R. M., Harrison, B. J., Fornito, A., Pujol, J., et al. (2008). Anterior cingulate glutamate-glutamine levels predict symptom severity in women with obsessive-compulsive disorder. *Australian & New Zealand Journal of Psychiatry, 42*(6), 467–477.

Zielinski, C. M., Taylor, M. A., & Juzwin, K. R. (1990). Neuropsychological deficits in obsessive-compulsive disorder. *Neuropsychiatry, Neuropsychology, and Behavioral Neurology, 4*(2), 110–126.

Zielinski, C. M., Taylor, M. A., & Juzwin, K. R. (1991). Neuropsychological deficits in obsessive-compulsive disorder. *Neuropsychiatry, Neuropsychology and Behavioral Neurology, 4*, 110–116.

Zitterl, W., Urban, C., Linzmayer, L., Aigner, M., Demal, U., Semler, B., et al. (2001). Memory deficits in patients with DSM-IV obsessive-compulsive disorder. *Psychopathology, 34*(3), 113–117.

Zohar, A. H. (1999). The epidemiology of obsessive-compulsive disorder in children and adolescents. *Child & Adolescent Psychiatric Clinics of North America, 8*(3), 445–460.

Zohar, J. (1997). Is there room for a new diagnostic subtype: The schizo-obsessive subtype? *CNS Spectrums, 2*, 49–50.

Zohar, J., Hermesh, H., Weizman, A., Voet, H., & Gross-Isseroff, R. (1999). Orbitofrontal cortex dysfunction in obsessive-compulsive disorder? I. Alternation learning in obsessive-compulsive disorder: Male-female comparisons. *European Neuropsychopharmacology, 9*(5), 407–413.

CHAPTER 13

Posttraumatic Stress Disorder

Marc E. Lavoie, Robert M. Roth, & Stéphane Guay

INTRODUCTION

Over approximately the past 20 years, posttraumatic stress disorder (PTSD) has been increasingly recognized as a significant personal and societal problem (Alonso et al., 2004; Kessler, 2000). With this recognition has come a burgeoning of research examining the neurobiological and cognitive characteristics of the disorder. Much of the early research on PTSD focused on military veterans, in particular those who served in World War II and the Vietnam War (Card, 1987; Foy & Card, 1987). More recently, considerable emphasis has been placed on understanding the etiology and consequences of PTSD in military personnel returning from operations in the Middle East termed "Operation Enduring Freedom" and "Operation Iraqi Freedom"(OEF/OIF; Vasterling, Verfaellie, & Sullivan, 2009). Research has also involved individuals with PTSD secondary to a variety of other common causes including rape, criminal victimization, motor vehicle accidents, and physical abuse in childhood or adulthood (Darves-Bornoz et al., 2008; Kessler, 2000).

In this chapter, we first provide an overview of the diagnostic criteria for PTSD and common assessment measures, as well as the epidemiology and course of the disorder. We then review the neuropsychological correlates of PTSD, including variables that may contribute to the heterogeneity of findings. We briefly address current treatment approaches to PTSD and what is known about their impact on neuropsychological functioning, as well as the potential role of neuropsychological assessment in treatment planning. Finally, we conclude with a discussion of brain imaging research that has informed our understanding of neural substrates and its associated cognitive limitations.

DIAGNOSIS AND ASSESSMENT

PTSD is a relatively recent diagnosis in psychiatric nosology, first appearing in the *Diagnostic and Statistical Manual of Mental Disorders, 3rd edition* (*DSM-III*) in 1980 (American Psychological Association, 1980). The diagnosis is multidimensional, and includes cognitive, emotional, and physiological symptoms. According to the *DSM-IV-TR* (American Psychological Association, 2000), development of PTSD follows personal exposure to a traumatic event that involved actual or threatened death or serious injury, or some other threat to the physical integrity; or witnessing an event that resulted in the death, injury, or threat to the physical integrity of another person; or learning about serious harm, threat of death or injury, or the unexpected or violent death of a family member or other close associate (Criterion A1). The person's response to the event must have involved intense fear, helplessness, or horror (Criterion A2). Characteristic symptoms resulting from the traumatic event are grouped into three symptom clusters including persistently re-experiencing the event in the form of intrusive recollections, recurrent distressing dreams, and acting and/or feeling as if the event were recurring; persistent avoidance of stimuli associated with the trauma and numbing of general responsiveness in the form of detachment from others or a restricted range of affect; and persistent symptoms of increased arousal manifested by difficulty falling or staying asleep, hypervigilance, an exaggerated startle response, irritability or anger outburst, and/or difficulty concentrating. The symptoms must result in clinically significant distress or functional impairment. Symptoms must be present for at least 1 month and are considered *acute* between 1 and 3 months after the traumatic event (diagnosed as Acute Stress Disorder) and *chronic* (and therefore PTSD) when lasting 3 months or longer.

There are several instruments available to facilitate the assessment and diagnosis of PTSD. The Structured Clinical Interview for *DSM-IV* Axis I Disorders (SCID; First, Spitzer, Gibbon, & Williams, 2002) and the Anxiety Disorders Interview Schedule for *DSM-IV* (ADIS; Brown, Di Nardo, & Barlow, 1994) are commonly employed diagnostic instruments allowing for the evaluation of PTSD along with other frequently comorbid conditions such as depression and other anxiety disorders. Whereas the SCID and ADIS were designed as relatively broad diagnostic tools, the Clinician-Administered PTSD Scale (CAPS; Blake et al., 1995) is the most commonly employed measure designed specifically for the assessment PTSD, at least in research settings. The CAPS is a structured clinical interview assessing the frequency and intensity of current and lifetime core and associated symptoms of PTSD, and the impact of these on social and occupational functioning. This instrument has been validated for use in a variety of populations including victims of motor vehicle accidents and war veterans (Weathers, Keane, & Davidson, 2001). The Modified PTSD Symptom Scale is a self-report measure developed to assess the severity and frequency of symptoms included in the clusters described by the *DSM-IV*, that is, re-experiencing, avoidance, numbing, and hyperarousal (Coffey, Dansky, Falsetti, Saladin, & Brady, 1998; Falsetti, Resnick, Resick, & Kilpatrick, 1993). In addition, the PTSD Checklist (PCL) is another self-report measure assessing symptoms of PTSD, but which also is available in three versions: Military (PCL-M), Civilian (PCL-C), and Specific (PCL-S), the latter being tied to an indentified specific stressor (Blanchard, Jones-Alexander, Buckley, & Forneris, 1996).

EPIDEMIOLOGY

Exposure to trauma is common in community populations. In fact, often more than half of adult samples report having experienced a traumatic event at some point in their lives (Darves-Bornoz et al., 2008; Kessler, Sonnega, Bromet, Hughes, & Nelson, 1995; Van Ameringen, Mancini, Patterson, & Boyle, 2008; Vrana & Lauterbach, 1994). Less than 10% of those who have experienced a traumatic event, however, go on to develop PTSD (Breslau, 2009; Perkonigg, Kessler, Storz, & Wittchen, 2000), with the lifetime prevalence rate of PTSD reported to range from 1.0%–9.2% in community samples of adults (Breslau et al., 1998; Helzer, Robins, & McEvoy, 1987; Kessler et al., 2005; Van Ameringen et al., 2008). Some of this variability is likely attributable to differences in assessment measures and the length of time elapsed between the experience of a traumatic event and diagnostic assessment.

Several variables have been reported to be associated with the risk for PTSD, with gender showing the strongest association. Although men are more likely than women to experience a traumatic event, with the exception of sexual assault, women are at least twice as likely to develop PTSD than men (Darves-Bornoz et al., 2008; Frans, Rimmo, Aberg, & Fredrikson, 2005; Koenen & Widom, 2009). This appears to hold true regardless of the type of traumatic experience (Frans et al., 2005), with the exception of inconsistent gender differences that are observed in studies of military personnel (Turner, Turse, & Dohrenwend, 2007). The reason for the gender discrepancy in prevalence of PTSD remains unclear (Olff, Langeland, Draijer, & Gersons, 2007).

PTSD is reported to have a chronic course in most individuals (Kessler, 2000; Van Ameringen et al., 2008). Several variables, however, have been reported to influence the course of the disorder, such as perceived social support (Koenen, Stellman, Stellman, & Sommer, 2003) and the presence of financial and social stressors (Galea, Tracy, Norris, & Coffey, 2008). The course of PTSD may also be complicated by the presence of comorbid disorders. In particular, PTSD has been associated with elevated rates of major depressive disorder and alcohol and substance use disorders (Kessler et al., 1995; Mills, Teesson, Ross, & Peters, 2006; Van Ameringen et al., 2008). Furthermore, there is evidence suggesting that persons who develop PTSD commonly report having had a pre-existing mental disorder (Koenen et al., 2008).

NEUROPSYCHOLOGICAL FUNCTIONING

Neuropsychological studies have been carried out with a variety of populations with PTSD, including combat veterans, victims of sexual or other physical violence, motor vehicle accident survivors, and Holocaust and disaster survivors. To date, no clear or typical neuropsychological profile has emerged for PTSD. This is at least partly attributable to the considerable methodological variations across studies, including sample characteristics and the specific measures employed. Nonetheless, there is evidence that neuropsychological deficits contribute to problems in occupational and social functioning in those with PTSD (Geuze, Vermetten, de Kloet, Hijman, & Westenberg, 2009) and may have implications for treatment. Here, we provide an overview of research on the performance of patients with PTSD in different domains of neuropsychological functioning.

Intellectual Functioning

Cross-sectional investigations have yielded inconsistent findings with respect to the relationship between PTSD and intellectual functioning (Bremner et al., 1993; Saigh, Yasik, Oberfield, Halamandaris, & Bremner, 2006; Sutker, Bugg, & Allain, 1991; Vasterling, Brailey, Constans, & Sutker, 1998; Vasterling et al., 2002; Zalewski, Thompson, & Gottesman, 1994). Some studies have reported a weakness in verbal relative to perceptual tasks (Gil, Calev, Greenberg, Kuglemass, & Lerer, 1990; Saigh et al., 2006; Vasterling et al., 1997). The inconsistency may be partly due to variability in the measures employed, with some studies using only estimates of IQ rather than comprehensive evaluations. Several studies have suggested, however, that higher premorbid intellectual functioning may offer some protection against the development of PTSD following trauma exposure (Breslau, Wilcox, Storr, Lucia, & Anthony, 2004; Kaplan et al., 2002; Macklin et al., 1998). This is further supported by evidence of lower IQ in both members of twin pairs where the trauma-exposed twin developed PTSD than in pairs where trauma was not associated with the development of PTSD (Gilbertson et al., 2006). It should be noted, however, that IQ scores reported in such studies have generally been in the average range in the PTSD samples. Furthermore, the extent to which pre-trauma IQ may protect against the development of PTSD may depend on the severity of the trauma, with more severe trauma mitigating any benefit of higher intellect (Thompson & Gottesman, 2008).

Attention and Executive Functions

PTSD in both children and adults is associated with a bias towards attending to trauma-relevant information at the expense of attention to trauma-irrelevant information (Constans, McCloskey, Vasterling, Brailey, & Mathews, 2004; Foa, Feske, Murdock, Kozak, & McCarthy, 1991; Moradi, Taghavi, Neshat Doost, Yule, & Dalgleish, 1999; Stanford, Vasterling, Mathias, Constans, & Houston, 2001) even if the latter are emotionally valanced (McNally, Kaspi, Riemann, & Zeitlin, 1990). Interestingly, a positron emission tomography (PET) study observed reduced anterior cingulate blood flow during emotional but not emotionally neutral Stroop stimuli in women with early childhood sexual abuse – related PTSD, consistent with difficulty suppressing attention towards the threatening words (Bremner et al., 2004b).

Numerous studies of PTSD have examined attention to emotionally neutral stimuli using more traditional neuropsychological measures. Evidence for deficient sustained and divided attention have been reported in some studies (Jenkins, Langlais, Delis, & Cohen, 2000; Koso & Hansen, 2006; Veltmeyer et al., 2005) but not others (Golier et al., 1997). Impaired auditory attention has been noted in some studies (Gilbertson, Gurvits, Lasko, Orr, & Pitman, 2001; Schoeman, Carey, & Seedat, 2009) and found to contribute to deficits in other cognitive domains (Gilbertson, et al., 2001).

Evidence for a disturbance of attention has also been garnered in studies using event-related potentials (ERP). In a meta-analysis of 15 ERP studies, patients with PTSD showed reduced amplitude and prolonged latency of the P300 in response to non-emotional target and distracter stimuli, suggesting reduced attentional resource availability (Karl, Malta, & Maercker, 2006a). Increased P300 amplitude was observed when distracters were trauma related, consistent with behavioral studies of attentional bias. Reduced P300 abnormality may, however, be related to only certain symptoms of PTSD, namely greater avoidance and numbing, and appears to be correlated with structural abnormality of the anterior cingulate cortex (Araki et al., 2005).

Executive functions have been examined in many studies of PTSD. Difficulty inhibiting inappropriate responses has been observed, most commonly during sustained attention tasks (Koso & Hansen, 2006; Vasterling, Brailey, Constans, & Sutker, 1998) rather than during the Stroop interference condition (Vasterling et al., 1998; Vasterling et al., 2002). Performance on tests of working memory has generally been intact in PTSD (Samuelson, Krueger, Burnett, & Wilson, 2010; Twamley, Hami, & Stein, 2004), despite neuroimaging evidence of disruption of brain activation during working memory tasks involving emotionally neutral stimuli (Shaw et al., 2009). Findings for tasks requiring cognitive flexibility, such as Part B of the Trail Making Test or the Wisconsin Card Sorting Task, have also most often failed to show a deficit (Samuelson et al., 2010; Schoeman et al., 2009; Twamley et al., 2009; Twamley et al., 2004), although some opposing findings have also emerged (Gilbertson et al., 2001; Schoeman et al., 2009; Uddo, Vasterling, Brailey, & Sutker, 1993) and one study found that poorer cognitive flexibility was associated with reduced frontal lobe volume in PTSD (Fennema-Notestine, Stein, Kennedy, Archibald, & Jernigan, 2002). Interestingly, at least one study has observed an association between PTSD and perseveration during object alternation (Koenen et al., 2001), a task sensitive to ventromedial prefrontal dysfunction, a region neuroimaging studies have implicated in the disorder and that is associated with impaired fear extinction recall (Milad et al., 2009).

Memory

Many symptoms of PTSD are hypothesized to be directly or indirectly related to disturbances of memory processes (Rubin, Berntsen, & Bohni, 2008; Rubin, Boals, & Berntsen, 2008). Repetitive intrusion of traumatic memories is one of the most distinctive symptoms of the disorder. The ability of patients with PTSD to learn and retain new neutral (i.e., non-emotional) information has therefore received considerable examination.

Deficits in both verbal and visual memory have been observed in PTSD (Bremner et al., 1993; Geuze et al., 2009; Gilbertson et al., 2001), although deficits in verbal memory are more frequently reported and appear to be more prominent for encoding rather than delayed recall (Johnsen & Asbjornsen, 2009; Samuelson et al., 2010; Yehuda, Golier, Tischler, Stavitsky, & Harvey, 2005). In addition, several studies have reported that PTSD is also associated with greater sensitivity to proactive (Uddo et al., 1993) and retroactive (Vasterling et al., 1998) interference. Some aspects of verbal memory impairment in PTSD may be chronic and susceptible to accelerated age-related decline, although the pattern of change over time may depend on the measure employed (Yehuda, et al., 2005; Yehuda et al., 2006). Failures to observe memory deficits have, however, also been reported (Crowell, Kieffer, Siders, & Vanderploeg, 2002; Pederson et al., 2004; Zalewski et al., 1994). Interestingly, one study reported evidence suggesting that memory impairment in PTSD may be related to poorer use of a serial encoding strategy during encoding of verbal information (Johnsen & Asbjornsen, 2009), although another study did not observe problems with either semantic or serial organizational strategy use (Jenkins, Langlais, Delis, & Cohen, 1998).

A recent meta-analysis of 27 studies of memory for emotionally neutral information showed small to moderate effect sizes that were larger for verbal than visual material, were present for both immediate and delayed recall, and held true for both civilian and military samples (Brewin, Kleiner, Vasterling, & Field, 2007). Furthermore, a number of studies have demonstrated that when verbal memory impairment is present, it is specifically related to PTSD and not simply to exposure to trauma (Gilbertson, et al., 2001; Jenkins et al., 1998; Vasterling et al., 1998).

Language

Expressive language, most commonly verbal fluency, has been assessed in several studies of PTSD using tests of word generation. The findings, however, have been mixed. Whereas a number of investigations have observed no difference between PTSD and comparison groups in either phonemic (Crowell et al., 2002; Schoeman et al., 2009; Twamley et al., 2004) or semantic (Crowell et al., 2002; Hart et al., 2008; Schoeman et al., 2009; Twamley et al., 2009) fluency, others have observed deficits in at least one of these (Twamley et al., 2009; Uddo et al., 1993). A recent study of children with a history of neglect reported deficits in verbal fluency, naming, and comprehension, but these did not differ between subsamples with and without PTSD (De Bellis, Hooper, Spratt, & Woolley, 2009), raising the possibility that at least in some cases language deficits are related to trauma exposure and not to PTSD.

Visuospatial and Visuoconstruction Skills

PTSD and comparison samples have generally not differed on measures of visuospatial and visuoconstruction skills such as copying abstract figures (Crowell et al., 2002; Schoeman et al., 2009; Twamley et al., 2009), three-dimensional block construction (Crowell et al., 2002), or judgment of line orientation (Hart et al., 2008). Some exceptions have been noted in both pediatric (De Bellis et al., 2009) and adult (Schoeman et al., 2009) samples, although in at least one study, the figure-copying deficit was largely accounted for by pre-trauma variables that included intelligence, education, childhood ADHD, and having a history of neurodevelopmental problems (Gurvits et al., 2002).

Psychomotor Speed

Numerous studies have evaluated psychomotor processing speed in patients with PTSD, most commonly using measures such as Digit Symbol and Part A of the Trail Making Test. Variable results have been observed, with some studies (Gilbertson et al., 2001; Hart et al., 2008; Twamley et al., 2009) but not others (Samuelson et al., 2010; Twamley et al., 2004) reporting slower speed in PTSD.

Motor Skills

Relatively few studies of PTSD have examined more basic motor processes. These have generally not observed deficits on tests involving motor coordination and fine motor movements (Crowell et al., 2002; De Bellis et al., 2009; Sullivan et al., 2003). When deficits have been observed, they have tended to be on measures that place a greater demand on executive functions, such as tasks involving motor sequencing (Gurvits et al., 2000; Gurvits et al., 1993).

Subjective Cognitive Functioning

Neuropsychological complaints of problems with memory, attention, and concentration have been reported to be among the most commonly reported health complaints in veterans of the Gulf War (Proctor et al., 1998). There is little empirical information, however, with respect to these subjective cognitive problems or their relationship to objective neuropsychological test performance. In a recent study, veterans with PTSD reported more attention and memory problems on the CAPS than veterans without PTSD, and the severity of subjective cognitive complaints was correlated with object memory test performance (Geuze et al., 2009).

POTENTIAL CONTRIBUTORS TO NEUROPSYCHOLOGICAL PERFORMANCE

Age and Gender

Neuropsychological deficits have been observed in children, adolescents, and adults with PTSD. There is some evidence that PTSD may be associated with a more accelerated age-related decline in memory (Golier et al., 2002), although data is very limited on the impact of PTSD in older individuals. Despite the significant relationship between gender and PTSD, there is little information as to whether gender is associated with a differential neuropsychological profile in those with PTSD because most studies have either matched patient and control groups on gender composition or only included one gender their study.

Chronicity

The vast majority of neuropsychological studies of PTSD have assessed patients long after trauma exposure and development of PTSD. Little is known with respect to whether the chronicity of PTSD affects cognitive functioning. At least one study suggests, however, that cognitive problems may be present even shortly after trauma exposure. Lagarde and colleagues (2010) observed deficits in memory and executive functions 1 month after trauma exposure in patients with PTSD relative to trauma-exposed non-PTSD controls.

Type and Severity of Trauma

Research to date suggests that the specific *type* of trauma experienced does not have a significant impact on neuropsychological functioning (Brewin et al., 2007). The *frequency* and *intensity* of trauma exposure appears to be more relevant, however, as severity of trauma has been reported to account for 23.3% of the variance in determining PTSD irrespective of trauma type (Frans et al., 2005) and contributes to the chronicity of the disorder (Kolassa et al., 2010).

Consistent with this, the severity of childhood abuse has been reported to be related to poorer functioning in at least some cognitive domains (Bremner, Vermetten, Afzal, & Vythilingam, 2004a; Twamley et al., 2009), and greater severity of current PTSD symptoms has been associated with worse cognitive functioning including psychomotor speed, attention, memory, working memory, and intelligence (Bremner et al., 2004a; Meewisse et al., 2005; Parslow & Jorm, 2007; Twamley et al., 2009). Furthermore, in a sample of veterans, poorer verbal memory was associated with the severity of the worst trauma episode but not to current PTSD symptom severity. This was interpreted as suggesting that the memory deficit may reflect the magnitude of the psychological response to trauma rather than current symptoms interfering with memory (Tischler et al., 2006).There is also some evidence that certain cognitive deficits may be associated with the severity of specific symptoms of PTSD (Twamley et al., 2009). These findings are generally consistent with recent evidence that greater trauma load is related to more severe structural abnormality in several brain regions as measured via MRI (Nardo et al., 2010).

Co-Occurring Psychiatric Disorders

PTSD is commonly comorbid with other psychiatric disorders such as major depression and alcohol and substance use disorders, but the impact of such comorbidities on neuropsychological functioning in those with PTSD has received limited empirical investigation. There is evidence to suggest that at least some cognitive difficulties in PTSD may be related to the presence of concomitant substance abuse or other psychiatric illnesses such as depression or anxiety disorder (Barrett, Green, Morris, Giles, & Croft, 1996; Burriss, Ayers, Ginsberg, & Powell, 2008; Hart et al., 2008). Other studies have found deficits in cognitive functioning even after controlling for depression, anxiety, and alcohol or substance abuse (Gurvits et al., 2002; Jenkins et al., 2000; Samuelson et al., 2006).

Traumatic Brain Injury

The presence of a history of traumatic brain injury (TBI) in patients with PTSD is of considerable concern given that even mild levels of TBI may be associated with cognitive deficits similar to those reported in association with PTSD (Vanderploeg, Curtiss, & Belanger, 2005). The relationship between PTSD and TBI remains, however, a matter of considerable debate (King, 2008; Stein & McAllister, 2009; Vasterling et al., 2009), which is complicated by the overlap of symptoms commonly reported in association with TBI and those in the *DSM-IV-TR* diagnostic criteria for PTSD (Parker, 2002), and the increased exposure to both by recent OEF/OIF veterans. Nonetheless, there is evidence suggesting that even mild TBI may increase the risk of developing PTSD. Although there have been some suggestions that longer duration of loss of consciousness or posttraumatic amnesia may be protective against PTSD (Bryant et al., 2009; Glaesser, Neuner, Lutgehetmann, Schmidt, & Elbert, 2004), this remains controversial.

Although there has been a recent burgeoning of research efforts on the effects of PTSD and TBI comorbidity, due in some measure to the attention paid to the effects of blast injury in OEF/OIF veterans, very few published neuropsychological studies to date have addressed the issue. Poorer processing speed and executive function has been reported in veterans with both PTSD and TBI relative to those with TBI alone (Nelson, Yoash-Gantz, Pickett, & Campbell, 2009). In contrast, other investigations have not observed an additive effect of concurrent PTSD and TBI on cognition. A study of patients with severe TBI found no relationship between memory test performance and PTSD symptom severity (Williams, Evans, Needham, & Wilson, 2002). No differences were observed between veterans having blast-related TBI with or without PTSD on measures of processing speed, sustained attention, memory, or executive function (Brenner et al., 2010).A meta-analysis concluded that concurrent TBI does not account for deficits in memory in PTSD (Brewin et al., 2007), although it must be noted that most studies reviewed either excluded patients with a history of TBI or did not address the issue.

Sleep Disturbance

Sleep disturbance in the form of insomnia or recurrent nightmares is identified within the symptom clusters of PTSD in the *DSM-IV-TR*, and is reported to be present in 70%–87% of patients with PTSD (Babson & Feldner, 2010; Foa et al., 1995; Leskin, Woodward, Young, & Sheikh, 2002; Ohayon & Shapiro, 2000). The presence of disordered sleep is associated with severity of PTSD symptoms (Belleville, Guay, & Marchand, 2009), and, when present in the first month following the traumatic event, has been reported to be highly predictive of the later development of PTSD (Mellman, Bustamante, Fins, Pigeon, & Nolan, 2003). Furthermore, poor sleep itself has been associated with cognitive difficulties including problems with attention, memory, and executive functions (Casement, Broussard, Mullington, & Press, 2006; Fernandez-Mendoza et al., 2010; Nilsson et al., 2005). Despite this, we are aware of only one study that has examined the relationship between sleep and cognition in PTSD, reporting that poorer sleep was associated with worse performance on the Paced Auditory Serial Additions Test (PASAT), a measure of information processing speed and working memory (Meewisse et al., 2005).

Medication Status

Several studies have reported the presence of neuropsychological deficits in unmedicated participants with PTSD (Geuze et al., 2009; Gilbertson et al., 2001; Stein, Kennedy, & Twamley,

2002). Other investigations have failed to observe significant differences in cognitive functioning based on medication status (Vasterling et al., 2002; Vasterling, Rogers, & Kaplan, 2000).

Litigation

Trauma resulting in the development of PTSD may be put forth as a basis for compensation in civil litigation and disability claims or in an attempt to deny criminal responsibility in defendants. Ongoing litigation is known to impact the likelihood of observing neuropsychological deficits after TBI (Belanger, Curtiss, Demery, Lebowitz, & Vanderploeg, 2005) and may be associated with poorer performance on formal measures of effort. Furthermore, patients with a history of trauma exposure appear to be more likely to develop PTSD even if assessed when still only contemplating litigation (Blanchard, Hickling, Taylor, Loos, Forneris, & Jaccard, 1996). As noted by Blanchard and colleagues (1996), it is unclear whether these individuals portray themselves as more symptomatic or that those with more severe trauma and/or physical injury are more likely to seek the services of a lawyer. Unfortunately, little attention has been paid to the impact of litigation on cognitive functioning in PTSD. In one study, failure on effort tests was associated with poorer neuropsychological test performance in patients with PTSD, and there was no relationship between cognitive functioning and PTSD when only those who showed adequate effort were considered (Demakis, Gervais, & Rohling, 2008). In a study of 799 patients with both concussion and PTSD seeking compensation or litigation, about half failed a memory malingering test and the failure rate was significantly higher in those with the concurrent presentation than those with concussion alone (Greiffenstein & Baker, 2008).

TREATMENT AND NEUROPSYCHOLOGICAL FUNCTIONING

A wide variety of treatments have been applied successfully to individuals with PTSD. These have most commonly consisted of psychotherapy, in particular cognitive and cognitive-behavioral therapy (Ehlers et al., 2010; Germain, Marchand, Bouchard, Drouin, & Guay, 2009; Powers, Halpern, Ferenschak, Gillihan, & Foa, 2010) and medications such as antidepressants and anxiolytics (Albucher & Liberzon, 2002; Sullivan & Neria, 2009). Considering reported overall efficacy and side effects profiles, trauma-focused psychotherapy (e.g., cognitive behavior therapy) and selective serotonin reuptake inhibitors have emerged as the preferred first-line treatments for PTSD (Foa, Keane, & Friedman, 2008). Mood stabilizers, atypical neuroleptics, adrenergic agents, and newer antidepressants also show promise but require further controlled trials to clarify their place in the pharmacopoeia for PTSD (Albucher & Liberzon, 2002). A small number of studies have also investigated other interventions such as repetitive transcranial magnetic stimulation (rTMS; Boggio et al. 2010; Osuch et al., 2009).

Unfortunately, very few studies have systematically examined the impact of treatment on neuropsychological functioning in PTSD. In one study, rTMS to the left or right dorsolateral prefrontal cortex was observed to improve symptoms of PTSD and mood but had no significant impact on cognition (Boggio et al., 2010). In addition, a study of 15 women found significant improvements in executive functions after 3 months of individual psychotherapy with a largely cognitive or cognitive-behavioral focus (Walter, Palmieri, & Gunstad, 2010). Verbal memory was found to significantly improve in those with PTSD after 9–12 months of treatment with paroxetine, and the degree of cognitive change was unrelated to change in the severity of PTSD symptoms (Vermetten, Vythilingam, Southwick, Charney, & Bremner, 2003). This was not a placebo-controlled trial, however, thus, other potential reasons for the change other than medication could not be ruled out.

Neuropsychological assessment has shown some promise, albeit limited, in contributing to treatment outcome prediction and evaluation. Poorer pretreatment verbal memory was observed to be associated with poorer response to cognitive-behavioral therapy in one study (Wild & Gur, 2008). This finding was noted to be independent of intelligence, attention, initial PTSD severity, depression, or alcohol/substance misuse.

NEUROBIOLOGICAL BASIS OF PTSD

Theoretical models of the neurobiology of PTSD have generally emphasized the role of the amygdala, frontal lobe, and hippocampus. For example, Rauch, Shin, and Phelps (2006) have argued that PTSD is related to exaggerated amygdala responses involved in the acquisition of fear associations and the expression of fear responses, deficient frontal–cortical function contributing to deficits in extinction and the capacity to suppress attention to trauma-related stimuli, deficient hippocampal function resulting in deficits in episodic learning and memory as well as diminished ability to appreciate cues indicating that given contexts are safe. Nemeroff and colleagues (2006) proposed that PTSD involves interactions between the thalamus (acting as a gateway for sensory input); the hippocampus (with its role in memory and processing of contextual fear cues); the amygdala (involved in fear conditioning); posterior brain regions such as the posterior cingulate cortex, parietal lobe, and motor cortex (having roles in visuospatial processing and threat assessment); and medial prefrontal cortex regions such as the anterior cingulate cortex, orbitofrontal gyrus, and subcallosal gyrus (involved in extinguishing maladaptive subcortical responses).

Over the past 10–15 years, human neuroimaging studies have begun to elucidate the structural and functional brain changes associated with PTSD. This work has been driven at least partly by evidence from animal neuroscience and human studies that have implicated several brain regions in processes likely of etiological relevance to PTSD, such as memory, stress response, emotion regulation, and fear conditioning (LeDoux, 1993; Milad & Quirk, 2002; Vermetten & Bremner, 2002).

Hippocampus

The hippocampus has been the subject of numerous structural magnetic resonance imaging (MRI) investigations in PTSD, not surprisingly given its important role in memory and the effects of stress on its integrity (Kim & Diamond, 2002; Lupien & Lepage, 2001). Findings across individual studies have revealed inconsistent results, with some reporting smaller hippocampal volume in adults with PTSD relative to trauma-exposed controls (Gurvits et al., 1996; Lindauer et al., 2005), and others finding no difference from comparison samples (Boone et al., 2001; Rogers et al., 2009). A recent meta-analysis of 39 studies reported hippocampal volume reduction in trauma-exposed adults relative to non-exposed comparison subjects irrespective of the presence of PTSD, although the right hippocampus was found to be smaller in trauma-exposed adults with PTSD relative to those without PTSD (Woon, Sood, & Hedges, 2010). The laterality of volume reduction appears variable, however, because a prior meta-analysis reported the left hippocampus to be smaller (Karl et al., 2006a). Furthermore, a meta-analysis of 12 studies that reported data on alcoholism found that a lifetime history of alcoholism contributes to, but does not account for, hippocampal volume reduction in PTSD (Hedges & Woon, 2010).

Several factors may impact the likelihood of observing hippocampal volume reduction in PTSD. Normal hippocampal volume was observed within 1 week and at 6 months following trauma exposure in a small sample of adults with PTSD (Boone et al., 2001), although another study observed smaller volume within about 4–6 months after trauma exposure (Wignall et al., 2004). Longer duration and greater severity of PTSD have been associated with smaller volumes (Felmingham et al., 2009; Gurvits et al., 1996), albeit not consistently (Bossini et al., 2008).In addition, there is little evidence to support the presence of hippocampal volume loss in trauma-exposed children (Carrion et al., 2001; De Bellis et al., 2002). Despite evidence that early-life stress is associated with later development of hippocampal abnormalities in animal models (Mirescu, Peters, & Gould, 2004), no hippocampal volume changes were observed in children with PTSD either at baseline or on a two-year follow-up scan (De Bellis, Hall, Boring, Frustaci, & Moritz, 2001). In contrast, another study reported that PTSD symptoms and cortisol level at baseline assessment predicted right hippocampal volume reduction over an ensuing 12–18-month interval in a sample of children (Carrion, Weems, & Reiss, 2007). Intriguingly, there is evidence suggesting that there may be critical childhood periods during which trauma exposure is more likely to be associated with smaller volume of the hippocampus and other brain regions in adulthood (Andersen et al., 2008); this may help explain some of the contradictory findings.

Along with possible volumetric changes, functional neuroimaging studies have begun to identify changes in the hippocampus during cognitive processing on non-emotional information in PTSD. Functional MRI (fMRI) studies have observed abnormalities during associative learning and memory (Geuze, Vermetten, Ruf, de Kloet, & Westenberg, 2008; Werner et al., 2009) and working memory (Moores et al., 2008) tasks. Two PET studies have reported reduced recruitment of the hippocampus during verbal memory tasks (Bremner et al., 2003a; Shin et al., 2004).

Amygdala

The amygdala has been implicated in fear conditioning (Delgado, Nearing, Ledoux, & Phelps, 2008; Olsson & Phelps, 2007), emotional memory (LeDoux, 1993), and the processing of visual signals of fear and anger (Hariri, Mattay, Tessitore, Fera, & Weinberger, 2003; Phan, Wager, Taylor, & Liberzon, 2002). Structural MRI findings for amygdala volume in PTSD have been mixed. Normal amygdala volumes have been reported for both adults (Boone et al., 2001; Bremner et al., 1997; Wignall et al., 2004) and children (De Bellis et al., 2001) with PTSD. One meta-analysis of seven studies indicated smaller left amygdala volume (Karl et al., 2006b) whereas another including nine studies failed to observe any difference between PTSD and comparison samples, although a trend towards smaller left volume was noted (Woon & Hedges, 2009). At least one study has observed that smaller amygdala volume bilaterally is correlated with greater symptom severity (Rogers et al., 2009).

Functional neuroimaging studies of the amygdala in PTSD have been far more consistent. Contrary to the evidence for reduced activity of the hippocampus, the amygdala seems to function in an overactive mode in PTSD, both in response to trauma- or fear-relevant material (Liberzon, Britton, & Phan, 2003; Shin et al., 2005; Williams et al., 2006), even when the stimuli are manipulated to prevent conscious recognition (Bryant et al., 2008). Overactivation of the amygdala in PTSD has also been reported in response to emotionally neutral stimuli (Brunetti et al., 2010), suggesting an overgeneralized emotional response tendency. Recent studies have also supported the hypothesis that fear conditioning is impaired in PTSD, observing abnormally increased amygdala response during fear acquisition and extinction learning (Bremner et al., 2005; Milad et al., 2009), as well as lesser activation medial prefrontal cortex and hippocampus during extinction recall (Milad et al., 2009). These findings may provide an explanation for the observation that greater symptom severity is associated with larger amygdala response to neutral stimuli (Brunetti et al., 2010) and during the encoding of fearful faces (Dickie, Brunet, Akerib, & Armony, 2008), as well as the difficulty of extinguishing fear responses even after an extended period of time without direct exposure to trauma-related cues in PTSD.

Anterior Cingulate Cortex

Accumulating evidence has implicated the anterior cingulate cortex (ACC) in PTSD. The ACC plays a role in a variety of self-regulatory functions such as selective attention, conflict monitoring, and the regulation of autonomic and emotional responses (Allman, Hakeem, Erwin, Nimchinsky, & Hof, 2001; Critchley et al., 2003; Phillips, Drevets, Rauch, & Lane, 2003). Reduced volume of the ACC in PTSD has been reported in a number of studies (Felmingham et al., 2009; Kitayama, Quinn, & Bremner, 2006; Rauch et al., 2003) as well as in a meta-analysis (Karl et al., 2006b). The observation that volume loss is correlated with symptom severity (Yamasue et al., 2003) as well as results from a recent study of combat-exposed twins suggest that volume loss in the ACC is an acquired abnormality rather than a vulnerability factor (Kasai et al., 2008). Functional abnormalities of the ACC have also been reported during a variety of tasks including those involving working memory (Shaw et al., 2009), recall of emotionally valanced word pairs (Bremner et al., 2003b), emotional but not emotionally neutral Stroop interference (Bremner et al., 2004b), and diminished response during symptom provocation (Hou et al., 2007; Lanius et al., 2007). Of particular relevance, recent functional neuroimaging studies have demonstrated abnormal connectivity between the ACC and other brain regions including the amygdala in PTSD (Gilboa et al., 2004), which may be consistent with a study showing that reduced gray matter density in the ACC is correlated with smaller amygdala volume in the disorder (Rogers et al., 2009).

Other Brain Regions

Structural and functional neuroimaging studies have implicated several other brain regions in PTSD, although these have received less empirical and theoretical attention than the regions reviewed earlier in this chapter. Reduced volume of the corpus callosum has been found in children with PTSD (De Bellis et al., 2002; Jackowski, de Araujo, de Lacerda, Mari, & Kaufman, 2009) and adults with child abuse – related PTSD (Kitayama et al., 2007). Both larger and smaller volume of the prefrontal cortex has been observed in pediatric PTSD (De Bellis et al., 2002; Richert, Carrion, Karchemskiy, & Reiss, 2006), the variability being related in part to which subregion was examined. A study of veterans with PTSD demonstrated reduced thickness of the superior and middle frontal cortex bilaterally, left inferior frontal gyrus, and left superior temporal gyrus (Golier et al., 2005).Reduced insula volume has been noted in one study and reported to be correlated with worse declarative memory (Chen, Li, Xu, & Liu, 2009). The cerebellum and pons have also been implicated (Carrion et al., 2009).

RISK OR CONSEQUENCE

The vast majority of neuropsychological and neuroimaging research on PTSD has involved participants with active symptoms of the disorder. Several studies have raised the question, however, as to whether neural changes observed in PTSD are a consequence of trauma, or if instead they reflect risk factors for developing PTSD following trauma exposure. This issue was first raised by an MRI study that showed that unaffected twins of veterans with PTSD also show reduced hippocampus volume relative to control subjects (Gilbertson et al., 2002). Other twin study findings have also been interpreted as being consistent with a vulnerability model, including observations of similar neurological soft signs (Gurvits et al., 2006) and abnormal resting dorsal ACC/mid-cingulate cortex metabolic rate (Shin et al., 2009) in twin-pair veterans with PTSD. Evidence of smaller left hippocampi in veterans with PTSD who developed the disorder after a single trauma relative to those who needed a subsequent event to develop the disorder may also support the vulnerability model (Tischler et al., 2006). On the other hand, differences between twins consistent with a trauma effect rather than vulnerability have been reported in studies of gray matter density in the hippocampus, ACC, and insula (Kasai et al., 2008) as well as for certain event-related potentials (Metzger et al., 2009; Metzger, Pitman, Miller, Paige, & Orr, 2008)

A number of neuropsychological studies of twin-pairs have suggested that at least some of the cognitive difficulties associated with PTSD may reflect vulnerability for the development of PTSD following trauma exposure rather than being the consequence of trauma (Gilbertson et al., 2006; Gilbertson et al., 2007; Kremen et al., 2007). Furthermore, as mentioned earlier, lower estimated premorbid intellectual functioning has been associated with higher risk for PTSD. In addition, a large study of young adults found that poorer pre-trauma neuropsychological functioning was associated with greater severity of PTSD symptoms following trauma exposure (Parslow & Jorm, 2007).

SUMMARY

The current literature on neuropsychological functioning in PTSD has yielded inconsistent findings, with evidence for deficits in most of the domains assessed in one study or another. The most consistent finding, however, appears to be that of a deficit in verbal memory, especially at the encoding stage of processing. Somewhat less consistent evidence has emerged for deficits in visual memory, attention, and aspects of executive function. Importantly, the test findings indicate that cognitive disturbance in PTSD extends beyond the processing of emotional information to also encompass emotionally neutral material. Overall, the pattern of findings is generally consistent with neuroimaging evidence for abnormalities of mesial temporal regions including the hippocampus and amygdala, as well as frontal lobe regions such as the anterior cingulate cortex.

There are several likely contributors to the heterogeneity of neuropsychological findings in PTSD, although few studies have examined these in detail. At this time, discrepancies in sample characteristics such as trauma severity and the presence of comorbid psychiatric disturbances appear to be especially salient and should be considered when interpreting the results of neuropsychological evaluations. Further research will be important to determine the consistency with which particular demographic and clinical characteristics impact cognitive functioning in the disorder.

A growing body of research suggests that at least some of the structural and functional brain abnormalities observed in PTSD may actually be present prior to trauma exposure, and may therefore potentially reflect pre-trauma vulnerability markers. At the neuropsychological level, the presence of lower intellectual functioning has been suggested by some authors to be such a marker. Nonetheless, the evidence reviewed also suggests that trauma exposure *per se* can impact neuropsychological functioning and brain morphology. The degree to which genetic/vulnerability factors versus trauma exposure and other environmental factors contribute to neuropsychological functioning in PTSD remains a matter of controversy requiring considerably more scientific inquiry.

In addition to etiological considerations, there is a very small body of preliminary evidence suggesting that neuropsychological assessment in PTSD may be helpful in assessing likely treatment responsiveness as well as treatment outcome. It has already been noted that one of the priorities for current research in PTSD is the understanding of brain mechanisms underlying the successful response to treatment (Nemeroff et al., 2006). Further large-scale studies are clearly needed to evaluate whether current empirically validated treatments for PTSD ameliorate neuropsychological functioning in those with the disorder as well as whether cognitive measures can meaningfully contribute to the prediction of treatment response.

REFERENCES

Albucher, R. C., & Liberzon, I. (2002). Psychopharmacological treatment in PTSD: A critical review. *Journal of Psychiatric Research, 36*(6), 355–367.

Allman, J. M., Hakeem, A., Erwin, J. M., Nimchinsky, E., & Hof, P. (2001). The anterior cingulate cortex: The evolution of an interface between emotion and cognition. *Annals of the New York Academy of Sciences, 935*, 107–117.

Alonso, J., Angermeyer, M. C., Bernert, S., Bruffaerts, R., Brugha, T. S., Bryson, H., et al. (2004). Disability and quality of life impact of mental disorders in Europe: Results from the European Study of the Epidemiology of Mental Disorders (ESEMeD) project. *Acta Psychiatrica Scandinavica*, suppl.(420), 38–46.

Andersen, S. L., Tomada, A., Vincow, E. S., Valente, E., Polcari, A., & Teicher, M. H. (2008). Preliminary evidence for sensitive periods in the effect of childhood sexual abuse on regional brain development. *Journal of Neuropsychiatry & Clinical Neurosciences, 20*(3), 292–301.

Araki, T., Kasai, K., Yamasue, H., Kato, N., Kudo, N., Ohtani, T., et al. (2005). Association between lower P300 amplitude and smaller anterior cingulate cortex volume in patients with posttraumatic stress disorder: A study of victims of Tokyo subway sarin attack. *Neuroimage, 25*(1), 43–50.

American Psychiatric Association. (1980). *Diagnostic and statistical manual of mental disorders* (3rd ed.). Washington, DC: American Psychiatric Press.

American Psychiatric Association. (2000). *Diagnostic and statistical manual of mental disorders* (revised, 4th ed.). Washington, DC: American Psychiatric Press.

Babson, K. A., & Feldner, M. T. (2010). Temporal relations between sleep problems and both traumatic event exposure and PTSD: A critical review of the empirical literature. *Journal of Anxiety Disorders, 24*(1), 1–15.

Barrett, D. H., Green, M. L., Morris, R., Giles, W. H., & Croft, J. B. (1996). Cognitive functioning and posttraumatic stress disorder. *American Journal of Psychiatry, 153*(11), 1492–1494.

Belanger, H. G., Curtiss, G., Demery, J. A., Lebowitz, B. K., & Vanderploeg, R. D. (2005). Factors moderating neuropsychological outcomes following mild traumatic brain injury: A meta-analysis. *Journal of the International Neuropsychological Society, 11*(3), 215–227.

Belleville, G., Guay, S., & Marchand, A. (2009). Impact of sleep disturbances on PTSD symptoms and perceived health. *Journal of Nervous & Mental Disease, 197*(2), 126–132.

Blake, D. D., Weathers, F. W., Nagy, L. M., Kaloupek, D. G., Gusman, F. D., Charney, D. S., et al. (1995). The development of a Clinician-Administered PTSD Scale. *Journal of Traumatic Stress, 8*(1), 75–90.

Blanchard, E. B., Hickling, E. J. Taylor, A. E., Loos, W. R., Forneris, C. A., & Jaccard, J. (1996). Who develops PTSD from motor vehicle accidents? *Behaviour Research & Therapy, 34*(1), 1–10.

Blanchard, E. B., Jones-Alexander, J., Buckley, T. C., & Forneris, C. A. (1996). Psychometric properties of the PTSD Checklist (PCL). *Behavioral Research and Therapy, 34*(8), 669–673.

Boggio, P. S., Rocha, M., Oliveira, M. O., Fecteau, S., Cohen, R. B., Campanha, C., et al. (2010). Noninvasive brain stimulation with high-frequency and low-intensity repetitive transcranial magnetic stimulation treatment for posttraumatic stress disorder. *Journal of Clinical Psychiatry, 71*(8), 992–999.

Boone, O., Brandes, D., Gilboa, A., Gomori, J. M., Shenton, M. E., & Pitman, R. K. (2001). Longitudinal MRI study of hippocampal volume in trauma survivors with PTSD. *American Journal of Psychiatry, 158*(8), 1248–1251.

Bossini, L., Maricla, T., Calossi, S., Lombardelli, A., Polizzotto, N. R., Galli, R., et al. (2008). Magnetic resonance imaging volumes of the hippocampus in drug-naive patients with post-traumatic stress disorder without comorbidity conditions. *Journal of Psychiatric Research, 42*(9), 752–762.

Bremner, J. D., Randall, P., Vermetten, E., Staib, L., Bronen, R. A., Mazure, C., et al. (1997). Magnetic resonance imaging-based measurement of hippocampal volume in posttraumatic stress disorder related to childhood physical and sexual abuse: A preliminary report. *Biological Psychiatry, 41*(1), 23–32.

Bremner, J. D., Scott, T. M., Delaney, R. C., Southwick, S. M., Mason, J. W., Johnson, D. R., et al. (1993). Deficits in short-term memory in posttraumatic stress disorder. *American Journal of Psychiatry, 150*(7), 1015–1019.

Bremner, J. D., Vermetten, E., Afzal, N., & Vythilingam, M. (2004a). Deficits in verbal declarative memory function in women with childhood sexual abuse-related posttraumatic stress disorder. *Journal of Nervous & Mental Disease, 192*(10), 643–649.

Bremner, J. D., Vermetten, E., Schmahl, C., Vaccarino, V., Vythilingam, M., Afzal, N., et al. (2005). Positron emission tomographic imaging of neural correlates of a fear acquisition and extinction paradigm in women with childhood sexual-abuse-related post-traumatic stress disorder. *Psychological Medicine, 35*(6), 791–806.

Bremner, J. D., Vermetten, E., Vythilingam, M., Afzal, N., Schmahl, C., Elzinga, B., Charney, D. S. (2004b). Neural correlates of the classic color and emotional stroop in women with abuse-related posttraumatic stress disorder. *Biological Psychiatry, 55*(6), 612–620.

Bremner, J. D., Vythilingam, M., Vermetten, E., Southwick, S. M., McGlashan, T., Nazeer, A., et al. (2003a). MRI and PET study of deficits in hippocampal structure and function in women with childhood sexual abuse and posttraumatic stress disorder. *American Journal of Psychiatry, 160*(5), 924–932.

Bremner, J. D., Vythilingam, M., Vermetten, E., Southwick, S. M., McGlashan, T., Staib, L. H., et al. (2003b). Neural correlates of declarative memory for emotionally valenced words in women with posttraumatic stress disorder related to early childhood sexual abuse. *Biological Psychiatry, 53*(10), 879–889.

Brenner, L. A., Terrio, H., Homaifar, B. Y., Gutierrez, P. M., Staves, P. J., Harwood, J. E., et al. (2010). Neuropsychological test performance in soldiers with blast-related mild TBI. *Neuropsychology, 24*(2), 160–167.

Breslau, N. (2009). The epidemiology of trauma, PTSD, and other posttrauma disorders. *Trauma Violence & Abuse, 10*(3), 198–210.

Breslau, N., Kessler, R. C., Chilcoat, H. D., Schultz, L. R., Davis, G. C., & Andreski, P. (1998). Trauma and posttraumatic stress disorder in the community: The 1996 Detroit Area Survey of Trauma. *Archives of General Psychiatry, 55*(7), 626–632.

Breslau, N., Wilcox, H. C., Storr, C. L., Lucia, V. C., & Anthony, J. C. (2004). Trauma exposure and posttraumatic stress disorder: A study of youths in urban America. *Journal of Urban Health, 81*(4), 530–544.

Brewin, C. R., Kleiner, J. S., Vasterling, J. J., & Field, A. P. (2007). Memory for emotionally neutral information in posttraumatic stress disorder: A meta-analytic investigation. *Journal of Abnormal Psychology, 116*(3), 448–463.

Brown, T. A., Di Nardo, P. A., & Barlow, D. H. (1994). *Anxiety disorders interview schedule for DSM-IV*. Albany, NY: Graywind Publications.

Brunetti, M., Sepede, G., Mingoia, G., Catani, C., Ferretti, A., Merla, A., et al. (2010). Elevated response of human amygdala to neutral stimuli in mild post traumatic stress disorder: Neural correlates of generalized emotional response. *Neuroscience, 168*(3), 670–679.

Bryant, R. A., Creamer, M., O'Donnell, M., Silove, D., Clark, C. R., & McFarlane, A. C. (2009). Post-traumatic amnesia and the nature of post-traumatic stress disorder after mild traumatic brain injury. *Journal of the International Neuropsychological Society, 15*(6), 862–867.

Bryant, R. A., Kemp, A. H., Felmingham, K. L., Liddell, B., Olivieri, G., Peduto, A., et al. (2008). Enhanced amygdala and medial prefrontal activation during nonconscious processing of fear in posttraumatic stress disorder: An fMRI study. *Human Brain Mapping, 29*(5), 517–523.

Burriss, L., Ayers, E., Ginsberg, J., & Powell, D. A. (2008). Learning and memory impairment in PTSD: Relationship to depression. *Depression & Anxiety, 25*(2), 149–157.

Card, J. J. (1987). Epidemiology of PTSD in a national cohort of Vietnam veterans. *Journal of Clinical Psychology, 43*(1), 6–17.

Carrion, V. G., Weems, C. F., Eliez, S., Patwardhan, A., Brown, W., Ray, R. D., et al. (2001). Attenuation of frontal asymmetry in pediatric posttraumatic stress disorder. *Biological Psychiatry, 50*(12), 943–951.

Carrion, V. G., Weems, C. F., & Reiss, A. L. (2007). Stress predicts brain changes in children: A pilot longitudinal study on youth stress, posttraumatic stress disorder, and the hippocampus. *Pediatrics, 119*(3), 509–516.

Carrion, V. G., Weems, C. F., Watson, C., Eliez, S., Menon, V., & Reiss, A. L. (2009). Converging evidence for abnormalities of the prefrontal cortex and evaluation of midsagittal structures in pediatric posttraumatic stress disorder: An MRI study. *Psychiatry Research, 172*(3), 226–234.

Casement, M. D., Broussard, J. L., Mullington, J. M., & Press, D. Z. (2006). The contribution of sleep to improvements in working memory scanning speed: A study of prolonged sleep restriction. *Biological Psychology, 72*(2), 208–212.

Chen, S., Li, L., Xu, B., & Liu, J. (2009). Insular cortex involvement in declarative memory deficits in patients with post-traumatic stress disorder. *BMC Psychiatry, 9*, 39.

Coffey, S. F., Dansky, B. S., Falsetti, S. A., Saladin, M. E., & Brady, K. T. (1998). Screening for PTSD in a substance abuse sample: Psychometric properties of a modified version of the PTSD Symptom Scale Self-Report. *Journal of Traumatic Stress, 11*(2), 393–399.

Constans, J. I., McCloskey, M. S., Vasterling, J. J., Brailey, K., & Mathews, A. (2004). Suppression of attentional bias in PTSD. *Journal of Abnormal Psychology, 113*(2), 315–323.

Critchley, H. D., Mathias, C. J., Josephs, O., O'Doherty, J., Zanini, S., Dewar, B. K., et al.(2003). Human cingulate cortex and autonomic control: Converging neuroimaging and clinical evidence. *Brain, 126*, 2139–2152.

Crowell, T. A., Kieffer, K. M., Siders, C. A., & Vanderploeg, R. D. (2002). Neuropsychological findings in combat-related posttraumatic stress disorder. *Clinical Neuropsychologist, 16*(3), 310–321.

Darves-Bornoz, J. M., Alonso, J., de Girolamo, G., de Graaf, R., Haro, J. M., Kovess-Masfety, V., et al. (2008). Main traumatic events in Europe: PTSD in the European study of the epidemiology of mental disorders survey. *Journal of Traumatic Stress, 21*(5), 455–462.

De Bellis, M. D., Hall, J., Boring, A. M., Frustaci, K., & Moritz, G. (2001). A pilot longitudinal study of hippocampal volumes in pediatric maltreatment-related posttraumatic stress disorder. *Biological Psychiatry, 50*(4), 305–309.

De Bellis, M. D., Hooper, S. R., Spratt, E. G., & Woolley, D. P. (2009). Neuropsychological findings in childhood neglect and their relationships to pediatric PTSD. *Journal of the International Neuropsychological Society, 15*(6), 868–878.

De Bellis, M. D., Keshavan, M. S., Shifflett, H., Iyengar, S., Beers, S. R., Hall, J., et al. (2002). Brain structures in pediatric maltreatment-related posttraumatic stress disorder: A sociodemographically matched study. *Biological Psychiatry, 52*(11), 1066–1078.

Delgado, M. R., Nearing, K. I., Ledoux, J. E., & Phelps, E. A. (2008). Neural circuitry underlying the regulation of conditioned fear and its relation to extinction. *Neuron, 59*(5), 829–838.

Demakis, G. J., Gervais, R. O., & Rohling, M. L. (2008). The effect of failure on cognitive and psychological symptom validity tests in litigants with symptoms of post-traumatic stress disorder. *Clinical Neuropsychologist, 22*(5), 879–895.

Dickie, E. W., Brunet, A., Akerib, V., & Armony, J. L. (2008). An fMRI investigation of memory encoding in PTSD: Influence of symptom severity. *Neuropsychologia, 46*(5), 1522–1531.

Ehlers, A., Bisson, J., Clark, D. M., Creamer, M., Pilling, S., Richards, D., et al. (2010). Do all psychological treatments really work the same in posttraumatic stress disorder? *Clinical Psychology Review, 30*(2), 269–276.

Falsetti, S. A., Resnick, H. S., Resick, P., & Kilpatrick, D. (1993). The modified PTSD symptom scale: A brief self-report measure of post-traumatic stress disorder. *The Behavior Therapist, 16*, 161–162.

Felmingham, K., Williams, L. M., Whitford, T. J., Falconer, E., Kemp, A. H., Peduto, A., et al. (2009). Duration of posttraumatic stress disorder predicts hippocampal grey matter loss. *NeuroReport, 20*(16), 1402–1406.

Fennema-Notestine, C., Stein, M. B., Kennedy, C. M., Archibald, S. L., & Jernigan, T. L. (2002). Brain morphometry in female victims of intimate partner violence with and without posttraumatic stress disorder. *Biological Psychiatry, 52*(11), 1089–1101.

Fernandez-Mendoza, J., Calhoun, S., Bixler, E. O., Pejovic, S., Karataraki, M., Liao, D., et al. (2010). Insomnia with objective short sleep duration is associated with deficits in neuropsychological performance: A general population study. *Sleep, 33*(4), 459–465.

First, M. B., Spitzer, R. L., Gibbon, M., & Williams, J. B. W. (2002). *Structured clinical interview for DSM-IV-TR Axis I disorders (SCID-I/P), patient edition*. Washington, D.C.: American Psychiatric Publishing, Inc.

Foa, E. B., Feske, U., Murdock, T. B., Kozak, m. j., & McCarthy, P. R. (1991). processing of threat-related information in rape victims. *journal of abnormal psychology, 100*(2), 156–162.

Foa, E. B., Keane, T. M., & Friedman, M. J. (2008). *Effective treatments for PTSD*, 2nd ed. New York: Guilford Press.

Foa, E. B., Riggs, D. S., Gershuny, B. S., Foa, E. B., Riggs, D. S., & Gershuny, B. S. (1995). Arousal, numbing, and intrusion: Symptom structure of PTSD following assault. *American Journal of Psychiatry, 152*(1), 116–120.

Foy, D. W., & Card, J. J. (1987). Combat-related post-traumatic stress disorder etiology: Replicated findings in a national sample of Vietnam-era men. *Journal of Clinical Psychology, 43*(1), 28–31.

Frans, O., Rimmo, P. A., Aberg, L., & Fredrikson, M. (2005). Trauma exposure and post-traumatic stress disorder in the general population. *Acta Psychiatrica Scandavica, 111*(4), 291–299.

Galea, S., Tracy, M., Norris, F., & Coffey, S. F. (2008). Financial and social circumstances and the incidence and course of PTSD in Mississippi during the first two years after Hurricane Katrina. *Journal of Traumatic Stress, 21*(4), 357–368.

Germain, V., Marchand, A., Bouchard, S., Drouin, M. S., & Guay, S. (2009). Effectiveness of cognitive behavioural therapy administered by videoconference for posttraumatic stress disorder. *Cognitive Behaviour Therapy, 38*(1), 42–53.

Geuze, E., Vermetten, E., de Kloet, C. S., Hijman, R., & Westenberg, H. G. M. (2009). Neuropsychological performance is related to current social and occupational functioning in veterans with posttraumatic stress disorder. *Depression & Anxiety, 26*(1), 7–15.

Geuze, E., Vermetten, E., Ruf, M., de Kloet, C. S., & Westenberg, H. G. M. (2008). Neural correlates of associative learning and memory in veterans with posttraumatic stress disorder. *Journal of Psychiatric Research, 42*(8), 659–669.

Gil, T., Calev, A., Greenberg, D., Kuglemass, S., & Lerer, B. (1990). Cognitive functioning in posttraumatic stress disorder. *Journal of Traumatic Stress, 3*, 29–45.

Gilbertson, M. W., Gurvits, T. V., Lasko, N. B., Orr, S. P., & Pitman, R. K. (2001). Multivariate assessment of explicit memory function in combat veterans with posttraumatic stress disorder. *Journal of Traumatic Stress, 14*(2), 413–432.

Gilbertson, M. W., Paulus, L. A., Williston, S. K., Gurvits, T. V., Lasko, N. B., Pitman, R. K., et al. (2006). Neurocognitive function in monozygotic twins discordant for combat exposure: Relationship to posttraumatic stress disorder. *Journal of Abnormal Psychology, 115*(3), 484–495.

Gilbertson, M. W., Shenton, M. E., Ciszewski, A., Kasai, K., Lasko, N. B., Orr, S. P., et al. (2002). Smaller hippocampal volume predicts pathologic vulnerability to psychological trauma. *Nature Neuroscience, 5*(11), 1242–1247.

Gilbertson, M. W., Williston, S. K., Paulus, L. A., Lasko, N. B., Gurvits, T. V., Shenton, M. E., et al. (2007). Configural cue performance in identical twins discordant for posttraumatic stress disorder: Theoretical implications for the role of hippocampal function. *Biological Psychiatry, 62*(5), 513–520.

Gilboa, A., Shalev, A. Y., Laor, L., Lester, H., Louzoun, Y., Chisin, R., et al. (2004). Functional connectivity of the prefrontal cortex and the amygdala in posttraumatic stress disorder. *Biological Psychiatry, 55*(3), 263–272.

Glaesser, J., Neuner, F., Lutgehetmann, R., Schmidt, R., & Elbert, T. (2004). Posttraumatic stress disorder in patients with traumatic brain injury. *BMC Psychiatry, 4*, 5.

Golier, J., Yehuda, R., Cornblatt, B., Harvey, P., Gerber, D., & Levengood, R. (1997). Sustained attention in combat-related posttraumatic stress disorder. *Integrative Physiological & Behavioral Science, 32*(1), 52–61.

Golier, J. A., Yehuda, R., De Santi, S., Segal, S., Dolan, S., & de Leon, M. J. (2005). Absence of hippocampal volume differences in survivors of the Nazi Holocaust with and without posttraumatic stress disorder. *Psychiatry Research, 139*(1), 53–64.

Golier, J. A., Yehuda, R., Lupien, S. J., Harvey, P. D., Grossman, R., & Elkin, A. (2002). Memory performance in Holocaust survivors with posttraumatic stress disorder. *American Journal of Psychiatry, 159*(10), 1682–1688.

Greiffenstein, M. F., & Baker, W. J. (2008). Validity testing in dually diagnosed post-traumatic stress disorder and mild closed head injury. *Clinical Neuropsychologist, 22*(3), 565–582.

Gurvits, T. V., Gilbertson, M. W., Lasko, N. B., Tarhan, A. S., Simeon, D., Macklin, M. L., et al.. (2000). Neurologic soft signs in chronic posttraumatic stress disorder. *Archives of General Psychiatry, 57*(2), 181–186.

Gurvits, T. V., Lasko, N. B., Repak, A. L., Metzger, L. J., Orr, S. P., & Pitman, R. K. (2002). Performance on visuospatial copying tasks in individuals with chronic posttraumatic stress disorder. *Psychiatry Research, 112*(3), 263–268.

Gurvits, T. V., Lasko, N. B., Schachter, S. C., Kuhne, A. A., Orr, S. P., & Pitman, R. K. (1993). Neurological status of Vietnam veterans with chronic posttraumatic stress disorder. *Journal of Neuropsychiatry & Clinical Neurosciences, 5*(2), 183–188.

Gurvits, T. V., Metzger, L. J., Lasko, N. B., Cannistraro, P. A., Tarhan, A. S., Gilbertson, M. W., et al. (2006). Subtle neurologic compromise as a vulnerability factor for combat-related posttraumatic stress disorder: Results of a twin study. *Archives of General Psychiatry, 63*(5), 571–576.

Gurvits, T. V., Shenton, M. E., Hokama, H., Ohta, H., Lasko, N. B., Gilbertson, M. W., et al. (1996). Magnetic resonance imaging study of hippocampal volume in chronic, combat-related posttraumatic stress disorder. *Biological Psychiatry, 40*(11), 1091–1099.

Hariri, A. R., Mattay, V. S., Tessitore, A., Fera, F., & Weinberger, D. R. (2003). Neocortical modulation of the amygdala response to fearful stimuli. *Biological Psychiatry, 53*(6), 494–501.

Hart, J. Jr., Kimbrell, T., Fauver, P., Cherry, B. J., Pitcock, J., Booe, L. Q., et al. (2008). Cognitive dysfunctions associated with PTSD: Evidence from World War II prisoners of war. *Journal of Neuropsychiatry & Clinical Neurosciences, 20*(3), 309–316.

Hedges, D. W., & Woon, F. L. (2010). Alcohol use and hippocampal volume deficits in adults with posttraumatic stress disorder: A meta-analysis. *Biological Psychology, 84*(2), 163–168.

Helzer, J. E., Robins, L. N., & McEvoy, L. (1987). Post-traumatic stress disorder in the general population: Findings of the epidemiologic catchment area survey. *New England Journal of Medicine, 317*, 1630–1634.

Hou, C., Liu, J., Wang, K., Li, L., Liang, M., He, Z., et al. (2007). Brain responses to symptom provocation and trauma-related short-term memory recall in coal mining accident survivors with acute severe PTSD. *Brain Research, 1144*, 165–174.

Jackowski, A. P., de Araujo, C. M., de Lacerda, A. L. T., Mari, J. D & Kaufman, J. (2009). Neurostructural imaging findings in children with post-traumatic stress disorder: Brief review. *Psychiatry & Clinical Neurosciences, 63*(1), 1–8.

Jenkins, M. A., Langlais, P. J., Delis, D. A., & Cohen, R. A. (1998). Learning and memory in rape victims with posttraumatic stress disorder. *American Journal of Psychiatry, 155*, 278–279.

Jenkins, M. A., Langlais, P. J., Delis, D. A., & Cohen, R. A. (2000). Attentional dysfunction associated with posttraumatic stress disorder among rape survivors. *Clinical Neuropsychologist, 14*(1), 7–12.

Johnsen, G. E., & Asbjornsen, A. E. (2009). Verbal learning and memory impairments in posttraumatic stress disorder: The role of encoding strategies. *Psychiatry Research, 165*(1–2), 68–77.

Kaplan, Z., Weiser, M., Reichenberg, A., Rabinowitz, J., Caspi, A., & Bodner, E. (2002). Motivation to serve in the military influences vulnerability to future posttraumatic stress disorder. *Psychiatry Research, 109*, 45–49.

Karl, A., Malta, L. S., & Maercker, A. (2006a). Meta-analytic review of event-related potential studies in post-traumatic stress disorder. *Biological Psychology, 71*(2), 123–147.

Karl, A., Schaefer, M., Malta, L. S., Dorfel, D., Rohleder, N., & Werner, A. (2006b). A meta-analysis of structural brain abnormalities in PTSD. *Neuroscience & Biobehavioral Reviews, 30*(7), 1004–1031.

Kasai, K., Yamasue, H., Gilbertson, M. W., Shenton, M. E., Rauch, S. L., & Pitman, R. K. (2008). Evidence for acquired pregenual anterior cingulate gray matter loss from a twin study of combat-related posttraumatic stress disorder. *Biological Psychiatry, 63*(6), 550–556.

Kessler, R. C. (2000). Posttraumatic stress disorder: The burden to the individual and to society. *Journal of Clinical Psychiatry, 61*(Suppl 5), 4–12.

Kessler, R. C., Berglund, P., Demler, O., Jin, R., Merikangas, K. R., & Walters, E. E. (2005). Lifetime prevalence and age-of-onset distributions of DSM-IV disorders in the National Comorbidity Survey Replication. *Archives of General Psychiatry, 62*, 593–602.

Kessler, R. C., Sonnega, A., Bromet, E., Hughes, M., & Nelson, C. B. (1995). Posttraumatic stress disorder in the National Comorbidity Survey. *Archives of General Psychiatry, 52*(12), 1048–1060.

Kim, J. J., & Diamond, D. M. (2002). The stressed hippocampus, synaptic plasticity and lost memories. *Nature Reviews Neuroscience, 3*(6), 453–462.

King, N. S. (2008). PTSD and traumatic brain injury: Folklore and fact? *Brain Injury, 22*(1), 1–5.

Kitayama, N., Brummer, M., Hertz, L., Quinn, S., Kim, Y., & Bremner, J. D. (2007). Morphologic alterations in the corpus callosum in abuse-related posttraumatic stress disorder: A preliminary study. *Journal of Nervous & Mental Disease, 195*(12), 1027–1029.

Kitayama, N., Quinn, S., & Bremner, J. D. (2006). Smaller volume of anterior cingulate cortex in abuse-related posttraumatic stress disorder. *Journal of Affective Disorders, 90*(2–3), 171–174.

Koenen, K. C., Driver, K. L., Oscar-Berman, M., Wolfe, J., Folsom, S., Huang, M. T., et al. (2001). Measures of prefrontal system dysfunction in posttraumatic stress disorder. *Brain & Cognition, 45*(1), 64–78.

Koenen, K. C., Moffitt, T. E., Caspi, A., Gregory, A., Harrington, H., & Poulton, R. (2008). The developmental mental-disorder histories of adults with posttraumatic stress disorder: A prospective longitudinal birth cohort study. *Journal of Abnormal Psychology, 117*(2), 460–466.

Koenen, K. C., Stellman, J. M., Stellman, S. D., & Sommer, J. F. Jr. (2003). Risk factors for course of posttraumatic stress disorder among Vietnam veterans: A 14-year follow-up of American Legionnaires. *Journal of Consulting and Clinical Psychology, 71*(6), 980–986.

Koenen, K. C., & Widom, C. S. (2009). A prospective study of sex differences in the lifetime risk of posttraumatic stress disorder among abused and neglected children grown up. *Journal of Traumatic Stress, 22*(6), 566–574.

Kolassa, I. T., Ertl, V., Eckart, C., Kolassa, S., Onyut, L. P., & Elbert, T. (2010). Spontaneous remission from PTSD depends on the number of traumatic event types experienced. *Psychological Trauma: Theory, Research, Practice, and Policy, 2*(3), 169–174.

Koso, M., & Hansen, S. (2006). Executive function and memory in posttraumatic stress disorder: A study of Bosnian war veterans. *European Psychiatry, 21*(3), 167–173.

Kremen, W. S., Koenen, K. C., Boake, C., Purcell, S., Eisen, S. A., Franz, C. E., et al. (2007). Pretrauma cognitive ability and risk for posttraumatic stress disorder: A twin study. *Archives of General Psychiatry, 64*(3), 361–368.

Lagarde, G., Doyon, J., Brunet, A., Lagarde, G., Doyon, J., & Brunet, A. (2010). Memory and executive dysfunctions associated with acute posttraumatic stress disorder. *Psychiatry Research, 177*(1–2), 144–149.

Lanius, R. A., Frewen, P. A., Girotti, M., Neufeld, R. W. J., Stevens, T. K., & Densmore, M. (2007). Neural correlates of trauma script-imagery in posttraumatic stress disorder with and without comorbid major depression: A functional MRI investigation. *Psychiatry Research, 155*(1), 45–56.

LeDoux, J. E. (1993). Emotional memory systems in the brain. *Behavioural Brain Research, 58*(1–2), 69–79.

Leskin, G. A., Woodward, S. H., Young, H. E., & Sheikh, J. I. (2002). Effects of comorbid diagnoses on sleep disturbance in PTSD. *Journal of Psychiatric Research, 36*(6), 449–452.

Liberzon, I., Britton, J. C., & Phan, K. L. (2003). Neural correlates of traumatic recall in posttraumatic stress disorder. *Stress, 6*(3), 151–156.

Lindauer, R. J. L., Vlieger, E.-J., Jalink, M., Olff, M., Carlier, I. V. E., Majoie, C. B. L. M., et al. (2005). Effects of psychotherapy on hippocampal volume in out-patients with post-traumatic stress disorder: A MRI investigation. *Psychological Medicine, 35*(10), 1421–1431.

Lupien, S. J., & Lepage, M. (2001). Stress, memory, and the hippocampus: Can't live with it, can't live without it. *Behavioural Brain Research, 127*(1–2), 137–158.

Macklin, M. L., Metzger, L. J., Litz, B. T., McNally, R. J., Lesko, N. B., Orr, S. P., et al. (1998). Lower precombat intelligence is a risk factor for posttraumatic stress disorder. *Journal of Consulting and Clinical Psychology, 66* 323–326.

McNally, R. J., Kaspi, S. P., Riemann, B. C., & Zeitlin, S. B. (1990). Selective processing of threat cues in posttraumatic stress disorder. *Journal of Abnormal Psychology, 99*(4), 398–402.

Meewisse, M. L., Nijdam, M. J., de Vries, G. J., Gersons, B. P., Kleber, R. J., van der Velden, P. G., et al.(2005). Disaster-related posttraumatic stress symptoms and sustained attention: Evaluation of depressive symptomatology and sleep disturbances as mediators. *Journal of Traumatic Stress, 18*(4), 299–302.

Mellman, T. A., Bustamante, V., Fins, A. I., Pigeon, W. R., & Nolan, B. (2003). REM sleep and the early development of posttraumatic stress disorder. *American Journal of Psychiatry, 159*, 1696–1701.

Metzger, L. J., Clark, C. R., McFarlane, A. C., Veltmeyer, M. D., Lasko, N. B., Paige, S. R., et al. (2009). Event-related potentials to auditory stimuli in monozygotic twins discordant for combat: Association with PTSD. *Psychophysiology, 46*(1), 172–178.

Metzger, L. J., Pitman, R. K., Miller, G. A., Paige, S. R., & Orr, S. P. (2008). Intensity dependence of auditory P2 in monozygotic twins discordant for Vietnam combat: Associations with posttraumatic stress disorder. *Journal of Rehabilitation Research & Development, 45*(3), 437–449.

Milad, M. R., Pitman, R. K., Ellis, C. B., Gold, A. L., Shin, L. M., Lasko, N. B., et al. (2009). Neurobiological basis of failure to recall extinction memory in posttraumatic stress disorder. *Biological Psychiatry, 66*(12), 1075–1082.

Milad, M. R., & Quirk, G. J. (2002). Neurons in medial prefrontal cortex signal memory for fear extinction. *Nature, 420*(6911), 70–74.

Mills, K. L., Teesson, M., Ross, J., & Peters, L. (2006). Trauma, PTSD, and substance use disorders: Findings from the Australian National Survey of Mental Health and Well-Being. *American Journal of Psychiatry, 163*(4), 652–658.

Mirescu, C., Peters, J. D., & Gould, E. (2004). Early life experience alters response of adult neurogenesis to stress. *Nature Neuroscience, 7*(8), 841–846.

Moores, K. A., Clark, C. R., McFarlane, A. C., Brown, G. C., Puce, A., & Taylor, D. J. (2008). Abnormal recruitment of working memory updating networks during maintenance of trauma-neutral information in post-traumatic stress disorder. *Psychiatry Research, 163*(2), 156–170.

Moradi, A. R., Taghavi, M. R., Neshat Doost, H. T., Yule, W., & Dalgleish, T. (1999). Performance of children and adolescents with PTSD on the Stroop colour-naming task. *Psychological Medicine, 29*(2), 415–419.

Nardo, D., Hogberg, G., Looi, J. C., Larsson, S., Hallstrom, T., & Pagani, M. (2010). Gray matter density in limbic and paralimbic cortices is associated with trauma load and EMDR outcome in PTSD patients. *Journal of Psychiatric Research, 44*(7), 477–485.

Nelson, L. A., Yoash-Gantz, R. E., Pickett, T. C., & Campbell, T. A. (2009). Relationship between processing speed and executive functioning performance among OEF/OIF veterans: Implications for postdeployment rehabilitation. *Journal of Head Trauma Rehabilitation, 24*(1), 32–40.

Nemeroff, C. B., Bremner, J. D., Foa, E. B., Mayberg, H. S., North, C. S., & Stein, M. B. (2006). Posttraumatic stress disorder: A state-of-the-science review. *Journal of Psychiatric Research, 40*(1), 1–21.

Nilsson, J. P., Soderstrom, M., Karlsson, A. U., Lekander, M., Akerstedt, T., Lindroth, N. E., et al. (2005). Less effective executive functioning after one night's sleep deprivation. *Journal of Sleep Research, 14*(1), 1–6.

Ohayon, M. M., & Shapiro, C. M. (2000). Sleep disturbances and psychiatric disorders associated with posttraumatic stress disorder in the general population. *Comprehensive Psychiatry, 41*(6), 469–478.

Olff, M., Langeland, W., Draijer, N., & Gersons, B. P. (2007). Gender differences in posttraumatic stress disorder. *Psychological Bulletin, 133*(2), 183–204.

Olsson, A., & Phelps, E. A. (2007). Social learning of fear. *Nature Neuroscience, 10*, 1095–1102.

Osuch, E. A., Benson, B. E., Luckenbaugh, D. A., Geraci, M., Post, R. M., & McCann, U. (2009). Repetitive TMS combined with exposure therapy for PTSD: A preliminary study. *Journal of Anxiety Disorders, 23*(1), 54–59.

Parker, R. S., & Parker, R. S. (2002). Recommendations for the revision of DSM-IV diagnostic categories for co-morbid posttraumatic stress disorder and traumatic brain injury. *Neurorehabilitation, 17*(2), 131–143.

Parslow, R. A., & Jorm, A. F. (2007). Pretrauma and posttrauma neurocognitive functioning and PTSD symptoms in a community sample of young adults. *American Journal of Psychiatry, 164*(3), 509–515.

Pederson, C. L., Maurer, S. H., Kaminski, P. L., Zander, K. A., Peters, C. M., Stokes-Crowe, L. A., et al. (2004). Hippocampal volume and memory performance in a community-based sample of women with posttraumatic stress disorder secondary to child abuse. *Journal of Traumatic Stress, 17*(1), 37–40.

Perkonigg, A., Kessler, R. C., Storz, S., & Wittchen, H. U. (2000). Traumatic events and post-traumatic stress disorder in the community: Prevalence, risk factors and comorbidity. *Acta Psychiatrica Scandinavica, 101*(1), 46–59.

Phan, K. L., Wager, T., Taylor, S. F., & Liberzon, I. (2002). Functional neuroanatomy of emotion: A meta-analysis of emotion activation studies in PET and fMRI. *Neuroimage, 16*(2), 331–348.

Phillips, M. L., Drevets, W. C., Rauch, S. L., & Lane, R. (2003). Neurobiology of emotion perception I: The neural basis of normal emotion perception. *Biological Psychiatry, 54*(5), 504–514.

Powers, M. B., Halpern, J. M., Ferenschak, M. P., Gillihan, S. J., & Foa, E. B. (2010). A meta-analytic review of prolonged exposure for posttraumatic stress disorder. *Clinical Psychology Review, 30*(6), 635–641.

Proctor, S. P., Heeren, T., White, R. F., Wolfe, J., Borgos, M. S., Davis, J. D., et al. (1998). Health status of Persian Gulf War veterans: Self-reported symptoms, environmental exposures and the effect of stress. *International Journal of Epidemiology, 27*(6), 1000–1010.

Rauch, S. L., Shin, L. M., & Phelps, E. A. (2006). Neurocircuitry models of posttraumatic stress disorder and extinction: Human neuroimaging research–past, present, and future. *Biological Psychiatry, 60*(4), 376–382.

Rauch, S. L., Shin, L. M., Segal, E., Pitman, R. K., Carson, M. A., McMullin, et al. (2003). Selectively reduced regional cortical volumes in post-traumatic stress disorder. *NeuroReport, 14*(7), 913–916.

Richert, K. A., Carrion, V. G., Karchemskiy, A., & Reiss, A. L. (2006). Regional differences of the prefrontal cortex in pediatric PTSD: An MRI study. *Depression & Anxiety, 23*(1), 17–25.

Rogers, M. A., Yamasue, H., Abe, O., Yamada, H., Ohtani, T., Iwanami, A., et al. (2009). Smaller amygdala volume and reduced anterior cingulate gray matter density associated with history of post-traumatic stress disorder. *Psychiatry Research, 174*(3), 210–216.

Rubin, D. C., Berntsen, D., & Bohni, M. K. (2008). A memory-based model of posttraumatic stress disorder: Evaluating basic assumptions underlying the PTSD diagnosis. *Psychological Review, 115*(4), 985–1011.

Rubin, D. C., Boals, A., & Berntsen, D. (2008). Memory in posttraumatic stress disorder: Properties of voluntary and involuntary, traumatic and nontraumatic autobiographical memories in people with and without posttraumatic stress disorder symptoms. *Journal of Experimental Psychology: General, 137*(4), 591–614.

Saigh, P. A., Yasik, A. E., Oberfield, R. A., Halamandaris, P. V., & Bremner, J. D. (2006). The intellectual performance of traumatized children and adolescents with or without posttraumatic stress disorder. *Journal of Abnormal Psychology, 115*(2), 332–340.

Samuelson, K. W., Krueger, C. E., Burnett, C., & Wilson, C. K. (2010). Neuropsychological functioning in children with posttraumatic stress disorder. *Child Neuropsychology, 16*(2), 119–133.

Samuelson, K. W., Neylan, T. C., Metzler, T. J., Lenoci, M., Rothlind, J., Henn-Haase, C., et al. (2006). Neuropsychological functioning in posttraumatic stress disorder and alcohol abuse. *Neuropsychology, 20*(6), 716–726.

Schoeman, R., Carey, P., & Seedat, S. (2009). Trauma and posttraumatic stress disorder in South African adolescents: A case-control study of cognitive deficits. *Journal of Nervous & Mental Disease, 197*(4), 244–250.

Shaw, M. E., Moores, K. A., Clark, R. C., McFarlane, A. C., Strother, S. C., Bryant, R. A., et al. (2009). Functional connectivity reveals inefficient working memory systems in post-traumatic stress disorder. *Psychiatry Research, 172*(3), 235–241.

Shin, L. M., Lasko, N. B., Macklin, M. L., Karpf, R. D., Milad, M. R., Orr, S. P., et al.(2009). Resting metabolic activity in the cingulate cortex and vulnerability to posttraumatic stress disorder. *Archives of General Psychiatry, 66*(10), 1099–1107.

Shin, L. M., Shin, P. S., Heckers, S., Krangel, T. S., Macklin, M. L., Orr, S. P., et al. (2004). Hippocampal function in posttraumatic stress disorder. *Hippocampus, 14*(3), 292–300.

Shin, L. M., Wright, C. I., Cannistraro, P. A., Wedig, M. M., McMullin, K., Martis, B., et al. (2005). A functional magnetic resonance imaging study of amygdala and medial prefrontal cortex responses to overtly presented fearful faces in posttraumatic stress disorder. *Archives of General Psychiatry, 62*(3), 273–281.

Stanford, M. S., Vasterling, J. J., Mathias, C. W., Constans, J. I., & Houston, R. J. (2001). Impact of threat relevance on P3 event-related potentials in combat-related post-traumatic stress disorder. *Psychiatry Research, 102*(2), 125–137.

Stein, M. B., Kennedy, C. M., & Twamley, E. W. (2002). Neuropsychological function in female victims of intimate partner violence with and without posttraumatic stress disorder. *Biological Psychiatry, 52*(11), 1079–1088.

Stein, M. B., & McAllister, T. W. (2009). Exploring the convergence of posttraumatic stress disorder and mild traumatic brain injury. *American Journal of Psychiatry, 166*(7), 768–776.

Sullivan, G. M., & Neria, Y. (2009). Pharmacotherapy in post-traumatic stress disorder: Evidence from randomized controlled trials. *Current Opinion in Investigational Drugs, 10*(1), 35–45.

Sullivan, K. A., Krengel, M., Proctor, S. P., Devine, S., Heeren, T., & White, R. F. (2003). Cognitive functioning in treatment-seeking Gulf War veterans: Pyridostigmine bromide use and PTSD. *Journal of Psychopathology and Behavioral Assessment, 2*(2), 95–103.

Sutker, P., Bugg, F., & Allain, A. N. (1991). Psychometric prediction of PTSD among POW survivors. *Psychological Assessment, 3*, 105–110.

Thompson, W. W., & Gottesman, I. J. (2008). Challenging the conclusion that lower pre-induction cognitive ability increases risk for combat-related posttraumatic stress disorder in 2,375 combat-exposed, Vietnam War veterans. *Military Medicine, 173*(6), 576–582.

Tischler, L., Brand, S. R., Stavitsky, K., Labinsky, E., Newmark, R., Grossman, R., et al. (2006). The relationship between hippocampal volume and declarative memory in a population of combat veterans with and without PTSD. *Annals of the New York Academy of Sciences, 1071*, 405–409.

Turner, J. B., Turse, N. A., & Dohrenwend, B. P. (2007). Circumstances of service and gender differences in war-related PTSD: Findings from the national Vietnam Veteran Readjustment Study. *Journal of Traumatic Stress, 20*(4), 643–649.

Twamley, E. W., Allard, C. B., Thorp, S. R., Norman, S. B., Hami Cissell, S., Hughes Berardi, K., et al. (2009). Cognitive impairment and functioning in PTSD related to intimate partner violence. *Journal of the International Neuropsychological Society, 15*(6), 879–887.

Twamley, E. W., Hami, S., & Stein, M. B. (2004). Neuropsychological function in college students with and without posttraumatic stress disorder. *Psychiatry Research, 126*(3), 265–274.

Uddo, M., Vasterling, J. J., Brailey, K., & Sutker, P. B. (1993). Memory and attention in combat-related post-traumatic stress disorder (PTSD). *Journal of Psychopathology and Behavioral Assessment, 15*(1), 43–54.

Van Ameringen, M., Mancini, C., Patterson, B., & Boyle, M. H. (2008). Post-traumatic stress disorder in Canada. *CNS Neuroscience & Therapeutics, 14*(3), 171–181.

Vanderploeg, R. D., Curtiss, G., & Belanger, H. G. (2005). Long-term neuropsychological outcomes following mild traumatic brain injury. *Journal of the International Neuropsychological Society, 11*(3), 228–236.

Vasterling, J. J., Brailey, K., Constans, J. I., Borges, A., & Sutker, P. B. (1997). Assessment of intellectual resources in Gulf War veterans: Relationship to PTSD. *Assessment, 4*, 51–59.

Vasterling, J. J., Brailey, K., Constans, J. I., & Sutker, P. B. (1998). Attention and memory dysfunction in posttraumatic stress disorder. *Neuropsychology, 12*(1), 125–133.

Vasterling, J. J., Duke, L. M., Brailey, K., Constans, J. I., Allain, A. N. Jr., & Sutker, P. B. (2002). Attention, learning, and memory performances and intellectual resources in Vietnam veterans: PTSD and no disorder comparisons. *Neuropsychology, 16*(1), 5–14.

Vasterling, J. J., Rogers, C., & Kaplan, E. (2000). Qualitative block design analysis in posttraumatic stress disorder. *Assessment, 7*(3), 217–226.

Vasterling, J. J., Verfaellie, M., & Sullivan, K. D. (2009). Mild traumatic brain injury and posttraumatic stress disorder in returning veterans: Perspectives from cognitive neuroscience. *Clinical Psychology Review, 29*(8), 674–684.

Veltmeyer, M. D., Clark, C. R., McFarlane, A. C., Felmingham, K. L., Bryant, R. A., & Gordon, E. (2005). Integrative assessment of brain and cognitive function in post-traumatic stress disorder. *Journal of Integrative Neuroscience, 4*(1), 145–159.

Vermetten, E., & Bremner, J. D. (2002). Circuits and systems in stress. I. Preclinical studies. *Depression and Anxiety, 15*(3), 126–147.

Vermetten, E., Vythilingam, M., Southwick, S. M., Charney, D. S., & Bremner, J. D. (2003). Long-term treatment with paroxetine increases verbal declarative memory and hippocampal volume in posttraumatic stress disorder. *Biological Psychiatry, 54*(7), 693–702.

Vrana, S., & Lauterbach, D. (1994). Prevalence of traumatic events and post-traumatic psychological symptoms in a nonclinical sample of college students. *Journal of Traumatic Stress, 7*(2), 289–302.

Walter, K. H., Palmieri, P. A., & Gunstad, J. (2010). More than symptom reduction: Changes in executive function over the course of PTSD treatment. *Journal of Traumatic Stress, 23*(2), 292–295.

Weathers, F. W., Keane, T. M., & Davidson, J. R. (2001). Clinician-Administered PTSD Scale: A review of the first ten years of research. *Depression & Anxiety, 13*(3), 132–156.

Werner, N. S., Meindl, T., Engel, R. R., Rosner, R., Riedel, M., & Reiser, M. (2009). Hippocampal function during associative learning in patients with posttraumatic stress disorder. *Journal of Psychiatric Research, 43*(3), 309–318.

Wignall, E. L., Dickson, J. M., Vaughan, P., Farrow, T. F. D., Wilkinson, I. D., Hunter, M. D., et al. (2004). Smaller hippocampal volume in patients with recent-onset posttraumatic stress disorder. *Biological Psychiatry, 56*, 832–836.

Wild, J., & Gur, R. C. (2008). Verbal memory and treatment response in post-traumatic stress disorder. *British Journal of Psychiatry, 193*(3), 254–255.

Williams, L. M., Kemp, A. H., Felmingham, K., Barton, M., Olivieri, G., Peduto, A., et al. (2006). Trauma modulates amygdala and medial prefrontal responses to consciously attended fear. *Neuroimage, 29*(2), 347–357.

Williams, W. H., Evans, J. J., Needham, P., & Wilson, B. A. (2002). Neurological, cognitive and attributional predictors of posttraumatic stress symptoms after traumatic brain injury. *Journal of Traumatic Stress, 15*(5), 397–400.

Woon, F. L., & Hedges, D. W. (2009). Amygdala volume in adults with posttraumatic stress disorder: A meta-analysis. *Journal of Neuropsychiatry & Clinical Neuroscience, 21*(1), 5–12.

Woon, F. L., Sood, S., & Hedges, D. W. (2010). Hippocampal volume deficits associated with exposure to psychological trauma and posttraumatic stress disorder in adults: A meta-analysis. *Progress in Neuro-Psychopharmacology & Biological Psychiatry, 34*, 1181–1188.

Yamasue, H., Kasai, K., Iwanami, A., Ohtani, T., Yamada, H., Abe, O., et al. (2003). Voxel-based analysis of MRI reveals anterior cingulate gray-matter volume reduction in posttraumatic stress disorder due to terrorism. *Proceedings of the National Academy of Sciences of the United States of America, 100*(15), 9039–9043.

Yehuda, R., Golier, J. A., Tischler, L., Stavitsky, K., & Harvey, P. D. (2005). Learning and memory in aging combat veterans with PTSD. *Journal of Clinical & Experimental Neuropsychology, 27*(4), 504–515.

Yehuda, R., Tischler, L., Golier, J. A., Grossman, R., Brand, S. R., & Kaufman, S. (2006). Longitudinal assessment of cognitive performance in Holocaust survivors with and without PTSD. *Biological Psychiatry, 60*(7), 714–721.

Zalewski, C., Thompson, W., & Gottesman, I. (1994). Comparison of neurological test performance in PTSD, generalized anxiety disorder, and control Vietnam veterans. *Assessment, 1*, 133–142.

CHAPTER 14

Somatoform Disorders

Jacqueline Remondet Wall, Jennifer Mariner, & Jeremy J. Davis

INTRODUCTION

Medicine is replete with stories of patients whose symptoms are not consistent with medical understanding, and for these cases, the diagnostic category of somatoform disorders (SFD) must be considered. Although specific symptom presentations are variable, practitioners readily recall patients with these concerns. Most providers have encountered persons with such perplexing presentations, and often, these memories are less than pleasant. Considering patients with unexplainable symptoms brings to mind three questions that are part of the diagnostic conundrum encountered: dualism verses monism when confronting issues of physical verses mental health, the dimension of intentionality of presentation, and the excess in number or intensity with which symptoms are shared. These questions lead to an enigma of accurate diagnosis, following which patients with somatoform conditions provide substantive challenge to creating successful treatment outcomes. For example, patients with SFDs frequently are those who disregard health care provider recommendations, seek multiple opinions seemingly searching for the "right" answer, or call providers after hours demanding service, and so forth. In fact, one study noted that when compared to other health conditions, SFDs are rated as one of the most difficult to treat (Hahn, 2001). Practitioners in neuropsychology are referred patients presenting with such symptoms, so a review of this condition, including its definition, information on epidemiology, etiology, pathology, neuropsychological pathology and sequelae, diagnostic considerations, and contemporary modes of treatment are provided.

DEFINITION

First introduced in the third edition of the *Diagnostic and Statistical Manual* (*DSM-III*) of the American Psychiatric Association (APA; 1980), the diagnostic category of SFDs was established as a classification to identify patients whose symptoms were not thought to represent pure physical/medical phenomena. The classification of persons with these symptoms was born out of attempts to increase the reliability in psychiatric diagnoses through greater operationalization and initially yielded a speculative diagnostic category (Hiller & Rief, 2005). However, its presentation has remained in subsequent editions of the *DSM*, and the condition is one of the diagnostic categories being considered for inclusion in the upcoming edition. In the current edition (*DSM-IV-TR*; APA, 2000), the professionally agreed-upon diagnostic criteria for the diagnosis of SFDs has been expanded from that offered in the previous edition

TABLE 14.1 Primary Symptom Differentiation Among SFDs

Diagnosis	Primary symptom presentation
Body dysmorphic disorder	Preoccupation that one's body is deformed or defective.
Conversion disorder	Deficits in voluntary motor or sensory functions for which there is no evident underlying physical etiology.
Hypochondriasis	Preoccupation with having a serious, yet undetected disease that persists in light of negative medical evaluation.
Pain disorder	Presence of pain for which psychological factors are judged to play an important role in onset, severity, or exacerbation.
Somatization disorder	Physical symptoms present before the age of 30 years; occur over several years; and include pain, gastrointestinal, sexual/reproductive, and pseudoneurological symptoms. These remain even though medical evaluation and treatment has been sought from multiple providers.
Undifferentiated somatoform disorder	One or more complaints that cause substantive distress or functional limitations that last more than 6 months.

to include SFD, body dysmorphic disorder (BDD), conversion disorder, hypochondriasis, pain, and undifferentiated somatization disorder. The primary symptoms associated with each of these syndromes are shown in Table 14.1. These disorders not only include symptoms that are unexplainable or are judged to be exaggerated but also present with questions about the presence of secondary gain, as well as the intentionality of attribution. Ranging in severity, intensity, and duration, these diagnoses all include those for which symptoms are not intentionally produced. For example, undifferentiated somatization disorder affects one organ system with milder symptoms than somatization disorder. Somatization disorder, though, must begin before age 30 and incorporate multiple organ systems across years even with the application of multiple assessments and interventions.

All of these conditions have at the root of their presentation symptoms thought to be related to psychological concerns. The SFDs are similar to, but unique from, the factitious disorders (e.g., factitious disorder with physical signs, with psychological signs, or both) and malingering (APA, 2000). In both factitious disorder and malingering, there is an intentional production or feigning of symptoms. However, in the factitious disorders it is for an internal reward such as attention and sympathy, whereas malingering symptoms are motivated by external incentives, such as the avoidance of unpleasant tasks or the receipt of financial rewards. Unique from malingering, SFDs share with factitious disorder syndromes a lack of awareness of the personal motivation associated with being ill. Given this, these categories are thought to have substantial overlap in symptom presentation. These considerations are important in the United States because undifferentiated somatic symptoms are cited as accounting for more than half of all clinic visits each year (Schappert, 1992). Via a survey, 3,000 primary care patients were asked to endorse whether they had experienced any of 15 common symptoms during the previous 4 weeks. The top 12 symptoms were reported by more than 20% of the sample. Additionally, the top five symptoms, in decreasing order of frequency, were: fatigue, limb pain, back pain, headache, and insomnia; all having a prevalence of 50% or higher (Kroenke, Spitzer, & Williams, 2002). Interestingly, these symptoms are also associated with the incidence of somatoform conditions, and it is into this mixture that the diagnostic problem arises. These symptoms, which may be attributed to physical or psychological factors, may perplex the practitioner, and it is generally when they have been present for more than 6 months or there is an extended history that there is a consideration of a somatoform condition. Even so, psychological, physical, and social variables must be considered to understand SFDs (Witthoft & Hiller, 2010).

Although a disorder found to be diagnosed more frequently in women, many studies find varying prevalence rates and the actual disproportionate representation has been questioned, with greater emphasis also being placed on socio-economic class and the presence of emotional distress (Ladwig, Marten-Mittag, Erazo, & Gündel, 2001). A portion of this is likely due to historical variables, but also to the factors that are associated with and/or cause the symptoms. Different etiological perspectives range from difficulties with early attachment and intra-psychic conflict to those emphasizing learning principles associated with symptom acquisition (Lamberty, 2008). Perhaps more interesting than the proposed etiological theories of this presentation are findings that cultural issues may be associated with symptom presentation. Although not entirely explanatory and beyond the scope of this chapter is the notion of culture and enculturation and how these factors may increase understanding of these conditions.

HISTORY OF THE DIAGNOSTIC CATEGORY, ITS CURRENT STATUS, AND FUTURE CONSIDERATIONS

Symptoms classified as SFDs have been described since the time of Hippocrates and have been the subject of close study by clinicians and researchers since the time of Charcot and Freud (Crimlisk & Ron, 1999; Micale, 2000). In 1859, though, Briquet was the first person to describe the condition known as SFD. Despite this lengthy history of scientific scrutiny, the definition and nosological status of these disorders still remain controversial (Brown, Cardena, Nijenhuis, Sar, & van der Hart, 2007; Mayou, Kirmayer, Simon, Kroenke, & Sharpe, 2005; Sharpe & Carson, 2001). Among the problems identified with current criteria for the SFDs, two main issues related to terminology and diagnosis have been highlighted by multiple authors.

In clinical situations and in research publications regarding somatoform conditions, a proliferation of terms and definitions with variable usage patterns hampers clinical communication and leads to difficulty generalizing research findings (Kroenke, 2007a). Somatoform conditions have been described with a wide range of terms including hysteria, hysterical conversion, Briquet syndrome, psychosomatic condition, psychophysiological disorder, conversion (disorder), dissociative conversion, and somatization (Crimlisk & Ron, 1999; Oken, 2007). Outside of neurology and psychiatry, each medical specialty appears to have its own label for symptoms and syndromes that defy medical explanation (Deary, 1999; Richardson & Engel, 2004; Wessely, Nimnuan, & Sharpe, 1999), which are collectively referred to as medically unexplained symptoms (Richardson & Engel, 2004) and functional somatic syndromes (Barsky & Borus, 1999). The observation of similarities across syndromes has led some authors to ponder the utility of a unified construct (Deary, 1999; Wessely et al., 1999), and Kroenke (2007b) suggested a conceptual model that places conditions involving somatic symptoms on a spectrum ranging from symptom-only conditions (i.e., the medically unexplained symptoms common in general practice) to SFD. Others have recommended reclassifying conversion disorder as a dissociative disorder (Brown et al., 2007); removing the SFDs category and creating a functional somatic syndromes category on Axis III (Mayou et al., 2005). Others, though, have recommended maintaining the current SFDs category but adding sub-types and broadening the diagnosis to include cases where clinically significant symptoms warrant a diagnosis (Hiller, 2006).

In addition to these definitional difficulties, it has also been suggested that current criteria for somatization disorder are too restrictive, fail to capture the large numbers of individuals who present with somatic symptoms, and result in overuse of the residual diagnostic category (APA, 2010a; Kroenke, 2007a). According to the *DSM-IV-TR* (APA, 2000), the prototypical SFDs are rare, with estimated prevalence rates of 0.2%–2% for somatization disorder and 0.1–3% for conversion disorder. These estimates appear low in comparison to the prevalence rates of somatic complaints and medically unexplained symptoms in primary care (Khan, Khan, Harezlak, Tu, & Kroenke, 2003; Lynch, McGrady, Nagel, & Zsembik, 1999) and neurology clinics (Carson et al., 2000; Fink, Hansen, & Søndergaard, 2005).

In an attempt to match diagnostic criteria with clinical observation, modified criteria have been proposed that reduce the number of symptoms required for a diagnosis. Escobar, Burnam, Karno, Forsythe, and Golding (1987) proposed a category entitled *abridged somatization;* it requires only four or more symptoms for males and six or more symptoms for females. Another set of modified criteria, termed *multisomatoform disorder,* is based on three or more symptoms regardless of gender (Kroenke et al., 1997). Lynch and colleagues (1999) compared these modified diagnostic criteria with *DSM-IV* criteria in a clinical sample. Results showed that 1% met criteria for *DSM-IV* somatization disorder, 6% met criteria for abridged somatization (Escobar et al., 1987), 24% met criteria for multisomatoform disorder (Kroenke et al., 1997), and 79% met criteria for *DSM-IV* undifferentiated SFD. The prevalence of SFDs in a neurology clinic showed a similar trend, with 35% of patients meeting criteria for any SFD and only 1% meeting criteria for somatization disorder according to *DSM-IV* criteria (Fink et al., 2005).

The *DSM-V*, currently in development, illustrates marked changes in thought regarding these conditions and potentially a new system that incorporates integration between physical and mental health symptoms (Creed, Guthrie, Fink, Henningsen, Rief, Sharpe, & White, 2010). In preparation for upcoming revisions to both the *DSM* and the International Classification of Diseases (ICD), a number of work groups and conferences were convened in order to clarify the problems with current diagnostic criteria and to reach consensus with regard to proposed revisions (Kroenke, Sharpe, & Sykes, 2007; Regier, 2007). Details of the debate and reviews of the proceedings undertaken to explore the issue are described elsewhere (APA, 2010a; Creed, 2009a, 2009b; Creed et al., 2010; Dimsdale, Patel, Xin, & Kleinman, 2007; Kroenke, 2007b; Kroenke & Sharpe, 2006). A summary of one series of workshops attended by international experts in somatoform conditions noted a "number of divergent views held within the areas of consensus" (Kroenke et al., 2007, p. 283). The recent proposal disseminated by the Somatic Symptoms Work Group of the APA strikes a balance between many of the divergent opinions (APA, 2010b). Four substantial changes have been proposed: 1) creating a group of diagnoses called *somatic symptom disorders* and subsuming SFDs, factitious disorders, and psychological factors affecting medical condition within it; 2) combining somatization disorder, undifferentiated SFD, and hypochondriasis into one diagnosis called *complex somatic symptom disorder* (CSSD); 3) reducing the importance of medically unexplained symptoms to the new CSSD diagnosis; and 4) modifying conversion disorder criteria to reduce the requirement to establish the presence of psychological factors to the condition. The proposed criteria are described in detail along with the rationale in documents prepared by the Somatic Symptoms Work Group (APA, 2010a, 2010b).

Recent notions have been proposed that establish new diagnostic categories outside of the *DSM* system for persons who present with excessive cognitive complaints that could be subsumed within the category of SFD (Delis & Wetter, 2007; Larrabee, 2007). These categories are for persons who present with exaggerated cognitive concerns, but these "impairments" are not identified as being produced volitionally, and are based on the diagnostic criteria for malingered neurocognitive dysfunction proposed by Slick, Sherman, and Iverson (1999). The proposed diagnostic criteria include identification of at least two symptoms out of nine, which incorporate the following: "cognitive complaints or poor test performance" that are considered unlikely given the presenting condition, inconsistencies between test performance and observed behavior, delay of onset of symptoms following injury event, evidence of poor effort on testing, and variability in presentation over time. It will be interesting to see if these criteria become established, and the reader is encouraged to examine them in more detail.

NEUROPSYCHOLOGICAL AND BEHAVIORAL SEQUELAE

SFDs are common in the fields of psychiatry and neurology, and it was Freud who introduced the term *conversion* to describe patients who presented with neurological symptoms for which no underlying diagnostic cause was evident (Kaplan, Sadock, & Gregg, 1994). Much like medicine, the neuropsychological literature contains case histories and studies describing how to identify persons for whom presenting complaints are surmised by practitioners to be without physiological explanation. Although the presentation of specific neurocognitive deficits in patients having somatoform conditions has been noted to be rare (Lamberty, 2008), the incidence of unexplainable symptoms in the field of neuropsychology is more common, and such cases are described in the literature (Axelrod, 2008; Cullum, Heaton, & Grant, 1991; Horton, 1992; Miller, 1984).

Early neuropsychological research in SFDs was inconsistent. Matthews, Shaw, and Klove (1966) compared patients presenting with a pseudoneurological presentation to a demographically matched group of persons with brain injury on a standardized neuropsychological battery. The brain injury group scored worse on 17 of 26 measures; a global impairment rating identified 72% of the brain injury group and only 6% of the pseudoneurological group. In contrast, 9 out of 10 participants diagnosed with somatization disorder were identified as having abnormal scores on a neuropsychological battery when evaluated using blind raters (Flor-Henry, Fromm-Auch, Tapper, & Schopflocher, 1981). Levy and Jankovic (1983) presented a case study of experimentally manipulated conversion symptoms that included reduced performance on neuropsychological measures. These studies may have limited application to present diagnostic considerations given the lack of effort assessment when they were performed (Bush et al., 2005).

Liebson, White, and Albert (1996) compared neuropsychological performance in a sample of outpatients diagnosed with somatization disorder, factitious disorder, dissociative disorder, or malingering with a comparison group that had neurological diagnoses including open and closed head injury, anoxic encephalopathy, and dementia. The authors measured effort via questionable responses (e.g., approximate answers), inconsistencies within and between tests (e.g., delayed recall better than immediate recall), and other embedded measures (e.g., less than chance performance on recognition memory tasks). Group differences were noted only in the number of approximate answers, which were lower in the group with neurological diagnoses.

Kemp et al. (2008) explored performance on effort measures in patients with medically unexplained symptoms and compared this group with two groups of simulators matched on age, gender, and estimated IQ. None of the participants in the medically unexplained symptoms group were involved in litigation, but 23 of 43 were involved in disability claims; their diagnoses included psychogenic nonepileptic seizures, functional movement disorders, and nonorganic sensory deficits. Participants completed five symptom validity measures. In the medically unexplained symptoms group, 11% of participants (5 of 43) failed two or more effort tests.

One of the few recent studies to examine cognitive profiles in individuals diagnosed with a SFD did not include symptom validity tests (Niemi, Portin, Aalto, Hakala, & Karlsson, 2002). A group of 10 patients diagnosed with either somatization disorder or undifferentiated SFD and 10 age- and education-matched control participants completed a battery of clinician- and computer-administered tasks and a psychiatric symptom checklist. The patient group showed higher self-reported somatic symptoms and had lower scores on measures of visuoconstruction, abstract verbal reasoning, immediate and delayed recall of paired words, and working memory. The results from this pilot study were thought to reflect cerebro-hypometabolism in the patient sample because mediating effects from other known disease processes were removed and deficits seen.

Along a similar vein, recent research with persons diagnosed with BDD has found evidence of cognitive compromise. Specifically, Hanes (1998) reported results of a study comparing neuropsychological evaluation results between patients diagnosed with BDD to 10 persons diagnosed with obsessive-compulsive disorder (OCD), 14 diagnosed with schizophrenia, and 24 non-psychiatric/non-neurological controls. Results from an ANCOVA controlling for age, premorbid intelligence, and depressive symptoms found significant effects for tests measuring executive functions. Post-hoc comparisons identified that those with BDD performed at lower levels than controls on these measures, but were comparable to the OCD patient group. These two groups, when compared to persons with schizophrenia, performed better on tests of memory and learning. The author concluded that these results supported the relationship between these two disorders and that there could be an implication of prefrontal cortical involvement, recognizing, though, the need for replication in a larger sample.

Another recent study also examined performance on neuropsychological tests without administering symptom validity tests in a sample of 20 patients diagnosed with somatization disorder (Trivedi, Sharma, Singh, Sinha, & Tandon, 2005). A comparison group of 15 relatives and friends of the patients was matched in age, gender, and education. The groups completed computerized versions of the Wisconsin Card Sorting Test (Heaton, 1981), Continuous Performance Test (Conners, 1997), and the Spatial Working Memory Test (Trivedi et al., 2005). The groups showed significant differences on portions of each of the measures. The patient group completed fewer categories and made more perseverative errors on the Wisconsin Card Sorting Test; made fewer correct responses, more missed responses, and had longer response time on the Continuous Performance Test; and had fewer correct responses at 20-second delay on the Spatial Working Memory Test.

PSYCHOLOGICAL DIAGNOSTIC TECHNIQUES

Minnesota Multiphasic Personality Inventory-2 (MMPI-2)

The Minnesota Multiphasic Personality Inventory-second edition (MMPI-2; Butcher, Dahlstrom, Graham, Tellegen, & Kaemmer, 1989) has an extensive body of research examining its utility in a wide range of conditions, including the SFDs. The clinical use and interpretation of the measure is comprehensively covered in various other studies (Greene, 2005; Graham, 2000) so the present discussion will focus on its use in the assessment of SFDs. The labels of two clinical scales—Scale 1 (Hypochondriasis) and Scale 3 (Hysteria)—suggest the intent of the developers of the measure to devise a tool for diagnosing conditions that are now grouped as SFDs in the *DSM-IV-TR* (McKinley & Hathaway, 1944). Interpretation of the MMPI through configuration or profile analysis was recommended not long after its initial description in the literature, and the relationship of the first three scales, the neurotic triad, figured prominently in many of the interpretable profiles (Gough, 1946; McKinley & Hathaway, 1944). One of the more commonly discussed two-point code types on the MMPI-2, the 1–3/3–1 profile (also known as the conversion valley or conversion V) first appeared in the early MMPI literature as the "depressive valley" (Gough, 1946, p. 30).

More recent research using the MMPI-2 has focused on a number of conditions outside the *DSM-IV-TR* somatoform disorders category that share clinical features and MMPI-2 profile similarities with somatoform conditions including chronic pain (Dush, Simons, Platt, Nation, & Ayres, 1994), multiple chemical sensitivity (Binder, Storzbach, & Salinsky, 2006), memory complaints (Gervais, Ben-Porath, Wygant, & Green, 2008), and postconcussive syndrome (Youngjohn, Burrows, & Erdal, 1995). Because evaluations involving these conditions are often conducted in a medicolegal context, much of the research has been aimed at developing measures of response bias and symptom validity. As a result of this search for additional indices of symptom exaggeration, a number of scales have been developed, including the Fake Bad Scale (FBS; Lees-Haley, English, & Glenn, 1991), the Response Bias Scale (Gervais, Ben-Porath, Wygant, & Green, 2007), and the Henry-Heilbronner Index (Henry, Heilbronner, Mittenberg, & Enders, 2006). Although use of these scales has been strongly supported in forensic contexts (Nelson, Hoelzle, Sweet, Arbisi, & Demakis, 2010), the routine clinical use of at least one, the FBS, has been challenged due to its proneness to misclassify individuals with legitimate physical symptoms from medical conditions (Butcher, Arbisi, Atlis, & McNulty, 2003). Despite a lively debate (Greve & Bianchini, 2004; Larrabee, 2003; Lees-Haley & Fox, 2004), the issue of whether MMPI-2 respondents with SFDs will consistently exceed cut scores on symptom exaggeration scales remains a question for further empirical examination.

Via a secondary analysis, Boone and Lu (1999) examined records from a group of patients who obtained clinical elevations on both Scales 1 (Hypochondriasis) and 3 (Hysteria) on the MMPI/MMPI-2. They identified a sample of 19 patients who obtained clinically significant, highest profile elevations on scales 1 and 3. After identifying this sample, the researchers examined scores on standard neuropsychological tests to see if non-credible performance was generated. Over two-thirds of this sample failed one or more symptom validity tests and demonstrated patterns of performance on other tests suggesting questionable performance validity.

MMPI-2 Restructured Format

The MMPI-2 Restructured Format (MMPI-2-RF; Ben-Porath & Tellegen, 2008) has been developed from the second edition with a goal of reducing item overlap, thereby improving scale homogeneity. Although research using the MMPI-2-RF remains limited in comparison to the thousands of publications on earlier versions of the instrument, several recent publications examine its psychometrics and utility in SFDs. Thomas and Locke (2010) used taxometrics, confirmatory factor analysis, and item response theory to examine the psychometric properties of the Somatic Complaints scale (RC1) in a clinical sample with diagnoses of epilepsy or nonepileptic seizures. Although the details of the methodology are beyond the scope of the present discussion, the article provides independent validation of the structure of RC1 and evidence that its optimal range of measurement fits the intended purpose of the scale as a measure of somatization at clinically significant levels.

Locke and colleagues (2010) examined MMPI-2-RF profiles of patients in an epilepsy monitoring unit who had been diagnosed with epilepsy or nonepileptic seizures (NES) and examined the classification accuracy of a number of clinical, validity, and specific problems scales. Epilepsy and NES groups were comparable in demographic variables except gender (more females in NES group); seizure history and psychiatric history were more extensive in the NES group; the groups were similar on measures of intellectual ability. Comparison of MMPI-2-RF profiles showed higher scores for the NES group on a number of scales including Infrequent Somatic Responses (Fs), Symptom Validity (FBS-r), Somatic Complaints (RC1), and on the specific problems scales, Malaise, Gastrointestinal Complaints, Head Pain Complaints, and Neurological Complaints. Using RC1 to predict group membership with a *T* score of 65 as a cut point, the sensitivity was 0.76 and specificity was 0.60. Thomas and Youngjohn (2009) compared the Restructured Clinical (RC) scales to MMPI-2 validity and clinical scales in a sample of individuals with a history of traumatic brain injury involved in litigation. Participants were grouped by injury severity (mild, mild complicated, and moderate/severe) and by passing or failing symptom validity tests. The MMPI-2 profiles of both mild and mild complicated groups showed a conversion V configuration. The RC scale elevations were not significantly different between groups of TBI severity, but participants who passed symptom validity tests had lower RC1 scores than participants who failed symptom validity tests. A discriminant function analysis using the RC scales correctly classified 80% of participants into groups based on symptom validity tests performance.

Other research on the RC scales and MMPI-2-RF has also examined issues related to symptom exaggeration and non-credible cognitive performance. Henry, Heilbronner, Mittenberg, Enders, and Stanczak (2008) compared the classification accuracy of RC1 with the FBS and the HHI in a sample comprising individuals involved in litigation or disability claims who failed symptom validity tests and control participants who had sustained a head injury. Logistic regression analyses showed the FBS and HHI to be better predictors of probable malingering than RC1. Wygant and colleagues (2009) examined MMPI-2-RF validity scales in samples of medical and head injury simulators and individuals involved in personal injury litigation or disability claims. In comparison to respective control participants, both medical and head injury simulators showed significant elevations on Infrequent Responses (F-r), Infrequent Psychopathology (Fp-r), and Infrequent Somatic Responses (Fs). Medical simulators also showed significantly greater elevations on FBS-r than control participants. In the civil forensic sample, differences were noted between litigants and claimants who passed symptom validity tests and those who failed one or more symptom validity tests on all four validity scales. As the number of failed symptom validity tests increased, the elevations on all validity scales increased. Somatic complaints have been found to correlate with subjective cognitive difficulty as reported by the MMPI-2-RF Cognitive Complaints scale (COG; Gervais, Ben-Porath, & Wygant, 2009). Gervais and colleagues (2009) recommend considering elevations on COG in addition to the other MMPI-2-RF validity scales and provide interpretive guidelines: COG elevations and normal limits scores on the infrequent response scales may reflect true cognitive difficulty or subjective cognitive difficulty related to emotional factors; elevations on COG and infrequent response scales suggest symptom over-reporting.

Although a growing body of research has shown the utility of the MMPI-2-RF in differentiating epileptic from nonepileptic seizures and in identifying individuals with history of mild TBI who failed symptom validity tests, other research in forensic settings has shown inconsistencies. Whether the MMPI-2-RF can aid in the differentiation of somatoform conditions from non-credible symptom reporting in the context of secondary gain remains a topic for further investigation.

Personality Assessment Inventory

The Personality Assessment Inventory (PAI; Morey, 1991) is 344-item, self-report inventory that contains 4 validity scales, 11 clinical scales, 5 treatment scales, and 2 interpersonal scales. The clinical scales are transformed to linear *T* scores based on a census-matched normative sample of adults. Of the clinical scales, the 24-item Somatic Complaints scale is relevant to the present discussion. It was designed to capture concerns with health, physical functioning, and related symptoms; the scale includes three subscales: Conversion, Somatization, and Health Concerns. According to the manual, *T* scores in the range of 60–69 on the Somatic Complaints scale indicate concerns with health that are not uncommon among older adults and patients in medical settings. Scores equal to or greater than 70 are suggestive of significant somatic concerns likely leading to impairment in fulfilling daily responsibilities. Scores greater than or equal to 88 are suggestive of many somatic symptoms involving a range of organs and are likely to reflect chronic conditions with functional limitations.

A number of recent studies of SFDs and related symptoms have included the PAI. Aikman and Souheaver (2008) reported on the use of the PAI in routine neuropsychological examinations of psychiatric outpatients. The Somatic Complaints scale was related to verbal memory measures on the Repeatable Battery for the Assessment of Neuropsychological Status (Randolph, 1998), whereas other PAI scales were unrelated to neurocognitive performance. Kurtz, Shealy, and Putman (2007) examined psychological profiles on the PAI and MMPI in a clinical sample of individuals with a history of traumatic brain injury. Individuals with a history of mild traumatic brain injury showed elevations on the Somatic Complaints and Depression scales of the PAI; individuals with a history of moderate to severe traumatic brain injury showed elevations on the Antisocial Features and Alcohol Problems scales. Wagner, Wymer, Topping, and Pritchard (2005) provided evidence for the use of the PAI as a measure of nonepileptic seizure activity. They reported adequate sensitivity (0.84) and specificity (0.73) in identifying nonepileptic seizures using the Somatic Complaints scale. Sumanti and colleagues (2006) examined the relationship of PAI profiles and performance on symptom validity tests in a sample of individuals involved in workers' compensation claims. Participants who showed signs of questionable symptom validity on cognitive measures also showed elevations on a number of PAI clinical scales, including Somatic Complaints, Depression, Anxiety, and Schizophrenia, compared to patients without evidence of exaggerated cognitive difficulty. In a more recent study of the relationship of PAI profiles and effort on cognitive tasks, Whiteside and colleagues (2010) demonstrated the association of the Somatic Complaints scale with performance on the Test of Memory Malingering (TOMM; Tombaugh, 1996). Using a Somatic Complaints scale cut score ($T = 87$) to predict TOMM performance resulted in good sensitivity (0.93) and adequate specificity (0.76). These studies provide initial support for the PAI in both routine clinical settings and in medicolegal contexts. Additional research may be useful to evaluate the utility of validity measures on the PAI or to identify new indices related to symptom exaggeration and effort.

Millon Clinical Multiaxial Inventory-III

The Millon Clinical Multiaxial Inventory-III (MCMI-III; Millon, 1997) is a 175-item self-report inventory that is among the more commonly used objective personality measures (Camara, Nathan, & Puente, 2000). The test was developed to follow *DSM-IV-TR* diagnostic criteria and also reflects Millon's theory of personality. The MCMI-III includes 28 scales grouped into five categories: Modifying Indices, Clinical Personality Patterns, Severe Personality Pathology, Clinical Syndromes, and Severe Syndromes. Scores on the Modifying Indices establish protocol validity and include four measures of response style: randomness (Validity), openness (Disclosure), social desirability (Desirability), and symptom exaggeration (Debasement). Among the Clinical Syndromes scales, the 12-item Somatoform scale was developed to assess somatic complaints including pain, fatigue, vague bodily complaints, and preoccupation with health (Jankowski, 2002). Strengths of the measure include its brevity compared to the MMPI-2 and PAI and its focus on personality characteristics and Axis II pathology. Limitations include the frequent revisions made to keep pace with the changing *DSM*, which limits the available research for any one version, and the conflation of Millon's dimensional personality model with the categorical approach of the *DSM*. The score transformation and supporting documentation have been described as suboptimal (Grove & Vrieze, 2009).

A burgeoning body of research with the MCMI-III has been noted (Craig, 1999; Groth-Marnat, 2003). Although research using the test in SFDs remains limited, a number of recent studies in the medical and neuropsychological literature are relevant. Manchikanti and colleagues (2002) examined MCMI-III profiles of patients with chronic pain diagnoses and found significant differences from control participants on three Clinical Syndrome scales: Anxiety, Somatoform, and Major Depression. A follow-up study showed that as the number of pain regions increased, the proportion of clinically significant elevations also increased on Anxiety and Somatoform scales, and on Major Depression and Dysthymia scales combined (Manchikanti, Pampati, Beyer, Damron, & Barnhill 2002). Ruocco, Swirsky-Sacchetti, and Choca (2007) compared MCMI-III profiles of individuals with a history of mild to moderate traumatic brain injury (TBI) with a psychiatric sample matched for age, gender, and ethnicity. About 92% of members of the TBI sample were involved in disability claims or litigation. Responses to validity scales suggested less endorsement of psychiatric symptoms and greater endorsement of socially desirable items among the participants with history of TBI. A larger percentage of participants in the TBI group showed clinically significant elevations on the Somatoform scale than the psychiatric group (33% versus 17%, respectively).

Garden, Sullivan, and Lange (2010) explored the relationship between self-reported post-concussive symptoms and MCMI-III profiles in a community-dwelling sample of people who were without prior history of neurological condition, including TBI. Post-concussive symptoms were common in the sample; more than 20% reported experiencing 6 of 13 symptoms at a moderate intensity, and significant correlations were found between total post-concussive symptoms and 16 of 24 clinical scales on the MCMI-III. Group comparisons after splitting the sample on the basis of ICD-10 criteria for post-concussive syndrome showed significant differences on a number of clinical scales including Anxiety (Cohen's $d = 0.8$), Somatoform ($d = 1.1$), Dysthymia ($d = 0.4$), and Major Depression ($d = 1.0$). In one of the few studies to include symptom validity tests, Ruocco and colleagues (2008) described the relationship between the MCMI-III Modifying Indices (i.e., Validity, Disclosure, Desirability, and Debasement) and effort measures in a litigating or compensation-seeking sample. The MCMI-III modifier indices were not correlated with the TOMM or Reliable Digit Span (Greiffenstein, Baker, & Gola, 1994). The MCMI-III profiles were not significantly different between individuals who passed the TOMM and those who failed it.

TREATMENT

Categorically, the somatoform disorders are among the most difficult to treat effectively. This is due in part to the aforementioned lack of diagnostic clarity (Dohrenwend & Skillings, 2009; Stuart, Noyes, Starcevic, & Barsky, 2008). Additionally, researchers have suggested high dropout rates and a paucity of double-blind randomized controlled clinical trials as obstacles in establishing effective treatments (Kroenke, 2007a; Stuart et al., 2008). Given the suspected prevalence rates, frustration for patient and clinician alike, and high costs of SFDs (e.g., excessive medical utilization; lost time at work; reduced quality of life), these treatment-resistant disorders have recently received much more attention (Abbass, Kisley, & Kroenke, 2009; Kroenke, 2007a; Stuart et al., 2008; Sumathipala, 2007).

Psychological Approaches to Treatment

Those treating persons with SFDs must recognize that these patients frequently hold strong beliefs that their symptoms are the result of a physical cause and, concomitantly, there is an inherent resistance to the notion of psychiatric/psychologic factors playing a role in the initiation or exacerbation of symptoms (Oyama, Paltoo, & Greengold, 2007). Given such, those writing about providing treatment to persons diagnosed with SFDs emphasize the need for developing a therapeutic alliance and then discussing disease management through use of medication and therapy. The modality that has received the most research attention is cognitive-behavioral therapy (CBT). Generally, CBT focuses on cognitive reframing of both physiological symptoms and health care expectations, leading to a more accurate appraisal of situations. In addition, behavioral strategies are implemented to alter sick role behaviors and medical help-seeking. Relaxation skills are taught and distraction techniques are employed to reduce functional impairment (Stuart et al., 2008). Changing distorted cognitive appraisals and maladaptive sick role behaviors are, then, central in the treatment process. In addition, selective attention to benign physiological events is addressed (Stuart et al., 2008).

Sumathipala (2007) conducted a meta-analysis of available treatment studies from 1974 to 2007. Nearly half of all the participants in reviewed studies received CBT, which was determined to be most effective addressing the physical complaints associated with SFDs. The reduction of physical distress held true regardless of whether psychological suffering was reduced. Looper and Kirmayer (2002) performed a literature review in which the studies were separated according to specific diagnoses. They concluded individual CBT is an effective treatment option to address hypochondriasis and BDD. Further, group CBT was shown to have moderate efficacy for BDD and somatization disorder.

According to the fear-avoidance model of pain, psychological factors may change the experience of pain, but no evidence suggests these factors cause pain. It is likely that selective attention (fear of injury/re-injury) is paid to physical sensations, thereby reducing activity levels to avoid further pain/reinjury (maladaptive pain behavior). However, inertia is associated with increased pain following activity, which confirms the patient's fears and reinforces avoidance of movement (Crombez, Beirens, Van Damme, Eccleston, & Fontaine, 2009; Eifert, Zvolensky, & Louis, 2008). Cognitive-behavioral approaches can therefore address the hypervigilance to physical sensations, as well as behaviorally oriented strategies to compete with the pain response (relaxation, distraction, autogenic training).

Dahl and Lundgren (2006) posited acceptance and commitment therapy (ACT) as an effective treatment for chronic somatic pain conditions. The premise is to work with the patient to change those aspects of the condition that are under his or her direct control and continue to engage in activities while accepting those aspects of the condition that are uncontrollable. Their work suggests ACT significantly reduces long-term disability from chronic pain conditions, and is postulated to be effective because of changes in attention to discomfort and subsequent reduced activity. However, it is unlikely that any one single treatment approach will sufficiently address a pain syndrome; rather, several approaches may need to be used in combination to achieve maximal results (Dohrenwend & Skillings, 2009). Simultaneous use of non-narcotic pharmacological analgesics, psychological services to address coping skills/beliefs about illness, and alternative therapies (e.g., massage therapy, acupuncture) may be used simultaneously.

One such treatment combination for somatic pain syndromes is functional relaxation, commonly used in European countries. This technique involves relaxation and psychosomatic education. Specifically, the participant is familiarized with proprioception, stimulation of the autonomic nervous system, and during relaxed expiration, is instructed to engage in movement of the small joints. Then, focused exploration of different physical sensations experienced during these movements occurs. The participant can either describe the physiological sensations verbally during a therapeutic interaction or non-verbally. Theoretically, modifying perceptual experiences positively impacts sense of self, encouraging cohesion, as well as improved body self-awareness (Lahmann, Loew, Tritt, & Nickel, 2008).

Taking into account that somatization is thought to be a physical expression of psychological distress, insight-oriented approaches to treatment merit consideration (Kozlowska, 2005). Abbass and colleagues (2009) completed a meta-analysis of short-term psychodynamic psychotherapies. These researchers found that insight-oriented modalities improved treatment adherence and social and occupational functioning, while simultaneously reducing health care usage and psychological/physical complaints.

Attachment theory has been implicated in the expression of somatoform disorders. Specifically, those persons with insecure attachments may be more prone to experience and report physical symptoms, whereas those persons with preoccupied attachments may have increased health care utilization (Ciechanowski et al., 2002). As such, treatment is aimed at improving interpersonal relationships, especially disputes with loved ones regarding health care–seeking behavior (Stuart et al., 2008). Particular techniques used include communication analysis and identification of interpersonal incidents. These are explored to elucidate dysfunctional communication patterns, and more adaptive, clear communication patterns are rehearsed via role play (Stuart et al., 2008).

Hypnosis has long been associated with hysteria and subsequent hysterical reactions; however, its popularity as a viable treatment option waned during the third wave of treatment. It is now beginning to re-emerge as a potential treatment option for a myriad of problems, including somatoform disorders. Hallquist, Deming, Matthews, and Chaves (2010) suggest the following possible uses of hypnosis in treating somatoform disorders: build rapport and diffuse stigma, direct suggestion of symptom mitigation, symptom induction to effect remission, deconstructing symptoms, and age regression to explore origins for symptoms (p. 619).

Hallquist and colleagues (2010) recently proposed the use of hypnosis prior to other psychological treatments such as CBT. They posit by including hypnosis early in treatment, the patient may be less inclined to feel the need to "prove" his or her symptoms are medical and have no psychological component. Further, this may provide the opportunity for the patient to develop sufficient rapport with the clinician and restore faith that he or she is being heard; thus, the patient may be more likely to be open to future psychological intervention.

Scant clinical trials have been conducted to evaluate the effectiveness of hypnosis for SFDs. In a small study comparing hypnosis with wait-list control, investigators found hypnosis to significantly improve motor function by both an objective measure and behavioral observations (Moene, Spinhoven, Hoogduin, & van Dyck, 2003). Considering that the process of conversion disorder and hypnosis both involve some level of dissociation (Brown, 2004), it would seem to follow that hypnosis may well be a viable, if understudied, avenue worthy of additional research attention.

Hypochondriasis is thought to be one of the more chronic and difficult to treat somatoform disorders. Recently, CBT emphasizing exposure with response prevention has shown promise as an effective treatment option (Martinez & Botella, 2005). Of particular importance is the establishment of a differential reinforcement schedule. To be successfully implemented, significant others of the patient must be educated if long-term success is to be achieved.

Pharmacological Approaches to Treatment

Despite the lack of a clear etiology of somatoform disorders, serotonin and its transporter 5-HTT have consistently been linked to disease expression (Han et al., 2008a) and others have surmised that serotonergic amino acids are biological correlates of multiple unexplained symptoms (Rief et al., 2004). Although it is not uncommon for an individual with a somatization disorder to have comorbid anxiety and/or depression, there is evidence that medications that alter the serotonin pathways may reduce somatoform symptoms irrespective of mood symptoms. Thus, Han and colleagues investigated the impact of fluoxetine and sertraline in undifferentiated somatoform disorder, using the 15 item Patient Health Questionnaire (PHQ-15, Kroenke, Spitzer, & Williams, 2002) to measure symptoms. These researchers randomly assigned 45 patients to groups receiving one medication or the other for a 12-week open label, parallel group trial. Although the study was conducted on a small group of participants and there was substantive withdrawal during the course of the research (29% of the original 45 participants), both fluoxetine and sertraline significantly reduced the total score on the PHQ-15 by almost 60%. In addition, decreased scores on other measures of general health and depression were noted.

Two potentially key findings emerged from this research. First, the improvements in somatic symptoms in this study are unlikely related to mood, as those with Axis I mood disorder diagnoses were excluded from the study. Second, the symptom reductions did not occur until the eighth week of the trial (Han et al., 2008a). Thus, it may be important for an adjunctive therapy to be used for psychoeducation to improve treatment adherence.

Han and colleagues (2008b) conducted a study similar to their aforementioned research using venlafaxine and mirtazapine. A group of 71 participants, randomly assigned to treatment condition, completed the study. Both groups displayed a significant reduction in scores on the PHQ-15, and no between-group differences were observed. Unlike previous research (Han, 2008a), where the effects were significant after the eighth week, the treatment effects for venlafaxine and mirtazapine were not observed until the 12th week (final) of the study.

Pregabalin and gabapentin are anticonvulsant medications that have been successfully used to treat neuropathic pain disorders. They are thought to exert both anxiolytic and analgesic effects. Specifically, by binding with calcium channels in a myriad of brain regions, the excitatory neurotransmitters responsible for pain production are inhibited (Kroenke, Krebs, & Bair, 2009).

Investigators conducted a small study (n=8) with inpatients diagnosed with the following: persistent somatoform pain disorder, hypochondriasis, undifferentiated SFD, and autonomic dysfunction somatoform disorder (Harnack et al., 2007). Five patients received 300 mg of pregabalin per day, two received the maximum dose of 600 mg per day, and one received a moderate dose of 450 mg per day. According to the researchers, "there was a clinically impressive response to the open label treatment with pregabalin" (Harnack et al., p. 537). Specifically, they reported a rapid onset (pain reduction within 1–2 weeks) and a side effect profile similar to unimodal antidepressants. Although this study was small, it may represent a promising treatment option pending further validation and study.

Recently, investigators conducted a double-blind clinical trial to assess the efficacy of fluoxetine in somatic pain disorder. Results suggest fluoxetine is superior to placebo in pain reduction in as few as 2 weeks (Luo et al., 2009). These results add further evidence that antidepressants may reduce pain in *non-depressed* patients; effects are observed with dosages lower than those typically used to treat depression, and analgesic response is observed more quickly (Mico, Ardid, Berrocoso, & Eschalier, 2006).

Pharmacological interventions have been shown to hold promise in treating BDD, although most have been open-label trials. Phillips & Hollander, (2008) suggest SSRI monotherapy significantly reduces symptoms and impairment in participants with BDD. Similarly, fluoxetine, citalopram, escitalopram, and fluvoxamine have been efficacious and are typically tolerated well (Phillips & Menard, 2009).

Although the pharmacokinetics are not definitively elucidated, levetiracetam is thought to work presynaptically. Specifically, it blocks calcium channel (high-voltage) and influences GABA -mediated responses. Given that levetiracetam has been previously shown to improve symptoms in social phobia, it is theorized it may well be an effective treatment option for BDD (Phillips & Menard, 2009). In an open-label trial, 17 participants were given 250 mg daily for week 1 and the dose was escalated to the maximum dose of 1,500 mg twice daily, to the extent it was tolerated. Results of this small study suggest levetiracetam *may* be effective in treating BDD, with significant reductions in symptom severity in completers. However, seven participants withdrew from the study due to side effects, including two for suicidal thinking (Phillips & Menard, 2009); therefore, it is difficult to support this as an effective, safe treatment option presently.

SUMMARY

Despite an extensive history of clinical observation and empirical scrutiny, the somatoform disorders elude precise definition and remain a diagnostic challenge. Clinical terminology is inconsistent, diagnostic criteria are thought to be too restrictive, and there is disagreement on the defining characteristics of these disorders. These conditions highlight the limitations of psychiatric nosology, and revisions to diagnostic formulations are currently in development. The difficulty explaining the bewildering array of symptoms presented by individuals with somatoform disorders—from sensory and motor impairment to alterations of consciousness and memory complaints—with medical disease models suggests that neuropsychologists will continue to be tasked with evaluating these patients. Furthermore, the incidence of medically unexplained (or functional) symptoms is high, suggesting that there will continue to be substantial numbers of patients to be evaluated.

Formal neuropsychological categorization of these conditions remains limited, and there is no expected presentation of cognitive symptoms for persons falling into the SFD category. However, assessment of patients with these symptoms remains an element of neuropsychological practice. This is quite true when the presentation incorporates cognitive concerns. Structured personality inventories have proven somewhat useful in identifying characteristics associated with these cases. Yet, behavioral observations, performance on interview, input from corroborative informants, and record review are likely the optimal way to identify persons with somatoform conditions. Although not comprehensively examined, performance validity tests will likely show benefit in identifying those who present with somatoform symptoms.

In addition to these diagnostic challenges, the SFDs are also difficult to treat in large part due to a paucity of research to guide evidence-based practice. Although research identifying effective treatment is growing, detailed treatment guidelines may be several years forthcoming (LaFrance, 2009). Despite these limitations, there are some generally agreed-upon strategies for treating patients with SFDs (Levenstein, 2009). The relationship between provider and patient is paramount (Eifert et al., 2008; LaFrance, 2009; Witthoft & Hiller, 2010). Identifying a "common cause" and aligning so that both provider and patient are on the same side may reduce resistance when psychotherapy is suggested and may prevent excessive medical testing. Regularly scheduled appointments discourage emergency department visits and lower the frequency of urgent office visits.

With regard to specific psychotherapies, cognitive and behavioral interventions have been shown to be the most efficacious approaches. Although specific components vary depending on the disorder, identification of triggers that precede or exacerbate symptoms is vital to facilitating improvement. Exposure and response prevention has also demonstrated effectiveness in reducing symptom severity and functional impairment, particularly for hypochondriasis. Supplementing psychological intervention with pharmaceuticals has been the most studied treatment approach. Cumulative evidence implicates serotonin in the expression and maintenance of SFDs. Addressing the biological substrate with pharmacotherapy may lead individuals with SFDs to engage more fully in psychotherapy and maximize the likelihood of long-term treatment gains.

In sum, clients presenting with symptoms that do not match our current understanding of pathology have presented and will continue to present to health care professionals. These patients will also continue to present with challenges to accurate diagnosis and successful treatment.

REFERENCES

Abbass, A., Kisley, S., & Kroenke, K. (2009). Short-term psychodynamic psychotherapy for somatic disorders: Systematic review and meta-analysis of clinical trials. *Psychotherapy and Psychosomatics, 78*, 265–274.

Aikman, G.G., & Souheaver, G.T. (2008). Use of the Personality Assessment Inventory (PAI) in neuropsychological testing of psychiatric outpatients. *Applied Neuropsychology, 15*, 176–183.

American Psychiatric Association (1980). *Diagnostic and statistical manual of mental disorders* (3rd ed.). Washington, DC: Author.

American Psychiatric Association (2000). *Diagnostic and statistical manual of mental disorders–text revision* (4th ed.). Washington, DC: Author.

American Psychiatric Association (2010a). Justification of criteria—somatic symptoms (draft 1/29/10). *Retrieved from http://www.dsm5.org/ProposedRevisions/Pages/proposedrevision.aspx?rid=6#*

American Psychiatric Association (2010b). Somatic symptom disorders (draft 8/20/10). *Retrieved from http://www.dsm5.org/ProposedRevisions/Pages/SomatoformDisorders.aspx*

Axelrod, B. N. (2008). Fabrication of psychiatric symptoms: Somatoform and psychotic disorders. In J. E. Morgan & J. J. Sweet (Eds.), *Neuropsychology of Malingering Casebook* (pp. 180–194). New York: American Academy of Neuropsychology.

Barsky, A. J., & Borus, J. F. (1999). Functional somatic syndromes. *Annals of Internal Medicine, 130*, 910–921.
Ben-Porath, Y. S., & Tellegen, A. (2008). *The Minnesota Multiphasic Personality Inventory-2 Restructured Form: Manual for administration, scoring, and interpretation*. Minneapolis: University of Minnesota Press.
Binder, L. M., Storzbach, D., & Salinsky, M. C. (2006). MMPI-2 profiles of persons with multiple chemical sensitivity. *The Clinical Neuropsychologist, 20*, 848–857.
Boone, K. B., & Lu, P. H. (1999). Impact of somatoform symptomatology on credibility of cognitive performance. *The Clinical Neuropsychologist, 13*(4), 414–419.
Brown, R. J. (2004). Psychological mechanism of medically unexplained symptoms: An integrative conceptual model. *Psychological Bulletin, 130*, 793–812.
Brown, R. J., Cardena, E., Nijenhuis, E., Sar, V., & van der Hart, O. (2007). Should conversion disorder be reclassified as a dissociative disorder in DSM–V? *Psychosomatics, 48*(5),369–378.
Bush, S. S., Ruff, R. M., Troster, A. I., Barth, J. T., Koffler, S. P., Pliskin, N. H., et al. (2005). Symptom validity assessment: Practice issues and medical necessity. *Archives of Clinical Neuropsychology, 20*, 419–426.
Butcher, J. N., Arbisi, P. A., Atlis, M. M., & McNulty, J. L. (2003). The construct validity of the Lees-Haley Fake Bad Scale (FBS): Does this scale measure malingering and feigned emotional distress? *Archives of Clinical Neuropsychology, 18*, 473–485.
Butcher, J. N., Dahlstrom, W. G., Graham, J. R., Tellegen, A., & Kaemmer, B. (1989). *Minnesota Multiphasic Personality Inventory-2: Manual for administration and scoring*. Minneapolis: University of Minnesota Press.
Camara, W. J., Nathan, J. S., & Puente, A. E. (2000). Psychological test usage: Implications in professional psychology. *Professional Psychology: Research and Practice, 31*(2), 141–154.
Carson, A. J., Ringbauer, B., Stone, J., McKenzie, L., Warlow, C., & Sharpe, M. (2000). Do medically unexplained symptoms matter? A prospective cohort study of 300 new referrals to neurology outpatient clinics. *Journal of Neurology, Neurosurgery & Psychiatry, 68*, 207–210.
Ciechanowski, P. S., Walker, E. A., Katon, W. J., & Russo, J. E. (2002). Attachment theory: A model for health care utilization and somatization. *Psychosomatic Medicine, 64*, 660–667.
Conners, C. K. (1997). *Conner's Rating Scales – Revised technical manual*. Toronto: Multi-Health Systems, Inc.
Craig, R. J. (1999). Overview and current status of the Millon Clinical Multiaxial Inventory. *Journal of Personality Assessment, 72*, 390–406.
Creed, F. (2009a). New research on medically unexplained symptoms – much remains to be done before DSM V and ICD-10 can provide a satisfactory new classification. *Journal of Psychosomatic Research, 66*, 359–361.
Creed, F. (2009b). The outcome of medically unexplained symptoms: Will DSM-V improve on DSM-IV somatoform disorders? *Journal of Psychosomatic Research, 66*, 379–381.
Creed, F., Guthrie, E., Fink, P., Henningsen, P., Rief, W., Sharpe, M., White, P. (2010). Is there a better term than "medically unexplained symptoms"? *Journal of Psychometric Research, 68*, 5–8.
Crimlisk, H. L., & Ron, M. A. (1999). Conversion hysteria: History, diagnostic issues, and clinical practice. *Cognitive Neuropsychiatry, 4*(3), 165–180.
Crombez, G., Beirens, K., Van Damme, S., Eccleston, C., & Fontaine, J. (2009). The unbearable lightness of somatization: A systematic review of the concept of somatization in empirical studies of pain. *Pain, 145*, 31–35.
Cullum, C. M., Heaton, R. K., & Grant, I. (1991). Psychogenic factors influencing neuropsychological performance: Somatoform disorders, factitious disorders, and malingering. In H. O. Doerr & A. S. Carlin (Eds.), *Forensic neuropsychology: Legal and scientific bases* (pp. 141–171). New York: Guilford Press.
Dahl, J., & Lundgren, T. (2006). *Living beyond your pain*. Oakland, CA: New Harbinger.
Deary, I. (1999). A taxonomy of medically unexplained symptoms. *Journal of Psychosomatic Research, 47*(1), 51–59.
Delis, D. C., & Wetter, S. R. (2007). Cogniform disorder and cogniform condition: Proposed diagnosis for excessive cognitive symptoms. *Archives of Clinical Neuropsychology, 22*, 589–604.
Dimsdale, J. E., Patel, V., Xin, Y., & Kleinman, A. (2007). Somatic presentations: A challenge for DSM-V. *Psychosomatic Medicine, 69*, 829.
Dohrenwend, A., & Skillings, J. L. (2009). Diagnosis specific management of somatoform disorders: Moving beyond "vague complaints of pain". *The Journal of Pain, 10*(11), 1128–1137.
Dush, D. M., Simons, L. E., Platt, M., Nation, P. C., & Ayres, S. Y. (1994). Psychological profiles distinguishing litigating and nonlitigating pain patients: Subtle, and not so subtle. *Journal of Personality Assessment, 62*, 299–313.
Eifert, G. H., Zvolensky, M. J., & Louis, A. (2008). Somatoform disorders. In J.E. Maddux & B. A. Winstead (Eds.)., *Psychopathology: Foundations for a contemporary understanding*. New York: Routledge Press.

Escobar, J. I., Burnam, M. A., Karno, M., Forsythe, A., & Golding, J. M. (1987). Somatization in the community. *Archives of General Psychiatry, 44*, 713–718.

Fink, P., Hansen, M.S., & Søndergaard, L. (2005). Somatoform disorders among first-time referrals to a neurology service. *Psychosomatics, 46*(6), 540–548.

Flor-Henry, P., Fromm-Auch, D., Tapper, M., & Schopflocher, D. (1981). A neuropsychological study of the stable syndrome of hysteria. *Biological Psychiatry, 16*, 601–626.

Garden, N., Sullivan, K. A., & Lange, R. T. (2010). The relationship between personality characteristics and postconcussion symptoms in a nonclinical sample. *Neuropsychology, 24*, 168–175.

Gervais, R. O., Ben-Porath, Y. S., & Wygant, D. B. (2009). Empirical correlates and interpretation of the MMPI-2-RF cognitive complaints (COG) scale. *The Clinical Neuropsychologist, 23*, 996–1015.

Gervais, R. O., Ben-Porath, Y. S., Wygant, D. B., & Green, P. (2007). Development and validation of a Response Bias Scale (RBS) for the MMPI-2. *Assessment, 14*, 196–208.

Gervais, R. O., Ben-Porath, Y. S., Wygant, D. B., & Green, P. (2008). Differential sensitivity of the Response Bias Scale (RBS) and MMPI-2 validity scales to memory complaints. *The Clinical Neuropsychologist, 22*, 1061–1079.

Gough, H. G. (1946). Diagnostic patterns on the Minnesota Multiphasic Personality Inventory. *Journal of Clinical Psychology, 2*, 23–37.

Graham, J. R. (2000). *MMPI-2: Assessing personality and psychopathology* (3rd ed.). New York: Oxford University Press.

Greene, R. L. (2005). *The MMPI-2: An interpretive manual* (2nd ed.). Boston: Allyn & Bacon.

Greiffenstein, M. F., Baker, W. J., & Gola, T. (1994). Validation of malingered amnesia measures with a large clinical sample. *Psychological Assessment, 6*, 218–224.

Greve, K. W., & Bianchini, K. J. (2004). Response to Butcher et al. (2003) "The construct validity of the Lees-Haley Fake-Bad Scale . . .". *Archives of Clinical Neuropsychology, 19*(3), 337–339.

Groth-Marnat, G. (2003). *Handbook of psychological assessment* (5th ed.). New York: John Wiley & Sons.

Grove, W. M., & Vrieze, S. I. (2009). An exploration of the base rate scores of the Millon Clinical Multiaxial Inventory-III. *Psychological Assessment, 21*, 57–67.

Hahn, S.R. (2001). Physical symptoms and physician-experienced difficulty in the patient-physician relationship. *Annals of Internal Medicine, 134*, 897–904.

Hallquist, M. N., Deming, A., Matthews, A., & Chaves, J. F. (2010). Hypnosis for medically unexplained symptoms and somatoform disorders. In S. J. Lynn, J. W. Rhue, & I. Kirsch (Eds.), *Handbook of Clinical Hypnosis, 615–639*. Washington, DC: American Psychological Association.

Han, C., Pae, C. U., Lee, B. H., Ko, Y. H., Masand, P. S., Patkar, A. A., et al. (2008a). Fluoxetine versus sertraline in the treatment of patients with undifferentiated somatoform disorder: A randomized, open-label, 12-week, parallel-group trial. *Progress in Neuro-Psychopharmacology & Biological Psychiatry, 32*, 437–444.

Han, C., Pae, C. U., Lee, B. H., Ko, Y. H., Masand, P. S., Patkar, A. A., et al. (2008b). Venlafaxine versus mirtazapine in the treatment of undifferentiated somatoform disorder. *Clinical Drug Investigations, 28*(4), 251–261.

Hanes, K. R. (1998). Neuropsychological performance in body dysmorphic disorder. *Journal of the International Neurological Society, 4*, 167–171.

Harnack, D., Scheel, M., Mundt, A., Kupsch, A., Heinz, A., & Ströhle, A. (2007). Pregabalin in patients with antidepressant treatment-resistant somatoform disorders. *Journal of Clinical Psychopharmacology, 27*(5) 537–539.

Heaton, R. K. (1981). *Wisconsin card sorting test manual*. Odessa, FL: Psychological Assessment Resources.

Henry, G. K., Heilbronner, R. L., Mittenberg, W., & Enders, C. (2006). The Henry-Heilbronner index: A 15-item empirically derived MMPI-2 subscale for identifying probable malingering in personal injury litigants and disability claimants. *The Clinical Neuropsychologist, 20*, 786–797.

Henry, G. K., Heilbronner, R. L., Mittenberg, W., Enders, C., & Stanczak, S. R. (2008). Comparison of the Lees-Haley fake bad scale, Henry-Heilbronner index, and restructured clinical scale 1 in identifying noncredible symptom reporting. *The Clinical Neuropsychologist, 22*, 919–929.

Hiller, W. (2006). Don't change a winning horse. *Journal of Psychosomatic Research, 60*, 345–347.

Hiller, W., & Rief, W. (2005). Why DSM–III was right to introduce the concept of somatoform disorders. *Psychosomatics, 46*, 105–108.

Horton, A. M. (1992). Pseudoneurological and psychosomatic disorders. In A. E. Puente and R. J. McCaffrey (Eds.), *Handbook of Neuropsychological Assessment* (pp. 335–352). New York: Plenum Press.

Jankowski, D. (2002). *A Beginner's Guide to the MCMI-III*. Washington, DC: American Psychological Association.

Kaplan, H. L., Sadock, B. J., & Gregg, J. A. (1994). *Kaplan and Sadock's synopsis of psychiatry - behavioral sciences - clinical psychiatry*. Baltimore, MD: Lippincott Williams & Wilkins.

Kemp, S., Coughlan, A. K., Rowbottom, C., Wilkinson, K., Teggart, V., & Baker, G. (2008). The base rate of effort test failure in patients with medically unexplained symptoms. *Journal of Psychosomatic Research, 65*, 319–325.

Khan, A. A., Khan, A., Harezlak, J., Tu, W., & Kroenke, K. (2003). Somatic symptoms in primary care: Etiology and outcome. *Psychosomatics, 44,* 471–478.

Kozlowska, K. (2005). Healing the disembodied mind: Contemporary models of conversion disorder. *Harvard Review in Psychiatry, 13*(1), 1–13.

Kroenke, K. (2007a). Efficacy of treatment for somatoform disorders: A review of randomized controlled trials. *Psychosomatic Medicine, 69,* 881–888.

Kroenke, K. (2007b). Somatoform disorders and recent diagnostic controversies. *Psychiatric Clinics of North America, 30,* 593–619.

Kroenke, K., Krebs, E. E., & Bair, M. J. (2009). Pharmacotherapy of chronic pain: A synthesis of recommendations from systematic reviews. *General Hospital Psychiatry, 31,* 206–219.

Kroenke, K., & Sharpe, M. (2006). Special mini-series on somatoform disorders: Preface. *Journal of Psychosomatic Research, 60,* 323.

Kroenke, K., Sharpe, M., & Sykes, R. (2007). Revising the classification of somatoform disorders: Key questions and preliminary recommendations. *Psychometrics, 48,* 277–285.

Kroenke, K., Spitzer, R. L., deGruy, F. V., Hahn, S. R., Linzer, M., Williams, J. B., et al. (1997). Multisomatoform disorder. An alternative to undifferentiated somatoform disorder for the somatizing patient in primary care. *Archives of General Psychiatry, 54,* 352–358.

Kroenke, K., Spitzer, R. L., & Williams, J. B. (2002). Validity of a new measure for evaluating the severity of somatic symptoms. *Psychosomatic Medicine, 64, (2),* 258–266.

Kurtz, J. E., Shealy, S. E., & Putnam, S. H. (2007). Another look at paradoxical severity effects in head injury patients with the personality assessment inventory. *Journal of Personality Assessment, 88*(1), 66–73.

Ladwig, K. H., Marten-Mittag, B., Erazo, N., & Gündel, H. (2001). Identifying somatization disorder in a population-based health examination survey: Psychosocial burden and gender differences. *Psychosomatics: A Journal of Consultation Liaison Psychiatry, 42, (6),* 511–518.

LaFrance, W. C. (2009). Somatoform disorders. *Seminars in Neurology, 29*(3), 234–246.

Lahmann, C., Loew, T. H., Tritt, K., & Nickel, M. (2008). Efficacy of functional relaxation and patient education in the treatment of somatoform heart disorders: A randomized, controlled clinical investigation. *Psychosomatics, 49*(5), 378–385.

Lamberty, G. J. (2008). *Understanding somatization in the practice of clinical neuropsychology.* New York: Oxford University Press.

Larrabee, G. J. (2003). Exaggerated MMPI-2 symptom report in personal injury litigants with malingered neurocognitive deficit. *Archives of Clinical Neuropsychology, 18*(6), 673–686.

Larrabee, G. J. (2007). Commentary on Delis and Wetter, cogniform disorder and cogniform condition: Proposed diagnosis for excessive cognitive symptoms. *Archives of Clinical Neuropsychology, 22,* 683–687.

Lees-Haley, P. R., English, L. T., & Glenn, W. J. (1991). A fake bad scale on the MMPI-2 for personal injury claimants. *Psychological Reports, 68,* 203–210.

Lees-Haley, P. R., & Fox, D. D. (2004). Commentary on Butcher, Arbisi, Atlis, and McNulty (2003) on the Fake Bad Scale. *Archives of Clinical Neuropsychology, 19*(3), 333–336.

Levenstein, L. (2009). The evidence for treatments for somatoform disorders: A view from the trenches. In M. Gresser (Ed.), *Somatic presentations of mental disorders: Refining the research agenda for DSM-V* (pp.165–169). Arlington, VA: American Psychological Association.

Liebson, E., White, R. F., Albert, M. L. (1996). Cognitive inconsistencies in abnormal illness behavior and neurological disease. *Journal of Nervous and Mental Disease, 184,* 122–125.

Levy, R. S., & Jankovic, J. (1983). Placebo-induced conversion reaction: A neurobehavioral and EEG study of hysterical aphasia, seizure, and coma. *Journal of Abnormal Psychology, 92,* 243–249.

Locke, D. E. C., Kirlin, K. S., Thomas, M. L., Osborne, D., Hurst, D. F., Drazkowski, J. F., Sirven, J. I., & Noe, K. H. (2010). The Minnesota Multiphasic Personality Inventory-2-Restructured Form in the epilepsy monitoring unit. *Epilepsy & Behavior, 17,* 252–258.

Looper, K. J. & Kirmayer, L. J. (2002). Behavioral medicine approaches to somatoform disorders. *Journal of Consultation and Clinical Psychology* (70), 810–827.

Luo, Y. L., Zhang, M. Y., Wu, W. Y., Li, C. B., Lu, Z., & Li, Q. W. (2009). A randomized double-blind clinical trial on analgesic efficacy of fluoxetine for persistent somatoform pain disorder. *Progress in Neuro-Psychopharmacology & Biological Psychiatry, 33,* 1522–1525.

Lynch, D. J., McGrady, A., Nagel, R., & Zsembik, C. (1999). Somatization in family practice: Comparing 5 methods of classification. *The Primary Care Companion to the Journal of Clinical Psychiatry, 1,* 85–89.

Manchikanti, L., Pampati, V., Beyer, C., Damron, K., & Barnhill, R. C. (2002). Evaluation of psychological status in chronic low back pain: comparison with general population. 149–155.

Martinez, M. P., & Botella, C. (2005). An exploratory study of the efficacy of a cognitive-behavioral treatment for hypochondriasis using different measures of change. *Psychotherapy Research, 15,* 392–408.

Matthews, C. G., Shaw, D. J., & Klove, H. (1966). Psychological test performances in neurologic and "pseudo-neurologic" subjects. *Cortex, 2*, 244–253.
Mayou, R., Kirmayer, L. J., Simon, G., Kroenke, K., & Sharpe, M. (2005). Somatoform disorders: Time for a new approach in DSM-V. *American Journal of Psychiatry, 162*, 847–855.
McKinley, J. C., & Hathaway, S. R. (1944). The Minnesota Multiphasic Personality Inventory: V. Hysteria, hypomania and psychopathic deviate. *Journal of Applied Psychology, 28*, 153–174.
Micale, M. S. (2000). The decline of hysteria. *The Harvard Mental Health Letter*, 4–6.
Mico, J. A., Ardid, D., Berrocoso, E., & Eschalier, A. (2006). Antidepressants and pain. *Trends in Pharmacological Science, 27*, 348–54.
Miller, L. (1984). Neuropsychological concepts of somatoform disorders. *International Journal of Psychiatry in Medicine, 14*, 31–46.
Millon, T. R. (1997). *Millon Clinical Multiaxial Inventory-III Manual* (2nd ed.). Minneapolis: Pearson.
Moene, F. C., Spinhoven, P., Hoogduin, K. A. L., & van Dyck, R. (2003). A randomized controlled trial of hypnosis-based treatment for patients with conversion disorder, motor type. *International Journal of Clinical and Experimental Hypnosis, 51*, 29–50.
Morey, L. (1991). *Personality Assessment Inventory*. Odessa, FL: Psychological Assessment Resources.
Nelson, N. W., Hoelzle, J. B., Sweet, J. J., Arbisi, P. A., & Demakis, G. J. (2010). Updated meta-analysis of the MMPI-2 symptom validity scale (FBS): Verified utility in forensic science. *The Clinical Neuropsychologist, 24*, 701–724.
Niemi, P. M., Portin, R., Aalto, S., Hakala, M., & Karlsson, H. (2002). Cognitive functioning in severe somatization—a pilot study. *Acta Psychiatrica Scandinavia, 106*, 461–463.
Oken, D. (2007). Evolution of psychosomatic diagnosis in DSM. *Psychosomatic Medicine, 69*, 830–831.
Oyama, O., Paltoo, C., & Greengold, J. (2007). Somatoform disorders. *American Family Physician, 76*, 1333–1338.
Phillips, K. A., & Menard, W. (2009). A prospective pilot study of levetiracetam for Body Dysmorphic Disorder. *CNS Spectrum, 14*(5), 252–260.
Phillips, K. A., & Hollander, E. (2008). Treating body dysmorphic disorder with medication: Evidence, misconceptions and a suggested approach. *Body Image, 5*, 13–27.
Randolph, C. (1998). *Repeatable Battery for the Assessment of Neuropsychological Status (RBANS) manual.* San Antonio, TX: The Psychological Corporation.
Regier, D. A. (2007). Somatic presentations of mental disorders: Refining the research agenda for DSM-V. *Psychosomatic Medicine, 69*, 827–828.
Richardson, R. D., & Engel, C.C. (2004). Evaluation and management of medically unexplained physical symptoms. *The Neurologist, 10*(1), 18–30.
Rief, W., Pilger, F., Ihle, D., Verkerk, R., Scharpe, S., & Maes, M. (2004). Psychobiological aspects of somatoform disorders: Contributions of monoaminergic transmitter systems. *Neuropsychobiology, 49*, 24–29.
Ruocco, A. C., Swirsky-Sacchetti, T., Choca, J. P. (2007). Assessing personality and psychopathology after traumatic brain injury with the Millon Clinical Multiaxial Inventory-III. *Brain Injury, 21*, 1233–1244.
Ruocco, A. C., Swirsky-Sacchetti, T., Chute, D. L., Mandel, S., Platek, S. M., & Zillmer, E. A. (2008). Distinguishing between neuropsychological malingering and exaggerated psychiatric symptoms in a neuropsychological setting. *The Clinical Neuropsychologist, 22*, 547–564.
Schappert, S. M. (1992). *Vital Health Statistics. National ambulatory medical care survey: 1989 summary, 13*(110), 1–87. Hyattsville, MD: US Department of Health and Human Services, National Center for Health Statistics.
Sharpe, M., & Carson, A. J. (2001). 'Unexplained' somatic symptoms, functional syndromes, and somatization: Do we need a paradigm shift? *Annals of Internal Medicine, 134*, 926–930.
Slick, D. J., Sherman, E. M. S & Iverson, G. L. (1999). Diagnostic criteria for malingered cognitive dysfunction: Proposed standards for clinical practice and research. *The Clinical Neuropsychologist, 13*, 545–561.
Stuart, S., Noyes, R., Starcevic, V., & Barsky, A. (2008). An integrative approach to somatoform disorders combing interpersonal and cognitive-behavioral theory and techniques. *Journal of Contemporary Psychotherapy, 38*, 45–53.
Sumanti, M., Boone, K. B., Savodnik, I., & Gorsuch, R. (2006). Noncredible psychiatric and cognitive symptoms in a workers' compensation "stress" claim sample *The Clinical Neuropsychologist, 20*, (4), 754–765.
Sumathipala, A. (2007). What is the evidence for the efficacy of treatments for somatoform disorders? A critical review of previous intervention studies. *Psychosomatic Medicine, 69*, 889–900.
Thomas, M. L., & Locke, D. E. C. (2010). Psychometric properties of the MMPI-2-RF Somatic Complaints (RC1) scale. *Psychological Assessment, 22*, 492–503.

Thomas, M. L., & Youngjohn, J.R. (2009). Let's not get hysterical: Comparing the MMPI-2 validity, clinical, and RC scales in TBI litigants tested for effort. *The Clinical Neuropsychologist, 23*, 1067–1084.

Tombaugh, T. N. (1996). *Test of memory malingering* (TOMM). North Tonowanda, NY: Multi-Health Systems.

Trivedi, J. K., Sharma, S., Singh, A. P., Sinha, P. K., & Tandon, R. (2005). Neurocognition in somatization disorder. *Hong Kong Journal of Psychiatry, 15*, 97–100.

Wagner, M. T., Wymer, J. H., Topping, K. B., & Pritchard, P. B. (2005). Use of the Personality Assessment Inventory as an efficacious and cost-effective diagnostic tool for nonepileptic seizures. *Epilepsy & Behavior, 7*, 301–304.

Wessely, S., Nimnuan, C., & Sharpe, M. (1999). Functional somatic syndromes: One or many? *The Lancet, 354*(9182), 936–939.

Whiteside, D., Clinton, C., Diamonti, C., Stroemela, J., Whitea, C. Zimberoff, A., et al. (2010). Relationship between suboptimal cognitive effort and the clinical scales of the Personality Assessment Inventory,*24*(2), 315–325.

Witthoft, M., & Hiller, W. (2010). Psychological approaches to origins and treatments of somatoform disorders. *Annual Review of Clinical Psychology, 6*, 257–284.

Wygant, D. B., Ben-Porath, Y. S., Arbisi, P. A., Berry, D. T. R., Freeman, D. B., & Heilbronner, R. L. (2009). Examination of the MMPI-2 restructured form (MMPI-2-RF) validity scales in civil forensic settings: Findings from simulation and known group samples. *Archives of Clinical Neuropsychology, 24*, 671–680.

Youngjohn, J. R., Burrows, L., & Erdal, K. (1995). Brain damage or compensation neurosis? The controversial post-concussion syndrome. *The Clinical Neuropsychologist, 9*, 112–123.

CHAPTER 15

Schizophrenia

Gerald Goldstein, Leslie H. Brown, Gretchen L. Haas, & Daniel N. Allen

INTRODUCTION

It can be suggested that there are two neuropsychologies of schizophrenia. One of them is experimental neuropsychology and involves basic scientific investigation of cognitive, perceptual, and motor processes that characterize schizophrenia and typically involves associated procedures that assess relevant anatomy, chemistry, physiology, or genetics. Thus, there is a wealth of studies in assessment methods initially involving reaction time and associated measures of attention (Zubin, 1975), and expanding to such areas as various forms of memory, perception, language, and conceptual abilities. This work is typically conducted in a laboratory setting, often with behavioral measure, such as reaction time, being studied simultaneously with neurobiological procedure such as event-related potentials or functional MRI. The major application of these procedures is research devoted to discovery of the neuropsychological bases of schizophrenia. Historically, such studies may have followed earlier research that was more clinical in nature that examined the nature of "schizophrenic thinking" or the disturbances of cognition that characterize schizophrenia. For example, at one time in the past there was a great deal of interest in syllogistic, logical reasoning in schizophrenia, or in the way individuals with schizophrenia generalize from experience. Currently, there appears to be greater interest in such basic processes as working or source memory, executive abilities, and various aspects of sustained attention. A group has recently been formed, called the Cognitive Neuroscience Test Reliability and Clinical Applications for Schizophrenia (CNTRACS) to support research devoted to these and related areas concerned with efforts to improve cognition and functional outcomes in schizophrenia. The areas under particular study are visual perception, goal maintenance, and relational encoding and retrieval.

The other neuropsychology of schizophrenia is clinical neuropsychology, and has to do with the use of neuropsychological and other cognitive tests to describe thought processes and to examine neurological correlates in the way in which clinical neuropsychologists typically do. Research and practice in this area is accomplished mainly with neuropsychological tests commonly used by practitioners in their office practices. Projective techniques, notably the Rorschach test and Human Figure Drawings, were commonly used, as were intelligence tests, mainly the Wechsler Scales. In later years, actuarial objective procedures such as the MMPI came into use as assessment tools for evaluation of schizophrenia. The projective tests, for the most part, have not survived the test of time because of inadequate validation, but the Wechsler scales remain in common use in the neuropsychological evaluation of schizophrenia.

David Wechsler himself had an interest in schizophrenia and those coming after him pursued this interest (Goldstein & Saklofske, 2010). In recent times, clinical neuropsychological tests have been frequently used for assessment of individuals with schizophrenia.

A number of issues related to the clinical neuropsychology of schizophrenia are discussed in Harvey and Keefe (2009), who describe the nature of cognitive impairment, its onset and course, and a number of matters related to assessment strategy. They indicate that assessment of neurocognitive function in schizophrenia is typically conducted using many of the same tests used in evaluation of other patient groups, such as the Wechsler scales, the Wisconsin Card Sorting Test, the Continuous Performance Test, and other familiar, commonly used neuropsychological tests. The major issues have to do with interpretation and the relationship between test performance and such considerations as premorbid level of function, severity of illness, effects of medication, neurocognitive profile, and relation to functional status. Harvey and Keefe, as well as numerous others covering the same topic, agree that schizophrenia, even before onset of the illness, is associated with significant cognitive deficits. Summarizing a great deal of discussion, the consensus appears to be that the deficit is generalized in nature and not restricted to some particular cognitive domain such as memory or language. What appears to be a unifying factor is slowness of information processing, but this condition is found to be important in numerous other conditions, notably traumatic brain injury (TBI). A consortium similar to CNTRACS called Measurement and Treatment Research to Improve Cognition in Schizophrenia (MATRICS) developed a consensus cognitive battery containing complex neuropsychological tests of the type commonly used in clinical assessment to support development in that type of procedure. Thus, we now have a structure that will support developments in specific laboratory assessment procedures coming from cognitive neuroscience and the more complex procedures associated with clinical neuropsychological assessment.

NEUROPATHOLOGY AND PATHOPHYSIOLOGY

This area is reviewed in a remarkably comprehensive volume entitled *Schizophrenia: Just the Facts* containing articles published in *Schizophrenia Research*, the *Journal of Psychiatric Research* and the *Asian Journal of Psychiatry*. The effort was coordinated by Rajiv Tandon, Matcheri S. Keshavan, and Henry Nasrallah and sponsored by Elsevier (2011). The reader is referred to that volume for an extensive coverage of that field. These authors group areas of relevant research into neuroanatomic alterations, white matter pathology and disconnectivity, functional neuroimaging studies, alterations in brain physiology, neurochemical alterations, and postmortem studies. The area of genetics is considered separately along with epidemiology and etiology. Thus, the biology of schizophrenia has been considered in a broad spectrum of areas with information pouring in from all of the major neurobiological disciplines.

It is now generally accepted that schizophrenia is a brain disorder with a substantial genetic component, but definitive etiology and the specific genes are not fully known, although they have been extensively researched. There is clear evidence of structural and functional brain abnormalities and limited acceptance of the dopamine hypothesis stating that schizophrenia is associated with an increase in dopamine (D_2) receptors in the brain, although recent research has led to substantial reconsideration of this theory. Dopamine is a neurotransmitter and plays important roles in numerous areas including cognition, movement, motivation, attention, memory, and learning. An important dopamine pathway goes to the prefrontal cortex.

Autopsy and structural neuroimaging studies have shown areas of tissue abnormality throughout the brain without any clear identification of an area or structure particularly relevant to understanding the etiology of schizophrenia. Neuropathologic examination of tissue has not identified any characteristic pathology in the sense that schizophrenia is not a neoplastic, infectious, vascular, traumatic, or other form of pathological disorder. The most general finding is that all brain matter is reduced with enlargement of the ventricles. There is evidence of such reduction in numerous structures including the hippocampus, amygdala, superior temporal gyri, prefrontal cortex, thalamus, anterior cingulate, and corpus callosum. Additionally, there is extensive evidence that the normal structural asymmetry between left and right hemisphere size is substantially reduced in schizophrenia, with individuals with schizophrenia having a larger right planum temporale, a structure in the temporal lobe. Both postmortem and in vivo neuroimaging studies have demonstrated these structural changes. MRI studies report finding enlarged lateral and third ventricles, decreased brain volume (mainly gray matter), reductions in volume of the temporal cortex, particularly the hippocampus and the superior temporal gyrus, and reduced size of the prefrontal cortex. By far the most commonly reported neuropathological finding in schizophrenia is enlarged ventricles. However, functional and structural neuroimaging studies have also identified more specific abnormalities in frontal–striatal and temporal–limbic regions, including cortical gray matter volume reductions (Ananth et al., 2002; Gur et al., 2000a; Gur et al., 2000b; Harvey et al., 1993; Sullivan, Mathalon, Lim, Marsh, & Pfefferbaum, 1998). Frontal lobe regions that have been shown to be functionally or structurally abnormal include the dorsolateral prefrontal cortex (Gur et al., 2000a; Ragland et al., 1998; Weinberger, Berman, Suddath, & Torrey, 1992), medial prefrontal cortex and anterior cingulate (Ananth et al., 2002; Haznedar et al., 1997), frontal eye fields (Sweeney et al., 1998), and orbital frontal cortex (Gur et al., 2000a; Malaspina et al., 1998). Abnormalities have also been reported for the superior temporal gyrus (Menon et al., 1995; Shenton et al., 1992; Sullivan et al., 1998) and medial temporal lobe structures (Arnold et al., 1995; Bogerts et al., 1990; Suddath, Christison, Torrey, & Weinberger, 1990).

Keshavan, Tandon, Boutros, and Nasrallah (2008), summarizing numerous studies, make the following conclusions about these anatomic alterations: Some of them are found at illness onset and so are not likely to be produced by medication. However, they might not be specific to schizophrenia and are sometimes seen, albeit to a lesser degree, in individuals with other psychotic disorders. They are highly heritable and progression is seen in some but not all patients, and when it does occur, it may do so into the chronic stages of the illness.

Regarding neurochemistry, the dopamine hypothesis proposes that an abnormality in the mesolimbic dopaminergic system is a key agent in the pathogenesis of schizophrenia. Evidence for this view came largely from the beneficial effects of drugs that block dopamine receptors. Additional support arose from observations of the negative side effects of dopaminergic agonists, which mimic some of the positive features of schizophrenia. Nevertheless, the dopamine hypothesis does not now have unqualified acceptance, largely because it was based on indirect evidence coming from medication response. One important new development involves a consideration of the molecular biology of the disorder using magnetic resonance spectroscopy (MRS). In chronic schizophrenia patients with a more severe course, and especially in males, there appears to be a progressive loss of frontal and posterior superior temporal gray matter. The question is what produced these changes. MRS is an MRI-related procedure that assesses brain metabolism at a molecular biology level. An initial answer (Pettegrew et al., 1991) was that these morphometric changes reflect a reduction in neuropil secondary to exaggerated synaptic pruning with resultant loss of synapses. Reduction in neuropil would be expected to increase neuronal density, and in fact increases have been reported in pyramidal cell density in schizophrenia (Selemon, 2004). Reductions have also been seen in dendritic spines from cortical pyramidal cells in the frontal cortex (Garey et al., 1998; Glantz & Lewis, 2001) and elsewhere in the cerebral cortex. Thus, the reduction in cortical volume could result from loss of neuropil and synapses and reflect an exaggeration of the normal synaptic pruning that occurs during adolescence.

Numerous lines of evidence support a neurodevelopmental role in schizophrenia. Recently, there has been some suggestion that in addition to growth abnormalities, there may be neurodegenerative processes occurring at least in some schizophrenia patients (Lieberman, 1999; Mathalon, Sullivan, Lim, & Pfefferbaurn, 2001) and that this progression may contribute to the cognitive decline observed in some patients (Flashman & Green, 2004; Lieberman, 1999). In two longitudinal MRS-cognitive studies, chronic schizophrenia patients were found to have reduced NAA/PCr-I-Cr in the left hemisphere compared to recent-onset schizophrenia patients and controls (Molina et al., 2005). The other revealed decreased NAA in the anterior cingulate gyrus in schizophrenia.

To summarize, schizophrenia is now thought to be a neurodevelopmental disorder characterized by initiation of an abnormal synaptic pruning process that destroys substantially more neurons than normal. The process appears to involve an abnormality in membrane phospholipid metabolism that produces decreased synthesis of membranes, primarily affecting synapses. This process manifests itself as abnormal synaptic pruning compared to that which normally takes place in adolescence, at least in nonhuman primates. ^{31}P MRS (phosphorus spectrum) studies of schizophrenia have consistently found alterations of membrane phospholipid metabolism, and ^{1}H MRS (hydrogen spectrum) studies have demonstrated loss of neuronal cells evidenced by reduced NAA. The process appears to involve a cycle of membrane breakdown reflected in the increase of a metabolite called phosphodiester (PDE) followed by attempts at repair reflected in elevation of phosphomonoester (PME). Dopamine becomes involved in this process because of an agent called dopamine-CAMP-regulated phosphoprotein (DARPP) that is involved in phosphorylation of membrane channels and receptors, apparently involved in cell repair. Phosphorylation is a process that activates or deactivates enzymes. There is the possibility that some individuals with schizophrenia, in addition to these developmental abnormalities, sustain a neurodegenerative process in later life. This group may constitute what has been described as "Kraepelinian" or "Very Poor Outcome" schizophrenia.

Genetic Factors

The currently most favored view concerning the basis for these neurobiological phenomena is that they are genetic in origin, but specific "schizophrenia genes" have not been identified. There has been an enormous amount of genetic research in schizophrenia ranging from earlier population or family descriptive studies of twins to state-of-the-art laboratory investigations. Weinberger et al., (1992) writes that there are several promising candidate genes. They are catechol 0-methyltransferase (*COMT*), dysbindin-1, neuregulin 1 (*NRG1*), metabotropic glutamate receptor 3 (*GRM-3*), glutamate decarboxylase 1, and disrupted in schizophrenia 1 (*DISC1*). *COMT* has probably been the most extensively studied. It affects prefrontal function by altering the regulation of dopamine activity in the brain stem. *GRM-3* plays a similar role by affecting glutamate synapses. *DISC1* affects hippocampal function, and dysbindin-1 appears to have a general influence on cognitive capacity. These genes are characterized as "susceptibility genes" that may influence development of the schizophrenic phenotype. This list was essentially repeated in a more recent review by Tandon, Keshavan, and Nasrallah (2008).

A detailed description of these and other genes and their possible relations to schizophrenia are presented in an extensive review by Harrison and Weinberger (2005). Although the most extensive work has been done with *COMT*, there is a particularly interesting susceptibility gene from the standpoint of the MRS-derived abnormal synaptic pruning theory. *NRG1* is of interest because of its role as a growth factor involved in neuronal migration, axon guidance, synaptogenesis, glial differentiation, and myelination. Harrison and Weinberger conclude that the various candidate or susceptibility genes converge on schizophrenia risk through influencing "synaptic plasticity and the development and stability of cortical microcircuitry" (Harrison & Weinberger, 2005, p. 1).

Summary

The neuropathological or neuroanatomic and neurochemical conceptualization of schizophrenia as illustrated by studies of visible structural abnormalities such as enlarged lateral ventricles and by the "dopamine hypothesis" are in large part outdated and have been replaced by advanced methodologies in microbiology, neuroimaging, and genetics. This work has not yet led to any definitive conclusions about the specific biology of schizophrenia, although there is abundant evidence of abnormalities in synaptic transmission and microcircuitry in the brain. These abnormalities, apparently influenced by multiple genetic factors, involve numerous genes and gene interactions.

NEUROPSYCHOLOGICAL AND BEHAVIORAL SEQUELAE

The Wechsler Intelligence Scales

Studies of the Wechsler scales in schizophrenia are very numerous, going back to research done with the Wechsler-Bellevue, the original version of the test (Goldstein & Saklofske, 2010). Earlier studies concentrated on the identification of a "schizophrenic profile" or pattern of subtest scores that had high levels of sensitivity and specificity for identification of schizophrenia. There has been particular interest in use of the Wechsler scales in studies of cognitive function in schizophrenia. Individuals with schizophrenia may have a wide range of general intellectual ability going from mental retardation to superior intelligence, but it was thought that there might be particular profiles characterizing the disorder. As a general statement, that was not found to be the case, but rather, there was a great deal of heterogeneity. It is well established that although individuals with schizophrenia are as a group lower in general intelligence (IQ) than the normal population, scores on intelligence tests are extremely variable, ranging from the intellectual disability to the superior level. Efforts to find the basis for this variability have included studies of demographic differences including gender, age and education, genetic differences, and differences related to symptom profile or clinical subtype, with inconclusive results. The studies of gender differences reported a superiority of males (Weiser et al., 2000), females (Voglmaier et al., 2005), or no difference (Andia et al., 1995). Other studies have focused on premorbid cognitive performance; type of schizophrenia, particularly with regard to deficit and nondeficit or positive and negative subtypes; and family history (Seckinger et al., 2004; Wolitzky et al., 2006).

Thus, intelligence test performance may be used in a conventional way to predict outcome and formulate case management strategies congruent with level of cognitive ability. With the advent of neuropsychological research with the Wechsler scales, they may also be helpful in identifying specific areas of brain dysfunction and may be particularly useful in identifying the possible consequences of other disorders, notably substance abuse, malnutrition, and related illnesses that are commonly found among individuals with schizophrenia.

Some clinicians have raised objection to use of intelligence tests with patients with schizophrenia because the thinking disorder associated with the disorder may lead to an underestimation of ability level. That does not appear to be a major cause for concern because in large-sample studies, the mean IQ of patients with schizophrenia turned out to be in the average intelligence range, with variability above and below that range. Indeed, a subgroup described as having "neuropsychologically normal schizophrenia" has been identified (Allen, Goldstein, & Warnick, 2003; Palmer et al., 1997) with some of the individuals in that group having superior intellectual levels.

Substance use disorder comorbid with schizophrenia has been a matter of substantial concern because the existence of both disorders in the same individual is not uncommon. The matter is a complicated one because of differences among substances with regard to cognitive function and age. With regard to alcoholism, a disorder that has known cognitive effects, it has been reported that these effects often do not produce substantial impairment going beyond the often significant effects of the schizophrenia itself. However, as individuals grow older, the progressive impairment associated with alcoholism creates an increasing distinction between individuals with schizophrenia with and without alcoholism (Allen, Goldstein, & Aldarando, 1999).

Premorbid intelligence has been a major consideration in understanding the developmental aspects of several disorders. In the area of schizophrenia, it has been demonstrated that individuals who go on to acquire schizophrenia exhibit lower IQ than the general population long before the onset of the illness (Allen, Frantom, Strauss, & van Kammen, 2005). Thus, impairment occurs during early childhood and deterioration occurs later in the course of the emerging illness. A distinction has been made between "good premorbid" and "poor premorbid" individuals with schizophrenia, these subgroups having differing courses and outcomes (Gittelman-Klein & Klein, 1969; Goldstein, Allen, & van Kammen, 1998).

The Wisconsin Card Sorting Test (WCST)

Aside from the Wechsler scales, the WCST is probably the most widely used test for assessment of patients with schizophrenia. It has been the instrument most strongly associated with the identification of executive dysfunction as a cardinal symptom of the disorder (Robinson, Heaton, Lehman, & Stilson, 1980). The test assesses ability to identify concepts based on experience and ability to shift conceptually. Impairment on this test has been specifically associated with dysfunction of the dorsolateral surface of the prefrontal region, with strong support from neuroimaging and cerebral blood flow studies. This evidence has been used to express the view that schizophrenia is a disorder associated specifically with frontal lobe dysfunction, but alternative lines of evidence have questioned the existence of such specificity. Nevertheless, abnormal performance on the WCST is typically impaired in schizophrenia, and it remains a good test for measuring conceptual abilities.

The Continuance Performance Test (CPT)

The CPT is, in essence, a clinical test produced by several pioneers in the field, notably David Shakow and Joseph Zubin, based on extensive research in reaction time done with patients with schizophrenia. The test measures vigilance or sustained attention that may be assessed at varying levels of complexity. For example, the subject can be asked to press a lever only when the letter Y is shown on a screen or to press the lever only when the letter Y is preceded by the letter A. Sometimes the letters or numbers presented are blurred or degraded in some way, making the task more difficult. Performance on the CPT typically documents the impairments of sustained attention and the distractibility that characterize schizophrenia. The work of Keith Nuechterlein and his group has made a particularly important contribution to the use of this procedure in schizophrenia research over many years, establishing it as a vulnerability indicator (Nuechterlein & Dawson, 1984). The CPT is available as an assessment instrument to clinicians in the form of published tests, notably the Conners version (Conners, 2000).

The Halstead-Reitan Battery (HRB)

The history of the use of the HRB in connection with schizophrenia is interesting. It can be said to have begun with a series of critical papers by Watson and colleagues at the St. Cloud VA Hospital (Watson, Thomas, Andersen, & Felling, 1968a; Watson, Thomas, Felling, & Andersen, 1968b). They are now known as the "St. Cloud studies." They were critical of the HRB because it did not distinguish between patients with schizophrenia and those with structural brain damage, a matter that at the time was considered to be a crucial problem in differential diagnosis (Goldstein, 1978). These studies were published at the time that schizophrenia was commonly viewed as a functional disorder produced by environmental circumstances during early life and before the "biological revolution," which rather clearly established schizophrenia as a brain disorder through extensive neuroimaging, neurochemical, and genetic studies. It is now not expected that patients with schizophrenia will typically perform normally on the HRB, but this finding is interpreted as reflecting the brain dysfunction associated with the illness. Thus, the St. Cloud group turned out to be correct in their observation but incorrect in its interpretation on the basis of, by now, many years of neurobiological research.

In the more recent past, two groups have produced extensive studies of the HRB based on large samples of patients with schizophrenia. Beginning in 1978, Robert Heaton and colleagues produced a large amount of research and theoretical formulations regarding neuropsychological status of neuropsychiatric patients in general (Heaton, Baade, & Johnson, 1978) and schizophrenia in particular (Heaton et al., 2001). Areas of specific concern were whether level or pattern of performance characterizes the cognitive deficits found in schizophrenia (Lehman, Chelune, & Heaton, 1979), the relation of schizophrenia to functional everyday living capacity (McSweeny et al., 1985; McClure et al., 2007), differences among subtypes of schizophrenia (Palmer et al., 2009), and individual differences associated with gender (Andia et al., 1995), aging (Harvey et al., 2010), and symptom profile (Gladsjo et al., 2004). A particularly exciting study was done by Palmer and collaborators entitled "Is it possible to be schizophrenic yet neuropsychologically normal?" (Palmer et al., 1997). This study introduced the still unresolved idea of "neuropsychologically normal schizophrenia," a relatively small subgroup of individuals with accurately diagnosed schizophrenia who perform normally or near normally on commonly used neuropsychological tests.

The second group involved Goldstein and various collaborators, who were concerned with similar matters evaluated with the HRB. Their interests were in age differences (Goldstein & Zubin, 1990), the influence of hospitalization and medication (Goldstein & Shemansky, 2000; Goldstein, Zubin, & Pogue-Geile, 1991), comorbidity with alcoholism (Allen, Goldstein & Aldorando, 1999), effects of premorbid ability (Allen, Goldstein & Warnick, 2003), and differences among clinical subtypes and symptom profiles (Allen et al., 2000a). However, in recent years, the major interest of this group has been in cognitive heterogeneity, the great variability seen in individuals with schizophrenia in cognitive function, and in a search for empirically valid subtypes.

Both of these groups, with the exception of a relatively small number of studies, used some version of the HRB as their assessment method and produced a substantial amount of data concerning performance of individuals with schizophrenia on that procedure. This material will not be reviewed here except in the context of several theoretical matters that will be discussed. Suffice it to say that there are extensive data supporting inferences derived from the HRB concerning neuropsychological function in schizophrenia.

MATRICS

Probably the most recently developed approach to assessment of schizophrenia is the MATRICS Consensus Cognitive Battery (Nuechterlein et al., 2008). The battery was developed by a panel of experts with the aim of constructing a procedure containing a series of repeatable measures that were highly sensitive to cognitive impairment in schizophrenia. It contains tests of working memory, speed of processing, reasoning and problem solving, social cognition, and other cognitive abilities. MATRICS is unique relative to the Wechsler scales and the HRB because it was specifically developed for the assessment of schizophrenia. It has only recently become available and has little research literature as yet based on experience of clinicians, but it may well be the prototype neuropsychological assessment instrument in the future for schizophrenia.

Other Neuropsychological Tests

It is probably accurate to say that most of the available neuropsychological tests have been used in assessment of individuals with schizophrenia, but it is equally accurate to say that none of them alone or in combination have produced results unique to schizophrenia. Scores ranging from those reflecting severe impairment to normal or near normal ranges are typically found in individual patients. These tests are sometimes used in experimental research to test specific hypotheses about individual cognitive functions such as memory (Paulsen et al., 1995) and executive function or problem-solving ability, but in clinical application of these tests, a wide range of performance levels is typically found. There is evidence that people with schizophrenia often do better on spatial-constructional tasks relative to attentional and problem-solving tasks, but there is also great variability in that regard. A difficulty in this area is that for any particular test, there may be a statistically significant difference between schizophrenia and normal control groups, but the magnitude of these differences generally does not generate sufficiently robust cutoff scores to produce sufficient sensitivity and specificity.

TWO MAJOR PROBLEMS: THE "GENERAL DEFICIT SYNDROME" AND COGNITIVE HETEROGENEITY

Chapman and Chapman (1973) have taken the view that in schizophrenia there is a generalized problem-solving deficit and that apparent differential deficit among cognitive abilities is often a matter of tasks representing these abilities being of differing difficulty levels. Various matched task procedures have been proposed to resolve that situation. However, application of these methods often shows that an apparent task deficit difference is actually a matter of differing difficulty levels between these tasks. Research of this type has promoted the view that the cognitive deficit in schizophrenia is generalized in nature, and profiles of various abilities that apparently show differential performance actually differ only in difficulty or complexity and not in regard to the specific abilities themselves. For example, if a difference was noted in schizophrenia patients between verbal and spatial memory tasks with verbal memory being worse, that does not mean that people with schizophrenia are characterized by a relative, differential impairment of verbal memory. It may simply mean that the verbal task used, as evaluated by studies of normal individuals, is more difficult than the spatial task. Studies or clinical assessments that do not consider multiple abilities but focus on only one, such as memory, for example, may conclude that schizophrenia is a disorder of memory. However, consideration of other abilities may well reveal comparable disabilities in those areas as well.

The far-reaching implication of these considerations is that cognitive deficit in schizophrenia is generalized, and will lead to performance on any difficult cognitive task that is worse than on any simpler task. The domain or other specifics of the task are irrelevant. If one accepts this view, it would appear that the conventional practice in neuropsychological assessment of reviewing the various cognitive domains such as memory, problem-solving, language, and attention may not be an optimal strategy for schizophrenia because test scores obtained from these domains may vary mainly on the basis of differing difficulty levels for the tasks selected for the domains and may not be an indication of functional differences among the domains themselves. Obviously, this situation is quite different from what is found in neurological patients, particularly those with focal lesions, in which individual domain evaluations can identify specific impairments in appropriate areas, such as aphasia in left temporal lobe lesions, relative to more intact function in other areas. This consideration might lead to the recommendation that the neuropsychological assessment of patients with schizophrenia should not be organized in correspondence with the traditional cognitive domains but with the characteristics of the schizophrenia itself. This process needs to take into account the matter of heterogeneity, to which we now turn our attention.

The experienced clinician working in a psychiatric setting treating patients with schizophrenia across the course of the disorder has most likely observed that performance on neuropsychological tests is markedly variable. Some patients perform at a very impaired level resembling what is seen in testable individuals with dementia, whereas others may produce a normal or near normal performance with an average or above average IQ. This variation often does not correspond with gender, age, or educational differences. Most patients show a level and pattern of impairment between these two extremes, demonstrating moderate deficits with no consistent discernible cognitive profile. Systematic documentation of this variability has mainly been made with the Wechsler scales or the HRB. Three groups of investigators had the advantage of access to large databases of patients with schizophrenia who took a neuropsychological test battery and who had available at least reasonably adequate documentation of health status, including reliable diagnoses of schizophrenia. The research produced had various aspects, but we will focus here on the matter of heterogeneity, which was studied by these groups in somewhat different ways.

The problem set forth by students of heterogeneity is that although some groups of characteristics may be exceedingly variable, there may be in that variability meaningful subtypes that may be evaluated with several methods. One method is a straightforward evaluation of the presence of patterns of these characteristics by their observation. For example, in a large population of males, it may be observed that there appears to be a subgroup of individuals with red hair, green eyes, and a freckled complexion. This method is commonly used in taxonomy, in which a population is classified in accordance with observable characteristics that appear to be associated with each other. A second method is numerical taxonomy, as described by Sokal and Sneath (1963), in which quantitative methods are used, mainly classification statistics such as cluster analysis. The goal of this method is to obtain empirically derived subtypes or clusters that group together mathematically, although there may not be directly observable similarity patterns.

The San Diego Group

The Heaton group at the University of California San Diego and the San Diego VA Hospital made, in our opinion, a major contribution to the concept of heterogeneity in schizophrenia in Palmer and colleagues' (1997) paper on "neuropsychologically normal schizophrenia." In this paper, it was reported that 27% of a large sample of individuals with schizophrenia were rated by experienced clinicians as neuropsychologically normal based upon an expanded version of the HRB. This finding flew in the face of the commonly held belief that cognitive dysfunction was an essential component of schizophrenia, existing in all patients with the disorder. This result was particularly provocative because of the common acceptance by clinical neuropsychologists that the HRB, particularly in the expanded version, including the Wechsler scales and other well established neuropsychological tests, is a highly sensitive and comprehensive instrument for identifying cognitive dysfunction. This paper led to a controversial series of studies that supported or refuted this view. However, it did establish the consideration that one important cutting point in organizing heterogeneity is the distinction between "neuropsychologically normal" and "neuropsychologically impaired" schizophrenia on the basis of performance on a number of cognitive tests and that there is a consensus concerning identification of cognitive dysfunction. Supportive of Palmer and colleagues' study, Paulsen and colleagues (1995), using the California Verbal Learning Test, found that 35% of their patients with schizophrenia produced a normal pattern on this sensitive memory test. In a review paper on the neuropsychology of schizophrenia, members of the San Diego group presented the general conclusion that there is substantial inter-patient heterogeneity in schizophrenia, although some degree or type of cognitive impairment is present in most if not all persons with the disorder.

The Topeka/Pittsburgh Group

The Goldstein group at the Topeka VA Hospital and later at the VA hospital in Pittsburgh took a numerical taxonomy approach to the problem of heterogeneity, using cluster analysis as its evaluation method. This work is reviewed in Seaton, Goldstein, and Allen (2001) and only the conclusions will be presented here. A cluster analysis of 136 males with schizophrenia who had completed portions of the HRB plus the WCST resulted in a five-cluster solution, each cluster demonstrating a different pattern. Cluster 1 had a flat profile, reflecting generalized moderate impairment. Cluster 2 had mainly normal scores with the exception of the WCST. Cluster 3 obtained severely impaired scores on all tests, particularly the Trail Making Test. Cluster 4 had a pattern characterized by relatively good performance on the WCST with very poor performance on the Halstead Category Test. Cluster 5 has a relatively good performance on the Trail Making Test with severe impairment on the other tests. Cluster 2 comes close to the "neuropsychologically normal" group in Palmer and colleagues' study, whereas the other clusters have varying levels and patterns indicating significant impairment. In a subsequent study, Allen, Goldstein, and Warnick (2003) made a further examination of this "neuropsychologically normal" group, finding that these patients were normal on most, but not all, tests, and it was recommended that the term "high functioning," commonly used in the diagnosis of autism to connote an IQ above 70, might be appropriate for schizophrenia as well. It was also reported that "neuropsychologically normal" status was associated with age, with these individuals typically being in their early 30s. Other studies evaluated the relationship between cluster membership and performance on the WCST (Goldstein, Beers, & Shemansky, 1996), various demographic considerations (Goldstein & Shemansky, 1995), and clinical subtypes (Seaton, Allen, Goldstein, Kelley, & van Kammen, 1999).

The Heinrichs Group

Another group also used cluster analysis to identify subgroups of schizophrenia based on an extensive battery of tests including WAIS-R subtests, the California Verbal Learning Test, the WCST, and the Purdue Pegboard. They reported a five-cluster solution including a normal cluster, but the other clusters had varying patterns and levels of impairment. In addition to this normal subgroup, one cluster demonstrated relatively specific impairment on the WCST, another had low scores on all measures used, another had low scores indicating impairment on the WCST and Purdue Pegboard, and the fifth cluster only demonstrated impairment on the Purdue Pegboard. These investigators named their clusters Normal, Executive, Dementia, Executive-Motor, and Motor. This solution was not greatly different from the one presented by Goldstein (1990). In subsequent studies, this group evaluated the stability of the cluster solution; utility of alternative solutions, one of which involved cognitively impaired, normal, and verbal memory subtypes (Ammari, Heinrichs & Miles, 2010); symptom severity and cognition as related to outcome (Heinrichs, Ammari, Miles, McDermid, Vaz, & Chopov, 2009); and life skills and clinical subtype differences (Heinrichs, Ammari, McDermid, Vaz, & Miles, 2008). The Heinrich group studies also attested to the usefulness of a heterogeneity model in assessment and prognosis related to schizophrenia.

Summary

The research of these three groups is remarkably concordant with regard to the documentation of cognitive heterogeneity in schizophrenia and its organization into subgroups. These subgroups should be more appropriately described as clusters rather than subtypes because the term subtype connotes an established form of a disorder with a known pathophysiology, clinical phenomenology, course and outcome. Nevertheless, at this point they appear to be clinically meaningful and should be helpful to the neuropsychologist in assessment work. In conducting neuropsychological assessment of patients with schizophrenia, it seems important to know that despite the fact that the patient has the disorder, neurocognitive function may be essentially normal, globally and severely impaired, or reflecting a cognitive profile that may in the future be associated with a number of specific brain systems. We have indicated our belief that this organization of assessment is better in the case of schizophrenia than an organization by the traditional cognitive domains. The clusters essentially cut across all domains and generally a patient impaired in memory may also be impaired on equally difficult tasks in the domains of language and executive abilities. The cognitive status of people with schizophrenia is not like those of people with aphasia, amnesia, or other classical neurobehavioral syndromes.

ADVANCED DIAGNOSTIC CONSIDERATIONS

Regarding the serious mental illnesses, neuropsychological tests are not generally used to diagnose schizophrenia, something done more adequately by structured interviews, but to provide information about significant aspects of schizophrenic thinking and functioning. There is no prototypic "schizophrenia diagnostic profile" but rather a great deal of heterogeneity as described previously in level and pattern of cognitive function. Contemporary use of neuropsychological tests in diagnostic work does not aim toward making the mental disorder diagnosis but rather toward detailing its cognitive organization and neuropsychological implications. Since general acceptance of the *DSM* system (American Psychiatric Association [APA], 2000), there is general consensus that diagnoses are best made by agreed-on assessment instruments, notably structured interviews such as the SCID (First, Spitzer, Gibbon, & Williams, 1997). That is, the diagnosis of schizophrenia should be made on the basis of criteria listed in *DSM-IV-TR*, including delusions, hallucinations, disorganized speech, disorganized or catatonic behavior, and negative symptoms such as affective flattening. At least two of these criteria must be present to make the diagnosis (APA, 2000). It is anticipated that the changes for schizophrenia to be made in the forthcoming *DSM-V* will be minor, although there has been a recommendation that the clinical subtypes should be eliminated. The reason for this recommendation is lack of clinical or research usefulness for the subtypes and the desire to develop dimensional assessments allowing for estimation of symptom severity.

The clinical neuropsychologist competent in psychiatric diagnosis may perform the appropriate procedures needed to make the diagnosis, but that is a separate matter from neuropsychological assessment. The literature reviewed previously on cognitive heterogeneity clearly indicates that there can be no prototypic neuropsychological profile that unequivocally identifies or diagnoses schizophrenia. In the absence of the availability of the SCID and a trained reliable interviewer, or as a supplement to the SCID, the clinician should be assured that the diagnosis meets *DSM-IV-TR* (to be *DSM-5* starting in 2013) criteria on the basis of clinical interviews with the patients and informants and review of the available records.

A particular area of concern for clinical neuropsychology is that referrals are often made when there is a question of whether the patient has a neurological or general medical disorder comorbid with the schizophrenia. Sometimes, the neuropsychological assessment can be helpful in suggesting that a patient, in addition to schizophrenia, has an undiagnosed medical condition such as a "silent stroke" or residuals of a traumatic brain injury. If the neuropsychological assessment is done for evaluation of this matter, some adjustment should be made in order to give tests pertinent to the disorder in question in addition to what is necessary for assessment of the schizophrenic condition. Comorbidity with alcoholism may also be evaluated with additional procedures, notably sensory-perceptual tests (Allen et al., 2000a; Goldstein et al., 2005).

TREATMENT

Historically, schizophrenia was managed, if not treated, by institutionalization in hospitals for the mentally ill. In some cases, individual or group psychotherapy was attempted during hospitalization. Most patients lived substantial portions of their lives within these institutions. Treatments also applied during hospitalization were frontal lobotomy, electroshock therapy, and insulin shock therapy. These methods are rarely used in contemporary treatment. Discharge to the community was rarely, if ever, a treatment goal, and the aim of treatment was typically to optimize hospital adjustment or to alleviate acute symptoms of anxiety, violence, or self-destructive or disruptive behaviors.

Given the chronic nature of schizophrenia and its impact on occupational and social functioning, treatment providers are increasingly adopting multimodal treatment approaches that include both pharmacological and psychosocial components (Tandon, Nasrallah, & Keshavan, 2010). Although which treatment will be most beneficial for a given individual is difficult to predict, treatment can be guided by the severity of symptoms, extent of functional impairments, and phase of illness. Despite the fact that schizophrenia is chronic and often disabling, many affected patients are able to function with support in the community through modern treatment regimes, in contrast to the long-term, custodial care that was considered state-of-the-art treatment a century ago.

Pharmacological Approaches

Medication for schizophrenia is still considered an essential component of treatment. The so-called first-generation antipsychotic (FGA) medications included drugs such as fluphenazine and haloperidol. These medications, which acted primarily as dopamine antagonists, can cause extrapyramidal side effects, a cluster of symptoms consisting of Parkinson-like movement difficulties. Furthermore, they carry a significant risk of tardive dyskinesia, a potentially irreversible movement disorder.

The side effect profile of FGAs prompted the innovation of the second-generation antipsychotics (SGAs), the first of which was clozapine in the late 1960s. To date, 13 SGAs have been identified, with some of the more commonly-used agents including olanzapine, risperidone, quetiapine, and ziprasidone. SGAs differ from FGAs in their mechanisms of action, typically targeting the $alpha_1$ adrenoceptor and/or the serotonergic 5-HT_2 receptor in addition to the dopaminergic D_2 receptors.

Recent emphasis has been placed on evidence-based approaches to the treatment of schizophrenia. Given the completion in recent years of several large-scale, pharmacological treatment trials for patients with schizophrenia—for example, the Clinical Antipsychotic Trials of Intervention Effectiveness (CATIE; Lieberman et al., 2005)—there have been strides in understanding the best potential uses of different antipsychotic medications. Most notably, the schizophrenia Patient Outcomes Research Team (PORT) has provided comprehensive guidelines for evidence-based pharmacological treatment practices, most recently providing an updated set of recommendations based on a literature review of over 400 medication treatment studies (Buchanan et al., 2010).

In terms of side effects, the literature suggests that FGAs generally tend to present a higher risk of extrapyramidal symptoms and tardive dyskinesia, whereas SGAs tend to present a higher risk of weight gain and related metabolic side effects. However, there is substantial heterogeneity in side effect profiles within each class of medication, which has implications for guiding individual treatment decisions. Given that FGAs and SGAs are similarly efficacious and both affect dopamine D_2 receptors, some have argued for abandoning this categorical distinction (Grunder, Hippius, & Carlsson, 2009).

There has been little evidence to support a difference in the efficacy of FGAs versus SGAs in treating symptoms or functional deficits in patients with schizophrenia (Tandon, Nasrallah, & Keshavan, 2010). Antipsychotic medications reduce overall symptoms of schizophrenia, particularly positive and disorganized symptoms. None of these medications has been shown to be effective in substantially improving the negative symptoms and neurocognitive deficits associated with the disorder. Clozapine, however, may be more effective in treating treatment-refractory schizophrenia (Bonham & Abbott, 2008). Given the low but potentially fatal risk of clozapine-induced agranulocytosis, PORT has recommended that other antipsychotics be prescribed prior to a possible trial of clozapine in first-episode patients (Buchanan et al., 2010). There is little evidence to suggest that medications other than antipsychotics are beneficial in treating schizophrenia. Although there continues to be a need for new pharmacological agents to treat patients who respond minimally or partially to antipsychotics—particularly those with persistent negative and neurocognitive symptoms—the paradigm shift in schizophrenia treatment made possible by modern antipsychotic medications should not be underestimated.

Somatic Approaches

Historically, somatic treatments such as electroconvulsive therapy (ECT) or "shock therapy," psychosurgery, and insulin shock therapy predated the use of psychosocial and pharmacological treatments. In modern practice, somatic treatments are rarely employed. However, ECT continues to be used in conjunction with other treatments, and may be indicated primarily for treatment-refractory individuals in conjunction with clozapine (Braga & Petrides, 2005), patients with catatonia (Thirthalli et al., 2009), or those with severe, comorbid mood symptoms. ECT has been shown to result in a short-term small benefit to global symptoms. However, the safety and efficacy of ECT may depend upon several factors, including dose, frequency, and electrode placement (The UK ECT Review Group, 2003). There is no body of evidence to support the longer-term therapeutic benefits above and beyond those of medications, benefits of ECT for treatment-refractory patients, or clear adverse effects (Buchanan et al., 2010; Matheson, Green, Loo, & Carr, 2010).

Repetitive transcranial magnetic stimulation (rTPS), a noninvasive method in which magnetic coils generate electric stimulation to the neocortex, has gained increasing popularity for treating neurologic and psychiatric disorders. For patients with schizophrenia, rTPS may be beneficial in reducing auditory hallucinations (Matheson et al., 2010). Accordingly, PORT has recommended the use of low-frequency rTMS over the left temporoparietal cortex for treating auditory hallucinations that have not responded to antipsychotic medications (Buchanan et al., 2010).

Psychosocial Approaches

Because medication treatment is not effective for all patients across phases of illness, psychosocial treatments tailored to the needs of individual patients is critical. Current empirically-supported psychosocial treatments include psychoeducation, cognitive-behavioral therapy (CBT), social skills training, token economy systems, supportive employment, case management in the community, and treatment of comorbid substance use problems (Dixon et al., 2010). In addition to these treatments, there is increasing interest in the use of cognitive remediation and other cognition-enhancing approaches for addressing the neurocognitive deficits in schizophrenia.

The literature on psychosocial interventions for schizophrenia indicate that their efficacy varies depending on four key dimensions: (1) the phase of illness (i.e., early acute versus the later, more stable phase of illness); (2) the specific focus or goals of treatment (e.g., enhancement of compliance with treatment, increasing socialization, versus reduction of positive symptoms); (3) the format of delivery (e.g., individual-, group-, or family-based); and (4) the theoretical model and the related intervention techniques (e.g., behavioral versus cognitive-behavioral; Goldstein, Allen, & Haas, 2007). A brief review of the current literature on efficacy of psychosocial treatments for schizophrenia follows.

Psychoeducational interventions are designed to inform the patient and family members about the nature of the disorder, the potential costs and benefits of medications, early warning signs of relapse, and other issues relevant to treatment. Psychoeducational interventions have been found to be effective in improving treatment adherence when used as a component of family intervention. Key aspects of beneficial family interventions—in addition to psychoeducation—include emotional support and coping, problem-solving, and crisis intervention. Family-based treatment packages with psychoeducational components have been found to reduce rates of rehospitalization and relapse (Pharoah, Mari, & Streiner, 2003; Pitschel -Walz et al., 2001). Furthermore, family-based treatments may result in fewer symptoms of psychosis, increased medication adherence, reduced levels of stress in patients, and improved perceptions of family relationships (Tandon, Nasrallah, & Keshavan, 2010).

Cognitive-behavioral therapy (CBT) can help patients identify delusional beliefs and learn to question and consider alternative cognitions. Cognitive theory postulates that faulty perceptions of events, based in part on early learning experiences, lead to negative mood states and can perpetuate consistent errors in thinking to which people with schizophrenia may be prone (Kern, Glynn, Horan, & Marder, 2009). CBT has been found to be beneficial for people with schizophrenia in reducing positive symptoms, improving overall functioning, and, to a lesser extent, reducing negative symptoms (e.g., Wykes, Steel, Everitt, & Tarrier, 2008; Zimmerman et al., 2005). However, the extent of the benefits likely varies according to length of therapy, skills of the therapists, and other nonspecific treatment effects (Tarrier & Wykes, 2004). PORT proposes in its 2009 psychosocial treatment recommendations that people with persistent psychotic symptoms of schizophrenia should be offered 4–9 months of group or individual CBT in conjunction with pharmacotherapy (Dixon et al., 2010).

Social skills training (SST) has been shown to be an effective psychosocial treatment approach, although whether skills generalize beyond the training setting remains an empirical question. For example, Hogarty and colleagues (1997) found that people in social skills interventions demonstrated improved personal adjustment and social functioning compared to those who received a combination of supportive psychotherapy and family psychoeducation. A recent meta-analysis by Kurtz and Mueser (2008) of 22 social skills training programs in schizophrenia found that social skills training programs can improve social skills knowledge, social and daily living skills, and community functioning and, to a lesser extent, can reduce rates of relapse. *Token economy interventions*, the historical precursor to SST, which use social learning principles to provide positive reinforcement, are effective in increasing the adaptive behaviors of patients with schizophrenia in inpatient treatment settings (Lippman & Motta, 1993).

Supported employment is an intervention that offers individually tailored job development and support, and research studies have consistently shown its effectiveness in helping people with schizophrenia to attain competitive employment, work more hours, and earn more wages than those not receiving supported employment.

Case management in the community is a treatment commonly offered to patients since deinstitutionalization in the 1960s moved the majority of mental health treatment away from inpatient hospitals and into community-based treatment. *Assertive Community Treatment*

(ACT) is an empirically supported variation that integrates case management with other clinical services. ACT teams consist of providers from different disciplines (including a medication prescriber) who work together to provide outreach and direct services to patients in the community. ACT has been shown to significantly reduce homelessness and hospitalizations among people with schizophrenia and may be especially beneficial for patients at risk for homelessness and repeated hospitalizations (Dixon et al., 2010).

Treatment of comorbid substance use problems is an empirically supported treatment for people with schizophrenia and may be a critical component of treatment given high rates of comorbid alcohol and substance use problems in this population. Although there is a dearth of randomized clinical trials in this area, the PORT team concluded in its 2009 treatment recommendations that the majority of motivational enhancement and/or cognitive-behavioral interventions for substance use in schizophrenia have resulted in greater treatment attendance, less substance use and relapse, and improved symptoms and functioning (Dixon et al., 2010). Furthermore, the PORT team recommends that these treatments be integrated with mental health care and specifically target engagement in treatment, coping skills training, and relapse prevention.

In addition to these treatments, *cognitive remediation* and other cognition-enhancing treatments may show promise for targeting the neurocognitive deficits in schizophrenia that persist through all stages of the illness, are relatively stable, and serve as a rate-limiting factor in functional recovery (Green, 1996). Although computer-based training exercises are often a common element of cognitive remediation, there are multiple methods and approaches, often combining computer tasks with other types of interventions such as supported employment or behavior therapy. For example, Hogarty et al. (2004) have targeted aspects of social cognition, whereas others have trained a variety of cognitive abilities including facial affect recognition, memory, attention, and the executive abilities associated with card sorting training. Some novel approaches include the computer-based auditory training exercises found to improve bottom-up sensory processing in schizophrenia (Adcock et al., 2009), as well as computerized adaptation training, a home-based, multimodal treatment including environmental supports such as medication containers and organization of belongings to bypass cognitive deficits and sequence and cue adaptive behaviors (Velligan et al., 2009). Although empirical questions remain about the size and duration of treatment effects, as well as whether potential benefits generalize to other cognitive tasks, cognitive remediation shows promise in improving cognitive performance, psychotic symptoms, and social and occupational functioning in schizophrenia (McGurk et al., 2007).

Summary

The treatment of schizophrenia can be particularly vexing if a multidimensional approach is not undertaken. Although pharmacological intervention remains the most essential feature of treatment, the literature over the years has continued to emphasize the use of psychosocial approaches in combination with physiological modifiers that come with medicinal support. These psychosocial approaches include psychoeducation, CBT, social skills training, token economy systems, supportive employment, case management in the community, and treatment of comorbid substance use problems, and must be tailored to the patient. Furthermore, fluidity of these interventions across a patient's life is critical as the phase of the illness, goal of the intervention(s), format of delivery, and theoretical model and intervention technique all serve as mediators. From a neuropsychological standpoint, growing interest in cognitive remediation as an intervention has been seen over recent years to address the neurocognitive deficits associated with the illness that do not fully respond to the combined efforts of pharmacological and psychosocial intervention. Although this line of research remains in its infancy in comparison to these other treatment modalities, outcomes thus far show promise.

CONCLUSIONS

Although schizophrenia, as well as many other psychiatric illnesses, was previously viewed as a functional disorder, it has now long been recognized as a brain disorder. Literature emerging over the past few decades has consistently demonstrated this fact. Documentation of underlying neuropathological features and genetic correlates are relatively vast and have been previously discussed in this chapter, albeit sparingly. Alongside this, there has been a growth in the appreciation of the role neuropsychology as a practice can play in the assessment and treatment of patients with schizophrenia. Although diagnostics remain based in structured interviewing and history taking, the neurocognitive sequelae that accompany the illness, which themselves can impede functional outcomes, emphasize the importance of neuropsychological practice. Cognitive heterogeneity of this group supports the role of individualized assessment so to better permit tailored interventions on a case-by-case basis, which may then guide cognitive remediation plans to better aid holistic intervention for patients. Consequently, as science continues to expand our understanding of schizophrenia and its variants, it should be reasonably expected that neuropsychology, both experimentally and clinically applied, will continue to grow in its role in the assessment and treatment of these patients.

ACKNOWLEDGMENT

This work was supported by the VA VISN-IV Mental Illness Research, Educational, and Clinical Center and the Research Service, VA Pittsburgh Healthcare System, Pittsburgh, PA.

REFERENCES

Adcock, R. A., Dale, C., Fisher, M., Aldebot, S., Genevsky, A., Simpson, G. V., et al. (2009). When top-down meets bottom-up: Auditory training enhances verbal memory in schizophrenia. *Schizophrenia Bulletin, 35,* 1132–1141.

Allen, D. N., Frantom, L. V., Strauss, G. P., & van Kammen, D. P. (2005). Differential patterns of premorbid academic and social deterioration in patients with schizophrenia. *Schizophrenia Research, 75,* 389–97.

Allen, D. N., Goldstein, G., & Aldarando, F. (1999). Neurocognitive dysfunction in patients diagnosed with schizophrenia and alcoholism. *Neuropsychology, 13,* 62–68.

Allen, D. N., Goldstein, G., Forman, S. D., Keshavan, M. S., van Kammen, D. P., & Sanders, R.D. (2000a). Neurologic examination abnormalities in schizophrenia with and without a history of alcoholism. *Neuropsychiatry, Neuropsychology and Behavioral Neurology, 13,* 184–187.

Allen, D. N., Goldstein, G., & Warnick, E. (2003). A consideration of neuropsychologically normal schizophrenia. *Journal of the International Neuropsychological Society, 9,* 56–63.

Ammari, N., Heinrichs, R. W., & Miles, A. A. (2010). An investigation of 3 neurocognitive subtypes in schizophrenia. *Schizophrenia Research, 121,* 32–38.

American Psychiatric Association (2000). Diagnostic and statistical manual of mental disorders (4th ed., text revision) Washington, DC: Author.

Ananth, H., Popescu, I., Critchley, H. D., Good, C. D., Frackowiak, R. S., & Dolan, R. J. (2002). Cortical and subcortical gray matter abnormalities in schizophrenia determined through structural magnetic resonance imaging with optimized volumetric voxel-based morphometry. *American Journal of Psychiatry, 159,* 1497–1505.

Andia, A. M., Zisook, S., Heaton, R. K., Hesselink, J., Jernigan, T., Kuck, J., et al. (1995). Gender differences in schizophrenia. *Journal of Nervous and Mental Disease, 183,* 522–528.

Arnold, S. E., Franz, B. R., Gur, R. C., Gur, R. E., Shapiro, R. M., Moberg, P. J., & Torojanowski, J. Q. (1995). Smaller neuron size in schizophrenia in hippocampal subfields that mediate cortical-hippocampal interaction. *American Journal of Psychiatry, 152,* 738–748.

Bogerts, B., Ashtari, M., Degreef, G., Alvir, J. M., Bilder, R. M., & Lieberman, J. A. (1990). Reduced temporal limbic structure volumes on magnetic resonance images in first episode schizophrenia. *Psychiatry Research, 35,* 1–13.

Bonham, C., & Abbott, C. (2008). Are second-generation antipsychotics a distinct class? *Journal of Psychiatric Practice, 14,* 225–237.

Braga, R. J., & Petrides, G. (2005). The combined use of electroconvulsive therapy and antipsychotics in patients with schizophrenia. *Journal of Electroconvulsive Therapy, 21,* 75–83.

Buchanan, R. W., Kreyenbuhl, J., Kelly, D. L., Noel, J. M., Boggs, D. L., Fischer, Bernard A., et al. (2010). The 2009 schizophrenia PORTpsychopharmacological treatment recommendations and summary statements. *Schizophrenia Bulletin, 36,* 71–93.

Chapman, L. J., & Chapman, J. P. (1973). The measurement of differential deficit. *Journal of Psychiatric Research*, *14*(1-4), 303–11.

Conners, C. K. (2000). *Continuous Performance Test II*. Toronto: Multi-Health systems.

Dixon, L. B., Dickerson, F., Bellack, A. S., Bennett, M., Dickinson, D., Goldberg, R.W., et al. (2010). The 2009 schizophrenia PORT psychosocial treatment recommendations and summary statements. *Schizophrenia Bulletin*, *36*, 48–70.

First, M., Spitzer, R., Gibbon, M., & Williams, J. B. (1997). Structured Clinical Interview for DSM-IV Axis I Disorders. Washington, DC: American Psychiatric Press.

Flashman, L. A., & Green, M. F. (2004). Review of cognition and brain structure in schizophrenia: Profiles, longitudinal course, and effects of treatment. *The Psychiatric Clinics of North America*, *27*(1), 1–18.

Garey, L. J., Ong, W. Y., Patel, T. S., Kanani, M., Davis, A., Mortimer, A. M., et al. (1998). Reduced dendritic spine density on cerebral cortical pyramidal neurons in schizophrenia. *Journal of Neurology, Neurosurgery, and Psychiatry*, *65(4)*, 446–453.

Gittelman-Klein, R., & Klein, D. F. (1969). Premorbid asocial adjustment and prognosis in schizophrenia. *Journal of Psychiatric Research*, *7*, 35–53.

Gladsjo, J. A., McAdams, .a., Palmer, B. W., Moore, D. J., Jeste, D. V., & Heaton, R. K. (2004) A six-factor model of cognition in schizophrenia and related psychotic disorders: relationships with clinical symptoms and functional capacity. *Schizophrenia Bulletin*, *30*, 739–754.

Glantz, L. A., & Lewis, D. A. (2001). Dendritic spine density in schizophrenia and depression. *Archives of General Psychiatry*, *58*, 203.

Goldstein, G. (1978). Cognitive and perceptual differences between schizophrenics and organics. *Schizophrenia Bulletin*, *4*, 160–185.

Goldstein, G. (1990). Neuropsychological heterogeneity in schizophrenia: A consideration of abstraction and problem solving abilities. *Archives of Clinical Neuropsychology*, *5*, 251–264.

Goldstein, G., Allen, D. N., & Haas, G. L. (2007). Schizophrenia. In D. E. Fujii & I. Ahmed (Eds.), *The spectrum of psychotic disorders: Neurobiology, etiology and pathogenesis*.Cambridge, UK: Cambridge University Press.

Goldstein, G., Allen, D. N., & van Kammen, D. P. (1998). Individual differences in cognitive decline in schizophrenia. *American Journal of Psychiatry*, *155*, 1117–1118.

Goldstein, G., Beers, S. R., & Shemansky, W. J. (1996). Neuropsychological differences between schizophrenic patients with heterogeneous Wisconsin Card Sorting Test performance. *Schizophrenia Research*, *21*, 13–18.

Goldstein, G., & Saklofske, D. (2010). The Wechsler Intelligence Scales in the assessment of psychopathology. In L. Weiss, D. Saklofske, D. Coalson, & R. Raiford (Eds.), *WAIS IV clinical use and interpretation: Scientist-practitioner perspectives*. New York:Academic Press.

Goldstein, G., Sanders, R. D., Forman, S. D., Tarpey, T., Gurklis, J. A., van Kammen, D. P., & Keshavan, M. S. (2005). The effects of antipsychotic medication on factor and cluster structure of neurologic examination abnormalities in schizophrenia. *Schizophrenia Research*, *75*, 55–64.

Goldstein, G., & Shemansky, W. J. (1995). Influences on cognitive heterogeneity in schizophrenia. *Schizophrenia Research*, *18*, 59–69.

Goldstein, G., & Zubin, J. (1990). Neuropsychological differences between young and old schizophrenics with and without associated neurological dysfunction. *Schizophrenia Research*, *3*, 117–126.

Goldstein, G., Zubin, J., & Pogue-Geile, M. F. (1991). Hospitalization and the cognitive deficits of schizophrenia: The influences of age and education. *Journal of Nervous & Mental Disease*, *179* , 202–206.

Green, M. F. (1996). What are the functional consequences of neurocognitive deficits in schizophrenia? *American Journal of Psychiatry*, *153*, 321–330.

Grunder, G., Hippius, H., & Carlsson, A. (2009). The 'atypicality' of antipsychotics: A concept re-examined and re-defined. *Nature Reviews Drug Discovery*, *8*, 197–202.

Gur, R. E., Cowell, P. E., Latshaw, A., et al. (2000a). Reduced dorsal and orbital prefrontal gray matter volumes in schizophrenia. *Archives of General Psychiatry*, *57*, 761–8.

Gur, R. E., Turetsky, B. I., Cowell, P. E., et al. (2000b). Temporolimbic volume reductions in schizophrenia. *Archives of General Psychiatry*, *57*, 769–75.

Harrison, P. J., & Weinberger, D. R., (2005). Schizophrenia genes, gene expression, and neuropathology: On the matter of their convergence. *Molecular Psychiatry*, *10*(1), 40–68.

Harvey, P. D., Reichenberg, A., Bowie, C. R., Patterson, T. L., & Heaton, R. K. (2010). The course of neuropsychological performance and functional capacity in older patients with schizophrenia: influences of previous history of long-term institutional stay. *Biological Psychiatry*, *67*, 933–939.

Harvey, I., Ron, M., du Bouley, G., Wicks, D., Lewis, S. W., & Murray, R. M. (1993). Reduction of cortical volume in schizophrenia on magnetic resonance imaging. *Psychological Medicine*, *23*, 591–604.

Harvey, P. D., & Keefe, R. S. E., (2009). Clinical neuropsychology of schizophrenia. In I. Grant, & K. M. Adams (Eds.), *Neuropsychological assessment of neuropsychiatric and neuromedical disorders (3rd ed.)*, (pp. 507–522). New York: Oxford University Press.

Haznedar, M. M., Buchsbaum, M. S., Luu, C., Hazlett, E. A., Siegel, B. V. Jr, Lohr, J., et al. (1997). Decreased anterior cingulate gyms metabolic rate in schizophrenia. *American Journal of Psychiatry. 154*, 682–4.

Heaton, R. K., Baade, L. E., & Johnson, K. L (1978). Neuropsychological test results associated with psychiatric disorders in adults. *Psychological Bulletin, 85*(1), 141–62.

Heaton, R. K., Gladsjo, J. A., Palmer, B. W., Kuck, J., Marcotte, T. D., & Jeste, D. V. (2001). Stability and course of neuropsychological deficits in schizophrenia. *Archives of General Psychiatry, 58*, 24–32.

Heinrichs, R. W., Ammari, N., McDermid, Vaz, S., & Miles, A. A. (2008). Are schizophrenia and schizoaffective disorder neuropsychologically distinguishable? *Schizophrenia Research, 99*, 149–154

Heinrichs, R. W., Ammari, N., Miles, A., McDermid Vaz, S., & Chopov, V. (2009). Psychopathology and cognition in divergent functional outcomes in schizophrenia. *Schizophrenia Research, 109*, 46–51.

Hogarty, G. E., Flesher, S., Ulrich, R., Carter, M., Greenwald, D., Pogue-Geile, M, et al. (2004). Cognitive enhancement therapy for schizophrenia: Effects of a 2-year randomized trial on cognition and behavior. *Archives of General Psychiatry, 61*(9), 866–76.

Hogarty, G. E., Greenwald, D., Ulrich, R.F., Kornblith, S. J., DiBarry, A. L., Cooley, S., et al. (1997). Three-year trials of personal therapy among schizophrenic patients living with or independent of family, I: Description of study and effects on relapse rates. *American Journal of Psychiatry, 154*, 1504–1513.

Kern, R. S., Glynn, S. M., Horan, W. P., & Marder, S. R. (2009). Psychosocial treatments to promote functional recovery in schizophrenia. *Schizophrenia Bulletin, 35*, 347–361.

Keshavan, M. S., Tandon, R., Boutros, N. N., & Nasrallah, H. A. (2008). Schizophrenia, "just the facts": what we know in 2008: Part 3: Neurobiology. *Schizophrenia Research, 106*, 89–107.

Kurtz, M. M., & Mueser, K. T. (2008). A meta-analysis of controlled research on social skills training for schizophrenia. *Journal of Consulting and Clinical Psychology, 76*, 491–504.

Lehman, R. A., Chelune, G. J., & Heaton, R. K. (1979). Level and variability of performance on neuropsychological tests. *Journal of Clinical Psychology, 35*, 8–63.

Lieberman, J. A. (1999). Is schizophrenia a neurodegenerative disorder? A clinical and neurobiological perspective. *Biological Psychiatry, 46*(6), 729–739.

Lieberman, J. A., Stroup, T. S., McEvoy, J. P., et al. (2005). Effectiveness of antipsychotic drugs in patients with chronic schizophrenia. *New England Journal of Medicine, 353*, 1209–1223.

Lippman, M. R., & Motta, R.W. (1993). Effects of positive and negative reinforcement on daily living skills in chronic psychiatric patients in community residences. *Journal of Clinical Psychology, 49*, 654–662.

Malaspina, D., Perera, G. M., Lignelli, A., Marshall, R. S., Esser, P. D., Storer, S., et al. (1998). SPECT imaging of odor identification in schizophrenia. *Psychiatry Research, 82*, 53–61.

Mathalon, D. H., Sullivan, E. V., Lim, K. O. & Pfefferbaurn, A. (2001). Progressive brain volume changes and the clinical course of schizophrenia in men: A longitudinal magnetic resonance imaging study. *Archives of General Psychiatry, 58* (2), 148–57.

Matheson, S. L., Green, M. J., Loo, C. & Carr, V. J. (2010). Quality assessment and comparison of evidence for electroconvulsive therapy and repetitive transcranial stimulation for schizophrenia: A systematic meta-review. *Schizophrenia Research, 118*, 201–210.

McClure, M. M., Bowie, C. R., Patterson, T. L., Heaton, R. K., Weaver, C., Anderson, H. & Harvey, P. D (2007). Correlations of functional capacity and neuropsychological performance in older patients with schizophrenia: evidence for specificity of relationships. *Schizophrenia Research. 89*, 330–338.

McGurk, S. R., Twamley, E. W., Sitzer, D. I., McHugo, G. J. & Mueser, K. T. (2007). A meta-analysis of cognitive remediation in schizophrenia. *American Journal of Psychiatry, 164*, 1791–1802.

McSweeny, A. J., Grant, I., Heaton, R. K., Prigatano, G. P. & Adams, K. M. (1985). Relationship of neuropsychological status to everyday functioning in healthy and chronically ill persons. *Journal of Clinical and Experimental Psychology, 7*, 281–291.

Menon, R. R., Barta, P. E., Aylward, E. H., Richards, S. S., Vaughn, D. D., Tien, A. Y., et al. (1995). Posterior superior temporal gyrus in schizophrenia: Grey matter changes and clinical correlates. *Schizophrenia Research, 16*, 127–35.

Molina, V., Sanchez, J., Reig, S., Sanz, J., Benito, C., Santamarta, C., et al. (2005). N-acetyl-aspartate levels in the dorsolateral prefrontal cortex in the early years of schizophrenia are inversely related to disease duration. *Schizophrenia Research, 73*(2-3), 209–219.

Nuechterlein, K. H., & Dawson, M. E. (1984). Information processing and attentional functioning in the developmental course of schizophrenic disorders. *Schizophrenia Bulletin, 10*, 160–203.

Nuechterlein, K. H., Green, M. F., Kern, R. S., Baade, L. E., Barch, D. M., Cohen, J. D., et al. (2008). The MATRICS consensus cognitive battery: Part 1. Test selection, reliability, and validity. *American Journal of Psychiatry, 165*, 203–213.

Palmer, B. W., Dawes, S. E., & Heaton, R. K. (2009). What do we know about neuropsychological aspects of schizophrenia? *Neuropsychology Review, 19*, 365–384.

Palmer, B. W., Heaton, R. K., Paulsen, J. S., Kuck, J., Braff, D., Harris, M. J., et al. (1997). Is it possible to be schizophrenic yet neuropsychologically normal? *Neuropsychology, 11*, 437–46.

Paulsen, J. S., Heaton, R. K., Sadek, J. R., Perry, W., Delis, D. C., Braff, D., et al. (1995). The nature of learning and memory impairments in schizophrenia. *Journal of the International Neuropsychological Society, 1*, 88–99.

Pettegrew, J. W., Keshavan, M. S., Panchalingam, K., Strychor, S., Kaplan, D. B., Tretta, M. G., et al. (1991). Alterations in brain high-energy phosphate and membrane phospholipid metabolism in first-episode, drug-naive schizophrenics. A pilot study of the dorsal prefrontal cortex by in vivo phosphorous 31 nuclear magnetic resonance spectroscopy. *Archives of General Psychiatry, 48*, 563–568.

Pharoah, F. M., Mari, J. J., & Streiner, D. (2003). Family interventions for schizophrenia. *Cochrane Database of Systematic Reviews* , CD000088. Retrieved [ ] from [ ] .

Pitschel-Walz, G., Leuct, S., Bäuml, J., Kissling, W., & Engel, R. R. (2001). The effect of family interventions on relapse and rehospitalisation in schizophrenia–A meta-analyis. *Schizophrenia Bulletin, 27*, 73–92.

Ragland, J. D., Gur, R. C., Glahn, D. C., Censits, D. M., Smith, R. J., Lazarev, M. G., et al. (1998). Frontotemporal cerebral blood flow change during executive and declarative memory tasks in schizophrenia: A positron emission tomography study. *Neuropsychology, 12*, 399–413.

Robinson, A. L., Heaton, R. K., Lehman, R. A., & Stilson, D. W. (1980). The utility of the Wisconsin Card Sorting Test in detecting and localizing frontal lobe lesions. *Journal of Consulting and Clinical Psychology, 48*, 605–14.

Seaton, B. E., Allen, D. N., Goldstein, G., Kelley, M. E., & van Kammen, D.P. (1999). Relations between cognitive and symptom profile heterogeneity in schizophrenia. *Journal of Nervous & Mental Disease, 187*, 414–419.

Seaton, B. E., Goldstein, G., & Allen, D. N. (2001). Sources of heterogeneity in schizophrenia: The role or neuropsychological functioning. *Neuropsychology Review, 11*, 45–67.

Seckinger, R. A., Goudsmit, N., Coleman, E., Harkavy-Friedman, J., Yale, S., Rosenfield, P.J., et al. (2004). Olfactory identification and WAIS-R performance in deficit and nondeficit schizophrenia. *Schizophrenia Research, 69*, 55–65.

Selemon, L. D., (2004). Increased cortical neuronal density in schizophrenia. *American Journal of Psychiatry, 161*(9), 1564.

Shenton, M. E., Kikinis, R., Jolesz, F. A., Pollak, S. D., LeMay, M., Wible, C. G., et al. (1992). Abnormalities of the left temporal lobe and thought disorder in schizophrenia?A quantitative magnetic resonance imaging study. *New England Journal of Medicine, 327*, 604–12.

Sokal, R. R., & Sneath, P. H., (1963). *Principles of numerical taxonomy.*, San Francisco: Freeman.

Suddath, R. L., Christison, G. W.,Torrey, E. F., & Weinberger, D. R. (1990). Cerebral anatomical abnormalities in monozygotic twins discordant for schizophrenia. *New England Journal of Medicine, 322*, 789–94.

Sullivan, E. V., Mathalon, D. H.,Lim, K. O., Marsh, L., & Pfefferbaum, A. (1998). Patterns of regional cortical dysmorphology distinguishing schizophrenia and chronic alcoholism. *Biological Psychiatry, 43*, 118–131.

Sweeney, J. A., Luna, B.,Srinivasagam, N. M., Keshavan, M. S., Schooler, N. R., Haas, G. L., et al. (1998). Eye tracking abnormalities in schizophrenia: Evidence for dysfunction in the frontal eye fields. *Biological Psychiatry, 44*, 698–708.

Tandon, R., Keshavan, M. S., & Nasrallah, H. (2008). Schizophrenia , "Just the facts": What we know in 2008. 2: Epidemiology and etiology. *Schizophrenia Research, 102*, 1–18.

Tandon, R., Keshavan, M. S., & Nasrallah, H. (2011). *Schizophrenia: Just the facts*. New York: Elsevier

Tandon, R., Nasrallah, H. A., & Keshavan, M. S. (2010). Schizophrenia, "just the facts": 5. Treatment and prevention past, present, and future. *Schizophrenia Research, 122*, 1–23.

Tarrier, N., & Wykes, T., (2004). Is there evidence that cognitive behaviour therapy is an effective treatment for schizophrenia? A cautious or cautionary tale? *Behaviour Research and Therapy, 42*, 1377–1401.

The UK ECT Review Group. (2003). Efficacy and safety of electroconvulsive therapy in depressive disorders: A systematic review and meta-analysis. *Lancet, 361*, 799–808.

Thirthalli, J., Phutane, V. H., Muralidharan, K., Kumar, C. N., Munishwar, B., Baspure, P., et al. (2009). Does catatonic schizophrenia improve faster with electroconvulsive therapy than other subtypes of schizophrenia? *World Journal of Biological Psychiatry, 10, 772–777.*

Velligan, D. I., Draper, M., Stutes, D., Maples, N., Mintz, J., Tai, S., et al. (2009). Multimodal cognitive therapy: Combining treatments that bypass cognitive deficits and deal with reasoning and appraisal biases. *Schizophrenia Bulletin, 35*, 884–893.

Voglmaier, M. M., Seidman, L. J., Niznikiewicz, M. A., Dickey, C. C., Shenton, M. E., & McCarlewy, R. W. (2005). A comparative profile analysis of neuropsychological function in men and women with schizotypal personality disorder. *Schizophrenia Research, 74*, 43–49.

Watson, C. G., Thomas, R. W., Andersen, D., & Felling, J. (1968a). Differentiation of organics from schizophrenics at two chronicity levels by use of the Reitan-Halstead organic test battery. *Journal of Consulting and Clinical Psychology, 32*, 679–684.

Watson, C. G., Thomas, R. W., Felling, J., & Andersen, D. (1968b). Differentiation of organics from schizophrenics with Reitan's sensory-perceptual disturbance tests. *Perceptual and Motor Skills, 26,* 1191–1198.

Weinberger, D. R., Berman, K. F., Suddath, I. L., & Torrey, E. F. (1992). Evidence of dysfunction of a prefrontal-limbic network in schizophrenia: A magnetic resonance imaging and regional cerebral blood flow study of discordant monozygotic twins. *American Journal of Psychiatry, 149,* 890–97.

Weiser, M., Reichenberg, A., Rabinowitz, J., Kaplan, Z., Mark, M., Nahon, D. (2000). Gender differences in premorbid cognitive performance in a national cohort of schizophrenic patients. *Schizophrenia Research, 45,* 185–190.

Wolitzky, R., Goudsmit, N., Goetz, R. R., Printz, D., Gil, R., Harkavy-Friedman, J., et al. (2006). Etiological heterogeneity and intelligence test scores in patients with schizophrenia. *Journal of Clinical and Experimental Neuropsychology, 28,* 161–177.

Wykes, T., Steel, C., Everitt, B., & Tarrier, N. (2008). Cognitive behavior therapy for schizophrenia effect sizes, clinical models, and methodological rigor. *Schizophrenia Bulletin, 34,* 523–537.

Zimmerman, G., Favrod, J., Trieu, V. H., & Pomini, V. (2005). The effect of cognitive behavioral treatment on the positive symptoms of schizophrenia spectrum disorders: A meta-analysis. *Schizophrenia Research, 77,* 1–9.

Zubin, J. (1975). Problem of attention in schizophrenia. In M. L. Kietzman, S. Sutton, & J. Zubin (Eds.), *Experimental approaches to psychopathology* (pp. 139–166). New York:Academic Press

CHAPTER 16

Personality Disorders

Chad A. Noggle, Melanie Rylander, & Stephen Soltys

INTRODUCTION

A personality disorder is defined as a pattern of enduring, pervasive, and inflexible thoughts and behaviors in and toward one's environment that causes interpersonal stress due to social and cultural inappropriateness (Trammel & Dean, 2011). The *Diagnostic and Statistical Manual of Mental Disorders, fourth edition, text revision* (*DSM-IV-TR*; American Psychiatric Association [APA], 2000) specifically states that the "essential feature of a Personality Disorder is an enduring pattern of inner experience and behavior that deviates markedly from the expectations of the individual's culture and is manifested in at least two of the following areas: cognition, affectivity, interpersonal functioning, or impulse control" (p. 686). The "enduring" nature of personality disorders is rooted in theory that suggests there are constitutional temperaments that, in concert with experience, lead to the development of a personality that becomes the habitual style with which the individual responds to external demands (Nestadt et al., 2010. This does not presume stability. Rather, Tyrer and colleagues (2007) as well as others (Durbin & Klein, 2006) have now suggested that personality status is relatively unstable and susceptible to the effects of time, developmental stage, and life circumstances, among other variables.

The literature has supported the concept that social factors, which include early adverse events, play a role in the development of personality disorders in conjunction with neurobiological characteristics. From a neuroscientific standpoint, the personality disorders as a group have received less empirical attention than Axis I presentations, with borderline personality disorder (BPD), antisocial personality disorder (ASPD), and schizotypal personality disorder (StPD) drawing the majority of research. In conducting the literature search for this chapter, it was difficult to find articles discussing many of the targeted domains (e.g., neuropathology, neurophysiology, neurochemistry, neuropsychology, etc.) for many of the individual personality disorders apart from these three. Thus, this chapter will naturally reflect the attention bias of the current literature.

The prevalence of personality disorders ranges from between 0.3% and 5.6% for any individual diagnostic category, with an overall prevalence of 4.4% to 13% (Coid, 2003; Lenzenweger, Lane, Loranger, & Kessler, 2007). Longevity and stability of the core features is critical to diagnosis of personality disorders, with features emerging in adolescence or earlier becoming solidified by early adulthood. Although in the majority of cases diagnosis is not made until after the age of 18, the *DSM-IV-TR* allows that "in those relatively unusual instances in which the individual's particular maladaptive personality traits appear to be pervasive, persistent, and unlikely to be limited to a particular developmental stage or episode of an Axis I disorder" (APA, 2000, p. 687), diagnosis may be made earlier.

The exception to this rule is ASPD, which cannot be diagnosed prior to the age of 18 regardless of the features presenting. Early on the development of the *DSM* series, it was noted that research had shown that a diagnosis of conduct disorder in a child or adolescent does not necessarily mean that the child will go on to develop ASPD. Many Axis I disorders presented in childhood with disruptive behavior although the psychiatric disorder underlying that behavior was not immediately apparent. Studies demonstrated that significant numbers of youth who were diagnosed with conduct disorder were later found to no longer qualify for a conduct disorder diagnosis (Lewis, Lewis, Unger, & Goldman, 1984). A study of the stability of disruptive behavior disorders suggested that the tendency to oppositional behavior is stable over time (a trait behavior) whereas the tendency to violate major social norms seen in conduct disorder is more the result of situational stressors that come and go, resulting in the conduct disorder behaviors waxing and waning (a state behavior; Cantwell & Baker, 1989). As a result, the prohibition on diagnosis of ASPD in individuals under the age of 18 was put into place to prevent the premature labeling of individuals as having an ASPD with ominous long-term implications.

Although personality disorders are relatively common in those seeking psychiatric services, presenting in upward of 30% of individuals presenting for services (Zimmerman, Rothschild, & Chelminski, 2005; Moran, Jenkins, Tylee, Blizard, & Mann, 2000; Hueston, Werth, & Mainous, 1999), they are rarely the main focus of consultations and notoriously underdiagnosed (Casey, Birbeck, McDonagh, et al., 2004; Zimmerman et al., 2005). This is often due to the fact that they present comorbidly with other mental disorders that receive the majority of the clinical attention (Cramer, Torgersen, Kringlen, 2006; Morse & Lynch, 2004). However, appropriate recognition and treatment of comorbid personality disorders is critical because their coexistence is known to worsen outcomes (Cramer et al., 2006; Morse & Lynch, 2004). Still, as many as 30% or more of individuals with a diagnosable personality disorders may present without a comorbid Axis I disorder (Zimmerman et al., 2005). As a grouping, the personality disorders are consistently recognized as being among the most chronic and financially burdensome of the psychiatric disorders (Comtois, Russo, Snowden, Srebnik, & Ries, 2003). Research has demonstrated poorer treatment outcomes and health status and higher rates of health care use and costs in patients with a comorbid personality disorder in addition to other chronic mental or medical disorders (Gross et al., 2002; Hueston et al., 1999; Moran, Rendu, Jenkins, Tylee, & Mann, 2001; Rendu, Moran, Patel, Knapp, & Mann, 2002).

Although research has long held that the features of personality disorder are multifaceted in their origin with relative contribution from hereditary temperamental traits and environmental and developmental events, relatively little is understood regarding their neurobiological bases (Ruocco et al., 2009). What is known, as previously suggested, is disproportionate in focus with greater attention paid to a few specific disorders (i.e., borderline, antisocial, schizotypal) as compared to others. In this chapter, a breakdown of the classification scheme of personality disorders is provided, including an overview of the clustering of presentations, followed by discussion of the neuroscientific features of individual disorders within the context of their cluster grouping. This includes discussion of the literature on underlying physiological, neurochemical, neuropathological, and neuroanatomical correlates. Discussion will also focus on the neuropsychological presentation of the various personality disorders as the literature permits. Emerging data are consistently linking personality disorders with neuropsychological deficits. Not surprisingly, this has been most commonly done in borderline, antisocial, and schizotypal personality disorders, although there are isolated studies that have evaluated clusters (e.g., B, C). Many of these findings have suggested disruptions of frontal-limbic systems at varying degrees. Although variability has been noted in the neurocognitive strengths and weaknesses demonstrated by patients, consensus has suggested that alterations in executive functioning, attention, working memory, verbal and visual memory, and cognitive efficiency and flexibility are common in various personality disorders. Findings will be discussed as they relate to specific disorders. Finally, diagnostic and treatment considerations will be outlined.

PERSONALITY AS A GENE-ENVIRONMENT DIATHESIS

Personality traits are stable ways in which individuals interpret and react to the environment around them and the situations in which they find themselves (APA, 2000). Cloninger (1987) defined temperament traits that are fundamental to personality development and will be discussed in detail in subsequent sections: harm avoidance, novelty seeking, and reward dependence. In the context of personality disorders, these personality traits are particularly inflexible and maladaptive in comparison to societal and cultural norms and expectations leading to functional and interpersonal deficits. Eskedal and Demetri (2006) have suggested that personality, like many other traits, has a biological blueprint that varies in how it takes shape based on one's environmental experience. In other words, the emerging phenotype is the combination of one's genotype and life experiences. The genetic basis of personality and specific personality disorders has been well documented in the literature with 30%–60% of the variance attributed to inherited factors (Siever, 2009).

However, genetic heritability is mostly related to specific components, or personality traits, that are central to each disorder, such as impulsivity and emotional irregularity, rather than the presence of the disorder itself. It may be the case that these heritable traits contribute to each individual's neuropsychological profile, rendering them susceptible to certain personality disorders depending on environmental factors. In this manner, it is the combination of genetic factors and environmental forces that coalesce into the final product of personality. The neurological systems and structures commonly linked with the establishment and maintenance of personality includes, but is not limited to, the prefrontal cortices, temporal lobes, and limbic system, including the amygdala and anterior cingulate cortex (ACC). Additionally, multiple neurochemical systems facilitate features of personality, emotionality, and behavior.

Although the neurobiological origin of personality and personality disorders is intriguing, twin studies have demonstrated that much variability in presentation is still explained by other factors. There are some findings that link their development to childhood temperament, environmental experiences, and trauma. Clark (2005) noted that childhood temperament may play an important role in the development of personality disorders, mostly based on three broad domains of temperament, including negative affectivity, positive affectivity, and disinhibition. Environmental experiences and trauma, such as a history of sexual abuse, are often observed in personality disorders, particularly with regard to BPD (APA, 2000). Additionally, it appears that factors such as age and gender may serve as mediators to some extent.

Nestadt and colleagues (2010) found that stability of personality disorders in adults changed over time in regard to outcomes on objective assessment. The authors reported moderate stability of antisocial, avoidant, borderline, histrionic, and schizotypal disorders over a span of 12–18 years and "appreciable" stability of obsessive-compulsive personality disorder (OCPD). In comparison, dependent, narcissistic, paranoid, and schizoid disorders were unstable over time. Nestadt and colleagues (2010) went further to examine the stability of particular traits of the disorders assessed. They found that with increased age, decreases were seen in the extent of irritability and aggressiveness exhibited by those with ASPD, social withdrawal and unwillingness to form relationships in those with avoidant personality disorder (APD), overreaction to minor angry outbursts and dependency in those with histrionic personality disorder (HPD), and stubbornness in those with OCPD. Increases over time were noted in individuals' desire for affection in those with APD, impulsivity and moodiness in BPD, and excessive work devotion in OCPD. Those traits that remained relatively stable over the course of the 12–18 years involved work inconsistency and fighting in those with ASPD, hypersensitivity to rejection in those with APD, unstable relationships in those with BPD, self-dramatizing in those with HPD, and emotional constriction and perfectionism in those with OCPD. The authors postulated that those features that remained stable represent the key elements of the presentation, and those features that changed are more susceptible to the influences of the environment. This is consistent with the conclusions of Grilo and colleagues (2004), who also suggested that although the features of the disorders may remain stable, the severity of individual traits may vary over time in severity.

Gender appears to mediate symptom manifestation and relative risk of particular personality disorders. Males are more commonly diagnosed with antisocial and narcissistic personality disorders, whereas females are diagnosed at higher rates with avoidant, dependent, paranoid, borderline, and histrionic personality disorders. However, some of this gender discrepancy may reflect cultural bias. In other words, clinicians may be more apt to attribute aggressive behavior in males to antisocial tendencies whereas this same behavior in women may be attributed to borderline pathology (APA, 2000).

The personality disorders are collectively grouped because they all adhere to the basic criterion of an inflexible and pervasive pattern of thought/cognition and behavior, arising in adolescence or early adulthood, that markedly deviates from societal and cultural expectations and results in significant distress or impairment in social, occupational, or other environmental domains, and that is not secondary to another mental disorder, substance abuse, or medical condition (APA, 2000). See the *DSM-IV-TR* and ICD-10 for general and disorder-specific diagnostic criteria.

When it comes to a more refined classification of the personality disorders, a three-cluster arrangement (i.e., A–C) has been used with individual presentations being so grouped based on an overlapping of their clinical dimensions. In all, the *DSM-IV-TR* (APA, 2000) recognizes a total of 10 distinct personality disorders across these three clusters. Cluster A includes paranoid personality disorder (PPD), schizoid personality disorder (SzPD), and StPD. Cluster B includes ASPD, BPD, HPD and narcissistic personality disorder (NPD). Finally, Cluster C includes APD, dependent personality disorder (DPD), and OCPD. In addition, there is a personality disorder not otherwise specified (NOS) option for clinicians to be used in those instances where, in individuals, features are consistent with the basic criteria of a personality disorder but does not meet the specific criteria of any of the other recognized personality disorders.

CLUSTER A DISORDERS

The Cluster A personality disorders are so grouped because they share the tendency toward odd or eccentric behaviors in combination with varying degrees of social deficits, cognitive distortions bordering on delusional, and perceptual distortions (sensing that another person is present or hearing a voice murmuring one's name) that are not to the point of auditory hallucinations. Some have used the term pre-psychotic to describe this grouping because they have all been considered to fall within the realm of what some refer to as the schizophrenia spectrum disorders.

Schizotypal Personality Disorder (StPD)

Clinical Features

Rosenthal and colleagues (1971) are attributed with the original identification and description of StPD, which was first included in the *DSM-III*. The presentation was conceptualized as a form of borderline schizophrenia that Rosenthal and colleagues observed in relatives of patients with schizophrenia who themselves did not meet the diagnostic criteria for schizophrenia or other Axis I psychotic disorders. Research has since further demonstrated a prominent overlap with schizophrenia along both genetic and biological lines as well as treatment responsiveness.

Clinically, individuals with StPD demonstrate odd behavior, magical thinking and unusual beliefs, ideas of reference, eccentric appearance or behavior, perceptual abnormalities, paranoia and suspiciousness, alterations in language characterized by circumstantialities, and asocial tendencies (APA, 2000). Keeping with Rosenthal's conceptualization of a "borderline" schizophrenia, the behavioral and cognitive deficits associated with StPD are less broad and severe. Individuals do not present with hallucinations in association with StPD. If hallucinations were present, a schizophrenia diagnosis would be considered. In such an instance where a schizophrenia diagnosis is made, a diagnosis of StPD cannot be made if the StPD features are present exclusively during the course of schizophrenia.

From a neuropsychological standpoint, StPD is associated with moderate impairment across a few cognitive domains in comparison to schizophrenia, which can present with moderate to severe deficits across a majority of domains (Nuechterlein et al., 2004). Neuropsychological correlates are discussed in greater detail in the following text.

Biological Correlates

The biological substrates of StPD demonstrate a convergence of genetics, neuroanatomy, neurochemistry, and neurophysiology. Consistent with their behavioral presentation, overlap is seen between StPD and schizophrenia. Their behavioral similarities may well be rooted in genetics. Numerous studies have demonstrate a genetic relationship between the two disorders (Fanous et al., 2001; Kendler et al. 1993A,B; Kety et al. 1994; Torgersen et al., 2002), suggesting StPD is part of a schizophrenia spectrum. Recall that StPD was first described by Rosenthal and colleagues (1971) based on his observation of the relatives of patients with schizophrenia.

Both disorders (i.e., StPD and schizophrenia) have been linked anatomically with reductions in superior temporal gyrus volume, although this tends to be more prominent in schizophrenia (Hazlett et al., 2008; Kawasaki et al., 2004; Takahashi et al., 2006). Reductions in Broadman's area 22 (BA22) has been suggested as specific to StPD compared to BPD (Goldstein et al., 2009; Zanarini et al., 1998) and potentially serves as a means of differentiating the two disorders anatomically. StPD has also demonstrated associations with volumetric reductions of gray matter in the middle and inferior temporal gyri (Downhill et al., 2001) as well as reductions in Heschl's gyrus (Dickey et al., 2002), amygdala (Suzuki et al., 2005), hippocampus (Dickey et al., 2007), striatum (Byne et al., 2001), thalamus (Shihabuddin et al. 2001), caudate nucleus (Koo et al., 2006; Levitt et al., 2002), and lateral ventricles (Buchsbaum et al., 1997). Some studies have failed to find such anatomical alterations (Dickey et al., 2002b). Abnormalities of the caudate nucleus are of particular interest cognitively given its connections with prefrontal and temporal systems. Consequently, caudate nucleus volume is linked with various cognitive outcomes.

Although temporal involvement is relatively similar in StPD and schizophrenia, primary differences may result from frontal involvement. The majority of research has reported far greater sparing of the frontal cortex in StPD compared to both schizophrenia (Buchsbaum et al., 2002; Hazlett et al., 2008; Kawasaki et al., 2004; Siever et al., 2002, Suzuki et al., 2005) and BPD (Hazlett et al., 2005; Lyoo et al., 1998; Tebartz van Elst et al., 2003). Greater volumetric reductions in these areas can be linked with greater symptom severity. For example, Goldstein and colleagues (2009) demonstrated an inverse relationship between STG volume and symptom severity, with lower volume being associated with greater symptom severity.

Neuropsychological Presentation

Not surprisingly given the extent of neurological abnormalities associated with StPD, neuropsychological deficits in StPD have been consistently reported. Again, although these deficits are not usually as severe or as broad in scope as those seen in association with schizophrenia, moderate impairments are often still observed across a few cognitive domains. Mitropoulou and colleagues (2005) reported modest impairments in neurocognition across a number of domains in their assessment of participants diagnosed with StPD. These deficits were specific to the domains of working memory, episodic memory, and delayed recall. In comparison, processing speed, susceptibility to cognitive interference, and overall intellectual functioning were relatively preserved. Of all the tests incorporated, the authors noted that the greatest differentiation between StPD participants and normal controls was seen in auditory working memory as assessed by the Paced Auditory Serial Addition Test, favoring controls over those with StPD. Many of these outcomes are corroborated by other studies. For example, deficits in working memory have been reported previously (Heinrichs & Zakzanis, 1998; Mitropoulou et al., 2002, 2005) and is one domain in which individuals with StPD perform as poorly as those with schizophrenia. Dickey and colleagues (2005) previously reported episodic memory deficits of a verbal modality in relation to StPD. Koo and colleagues (2006) found deficits in verbal learning performance on the California Verbal Learning Test in relation to StPD. McClure et al. (2007) demonstrated similar deficits within the visual-spatial modality. Deficits in episodic memory have been acknowledged as the most widely replicated and pronounced deficits associated with StPD (McClure et al., 2010).

Executive function deficits are also commonly reported in relation to StPD. Koo and colleagues (2006) found individuals with StPD performed significantly worse on the Wisconsin Card Sorting (WCST) than controls. The authors found that volumetric reductions of the caudate nucleus was associated with greater executive dysfunction in both females in their study (Koo et al., 2006) as well as males in a previous study (Levitt et al., 2002). Associations have also been established between caudate nucleus volume and working memory (Levitt et al., 2002), concept formation (Volgmaier et al., 1997, 2000), verbal learning (Koo et al., 2006), and general clinical symptoms (Scheepers et al., 2001) in StPD. Regarding verbal learning, females with StPD tend to show fewer deficits than males (Voglmaier et al., 2005). Although the role of the caudate nucleus may not be obvious to some within these cognitive domains, its presumed role in the case of these deficits is through a disruption of the connectivity between basal ganglion-subcortical regions and prefrontal lobes mediated by the thalamus. As suggested by Koo and colleagues (2006), the fact that the neuropsychological profiles associated with StPD appear prefrontal in nature in the absence of prefrontal volume reductions implies that the deficits arise elsewhere in the fronto–subcortico–thalamic circuitry or are mediated by a volume-sparing mechanism within the prefrontal cortex, such as alterations in neurotransmission or protein expression.

Although further research on medicinal interventions with specific focus on reducing neurocognitive deficits in StPD is needed, administration of pergolide has been linked with improvements in processing speed, executive functioning, working memory, and verbal learning (McClure et al., 2010). As previously suggested, volumetric reductions of the STG are also seen in relation to StPD. The functional outcome of this is oddities of speech with greater speech disturbance associated with smaller STG volume (Dickey et al., 2003). Additionally, STG reductions have been correlated with auditory information processing deficits (Engelien et al., 1995; Rajarethinam et al., 2000).

Mitropoulou et al. (2005) have suggested that insight into the social isolative tendencies of individuals with StPD may also correspond with their neurocognitive profile. The authors suggest modest support can be found for the hypothesis that deficits in information processing and the inability to titrate effort to situational demands could possibly lead to increases in social isolation, a core characteristic of the schizophrenia spectrum disorders, including StPD. This hypothesis is in need of further scientific investigation.

Paranoid Personality Disorder (PPD)

As the name suggests, PPD is characterized by a general pattern of mistrust toward others that is pervasive in nature (APA, 2000). Associated features of hypersensitivity to criticism and rigidly held maladaptive beliefs about others' motives are seen, which contribute to the individual's persona of emotional coldness and hostility (Edens, Marcus, & Morey, 2009). Prevalence is estimated to range from 0.5%–2.5% in the general population but is four times as likely in the outpatient psychiatric settings, and highest rates present within the inpatient setting, with estimates ranging from 10%–30% (APA, 2000). Grant and colleagues (2004) reported that minorities including African Americans, Hispanics, and Native Americans were at greater risk for having PPD than Caucasians and that the presentation was more common among younger people (18–29), those with lower socioeconomic status, and singles (i.e., either divorced or never married).

As a result of the core features of the disorder, individuals present with relatively higher rates of internalizing disorders (e.g., depression and anxiety), criminality, and violence (Johnson et al., 2000; Johnson, Cohen, Kasen, & Brook, 2005). One may describe individuals as feeling backed into a corner by life. One can only assume how emotionally draining this would be. Consequently, quality of life is significantly impaired and over time there is significant risk for suicide (Overholser, Stockmeier, & Dilley, 2002) that we may reasonably presume is seen as a means of escape.

Criticism of the *DSM-IV-TR* criteria can be found. Bernstein and Useda (2007) have suggested that there is an overemphasis on mistrust and suspiciousness, likely due to the fact this is seen as best falling in line with the concept of being "paranoid." Rather, the authors suggest greater emphasis should be placed on individuals' antagonistic, aggressive, and hypervigilant tendencies and accompanying behavioral, cognitive, and emotional rigidity. Bögels and Mansell (2004) have suggested that this hypervigilance, manifested as social distrust and phobia, stems from a misattribution of social cues and attentional biases. A potential underlying neurological substrate for this has not been proposed. One may offer a general assumption that dysfunction in prefrontal and temporal regions may be seen, as this holds true across those personality disorders in which such studies have been undertaken. Similarly, no real attention has been given to the neuropsychological features of PPD. Once more, it may be reasonable to expect domain-based features similar to those seen in StPD if prefrontal and temporal dysfunction is presumed. It could be hypothesized that deficits in executive functioning, episodic memory, and working memory might be found, but currently there is a lack of corroborating, empirical evidence.

The dearth of literature on PPD from a neurological standpoint may be a by-product of the criticisms offered by some regarding the key features of the disorder and whether PPD is truly a discrete disorder. PPD demonstrates a high comorbidity with other personality disorders including schizotypal, schizoid, borderline, narcissistic, and avoidant personality disorders. Widiger and Trull (1998) have estimated that as many as 75% of all individuals diagnosed with PPD present comorbidly with one of these other personality disorders, which may suggest that PPD represents a dimension of these other disorders in lieu of an independent disorder. Others have suggested that the presentation arises from a combination of genetic predisposition and experienced trauma (Dunn et al., 2004; Golier et al., 2003; Halles et al., 2004). The summative findings of these studies have shown increased risk of PPD in individuals with a history of abuse as a child or even as an adult (Dunn et al., 2004; Golier et al., 2003; Halles et al., 2004), or a diagnosis of PTSD (Golier et al., 2003; Dunn et al., 2004).

Beyond their higher rate of comorbidity, there is particularly significant clinical overlap seen between PPD and StPD. As is the case with StPD, some have suggested PPD represents a schizophrenic spectrum disorder. Whereas ample research exists (some previously described) investigating the genetic relationship between StPD and schizophrenia, relatively little is found along these lines with PPD. Previously, there have been studies that have suggested increased prevalence of PPD in first-degree relatives of individuals with schizophrenia (Baron et al., 1985; Kendler & Gruenberg, 1982) whereas others have failed to find significant relationships (Coryell & Zimmerman, 1989; Kendler, Masterson, & Davis, 1985). Kendler and colleagues (1985) actually found a greater frequency of PPD in the first-degree relatives of individuals with delusional disorders than those with schizophrenia, although both rates were relatively low, 4.8% and 0.8%, respectively.

Schizoid Personality Disorder (SzPD)

Clinical Features

The *DSM-IV-TR* (APA, 2000) describes SzPD as a pervasive pattern of detachment from social relationships and a restricted range of expression of emotions in interpersonal settings, beginning by early adulthood and presenting in a variety of contexts. Further, they exhibit a general indifference to the views and opinions of others. In comparison to StPD, in which there is felt to be a desire for interpersonal relationships that is inhibited by their discomfort in social interactions and oddness of behavior, individuals with SzPD appear to have a blatant lack of interest in developing relationships with others.

SzPD was first introduced in the *DSM-II* and further refined in *DSM-III* to distinguish it from newly included disorders added at that time (i.e. StPD and APD). Guntrip (1968) is widely recognized as providing the most comprehensive conceptualization of the underlying features of the presentation which includes an inner-directed mindset where individuals are focused on themselves and their inner world. This leads to a lack of interest in others and progressive withdrawal from the external environment. An individual?s capacity to interact in our world and the social skills used to do so successfully are constantly being refined through environmental interactions. As individuals with SzPD continue to withdrawal, the gap between their functional skill level and that which is required to successfully navigate the external world becomes wider. Consequently, over time individuals with SzPD tend to regress even further leading to an overall cycle of decline. This over time can give way to depersonalization and a loss of affect. Nevertheless, within their mindset they may hold a sense of superiority and even demonstrate aspects of narcissism (Guntrip, 1968). This too is a manifestation of their inner-directed focus as they are not comparing themselves to the external world as most do, but rather, conceptualize themselves as the master of their own internal domain. Consequently, disparities between their outward appearance and their internal self can be quite prominent. While an individual may be very passive and shy outwardly, they may for example view themselves as a great romantic internally and highly desired by potential partners (Akhtar, 1987; Guntrip, 1968).

Biological Correlates

The biological origins and contributions to the development of SzPD are not well understood as they are significantly understudied. Genetic predisposition has been reported. Similar to schizotypal disorder, increased rates of SzPD have been reported in first-degree relatives of patients with schizophrenia (Kendler, Myers, Torgersen, Neale, & Reichborn-Kjennerud, 2007). Recall that in comparison to StPD and SzPD, PPD has shown a greater correlation to family history of delusional disorders than schizophrenia, even though some still consider PPD a schizophrenia spectrum disorder whereas others refer to it as a delusional spectrum disorder. This contention has led some to simply refer to the Cluster A grouping as prepsychotic spectrum disorders.

From a neurobiological standpoint, abnormalities in opiate, oxytocin, and dopaminergic signaling have been proposed as a possible etiological factor (Depue, 2009). This has stemmed from the research demonstrating the role of opiates and dopamine in reward dependence. Reward dependence was originally defined as a heritable tendency to respond intensely to signals of reward, particularly signals of social approval (Cloninger, 1993). An individual's capacity to experience satisfaction and reward in response to social closeness underlies the ability to maintain interpersonal relationships and social organization. The neurobiology underlying bonding and attachment is thought to involve the endogenous opiate system (Depue, 2009). Opiate neurons originating in the arcuate nucleus in the hypothalamus have broad-reaching projections both within the central nervous system and systemically including the VTA and NAC (Depue, 2009). Other brain regions hypothesized to be involved include the amygdala, anterior insula, and ACC. Reward dependence is mediated mainly through the μ-opiate receptor. Animals will self-administer opiates in a dose-dependent manner, which supports their role in reward and reinforcement. Animal studies have also demonstrated that μ-receptor agonists increase maternal social interaction, grooming, licking, lactation, and sexual activity. The rewarding and reinforcing effects of opiates may be mediated via arcuate nuclear projections to the VTA and NAC (Depue, 2009). The location of these projections is similar to that observed in the dopaminergic reward pathway. To date, no studies have examined the role of opiates in these patient populations. Reward dependence may be further mediated by oxytocin. Animal studies have shown that distress induced by social isolation can be decreased with oxytocin administration. As mentioned, oxytocin has been shown to be involved in several animal behaviors involved in social bonding (Depue, 2009). Despite the theoretical basis, no studies have examined the role of oxytocin in this patient population.

Blum and colleagues (1997) used a combination of the DRD_2, DAT_1, and DβH B_1 gene polymorphisms by way of multivariate disorder regression analysis and were able to account for roughly 7.6% of the genetic variance, which they felt might be anticipated if there are multiple genes and other factors like gender involved in the manifestation of the disorder. When taking into consideration the limitations inherent to their low sample size, the authors suggested these results indicated a role of dopamine in SzPD. The prevalence of SzPD is fairly low. Whether this reflects a true epidemiologic phenomenon or the lower likelihood of SzPD patients seeking clinical help is unknown. Regardless, the low sample size is an issue that commonly impedes studies.

However, it could be the case that abnormalities in opiate, oxytocin, and dopaminergic signaling leads to a diminished reward experience for social interaction and thus, over time, individuals do not seek out such interactions (Blum et al., 1997; Blum, Cull, Braverman, Comings, 1996a; Blum, Sheridan, Wood, Braverman, Chen, et al., 1996b).

Neuropsychological Presentation

As is seen within the realm of neurobiology, there is a dearth of studies looking at the neuropsychological features associated with SzPD. A study by Wolff and Barlow (2006) was the lone article that could be found that seemed to appropriately address the subject matter. In their study, they compared children and adolescents who seemed to meet the diagnostic criteria for SzPD to children and adolescents with high-functioning autism as well as normal controls. Their justification for using children and adolescents, aside from being part of a child psychiatry department, was that the concept of SzPD suggests an enduring pattern of behavior and cognition that is likely developmental in nature. The results revealed that participants diagnosed with SzPD demonstrated deficits in digit span, free auditory recall, visual memory and retention, and visual association. Children with SzPD did not demonstrate tendencies toward perseveration or repetition. Overall, on the WISC, children with SzPD demonstrated a significantly wider scatter on subtest performance than did normal controls but less so than children with autism. When it came to auditory recall, they seemed not to benefit as much in recall from meanings that were provided compared to normal controls. The authors felt this reflected their preoccupations with their inner world rather than with the need to make sense of their environment. In regard to outcomes on performance subtests, such as the Picture Arrangement Task, children with SzPD scored especially poorly. This outcome is salient because the task requires them to appreciate logical, temporal sequences of events and their outcomes. Consistency was seen between their functional outcomes on this task and their measured capacities in behavioral domains. Specifically, when it came to their use of emotional constructs to describe people, they tended to introduce a greater frequency of emotional irrelevancies. They tended to use fewer emotional constructs than both normal controls and children with autism. For example, when describing their mother and other emotionally significant people, they tended to describe their clothes and physical appearance as opposed to describing their character, actions, or even their emotional presentation consistent with a detachment and concreteness in social relationships.

Collectively, these outcomes could be explained by dysfunctions of a prefrontal and temporal-limbic origin. Tasks investigating working memory were not incorporated, but it may be reasonably presumed that this could pose an area of potential dysfunction. Similarly, executive dysfunction could serve as an additional area of impairment, but empirical evidence to support this has not yet been sought.

CLUSTER B DISORDERS

As a group, Cluster B personality disorders are the personality disorders most frequently seen in psychiatric patients (Coid, Yang, Tyrer, Roberts, & Ullrich, 2006; Torgersen, Kringlen, & Cramer, 2001; Zimmerman et al., 2005; Zimmerman, Chelminski, & Young, 2008). They present with higher rates of comorbid Axis I disorders, long-term impairment, societal costs, and lower quality of life (Moran et al., 2000; Soeteman, Hakkaart-van Roijen, Verheul, & Busschbach, 2008; Soeteman, Verheul, & Busschbach, 2008). Characteristically, Cluster B personality disorders present with features of impulsiveness, aggressiveness, unstable affective regulation, and poor emotional processing, leading to these individuals being described as overly dramatic or emotional. As a group, the Cluster B personality disorders have likely received the greatest attention empirically. Admittedly, much of the focus here has been placed on BPD and ASPD. With this attention has come refinement of our understanding not only of the behavioral and emotional features that characterize the disorders but also underlying neurobiological features and resulting neuropsychological sequelae. This discussion is heavily weighted to BPD and ASPD given the disparity in available literature between these presentations and both narcissistic and histrionic personality disorders.

Although discussion is offered specific to each disorder, research has suggested group characteristics from both biological and neuropsychological standpoints. Clinical features suggest that Cluster B personality disorders are characterized by high novelty seeking and extremes in harm avoidance and reward dependence (Cloninger 1987). Novelty seeking is defined as a heritable tendency to engage in exploration of novel stimuli. It is also characterized by impulsive decision making, intense responses to cues for potential rewards, and active avoidance of frustration. Individuals high in novelty seeking tend to be impulsive, exploratory, fickle, excitable, quick-tempered, and extravagant. Generally, they engage quickly in new activities, but are easily bored (Cloninger 1987). Harm avoidance is defined as a heritable tendency to respond intensely to potential aversive stimuli (Cloninger 1987). Individuals high in harm avoidance tend to worry excessively about potential negative outcomes and experience high levels of negative affect. Those low in harm avoidance may frequently act recklessly with minimal attention to consequences. ASPD has been associated with high novelty seeking, low harm avoidance, and low reward dependence. BPD has been associated with both high novelty seeking and harm avoidance, which contributes to the erratic and conflicting behavior often observed. HPD has been associated with high novelty seeking, low harm avoidance, and high reward dependence.

Harm avoidance is thought to be mediated by interactions between serotonin pathways, the central corticotrophin releasing hormone system, and the peripheral glucocorticoid system (Cloninger & Svrakic, 2009; Depue, 2009). Numerous researchers have identified a link between low serotonin activity and aggressive behavior, which is indicative of individuals with low harm avoidance. Several genetic polymorphisms involving serotonin receptors, the serotonin transporter, and tryptophan hydroxylase (the rate limiting enzyme in 5HT synthesis) have been identified and linked with low serotonergic activity (Cloninger & Svrakic, 2009). Abnormalities in monoamine oxidase (MAO) have also been reported, with Cluster B patients showing a higher prevalence of the low activity variant MAO_A-LPR isoform than controls. MAO_A is the prevailing isoform in the CNS and critically involved in the metabolism of monoamine neurotransmitters, including serotonin and, to a lesser extent, norepinephrine and dopamine. If one thinks about the role these neurotransmitters play in cognition and behavioral and emotional regulation, one can imagine the potential for an array of functional impairments resulting from altered transmitter metabolism. Disruptions in these neurotransmitter systems have been associated with hyperactivity, disinhibition, addictive tendencies, hypersexuality, aggression, and mental retardation (Brunner et al., 1993; Murphy et al., 1990).

Anatomically, Cluster B personality disorders are most associated with abnormalities of frontal and temporal regions, with specific anomalies attributed but not limited to the orbitofrontal cortex (OFC), dorsolateral cortex, ventromedial cortex, insula, and limbic system (e.g., amygdala). The serotonergic system has modulating effects on the amygdala, which is thought to mediate fear responses to actual and perceived threats. Serotonergic projections from the ACC inhibit amygdala activation, and individuals rated high in harm avoidance (HA) were shown to have reduced amygdala-ACC connections. Individuals high in HA are noted to have amygdala hyperactivity in response to environmental stimuli (Cloninger & Svrakic, 2009). Glucocorticoid projections from the central and extended amygdala extend to several brain regions involved in emotion, memory, and autonomic arousal, including the hippocampus, hypothalamus, and locus ceruleus (Depue, 2009). Serotonin modulates the central and peripheral glucocorticoid system, which is activated in both acute and chronic stress via enhancing expression of glucocorticoid receptors and therefore facilitating negative feedback (Depue, 2009). Deficits in serotonin activity can therefore result in decreased negative feedback and heightened glucocorticoid activity in response to an environmental stressor.

Associations have also been made between prefrontal systems and impulsivity. Much of this has arisen from lesion studies such as those occurring as a result of traumatic brain injury. The frontal lobes and temporal poles demonstrate a higher propensity for injury given their proximity and orientation to the cranial fossa. As a result of trauma to prefrontal regions, increased impulsivity and poor behavioral control is often seen (Damasio, 1994). Consequently, prefrontal dysfunction has been suggested as the origin of impulsivity in Cluster B personality disorders. Disorder specific features are discussed subsequently.

Behaviorally, the Cluster B personality disorders demonstrate clinical overlap with bipolar disorders. Both bipolar and cluster B personality disorders share various clinical features, impulsivity being the most commonly reported feature (Henry, Mitropoulou, New, Koenigsberg, Silverman, & Siever, 2001; Fan & Hassel, 2008). These shared features have led some to suggest the inclusion of Cluster B personality disorders as part of the bipolar spectrum similar to the way Cluster A personality disorders have been suggested as being part of the schizophrenia or delusional spectra (Henry et al., 2001; Perugi & Akiskal, 2002; Swann, Lijffijt, Lane, Steinberg, & Moeller, 2009). Not surprisingly, research has demonstrated a relatively high comorbidity of Cluster B personality disorders and bipolar disorder (Fan & Hassell, 2008; Gunter et al., 2008; Mueser, Crocker, Frisman, Drake, Covell, & Essock, 2006). Clinically, this becomes more problematic because features of addiction and suicidal ideation in relation to bipolar disorder present at greater rates and severity when individuals present with a concurrent personality disorder (Kay, Altshuler, Ventura, & Mintz, 2002; Garno, Goldberg, Ramirez, & Ritzler, 2005; Swann, Dougherty, Pazzaglia, Pham, Steinberg, & Moeller, 2005).

Functionally, studies have fairly consistently associated a variety of neuropsychological deficits with Cluster B personality disorders. Again, the vast majority of studies have been with ASPD and BPD. Nevertheless, the consensus has suggested that compared with healthy controls, deficits corresponding with prefrontal-temporal processes are commonly found (Morgan & Lilienfeld 2000; Dolan & Park, 2002; Bazanis et al., 2002). This corresponds with difficulties in a variety of specific deficits, with executive dysfunction and memory issues being the most commonly cited. Reversal learning, as exemplified by performance on the Iowa Gambling Task (IGT), has also been seen across the Cluster B disorders (Ruocco et al., 2009). The authors reported, "It is possible that these patients have a selective difficulty with flexible learning, particularly in situations which present salient reward and punishment contingencies." As is the case regarding neurobiological features, specific neuropsychological findings are presented in the following as they correspond with individual disorders within this cluster.

Antisocial Personality Disorder (ASPD)

ASPD is one of the most studied personality disorders. Although ASPD is the recognized term, as set forth by the *DSM-IV-TR* (APA, 2000), the disorder and its core features has also been referred to as psychopathy, sociopathy, or dissocial personality disorder. Relative interest in the presentation is seen both within the scientific community as well as in mainstream society. Regarding the former, interest has been generated by the core features of the disorder, which deviate from normalcy to such a degree that individuals violate societal and interpersonal rules through means of violence and aggression, property damage, truancy, and so forth (Dishion & Patterson, 2006). Although only presenting in approximately 1% of the general population, the presentation is estimated to account for nearly 25% of prisoners and 15% of substance abusers, making it a prominent public issue (Hare, 1991, 2003; Alterman and Cacciola, 1991; Alterman et al., 1998). From a mainstream society standpoint, ASPD has likely been portrayed in more movies than any other personality disorder. Interests in serial killers or other extreme deviants, which constitutes a small portion of this grouping, has long held the interest of the media and society as a whole as individuals seek to understand and get a glimpse of these individuals which society views as "evil" at their core. Again, although these extremes of the disorder is what mainstream society would likely think of when considering ASPD, this is only a small portion of the holistic group. The features and characteristics of the disorder are more generalized and manifest in varying ways.

Clinical Features

The *DSM-IV-TR* (APA, 2000, p. 701) reports the essential feature of ASPD as being a "pervasive pattern of disregard for, and violation of, the rights of others that begins in childhood or early adolescence and continues into adulthood." As suggested previously and outlined in the diagnostic criteria, ASPD presents with a combination of antisocial behavior (acts that purposely violate rules and the rights of other, aggression resulting in interpersonal harm, or property damage) and psychopathic personality features (shallow affect, manipulative; Cooke, Michie, & Hart, 2005). There is a general lack of emotional responsiveness or experience of social events, which leads to a detached, predatory style as a means of meeting the person's own needs without concern of consequences or the potential of harm to others (Patrick, 2001). Although some describe ASPD as a disorder without psychosis or anxiety (Lijffijt et al., 2009), others have suggested that anxiety, through its relation with behavioral inhibition, at least early on, serves as a mediator of antisocial behaviors (Kerr et al., 1997). Others have discussed anxiety as precursor to depression (Burke et al., 2005), which itself contributes to the development of antisocial behaviors. Admittedly, results have been mixed and at best, some have suggested a nondirectional link between these traits and the development of antisocial features (Diamantopoulou, Verhulst, & van der Ende, 2010) in which possible irritability and hopelessness that stems from depression contributes to a reduced concern or indifference to the consequences of antisocial behaviors (Kasen et al., 2001). Still, one might argue that the perception of "anxiety" in childhood could be otherwise described as early signs of emotional dysregulation and the emergence of "depression" may be the misperception of developing callousness and affective flattening.

Although diagnosis is not permitted until 18 years of age, making it the only disorder that has such a concrete age restriction, individuals present with a diagnostic history of oppositional defiant disorder or conduct disorder originating in childhood and adolescence with the latter arising prior to age 15, representing a requisite of diagnosis. Still, only about 25% of children and adolescents presenting with conduct disorder are eventually diagnosed as having ASPD (APA, 2000). Dishion and Patterson (2006) report that both ASPD in adults and antisocial traits in adolescents demonstrate a childhood onset of aggression and disruptive behaviors. Loeber and colleagues (2000) summarized ASPD as a culmination of the combination of behavioral and affective problems that can be traced back to adolescence and early childhood (Diamantopoulou et al., 2010).

The fact that only 25% of adolescents with conduct disorder are eventually diagnosed with ASPD has been attributed to the failure of clinicians to recognize other disorders that are causing disruptive behavior (Lewis et al., 1984), to transient increases in stressors that result in children with oppositional defiant disorder transiently increasing the degree of their disruptiveness (Cantwell & Baker, 1989), and to changes in the child's environment leading to dispelling of the features (Lahey, Waldman, & McBurnett, 1999). Differentiation has been made based on the longevity of the features from a developmental standpoint. Greater heritability is associated with what Moffitt (1993) termed life-course persistent antisocial behavior, in which features develop in childhood and persist. These individuals present with greater degrees of aggressiveness and callousness as well as more pronounced neuropsychological deficits and parental psychopathology and are consequently diagnosed as having ASPD (Aguilar et al., 2000; Frick et al., 2003; Moffitt & Caspi, 2001). The other course Moffitt referred to was adolescence-limited: an emergence of antisocial features arising during adolescence but diminishing over time. A childhood-limited group has also been suggested (Odgers et al., 2008) with disruptive features declining prior to adolescence. In both these limited courses, a later diagnosis of ASPD would not be made.

The emergence of these externalizing features early on contributes to pronounced social and academic difficulties (Farrington, 1995). Of the various features that emerge in childhood and adolescence, aggression against others appears to be one of the traits most predictive of adult pathology and diagnosis of ASPD. Olweus (1979) reported previously that aggression presents similarly to IQ in regards to its longitudinal stability. Aggression and other antisocial behaviors readily constitute one of the most common referrals for youth mental health services in the United States (Kazdin et al., 2006). Consequently, the societal cost of ASPD starts in these early years with children and adolescents presenting with conduct disorder costing roughly $10,000+ more per year than peers without such features as a result of health care, academic, and juvenile justice services (Foster & Jones, 2005).

Frick and colleagues (1993) have reported antisocial behaviors manifest in both overt and covert ways. Overt features include physical and verbal aggression such as fighting and bullying, whereas covert features consist of behaviors rooted in deceitfulness such as lying and stealing. Although overt features are more likely to receive attention within the school and home, persistence of covert features remain highly predictive of longitudinal dysfunction (Lee & Hinshaw, 2004). Yet, when comparing overt and covert features, there appears to be a stronger genetic inheritability of overt features compared to covert (Burt, 2009). Manifestation of overt versus covert features may also be affected by gender with girls presenting with less aggressive tendencies compared to boys, but still operating fairly equally along covert lines (Moffitt et al., 2001; Silverthorn and Frick, 1999). However, given the tendency for overt features to receive greater attention as they constitute what seems to be a greater threat to others, boys tend to be diagnosed with conduct disorder as great as four times as much as girls (Cohen et al., 1993). This pattern holds true for children and adolescence in general with boys tending to meet conflict with their peers through more externalized and aggressive means whereas girls tend to take a more passive/covert path by attacking the individual's social standing by attempting to dismantle the individual's peer status through rumors and other verbal attacks. These discrepancies, however, may be age dependent, as Lee and colleagues (2007) have noted that in early childhood no significant difference exists between boys and girls in terms of their rate of physical aggression, but by middle childhood to preadolescence, girls become more covert in their aggressiveness. This causes an increase in the covert aggression of girls over time (Hipwell et al., 2002)

Again, not all roads of childhood and adolescent antisocial and conduct behavior lead to eventual diagnosis of ASPD. Richters (1997) has described the concepts of multifinality and equifinality, which in summary suggest that an array of factors influence these behaviors and are influenced by these behaviors. This multidirectional interaction of the environment in combination with the individual's genetic temperamental makeup creates the final byproduct, which in some cases equates to ASPD. In summation, the development of ASPD may depend on a biological predisposition and environmental factors that promote stability of the antisocial features. Such factors include attachment, parental involvement, and peer status (Shaw et al., 1998; Campbell, 1995; Pettit, Bates, & Dodge, 1993; McFadyen-Ketchum, Bates, Dodge, & Pettit, 1996;. Gardner, 1994; Deater-Deckard, 2001; Dishion & Piehler, 2007; Dodge, Bates, & Petit, 1990).

Although aggression, lying, and other overt and covert features receive the greatest attention when conceptualizing ASPD, emotional state and responsiveness should not be underestimated. Individuals with ASPD present with a callousness that is a cornerstone of the disorder. If an individual can think about committing a wrong against someone, the consideration itself can lead to emotional reactivity ranging from fear of potential consequences (e.g., legal punishment, social detriment) and what could be termed empathic foresight, in other words, imagining the harm physically, emotionally, and so on, experienced by the individual(s) to be acted against. This empathy serves as an inhibitory mechanism. Consequently, if this is not experienced, as is the case in the callousness of ASPD, one may suggest a big wall that keeps an individual away from those inappropriate behaviors has been removed. Truly, empathy, at its core, promotes social affiliation and prosocial behavior, and its absence is consistently correlated with antisocial behavior (Enebrink, Andershed, & Langstrom, 2005. Beyond aggression, callousness and unemotional traits may be the best predictor of which children and adolescents will continue to demonstrate antisocial features (Frick, Cornell, Barry, Bodin, & Dane, 2003). Some have even suggested that this callousness is the key ingredient of ASPD. Violence and aggression may characterize an act, but empathy is what prevents the foot from pushing down on the pedal. It is this absence of empathy (callousness) that impedes the decision-making process that would otherwise steer the individual away from committing these acts (Kimonis, Frick, Fazekas, & Loney, 2006; Shirtcliff et al., 2009). This callousness may be partially promoted by environmental experiences but has also been linked to biological mechanisms in the form of under-arousal. Additionally, dysfunction of self-regulation, emotional regulation, and neurocognitive control contributes to this process. The summative conclusion of these neurobiological findings suggests a physiological dysfunction as a major source of ASPD. Yet, it is difficult to determine to what extent the neurological picture is innate and what is itself shaped by the environment and experience.

Biological Correlates

Although the origins of ASPD cannot be explained by biological factors alone, the literature is rich with links to possible genetic, structural, chemical, and other physiological factors (Raine, Baker, & Liu, 2006; Raine & Yang, 2006).

Genetically, although there is the expected variability in outcomes across studies, examination of the heritability of antisocial behavior has resulted in estimations of moderate heritability falling between 30% and 60% across twin and adoption studies (Blonigen et al., 2003, 2006; Rhee & Waldman, 2002). Unexplained variance is consistent with research that suggests that ASPD is the by-product of environmental experiences acting on a genetic diathesis (Cadoret, Yates, Troughton, Woodworth, & Stewart, 1995; Caspi et al., 2002). Early thoughts on ASPD often attributed the etiology of ASPD entirely to maltreatment and abuse. This has since been refuted. Caspi and colleagues (2002) conducted a longitudinal study over the course of 18 years to evaluate the potential for the development of antisocial behavior and the potential contribution of environmental experiences (e.g., maltreatment) and genetic mediators, with benchmark assessments starting at age 3 and being done every 2 years up until age 15 and then every 3 years, concluding at the age of 21. Within their sample, they found 8% experienced "severe" maltreatment, 28% experienced "probable" maltreatment, and 64% experienced no maltreatment. The researchers found that a functional polymorphism in the gene occurring in the neurotransmitter metabolizing enzyme monoamine oxidase A (MAO_A) was found to moderate the effect of maltreatment significantly. Specifically, those with a low MAO_A activity genotype developed antisocial behavior at a significantly higher rate. Eighty-five percent of those with this genotype who had experienced maltreatment developed antisocial behavior. In comparison, those who had a high MAO_A activity genotype did not present with elevations in antisocial behavior in the presence of maltreatment. The implications of the study are twofold. First, it clearly demonstrates the interaction between biology and experiences. Second, it specifically suggests a role of MAO_A activity as a moderator of an individual's response to maltreatment and subsequent development of ASPD. MAO_A is the prevailing isoform in the CNS and is critically involved in the metabolism of monoamine neurotransmitters, including serotonin and, to a lesser extent, norepinephrine and dopamine. Regarding serotonin in particular, genes responsible for its regulation have been associated with aggression (i.e., 5-HT). Studies have been undertaken in both rodent and primate studies. For example, Holmes and colleagues (2002) reported that increased aggression in mice was associated with lower levels of 5-HT in limbic and hypothalamic regions. In the reverse, elevated 5-HT transmission is associated with increased aggression and suicidal ideation among depressed, anxious, bipolar, and psychotic patients (Carrillo et al., 2009). 5-HT availability in the brain is regulated by *5-HTTLPR*, which is the serotonin transporter gene located on chromosome 17q12 and has particular influence over the amygdala (Lesch et al., 1996), accounting for approximately 10% of its activity (Munafò et al., 2008). Similar to studies with MAO_A , links have been made between *5-HTTLPR* and early environmental experience. Reif and colleagues (2007) found a significant relationship between childhood adversity and the *5-HTTLPR* genotype.

Functional disruptions of the hypothalamic-pituitary-adrenal (HPA) axis, amygdala, hippocampus, cerebellum, and left neocortex have all been associated with early maltreatment (Teicher et al., 2003), although the mechanism by which these functional alterations come about are unknown. Links have also been made between ASPD and abnormalities of the prefrontal cortex, temporal cortex, insula, and anterior/posterior cingulate gyrus (Kiehl, 2006; Raine & Yang, 2006).

The prefrontal region has received the greatest attention due to the role this region plays in behavioral control and inhibition and the linkage of personality changes following brain injury to this area. Deficits associated with antisocial behavior often follow patterns of lateralization. Yang and Raine (2009), in a meta-analysis, found a significant association between antisocial behaviors and lateralized prefrontal impairment. They indicated that increased antisocial behavior was significantly associated with structural and functional reductions in the right OFC, the right ACC, and the left dorsolateral prefrontal cortex (DLPFC). Similarly, while right-sided abnormalities of the OFC and ACC led to deficits in social conduct, emotional processing, personality, and decision-making in a study by Tranel and colleagues (2002), left-sided lesions carried no real deficits in these areas. Similar discrepancies are observed on lateralization of DLPFC impairment, with left-sided abnormalities contributing to potential antisocial constructs but not when the right is abnormal (Angrilli et al., 1999). The summation of these features leads to a general reduction of frontal lobe gray matter volume (Lyoo et al., 1998; Raine et al., 2000). Ventromedial (VM) abnormalities have not been consistently reported.

From a clinical symptom standpoint, lying and deception appears related to similar abnormalities of the OFC, VM, and DLPFC (Lee et al., 2005; Nunez, Casey, Egner, Hare, & Hirsch, 2005; Spence et al., 2001). Lying and deception in comparison is linked more with the ACC, thalamus, caudate nucleus, and insula (Nunez et al., 2005; Abe, Suzuki, Mori, Itoh, & Fujii, 2007; Kozel, Johnson, Mu, Grenesko, Laken, & George, 2005). Additional studies have also implicated the temporal lobes and parietal lobes without greater specificity than a general regional indictment (Kozel et al., 2005). When it comes to a lack of empathy or callousness, the insula and ACC have been the most commonly reported sites of dysfunction (Fehr & Rockenbach, 2004; Kiehl et al., 2001; Sterzer et al., 2007). ACC hypoactivity has simultaneously been associated with low basal cortisol levels, which together may well explain the lack of a stimulated stress response and thus physiological capacity for callousness as well as a general underarousal of the physical system (Baker et al., 2009). This lack of system arousal corresponds with an altered resting heart rate level, which in a meta-analysis by Ortiz and Raine (2004) was reported as a commonly replicated risk factor for individuals with antisocial behaviors. Given that the autonomic nervous system serves as the propelling force behind the naturalistic retreat from aversive and dangerous situations, this permits individuals to face threat without fear.

The striatum contributes to reward seeking and impulsivity and has been reported as having increased volume in ASPD (Barkataki, Kumari, Das, Taylor, & Sharma, 2006). Finally, reductions of the amygdala have been linked with lowered fear conditioning, emotional recognition, and even general cooperativeness (Birbaumer et al., 2005; Rilling et al., 2007; Sterzer et al., 2005).

Neuropsychological Presentation

The neuropsychological profile associated with ASPD can be generally defined as frontal in nature. Not surprisingly, given their diminished prefrontal activity, individuals with ASPD tend to exhibit deficits in executive functioning (Morgan & Lilienfeld, 2000; Dolan & Park, 2002; Bazanis et al., 2002), including decision making (Bechara et al., 2000) and perseveration (Newman et al., 1998). However, in some areas of executive functioning, individuals with ASPD may actually demonstrate heightened capabilities, such as planning (Blair et al., 2006, Dvorak-Bertsch et al., 2007; Hiatt et al., 2004, Vitale et al., 2007).

Prefrontal dysfunction also serves as the basis for deficits in cognitive flexibility commonly noted in ASPD (Dolan & Park, 2002; Morgan & Lilienfeld, 2000), although mixed results are seen across the literature in the realms of attention and working memory, as well as other aspects of executive functioning (Rogers, 2006). Mol and colleagues (2009) found no difference between ASPD and normal controls on the WCST, which is a classic test of prefrontal functioning.

Impairments in error monitoring and task switching have been associated with the disorder (Kiehl et al., 2000a). Noted deficits in response inhibition, modulation, and reversal are also commonly seen (Kiehl et al., 2000b; Lapierre et al., 1995; Mitchell et al., 2002; Newman & Schmitt, 1998. Individuals with ASPD may have inconsistent difficulty on measures such as the Go/No-Go test, Iowa Gambling task, and Porteus Mazes. Outcomes on the Stoop Color-Word test have been insignificant, with no indication of interference on the classic version or the counting number Stroop tasks (Blair et al., 2006; Dvorak-Bertsch et al., 2007; Hiatt et al., 2004).

Memory deficits, both in verbal and visual capacities, have been commonly noted and linked with lower temporolimbic activity, particularly in the hippocampus (Morgan & Lilienfeld 2000; Dolan & Park, 2002; Bazanis et al., 2002). Selective difficulties are also noted in recall of emotional words due to a reduced capacity for processing emotional words (Loney et al., 2003). This likely stems from dysfunction of the amygdala, which associates emotionality to memories, thereby increasing contextual recall, possibly explaining the emotional disconnect of individuals with ASPD, which serves as a foundation for many of their clinical features including diminished fear and defensive response (Sutton et al., 2002). Individuals with ASPD demonstrate deficits in processing facial affect (Woodbury-Smith et al., 2005). No difference was found in blink-reflex magnitude in processing positive and negative stimuli in individuals with ASPD (Levenston et al., 2000). However, others have not found deficits in memory of affective stimuli. Kiehl and colleagues (2001) found that individuals with ASPD had better memory for affective stimuli compared to non-affective stimuli, similar to what is found in healthy controls. This is not to suggest, however, that their perception of affective context is to the same degree of healthy controls. Furthermore, deficits have been noted in conjunction with ASPD even in the processing of neutral stimuli (Hiatt, Schmitt, & Newman, 2004; Vitale, Brinkley, Hiatt, & Newman, 2007). Kosson (1996) suggested this global decrease in processing may be thus best explained as a reduced attentional capacity or breadth.

Language and communication serve as another area in which abnormalities have been found in the performance of those with ASPB. Jutaie and colleagues (1987) noted in their study of event-related potentials (ERP) that ASPD presented with an atypical lateralization of the cerebral hemispheres in relation to language functioning. Additional studies have specified difficulties are most noticeable when performing semantic processing tasks (Gillstrom & Hare, 1988). Hare and Jutai (1988) noted individuals with ASPD demonstrated more errors in abstract semantic categorization compared to normal controls. In another study, ASPD was associated with particular deficits in abstract information processing and discrimination that were tied with late negativity maximal waveforms over the frontal midline sites (Kiehl et al., 1999a, 1999b). Finally, individuals with ASPD demonstrate deficient processing of emotional language and stimuli (Blair et al., 2002; Day & Wong, 1996; Herve et al., 2003). Skin conductance studies previously undertaken showed a lack of response in individuals with ASPD when presented with loud noxious tones (Hare et al., 1978), pain associated with needle insertion (Hare, 1978), and seeing disturbing photos of mutilated faces (Mathis, 1970). Their lack of arousal change to stimuli may also explain group difficulties in orienting processes (Hare, 1978).

Borderline Personality Disorder (BPD)

Clinical Features

BPD is characterized by persistent problems with emotional , behavioral, cognitive, and interpersonal functioning (APA, 2000). Paris (2007) notes that BPD is a heterogeneous, multifaceted condition characterized by various domains of features including instability, impulsivity, instability in interpersonal relationships, and cognitive defects, each of which may reflect a different diatheses from a psychobiological perspective. Emotional lability, deliberate self-harm, cognitive dissociation, substance abuse, risky sexual behavior, chaotic interpersonal relationships, and disrupted eating behaviors can all present in association with BPD (APA, 2000; Frankenburg & Zanarini, 2004; Skodol et al., 2005). Additionally, BPD is strongly linked with suicidal ideation and attempts, with approximately 10% of this grouping committing suicide, which is 50 times higher than the rate seen in the general population (APA, 2000).

Epidemiological research suggests BPD affects from 1%–6% of the general population, approximately 10% of those who seek outpatient services, and as many as 20% of those who undergo inpatient treatment (Grant et al., 2008). No significant difference in prevalence has been reported between males and females (Grant, Chou, Goldstein, Huang, & Stinson, 2008). The possible biological roots of this disorder are best exemplified by the fact that clinical features can be observed as early as late childhood or adolescence (Miller, Muehlenkamp, & Jacobson, 2008) although rarely diagnosed prior to 18 years of age. However, over time, improvement can be seen, with some returning to a state of normal functioning by 40 years of age (Paris, 2002). Furthermore, BPD demonstrates increased comorbidity with several Axis I disorders including mood, anxiety, and substance use disorders as well as eating disorders (APA, 2000; Zanarini et al., 1998; Trull, Sher, Minks-Brown, Durbin, & Burr, 2000).

Biological Correlates

For many years, BPD was viewed as a functional disorder that served as the by-product of environmental experiences. The biological movement, with emerging interests of genetic contributions and neurological correlates, brought a revisiting of this hypothesis. Torgersen and colleagues (2000) in their assessment of the potential genetic contributions to BPD then found an inheritability profile of approximately 65%. Today, the foundations of BPD is best conceptualized by Linehan's (1993) biosocial theory, although other theories exist (Fonagy, Target, & Gergely, 2000; Judd & McGlashan, 2003). Linehan suggests BPD is result of specific environmental influences acting on biological vulnerabilities that correspond with broad dysregulation of emotional responding mechanisms (e.g., limbic system). Cicchetti (2008) specifies that mechanisms of any aspect of developmental psychopathology include an integration of genetic, neural, behavioral, familial, and social factors. Consistent with Cicchetti's suggestion, the biological dysfunction of BPD crosses structural, neurochemical, and genetic lines.

Anatomically, abnormal volume in the fronto-limbic regions appear to underlie the affective symptoms characteristic of BPD (Soloff et al., 2008). Whereas Lyoo and colleagues (1998) previously reported general reductions in overall frontal lobe volume, additional studies have since refined the anatomical picture of BPD. Tebartz van Elst et al. (2003) initially identified specific volumetric reduction in both the left OFC and the right ACC but later found no difference using voxel-based morphometric MRI (Rusch et al., 2003). Additionally, dysfunctions have been cited in relation to the DLPFC, hippocampus, and amygdala. Driessen and colleagues (2000) found that the hippocampus and amygdala may be as much as 16% smaller in individuals with BPD. Tebartz van Elst and colleagues (2007) found a significant reduction in amygdala volume in conjunction with increased left amygdala creatine concentration. Others have not found such volumetric reductions in relation to the amygdala (Brambilla, Soloff, Sala, Nicoletti, Keshavan, & Soares, 2004). These authors also failed to find differences in the caudate, temporal lobes, DLPFC, and total brain volumes in BPD patients. They did find diminished hippocampal volume in addition to increased putamen volume

The undersized prefrontal cortex is thought to potentially be unable to fully regulate the limbic system (de la Fuente et al., 1997). This leads to overactivity of the limbic system as exemplified by patients with BPD demonstrating hypersensitivity to emotionally based or fearful stimuli and situations (Donegan, Sanislow, Blumberg, Fulbright, & Lacadie, 2003; Herpertz, Dietrich, Wenning, Krings, & Erberich, 2001). For example, Herpetz and colleagues (2001) found heightened amygdala activity in response to negatively valanced pictures. Donegan and colleagues (2003) found a similar hyperactivity of the amygdala to facial expressions of emotion. The ACC also appears to exhibit deficits in its modulation of emotional responsiveness. Functionally, BPD is associated with hypometabolism of glucose in both the frontal cortex and the limbic system. Reduced uptake of glucose by the OFC is associated with diminished regulation of impulsive behavior (Soloff, Meltzer, Becker, Greer, Kelly, & Constantine, 2003).

Some have suggested the reductions in hippocampal volume may be mediated by an elevated activity of the HPA axis (Sapolsky, 2000) and the negative impact of a state of stress on the structure. Extensive research supports the notion that early abuse and neglect mediates volumetric reductions of the hippocampus and BPD (Feder, Robbins, & Ostermeyer, 2003). Although the link between early trauma effects on the developing brain and the hippocampus in particular is not fully understood, the predominance of glucocorticoid receptors in the hippocampus is believed to make it susceptible to stress effects that inhibit its development (Sapolsky, McEwen, & Rainbow, 1983). Again, this path may go through the HPA axis, which itself is made prone to hyperactivity following childhood abuse or maltreatment leading to increased ACTH and cortisol response (Rinne et al., 2002). Early stress may also impede hemispheric lateralization, adversely affecting integration of the right and left hemispheres (Schiffer, Teicher, & Papanicolaou, 1995) and may explain why splitting is used by patients with BPD as a defense mechanism (Gabbard, 2005).

From a neurochemical standpoint, serotonin, dopamine, and vasopressin have received the most attention, although acetylcholine, noradrenaline, and gamma-aminobutyric acid have also been discussed. The relationship of these chemicals have been mostly discussed in relation to behavioral genetics, although studies have been fraught with methodological errors that call much of these results into question. As suggested, Torgesen and colleagues (2000) have likely most thoroughly demonstrated the relative contribution of genetics in the manifestation of BPD. In their study of 92 monozygotic and 129 dizygotic twins, 69% of the variance in symptoms was attributable to additive genetic effects and 31% of the variance was attributed to non-shared environmental effects, with no shared environmental effects. Additionally, a 38% concordance rate among monozygotic twins and an 11% concordance rate among dizygotic twins was found.

Associations along genetic lines has also found links between 5-HT candidate genes. Greenberg and colleagues (2000) found a relationship between BPD and polymorphisms of the *5-HTT* transporter gene that appears to correspond with fewer *5-HTT* platelet-binding sites. This has been reiterated by Retz et al. (2004), who specifically reported potential connections with the short allele of the gene-linked polymorphic region of the serotonin transporter (5-HTTLPR). This had been hypothesized by Lyons-Ruth and colleagues (2007) when they demonstrated an association between the short allele and BPD in young adults with lower socioeconomic status, suggesting the combination of this genetic factor and environmental stressors contribute to disorder manifestation. The 5-HTTLPR polymorphism causes a faster uptake of 5-HT, leading to depleted serotonin levels within the synaptic clefts and in turn increased risk of depression, particularly following maltreatment as a child (Caspi et al., 2002). Of further interest is Hariri and colleagues' (2002) findings that this particular polymorphism corresponds with hyperactivity of the amygdala when encountering fearful stimuli. Aggression, affective instability, mood disorders, suicidal ideation, and self-injury have been linked with polymorphisms of 5-HT (Gurvits, Koenigsberg, & Siever, 2000; Kamali, Oquendo, & Mann, 2002).

Discussed in conjunction with low 5-HT activity is associated tendency for high vasopressin activity in the CNS (Coccaro, Kavoussi, Hauger, Cooper, & Ferris, 1998). Delville and colleagues (1996) have proposed these systems' combined interaction serves to promote aggression. Additionally, MAO_A, with its propensity for interacting with environmental experiences, particularly child maltreatment, has also been linked with aggression and may together with 5-HT and vasopressin create aggressive tendencies (Caspi et al., 2002). Additionally, MAO_B has been associated with BPD (Zuckerman & Kulman, 2000). The noradrenergic (NE) system has also been proposed as being linked with BPD although direct links have not been associated with the disorder itself.

Similar to serotonin, dopamine has been associated with many of the emotional, behavioral, and cognitive features of BPD (Friedal, 2004) although studies are far more limited in quantity and refinement compared to that which has been done with serotonin. Joyce and colleagues (2006) have found a significant association between a polymorphism of the DAT (the 9-repeat allele of the DAT) and the presence of comorbid BPD in a sample of outpatients with major depressive disorder. They also suggested a link between arrangements of the DA transporter gene and the manifestation of BPD that can produce either decreased cortical dopaminergic activity associated with impulsivity or increased meso-limbic dopaminergic activity associated with psychotic-like features seen in the disorder. However, this same polymorphism as been linked with externalizing behaviors such as ADHD and conduct disorder (Kim, Kim, & Cho, 2006; Young et al., 2002). Given the greater consistency of impulsivity being seen across patients compared to psychotic-like features, a hypodopaminergic system seems more plausible, although less so than in ADHD given the absence of hyperactivity.

Finally, speculation about the role of oxytocin has gained increased attention in the literature of late, and preliminary data suggest that it may have a role in attenuating negative affect and facilitating emotional regulation (Simeon et al., 2011).

Neuropsychological Presentation

Several neuropsychological deficits have been reported in conjunction with BPD, with executive dysfunction constituting the most common finding. As suggested earlier, impulsivity is often observed behaviorally (Parker & Bagby, 1997; Stein, 1995). Cognitively, this has been noted in the realms of cognitive inhibition (Berlin & Rolls, 2004; Nigg, Silk, Stavro, & Miller, 2005; Rentrop et al., 2008), decision making and planning (Haaland & Landro, 2007; Kirkpatrick et al., 2007), and cognitive flexibility and fluency (Beblo et al., 2006; Dinn et al., 2004). Beyond this domain, verbal, visual, and auditory memory; attention; visual perception; visuomotor speed; visuospatial functioning; language; and cognitive inhibition deficits have also be noted (Beblo et al., 2006; Kirkpatrick et al., 2007; Monarch, Saykin, & Flashman, 2004; Posner et al., 2002; Swirsky-Sacchetti et al., 1993; Travers & King, 2005), although findings are admittedly inconsistent and may very well be due to clinical features of the sample studied (e.g., presence or absence of dissociative features). Additionally, neuropsychiatric abnormalities including neurological soft signs have been found in BPD patients (Stein et al., 1993; van Reekum, Conway, Gansler, White, & Bachman, 1993). Interestingly, these soft signs have been more prevalent on the left side, indicting right hemispheric dysfunction, and have been consistently linked with frontal lobe pathology and subsequent impairment of executive functioning (Stein et al., 1993).

Haaland and Landro (2009) completed one of the most comprehensive and methodologically sound studies of neuropsychological assessment with patients diagnosed with BPD with and without dissociative features, comparing them to normal controls and each other. Among their findings, executive functioning deficits were found between both clinical group subsets compared to normal controls. This was noted cumulatively across tasks, which included the Stroop test, Tower of London, WCST, Trail Making Test, Controlled Oral Word Association, and the Iowa Gambling Task. Further, dissociative traits were associated with significantly greater impairment in executive functioning. Beyond this domain, the authors found no other significant impairments associated with BPD without dissociative features in the areas of attention, working memory, verbal long-term memory, nonverbal long-term memory, or general cognitive functioning. When comparing BPD participants with and without dissociative traits, those with dissociative features performed significantly worse on measures of working memory, verbal long-term memory, and general cognitive functioning. When patients with BPD with dissociative features were compared to the healthy controls, global differences were seen across all domains. The findings from this study are thus twofold. First, executive function deficits are hallmarks of BPD compared to controls regardless of the presence of dissociative traits. Second, when BPD presents with dissociative traits, the extent of neuropsychological impairment becomes more severe and broad in scope when compared to controls and even to others with BPD without dissociative features. Travers and King (2005) completed a review of 14 neuropsychological studies of BPD, finding that 71% of the studies indicated significant impairment across a wide range of cognitive domains. Similarly, two other reviews have been completed. Niederhofer (2004) reported that in a review of 10 studies, BPD patients performed more poorly than healthy controls in attention, cognitive flexibility, learning, memory, planning, speeded processing, and visuospatial abilities. Niederhofer also noted that nonverbal functions were predominately affected and more strongly lateralized to the right hemisphere. Although LeGris and van Reekum (2006) noted that 83% of studies of BPD patients found impairments compared to healthy controls, they merely reported that this percentage included studies that found impairments in one or more cognitive domains.

Findings of executive dysfunction are not surprising when considering the aforementioned anatomical correlates of volumetric reductions of the prefrontal regions of the brain (Lyoo et al., 1998; Raine et al., 2000). Furthermore, the amygdala and limbic system may serve as an indirect source of this dysfunction. BPD is associated with hyperactivity of the amygdala. Whereas moderate activation of the amygdala can aid cognition (McGough, Roozendaal, & Cahill, 2000), over-activity in BPD impedes cognitive functioning within realms of executive control as well as areas of working memory (Lupien, Gillin, & Hauger, 1999).

When it comes to memory, mixed results abound. For example, although verbal memory deficits have been previously reported (Swirsky-Sacchetti et al., 1993), Beblo and colleagues (2006) did not find such deficits. As suggested by the more recent studies (Haaland & Landro, 2009), it may be the case that differences between studies could be attributed to differing ratios of BPD subjects with dissociation (higher memory impairment) versus BPD subject without dissociation (lower memory impairment).

Similarly, immediate memory spans and fluency measures are usually without impairment (Beblo et al., 2006; Dinn et al., 2004). Dinn and colleagues (2004) also revealed unimpaired verbal working and delayed memory performances. Although there are previous studies that found working and delayed memory deficits (O'Leary et al., 1991), again, the variability across studies may well be explained by the presence or absence of dissociative traits in participants. Visual memory tests, on the other hand, have been linked with BPD more readily and have been suggested as a manifestation of poor organizational skills (Ruocco, 2005).

Histrionic Personality Disorder (HPD)

Clinical Features

HPD is characterized by a pervasive pattern of excessive emotionality and attention seeking, beginning by early adulthood, which presents in a variety of contexts and situations (APA, 2000). The means by which they attempt to gain this attention can be varied and include behaving in a sexually provocative manner, being overly concerned with appearance, and acting in an overly dramatic manner such as in their greeting of others and telling stories. The pathological need for attention from others may well stem from low self-esteem and a need for affirmation about their social status and appeal. Consequently, individuals with HPD tend not to like when someone else is the center of attention and thus may try to one-up those around them.

Individuals with HPD need attention from others to feel good about themselves and are especially uncomfortable in situations in which someone else is the center of attention. They are often overly concerned with appearance as a means of drawing attention to themselves. In comparison to narcissistic personality disorder (NPD) in which individuals wish to only present a sense of superiority, individuals with HPD are willing to present themselves in an inferior light if it is necessary to obtain the desired amount of attention.

Prevalence rates suggest a relative occurrence between 0.2% (Samuels et al., 2002) and 1.8% (Grant et al., 2004) within the general population. Within the outpatient setting, occurrences are around 9.1% (Carter et al., 1999). There is also a significant potential for comorbidity of HPD with particular Axis I presentations. For example, roughly 20%–25% of individuals with HPD present with comorbid somatoform disorders (Garyfallos et al., 1999) while 15%–30% present with comorbid depression (Corruble et al., 1996). Substantial overlaps with BPD have led some to suggest that the two fall on the same spectrum, with the BPD being conceptualized as a more severe form of HPD (Kernberg, 1988). Higher comorbidity and overlap is also seen between HPD and the other Cluster B disorders.

Biological Correlates

From a genetic predisposition standpoint, HPD has demonstrated a heritability index of 0.67 (Torgersen et al., 2000). Beyond this, little is known about the underlying neurobiology of HPD either from a anatomical, chemical, or physiological standpoint. Cluster B disorders are associated with a MAO_A-LPR as well as anatomical abnormalities of the frontal and temporal regions. However, it is recognized that within these "cluster" studies there is often a predominance of BPD and ASPD relative to HPD and NPD. Although there is evidence suggesting a generalized picture of the anatomy of cluster B disorders, it would be a presumption to conclude that these systems are associated with HPD.

Neuropsychological Presentation

As is the case with biological correlates, the literature on the neuropsychological features of HPD is tremendously sparse, if not nonexistent. Given the involvement of frontal and temporal regions in other Cluster B personality disorders, one might assume that assessment deficits in executive functioning, attention, or memory impairments (working, verbal, visual, or auditory) would be found. Yet, without empirical investigation along these lines, this cannot be ascertained.

Narcissistic Personality Disorder (NPD)

Clinical Features

NPD represents a pervasive pattern of grandiosity, need for admiration, and lack of empathy (APA, 2000). Grandiosity is seen in the individual's self-perception of importance, superiority, or being special. They often present as cocky, prideful, and outspoken. Some have suggested a covert/shy variant of NPD, where the individual can inhibit his or her external portrayal of their distorted, grandiose self-concept. The overt NPD may suggest how much better he or she are compared to another person, whereas the covert will simply think it to him- or herself. Nevertheless, the old saying "actions speak louder than words" holds true, and even in the case of covert NPD, their true colors can be seen in their concern for others' feelings, rigidity to their own way of thinking, and affective response to things not going their way.

Individuals with NPD expect and to some extent demand attention and admiration. They have a nose-in-the-air approach to life, which in combination with their self-perception of importance leads them to view others as not worth their time, and thus, they are generally unwilling to recognize or concern themselves with the feelings of others. In reality, the disorder may be an overcompensation for poor and fragile self-esteem. The *DSM-IV-TR* (2000) acknowledges this as an associated feature along with sensitivity and intense reactions of humiliation, emptiness, or disdain to criticism or defeat, and vocational irregularities due to difficulties tolerating criticism or competition. NPD has been considered particularly resistant to change (Millon, 1981).

Prevalence rates within the general population range from more than 1% to just over 5% based on a combination of studies (Torgersen et al., 2001; Klein et al., 1995). These rates climb to 2%–16% within the clinical population (Gunderson, Ronningstam, & Smith, 1991). Gender differences have not been consistently found, with some reporting equal rates across sexes (Plakun, 1990), whereas the *DSM-IV-TR* (2000) suggests a greater prevalence in males, who account for 50%–75% of diagnoses. There is some tendency toward comorbidity with antisocial features (Gunderson & Ronningstam, 2001). Additionally, higher rates have been found in relation to BPD, depression, and specific substance abusers, although in this latter group, symptoms can be a residual effect of the substances themselves (e.g., cocaine; Sato et al., 1997; Turley et al., 1992). In fact, NPD presents as one of the most commonly occurring personality disorders among bipolar patients (Brieger, Ehrt, & Marneros, 2003). NPD has also shown associations with histrionic, antisocial, obsessive-compulsive, schizotypal, and borderline personality disorders (Fossati, Maffei, Bagnato, et al., 2000; Grilo, Anez, & McGlashan, 2002; Marinangeli, Butti, Scinto, et al., 2000; Grilo, Sanislow, & McGlashan, 2002).

There is also significant overlap between NPD and BPD. Both share a sensitivity to criticism and a sense of entitlement (Gunderson, 2001). Additionally, both demonstrate affective dysregulation, impulsivity, and instability in relationships (Holdwick et al., 1998). These many similarities have led some to suggest that the two fall along the same spectrum (Gunderson & Ronningstam, 2001) with inflated self-concept and grandiose features defining the NPD pole (Holdwick et al., 1998). NPD and ASPD share the characteristics of a lack of empathy and interpersonal exploitation (Blais et al., 1997).

As with other personality disorders, research has suggested a developmental trajectory for NPD with features being observed as early as childhood. Kernberg (1998) reported possessiveness, omnipotent control, grandiose features, self-absorption, and lack of empathy may all be observed as early as childhood and remain persistent over time, eventually being diagnosed as NPD, although many grow out of these early behaviors.

Biological Correlates

Torgersen and colleagues (2000) reported nearly 80% of the variation in NPD traits could be attributed to genetics whereas a heritability index of 0.45 has also been reported (Jang et al., 1996). Fonagy and colleagues (2003) suggested that the combination of genetic heritability and an incongruence between a child's emotional state and the caregiver's mirroring and misperception leads to the development of NPD. At the heart of the parent-child dysfunctional relationship as proposed by Fonagy and colleagues (2003), the child is attended to in an intense manner and used as a means of regulating the parents self-esteem themselves, yet not valued as their own individual.

Although from an anatomical or other physiological standpoint it might be assumed that NPD would have similarities with both BPD and ASPD, given a lack of empirical investigations into the matter, this would be purely hypothetical.

Neuropsychological Presentation

As with HPD, there is a lack of literature regarding the neuropsychological correlates of NPD. Again, given the prominent overlap between NPD and both BPD and ASPD, it is reasonable to expect similarities in neuropsychological functioning. Given that features of executive dysfunction are seen across the Cluster B disorders, it would seem likely that they would to some extent be seen in NPD as well, but this has not been established empirically. Similarly, additional deficits seen in these comparable disorders may well be deficient in NPD as well.

CLUSTER C DISORDERS

In discussing the Cluster C disorders, a different format must be followed due to the fact that no disorder that has received significant attention in the literature. Rather, the few investigations that have been undertaken tend to group the disorders as a whole. The dearth of literature within this group is particularly interesting given the fact that Cluster C disorders are the most prevalent personality disorders both in the general population and outpatient clinical population (Torgersen, Kringlen, & Cramer, 2001). Just as is the case with other personality disorders, the co-occurrence of Cluster C disorders with Axis I presentations is associated with poorer outcomes (Hardy et al., 1995; Reich & Vasile, 1993). As a group, individuals with Cluster C disorders are commonly viewed as anxious/nervous, overly cautious, fearful, or overly inhibited. Specific clinical features are discussed in the following in association with each specific disorder.

Biological Correlates and Neuropsychological Presentation

Cluster C disorders are characterized by high harm avoidance and low novelty seeking (Cloninger, 1987). What limited research is available suggests a potential role of the serotonergic system by way of polymorphisms of the serotonin transporter gene (*5-HTT*), specifically of 5-HTTLPR. Jacob and colleagues (2004) found that patients with a Cluster C diagnosis who were carriers of the 5-HTTLPR short allele exhibited higher scores for neuroticism and harm avoidance than noncarriers. The short allele is known to cause amygdala hyperactivity and thus has the potential to set into a motion a cascade of actions that causes increased anxiety. The hyperactivity of the amygdala, among other things, serves to activate the autonomic nervous system, which sets into motion the fight -or- flight response. Although this is advantageous in times of threat, continued activation serves to a create a persisting state of resting anxiety or nervousness or the potential for such. Not surprisingly, Jacob and colleagues (2004) found that carrying the low-activity 5-HTTLPR allele corresponded with increased anxiety and heightened amygdala activity. Previous studies have also revealed one or two copies of the low-activity short allele of 5-HTTLPR corresponds with greater neuronal activity of the amygdala (Hariri et al., 2002).

It has been suggested that coupling the low-activity short allele with reduced frontal activity that would otherwise hold overactivity of the amygdala in check may be a biological basis for developing Cluster C disorders (Davidson, 2002). Allelic variation in 5-HTT function has previously been found to account for 8% of the inherited variance in anxiety-related personality traits (Lesch, Bengel, Heils, Sabol, Greenberg, & Petri, et al., 1996). Still, it has been suggested that among all the personality disorders, cluster C is more strongly influenced by environmental experiences, which carry an impact on the CNS via epigenetics (Jacob et al., 2004). The literature on Axis I anxiety disorders has noted neurological anomalies including the septo-hippocampal circuit, the brain stem periaqueductal gray-medial hypothalamic circuit, the basal ganglia, the frontal-striatal circuitry, the hippocampus, the amygdala, the anterior cingulate cortex, and the prefrontal cortices. Given that anxiousness is a core feature across the Cluster C disorders, neuropsychological deficits would likely be in the areas of executive function, working memory, possibly attention, and memory dysfunction (both verbal and visual). Nevertheless, with no appropriate sample of research studies available for review, this can only be hypothesized.

Avoidant Personality Disorder (APD)

Clinical Features

According to the *DSM-IV-TR* (2000), APD is characterized by a pervasive pattern of social inhibition, feelings of inadequacy or inferiority, and hypersensitivity to negative evaluation.

Whereas APD is the accepted name in the *DSM-IV-TR*, the ICD-10 (World Health Organization, 1993) refers to the disorder as anxious personality disorder. Individuals present as overly shy and timid. They are sensitive to and fearful of criticism. They have a tremendous amount of self-doubt and lack self-confidence in new situations or in social settings where they do not know people. This can inhibit them socially, educationally, and occupationally because they are not willing to branch out and meet new people or do new things. They may resist promotion in a job for fear of being able to handle new responsibilities.

APD is recognized as one of the more common personality disorders with reported estimated prevalences ranging from 2.25% (Jackson et al., 2004) to 2.36% (Grant et al., 2004). These numbers differ from the prevalence rates offered by the *DSM-IV-TR* (APA, 2000) which originally suggested a prevalence of 0.5%–1% of the general population. Within the clinical setting, rates have ranged from 5%–35%, with high comorbidity with anxiety and mood disorders (Grant et al., 2005; Mattia & Zimmerman, 2001; Rossi et al., 2001; Skodol et al., 1999). Some family studies have also found a familial relationship of APD with schizophrenia, which has led some to suggest APD is part of the schizophrenia spectrum disorders (i.e., Cluster A disorders; Asarnow et al., 2001; Kendler et al., 1993). Further, there tends to be a higher prevalence in females versus males (Grant et al., 2004).

Studies of the developmental trajectory of the disorder often suggest an emergence in childhood, presenting as shyness and social anxiety, which leads to isolation (Bernstein & Travaglini, 1999). However, many children who demonstrate such traits grow out of them. It is also the case that features that present in adolescence and even young adulthood that resemble APD may be developmental stage dependent. Thus, it is critical during clinical evaluation to determine the pervasiveness of the disorder and traits.

Dependent Personality Disorder (DPD)

Clinical Features

DPD first appeared in the *DSM-III*. As outlined by the *DSM-IV-TR* (2000), DPD is characterized by a pervasive pattern of excessive neediness, including a need to be taken care of, that leads to submissiveness to others and fear of separation. It may be likened to a child who is clingy. Bornstein (1995) reported that there is tendency for such behaviors to be underreported by the patients themselves because they remain consciously aware of the fact that such dependency is seen as immature and a weakness. As a result, psychosocial factors such as living arrangements and interviews with loved ones can be useful diagnostic information (e.g., a 40 year old still living with his or her parents for not otherwise explainable reasons). Further, there is considerable predictability of long-term features based on clinical presentation at the time of early adulthood. Abrams and Horowitz (1996) reported that individuals who demonstrate DPD symptoms at this developmental benchmark (i.e., early adulthood) demonstrate similarly high DPD symptoms later in life. Further, dependency has a tendency to increase with age because functional limitations cause dependency to some degree (Baltes, 1996). Although some positive outcomes have been found in relation to cognitive-behavioral therapy (Rathus et al., 1995) and SSRIs (Zaretsky et al., 1997), these findings have not been consistently replicated (Rector, Bagby, Segal, Joffe, & Levitt, 2000). In regard to the latter, positive outcomes are potentially more a by-product of reducing comorbid depression, which is known to increase dependency (Bornstein, 1995), as opposed to necessarily treating DPD itself, although further empirical research is needed to evaluate the link between SSRIs and reduction of DPD features.

DPD is one of the more rarely diagnosed PDs. Within the outpatient population, rates are reported below 10%, but rates are as high as 25% in the inpatient setting (Klein, 2003) and DPD is 40% more common in women compared to men (Bornstein, 1997. The clinical features of DPD show a genetic predisposition. Torgerson and colleagues (2000) reported that 30% of the variability in DPD was due to genetic influence. As with other disorders, the accepted proposal for the etiology of DPD is that it is related to environmental and experiential factors acting in combination with genetic heritability with the end result of the clinical features. Most research has focused on parenting style and cultural influence in the development of DPD. Regarding the latter, Eastern cultures have been associated with a greater tendency toward dependency because they emphasize interpersonal and societal ties in lieu of individual achievement, whereas Western culture places emphasis on competition, freedom, and independence (Cross, Bacon, & Morris, 2000).

In terms of parenting styles, Head and colleagues (1991) reported an authoritarian or overprotective parent raises the risk of DPD because the child is not afforded the opportunity to gradually learn independence or to speak his or her own views or wishes by implying that he or she either is susceptible to harm (overprotective) or that others in power will inform him or her as to how to think or behave (authoritarian). This may over time engrain a perception of diminished competence and automatic thoughts of failure before attempt (Freeman & Leaf, 1989). Further, in the case of parenting, if the individual's parents or caregiver then steps in and addresses the matter for the patient, in essence the problematic behavior becomes further conditioned because it has been rewarded. Thus, removing the reward for dependency and instead rewarding independence may provide a means of extinguishing the dependency, although, again, this has mixed outcomes therapeutically.

Obsessive-Compulsive Personality Disorder (OCPD)

Clinical Features

OCPD has long been one of the more debated disorders because individuals in many ways feel they benefit from the core features of the disorder. In reality, as society has continued to promote and reward increased productivity and accomplishment, the past "line in the sand" regarding what features constitute pathology, has been covered up and redrawn several times. What is of importance to remember in this area is that the features must cause a disturbance in functioning. It can be easy to misconstrue the core features to an extent that the disorder is either made nonexistent or that it becomes a catch-all. There is a difference between OCPD and highly motivated professionals that can and should be realized by adherence to the diagnostic criteria. OCPD, also referred to as anankastic personality disorder by the ICD-10, is characterized by a pervasive "preoccupation with orderliness, perfectionism, and mental and interpersonal control, at the expense of flexibility, openness, and efficiency" (APA, 2000, p. 725). It can be easy to see some of the traits, such as perfectionism and orderliness, in a positive light, but in reality, this is dysfunctional because it actually prevents things from getting done in many ways. For example, the preoccupation with perfectionism could lead to a report for work never being turned in due to the need to review and revise it over and over again. A decision may not be arrived at because of concern that a better option is available that has not been considered yet. In the case of extreme devotion to work, although this may aid the individual in professional promotion, it is done at the expense of his or her social life. Self-concept and self-esteem is dependent upon success and recognition and not internally maintained.

Caballo and colleagues (2004) have suggested that features of OCPD can be described along emotional, behavioral, and cognitive lines. They noted that emotionally, individuals with OCPD have difficulties expressing emotions, including love, affection, and tenderness, whereas anger, irritability, and indignation are more easily expressed. These latter traits can often manifest in relation to a situation or person with which the individual has little patience, such as persons who are impulsive and not well organized or goal oriented. The emotions previously mentioned that are difficult for them to display, as well as features such as tearfulness, are controlled for and regulated due to the perception of portraying weakness, immaturity, or even irresponsibility. There is a persistence of tension that inhibits the individual's ability to relax and feel at ease. The tension related to the obsession of achievement and recognition, such as in the workplace, is only eased by engaging in the compulsive action of working long hours because this is the only thing seen as working toward their end goal, even though they constantly set new goals if and when those goals are achieved.

Behaviorally, Caballo and colleagues (2004) note that OCPD is characterized by rigidity, structure, and organization. There is a hyperfocus on planning, details, and work. Yet, there is a tendency toward procrastination, often due to poor decision making and excessive pre-action planning coupled with delays secondary to perfectionistic tendencies. There is a strict adherence to social norms. Although there is an emotional distance toward others socially, if such interactions are seen as serving a secondary gain from a status standpoint, they engage more readily, but there is lack of genuineness. There is a tendency for people with OCPD to criticize others but act in a highly respectful way toward those in authority, particularly those who they perceive as being able to elevate their status. Personal appearance tends to be very formal and conservative.

Finally, from a cognitive standpoint, Caballo and colleagues (2004) suggest OCPD is marked by rigidity in thinking, dichotomous thinking, and tending not to be receptive of thoughts divergent of their own or a different way of doing things. Still, they fear consequences of choices and thus struggle with making decisions because making a wrong decision can place them in an unfavorable light and be viewed by others as irresponsible. This rigidity in thought contributes to a lack of creativity and imagination. There is a lack of trust in others' capabilities, which leads to a resistance in delegating responsibilities. Details are overly concentrated on, which can lead to a loss of the big picture. They are never really satisfied with the performance.

The etiology of OCPD is unknown. Unlike other personality disorders, to date there have not been thorough investigations into genetic contributions or other biological correlates. A select finding offered by Samuels and colleagues (2000) reported that OCPD occurs more frequently in relatives of individuals with OCD than in relatives of controls. There has also been increased prevalence reported in relatives of individuals with eating disorders (Bellodi et al., 2001). Beyond these isolated genetic findings, Millon (1996) has proposed parenting style and the childhood and adolescence home environment as potential precursors. Overcontrol of parents may instill an sense of belief in the child that he or she must perform in particular ways to avoid punishment or reprimand. Simultaneously, the parents, trying to lead by example, may portray themselves in a perfectionistic way, modeling that behavior to the child who then integrates this into his or her personal characteristics. In this scenario, if positive regard and acknowledgment is then just granted for the child's own drive toward perfection, then this becomes engrained. The child then desires perfection while fearing anything less. Culture can also figure into this as evidenced by the fact that OCPD is far more prevalent in Western culture (Beck, Freeman, & Davis, 2004), which is likely due to the fact that many of the traits are rewarded in our societal infrastructure by way of occupational promotion, which brings with it greater security and even monetary reward.

The prevalence of OCPD has been reported to fall somewhere between 1% and 6% in the general population based on various studies undertaken (APA, 2000; Maier et al., 1992), with only subtle influxes seen in the outpatient psychiatric population (3%–10%) according to Widiger and Sanderson (1997). OCPD is twice as likely in males than females (APA, 2000). Beyond the link with obsessive-compulsive disorder and eating disorders, increased risk of OCPD in depressive and other anxiety disorders has also been suggested (APA, 2000).

DIAGNOSTIC PRACTICES AND CONSIDERATIONS

Structured interviews such as the SCID, which adhere to *DSM* criteria, remain the most acceptable form of diagnosis when it comes to personality disorders and the array of mental illnesses (First, Spitzer, Gibbon, & Williams, 1997). Such structured approaches offer particular reliability and validity to the assessment because some disorders may only be noted over the course of time or by establishing a formal psychiatric and social history. Establishment of the individual's history of interpersonal relationships, early development and home life, educational history, occupational history, psychiatric and substance abuse history, and legal history are essential. Consideration of potential comorbid personality disorders or Axis I disorders should be made.

Neuropsychological assessment may serve as an adjunct to treatment by describing neurocognitive strengths and weaknesses, which may serve as foci of intervention to aid in ensuring an optimal functional status. Neuropsychological assessment is particularly useful in those instances when comorbid neurological or medical conditions are present, such as in the instance where there is a history of brain injury reported, which may account for personality dysfunction. Still, in this instance, thorough history taking would prove essential to describing such a history and discussing potential personality changes following insult. Neuropsychological assessment can also prove useful in those instances of substance abuse, which presents at higher rates of comorbidity with various personality disorders and may attribute to personality changes. The stability of the symptoms is an important factor in diagnosis, particularly with regard to differential diagnosis.

Although various cognitive domains are implicated at varying degrees across the personality disorders, there is not a prototypical profile for any of the disorders that would support an actuarial approach to diagnosis by way of neuropsychological assessment. Furthermore, although neurobiological correlates have been described, they are not incorporated into the differential diagnosis process. In addition to these diagnostic criteria and structured interviews such as the SCID, various psychometrically based measures are available that can aid in the objective assessment of personality and personality features. Table 16.1 includes some of the potential tools. They are divided into groupings including personality inventories and scales of mood and psychiatric states.

Still, there are some that have suggested going away from the categorical approach to diagnosing personality disorders and moving instead toward a dimensional approach that would adhere to the five-factor model of personality, which would treat personality disorders as following along a shared continuum (Clark, Livesley, & Morey, 1997; Widiger & Frances, 1994). One of the primary advantages that would come from such an approach is that group dimensions could be established by way of factor analysis as opposed to the committee decisions scheme currently employed (Clark et al., 1997). Admittedly, this has not yet been well received.

METHODS OF INTERVENTION AND TREATMENT

Treatment for patients with personality disorders is often long term and can be quite frustrating for the clinician because there is a tendency toward greater resistance on the part of the patient compared to Axis I disorders given the egosyntonic nature of Axis II pathology. The method of treatment is often multifaceted. A combination of therapeutic and behavioral interventions in combination with pharmacological interventions many times is warranted. Additionally, given the high rate of comorbidity with Axis I disorders as well as other Axis

TABLE 16.1 Objective Measures of Personality and Related Features

Personality Inventories
• Millon Clinical Multiaxial Inventory-III (MCMI-III)
• Minnesota Multiphasic Personality Inventory (MMPI-2/MMPI-RF)
• NEO Personality Inventory-3 (NEO-PI-3)
• Personality Assessment Inventory (PAI)
• Personality Diagnostic Questionnaire—4th Edition (PDQ-4)
• Personality Inventory for Youth (PIY)
• Structured Clinical Interview for *DSM-IV* Disorders (SCID)
• Structured Clinical Interview for *DSM-IV-TR* Axis II Personality Disorders (SCID-II)
• Structured Interview for *DSM-IV* Personality
• The ICD-10 International Personality Disorder Examination (IPDE)
Related Symptom Measures
• Beck Depression Inventory-II (BDI-II)
• Beck Anxiety Inventory (BAI)
• Brief Symptoms Inventory (BSI)
• Cognitive Distortions Scale (CDS)
• Dissociative Experiences Scale (DES)
• Psychopathy Checklist-Revised (PCL-R)
• Symptom Check List-90-R (SCL-90-R)

II disorders, treatment is often complex. Not surprisingly, the personality disorders are consistently recognized as being among the most chronic and financially burdensome of the psychiatric disorders (Comtois et al., 2003). As previously suggested, research has demonstrated poorer treatment outcomes and health status and higher rates of health care use and costs in patients with a comorbid personality disorder in addition to other chronic mental or medical disorders (Gross et al., 2002; Hueston, Werth, & Mainous, 1999; Moran, Rendu, Jenkins, Tylee, & Mann, 2001; Rendu, Moran, Patel, Knapp, & Mann, 2002).

Many have suggested early identification and intervention is key. For example, in discussing ASPD, it has been reported that to prevent serious negative outcome associated with the disorder, early identification of psychopathic traits is crucial because attempts to alleviate and treat psychopathy in adulthood have been unsuccessful in the past (Lynam, 1996, 1997). Intervention, regardless of when it is started, starts with assessment. Either through structured interviewing or other forms of objective assessment, prior to treatment being implemented, the nature of the individual's symptom profile must be fully understood so an initial course of intervention may be conceptualized.

Therapeutic treatment approaches have included CBT, group therapy, family therapy, and psychodynamic therapy. The focus of such therapies is on developing a more adaptive lifestyle and better interpersonal relationships. However, given the variations in clinical presentation and core features, each personality disorder cluster should be approached in a different therapeutic fashion and with specific treatment interventions. It is beyond the scope of this chapter to discuss individual approaches to therapy on a disorder by disorder basis. Rather, Livesly (2005) offered an effective review and synthesis of the literature on the therapeutic treatment of personality disorders, outlining the basic components involved. He noted that the following basic principles must be kept in mind for appropriate treatment of the personality disorders through therapeutic modalities: (1) comprehensive treatment requires a combination of interventions to treat the range of psychopathology typically associated with personality disorder; (2) multiple interventions should be delivered in an integrated and coordinated way; (3) treatment involves general strategies to manage and treat core self- and interpersonal pathology and specific strategies to treat individual differences in problems and psychopathology; (4) the most appropriate stance for treating personality disorders is to provide support, empathy, and validation; (5) treatment should maximize the effects of common factors; (6) treatment progress can and should be described as a series of phases (i.e., safety and managing crises, containment, control and regulation); (7) change occurs through a series of stages, and interventions should be appropriate to the patient's stage of change; (8) the work of therapy is a collaborative description of patient problems and psychopathology and their effect on the patient's life and relationships; and (9) the features of personality disorder differ in stability and potential for change.

Livesly (2005) also suggested general therapeutic strategies in working with personality disorders. First, he reported a necessity to build and maintain a collaborative relationship. Using both Luborsky's two-component description of the alliance and Safran and Muran's work on repairing alliances, Livesly (2005) notes that the clinician must not only instill hope and gain the confidence of the patient, but also promote the patient's participation in a joint search for understanding, help the patient learn skills for use outside of treatment, encourage the patient–therapist bond, and emphasize the collaborative nature of treatment. Second, the clinician must maintain a consistent treatment process. Livesly (2005) acknowledges this can be a challenge in working with patients with personality disorders but that meeting this goal requires setting limits without damaging empathy by confronting attempts to change the frame of therapy. He noted that this requires recognizing the reasons for the challenge to the therapeutic frame and discussing how it can adversely affect therapy. The third strategy involves establishing and maintaining a validating treatment process. Livesly (2005) notes that the goal here is to promote self-validation and the development of a more adaptive self-structure by helping the patient distinguish the experience, the reasons behind it, and what can be drawn from it. The final strategy is to build and maintain motivation for change. Too easily, individuals can fall back into their same pattern and then perceive that failed attempt at change as a sign that change is impossible. Livesly (2005) suggests that when motivation is poor, maintaining a supportive stance and attempting to build motivation by exploring the consequences of maladaptive behavior is often the best course of action. For a detailed review of these various principles and concepts, see Livesly (2005).

Beyond therapy, pharmacological interventions are often used as a supplement. Antipsychotics, antidepressants, benzodiazepines, and mood stabilizers have received the greatest attention along these lines. In many instances, pharmacological intervention has been previously directed at treating comorbid Axis I features, whereas psychotherapy was seen as the primary treatment for the Axis II features. Further, researchers suggested that any improvement seen in PDs related to pharmacological treatment stemmed from a resolution of Axis I traits as opposed to treating the Axis II disorder. Contemporary literature has reported in the contrary.

Antipsychotics

Antipsychotics are selectively used across some of the personality disorders with positive effects. For example, reductions in delusions, anger, hostility, obsessive-compulsive features, and phobic anxiety were found in patients with BPD or StPD receiving thiothixene compared to placebo (Goldberg et al., 1986). Positive outcomes have actually been reported across the Cluster A disorders with the use of neuroleptics, with no difference based on the specific agent used (Coccaro, 1993). In this grouping, these agents have a specific affinity for reducing perceptive-cognitive dysfunction and psychotic decompensation. Neuroleptics have also been shown to reduce paranoia, anger, and dissociation (Ingenhoven et al., 2010) although impulsive-behavioral dyscontrol, depressed mood, anxiety, and mood lability were not significantly reduced. Both standard antipsychotics (Chengappa et al., 1999; Allain et al., 2000) and atypical antipsychotics (Khouzam & Donnelly, 1997; Zanarini & Frankenburg, 2001) have demonstrated a capacity in reducing aggression in BPD.

Antidepressants

Several studies have investigated the role of antidepressants with serotonergic actions (e.g., TCAs, MAOIs, and SSRIs) in the treatment of personality disorders. With their efficacy in reducing anger, impulsivity, and/or aggression (Cocarro & Kavoussi, 1997; Saltzman et al., 1995; Rinne, van den Brink, Wouters, & van Dyck, 2002), they have been successfully used across the various clusters, with particular interest in their use within Cluster B disorders. Tang and colleagues (2009) found that paroxetine, as an example, reduced neuroticism and increased extraversion as assessed by the NEO Five Factor Inventory, thus suggesting a potential role for treatment of features seen in Clusters A and C disorders. Gabbard (2005) has further suggested that the use of SSRIs may facilitate psychotherapy by reducing "affective noise"—such as intense anger, hypervigilant anxiety, or dysphoria—that prevents patients from reflecting on their internal world and the inner experiences of others. Additionally, SSRIs have been noted to reduce hyperreactivity of the HPA axis by reducing hypersecretion of CRF, which could suggest a role in reducing tension in Cluster C patients (Nemeroff & Owens, 2004).

Benzodiazepines

Studies have demonstrated a decrease in anxiety and hostility in relation to benzodiazepine use (Faltus, 1984; Soloff, 1994). However, at the same time, concerns that these agents may cause behavioral disinhibition and subsequent episodes of anger and aggression have also been voiced (Cowdry & Gardner, 1988), though use of longer acting agents may negate this. As a class, benzodiazepines have demonstrated efficacy in reducing features of anxiety and may have a role in the treatment of Cluster C disorders as well as treating anxiety features across other clusters.

Mood Stabilizers

Lithium has been shown to reduce aggression in adults with BPD (Hori, 1998), as well as in prison populations, which are known to have an increased prevalence of ASPD (Tupin et al., 1973; Sheard et al., 1976). Phenytoin and carbamazepine have demonstrate anti-aggressive tendencies (Barratt et al., 1997; Cowdry & Gardner, 1988). Carbamazepine has also demonstrated efficacy in borderline patients (Gardner & Crowdry, 1986). Studies have also shown valproate to be helpful in limiting aggressive outbursts in borderline patients. Ingenhoven and colleagues (2010) reported reductions in impulsivity and behavioral dyscontrol as well as depressed mood, anger, and anxiety related to the use of mood stabilizers. As noted by Rylander and Soltys (2012), one of the difficulties in using mood stabilizers to rationally target temperament domains mediated by specific neurotransmitter pathways is our lack of knowledge of how these medications influence neurotransmission, though interactions with serotonergic and glucocorticoid systems are suggested.

SUMMARY

Personality disorders represent patterns of enduring, pervasive, and inflexible thoughts and behaviors in and toward one's environment that cause interpersonal stress due to social and cultural inappropriateness. As a grouping, they represent some of the most treatment-resistant disorders recognized by the *DSM-IV-TR* and consequently one of the most financially burdensome. Interestingly, although they may present in upward of 30% of individuals seen for psychiatric care, they are rarely the main focus of consultations and are notoriously underdiagnosed. Inherent to the disorders, they are termed personality disorders because they reflect a deviation from normalcy of who the person is at his or her core.

Evidence has emerged suggesting the role of various neurobiological correlates of these disorders. Across all types, genetic outcomes suggests a heritability of these presentations. Beyond this, much of the literature is isolated to specific disorders (mainly schizotypal, borderline, and antisocial personality disorders). Although this research may be used to make assumptions about the other personality disorders, the dearth of this information suggests avenues for research in years to come. Similarly, there is a sparseness of the neuropsychological data related to the disorders aside from those noted as being more heavily researched. Consensus would suggest that across most if not all of the personality disorders, there is a tendency toward executive function deficits with additional potential for abnormalities in working memory, attention, and broader domains of visual and verbal memory being seen at varying degrees. Still, in no personality disorder, including those well researched, has there been an emergence of a prototypical profile. Consequently, neuropsychological assessment may be used to define the individual characteristics of patients as it corresponds with their neurocognitive functioning, which carries implications for their functional status on a day-to-day basis. As the neuroscientific literature continues to expand into these disorders, neuropsychology, neuropsychiatry, and the behavioral neuroscience will be looked to in order to provide a refined understanding of the biology of these disorders, which may serve as the gateway to further advances in the manner in which we treat these disorders.

REFERENCES

Abe, N., Suzuki, M., Mori, E., Itoh, M., & Fujii, T. (2007). Deceiving others: Distinct neural responses of the prefrontal cortex and amygdala in simple fabrication and deception with social interactions. *Journal of Cognitive Neuroscience, 19*, 287–295.

Abrams, R. C., & Horowitz, S. V. (1996). Personality disorders after age 50: A meta-analysis. *Journal of Personality Disorders, 10*, 271–281.

Aguilar, B., Sroufe, L. A., Egeland, B., & Carlson, E. (2000). Distinguishing the early onset/persistent and adolescence-onset antisocial behavior types: From birth to 16 years. *Development and Psychopathology, 12*(2), 109–132.

Akhtar, S. (1987). Schizoid personality disorder: A synthesis of developmental, dynamic, and descriptive features. *American Journal of Psychotherapy, 151*, 499–518.

Allain, H., Dautzenberg, P. H., Maurer, K., Schuck, S., Bonhomme, D., & Gerard, D. (2000). Double blind study of tiapride versus haloperidol and placebo in agitation and aggressiveness in elderly patients with cognitive impairment. *Psychopharmacology, 148*, 361–366.

Alterman, A. I., & Cacciola, J. S. (1991). The antisocial personality disorder diagnosis in substance abusers: Problems and issues. *Journal of Nervous and Mental Disease, 179*(7), 401–409.

Alterman, A. I., McDermott, P. A., Cacciola, J. S., Rutherford, M. J., Boardman, C. R., McKay, J. R., et al. (1998). A typology of antisociality in methadone patients. *Journal of Abnormal Psychology, 107*(3), 412–422.

American Psychiatric Association. (2000). *Diagnostic and statistical manual of mental disorders* (4th ed., text rev.). Washington, DC: Author.

Angrilli, A., Palomba, D., Cantagallo, A., Maietti, A., & Stegagno, L. (1999). Emotional impairment after right orbitofrontal lesion in a patient without cognitive deficits. *Neuroreport, 10*(8), 1741–1746.

Asarnow, R. F., Nuechterlein, K. H., Fogelson, D., Subotnik, K. L., Payne, D. A., Russell, A. T., et al. (2001). Schizophrenia and schizophrenia-spectrum personality disorders in the first degree relatives of children with schizophrenia. *Archives of General Psychiatry, 58*, 581–588.

Baker, L. A., Tuvblad, C., Reynolds, C., Zheng, M., Lozano, D. I., & Raine, A. (2009). Resting heart rate and the development of antisocial behavior from age 9 to 14: Genetic and environmental influences. *Development and Psychopathology, 21*(3), 939–960.

Baltes, M. M. (1996). *The many faces of dependency in old age*. New York: Cambridge University Press.

Barkataki, I., Kumari, V., Das, M., Taylor, P., & Sharma, T. (2006). Volumetric structural brain abnormalities in men with schizophrenia or antisocial personality disorder. *Behavioral Brain Research, 15*, 239–247.

Baron, M., Gruen, R., Asnis, L., & Lord, S. (1985). Familial transmission of schizotypal and borderline personality disorders. *American Journal of Psychiatry, 142*, 927–934.

Barratt, E. S., Stanford, M. S., Felthous, A. R., & Kent, T. A. (1997). The effects of phenytoin on impulsive and premeditated aggression: A controlled study. *Journal of Clinical Psychopharmacology, 17*, 341–349.

Bazanis, E., Rogers, R. D., Dowson, J. H., Taylor, P., Meux, C., Staley C, et al. (2002). Neurocognitive deficits in decision-making and planning of patients with DSM-III-R borderline personality disorder. *Psychological Medicine, 32*(8), 1395–1405.

Beblo, T., Mensebach, C., Wingenfeld, K., Rullkoetter, N., & Driessen, M. (2006). Assessing learning with and without interference. *Zeitschrift für Neuropsychologie, 17*, 219–223.

Beblo, T., Saavedra, A. S., Mensebach, C., Lange, W., Markowitsch, H. J., Rau, H., et al. (2006). Deficits in visual functions and neuropsychological inconsistency in borderline personality disorder. *Psychiatry Research, 145*, 127–135.

Bechara, A., Tranel, D., & Damasio, H. (2000). Characterization of the decision-making deficit of patients with ventromedial prefrontal cortex lesions. *Brain, 123*, 2189–2202.

Beck, A. T., Freeman, A., & Davis, D. D. (2004). *Cognitive therapy of personality disorders* (2nd ed.). New York: Guilford.

Bellodi, L., Cavallini, M. C., Bertelli, S., Chiapparino, D., Riboldi, C., & Smeraldi, E. (2001). Morbidity risk for obsessive-compulsive spectrum disorders in first-degree relatives of patients with eating disorders. *American Journal of Psychiatry, 158*, 563–569.

Berlin, H. A., & Rolls, E. T. (2004). Time perception, impulsivity, emotionality, and personality in self harming borderline personality disorder patients. *Journal of Personality Disorders, 18*, 358–378.

Berlin, H. A., Rolls, E. T., & Kischka, U. (2004). Impulsivity, time perception, emotion and reinforcement sensitivity in patients with OFC lesions. *Brain, 127*, 1108–1126.

Bernstein, D. P., & Travaglini, L. (1999). Schizoid and avoidant personality disorders. In T. Millon, P. H. Blaney, & R. D. Davis (Eds.), *Oxford textbook of psychopathology*, 586–601. New York: Oxford University Press.

Bernstein, D. P., & Useda, J. D. (2007). Paranoid personality disorder. In W. T. O'Donohue, K. A. Fowler, & S. O. Lilenfeld (Eds.), *Personality disorders: Toward the DSM-V* (pp. 41–62). Thousand Oaks, CA: Sage.

Birbaumer, N., Veit, R., Lotze, M., Erb, M., Hermann, C., Grodd, W., et al. (2005). Deficient fear conditioning in psychopathy: A functional magnetic resonance imaging study. *Archives of General Psychiatry, 62*(7), 799–805.

Blair, K. S., Newman, C., Mitchell, D. G., Richell, R. A., Leonard, A., Morton, J., et al. (2006). Differentiating among prefrontal substrates in psychopathy: Neuropsychological test findings. *Neuropsychology, 20*, 153–165.

Blair, R. J. R., & Coles, M. (2000). Expression recognition and behavioural problems in early adolescence. *Cognitive Development, 15*, 421–434.

Blair, R. J. R., Mitchell, D. G., Richell, R. A., Kelly, S., Leonard, A., Newman, C., et al. (2002). Turning a deaf ear to fear: Impaired recognition of vocal affect in psychopathic individuals. *Journal of Abnormal Psychology, 111*(4), 682–686.

Blais, M. A., Hilsenroth, M. J., & Castelbury, F. D. (1997). Content validity of the DSM-IV borderline and narcissistic personality disorder criteria sets. *Comprehensive Psychiatry, 38*(1), 31–37.

Blonigen, D. M., Carlson, S. R., Krueger, R. F., & Patrick, C. J. (2003). A twin study of self-reported personality traits. *Personality and Individual Differences, 35*, 179–197.

Blum, K., Braverman, E. R., Wu, S., Cull, J. G., Chen, T. J. H., Gill, J., et al. (1997). Association of polymorphisms of dopamine D2 receptor (DRD2), and dopamine transporter (DAT1) genes with schizoid/avoidant behaviors(SAB). *Molecular Psychiatry, 2*, 239–246.

Blum, K., Cull, J. G., Braverman, E. R., & Comings, D. E. (1996a). Reward deficiency syndrome. *American Scientist, 84*, 132–145.

Blum, K., Sheridan, P. J., Wood, R. C., Braverman, E. R., Chen, T. J. H., Cull, J. G., et al. (1996b). The D2 dopamine receptor gene as a predictor of "reward deficiency syndrome" (RDS) behavior: Bayes' Theorem. *Journal of the Royal Society of Medicine, 87*, 396–400.

Bögels, S. M., & Mansell, W. (2004). Attention processes in the maintenance and treatment of social phobia: Hypervigilance, avoidance, and self-focused attention. *Clinical Psychology Review, 24*(7), 827–856.

Bornstein, R. F. (1995). Comorbidity of dependent personality disorder and other psychological disorders: An integrative review. *Journal of Personality Disorders, 9*(4), 286–303.

Bornstein, R. F. (1997). Dependent personality in the DSM-IV and beyond. *Clinical Psychology: Science and Practice, 4*(2), 175–187.

Brambilla, P., Soloff, P. H., Sala, M., Nicoletti, M. A., Keshavan, M. S., & Soares, J. C. (2004). Anatomical MRI study of borderline personality disorder patients. *Psychiatry Research, 131*, 125–133.

Brieger, P., Ehrt, U., & Marneros, A. (2003). Frequency of comorbid personality disorders in bipolar and unipolar affective disorders. *Comprehensive Psychiatry, 44*, 28–34.

Brunner, H. G., Nelen, M., Breakefield, X. O., Ropers, H. H., & van Oost, B. A. (1993). Abnormal behavior associated with a point mutation in the structural gene for monoamine oxidase A. *Science, 262*, 578–580.

Buchsbaum, M. S., Shihabuddin, L., Hazlett, E. A., Schroder, J., Haznedar, M. M., Powchik, P., et al. (2002). Kraepelinian and non-Kraepelinian schizophrenia subgroup differences in cerebral metabolic rate. *Schizophrenia Research, 55*, 25–40.

Buchsbaum, M. S., Yang, S., Hazlett, E., Siegel, B. V. Jr., Germans, M., Haznedar, M., et al. (1997). Ventricular volume and asymmetry in schizotypal personality disorder and schizophrenia assessed with magnetic resonance imaging. *Schizophrenia Research, 27*, 45–53.

Burke, J. D., Loeber, R., Lahey, B. B., & Rathouz, P. J. (2005). Developmental transitions among affective and behavioral disorders in adolescent boys. *Journal of Child Psychology and Psychiatry, 46*, 1200–1210.

Burt, S. A. (2009). Are there meaningful etiological differences within antisocial behavior? Results of a meta-analysis. *Clinical Psychology Review, 29*(2), 163–178.

Byne, W., Buchsbaum, M. S., Kemether, E., Hazlett, E. A., Shinwari, A., Mitropoulou, V., et al. (2001). Magnetic resonance imaging of the thalamic mediodorsal nucleus and pulvinar in schizophrenia and schizotypal personality disorder. *Archives of General Psychiatry, 58*, 133–140.

Caballo, V. E., López-Gollonet, C., & Bautista, R. (2004). *Obsessive-compulsive personality disorder. In V. E. Caballo (Ed.), Handbook of personality disorders: Description, assessment and treatment (pp. 231–247).* Madrid, Spain: Ed. Síntesis.

Cadoret, R. J., Yates, W. R., Troughton, E., Woodworth, G., & Stewart, M. A. (1995). Genetic-environmental interaction in the genesis of aggressivity and conduct disorders. *Archives of General Psychiatry, 52*, 916–924.

Campbell, S. B. (1995). Behavior problems in preschool children: A review of recent research. *Journal of Child Psychology and Psychiatry, 36*, 113–149.

Cantwell, D. P., & Baker, L. (1989). Stability and natural history of DSM-III childhood diagnoses. *Journal of the American Academy of Child and Adolescent Psychiatry, 28*(5), 691–700.

Carrillo, M., Ricci, L. A., Coppersmith, G. A., & Melloni, R. H. Jr. (2009). The effect of increased serotonergic neurotransmission on aggression: A critical meta-analytical review of preclinical studies. *Psychopharmacology, 205*(3), 349–368.

Carter, J. D., Joyce, P. R., Mulder, R. T., Sullivan, P. F., & Luty, S. E. (1999). Gender differences in the frequency of personality disorders in depressed outpatients. *Journal of Personality Disorders, 13*(1), 67–74.

Casey, P., Birbeck, G., McDonagh, C., Horgan, A., Dowrick, C., Dalgard, O., et al. (2004). Personality disorders, depression and functioning: Results from the ODIN study. *Journal of Affective Disorders, 82*, 277–283.

Caspi, A., McClay, J., Moffitt, T. E., Mill, J., Martin, J., Craig, I. W., et al. (2002). Role of genotype in the cycle of violence in maltreated children. *Science, 297*, 851–854.

Chengappa, K. N., Ebeling, T., Kang, J. S., Levine, J., & Parepally, H. (1999). Clozapine reduces severe self-mutilation and aggression in psychotic patients with borderline personality disorder. *Journal of Clinical Psychiatry, 60*, 477–484.

Cicchetti, D. (2008). A multiple-levels-of-analysis perspective on research in developmental psychopathology. In T. P. Beauchaine & S. P. Hinshaw (Eds.), *Child psychopathology(pp. 27–57)*. Hoboken, NJ: Wiley.

Clark, L. A. (2005). Temperament as a unifying basis for personality and psychopathology. *Journal of Abnormal Psychology, 114*, 505–521.

Clark, L. A., Livesley, W. J., Morey, L. (1997). Personality disorders assessment: The challenge of construct validity, *11*(3), 205–231.

Cloninger, C. R. (1987). A systematic method for clinical description and classification of personality variants: A proposal. *Archives of General Psychiatry, 44*, 573–588.

Cloninger, C. R. (2009). Evolution of human brain functions: The functional structure of human consciousness. *Australian and New Zealand Journal of Psychiatry, 43*, 994–1006.

Cloninger, C. R., Svrakic, D. M., & Przybeck, T. R. (1993). A psychobiological model of temperament and character. *Archives of General Psychiatry, 50*, 975–990.

Coccaro, E. F. (1993). Psychopharmacologic studies in patients with personality disorders: Review and perspective. *Journal of Personality Disorders, Supplement*, 181–192.

Coccaro, E. F., & Kavoussi, R. J. (1997). Fluoxetine and impulsive aggressive behavior in personality disordered subjects. *Archives of General Psychiatry, 54*, 1081–1088.

Coccaro, E. F., Kavoussi, R. J., Hauger, R. L., Cooper, T. B., & Ferris, C. F. (1998). Cerebrospinal fluid vasopressin levels correlates with aggression and serotonin function in personality disordered subjects. *Archives of General Psychiatry, 55*, 708–714.

Cohen, P., Cohen, J., Velez, S. C. N., Hartmark, C., Johnson, J., Rojas, M., et al. (1993). An epidemiological study of disorders in late childhood and adolescence—I. Age- and gender-specific prevalence. *Journal of Child Psychology and Psychiatry and Allied Disciplines, 34*, 851–867.

Coid, J. W. (2003). Epidemiology, public health and the problem of personality disorder. *British Journal of Psychiatry, 182*(Suppl. 44), 3–10.

Coid, J. W., Yang, M., Tyrer, P., Roberts, A., & Ullrich, S. (2006). Prevalence and correlates of personality disorder in Great Britain. *British Journal of Psychiatry, 188*, 423–431.

Comtois, K. A., Russo, J., Snowden, M., Srebnik, D., Ries, R., & Roy-Byrne, P. (2003). Factors associated with high use of public mental health services by persons with borderline personality disorder. *Psychiatric Services, 54*, 1149–1154.

Cooke, D. J., Michie, C., & Hart, S. D. (2005). Facets of clinical psychopathy: Toward clearer measurement. In C. J. Patrick (Ed.), *Handbook of psychopathy*. New York: The Guilford Press.

Corruble, E., Ginestet, D., & Guelfi, J. D. (1996). Comorbidity of personality disorders and unipolar major depression: A review. *Journal of Affective Disorders, 37*(2–3), 157–170.

Cowdry, R. W., & Gardner, D. L. (1988). Pharmacotherapy of borderline personality disorder: Alprazolam, carbamazepine, trifluoperazine, and tranylcypromine. *Archives of General Psychiatry, 45*, 111–119.

Cramer, V., Torgersen, S., & Kringlen, E. (2006). Personality disorders and quality of life: A population study. *Comprehensive Psychiatry, 47*, 178–184.

Cross, S. E., Bacon, P. L., & Morris, M. L. (2000). The relational-interdependent self-construal and relationships. *Journal of Personality and Social Psychology, 78*, 791–808.

Damasio, A. R. (1994). *Descartes' error: Error, reason, and the human brain*. New York: Grosset/Putnam.

Davidson, R. J. (2002). Anxiety and affective style: Role of prefrontal cortex and amygdala. *Biological Psychiatry, 51*, 68–80.

Day, R., & Wong, S. (1996). Anomalous perceptual asymmetries for negative emotional stimuli in the psychopath. *Journal of Abnormal Psychology, 105(4):648–652.*

Deater-Deckard, K. (2001). Annotation: Recent research examining the role of peer relationships in the development of psychopathology. *Journal of Child Psychology and Psychiatry, 42*, 565–579.

de la Fuente, J. M., Goldman, S., Stanus, E., Vizuete, C., Morlán, I., Bobes, J., et al. (1997). Brain glucose metabolism in BPD. *Journal of Psychiatric Research, 31*, 531–541.

Delville, Y., Mansour, K. M., & Ferris, C. F. (1996). Serotonin blocks vasopressin-facilitated offensive aggression: Interactions within the ventrolateral hypothalamus of golden hamsters. *Physiology & Behavior, 59*(4–5), 813–816.

Depue, R. A. (2009). Genetic, environmental, and epigenetic factors in the development of personality disturbance. *Development and Psychopathology, 21*, 1031–1063.

Diamantopoulou, S., Verhulst, F. C., & van der Ende, J. (2010). Testing developmental pathways to antisocial personality problems. *Journal of Abnormal Child Psychology, 38*, 91–103.

Dickey, C. C., McCarley, R. W., Niznikiewicz, M. A., Voglmaier, M. M., Seidman, L. J., Kim, S., et al. (2005). Clinical, cognitive, and social characteristics of a sample of neuroleptic-naive persons with schizotypal personality disorder. *Schizophrenia Research, 78*, 297–308.

Dickey, C. C., McCarley, R. W., & Shenton, M. E. (2002). The brain in schizotypal personality disorder: A review of structural MRI and CT findings. *Harvard Review of Psychiatry, 10*, 1–15.

Dickey, C. C., McCarley, R. W., & Voglmaier, M. M. (2003). An MRI study of superior temporal gyrus volume in women with schizotypal personality disorder. *American Journal of Psychiatry, 160*, 2198–2201.

Dickey, C. C., McCarley, R. W., Voglmaier, M. M., Frumin, M., Niznikiewicz, M. A., Hirayasu, Y., et al. (2002). Smaller left Heschl's gyrus volume in patients with schizotypal personality disorder. *American Journal of Psychiatry, 159*, 1521–1527.

Dickey, C. C., McCarley, R. W., Xu, M. L., Seidman, L. J., Voglmaier, M. M., Niznikiewicz, M. A., et al. (2007). MRI abnormalities of the hippocampus and cavum septi pellucidi in females with schizotypal personality disorder. *Schizophrenia Research, 89*, 49–58.

Dinn, W. M., Harris, C. L., Aycicegi, A., Greene, P. B., Kirkley, S. M., & Reilly, C. (2004). Neurocognitive function in borderline personality disorder. *Progress in Neuropsychopharmacology and Biological Psychiatry, 28*, 329–341.

Dishion, T., & Patterson, G. (2006). The development and ecology of antisocial behavior in children and adolescents. In D. Cicchetti & D. J. Cohen (Eds.), *Developmental psychopathology: Vol. 3. Risk, disorder, and adaptation* (pp. 503–541). Hoboken, NJ: Wiley.

Dishion, T., & Piehler, T. (2007). Peer dynamics in the development and change of child and adolescent problem behavior. In A. Masten (Ed.), *Multilevel dynamics in developmental psychopathology: Pathways to the future* (pp. 151–180). New York: Taylor & Francis/Erlbaum.

Dodge, K., Bates, J., & Pettit, G. (1990). Mechanisms in the cycle of violence. *Science, 250*, 1678–1689.

Dolan, M., & Park, I. (2002). The neuropsychology of antisocial personality disorder. *Psychological Medicine, 32*(3), 417–427.

Donegan, N. H., Sanislow, C. A., Blumberg, H. P., Fulbright, R. K., Lacadie, C., Skudlarski, P., et al. (2003). Amygdala hyperreactivity in borderline personality disorder: Implications for emotional dysregulation. *Biological Psychiatry, 54*, 1284–1293.

Downhill, J. E., Buchsbaum, M. S., Hazlett, E. A., Barth, S., Lees Roitman, S., Nunn, M., et al. (2001). Temporal lobe volume determined by magnetic resonance imaging in schizotypal personality disorder and schizophrenia. *Schizophrenia Research, 48*, 187–199.

Driessen, M., Herrmann, J., Stahl, K., Zwaan, M., Meier, S., Hill, A., et al. (2000). Magnetic resonance imaging volumes of the hippocampus and the amygdala in women with borderline personality disorder and early traumatization. *Archives of General Psychiatry, 57*, 1115–1122.

Dunn, N. J., Yanasak, E., Schillaci, J., Simotas, S., Rehm, L. P., Souchek, J., et al. (2004). Personality disorders in veterans with posttraumatic stress disorder and depression. *Journal of Traumatic Stress, 17*(1), 75–82.

Durbin, C. E., & Klein, D. N. (2006). Ten-year stability of personality disorders among outpatients with mood disorders. *Journal of Abnormal Psychology, 115*(1), 75–84.

Dvorak-Bertsch, J. D., Sadeh, N., Glass, S. J., Thornton, D., & Newman, J. P. (2007). Stroop tasks associated with differential activation of anterior cingulate do not differentiate psychopathic and non psychopathic offenders. *Personality and Individual Differences, 42*, 585–595.

Edens, J. F., Marcus, D. K., & Morey, L. C. (2009). Paranoid personality has a dimensional latent structure: Taxometric analyses of community and clinical samples. *Journal of Abnormal Psychology, 118*(3), 545–553.

Enebrink, P., Andershed, H., & Langstrom, N. (2005). Callous-unemotional traits are associated with clinical severity in referred boys with conduct problems. *Nordic Journal of Psychiatry, 59*(6), 431–440.

Engelien, A., Silbersweig, D., Stern, E., Huber, W., Doring, W., Frith, C., et al. (1995). The functional anatomy of recovery from auditory agnosia: A PET study of sound categorization in a neurological patient and normal controls. *Brain, 118*, 1395–1409.

Eskedal, G. A., & Demetri, J. M. (2006). Etiology and treatment of Cluster C personality disorders. *Journal of Mental Health Counseling, 28*, 1–17.

Faltus, F. J. (1984). The positive effect of alprazolam in the treatment of three patients with borderline personality disorder. *American Journal of Psychiatry, 141*(6), 802–803.

Fan, A. H., & Hassell, J. (2008). Bipolar disorder and comorbid personality psychopathology: A review of the literature. *Journal of Clinical Psychiatry, 69*, 1794–1803.

Fanous, A., Gardner, C., Walsh, D., & Kendler, K. S. (2001). Relationship between positive and negative symptoms of schizophrenia and schizotypal symptoms in nonpsychotic relatives. *Archives of General Psychiatry, 58*, 669–673.

Farrington, D. P. (1995). The development of offending and antisocial behaviour from childhood: Key findings from the Cambridge Study in Delinquent Development. *Journal of Child Psychology and Psychiatry, 36*, 929–964.

Feder, A., Robbins, S. W., & Ostermeyer, B. (2003). Personality disorders. In M. D. Feldman & J. F. Christensen. *Behavioral medicine in primary care* (2nd ed., pp. 231–252). New York: Lange Medical Books/McGraw-Hill Medical.

Fehr, E., & Rockenbach, B. (2004). Human altruism: Economic, neural, and evolutionary perspectives. *Current Opinion in Neurobiology, 14*(6), 784–790.

First, M., Spitzer, R., Gibbon, M., & Williams, J. B. (1997). *Structured clinical interview for DSM-IV Axis I disorders*. Washington, DC: American Psychiatric Press.

Fonagy, P., Target, M., & Gergely, G. (2000). Attachment and borderline personality disorder: A theory and some evidence. *Psychiatric Clinics of North America, 23*(1), 103–122.

Fonagy, P., Target, M., Gergely, G., Allen, J. G., & Bateman, A. W. (2003). The developmental roots of borderline personality disorder in early attachment relationships: A theory and some evidence. *Psychoanalytic Inquiry: A Topical Journal for Mental Health Professionals, 23*(3), 412–459.

Fossati, A., Maffei, C., Bagnato, M., Battaglia, M., Donati, D., Donini, M., et al. (2000). Patterns of covariation of DSM-IV personality disorders in a mixed psychiatric sample. *Comprehensive Psychiatry, 41*, 206–215.

Foster, E. M., & Jones, D. E. (2005). The high cost of aggression: Public expenditures resulting from conduct disorder. *American Journal of Public Health, 95*(10), 1767–1772.

Frankenburg, F. R., & Zanarini, M. C. (2004). The association between borderline personality disorder and chronic medical illnesses, poor health-related lifestyle choices, and costly forms of health care utilization. *Journal of Clinical Psychiatry, 65*, 1660–1665.

Freeman, A., & Leaf, R. C. (1989). Cognitive therapy applied to personality disorders. In A. Freeman, K. M. Simon, L. E. Beutler, & H. Arkowitz (Eds.), *Comprehensive handbook of cognitive therapy* (pp. 403–434). New York: Plenum Press.

Frick, P. J., Cornell, A. H., Barry, C. T., Bodin, S. D., & Dane, H. E. (2003). Callous-unemotional traits and conduct problems in the prediction of conduct problem severity, aggression, and self-report of delinquency. *Journal of Abnormal Child Psychology, 31*(4), 457–470.

Frick, P. J., Cornell, A. H., Bodin, S. D., Dane, H. E., Barry, C. T., & Loney, B. R. (2003). Callous-unemotional traits and developmental pathways to severe conduct problems. *Developmental Psychology, 39*(2), 246–260.

Frick, P. J., Lahey, B. B., Loeber, R., Tannenbaum, L., Van Horn, Y., Christ, M. A. G., et al. (1993). Oppositional defiant disorder and conduct disorder: A meta-analytic review of factor analyses and cross-validation in a clinic sample. *Clinical Psychology Review, 13*(4), 319–340.

Friedel, R. O. (2004). Dopamine dysfunction in BPD: A hypothesis. *Neuropsychopharmacology, 29*, 1029–1039.

Gabbard, G. O. (2005). Mind, brain, and personality disorders. *American Journal of Psychiatry, 162*, 648–655.

Gardner, D. L., & Cowdry, R. W. (1986). Positive effects of carbamazepine on behavioral dyscontrol in borderline personality disorder. *American Journal of Psychiatry, 143*(4), 519–522.

Gardner, F. E. (1994). The quality of joint activity between mothers and their children with behavior problems. *Journal of Child Psychology and Psychiatry, 35*, 935–948.

Garno, J. L., Goldberg, J. F., Ramirez, P. M., & Ritzler, B. A. (2005). Bipolar disorder with comorbid cluster B personality disorder features: Impact on suicidality. *Journal of Clinical Psychiatry, 66*(3), 339–345.

Garyfallos, G., Adamopoulou, A., Karastergiou, A., Voikli, M., Ikonomidis, N., Donias, S., et al. (1999). Somatoform disorders: Comorbidity with other DSM-III-R psychiatric diagnoses in Greece. *Comprehensive Psychiatry, 40*(4), 299–307.

Gillstrom, B. J., & Hare, R. D. (1988). Language-related hand gestures in psychopaths. *Journal of Personality Disorders, 21*, 21–27.

Goldberg, S. C., Schulz, S. C., Schulz, P. M., Resnick, R. J., Hamer, R. M., & Friedel, R. O. (1986). Borderline and schizotypal personality disorders treated with low-dose thiothixene vs placebo. *Archives of General Psychiatry, 43*(7), 680–686.

Goldstein, K. E., Hazlett, E. A., New, A. S., Haznedar, M. M., Newmark, R. E., Zelmanova, Y., et al. (2009). Smaller superior temporal gyrus volume specificity in schizotypal personality disorder. *Schizophrenia Research, 112*(1–3), 14–23.

Golier, J. A., Yehuda, R., Bierer, L. M., Mitropoulou, V., New, A. S., Schmeidler, J., et al. (2003). The relationship of borderline personality disorder to posttraumatic stress disorder and traumatic events. *American Journal of Psychiatry, 160*, 2018–2024.

Grant, B. F., Chou, S. P., Goldstein, R. B., Huang, B., Stinson, F. S., Saha, T. D., et al. (2008). Prevalence, correlates, disability, and comorbidity of DSM IV borderline personality disorder: Results from the Wave 2 National Epidemiologic Survey on Alcohol and Related Conditions. *Journal of Clinical Psychiatry, 69*(4), 533–545.

Grant, B. F., Hasin, D. S., Stinson, F. S., Dawson, D. A., Chou, S. P., Ruan, W. J., et al. (2004). Prevalence, correlates, and disability of personality disorders in the United States: Results from the national epidemiologic survey on alcohol and related conditions. *Journal of Clinical Psychiatry, 65*(7), 948–958.

Grant, B. F., Hasin, D. S., Stinson, F. S., Dawson, D. A., Chou, S. P., Ruan, W. J., Pickering, R. P., et al. (2004). Prevalence, correlates, and disability of personality disorders in the United States: results from the National Epidemiologic Survey on Alcohol and Related Conditions. *J Clin Psychiatry, 65*: 948–958.

Greenberg, B. D., Li, Q., Lucas, F. R., Hu, S., Sirota, L. A., Benjamin, J., et al. (2000). Association between the serotonin transporter promoter polymorphism and personality traits in a primarily female population sample. *American Journal of Medical Genetics (Neuropsychiatric Genetics), 96*, 202–216.

Grilo, C. M., Anez, L. M., & McGlashan, T. H. (2002). DSM-IV axis II comorbidity with borderline personality disorder in monolingual Hispanic psychiatric outpatients. *Journal of Nervous and Mental Disease, 190*(5), 324–330.

Grilo, C. M., Sanislow, C. A., Gunderson, J. G., Pagano, M. E., Yen, S., Zanarini, M. C., et al. (2004). Two-year stability and change of schizotypal, borderline, avoidant, and obsessive-compulsive personality disorders. *Journal of Consulting and Clinical Psychology, 72*(5), 767–775.

Grilo, C. M., Sanislow, C. A., & McGlashan, T. H. (2002). Co-occurrence of DSM-IV personality disorders with borderline personality disorder. *Journal of Nervous and Mental Disease, 190*, 552–554.

Gross, R., Olfson, M., Gameroff, M., Shea, S., Feder, A., Fuentes, M., et al. (2002). Borderline personality disorder in primary care. *Archives of Internal Medicine, 162*, 53–60.

Gunderson, J. G. (2001). *Borderline personality disorder: A clinical guide.* Washington, DC: American Psychiatric Publishing.

Gunderson, J. G., & Ronningstam, E. (2001). Differentiating narcissistic and antisocial personality disorders. *Journal of Personality Disorders, 15*(2), 103–109.

Gunderson, J. G., Ronningstam, E., & Smith, L. (1991). Narcissistic personality disorder: A review of data on DSM-III-R descriptions. *Journal of Personality Disorders, 5*, 167–177.

Gunter, T. D., Arndt, S., Wenman, G., Allen, J., Loveless, P., Sieleni, B., et al. (2008). Frequency of mental and addictive disorders among 320 men and women entering the Iowa prison system: Use of the MINI-Plus. *Journal of the American Academy of Psychiatry and the Law, 36*, 27–34.

Guntrip, H. J. S. (1968). *Schizoid phenomena, object-relations, and the self.* New York: International Universities Press.

Gurvits, I. G., Koenigsberg, H. W., & Siever, L. (2000). Neurotransmitter dysfunction in patients with borderline personality disorder. *Psychiatric Clinics of North America, 23*, 27–40.

Haaland, V. O., & Landro, N. I. (2007). Decision making as measured with the Iowa Gambling Task in patients with borderline personality disorder. *Journal of the International Neuropsychological Society, 13*(4), 699–703.

Haaland, V. O., & Landro, N. I. (2009). Pathological dissociation and neuropsychological functioning in borderline personality disorder. *Acta Psychiatrica Scandinavica, 119*, 383–392.

Halles, D. L., & Miles, D. R. (2004). Personality disturbances in drug-dependent women: Relationship to childhood abuse. *American Journal of Drug and Alcohol Abuse, 30*(2), 269–286.

Hardy, G. E., Barkham, M., Shapiro, D. A., Stiles, W. B., Rees, A., & Reynolds, S. (1995). Impact of cluster C personality disorders on outcomes of contrasting brief psychotherapies for depression. *Journal of Consulting and Clinical Psychology, 63*, 997–1004.

Hare, R. D. (1978). Electrodermal and cardiovascular correlates of psychopathy. In R. D. Hare & D. Schalling (Eds.), *Psychopathic behavior: Approaches to research* (pp. 107–143). Chichester, UK: Wiley.

Hare, R. D. (2003). *Manual for the Hare Psychopathy Checklist-Revised* (2nd ed.). Toronto, Canada: Multi-Health Systems.

Hare, R. D., Frazelle, J., & Cox, D. N. (1978). Psychopathy and physiological responses to threat of an aversive stimulus. *Psychophysiology, 152*, 165–172.

Hare, R. D., Hart, S. D., & Harpur, T. J. (1991). Psychopathy and the DSM-IV criteria for antisocial personality disorder. *Journal of Abnormal Psychology, 100*, 391–398.

Hare, R. D., & Jutai, J. W. (1988). Psychopathy and cerebral asymmetry in semantic processing. *Personality and Individual Differences, 9*, 329–337.

Hariri, A. R., Mattay, V. S., Tessitore, A., Kolachana, B., Fera, F., Goldman, D., et al. (2002). Serotonin transporter genetic variation and the response of the human amygdala. *Science, 297*, 400–403.

Hazlett, E. A., Buchsbaum, M. S., Haznedar, M. M., Newmark, R., Goldstein, K. E., Zelmanova, Y., et al. (2008). Cortical gray and white matter volume in unmedicated schizotypal and schizophrenia patients. *Schizophrenia Research, 101*, 111–123.

Hazlett, E. A., New, A. S., Newmark, R., Haznedar, M. M., Lo, J. N., Speiser, L. J., et al. (2005). Reduced anterior and posterior cingulate gray matter in borderline personality disorder. *Biological Psychiatry, 58*, 614–623.

Head, S. B., Baker, J. D., & Williamson, D. A. (1991). Family environment characteristics and dependent personality disorder. *Journal of Personality Disorders, 5*, 256–263.

Heinrichs, R. W., & Zakzanis, K. K. (1998). Neurocognitive deficit in schizophrenia: A quantitative review of the evidence. *Neuropsychology, 12*, 426–445.

Henry, C., Mitropoulou, V., New, A. S., Koenigsberg, H. W., Silverman, J., & Siever, L. J. (2001). Affective instability and impulsivity in borderline personality and bipolar II disorders: Similarities and differences. *Journal of Psychiatric Research, 35*, 307–312.

Herpertz, S. C., Dietrich, T. M., Wenning, B., Krings, T., Erberich, S. G., Willmes, K., et al. (2001). Evidence of abnormal amygdala functioning in borderline personality disorder: A functional MRI study. *Biological Psychiatry, 50*(4), 292–298.

Herve, H. F., Hayes, P., & Hare, R. D. (2003). Psychopathy and sensitivity to the emotional polarity of metaphorical statements. *Personality and Individual Differences, 357*, 1497–1507.

Hiatt, K. D., Schmitt, W. A., & Newman, J. P. (2004). Stroop tasks reveal abnormal selective attention among psychopathic offenders. *Neuropsychology, 18*, 50–59.

Hipwell, A. E., Loeber, R., Stouthamer-Loeber, M., Keenan, K., White, H. R., & Kroneman, L. (2002). Characteristics of girls with early onset disruptive and antisocial behavior. *Criminal Behavior and Mental Health, 12*, 99–118.

Holdwick, D. J., Hilsenroth, M. J., Castlebury, F. D., & Blais, M. A. (1998). Identifying the unique and common characteristics among the DSM-IV antisocial, borderline and narcissistic personality disorder. *Comprehensive Psychiatry, 39*(5), 277–286.

Holmes, A., Murphy, D. L., & Crawley, J. N. (2002). Reduced aggression in mice lacking the serotonin transporter. *Psychopharmacology, 161*(2), 160–167.

Hori, A. (1998). Pharmacotherapy for personality disorders. *Psychiatry and Clinical Neurosciences, 52*(1), 13–19.

Horn, N., Dolan, M., Elliot, R., Deakin, J. F. W., & Woodruff, P. W. (2003). Response inhibition and impulsivity: An FMRI study. *Neuropsychologia, 41*, 1959–1966.

Hueston, W. J., Werth, J., & Mainous, A. G. III (1999). Personality disorder traits: Prevalence and effects on health status in primary care patients. *International Journal of Psychiatry in Medicine, 29*, 63–74.

Ingenhoven, T., Lafay, P., Rinne, T., Passchier, J., & Duivenvoorden, H. (2010). Effectiveness of pharmacotherapy for severe personality disorders: Meta-analyses of randomized controlled trials. *Journal of Clinical Psychiatry, 71*(1), 14–25.

Jackson, H. J., & Burgess, P. M. (2004). Personality disorders in the community: Results from the Australian National Survey of Mental Health and Well-being Part III. Relationships between specific type of personality disorder, Axis 1 Mental disorders and physical conditions with disability and health consultations. *Social Psychiatry and Psychiatric Epidemiology, 39*(10), 765–776.

Jackson, P. L., Brunet, E., Meltzoff, A. N., & Decety, J. (2006). Empathy examined through the neural mechanisms involved in imagining how I feel versus how you feel pain. *Neuropsychologia, 44*(5), 752–761.

Jackson, P. L., Meltzoff, A. N., & Decety, J. (2005). How do we perceive the pain of others? *A window into the neural processes involved in empathy. Neuroimage, 24*(3), 771–779.

Jacob, C. P., Muller, J., Schmidt, M., Hohenberger, K., Gutknecht, L., Reif, A., et al. (2005). Cluster B personality disorders are associated with allelic variation of monoamine oxidase A activity. *Neuropsychopharmacology, 30*(9), 1711–1718.

Jacob, C. P., Strobel, A., Hohenberger, K., Ringel, T., Gutknecht, L., Reif, A., et al. (2004). Association between allelic variation of serotonin transporter function and neuroticism in anxious cluster C personality disorders. *American Journal of Psychiatry, 161*(3), 569–572.

Jang, K. L., Livesley, W. J., Vernon, P. A., & Jackson, D. N. (1996). Heritability of personality disorder traits: A twin study. *Acta Psychiatrica Scandinavica, 94*, 438–444.

Johnson, J. G., Cohen, P., Kasen, S., & Brook, J. S. (2005). Personality disorder traits associated with risk for unipolar depression during middle adulthood. *Psychiatry Research, 136*, 113–121.

Johnson, J. G., Cohen, P., Smailes, E. M., Kasen, S., Oldham, J. M., & Skodol, A. E. (2000). Adolescent personality disorders associated with violence and criminal behavior during adolescence and early adulthood. *American Journal of Psychiatry, 157*, 1406–1412.

Joyce, P. R., McHugh, P. C., McKenzie, J. M., Sullivan, P. F., Mulder, R. T., Luty, S. E., et al. (2006). A dopamine transporter polymorphism is a risk factor for borderline personality disorder in depressed patients. *Psychological Medicine, 36*, 807–813.

Judd, P. H., & McGlashan, T. H. (2003). *A developmental model of BPD: Understanding variations in course and outcome.* Arlington, VA: American Psychiatric Press.

Jutai, J. W., Hare, R. D., & Connolly, J. F. (1987). Psychopathy and event-related brain potentials: ERPs associated with attention to speech stimuli. *Personality and Individual Differences, 82*, 175–184.

Kamali, M., Oquendo, M. A., & Mann, J. J. (2002). Understanding the neurobiology of suicidal behavior. *Depression and Anxiety, 14*, 164–176.

Kasen, S., Cohen, P., Skodol, A. E., Johnson, J. G., Smailes, E., & Brook, J. S. (2001). Childhood depression and adult personality disorder: Alternative pathways of continuity. *Archives of General Psychiatry, 58*, 231–236.

Kawasaki, Y., Suzuki, M., Nohara, S., Hagino, H., Takahashi, T., Matsui, M., et al. (2004). Structural brain differences in patients with schizophrenia and schizotypal disorder demonstrated by voxel-based morphometry. *European Archives of Psychiatry and Clinical Neuroscience, 254*, 406–414.

Kay, J. H., Altshuler, L. L., Ventura, J., & Mintz, J. (2002). Impact of axis II comorbidity on the course of bipolar illness in men: A retrospective chart review. *Bipolar Disorders, 4*(4), 237–242.

Kazdin, A. E., Whitley, M., & Marciano, P. L. (2006). Child–therapist and parent–therapist alliance and therapeutic change in the treatment of children referred for oppositional, aggressive and antisocial behavior. *Journal of Child Psychology and Psychiatry, 47*(5), 436–445.

Kendler, K. S., & Gruenberg, A. M. (1982). Genetic relationship between paranoid personality disorder and the "schizophrenia spectrum" disorders. *American Journal of Psychiatry, 139*, 1185–1186.

Kendler, K.S., Masterson, C.C., & Davis, K. L. (1985). Psychiatric illness in first-degree relatives of patients with paranoid psychosis, schizophrenia and medical illness. *British Journal of Psychiatry, 147*, 524–531.

Kendler, K. S., McGuire, M., Gruenberg, A. M., O'Hare, A., Spellman, M., & Walsh, D. (1993). The Roscommon Family Study. I. Methods, diagnosis of probands, and risk of schizophrenia in relatives. *Archives of General Psychiatry, 50*(7), 527–540.

Kendler, K. S., McGuire, M., Gruenberg, A. M., O'Hare, A., Spellman, M., & Walsh, D. (1993). The Roscommon Family Study. III. Schizophrenia-related personality disorders in relatives. *Archives of General Psychiatry, 50*(10), 781–788.

Kendler, K. S., Myers, J., Torgersen, S., Neale, M. C., & Reichborn-Kjennerud, T. (2007). The heritability of cluster A personality disorders assessed by both personal interview and questionnaire. *Psychological Medicine, 37*, 655–665.

Kernberg, O. F. (1988). *Severe personality disorder: Psychotherapeutic strategies*. New Haven, CT: Yale University Press.

Kernberg, P. (1998). Narcissistic personality disorder in children. In E. Ronningstam (Ed.), *Disorders of narcissism: Diagnostic, clinical and empirical implications* (pp. 103–120). Washington, DC: American Psychiatric Press.

Kerr, M., Tremblay, R. E., Pagani, L., & Vitaro, F. (1997). Boys' behavioral inhibition and risk for later delinquency. *Archives of General Psychiatry, 54*, 809–816.

Kety, S. S., Wender, P. H., Jacobsen, B., Ingraham, L. J., Jansson, L., Faber, B., et al. (1994). Mental illness in the biological and adoptive relatives of schizophrenic adoptees. Replication of the Copenhagen Study in the rest of Denmark. *Archives of General Psychiatry, 51*(6), 442–455.

Khouzam, H., & Donnelly, N. (1997). Remission of self-mutilation in a patient with borderline personality disorder during risperidone therapy. *Journal of Nervous and Mental Disease, 185*, 348–349.

Kiehl, K. A. (2006). A cognitive neuroscience perspective on psychopathy: Evidence for paralimbic system dysfunction. *Psychiatry Research, 142*(23), 107–128.

Kiehl, K. A., Hare, R. D., McDonald, J. J., Brink, J. (1999a) Semantic and affective processing in psychopaths: an event-related potential (ERP) study. *Psychophysiology, 36*(6): 765–774.

Kiehl, K. A., Liddle, P. F., & Hopfinger, J. B. (2000a). Error processing and the rostral anterior cingulate: An event-related fMRI study. *Psychophysiology, 37*, 216–223.

Kiehl, K. A., Liddle, P. F., Smith, A. S., Mendrek, A., Forster, B. B., & Hare, R. D. (1999b). Neural pathways involved in the processing of concrete and abstract words. *Human Brain Mapping, 7*, 225–233.

Kiehl, K. A., Smith, A. M., Hare, R. D., & Liddle, P. F. (2000b). An event-related potential investigation of response inhibition in schizophrenia and psychopathy. *Biological Psychiatry, 483*, 210–221.

Kiehl, K. A., Smith, A. M., Hare, R. D., Mendrek, A., Forster, B. B., Brink, J., et al. (2001). Limbic abnormalities in affective processing by criminal psychopaths as revealed by functional magnetic resonance imaging. *Biological Psychiatry, 50*(9), 677–684.

Kim, J., Kim, B., & Cho, S. (2006). The dopamine transporter gene and the impulsivity phenotype in attention deficit hyperactivity disorder: A case-control association study in a Korean sample. *Journal of Psychiatric Research, 40*, 730–737.

Kimonis, E. R., Frick, P. J., Fazekas, H., & Loney, B. R. (2006). Psychopathy, aggression, and the processing of emotional stimuli in non-referred girls and boys. *Behavioral Sciences and the Law, 24*(1), 21–37.

Kirkpatrick, T., Joyce, E., Milton, J., Duggan, C., Tyrer, P., & Rogers, R. D. (2007). Altered emotional decision-making in prisoners with borderline personality disorder. *Journal of Personality Disorders, 21*, 243–226.

Klein, D. N. (2003). Patients' versus informants' reports of personality disorders in predicting 7-year outcome in outpatients with depressive disorders. *Psychological Assessment, 15*, 216–222.

Klein, D. N., Riso, L. P., Donaldson, S. K., Schwartz, J. E., Anderson, R. L., Ouimette, P. C., et al. (1995). Family study of early-onset dysthymia: Mood and personality disorders in relatives of outpatients of dysthymia and episodic major depression and normal controls. *Archives of General Psychiatry, 52*, 487–496.

Koo, M. S., Levitt, J. J., McCarley, R. W., Seidman, L. J., Dickey, C. C., Niznikiewicz, M. A., et al. (2006). Reduction of caudate nucleus volumes in neuroleptic-naïve female subjects with schizotypal personality disorder. *Biological Psychiatry, 60*(1), 40–48.

Kosson, D. S. (1996). Psychopathy and dual-task performance under focusing conditions. *Journal of Abnormal Psychology, 105*, 391–400.

Kozel, F. A., Johnson, K. A., Mu, Q., Grenesko, E. L., Laken, S. J., George, M. S. (2005). Detecting Deception Using Functional Magnetic Resonance Imaging. *Biological Psychiatry, 58*(8), 605–613.

Kozel, F. A., Padgett, T. M., & George, M. S. (2004). A replication study of the neural correlates of deception. *Behavioral Neuroscience, 118*, 852–856.

Lahey, B. B., Waldman, I., & McBurnett, K. (1999). The development of antisocial behavior: An integrative causal model. *Journal of Child Psychology and Psychiatry, 40*, 669–682.

Lapierre, D., Braun, C. M. J., & Hodgins, S. (1995). Ventral frontal deficits in psychopathy: Neuropsychological test findings. *Neuropsychologia, 332*, 139–151.

Lee, K., Baillargeon, R. H., Vermunt, J. K., Wu, H., & Tremblay, R. E. (2007). Age differences in the prevalence of physical aggression among 5–11-year-old Canadian boys and girls. *Aggressive Behavior, 33*(1), 26–37.

Lee, S. S., & Hinshaw, S. P. (2004). Severity of adolescent delinquency among boys with and without attention deficit hyperactivity disorder: Predictions from early antisocial behavior and peer status. *Journal of Clinical Child and Adolescent Psychology, 33*(4), 705–716.

Lee, T. M. C., Ho-Ling, L., Chan, C. C. H., Yen-Bee, N., Fox, P. T., & Gao, J. (2005). Neural correlates of feigned memory impairment. *Neuroimage, 28*, 305–313.

LeGris, J., & van Reekum, R. (2006). The neuropsychological correlates of borderline personality disorder and suicidal behaviour. *Canadian Journal of Psychiatry, 51*, 131–142.

Lenzenweger, M. F., Lane, M. C., Loranger, A. W., & Kessler, R. C. (2007). DSM-IV personality disorders in the National Comorbidity Survey Replication. *Biological Psychiatry, 62*, 553–564.

Lesch, K. P., Bengel, D., Heils, A., Sabol, S. Z., Greenberg, B. D., Petri, S., et al. (1996). Association of anxiety-related traits with a polymorphism in the serotonin transporter gene regulatory region. *Science, 274*(5292), 1527–1531.

Levenston, G. K., Patrick, C. J., Bradley, M. M., & Lang, P. J. (2000). The psychopath as observer: Emotion and attention in picture processing. *Journal of Abnormal Psychology, 109*(3), 373–385.

Levitt, J. J., McCarley, R. W., Dickey, C. C., Voglmaier, M. M., Niznikiewicz, M. A., Seidman, L. J., et al. (2002). MRI study of caudate nucleus volume and its cognitive correlates in neuroleptic-naive patients with schizotypal personality disorder. *American Journal of Psychiatry, 159*, 1190–1197.

Lewis, D. O., Lewis, M. L., Unger, L., & Goldman, C. (1984). Conduct disorder and its synonyms: Diagnoses of dubious validity and usefulness. *American Journal of Psychiatry, 141*, 514–519.

Lijffijt, M., Moeller, F. G., Boutros, N. N., Burroughs, S., Steinberg, J. L., Lane, S. D., et al. (2009). A pilot study revealing impaired P50 gating in antisocial personality disorder. *Journal of Neuropsychiatry and Clinical Neurosciences, 21*(3), 328–331.

Linehan, M. (1993). *Cognitive–behavioral treatment of borderline personality disorder*. New York: Guilford Press.

Livesly, W. J. (2005). Principles and strategies for treating personality disorder. *Canadian Journal of Psychiatry, 50*(8), 442–450.

Loeber, R., Burke, J. D., Lahey, B. B., Winters, A., & Zera, M. (2000). Oppositional defiant disorder and conduct disorder: A review of the past 10 years, part I. *Journal of the American Academy of Child and Adolescent Psychiatry, 39*(12), 1468–1484.

Loney, B. R., Frick, P. J., Clements, C. B., Ellis, M. L., & Kerlin, K. (2003). Callous-unemotional traits, impulsivity, and emotional processing in adolescents with antisocial behavior problems. *Journal of Clinical Child and Adolescent Psychology, 321*, 66–80.

Luborsky, L. (1984). *Principles of psychoanalytic psychotherapy*. New York: Basic Books.

Lupien, S. J., Gillin, C. J., & Hauger, R. L. (1999). Working memory is more sensitive than declarative memory to the acute effects of corticosteroids: A dose-response study in humans. *Behavioral Neuroscience, 113*, 420–430.

Lynam, D. R. (1996). The early identification of chronic offenders: Who is the fledgling psychopath? *Psychological Bulletin, 120*, 209–234.

Lynam, D. R. (1997). Pursuing the psychopath: Capturing the fledgling psychopath in a nomological net. *Journal of Abnormal Psychology, 106*, 425–438.

Lyons-Ruth, K., Holmes, B. M., Sasvari-Szekely, M., Ronai, Z., Nemoda, Z., & Pauls, D. (2007). Serotonin transporter polymorphism and borderline or antisocial traits among low-income young adults. *Psychiatric Genetics, 17*, 339–343.

Lyoo, I. K., Han, M. H., & Cho, D. Y. (1998). A brain MRI study in subjects with borderline personality disorder. *Journal of Affective Disorders, 50*(2–3), 235–243.

Maier, W., Lichtermann, D., Klingler, T., Heun, R., & Hallmayer, J. (1992). Prevalences of personality disorders (DSM-III-R) in the community. *Journal of Personality Disorders, 6*, 187–196.

Marinangeli, M. G., Butti, G., Scinto, A., Di Cicco, L., Petruzzi, C., Daneluzzo, E., et al. (2000). Patterns of comorbidity among DSM-III-R personality disorders. *Psychopathology, 33*, 69–74.

Mathis, H. (1970). *Emotional responsivity in the antisocial personality* (Unpublished doctoral dissertation). George Washington University, Washington, DC.

Mattia, J. I., & Zimmerman, M. (2001). Epidemiology. In Handbook of Personality Disorders, Livesley, W. J. (ed.). Guilford Press, New York.

McClure, M. M., Harvey, P. D., Goodman, M., Triebwasser, J., New, A., Koenigsberg, H. W., et al. (2010). Pergolide treatment of cognitive deficits associated with schizotypal personality disorder: Continued evidence of the importance of the dopamine system in the schizophrenia spectrum. *Neuropsychopharmacology, 35*, 1356–1362.

McClure, M. M., Romero, M. J., Bowie, C. R., Reichenberg, A., Harvey, P. D., & Siever, L. J. (2007). Visual spatial learning and memory in schizotypal personality disorder: Continued evidence for the importance of working memory in the schizophrenia spectrum. *Archives of Clinical Neuropsychology, 22*, 109–116.

McFayden-Ketchum, S. A., Bates, J. E., Dodge, K. A., & Pettit, G. S. (1996). Patterns of change in early childhood aggressive–disruptive behavior: Gender differences in predictions from early coercive and affectionate mother–child interactions. *Child Development, 67*, 2417–2433.

McGough, J. L., Roozendaal, B., & Cahill, L. (2000). Modulation of memory storage by stress hormones and the amygdaloid complex. In M. S. Gazzaniga (Ed.), *The new cognitive neuroscience* (pp. 1081–1098). Cambridge, MA: MIT Press.

Miller, A. L., Muehlenkamp, J. J., & Jacobson, C. M. (2008). Fact or fiction: Diagnosing borderline personality disorder in adolescents. *Clinical Psychology Review, 28*(6), 969–981.

Millon, T. (1981). *Disorders of personality DSM-III: Axis II*. New York: Wiley & Sons.

Millon, T. (1996). *Disorders of personality: DSM-IV and beyond*. New York: Wiley.

Mitchell, D., Colledge, E., Leonard, A., & Blair, R. J. R. (2002). Risky decisions and response reversal: Is there evidence of orbitofrontal cortex dysfunction in psychopathic individuals? *Neuropsychologia, 40*(12), 2013–2022.

Mitropoulou, V., Harvey, P. D., Maldari, L. A., Moriarty, P. J., New, A. S., Silverman, J. M., et al. (2002). Neuropsychological performance in schizotypal personality disorder: Evidence regarding diagnostic specificity. *Biological Psychiatry, 52*, 1175–1182.

Mitropoulou, V., Harvey, P. D., Zegarelli, G., New, A. S., Silverman, J. M., & Siever, L. J. (2005). Neuropsychological performance in schizotypal personality disorder: Importance of working memory. *American Journal of Psychiatry, 162*, 1896–1903.

Moffitt, T. E. (1993). Adolescence-limited and life-course-persistent antisocial behavior: A development taxonomy. *Psychological Review, 100*, 674–701.

Moffitt, T. E. (2003). Life-course persistent and adolescence-limited antisocial behavior: A 10-year research review and a research agenda. In B. B. Lahey, T. E. Moffitt, & A. Caspi (Eds.), *Causes of conduct disorder and juvenile delinquency* (pp. 49–75). New York: Guilford Press.

Moffitt, T. E., & Caspi, A. (2001). Childhood predictors differentiate life-course persistent and adolescence-limited antisocial pathways among males and females. *Development and Psychopathology, 13*(2), 355–375.

Moffitt, T. E., Caspi, A., Rutter, M., & Silva, P. A. (2001). Sex differences in antisocial behavior: Conduct disorder, delinquency, and violence in the Dunedin Longitudinal Study. New York: Cambridge University Press.

Mol, B., Van Den Bos, P., & Derks, Y. (2009). Executive functioning and the two-factor model of psychopathy: No differential relation? *International Journal of Neuroscience, 119*, 124–140.

Monarch, E. S., Saykin, A. J., & Flashman, L. A. (2004). Neuropsychological impairment in borderline personality disorder. *Psychiatric Clinics of North America, 27*, 67–82.

Moran, P., Jenkins, R., Tylee, A., Blizard, R., & Mann, A. (2000). The prevalence of personality disorders among UK primary care attenders. *Acta Psychiatrica Scandinavica, 102*, 52–57.

Moran, P., Rendu, A., Jenkins, R., Tylee, A., & Mann, A. (2001). The impact of personality disorder in UK primary care: A 1-year follow-up of attenders. *Psychological Medicine, 31*, 1447–1454.

Morgan, A. B., & Lilienfeld, S. O. (2000). A meta-analytic review of the relation between antisocial behaviour and neuropsychological measures of executive function. *Clinical Psychology Review, 20*(1), 113–136.

Morse, J. Q., & Lynch, T. R. (2004). A preliminary investigation of self-reported personality disorders in late life: Prevalence, predictors of depressive severity, and clinical correlates. *Aging & Mental Health, 8*, 307–315.

Mueser, K. T., Crocker, A. G., Frisman, L. B., Drake, R. E., Covell, N. H., & Essock, S. M. (2006). Conduct disorder and antisocial personality disorder in persons with severe psychiatric and substance use disorders. *Schizophrenia Bulletin, 32*, 626–636.

Munafò, M. R., Brown, S. M., & Hariri, A. R. (2008). Serotonin transporter (5-HTTLPR) genotype and amygdala activation: A meta-analysis. *Biological Psychiatry, 63*(9), 852–857.

Murphy, D. L., Sims, K. B., Karoum, F., de la Chapelle, A., Norio, R., Sankila, E. M., et al. (1990). Marked amine and amine metabolite changes in Norrie disease patients with an X-chromosomal deletion affecting monoamine oxidase. *Journal of Neurochemistry, 54*, 242–247.

Nemeroff, C. B., & Owens, M. J. (2004). Pharmacologic differences among the SSRIs: Focus on monoamine transporters and the HPA axis. *CNS Spectrums, 9*, 23–31.

Nestadt, G., Di, C., Samuels, J. F., Bienvenu, O. J., Reti, I. M., Costa, P., et al. (2010). The stability of DSM personality disorders over twelve to eighteen years. *Journal of Psychiatric Research, 44*(1), 1–17.

Newman, D. L., Moffitt, T., Caspi, A., & Silva, P. A. (1998). Comorbid mental disorders: Implications for treatment and sample selection. *Journal of Abnormal Psychology, 107*, 305–311.

Niederhofer, H. (2004). Left-handedness in a sample of nine patients with borderline personality disorder. *Perceptual and Motor Skills, 99*, 849–852.

Nigg, J. T., Silk, K. R., Stavro, G., & Miller, T. (2005). Disinhibition and borderline personality disorder. *Development and Psychopathology, 17*, 1129–1149.

Nuechterlein, K. H., Barch, D. M., Gold, J. M., Goldberg, T. E., Green, M. F., & Heaton, R. F. (2004). Identification of separable cognitive factors in schizophrenia. *Schizophrenia Research, 72*(1), 29–39.

Nunez, M. J., Casey, B. J., Egner, T., Hare, T., & Hirsch, J. (2005). Intentional false responding shares neural substrates with response conflict and control. *Neuroimage, 25*, 267–277.

Odgers, C. L., Moffitt, T. E., Broadbent, J. M., Dickson, N., Hancox, R. J., Harrington, H., et al. (2008). Female and male antisocial trajectories: From childhood origins to adult outcomes. *Development and Psychopathology, 20*(2), 673–716.

O'Leary, K. M., Brouwers, P., Gardner, D. L., & Cowdry, R. W. (1991). Neuropsychological testing of patients with borderline personality disorder. *American Journal of Psychiatry, 148*, 106–111.

Olweus, D. (1979). Stability of aggressive reaction patterns in males: A review. *Psychological Bulletin, 86*(4), 852–875.

Ortiz, J., & Raine, A. (2004). Heart rate level and antisocial behavior in children and adolescents: A meta-analysis. *Journal of the American Academy of Child and Adolescent Psychiatry, 43*(2), 154–162.

Overholser, J. C., Stockmeier, C., & Dilley, G. (2002). Personality disorders in suicide attempters and completers: Preliminary findings. *Archives of Suicide Research, 6*, 123–133.

Paris, J. (2002). Chronic suicidality among patients with BPD *Psychiatric Services, 53*, 738–742.

Paris, J. (2007). The nature of BPD: Multiple dimensions, multiple symptoms, but one category. *Journal of Personality Disorders, 21*, 457–473.

Parker, J. D. A., & Bagby, R. M. (1997). Impulsivity in adults: A critical review of measurement approaches. In C. D. Webster & M. A. Jackson (Eds.), *Impulsivity: Theory, assessment, and treatment* (pp. 142–157). New York: Guilford Press.

Parvizi, J., Van Hoesen, G. W., Buckwalter, J., & Damasio, A. R. (2006). Neural connections of the posteromedial cortex in the macaque. *Proceedings of the National Academy of Sciences of the United States of America, 103*, 1563–1568.

Patrick, C. J. Emotional processes in psychopathy. (2001). *In A. Raine & J. Sanmartín (Eds.), Violence and psychopathy*, (pp. 57–78). New York: Kluwer Academic/Plenum Publishers.

Perugi, G., & Akiskal, H. S. (2002). The soft bipolar spectrum redefined: Focus on the cyclothymic, anxious-sensitive, impulse-dyscontrol, and binge-eating connection in bipolar II and related conditions. *Psychiatric Clinics of North America, 25*(4), 713–737.

Petitt, G. S., Bates, J. E., & Dodge, K. A. (1993). Family interaction patterns and children's conduct problems at home and school: A longitudinal perspective. *School Psychology Review, 22*, 403–420.

Plakun, E. M. (1990). Empirical overview of narcissistic personality disorder. In E.M. Plakun (Ed.), *New perspectives on narcissism* (pp. 101–149). Washington, DC: American Psychiatric Press.

Raine, A., Baker, L., & Liu, J. (2006). Biological risk factors for antisocial and criminal behavior. In A. Raine (Ed.), *Crime and schizophrenia: Causes and cures* (pp. 83–108). New York: Nova Science.

Raine, A., Lencz, T., Bihrle, S., LaCasse, L., & Colletti, P. (2000). Reduced prefrontal gray matter volume and reduced autonomic activity in antisocial personality disorder. *Archives of General Psychiatry, 57*, 119–127.

Raine, A., & Yang, Y. (2006). Neural foundations to moral reasoning and antisocial behavior. *Social, Cognitive, and Affective Neuroscience, 1*, 203–213.

Rajarethinam, R. P., DeQuardo, J. R., Nalepa, R., & Tandon, R. (2000). Superior temporal gyrus in schizophrenia: A volumetric magnetic resonance imaging study. *Schizophrenia Research, 41*, 303–312.

Rathus, J. H., Sanderson, W. C., Miller, A. L., & Wetzler, S. (1995). Impact of personality functioning on cognitive behavioral treatment of panic disorder: A preliminary report. *Journal of Personality Disorders, 9*(2), 160–168.

Rector, N. A., Bagby, R. M., Segal, Z. V., Joffe, R. T., & Levitt, A. (2000). Self-criticism and dependency in depressed patients treated with cognitive therapy or pharmacotherapy. *Cognitive Therapy and Research, 24*, 571–584.

Reich, J. H., & Vasile, R. G. (1993). Effect of personality disorders on the treatment outcome of axis I conditions: An update. *Journal of Nervous and Mental Disease, 181*, 475–484.

Reif, A., Rösler, M., Freitag, C. M., Schneider, M., Eujen, A., Kissling, C., et al. (2007). Nature and nurture predispose to violent behavior: Serotonergic genes and adverse childhood environment. *Neuropsychopharmacology, 32*(11), 2375–2383.

Rendu, A., Moran, P., Patel, A., Knapp, M., & Mann, A. (2002). Economic impact of personality disorders in UK primary care attenders. *British Journal of Psychiatry, 181*, 62–66.

Rentrop, M., Backenstrass, M., Jaentsch, B., Kaiser, S., Roth, A., Unger, J., et al. (2008). Response inhibition in borderline personality disorder: Performance in a Go/Nogo task. *Psychopathology, 41*(1), 50–57.

Retz, W., Retz-Junginger, P., Supprian, T., Thome, J., & Rösler, M. (2004). Association of serotonin transporter promoter gene polymorphism with violence: Relation with personality disorders, impulsivity, and childhood ADHD psychopathology. *Behavioral Sciences and the Law, 22*, 415–425.

Rhee, S. H., & Waldman, I. D. (2002). A meta-analytic review of twin and adoption studies examining antisocial behavior. *Psychological Bulletin, 128*, 490–529.

Richters, J. E. (1997). The Hubble hypothesis and the developmentalist's dilemma. *Development and Psychopathology, 9*, 193–229.

Rilling, J. K., Glenn, A. L., Jairam, M. R., Pagnoni, G., Goldsmith, D. R., Elfenbein, H. A., et al. (2007). Neural correlates of social cooperation and non-cooperation as a function of psychopathy. *Biological Psychiatry, 61*(11), 1260–1271.

Rinne, T., van den Brink, W., Wouters, L., & van Dyck, R. (2002). SSRI treatment of borderline personality disorder: A randomized, placebo-controlled clinical trial for female patients with borderline personality disorder. *American Journal of Psychiatry, 159*, 2048–2054.

Rogers, R. D. (2006). The functional architecture of the frontal lobes: Implications for research with psychopathic offenders. In C. J. Patrick (Ed.), *Handbook of psychopathy* (pp. 313–334). London: The Guilford Press.

Rosenthal, D., Wender, P. H., Kety, S. S., Welner, J., & Schulsinger, F. (1971). The adopted-away offspring of schizophrenics. *American Journal of Psychiatry, 128*, 307–311.

Rossi, A., Marinangeli, M. G., Butti, G., Scinto, A., DiCicco, L., Kalyvoka, A., et al. (2001). Personality disorders in bipolar and depressive disorders. *Journal of Affective Disorders, 65*(1), 3–8.

Ruocco, A. C. (2005). The neuropsychology of borderline personality disorder: A meta-analysis and review. *Psychiatry Research, 137*, 191–202.

Ruocco, A. C., McCloskey, M., Lee, R., & Coccaro, E. F. (2009). Indices of orbitofrontal and prefrontal function in cluster B and cluster C personality disorders. *Psychiatry Research, 170*(2–3), 282–285.

Rusch, N., Tebartz van Elst, L., Ludaescher, P., Wilke, M., Huppertz, H. J., Thiel, T., et al. (2003). A voxel-based morphometric MRI study in female patients with borderline personality disorder. *Neuroimage, 20*, 385–392.

Rylander, M., & Soltys, S. (2012). The psychopharmacology of temperament. In C. A. Noggle & R. S. Dean (Eds.), *The neuropsychology of psychopharmacology*. New York: Springer.

Salzman, C., Wolfson, A. N., Schatzberg, A., Looper, J., Henke, R., Albanese, M., et al. (1995). Effect of fluoxetine on anger in symptomatic volunteers with borderline personality disorder. *Journal of Clinical Psychopharmacology, 15*, 23–29.

Samuels, J., Eaton, W. W., Bienvenu, O. J., Brown, C. H., Costa, P. T., & Nestadt, G. (2002). Prevalence and correlates of personality disorders in a community sample. *British Journal of Psychiatry, 180*, 536–542.

Samuels, J., Nestadt, G., Bienvenu, O. J., Costa, P. T. Jr., Riddle, M. A., Liang, K. Y., et al. (2000). Personality disorders and normal personality dimensions in obsessive-compulsive disorder. *British Journal of Psychiatry, 177*, 457–462.

Sapolsky, R. M. (2000). The possibility of neurotoxicity in the hippocampus in major depression: A primer on neuron death. *Biological Psychiatry, 48*, 755–765.

Sapolsky, R. M., McEwen, B. S., & Rainbow, T. C. (1983). Quantitative autoradiography of [3H] corticosterone receptors in rat brain. *Brain Research, 271*, 331–334.

Sato, T., Sakado, K., Uehara, T., Sato, S., Nishioka, K., & Kasahara, Y. (1997). Personality disorders using DSM-III-R in a Japanese clinical sample with major depression. *Acta Psychiatrica Scandinavica, 95*, 451–453.

Scheepers, F. E., Gispen de Wied, C. C., Hulshoff Pol, H. E., & Kahn, R. S. (2001). Effect of clozapine on caudate nucleus volume in relation to symptoms of schizophrenia. *American Journal of Psychiatry, 158*, 644–646.

Schiffer, F., Teicher, M. H., & Papanicolaou, A. C. (1995). Evoked potential evidence for right-brain activity during the recall of traumatic memories. *Journal of Neuropsychiatry and Clinical Neurosciences, 7*, 169–175.

Shaw, D. S., Winslow, E. B., Owens, E. B., Vondra, J. I., Cohn, J. F., & Bell, R. Q. (1998). The development of early externalizing problems among children from low-income families: A transformational perspective. *Journal of Abnormal Child Psychology, 26*, 95–107.

Sheard, M., Marini, J., Bridges, C., & Wagner, E. (1976). The effect of lithium on impulsive aggressive behavior in man. *American Journal of Psychiatry, 133*, 1409–1413.

Shihabuddin, L., Buchsbaum, M. S., Hazlett, E. A., Silverman, J., New, A., Brickman, A. M., et al. (2001). Striatal size and relative glucose metabolic rate in schizotypal personality disorder and schizophrenia. *Archives of General Psychiatry, 58*, 877–884.

Shirtcliff, E. A., Vitacco, M. J., Graf, A. R., Gostisha, A. J., Merz, J. L., & Zahn-Waxler, C. (2009). Neurobiology of empathy and callousness: Implications for the development of antisocial behavior. *Behavioral Sciences and the Law, 27*(2), 137–171.

Siever, L. (2009). The neurobiology of personality disorders: Implications for psychoanalysis. *Journal of the American Psychoanalytical Association, 57*, 361–398.

Silverthorn, P., & Frick, P. J. (1999). Developmental pathways to antisocial behavior: The delayed-onset pathway in girls. *Development and Psychopathology, 11*(1), 101–126.

Simeon, D., Bartz, J., Hamilton, H., Crystal, S., Braun, A., Ketay, S., et al. (2011). Oxytocin administration attenuates stress reactivity in borderline personality disorder: A pilot study. *Psychoneuroendocrinology, 36*(9), 1418–1421.

Skodol, A. E., Oldham, J. M., Bender, D. S., Dyck, I. R., Stout, R. L., Morey, L. C., et al. (2005). Dimensional representations of DSM-IV personality disorders: Relationships to functional impairment. *American Journal of Psychiatry, 162*, 1919–1925.

Skodol, A. E., Stout, R. L., McGlashan, T. H., Grilo, C. M., Gunderson, J. G., Shea, M. T., et al. (1999). Co-occurrence of mood and personality disorders: A report from the Collaborative Longitudinal Personality Disorders Study (CLPS). *Depression and Anxiety, 10*(4), 175–182.

Soeteman, D. I., Hakkaart-van Roijen, L., Verheul, R., & Busschbach, J. J. V. (2008). The economic burden of personality disorders in mental health care. *Journal of Clinical Psychiatry, 69*, 259–65.

Soeteman, D. I., Verheul, R., & Busschbach, J. J. V. (2008). The burden of disease in personality disorders: Diagnosis-specific quality of life. *Journal of Personality Disorders, 22*, 259–268.

Soloff, P. H., Meltzer, C. C., Becker, C., Greer, P. J., Kelly, T. M., & Constantine, D. (2003). Impulsivity and prefrontal hypometabolism in BPD. *Psychiatry Research, 123*, 153–163.

Soloff, P. H. (1994). Is there any drug treatment of choice for the borderline patient? *Acta Psychiatrica Scandinavica, 89*(S-379), 50–55.

Soloff, P. H., Nutche, J., Goradia, D., & Diwadkar, V. (2008). Structural brain abnormalities in borderline personality disorder: A voxel-based morphometry study. *Psychiatry Research, 164*, 223–236.

Spence, S. A., Farrow, T. D., Herford, A. E., Wilkinson, I. D., Zheng, Y., & Woodruff, P. W. R. (2001). Behavioural and functional anatomical correlates of deception in humans. *Neuroreport, 12*, 2849–2853.

Stein, D. J., Hollander, E., Cohen, L., Frenkel, M., Saoud, J. B., DeCaria, C., et al. (1993). Neuropsychiatric impairment in impulsive personality disorders. *Psychiatry Research, 48*, 257–266.

Stein, D. J., Towney, J., & Hollander, E. (1995). The neuropsychiatry of impulsive aggression. In E. Hollander & D. J. Stein (Eds.), *Impulsivity and aggression* (pp. 91–105). New York: Wiley.

Sterzer, P., Stadler, C., Krebs, A., Kleinschmidt, A., & Poustka, F. (2005). Abnormal neural responses to emotional visual stimuli in adolescents with conduct disorder. *Biological Psychiatry, 57*(1), 7–15.

Sterzer, P., Stadler, C., Poustka, F., & Kleinschmidt, A. (2007). A structural neural deficit in adolescents with conduct disorder and its association with lack of empathy. *Neuroimage, 37*(1), 335–342.

Sutton, S. K., Vitale, J. E., & Newman, J. P. (2002). Emotion among women with psychopathy during picture perception. *Journal of Abnormal Psychology, 111*(4), 610–619.

Suzuki, M., Zhou, S. Y., Takahashi, T., Hagino, H., Kawasaki, Y., Niu, L., et al. (2005). Differential contributions of prefrontal and temporolimbic pathology to mechanisms of psychosis. *Brain, 128*, 2109–2122.

Swann, A. C., Dougherty, D. M., Pazzaglia, P. J., Pham, M., Steinberg, J. L., & Moeller, F. G. (2005). Increased impulsivity associated with severity of suicide attempt history in patients with bipolar disorder. *American Journal of Psychiatry, 162*, 1680–1687.

Swann, A. C., Lijffijt, M., Lane, S. D., Steinberg, J. L., & Moeller, F. G. (2009). Trait impulsivity and response inhibition in antisocial personality disorder. *Journal of Psychiatric Research, 43*, 1057–1063.

Swirsky-Sacchetti, T., Gorton, G., Samuel, S., Sobel, R., Genetta-Wadley, A., & Burleigh, B. (1993). Neuropsychological function in borderline personality disorder. *Journal of Clinical Psychology, 49*, 385–396.

Takahashi, T., Suzuki, M., Zhou, S. Y., Tanino, R., Hagino, H., Kawasaki, Y., et al. (2006). Morphologic alterations of the parcellated superior temporal gyrus in schizophrenia spectrum. *Schizophrenia Research, 83*, 131–143.

Tang, T., DeBubeis, R., Hollon, S., Amsterdam, J., Shelton, R., & Schalet, B. (2009). Personality change during depression treatment. *Archives of General Psychiatry, 66*(12), 1322–1330.

Tebartz van Elst, L., Hesslinger, B., Thiel, T., Geiger, E., Haegele, K., Lemieux, L., et al. (2003). Frontolimbic brain abnormalities in patients with borderline personality disorder: A volumetric magnetic resonance imaging study. *Biological Psychiatry, 54*, 163–171.

Tebartz van Elst, L., Ludaescher, P., Thiel, T., Büchert, M., Hesslinger, B., Bohus, M., et al. (2007). Evidence of disturbed amygdalar energy metabolism in patients with borderline personality disorder. *Neuroscience Letters, 417*, 36–41.

Teicher, M. H., Andersen, S. L., Polcari, A., Anderson, C. M., Navalta, C. P., & Kim, D. M. (2003). The neurobiological consequences of early stress and childhood maltreatment. *Neuroscience and Biobehavioral Reviews, 27*(1–2), 33–44.

Torgersen, S., Edvardsen, J., Øien, P. A., Onstad, S., Skre, I., Lygren, S., et al. (2002). Schizotypal personality disorder inside and outside the schizophrenic spectrum. *Schizophrenia Research, 54*, 33–38.

Torgersen, S., Kringlen, E., & Cramer, V. (2001). The prevalence of personality disorders in a community sample. *Archives of General Psychiatry, 58*, 590–596.

Torgersen, S., Lygren, S., Øien, P. A., Skre, I., Onstad, S., Edvardsen, J., et al. (2000). A twin study of personality disorders. *Comprehensive Psychiatry, 41*, 416–425.

Trammel, B., & Dean, R. S. (2011). Personality disorders. In C.A. Noggle, R.S. Dean, & A.M. Horton Jr. (Eds.), *The Encyclopedia of Neuropsychological Disorders* (pp. 585–586). New York: Springer.

Tranel, D., Bechara, A., Denburg, NL. (2002). Asymmetric functional roles of right and left ventromedial prefrontal cortices in social conduct, decision-making, and emotional processing. *Cortex, 38*(4): 589–612.

Travers, C., & King, R. (2005). An investigation of organic factors in the neuropsychological functioning of patients with borderline personality disorder. *Journal of Personality Disorders, 19*, 1–18.

Trull, T. J., Sher, K. J., Minks-Brown, C., Durbin, J., & Burr, R. (2000). Borderline personality disorder and substance use disorders: A review and integration. *Clinical Psychology Review, 20*, 235–253.

Tupin, J. P., Smith, D. B., Clanon, T. L., Kim, L. I., Nugent, A., & Groupe, A. (1973). The long-term use of lithium in aggressive prisoners. *Comprehensive Psychiatry, 14*, 311–317.

Turley, B., Bates, G., Edwards, J., & Jackson, H. (1992). MCMI-II personality disorders in recent-onset bipolar disorders. *Journal of Clinical Psychology, 48*(3), 320–329.

Tyrer, P., Coombs, N., Ibrahimi, F., Mathilakath, A., Bajaj, P., Ranger, M., et al. (2007). Critical developments in the assessment of personality disorder. *British Journal of Psychiatry, 190*, 51–59.

van Reekum, R., Conway, C. A., Gansler, D., White, R., & Bachman, D. L. (1993). Neurobehavioral study of borderline personality disorder. *Journal of Psychiatry and Neuroscience, 18*, 121–129.

Vitale, J. E., Brinkley, C. A., Hiatt, K. D., & Newman, J. P. (2007). Abnormal selective attention in psychopathic female offenders. *Neuropsychology, 21*(3), 301–312.

Voglmaier, M. M., Seidman, L. J., Niznikiewicz, M. A., Dickey, C. C., Shenton, M. E., & McCarley, R. W. (2005). A comparative profile analysis of neuropsychological function in men and women with schizotypal personality disorder. *Schizophrenia Research, 74*, 43–49.

Voglmaier, M. M., Seidman, L. J., Niznikiewicz, M. A., Dickey, C. C., Shenton, M. E., & McCarley, R. W. (2000). Verbal and nonverbal neuropsychological test performance in subjects with schizotypal personality disorder. *Am J Psychiatry*, 157:787–793.

Voglmaier, M. M., Seidman, L. J., Salisbury, D., McCarley, R. W. (1997). Neuropsychological dysfunction in schizotypal personality disorder: A profile analysis. *Biol Psychiatry*, 41:530–540.

Widiger, T. A., & Frances, A. (1994). Towards a dimensional model for the personality disorders. In P. Costa & T. A. Widiger (Eds.), *Personality disorders and the five-factor model of personality* (pp. 19–39). Washington, DC: American Psychological Association.

Widiger, T. A., & Sanderson, C. J. (1997). Personality disorders. In A. Tasman, J. Kay, & A. Lieberman (Eds.), *Psychiatry* (*Vol. 2*, pp. 1291–1317). Philadelphia, PA: Saunders.

Widiger, T. A., & Trull, T. J. (1998). Performance characteristics of the DSM-III-R personality disorder criteria set. In T. A. Widiger, A. J. Frances, H. A. Pincus, T. Ross, M. B. First, W. W. Davis, et al. (Eds.), *DSM-IV sourcebook I* (*Vol. 4*, pp. 357–373). Washington, DC: American Psychiatric Association.

Wolff, A., & Barlow, A. (2006). Schizoid personality in childhood: A comparative study of schizoid, autistic, and normal children. *Journal of Child Psychology and Psychiatry, 20*(1), 29–46.

Woodbury-Smith, M. R., Clare, I. C. H., Holland, A. J., Kearns, A., Staufenberg, E., & Watson, P. (2005). A case-control study of offenders with high functioning autistic spectrum disorders. *Journal of Forensic Psychiatry & Psychology, 16*, 747–763.

Yang, Y., & Raine, A. (2009). Prefrontal structural and functional brain imaging findings in antisocial, violent, and psychopathic individuals: A meta-analysis. *Psychiatry Research, 174*(2), 81–88.

Young, S. E., Smolen, A., Corley, R. P., Krauter, K. S., DeFries, J. C., Crowley, T. J., et al. (2002). Dopamine transporter polymorphism associated with externalizing behavior problems in children. *American Journal of Medical Genetics, 114*, 144–149.

Zanarini, M. C., & Frankenburg, F. R. (1997). Pathways to the development of borderline personality disorder. *Journal of Personality Disorders, 11*, 93–104.

Zanarini, M. C., Frankenburg, F. R., Dubo, E. D., Sickel, A. E., Trikha, A., Levin, A., et al. (1998). Axis I comorbidity of borderline personality disorder. *American Journal of Psychiatry, 155*, 1733–1739.

Zanarini, M. C., Frankenburg, F. R., Dubo, E. D., Sickel, A. E., Trikha, A., Levin, A., et al. (1998). Axis II comorbidity of borderline personality disorder. *Comprehensive Psychiatry, 39*, 296–302.

Zanarini, M. C., & Frankenburg, F. R. (2001). Attainment and maintenance of reliability of axis I and II disorders over the course of a longitudinal study. *Compr Psychiatry, 42*, 369–374.

Zaretsky, A. E., Fava, M., Davidson, K. G., Pava, J. A., Matthews, J., & Rosenbaum, J. F. (1997). Are dependency and self-criticism risk factors for major depressive disorder? *Canadian Journal of Psychiatry, 42*, 291–297.

Zimmerman, M., Chelminski, I., & Young, D. (2008). The frequency of personality disorders in psychiatric patients. *Psychiatric Clinics of North America, 31*, 405–420.

Zimmerman, M., & Coryell, W. (1989). DSM-III personality disorder diagnoses in a nonpatient sample demographic correlates and comorbidity. *Archives of General Psychiatry, 46*(8), 682–689.

Zimmerman, M., Rothschild, L., & Chelminski, I. (2005). The prevalence of DSM–IV personality disorders in psychiatric outpatients. *American Journal of Psychiatry, 162*, 1911–1918.

Zuckerman, M. & Kulman, D. M. (2000). Personality and risk-taking: Common biosocial factors. *Journal of Personality, 68*(6), 999–1029.

CHAPTER 17

Alzheimer's Disease

Douglas Watt, Deborah Ely Budding, & Leonard F. Koziol

INTRODUCTION

As the United States and most other Western societies show an increasing demographic presence of citizens over 65, there is increasing concern that the diseases of aging will pose enormous challenges to health care systems and their long-term financial viability. Among the most worrisome of those challenges is that posed by the increasing incidence of dementing disorders, particularly the most common of those, Alzheimer's disease, responsible for roughly 60%–80% of all dementias (Jalbert, Daiello, & Lapane, 2008). Although the disease was originally considered a rare presenile condition as initially described by Alois Alzheimer in 1906, by the 1960s and early 1970s, many elderly patients were found with the disease's histopathology at autopsy (Katzman, 1976). Not unlike autism at the other end of the neurodevelopmental continuum, Alzheimer's disease has rapidly expanded from an initially rare and exotic degenerative condition to a worldwide epidemic. Conservatively, at least 5.5 million persons in the United States are thought to be suffering from the disease, with current total associated costs over $100 billion per year in the United States alone (not counting unpaid family caregiver contributions), while worldwide costs for an estimated 35+ million sufferers approach a half trillion dollars per annum (Wimo, Winblad, & Jansson, 2010). Estimated costs by 2030 are expected to triple in the context of the aging of the baby boomer generation.

Enormous changes have taken place in our understanding of Alzheimer's disease over the last 15–20 years. Although the traditional view 20 years ago implied a neat demarcation between normal aging and Alzheimer's disease, this notion has been largely discredited. Additionally, traditional use of the term "Alzheimer's disease" has been restricted to patients with established dementia, whereas recent work suggests a heuristic extension of the term to a prodromal phase (in patients with milder cognitive impairment), and even to a preclinical phase of the illness (where subjects are still mostly cognitively normal, but long-term changes are laying the groundwork for neurodegeneration and cognitive decline). Underscoring the disease's intrinsic connections to aging, AD appears to roughly double in incidence every 5 years after the age of 65 (at least in most societies if not in all), and age is still considered the most significant risk factor for the disease (Profenno, Porsteinsson, & Faraone, 2010). For many reasons, Alzheimer's disease is increasingly in the public awareness, but it is still viewed as a destructive juggernaut, largely untreatable, and also largely unrelated to lifestyle and life history, unfortunate assumptions which may undercut both early treatment as well as prevention. Unfortunately, the disease is typically not diagnosed in this country until patients are (on average) mildly to moderately demented (Querfurth & LaFerla, 2010). Even when it is diagnosed, in some cases patients receive no treatment at all, or only cholinergic monotherapy, which is at best modestly and at worst minimally effective (Mangialasche, Solomon, Winblad, Mecocci, & Kivipelto, 2010; Cancelli, Beltrame, Gigli, & Valente, 2009). The modest effectiveness of cholinergic therapy further contributes to diagnostic and therapeutic passivity, seeming to confirm a pessimistic view of the illness as largely untreatable, and lacking a single, currently available, "disease-modifying"[1] pharmacological intervention. Additional problems arise around the regrettably common induction of delirium in patients in cognitive decline from AD, often iatrogenically from various CNS depressant medicines, hospital-borne infections, surgery, and general anesthesia (Han, Wilson, & Ely, 2010). Recent research suggests that in addition to the conventional recognition that Alzheimer's disease constitutes a risk factor for delirium (see Chapter 19), delirium may accelerate AD (Fong et al., 2009). Delirium may also constitute a primary risk factor for AD, suggesting that careful efforts in the direction of delirium prevention may be an underappreciated but crucial aspect of preventing Alzheimer's disease (see Chapter 19).

A major reason for the systematic failure of early diagnosis in this country is an insufficient level of attention paid to cognitive and mental status in the elderly on the part of many if not most medical practitioners and primary care physicians (PCP), combined with our inability to find a relatively inexpensive and noninvasive biomarker (see the section on biomarkers). Additionally, the popular Mini Mental State Exam, in widespread use by PCPs as a screening instrument, both underestimates overall cognitive deficit and is a grossly inadequate screen of short-term memory functions, the neurocognitive domain essential to early diagnosis of AD. A better alternative to the Mini Mental State Exam, the Montréal Cognitive Assessment (MoCA), has not yet achieved widespread popularity or use (Nasreddine et al., 2005). Although there are several sensitive and specific biomarkers for Alzheimer's disease currently available—particularly, characteristic CSF proteins and functional imaging findings (see the section on biomarkers)—these clinical bioassays, along with traditional neuropsychological assessment (which quickly exposes even milder amnestic syndromes), are all significantly underused in relationship to at-risk populations (patients presenting with evidence for mild cognitive impairment or with other known risk factors). These trends of therapeutic pessimism and diagnostic and therapeutic passivity present a frankly worrisome picture in relationship to clinical care for AD in this country (Casey, Antimisiaris, & O'Brien, 2010).

Last but certainly not least, there is some evidence that lifestyle and life history variables of a wide variety may play a major role in determining who develops the sporadic or nonfamilial form of the disease (Archer et al., 2010; Lahiri & Maloney, 2010). Lifestyle variables potentially relevant to the prevention of Alzheimer's disease may include all lifestyle factors that reduce or improve the management of oxidative stress (OS) and/or systemic inflammation (Holmes et al., 2009). This would include regular aerobic exercise, diets rich in polyphenols (pleiotropic chemical substances found in all fruits and vegetables, simplistically described as antioxidants), healthy omega-3/omega-6 ratios, avoiding obesity, an absence of severe chronic stress or recurrent major depression, and decent quality sleep (Liang et al., 2010; Polidori et al., 2009; Dyall, 2010; Jicha & Markesbery, 2010; Plassman, Williams, Burke, Holsinger, & Benjamin, 2010; Pasinetti, Chen, Janle, & Cheng, 2010). Each of these issues has at least some research demonstrating significant modulation of downstream risk for Alzheimer's disease, although a recent NIH panel statement pessimistically concluded that evidence for prevention by diet and lifestyle factors was "of low scientific quality." These difficulties in relationship to prevention, diagnosis, and treatment may emerge in part from a serious under-education of medical professionals about AD. Indeed, relative to other common diseases of aging (heart disease, arthritis, cancers, diabetes, etc.), AD typically receives very modest attention in medical school curricula. Thus, the current health care environment—in which preventive efforts in relationship to other diseases of aging through the modification of lifestyle factors is seriously sub-optimal—is also by implication presumably failing in relationship to the potential prevention of Alzheimer's disease (Kivipelto, 2010). The current health

[1]"Disease-modifying" might be operationally defined as an intervention in a patient with an existing dementia that after 1 year of therapy improves his or her cognitive and behavioral status relative to his or her status at the initiation of treatment.

care environment may also be failing at instituting early optimal treatment once cognitive decline has started.

ADVANCED DIAGNOSTIC CONSIDERATIONS AND PRACTICES

One of the biggest impediments to accurate and early diagnosis of this disease is the still widespread cultural myth that progressive loss of short-term memory is simply part of normal aging or due to arthrosclerosis ("hardening of the arteries"). These widespread assumptions prevent many patients and their families from seeking diagnostic workups when the illness may be at an earlier (and more treatable) stage. Although several other clinical phenotypes have been found to be associated with an underlying histopathology of Alzheimer's disease,[2] far and away the most common phenotype is an insidious-onset, slowly progressive amnestic decline (Machulda et al., 2009). In addition, patients even in relatively early stages of the illness experience difficulties with executive functions, dysnomia (word finding difficulties) and loss of verbal fluency without classical aphasia, and personality/affective changes, typically in the direction of emotional disinhibition and rarely in the direction of apathy (Mahieux et al., 2009; Mayeux, 2010). Indeed, apathy as a primary problem and first symptom (not to be confused with apathetic depressions) is unusual in early AD and raises the index of suspicion for a frontotemporal dementia (see Chapter 18). Recent work also suggests that pure Alzheimer's disease may be actually less common than thought because it is found often within admixtures of two or more primary neuropathologies, particularly admixtures of AD with vascular disease, as well as with Lewy body disease pathology (Schneider, Arvanitakis, Leurgans, & Bennett, 2009), suggesting that a sizable fraction of patients (approximately 45%) presenting with apparent clinical AD may suffer from a mixed etiology dementia. A high percentage of the very old (85 years and older) with dementia have a mixed etiology process (Jellinger & Attems, 2010).

Although through the 1960s and 1970s, Alzheimer's disease was a diagnosis of exclusion (ruling out other causes for a dementia), that is no longer an adequate basis for clinical diagnosis. Since the mid-1980s, diagnosis of AD has been largely hinged to two different sets of criteria, one from the *Diagnostic and Statistical Manual of Mental Disorders, Fourth Edition, Text Revision* (*DSM-IV-TR*) and another from the National Institute of Neurological Disorders and Stroke–Alzheimer's Disease and Related Disorders (NINDS–ADRDA) work group (Dubois et al., 2007) (Table 17.1). Although the two sets of criteria are not grossly in conflict, they are quite different when examined in detail. Suggestions for revision of the NINDS–ADRDA criteria have been recently presented in the context of increasing appreciation that earlier criteria were out of date and nonspecific (poorly discriminating, for example, Alzheimer's disease from frontotemporal dementias), while *DSM-IV-TR* criteria, also acknowledged as out of date, are in the process of being revised by the *DSM-V* work group. Both the newer proposed NINDS-ADRDA criteria and *DSM-IV-TR* and *DSM-V* are given in the following. A notable difference in two groups of criteria is the absence of any biomarker reference in *DSM-IV-TR* versus specific biomarker references in the draft of *DSM-V*.

The *DSM-IV-TR* criteria require development of multiple cognitive deficits including both impairment in memory or the ability to learn new information and one more of the following cognitive disturbances: aphasia, apraxia, agnosia, or executive dysfunction (APA, 2000). Additionally, the *DSM-IV-TR* stipulates that the cognitive deficits must cause significant impairment in social or occupational functioning, represent a significant decline from a previous level of functioning, present as a gradual onset and continuous decline, and not purely related to or better explained by delirium, other CNS conditions, or other Axis I disorders (APA, 2000). Although *DSM-IV-TR* criteria are widely treated as a gold standard by psychiatric clinicians, there are serious problems with these criteria: (1) perceptual agnosias rarely appear in Alzheimer's disease until cognitive decline is fairly advanced and are almost

[2]Several other clinical phenotypes associated with Alzheimer's disease pathology include posterior cortical atrophy (typically with Balint syndrome), semantic dementia, primary progressive aphasia, and dysexecutive presentations. Semantic dementia, PPA, and dysexecutive syndromes of course are also seen in the frontotemporal lobar degeneration diseases (see Chapter 18).

TABLE 17.1 NINDS-ADRDA Diagnostic Criteria for Alzheimer's Disease (Revised)

Probable AD: A plus one or more supportive features B, C, D, or E core diagnostic criteria

A. Presence of an early and significant episodic memory impairment that includes the following features:
- Gradual and progressive change in memory function reported by patients or informants over more than 6 months
- Objective evidence of significantly impaired episodic memory on testing: this generally consists of recall deficit that does not improve significantly or does not normalize with cueing or recognition testing and after effective encoding of information has been previously controlled
- The episodic memory impairment can be isolated or associated with other cognitive changes at the onset of AD or as AD advances

Supportive features

B. Presence of medial temporal lobe atrophy
- Volume loss of hippocampi, entorhinal cortex, and amygdala evidenced on MRI with qualitative ratings using visual scoring (referenced to well-characterized population with age norms) or quantitative volumetry of regions of interest (referenced to well-characterized population with age norms)

C. Abnormal cerebrospinal fluid biomarkers
- Low amyloid beta1–42 concentrations, increased total tau concentrations, increased phospho-tau concentrations, or combinations of the three
- Other well-validated markers to be discovered in the future

D. Specific pattern on functional neuroimaging with PET
- Reduced glucose metabolism in bilateral temporal parietal regions
- Other well-validated ligands, including those that will foreseeably emerge such as Pittsburg compound B or FDDNP

E. Proven AD autosomal dominant mutation within the immediate family

Exclusion criteria

History
- Sudden onset
- Early occurrence of the following symptoms: gait disturbances, seizures, behavioral changes

Clinical features
- Focal neurological features including hemiparesis, sensory loss, visual field deficits
- Early extrapyramidal signs

Other medical disorders severe enough to account for memory and related symptoms
- Non-AD dementia
- Major depression
- Cerebrovascular disease
- Toxic and metabolic abnormalities, all of which may require specific investigations
- MRI FLAIR or T2 signal abnormalities in the medial temporal lobe that are consistent with infectious or vascular insults

Criteria for definite AD

AD is considered definite if the following are present:
- Both clinical and histopathological (brain biopsy or autopsy) evidence of the disease, as required by the NIA-Reagan criteria for the post-mortem diagnosis of AD; criteria must both be present
- Both clinical and genetic evidence (mutation on chromosome 1, 14, or 21) of AD; criteria must both be present

Source: (Dubois et al., 2007).

never seen in early stage and rarely in middle-stage patients; (2) the language disturbance associated with AD is relatively subtle early in the illness, and often cannot be discerned without neuropsychological assessment, where it is typically manifest as dysnomia and verbal fluency difficulties but almost never an outright aphasia; (3) the definition of apraxia here is awkward and atypical (usually it is defined as a loss of skilled movement); (4) the definition of memory impairment in *DSM-IV-TR* badly blurs the distinction between short-term (episodic) memory and long-term memory. Indeed, a failure of long-term memory (very rarely seen in early-stage AD) would meet criteria. These criteria are currently being revised in *DSM-5* (see the following).

In response to increasing recognition of a prodromal stage of Alzheimer's disease characterized by milder cognitive impairment and a primary amnestic syndrome but milder or minimal difficulties in other major cognitive domains, *DSM-IV-TR* included the notion of mild cognitive impairment (MCI) as an extension of cognitive disorder, not otherwise specified (294.9). MCI has been variably defined by different sources, but typically is taken to mean significantly greater cognitive difficulties than seen in normal aging but with generally unaffected activities of daily living/level of function; affected people do not meet currently accepted dementia diagnostic criteria (Dubois et al., 2007). In response to concerns that an MCI diagnosis was too nonspecific, and to accommodate research findings showing enormous variation in rates of progression of MCI to dementia (Jelic, Kivipelto, & Winblad, 2006), suggesting a widely heterogeneous group falling under the MCI umbrella, there has been a recent emphasis on the diagnosis of MCI, amnestic subtype as a more reliable prodromal stage marker for Alzheimer's disease, showing a primary impairment of short-term or episodic memory compared to other, better preserved domains (Sachdev, Ganguli, & Petersen, 2010).

Provisional *DSM-5* criteria notably subsume both dementia as well as MCI, replacing them with concepts of minor and major neurocognitive disorder. Both subtypes must correspond with a gradual and consistent trajectory of decline in areas of deficiency and are not wholly or primarily attributable to other disorders, although high comorbidity is acknowledged. Criteria also emphasize more quantitative techniques in determining the existence of short-term memory deficits, a step in the right direction, although more specific biomarker criteria have been omitted from the working draft of these criteria as of November 2010. The full criteria can be found at: www.dsm5.org/ProposedRevisions/Pages/proposedrevision.aspx?rid=421.

In regard to Alzheimer's disease, which is seen as constituting the major subtype, criteria for major neurocognitive disorder must be met. Individuals must demonstrate impairments in memory and at least one other domain with executive dysfunction being the most often seen. As the disease progresses, additional domains show deficiency. The criteria specify that these deficits must be significant cognitive declines from a previous level of performance as evidenced by reports by the patient or a knowledgeable informant, or observation by the clinician, of clear decline in specific abilities as outlined for specific domains. Further, individuals must demonstrate clear deficits in objective assessment of the relevant domain (typically greater than 2.0 SD below the mean [or below the 2.5th percentile] of an appropriate reference population [e.g., age, gender, education, premorbid intellect, and culturally adjusted]). Finally, these deficits must be of such significance that they sufficiently interfere with independence whereby individuals require assistance in instrumental activities of daily living or in complete tasks such as financial management.

In comparison, the minor subtype must meet the criteria for minor neurocognitive disorder. This subtype, which is seen as encompassing MCI of the amnestic type, presents with memory impairment, but no other impairments are required. This decline is minor but still noticeable as evidenced by the reports of the patient or a knowledgeable informant, or observation by the clinician. Deficits must also be documented on cognitive assessment (typically 1.0–2.0 SD below the mean [or in the 2.5th to 16th percentile] of an appropriate reference population (e.g., age, gender, education, premorbid intellect, and culturally adjusted). When serial measurements are available, a significant (i.e., 0.5 SD) decline from the patient's own baseline would serve as more definitive evidence of decline. Although these deficits are a noticeable divergence from previous functional levels, the cognitive deficits are not sufficient to interfere with independence (instrumental activities of daily living are preserved), although greater effort and compensatory strategies may be required to maintain independence. Clear supporting evidence for the Alzheimer's etiology such as biomarker testing outcomes or imaging is also needed.

Recommended Clinical Work-Up for Patients in Suspected Cognitive Decline

After wading through such disparate sets of criteria, clinicians might rightly conclude that the diagnostic process would seem to be a very confusing and uncertain enterprise indeed!

However, the current standard of care suggests that any patient thought to potentially be suffering from cognitive decline receive consideration for the following work-ups:

1. Some form of neurocognitive assessment (formal neuropsychological assessment preferred but if full neuropsychological assessment not feasible, screening with Montréal Cognitive Assessment or Mattis Dementia Rating Scale II or similar instrument preferred over MMSE)
2. Careful clinical history taking with both patient and family
3. Structural imaging (CT or MRI, MRI preferable if clinically feasible)
4. Laboratory studies (CBC, metabolic panels, thyroid function, B12, folate, urinalysis, and other studies as indicated) to rule out metabolic issues, infections, and other reversible causes for cognitive deficits
5. Options for functional imaging (PET or SPECT)
6. Options for CSF assays (tau, phosphorylated tau, beta-amyloid 42)

Biomarkers for AD

Biomarkers can comprise either physiologic, anatomic, or biochemical alterations, indicating at least some effect of the complex degenerative cascades in AD (see table of factors contributing to neurodegenerative matrix in the section on Neuropathology and Pathophysiology). Biomarkers provide critical value in relationship to diagnosis, treatment, and research, in at least four basic ways: (1) objective biological measures in the diagnostic enterprise; (2) crucial staging information; (3) an objective metric for testing potential treatments (an effective *clinical treatment* should reduce biomarkers of disease state whereas a *preventive treatment* should reduce preclinical biomarkers); and (4) the progression and timing of various biomarkers can give insights into the nature of complex neurodegenerative cascades (Brys et al., 2009; Hampel et al., 2008).

There is good evidence of a consistent sequence of biomarkers in AD, broken down into two stages—a preclinical stage and a clinical stage—as well as a progressive sequence within the clinical stage biomarkers. A first major biomarker, occurring during the preclinical stage, is deposition of amyloid protein in the brain.[3] This can be imaged with Pittsburgh binding compound PET scans (PiB-PET), using a radioligand that binds to extracellular plaque deposition (Jack et al., 2010). This deposition takes place in the preclinical stages, during which patients are typically cognitively intact for their age. This extracellular deposition is associated with the gradual lowering of beta-amyloid in CSF, presumably in the context of declining CNS clearance, while decreasing CSF amyloid and positive PiB PET findings are well correlated (Jack et al., 2010). Recent work shows that even at this preclinical stage, there may be cortical thinning in regions of amyloid deposition, yet without significant cognitive sequelae (Dickerson et al., 2009). It is not known, however, if patients can have significant amyloid deposition indefinitely without eventually demonstrating cognitive decline/neural degeneration. However, cognitive reserve (defined in terms of education and premorbid cognitive ability) does appear to buffer effects of amyloid deposition (Rentz et al., 2010). It is also not known whether more subtitle cognitive changes may be intrinsic to the preclinical stages, and how preclinical stages eventually give way to more discernible neural and cognitive loss.

Additional biomarkers associated with a neurodegenerative cognitive decline include increases in CSF tau, phosphorylated tau, and isoprostane (a measure of OS on lipid membranes), along with characteristic alterations on PET scans (typically decreasing temporoparietal metabolism or decreasing temporoparietal perfusion on SPECT). CSF tau is widely regarded as a nonspecific marker of neuronal damage, and it is elevated in stroke and head trauma as well as AD. CSF tau increases modestly as the disease enters clinical phases (MCI) and then increases further as patients become mildly demented, as does phosphorylated tau

[3]Although amyloid deposition is often referenced as the first biomarker, coincident with declining CSF amyloid concentrations (suggesting failing CNS clearance of amyloid), markers for CNS protein and nucleic acid OS are elevated prior to amyloid deposition and CSF amyloid alterations (Pratico, 2010).

and isoprostane, while CSF amyloid (small oligomers) typically declines further. In other words, all four of these CSF biomarkers (tau, phosphorylated tau, amyloid, and isoprostane) discriminate preclinical from clinical patients, as well as potentially discriminate early from later stage clinical disease (Brys et al., 2009). The combination of elevated tau, elevated phosphorylated tau, and decreased amyloid is particularly diagnostic, and an elevated tau/amyloid CSF ratio predicts progression in MCI (Jack et al., 2010). A more recent biomarker involves imaging glial activation, which indexes CNS inflammation, increasingly thought to contribute to cognitive decline (Ager et al., 2010). Glial activation inversely correlates with MMSE scores, arguing that CNS inflammation contributes to degenerative cascades (Edison et al., 2008). Curiously, whereas isoprostane (lipid membrane OS) progressively increases from aged controls into various clinical stages, other aspects of OS (indexed by 8OHG [oxidized nucleic acids]) and oxidized protein (nitrotyrosine) may decline as amyloid deposition and tangling advance, suggesting that AD may emerge from compensatory mechanisms aimed at protecting intracellular domains from OS (Jomova, Vondrakova, Lawson, & Valko, 2010). Elevated 8OHG is found in preclinical familial AD and in Down syndrome, underlining that OS may be the earliest event in a complex degenerative cascade (see section on Neuropsychological and Behavioral Sequelae). Evidence suggests a primary mitochondrial source for OS, with aging associated with increased OS, and with mitochondrial declines and increased OS possibly driving upregulation of amyloid processing (Aliev et al., 2010; Mancuso et al., 2007). Regrettably, most of these biomarkers are either costly (imaging) or invasive (CSF), limiting their use. A well-validated serum biomarker has yet to be found and this remains, in the judgment of many, a desired Holy Grail for making early diagnosis both more accurate and cost-effective (Schneider, Hampel, & Buerger, 2009).

NEUROPSYCHOLOGICAL AND BEHAVIORAL SEQUELAE

Manifestations of this disease vary enormously, dependent on staging, premorbid personality, and perhaps other variables. Alzheimer's disease (in its most common clinical phenotype) generates a slowly progressive amnestic syndrome, accompanied by dysnomia, declining verbal fluency, and increasing working memory and executive deficits, along with declining affective regulation and behavioral control. As the disease progresses, patients become progressively disabled and eventually require total care. Preclinical stages (discussed in the following) consist of altered biomarkers but no evidence for significant cognitive or personality/affective changes, although this latter issue has been more poorly researched. Early clinical stages (MCI to mild dementia) are characterized by significantly milder cognitive impairment, primarily in short-term memory. As the disease enters middle stages, behavioral regulation and organization often becomes much more impaired, and patients require increasing environmental structure and support. There is some anecdotal evidence that behavioral regulation may collapse more severely in patients with histories of trauma or severe Axis II issues (von Gunten, Pocnet, & Rossier, 2009). Later stages are often associated with a global cognitive collapse and a chronic confusional state, often with a circadian worsening (sundowning), but this should not be conflated with a milder dementia or even MCI with a superimposed and reversible delirium.

NEUROPATHOLOGY AND PATHOPHYSIOLOGY OF AD

Histopathologically, Alzheimer's disease (at the stage of causing a full-blown dementia) is characterized by widespread accumulation of extracellular amyloid plaques structures (neuritic or "senile" or "compact" plaques, not to be confused with diffuse plaque, a more preclinical marker) and intracellular accumulations of hyperphosphorylated tau proteins referred to as neurofibrillary tangles (Braskie et al., 2008). The disease is characterized by progressive synaptic loss—in early stages, probably much more critical to the disease's effects than neuronal loss—with both of these ultimately driving progressive atrophy (Terry et al., 1991). Tangling is far better correlated with regional atrophy than plaque concentrations, but synaptic loss exceeds what tangling alone might account for (Querfurth & LaFerla, 2010). There is also increasing central inflammation. Although traditionally viewed as a cortical dementia, in its earlier stages, degeneration is greatest in paralimbic and reticular areas (with dorsal raphe [DR], basal forebrain [BF] and hippocampal [HC]/entorhinal areas as sites of the early extensive tangling and heavy synaptic loss). Tangling in DR precedes even BF and entorhinal tangling (Grinberg et al., 2009).

However, despite many decades of research into its fundamental biology, the cause or causes of Alzheimer's disease still remains a mystery, and recent evidence increasingly suggests that amyloid plaque and tangling are markers and not causes (Armstrong, 2009). Tangling appears to be much closer to synaptic and neural loss than plaque deposition, and closely tracks regional atrophy and synaptic loss, despite being thought largely downstream of amyloidosis. Many lines of evidence suggest that AD may emerge from a convergence of many interactive factors, including increased oxidative stress, inflammation, and the accumulation and/or clearance failure of characteristic pathogenic proteins, along with increasing deleterious synaptic effects from those proteins and from associated inflammation (De Strooper, 2010; Mondragon-Rodriguez et al., 2010; Palop & Mucke, 2010).

AD appears to start with a preclinical phase, characterized by diffuse extracellular plaque deposition, appearing years or even decades before any discernible cognitive decline (Jack et al., 2010). The deposition appears in regions with the highest cortical connectivity (receiving extensive projections from the cortex), and curiously, overlaps extensively with the default network (Buckner et al., 2009). However, plaque deposition does not predict regional tangle concentrations or regional synaptic loss and atrophic change. These are in fact poorly correlated, with amyloid plaque concentrations greatest prefrontally and in the posterior medial cortex, whereas neurofibrillary tangling begins initially in the serotonergic brainstem nuclei, hippocampal/entorhinal regions, and cholinergic basal forebrain regions (a pattern that correlates with the clinical disease phenotype). Plaque forms in most regions receiving heavy cortical projections (including BG), whereas tangling occurs in regions sending many projections to cortex, a largely unexplained and mysterious correlation. Reasons for the poor regional correlation between plaques and tangles are unknown, as is the basis for the long (and variable) delay from a preclinical deposition of amyloid, to the beginnings of MCI and a clinical decline phase.

Familial Alzheimer's disease, although a relatively small fractional slice of the total Alzheimer's disease pie (at most 1%–2%), has informed etiological thinking about AD in its much more common sporadic or nonfamilial form because the two forms of the disease are mostly indistinguishable. Familial AD requires one of three mutations: mutation of the amyloid precursor protein, or of one of two presenilins that are components of the gamma secretase complex (involved in the cleaving of the amyloid precursor protein [APP] in a specific location to form beta-amyloid after an initial beta-secretase cleavage; Ryan & Rossor, 2010). On the other hand, alpha-secretase cleavage of APP precludes generation of beta-amyloid. Given the genetic basis of familial AD, and that extracellular accumulations of beta amyloid fibrils are essential to the diagnosis of the disease, the amyloid cascade model has been dominant in both recent theory construction and as primary rationale in drug therapy design. A basic assumption of the amyloid cascade model is that beta-amyloid protein drives a destructive cascade that leads eventually to neurodegeneration of a progressive nature (Hardy, 1992). However, the precise sequence of events in a degenerative cascade is still incompletely understood, including what might contribute to abnormal amyloid metabolism and deposition and/or clearance failure in the first place (Castellani et al., 2009). Indeed, in its original form, a simple amyloid cascade model cannot explain why AD is a primary disease of aging. As many authors have emphasized, major challenges to the original form of the amyloid hypothesis are: (1) Both global and regional atrophy and both global and domain-related cognitive declines have been understood for decades to be much better correlated with the regional spread and density of the other histopathological histopathological marker, neurofibrillary tangling (NFT); and (2) there is considerable delay between the appearance of diffuse plaque and the appearance of tangling, with the latter better correlated with onset and progression of cognitive decline, whereas the former is often present for many years, even decades, without major cognitive symptoms. Additional serious challenges to classic plaque-centered etiologic theories emerge from a 2008 *Lancet* study (Holmes et al., 2008), which demonstrated that plaque immunization initiated in patients that were mildly to moderately demented, although often successful in clearing plaque structures from the brain, made no difference whatsoever in slowing cognitive decline (patients with extensive clearing out of plaque structures showed *no* neuroprotective benefit from the treatment). Additionally, recent drug trials derived from the amyloid hypothesis have been consistently (even spectacularly) negative, including the recent failure of two amyloid-lowering drugs (Tarenflurbil and Semagacestat, both gamma-secretase inhibitors, with the latter drug actually making patients cognitively worse), raising major questions about whether reducing amyloidogenesis and/or extracellular plaque accumulations has any substantive therapeutic value, once past preclinical stages (in which plaque accumulation predates cognitive decline; Prins, Visser, & Scheltens, 2010; Extance, 2010).

Over the last 10–15 years, a substantial modification of the original amyloid hypothesis has been the discovery of destructive effects of smaller (soluble) amyloid oligomers, thought to figure heavily in synaptic loss (Querfurth & LaFerla, 2010). A similar view of oligomers of phosphorylated tau protein has also emerged, showing that these depress synaptic function as well (Gong, Grundke-Iqbal, & Iqbal, 2010). However, this newer emphasis on soluble toxic proteins (versus the classic emphasis on histopathologically visible larger protein aggregations) still leaves a critical question unanswered, namely, how and why are these pathogenic proteins appearing in the brain and why are they not being cleared out? The traditional view of amyloid as a toxic junk protein begs the question as to its adaptive functions. Although still poorly understood, amyloid and its precursor protein have been linked to: (1) neuronal development and the establishment of neuronal columns (cell-matrix adhesion); (2) possible roles in antimicrobial and antioxidant defense; (3) response to ischemic-hypoxic injury; (4) calcium channel homeostasis; and (5) roles in neuroplasticity. This suggests that amyloid dysmetabolism may emerge from age-related immuno-challenges, CNS OS or other damage associated with aging, and neuroplasticity challenges faced by an aging brain (Baiden-Amissah et al., 1998). Beta-amyloid processing is also upregulated in the context of brain injury (stroke and head trauma) and by cholinergic and aminergic deafferentation (Johnson, Stewart, & Smith, 2010; Beach et al., 2008).

Recent work suggests that not only do pathogenic proteins contribute to CNS inflammation and OS, but that CNS markers for OS (particularly nucleic acid oxidation) actually precede the appearance of classic plaques and tangles (Pratico, 2010). These markers for increased CNS OS precede even diffuse plaque deposition, which typically predates tangling considerably, suggesting that OS might be the first falling domino. Additional evidence for a primary role for OS include: (1) absence of markers of OS in regions largely untouched by AD (such as the cerebellum and basal ganglia; (2) some OS markers actually decline with increasing plaque and tangle count; for example, neurons with NFT show a 40%–56% decrease in relative 8OHG levels (marker for nucleic acid OS) compared with neurons free of NFT; (3) most negative and positive risk factors for AD modulate OS, such as exercise, polyphenol dietary intake, stroke and reperfusion injury, head trauma, and so forth; and (4) there are close reciprocal relationships between OS and inflammation (inflammation causing OS and OS causing inflammation; Nunomura et al., 2001). This suggests the possibility that the classical markers for AD (plaques and tangles) may emerge in part from antioxidant defense (Patten, Germain, Kelly, & Slack, 2010).

Recent work supporting this view of the disease includes work on "inflammaging," a term coined by Franceschi and colleagues to characterize how aging is accompanied by a low-grade chronic up-regulation of certain pro-inflammatory responses (2007). Inflammaging differs significantly from acute (classical/regional) inflammation and reflects increased innate immunity as compensatory for declining adaptive immunity. Unlike classic acute inflammation, inflammaging is low grade, chronic, and systemic, and initially asymptomatic. Given that both inflammation and OS (classic factors in the biology of aging) appear to cause upregulation of amyloid processing, various amyloid moieties may in turn potentiate both inflammation and OS, and that hyperphosphorylation of tau (tangling) may also be driven by defenses against OS (such as upregulation of heme oxygenase), these interactions potentially form large positive feedback loops driving an aging brain into a progressive neurodegenerative failure. Although linear causality (A causes B which causes C) is the dominant model of causality in science, a circular causality model (A causes B which causes C which potentiates A), emphasizing a more recursive image of biological systems, may be a more realistic paradigm for understanding biological dysfunction and disease. Table 17.2 emphasizes multiple factors contributing to neurodegenerative cascades. What were originally adaptive mechanisms (such as inflammation, recruitment of amyloid pathways by various stresses and neuroplasticity challenges, and phosphorylation) may become pathogenic in the context of chronic synergistic recruitment, biological stress, and neuroplasticity challenge. This suggests an image of Alzheimer's disease in which a host of individually adaptive and compensatory mechanisms jointly conspire to drive the brain into a neurodegenerative process (Mondragon-Rodriguez et al., 2010). Given that these interactions between individually adaptive processes occur past a reproductive period, they would clearly escape selection pressure.

Rather than a single factor model, Table 17.2 emphasizes a neurodegenerative matrix of factors. This model suggests that an optimal neuroprotective therapy might profitably intercede at multiple points within the neurodegenerative cascades (depending on the stage of the process), as opposed to the current penchant for a single drug or therapy that would "cure" or stop Alzheimer's disease. We believe that it is unlikely (albeit possible) that we will find such a silver bullet for a disease involving so many biologic factors, and one that is so closely intertwined with the biology of aging itself, particularly once the disease is well established. Instead, this table argues for a looping matrix of factors, involving the interaction of pathogenic proteins, disinhibited inflammation, and oxidative stress. A deeper unraveling of Alzheimer's disease may require a much deeper understanding of the dynamics of cell signaling and internal cellular regulation, given the centrality of cell signaling to our responses to cellular stress. Although recently developed disease-modifying treatments emphasize anti-amyloid therapies, we suspect that future efforts may aim more directly at reducing CNS inflammation and oxidative stress, and at directly protecting and promoting synaptic function, particularly in view of evidence that synaptic loss is emerging as the major biological correlate of cognitive decline.

CONTEMPORARY MODES OF TREATMENT

Early treatment efforts (1980s through the 1990s) focused mainly on development of what proved to be largely symptomatic treatments, cholinesterase inhibitors, based on early cholinergic deficit models of AD (Poirier et al., 1995; Emre, Geula, Ransil, & Mesulam, 1992; McKhann et al., 1984). Cholinergic monotherapy is often the only therapy many Alzheimer's patients ever receive. However, such monotherapy is now widely acknowledged as modestly—and in some cases minimally—effective. Memantine, a noncompetitive NMDA antagonist, is also FDA-approved for the treatment of Alzheimer's disease, and is conventionally regarded as a drug for middle to later stage patients. Unfortunately, relatively few early-stage patients are put on the combination of cholinesterase inhibitors and memantine, which recent research suggests may be more neuroprotective at any stage of the disease than cholinesterase inhibitors alone, suggesting that reserving memantine for patients as they become more seriously demented may be unwise (Atri, Shaughnessy, Locascio, & Growdon, 2008; Mangialasche et al., 2010), although there is counter-opinion on this point. Neither of these prescription drugs is individually considered strongly disease-modifying, but their joint effect may be *modestly* disease-modifying. Currently, there is no single agent or drug that meets the criteria of disease-modifying, although some future combination of neuroprotective agents may meet these important criteria. Unfortunately, combination therapies (particularly prescription drugs plus several nutraceuticals) have been poorly studied (Chow et al., 2010; Chen et al., 2010).

Recent research has focused on developing disease-modifying agents. These have largely been aimed at amyloid processing and, to a much lesser extent, at neurofibrillary tangling. In general, these efforts have been spectacularly unsuccessful, at least so far (Extance, 2010). Tramiprosate, an amyloid binding compound (aimed at the prevention of fibrils and oligomers), recently failed its first phase III trial. Tarenflurbil, a gamma secretase modulator, also recently failed its first phase III trial. An attempt at amyloid immunization, although successful at reducing extracellular plaque deposits, did not make any difference in altering cognitive decline in patients who were already mildly to moderately demented (Holmes et

TABLE 17.2 Factors Contributing to a Neurodegenerative Matrix in AD

Biomarker	Produced by	Producing	Clinical/Other Correlates
Beta amyloid plaque (extracellular Aβ)	Aging, genes, ↓ BBB fx, ↓ clearance, oxidative stress	Inflammation, (glial activation), OS	Subtle regional atrophic changes. Second biomarker to appear
Small aggregate amyloid (oligomeric Aβ)	β/γ secretases, inflammation, oxidative stress	Synaptic loss and dysfunction, OS, INFLAM	Synaptic loss (NMDA, AMPA), loss of LTP, increased LTD
Inflammation (INFLAM) (esp. ↑ innate immunity)	Amyloid fibrils, ↓ ACh, ↑ rAGE signaling, aging, OS	Synaptic dysfunction, ? apoptosis, ↑ Aβ, OS	Contributes directly to cognitive dysfunction via multiple effects
Central insulin resistance (in CNS)	Inflammation (NFk-b)	↓energy, HC damage, ↑ kinases (→ tangles)	Promotes synaptic dysfunction and loss, promotes amyloidosis
Oxidative stress (OS), (MITO, lipid membranes)	Aging, Aβ oligomers in MITO, metal ions, INFLAM	Synaptic and neural loss, INFLAM, Aβ, tangling	Appears before plaques/ tangling. Membrane OS increases with disease; DNA OS markers do not.
Excitotoxicity and Ca++ dysfunction	Oligomers (Aβ) in MITO, and at calcium channels	Probable synaptic dysfunction, apoptosis	Synaptic dysfunction, eventually SL/NL
Neurotrophin and neuro-transmitter depletion	Oligomers (Aβ) → receptor internalization, tau pathology → microtubule dysfunction, INFLAM	ACh loss → ↑ Aβ, BDNF/ NGF declines	Synaptic dysfunction, promotion of both SL and apoptosis
Neurofibrillary tangling and tau aggregates	Oxidative stress (OS) → ↑ kinases, insulin resistance	Basal forebrain (ACh) loss, SL, apoptosis	Tracks atrophic change (SL/NL) and declining cognitive function closely.
Atrophy HC/EC → lateral temporal lobe → frontal and parietal convexities	Multifactorial—many factors listed here contribute	Proceeds functional declines (slightly)	Major biomarker for degenerative changes in clinical stages of AD.
Cognitive loss, especially STM, then language and executive function	Synaptic loss early, SL plus NL later (apoptosis)	Declining function, compensatory neuroplasticity effort	Primary functional measure, necessary for diagnosis

SL, synaptic loss; NL, neural loss (neuronal cell death); Aβ, beta-amyloid; BBB fx, blood brain barrier function; MITO, mitochondria; ACh, acetylcholine; NGF, nerve growth factor; BDNF, brain derived neurotrophic factor; rAGE, receptors for advanced glycation end products (which promote inflammation); HC, hippocampus; EC, entorhinal cortex; apoptosis, programmed cell death; NFk-b, nuclear factor kappa B (transcription factor involved in inflammatory signaling); oligomers, several molecules of beta-amyloid stuck together; kinases, enzymes promoting phosphorylation and tangling; NMDA/AMPA, subtypes of glutamate receptor; LTP, long-term potentiation; LTD, long-term depression.

al., 2008). Collectively, this group of results argues that once cognitive decline has started, efforts aimed at reducing amyloid processing or clearing plaque structures may be futile. Currently, there is no clear understanding of how one might protect neurons from the anti-synaptic and other intracellular effects of oligomeric (small molecule) amyloid, increasingly thought to be a major factor in cognitive decline and synaptic loss, and thought to be more directly destructive to synaptic function than large extracellular plaque structures (Querfurth & LaFerla, 2010). Reducing CNS inflammation has also been an elusive target, although etanercept may show potential, and omega-3 and curcuminoids and other polyphenols may also help (Tobinick, 2010; Candore et al., 2010; Aftab & Vieira, 2010; Jicha & Markesbery, 2010).

Although latrepirdine, an older Russian antihistamine, suggested disease-modifying effects in its first large-scale trial in 2008 and was speculated to have a protective effect on mitochondria in relationship to oligomeric amyloid, it failed to show efficacy at recent replication trials in relationship to mild to moderate dementia patients, a major disappointment in the Alzheimer's research community (Doody et al., 2008). Further studies are underway. Methylene blue (Rember), a treatment aimed at tangling, also did not show success in a phase II trial (Neugroschl & Sano, 2010). A promising compound in phase II trials, AL-108 (Davunetide), derived from a larger neuroprotective neuropeptide, appears to show significant cognitive enhancing effects in early trials with MCI patients, and may reverse tangling and synaptic decline; it is awaiting a phase III trial (Mangialasche et al., 2010). Although a single disease-modifying drug has not been found, current treatment options include cholinesterase inhibitors and memantine, omega-3 supplementation and other "nutraceuticals" including curcuminoids (from the Indian spice turmeric), green tea extract (containing the polyphenol EGCG), and resveratrol (Cornelli, 2010). Other dietary polyphenols (there may be as many as 6000 polyphenols in the human diet) may also be neuroprotective (Darvesh, Carroll, Bishayee, Geldenhuys, & Van der Schyf, 2010; Polidori et al., 2009). Additional treatment considerations include family education, family psychotherapy and counseling, exercise programs, and increased daytime structure (Cho et al., 2010; Howe, 2009). Exercise is also thought neuroprotective, but changing lifelong patterns of sedentary behavior and frequent orthopedic and gait issues often make this impractical and difficult to implement.

We believe that a multifactorial, multiagent model of intervention emphasizing both biological and psychological components is likely to be more effective in maintaining cognition, quality of life, and patients' functioning in the community than simply placing patients on a cholinesterase inhibitor (often done only after patients are quite demented), and then doing little else until they require nursing home placement. Unfortunately, this type of hands-on care, with ongoing monitoring of cognitive and behavioral status and increased social support, is still much more the exception than the rule. Given that numerous comorbidities (especially diabetes, infections, delirium, and depression) may all accelerate AD, aggressive efforts to contain, treat, and otherwise minimize these AD accelerants are both badly needed and generally grossly underappreciated. We would also argue that neuropsychologists will likely see their role shift from primary diagnosticians toward treatment monitors and managers through evaluating patient response to therapy and being more involved in ongoing hands-on care, particularly as using biomarkers to establish initial diagnosis becomes more commonplace. At some point, we anticipate that there will be a blood test for AD in its early or perhaps even preclinical stages, an enormous boon to early detection and treatment[4] (although we strongly suspect it will have to be a matrix measure and not a single protein). In the interim, much more attention to cognitive status on the part of primary care doctors would seem to be a critical first step towards reversing the current state of late diagnosis and relative therapeutic passivity towards Alzheimer's disease, one of the most critical of all the diseases of aging.

[4] Serum cytokine assays can reliably detect the disease once patients have mild dementia from AD, but this is in a sense too late (Gomez & Moscato, 2008).

REFERENCES

Aftab, N., & Vieira, A. (2010). Antioxidant activities of curcumin and combinations of this curcuminoid with the other phytochemicals. *Phytotherapy Research, 24,* 500–502.

Ager, R. R., Fonseca, M. I., Chu, S. H., Sanderson, S. D., Taylor, S. M., Woodruff, T. M., et al. (2010). Microglial C5aR (CD88) expression correlates with amyloid-beta deposition in murine models of Alzheimer's disease. *Journal of Neurochemistry, 113,* 389–401.

Aliev, G., Palacios, H. H., Gasimov, E., Obrenovich, M. E., Morales, L., Leszek, J., et al. (2010). Oxidative Stress Induced Mitochondrial Failure and Vascular Hypoperfusion as a Key Initiator for the Development of Alzheimer Disease. *Pharmaceuticals, 3,* 158–187.

American Psychiatric Association. (2000). *Diagnostic and Statistical Manual of Mental Disorders*: DSM-IV-TR. Washington, DC: American Psychological Association.

Archer, H. A., Kennedy, J., Barnes, J., Pepple, T., Boyes, R., Randlesome, K., et al. (2010). Memory complaints and increased rates of brain atrophy: Risk factors for mild cognitive impairment and Alzheimer's disease. *International Journal of Geriatric Psychiatry,* 22(3), 1119–1126.

Armstrong, R. A. (2009). The molecular biology of senile plaques and neurofibrillary tangles in Alzheimer's disease. *Folia Neuropathologica, 47*(4), 289–299.

Atri, A., Shaughnessy, L. W., Locascio, J. J., & Growdon, J. H. (2008). Long-term course and effectiveness of combination therapy in Alzheimer's disease. *Alzheimer's disease and associated disorders,* 22(3), 209–221.

Baiden-Amissah, K., Joashi, U., Blumberg, R., Mehmet, H., Edwards, A. D., & Cox, P. M. (1998). Expression of amyloid precursor protein (APP) in the neonatal brain following hypoxic ischaemic injury. *Neuropathology and applied neurobiology, 24,* 346–352.

Beach, T., Potter, P., Sue, L., Newell, A., Poston, M., Cisneros, R., et al. (2008). Cortical Cholinergic Lesion Causes A Deposition: Cholinergic-Amyloid Fusion Hypothesis. *Advances in Alzheimer's and Parkinson's Disease,* 411–427.

Braskie, M. N., Klunder, A. D., Hayashi, K. M., Protas, H., Kepe, V., Miller, K. J., et al. (2008). Plaque and tangle imaging and cognition in normal aging and Alzheimer's disease. *Neurobiology of Aging, 31,* 1669–1678.

Brys, M., Pirraglia, E., Rich, K., Rolstad, S., Mosconi, L., Switalski, R., et al. (2009). Prediction and longitudinal study of CSF biomarkers in mild cognitive impairment. *Neurobiology of Aging, 30,* 682–690.

Buckner, R. L., Sepulcre, J., Talukdar, T., Krienen, F. M., Liu, H., Hedden, T. et al. (2009). Cortical hubs revealed by intrinsic functional connectivity: Mapping, assessment of stability, and relation to Alzheimer's disease. *Journal of Neuroscience, 29*(6), 1860–1873.

Cancelli, I., Beltrame, M., Gigli, G. L., & Valente, M. (2009). Drugs with anticholinergic properties: Cognitive and neuropsychiatric side-effects in elderly patients. *Neurological Sciences, 30,* 87–92.

Candore, G., Bulati, M., Caruso, C., Castiglia, L., Colonna-Romano, G., Di, B. D., et al. (2010). Inflammation, cytokines, immune response, apolipoprotein E, cholesterol, and oxidative stress in Alzheimer's disease: therapeutic implications. *Rejuvenation. Res, 13,* 301–313.

Casey, D. A., Antimisiaris, D., & O'Brien, J. (2010). Drugs for Alzheimer's disease: Are they effective? *Pharmacy and Therapeutics, 35,* 208.

Castellani, R. J., Lee, H., Siedlak, S. L., Nunomura, A., Hayashi, T., Nakamura, M., et al. (2009). Reexamining Alzheimer's disease: Evidence for a protective role for amyloid-β protein precursor and amyloid-β. *Journal of Alzheimer's Disease, 18,* 447–452.

Chen, T. F., Huang, R. F., Lin, S. E., Lu, J. F., Tang, M. C., & Chiu, M. J. (2010). Folic Acid potentiates the effect of memantine on spatial learning and neuronal protection in an Alzheimer's disease transgenic model. *Journal of Alzheimer'sDisease, 20,* 607–615.

Cho, J. Y., Um, H. S., Kang, E. B., Cho, I. H., Kim, C. H., Cho, J. S., et al. (2010). The combination of exercise training and alpha-lipoic acid treatment has therapeutic effects on the pathogenic phenotypes of Alzheimer's disease in NSE/APPsw-transgenic mice. *International Journal of Molecular Medicine, 25,* 337–346.

Chow, V. W., Savonenko, A. V., Melnikova, T., Kim, H., Price, D. L., Li, T., et al. (2010). Modeling an anti-amyloid combination therapy for Alzheimer's disease. *Science Translational Medicine, 2,* 13ra1.

Cornelli, U. (2010). Treatment of Alzheimer's disease with a cholinesterase inhibitor combined with antioxidants. *Neurodegenerative Diseases, 7,* 193–202.

Darvesh, A. S., Carroll, R. T., Bishayee, A., Geldenhuys, W. J., & Van der Schyf, C. J. (2010). Oxidative stress and Alzheimer's disease: Dietary polyphenols as potential therapeutic agents. *Expert Review of Neurotherapeutics, 10,* 729–745.

De Strooper, B. (2010). Proteases and proteolysis in Alzheimer's disease: A multifactorial view on the disease process. *Physiological Reviews, 90,* 465.

Dickerson, B. C., Bakkour, A., Salat, D. H., Feczko, E., Pacheco, J., Greve, D. N., et al. (2009). The cortical signature of Alzheimer's disease: Regionally specific cortical thinning relates to symptom severity in very mild to mild AD dementia and is detectable in asymptomatic amyloid-positive individuals. *Cerebral Cortex, 19*(3), 497–510.

Doody, R. S., Gavrilova, S. I., Sano, M., Thomas, R. G., Aisen, P. S., Bachurin, S. O., et al. (2008). Effect of dimebon on cognition, activities of daily living, behaviour, and global function in patients with mild-to-moderate Alzheimer's disease: A randomised, double-blind, placebo-controlled study. *The Lancet, 372*, 207–215.

Dubois, B., Feldman, H. H., Jacova, C., Dekosky, S. T., Barberger-Gateau, P., Cummings, J., et al. (2007). Research criteria for the diagnosis of Alzheimer's disease: Revising the NINCDS-ADRDA criteria. *Lancet Neurology, 6*, 734–746.

Dyall, S. C. (2010). Amyloid-beta peptide, oxidative stress and inflammation in Alzheimer's disease: Potential neuroprotective effects of omega-3 polyunsaturated fatty acids. *International Journal of Alzheimer's Disease*, 10.4061/2010/274128.

Edison, P., Archer, H. A., Gerhard, A., Hinz, R., Pavese, N., Turkheimer, F. E., et al. (2008). Microglia, amyloid, and cognition in Alzheimer's disease: An [11C](R) PK11195-PET and [11C] PIB-PET study. *Neurobiology of Disease, 32*, 412–419.

Emre, M., Geula, C., Ransil, B. J., & Mesulam, M. M. (1992). The acute neurotoxicity and effects upon cholinergic axons of intracerebrally injected beta-amyloid in the rat brain. *Neurobiology of Aging, 13*, 553–559.

Extance, A. (2010). Alzheimer's failure raises questions about disease-modifying strategies. *Nature Reviews Drug Discovery, 9*, 749–751.

Fong, T. G., Jones, R. N., Shi, P., Marcantonio, E. R., Yap, L., Rudolph, J. L., et al. (2009). Delirium accelerates cognitive decline in Alzheimer's disease. *Neurology, 72*, 1570–1575.

Franceschi, C., Capri, M., Monti, D., Giunta, S., Olivieri, F., Sevini, F., et al. (2007). Inflammaging and anti-inflammaging: A systemic perspective on aging and longevity emerged from studies in humans. *Mechanisms of Ageing and Development, 128*, 92–105.

Gomez, R. M., & Moscato, P. (2008). Identification of a 5-protein biomarker molecular signature for predicting Alzheimer's disease. *PLoS One, 3*, e3111.

Gong, C. X., Grundke-Iqbal, I., & Iqbal, K. (2010). Targeting Tau Protein in Alzheimer's Disease. *Drugs & Aging, 27*, 351–365.

Grinberg, L. T., Rub, U., Ferretti, R. E., Nitrini, R., Farfel, J. M., Polichiso, L., et al. (2009). The dorsal raphe nucleus shows phospho-tau neurofibrillary changes before the transentorhinal region in Alzheimer's disease. *A precocious onset? Neuropathology and Applied Neurobiology, 35*, 406–416.

Hampel, H., Burger, K., Teipel, S. J., Bokde, A. L., Zetterberg, H., & Blennow, K. (2008). Core candidate neurochemical and imaging biomarkers of Alzheimer's disease. *Alzheimers & Dementia, 4*, 38–48.

Han, J. H., Wilson, A., & Ely, E. (2010). Delirium in the older emergency department patient: A quiet epidemic. *Emergency Medicine Clinics of North America, 28*, 611–631.

Hardy, J. (1992). An 'anatomical cascade hypothesis' for Alzheimer's disease. *Trends in Neurosciences, 15*, 200–201.

Holmes, C., Boche, D., Wilkinson, D., Yadegarfar, G., Hopkins, V., Bayer, A., et al. (2008). Long-term effects of Abeta42 immunisation in Alzheimer's disease: Follow-up of a randomised, placebo-controlled phase I trial. *Lancet, 372*, 216–223.

Holmes, C., Cunningham, C., Zotova, E., Woolford, J., Dean, C., Kerr, S., et al. (2009). Systemic inflammation and disease progression in Alzheimer's disease. *Neurology, 73*, 768–774.

Howe, E. (2009). Treatment initiatives for patients with Alzheimer's disease. *Psychiatry (Edgmont), 6*, 40–47.

Jack, C. R. Jr., Knopman, D. S., Jagust, W. J., Shaw, L. M., Aisen, P. S., Weiner, M. W., et al. (2010). Hypothetical model of dynamic biomarkers of the Alzheimer's pathological cascade. *Lancet Neurology, 9*, 119–128.

Jalbert, J. J., Daiello, L. A., & Lapane, K. L. (2008). Dementia of the Alzheimer type. *Epidemiologic Reviews, 30*, 15.

Jelic, V., Kivipelto, M., & Winblad, B. (2006). Clinical trials in mild cognitive impairment: Lessons for the future. *Journal of Neurology, Neurosurgery and Psychiatry, 77*, 429–438.

Jellinger, K. A., & Attems, J. (2010). Prevalence of dementia disorders in the oldest-old: An autopsy study. *Acta Neuropathologica, 119*, 421–433.

Jicha, G. A., & Markesbery, W. R. (2010). Omega-3 fatty acids: Potential role in the management of early Alzheimer's disease. *Journal of Clinical Interventions in Aging, 5*, 45–61.

Johnson, V. E., Stewart, W., & Smith, D. H. (2010). Traumatic brain injury and amyloid-β pathology: A link to Alzheimer's disease? *Nature Reviews Neuroscience, 11*, 361–370.

Jomova, K., Vondrakova, D., Lawson, M., & Valko, M. (2010). Metals, oxidative stress and neurodegenerative disorders. *Molecular and cellular biochemistry, 1–14*..

Katzman, R. (1976). Editorial: *The prevalence and malignancy of Alzheimer disease. A major killer. Archives of Neurology, 33*(4), 217–218.

Kivipelto, M. (2010). Alzheimer prevention: Walk the talk. *Alzheimer's and Dementia, 6*, S115.

Lahiri, D. K., & Maloney, B. (2010). The "LEARn" (Latent Early-life Associated Regulation) model integrates environmental risk factors and the developmental basis of Alzheimer's disease, and proposes remedial steps. *Experimental Gerontology, 45*, 291–296.

Liang, K. Y., Mintun, M. A., Fagan, A. M., Goate, A. M., Bugg, J. M., Holtzman, D. M., et al. (2010). Exercise and Alzheimer's disease biomarkers in cognitively normal older adults. *Annals of Neurology, 68*, 311–318.

Machulda, M. M., Senjem, M. L., Weigand, S. D., Smith, G. E., Ivnik, R. J., Boeve, B. F., et al. (2009). Functional magnetic resonance imaging changes in amnestic and nonamnestic mild cognitive impairment during encoding and recognition tasks. *Journal of the International Neuropsychological Society, 15*, 372–382.

Mahieux, F., Onen, F., Berr, C., Volteau, M., Habert, M. O., Legrain, S., et al. (2009). Early detection of patients in the pre demented stage of Alzheimer's disease: The Pre-Al Study. *Journal of Nutrition Health and Aging, 13*, 21–26.

Mancuso, C., Scapagini, G., Currò, D., Giuffrida Stella, A. M., De Marco, C., Butterfield, D. A., et al. (2007). Mitochondrial dysfunction, free radical generation and cellular stress response in neurodegenerative disorders. *Front Biosci, 12*, 1107–1123.

Mangialasche, F., Solomon, A., Winblad, B., Mecocci, P., & Kivipelto, M. (2010). Alzheimer's disease: clinical trials and drug development. *The Lancet Neurology, 9*, 702–716.

Mayeux, R. (2010). Early Alzheimer's Disease. *New England Journal of Medicine, 362*, 2194–2201.

McKhann, G., Drachman, D., Folstein, M., Katzman, R., Price, D., & Stadlan, E. M. (1984). Clinical diagnosis of Alzheimer's disease: Report of the NINCDS-ADRDA Work Group on Alzheimer's Disease. *Neurology, 34*, 939–944.

Mondragon-Rodriguez, S., Basurto-Islas, G., Lee, H. G., Perry, G., Zhu, X., Castellani, R. J., et al. (2010). Causes versus effects: The increasing complexities of Alzheimer's disease pathogenesis. *Expert Review of Neurotherapeutics, 10*, 683–691.

Nasreddine, Z. S., Phillips, N. A., Bédirian, V., Charbonneau, S., Whitehead, V., Collin, I., et al. (2005). The Montreal Cognitive Assessment, MoCA: A brief screening tool for mild cognitive impairment. *Journal of the American Geriatrics Society, 53*, 695–699.

Neugroschl, J., & Sano, M. (2010). Current treatment and recent clinical research in Alzheimer's disease. *Mt.* Sinai Journal of Medicine, 77, 3–16.

Nunomura, A., Perry, G., Aliev, G., Hirai, K., Takeda, A., Balraj, E. K., et al. (2001). Oxidative damage is the earliest event in Alzheimer's disease. *Journal of Neuropathology & Experimental Neurology, 60*(8), 759–767.

Palop, J. J., & Mucke, L. (2010). Amyloid-β-induced neuronal dysfunction in Alzheimer's disease: From synapses toward neural networks. *Nature Neuroscience, 13*, 812–818.

Pasinetti, G. M., Chen, T. Y., Janle, E. M., & Cheng, A. (2010). Role of grape-derived polyphenols in the prevention of Alzheimer's disease and the promotion of healthy aging. *The FASEB Journal, 24*, 230–237.

Patten, D. A., Germain, M., Kelly, M. A., & Slack, R. S. (2010). Reactive oxygen species: Stuck in the middle of neurodegeneration. *Journal of Alzheimer's Disease, 20* Suppl 2, S357–S367.

Plassman, B. L., Williams, J. W., Burke, J. R., Holsinger, T., & Benjamin, S. (2010). Systematic review: Factors associated with risk for and possible prevention of cognitive decline in later life. *Annals of Internal Medicine, 153*, 182.

Poirier, J., Delisle, M. C., Quirion, R., Aubert, I., Farlow, M., Lahiri, D., et al. (1995). Apolipoprotein E4 allele as a predictor of cholinergic deficits and treatment outcome in Alzheimer's disease. *Proceedings of the National Academy of Sciences of the United States of America, 92*, 12260.

Polidori, M. C., Pratico, D., Mangialasche, F., Mariani, E., Aust, O., Anlasik, T., et al. (2009). High fruit and vegetable intake is positively correlated with antioxidant status and cognitive performance in healthy subjects. *Journal of Alzheimers Disease, 17*, 921–927.

Pratico, D. (2010). The neurobiology of isoprostanes and Alzheimer's disease. *Biochimica et Biophysica Acta, 1801*, 930–933.

Prins, N. D., Visser, P. J., & Scheltens, P. (2010). Can novel therapeutics halt the amyloid cascade? *Alzheimer's Research & Therapy, 2*, 5.

Profenno, L. A., Porsteinsson, A. P., & Faraone, S. V. (2010). Meta-analysis of Alzheimer's disease risk with obesity, diabetes, and related disorders. *Biological Psychiatry, 67*, 505–512.

Querfurth, H. W., & LaFerla, F. M. (2010). Alzheimer's disease. *New England Journal of Medicine, 362*, 329–344.

Rentz, D. M., Locascio, J. J., Becker, J. A., Moran, E. K., Eng, E., Buckner, R. L., et al. (2010). Cognition, reserve, and amyloid deposition in normal aging. *Annals of Neurology, 67*, 353–364.

Ryan, N. S., & Rossor, M. N. (2010). Correlating familial Alzheimer's disease gene mutations with clinical phenotype. *Biomarkers in Medicine, 4,* 99–112.

Sachdev, P. S., Ganguli, M., & Petersen, R. C. (2010). How can we best categorize cognitive impairment in nondemented older adults? *American Journal of Geriatric Psychology, 18,* 657.

Schneider, J. A., Arvanitakis, Z., Leurgans, S. E., & Bennett, D. A. (2009). The neuropathology of probable Alzheimer's disease and mild cognitive impairment. *Annals of Neurology, 66,* 200–208.

Schneider, P., Hampel, H., & Buerger, K. (2009). Biological marker candidates of Alzheimer's disease in blood, plasma, and serum. *CNS Neuroscience & Therapeutics, 15,* 358–374.

Terry, R. D., Masliah, E., Salmon, D. P., Butters, N., DeTeresa, R., Hill, R., et al. (1991). Physical basis of cognitive alterations in Alzheimer's disease: Synapse loss is the major correlate of cognitive impairment. *Annals of Neurology, 30,* 572–580.

Tobinick, E. (2010). Perispinal etanercept: A new therapeutic paradigm in neurology. *Expert review of Neurotherapeutics, 10,* 985–1002.

von Gunten, A., Pocnet, C., & Rossier, J. (2009). The impact of personality characteristics on the clinical expression in neurodegenerative disorders—A review. *Brain Research Bulletin, 80,* 179–191.

Wimo, A., Winblad, B., & Jansson, L. (2010). The worldwide societal costs of dementia: 2009 revisited. *Alzheimer's & Dementia, 6,* 103.

CHAPTER 18

Frontal-Subcortical Dementias

Leonard F. Koziol, Douglas Watt, & Deborah Ely Budding

INTRODUCTION

Whereas Alzheimer's disease (AD), the most common form of dementing illness, is typically characterized by initial deterioration within limbic and reticular structures (hippocampal/entorhinal regions and basal forebrain cholinergic systems) with later involvement of the neocortex (particularly in temporal and parietal cortices), a second and diverse group of dementias do not initially present with a primary amnestic syndrome or initial pathology in regions affected in AD. Instead, these conditions are characterized by variable but primary changes in personality, working memory, attentional and executive function, and affective regulation and behavioral organization. These conditions constitute a large and heterogeneous group of conditions termed frontal-subcortical dementias (Bonelli & Cummings, 2008; Stewart, 2006; Bak, Crawford, Berrios, & Hodges, 2010). Unlike most typical presentations of AD, this group of dementias is typically characterized by primary deterioration in the prefrontal cortices, in various regions of the basal ganglia, within the white matter tracts connecting these regions, or in other associated subcortical systems in a functional partnership with prefrontal systems. As a result, these dementias can have very diverse etiologies, with clinical phenotypes mapping onto any number of etiologic substrates, making correlation of clinical syndrome and underlying etiology often difficult and challenging (Manes et al., 2010; Chow et al., 2008). Any disease process that affects the frontal lobes and/or their connections to subcortical structures, including basal ganglia, cerebellum, thalamus, or reticular activating systems, can generate a frontal system dementia phenotype. Additional complexities emerge from a host of low-grade encephalopathic conditions (see Chapter 19) that produce a subsyndromal presentation of confusional states that can closely mimic several behavioral and cognitive phenotypes of these frontal-subcortical dementias, with varying degrees of apathy versus behavioral and affective disinhibition along with cognitive disorganization, but shy of a full-blown delirium. These wide-ranging mild encephalopathic conditions can also mimic the neurocognitive phenotype of these frontal-subcortical dementias. Because of this enormous diversity of etiologies, the differential diagnosis of any condition presenting with the cognitive and behavioral phenotype of a frontal-subcortical dementia is particularly challenging to the clinician, even if one is confident that the etiology is neurodegenerative (Duff et al., 2010) and not due to a low-grade reversible encephalopathy. Thus, this group of frontal-subcortical dementias has highly diverse neuropathologies associated with a group of common clinical syndromes; diverse treatment implications, depending on neuropsychological phenotype and behavioral issues; as well as underlying etiology.

TABLE 18.1 Abbreviated List of Common Causes of Frontal-Subcortical Dementia

AIDS dementia complex
Chronic alcoholism (with or without thiamine deficiency)
Anoxic encephalopathy
Carbon monoxide poisoning
Closed head injuries
Cerebrovascular disease (both cortical as well as subcortical)
Creutzfeldt–Jakob disease and other prion diseases
Frontotemporal lobar degeneration (four distinct diseases at a histological level)
Huntington disease
Lyme disease
Multiple sclerosis
Neurosyphilis
Normal pressure hydrocephalus
Parkinson disease (both brainstem and diffuse Lewy body disease)
Progressive supranuclear palsy
Multiple system atrophy (striatonigral degeneration)
Corticobasal Degeneration
Tumors
Wilson's disease
Other moderate to severe metabolic diseases
Any advanced dementing process (AD included)
Milder versions of virtually any medical condition that would cause delirium if more severe
Schizophrenia/schizoaffective disorders
Severe chronic substance abuse of almost any psychoactive drug

NEUROPATHOLOGY AND PATHOPHYSIOLOGY

The neuropathology and pathophysiology of this group of conditions depends on the underlying etiology. This often cannot be definitively established premortem, particularly in the case of neurodegenerative disorders (see the following), where postmortem brain biopsy and histopathology are required for definitive identification of underlying etiology. The likely primary causes (at a bare minimum) for this type of dementia are included in Table 18.1.

Space limitations preclude detailed discussions of each of these neuropathologies, and we will instead provide highly abbreviated summaries of each major etiology and its relevant neuropathology.

In AIDS, where there is a significant neurotoxic effect from the virus, this is typically combined with damage associated with the subject's own immune system and inflammatory responses, and these joint influences produce subsequent degeneration of white matter and gray matter (Navia & Rostasy, 2005). Histopathologically, AIDS dementia complex is typically associated with infiltration of monocytes and macrophages (classes of immune cell) into the CNS, as well as with gliosis, pallor of myelin sheaths, and with abnormalities of dendritic processes and both synaptic and neuronal loss (Abdulle et al., 2007; Anthony & Bell, 2008). In some cases, the degree of clinical dementia correlates poorly with these classic markers, suggesting that synaptic loss may be due to elevated cytokines, or perhaps other poorly understood neurotoxic effects of the virus, particularly its protein coat (Xing et al., 2009).

Alcoholism with severe thiamine deficiency—typically associated with binge drinking and severe nutritional compromise—initially results in acute Wernicke encephalopathy, a confusional state often presenting with sluggish eye movements (ophthalmoplegia) and ataxia, and greatly affecting medial thalamic nuclei, mammillary bodies, periaqueductal and periventricular brainstem nuclei, cranial nerves, and superior cerebellar vermis (Pitel et al., 2010). If the thiamine deficiency state is not rectified relatively rapidly, a Korsakoff dementia ensues (Shimamura, Jernigan, & Squire, 1988). Classic structural findings have emphasized atrophy of mamillary bodies and of the heteromodal (older) diencephalon, particularly medial dorsal, pulvinar, and anterior thalamus (Mair, Warrington, & Weiskrantz, 1979), but these are very difficult regions to image clinically because of their small size, and atrophy is typically confirmed only on postmortem examination. More recent studies have considered specific effects on cerebellar regions and associated effects on neurocognitive functions (Wijnia & Goossensen, 2010). Chronic alcoholism without thiamine deficiency tends to produce generalized atrophic change in the cerebellum and cerebellar vermis in particular, with loss of Purkinje cells (Zahr, Pitel, Chanraud, & Sullivan, 2010) and typically milder amnestic difficulties, whereas degeneration of medial/heteromodal thalamic systems in severe thiamine deficiency can create severe amnestic syndromes, often confounding any easy discrimination from AD.

Anoxic encephalopathy causes widespread and severe oxidative stress in mitochondria upon reperfusion with oxygenated blood and appears functionally identical to global ischemic injury (leading to the term hypoxic-ischemic insult). This can be generated by any number of common conditions, including common cardiac arrest, asphyxiation, and carbon monoxide poisoning. However, the brain's vulnerability to this severe oxidative stress in mitochondria appears to be regionally uneven, such that certain brain regions appear to take a greater hit, including particularly the globus pallidus, the hippocampus, and perhaps the substantia nigra (Lou, Jing, Selim, Caplan, & Ding, 2009). Additionally, contributions may be mediated by glutamatergic excitotoxicity and microglial activation/inflammatory signaling. The presence of amnestic features, particularly in elder victims of ischemic hypoxic injury, obviously complicates discrimination from AD, suggesting that a careful history is essential to discern a sudden onset of behavioral and amnestic difficulties after a presumed primary ischemic-hypoxic event.

Closed head injury (CHI) is a complex and heterogeneous syndrome, characterized by enormous regional variability of effect, an equally enormous spectrum of severity, and protean effects on behavior, cognition, and emotion/affective regulation (Silver, Hales, & Yudofsky, 2010). However, because of the frequent presence of diffuse axonal injury, inflammatory processes, and excitotoxicity in mild as well as moderate head trauma, a single moderate to severe CHI (as well as serial milder CHIs) can result in a frontal-subcortical dementia syndrome. Longer-term changes associated with serial CHIs can result in chronic traumatic encephalopathy (CTE), which is associated with cerebral atrophy, cavum septi pellucidi with fenestrations, atrophy of mamillary bodies, widespread tau immunoreactive inclusions (intraneuronal and glial tangles and neuropil neurites), and, in some cases, a TDP-43 proteinopathy (see the following discussion of the frontotemporal dementias, McKee et al., 2010; Gavett, Stern, & McKee, 2011). This disorder has prominent features of affective dysregulation, with poor memory and executive functioning and a wide variety of behavioral and affective regulatory disturbances (irritability, impulsiveness, apathy, depression, and suicidality). CTE can also show parkinsonism and, occasionally, motor neuron disease and should be considered in the differential diagnosis of anyone with possibly recurrent head trauma.

Cerebrovascular disease can similarly have very protean and diverse neurocognitive manifestations, depending on whether the primary pathology is microvascular (typically affecting white matter), or in a larger vessel, and also depending, of course, on the locations most affected by vascular disease and white matter loss. White matter ischemic change, commonly found on structural imaging studies, is classically seen on MRI as white matter hyperintensities (WMH). WMH tend to develop in "watershed" areas supporting the traditional assumption that they represent a marker of small vessel vascular disease, possibly from damage due to chronic hypoperfusion. Recent work suggests they may have fundamental connections to AD and not simply to classic vascular disease risk factors (hypertension, diabetes, dyslipidemia, smoking, sedentary lifestyle, etc.), given evidence that amyloid angiopathy is a primary, but not exclusive, factor in microangiopathy and white matter loss (Brickman et al., 2009).

Creutzfeldt–Jakob disease (CJD) is a prion disease where the infectious agent is a pathologically folded protein. It is thought to be the most common of the so-called transmissible spongiform encephalopathies, characterized by rapid progression and an invariably fatal outcome almost always within 1 year, and occasionally within a matter of a few months (Appleby & Lyketsos, 2011). All prion diseases are caused by central accumulation of a misfolded isoform of the human prion protein (PrP), a constituent of neuronal membranes, with five known major types: kuru, CJD, Gerstmann-Sträussler-Scheinker syndrome (GSS), fatal insomnia (FI), and variant CJD (vCJD). These subtypes have some differences in their classic clinical phenotypes and somewhat different brain histopathologies that allow their postmortem discrimination. First symptoms can include a wide variety of behavioral difficulties (including disinhibition or apathy), along with myoclonus, ataxia, declining ambulation, and vulnerability to seizures. One can acquire CJD through a mutation of the prion protein (5%–10% of cases), or through eating or otherwise absorbing prions, including from exposure to contaminated human growth hormone products (typically derived from human pituitaries), blood transfusions, other blood products such as immunoglobulins, corneal grafts, or other organ donation (Spero & Lazibat, 2010). CJD or one of the other prion diseases should be considered whenever someone has a rapidly progressive dementia, particularly with myoclonus, and diagnosis of CJD can be made more probable in the context of characteristic triphasic waves on EEG, spinal taps with characteristic proteins (14-3-3 protein), and high signal intensity in putamen and caudate on T2 MRI images. Histopathologically, the brain of patients with CJD shows neuronal loss, reactive astrocytic proliferation and classic spongiform appearance in the gray matter with round vacuoles (holes) in multiple cortical layers, and occasionally cerebellar involvement as well.

Frontotemporal dementias (now referred to as frontotemporal lobar degeneration [FLTD]), characterized structurally by increased atrophic change in frontotemporal regions, constitute a group of four discrete illnesses at a histopathological level, including a tauopathy (demonstrating neurofibrillary tangling, but without amyloid deposition), a disease demonstrating Pick's bodies, and a disease showing ubiquitin inclusions and deposition of TAR DNA-binding protein 43 (TDP-43), and a version lacking distinctive histopathology (Geser, Martinez-Lage, Kwong, Lee, & Trojanowski, 2009). TDP-43 protein appears to also play a role in amyotrophic lateral sclerosis as well as in a significant percentage of FTD. Although initially assumed to be specific to ALS and FTLD, TDP-43 pathology has now been found in other diseases involving tau pathology, including Guam Parkinson dementia complex and, most intriguingly, AD. TDP-43 pathology has recently been detected in one-quarter to one-half of AD cases, particularly in those with more severe Alzheimer's histopathology, as well as in those with hippocampal sclerosis (Wilson, Dugger, Dickson, & Wang, 2011). The comorbidity of this histopathology with more advanced AD is still mysterious and unexplained. TAR DNA-binding protein 43 is thought to be involved in transcriptional repression, gene splicing, and RNA metabolism during cellular stress responses (Wilson et al., 2011). Mutations of tau protein are associated with tauopathy/tangling histopathologies, whereas mutations of progranulin, a growth factor involved in the regulation of apoptosis and inflammation, can show ubiquitin positive inclusions (Baker et al., 2006). Clinical phenotypes for each of these four histopathologies are diverse and can include a primary progressive aphasia, a semantic dementia, classic frontal behavioral variants with primary disinhibition or apathy, and a motor neuron (ALS) phenotype, or patients can present with admixtures of these clinical phenotypes. This makes the large family of frontotemporal lobar degenerative disorders perhaps the most heterogeneous and confusing family of neurodegenerative dementing disorders, and still very poorly understood, particularly relative to both AD.

Huntington's disease (HD) is characterized by progressive atrophy of caudate and putamen and failure of basal ganglia inhibitory operations due to primary loss of indirect pathway functions (Yang & Chan, 2011). It is an autosomal dominant disorder with complete penetrance and is associated with poly-glutamine (nCAG) repeats, with the number of CAG repeats influencing age of onset, and encoding poly-glutamine residues at the terminal end of huntingtin (HTT) protein on chromosome 4. Since the discovery of the mutated *HTT* gene in 1993, how aggregated and mutant HTT protein contributes to neurodegeneration remains mysterious, and no disease-modifying therapy is available. Choreiform and other involuntary movement is regarded as the classical marker in adult onset HD, with tremor and myoclonus (and even parkinsonism—an opposite problem to chorea) seen in more juvenile (early-onset) variants (Thompson et al., 2010). Problems are also seen with eye movement (defective pursuit and tracking), gait abnormalities, and, as the disease progresses, speech motor abnormalities. Behavioral disinhibition and psychosis are not uncommon as the disease advances, consistent with failure of the inhibitory indirect pathway, but depression and apathy are also seen.

Tardive dyskinesia is probably the illness most commonly misdiagnosed as HD (Bhidayasiri & Boonyawairoj, 2011).

NEUROPSYCHOLOGICAL AND BEHAVIORAL SEQUELAE

Characteristics of the Neuropsychological Presentation

In order to understand the often protean neuropsychological and behavioral effects of these various dementing conditions, it is essential to understand the functions of cortico-striatal-pallidal-thalamic-cortical circuitry, as these relatively segregated circuitries help link characteristic neuropsychological and behavioral deficits to the relevant frontostriatal systems (Chase, 2010). In general, these dementias are characterized by various forms of executive dysfunction and associated disorganization and behavioral change. These dementias also can present with slowed declarative learning and poor recall, complicating their discrimination from AD. However, recollection is usually significantly improved in recognition paradigms, implying that retrieval of newly presented information can be disrupted, but not necessarily the encoding or retention (storage) of that data (Swartz, Stuss, Gao, & Black, 2008). Generalized mental slowing, or bradyphrenia, is common (Kehagia, Barker, & Robbins, 2010). There are difficulties in mentally manipulating acquired knowledge (working memory), and with a wide variety of executive deficits. Performance deficits on all tasks of spontaneous word generation or fluency are common (Davis et al., 2010). Disturbances in visuospatial functioning have also been reported (Fukui et al., 2009).

The psychological and behavioral presentation is often characterized by apathy, or, in contrast, lability and disinhibition. Occasionally, patients can display fluctuating admixtures of apathy and abulia alternating with lability, impulsiveness, and poor affective regulation (Chaudhuri, Ondo, Chaudhuri, & Reddy, 2010). These affective and mood changes may or may not be accompanied by depression (Kirsch-Darrow, Fernandez, Marsiske, Okun, & Bowers, 2006). Indeed, a primary apathy state can partially mimic and be misdiagnosed as an apathetic or retarded depression, a difficult clinical distinction to draw. Nevertheless, there is frequently a loss of interest in the environment and a lack of initiative in this group of frontal-subcortical dementias. Irritable mood is also often apparent. Patients are frequently unaware of these affective changes, suggesting failure of self-monitoring and insight. In fact, they may even deny any deficits or difficulties of any kind, underscoring the importance of collateral sources of history and background in relation to these patients (Prigatano, Maier, & Burns, 2010). The onset of these conditions is often marked by relatively insidious changes in the direction of apathy or loss of emotional control (Ceravolo, Frosini, Rossi, & Bonuccelli, 2010).

This group of frontal-subcortical dementias often lacks the striking instrumental deficits of anterograde amnesia and other posterior cortical deficits that are characteristic of AD past its earliest stages. Instead, it is the deterioration in anterior brain systems and/or their associated subcortical partners that generates the picture of changes in personality and executive functions. The frontal-subcortical system is composed of distinct subsystems subsumed by various specific cortico-striatal-pallidal-thalamic-cortical tracts, such that there really is no single "frontal lobe syndrome." Instead, most frontal-subcortical dementias are characterized by disturbances in multiple frontostriatal systems, resulting in behavioral presentations that are often varied or mixed (Bonelli & Cummings, 2008). Although some patients with frontal-subcortical dementias demonstrate movement disorder because motor circuits can be affected, a movement disorder is not a precondition for subcortical dementia because in numerous instances, motor circuitry is initially spared in the beginning stages of the disease process (Huey et al., 2009; Kertesz & McMonagle, 2010).

THE *DSM* AND FRONTAL-SUBCORTICAL DEMENTIAS: A Biased Description of Dementia?

The *Diagnostic and Statistical Manual of Mental Disorders*, also known as the *DSM*, is a behaviorally defined diagnostic classification system that is not anatomically organized (American

Psychiatric Association [APA], 2007). The disorders listed within the *DSM* are not categorized according to principles of known brain–behavior relationships. Instead, diagnosis is syndromal, and made on the basis of observing and/or reporting a cluster of behavioral symptoms or mental status changes. Curiously, the *DSM* does not even list a specific category of frontal-subcortical dementia. However, it does categorize "Dementia Due to Other General Medical Conditions," which can include dementia due to HIV disease, dementia due to head trauma, dementia due to Parkinson disease, dementia due to Huntington disease, dementia due to Pick's disease, and dementia due to CJD. There is also a general category that includes medical conditions such as "normal pressure hydrocephalus, hypothyroidism, brain tumor, vitamin B12 deficiency, and intracranial radiation." Notably, the current working draft of the *DSM-5* criteria has eliminated the frontal dementia concept along with the entire dementia concept (Sachdev, Andrews, Hobbs, Sunderland, & Anderson, 2009). Regardless, from our perspective, this approach to dementia classification has several major problems.

Clearly, a first concern is that the listing of possible etiologies is very incomplete and leaves out numerous disorders appearing even in our admittedly truncated list, such as the frontotemporal lobar degeneration family, corticobasal degeneration, progressive supranuclear palsy, and numerous other conditions. Additionally, *DSM-IV-TR* criteria for all forms of dementia are heavily canted in the direction of an AD phenotype, emphasizing memory impairment and posterior cortical deficits such as aphasia, apraxia, or agnosia (as well as possible executive deficits that are often seen in both frontal-subcortical dementias as well as in AD). Thus, *DSM-IV-TR* criteria intrinsically short the critical personality, behavioral, and affective alterations (described earlier) central to the frontal-subcortical syndrome description. Therefore, if a patient presents with personality and affective changes and associated executive changes indicative of a possible early-stage frontal-subcortical dementia process, particularly when these disturbances are relatively mild, but does not demonstrate amnestic difficulties, a literal-minded application of the *DSM-IV-TR* criteria for dementia would encourage diagnostic error (in this case, a false-negative result).

This set of issues is particularly seen in the *DSM-IV-TR* listing for vascular dementia, which is basically identical to the criteria for dementia due to AD (excepting motor difficulties or radiologic evidence of vascular disease), whereas many patients with moderate to severe white matter ischemic change (what used to be called Binswanger's disease) or with multiple cortical infarcts develop a mild dementia that looks quite different from AD. An additional complication is that many patients diagnosed with vascular dementia probably have mixed vascular AD processes (Craft, 2009; Li et al., 2010a; see Chapter 17).

Major neurocognitive disorder (including what was formerly known as dementia) is a disorder with greater cognitive deficits in at least one (typically two or more) of the following domains: (1) complex attention, (2) executive ability (planning, decision making, working memory, responding to feedback/error correction, overriding habits, mental flexibility), (3) learning and memory (immediate memory, recent memory [including free recall, cued recall, and recognition memory]) (4) language (expressive language [including naming, fluency, grammar, and syntax] and receptive language), (5) visuoconstructional-perceptual ability (construction and visual perception), and (6) social cognition (recognition of emotions, theory of mind, behavioral regulation). For the entire rationale and criteria, please see the neurocognitive disorders proposal for *DSM-5* at the *DSM-5* website (www.dsm5.org/ProposedRevisions/Pages/proposedrevision.aspx?rid=421.). Readers will find that evidence for significant decline in one or more of the previous domains is required and should be determined by reports by the patient or a knowledgeable informant or observation by the clinician and demonstrated on objective assessment of the relevant domain (typically greater than 2.0 SD below the mean [or below the 2.5th percentile] of an appropriate reference population [i.e., age, gender, education, premorbid intellect, and culturally adjusted]). The cognitive deficits must be sufficient to interfere with functional independence and not be wholly attributable to delirium or other CNS or Axis I disorder. Important changes from the *DSM-IV-TR* criteria include change in nomenclature (MNCD or dementia), not necessarily requiring memory to be one of the impaired domains, and allowing cognitive deficit limited to one domain. In the introductory text, we offer a table that offers more details about the assessment of each domain in the form of specific symptoms of decline that can be elicited or observed, and assessment procedures that can be used to document the cognitive impairment and quantify its severity.

THE FUNCTIONAL NEUROANATOMY OF FRONTAL-SUBCORTICAL DEMENTIAS

A basic understanding of anterior brain circuitry is essential for conceptualizing frontal-subcortical dementia symptom presentations. The frontal lobes can be divided into several separate regions, which include the prefrontal cortex, the supplementary and premotor cortices, the frontal eye fields, and the primary motor cortex. The prefrontal cortex is further subdivided into three regions. These major subdivisions include dorsolateral prefrontal cortex, lateral and medial subdivisions of the orbitofrontal cortex, and anterior cingulate/medial frontal cortex (Blumenfeld, 2002). Dependent upon specific functional neuroanatomic considerations, these regions can be divided into further subdivisions. However, the divisions listed here are sufficient to establish a framework for the clinical practitioner with a practical diagnostic focus. Each of these frontal regions send white matter projections to the basal ganglia, a collection of bilaterally represented gray matter nuclei located deep within the white matter of the cerebral hemispheres. These nuclei lie at the core of the cerebral hemispheres and are central to the basal forebrain (Alexander, DeLong, & Strick, 1986).

The term basal ganglia most commonly refers to four structures (Middleton, 2003). These structures comprise the striatum (caudate and putamen), the globus pallidus (internal and external subdivisions), the substantia nigra, and the subthalamic nucleus. These structures in turn feature a number of important subdivisions, such as the nucleus accumbens and olfactory tubercle. A number of texts address these areas in detail; interested readers should consult these for more information (Middleton, 2003; Utter & Basso, 2008; Koziol & Budding, 2009). The frontal cortices and other cortical regions are connected to the basal ganglia in a highly specific manner: The cortex projects to the striatum, the striatum projects to the globus pallidus, which projects to the thalamus, and then back to the cortex to the same region where the circuit originated. This simplified circuitry is depicted in Figure 18.1.

Each basal ganglia circuit features two essential connectional profiles: the direct and indirect pathways. These connectional systems essentially enable the basal ganglia to function as a gating system or variable "brake" upon the cerebral cortex (Anderson, Fincham, Qin, & Stocco, 2008). When the cerebral cortex—which always has an excitatory, activational influence on either pathway—activates a direct pathway, the striatum releases the tonic inhibitory control that the globus pallidus exerts on the thalamus. Thus disinhibited, the thalamus

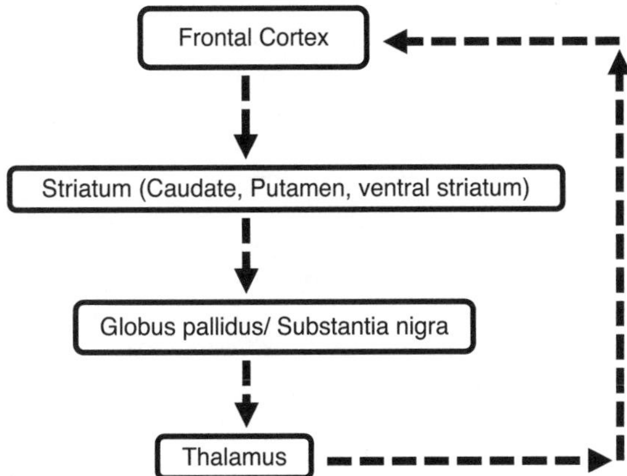

FIGURE 18.1 Fronto-subcortical connections. The diagram outlines the primary components of the fronto-subcortical circuitry.

activates cortex, resulting in perceptual activation in sensory circuits and motor activation in motor circuits. When the cortex activates the indirect pathway, the inhibitory influence the globus pallidus exerts upon the thalamus is increased. This inhibits the thalamus so it can no longer exert an excitatory influence on the cortex. Perceptions are thus inhibited in sensory circuits, and behavioral release is inhibited in motor circuits. In essence, this circuitry allows the basal ganglia to tell which regions of the highly compartmentalized cortex when they should and should not become active. This process allows attention (perception) and action (motor behavior) to be focused in a particular direction while precluding attention and action from being focused in other directions (Hikosaka & Isoda, 2010; Houk et al., 2007).

Seven differentiated, prototypical circuits have been identified that connect the frontal lobes and the remainder of the cortex to the basal ganglia and thalamus. Each circuit is named according to its point of origin and follows the same projection pattern while remaining segregated from the other circuits (Alexander et al., 1986; Bonelli & Cummings, 2007). These circuits include: (1) the dorsolateral prefrontal circuit, (2) the orbitofrontal circuit, (3) the medial/anterior cingulate circuit, (4) the skeletal-motor circuit, and (5) the oculomotor circuit. Subsequent to Alexander's classic work, posterior sensory circuits, including the temporal and parietal circuits, have been revealed that follow the same connectional pattern (Middleton & Strick, 2001). These posterior circuits are mentioned so that the reader understands that the basal ganglia play a role in all attentional (perceptual) and behavioral (motor) selections.

Each of these segregated and discrete circuits have separate functions. The skeletal-motor circuit mediates movement, the oculomotor circuit originates in the frontal eye fields and controls visual search eye movements, the dorsolateral prefrontal circuit mediates the activation of cognitive activity, the orbitofrontal circuit plays an important role in mediating adaptive social behavior and in empathy and the internalization of social rules and contingencies, and the medial/anterior cingulate circuit governs motivation (Levy & Krebs, 2006). The temporal and parietal circuits are involved in perception and certain types of categorization and information-integration learning (Ashby & O'Brien, 2007; Seger, 2008). We will focus upon the anterior circuits, specifically, the dorsolateral, orbitofrontal, and anterior cingulate/medial tracts to assist in understanding the role of this projection system in the most common frontal-subcortical dementias.

Parkinson disease is in part characterized by difficulties initiating and stopping movements, and by perseveration that makes switching from one movement to another difficult. This occurs because of deterioration within the substantia nigra pars compacta, which deprives the striatum of dopamine essential for activating the direct pathway (Bamford & Cepeda, 2009). As a result, the striatum cannot inhibit the control the globus pallidus has over the thalamus, and motor behavior cannot easily be released. HD is characterized by release of fragments of purposeful movements. In the early, initial stages of this disease, the striatum is primarily affected, resulting in alterations in certain neuropeptides within the indirect pathway (Thompson et al., 2010). This results in an inability to activate the globus pallidus, so that thalamic activity can no longer be suppressed, which is manifest by the release of fragments of purposeful, unwanted movements. These two classic basal ganglia diseases thus reflect opposite problems with frontostriatal function, and initially primarily involve motor circuitry, but past earlier stages, show a deepening involvement of other frontostriatal circuits beyond primary motor loops.

Because all cortical-striatal circuits run in parallel and are governed by the same organizational principles and functional mechanisms, the inability to translate intention to action that manifests in motor problems in these patients would be predicted to manifest in a variety of other pathologies when other circuits are involved (Ligot et al., 2010). These two disease processes are always characterized by cognitive and personality changes because deterioration in these pathologies involves degeneration in other frontal-subcortical circuits as well. This is why both of these classic movement disorders are characterized by features of frontal-subcortical dementia. The next sections will focus upon the functions of the dorsolateral, orbital, and anterior cingulate/medial circuits in order to assist in applying these (oversimplified) principles of movement to cognitive and affective functions. The functions of these circuits have previously been described in detail by Koziol and Budding (2009) and can be reviewed in further detail in that publication. The following section includes the detailed projection patterns of these individual tracts so that the reader can appreciate the segregated nature of these connections, while applying the basic principles of movement disorders to analogues or deficits in cognitive, affective and motivational, and social/behavioral function. This discussion will be concluded with a case presentation that illustrates the application of these principles to clinical practice.

THE DORSOLATERAL PREFRONTAL CIRCUIT

The dorsolateral prefrontal (DLPF) circuit originates on the lateral surface/convexity of the prefrontal lobes. Neurons in this region project to the dorsolateral head of the caudate nucleus. Fibers from this region of the caudate project to the lateral aspect of the mediodorsal Gpi and to the rostrolateral SNpr as part of the direct pathway. The indirect route projects from the caudate to the dorsal Gpe, which projects to the lateral STN. Output of the DLPF circuit from the basal ganglia projects to the ventral anterior and to the mediodorsal thalamus. The circuit is closed by the mediodorsal thalamus projecting back to the region of origin of the circuit (Lichter & Cummings, 2001). This thalamic projection defines the prefrontal lobe (Fuster, 1997). The DLPF circuit is responsible for executive cognitive activity. Executive function can be described as the capacity to generate adaptive behavior autonomously, in the absence of external direction, support, or guidance. The capacities necessary to accomplish the behavior include the ability to focus attention, inhibit inappropriate responses, provide the working memory required for the frontal lobe's planning and organizational functions, and to program behaviors in order to solve problems that do not have an immediate, stimulus-based solution. When affect is disturbed in patients with damage to this circuit, the most common presentations are apathy and depression. Most neuropsychological and cognitive tests access or go through this specific circuit (Ardila, 2008; Malloy & Richardson, 2001; Stewart, 2006).

ORBITOFRONTAL CIRCUITRY

The orbitofrontal circuit (OFC) has two divisions—the lateral and medial divisions—that can be considered two circuitries based upon their projection patterns. The medial OFC originates in ventromedial prefrontal cortex and projects to the medial nucleus accumbens, ventral regions of the pallidum, and back to medial-dorsal thalamus and medial OFC. This region of the OFC has reciprocal connections with the limbic system and insula (Frank & Claus, 2006). Medial OFC circuitry is believed to integrate and modulate visceral drives and the internal milieu (Lichter & Cummings, 2001). This circuitry is not directly assessed through neuropsychological and/or psychological testing. Aspects of this circuitry would be evaluated informally, through history and observation, in regard to alimentary, gustatory, and olfactory behaviors (Ibarretxe Bilbao et al., 2010; Li et al., 2010b). These functions could play roles in areas of adaptation more traditionally understood as related to personality functioning. Changes in eating patterns or in the sense of smell can betray involvement of medial circuitry. Personality changes include anergy and anhedonia (Mega & Cummings, 2001).

The lateral OFC also originates in the ventromedial prefrontal cortex, sending projections to the ventromedial striatum/caudate. This region projects to the most medial region of the mediodorsal Gpi and to rostromedial SNpr. The ventral anterior and mediodorsal nuclei are the thalamic targets that project back to OFC (Lichter & Cummings, 2001). Lateral OFC circuit involvement results in the "Phineas Gage" syndrome. The primary deficits are related to personality changes including disinhibition, impulsivity, irritability, and emotional lability. In terms of social behavior, tactlessness and undue familiarity are often described (Ardila, 2008; Chow & Cummings, 2007; Mega & Cummings, 2001). This circuitry is important for the temporal ordering of behavior in determining the proper time and place for expressing behaviors (Fuster, 1997). As a result, damage to this circuit often results in socially inappropriate behavior. This circuit plays an important role in sustaining motivated behaviors in the absence of external cues or contingencies. It assists in allowing the individual to maintain behavior without immediate, tangible reinforcement, or environmental influence. It is involved in inhibiting responding to external distractions and other interfering influences. Therefore, attention is disturbed as manifest by impairment in inhibitory/exclusionary functions (Fuster, 1997).

Deficits involving this region often result in social disinhibition and socially inappropriate behaviors because instincts are disinhibited. Patients with OFC involvement are often "stimulus bound." This has been termed the environmental dependency syndrome or utilization behavior (Lhermitte, Pillon, & Serdaru, 1986; Lhermitte, 1986). Involvement within this circuit is often broadly characterized by dysregulation of affect, judgment, and social behavior. The affective tone is frequently characterized by euphoria or mania (Cummings & Miller, 2007).

Few neuropsychological test measures of orbitofrontal functions in humans exist (Malloy & Richardson, 2001). Inferences about the integrity of this circuitry are thus frequently drawn from observation or report. Therefore, the methodologies for evaluating involvement of this region are vulnerable to all the biases that can affect self-report and observational report instruments. Patients with focal OFC pathology can perform adequately on many neuropsychological tests because discrete lesions in this region do not necessarily affect cognitive function (Ardila, 2008). However, competing programs and go/no-go tasks can be useful for identifying the disinhibition frequently characteristic of people with OFC pathology.

THE ANTERIOR CINGULATE/MEDIAL FRONTAL CIRCUITS

The medial frontal circuit originates in the anterior cingulate, which projects primarily to the nucleus accumbens and related regions of the ventral striatum, including the olfactory tubercle (which is technically part of the basal ganglia according to detailed classification systems and has functions largely identical to the nucleus accumbens). These regions can be considered the limbic striatum (Heimer, Van Hoesen, Trimble, & Zahm, 2008). This circuit returns near its point of origin through the rostrolateral globus pallidus and the dorsomedial nucleus of the thalamus to the anterior cingulate area. Dysfunction in this circuit is characterized primarily by apathy and motivational deficits. Patients appear indifferent and to lack interest. Observed deficits are not primarily cognitive as they are in the dorsolateral syndrome. Rather, MFC circuit involvement results in what is known as a-motivational syndrome. In its most extreme form, this is characterized by akinetic mutism, classically associated with bilateral cingulate lesions (Mega & Cummings, 2001). Severe forms of akinetic mutism can be seen in subcortical injury, specifically to systems closely affiliated with the cingulate including particularly bilateral ventral basal ganglia insults, lesions of the ventral tegmental area, or full lesions of midbrain periaqueductal gray (Watt, Pincus, & Panksepp, 2004). Patients with this condition are literally mute and show minimal to no response to those stimuli that were previously sources of reward and reinforcement. In less extreme forms, spontaneous speech is diminished, verbalizations are brief, and there is little drive and motivation. Apathetic depressions obviously involve lesser disruption of this same paralimbic-subcortical network (Kirsch-Darrow et al., 2006).

Because of these aspects of the presentation, cognitively capable patients with reasonably intact cognitive profiles can often escape detection through traditional neuropsychological tests, while the presenting difficulties might be attributed to psychological or emotional variables. This helps to foster the misleading notion that cognitive and emotional functions are separate, and that problems with motivation and drive are not brain-related. In brain–behavior relationship reality, these types of executive deficits result from interactions between brain circuitries, although neuropsychological test psychometric scores are not particularly useful for identifying and characterizing these possible interactions. In this regard, deficits in executive functioning can and do occur for reasons other than cognitive pathology (Ardila, 2008; Chow & Cummings, 2007). As is the case with OFC pathology, go/no-go task performance is often pathognomonic of involvement, although due to performance overlap, these types of competing programs tasks lack highly specific localization capability. There are currently no commercially available neuropsychological procedures that are specific to identifying apathy and/or motivation.

FRONTAL SYSTEM SYNDROMES

These circuitries help demonstrate that there is no one frontal lobe syndrome. Instead, there are multiple frontal system syndromes. Each broad type of frontal lobe syndrome is characterized by the specific behavior patterns described previously. Particularly at the level of the cortical convexity, lesions can be very discrete and can result in distinct cognitive and behavioral presentations. A lesion anywhere within the looped architecture of any specific circuit will generate a similar if not identical symptom picture. However, it is not unusual for more than one circuit to be involved in a patient's clinical presentation, and this is manifest by a mixture of behaviors and symptoms that would characterize malfunctions of several circuits (Chow & Cummings, 2007; Malloy & Richardson, 2001).

Although more than one circuit is often involved in a patient's presentation, the functioning of every circuit cannot be approached through using the same assessment methodologies. For example, if dorsolateral pathology in particular is not involved, it can be very difficult and sometimes impossible to identify deficits using classic neuropsychological tests. When this occurs, a neuropsychologist might conclude that the patient's executive functioning is perfectly normal. This conclusion is not necessarily justified. Instead, it may very well be that the testing procedures did not access regions demonstrating pathology. This fact contributes significantly to the problems with ecological validity frequently noted in relation to neuropsychological evaluation (Sbordone, 2001; Odhuba, van den Broek, & Johns, 2005; Silver, 2000; Sbordone, 2010). Simply put, as they exist today, neuropsychological tests do not measure every possible brain-related function, particularly in more affective and personality domains. In addition, an important principle of this distributed circuitry is that lesions in areas to which these circuits project can have a strikingly similar (if not identical) presentation (Mega & Cummings, 2001). The psychometric properties of neuropsychological tests are simply not sensitive to making these differential localization discriminations. For example, lesions of the dorsolateral prefrontal cortex, a lesion within the dorsolateral head of the caudate, or a lesion in the medial dorsal region of the internal section of the globus pallidus can all generate a very similar symptom picture (Cummings & Miller, 2007; Grau-Olivares, Arboix, Bartres-Faz, & Junque, 2007a; Grau-Olivares et al., 2007b; Bombois et al., 2007; Lee & Chui, 2007; Su, Chen, Kwan, Lin, & Guo, 2007).

These frontal-basal ganglionic circuits are organized around different channels or modules of function. Despite the fact that these circuits originate in widespread regions of the frontal cortices and project deep inside the basal forebrain to a spatially restricted region, the integrity and segregation of each of these circuits is maintained. However, because of the spatial extent of the convexity, lesions in very circumscribed cortical regions can result in very specific frontal lobe syndromes, with fairly well-delineated cognitive, affective, and behavioral manifestations. As lesions descend deeper into anterior brain regions toward the basal forebrain, however, the spatial constriction of the area greatly increases the likelihood that one lesion would impact on more than one circuit. At this deeper level, behavioral manifestations become more mixed, with one lesion generating the effects and features of multiple circuitries (Su et al., 2007; Lee & Chui, 2007; Bombois et al., 2007). In fact, descending deep into the brain, it becomes difficult to imagine a single lesion impacting only upon a single circuit (Middleton, 2003). The involvement of multiple circuits with mixed cognitive, affective, and motivational features becomes the rule rather than the exception because the spatial geography or territory becomes increasingly constricted and shared. Therefore, in considering frontal system syndromes, it is critical to remember that neuropsychological tests do not measure all relevant cognitive, affective, motivational, and behavioral functions; that the involvement of multiple frontal system circuitries is common; and that the various and differing multiple etiologies of frontal-subcortical pathologies are not neuropsychologically friendly with respect to differential diagnostic interpretations. As a result, it is best to consider, interpret, and report neuropsychological test results in cognitive and behavioral terms (Alvarez & Emory, 2006). The following case example illustrates many of these issues.

FRONTAL SYSTEMS DEMENTIA: A CASE EXAMPLE

This is a case of a 70-year-old right-handed male with a doctorate degree who was functioning in an independent health care practice. At the time of evaluation, his family reported a 1.5-year history of insidiously deteriorating function. Personality and emotional changes included a high degree of anxiety, easily provoked crying, frustration and irritability, and an unusual indifference to things that would formerly engage him. In addition, he began to develop a blank facial expression. Cognitive changes included memory lapses, forgetfulness, and failures in information retrieval. He became easily distractible. At times, he exhibited obsessive-like fixations on aspects of tasks to the exclusion of grasping the broader picture, leading to increasing interpersonal difficulty. He became concrete in his thinking, failing to see the whole picture within the appropriate context. He exhibited difficulties with time estimation and management. He became impulsive with episodes of behavioral dyscontrol (e.g., hitting the dog or the cat). He increasingly needed to be reminded about things, even eating. In fact, he needed to have food put in front of him or he would not initiate eating independently. While previously a reasonably neat person, his desk and office became visibly disorganized. The patient himself complained of indistinct-onset memory problems that he felt were gradually becoming worse. He was not highly concerned about this symptom, but was bothered that his work efficiency had decreased. He did not notice changes in his mood. He denied experiencing emotional changes. He denied experiencing problems with his attention or concentration. He denied problems with speech or language, and these types of instrumental cognitive changes were not observed during interview conversation or discourse.

He was cooperative in relation to the evaluation. He was friendly, eager to engage, and not observably anxious. His mood was euthymic. When experiencing difficulties in completing certain cognitive tasks, he showed no concern about this, and either denied or benignly rationalized them. His disinhibition was readily evident. While completing several testing tasks, he would insist on calling his family, which he did on his cell phone, right in the middle of the task administration. As the evaluation session progressed, he became irritable and agitated about the time the session was taking, but he was able to continue working to avoid a return appointment. When answering questions, either about personal history information or formal test questions, he had a tendency to associate to something that interested him instead of strictly adhering to what was asked, and he was unaware that his replies were off target. He was also unable to return to the central theme of what was originally asked. His test results are presented in Table 18.2

Perhaps the most obvious differential diagnosis here would be between a frontotemporal lobe dementia versus depression. However, although there is behavioral evidence of affective change in terms of irritability, lack of initiation, and apathy, there are really no substantive observations of depression, at least not in terms of meeting the behaviorally defined diagnostic criteria for that condition as listed within the *DSM-IV-TR*. However, there is behavioral evidence of dorsolateral, orbitofrontal, and anterior cingulate/medial circuitry involvement. For example, there are indications of executive function changes not only in terms of cognitive activity, but in terms of the appropriate inhibition and motivation that are necessary for placing circumstances within proper context for proper social and professional judgment as well. Forgetfulness, retrieval problems, distractibility, and diminished insight implicate involvement of the dorsolateral system (working memory deficits are often perceived by patients or evidenced by observing family members as forgetfulness and distractibility). Disinhibition is readily evident in terms of impulsive behavior, episodic dyscontrol, and even irritability. Attention is poorly controlled at least in terms of an inability to maintain a focused stream of response in responding to questions. Anxiety, irritability, crying spells, and appetitive disturbance all imply involvement of lateral and medial orbitofrontal tracts. Apathy, lack of concern over the relevance of behaviors, and lack of purposeful behavioral initiation all implicate involvement of anterior cingulate/medial pathways that project into

TABLE 18.2 Case Example: Neuropsychological Data/Test Performance

Gordon Diagnostic System	raw	z
Vigilance task		
correct =	26	−5.1
commis =	8	−3.0
latency =	290	+1.2
Distractibility task		
correct =	7	−2.6
commis =	9	−2.3
latency =	440	−0.1

Digit Vigilance Test

iTotal Time = 362. T = 63

Total Errors = 48. T = 24

Wisconsin Card Sorting Test	raw	T
Categories	6	
Responses	101	
Errors	22	54
Percent Persev Err	12	53
Fail Maintain Set	1	
Trials to 1st cat	10	

MOANS Age and Ed Corrected Scaled Scores	Raw	SS
Control'd Oral Word Assoc	36	7.1
Boston Naming Test	60	14.7
Token Test	44	10.2
Stroop Word	77	4.4
Stroop Color	46	3.9
Stroop Color/Word	31	8.5
Trails A	33	9.9
Trails B	73	9.2
Judgement of Line Orient	24	10.1

Mattis Dementia Rating Scale-2	raw score	AMSS	AEMSS
Attention =	37	13	
Initiation/Perseveration =	37	13	
Constructions =	36	10	
Conceptualization =	39	13	
Memory =	25	13	
Total Score =	143	14	13

Word Association (3 stimuli, 1 min each)

Letters = 36 (MAE COWA %tile = 99)

Categories = 46

Animals only = 22. T = 40

Frontal Systems Behavioral Scale

Ratings were done by daughter "Before" illness 2 years ago and "At Present Time."

Higher T scores are more troublesome relative to normal controlpopulation.

Ratings done by daughter	Before illness T score	Current T score
Apathy	53	79
Disinhibition	62	89
Executive	70	107
Total	65	101

(continued)

TABLE 18.2 Case Example: Neuropsychological Data/Test Performance *(Continued)*

<u>WAIS-III</u>

Index Scores

Processing Speed = 106

Performances subtest scaled scores

DSy = 12
SmS = 10

Dsym percentible levels:
Incident learn pairing > 50
Incident free recall = 2-5
Copy > 50

<u>Ravens Colored Matrices</u>

Correct = 29. Percentile = 90

<u>Facial Recognition</u> (short form, extrapolated)

Correct = 47. Percentile = 71

<u>WMS-III</u>

Primary Index Scores

Auditory Immed =	97
Visual Immed =	88
Immed Mem =	91
Auditory Delay =	99
Visual Delayed =	94
Aud Recog Del =	100
General Mem =	96

Subtest scaled scores

Log Mem I =	12
Faces I =	7
Verb PA I =	7
Fam Pic I =	9
LNS =	
Spa Span =	
Log Mem II =	12
Faces II =	11
Verb PA II =	8
Fam Pic II =	7
Aud Rec Del =	10
Inf & Orien =	(72 %tile level)
LM Thermatic I =	15
LM Thermatic II =	15
Ment Contr =	11

<u>Rey Auditory Verbal Learning Test(recall of 15 word list)</u>

<u>Trail:</u>	<u>I</u>	<u>II</u>	<u>III</u>	<u>IV</u>	<u>V</u>	<u>Int</u>	<u>VI</u>	trial VI <u>Recog</u>	30° <u>Rcl</u>	30° <u>Recog</u>
	5	6	7	8	8	3	6	14	6	14
ss*:	10					9	8		9	11

*MOANS age & education adjusted; Learning Over Trials ss = 8.

the basal forebrain, limbic basal ganglia, and deep mesodiencephalon. Therefore, history review provides many important clues for a possible diagnosis of frontal-subcortical dementia. Psychometric test findings need to be interpreted using these behavioral observations and their neuroanatomic implications as anchor points.

The patient's test results were revealing, with several subtle interpretive issues. On the Raven's matrices, he performed at the 90th percentile ranking, with the implication that global concept formation remained intact. He did score at a level consistent with expectation in view of his educational history, although to be sure, the "colored" version of this task is decidedly easier than the standard matrices. Nevertheless, one would not predict significant global cognitive deficits in a case of early onset dementia, and this conclusion would be supported by his performance on the Mattis Dementia Rating Scale-II. Similarly, there were no indications of instrumental cognitive deficits such as aphasic speech, agnosia or other perceptual disturbance, or apraxia, with the possible exception of mild dyscalculia because he made errors with simple mental subtraction, implying a loss of calculation efficiency and accuracy. Performances on measures of "processing speed" were also generally within normal limits. However, it was suspicious that on the incidental recall paradigm of the Digit Symbol subtest, his score fell between the 2nd–5th percentile ranking, implying either inattention and/or deficits in the initial encoding of information.

Although speech was fluent and without paraphasias in spontaneous conversation or in naming upon object confrontation, his abilities to associate and retrieve words to categories (animal naming fluency) and letters (FAS) were both below the level of expectation for a person of his intellectual and educational backgrounds, and this finding frequently occurs in patients with involvement of anterior brain regions.

Multiple aspects of the attentional matrix were affected. Fluctuations in performances on immediate recall tasks clearly implied he was not able to consistently encode the same range of information as his peers, with scores ranging from above average to a standard deviation below the mean. Therefore, this information that was missed would obviously not be available to executive working memory to assist in guiding behavior. His performance on two tasks of sustained monitoring was poor, characterized by numerous errors of omission (inattention) as well as significant errors of commission (disinhibition). An attentional shifting task required him to switch the focus of attention from one idea to another; his performance was well within normal limits on this task (Wisconsin Card Sorting Test), which is presumably heavily dependent upon the input of dorsolateral cognitive circuitry.

This patient's most notable deficits were observed in relation to a word list learning task. He acquired new information slowly, and he learned less information than his peers. He exhibited the shallow learning slope often characteristic of "frontal system" patient populations. Although voluntary (unstructured) retrieval was poorer than expected, significant improvement was observed upon recognition, again indicative of a frontal system pattern. In this regard, although information retrieval for newly learned information was sometimes incomplete, there was no clear or convincing evidence that he ever forgot what he learned during the assessment, again implying involvement of anterior brain regions. Rating scale data was provided by his daughter, who had contact with him on a daily basis. On the Frontal Lobe Personality Scale, significant deterioration in behavioral functioning was reported within dimensions of apathy, disinhibition, and executive functioning, characteristic of patients with involvement of frontal-subcortical circuitry.

Overall, the patient exhibited abnormal changes in behavioral (executive) and emotional functioning, accompanied by deficits within certain attentional functions. All of these deficits were considered mild to moderate in severity. Strictly cognitive changes were considerably milder. His disinhibition clearly implied ventral orbital and medial prefrontal involvement. Although the neuropsychologist who completed the evaluation recognized that these findings were not highly specific as to etiology, frontotemporal dementia (FTD) was strongly suspected. This certainly represented a reasonable diagnostic conclusion, but later histopathology did not confirm this, and suggested a significantly rarer prion disorder. For example, as summarized by Salmon and Bondi (2009), FTD patients have greater deficits in executive functions than in other cognitive abilities, whereas AD patients have executive disturbances that are proportional to their instrumental cognitive deficits in language and visuospatial abilities. On the other hand, FTD patients have been characterized as exhibiting significantly worse performance on word generation subtests sensitive to frontal lobe dysfunction (as on letter and category fluency tasks) but as functioning much better on tests sensitive to medial temporal lobe memory system impairment and parietal association cortices that support instrumental cognitive abilities (Salmon & Bondi, 2009).

Subsequent MRI of the brain revealed a pronounced degree of periventricular ischemic white matter changes of a confluent nature bilaterally, much more than might be expected for his age. The confluent character of these changes was consistent with involvement of multiple prefrontal-subcortical circuits. In other words, this patient's primary pathology on imaging was not cortical. Instead, abnormalities were observed within the white matter tracts connecting the frontal lobes with the direct and indirect pathways of the striatum. The patient's condition took a progressively downward course; he was bedridden within a few months, lost all ability to speak, developed aspects of decerebrate posture/rigidity, and died approximately 5 months after this neuropsychological evaluation. Autopsy confirmed a diagnosis of the sporadic form of CJD, not any one of the frontotemporal lobar degeneration diseases discussed earlier. This illustrates that the actual postmortem histopathology, clearly the gold standard for diagnosis for the underlying neurological illness, is often very difficult to estimate based even on the most careful and detailed assessment of clinical phenotype, and that any given clinical phenotype maps to several histopathologies, even though a given histopathology may prefer or gravitate toward a limited range of clinical phenotypic manifestations.

To summarize, these test results are significant for several reasons. This case exemplifies the diagnostic issues that need to be considered in frontal-subcortical dementias, particularly at the subcortical level. Important considerations include the fact that disturbances in frontal-basal ganglia circuitry can generate a similar cognitive and behavioral presentation regardless of the level at which cortico-striatal-pallidal-thalamo-cortial circuitry is affected. Neuropsychological tests do not assess all relevant cognitive, affective, and motivational influences on behavior, so that test profiles need to be interpreted within the context of both neuroanatomical and behavioral frameworks. This approach requires information from multiple sources. Test results need to be interpreted and reported in cognitive and behavioral descriptive terminology instead of strictly in terms of neuroanatomical reference points (Alvarez & Emory, 2006). Finally, neuropsychological test results cannot be interpreted by using the points of reference established through behaviorally defined, *DSM*-type diagnostic systems. Our current state of knowledge dictates that neuropsychological test data are to be employed as one source of information, integrated with data from other points of reference, in order to assist in guiding diagnostic conclusions. This will remain the case until the field of neuropsychology can further develop methodologies for assessing segregated frontal-subcortical circuitries that contribute to the expression of cognitive, affective, motivational, and social functioning.

REFERENCES

Abdulle, S., Mellgren, A., Brew, B. J., Cinque, P., Hagberg, L., Price, R. W., et al. (2007). CSF neurofilament protein (NFL) a marker of active HIV-related neurodegeneration. *Journal of Neurology, 254,* 1026–1032.

Alexander, G. E., DeLong, M. R., & Strick, P. L. (1986). Parallel organization of functionally segregated circuits linking basal ganglia and cortex. *Annual Review of Neuroscience, 9,* 357–381.

Alvarez, J. A., & Emory, E. (2006). Executive function and the frontal lobes: A meta-analytic review. *Neuropsychological Review, 16,* 17–42.

American Psychiatric Association. (2007). *Diagnostic and statistical manual of mental disorders.* Washington, DC: Author.

Anderson, J. R., Fincham, J. M., Qin, Y., & Stocco, A. (2008). A central circuit of the mind. *Trends in Cognitive Sciences, 12,* 136–143.

Anthony, I. C., & Bell, J. E. (2008). The neuropathology of HIV/AIDS. *International Review of Psychiatry, 20,* 15–24.

Appleby, B. S., & Lyketsos, C. G. (2011). Rapidly progressive dementias and the treatment of human prion diseases. *Expert Opinion on Pharmacotherapy, 12,* 1–12.

Ardila, A. (2008). On the evolutionary origins of executive functions. *Brain and Cognition. 68*(1), 92–99.

Ashby, F. G., & O'Brien, J. B. (2007). The effects of positive versus negative feedback on information-integration category learning. *Perception and Psychophysics, 69,* 865–878.

Bak, T. H., Crawford, L. M., Berrios, G., & Hodges, J. R. (2010). Behavioural symptoms in progressive supranuclear palsy and frontotemporal dementia. *Journal of Neurology, Neurosurgery & Psychiatry, 81,* 1057.

Baker, M., Mackenzie, I. R., Pickering-Brown, S. M., Gass, J., Rademakers, R., Lindholm, C. et al. (2006). Mutations in progranulin cause tau-negative frontotemporal dementia linked to chromosome 17. *Nature, 442*, 916–919.

Bamford, N. S., & Cepeda, C. (2009). The Corticostriatal Pathway in Parkinson's Disease. In Tseng, K. Y. (Ed.), *Cortico-Subcortical Dynamics in Parkinson's Disease*, (pp. 87–104). New York: Humana Press.

Bhidayasiri, R., & Boonyawairoj, S. (2011). Spectrum of tardive syndromes: clinical recognition and management. *Postgraduate Medical Journal, 87*, 132.

Blumenfeld, H. (2002). *Neuroanatomy through clinical cases*. Sunderland, MA: Sinauer Associates.

Bombois, S., Debette, S., Delbeuck, X., Bruandet, A., Lepoittevin, S., Delmaire, C., et al. (2007). Prevalence of subcortical vascular lesions and association with executive function in mild cognitive impairment subtypes. *Stroke, 38*, 2595–2597.

Bonelli, R. M., & Cummings, J. L. (2007). Frontal-subcortical circuitry and behavior. *Dialogues in Clinical Neuroscience, 9*, 141.

Bonelli, R. M., & Cummings, J. L. (2008). Frontal-subcortical dementias. *Neurologist, 14*, 100–107.

Brickman, A. M., Siedlecki, K. L., Muraskin, J., Manly, J. J., Luchsinger, J. A., Yeung, L. K. et al. (2009). White matter hyperintensities and cognition: Testing the reserve hypothesis. *Neurobiology of Aging*. *32*(9), 1588–1598.

Ceravolo, R., Frosini, D., Rossi, C., & Bonuccelli, U. (2010). Impulse control disorders in Parkinson's disease: Definition, epidemiology, risk factors, neurobiology and management. *Parkinsonism & Related Disorders, 15*, S111–S115.

Chase, T. N. (2010). Apathy in neuropsychiatric disease: Diagnosis, pathophysiology, and treatment. *Neurotoxicity Research*. *19*(2), 266–278.

Chaudhuri, K. R., Ondo, W., Chaudhuri, K. R., & Reddy, P. (2010). Parkinsonian syndromes. In *Movement Disorders in Clinical Practice* (pp. 33–47). London:Springer.

Chow, T. W., & Cummings, J. L. (2007). Frontal-subcortical circuits. In B.L. Miller & J. L. Cummings (Eds.), *The human frontal lobes: Functions and disorders* (2nd ed., pp. 25–43). New York: Guilford Press.

Chow, T. W., Izenberg, A., Binns, M. A., Freedman, M., Stuss, D. T., Scott, C. J. et al. (2008). Magnetic resonance imaging in frontotemporal dementia shows subcortical atrophy. *Dementia and Geriatric Cognitive Disorders, 26*, 79–88.

Craft, S. (2009). The role of metabolic disorders in Alzheimer's disease and vascular dementia: Two roads converged. *Archives of Neurology, 66*, 300.

Cummings, J. L., & Miller, B. L. (2007). Conceptual and clinical aspects of the frontal lobes. In B.L.Miller & J. L. Cummings (Eds.), *The human frontal lobes: Functions and disorders* (2nd ed., pp. 12–24). New York: The Guilford Press.

Davis, C., Heidler-Gary, J., Gottesman, R. F., Crinion, J., Newhart, M., Moghekar, A. et al. (2010). Action versus animal naming fluency in subcortical dementia, frontal dementias, and Alzheimer's disease. *Neurocase, 16*, 259–266.

Duff, K., Paulsen, J. S., Beglinger, L. J., Langbehn, D. R., Wang, C., Stout, J. C. et al. (2010). "Frontal" behaviors before the diagnosis of Huntington's disease and their relationship to markers of disease progression: Evidence of early lack of awareness. *Journal of Neuropsychiatry and Clinical Neurosciences, 22*, 196–207.

Frank, M. J., & Claus, E. D. (2006). Anatomy of a decision: Striato-orbitofrontal interactions in reinforcement learning, decision making, and reversal. *Psychological Review, 113*, 300–326.

Fukui, T., Lee, E., Kitamura, M., Hosoda, H., Bokui, C., Ikusu, K. et al. (2009). Visuospatial dysfunction may be a key in the differentiation between Alzheimer's disease and subcortical cognitive impairment in moderate to severe stages. *Dementia and Geriatric Cognitive Disord, 28*, 288–294.

Fuster, J. M. (1997). *The prefrontal cortex: Anatomy, physiology and neuropsychology of the frontal lobe*. (3rd ed.) Philadelphia: Lippincott-Raven.

Gavett, B. E., Stern, R. A., & McKee, A. C. (2011). Chronic traumatic encephalopathy: A potential late effect of sport-related concussive and subconcussive head trauma. *Clinics in Sports Medicine, 30*, 179–188.

Geser, F., Martinez-Lage, M., Kwong, L. K., Lee, V. M. Y., & Trojanowski, J. Q. (2009). Amyotrophic lateral sclerosis, frontotemporal dementia and beyond: The TDP-43 diseases. *Journal of Neurology, 256*, 1205–1214.

Grau-Olivares, M., Arboix, A., Bartres-Faz, D., & Junque, C. (2007a). Neuropsychological abnormalities associated with lacunar infarction. *Journal of the Neurological Sciences, 257*, 160–165.

Grau-Olivares, M., Bartres-Faz, D., Arboix, A., Soliva, J. C., Rovira, M., Targa, C. et al. (2007b). Mild cognitive impairment after lacunar infarction: voxel-based morphometry and neuropsychological assessment. *Cerebrovascular Diseases, 23*, 353–361.

Heimer, L., Van Hoesen, G. W., Trimble, M., & Zahm, D. S. (2008). *Anatomy of neuropsychiatry: The new anatomy of the basal forebrain and its implications for neuropsychiatric illness*. San Diego, CA: Academic Press.

Hikosaka, O. & Isoda, M. (2010). Switching from automatic to controlled behavior: Cortico-basal ganglia mechanisms. *Trends in Cognitive Sciences, 14,* 154–161.

Houk, J. C., Bastianen, C., Fansler, D., Fishbach, A., Fraser, D., Reber, P. J. et al. (2007). Action selection and refinement in subcortical loops through basal ganglia and cerebellum. *Philosophical Transactions of the Royal Society of London. Series B, Biological Sciences, 362,* 1573–1583.

Huey, E. D., Goveia, E. N., Paviol, S., Pardini, M., Krueger, F., Zamboni, G. et al. (2009). Executive dysfunction in frontotemporal dementia and corticobasal syndrome. *Neurology, 72,* 453–459.

Ibarretxe Bilbao, N., Junque, C., Marti, M. J., Valldeoriola, F., Vendrell, P., Bargallo, N. et al. (2010). Olfactory impairment in Parkinson's disease and white matter abnormalities in central olfactory areas: A voxel based diffusion tensor imaging study. *Movement Disorders, 25,* 1888–1894.

Kehagia, A. A., Barker, R. A., & Robbins, T. W. (2010). Neuropsychological and clinical heterogeneity of cognitive impairment and dementia in patients with Parkinson's disease. *Lancet Neurology, 9,* 1200–1213.

Kertesz, A., & McMonagle, P. (2010). Behavior and cognition in corticobasal degeneration and progressive supranuclear palsy. *Journal of the Neurological Sciences, 289,* 138–143.

Kirsch-Darrow, L., Fernandez, H. F., Marsiske, M., Okun, M. S., & Bowers, D. (2006). Dissociating apathy and depression in Parkinson disease. *Neurology, 67,* 33.

Koziol, L. F. & Budding, D. E. (2009). *Subcortical structures and cognition : Implications for neuropsychological assessment.* New York: Springer.

Lee, A. Y., & Chui, H. (2007). Vascular disease and the frontal lobes. In B. L. Miller & J. L. Cummings (Eds.), *The human frontal lobes: Functions and disorders* (2nd ed., pp. 447–471). New York: Guilford Press.

Levy, F., & Krebs, P. R. (2006). Cortical-subcortical re-entrant circuits and recurrent behaviour. *Australian and New Zealand Journal of Psychiatry, 40,* 752–758.

Lhermitte, F. (1986). Human autonomy and the frontal lobes. Part II: Patient behavior in complex and social situations: The "environmental dependency syndrome". *Annals of Neurology, 19,* 335–343.

Lhermitte, F., Pillon, B., & Serdaru, M. (1986). Human autonomy and the frontal lobes. Part I: Imitation and utilization behavior: A neuropsychological study of 75 patients. *Annals of Neurology, 19,* 326–334.

Li, J., Zhang, M., Xu, Z. Q., Gao, C. Y., Fang, C. Q., Deng, J. et al. (2010a). Vascular risk aggravates the progression of Alzheimer's disease in a Chinese cohort. *Journal of Alzheimer's Disease, 20,* 491–500.

Li, W., Lopez, L., Osher, J., Howard, J. D., Parrish, T. B., & Gottfried, J. A. (2010b). Right orbitofrontal cortex mediates conscious olfactory perception. *Psychological Science. 21*(10), 1454–1463

Lichter, D. G., & Cummings, J. L. (2001). *Frontal-subcortical circuits in psychiatric and neurological disorders.* New York: The Guilford Press.

Ligot, N., Krystkowiak, P., Simonin, C., Goldman, S., Peigneux, P., Van Naemen, J. et al. (2010). External globus pallidus stimulation modulates brain connectivity in Huntington's disease. *Journal of Cerebral Blood Flow & Metabolism. 31,* 41–46

Lou, M., Jing, C., Selim, M. H., Caplan, L. R., & Ding, M. (2009). Delayed substantia nigra damage and leukoencephalopathy after hypoxic-ischemic injury. *Journal of the Neurological Sciences, 277,* 147–149.

Mair, W. G., Warrington, E. K., & Weiskrantz, L. (1979). Memory disorder in Korsakoff's psychosis: A neuropathological and neuropsychological investigation of two cases. *Brain, 102,* 749–783.

Malloy, P. F., & Richardson, E. D. (2001). Assessment of frontal lobe function. In S.P.Salloway, P. F. Malloy, & J. D. Duffy (Eds.), *The frontal lobes and neuropsychiatric illness* (pp. 125–138). Washington, D.C.: American Psychiatric Publishing.

Manes, F. F., Torralva, T., Roca, M., Gleichgerrcht, E., Bekinschtein, T. A., & Hodges, J. R. (2010). Frontotemporal dementia presenting as pathological gambling. *Nature Reviews Neurology. 6*(6), 347–52

McKee, A. C., Gavett, B. E., Stern, R. A., Nowinski, C. J., Cantu, R. C., Kowall, N. W. et al. (2010). TDP-43 proteinopathy and motor neuron disease in chronic traumatic encephalopathy. *Journal of Neuropathology & Experimental Neurology, 69,* 918.

Mega, M. S., & Cummings, J. L. (2001). Frontal subcortical circuits: Anatomy and function.. In S.P.Salloway (Ed.), *The frontal lobes and neuropsychiatric illness.*(pp. 15–32), Washington, DC: American Psychiatric Publishing.

Middleton, F. A. (2003). Fundamental and clinical evidence for basal ganglia influences on cognition. In M. Bedard, Y. Agid, S. Chouinard, S. Fahn, & A. Korczyn (Eds.), Mental and Behavioral Dysfunction in Movement Disorders (pp. 13–33). Totowa, NJ: Human Press, Inc.

Middleton, F. A., & Strick, P. L. (2001). A revised neuroanatomy of frontal-subcortical circuits. In D. G. Lichter, J. L. Cummings (Eds.), Frontal-Subcortical Circuits in Psychiatric and Neurological Disorders, (pp. 44–58). New York: Guilford Press.

Navia, B. A., & Rostasy, K. (2005). The AIDS dementia complex: Clinical and basic neuroscience with implications for novel molecular therapies. *Neurotoxicity Research, 8,* 3–24.

Odhuba, R. A., van den Broek, M. D., & Johns, L. C. (2005). Ecological validity of measures of executive functioning. *British Journal of Clinical Psychology, 44,* 269–278.

Pitel, A. L., Zahr, N. M., Jackson, K., Sassoon, S. A., Rosenbloom, M. J., Pfefferbaum, A. et al. (2010). Signs of preclinical Wernicke's encephalopathy and thiamine Levels as predictors of neuropsychological deficits in alcoholism without Korsakoff's syndrome. *Neuropsychopharmacology. 36*(3), 580–588.

Prigatano, G. P., Maier, F., & Burns, R. S. (2010). Anosognosia and Parkinson's. *Advances in the Study of Anosognosia.* In G. Prigatano (Ed.) The Study of Anosognosia (pp. 159–170). New York: Oxford.

Sachdev, P., Andrews, G., Hobbs, M. J., Sunderland, M., & Anderson, T. M. (2009). Neurocognitive disorders: Cluster 1 of the proposed meta-structure for DSM-V and ICD-11. *Psychological Medicine, 39,* 2001–2012.

Salmon, D. P., & Bondi, M. W. (2009). Neuropsychological assessment of dementia. *Annual Review of Psychology, 60,* 257–282.

Sbordone, R. J. (2001). Limitations of neuropsychological testing to predict the cognitive and behavioral functioning of persons with brain injury in real-world settings. *Neuro Rehabilitation, 16,* 199–201.

Sbordone, R. J. (2010). Neuropsychological tests are poor at assessing the frontal lobes, executive functions, and neurobehavioral symptoms of traumatically brain-injured patients. *Psychological Injury and Law, 3,* 25–35.

Seger, C. A. (2008). How do the basal ganglia contribute to categorization? Their roles in generalization, response selection, and learning via feedback. *Neuroscience & Biobehavioral Review, 32,* 265–278.

Shimamura, A. P., Jernigan, T. L., & Squire, L. R. (1988). Korsakoff's syndrome: radiological (CT) findings and neuropsychological correlates. *Journal of Neuroscience, 8,* 4400–4410.

Silver, C. H. (2000). Ecological validity of neuropsychological assessment in childhood traumatic brain injury. *Journal of Head Trauma Rehabilitation, 15,* 973–988.

Silver, J. M., Hales, R. E., & Yudofsky, M. B. A. S. (2010). Neuropsychiatric aspects of traumatic brain injury. In M. B. A. S. Yudofsky & R. E. Hales (Eds.), *Essentials of Neuropsychiatry and Behavioral Neurosciences* (pp. 223–274). Arlington, VA: Amer Psychiatric Pub Inc.

Spero, M., & Lazibat, I. (2010). Creutzfeldt-Jakob disease: case report and review of the literature. *Acta Clinica Croatica, 49,* 181–187.

Stewart, J. T. (2006). The frontal/subcortical dementias: Common dementing illnesses associated with prominent and disturbing behavioral changes. *Geriatrics, 61,* 23–27.

Su, C. Y., Chen, H. M., Kwan, A. L., Lin, Y. H., & Guo, N. W. (2007). Neuropsychological impairment after hemorrhagic stroke in basal ganglia. *Archives of Clinical Neuropsychology, 22,* 465–474.

Swartz, R. H., Stuss, D. T., Gao, F., & Black, S. E. (2008). Independent cognitive effects of atrophy and diffuse subcortical and thalamico-cortical cerebrovascular disease in dementia. *Stroke, 39,* 822–830.

Thompson, J. C., Poliakoff, E., Sollom, A. C., Howard, E., Craufurd, D., & Snowden, J. S. (2010). Automaticity and attention in Huntington's disease: When two hands are not better than one. *Neuropsychologia, 48,* 171–178.

Utter, A. A., & Basso, M. A. (2008). The basal ganglia: An overview of circuits and function. *Neuroscience & Biobehavioral Reviews, 32,* 333–342.

Watt, D. F., Pincus, D. I., & Panksepp, J. (2004). *Textbook of biological psychiatry.*

Wijnia, J. W., & Goossensen, A. (2010). Cerebellar neurocognition and Korsakoff's syndrome: An hypothesis. *Medical Hypotheses. 75*(2), 266–268

Wilson, A. C., Dugger, B. N., Dickson, D. W., & Wang, D. S. (2011). TDP-43 in aging and Alzheimer's disease. A review. *International Journal of Clinical and Experimental Pathology, 4,* 147.

Xing, H. Q., Hayakawa, H., Izumo, K., Kubota, R., Gelpi, E., Budka, H. et al. (2009). In vivo expression of proinflammatory cytokines in HIV encephalitis: An analysis of 11 autopsy cases. *Neuropathology, 29,* 433–442.

Yang, S. H., & Chan, A. W. (2011). *Transgenic animal models of Huntington's disease. Current topics in behavioral neurosciences. 7,* 61–85

Zahr, N., Pitel, A. L., Chanraud, S., & Sullivan, E. (2010). Contributions of studies on alcohol use disorders to understanding cerebellar function. *Neuropsychology Review, 20,* 280–289.

CHAPTER 19

Delirium

Douglas Watt, Deborah Ely Budding, & Leonard F. Koziol

INTRODUCTION

Although there are literally dozens of chapters on delirium and confusional states in virtually every psychiatric textbook, the syndrome remains badly neglected in terms of fundamental research attention within clinical neuroscience and poorly understood and managed in terms of routine clinical care (Khan, Kahn, & Bourgeois, 2009). Indeed, relative to its very commonplace occurrence, delirium might be the most neglected syndrome in all of neurology and psychiatry—if not all of medicine—in terms of relative research attention it garners. Fundamental questions about delirium remain unanswered in many traditional textbook treatments, centrally the mystery of how delirium represents a final common pathway uniting etiologies as diverse as renal failure, infection, anticholinergic drug ingestion, alcohol withdrawal, head trauma, and right parietal stroke. Delirium is consistently underdiagnosed, all too frequently blamed on a dementia (instead of appreciating its superposition and reversible etiologies), and too often iatrogenically created by a number of medical interventions and untoward events (frequent and less-than-optimally circumspect use of benzodiazepines, opiates, and anticholinergics in elderly patients; surgeries; severe sleep deprivation in most intensive care units [ICU]; and hospital-based infections). Confusional states are also a frequent manifestation of neurodegenerative dementias that have moved well into their middle stages, prior to even later-stage minimally conscious and vegetative states (Isenberg & Garcia, 2008). Although a principled distinction is typically drawn between these chronic confusional states (in later stages of Alzheimer's disease [AD]) and more acute deliriums, they are symptomatically and behaviorally indistinguishable (Hufschmidt, Shabarin, & Zimmer, 2009). The moderately to severely demented population is widely regarded as untreatable because their mental status is assumed to be structurally based in serious generalized (and regional) atrophy. These chronically confusional patients, who may number in the millions in this country, are seen as largely hopeless, and in terms of both research and treatment, are virtually abandoned. The assumption that such chronic confusional states are structurally determined remains uncritically accepted and yet untested by concerted research or treatment efforts. Developing a deeper understanding of delirium in neural network terms might open treatment frontiers for this large group of tragic and abandoned individuals, and presumably would also suggest ways of protecting others from the disorder who are at elevated risk for its more acute forms, as well as more effective ways of treating the disorder once it has been manifest.

Unfortunately, accurate, rapid diagnosis of confusional states occurs far too infrequently within our medical system despite their common occurrence (Moraga & Rodriguez-Pascual, 2007; Arend & Christensen, 2009; Holmes & House, 2000). Previous studies have shown that somewhere between 32% and 66% of cases are not recognized by attending physicians, yet delirium complicates 15%–25% of all acute hospital admissions, affecting up to 50% of hospitalized older patients and 60%–85% of ICU patients (Inouye & Ferrucci, 2006; Inouye, 1999; Fann, 2000; McNicoll et al., 2003). We believe that there is an unacknowledged context for this. This diagnostic failure occurs within the larger context of the neglect of virtually all cognitive disorders within medical practice in the United States, even in the elderly, where cognitive disorders are common. This likely reflects a mix of factors: (1) insufficient attention to mental status in medical circles, both in acute inpatient (IP) care and in outpatient (OP) primary care; (2) when there is attention to mental status, cognitive issues in elderly patients are often painted with overly broad brushstrokes (everything is "dementia," a term used synonymously with Alzheimer's disease, a problematic equivalence); and (3) when there is any actual assessment of cognition, clinicians often rely on the MMSE, regarded as an adequate assessment tool for both identifying and R/O early dementing disorders, when evidence suggests just the opposite (Luetz et al., 2010; Kahokehr, Siegert, & Weatherall, 2004). Additionally, a continued pessimism about the treatment of Alzheimer's disease promotes both diagnostic and treatment passivity about age-related cognitive disorders (see Chapter 17). Last but certainly not least, there is generally an inadequate emphasis in medical school education on neurocognitive disorders.

ADVANCED DIAGNOSTIC CONSIDERATIONS AND PRACTICES

This next major section on diagnostic considerations and practices contains three subsections, including a brief discussion of delirium as a disorder of more than simply attention, a critical analysis of the *DSM-IV-TR* criteria, and presentation of a continuum of disorders of consciousness including delirium, as well as an outline of a continuum of severity within delirium itself and a brief treatment of the large "etiology space" for the syndrome. These issues jointly provide context to the diagnostic process.

Confusional States as Global Cognitive Disorders

Although confusional states are widely regarded as "disorders of attention," a view originally initiated by Geschwind (1982), we believe that this is potentially somewhat misleading. Virtually all global-state cognitive operations (attention, working memory, executive functions) collapse in direct proportion to the severity of any confusional state, and given that these processes are foundational for virtually all other cognitive operations, their joint collapse brings down the entire cognitive apparatus, often resulting in severe language and perceptual failure, particularly as deliriums become more severe (Mesulam, 1990; Mesulam & Geschwind, 1976). Attention, working memory, and behavioral organization (executive functions) are functionally deeply interdigitating, and difficult to neatly separate (Watt & Pincus, 2004; Merker, 2007). Working memory functions partially as a supervisor for attentional selection, whereas attention funnels content into working memory (Hazy, Frank, & O'Reilly, 2006). Executive functions (the selection of both behavioral goals and strategies) are intimately dependent on both working memory and attention, while exercising major influence on them as well. Thus, a one-dimensional view of delirium as a simple disorder of attention is misleading and not heuristic.

DSM-IV-TR Criteria: Room for Improvement?

DSM-IV-TR criteria for delirium are generally presented as the gold standard for diagnosis (APA, 2000). However, we believe that there are significant problems with the criteria as they are currently formulated. *DSM-IV-TR* criteria are as follows: (1) a disturbance of consciousness indicated by reduced awareness of the environment, along with diminished ability to focus, sustain, or shift attention; (2) a change in cognition (which may include deficits of memory, language, or orientation) or onset of a perceptual disturbance not better accounted for by a dementia; (3) development over a short period with a tendency to fluctuate during the course of the day; and (4) evidence from history, physical examination, or laboratory findings that the disturbance is caused by the direct physiological consequences of a general medical condition. Despite their widespread acceptance, these criteria feature a number of significant and poorly appreciated problems. For example, the first criterion does not provide an adequate operational definition for how a "disturbance of consciousness or attention" might be indexed or manifest. We would argue that a very useful and simple criterion here is the failure to register incoming stimuli into some form of working memory on a consistent basis, with the associated collapse of stable representation of those stimuli in working memory, along with loss of the organized segues within working memory that define a coherent train of thought. The second criterion is overly complicated and duplicative; attentional registration of stimuli and closely associated functions of working memory and executive functions define a base for the cognitive pyramid. If that base collapses, many other cognitive operations would be expected to deteriorate. However, the current wording of the second criterion is confusing and does not make this point explicitly enough, while obviously implying it. Regarding the third criterion, a short period can mean weeks or longer in the case of slowly progressive metabolic disorders. The fourth criterion neglects that fact that many etiologies are mixed and multi-factorial. This criterion places clinicians in a "catch 22" by requiring them to find an etiology before technically diagnosing a delirium, and failing also to provide a sufficiently complete listing of major etiology categories. The first author has personally seen over 2,500 instances of delirium, and despite careful and in many cases exhaustive work-ups, unequivocal etiologies are not always found (approximately 1%–2% of the time). A literal interpretation of the fourth criterion would mean that these cases would not allow for diagnosis of delirium because one could not find a cause for it! This simply does not make sense, and the criteria should include the possibility of "delirium due to unknown etiology" (see discussion of this in the following section).

Additionally, the *DSM-IV-TR* criteria fail to adequately appreciate the enormous range of severity within the full spectrum and panoply of confusional states. This spectrum runs the gamut from very severe deliriums where patients are minimally conscious, to low-grade encephalopathic states that are frequently missed completely. The very severe delirium may represent a mild version of "minimally conscious state" where virtually all basic cognitive processes appear severely degraded, underlining that coma, stupor, and minimally conscious states all border delirium in a taxonomy of diseases of consciousness. On the other hand, patients presenting with relatively low-grade encephalopathic states (which a significant percentage of the general population may have suffered at one time or another) show major working memory and cognitive efficiency decrements relative to baseline while remaining superficially lucid and mostly oriented, although often subtly quite disorganized and clearly unsafe to drive an automobile. These milder encephalopathic states often cannot be identified without at least bedside if not quantitative neurocognitive assessment. Failing to identify these states means that attending clinicians potentially remain unaware of reversible factors degrading a patient's mental status (Ouimet et al., 2007). This wide spectrum of severity is poorly represented in the *DSM-IV-TR* criteria, and there is evidence that milder confusional states, particularly where patients are quietly confusional and not agitated or hallucinating, are frequently missed by attending clinicians, sometimes with negative and occasionally grave consequences (Collins, Blanchard, Tookman, & Sampson, 2010; King & Gratrix, 2009). Unfortunately, the diagnostic criteria being proposed and under consideration for the *DSM-5* appear to suffer from the same drawbacks.

An additional source of confusion about confusional states (no pun intended) relates to the frequent and sloppy use of the term confusion itself. How many times have clinicians read (or written), "the patient is alert but confused." Such terms are woefully nonspecific and these descriptions often appear in relation to patients who are simply forgetful and amnestic, as opposed to confusional or actively psychotic. Unfortunately, such nonspecific terms (confused or confusion) pass the work of clarification to the next clinician in the communication chain. Further, in addition to these intrinsically vague descriptors, the syndrome has acquired an enormous number of other labels over the decades including:

- Acute brain failure
- Acute brain syndrome

- Acute brain syndrome with psychosis
- Acute organic reaction
- Acute organic syndrome
- Acute reversible psychosis
- Acute secondary psychosis
- Cerebral insufficiency
- Dysergastic reaction
- Exogenous psychosis
- Infective-exhaustive psychosis
- ICU psychosis
- Metabolic encephalopathy
- Oneiric (dreamlike) state
- Organic brain syndrome
- Reversible cerebral dysfunction
- Reversible cognitive dysfunction
- Reversible dementia
- Reversible toxic psychosis
- Toxic confusional state
- Toxic encephalopathy

Such variable terminology potentially creates more diagnostic confusion, even if clinicians are well-informed about such variable nomenclature, but especially if they are not.

Delirium Within a Taxonomy of Disorders of Consciousness: Stages and Levels of Confusional State

Current *DSM-IV-TR* criteria, which emphasize delirium as a "disturbance of consciousness," beg the question as to where delirium might fit within a more comprehensive taxonomy of diseases of consciousness. We offer the following as a rough heuristic, with disorders of consciousness ranging from the most severe to the least severe (Watt & Pincus, 2004):

- Coma
- Persistent vegetative state
- Stupor (obtunding of consciousness)
- Akinetic mutism
- Minimally conscious state
- Delirium/confusional states

Such a taxonomy would provide a continuum, with "gray zones" or transitional regions demarcating one disorder from the next. This approach would further allow for a continuum of severity in relationship to delirium itself, which, as we just noted, is not currently acknowledged at all in *DSM-IV-TR*. We therefore offer the following descriptive outline detailing a continuum of severity from mildest to most severe:

1. Mildest possible encephalopathy: lowered cognitive efficiency and speed of processing, poor working memory, other mild cognitive disruption (especially in short-term memory and executive function) but with preserved orientation to place and situation (basic lucidity). Patients at this level are probably better diagnosed with reversible mild cognitive impairment rather than delirium proper. However, as the physiological condition(s) underlying this mildest possible manifestation of encephalopathy worsen (or as additional etiologies are added to the clinical picture), patients begin to segue into the stages of delirium proper. Patients at this stage are frequently misdiagnosed with early-stage dementing disorders if they are undergoing neuropsychological testing. Conversely, without such formal cognitive assessment, this stage (essentially a preclinical or prodromal stage of delirium proper) is rarely detected. Mental status exams may pick up on this condition if

they include more challenging probes such as backward serial sevens or go/no-go testing. This stage of the process is often clinically almost invisible, except to the exceptionally sensitive observer who realizes that the patient is cognitively off without being more severely impaired. Insightful and introspective patients may also report that they feel "fuzzyheaded," "can't focus," "are not sharp," "not themselves," "feel spacey," or other similar descriptions.
2. Mild confusional states show increasing cognitive disorganization relative to the first stage: there is now more obvious task derailing and basic registration failures of relatively simple stimuli starting to appear within working memory function. Patients are still mostly oriented to situation/place. However, the degree of disorganization is now sufficient to preclude performing any attentional-demanding tasks, and this level of deficit can be detected in many mental status exams. Patients can no longer successfully complete such relatively simple working memory tasks as months of the year backwards or serial arithmetic, and make multiple errors. Simple digit span forward performance can be preserved, but often in concert with remarkably poorer digit span backward (large gap between digits forward and digits backward). Increased anxiety or hypoactivity may be visible.
3. Mild to moderate confusional states: basic orientation to environment may fluctuate, with patients occasionally aware of where they are but at least intermittently showing disorientation to place, in concert with increasing and now obvious collapse of working memory and task organization. Thinking is more obviously disorganized, with difficulty following any train of thought. In some cases, patients now cannot consistently register questions, and may produce non sequiturs. Even digit span forward performance starts to collapse. Agitation or behavioral slowing may be more obvious.
4. Moderate confusional states: orientation to situation/place now consistently impaired, registration of incoming stimuli consistently poor with registration failures becoming endemic/constant, increasing language disorganization, possible hallucinatory phenomena. Patients demonstrate severe behavioral disorganization, with almost no task organization possible. Most attempts at cognitive assessment are now virtually impossible given patients' poor registration of questions and tasks.
5. Severe confusional states: complete failure of registration, lack of orientation to the environment, unintelligible or mute language production, loss of orienting to salient stimuli, approximating a minimally conscious state.

Such a staging or continuum of confusional states contrasts the *DSM-IV-TR*'s current "one size fits all" assumption, which has encouraged the mistaken belief in the relative uniformity of syndrome manifestation. We believe that such assumptions play a major role in the frequent failure to diagnose many milder confusional states. We would also argue that the mildest manifestation of this continuum, namely "low-grade encephalopathy" (a state probably too mild be considered part of delirium proper), is often misdiagnosed upon neuropsychological testing as a prodromal or early stage of a frontal system neurodegenerative disorder due to the appearance of working memory and executive function deficits. This underlines the importance of clinicians making a concerted effort to determine whether or not a patient undergoing neuropsychological assessment is truly at a representative baseline, because prodromal stages of confusional states (what one might term subclinical delirium) still merit a review of potential (generative) etiologies, another source of confusion and clinical difficulty to which we will now turn our attention.

Etiologies for Delirium and Confusional States

In older literature, delirium was referred to as the "Pan-Agent Syndrome" (Lipowski, 1980), an instructive term that curiously appears to have fallen completely off the map for uncertain reasons. The term underscores that almost any physiological difficulty or medical condition can be etiologic for a confusional state. Understanding the large etiology space of delirium, and thus conducting a careful etiology review, is perhaps the most critical clinical task in relationship to the delirious patient because currently, identifying and reversing etiologies is regarded as the primary treatment intervention (along with various forms of supportive care and behavioral management; Kamholz, 2010). Unfortunately, students and clinicians are often required to memorize long lists of potential etiologies, without these lists containing any kind of heuristic integration or conceptual organization. One of these traditional lists might look something like this:

- Wernicke encephalopathy
- Withdrawal from any addicting substance (especially alcohol, barbiturates, and sedative hypnotics)
- Hypertensive encephalopathy
- Hypoglycemia
- Hypoxemia or hypoxia
- Hypoperfusion of the CNS
- Intracranial bleeding or cerebral-vascular accident or space-occupying lesion (tumor)
- Infection, systemic or central
- Poisons or medicines of various kinds
- Virtually any major form of metabolic derailment: acidosis, alkalosis, electrolyte disturbance, hepatic or renal failure, congestive heart failure, and so forth
- Trauma (virtually any massive injury, CHI, heatstroke, surgery, severe burns)
- Severe endocrinopathies
- Severe allergic reactions with subsequent anaphylactic shock
- Various deficiency states, particularly vitamin B12, niacin, and thiamine
- Serious dehydration and malnourishment and moderate to severe sleep deprivation

Although such long lists are impressive, they may not be optimally heuristic, particularly for trainees and students. First of all, they place an enormous mnemonic load on young clinicians to learn all these seemingly arbitrary correlations. This problem, in turn, leads to the creation of multiple "catchy mnemonics." A popular example is "I WATCH DEATH," in which "I" stands for infection, "W" stands for withdrawal, and so forth. Although replete with the ubiquitous dark humor often necessary for medical school survival, these are not optimally heuristic either (in this particular mnemonic, for example, how is one supposed to remember that "H" stands for both heavy metals and hypoxia?). We would argue that simple heuristics can profitably replace such imposing lists. The many disparate etiologies can be summed under three major headings: (1) a wide variety of metabolic and physiological problems, particularly infection; (2) disruption of CNS neuromodulatory envelopes (by either drug/toxin ingestion or drug withdrawal); and (3) structural insults to the CNS itself (stroke, head trauma, etc.).

Adding to the conceptual and memorization overload, a recent summary table for drugs that cause delirium included 13 classes of drugs and more than 60 compounds (Short & Winstead, 2007). This, in our judgment, is also not optimally heuristic, and such a table taken literally would suggest (unwisely) that nonsteroidal anti-inflammatories are as likely to cause delirium as opiates, which is absolutely not the case. Instead of such a long laundry list of possible deliriogenic drugs, clinical experience suggests that a handful of pharmacological agent classes cause the lion's share of problems and are the most consistently deliriogenic. This shorter list would centrally include opiates, benzodiazepines, and anticholinergics (Cancelli, Beltrame, Gigli, & Valente, 2009). Additionally, anti-parkinsonian medicines (dopamine precursors and agonists) can be potently deliriogenic as well, particularly as dosages rise, and baseline cognitive deficits increase due either to advancing Parkinson disease or concomitant and frequently undiagnosed Alzheimer's disease (Rabey, 2010; Sastre & Pena, 2009). Although many other medicines have been occasionally associated with delirium, including lithium (especially at levels over 1.0); various anticonvulsants (particularly phenytoin [Dilantin]), anti-spasmodics, and muscle relaxants; and virtually any other CNS depressant, the vast majority of medicine-induced deliriums (or where medicines are at least a significant cofactor in the generation of delirium) are associated with opiates, anticholinergics, and benzodiazepines. In terms of over-the-counter medicines, diphenhydramine (Benadryl) is far and away the most common culprit, and its inclusion in many cold remedies and over-the-counter sleep aids, along with a popular assumption of an almost unlimited safety envelope for this medicine, contribute to a significant role for diphenhydramine in delirium genesis in this country (Cancelli et al., 2009). Other first-generation antihistamines (virtually all of which have significant anticholinergic properties) are also problematic for this reason. Thus, careful survey of patient over-the-counter medicine use (and not simply prescription medicine usage), becomes essential for successful etiology review.

Another important issue concerns the assumption that peripherally acting anticholinergics (such as tolterodine [Detrol] or darifenacin [Enablex]) cannot be deliriogenic. In our experience, this is simply not true for at least two reasons: First, the blood–brain barrier is seldom intact in older patients with vascular disease (Wardlaw, Sandercock, Dennis, Starr, & Kalimo, 2003; Topakian, Barrick, Howe, & Markus, 2010). Additionally, emerging evidence argues for significant blood–brain barrier dysfunction in even early-stage Alzheimer's disease (see Chapter 17; Bowman et al., 2007; Bell & Zlokovic, 2009). Indeed, there is evidence that bacterial infection, one of the most common etiologies of delirium, may itself generate alterations in the blood–brain barrier (Banks, 2009). Pro-inflammatory cytokines appear to alter the blood–brain barrier, dynamically modulating its permeability to various immune molecules and cells. Pro-inflammatory cytokines are increasingly appreciated as having a massive regulatory influence on the brain itself, well past their traditional designation as simple immune-signaling molecules (Banks & Erickson, 2010; Giunta, 2008). Indeed, sleep, CNS arousal, regulation of neuroplasticity and trophic factors, core motivational systems, and probably multiple neurotransmitter systems all appear directly affected by pro-inflammatory signaling (Mitchell, Yang, Berk, Tran, & Iadarola, 2009; Whitney, Eidem, Peng, Huang, & Zheng, 2009). Given the evidence for increased CNS inflammation in Alzheimer's disease itself, the presence of infection and associated up-regulation of pro-inflammatory signaling in the periphery may have an enhanced deleterious effect on the mental status of any patient with Alzheimer's disease. Additional interactions include a serious disinhibition of inflammatory signaling in glial cells in the absence of sufficient (inhibitory) cholinergic modulation (van Gool, van de Beek, & Eikelenboom, 2010). This suggests that the cholinergic deprivation associated with basal forebrain neurofibrillary tangling and the suppressive synaptic effects of amyloid oligomers on the cholinergic system create a disinhibited CNS sensitivity to peripheral inflammation (Querfurth & LaFerla, 2010). This may help explain why even early-stage Alzheimer's patients are exquisitely sensitive to peripheral infection and why urinary tract infections (UTI) cause so many confusional states in patients in (often unrecognized) cognitive decline.

Another basic problem in relationship to etiology review is the tendency for clinicians to conclude a review upon discovering one suspicious factor. This is problematic, given evidence that a significant fraction of deliriums are multifactorial. For example, a patient might have moderate to severe congestive heart failure, have been given a dose of Ativan for claustrophobia prior to an MRI, have mild lower extremity cellulitis, and be moderately sleep deprived. Within this multifactorial context, it is almost impossible to assign etiologic priority to one of these potential culprits. Although poorly understood or modeled in the delirium literature, there is reason to believe that each of these various classic etiologies for delirium may have synergistic interactions with other etiologies. In other words, someone might be able to tolerate one degrading process impacting CNS function, but as additional processes are added or superimposed, neural compensation is stretched past some poorly defined compensatory envelope, with delirium as the ensuing result.

CONTEMPORARY MODES OF TREATMENT

Treatment of delirium is at this point largely predicated on identifying and attempting to reverse underlying etiologies, while providing supportive care (by necessity inpatient), managing any emerging agitation, and ensuring patient safety. The previous section emphasized a few of the complexities and pitfalls accompanying the first step of this process (finding an etiology/etiologies). We would now like to address some additional issues, particularly agitation management and avoiding symptom exacerbation (which is a regrettably common problem). It is all too easy for management of a delirious patient to "pour gas on the fire" in one fashion or another, particularly around the management of agitation (Nicholson & Henderson, 2009; Mac Sweeney et al., 2010).

Delirium is an intrinsically frightening and bewildering state and also involves a basic degradation of affective regulation (probably intrinsic to the executive and cognitive collapse), biasing affective activation in the negative direction while simultaneously degrading capacities to manage negative emotion. These dynamics make agitation and the induction of paranoid states much more likely, perhaps particularly in those with significant Axis II issues. Managing agitation is thus one of the most challenging and commonplace treatment tasks. Although the use of benzodiazepines and haloperidol (Haldol), often administered together, is a commonplace intervention, outside of deliriums associated with substance withdrawal, the widespread use of benzodiazepines is, in our judgment, inadvisable, and actually has no single controlled study supporting its widespread usage. A recent Cochrane database review concluded that there was actually no empirical support for this widespread practice and that therefore, it could not be recommended (Lonergan, Luxenberg, & Areosa, 2009). Of course, in deliriums precipitated by withdrawal from alcohol and other GABAergic drugs, benzodiazepines actually treat the delirium and quickly restore better cognitive function, and also have indications in delirium associated with neuroleptic malignant syndrome, but outside of these two conditions (where benzodiazepines actually treat the underlying pathophysiology and improve cognitive status), they consistently degrade the cognitive status of virtually any patient suffering from delirium. Indeed, in patients with early-stage Alzheimer's disease, benzodiazepines are actually potent *deliriogenic* drugs, suggesting that their widespread use may actually significantly protract and/or deepen deliriums in many patients suffering from nonwithdrawal related confusional states. Additionally, although neuroleptics may reduce agitation, they also can protract confusional states, and in some cases, maintain them almost indefinitely. Many neuroleptics, including popular atypicals such as olanzapine (Zyprexa), may have significant anticholinergic effects. Additionally, haloperidol, because of its extremely potent D_2 antagonism, has a higher risk of generating parkinsonian or dystonic crises, which in turn may necessitate the use of anticholinergic drugs, creating additional opportunities for iatrogenesis and the deepening and protraction of the confusional state. One obviously wants to take great pains to avoid creating such vicious circles. Agitation often can be managed through other interventions and clearly is reduced when nursing and other clinical staff are experienced by patients as supportive and available. We would argue that the use of virtually any CNS depressant medicine is potentially problematic, but that quetiapine (Seroquel) or trazodone (Desyrel) may have some safety advantages over Haldol and other more potent D_2 blockers in controlling dangerous levels of agitation (Maldonado, 2008). Although increasing dopaminergic tone may be deliriogenic in some deliriums, there are currently no clinical heuristics for determining which deliriums might be characterized by such a neuromodulatory issue, and a reflexive use of neuroleptics in deliriums not characterized by hyperdopaminergic tone may significantly protract deliriums where this alteration is not present. In other words, treating delirium with neuroleptics is, at best, a mixed bag. An additional drug with great promise in treating (and preventing) agitation, although not in common use yet, is dexmedetomidine (Precedex), a novel alpha-2 adrenergic agonist, which promotes sympathetic de-arousal and reduces agitation without many of the potentially more serious side effects of neuroleptics and other CNS depressant drugs (Riker et al., 2009; Maldonado et al., 2009; Boyer, 2010). Unlike many more classic CNS depressants and neuroleptics, there is no evidence that dexmedetomidine increases cognitive impairment (Hall, Schweickert, & Kress, 2009). Unfortunately, many physicians know very little about it, and therefore it is not in frequent use.

Delirium prevention may be equally important, particularly in view of how many hospitalized patients go on to subsequently develop delirium after admission (approximately 15%–25%) (Inouye et al., 2007). Delirium has many serious morbidities, including an increased risk of all-cause mortality, precipitation (or acceleration) of cognitive decline, increased risk for falls (which have their own major morbidities), protraction of hospital lengths of stay, and so forth. Inouye and colleagues (1999) have demonstrated that relatively simple approaches to delirium prevention can significantly reduce incidence of delirium in hospitalized patients.

These low-tech interventions emphasize reducing sensory deprivation and immobility, reorienting patients in a supportive way, non-pharmacologic sleep restoration protocols, and minimizing and treating dehydration. Evidence suggests that sleep deprivation is capable of sustaining delirium initiated by other etiologies, and in moderate to severe forms, sleep deprivation becomes a primary etiology itself. For example, sleep disorders have been consistently associated with a variety of deficits in aspects of attention and executive function (Figueroa-Ramos, Arroyo-Novoa, Lee, Padilla, & Puntillo, 2009; Malhotra & Desai, 2010). Delirium frequently causes inversion of the sleep cycle (patients awake at night and napping during the day) through poorly understood circadian mechanisms, suggesting that careful restoration of viable sleep homeostasis may be important in resolving delirium. Many sedating or sleep-promoting drugs may potentiate delirium, and there are no absolutely safe choices in terms of medicines to promote sleep, although some prefer low-dose trazodone as a first option (Inouye, 2006). Other options might include mirtazapine (Remeron) or low-dose quetiapine (Pandi-Perumal, Monti, & Monjan, 2009). However, virtually any CNS depressant should be considered a mixed bag with potential for protracting and promoting delirium, and should be used with considerable caution and at a lowest possible effective dose.

Complex Reciprocal Relationships Between Alzheimer's Disease and Delirium

It has been understood for quite some time that Alzheimer's disease, including even its earliest stages, predisposes to delirium (Fick, Kolanowski, Beattie, & McCrow, 2009; Jones et al., 2010). Other neurodegenerative dementing disorders and vascular dementias probably do as well, although this question has been poorly researched. The mechanisms for this are still poorly understood (Simic et al., 2009). Alzheimer's disease may predispose to delirium not by virtue of its amnestic syndrome per se, but by virtue of its early decrements in attentional and working memory functions, lowering the threshold for the induction of confusional states from a wide variety of etiologies. These early stage decrements in attentional and working memory functions, although perhaps less appreciated compared to the classic amnestic syndrome of Alzheimer's disease, are critical components of the presentation of this disease in neuropsychological work-ups, even early in the disease process (Duchek et al., 2009). In addition, there is a frontal variant of Alzheimer's disease that can present with primary symptoms in these types of attentional and working memory/executive dysfunctions (Johnson, Brun, & Head, 2007). Early-stage decrements in attentional and working memory functions are still poorly mapped in terms of causes, but are multifactorial, and probably etiologically associated with: (1) early neurofibrillary tangling of the cholinergic basal forebrain and hippocampal/entorhinal areas (Mesulam, 1995), (2) primary synaptic effects of amyloid oligomers, and (3) effects of CNS inflammation (Murray et al., 2010). Recent work has suggested that the hippocampus plays a critical role in working memory as well the acquisition and retention of newly presented information commonly referred to as short-term memory (Shrager, Levy, Hopkins, & Squire, 2008; Squire, 2009). The up-regulation or disinhibition of pro-inflammatory signaling in the brain, including a larger reaction to peripheral inflammation in someone suffering from Alzheimer's disease (Hansson, 2009; Bona et al., 2010), may also be driven by cholinergic deprivation (Bona et al., 2010). A useful predictive algorithm may be that predisposing variables such as Alzheimer's disease and other dementias or advanced age may interact with acute biological stressors to determine overall risk of delirium (Inouye & Charpentier, 1996). In those with high baseline vulnerability, minimal stressors may be sufficient, whereas in healthy younger adults, a much larger insult/stressor may be required to create a confusional state.

Early treatment with cholinesterase inhibitors as well as other pro-CNS arousal agents may potentially raise the threshold for the induction of delirium in patients with prodromal and early-stage Alzheimer's disease. However, this has received limited research attention, and some studies of cholinesterase inhibitors have failed to confirm significant preventive value (Gamberini et al., 2009). There have also been some studies showing a protective effect by pre-medicating patients with low-dose neuroleptics, although this is more controversial and potentially more risky. Additional predisposition to delirium within even early stage

Alzheimer's disease may be due to upregulation of inflammatory cascades in brains, possibly by making the CNS response to infection more dramatic (Bona et al., 2010). Dysfunction in the blood–brain barrier has been recently linked to Alzheimer's disease, and pro-inflammatory cytokines are also critical modulators and modifiers of blood–brain barrier dynamics. However, these questions have as yet been relatively poorly researched, and any version of a psychopharmacology to reduce or even prevent delirium has to be considered in its infancy. Research into potentially promising candidates such as nicotine, modafinil (Provigil), and other pro-CNS arousal drugs such as stimulating antidepressants has been minimal.

Recent work suggests, however, that the relationship between cognitive decline and delirium may be strongly reciprocal: in addition to Alzheimer's disease lowering the threshold for and thus predisposing to delirium, delirium may accelerate already present or nascent Alzheimer's disease sitting quietly in the background, in addition to functioning as a risk factor for the eventual induction of cognitive decline in patients without discernible AD (Fong et al., 2009; Jones et al., 2010). Given that extracellular plaque deposition may proceed actual cognitive decline by many years, and that this preclinical stage of AD cannot be discerned without either CSF amyloid or PET PIB ligand assays, many relatively cognitively intact patients may have the earliest stages of AD already present, and thus, delirium may trigger progression into more clinical stages of overt cognitive decline. However, these issues have not been adequately researched.

Our continued systemic and widespread failure of early diagnosis of Alzheimer's disease is frequently exposed in medical inpatient settings, where patients in undiagnosed cognitive decline undergo the cognitive collapse of delirium. These patients can take weeks or even months to get back to an approximation of their original baseline. In this sense, delirium can indicate the presence of Alzheimer's disease in patients who otherwise might not be diagnosed, and who therefore would not get a chance to begin some form of neuroprotective therapy until significantly later in their illnesses (when it typically is significantly less beneficial). This potential benefit has to be balanced against the emerging evidence that even one episode of delirium may accelerate cognitive decline (Fong et al., 2009), possibly canceling out putative benefits for early initiation of neuroprotective therapy (Jackson, Gordon, Hart, Hopkins, & Ely, 2004). Protracted and severe deliriums may take a long-term toll on the aging brain, again particularly in patients already in cognitive decline, possibly by accelerating apoptosis and by potentiating inflammatory and atrophic processes, although precise mechanisms remain uncharted. The older traditional view that patients will simply return to their previous baseline after deliriums not due to structural insult (e.g., induced by drugs, infection, and metabolic problems) without long-term sequelae now appears to be mistaken.

Initial screenings of potentially confusional patients can be done without exhaustive neuropsychological test batteries, and indeed, such an exhaustive battery in a patient with a delirium is undesirable and even punitive to the patient. Any cognitive probe loading working memory, task organization, and complex attention is likely to be quite sensitive to even mild confusional states and expose them often quite dramatically, whereas a heavy reliance on structured clinical interviewing leads almost inevitably to an underestimation of cognitive deficit. Common bedside mental status probes potentially revealing confusional states include serial arithmetic tasks, go/no-go tasks, continuous performance tasks, as well as a wide variety of more formal working memory and executive probes. We would suggest a variety of relatively easy as well as more difficult tasks of these basic functions so that the severity of deficit is clearly exposed. In view of all these considerations, neuropsychologists should play a critical role in the careful assessment of the confusional patient both during and after a confusional state, suggesting a need for significantly greater presence by neuropsychologists in medical settings and inpatient services than traditionally used.

NEUROPATHOLOGY AND PATHOPHYSIOLOGY

Toward a Neural Network Theory of Delirium

As we mentioned in the introduction, a compelling and yet unanswered question in the literature relates to the manner in which delirium reflects a final common pathway for etiologies as diverse as commonplace infections (such as UTI and pneumonia), stroke, head trauma, anticholinergics, benzodiazepines or opiates, renal failure, and serious sleep deprivation. It is instructive to remind readers that the literature on delirium has had a long history of attempting to nominate single biological factors as universally generative. This has included early hypotheses asserting that deliriums were disorders of oxidative metabolism as well as later notions emphasizing inflammation, neurotransmitter deficiencies, and disorders in cell signaling (Lipowski, 1980; Maldonado, 2008).

We would suggest the simple heuristic that all etiologies for delirium have to impact the functioning of neural networks that underpin the large-scale and highly integrative global cognitive operations involved in attention, working memory, and executive functions, cognitive operations that clearly relate to large overlapping neural systems. This suggests that all etiologies for delirium would have to functionally impact distributed networks involving prefrontal, parietal, and cingulate regions in the cortex, associated basal ganglia, cerebellar and thalamic nuclei, and multiple reticular-activating system regions and their complex connectivities. Such a global network probably forms the comprehensive lesion correlates for focal brain injuries causing delirium, although the edema and inflammatory cascades associated with virtually any stroke location or CNS lesion (if substantial enough) can produce delirium as well from virtually any central lesion location. Drug ingestion or drug withdrawal, particularly common deliriogenic medicines, would presumably impact complex multifactorial neuromodulatory envelopes regulating such a large-scale network, while metabolic problems, when severe enough, would presumably undercut the physiologic function of neurons within such a network (because neurons are perhaps the most metabolically demanding and energy-intensive systems in the body). Critical modulatory systems regulating global state control include all of the classic amines (dopamine, serotonin, norepinephrine, and acetylcholine), GABA and glutamate, as well as multiple neuropeptides and hormones (although the precise contributions of these latter two large groups of modulators to cognitive function are relatively poorly mapped). However, hormones and neuropeptides may be particularly critical to the regulation of more ancient brain regions, suggesting that exclusively amine-centered conceptions of delirium may slight the critical importance of these ancient modulatory systems (Panksepp, Nelson, & Bekkedal, 1997). Additionally, cytokines clearly function as CNS modulators, suggesting a very large interactive network of modulatory systems relevant to delirium. This is consistent with evidence that virtually any severe boosting or blocking of any modulatory system that we can manipulate generates delirium. We believe that the amine-centered conceptions of delirium emerge in part because of our better ability to manipulate those systems, compared to neuropeptides, CNS cytokines, and hormones. We suspect that this has unfortunately led to an amine-centered bias in the etiological thinking of psychiatry in general.

We also believe that the adaptive functioning of such a global network probably requires characteristic neurodynamics, which index communication within the global network. Such communication might be indexed through the measurement of synchronous oscillations in various EEG bands. These neurodynamic relationships between distributed systems involved in intact attention and behavioral organization may require certain kinds of synchronous oscillations, particularly at higher gamma and beta frequencies but probably in delta and theta bands as well, although detailed understanding of these issues is still limited (Freeman, 2003). These synchronous oscillations (where neurons widely spatially distributed appear to be firing in synchrony) may thus index intact communication between dorsolateral prefrontal, parietal, and anterior cingulate regions, an optimum and balanced "symphony of neuromodulators," and intact physiologic resources within the brain. There are likely to be equally critical subcortical contributions coming from thalamic, collicular, striatal, and reticular activating system resources as well, although the neurodynamic rhythms organizing communication between these systems and the forebrain is significantly less mapped. However, it is clear that subcortical lesions in several key locations clearly can and do disrupt cortical neurodynamics (Steriade, 2004).

Although a cholinergic-centered hypothesis about delirium has become quite popular, and has been updated in terms of a proposed underlying cholinergic deficiency and/or dopaminergic excess in all deliriums (Trzepacz & Van der Mast, 2002), it is difficult to square such appealing modulatory explanations with evidence that bacterial infections are probably statistically the most common etiology for the induction of confusional states, effects presumably traduced through pro-inflammatory cytokines, which appear to impact on many neural systems including sympathetic/parasympathetic balance, glutamate, dopamine, and serotonin (Whitney et al., 2009) at a minimum. Several recent studies have shown that serum anticholinergic activity are not well correlated with delirium, while EEG slowing is (Thomas et al., 2008). Additionally, there is increasing appreciation for hormones, cytokines, and peptides as critical modulators of cognitive function versus older exclusively aminergic perspectives. From these considerations, we would argue for the value of a complex multi-note modulatory symphony where balance between systems is critical vs. a one-note cholinergic theory or a two-note ACh-DA theory (Trzepacz & Meagher, 2010). Walter Freeman (2003; a pioneer of electroneurophysiology in this country) has bemoaned the gravitation within American psychiatry to "a neo-phrenology of neuromodulators," a penchant for simple neuromodulatory deficit/excess conceptions that gave us the simplistic notion that depression was a "shortage of serotonin" and schizophrenia "an excess of dopamine" The limitations of these points of view are now widely apparent. This suggests caution about uncritically embracing any simple univalent cholinergic hypothesis for delirium, or even its current revised form (in which delirium reflects either an excess of dopamine and/or a shortage of acetylcholine). However, both dopamine and acetylcholine are particularly critical to the instantiation of the large-scale distributed network that we have outlined, and thus, this popular theory contains a very important and large grain of truth.

Additionally, we believe that a true understanding of delirium cannot emerge through simply focusing on single molecules, however important those particular transmitter systems may be, but can only come from focusing on the large-scale networks that underlie organized behavior and thought, because these are the proper antecedent biological systems, with consciousness and behavior as dependent concomitants. In that sense, coherent explanation for delirium can only emerge by studying the neurodynamics of large-scale neural systems and not through a monocular focus on single transmitter systems. Indeed, single neuromodulatory systems become relevant (at least in terms of producing a detectible change in behavior or mental status) only through their direct role in the neural modulation of these same large-scale networks. Although this may seem like a semantic distinction, we believe that this network hypothesis for delirium generates a clear prediction that separates it from traditional molecular views focusing on single or even several aminergic systems: The prediction would be that all etiologies for confusional states should produce detectable disruptions in synchronous oscillations in various frequency bandwidths linking critical cortical and subcortical structures involved in attention and working memory, and in behavioral organization and planning. This prediction is consistent with existing EEG work on delirium and suggests that properly calibrated magnetoencephalography (MEG) might be able to reliably detect delirium. However, to our knowledge there has never been a single MEG study of delirium.

We would therefore advocate for the view that delirium may reflect a final common pathway showing disruption of the neurodynamic relationships between several cortical and subcortical systems, with intact communication between these systems underpinning working memory and intact attentional and executive function. This suggests that a very widely distributed neural architecture of systems is implicated in delirium, and clinical evidence suggests that one can induce a delirium from lesioning virtually any portion of this distributed network, particularly in a vulnerable elderly individual (in cognitive decline). These critical neurodynamics in an extended network can putatively be disrupted by: (1) a large array of metabolic and physiological issues; (2) by structural insults to a wide variety of structures and pathways; and (3) by disruption of numerous neuromodulatory envelopes integrating communication within these widely distributed networks. However, we do not believe that it makes sense to think that one or two neuromodulatory systems have some kind of functional hegemony or dominance for this process. Instead of focusing on one or two molecular systems, this hypothesis of common degrading neurodynamic effects underlying the diversity of etiologies suggests how vulnerable certain aspects of forebrain neurodynamics may be, and that those critical cortical neurodynamics in an extended cortical and subcortical network can indeed be collapsed by a very large number of influences. We believe that this distributed network model for delirium is more heuristic than looking concretely for a single underlying biological factor or "faultline." Linking delirium to oscillatory envelopes structuring communication between widely distributed cortical and subcortical epicenters also underlines the connection of delirium to other more severe diseases of consciousness such as stupor, minimally conscious state, and coma, where consciousness is lost or more severely impaired and where these thalamocortical neurodynamics are presumably, in direct proportion, even more profoundly disrupted. Clearly, delirium is a complex of symptoms, and not simply global cognitive disruption, but any patient presenting with sleep-wake cycle disturbances, agitation, and sensory alterations but who is fundamentally lucid and registering stimuli on a consistent basis and showing a coherent train of thought (indexing intact attentional function and working memory) would never be (properly) diagnosed with a confusional state.

REFERENCES

American Psychiatric Association, (2000). Diagnostic and Statistical Manual of Mental Disorders: DSM-IV-TR. Washington, DC: American Psychological Association.

Arend, E., & Christensen, M., (2009). Delirium in the intensive care unit: A review. *Nursing in Critical Care, 14*, 145–154.

Banks, W. A., (2009). The blood-brain barrier in psychoneuroimmunology. *Immunology and Allergy Clinics of North America, 29*, 223–228.

Banks, W. A, & Erickson, M. A., (2010). The blood-brain barrier and immune function and dysfunction. *Neurobiology of Disease, 37*, 26–32.

Bell, R. D., & Zlokovic, B. V., (2009). Neurovascular mechanisms and blood-brain barrier disorder in Alzheimer's disease. *Acta Neuropathologica, 118*, 103–113.

Bona, D. D., Scapagnini, G., Candore, G., Castiglia, L., Colonna-Romano, G., Duro, G., et al. (2010). Immune-inflammatory responses and oxidative stress in Alzheimer's disease: Therapeutic implications. *Current Pharmaceutical Design, 16*, 684–691.

Bowman, G. L., Kaye, J. A., Moore, M., Waichunas, D., Carlson, N. E., & Quinn, J. F. (2007). Blood-brain barrier impairment in Alzheimer's disease: Stability and functional significance. *Neurology, 68*, 1809–1814.

Boyer, J. (2010). Calming patient agitation with dexmedetomidine. *Nursing in Critical Care, 5*(1), 30–34.

Cancelli, I., Beltrame, M., Gigli, G. L., & Valente, M. (2009). Drugs with anticholinergic properties: Cognitive and neuropsychiatric side-effects in elderly patients. *Neurological Sciences, 30*, 87–92.

Collins, N., Blanchard, M. R., Tookman, A., & Sampson, E. L. (2010). Detection of delirium in the acute hospital. *Age and Ageing, 39*, 131–135.

Duchek, J. M., Balota, D. A., Tse, C. S., Holtzman, D. M., Fagan, A. M., & Goate, A. M. (2009). The utility of intraindividual variability in selective attention tasks as an early marker for Alzheimer's disease. *Neuropsychology, 23*, 746–758.

Fann, J. R. (2000). The epidemiology of delirium: A review of studies and methodological issues. *Seminars in Clinical Neuropsychiatry, 5(2)*, 64–74.

Fick, D. M., Kolanowski, A., Beattie, E., & McCrow, J. (2009). Delirium in early-stage Alzheimer's disease: Enhancing cognitive reserve as a possible preventive measure. *Journal of Gerontological Nursing, 35*, 30–38.

Figueroa-Ramos, M. I., Arroyo-Novoa, C. M., Lee, K. A., Padilla, G., & Puntillo, K. A. (2009). Sleep and delirium in ICU patients: A review of mechanisms and manifestations. *Intensive Care Medicine, 35*, 781–795.

Fong, T. G., Jones, R. N., Shi, P., Marcantonio, E. R., Yap, L., Rudolph, J. L., et al. (2009). Delirium accelerates cognitive decline in Alzheimer's disease. *Neurology, 72*, 1570–1575.

Freeman, W. J. (2003). Neurodynamic models of brain in psychiatry. *Neuropsychopharmacology, 28 Suppl* 1S54–S63.

Gamberini, M., Bolliger, D., Lurati Buse, G. A., Burkhart, C. S., Grapow, M., Gagneux, A., et al. (2009). Rivastigmine for the prevention of postoperative delirium in elderly patients undergoing elective cardiac surgery-A randomized controlled trial. *Critical Care Medicine, 37*, 1762–1768.

Geschwind, N. (1982). Disorders of attention: A frontier in neuropsychology. *Philosophical Transactions of the Royal Society of London. Series B, Biological Sciences, 298*, 173–185.

Giunta, S. (2008). Exploring the complex relations between inflammation and aging (inflamm aging): Anti-inflamm-aging remodelling of inflamm-aging, from robustness to frailty. *Inflammation Research, 57*, 558–563.

Hall, J. B., Schweickert, W., & Kress, J. P. (2009). Role of analgesics, sedatives, neuromuscular blockers, and delirium. *Critical Care Medicine, 37*(10), S416–S421.

Hansson, G. K. (2009). Inflammatory mechanisms in atherosclerosis. *Journal of Thrombosis and Haemostasis, 7 Suppl 1*, 328–331.

Hazy, T. E., Frank, M. J., & O'Reilly, R. C. (2006). Banishing the homunculus: Making working memory work. *Neuroscience, 139*, 105–118.

Holmes, J. D., & House, A. O. (2000). Psychiatric illness in hip fracture. *Age and Ageing, 29*, 537–546.

Hufschmidt, A., Shabarin, V., & Zimmer, T. (2009). Drug-induced confusional states: The usual suspects? *Acta Neurologica Scandinavica, 120*, 436–438.

Inouye, S. K. (1999). Predisposing and precipitating factors for delirium in hospitalized older patients. *Dementia and Geriatric Cognitive Disorders, 10*, 393–400.

Inouye, S. K. (2006). Delirium in older persons. *New England Journal of Medicine, 354*, 1157–1165.

Inouye, S. K., Bogardus, S. T. Jr., Charpentier, P. A., Leo-Summers, L., Acampora, D., Holford, T. R., et al. (1999). A multicomponent intervention to prevent delirium in hospitalized older patients. *New England Journal of Medicine, 340*, 669–676.

Inouye, S. K., & Charpentier, P. A. (1996). Precipitating factors for delirium in hospitalized elderly persons. Predictive model and interrelationship with baseline vulnerability. *JAMA: The Journal of the American Medical Association, 275*, 852–857.

Inouye, S. K., & Ferrucci, L. (2006). Elucidating the pathophysiology of delirium and the interrelationship of delirium and dementia. *Journals of Gerontology Series A: Biological Sciences and Medical Sciences, 61*, 1277–1280.

Inouye, S. K., Zhang, Y., Jones, R. N., Kiely, D. K., Yang, F., & Marcantonio, E. R. (2007). Risk factors for delirium at discharge: Development and validation of a predictive model. *Arch. Intern. Med, 167*, 1406–1413.

Isenberg, K. E. Garcia, K. (2008). Syndromes of brain dysfunction presenting with cognitive impairment or behavioral disturbance: Delirium, dementia, and mental disorders caused by a general medical condition. In Fatemi , S. H., Clayton P. J., (Eds), *The Medical Basis of Psychiatry*, (pp 17–37). Tototowa, New Jersey: Humana Press.

Jackson, J. C., Gordon, S. M., Hart, R. P., Hopkins, R. O., & Ely, E. W. (2004). The association between delirium and cognitive decline: A review of the empirical literature. *Neuropsychology Review, 14*, 87–98.

Johnson, J., Brun, A., & Head, E. (2007). Frontal variant of Alzheimer's disease. *The human frontal lobes: Functions and disorders*, 429–446.

Jones, R. N., Fong, T. G., Metzger, E., Tulebaev, S., Yang, F. M., Alsop, D. C., et al. (2010). Aging, brain disease, and reserve: Implications for delirium. *American Journal of Geriatric Psychiatry, 18*, 117–127.

Kahokehr, A., Siegert, R. J., & Weatherall, M. (2004). The frequency of executive cognitive impairment in elderly rehabilitation inpatients. *Journal of Geriatric Psychiatry and Neurology, 17*, 68–72.

Kamholz, B. (2010). Update on delirium: Diagnosis, management, and pathophysiology. *Psychiatric Annals, 40*, 52–62.

Khan, R. A., Kahn, D., & Bourgeois, J. A. (2009). Delirium: Sifting through the confusion. *Current Psychiatry Reports, 11*, 226–234.

King, J., & Gratrix, A. (2009). Delirium in intensive care. *Continuing Education in Anaesthesia, Critical Care & Pain, doi: 10.1093/bjaceaccp/mkp023.*

Lipowski, Z. J. (1980). *Delirium: Acute brain failure in man*, Springfield, IL: Charles C. Thomas Publisher

Lonergan, E., Luxenberg, J., & Areosa, S. A. (2009). Benzodiazepines for delirium. *Cochrane Database of Systematic Reviews*, CD006379.

Luetz, A., Heymann, A., Radtke, F. M., Chenitir, C., Neuhaus, U., Nachtigall, I., et al. (2010). Different assessment tools for intensive care unit delirium Which score to use? *Critical Care Medicine, 38*, 409–418.

Mac Sweeney, R. M., Barber, V., Page, V., Ely, E. W., Perkins, G. D., Young, J. D., et al. (2010). A national survey of the management of delirium in UK intensive care units. *QJM, 103*, 243–251.

Maldonado, J. R. (2008). Pathoetiological model of delirium: A comprehensive understanding of the neurobiology of delirium and an evidence-based approach to prevention and treatment. *Critical Care Clinics, 24*, 789–856.

Maldonado, J. R., Wysong, A., van der Starre, P. J. A., Block, T., Miller, C., & Reitz, B. A. (2009). Dexmedetomidine and the reduction of postoperative delirium after cardiac surgery. *Psychosomatics, 50*, 206–217.

Malhotra, R. K., & Desai, A. K. (2010). Healthy brain aging: What has sleep got to do with it? *Clinics in Geriatric Medicine, 26*, 45–56.

McNicoll, L., Pisani, M. A., Zhang, Y., Ely, E. W., Siegel, M. D., & Inouye, S. K. (2003). Delirium in the intensive care unit: Occurrence and clinical course in older patients. *Journal of the American Geriatrics Society, 51*, 591–598.

Merker, B. (2007). Consciousness without a cerebral cortex: A challenge for neuroscience and medicine. *Behavioral and Brain Sciences, 30*, 63–81.
Mesulam, M. M., (1990). Large-scale neurocognitive networks and distributed processing for attention, language, and memory. *Annals of Neurology, 28*, 597–613.
Mesulam, M. M., (1995). Cholinergic pathways and the ascending reticular activating system of the human brain. *Annals of the New York Academy of Sciences, 757*, 169–179.
Mesulam, M. M., & Geschwind, N. (1976). Disordered mental states in the postoperative period. *Urologic Clinics of North America, 3*, 199–215.
Mitchell, K., Yang, H. Y. T., Berk, J. D., Tran, J. H., & Iadarola, M. J. (2009). Monocyte chemoattractant protein-1 in the choroid plexus: A potential link between vascular proinflammatory mediators and the CNS during peripheral tissue inflammation. *Neuroscience, 158*, 885–895.
Moraga, A. V., & Rodriguez-Pascual, C. (2007). Acurate diagnosis of delirium in elderly patients. *Current Opinion in Psychiatry, 20*, 262–267.
Murray, C., Sanderson, D. J., Barkus, C., Deacon, R. M. J., Rawlins, J. N. P., Bannerman, D. M., et al.(2010). Systemic inflammation induces acute working memory deficits in the primed brain: Relevance for delirium. *Neurobiology of Aging. doi:10.1016/j.neurobiolaging.2010.04.002.*
Nicholson, T. R., & Henderson, M., (2009). Management of delirium. *British Journal of Hospital Medicine (London), 70*, 217–221.
Ouimet, S., Riker, R., Bergeron, N., Cossette, M., Kavanagh, B., & Skrobik, Y. (2007). Subsyndromal delirium in the ICU: Evidence for a disease spectrum. *Intensive Care Medicine, 33*, 1007–1013.
Pandi-Perumal, S. R., Monti, J. M., & Monjan, A. A. (2009). *Principles and practice of geriatric sleep medicine.* Cambridge:Cambridge University Press.
Panksepp, J., Nelson, E., & Bekkedal, M. (1997). Brain systems for the mediation of social separation-distress and social-reward. Evolutionary antecedents and neuropeptide intermediaries. *Annals of the New York Academy of Sciences, 807*, 78–100.
Querfurth, H. W., & LaFerla, F. M. (2010). Mechanisms of Disease. *New England Journal of Medicine, 362*, 329–344.
Rabey, J. M. (2010). Hallucinations and psychosis in Parkinson's disease. *Parkinsonism & Related Disorders, 15*, S105–S110.
Riker, R. R., Shehabi, Y., Bokesch, P. M., Ceraso, D., Wisemandle, W., Koura, F., et al. (2009). Dexmedetomidine vs midazolam for sedation of critically ill patients: A randomized trial. *JAMA: The Journal of the American Medical Association, 301*, 489–499.
Sastre, J. S., & Pena, A. S. (2009). Delirium psychoses caused by antiparkinsonian drugs. *European Neuropsychopharmacology. 19*, S523–S524.
Short, M. R., & Winstead, P. S. (2007). Delirium dilemma. *Orthopedics, 30*, 273–276.
Shrager, Y., Levy, D. A., Hopkins, R. O., & Squire, L. R. (2008). Working memory and the organization of brain systems. *Journal of Neuroscience, 28*, 4818.
Simic, G., Stanic, G., Mladinov, M., Jovanov-Milosevic, N., Kostovic, I., & Hof, P. R. (2009). Does Alzheimer's disease begin in the brainstem? *Neuropathology and Applied Neurobiology, 35*, 532–554.
Squire, L. R. (2009). Memory and Brain Systems: 1969–2009. *Journal of Neuroscience, 29*, 12711.
Steriade, M. (2004). Acetylcholine systems and rhythmic activities during the waking-sleep cycle. *Progress in Brain Research, 145*, 179–196.
Thomas, C., Hestermann, U., Kopitz, J., Plaschke, K., Oster, P., Driessen, M., et al. (2008). Serum anticholinergic activity and cerebral cholinergic dysfunction: An EEG study in frail elderly with and without delirium. *BMC Neuroscience, 9*, 86.
Topakian, R., Barrick, T. R., Howe, F. A., & Markus, H. S. (2010). Blood-brain barrier permeability is increased in normal-appearing white matter in patients with lacunar stroke and leucoaraiosis. *Journal of Neurology, Neurosurgery & Psychiatry, 81*, 192–197.
Trzepacz, P., & Meagher, D. (2010). Neuropsychiatric aspects of delirium. In S. C. Yudofsky, & R. E. Hales (Eds.), *Essentials of neuropsychiatry and behavioral neurosciences*, (pp. 149–222. Arlington, VA: American Psychiatric Publishing.
Trzepacz, P., & Van der Mast, R., (2002). The neuropathophysiology of delirium. *Delirium in Old Age*, 51–90.
van Gool, W. A., van de Beek, D., & Eikelenboom, P. (2010). Systemic infection and delirium: When cytokines and acetylcholine collide. *Lancet, 375*, 773–775.
Wardlaw, J. M., Sandercock, P. A. G., Dennis, M. S., Starr, J., & Kalimo, H. (2003). Is breakdown of the blood-brain barrier responsible for lacunar stroke, leukoaraiosis, and dementia? *Stroke, 34*, 806–812.
Watt, D. F., & Pincus, D. I. (2004). Neural substrates of consciousness: implications for clinical psychiatry. In J. Panksepp (Ed.), *Textbook of Biological Psychiatry*, (pp. 75–110). Hoboken, NJ: Wiley
Whitney, N. P., Eidem, T. M., Peng, H., Huang, Y., & Zheng, J. C. (2009). Inflammation mediates varying effects in neurogenesis: Relevance to the pathogenesis of brain injury and neurodegenerative disorders. *Journal of Neurochemistry, 108*, 1343–1359.

CHAPTER 20

Eating Disorders

Catherine Cook-Cottone & Amanda Smith

THE NEUROPSYCHOLOGY OF EATING DISORDERS

Eating disorders are complex psychiatric disorders that are influenced by behavioral (e.g., caloric restriction, binging/purging, excessive exercise), psychopathological (e.g., fear of fatness, drive for thinness, body image disturbance), and neuropathological (hormonal imbalance, cerebral pathology) factors (Cook-Cottone, in press; Cook-Cottone, 2009; Hurley & Taber, 2008; Uher & Treasure, 2005). These risk factors can evolve into eating-related symptomology used to manage stress, anxiety, and emotions (Cook-Cottone, 2006; 2009). Unique to these disorders, symptoms are focused on food, eating behaviors, and the body. Accordingly, patients with eating disorders display a unique set of behaviors that include an intense preoccupation with thinness and a fear of gaining weight, often in place of age-appropriate concerns and worries (Cook-Cottone, 2006). As a result of prolonged states of malnutrition, significant medical complications are often present and can complicate psychological and neuropsychological symptoms (Herzog & Eddy, 2007). Additionally, comorbid diagnoses (e.g., mood, anxiety, impulse-control, and substance abuse disorders) are common, with the greatest risk of suicide among patients with anorexia nervosa (AN) and major depression (Hurley & Taber, 2008).

More than 90% of eating disorders occur in females regardless of its manifestation as AN or bulimia nervosa (BN; American Psychiatric Association [APA], 2000). Although eating disorders have the highest female-to-male ratio of any major psychiatric disorder (APA, 2000), a growing number of males are also affected. Recent research suggests that the rate of subthreshold binge eating disorder is higher in males than females (Hurley & Taber, 2008). The consequences of eating-disordered behaviors are clear, with comparatively high mortality rates (APA, 2000). Causality is complicated by major cultural shifts such as the proliferation and sophistication of media, food availability, and shifts toward a more sedentary lifestyle (Cook-Cottone, 2006). For example, food availability data from 1909–2007 show increases in per capita availability of several product classes: added oils increased from 16.1 to 39.4 kg/y, meat increased from 56.3 to 91.2 kg/y, cheese increased from 1.7 to 14.9 kg/y, frozen dairy products increased from 0.7 to 11.5 kg/y, and sweeteners increased from 54.1 to 62.0 kg/y (Barnard, 2010). At the same time, per capita media advertising has increased many times over and targets children for fast food consumption, adults for diet products, and nearly always extols a very thin, lean, and attractive ideal as the route to happiness (Cook-Cottone, 2006). These changes may, in part, explain increases in the prevalence of eating disorders.

The question remains—if nearly everyone is exposed to the environmental risks, why is it that only a small subset of individuals becomes clinically ill with eating disorders? Despite the growing prevalence of eating disorders in males and females, the pathophysiology of eating disorders remains largely unknown partly due to only a few neuropsychological studies existing on eating disorders (Duchesne et al., 2004; Tchanturia, Campbell, Morris, & Treasure, 2005). Interestingly, there have been fewer neuropsychological studies of eating disorders than of any major psychiatric disorder and more research on the neurobiological correlates of AN than BN (Fairburn & Harrison, 2003; Tchanturia et al., 2005). Although eating disorders lack a neurofunctional model, a growing body of evidence suggests a unique set of neuropathological and neuropsychological factors that contribute to the onset and maintenance of eating disorders (Cavedini et al., 2004; Cook-Cottone, 2009).

ADVANCED DIAGNOSTIC CONSIDERATIONS AND PRACTICES

The current *Diagnostic and Statistical Manual of Mental Disorders, fourth edition, text revision* (*DSM-IV-TR*; APA, 2000) recognizes three major eating disorders: AN, BN, and eating disorder not otherwise specified (EDNOS). The current diagnostic system evaluates eating disorders based on weight, behavioral, and psychopathological constructs (Mitchell, Cook-Myers, & Wonderlich, 2005). It is important to note that criteria set for AN are not always determined based on empirical evidence. For instance, the criterion that AN patients are less than 85% of expected weight for height was not established based on scientific evidence. As such, these criteria may be too restrictive, leaving the majority of eating disorder patients to fall in the category of EDNOS (i.e., 49%–71%; Mitchell et al.).

AN is typically classified as an intense fear of gaining weight, distorted body image, amenorrhea (in females) and pursuit of an abnormally low body weight (i.e., below 85% of normal weight for age and height) through the restriction of food intake, whereas BN is viewed as a lack of control over frequent episodes of binging and compensatory purging (e.g., self-induced vomiting, use of laxatives). Patients with BN may or may not have abnormally low body weight, creating a unique challenge in its identification. Lastly, the diagnosis of EDNOS is traditionally used when a patient exhibits some features of AN or BN but does not meet full diagnostic criteria. Additionally, the current diagnostic system includes binge eating disorder (BED) within the EDNOS category (Hurley and Taber, 2008). BED is in consideration for inclusion as a major eating disorder in the *DSM-5* given this disorder's unique symptomatic presentation, etiology, and maintenance factors (Wonderlich, Gordon, Mitchell, Crosby, & Engel, 2009). Research criteria include recurrent episodes of binge eating in which a lack of control over eating behaviors is observed within a discrete period of time with no compensatory mechanisms to purge the food.

A hierarchy is presented in the current *DSM-IV-TR* used to rule out more severe pathology (APA, 2000). Medical disorders, medication, and substance abuse are to be ruled out before making other less severe diagnoses. In AN, general medical conditions (e.g., gastrointestinal disease, brain tumors, occult malignancies, superior mesenteric artery syndrome [i.e., postprandial vomiting]) should be ruled out. Additionally, the existence or coexistence of other psychiatric disorders such as major depressive disorder (in relation to weight loss), schizophrenia (abnormal eating behavior), social phobia (embarrassment with eating in public), obsessive-complusive disorder (OCD; observation of obsessions or compulsions related to food), and body dysmorphic disorder (preoccupied with an imagined defect in body appearance) should be thoroughly explored. Futhermore, it is important to differentiate BN from AN with a subtype of binge-eating/purging. Finally, unique considerations should be taken when evaluating children and adolescents for eating disorders. Bravender and colleagues (2010) suggest that a lower and more developmentally sensitive threshold for frequency and occurrence of eating disorder behaviors be determined, behavioral indicators for psychological features be considered outside of self-report, and information regarding symptomology be gathered from multiple informants.

Clear distinctions among the eating disorders are not always possible in clinical settings. Recent empirical evidence points to the tendency of diagnostic migration; the shifting of symptomology between AN and BN and clouding the nosology of separate disorders (Milos, Spindler, Schnyder, & Fairburn, 2005; Thomas, Vartanian, & Brownell, 2009; Wonderlich,

Joiner, Keel, Williamson, & Crosby, 2007). Fairburn and Bohn (2005) promote a trans-diagnostic perspective of eating disorders such that a single unitary category is created, merging AN, BN, and EDNOS in to one category. Additionally, Uher and Treasure (2005) provide empirical evidence suggesting that deficits in similar brain regions (i.e., medial prefrontal cortex) are at play in both AN and BN, implicating the trans-diagnostic model at the neural level. In response, Birmingham, Touyz, and Harbottle (2009) argue against such models, stating that the distinctions among AN, BN, and ENDOS would prevent clinical specificity and sensitivity of diagnosis. Some argue for subcategories. Steiger and Bruce (2007) have recommended three subcategories of BN: psychologically intact-perfectionistic, overregulated-compulsive, and dysregulated-impulsive. Associated risk and outcomes may support these distinctions. For example, individuals with the dysregulated-impulsive BN sub-phenotype may display more comorbid psychopathology (e.g., depression, self-mutilation, and/or substance abuse), developmental disturbance (e.g., child abuse or attachment difficulties), and thus have poorer treatment outcomes (Steiger & Bruce, 2007).

NEUROPSYCHOLOGICAL AND BEHAVIORAL SEQUELAE

Neuropsychological research is conducted through a combination of psychometric tests and qualitative exams of functioning (i.e., sensory-motor, emotional, and cognitive) in order to examine the relationship between psychological functioning and the expression of behavior (Cook-Cottone, in press). Broadly speaking, these tests are used to assist in diagnosis and documentation of psychiatric disorders. To this end, neuropsychological evaluations serve as auxiliary tools in the clinical practice and empirical study of patients with eating disorders while also serving in the development of treatment plans (Tchanturia et al., 2005). Due to physiological complications relevant to eating disorder symptoms (e.g., malnutrition and electrolyte imbalances), neurobiological functioning of the brain is affected. In AN, cognitive deficits are evident due to the low weight along with a decrease in gray and white brain matter associated with starvation (Bosanac et al., 2007; Hamsher, Halmi, & Benton, 1981). Additionally, neuroimaging studies have identified ventricular enlargement and cortical atrophy in AN (Herholz, 1996). Causality is complicated, and researchers debate the basis of the apparent cognitive deficits. Some contend that preexisting cognitive deficits place children at a higher risk for an eating disorder, whereas others point to the fact that upon re-feeding, some cognitive deficits are ameliorated (Duchesne et al., 2004; Lena, Fiocco, & Leyenaar, 2004). Seed, Dixon, McCluskey, and Young (2000) indicate that the effects of starvation alter glucocorticoid functioning that impacts the central nervous system and specifically stimulus perception and information processing. Due to the high number of glucocorticoid receptors, the hippocampus may be uniquely impaired affecting learning, memory, and attention (Seed et al., 2000).

Complexity of Conducting Neuropsychological Research Within the Eating Disorder Population

Because the cause of eating disorders is relatively unknown, neurological dysfunction has been investigated through neuropsychological tests, with the goal to better understand the risk to and etiology of eating disorder symptomology (Duchesne et al., 2004). Research of this kind has added substantially to the understanding of eating disorders (Tchanturia et al., 2005). However, the generalizability and interpretability from which these results stem should be examined under certain precautions (Tchanturia et al., 2005).

Several confounding variables exist when examining neuropsychological studies of eating-disordered patients (Cook-Cottone, 2009). One issue involves the lack of homogeneity in a classification system, making the comparison of study outcomes difficult (Duchesne et al., 2004). Specifically, Tchanturia and colleagues (2005) indicated that 44% of the studies they reviewed used diagnostic criteria from *DSM-II* and *DSM-III*, neither of which indicates the separation between subtypes in eating disorders. Additionally, there is a lack in consensus regarding how to define different levels of severity (e.g., mild, moderate, severe) and stages of illness (e.g., remission, recovery, relapse). Bachner-Melman, Zohar, and Ebstein (2006) state that the operational definition of recovery varies, sometimes encompassing and other times excluding biological, behavioral, and psychological criteria. Therefore, treatment response becomes a definition of empirical preference or clinical interpretation. Furthermore, debate exists regarding the utility and function of certain neuropsychological tests. For instance, the subtest of Digit Symbol on the Weschler Adult Intelligence Scale–Revised (WAIS-R) is viewed by some as a test of psychomotor speed and others a test of attention (Duchesne et al., 2004).

Methodological problems are additionally inherent, negatively impacting the reliability and validity of study results (Cook-Cottone, 2009). Eating disorders are typically treatment-resistant, and therefore it is rare that patients seek help voluntarily (Pike, Walsh, & Roberto, 2006). As such, recruitment, retention, compliance with treatment protocol, and completion of follow-up assessments are complicated with participants dropping out or participating inconsistently, plaguing clinical trials with small sample sizes (Chavez & Insel, 2007; Duchesne et al., 2004). Therefore, the power to determine statistical significance drastically diminishes, leaving researchers interpreting findings that may actually be a result of chance (Bulik, Berkman, Brownley, Sedway, & Lohr, 2007). Additionally, Striegel-Moore and Bulik (2007) indicate that samples drawn from populations of affluent young white females may be biased by who has sought or could seek out treatment and not by who is in need of treatment. Thus, the true demographic variables of those with eating disorders may be more varied than current research illustrates. Lastly, the high incidence of medical complications increase dropout rates as patients' severity of illness may require inpatient admission (Pike et al., 2006). Neuropsychological research in the area of eating disorders should be viewed within the context of these substantial methodological challenges (Cook-Cottone, 2009).

ANOREXIA NERVOSA

The cognitive deficits related to AN symptomology have been conceptualized by some as a result of inadequate nutrition and the consequence of starvation. In states of starvation, the body responds by producing an increased amount of cortisol (i.e., hypercortisolism), which can lead to the loss of gray matter and associated cognitive deficits (Hendren, DeBacker, & Pandina, 2000). As a result of these psychobiological disturbances, symptom expression is often marked by rigid, repetitive, obsessive, hypo-affective, aggressive, and inflexible behavior (Cook-Cottone, 2009). Additionally, some researchers have drawn a comparison between AN and pervasive disorders such as OCD and autism spectrum disorder (ASD) due to the similarities in obsessional, perfectionistic, and compulsive tendencies (Gillberg, Rastam, Wentz, & Gillberg, 2007; Steinglass, Walsh, & Stern, 2006).

Neuropsychological Correlates of Anorexia Nervosa

Debate exists regarding the intellectual functioning of patients with AN (Cook-Cottone, 2009). Although AN has historically been associated with high IQ (Gillberg et al., 2007) more recent findings indicate IQ to be average in patients with AN. Gillberg and colleagues (2007) indicate AN is typically associated with a higher level of intellectual functioning; however, other research has dismissed this belief, illustrating equivocal differences between eating disorder patients and healthy controls (Galderisi et al., 2003).

Despite inconclusive results regarding the intellectual functioning of patients with AN, specific neuropsychological processes have been implicated. In particular, visuospatial and visio-construction deficits are apparent (Duchesne et al., 2004). It is therefore suggested that deficits may be due to right parietal lobe dysfunction and help to explain, in part, disturbances in body image. Regardless, improvement in visuospatial functioning is associated with weight gain but may preexist the onset of AN and therefore contribute to the progression of the disorder (Lena et al., 2004).

Psychomotor speed and speed of processing is conceptualized as the ability to complete tasks quickly and accurately. Although findings are inconsistent, it appears that processing speed increases with weight gain (Duchesne et al., 2004). Additionally, somatosensory processing and particularly haptic perception (palpating objects when eyes are closed) in patients with AN was examined. Grunwald and colleagues (2001) reported that adolescents with AN explored objects for a significantly shorter period of time than healthy control subjects; however, the patients' ability to replicate objects in drawings was notably worse. These findings remained true even after weight gain. Such findings are hypothesized to be a result of tactual-spatial processing and a deficit in the right parietal-occipital regions.

The cognitive process of attention has also been examined in AN populations. Excessive concerns regarding eating, body weight, and shape inherently observed in patients with AN were theorized as a function of selective attention (Duchesne et al., 2004). Selective attention is thought to be a result of cognitive schemas built around food and body image. Inconclusive results are indicated because some researchers have found that when compared to normal controls, patients with AN demonstrate significant attentional bias toward words associated with eating and body shape over neutral words (Cooper & Fairburn, 1992; Long, Hinton, & Gillespie, 1994), whereas others indicate no such difference (Lovell, Williams, & Hill, 1997). It appears that attentional problems exist during periods of weight deficit and may improve upon refeeding (Cook-Cottone, 2009). Additionally, vigilance (or sustained attention) in AN has been investigated and results have been no more conclusive. Specifically, some researchers indicate AN patients have difficulty detecting target noise in a vigilance task showing deficits (Seed et al., 2000), whereas others have illustrated no deficits (Bradley et al., 1997).

Memory deficits have been found in patients with AN and do not appear to change with weight gain, therefore suggesting these deficits may precede the eating disorder and contribute to its symptomology (Lena et al., 2004). Various aspects of memory have been examined. Duchesne and colleagues (2004) indicate mixed results regarding short and long term memory because some researchers indicate normal verbal and visual memory (Lauer, Gorzewski, Gerlinghoff, Backmund, & Zihl, 1999; Seed et al., 2000), whereas others report worse performance than controls (Bayless et al., 2002). Duchesne and colleagues (2004) indicate that working memory remains stable throughout the illness, although this area of research is in need of replication.

The learning capacity of patients with AN may be affected uniquely, and there have been a substantial range of outcomes reported. For example, Duchesne and colleagues (2004) report that explicit learning (i.e., visual and auditory learning) is preserved among most patients with AN. Conversely, Seed and colleagues (2000) indicate that auditory verbal learning is impaired in patients with AN because their subjects tended to recall a significantly smaller proportion of learned items compared to controls. Of note, no differences were found on tests of visual episodic memory and visual associative learning. One area of research that has implications for risk as well as the maintenance of symptoms is in the area of implicit learning. Implicit learning capacity (non-declarative aspects of decision making, cognitive flexibility, set shifting) has been reported as impaired in patients with AN and appears persistent, despite otherwise normal cognitive functioning (Holliday, Tchanturia, Landau, Collier, & Treasure, 2005; Steinglass et al., 2006). Across researchers, the fronto-striatal and basal ganglia circuits have been implicated (Cook-Cottone, 2009). The ability to set-shift is necessary in order to adapt behaviors to those of the environment (Holliday et al., 2005). This can be seen clinically in patients with AN as a tendency to be concrete and rigid in their thinking and to struggle to change past patterns of thinking. Often, despite much information to the contrary, those with AN remain focused on food, weight, and size as a means to control anxieties and are unable to see other strategies as potentially effective.

Emotional processing presents as an important functional area for those with AN with conflicting thoughts as to its role in the risk and maintenance of symptoms (Cook-Cottone, 2009). For some time, a lack of conscious awareness to one's own emotion, known as alexithymia, has been observed in patients with AN (Subic-Wrana, Bruder, Thomas, Lane, & Kohle, 2005). It is theorized that this may result from the pattern of cognitive deficits related to introspective awareness (Lena et al., 2004). Evidence suggests that the anterior cingulate cortex may mediate this process because it plays an instrumental role in emotional awareness (Lane et al., 1998). On the other hand, Subic-Wrana and colleagues (2005) indicate that eating-disordered patients have a tendency to score higher on some measures of emotional awareness than other diagnostic groups. Therefore, additional work is needed to determine whether the deficit in emotional awareness indicated by Lena and colleagues (2004) is identical to impairment in emotional awareness in psychosomatic disorders (Subic-Wrana et al., 2005).

In addition to a lack of emotional awareness, AN patients have been characterized as displaying difficulties with empathy (Råstam, Gillberg, & Wentz, 2003). It is believed that the neurological systems responsible for empathy may be an especially critical piece in the etiological puzzle. To explain, empathy has been recognized as the ability to understand what others are thinking and feeling (Decety & Ickes, 2009). The studies that have examined the role of empathy in AN have been limited by narrowly defined populations (e.g., an urban Swedish community) and the examination of a variety of symptomology (e.g., OCD, obsessive-compulsive personality disorder, ASD; Råstam et al., 2003; Wentz et al., 2005). Results from these studies have indicated that patients with AN typically display similar characteristics of empathy to those of patients with ASD (Gillberg, 2007). However, replication of these studies is essential in order to systematically evaluate the role of empathy in adolescents with AN. It has been alternatively theorized that the symptoms in AN may work to decrease empathy and increase a focus on self and, therefore, function to simplify complex relational experiences (Cook-Cottone, 2009). Studies are needed to explore empathy in relation to symptom severity as well as recovery and improved functioning.

BULIMIA NERVOSA

There has been comparably less neuropsychological research conducted in the area of BN (Duchesne et al., 2004). This may be a result of: (1) the focus of the etiological picture of BN on cultural, behavioral, and mood-based factors leaving neuropsychological factors less researched (Cook-Cottone, 2009), and/or (2) reflection of the lack of homogeneity within the BN population. Despite the lack of research to date, researchers believe that there are neurological factors associated with the disorder (Steiger & Bruce, 2007). Neuropsychological dysfunction and disorders commonly associated with BN include panic disorder, dramatic-erratic personality disorders, alcohol and substance abuse and dependence, novelty seeking, impulsivity, and affect instability (Steiger & Bruce, 2007).

Neuropsychological Correlates of Bulimia Nervosa

Impulsive behaviors (e.g., binge-eating, suicide, and self-harming behavior) are common among patients with BN. For example, on a test of impulsivity (e.g., the Motoric subscale of the Barratt Impulsivity Scale-II; Barratt, 1994) Rosval and colleagues (2006) found that patients with BN and AN binge-purge type scored higher than controls and AN restricting type. Additionally, patients with BN tended to concentrate on completing the Symbol Digit Modalities Test with speed rather than with accuracy (Smith, 1973; Lena et al., 2004). It is postulated that impulsive tendencies may lead to eating behaviors that are sporadic and out of control (Lena et al., 2004). Impulsivity is accompanied by a lack of inhibition or control and, therefore, believed to moderate effect over food intake (Duchesne et al., 2004; Dukarm, 2005; Rosval et al., 2006).

The most frequently assessed neurological processes in individuals with BN are attention and executive functioning; however, findings are mixed (Duchesne et al., 2004; Lena et al., 2004). Although researchers have reported sustained attention to be reduced in patients with BN, there has been no consistent replication of these findings (Duchesne et al., 2004). Notably, both BN and attention deficit hyperactivity disorder (ADHD) share diagnostic features that include the lack of impulse control (Dukarm, 2005). Dukarm (2005) reported responsiveness of BN to psychostimulant medication commonly used to treat ADHD. Further, like AN patients, individuals with BN tend to show a similar attentional bias toward words associated with body weight and shape, and improvements have been seen with treatment (Dobson & Dozois, 2004; Duchesne et al., 2004).

Although limited research has been conducted, other areas of cognitive functioning have been explored. Deficits in visuospatial processing, abstract concept formation, problem-solving, and psychomotor speed have all been found in BN patients when compared to healthy controls (Duchesne et al., 2004; Lena et al., 2004). Additionally, it was noted that deficits in speed of processing information improved with treatment (Duchesne et al., 2004). Lastly, certain areas of the brain have been associated with reactivity to food stimuli in BN (Tchanturia, et al., 2005). Decreased activity to food images in the lateral prefrontal cortex, an area of the brain known to be involved in inhibition and suppression of undesirable behavior, was noted in BN patients (Tchanturia et al., 2005). These findings have been interpreted as contributing to the lack of control over eating experienced by BN patients.

NEUROPATHOLOGY AND PATHOPHYSIOLOGY OF EATING DISORDERS

Neuropathology and pathophysiology examine the central and peripheral nervous systems along with the biochemical and physiological manifestations of eating disorders, respectively. The following sections collectively examine the neuropathology and pathophysiology of AN and BN.

Neuropathology of Eating Disorders

Brain Imaging Techniques in Eating Disorders

In order to evaluate the neuropathology of eating disorders, brain imaging technology provides a glimpse into areas of the brain that previously have gone unassessed (Kaye, 2008). Complex neurocircuits, brain structures, and their associated behavioral components can now be evaluated and examined in eating disorders in the following ways: Structural alterations as a result of eating disorder behavior can be assessed through CT and MRI. Positron emission tomography (PET) and single photon emission computed tomography (SPECT) are often used to study glucose metabolism and serotonin activity. Most recently, researchers have used functional MRI (fMRI) techniques to examine blood flow in the brain in response to particular stimuli. Despite these advanced techniques, inconsistencies exist in the brain regions, neurocircuitry, and behavioral correlates associated with eating disorders. This may in part be due to methodological limitations (e.g., small sample sizes) but may also imply the complexity and variability of the neuroanatomy and neuropathology of eating disorders that researchers have only begun to understand and categorize.

Hunger, Satiety, and Reward Systems in Eating Disorders

The study of the biochemical manifestations of eating disorders begins with a look at the in utero influences on eating behavior and brain development (Hurley & Taber, 2008). Fisher and Birch (2001) found that children develop certain food preferences during the fetal and nursing periods that are dependent on the food their mother ingests. Specifically, the development of certain brain areas (i.e., the anterior cingulate; the dorsolateral, prefrontal, and orbitofrontal cortices; the amygdala; the hippocampus; and the insula) are critical to the sensation of taste and smell along with the reward system in which eating and control over food are intrinsically linked (Hurley & Taber, 2008). Specifically, it has been suggested that the insula and frontal operculum provide the brain with a representation of food, separate from hunger (Kaye, 2008). Therefore, these areas of the brain may contribute to the reward value of food. Additionally, evidence points toward the role of the insular-striatal circuits in causing altered taste processing in patients with AN (Wagner et al., 2006). Moreover, when satiated, AN patients exhibited a decrease in the left inferior parietal cortex in comparison to when the AN patients were hungry, when less activation of the right visual occipital cortex was seen (Santel, Baving, Krauel, Münte, & Rotte, 2006). These results help to illustrate brain structures implicated in the attentional mechanism utilized to restrict eating despite hunger. Within BN populations, alterations in the firing patterns of the vagus nerve (cranial nerve X) may result from the voluntary binge eating and purging behavior (Faris et al., 2006). However, due to the depressive symptoms inherent to BN, increased in the vagal nerve activity may result.

In attempts to evaluate the role of the anterior ventral striatum in regard to reward and loss in AN, Wagner and colleagues (2007) compared 13 healthy women to 13 women who had recovered from restricting type AN. The anterior ventral striatum along with the caudate putamen are components of the limbic system. These areas may be impacted by dopamine dysfunction, and dysregulation of reward and affect may result. Findings from this study indicated hemodynamic activation of the caudate and the inability to distinguish between reward and loss, a process typically mediated by the anterior ventral striatum; that is, in comparison to control subjects, those who have recovered from AN may struggle to identify the emotional significance of particular stimuli.

Brain Lesions and Eating Disorders

A number of case studies describe eating disorder behavior as a result of brain tumors or head injuries (Uher & Treasure, 2005). Specifically, there appears to be a connection to hypothalamic lesions that resulted in abnormal eating behavior and unprovoked vomiting (symptoms also seen in AN). Additionally, brainstem tumors appear to initiate the fear of fatness, which improved after removal. Finally, hemispheric lesions have also been connected to eating disorder behavior. Specifically, damage to the frontal and temporal lobes in the right hemisphere was associated with weight and shape preoccupations, and in some cases, binging and purging symptomology typically observed in BN was noted. Finally, Houy, Debono, Dechelotte, and Thibaut (2007) present a case study in which a cavernoma located on the frontal side of the right sylvian fissure was removed. Upon removal of the tumor, it was reported that previous preoccupations and body image distortions were significantly reduced. These results extend the impact of disordered eating behavior beyond that of the hypothalamus, suggesting that other brain areas may play an important role in the neuropathological components to eating disorders.

Other Neuroanatomy Consequences of Eating Disorders

From a neuroanatomical perspective, several significant consequences appear to result from eating disorder behavior. For instance, Lena and colleagues (2004) suggest that sulcal widening, ventricular dilation, and cortical atrophy are evident in patients with AN. Additionally, decreases in global volumes of gray matter, particularly the anterior cingulated cortex, are suggested to be an irreversible component of brain changes associated with AN (Lambe, Katzman, Mikulis, Kennedy, & Zipursky, 1997; Mühlau et al., 2007). Regional cerebral blood flow (rCBF) is typically used as a marker of cerebral metabolism and neuronal activity (Key, O'Brien, Gordon, Christie, & Lask, 2006). In early onset AN, a connection with abnormalities in unilateral hypoperfusion (decreased blood flow to a given tissue or organ) in the temporal lobe has been identified (Chowdhury et al., 2003; Key et al., 2006). Despite findings of decreased rCBF in AN patients and controls, no differences were observed between subtypes of AN (i.e., restricting vs. binge eating/purging types), therefore indicating rCBF to be impacted regardless (Yonezawa, Otagaki, Miyake, Okamoto, & Yamawaki, 2008).

Pathophysiology of Eating Disorders

Impact on Sex Hormones

Eating disorders typically commence with the discontinuation or interruption of eating (Goodwin, 1990). As a result, several biochemical processes are altered, impacting the physiological processes of the body. In females, menstrual dysfunction can range from anovulation to oligomenorrhea and, at its worst, amenorrhoea (i.e., the loss of a regular menstrual cycle; Gary, 2001). The development of amenorrhoea is the body's natural response to severe levels of starvation. Prolonged starvation can cause hypothalamic abnormalities and result in the failure of the release of gonadotropin-releasing hormone from the pituitary. As such, the production of luteinizing hormone (LH) and follicular-stimulating hormone (FSH) is decreased and therefore not capable of stimulating the ovaries. Therefore, the ovaries do not release estrogen or progesterone, further inhibiting the pituitary gland by negating the inherent positive feedback loop. In males, changes are observed in gonadal but not pituitary hormone levels, and therefore negatively impact testosterone levels and result in decreased testicular volume, oligospermia, and reduced sexual functioning (Gary, 2001). However, in both males and females, refeeding appears to reverse any changes in the secretion of sex hormones (Goodwin, 1990).

Hormonal and Neuropeptide Abnormalities

Eating disorders have been linked to the dysregulation of several endocrine glands, including the hypothalamus, pituitary, adrenal, and gonads (Gary, 2001; Kaye, 2008). Specifically, the secretion of cortisol, thyroid, and growth hormone are affected. Particular to cortisol secretion, the hypothalamic-pituitary-adrenal (HPA) axis is implicated. The HPA axis plays a critical role in the stress response as corticotrophin-releasing hormone (CRH) in the central nervous system (in the hypothalamus) stimulates the production of adrenocorticotrophic hormone (ACTH). ACTH then acts to stimulate the production of cortisol in the adrenal glands (Licinio, Wong, & Gold, 1996). The release of CRH in the central nervous system activates the sympathetic system to increase heart rate and blood pressure while inhibiting vegetative functions (e.g., feeding and reproduction). At the peripheral level, cortisol is released to increase the promotion of gluconeogenesis (breakdown of protein), increase glucose and insulin, increase body fat, and suppress immunity. In their review, Licinio and colleagues (1996) found 17 out of 20 articles indicate elevated central cortisol levels, concluding that hypercortisolism is prevalent in AN. Refeeding, not weight restoration, appears to result in normal levels of cortisol (Goodwin, 1990).

Mechanisms for controlling food are also affected. Neuropeptides in the central nervous system and gastrointestinal peptide section in the peripheral nervous system interact to modulate feeding behavior (Kaye, 2008). In AN populations, altered concentrations of the neuropeptides DRH, neuropeptide Y (NPY), beta-endorphin, and leptin are impacted. In particular, leptin is secreted by fat cells, which regulate appetite and energy expenditure (Steiger & Bruce, 2007). Both AN and BN patients tend to have low leptin levels, although despite this deficiency, the levels of plasma leptin in AN patients were higher than expected (Klein & Walsh, 2004). The peptide cholecystokinin (CCK) is secreted by the gut to assist in appetite regulation. Specifically, CCK acts on the hypothalamus to produce satiety and are decreased in patients with BN (Klein & Walsh, 2004; Steiger & Bruce, 2007). Moreover, in AN, NPY appears to be significantly elevated in comparison to healthy controls (Kaye, Berrettini, Gwirtsman, & George, 1990). NPY acts to simulate eating behavior, and, therefore, its overproduction in underweight individuals is unclear. It is hypothesized that NPY may play a role in the obsessional and paradoxical interest in dietary intake and food preoccupation inherent to AN. Finally, ghrelin appears to be implicated in BN. Ghrelin affects growth hormone secretion, long-term regulation of energy balance and glucose homeostasis, and short-term regulation of appetite (Cook-Cottone, 2009).

Neuroendocrine Changes

It has been suggested that the inconsistent results of neuropsychological studies may be related to neuroendocrine changes (Galderisi et al., 2003). The impact of starvation induces glucocorticoid alterations that may play a role in central nervous system functions (e.g., perception and information processing; Cook-Cottone, 2009). Glucocorticoid receptors are located in the hippocampus, making this area particularly sensitive to increased levels of glucocorticoids (Seed et al., 2000). High cortisol levels have been associated with impaired performance on tasks typically mediated by the hippocampus (e.g., learning memory, attention).

Altered Neurotransmitter Function

Research has been conducted to examine the functioning of neurotransmitter systems in eating-disordered patients (Jacobi, Hayward, deZwaan, Kraemer, & Agras, 2004; Ribasés et al., 2008). Evidence suggests that as eating disorder symptoms increase, serotonergic responsiveness decreases. Serotonin (i.e., 5-HT) is a monoamine neurotransmitter synthesized in serotonergic neurons in the central nervous system and the enterochromaffin cells of the gastrointestinal tract (Cook-Cottone, 2009). The 5-HT system regulates mood, impulsivity, social behavior, and eating behavior, and at lower levels contributes to compulsive or binge-eating behaviors (Steiger & Bruce, 2007). Additionally, meal consumption typically enhances the release of 5-HT to assist in appetite regulation, and, therefore, alterations in 5-HT could result from caloric restriction (Kaye, 2008; Steiger & Bruce, 2007).

Bailer and colleagues (2004) looked to expand the role of 5-HT activity as it contributes to the etiology of eating disorders and not simply as a secondary result of malnutrition. Prior studies have illustrated altered functioning of the 5-HT system after the recovery of an eating disorder (Kaye, Gwirtsman, George, & Ebert, 1991). Additionally, it is evident that certain eating disorder traits (e.g., perfectionism, obsessionality, anxiety) persist after the recovery of AN (Bulik, Sullivan, Fear, & Joyce, 1997). In an examination of 10 recovered AN (binging-purging subtype) patients, PET scans were used so that in vivo study of the 5-HT functioning could be examined. Results confirmed the hypothesis that disturbances in brain 5-HT neuronal functioning persist even after recovery, and therefore, this system is implicated as playing a role in the etiology of AN. Specifically, receptor activity in the left subgenual cingulate as well as in the left parietal and right occipital cortex appear to be altered.

The function of dopamine (DA) in eating disorder behavior has also been examined. Reduced levels of DA are apparent in patients with AN, which appear to persist after recovery (Kaye, 2008). It is also suggested that as a key neurotransmitter in the reward system, DA dysfunction may contribute to altered reward, affect, decision making, and executive control.

Other Medical Complications and Long-Term Consequences of Eating Disorders

In states of malnutrition, it appears logical for patients to become more susceptible to infection (Chandra & Kumari, 1994). However, despite deficits in caloric intake, eating-disordered patients do not appear to be at any more risk of developing the common cold, and infection is not usually the cause of death (Korndorfer et al., 2003). In their study, Saito, Nomura, Hotta, and Takano (2007) further explore this phenomenon. It is hypothesized that an increase in CD4+ T-lymphocyte (CD4) may mediate the effects of illness on AN patients. Results indicate that, in fact, CD4 lymphocytes increased while other nutritional markers (e.g., total lymphocyte count, body mass index, insulin-like growth factor-1, and serum zinc) all decreased, therefore explaining in part why AN patients are capable of resisting infection despite their poor nutritional habits.

There is a negative impact on fluid and electrolyte balances resulting from prolonged states of malnutrition and dehydration. These disturbances are especially significant when an eating-disordered patient is engaging in binging and purging behaviors. Specifically, biochemical problems associated with purging may involve loss in sodium, water, potassium, phosphate, magnesium, and glucose levels (Connan, Lightman, & Treasure, 2000). Moreover, laxative abuse can result in metabolic acidosis and contribute to serious medical complications. Cardiovascular abnormalities are the most serious and life-threatening complication of eating disorders, and if not treated may result in fatality. After prolonged starvation, the sympathetic tone in the heart and blood vessels decrease, creating difficulty in the heart's ability to efficiently transport blood to the body's organs (Gary, 2001). Bradycardia, tachycardia, or orthostatic hypotension may result. In AN populations, it is common for patients to have heartbeats below 60 beats per minute and blood pressure levels consistent with hypotension. In conjunction, associated electrolyte imbalances may contribute to arrhythmias as the conduction of nerve impulses are impaired. Gastrointestinal, hematologic, and integumentary abnormalities can result. Finally, neurological complications in AN patients tend to transpire as general muscle weaknesses (Chowdhury & Lask, 2000).

Long-term complications may involve any of the body's systems but appear to most often be associated with bone and tooth decay that is typically irreversible (Gary, 2001). The onset of eating disorders tends to occur during adolescence, a time period critical to both cognitive and physical development. Therefore, the commencement of an eating disorder during this time may interfere with the development of bone mass, which over time could contribute to osteoporosis and a higher risk for bone fractures.

CONTEMPORARY MODES OF TREATMENT

Because eating disorders are often treatment resistant, it is essential to explore alternative modes of treatment when intervening with patients with eating disorders. In particular, the ego-syntonic nature of AN makes it one of the most intractable disorders to treat (Pike et al., 2006). Patients with eating disorders rarely seek out treatment voluntarily, and if they do, they want to feel better emotionally yet continue to fear weight gain and loss of control.

Treatment of AN or BN rarely takes a linear course toward recovery. Instead, the recovery process varies as the patient's motivation throughout the course of treatment changes. Effective approaches integrate thoughtful practice and implementation of evidence-treatment modalities in order to meet the needs of the client.

Inpatient and Outpatient Treatment

Generally, those with eating disorders are treated on an outpatient basis with an integrated treatment team that includes a medical doctor, a nutritionist, and a mental health professional (Cook-Cottone, 2009). Inpatient treatment is used when the patient meets medical criteria or has persistent symptoms that are not responding to outpatient treatment. Medical criteria include extremely low weight (less than 75% of expected weight for height), cardiac symptoms, dehydration, and electrolyte imbalances. Inpatient treatment for AN and BN is used to treat the most ill patients. Although a large percentage of those hospitalized respond to treatment by gaining weight or eliminating binge-purge behavior, relapse rates are high, ranging from 30%–60% (Pike et al., 2006). Traditionally, cognitive-behavioral therapy (CBT) has been illustrated as having the strongest support in preventing relapse among adults. Traditional treatment for BN involves CBT (Pike et al., 2006). To illustrate, Fairburn, Marcus, and Wilson (1993) presented an effective 20-session treatment program, delivered in three phases (i.e., review of the role cognition plays in behavior, cognitive restructuring of thoughts, and relapse prevention). Also, interpersonal psychotherapy focusing on interpersonal contexts that initiated and help maintain eating disorder behavior has been found to be effective for BN and AN (Pike et al., 2006). More recently, additional treatment modalities have been explored for use in both inpatient and outpatient settings and prove promising. These are reviewed here.

Motivational Enhancement Therapy

Patients with eating disorders tend to display low levels of motivation to change (Kotler, Boudreau, & Devlin, 2003). Even the most state-of-the-art treatment modalities prove themselves ineffective if the patient is not ready for change. Although maladaptive, patients report that their symptoms help them feel safe and in control and that they feel vulnerable without them. Motivational enhancement therapy (MET) targets both denial and resistance to change. Treatment begins with an assessment of the client's current stage of change (i.e., pre-contemplation, contemplation, preparation, and maintenance). Treatment interventions are typically brief (e.g., approximately four sessions) and are intended to increase early engagement and thereby improve treatment outcome. There is support for MET in both inpatient and outpatient settings (Feld, Woodside, Kaplan, Olmstead, & Carter, 2001; Geller, Zaitsof, & Srikameswaran, 2005; Treasure et al., 1999; Vansteenkiske, Soenens, & Vandereychen, 2005).

Family-Based Treatment for Anorexia Nervosa

The Maudsley method of family therapy has been supported for treating adolescents with AN in an outpatient setting (Pike et al., 2006). Several variations on the delivery method of the Maudsley model exist, which include conjoint family therapy (CFT; families treated as an unit) and separate family therapy (SFT; patient treated separately from family; Smith & Cook-Cottone, in prep). Specifically, in highly critical families, SFT appears to be more effective, whereas in families rated as less critical, CFT was more effective.

Processing and Symptom-Targeted Interventions

Treasure, Tchanturia, and Schmidt (2005) indicate the utility of neuroscience research in targeting treatment planning on the etiological factors (i.e., intra- and interpersonal) that maintain eating disorders. In 2008, Lopez, Roberts, Tchanturia, and Treasure provided AN patients a three-session, pre-therapy procedure that included neuropsychological assessment; feedback, formulation and target setting; and reflection. With the clinician, the patients explored the impact of the findings in various aspects of their lives and set goals (e.g., about how the client can work to think with more flexibility). Qualitative information indicated promise for the integration of such an intervention to be used in practice. In another targeted intervention, Fairburn, Cooper, and Shafran (2008) present an enhanced model of CBT for eating disorders (CBT-E) created to fit the specific psychopathology of the individual and not the symptoms associated with diagnosis. The goal is to engage the patient, personalize the formulation of the CBT treatment, provide education, and introduce in-session weighing and regular eating. Symptom-maintaining cognitions also are explored. For those who do not initially respond, there is a review progress to identify barriers to change. In a sample of 154 patients, substantial changes in eating behavior were observed and maintained over a 20-week follow-up period (Fairburn et al., 2009).

Dialectical Behavioral Therapy (DBT)

The goals of DBT for eating disorders is to reduce eating disorder behaviors, teach patients more adaptive ways to regulate emotions and, most importantly, to tolerate negative or uncomfortable emotions (Polivy & Herman, 1993). There are four modules: mindfulness skills, distress tolerance, emotional regulation, and interpersonal effectiveness. Several researchers have adapted DBT for populations with eating disorders with good results (Kotler et al., 2003; Safer, Telch, & Chen, 2009; Telch, Agras, & Linehan, 2000, 2001; Wiser & Telch; 1999; Wisniewski & Kelly, 2003).

Integrated Yoga and Psychotherapy

Consistent with DBT theory, recent work has explored the integration of yoga practice into psychotherapy work as a technique to build mindfulness and connect patients in a healthy way with their bodies. Cook-Cottone, Beck, and Kane's (2008) group treatment sessions integrated DBT techniques, media literacy, interactive discourse, meditation, and yoga practice, decreasing participants' desire to be thinner, concern with dieting, and fear of gaining weight. In a controlled study, Carei, Fyfe-Johnson, Breuner, and Brown (2009) explored the benefits of yoga in the treatment of AN, BN, and EDNOS. Subjects were randomly assigned to two different treatment arms: psychotherapy with yoga twice a week and psychotherapy with no yoga. Results indicated significantly larger decreases in eating disorder symptoms in the yoga group.

SUMMARY

Often considered disorders of our culture, eating disorders are not fully explained by cultural models. Neurological studies suggest that there may be characteristics unique to those with eating disorders that create vulnerability. Those with eating disorders generally struggle with food intake (restriction or binging), have an excessive focus on body image and thinness, and are comforted by their symptoms. There are significant physiological and neuropathological complications. Further, those with eating disorders show attentional biases to food and body-focused stimuli and perhaps overall attention deficits, are perfectionistic and rigid in their thinking, struggle with emotional regulation, and may have disturbances in processes related to empathy. Further, the neurological differences between AN and BN are substantial (Cassin & von Ranson, 2005). Those with AN can be rigid and inflexible in thinking, show more obsessive-compulsive traits, and handle stress through constriction of experience. Those with BN are more impulsive and emotionally dysregulated. The most promising interventions target the unique processing styles of patients and provide patients with a healthy cognitive framework, acceptance of neuropsychological challenges, and a method for emotional regulation and distress tolerance. Although much has been learned about the etiology, trajectory, and recovery of eating disorders, much more research is needed.

REFERENCES

American Psychiatric Association. (2000). *Diagnostic and statistical manual of mental disorders* (4th ed., text revision). Washington, DC: Author.

Bachner-Melman, R., Zohar, A. H., & Ebstein, R. P. (2006). An examination of cognitive versus behavioral components of recovery form anorexia nervosa. *The Journal of Nervous and Mental Disease, 194,* 697–703.

Bailer, U. F., Price, J. C., Meltzer, C. C., Mathis, C. A., Frank, G. K., Weissfeld, L., et al. (2004). Altered F-HT_2A receptor binding after recovery from bulimia-type anorexia nervosa: Relationships to harm avoidance and drive for thinness. *Neuropsychopharmacology, 29,* 1143–1155.

Barnard, N. D. (2010). Trends in food availability, 1909–2007. *American Journal of Clinical Nutrition, 91*(5),1530 S–1536 S.

Barratt, E. (1994). Impulsiveness and aggression. (pp. 61–79). In Monahan, J., & Steadman, H. (Eds.). *Violence and mental disorder: Developments in risk assessment.* Chicago: University of Chicago Press.

Bayless, J. D., Kanz, J. E., Moser, D. J., McDowell, B. D., Bowers, W. A., Andersen, A. E., et al. (2002). Neuropsychological characteristics of patients in a hospital-based eating disorder program. *Annual of Clinical Psychology, 14*, 203–207.

Birmingham, C. L., Touyz, S., & Harbottle, J. (2009). Are anorexia nervosa and bulimia nervosa separate disorders? Challenging the 'transdiagnostic' theory of eating disorders. *European Eating Disorder Review, 17*, 2–13.

Bosanac, P., Kulender, S., Stojanovska, L., Hallam, K., Norman, T., McGrath, C., et al. (2007). Neuropsychological study of underweight and weight recovered anorexia compared with bulimia nervosa and normal controls. *International Journal of Eating Disorders, 40*, 613–621.

Bradley, S. J., Taylor, M. J., Rovet, J. F., Goldberg, E., Hood, J., Washsmuth, R., et al (1997). Assessment of brain function in adolescent anorexia nervosa before and after weight gain. *Journal of Clinical and Experimental Neuropsychology, 19*, 20–33.

Bravender, T., Bryant-Waugh, R., Herzog, D., Katzman, D., Kriepe, R. D., Lask, B. (2010). Classification of eating disturbance in children and adolescents: Proposed changes for the DSM-V. *European Eating Disorder Review, 18*, 79–89.

Brownley, K. A., Berkman, N. D., Sedway, J. A., Lohr, K. N., & Bulik, C. M. (2007). Binge eating disorder treatment: A systematic review of randomized controlled trials. *International Journal of Eating Disorders, 40*, 337–348.

Bulik, C. M., Berkman, N. D., Brownley, K. A., Sedway, J. A., & Lohr, K. N. (2007). Anorexia nervosa treatment: A systematic review of randomized control trials. *International Journal of Eating Disorders, 40*, 310–320.

Bulik, C. M., Sullivan, P. F., Fear, J. L., & Joyce, P. R. (1997). Eating disorders and antecedent anxiety disorders: A controlled study. *Acta Psychiatrica Scandinavica, 96*, 101–107.

Carei, T. R., Fyfe-Johnson, A. L., Breuner, C. C., & Brown, M. A. (2009). Randomized controlled clinical trial of yoga in the treatment of eating disorders. *Journal of Adolescent Health, 46*(4), 346–351.

Cassin, S., & von Ranson, K. (2005). Personality and eating disorders: A decade in review. *Clinical Psychology Review, 25*(7), 895–916.

Cavedini, P., Bassi, T., Ubbiali, A., Cosolari, A., Giordani, S., Zorzi, C., et al. (2004). Neuropsycholoigical investigation of decision making in anorexia nervosa. *Psychiatric Research, 127*, 259–266.

Chandra, R. K., & Kumari, S. (1994). Nutrition and immunity: An overview. *Journal of Nutrition, 124*(8), 1433s–1435s.

Chavez, M., & Insel, T. R. (2007). Eating disorders: National Institute of Mental Health's perspective. *American Psychologist, 62*(3), 159–166.

Chowdhury, U., & Lask, B. (2000). Neurological correlates of eating disorders. *European Eating Disorder Review, 8*, 126–133.

Chowdhury, U., Gordon, I., Lask, B., Watkins, B., Watt, H., & Christie, D. (2003). Early onset anorexia nervosa: Is there evidence of a limbic system imbalance? *International Journal of Eating Disorders, 33*, 388–396.

Connan, F., Lightman, S., & Treasure, J. (2000). Biochemical and endocrine complications. *European Eating Disorders Review, 8*, 144–157.

Cook-Cottone, C. P. (2006). The attuned representation model for the primary prevention of eating disorders: An overview for school psychologists. *Psychology in the Schools, 43*, 223–230.

Cook-Cottone, C. (2009). The neuropsychology of eating disorders in women. In E. Fletcher-Janzen (Ed.), *Neuropsychology of women.* New York: Springer Publishing.

Cook-Cottone, C. P. (in press). Eating disorders. In A. S. Davis (Ed.), *Handbook of pediatric neuropsychology.* New York, NY: Springer Publishing.

Cook-Cottone, C., Beck, M., & Kane, L. (2008). Manualized-group treatment for eating disorders: Attunement in mind, body and relationship (AMBR). *The Journal for Specialists in Group Work, 33*(1), 61–83.

Cooper, M. J., & Fairburn, C. G. (1992). Selective processing of eating, weight, and shape related words in patients with eating disorders and dieters. *British Journal of Clinical Psychology, 31*, 363–365.

Decety, J., & Ickes, W. (2009). *The social neuroscience of empathy.* Cambridge, MA: The MIT Press.

Dobson, K. S., & Dozois, D. J. A. (2004). Attentional biases in eating disorders: A meta-analytic review of Stroop performance. *Clinical Psychology Review, 23*, 1001–1022.

Duchesne, M., Mattos, P., Fontenelle, L., Veiga, H., Rizo, L., Appolinario, J. C. (2004). Neuropsychology of eating disorders: A systematic review of the literature. *Review of Brazilian Psychiatry, 26*, 107–117.

Dukarm, C. P. (2005). Bulimia nervosa and attention deficit hyperactivity disorder: A possible role for stimulant medication. *Journal of Women's Health, 14*, 345–350.

Fairburn, C. G., & Bohn, K. (2005). Eating disorder NOS (EDNOS): An example of the troublesome "not otherwise specified" (NOS) category in DSM-IV. *Behaviour Research and Therapy, 43*, 691–701.

Fairburn, C. G., Cooper, Z., Doll, H. A., O'Conner, M. E., Bohn, K., Hawker, D. M., et al (2009). Transdiagnostic cognitive-behavioral therapy for patients with eating disorders: A two- site trial with 60-week follow up. *American Journal of Psychiatry, 166*(3), 311–319.

Fairburn, C. G., Cooper, Z., & Shafran, R. (2008). Enhanced cognitive behavior therapy for eating disorders ("CBT-E"): An overview. In C. G. Fairburn (Ed.), *Cognitive behavior therapy and eating disorders* (pp. 23–34). New York, NY: Guilford Press.

Fairburn, C. G., & Harrison, P. J. (2003). Eating Disorders. *The Lancet, 361*, 407–416.

Fairburn, C. G., Marcus, M. D., & Wilson, G. T. (1993). Cognitive-behavioral therapy for binge eating and bulimia nervosa: A comprehensive treatment manual. In C. G. Fairburn & G. T. Wilson (Eds.), *Binge eating: Nature, assessment, and treatment*. New York: Guilford Press.

Faris, P., Eckert, E., Kim, S-W., Meller, W. H., Pardo, J. V., Goodale, R. L., et al. (2006). Evidence for a vagal pathophysiology for bulimia nervosa and the accompanying depressive symptoms. *Journal of Affective Disorders, 92*, 79–90.

Feld, R., Woodside, D. B., Kaplan, A. S., Olmstead, M. P., & Carter, J. C. (2001). Pretreatment motivational enhancement therapy for eating disorders: A pilot study. *International Journal of Eating Disorders, 29*(4), 393–400.

Fisher, J. O., & Birch, L. L. (2001). Early experience with food and eating: Implications for the development of eating disorders. In J. K. Thompson and L. Smolak (Eds.), *Bodyimage, eating disorders and obesity in youth: Assessment, prevention and treatment*. Washington, DC: American Psychological Association.

Galderisi, S., Mucci, A., Monteleone, P., Sorrentino, D., Piegari, G., & Maj, M. (2003).Neurocognitive functioning in subjects with eating disorders: The influence ofneuroactive steroids. *Biological Psychiatry, 53*, 921–927.

Gary, A. (2001). Pathphysiology of eating disorders. In J. J. Robert-McComb (Ed.), *Eating disorders in women and children: Prevention, stress management and treatment*. Washington, DC: CRC Press.

Geller, J., Zaitsoff, S. L., & Srikameswaran, S. (2005). Tracking readiness and motivation forchange in individuals with eating disorders of the course of treatment. *Cognitive Therapyand Research, 29*(5), 611–625.

Gillberg, I. C. (2007). Non-autism childhood empathy disorders. In T. Farrow & P. Woodruff (Eds.), *Empathy in mental illness* (pp. 111–125). Cambrige, UK: Cambridge University Press.

Gillberg, I. C., Rastam, M., Wentz, E., & Gillberg, C. (2007). Cognitive and executivefunctions in anorexia nervosa ten years after onset of eating disorder. *Journal of Clinical and Experimental Neuropsychology, 29*, 170–178.

Goodwin, G. M. (1990). Neuroendocrine function and the biology of the eating disorders. *Human Psychopharmacology, 5*, 249–253.

Grunwald, N., Ettrich, C., Krause, W., Assmann, B., Dhne, A., Weiss, T., et al. (2001). Haptic perception in anorexia before and after weight gain. *Journal of Clinical and Experimental Neuropsychology, 23*, 520–529.

Hamsher, K. D., Halmi, K. A., & Benton, A. L. (1981). Prediction of outcome inanorexia nervosa from neuropsychological status. *Psychiatry Research, 4*, 79–88.

Hendren, R., DeBacker, I., & Pandina, J. (2000). Review of neuroimaging studies ofchild and adolescent psychiatric disorders from the past 10 years. *Journal of American Child and Adolescent Psychiatry, 39*, 815–828.

Herholz, K. (1996). Neuroimaging in anorexia nervosa. *Psychiatry Research, 62*(1), 105–110.

Herzog, D. B., & Eddy, K. T. (2007). Diagnosis, epidemiology, and clinical course of eating disorders. In J. Yager & P. S. Powers (Eds), (pp. 1–29). Washington, DC: American Psychiatric Publishing, Inc.

Holliday, J., Tchanturia, K., Landau, S., Collier, D., & Treasure, J. (2005). Is impaired set-shifting an endophenotype of anorexia nervosa? *The American Journal of Psychiatry, 162*(12), 2269–2275.

Houy, E., Debono, B., Dechelotte, P., & Thibaut, F. (2007). Anorexia nervosa associated with right frontal brain lesion. *International Eating Disorders, 40*, 758–761.

Hurley, R. A., & Taber, K. H. (2008). Imaging of eating disorders: Multiple techniques todemonstrate the dynamic brain. *Journal of Neuropsychiatry and Clinical Neuroscience,20*(3), 252–260.

Jacobi, C., Hayward, C., deZwaan, M., Kraemer, H. C., & Agras, W. S. (2004). Coming to termswith risk factors for eating disorders: Application of risk terminologies and suggestionsfor a general taxonomy. *Psychological Bulletin, 130*, 19–65.

Kaye, W. H. (2008). Neurobiology of anorexia and bulimia nervosa. *Physiology and Behavior, 94*, 121–135.

Kaye, W. H., Berrettini, W., Gwirtsman, H., & George, D. (1990). Altered cerebrospinal fluid neuropeptide Y and peptide YY immunoreactivity in anorexia and bulimia nervosa. *Archives of General Psychiatry, 47*(6), 548–556.

Kaye, W. H., Gwirtsman, H. E., George, D. T., & Ebert, M. H. (1991). Altered serotonin activity inanorexia nervosa after long-term weight restoration. Does elevated cerebrospinal fluid 5-hydroxyindoleacetic acid level correlate with rigid and obsessive behavior? *Archives of General Psychiatry, 48*, 556–562.

Key, A., O'Brien, A., Gordon, I., Christie, D., & Lask, B. (2006). Assessment of neurobiology in adults with anorexia nervosa. *European Eating Disorders Review, 14*, 308–314.

Klein, D. A., & Walsh, B. T. (2004). Eating disorders: Clinical features and pathophysiology. *Physiology and Behavior, 81*, 359–374.

Korndorfer, S. R., Lucas, A. R., Suman, V. J., Crowson, C. S., Krahn, L. E., & Melton, L. J. (2003). Long-term survival of patients with anorexia nervosa: A population-based study in Rochester, Minn. *Mayo Clinic Proceedings, 78*, 278–284.

Kotler, L. A., Boudreau, G. S., & Devlin, M. J. (2003). Emerging psychotherapies for eating disorders. *Journal of Psychiatric Practice, 9*(6), 431–441.

Lambe, E. K., Katzman, D. K., Mikulis, D. J., Kennedy, S. H., & Zipursky, R. B. (1997). Cerebral gray matter volume deficits after weight recovery from anorexia nervosa. *Archives of General Psychiatry, 54*, 537–542.

Lane, R., Reiman, E., Axelrod, B., Yun, L. S., Holmes, A. H., & Schwartz, G. (1998). Neural correlates of levels of emotional awareness: Evidence of an interaction between emotion and attention in the anterior cingulated cortex. *Journal of Cognitive Neuroscience, 10*, 225–235.

Lauer, C. J., Gorzewski, B., Gerlinghoff, M., Backmund, H., & Zihl, J. (1999). Neuropsychological assessments before and after treatment in patients with anorexia and bulimia nervosa. *Journal of Psychiatric Research, 33*, 129–138.

Lena, S. M., Fiocco, A. J., & Leyenaar, J. K. (2004). The role of cognitive deficits in the development of eating disorders. *Neuropsychology Review, 14*, 99–113.

Licinio, J., Wong, M. L., & Gold, P. W. (1996). The hypothalamic-pituitary-adrenal axis in anorexia nervosa. *Psychiatry Research, 62*, 75–83.

Long, C. G., Hinton, C., & Gillespie, N. K. (1994). Selective processing of food and body size words: Application of the Stroop Test with obese restrained eaters, anorexics and normals. *International Journal of Eating Disorders, 15*, 279–283.

Lopez, C., Roberts, M. E., Tchanturia, K., & Treasure, J. (2008). Using neuropsychological feedback therapeutically in treatment for anorexia nervosa: Two illustrative case reports. *European Eating Disorders Review, 16*, 411–421.

Lovell, D. M., Williams, J. M., & Hill, A. B. (1997). Selective processing of shape-related words in women with eating disorders and those who have recovered. *British Journal of Clinical Psychology, 36*, 421–432.

Milos, G., Spindler, A., Schnyder, U., & Fairburn, C. G. (2005). Instability of eating disorder diagnosis: Prospective study. *British Journal of Psychiatry, 187*, 573–578.

Mitchell, J. E., Cook-Myers, T., & Wonderlich, S. A. (2005). Diagnostic criteria for anorexia nervosa: Looking ahead to DSM-IV. *International Journal of Eating Disorders, 37*(S1), S95–S97.

Mühlau, M., Gaser, C., Ilg, R., Conrad, B., Leibl, C., Cebulla, M. H., et al. (2007). Gray matter decrease of the anterior cingulated cortex in anorexia nervosa. *American Journal of Psychiatry, 164*(12), 1850–1857.

Pike, K. M., Walsh, T., & Roberto, C. (2006). Anorexia nervosa. In J. E. Fisher & W. T.O'Dononue (Eds.), *Practitioner's guide to evidence-based psychotherapy* (pp. 45–56).New York: Springer.

Polivy, J., & Herman, C. P. (1993). Etiology of binge eating: Psychological mechanisms. In C. G.Fairburn & G. T. Wilson (Eds.), *Binge eating: Nature, assessment, and treatment* (pp. 173–205). New York: Guilford Press.

Råstam, M., Gillberg, I. C., & Wentz, E. (2003). Outcome of teenage-onset anorexia nervosa in aSwedish community-based sample. *European Child and Adolescent Psychiatry, 12*(Suppl. 1), 178–190.

Ribasés, M., Fernández-Aranda, F., Gratacòs, M., Mercader, J. M., Casasnovas, C.,Núnez, A., et al. (2008). Contribution of the serotoninergicsystem to anxious traits that may be partially responsible for the phenotypicalvariability of bulimia nervosa. *Journal of Psychiatric Research, 42*, 50–57.

Rosval, L., Steiger, H., Bruce, K., Isreal, M., Richardson, J., & Aubut, M. (2006).Impulsivity in women with eating disorders: Problem of response inhibition,planning, or attention? *International Journal of Eating Disorders, 39*, 590–593.

Safer, D. L., Telch, C. F., & Chen, E. Y. (2009). *Dialectical behavior therapy for binge eatingand bulimia*. New York: Guilford Press.

Saito, H., Nomura, K., Hotta, M., & Takano, K. (2007). Malnutrition induces dissociated changes in lymphocyte count and subset proportions in patients with anorexia nervosa. *International Journal of Eating Disorders, 40*, 575–579.

Santel, S., Baving, L., Krauel, K., Münte, T. F., & Rotte, M. (2006). Hunger and satiety in anorexia nervosa: fMRI during cognitive processing of food pictures. *Brain Research, 1114*, 138–148.

Seed, J. A., Dixon, R. A., McCluskey, S. E., & Young, A. H. (2000). Basal activity of the hypothalamic-pituitary-adrenal axis and cognitive function in anorexia nervosa. *European Archives in Psychiatry and Clinical Neuroscience, 250*, 11–15.

Smith, A. (1973). *Symbol Digits Modality Test.* Los Angeles: Western Psychological Services.

Smith, A., & Cook-Cottone, C. P. *An examination of the theoretical, empirical, and applied facets of family therapy as an effective intervention for anorexia nervosa in adolescents.* Manuscript in preparation.

Steiger, H., & Bruce, K. R. (2007). Phenotypes, endophenotypes, and genotypes inbulimia spectrum eating disorders. *La Revue Canadienne de Psyciatrie, 52*, 220–227.

Steinglass, J. E., Walsh, B. T., & Stern, Y. (2006). Set shifting deficit in anorexia nervosa. *Journal of the International Neuropsychological Society, 12*, 431–435.

Striegel-Moore, R. H., & Bulik, C. M. (2007). Risk factors for eating disorders. *The American Psychologist, 62*, 181–198.

Subic-Wrana, C., Bruder, S., Thomas, W., Lane, R. D., & Kohle, K. (2005). Emotional awareness in inpatients of a psychosomatic ward: A comparison of two differentmeasures of alexithymia. *Psychosomatic Medicine, 67*, 483–489.

Tchanturia, K., Campbell, I. C., Morris, R., & Treasure, J. (2005). Neuropsychologicalstudies in anorexia nervosa. *International Journal of Eating Disorders, 37*, S72–S76.

Telch, C. F., Agras, W. S., & Linehan, M. M. (2000). Group dialectical behavior therapy for binge eating disorder: A preliminary, uncontrolled trial. *Behavior Therapy, 31*, 569–582.

Telch, C. F., Agras, W. S., & Linehan, M. M. (2001). Dialectical behavior therapy for binge eating disorders. *Journal of Consultation and Clinical Psychology, 69*, 1061–1065.

Thomas, J. J., Vartanian, L. R., & Brownell, K. D. (2009). The relationship between eating disorder not otherwise specified (EDNOS) and officially recognized eating disorders: Meta-analysis and implications for DSM. *Psychological Bulletin, 135*(3), 407–433.

Treasure, J. L., Katzman, M., Schmidt, U., Troop, N., Todd, G., & de Silva, P. (1999). Engagement and outcome in the treatment of bulimia nervosa: First phase of a sequential design comparing motivation enhancement therapy and cognitive behavioural therapy. *Behaviour Research and Therapy, 37*(5), 405–418.

Treasure, J., Tchanturia, K., & Schmidt, U. (2005). Developing a model of treatment for eating disorder: Using neuroscience research to examine the how rather than the what of change. *Counselling and Psychotherapy Research, 5*(3), 191–202.

Uher, R., & Treasure, J. (2005). Brain lesions and eating disorders. *Journal of Neurology and Neurosurgery Psychiatry, 76*, 852–857.

Vansteenkiske, M., Soenens, B., & Vandereychen, W. (2005). Motivation to change in eating disorder patients: A conceptual clarification on the basis of self-determination theory. *International Journal of Eating Disorders, 37*(3), 207–219.

Wagner, A., Aizenstein, H., Venkatraman, V. K., Fudge, J., May, J. C., Frank, G. K., et al. (2007). Altered reward processing in women recovered from anorexia nervosa. *American Journal of Psychiatry, 164*(12), 1842–1849.

Wagner, A., Greer, P., Bailer, U. F., Frank, G. K., Henry, S. E., Putnman, K., et al. (2006). Normal brain tissue volumes after long-term recovery in anorexia and bulimia nervosa. *Biological Psychiatry, 69*, 291–293.

Wentz, E., Lacey, J. H., Waller, G., Råstam, M., Turk, J., & Gillberg, C. (2005). Childhood onsetneuropsychiatric disorders in adult eating disorder patients–A controlled pilot study. *European and Child & Adolescent Psychiatry, 14*, 431–437.

Wiser, S., & Telch, C. F. (1999). Dialectical behavior therapy for binge-eating disorder. *Journal of Clinical Psychology, 55*, 755–768.

Wisniewski, L., & Kelly, E. (2003). The application of dialectical behavior therapy to the treatment of eating disorders. *Cognitive and Behavioral Practice, 10*, 131–138.

Wonderlich, S. A., Gordon, K. H., Mitchell, J. E., Crosby, R. D., & Engel, S. G. (2009). The validity and clinical utility of binge eating disorder. *International Journal of Eating Disorders, 42*, 687–705.

Wonderlich, S. A., Joiner, T. E., Keel, P. K., Williamson, D. A., & Crosby, R. D. (2007). Eating disorder diagnosis: Empirical approaches to classification. *American Psychologist, 62*(3), 167–180.

Yonezawa, H., Otagaki, Y., Miyake, Y., Okamoto, Y., & Yamawaki, S. (2008). No differences are seen in the regional cerebral blood flow in the restricting type of anorexia nervosa compared with the binge eating/purging type. *Psychiatry and Clinical Neurosciences, 62*,26–33.

SECTION III

Interventions and Treatment

CHAPTER 21

Neuropsychological Assessment Within the Psychiatric Setting

Raymond S. Dean & Chad A. Noggle

INTRODUCTION

Beyond emotional and behavioral sequelae, an array of psychiatric illnesses demonstrates cognitive dysfunction as a premorbid or core clinical feature (Mesholam-Gately, Giuliano, Faraone, Goff, & Seidman, 2009; Torres, Boudreau, & Yatham, 2007; Wood, Allen, & Pantelis, 2009). The etiology of these cognitive deficits varies. Although results have been mixed, neurocognitive deficits have been correlated with psychiatric treatment itself (i.e., medication; Woodward, Purdon, Meltzer, & Zald, 2007), increased severity of psychiatric features (Martinez-Aran et al., 2004), and comorbidity (Chui et al., 2008; Yucel, Lubman, Solowij, & Brewer, 2009). Interestingly, cognitive impairments are more strongly linked than psychiatric symptoms with functional outcomes and quality of life over the long term (Allott, Liu, Proffitt, & Killackey, 2011b; Fett et al., 2011; Wingo, Harvey, & Baldessarini, 2009). Neuropsychological assessment represents a highly effective way of determining the nature and extent of such cognitive deficits. Nevertheless, neuropsychological assessment is consistently reported as one of the most underused resources within the psychiatric setting. This is likely a by-product of both the medical community's lack of knowledge as to what such assessments can add to diagnosis and treatment in psychiatric disorders and a sparseness of neuropsychologists who specialize in this specific population.

At its clinical core, neuropsychology has traditionally involved the measurement of brain function and volitional behavior. The field represents an interaction between psychology and other neurosciences. Within the general field of neuropsychology, neuropsychological assessment is designed to provide standardized observations of behavior known to depend on the integrity of the central nervous system. The present diagnostic use of this assessment procedure is based on extensive clinical research in which cognitive, sensorimotor, and emotional functioning were correlated with brain damage recognized at surgery or autopsy and now refined through its relationship with functional imaging outcomes. Within the psychiatric setting, neuropsychological assessment can often help clarify psychopathology in clinical situations in which the neurological evidence of brain dysfunction is inconsistent and the amount of functional impairment is not fully appreciated. Thus, it provides a theoretic framework in which both neurological and behavioral data are integrated into a comprehensive view of the patient's level of functioning. This chapter will outline the relevant information related to the use of neuropsychological assessment within the psychiatric setting.

HISTORICAL FOUNDATIONS

Neuropsychology is best conceptualized as a mixture of behavioral neurology, clinical and experimental psychology, and objective measurement of human behavior. This is evident in many of the procedures making up presently available neuropsychological test batteries. With few exceptions, current assessment procedures are either standardized versions of preexisting clinical procedures or adaptations of neuropsychological laboratory procedures for clinical use. Often seen as an expansion of the neurological examination, neuropsychological assessment emphasizes standardized behavioral observations and interpretations that rely on normative standards and critical value cutting scores. This approach has been shown to be of value in diagnosing neurological disorders and defining the behavioral effects of brain damage. In retrospect, one can criticize 19th and early 20th century methods that based conclusions about normal brain functioning on case studies of patients with diseased brains. Nevertheless, these early reports led to our present understanding of the relationship between clinically expressed behaviors and cerebral functions. The notion of a direct correspondence between behavior and localized microstructures of the brain seems naïve by present standards. We now recognize that the magnitude, site, and chronicity of a brain lesion; developmental history; and individual differences in brain structure and chemistry all interact to make highly specific localization tenuous. The inflexible notions of a one-to-one correspondence between observable behavior and structures of the brain have been rejected by most neuroscientists. However, a quantitative-actuarial approach remains that concentrates on the differential diagnosis of neurologically related conditions and their behavioral correlates. The emphasis on differential diagnosis in neuropsychological assessment is relatively recent in the history of the field and grows out of a need to describe the behavioral effects of neurological and psychiatric presentations more objectively. Although the neurologist or radiologist may be able to document and localize lesions, rarely is it possible to make specific predictions about a patient's behavioral functioning in his or her premorbid environment. Thus, neuropsychological assessment provides information useful in aftercare planning and following progressive disorders.

The scientific approach to identifying individual differences of the late 19th and early 20th centuries continues to influence psychometric theory in general and neuropsychological assessment specifically. From this perspective, various aspects of human behavior (e.g., memory) are viewed on a continuum rather than as a normal-abnormal dichotomy, with the majority of individuals clustering around a midpoint on a given ability spectrum. This approach to neuropsychological assessment has resulted in the scaling of functions and the interpretation of individual behavior relative to normal cohorts.

Historical Role of Neuropsychology Within the Psychiatric Setting

In the past, one of the most frequent referral questions asked of the neuropsychologist in the psychiatric setting involved differential diagnosis of "organic" and "functional" mental disorders stemming from the relatively extinct conceptualization that the two are/were mutually exclusive (Leonberger, 1989). Even though these terms hold a good deal of tradition in the psychiatric literature, we now realize these distinctions are better understood as a continuum rather than a nosologic dichotomy. Kandel (1998) best outlined the shift away from this dichotomous view in suggesting that the relevant clinical questions were to what degree is the biological process of a psychiatric disorder determined by genetic and developmental factors, to what degree is it environmentally or socially determined, and to what degree is it determined by a toxic or infectious agent, as opposed to whether it is functional or organic. This came as a result of advances in neuroscientific investigation that have challenged the normality of biochemical and structural brain features of numerous psychiatric disorders hitherto described as having a functional locus. With scientific advancements, we now recognize the more holistic, functional impact of the neurological substrates of psychiatric disorders. Neurocognitive compromise is just one functional domain now recognized as a common premorbid or core feature of various psychiatric illnesses. However, identification of the cognitive deficits associated with psychiatric disorders is beyond the capabilities of neuroimaging or traditional psychiatric or neurological evaluations, hence the role of neuropsychology in care.

CONTEMPORARY ROLE OF NEUROPSYCHOLOGY IN THE PSYCHIATRIC SETTING

Neuropsychological assessment comprises tasks examining a comprehensive array of behaviors that are compared with normative standards and those occurring in known neurological conditions. Such information permits recognition of "minor" behavioral/cognitive impairment, often the early sign of neurological disorders, including mental illnesses, which cumulative literature over the past few decades has clearly linked with neurological substrates. Of use in differential diagnosis, these data also provide the clinician with information concerning the extent of a patient's behavioral impairment. Neuropsychological assessment provides the objectivity necessary in following the course of progressive or chronic disorders and offers the clinician a monitoring capability not available with other procedures. It also offers the opportunity for reassessment, which may be necessary in relation to: (1) questionable validity on previous testing related to poor attention or motivation; (2) decline or improvement in cognition; (3) functional decline; (4) effects of a neurological event; (5) effects of substance abuse; (6) assessment of effects of cognitive interventions; (7) medication effects; and (8) test-retest for research purposes (Marcopulos et al., 2008). Neuropsychological examinations involve measures of cognitive, sensorimotor, and emotional functioning. Some of the tests are the same as those routinely administered in clinical evaluation. For example, the Minnesota Multiphasic Personality Inventory-2 (MMPI-2) and the Wechsler Intelligence Scales have been included as part of most neuropsychological evaluations after extensive research concerning the neurological correspondence of these measures. These tests have allowed a more comprehensive view of the patient's level of functioning. The tests used may vary somewhat with the individual laboratory or practitioner, but the functions presented in Figure 21.1 outline the areas of a comprehensive assessment.

In the case of psychopathology, neuropsychological assessment is used as an adjunct to the diagnostic practices of structured clinical interviewing and objective assessment of personality and psychiatric traits (e.g., depression). Neuropsychological assessments provide a means of objectively identifying potential brain dysfunction, including mild or subtle cognitive disturbances that are commonly identified as premorbid or core features of various psychiatric illnesses (Mesholam-Gately et al., 2009; Torres et al., 2007; Wood et al., 2009). Further, neuropsychological assessment can aid in delineating to what extent identified cognitive deficits contribute to other behavioral or psychosocial outcomes.

Having graduated from the outdated debate of functional versus organic, the role of neuropsychology within the psychiatric setting can take many shapes. However, if we were to specify the primary purpose or role of neuropsychology within the psychiatric setting, it would be to outline patients' unique neurocognitive profiles as they relate to and impact everyday functioning. This includes determination of their neurocognitive strengths as well as the nature and extent of any neurocognitive deficits. Consequently, neuropsychological assessment in the psychiatric setting is not intended for differential diagnoses, a task still best handled though structured diagnostic interviews and history-taking.

The role of neuropsychological assessment seems natural given that neurocognitive deficits are often noted in the absence of gross brain pathology and "normal" performance on traditional mental status examinations (e.g., the Mini-Mental Status Examination [MMSE]), requiring more refined, objective/actuarial assessment of performance. Neuropsychological assessment also offers the benefit of repeated assessment because functional changes can be seen over time (Woods, Delis, Scott, Kramer, & Holdnack, 2006). As a result, patients are likely best served by being assessed within the first year following psychiatric symptom onset, particularly in presentations such as schizophrenia. This permits immediate initiation of cognitive remediation strategies, if warranted. Early intervention is key because prolongation of untreated cognitive deficits can increase overall functional impairment. Over time, deficits can transform, requiring modifications of the interventions needed, which starts with reassessment. Reassessment should be undertaken as appropriate given the extent of neuro-

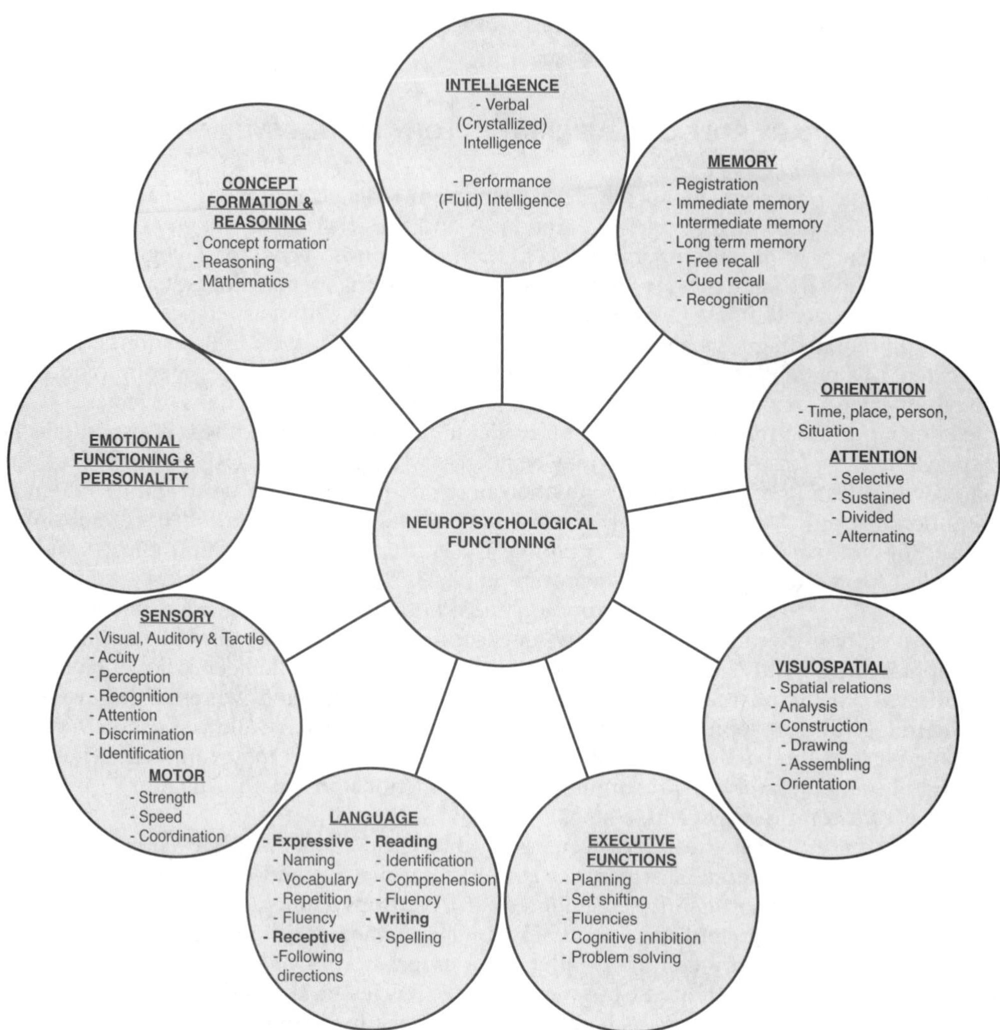

FIGURE 21.1 Neuropsychological domains.

cognitive involvement or in response to perceived changes in functional status. The various reasons for reassessment are noted previously.

When pursuing neuropsychological assessment within the psychiatric setting, it should be comprehensive because no unitary profile exists for the various disorders and presentations. Although the executive functions are some of the most commonly indicted deficits in the neurocognitive domain, even these deficits can be relatively nonspecific given that executive functioning is reliant upon lower-order cognitive skills. In reality, diffuse neurological dysfunction as opposed to more focal pathology better explains the poor neuropsychological performance commonly seen in conjunction with psychiatric manifestations, suggesting the need for comprehensive assessment (Alarcon, Libb, & Boll, 1994; Walterfang, Wood, Velakoulis, & Pantelis, 2006).

It is also the case that variability in effort and attention can be commonly seen within this clinical grouping, suggesting a need for a range of tests being used to better judge consistency in domain and test performance (Keefe, 1995). To reduce examinee burden, the clinician can add measures as the assessment proceeds if areas of noticeable difficulty arise, particularly when behavioral observations suggest potential waning of attention, engagement, or motivation. Still, test selection is much the same as with other presentations. Assessments should: (1) include measures of premorbid functioning, (2) assess a wide range of cognitive domains,

TABLE 21.1 Brief and Comprehensive Neuropsychological Assessment

Type of Evaluation	Tests
Neuropsychological screen	• Wechsler Abbreviated Scale of Intelligence (WASI) • Wechsler Test of Adult Reading (WTAR) • Repeatable Battery of Neuropsychological Status (RBANS) • Trails A and B *or* Comprehensive Trail Making Test (CTMT) • Stroop • Wisconsin Card Sorting Test • Grooved Pegboard
Comprehensive neuropsychological evaluation	• Wechsler Adult Intelligence Scale-IV (WAIS-IV) *or* Woodcock-Johnson-III-Tests of Cognitive Abilities (WJ-III-COG) • Wechsler Test of Adult Reading (WTAR) • California Verbal Learning Test-II (CVLT-II) • Wechsler Memory Scale-IV (WMS-IV) • Rey Complex Figure Test • Trails A and B *or* Comprehensive Trail Making Test (CTMT) • Stroop • Wisconsin Card Sorting Test • MAE Token Test • Boston Naming Test • Verbal Fluencies (e.g., COWAT & animals) • Continuous Performance Test-II • Wechsler Individual Achievement Test-III (WIAT-III) *or* Woodcock-Johnson-III-Tests of Achievement-III (WJ-III-ACH) *or* Kaufman Functional Academic Skills Test (K-FAST) • Test of Memory Malingering (TOMM) *or* Word Memory Test • Halstead-Reitan Sensory-Motor Battery *or* Dean-Woodcock Sensory-Motor Battery • Grooved Pegboard • Behavior Rating Inventory of Executive Functioning (BRIEF) • Minnesota Multiphasic Personality Inventory-II-Restructured Format (MMPI-2-RF) • Beck Anxiety Inventory (BAI) • Beck Depression Inventory (BDI)

(3) evaluate for potential malingering, (4) be mindful of examinee burden, and (5) be at the functional level of the client (Marcopulos et al., 2008). Interpretation must not simply focus on quantitative outcomes but also the qualitative input and output because task failure can stem from various cognitive processes and not necessarily a unitary function.

Table 21.1 includes a potential battery for a comprehensive neuropsychological assessment as well as a neuropsychological screening battery.

Premorbid and Neurodevelopmental History

The impact of neurocognitive deficits within psychiatric disorders is dependent on the individual's life stage, both in terms of chronological age and environmental demands of normal neurocognitive functioning. As a result, a detailed developmental and premorbid history is critical to fully appreciate and conceptualize the potential impact of the psychiatric disorder and to understand the interrelationship between cognitive, behavioral, biological, and environmental factors. Testa and Pantelis (2009) have noted that the age at which organic brain insult occurs mediates both behavioral and cognitive outcomes as well as the potential for recovery and rehabilitation. Disruptions in neurodevelopment have been proposed as the basis for psychiatric disorder manifestation with functional disturbances presenting in those domains where skill attainment and refinement occurs at the time point when the neurodevelopmental disruption takes place (Pantelis, Yucel, Wood, McGorry, & Velakoulis, 2003; Testa & Pantelis, 2009). This results in either developmental delay, arrest, or deterioration (Testa & Pantelis, 2009; Wood, Pantelis, Yung, Velakoulis, & McGorry, 2009). Within the psychiatric setting, disorder onset peaks in adolescence or early adulthood (Kessler & Wang, 2008); thus, it is not surprising that the executive functions are the most commonly impaired domain because they continue to develop during the time when psychiatric disorder onset is at its peak.

As is true in psychiatry and other clinical medical sciences, a patient's presenting symptoms must be interpreted relative to his or her medical, social, and family history. Although it is often difficult to examine the effect of education, socioeconomic status, and occupation on the individual, each has been shown to be related to performance on psychological measures in general and measures of neuropsychological functioning specifically, and may modify the interpretation of these measures. Prigatano and Parsons (1976) report a considerable relationship between the results of measures of neuropsychological functioning and the level of education for patients from a general medical service. However, the relationship between these variables for neurological and psychiatric patients is not as clear. Dean (1985, 1986, 1987) has argued that the adult patient's premorbid occupation and the concomitant opportunity to refine academic skills may be a potent predictor of neuropsychological functioning. Indeed, there seems to be a substantial relationship between socioeconomic status, when measured by occupation, and normal individuals' general cognitive abilities. The effect of race on neuropsychological functioning is not as clear. Although some have hypothesized a genetic component for race on such measures, the interaction of socioeconomic differences and aspects of cultural transmission make interpretation of these data for the individual patient tenuous.

As one would expect, the effects of age on neuropsychological performance are clearest at the two extremes, with batteries developed exclusively for adults and exclusively for children. Although diminution in neuropsychological functions is known to exist with advancing years, the extent to which these results are dependent on past learning and experience is not clear. In one early study, Reed and Reitan (1963) reported a moderate negative correlation between age and scores on the neuropsychological battery. However, this summary statistic obscures the more interesting result that little dependable change in neuropsychological functioning was observed for abilities that depended most directly on past learning. This replicated finding was as clear as the decline with advancing years of performance on tasks requiring mental flexibility, new learning, and memory when not based on old associations.

Finally, in taking a patient's developmental and premorbid history, it is important to assess for preexisting and comorbid conditions. Histories of attention deficit hyperactivity disorder, learning disabilities, externalizing disorders, pervasive developmental disorders, or more general intellectual disabilities are seen in a number of psychiatric patients (Proffitt, Brewer, & McGorry, 2006; Proffitt, Allott, McGorry, & Brewer, 2009) and must be considered clinically. When assessed within children or adolescents, this can also serve as a prognostic indicator for continued psychiatric symptomology into adulthood. As a result, including measures of personality constructs and psychiatric symptoms can supplement the neuropsychological formulation (Ready, Stierman, & Paulsen, 2001), which itself can help delineate the relative impact of comorbidities (Allott, Brewer, McGorry, & Proffitt, 2011a).

Clearly, the patient's developmental and medical history provides insight into his or her neuropsychological performance. Thus, the patient's present functioning level must be evaluated in light of seemingly unrelated factors. Although a head injury with loss of consciousness at age 12 may appear of little relevance in the now 40-year-old patient who presents with memory loss, the interpretation of inconsistencies in the patient's neuropsychological examination may be attributed in part to such an early closed-head injury. The same can be said for the 40-year old patient who first developed psychotic features at the age of 12, though the two cases are not directly comparable. Without knowledge of the patient's history, the neuropsychological formulation becomes less reliable. This is further suggested when considering the rate of comorbidities observed within this population.

Competing Factors in Assessment and Interpretation

Within the psychiatric setting, various factors must be taken into account to ensure the reliability of the assessment and results interpretation. Motivation, emotional expression, and sustained attention are all relevant to assessment outcomes. As noted by Chaytor and Schmitter-Edgecombe (2003), fluctuations in mentation are not uncommon in psychiatric illnesses and may impede performance consistency over the course of a multi-hour assessment. To compensate for this, the authors suggest assessment may be best completed over more than one session

Motivation

The practicing neuropsychologist must always be mindful of potential confounds to assessment results. Exaggeration and malingering have been well discussed in the literature when it comes to forensic proceedings. These same issues can arise within the psychiatric setting, particularly when there is a forensic component to the assessment. An in-depth review of forensic neuropsychology within the psychiatric setting is beyond the scope this chapter. Rather, interested readers are encouraged to review some of the existing literature on this subject matter (e.g., Horton & Hartlage, 2010; Larrabee, 2011). We classify this under the general principle of motivation.

Because neuropsychological assessment is an interactive process, the results are dependent on the patient's motivation. The interpretation of neuropsychological functioning is predicated on the assumption that the patient has tried to cooperate. Although the patient's motivation is continuously monitored during the examination and reinforcement is provided, secondary gains may influence the patient's performance. Measures such as the Word Memory Test, Test of Memory Malingering, and even the validity scales of the MMPI are designed to predict purposeful aberrations in performance, providing some picture of the patient's response sets. At the same time, a deliberate effort to influence neuropsychological test results in any consistent manner is difficult for the patient. Malingering and factitious disorders can be detected with considerable accuracy. Even if there is not a forensic application to the assessment, patients within the psychiatric setting can have a tendency to exaggerate cognitive deficits as a means of demonstrating the degree of affliction they are experiencing related to their psychiatric presentation. Further, mental fluctuations related to their psychiatric state can manifest as poor outcomes on measures of effort and thus call assessment outcomes into question.

Emotion

Another issue within this setting is the impact of emotionality on test performance and, consequently, assessment outcomes. Neuropsychological examination requires the patient's cooperation and concentration. Emotional disturbance may be important to consider in measuring neuropsychological function. Most research here has examined the relationship between measures of emotional disturbance and the results of neuropsychological tests. In general, results seem to vary with the degree that schizophrenics are included in the sample. The most consistent finding has been the lack of a reliable relationship between neuropsychological test performance and independent measures of depression, anxiety, or general emotional disturbance when schizophrenics are excluded from consideration. Unlike other psychiatric groups, for schizophrenics the relationship between clinical measures of disturbance and neuropsychological test findings is significant. Although some inconsistencies exist among studies, this may be largely attributable to differences in diagnostic criteria.

With chronic schizophrenics, as opposed to those with paranoid illnesses, the degree of psychosis seems negatively related to normal neuropsychological functioning. Some evidence suggests that improvement in neuropsychological functioning in chronic schizophrenics is concomitant with improvement of their clinical status. The association between the level of emotional disturbance and neuropsychological impairment in chronic schizophrenics is more like that found in neurological patients.

In a series of studies with neurological patients, Dikeman and Reitan (1976) found evidence of a relationship between the degree of impairment on tests of neuropsychological functioning and measures of emotional dysfunction in patients with documented cortical lesions. This finding has been replicated in a number of different neurological disorders. It is not possible to assume from these data that such emotional disturbance causes neuropsychological impairment. In fact, some data suggest that the degrees of emotional disturbance and of neuropsychological impairment are both related to the amount and location of neurological damage.

Neurological Comorbidity

Epidemiological research carried out in neurological care settings suggests that the prevalence for a psychiatric disorder increases following neurological impairment and exceeds the prevalence found in the general population and primary care settings (Carson et al., 2000; Fink et al., 2003; Ghoge et al., 2003; Lyketsors & Olin, 2002; Schiffer, 1983). This is substantial because epidemiologic estimates of mental disorders in neurological treatment and clinical care settings suggest 42%–55% prevalence (Sartorius, Ustun, Lecrubier, & Wittchen, 1996 ; Carson, Ringbauer, MacKenzie, Warlow, & Sharpe, 2000; Fink Hansen, Sondergaard, & Frydenberg, 2003). This has been documented across numerous neurological conditions, including but not limited to Parkinson disease (Schuurman et al., 2002), traumatic brain injury (Jorge et al., 2004), cerebrovascular disease (Ghoge et al., 2003), and Alzheimer disease (Lyketsos & Olin, 2002). In some instances, psychiatric manifestations can even serve as the earliest markers of disease onset (e.g., Alzheimer disease). Although attention is most commonly given to the primary neurological condition, research has demonstrated that the presence of comorbid psychiatric features negatively impacts neuropsychological functioning (Carson et al., 2000; Ramasubbu & Patten, 2003). Consequently, when psychiatric symptoms are observed, the neuropsychologist must consider and rule out the presence of additional neurological sequelae. Further, even when a neurological disorder is identified, it is important to consider the presence and relative contribution of comorbid psychiatric features.

Substance Use and Abuse

The rate of substance use and abuse is high within the psychiatric population compared to the general population (Mueser et al., 1990). Within the context of neuropsychological assessment, this poses a potential confound when it comes to interpretation. Alcohol and illicit substances may all demonstrate a negative effect acutely on neurocognitive functioning. However, literature regarding the long-term effects has shown mixed results. Whereas some studies have demonstrated a negative effect on neurocognition in association with a history of illicit drugs (Serper, Copersino, Richarme, Vahan, & Cancro, 2000) and alcohol (Allen et al., 2000) in psychiatric patients (mainly schizophrenia patients), others have failed to find a negative impact of illicit drugs (Pencer & Addington, 2003) or alcohol (Nixon, Hallford, & Tivis, 1996). In many respects, the effects, whether acute or long-term, are dependent upon type, amount, and duration of use. Given the rate of use within the psychiatric population, a thorough substance use history, including type of substance(s) used, duration of use, amount used, and time since last use, must be established and taken into consideration.

Psychotropic Medications

Although modern-day psychotropic agents have a lower risk profile compared to older agents, most still carry potential implications for neurocognitive functioning. A detailed review of the various drug classes used across the different psychiatric disorders is beyond this chapter. However, clinicians working within this population should educate themselves about the potential neurocognitive effects of these agents themselves. Those most commonly associated with neurocognitive deficits include benzodiazepines, anticonvulsants, and antipsychotics, although there is an emerging literature even related to negative effects of the selective serotonin reuptake inhibitors (SSRI) and SNRIs as well.

INTERPRETATION AND INTERVENTION FOLLOWING NEUROPSYCHOLOGICAL ASSESSMENT

Neuropsychological practice within the psychiatric setting must go beyond descriptions and formulations of phenomenology. The relative importance of neuropsychology within this clinical setting is seen when the data obtained through assessment are used to develop appropriate cognitive remediation strategies. When done, the combination of neuropsychological assessment and functional intervention is among the most impactful services. This is particularly true given that functional outcomes, level of disability, and quality of life have all been linked more so with cognitive impairment in psychiatric disorders than with psychiatric symptomology itself (Allott et al., 2011b; Fett et al., 2011; Wingo et al., 2009). Nevertheless, neuropsychological assessment and treatment remain uncommon within the psychiatric setting and have been recognized as unmet needs in psychiatric rehabilitation settings.

The intervention process starts with interpretation of the assessment results, as is the case with any neuropsychological evaluation. This should include not only a discussion of cognitive strengths and weaknesses but also the functional implications of any impairments and recommendations to circumvent those difficulties to maximize functioning (Marcopulos et al., 2008). As previously noted, interpretation cannot only focus on the quantitative results but must also take into account the qualitative input and output. This is best done through behavioral observation throughout the course of the assessment. This can help explain variations in specific tests in the case of environmental distracters as well as offer qualitative judgment of the individual's capacity for sustained effort.

Recent research has evaluated the utility and effectiveness of neuropsychological interventions to either rehabilitate or compensate for the cognitive deficits associated with various psychiatric illnesses (Twamley, Savla, Zurhellen, Heaton, & Jeste, 2008). Preliminary findings suggest that these cognitive-behavioral strategies are more effective than medicinal interventions (Crespo-Facorro et al., 2009; Woodward, Purdon, Meltzer, & Zald, 2005) and have been used across depression (Naismith, Redoblado-Hodge, Lewis, Scott, & Hickie, 2010), anxiety disorders (Buhlmann et al., 2006), bipolar disorders (Tufrey & Coulston, 2010), and psychotic disorders (Medalia & Freilich, 2008; Wexler & Bell, 2005). Timing can be critical and strategies may need to be changed from an intervention standpoint as cognitive alterations are potentially seen. For example, Addington (2007) noted that interventions have the greatest long-term impact when initiated in the first several years after onset of schizophrenia, which is when the greatest functional deterioration occurs. Table 21.2 includes some of the empirically based interventions and programs to aid in the rehabilitation and compensation for neurocognitive deficits arising from psychiatric manifestations.

Cognitive remediation may serve as a specialized extension of more practical interventions. An array of general tips for neurocognitive improvement can be found within multiple sources. Figure 21.2 outlines the different domains and skills for practical intervention with general tips that pertain to each.

These recommendations are in addition to other psychosocial interventions ranging from somatic treatments, psychotherapeutic offerings, and environmental modifications. Regarding the latter, while keeping in mind outcomes from neuropsychological assessment, counseling regarding employment placement and educational pursuits can and should be offered. This can aid in reducing limitations in everyday functioning, which can improve quality of life.

TABLE 21.2 Cognitive Remediation Programs

Program	Reference
Cognitive adaptive training	Velligan , Prihoda, Ritch, Maples, Bow-Thomas, & Dassori (2002)
Cognitive enhancement therapy	Hogarty & Fleshner (1999)
Cognitive remediation therapy	Wykes et al. (2007)
Integrated psychological therapy	Brenner et al. 1994
Neurocognitive enhancement therapy	Bell, Bryson, Greig, Corcoran, & Wexler (2001)
Neuropsychological educational approach to rehabilitation	Medalia & Revheim (1999)
PositScience	Fisher, Holland, Subramaniam, & Vinogradov (2010)

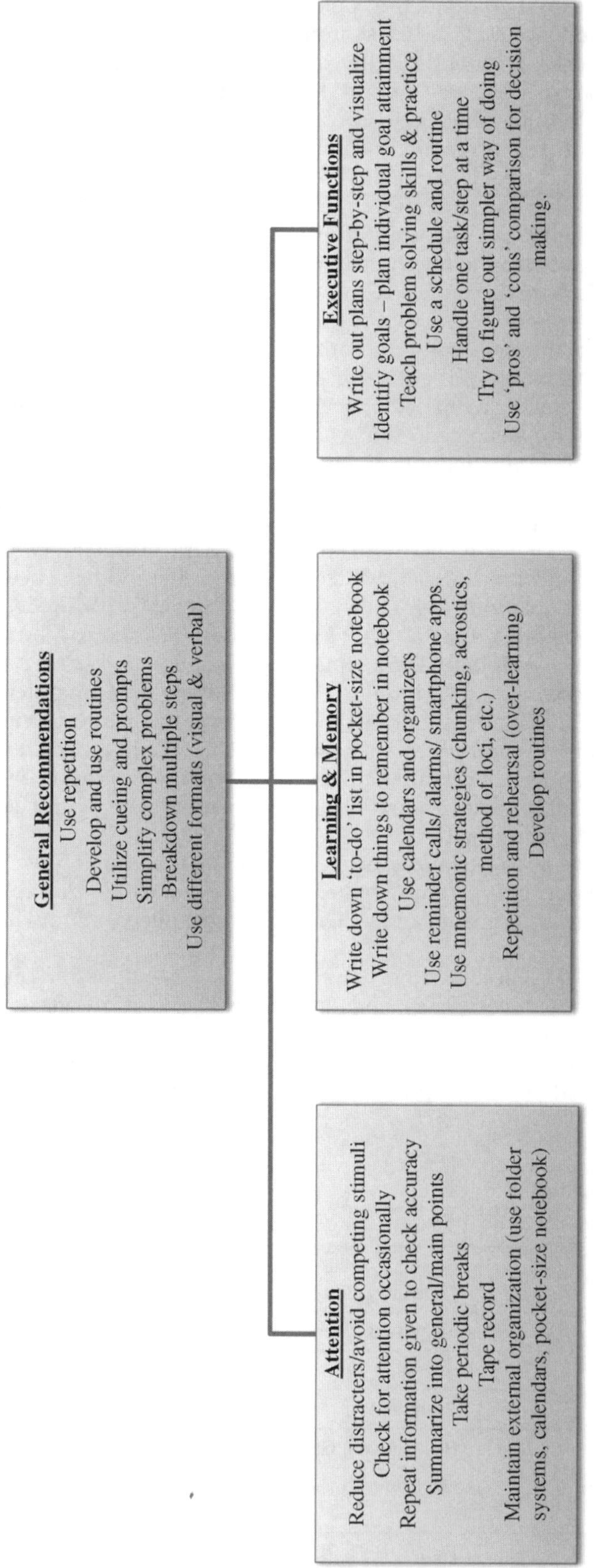

FIGURE 21.2 General recommendations for neuropsychological difficulties.

SUMMARY

As our conceptualization of psychiatric illnesses has changed, so too has the role of neuropsychology within this setting. Research has clearly demonstrated that across the majority of psychiatric disorders and presentations, neurocognitive deficits are often seen. Further, these neurocognitive deficits, not psychiatric symptoms, are better predictors of long-term outcomes and quality of life. Graduated from the outdated concept of functional versus organic dysfunction, neuropsychology finds itself as a clinical practice and science with the capacity not only to identify these deficits when they occur through neuropsychological assessment, but also to develop strategies for rehabilitation or compensation to reduce burden on everyday functioning.

REFERENCES

Addington, J. (2007). The promise of early intervention. *Early Intervention in Psychiatry, 1,* 294–307.

Alarcon, R. D., Libb, J. W., & Boll, T. J. (1994). Neuropsychological testing in obsessive-compulsive disorder: A clinical review. *Journal of Neuropsychiatry and Clinical Neurosciences, 6,* 217–228.

Allen, D. N., Goldstein, G., Forman, S. D., Keshavan, M. S., van Kammen, D. P., & Sanders, R. D. (2000). Neurologic examination abnormalities in schizophrenia with and without a history of alcoholism. *Neuropsychiatry, Neuropsychology and Behavioral Neurology, 13,* 184–187.

Allott, K., Brewer, W., McGorry, P. D., & Proffitt, T.-M. (2011a). Referrers' perceived utility and outcomes of clinical neuropsychological assessment in an adolescent and young adult public mental health service. *Australian Psychologist, 46,* 15–24.

Allott, K., Liu, P., Proffitt, T.-M., & Killackey, E. (2011b). Cognition at illness onset as a predictor of later functional outcome in early psychosis: Systematic review and methodological critique. *Schizophrenia Research, 125,* 221–235.

Bell, M., Bryson, G., Greig, T., Corcoran, C., & Wexler, B. E. (2001). Neurocognitive enhancement therapy with work therapy effects on neuropsychological test performance. *Archives of General Psychiatry, 58,* 763–768.

Brenner, H. D., Roder, V., Hodel, B., & Kienzle, N. (1994). *Integrated psychological therapy for schizophrenic patients* (IPT). Seattle, WA: Hogrefe & Huber.

Buhlmann, U., Deckersbach, T., Englehard, I., Cook, L. M., Rauch, S. L., Kathmann, N., et al. (2006). Cognitive retraining for organizational impairment in obsessive-compulsive disorder. *Psychiatry Research, 144,* 109–116.

Carson, A. J., Ringbauer, B., MacKenzie, L., Warlow, C., & Sharpe, M. (2000). Neurological disease, emotional disorder, and disability: They are related: A study of 300 consecutive new referrals to a neurology outpatient department. *Journal of Neurology, Neurosurgery, and Psychiatry, 68*(2), 202–205.

Chaytor, N., & Schmitter-Edgecombe, M. (2003). The ecological validity of neuropsychological tests: A review of the literature on everyday cognitive skills. *Neuropsychology Review, 13,* 181–197.

Chui, H. T., Christensen, B. K., Zipursky, R. B., Richards, B. A., Hanratty, M. K., Kabani, N. J., et al. (2008). Cognitive function and brain structure in females with a history of adolescent-onset anorexia nervosa. *Pediatrics, 122,* E426–E427.

Crespo-Facorro, B., Rodriguez-Sanchez, J. M., Perez-Iglesias, R., Mata, I., Ayesa, R., Ramirez-Bonilla, M., et al. (2009). Neurocognitive effectiveness of haloperidol, risperidone, and olanzapine in first-episode psychosis: A randomized, controlled 1-year follow-up comparison. *Journal of Clinical Psychiatry, 70,* 717–729.

Dean, R. S. (1985). Perspectives on the future of neuropsychological assessment. In B. S. Plake & J. C. Witt (Eds.), *Buros-Nebraska series on measurement and testing.* (pp. 203–244). Hillsdale, NJ: Lawrence Erlbaum.

Dean, R. S. (1986). Neuropsychological aspects of psychiatric disorders. *Child Neuropsychology, 2,* 83–112.

Dean, R. S. (1987). Psychometric principles of individual measures of intelligence. In R. S. Dean (Ed.), *Assessing human intelligence.* (pp. 269–288). Springfield, IL: C. C. Thomas.

Dikeman, S. & Reitan, R.M. (1976). Psychological deficits and recovery of functions after head injury. *Transactions of the American Neurological Association, 101,* (72–77).

Fett, A.-K. J., Viechtbauer, W., Dominguez, M.-D.-G., Penn, D. L., Van Os, J., & Krabbendam, L. (2011). The relationship between neurocognition and social cognition with functional outcomes in schizophrenia: A meta-analysis. *Neuroscience and Biobehavioral Reviews, 35*(3), 573–588.

Fink, P., Hansen, M. S., Sondergaard, L., & Frydenberg, M. (2003). Mental illness in new neurological patients. *Journal of Neurology, Neurosurgery, and Psychiatry, 74*(6), 817–821.

Fisher, M., Holland, C., Subramaniam, K., & Vinogradov, S. (2010). Neuroplasticity-based cognitive training in schizophrenia: An interim report on the effects 6 months later. *Schizophrenia Bulletin, 36*(4), 869–879.

Ghoge, H., Sharma, S., Sonawalla, S., & Parikh, R. (2003). Cerebrovascular disease and depression. *Current Psychiatry Reports, 5*, 231–238.

Hogarty, G. E., & Flesher, S. (1999). Practice principles of cognitive enhancement therapy of schizophreniа*Schizophrenia Bulletin, 25*(4), 693–708.

Horton, A. M. Jr., & Hartlage, L. (2010). *Handbook of forensic neuropsychology* (2nd ed.). New York: Springer.

Jorge, R. E., Robinson, R.G. Moser, D., Tateno, A., Crespo-Facorro, B., & Arndt, S. (2004). Major depression following traumatic brain injury. *Archives of General Psychiatry, 61*, 42–50.

Kandel, E. (1998). A new intellectual framework for psychiatry. *American Journal of Psychiatry, 155*, 457–469.

Keefe, R. S. E. (1995). The contribution of neuropsychology to psychiatry. *American Journal of Psychiatry, 152*, 6–15.

Kessler, R. C., & Wang, P.S. (2008). The descriptive epidemiology of commonly occurring mental disorders in the United States. *Annual Review of Public Health, 29*, 115–29.

Larrabee, G. (2011). *Forensic neuropsychology: A scientific approach*. Boston: Oxford University Press.

Leonberger, F.T. (1989). The question of organicity: Is it still functional? *Professional Psychology: Research and Practice, 20*, 411–414.

Lyketsos, C. G., & Olin, J. (2002). Depression in Alzheimer's disease: Overview and treatment. *Biological Psychiatry, 52*, 243–252.

Marcopulos, B. A., Fujii, D., O'Grady, J., Shaver, G., Manley, J., & Aucone, E. (2008). *Providing neuropsychological services for persons with schizophrenia: A review of the literature and prescription for practice. In J. E. Morgan & J. H. Rickers (Eds.), Textbook of clinical neuropsychology* (pp. 743–761). New York, NY: Taylor & Francis.

Martinez-Aran, A., Vieta, E., Reinares, M., Colom, F., Torrent, C., Sanchez-Moreno, J., et al. (2004). Cognitive function across manic or hypomanic, depressed, and euthymic states in bipolar disorder. *American Journal of Psychiatry, 161*, 262–270.

Medalia, A., Dorn, H., & Watras-Gans, S. (2000). Treating problem-solving deficits on an acute psychiatric inpatient unit. *Psychiatry Research, 97*, 79–88.

Medalia, A., & Freilich, B. (2008). The Neuropsychological Educational Approach to Cognitive Remediation (NEAR) model: Practice principles and outcome studies. *American Journal of Psychiatric Rehabilitation, 11*, 123–143.

Medalia, A., & Revheim, N. (1999). Computer assisted learning in psychiatric rehabilitation. *Psychiatric Rehabilitation Skills, 3*(1), 77–98.

Medalia, A., Revheim, N., & Casey, M. (2000). Remediation of memory disorders in schizophrenia. *Psychological Medicine, 30*, 1451–1459.

Medalia, A., Revheim, N., & Casey, M. (2001). The remediation of problem-solving skills in schizophrenia. *Schizophrenia Bulletin, 27*(2), 259–267.

Mesholam-Gately, R., Giuliano, A. J., Faraone, S. V., Goff, K. P., & Seidman, L. J. (2009). Neurocognition in first-episode schizophrenia: A meta-analytic review. *Neuropsychology, 23*, 315–336.

Mueser, K. T., Yarnold, P. R., Levinson, D. F., Singh, H., Bellack, A. S., Kee, K., et al. (1990). Prevalence of substance abuse in schizophrenia: Demographic and clinical correlates. *Schizophrenia Bulletin, 16*(1), 31–56.

Naismith, S. L., Redoblado-Hodge, M. A., Lewis, S. J. G., Scott, E. M., & Hickie, I. B. (2010). Cognitive training in affective disorders improves memory: A preliminary study using the NEAR approach. *Journal of Affective Disorders, 121*, 258–262.

Nixon, S. J., Hallford, H. G., & Tivis, R. D. (1996). Neurocognitive function in alcoholic, schizophrenic, and dually diagnosed patients. *Psychiatry Research, 64*, 35–45.

Pantelis, C., Yucel, M., Wood, S. J., McGorry, P. D., & Velakoulis, D. (2003). Early and late neurodevelopmental disturbances in schizophrenia and their functional consequences. *Australian and New Zealand Journal of Psychiatry, 37*, 399–406.

Pencer, A., & Addington, J. (2003). Substance use and cognition in early psychosis. *Journal of Psychiatry and Neuroscience, 28*, 48–54.

Prigatano, G. P., & Parsons, O. A. (1976). Relationship of age and education to Halstead Test performance in different patient populations. *Journal of Consulting and Clinical Psychology, 44*(4), 527–533.

Proffitt, T.-M., Allott, K. A., McGorry, P. D., & Brewer, W. J. (2009). The Orygen Clinical Neuropsychology Unit: Identifying and managing cognitive dysfunction in youth experiencing early psychosis [Abstract]. *Schizophrenia Bulletin, 35*(Suppl. 1), 299.

Proffitt, T.-M., Brewer, W. J. & McGorry, P. D. (2006). A neuropsychological approach to case formulation and treatment planning in early psychosis: Integrating the "cognitive" into bio-psycho-social models of mental health and mental illness in adolescence [Abstract]. *Acta Psychiatrica Scandinavica, 114*(Suppl. 431), s40.

Ramasubbu, R., & Patten, S. B. (2003). Effect of depression on stroke morbidity and mortality. *Canadian Journal of Psychiatry, 48*(4), 250–257

Ready, R. E., Stierman, L., & Paulsen, J. S. (2001). Ecological validity of neuropsychological and personality measures of executive functions. *Clinical Neuropsychologist, 15*, 314–323.

Reed, H. B. C., & Reitan, R. M. (1963). Changes in psychological test performance associated with the normal aging process. *Journal of Gerontology, 18*, 271–274.

Sartorius, N., Ustun, T. B., Lecrubier, Y., & Wittchen, H. U. (1996). Depression comorbid with anxiety: Results from the WHO study on psychological disorders in primary health care. *British Journal of Psychiatry, 30*, 38–43.

Schiffer, R. B. (1983). Psychiatric aspects of clinical neurology. *American Journal of Psychiatry, 140*, 205–207.

Schuurman, A. G., van den Akker, M., Ensinck, K. T., Metsemakers, J. K., Knottnerus, J. A., Leentjens, A. F., et al. (2002). Increased risk of Parkinson's disease after depression: A retrospective cohort study. *Neurology, 58*, 1501–1504.

Serper, M. R., Copersino, M. L., Richarme, D., Vahan, N., & Cancro, R. (2000). Neurocognitive functioning in recently abstinent, cocaine-abusing schizophrenic patients. *Journal of Substance Abuse, 11*(2), 205–213.

Testa, R., & Pantelis, C. (2009). The role of executive functions in psychiatric disorders. In S.J. Wood, N.B. Allen, & C. Pantelis (Eds.), *The Neuropsychology of Mental Illness* (pp. 117–137). Cambridge, UK: Cambridge University Press.

Torres, I. J., Boudreau, V. G., & Yatham, L. N. (2007). Neuropsychological functioning in euthymic bipolar disorder: A meta-analysis. *Acta Psychiatrica Scandinavica, 116*(Suppl. 434), 17–26.

Tufrey, K., & Coulston, C. (2010). Cognitive remediation for bipolar disorder: Adapting from models used in schizophrenia and acquired brain injury. *Acta Neuropsychiatrica, 22*, 311–313.

Twamley, E. W., Savla, G. N., Zurhellen, C. H., Heaton, R. K., & Jeste, D. V. (2008). Development and pilot testing of a novel compensatory cognitive training intervention for people with psychosis. *American Journal of Psychiatric Rehabilitation, 11*, 144–163.

Velligan, D. I., Prihoda, T. J., Ritch, J. L., Maples, N., Bow-Thomas, C. C., & Dassori, A. (2002). A randomized single-blind pilot study of compensatory strategies in schizophrenia outpatients. *Schizophrenia Bulletin, 28*(2), 283–292.

Walterfang, M., Wood, S. J., Velakoulis, D., & Pantelis, C. (2006). Neuropathological, neurogenetic and neuroimaging evidence for white matter pathology in schizophrenia. *Neuroscience and Biobehavioral Reviews, 30*, 918–948.

Wexler, B. E., & Bell, M. D. (2005). Cognitive remediation and vocational rehabilitation for schizophrenia. *Schizophrenia Bulletin, 31*, 931–941.

Wingo, A. P., Harvey, P. D., & Baldessarini, R. J. (2009). Neurocognitive impairment in bipolar disorder patients: Functional implications. *Bipolar Disorders, 11*, 113–135.

Wood, S. J., Allen, N. B., & Pantelis, C. (Eds.). (2009). *The neuropsychology of mental illness*. Cambridge, UK: Cambridge University Press.

Wood, S. J., Pantelis, C., Yung, A. R., Velakoulis, D., & McGorry, P. D. (2009). Brain changes during the onset of schizophrenia: Implications for neurodevelopmental theories. *Medical Journal of Australia, 190*, S10–S13.

Woods, S. P., Delis, D. C., Scott, J. C., Kramer, J. H., & Holdnack, J. A. (2006). The California Verbal Learning Test–second edition: Test-retest reliability, practice effects, and reliable change indices for the standard and alternate forms. *Archives of Clinical Neuropsychology, 21*, 413–420.

Woodward, N. D., Purdon, S. E., Meltzer, H. Y., & Zald, D. H. (2005). A meta-analysis of neuropsychological change to clozapine, olanzapine, quetiapine, and risperidone in schizophrenia. *International Journal of Neuropsychopharmacology, 8*, 457–472.

Woodward, N. D., Purdon, S. E., Meltzer, H. Y., & Zald, D. H. (2007). A meta-analysis of cognitive change with haloperidol in clinical trials of atypical antipsychotics: Dose effects and comparison to practice effects. *Schizophrenia Research, 89*, 211–224.

Wykes, T., Newton, E., Landau, S., Rice, C., Thompson, N., & Frangou, S. (2007). Cognitive remediation therapy (CRT) for young early onset patients with schizophrenia: An exploratory randomized controlled trial. *Schizophrenia Research, 94*(1), 221–230.

Wykes, T., Reeder, C., Corner, J., Williams, C., & Everitt, B. (1999). The effects of neurocognitive remediation on executive processing in patients with schizophrenia. *Schizophrenia Bulletin, 25(2):291–307*.

Yucel, M., Lubman, D. I., Solowij, N., & Brewer, W. J. (2009). Neurobiological and neuropsychological pathways into substance abuse and addictive behavior. In S. J. Wood, N. B. Allen, & S. Pantelis (Eds.), *The neuropsychology of mental illness* (pp. 326–341). Cambridge, UK: Cambridge University Press.

CHAPTER 22

Psychological Assessment: From Interviewing to Objective and Projective Measurement

Mauricio A. Garcia-Barrera, Esther Direnfeld, Jeff Frazer, & William R. Moore

INTRODUCTION

Best practice guidelines in psychological assessment include client evaluation models that are staged within a multi-step, multi-method, and multidimensional process (Baron, 2003; Garcia-Barrera & Kamphaus, 2006; Kamphaus & Reynolds, 2003; Lezak, Howieson, & Loring, 2004; McConaughy, 2005; Sattler, 2008). A multi-step assessment process involves a series of components often organized a priori to facilitate hypothesis generation and testing. Each component serves as a pillar for the next, and there is a sense of strategic sequencing; however, both structure and flexibility play equally important roles. Although there is not a fixed model for psychological assessment, understanding each one of these steps will certainly help the clinician to organize an assessment plan that would serve as an instrument to better understand the client, with the ultimate goal of making informed decisions about his or her current status and service needs. A clinical psychological assessment should facilitate generating a series of recommendations that provides the client, caregivers and families, and other professionals with tools to initiate both short-term and long-term intervention programs. Due to the potential implications of psychological assessment, state and provincial psychology boards in North America regulate this activity. This chapter summarizes best practice guidelines in psychological assessment, from the intake interview to testing using both objective and subjective measures.

INTAKE INTERVIEW

A clinical evaluation process starts with a referral followed by a formal intake, which may have the format of an interview. As is the case for any type of interview, the main goal is to obtain as much information as possible about the referral to elucidate if the assessment question is appropriate for the clinician's area of expertise, and if the evaluation itself is an appropriate process for the client. Furthermore, the intake interview is an opportunity for the client and caregivers to better understand the characteristics of a psychological assessment process; the nature of the questionnaires, rating scales, and tests that might be administered; the potential goals and limits of the evaluation; the type of assessment that best fits the needs of the client; and the role that each participant may play in the process. An ideal intake interview takes place during a visit to the clinician's office or any other appropriate setting, facilitating a personal one-to-one interaction toward early establishment of rapport; however, in some cases a phone interview can serve this purpose. When possible, both clinician and referral source should interact to create a common vocabulary, which ultimately facilitates understanding the client's needs (Sattler, 2008). If the evaluation is deemed appropriate, a written and signed consent from the parties involved formally initiates the assessment process. The written consent is a contract demonstrating this agreement. If parties do not agree to the assessment conditions, a brief report and recommendations to the referral source may follow. Often, the clinician may be interested in accessing previous records to better understand the case, as the assessment data provide only cross-sectional information. Discussion about the most efficient way to obtain these records should be included during the intake, followed by written consent in release forms.

REVIEW OF RECORDS

Significant variability in accessibility to clinical records is often observed in assessment practice. In most cases, records are obtained upon client's authorization and upon requesting them directly from the original sources. In any psychological assessment, records provide us with a documented, multi-setting, and hopefully multidimensional registry of variables that must be taken into account during the assessment process. This information can serve as a guideline during the clinical interview process and for the design of the assessment itself. Desirable records vary depending upon the case and referral questions, but often include previous psychological and psychiatric records, with a particular emphasis on any previous assessment and diagnostic reports. In neuropsychological assessment, other medical records may be of benefit (e.g., hospitalization records, neuroradiology and neurosurgery notes); in pediatric assessment, school records may become relevant to hypotheses generation; finally, in forensic assessment, access to legal records is often deemed appropriate.

Reviewing records can be approached using either an exploratory or a guided approach. An *exploratory* approach includes a thorough review of all the materials collected, without preconceived ideas about the kind of information the clinician is looking for; it is exploratory in nature, facilitating an unbiased comprehension of a case when there is not a clear guiding question. In contrast, a *guided* approach is confirmatory in nature; it includes a search for a specific behavioral pattern to facilitate hypotheses testing. This kind of approach may be strategic when there is a specific referral question at hand, often in terms of a particular psychopathology.

THE CLINICAL INTERVIEW

The clinical interview is perhaps the most important milestone in the assessment process (Groth-Marnat, 2009; McConaughy, 2005; Strauss, Sherman, & Spreen, 2006), and has been classified as a core pillar of any type of psychological assessment (Sattler, 2008). Consequently, clinical interviewing has been reported as the most often used assessment procedure among clinical psychologists (83% out of 412 surveyed) and across settings (ranked 1 to 4 among 37 options; Watkins, Campbell, Nieberding, & Hallmark, 1995). It has been also ranked as the number 1 social-emotional assessment procedure among child and adolescent psychologists in the United States (Cashel, 2002). Moreover, training internship facilities have often included assessment interviews as a regular topic in their didactic seminars (Elbert & Holden, 1987).

Merrell (2008) emphasized the unique opportunity that the clinical interview offers to establish rapport while having a face-to-face interpersonal communication with the client, as well as the benefits of its flexible and often unstructured format as opposed to the strict structure often required in formal testing. To adequately perform the role of interviewer, professional training and experience are of most relevance; a common observation when supervising novices is the impact of clinical interviewing skills in facilitating the assessment process. Reliability of the information provided by the client is directly associated with the quality of the interviewer because a clinician's verbal and nonverbal communication during the interview process can lead the clients to somewhat distort their valuable information because they may detect the clinician's biases, judgments, and cultural differences. However, data collected during a clinical interview can be at times unreliable and vulnerable to distortion despite the clinician's best efforts (McConaughy, 2005). Interviewing other potential informants and using structured background questionnaires often compensates for these limitations. Finally, because it serves to establish rapport and trust, clinical interviews facilitate the bridge between assessment and intervention (Merrell, 2008).

Background Questionnaires

Questionnaires are often used to gather specific information regarding the client's developmental, medical, work, and academic history. Questions regarding the client's current functioning at different settings are often part of these questionnaires. Most published background questionnaires are highly structured, although it is often the case that clinicians develop their own structured or semistructured questionnaires according to the needs at their clinical practice or settings. It is recommended that questionnaires are not used to replace the clinical interview; rather, their administration prior to the in-person interview can facilitate its planning (Strauss et al., 2006). There are several published examples of detailed semistructured background questionnaires for both children (Baron, 2003, pp. 61–65) and adults (Strauss et al., 2006, pp. 68–74). Among some commercialized forms, the Behavior Assessment System for Children–Second Edition (BASC-2) (Reynolds & Kamphaus, 2004) includes a pediatric structured developmental history (SDH), which provides a detailed review of medical, developmental, academic, social, psychological, and familiar history of the client.

Unstructured Interviews

The highly flexible format of unstructured interviews allows the clinician to communicate with the client using open-ended questions in a conversational style. The lack of structure requires a skilled clinician to keep control over the communication flow by moderating shifts in the direction of the interview, signaling and changing the flow at times, and deciding what could be considered a satisfying response or not. Some psychologists may consider this format too intrusive and would leave the clients free to express themselves without cues or guidance. A skillful clinician may be able to let the client take full control of the interview while making observations and taking notes not only about the information being provided but also about his or her communication style, emotionality, nonverbal signals, and overall behavior (Greenspan & Greenspan, 2003).

Facilitation of rapport and client trust in the process is one of the main strengths of unstructured interview methods; however, limited reliability of the information obtained is a significant issue (Kamphaus & Frick, 2002), potentially worsened by sources of bias such as the clinician's own beliefs, hypotheses, and inferences about the case, and even his or her theoretical orientation (Houts, 1984). Adding guidelines and strategies to interviews generally improves their reliability and validity indexes (Groth-Marnat, 2009). However, if the format was designed to be unstructured, strategy use increases interrater reliability at the cost of decreasing intra-rater reliability (Dougherty, Ebert, & Callender, 1986).

Semistructured Interviews

Often referred to as the most traditional interview method, semistructured interview formats are flexible and yet contained within a framed set of questions. There are relatively few valid and reliable semistructured interviews available for clinical assessment. An example of one such instrument is the Semistructured Clinical Interview for Children and Adolescents (SCICA; McConaughy & Achenbach, 1994), designed for use with children and adolescents aged 6 to 18, which is a component of the Achenbach System of Empirically Based Assessment (ASEBA; Achenbach, 1986, 2001; Achenbach & Rescorla, 2000, 2001; McConaughy & Achenbach, 2001). The SCICA comprises two sections: the first includes a semistructured interview using open-ended questions from a list of six areas (activities and interests, school and homework, friendship and relations, home situation and family relations, self-awareness and feelings, and adolescent issues); the second section includes a child's self-report form (125 items) and an interviewer observations form (120 items) to rate the child's behavior during the interview using a 4-point Likert scale. These ratings yield profile information on five behavioral scales: Anxious, Withdrawn/Depressed, Language/Motor Problems, Attention Problems, and Self-Control Problems. Three more scales are derived from the child's self-report: Anxious/Depressed, Aggressive/Rule-Breaking, and Somatic Complaints (McConaughy, 2005).

Other examples of broad-band semistructured interview instruments include the Child and Adolescent Psychiatric Assessment (CAPA; Angold & Costello, 2000), the Preschool Age Psychiatric Assessment (PAPA; Egger & Angold, 2004), the Interview Schedule for Children and Adolescents (ISCA; Sherrill & Kovacs, 2000), and the Pictorial Instrument for Children and Adolescents (PICA-III-R; Ernst, Cookus, & Moravec, 2000). Examples of narrow-band semistructured interviews include the Anxiety Diagnostic Interview for *DSM-IV*–Child and Parent versions (ADIS-C/P; Silverman & Albano, 1996) and the Schedule for Affective Disorders and Schizophrenia for School-Aged Children (K-SADS; Ambrosini, 2000).

Structured Interviews

Structured interviews have become quite popular given their psychometric strength (Kamphaus & Frick, 2002), yet they often become outdated because they rely on the *Diagnostic and Statistical Manual of Mental Disorders* (*DSM*) diagnostic criteria (Verhulst, 1995). A clinically useful and comprehensive structured interview that can be used to diagnose a wide range of mental health disorders according to the definitions and criteria of ICD-10 and *DSM-IV-TR* is the World Health Organization (WHO) Composite International Diagnostic Interview (CIDI; WHO, 1990). The CIDI is currently in its second version (WHO, 1997) and has been adapted in a third version for the World Mental Health Surveys that includes both a pencil and paper version as well as a computer-assisted one (Kessler & Ustun, 2004). The CIDI has been used extensively in epidemiological research (Kessler & Ustun, 2004) and thus its psychometric properties have been verified. Wittchen (1994) found high interrater reliability and moderate test-retest reliability. Research of the validity, namely concurrent validity, of the CIDI has revealed moderate to low indices, depending on the version, language, and diagnoses (Rogers, 2001). The CIDI has been translated into Spanish (Quintana, Gastal, Jorge, Miranda, & Andreoli, 2007), Persian (Amini et al., 2006), Turkish, and Dutch (Schrier et al., 2012), to name a few. A major benefit of the utility of the CIDI is its applicability across many cultures and languages for assessing mental health disorders.

Two of the most used structured interview instruments in pediatric assessment are the Diagnostic Interview for Children and Adolescents, Fourth Edition (DICA-IV; Herjanic & Reich, 1997; Reich, 2000) and the Diagnostic Interview Schedule for Children, Fourth Edition (DISC-IV; Shaffer, Fisher, Lucas, Dulcan, & Schwab-Stone, 2000). The DICA-IV has been used in several studies, and subsequently, its psychometric properties have been examined extensively. Findings include moderate to high indices of interrater agreement (Ezpeleta et al., 1997), test-retest reliability (Boyle et al., 1993), parent-child agreement (Reich, Herjanic, Welner, & Gandhy, 1982), and sensitivity to differentiate clinical from nonclinical samples (Merrell, 2008). Although efforts have been made to evaluate the clinical validity of this instrument (Welner, Reich, Herjanic, Jung, & Amado, 1987), caution regarding the minimal level of validity evidence available for the DICA has also been raised (Hodges, 1993; Kamphaus & Frick, 2002; Merrell, 2008). The DISC-IV requires minimal training for its administration, making it an appealing instrument for epidemiological and screening research studies. Among its strengths, it is also noted that the DISC-IV is available in Spanish and English and that its psychometric properties (reliability and validity) are fairly strong (Kamphaus & Frick, 2002; Merrell, 2008; Shaffer et al., 2000).

HYPOTHESIS TESTING IN PSYCHOLOGICAL ASSESSMENT

The following section includes a discussion about the dominant multidimensional and multimethod approaches to psychological assessment, involving projective and objective techniques (see Figure 22.1 for a flow chart of the assessment process). A brief introduction to reliable, valid, and mainstream instruments commonly used in psychological assessment is also included. Table 22.1 includes a summary of a range of projective and objective instruments, their components, age range for administration, and languages available.

Using Projective and Objective Assessment Techniques

In the realm of psychological assessment, especially in relation to personality assessment, a historical distinction between objective and projective assessment methods has been made (Butcher, 2010). In general, objective tests are more frequently used across a variety of assessment domains. In personality assessment in particular, objective tests commonly include but are not limited to behavioral rating inventories and structured instruments. For example, objective personality tests ask clients to consider example adjectives, propositions, or questions and then indicate the extent to which these items are characteristic of a given subject's personality. Typically, responses are limited to a provided set of options. More generally, objective tests also include performance-based measures, comprising the majority of psychological and neuropsychological assessment batteries. Such tasks purportedly capture a multitude of cognitive processes (e.g., attention, memory, overall cognitive status, etc.). Importantly, these performance-based measures, in addition to behavior ratings and clinical interviews, are considered objective because the psychologist administering them is not required to rely heavily on clinical judgment to interpret the findings. The scope of response options in most objective instruments is typically limited or circumscribed (e.g., true vs. false, yes vs. no, Likert scale-like ratings, reaction times, percent correct), responses on objective measures are straightforward for the most part, and they can thus be interpreted according to a pre-specified scoring key. Therefore, the main feature is that little or no subjective interpretation is required.

On the other hand, projective tests require subjects to freely generate responses to less structured stimuli. As a result of the stimuli being more ambiguous than those used in objective tests, the range of possible responses tends to be more varied with projective tests (Lilienfeld, Wood, & Garb, 2000). Thus, these types of tasks typically require substantial clinical interpretation. According to Frank (1939), the term projective is applied to these types of tasks because clients project aspects of their own personalities while interpreting the ambiguous and unstructured stimuli. This hypothesis is based on the assumption that personality characteristics, needs, and life experiences converge to influence these interpretations, a concept known as apperception (Sundberg, 1977). Therefore, some authors suggest that projective techniques ". . . through their indirection and concealed intent, encourage respondents to reveal their unconscious feelings and attitudes without being aware that they are doing so" (Will, Eadie, & MacAskill, 1996, p. 38). As a consequence, the hypothesized advantage of these methods is that they "bypass conscious defenses" and therefore allow access to unconscious information (Lilienfeld et al., 2000; p. 29).

According to Lindzey's (1959) taxonomy, projective techniques can be divided into association techniques (e.g., Rorschach inkblot tests and word association tests), construction techniques (e.g., human figure drawings and story creation methods, such as the Thematic Apperception Test [TAT]), completion techniques (e.g., sentence completion), arrangement or selection techniques (e.g., the Szondi Test and the Luscher Color Test), and expression techniques (e.g., doll play, puppetry, and handwriting analysis). However, the apparent differences among these tasks have led some authors to argue that the all-encompassing "projective" label should be adapted to reflect the diversity between these types of tasks (Meyer & Kurtz, 2006). For example, they argue that "applying a global and undifferentiated term to such a diverse array of assessment tasks seems akin to physicians classifying medical tests as either 'visual tests' or 'nonvisual tests'" (Meyer & Kurtz, 2006; p. 224).

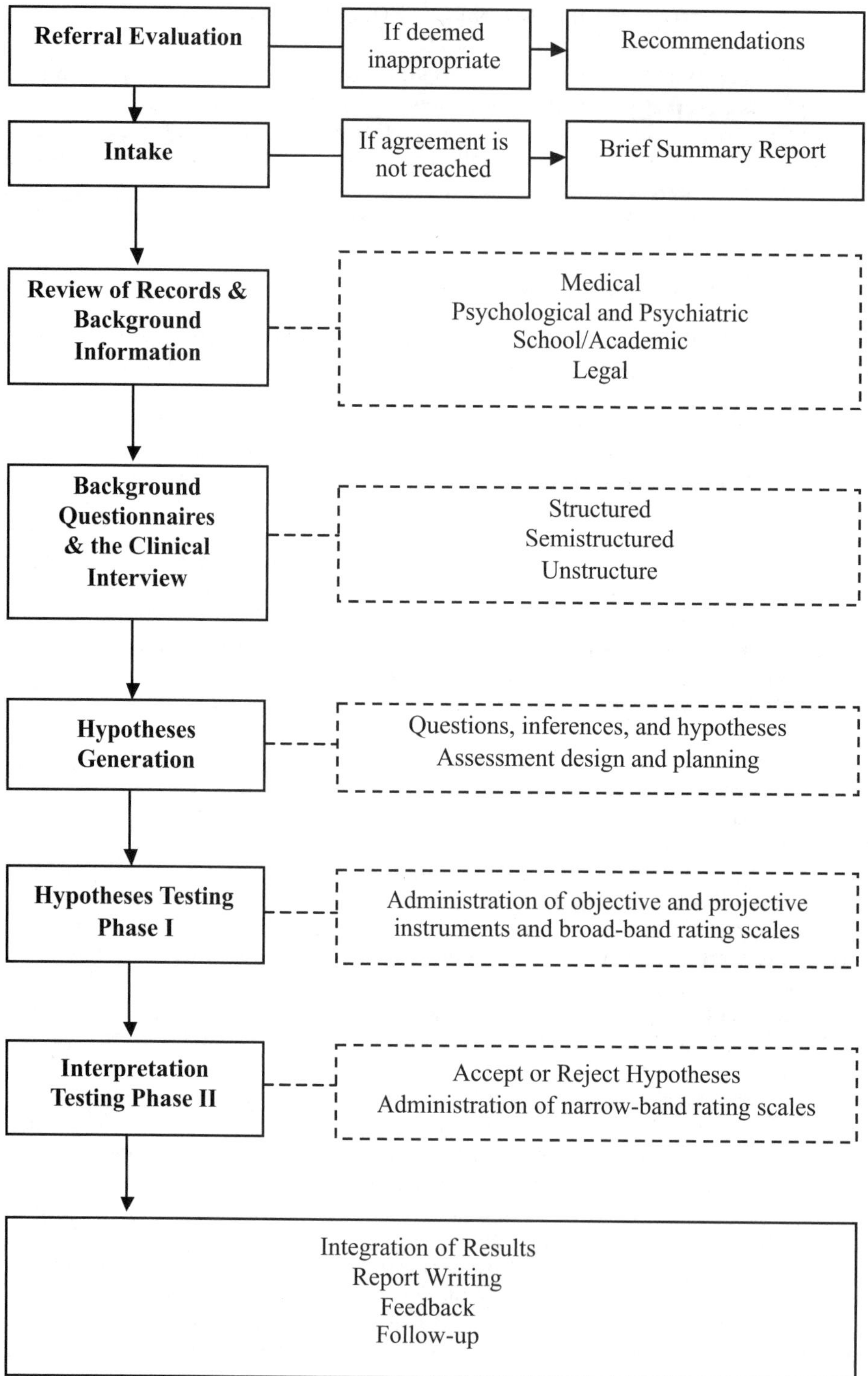

FIGURE 22.1 Flow chart of a multi-stage and multi-method psychological assessment.

TABLE 22.1 Summary Table for Empirically Supported Measures

Name/Authors	Description	Components	Age Range	Languages
Projective Measures				
The Rorschach Test (Rorschach, 1942)	Examinees are shown 10 cards with bilateral inkblots (black or colored), and asked to say what they see in a given card. Administration of both phases takes approximately 45 minutes.	Examiner-administered	18–65+	Cards do not have language printed on them
Thematic Apperception Test (Murray, 1943)	A variety of black-and-white pictures (approximately 8–12) are used to assess one's personality and thought processes. Takes approximately 40 minutes to complete.	Examiner-administered; a selection of pictures varies for adult males and females, and boys and girls	Children and adults. Extensions available for seniors.	Cards do not have languages printed on them; however, different cards are available for Chinese, African-American, and Hispanic populations
Robert's Apperception Test for Children (Roberts & Gruber, 2005)	A more structured projective test in which examinees are asked to narrate a story about what is occurring in 16 cards. Administration and scoring time is approximately 30–40 minutes.	Examiner-administered; different cards available for males and females, Caucasians, Hispanics, African-Americans, children, and teens	6–18	English
Objective Measures				
Behavioral Assessment System for Children – 2 (Reynolds & Kamphaus, 2004)	The questionnaire contains 134–185 items rated on a 4-point Likert scale ranging from 1 (never) to 4 (almost always). Completion time per questionnaire is approximately 10–30 minutes, depending on the form in use.	1. Structure developmental interview 2. Self-report questionnaire (ages 6–7, 8–11, 12–21) 3. Self-report of personality (ages 18–25, college age) 4. Parent report questionnaires (ages 2–5; 6–11; 12–21) 5. Teacher report questionnaires (ages 2–5, 6–11, 12–18) 6. Student observation system	2–25 (not all components are available for each age)	1. English 2. Spanish (United States) 3. Spanish (Spain) 4. Spanish (Colombia)

(continued)

TABLE 22.1 ***(Continued)*** **Summary Table for Empirically Suppoted Measures**

Name/Authors	Description	Components	Age Range	Languages
California Psychological Inventory – 3rd Edition (Gough & Bradley, 1996/ 2002)	A 434-item true/ false questionnaire derived partly from the MMPI, generating scores on 20 "folk concept" scales. Administration takes approximately 45 minutes.	Self-report regular form (CPI 434), short form (CPI 260)	Adolescents to adults	1. English 2. French 3. Italian 4. Japanese 5. Greek 6. Spanish
Conners' Comprehensive Behavior Rating Scale (Conners, 2008)	A useful screening tool to understand the child more comprehensively, and includes scales that screen for *DSM-IV-TR* disorders. Approximately 5–25 minutes.	Raters: 1. Parent rating scale (CBRS-P) 2 Teacher rating scale (CBRS-T) 3 Self-report scale (CBRS-SR) 4 Conners' clinical index (Conners' CI) 5 Conners' early childhood (Conners' EC) Teacher/ childcare provider (for ages 2–6 years; Conners, 2009).	Ages 6–18 (self-report available for ages 8–18 only)	1. English 2. Spanish 3. French
State-Trait Anxiety Inventory (Spielberger, 1983)	A 40-item questionnaire that differentiates between anxiety that an individual is experiencing at the moment of the interview (state anxiety) and how anxious an individual generally feels (trait anxiety). Administration takes approximately 10–20 minutes.	Self-report	High school age and adults	1. English 2. Spanish 3. Turkish 4. Japanese 5. Arabic

(continued)

TABLE 22.1 ***(Continued)*** **Summary Table for Empirically Suppoted Measures**

Name/Authors	Description	Components	Age Range	Languages
Achenbach System of Empirically Based Assessment (Achenbach & Rescorla, 2001)	A questionnaire in which individuals' activities, adaptive functioning, behavioral and emotional problems are assessed. Completion time is approximately 20 minutes.	1. Child behavior checklist 2. Teacher report forms (6–18) 3. Caregiver-teacher report form (daycare providers or preschool teachers for ages 1.5–5) 4. Youth self-report (11–18) 5. Young adult self-report (18–30) 6. Adult self-report (18–59) 7. Adult behavior checklist (18–59) 8. Older adult self-report (60–90+) 9. Older adult behavior checklist (60–90+) 10. Direct observation form (5–14) 11. Test observation form (2–18)	1.5–90+ years	1. English 2. Spanish (United States) 3. Chinese 4. Spanish (Chilean) 5. Hebrew 6. Arabic (Saudi Arabia) 7. Italian
Minnesota Multiphasic Personality Inventory (Butcher et al., 1989/2001)	A comprehensive questionnaire of personality in which examinees answer 567 true/false items.	Self-report.1 Full-form2 Short form	Adults; MMPI-A (3rd Ed.): ages 14–18	1. English 2. Chinese 3. Hebrew 4. Urdu (Pakistan) 5. Spanish (Chile) 6. Spanish (Mexico) 7. Japanese
Beck Depression Inventory-II (Beck et al., 1996)	A 21-item questionnaire assessing intensity and severity of depression and associated symptoms occurring within 2 weeks of the assessment. Administration is approximately 5–10 minutes.	Self-report	Adults (18+). This can be used with adolescents (e.g., 14–18 years old)	1 English 2 Spanish 3 Chinese 4 Italian

(continued)

TABLE 22.1 ***(Continued)*** **Summary Table for Empirically Suppoted Measures**

Name/Authors	Description	Components	Age Range	Languages
Beck Anxiety Inventory (Beck & Steer, 1990)	A 21-item questionnaire that measures the cognitive, somatic, and physiologic aspects of anxiety that examinees have experienced in the past week. Takes approximately 10 minutes to complete.	Self-report	Adults; however, can be used with adolescents.	1 English 2 Spanish 3 Chinese 4 Arabic 5 Turkish
Millon Clinical Multiaxial Inventory-III (Millon, Millon, Davis, & Grossman, 2006)	A 175-item true/false questionnaire, which examines one's personality and associated disorders. Completion is approximately 25–30 minutes	Self-report	Adults and adolescents	1. English 2. Spanish 3. French-Canadian 4. Italian

In addition, these authors suggest that the use of a categorical dichotomy, that is, projective versus objective, is misleading and carries unfavorable connotations. For instance, compared to projective methods, objective test methods tend to be associated with presumed advantages, including the assumption that they are more accurate. However, as Meyer and Kurtz (2006) suggest, these measurement techniques are not impervious to subjective biases; in fact, scoring errors can occur for objective and projective tests alike (Allard & Faust, 2000). Further, Meyer, and Kurtz (2006) aptly point out that even objective personality tests involve projection in the sense of the original term. Although interpretation of responses may be objective, it is nonetheless the responsibility of the test-taker to interpret the meaning of a given item and then make a relatively subjective evaluation of the extent to which it describes his or her own personality. In addition, test-takers must make a decision about how truthfully to respond. Therefore, subjective biases may be linked with both objective and projective test methods.

Regardless of definitional concerns, projective assessment methods have received considerable criticisms in the literature, which has led to significant controversy regarding their usage in clinical assessments. In fact, this debate has remained active for several decades (Knoff, 1983). Some of the limitations associated with projective measurements include the fact that they require extensive practice in terms of administration and interpretation, are quite time-consuming to administer even after training (Piotrowski & Belter, 1999), and more importantly, several authors have speculated that projective techniques are of limited if not poor utility due to questionable reliability and validity (Anastasi & Urbina, 1997). In particular, scoring procedures for projective tests can be unreliable, and the norms provided for such techniques have often been criticized as being nonexistent, poor, or misleading (Lilienfeld et al., 2000). For example, the norms for the Rorschach comprehensive (scoring) system have been shown to lead to erroneous inferences of serious psychopathology in several studies (Hamel, Shaffer, & Erdberg, 2000), leading many authors to question the empirical basis of these norms (Garb, Wood, Lilienfeld, & Nezworski, 2002). Historically, such criticisms of the Rorschach have led certain authors to oppose the use of the Rorschach quite vehemently, even suggesting that "the rate of scientific progress in clinical psychology might well be measured by the speed and thoroughness with which it gets over the Rorschach" (Jensen, 1965; p. 238). More recently, Hunsley and Bailey (1999) concluded that "there is currently no scientific basis for justifying the use of Rorschach scales in psychological assessment" (p. 266). However, these criticisms may be somewhat premature, given that other investigators have suggested that the validity and reliability of projective tests has perhaps not been studied sufficiently (Meyer & Archer, 2001). In support of this notion, many authors have reported difficulties in measuring the validity of projective tests due to a lack of adequate external criteria against which to judge them (Klopfer & Taulbee, 1976), although this does highlight another important advantage of more objective techniques.

Nonetheless, other studies have focused on the incremental validity of projective techniques to examine whether such techniques may augment information gathered using other assessment measures. Although many authors have surmised that projective measures provide incremental validity in the assessment of personality and psychopathology above and beyond objective measures, perhaps because they provide additional insights about unconscious information (Weiner, 1999), reviews have generally found that clinical judgments made by psychologists do not become more valid when projective data are added (Garb, 2003). In addition, results regarding incremental validity are mixed or negative in terms of the use of an array of projective techniques when diagnosing mood and most personality disorders. However, results do seem to support the incremental validity of projective tests, especially the Rorschach, for diagnosing thought disorder (Wood, Lilienfeld, Garb, & Nezworski, 2000), as well as for evaluating dependent personality traits (Garb et al., 2002). In contrast, other research has supported the use of the TAT to detect borderline personality disorder, as well as projective drawing techniques to screen for mental disorders among children (Garb et al., 2002).

Despite these less-than-supportive results, and the increasingly negative opinions about projective techniques, a recent study shows that these measures are still among the top 10 techniques reportedly used by school psychologists (Hojnoski, Morrison, Brown, & Matthews, 2006). Similarly, survey studies have reported that nearly half of the directors of graduate level clinical psychology programs and almost two-thirds of the directors of clinical psychology internships believe that formal training in projective techniques has merit (Durand, Blanchard, & Mindell, 1988). Thus, these techniques nonetheless appear to be useful, at least according to professional judgment. This argument has largely been put forth on the basis of the unique features inherent in such methods. Specifically for personality assessments, many authors have argued that information obtained on a variety of objective measures may be limited by an individual's willingness to respond honestly, perhaps even revealing unflattering characteristics; his or her ability to make accurate (subjective) judgments of him- or herself; and also by the level of insight that he or she may or may not have with respect to unconscious processes (Ganellen, 2007). In some instances, individuals may be familiar with the constructs being measured (e.g., psychopathy) and may not want to reveal these characteristics, they may not understand the intended meaning of some items (e.g., "reckless disregard for the safety of self or others"), or they may not be aware that they have these characteristics. Likewise, information obtained from informants such as family members, teachers, and others may be biased for similar reasons. Parents may lack sufficient knowledge to answer specific questions about their children, or they may not wish to portray their children in a particular light. However, projective techniques purportedly overcome these obstacles by tapping into information about an individual indirectly, by way of unconscious patterns of thinking, behaviors, and emotional responses that contribute to responses on projective measures. The underlying assumption is that by means of these control methods, this type of information cannot therefore be subjected to conscious biasing by either controlling or filtering (Ganellen, 2007). It is noted that these arguments do not imply that projective techniques are superior to objective methods universally, but rather, that projective assessment methods may have advantages in some cases. As stated by Meyer and Archer (2001), for example, "[similar to] all tests, the Rorschach is more valid for some purposes than others" (p. 499).

In summary, projective methods may provide relevant information about normal and abnormal personality characteristics and patterns of thinking, behaving, feeling, and interpersonal functioning that may augment information obtained using other (objective) methods (Ganellen, 2006). Thus, projective and objective techniques may simply represent different methods for gathering information, and each method has both strengths and weaknesses. Ultimately, it is the clinician's judgment to identify the best set of instruments to employ during each and every psychological evaluation.

Examples of Projective Instruments

The Rorschach

This performance-based test includes a set of 10 cards with bilateral inkblots (black or colored), first shown to the examinees while they are asked to describe what they see in a given card. In a second stage, examinees are asked to identify where on the card the main elements of their description or story occurred. The Rorschach assesses how an individual conveys meaning to different situations and perceptual experiences based on past experiences. The way in which one formulates responses to the Rorschach is thought to be representative of how the person will organize his or her responses to ambiguous situations needing organization and judgment. Historically, it has been used as a way to identify psychological processes associated with thought and perceptual disturbances. The scoring system devised by Exner (2003) is the most commonly used, and administration of both phases takes approximately 45 minutes.

Several studies have looked at the psychometric properties of this classic test, in both adult (Meyer, 2004) and pediatric populations (Weiner, 1986). Using the Rorschach comprehensive system in adult samples, interrater reliability has been found to be quite high (*r* above 0.82; Meyer et al., 2002); test-retest reliability has also been found to be adequate, ranging from 0.46 to 0.84 (Meyer & Archer, 2001); furthermore, interpreter agreement has been reported to be between 0.76 and 0.89 among well-trained and experienced clinicians (Meyer, Mihura, & Smith, 2005). Data on studies with younger populations have not been as consistent or as promising, with the highest stability obtained in groups of children 14 years of age and older (Exner, 2003). There is controversy concerning whether the Rorschach is a valid test, with some meta-reviews reporting adequate validity coefficients (Meyer, 2004) and others stating validity is low (Garb, Florio, & Groove, 1998). In addition, some researchers have found that the Rorschach Perceptual Thinking Index can distinguish between those with a primary psychotic disorder and mood disorder, and that it was able to classify participants into each group better than the Minnesota Multiphasic Personality Inventory–2nd edition (MMPI-2; Dao, Prevatt, & Horne, 2008). Others have found that scores on certain scales of the Rorschach (e.g., object relations) significantly correlate with performance on similar scales in the TAT (Ackerman, Hilsenroth, Clemence, Weatherill, & Fowler, 2001). Finally, one of the most relevant strengths of this test is that it appears not to be culturally bound (Meyer, Erdberg, & Shaffer, 2007).

Thematic Apperception Test

The TAT uses a set of black and white pictures (approximately 8–12) depicting interpersonal situations, a single person, landscapes, or nothing, and is used to assess one's personality and thought processes. The examinee must narrate a story based on what he or she thinks is happening in the picture, what caused the picture's event, and what the characters in the picture are feeling. The TAT takes approximately 40 minutes to complete. In comparison to the Rorschach, the TAT is more structured in administration and scoring. However, administration procedures and interpretation are subject to variability because there is no agreed-upon standardized system for its administration (Groth-Marnat, 2009). In addition, test results are sensitive to situational variables (Meyer, 2004), making the data about its reliability and validity scarce. A study reported interrater reliability range between 0.36 and 0.82 (Ackerman, Clemence, Weatherill, & Hilsenroth, 1999), and a meta-analysis found positive correlations between the TAT and behavioral outcomes in the 0.19–0.22 range (Spangler, 1992). Extensions of the TAT include the Senior's Apperception Test (Bellak & Abrams, 1997) and the Children's Apperception Test (Bellak & Abrams, 1997). Meyer (2004) presents an extensive review of the psychometric properties of the TAT.

Robert's Apperception Test for Children

The Robert's Apperception Test for Children (RACT-2) is a more structured projective test in which children's views are examined to obtain an extensive perspective of their personality and social understanding. Further, this tool gives examiners a broader view of individuals' functioning regarding social abilities, personality, and coping abilities. Examinees are shown 16 cards and asked to narrate a story about what is occurring. The administration and scoring time for the RATC-2 is approximately 30–40 minutes. Most of the psychometric external validity evidence of the RATC-2 has been conducted in doctoral dissertations (Merrell, 2008). One published study (Palomares, Crowley, Worchel, Olson, & Rae, 1991) used confirmatory principal component factor analysis to examine the underlying structure of the RATC-2. Consistent with the factor structure reported in the original manual, authors found that the three-factor model demonstrated the best fit in both the standardization sample and in a sample of chronically ill children. Further, a profile analysis of their clinical sample demonstrated that performance in the RATC-2 served to distribute the children between two categories, an adaptive copying skills group and a maladaptive group (Palomares et al., 1991). We failed to identify external validation studies using the RATC-2, and this lack of evidence has been already reported elsewhere (Merrell, 2008).

Examples of Broad-Band Objective Instruments

Minnesota Multiphasic Personality Inventory–2nd Edition

The MMPI-2 is a comprehensive, self-administered questionnaire of personality in which examinees answer 567 true/false items concerning recent physical, neurological, and psychiatric symptoms, generating scores on various components of clinical psychopathology and personality (e.g., depression, personality types, reliability, etc.). Scores indicate whether examinees are in the normal, borderline, or clinical range of functioning, generally suggesting whether a *DSM-IV-TR* Axis I disorder is present in an individual. When taken by hand, the MMPI-2 takes approximately 90 minutes to complete. The MMPI-2 psychometric properties have been extensively studied (Butcher, 2010). Reliability examination using a 2-week test-retest reliability interval for content scales ranges from 0.67–0.92 in a male sample and from 0.58–0.91 in a female sample (Butcher, Dahlstrom, Graham, Tellegen, & Kraemmer, 1989). Over a mean interval of 1.88 years, test-retest reliability in mental health patients was found to range from 0.48–0.69 for the basic profile scales, and 0.56–0.78 for the content scales (Munley, 2002). Validity and reliability analyses of the MMPI have been constrained by the high inter-correlations among items and scales, in part derived from the fact that several scales share the same items (Groth-Marnat, 2009). With the most recent edition of the inventory, there is controversy as to the validity of the fake-bad scale, which assesses symptom malingering. In addition, the Restructured Clinical Scales have been found to have poor sensitivity in mental health problems (Butcher, 2010). However, others have found that the MMPI-2 (Psyc-5 scales) can significantly predict *DSM-IV-TR*–based personality psychopathology symptoms (Bagby, Sellbom, Costa, & Widiger, 2008).

Millon Clinical Multiaxial Inventory–3rd Edition

The Millon Clinical Multiaxial Inventory–3rd edition (MCMI-III) is a 175-item true/false self-administered questionnaire that examines personality and associated disorders. This questionnaire generates scale scores closely related to Millon's theory of personality and psychopathology found in the *DSM-IV-TR* (1994). In fact, the emphasis of this assessment tool is mostly on *DSM-IV-TR* (1994) Axis-II disorders; however, it does examine likelihood of Axis I disorders. The time to complete the questionnaire is approximately 25–30 minutes. Authors reported scale internal consistency ranging from 0.66–0.90. Test-retest reliability, measured by a delay of 5–14 days, ranged from 0.82–0.96, although review of independent datasets using the MCMI-II has demonstrated higher levels of variability (Craig, 1999). High correlations have been found between the MCMI-III, the MMPI-2, and BDI (Groth-Marnat, 2009).

California Psychological Inventory–3rd Edition

The California Psychological Inventory (CPI) is a self-administered questionnaire including 434 true/false statements derived partly from the MMPI. It generates scores on 20 scales representing common everyday life interpersonal issues, such as dominance, self-control, and socialization, among others. Compared to the MMPI, this tool focuses more on the normal aspects of an individual's personality; however, it can be used to examine psychopathology. The administration time is approximately 45–75 minutes, although a recent short form (260 items) has been introduced (Gough & Bradley, 2005), abbreviating time to completion down to approximately 30 minutes. In terms of its psychometric properties, test-retest reliability over a 1-year period (long form) has been found to range between 0.51 (flexibility) and 0.84 (femininity/masculinity), with a median internal consistency of 0.76 on the CPI 434 (Gough, 1996/2002), and from 0.39 (communality) to 0.87 (dominance) for the CPI 260 (Gough & Bradley, 2005). Correlations between the two forms have been found to be very high, ranging between r = 0.81 and r = 0.97 (Gough & Bradley, 2005).

Behavioral Assessment System for Children–2nd Edition

The Behavior Assessment System for Children (BASC) is a multidimensional rating scale of externalizing, internalizing, and adaptive skills that includes questionnaires for parents and teachers of children and adolescents between the ages of 2 and 21 and self-report forms (ages 8–21). The BASC is among the most widely used measures of child behavior in the United States (Reynolds & Kamphaus, 2004), it has been cross-culturally validated in Colombia by Pineda and colleagues (Pineda et al., 1999), and it has also been broadly validated and published in Spain, among other countries. The questionnaires included in the most recent edition, BASC-2, contain about 100–176 items rated on a *4-point Likert* scale ranging from 1 (never) to 4 (almost always). Completion time per questionnaire is approximately 10–30 minutes, depending on the form in use.

The BASC has been recognized for its psychometric strength, especially if the intrinsic source variance observed across raters and settings is taken into account (Merrell, 2008). Test-retest reliability of its scales is generally consistent across time (e.g., ICC: 0.62–9.3; Nowinski, Furlong, Rahban, & Smith, 2008). In addition, this test has been found to distinguish between healthy individuals and a clinically referred group (Nowinski et al., 2008). Internal consistency generally has been found to be very good in the self-report scales (median internal consistency coefficients are in the 0.80s), and test-retest reliability (1–2 months) has been found to be in the range of r = 0.70. Test-retest reliability for the parent-report forms are adequate (r = 0.66 and higher for a 1–7 week delay), and interrater reliability is moderate across ages, with a trend to higher interrater reliability for parent report scales than for teacher report forms (Reynolds & Kamphaus, 2004). Correlations with the Achenbach self-report scales have been found to be good, r = 0.65 or higher.

The validity of the BASC as an assessment tool in school settings has been largely studied, and positive reviews have emerged in the literature (Sandoval & Echandia, 1994). The BASC has been shown to be a valid and robust diagnostic tool to be implemented in a multi-method and multidimensional assessment of attention deficit hyperactivity disorder (ADHD; Garcia-Barrera & Kamphaus, 2006; Pineda et al., 2005). In the context of neuropsychological assessment, a special interest in the frontal lobe/executive control (FLEC) BASC scale has been emerging in the literature (Jarratt, Riccio, & Siekierski, 2005; Mahone, Zabel, Levey, Verda, & Kinsman, 2002; Riccio et al., 1994). Sullivan and Riccio (2006) administered the original 18-item BASC FLEC scale to a community sample of 92 children with or without ADHD. These authors found the BASC FLEC to be sensitive to the identification of behaviors associated with executive dysfunctions in children with ADHD and other disorders. Interestingly, correlations with the Behavior Rating Inventory of Executive Function (BRIEF; Gioia, Isquith, Guy, & Kenworthy, 2000) scales ranged from 0.45 (organization of materials) to 0.83 (global executive composite). More recently, Garcia-Barrera, Kamphaus, & Bandalos (*in press*) examined the psychometric properties of a 25-item executive function screener from the original BASC-Teacher form for children 6–11. A four-factor model (attentional control, behavioral control, emotional control, and problem-solving) demonstrated the best fit and was held invariant after stepwise examination of configural, metric, and scalar measurement equivalence analyses across age and gender were performed (Garcia-Barrera et al., in press).

Achenbach System of Empirically Based Assessment (ASEBA)

The ASEBA is a questionnaire in which individuals' activities, adaptive functioning, and behavioral and emotional problems are assessed. This system can be used to identify individuals that may benefit from future intervention (Achenbach et al., 2008). Items are rated on a scale ranging from 0 (not true) to 2 (very true/often true), based on how the examinee has felt or what others have observed in the 6 months prior to assessment (2 months for 60–90+). The questionnaires (school-aged versions) consist of 113 items, with 2 open-ended questions describing school difficulties. For the school-aged version, scores are generated for scales of internalizing, externalizing, total problem, school problems, and *DSM*-oriented scales. There are some similar items on the preschool versions; however, item content mostly differs between the preschool and school-aged version. In the versions for younger children, there are 82 similar items, plus 17 specific, and its completion time is approximately 20 minutes.

Internal consistency for the ASEBA is good, with interrater reliability averaging approximately 0.6 for ages 1–19 years old (Rescorla, 2005) for those who play similar roles in examinees' lives. Internal consistency for all composite scores on the self-report forms is above 0.90, and test-retest reliabilities are adequate (generally in the 0.50 range for 7 months). Researchers have found that self-report problems were good predictors of adult problems. Test-retest reliability for the teacher form has been found to be somewhat variable (ranges from 0.31–0.91 over an 8-day–4-month period).

Conner's Comprehensive Behavior Rating Scales

This questionnaire enables numerous observers to assess various areas of emotional, behavioral, and academic functioning in children that have occurred in the month prior to assessment. It is useful as a screening tool to understand the child more comprehensively and includes scales that screen for *DSM-IV-TR* disorders. Items are rated on a 4-point Likert scale, ranging from 0 (not true at all/it never happened) to 4 (very much true/it happened very often). Time to complete the questionnaire ranges from approximately 5–25 minutes. Correlations between the Conner's Comprehensive Behavior Rating Scales (CBRS) and other scales are poor to good depending on the form and test. For example, the CBRS Emotional Distress Scale (self-report), has a correlation of r = 0.28 with the BASC-2: Adolescent: Depression Scale. The *DSM-IV-TR* scale correlates very highly with the ASEBA: Aggressive Behavior Scale, r = 0.93. Internal consistency coefficients for the CBRS are good and range from 0.69–0.97 (mean = 0.84). Test-retest reliability coefficients over a 2- to 4-week period range between 0.56–0.97 (mean = 0.82). Interrater reliability coefficients range from 0.50–0.89 (mean = 0.73).

Examples of Narrow-Band Objective Instruments

Beck Depression Inventory-II

The Beck Depression Inventory-II (BDI-II) is a 21-item, self-administered questionnaire assessing intensity and severity of depression and associated symptoms (e.g, emotional difficulties, behavior, thought, somatic symptoms) occurring within 2 weeks of the assessment. Behavior is rated on increasing severity of symptoms, generating a summed total score. Higher scores indicate greater impairment associated with depression. Scores of 20 or higher generally indicate moderate depression. Regardless of score, strong endorsements of certain items, such as the suicidal intent item (#9), should always be discussed with the individual if endorsed in order to clarify past, current, or future suicidal intent. The BDI-II administration is approximately 5–10 minutes.

In terms of its reliability and validity, test-retest reliability has been found to be poor to good (e.g., ICC = 0.73, Wiebe & Penley 2005; Beck, Steer, & Brown, 1996), although some studies have found a significant decline in scores over time (Wiebe & Penley, 2005). The BDI-II has a relatively high internal consistency in a variety of populations, ranging from 0.89–0.94 (Arnau, Meagher, Norris, & Bramson, 2001; Beck et al., 1996; Steer, Clark, Kumar, & Beck, 2008). In addition, it has moderate correlations with other depression scales (e.g., Beck Hopelessness Scale, r = 0.68, Depression-Anxiety Stress Scale, r = 0.88) and numerous studies have found that it discriminates well between depression and anxiety (Beck et al., 1996), whereas others have found that the BDI-II correlates with measures of anxiety (Steer et al., 2008).

Beck Anxiety Inventory

The Beck Anxiety Inventory (BAI) is a 21-item, self-administered questionnaire that measures the cognitive, somatic, and physiologic aspects of anxiety that examinees have experienced in the past week. This questionnaire is meant to differentiate anxiety from depression. Each item is rated on a 4-point Likert scale measuring intensity of anxiety symptoms, ranging from 0 (not at all bothered) to 3 (severely bothered). Higher scores reflect greater levels of anxiety. Scores of 16 or higher generally indicate moderate levels of anxiety. The BAI takes approximately 10 minutes to complete.

Test-retest reliability of the BAI has been found to be adequate over a delay of 1 week to a delay of 1 month (ranging from 0.67–0.81). Internal consistency has also been found to be very high (alphas of 0.9 or higher). Those with certain forms of anxiety may score higher than other on the test (Beck & Steer, 1990). In addition, higher mean scores have generally been found in those with anxiety disorders than those with a mood disorder or no disorder. Moderate correlations have been found with other anxiety instruments such as the Hamilton Rating Scale for Anxiety (r = 0.51) and the State Trait Anxiety Inventory (r = 0.47 or higher; Spielberger, 1983). Some researchers, however, have stated that some aspects of anxiety are not well represented in this scale, and some symptoms that overlap with mood disorders (e.g., restlessness) are not included. In addition, some have found that the BAI significantly correlates with measures of depression such as the BDI-II in various age groups (r = 0.62; Steer et al., 2008; r = 0.59; Steer, Clark, Beck, & Ranieri, 1998). Internal consistencies are high (coefficient alpha 0.91–0.92 for adolescents and adults; Steer et al., 2008).

State-Trait Anxiety Inventory

A 40-item questionnaire, rated on a 4-point Likert scale, ranging from 1 (not at all) to 4 (very much so) for state anxiety and from 1 (almost never) to 4 (almost always) for trait anxiety items. This questionnaire differentiates between anxiety an individual is experiencing at the moment of the interview (state anxiety) and how anxious an individual generally feels (trait anxiety). Half the items assess state anxiety and half the items assess trait anxiety. Completion time is approximately 10–20 minutes.

Test-retest reliability coefficients for the T-Anxiety scale are relatively high (ranging from 0.65–0.94; Spielberger & Sydeman, 1994; Barnes, Harp, & Jung, 2002). Test-retest reliability coefficients for the S-Anxiety scale are generally lower (ranging from 0.33–0.96). Mean internal consistency coefficients have been found to be 0.89 and 0.91 for both trait and state anxiety scales, respectively. There is a strong association with the ASQ and MAS (0.73–0.85). In addition, higher mean scores have been found for individuals with anxiety difficulties compared to healthy individuals.

SUMMARY

Psychological assessment is a dynamic process that involves multiple steps, techniques, and dimensions. From the clinical interview to the utilization of objective or projective measures, psychological assessment is a hypothesis-driven method. Today, although both objective and projective measures remain commercially available and are utilized by practitioners on a regular basis, objective measures are far more commonly used due to the considerable criticisms in the literature of their projective counterparts. Within the clinical setting, psychological assessment can clarify a clinical picture that is otherwise quite vexing to the practicing psychologist. Psychological assessment can refine diagnostic formulations and, in turn, improve treatment recommendations, thereby benefiting the patient and any other providers involved in his or her care. For this very reason, the clinical utility of these techniques is of unquestionable importance.

REFERENCES

Achenbach, T. M. (1986). *The Direct Observation Form of the Child Behavior Checklist* (rev. ed.). Burlington, VT: University of Vermont, Research Center for Children, Youth, and Families.

Achenbach, T. M. (2001). *Youth Self-Report for Ages 11–18*. Burlington, VT: University of Vermont, Research Center for Children, Youth, and Families.

Achenbach, T. M., Becker, A., Döpfner, M., Heiervang, E., Roessner, V., Steinhausen, H., et al. (2008). Multicultural assessment of child and adolescent psychopathology with ASEBA and SDQ instruments: Research findings, applications, and future directions. *The Journal of Child Psychology and Psychiatry, 49*(3), 251–275.

Achenbach, T. M., Newhouse, P. A., & Rescorla, L. A. (2004). *Manual for the ASEBA Older Adult Forms & Profiles*. Burlington, VT: Research Center for Children, Youth, and Families, University of Vermont.

Achenbach, T. M., & Rescorla, L. A. (2000). *Manual for ASEBA Preschool Forms & Profiles*. Burlington, VT: Research Center for Children, Youth, and Families, University of Vermont.

Achenbach, T. M., & Rescorla, L. A. (2001). *Manual for the ASEBA School-Age Forms & Profiles*. Burlington, VT: Research Center for Children, Youth, and Families, University of Vermont.

Achenbach, T. M., & Rescorla, L. A. (2002). *Manual for the ASEBA Adult Forms & Profiles*. Burlington, VT: Research Center for Children, Youth, and Families, University of Vermont.

Ackerman, S. J., Clemence, A. J., Weatherill, R., & Hilsenroth, M. J. (1999). Use of the TAT in the assessment of DSM-IV Cluster B personality disorders. *Journal of Personality Assessment, 73*(3), 422–448.

Ackerman, S. J., Hilsenroth, M. J., Clemence, A. J., Weatherill, R., & Fowler, J. C. (2001). Convergent validity of Rorschach and TAT scales of object relations. *Journal of Personality Assessment, 77*(2), 295–306.

Allard, G., & Faust, D. (2000). Errors in scoring objective personality tests. *Assessment, 7*(2), 119–129.

Ambrosini, P. J. (2000). Historical development and present status of the schedule for affective disorders and schizophrenia for school-age children (K-SADS). *Journal of the American Academy of Child and Adolescent Psychiatry, 39*(1), 49–58.

American Psychiatric Association. (2000). *Diagnostic and statistical manual of mental disorders (4th ed.), text revision*. Washington, DC: Author.

Amini, H., Alaghband-rad, J., Sharifi, V., Davari-Ashtiani, R., Kaviani, H., Shahrivar, Z., et al. (2006). [Validity of a Farsi translation of the composite International Diagnostic Interview (CIDI) to diagnose schizophrenia and bipolar disorder]. *Tehran University Medical Journal, 64*(8), 31–42.

Anastasi, A., & Urbina, S. (1997). *Psychological tests*. Upper Saddle River, NJ: Prentice Hall.

Angold, A., & Costello, E. J. (2000). The Child and Adolescent Psychiatric Assessment (CAPA). *Journal of the American Academy of Child and Adolescent Psychiatry, 39*(1), 39–48.

Arnau, R. C., Meagher, M. W., Norris, M. P., & Bramson, R. (2001). Psychometric evaluation of the Beck Depression Inventory-II with primary care medical patients. *Health Psychology, 20*(2), 112–119.

Bagby, R. M., Sellbom, M., Costa, P. T. Jr., & Widiger, T. A. (2008). Predicting Diagnostic and Statistical Manual of Mental Disorders-IV personality disorders with the five-factor model of personality and the personality psychopathology five. *Personality and Mental Health, 2*(2), 55–69.

Barnes, L. L. B., Harp, D., & Jung, W. S. (2002). Reliability generalization of scores on the Spielberger State-Trait Anxiety Inventory. *Educational and Psychological Measurement, 62*(4), 603–618.

Baron, I. S. (2003). *Neuropsychological evaluation of the child*. New York: Oxford University Press.

Beck, A. T., & Steer, R. A. (1990). *Manual for the Beck Anxiety Inventory*. San Antonio, TX: Psychological Corporation.

Beck, A. T., Steer, R. A., & Brown, G. K. (1996). *BDI-II, Beck Depression Inventory: Manual*. San Antonio, TX: Psychological Corporation.

Bellak, L., & Abrams, D. M. (1997). *The TAT, CAT, and SAT in clinical use* (6th ed.). Boston, MA: Allyn & Bacon.

Boyle, M. H., Offord, D. R., Racine, Y., Sanford, M., Szatmari, P., Fleming, J. E., et al. (1993). Evaluation of the Diagnostic Interview for Children and Adolescents for use in general population samples. *Journal of Abnormal Child Psychology, 21*(6), 663–681.

Butcher, J. N. (2010). Personality assessment from the nineteenth to the early twenty-first century: Past achievements and contemporary challenges. *Annual Review of Clinical Psychology, 6*, 1–20.

Butcher, J. N., Dahlstrom, W. G., Graham, J. R., Tellegen, A., & Kraemmer, B. (1989). *Manual for administration and scoring: MMPI-2*. Minneapolis: University of Minnesota Press.

Butcher, J. N., Graham, J. R., Ben-Porath, Y. S., Tellegen, A., Dahlstrom, W. G., & Kraemmer, B. (2001). *Minnesota Multiphasic Personality Inventory-2: Manual for administration and scoring* (2nd ed.). Minneapolis: University of Minnesota Press.

Butcher, J. N., Williams, C. L., Graham, J. R., Archer, R. P., Tellegen, A., Ben-Porath, Y. S., et al. (1992). *MMPI-A (Minnesota Multiphasic Personality Inventory-Adolescent): Manual for administration, scoring, and interpretation* (rev. ed.). Minneapolis: University of Minnesota Press.

Cashel, M. L. (2002). Child and adolescent psychological assessment: Current clinical practices and the impact of managed care. *Professional Psychology: Research and Practice, 33*(5), 446–453.

Conners, C. K. (2008). *Conners' Comprehensive Behavior Rating Scales manual*. Toronto: Multi-Health Systems.

Conners, C. K. (2009). *Conners' Early Childhood manual*. Toronto: Multi-Health Systems.

Dao, T. K., Prevatt, F., & Horne, H. L. (2008). Differentiating psychotic patients from nonpsychotic patients with the MMPI-2 and Rorschach. *Journal of Personality Assessment, 90*(1), 93–101.

Dougherty, T. W., Ebert, R. J., & Callender, J. C. (1986). Policy capturing in the employment interview. *Journal of Applied Psychology, 71*(1), 9–15.

Durand, V. M., Blanchard, E. B., & Mindell, J. A. (1988). Training in projective testing: A survey of clinical training directors and internship directors. *Professional Psychology: Research and Practice, 19,* 236–238.

Egger, H. L., & Angold, A. (2004). The Preschool Age Psychiatric Assessment (PAPA): A structured parent interview for diagnosing psychiatric disorders in preschool children. In R. DelCarmen-Wiggins & A. Carter (Eds.), *Handbook of infant, toddler, and preschool mental health assessment* (pp. 223–243). New York: Oxford University Press.

Elbert, J. C., & Holden, E. W. (1987). Child diagnostic assessment: Current training practices in clinical psychology internships. *Professional Psychology: Research and Practice, 18,* 587–596.

Ernst, M., Cookus, B. A., & Moravec, B. C. (2000). Pictorial Instrument for Children and Adolescents (PICA-III-R). *Journal of the American Academy of Child and Adolescent Psychiatry, 39*(1), 94–99.

Exner, J. E. Jr. (2003). *The Rorschach: A comprehensive system* (4th ed.). New York: Wiley.

Ezpeleta, L., de la Osa, N., Domenech, J. M., Navarro, J. B., Losilla, J. M., & Judez, J. (1997). Diagnostic agreement between clinicians and the Diagnostic Interview for Children and Adolescents–DICA-R–in an outpatient sample. *Journal of Child Psychology and Psychiatry and Allied Disciplines, 38*(4), 431–440.

Frank, L. K. (1939). Projective methods for the study of personality. *Journal of Psychology, 8*(2), 389–413.

Ganellen, R. J. (2006). Rorschach assessment of normal and abnormal personality. In S. Strack (Ed.), *Differentiating normal and abnormal personality* (pp. 473–500). New York: Springer-Verlag.

Ganellen, R. J. (2007). Assessing normal and abnormal personality functioning: Strengths and weaknesses of self-report, observer, and performance-based methods. *Journal of Personality Assessment, 89*(1), 30–40.

Garb, H. N. (2003). Incremental validity and the assessment of psychopathology in adults. *Psychological Assessment, 15*(4), 508–520.

Garb, H. N., Florio, C. M., & Grove, W. M. (1998). The validity of the Rorschach and the Minnesota Multiphasic Personality Inventory: Results from meta-analyses. *Psychological Science, 9*(5), 402–404.

Garb, H. N., Wood, J. M., Lilienfeld, S. O., & Nezworski, M. T. (2002). Effective use of projective techniques in clinical practice: Let the data help with selection and interpretation. *Professional Psychology: Research and Practice, 33,* 454–463.

Garcia-Barrera, M. A., & Kamphaus, R. W. (2006). Diagnosis of attention-deficit/hyperactivity disorder and its subtypes. In R. W. Kamphaus & J. M. Campbell (Eds.), *Psychodiagnostic assessment of children: Dimensional and categorical approaches* (pp. 319–355). Hoboken, NJ: John Wiley & Sons.

Garcia-Barrera, M. A., Kamphaus, R. W., & Bandalos, D. (in press). Theoretical and statistical derivation of a screener for the behavioral assessment of executive functions in children. *Psychological Assessment.*

Gioia, G. A., Isquith, P. K., Guy, S. C., & Kenworthy, L. (2000). *Brief: Behavior Rating Inventory of Executive Functions.* Odessa, FL: Psychological Assessment Resources.

Gough, H. G. (2000). The California Psychological Inventory. In C. E. Watkins Jr., & V. L. Campbell (Eds.), *Testing and Assessment in Counseling Practice* (2nd ed., pp. 45–72). Mahwah, NJ: Lawrence Erlbaum Associates.

Gough, H. G., & Bradley, P. (1996/2002). *California Psychological Inventory manual* (3rd ed.). Mountain View, CA: CPP, Inc.

Gough, H. G., & Bradley, P. (2005). *CPI 260 manual.* Mountain View, CA: Consulting Psychologists Press.

Greenspan, S. I., & Greenspan, N. T. (2003). *The clinical interview of the child* (3rd ed.). Washington, DC: American Psychiatric Publishing.

Groth-Marnat, G. (2009). *Handbook of psychological assessment* (5th ed.). Hoboken, NJ: John Wiley and Sons, Inc.

Hamel, M., Shaffer, T. W., & Erdberg, P. (2000). A study of nonpatient preadolescent Rorschach protocols. *Journal of Personality Assessment, 75*(2), 280–294.

Haro, J. M., Arbabzadeh-Bouchez, S., Brugha, T. S., de Girolamo, G., Guyer, M. E., Jin, R., et al. (2006). Concordance of the Composite International Diagnostic Interview version 3.0 (CIDI 3.0) with standardized clinical assessments in the WHO World Mental Health surveys. *International Journal of Methods in[vv$(so_hide)=1] Psychiatric Research, 15*(4), 167–180.

Hodges, K. (1993). Structured interviews for assessing children. *Journal of Child Psychology and Psychiatry, 34*(1), 49–68.

Hojnoski, R. L., Morrison, R., Brown, M., & Matthews, W. J. (2006). Projective test use among school psychologists: A survey and critique. *Journal of Psychoeducational Assessment, 24*(2), 145–159.

Houts, A. C. (1984). Effects of clinician theoretical orientation and patient explanatory bias on initial clinical judgments. *Professional Psychology: Research and Practice, 15*(2), 284–293.

Hunsley, J., & Bailey, J. M. (1999). The clinical utility of the Rorschach: Unfulfilled promises and an uncertain future. *Psychological Assessment, 11*(3), 266–277.

Jarratt, K. P., Riccio, C. A., & Siekierski, B. M. (2005). Assessment of Attention Deficit Hyperactivity Disorder (ADHD) using the BASC and BRIEF. *Applied Neuropsychology, 12*(2), 83–93.

Jensen, A. R. (1965). A review of the Rorschach. In O. K. Buros (Ed.), *Sixth mental measurements yearbook* (pp. 501–509). Highland Park, NH: Gryphon.

Kamphaus, R. W., & Frick, P. J. (2002). *Clinical assessment of child and adolescent personality and behavior* (2nd ed.). Boston: Allyn and Bacon.

Kamphaus, R. W., & Reynolds, C. R. (2003). *Handbook of psychological and educational assessment of children: Personality, behavior, and context* (2nd ed.). New York: Guilford Press.

Kessler, R. C., & Ustun, T. B. (2004). The World Mental Health (WMH) survey initiative version of the World Health Organization (WHO) Composite International Diagnostic Interview (CIDI). *International Journal of Methods in Psychiatric Research, 13*(2), 93–121.

Klopfer, W. G., & Taulbee, E. S. (1976). Projective tests. *Annual Review of Psychology, 27*, 543–567.

Knoff, H. M. (Ed.). (1983). Projective/personality assessment in the schools [Special issue]. *School Psychology Review, 12*(4).

Lezak, M. D., Howieson, D. B., & Loring, D. W. (2004). *Neuropsychological Assessment*. New York: Oxford University Press.

Lilienfeld, S. O., Wood, J. M., & Garb, H. N. (2000). The scientific status of projective techniques. *Psychological Science in the Public Interest, 1*(2), 27–66.

Lindzey, G. (1959). On the classification of projective techniques. *Psychological Bulletin, 56*(2), 158–168.

Mahone, E. M., Zabel, T. A., Levey, E., Verda, M., & Kinsman, S. (2002). Parent and self-report ratings of executive function in adolescents with myelomeningocele and hydrocephalus. *Child Neuropsychology, 8*(4), 258–270.

McConaughy, S. H. (2005). *Clinical interviews for children and adolescents: Assessment to intervention*. New York: The Guilford Press.

McConaughy, S. H., & Achenbach, T. M. (1994). *Manual for the semistructured clinical interview for children and adolescents*. Burlington, VT: University of Vermont, Department of Psychiatry.

McConaughy, S. H., & Achenbach, T. M. (2001). *Manual for the semistructured clinical interview for children and adolescents* (2nd ed.). Burlington, VT: University of Vermont, Research Center for Children, Youth, and Families.

Merrell, K. W. (2008). *Behavioral, social, and emotional assessment of children and adolescents* (3rd ed.). New York: Lawrence Erlbaum Associates.

Meyer, G. J. (2004). The reliability and validity of the Rorschach and Thematic Apperception Test (TAT) compared to other psychological and medical procedures: An analysis of systematically gathered evidence. In M. J. Hilsenroth and D. L. Segal (Eds.), *Personality assessment, Volume 2* (pp. 315–342). Hoboken, NJ: John Wiley & Sons, Inc.

Meyer, G. J., & Archer, R. P. (2001). The hard science of Rorschach research: What do we know and where do we go? *Psychological Assessment, 13*, 486–502.

Meyer, G. J., Erdberg, P., & Shaffer, T. W. (2007). Towards international normative reference data for the Comprehensive System [special issue]. *Journal of Personality Assessment, 89*(Suppl. 1), S201–S216.

Meyer, G. J., Hilsenroth, M. J., Baxter, D., Exner, J. E., Fowler, J. C., Piers, C. C., et al. (2002). An examination of interrater reliability for scoring the Rorschach Comprehensive System in eight data sets. *Journal of Personality Assessment, 78*(2), 219–274.

Meyer, G. J., & Kurtz, J. E. (2006). Advancing personality assessment terminology: Time to retire "objective" and "projective" as personality test descriptors. *Journal of Personality Assessment, 87*(3), 223–225.

Meyer, G. J., Mihura, J., & Smith, B. (2005). The interclinician reliability of the Rorschach interpretation in four data sets. *Journal of Personality Assessment, 84*(3), 296–314.

Millon, T., Millon, C., Davis, R., & Grossman, S. (2006). *MCMI-III manual* (3rd ed.). Minneapolis: NCS Pearson.

Munley, P. H. (2002). Comparability of MMPI-2 scales and profiles over time. *Journal of Personality Assessment, 78*(1), 145–160.

Murray, H. A. (1943). *Thematic Apperception Test manual*. Cambridge, MA: Harvard University Press.

Nowinski, L. A., Furlong, M. J., Rahban, R., & Smith, S. R. (2008). Initial reliability and validity of the BASC-2, SRP, College Version. *Journal of Psychoeducational Assessment, 26*(2), 156–167.

Palomares, R. S., Crowley, S. L., Worchel, F. F., Olson, T. K., & Rae, W. A. (1991). The factor analytic structure of the Roberts Apperception Test for Children: A comparison of the standardization sample with a sample of chronically ill children. *Journal of Personality Assessment, 56*, 414–425.

Pineda, D. A., Aguirre, D. C., Garcia, M. A., Lopera, F. J., Palacio, L. G., & Kamphaus, R. W. (2005). Validation of two rating scales for ADHD diagnosis in Colombian children. *Pediatric Neurology, 33*(1), 15–25.

Pineda, D. A., Kamphaus, R. W., Mora, O., Restrepo, M. A., Puerta, I. C., Palacio, L. G. et al. (1999). A system of multidimensional behavior assessment. A scale for parents of children from 6 to 11 years of age. Colombian version. Article in Spanish. *Rev Neurol. 28*(7), 672–681.

Piotrowski, C., & Belter, R. W. (1999). Internship training in psychological assessment: Has managed care had an impact? *Assessment, 6*, 381–390.

Quintana, M. I., Gastal, F. L., Jorge, M. R., Miranda, C. T., & Andreoli, S. B. (2007). Validade e limitações da versão brasileira do Composite International Diagnostic Interview (CIDI 2.1). [Validity and limitations of the Brazilian versions of the Composite International Diagnostic Interview (CIDI 2.1).] *Revista Brasileira de Psiquiatria, 29*(1), 18–22.

Reich, W. (2000). Diagnostic interview for children and adolescents (DICA). *Journal of the American Academy of Child and Adolescent Psychiatry, 39*(1), 59–66.

Reich, W., Herjanic, B., Welner, Z., & Gandhy, P. R. (1982). Development of a structured psychiatric interview for children: Agreement on diagnosis comparing child and parent interviews. *Journal of Abnormal Child Psychology, 10*(3), 325–336.

Rescorla, L. A. (2005). Assessment of young children using the Achenbach System of Empirically Based Assessment (ASEBA). *Mental Retardation and Developmental Disabilities Research Reviews, 11*(3), 226–237.

Reynolds, C. R., & Kamphaus, R. W. (2004). *Behavior assessment system for children* (2nd ed.). Minneapolis: Pearson Assessments.

Riccio, C. A., Hall, A. J., Morgan, A., Hynd, G. W., Gonzalez, J. J., & Marshall, R. M. (1994). Executive function and Wisconsin Card Sorting Test: Relationship with behavioral rating and cognitive ability. *Developmental Neuropsychology, 10*(3), 215–229.

Roberts, G. E., & Gruber, C. P. (2005). *Roberts-2 manual*. Los Angeles: Western Psychological Services.

Rogers, R. (2001). *Handbook of diagnostic and structured interviewing*. New York: The Guilford Press.

Rorschach, H. (1942). *Psychodiagnostics* (5th ed.). Berne, Switzerland: Verlag Hans Huber.

Sandoval, J., & Echandia, A. (1994). Behavior Assessment System For Children. *Journal Of School Psychology, 32*(4), 419–425.

Sattler, J. M. (2008). *Assessment of children: Cognitive Foundations* (5th ed.). San Diego: Jerome M. Sattler.

Shaffer, D., Fisher, P., Lucas, C. P., Dulcan, M. K., & Schwab-Stone, M. E. (2000). NIMH Diagnostic Interview Schedule for Children-version IV (NIMH DISC-IV): Description, differences from previous versions, and reliability of some common diagnoses. *Journal of the American Academy of Child and Adolescent Psychiatry, 39*(1), 28–38.

Sherrill, J. T., & Kovacs, M. (2000). Interview Schedule for Children and Adolescents (ISCA). *Journal of the American Academy of Child and Adolescent Psychiatry, 39*(1), 67–75.

Schrier, A. C., de Wit, M. A., Coupé, V. M., Fassaert, T., Verhoeff, A. P., Kupka, R. W., et al. (2012). Comorbidity of anxiety and depressive disorders: A comparative population study in Western and non-Western inhabitants in the Netherlands. *International Journal of Social Psychiatry*.

Silverman, W. K., & Albano, A. M. (1996). *The Anxiety Disorder Interview Schedule for Children for DSM-IV: Child and parent versions*. San Antonio, TX: Psychological Corporation.

Spangler, W. D. (1992). Validity of questionnaire and TAT measures of need for achievement: Two meta-analyses. *Psychological Bulletin, 112*, 140–154.

Spielberger, C. D. (1983). *Manual for the State-Trait Anxiety Inventory*. Palo Alto, CA: Consulting Psychologists Press.

Spielberger, C. D., & Sydeman, S. J. (1994). State-Trait Anxiety Inventory and State-Trait Anger Expression Inventory. In M. E. Maruish (Ed.), *The use of psychological testing for treatment planning and outcome assessment* (pp. 292–321). Hillside, NJ: L. Erlbaum Associates.

Steer, R. A., Clark, D. A., Beck, A. T., & Ranieri, W. F. (1998). Common and specific dimensions of self-reported anxiety and depression: The BDI-II versus the BDI-IA. *Behaviour Research and Therapy, 37*(2), 183–190.

Steer, R. A., Clark, D. A., Kumar, G., & Beck, A. T. (2008). Common and specific dimensions of self-report and depression in adolescent outpatients. *Journal of Psychopathology and Behavioural Assessment, 30*(3), 163–170.

Strauss, E., Sherman, E. M. S., & Spreen, O. (2006). *A compendium of neuropsychological tests: Administration, norms, and commentary* (3rd ed.). New York: Oxford University Press.

Sullivan, J. R., & Riccio, C. A. (2006). An empirical analysis of the BASC Frontal Lobe/Executive Control scale with a clinical sample. *Archives of Clinical Neuropsychology, 21*(5), 495–501.

Sundberg, N. (1977). *Assessment of persons*. Englewood Cliffs, NJ: Prentice Hall.

Verhulst, F. C. (1995). Recent developments in the assessment and diagnosis of child psychopathology. *European Journal of Psychological Assessment, 11*, 203–212.

Watkins, C. E., Campbell, V. L., Nieberding, R., & Hallmark, R. (1995). Contemporary practice of psychological assessment by clinical psychologists. *Professional Psychology: Research and Practice, 26*(1), 54–60.

Weiner, I. B. (1986). Assessing children and adolescents with the Rorschach. In H. M. Knoff (Ed.), *The Assessment of Child and Adolescent Personality* (pp. 141–172). New York: Guilford Press.

Weiner, I. B. (1999). What the Rorschach can do for you: Incremental validity in clinical applications. *Assessment, 6*(4), 327–338.

Welner, Z., Reich, W., Herjanic, B., Jung, K. G., & Amado, H. (1987). Reliability, validity, and parent-child agreement studies of the Diagnostic Interview for Children and Adolescents (DICA). *Journal of the American Academy of Child and Adolescent Psychiatry, 26*, 649–653.

Wiebe, J. S., & Penley, J. A. (2005). A psychometric comparison of the Beck Depression Inventory-II in English and Spanish. *Psychological Assessment, 17*(4), 481–485.

Will, V., Eadie, D., & MacAskill, S. (1996). Projective and enabling techniques explored. *Marketing Intelligence and Planning, 14*(6), 38–43.

Wittchen, H.-U. (1994). Reliability and validity studies of the WHO-Composite International Diagnostic Interview (CIDI): A critical review. *Journal of Psychiatric Research, 28*(1), 57–84.

Wood, J. M., Lilienfeld, S. O., Garb, H. N., & Nezworski, M. T. (2000). The Rorschach test in clinical diagnosis: A critical review, with a backward look at Garfield (1947). *Journal of Clinical Psychology, 56*(3), 395–430.

World Health Organization (1990). *Composite International Diagnostic Interview* (CIDI). Geneva: Author.

World Health Organization (1997). *Composite International Diagnostic Interview (CIDI), version 2.0*. Geneva: Author.

CHAPTER 23

The Psychopathology and Functional Neuroanatomy of Psychotherapy

Javan Horwitz, Emily Gilmore, Natalie Horwitz, John McConnell, & Rhonda Johnson

INTRODUCTION

A long-standing controversy in science and the sub-field of psychology has been how the influences of nature and nurture contribute to and explain abnormal behavior. Even Freud in 1895 concluded that changes in client's functioning following psychotherapy likely have some biological foundations. Over time, research has demonstrated that both nature and the environment contribute to psychopathology, although biological and psychological models have continued to emphasize primarily one or the other in their etiological models. More recently, models have been constructed to include the influences of both factors, such as diathesis-stress models, which generally state that a biological predisposition is exacerbated by an environmental influence (e.g., a stressful event), resulting in the production of pathology.

Nearly 60 years ago, Eysenck (1952) concluded, after reviewing existing outcome research, that psychotherapy was ineffective and even harmful. Eysenck's report stated that roughly two-thirds of patients did not improve following psychotherapy. Further, Eysenck concluded, "the more psychotherapy, the smaller the recovery rate" (p. 322). In the 1950s, these appeared to be daunting conclusions for the future practice of psychotherapy. However, Eysenck's report lacked the rigorousness of subsequent meta-analyses. In review of almost 400 controlled studies of psychotherapy, Smith and Glass (1977) found that individuals who received psychotherapy were better off than 75% of individuals who did not receive such care. Moreover, they found that there were no differences among therapeutic super-classes (i.e., behavioral vs. nonbehavioral). In a further meta-analytic review two decades later, Wampold and colleagues (1997) also concluded that there were "no differential outcomes despite technical diversity" (Stiles, Shapiro, & Elliott, 1986, p. 165).

Thus, the preponderance of evidence indicates that clients of any psychotherapy are better off than those who do not receive care for their concerns. Moreover, little evidence exists to show that bona fide psychotherapies pitted against each other elicit superior benefits for clients. Years of psychotherapy outcome research has clarified that common factors inherent in all psychotherapy likely explain a great deal of variance in symptom reduction, behavioral change, and neuroplasticity. As Lambert and Ogles (2004) concluded, "it appears that what can be firmly stated is that factors common across treatments are accounting for a substantial amount of improvement found in psychotherapy patients" (p. 172). Given that specific therapeutic modalities play only a small role in psychotherapy outcomes, it would benefit future research using neuroimaging techniques to focus most of their efforts on how any psychotherapy produces meaningful neurological changes. Spending a great deal of time investigating whether varying techniques produce differential neurological changes may possibly be fruitless. Preliminary work has already clarified that there are common neurological changes in the brain from varying psychotherapies (Roffman, Marci, Glick, Dougherty, & Rauch, 2005). Even if advanced neuroimaging techniques may someday be able to clarify specific neurological changes resulting from various techniques, these findings will not likely translate into differential outcomes for clients. In other words, whether or not various psychotherapy techniques have different neurological correlates, the overall outcome may be the same. In the final analysis, neuroimaging will likely show at a neurological level what years of outcome research have revealed at the psychosocial level; that is, psychotherapy that builds meaningful relationships with clients, regardless of its technical diversity, produces positive outcomes (Norcross, 2002).

LIMITATIONS WITH CURRENT STUDIES

Despite the numerous neuroimaging studies on psychotherapy, several significant problems exist with the current research. Heterogeneity throughout the studies (e.g., number of therapists, session number, delivery of psychotherapy individually or in a group) makes comparison and derivation of conclusions difficult (Roffman et al., 2005). Further, despite some therapies that are manual or time-limited being better adaptable to research designs (e.g., behavior therapy [BT], cognitive-behavior therapy [CBT], and interpersonal therapy [IPT]), specific adherence to these structures may not be perfect (Roffman et al., 2005). Additionally, there is a poor operationalization of specific psychotherapeutic styles and at times purported CBT, for example, may actually more closely resemble BT (Roffman et al., 2005).

In addition to these limitations with psychotherapy and research design, current neuroimaging is heterogeneous and our understanding of functional imaging is still controversial. Regarding heterogeneity, imaging may differ based on resolution of the image (e.g., voxel-based versus region of interest studied), mechanism of the device, and other patient-related limitations (Roffman et al., 2005). Additionally, study design may affect when imaging occurs during the experiment and what environmental factors may confound these results. Finally, despite the knowledge that glucose metabolism and cerebral blood flow are visualized during neurological imaging and this relates to brain activity, the neuroscientific field's understanding of these outputs is weak at best (Roffman et al., 2005).

Given these limitations to current neuroimaging and the nature of psychotherapy and its effects on clients, conclusions derived from studies should be interpreted with caution and understood as preliminary findings until the issues discussed above can be better addressed.

NATURE OF PSYCHOPATHOLOGY UNDER A NEUROPHYSIOLOGICAL PARADIGM

According to the neurophysiological paradigm, psychopathology arises primarily from two factors: (1) reduced capacity for learning and flexibility (plasticity) and (2) homeostatic dysregulation and dissociation between systems in the brain.

Adaptability, and consequently mental health, is based on the degree of mental flexibility or neuroplasticity of the brain, that is, the brain's ability to change in response to experiences (Cozolino, 2010; Kay, 2009). All behaviors are the result of intercellular interactions between neurons and neuronal networks (Kay, 2009). Plasticity represents the brain's ability to create new neurons and neural connections, and to strengthen existing neural networks (Kay, 2009). Continued plasticity allows individuals to assess the present based on past experience, to anticipate future events, and to regulate emotions (Kay, 2009). In other words, learning is the key to continued adaptability.

The amygdala plays a pivotal role in the formation of stimulus-reinforcement (S-R) learning, a type of learning in which associations are formed between neutral events and punishments or rewards, such that a specific or general stimuli allows the limbic system to predict a negative or positive outcome (LeDoux, 2000). For this purpose, the amygdala assigns emotional valences to stimuli and encodes these in the subcortical memory circuit, which plays a vital role in fear acquisition and maintenance.

New research also indicates that "the brain is constantly changing through the creation of new cells and circuits, especially within the hippocampus" (Kay, 2009, p. 293). The hippocampus is a cortical structure that assists in regulating and interpreting input from the amygdala. The prefrontal cortex (PFC) is also thought to influence brain responses to emotional stimuli by regulating primary affective responses, such as those initiated in the amygdala.

Another anatomical distinction that has received some attention pertaining to functional differences in approach and avoidance behaviors is that between right and left cerebral hemispheres (Kay, 2009). Approach-related behaviors and the expression of positive emotions has been attributed to activity in left frontal regions, and avoidance and withdrawal behaviors and the expression of negative emotions have been localized to activity in the right frontal regions. Key to psychopathology is the asymmetry between the regulation or activation of these regions, that is, the balance in activity between right and left brain areas.

Orbital-frontal regions have been linked to the updating of associations formed between neutral (sensory) stimuli and unconditioned (aversive) stimuli during fear acquisition, with changes in punishment and reward contingencies in the environment (Rolls, 2000). Counter to this, ventral regions may serve in part of the process involved in extinguishing these associations following changes in punishment/reward contingencies. Due to the dynamic nature of the brain, other areas are also involved in the alteration of these neural networks. Specifically, the medial PFC plays a role in representing and monitoring subjectively experienced emotional states, another key aspect of appraisal (Amodio & Frith, 2006). There is also evidence that the ventrolateral PFC is critical in the selective attention processes during the presentation of threat (Monk et al, 2006). Lastly, the anterior cingulated cortex has also been implicated in emotion regulation during challenging situations by responding to conflict and facilitating subsequent response selection (Lewis & Stieben, 2004).

Consequently, the learning and flexibility (plasticity) of various stimuli in the environment has some influence on the phenotypic expression by alteration of neurons and neuronal pathways involved primarily in the frontal and temporal-limbic zones. Overstimulation or reinforcement of certain pathways may result in a highly activated or highly inhibited system resulting in a reduced capacity for learning, negative (reduced) plasticity, dysregulation of homeostasis, or dissociation between neural network systems.

NEUROBIOLOGY OF PSYCHOTHERAPY

Although a relatively new area of research, studies of neurobiology have shown that psychotherapy affects brain structure and function (Kay, 2009). One of the ways that psychotherapy impacts the brain is through stimulus-response learning, described previously, which serves as the basis for many behavioral therapy techniques (Kay, 2009). S-R learning results in changes at the synaptic level through long-term potentiation, such that "decreasing input stimulus from a presynaptic cell [is needed] to elicit an increasingly stronger postsynaptic response" (Kay, 2009). In short, the more often a neural network is activated, the stronger and more effective the connection becomes, resulting in a network that is easier to activate with less stimulus. In other words, there is a lower threshold for activation in these reinforced circuits. This conclusion parallels the cognitive psychology tenet that automatic thoughts represent the core beliefs (thoughts, networks) that are activated most often. Similarly, cognitive models build on S-R changes; cognitions are simply the meaning we derive from patterns of S-R and the resulting connections are established and fortified. For example, if a person eats a new food (stimulus) and becomes ill (reinforcement), he or she might conclude that the new food made him or her sick (resulting cognition). At times, these associations may become aberrant, resulting in the catalysis and maintenance of psychopathology. These stored experiences serve as the basis for one's perceptions of future stimuli, resulting in a bias for similar imminent occurrences (Kay, 2009). Given the malleability of the neural networks, new

S-R events can be used to alter the current pathways and associated cognitions in order to treat psychopathology.

The preponderance of research in this area of neurobiology and psychotherapy demonstrates that the primary mechanism of action of most therapy approaches appears to be associated with stimulating growth and restructuring of neural networks (Cozolino, 2010; Kay, 2009; Kumari, 2006; Green, 2003). In essence, psychotherapy results in an enhancement of neural plasticity. As described previously, plasticity of the brain fosters survival by allowing the brain to integrate information from novel experiences by creating new connections between neurons or by strengthening existing connections and networks (Cozolino, 2010; Kay, 2009). Researchers believe that each time a network is stimulated, that network is strengthened or *primed,* to use a cognitive psychology term. Likewise, non-stimulated networks in a biological system will erode over time due to the organism's tendency to move toward homeostasis, or least energy state.

Because the brain is made up of hundreds of interrelated systems, it is vital that the strength of these connections maintain homeostatic balance. If one process or system becomes too strong without counter-development of the complementary system, an injury or dysfunction occurs. In fact, many systems operate by a delicate balance between activation and inhibition; thus, dyspraxia results from a dysfunction between the systems that control motor activation and motor inhibition. This finding is further supported by observation of the neurodegenerative process of dementia, where primitive reflexes reappear as the cortex gradually loses its inhibitory ability (Cozolino, 2010). Similarly, an organism exposed to chronic stress and deprivation can manifest brain atrophy, deficits, and/or the permanent or temporary use of more primitive behaviors, a process Freud would call regression (Cozolino, 2010). In turn, these dysregulations produce not only physiological symptoms, alteration in neurochemistry, and microstructural changes, but can also manifest functionally as mental illness.

Neurogenesis occurs in the regions involved in ongoing learning, including the hippocampus, amygdala, and frontal and temporal lobes (Cozolino, 2010). Most psychopathologies can be linked to dysfunction in the frontal or temporal lobes, rather than parietal or occipital, which may support the view that the neurobiology of psychopathology is related to neuroplasticity and dysregulation of the systems involved. Researchers hypothesize that the neurobiological correlate of mental illness is a lack of balance and integration of complementary systems in the brain, such as left-right imbalance, cortical-subcortical disintegration, or dorsal-ventral dissociation (Cozolino, 2010; Kay, 2009; Kumari, 2006). It is believed that stress disrupts the integration of these systems and that psychotherapy interventions create and restore coordination among these networks (Cozolino, 2010). This hypothesis appears to be consistently supported by neuroimaging studies, despite their previously discussed experimental limitations and nature of psychotherapy interventions (Cozolino, 2010; Kay, 2009; Kumari, 2006).

Given the confluence of most studies revealing similar functional neuroanatomy involvement within the context of previously discussed confounds and limitations—which concurs with previous research demonstrating that there is no significant difference in outcome between milieus of psychotherapy—various psychotherapies and their correlation to mental illness will be addressed rather than addressing each diagnostic criteria of mental illness separately. The focus of the information presented will be on more empirically validated psychotherapy with a more terse review of other psychotherapeutic techniques.

BEHAVIORAL AND COGNITIVE-BEHAVIORAL THERAPIES

Evolution selects traits and behaviors that are more likely to ensure survival, such as avoiding dangerous and life-threatening stimuli (Cozolino, 2010). "The neural circuitry involved in fear and anxiety include [both] the primitive subcortical regions and [the] cortex, which means we can become afraid of anything," from predators to hypothetical future situations (Cozolino, 2010, p. 239). Anxiety and fear are two of the conscious emotional cues that alert individuals of a perceived impending threat, but the body also engages in continuous, often subconscious, scanning (Cozolino, 2010). This ability is due to two interrelated neural circuits that regulate fear (Cozolino, 2010). The subcortical system rapidly sends information from the sensory systems through the thalamus, which compares the perceptions to a rough template before sending information onto the amygdala, which immediately translates this input into physiological responses through the autonomic nervous system (Cozolino, 2010). Simultaneously, the slower cortical system sends sensory input to the hippocampus and cortex for further evaluation. This cortical memory circuit compares information to memories of similar situations—temporarily contextualizing the event—and then decides how to proceed (Cozolino, 2010). Because bodily sensations arise from subcortical (limbic) appraisal of threat, such as traumatic memories being stored in these primitive circuits with less cortical and left hemisphere involvement, anxiety and fear can appear seemingly out of nowhere before an individual's cortical processing has an opportunity to make sense of or rationalize the responses (Cozolino, 2010).

The effectiveness of CBT, prolonged exposure, and cognitive processing therapy is hypothesized to be due to the use of "conscious linguistic structures of the slow[er] circuit to modify or inhibit dysfunctional reflexes and emotional appraisals of the fast[er] circuit" (Cozolino, 2010, p. 243).

Posttraumatic Stress Disorder

A series of studies by Baxter and colleagues (1992) demonstrated that exposure and response prevention therapies resulted in a decreased activity in the right caudate nucleus on a positron emission tomography (PET) scan (Kay, 2009). Posttraumatic stress disorder (PTSD) has been linked to higher levels of activation in the right hemisphere, limbic system, and medial-frontal structures (Cozolino, 2010). It is hypothesized that PTSD, like many other anxiety disorders, results from the dysregulation and overgeneralization of threat appraisal and response system (Cozolino, 2010). During times of lower hippocampal-cortical involvement (such as sleeping or intoxication), the amygdala is less inhibited; surges of noradrenaline (NE) during periods of safety result in the traumatic association being brought into awareness, overshadowing current non-threatening experiences (Cozolino, 2010). A study by Bechara and colleagues (1995) demonstrated that amygdala- and hippocampus-mediated memory systems are dissociable from one another, which means that some memories can be stored without conscious awareness or cortical control, whereas others can be stored consciously without emotional encoding (Cozolino, 2010, p. 248).

Because fear is an evolutionary system designed to prevent death, these pathways are hyper-potentiated, more easily triggered by subsequent stressors. Rauch and colleagues (1996) confirmed this theory when they found less regional cerebral blood flow in and around Broca's area during trauma memory recollection via PET scans. The hyperarousal is a result of dysregulation of the amygdala and autonomic nervous system (ANS) consistent with subcortical activation from trauma-associated stimuli, leading to an increase in intrusive thoughts and expression of emotional symptoms that produces avoidance strategies to temporarily reduce nervous system arousal (Cozolino, 2010).

Just like activation is associated with strengthening of the nervous system, or positive plasticity, sustained stress results in negative plasticity (i.e., hippocampal atrophy; Kay, 2009). It is well known that high amounts of stress impairs protein synthesis and other neuroplastic processes required for memory encoding, yet increased noradrenaline, such as in the case of traumatic memory encoding, results in stronger memories. In patients with PTSD, the hippocampus was found to be 12% smaller than in a sample of individuals without PTSD (Kay, 2009). The emotional symptoms associated with PTSD (e.g., aggression, intrusive memory recollection, etc.) are considered the consequence of a chronically stressed system (Cozolino, 2010).

Prolonged-exposure (PE) therapy is another type of therapy that is empirically validated and used in the treatment of PTSD. In PE, patients are asked to verbally describe their traumatic event(s) in first-person, present tense, using as much detail as possible. Patients are then asked to listen to the tape of this narrative several times per week until the next appointment, at which time the story is retold. It is hypothesized that the verbal processing of the traumatic event that occurs in PE stimulates increased cortical processing in the hippocampus during a period of subcortical (emotional) activation, thus supporting integration of subcortical and cortical circuitry in order to permit greater cortical inhibition of limbic stimulation. In short, PE is thought to allow for increased habituation, resulting in quicker parasympathetic responses to hyperactive sympathetic activation (Cozolino, 2010; Kay, 2009).

Panic Disorder

Similarly, CBT is thought to treat panic disorder through modification of information processing through the hippocampus and PFC (Kumari, 2006). Specifically, panic attacks are generated by anticipatory anxiety responses from the limbic system, combined with avoidance behaviors controlled by the PFC (Kumari, 2006). A study of psychopharmacology and CBT showed similar neural changes in frontal and temporal regions with both approaches, but interestingly faster changes were noted with CBT (Kumari, 2006).

Phobias

Phobias are associated with increased cerebral blood flow to the visual association cortex and decreased flow to the hippocampus, posterior cingulate, and orbitofrontal, prefrontal, and temporal cortices (Kumari, 2006). A comparative study of CBT treatment of social phobia and citalopram demonstrated that both treatments decreased activity bilaterally in the amygdala and hippocampus (Furmark et al., 2002). On the other hand, an fMRI imaging study of CBT treatment of a specific phobia (spiders) showed a reduction in the previously hyperactive insula and anterior cingulate areas (Straube, Glauer, Dilger, Mentzel, & Miltner, 2006). Neural response in the right frontal cortex is directly related to the use of cognitive strategies for coping (Johanson et al., 1998); CBT modifies the dorsolateral PFC and para-hippocampal gyrus to decondition contextual fear and maladaptive thinking (Paquette et al., 2003).

Obsessive-Compulsive Disorder

Correspondingly, response-prevention, a specific type of obsessive-compulsive disorder (OCD) treatment, also is hypothesized to work through habituation, inhibition, and extinction principles. Symptoms of OCD have been linked to increased activation in the medial parts of the frontal cortex and the caudate nucleus (Rauch et al., 1994) with cortico-striato-thalamic circuit producing OCD symptoms (Jenike, 2000). Behavior therapy with OCD was correlated with changes in caudate functioning (Schwartz, Stoessel, Baxter, Martin, & Phelps, 1996).

Depression

Research has demonstrated anxiety and depression are both correlated with changes in metabolic balance between different brain regions; more specifically, depression is associated with lower activation in the left PFC and higher activation in the right PFC (Baxter et al., 1985). Although both therapy and psychopharmacology have demonstrated similar effectiveness in multiple studies, it is likely that they work through different mechanisms to effect similar changes (Kay, 2009). For example, in a sample of individuals with depression, CBT has been shown to increase activity in the anterior cingulate, frontal, and hippocampal regions and to decrease activity in the thalamus and ventrolateral PFC, whereas venlafaxine (a common antidepressant) was shown to increase activity in the posterior cingulate (Kay, 2009). CBT is thought to alter the relationship between neural networks, impacting the balance of activation and inhibition across systems (Cozolino, 2010). In general, cognitions activate cortical processing in the left hemisphere and assist with inhibiting the right hemisphere (Cozolino, 2010). "The reestablishment of hemispheric and top down regulation allows for increase in positive attitudes and a sense of safety that counteracts the depressing and frightening effects of right hemisphere and subcortical [e.g. amygdala] dominance" (Ochsner & Gross, 2008). These studies highlight the importance of both neurochemical functioning, connectivity between neural circuits, and plasticity that is involved in these complex and dynamic processes.

Schizophrenia, Dementia, and Traumatic Brain Injury

One type of behavioral therapy is social skills training, which breaks complex behaviors into simpler steps, allowing the patient to learn and slowly integrate with additional steps through observation, role-playing (structured practice), and in vivo practice. In patients with schizophrenia, this intervention has resulted in long-term results due to the implementation of the S-R learning principles to develop new neural pathways in the brain (Green, 2003).

Another intervention used to address the neurocognitive deficits associated with schizophrenia is cognitive retraining, also called neurocognitive rehabilitation or cognitive remediation (Green, 2003). Short-term improvements on problem-solving and executive functioning tasks, such as the Wisconsin Card Sorting Test, have been demonstrated in samples with schizophrenia (Green, 2003). Individuals who completed 12 weeks of cognitive remediation therapy had increased frontal activity on an fMRI during a working memory task (Kumari, 2006). Cognitive remediation is also used with populations diagnosed with dementia and traumatic brain injury due to the associated improvements in frontal activity, essential with modulation of the difficulties experienced by individuals with these disorders. Unfortunately, neuroimaging findings are limited at this time with these groups.

OTHER PSYCHOTHERAPIES

Interpersonal Therapy (IPT)

Interpersonal therapy (IPT) is similar to the previously discussed cognitive and behavioral therapies in that it is time limited; however, IPT focuses on building interpersonal skills and developing interpersonal context. In other words, unlike other therapies that focus on the intrapsychic process, interpersonal therapy focuses on the interpersonal process.

Two studies of IPT found that this treatment resulted in normalization of the PFC, anterior cingulate, and temporal lobe according to PET; single photon emission computed tomography (SPECT) imaging also showed increased basal ganglia activity for both venlafaxine and interpersonal therapy but increased activity in the limbic system for interpersonal therapy only (Kay, 2009).

These findings are consistent with previously discussed cognitive therapies resulting in greater recruitment or involvement of the fronto-temporo-limbic systems, with greater activation of these areas noted on imaging due to therapy in comparison to medication alone.

Psychodynamic Therapy

Psychodynamic therapy is a briefer milieu of psychoanalysis that attempts to uncover unconscious psychic processes that are thought to contribute to psychic tension and thereby underlie mental illness. Like IPT, there is a strong focus on the relationship between the therapist and the patient.

In one case study, SPECT imaging indicated that one individual diagnosed with depression who participated in psychodynamic psychotherapy demonstrated an increased uptake of serotonin in the PFC and thalamus (Kay, 2009). A second SPECT case study also found similar changes in the serotonin transporter mechanism of a psychodynamic therapy patient (Kay, 2009). However, a third study of psychodynamic therapy with 19 subjects showed similar improvements in serotonin transporter concentration, but only in those with atypical depression (Kay, 2009). Thus, noted differences result from neurochemical and neuroanatomical differences; however, similar regions consistently demonstrate involvement.

Psychodynamic therapy brings about these noted changes due to the integration and balance between two neurobiological systems, resulting in a resolution of the emotional dysfunction. Whereas Freud conceptualized these systems as conscious and unconscious thoughts, neuropsychologists might refer to these as conscious and subconscious cortical and subcortical processing networks. "Freud focused on the role of overwhelming emotion as the cause of [psychopathology]," whereas a neuropsychologist might view the same response as limbic dysregulation (Cozolino, 2010, p. 33). From a psychodynamic perspective, phobias represent neural associations between a specific (or general) stimuli and the powerful emotion of fear, such that every encounter with the stimuli evokes a sudden anxiety response that may defy a logical progression. Freud hypothesized that ambiguous and unstructured situations provide insight into one's unconscious (neural organization); therefore, psychodynamic therapists use projective measures and free association techniques to help patients identify these connections, or defenses resulting in an integration of emotions and awareness (i.e., frontolimbic connections; Cozolino, 2010). From a neurological perspective, these defenses correlate to the neural networks that have resulted from exposure to a stressor and continue to shape one's perceptions of novel events based on prior consolidated experiences.

Humanistic/Person-Centered Therapy

Humanistic therapy is nondirective milieu that emphasizes empathy and self-directed growth through unconditional positive regard. This environment sets up a social environment that fosters biochemical changes in the brain capable of new growth and development (Cozolino, 2010). Research has shown that "social interactions in early life stimulate neurotransmitters and neural growth hormones" (Cozolino, 2010, p. 38). For example, animal studies have demonstrated that birds learn to vocalize songs better in the presence of other birds (Cozolino, 2010). At this time, the research is sparse related to neuroimaging studies that involve humanistic therapy and its effects on the human brain.

Family Systems Therapy

Family systems therapy focuses on family relationships as an emphasis for change. As previously discussed, neural networks are stimulated by social interactions, as well as the environment (Cozolino, 2010). Family systems represent one of the social networks individuals are most frequently exposed to. As a result, the patterns of neural stimulation that develop through family relationships may be stronger or overlearned as compared to others. These patterns are based on the rules and structure developed within the family system related to dealing with stress and anxiety that exists within that system (Cozolino, 2010). As with other types of therapy, family systems is hypothesized to work by improving homeostasis or connectivity across hemispheres or cortical-subcortical zones (Cozolino, 2010). Again, research is not available that focuses on family systems therapy, neuroimaging, and the brain.

Gestalt Therapy

Gestalt therapy emphasizes connections, the body, and the here and now. Gestalt work involves an increased awareness of the muscles, posture, and breathing, which is thought to enable an integration of conscious cortical processing with automatic, nonverbal, and unconscious processes primarily organized in right hemisphere and subcortical neural networks (Cozolino, 2010). Again, neuroimaging studies with this form of therapy are preliminary at this time.

IMPLICATIONS FOR PRACTICE

Accountability in psychotherapy has become an increasingly important issue due to pressure from managed care, third-party payers, and governmental agencies as well as internal pressures from professional organizations representing various mental health workers (Lambert, 2004). Increased accountability in psychotherapy has emerged as specific field within psychological research and has been broadly defined as evidence-based practice, that is, integrating sound science and clinical expertise with the practice of psychotherapy (McCabe, 2004). Evidence-based practice is concerned if psychotherapy works on several levels: efficacy (i.e., statistically significant changes in randomized controlled trials), effectiveness (i.e., productive in real-world settings), and patient-focused (i.e., clinically meaningful changes in idiographic cases) (Howard, Moras, Brill, Martinovich, & Lutz, 1996). Thus, therapists must continue to take an idiographic approach by monitoring their clients' progress through the use of outcome measures (Lambert, Hansen, & Finch, 2001; Lambert et al., 2003). Therapists that track their own clients' progress function as local–clinical scientists (Stricker & Trierweiler, 1995). Researchers have shown that such monitoring with self-report data produces clinically significant and meaningful changes in therapeutic outcomes because feedback allows therapists to adjust their techniques accordingly (Lambert et al., 2003). If neuroimaging could be made less invasive and more cost-effective, then therapists could begin using neuroimaging during psychotherapy. In this sense, not only could neuroimaging tell researchers how psychotherapy changes the brain in empirical applications, but it also could help clinicians clarify client changes within the therapeutic context. Receiving immediate in vivo feedback about client progress at the neurological level could help therapists adjust their techniques to better fit their clients and their presenting problems.

SUMMARY

Although differences exist with specific disorders, psychotherapies, and neurological changes observed, generally fronto-temporo-limbic systems are consistently involved in both the disorder presentation and the associated treatments. Due to the dynamic interconnectivity with these circuits and the field's current limitations with dynamic imaging, it is likely that these specific structures involved dominate the disorder presentation or treatment; however, the rest of the frontal and temporal limbic systems are also likely involved in some dynamic fashion.

Traditionally, the gold standard for psychotherapy and neuroimaging outcome research involves using pre-test/post-test designs, which liken psychotherapy to a black-box where clients go in distressed and come out feeling better. The problem inherent in randomized controlled trials (RCT) is that they often do not contain methods to verify if clients received the prescribed treatment (Greenberg & Foerster, 1996). RCTs are therefore subject to alternative explanations because it is often unclear whether clients actually received the treatment in the intended way, especially if researchers did not use integrity checks (Kendall, Holmbeck, & Verduin, 2004). However, there is another growing body of research concerned with explicating models of psychotherapy that best produce significant and clinically meaningful client changes across the entire course of psychotherapy (Greenberg, 1986, 2007). Such research is concerned with the process of changing, rather than just the outcome of psychotherapy. By clarifying what happens in the moment-to-moment interactions between counselors and clients, researchers may be in better positions to specify the active ingredients and processes that produce meaningful neurological outcomes (Greenberg, 1986). Using imaging techniques in vivo as psychotherapists provide treatment could be helpful in clarifying not only the neurological outcomes, but also the processes by which they occur. Researchers often accomplish process research through task-analysis (i.e., an iterative process of developing rational and empirical models of specific processes that best produce client changes; Greenberg, 2007). Through a task-analytic approach, researchers can more clearly compare persons who receive a specific active ingredient to those who do not, rather than pitting treatment groups versus nontreatment and/or control groups (Greenberg, 2007). As psychotherapy research using neuroimaging continues to accumulate, it would be beneficial to not only measure outcomes, but also track the therapeutic process.

In summary, psychotherapy remains an effective means of treatment for patients with neuropsychiatric disorders. While psychotherapy is not often conceptualized as having a "biological" effect to the extent that pharmacological treatment does, growing evidence supports the neurophysiological effects of psychotherapeutic intervention. While research has focused on more popular forms of therapy such as CBT, other modalities have consistently demonstrated efficacy in the treatment of psychiatric manifestations. Consequently, one might reasonably assume that these other methods also stimulate neurobiological changes. As our understanding of the neurological roots of psychiatric disorders continues to grow, it may be easy to fall into a mindset that medicinal intervention is the primary means of treatment, but the evidence remains clear that psychotherapy is not only useful, but it can truly change an individual's brain for the better.

REFERENCES

Amodio, D. M., & Frith, U. (2006). Meeting of the minds: The medial frontal cortex and social cognition. *National Review of Neuroscience, 7*(4), 268–277.

Baxter, L., Phelps, M., Mazziotta, J., Schwartz, J., Gerner, R., Selin, C., et al. (1985). Cerebral metabolic rates for glucose in mood disorders: Studies with positron emission tomography and flourodeoxyglucose F 18. *Archives of General Psychiatry, 42*(5): 441–447.

Baxter, L. R., Schwartz, J. M., Bergman, K. S., Szuba, M. P, Guze, B. H., Mazziotta, J. C., et al. (1992). Caudate glucose metabolic rate changes with both drug and behavior therapy for obsessive-compulsive disorder. *Archives of General Psychiatry, 49*(6), 681–689.

Bechara, A., Tranel, D., Damasio, H., Adolphs, R., Rockland, C., & Damasio, A. (1995). Double dissociation of conditioning and declarative knowledge relative to the amygdala and hippocampus in humans. *Science, 269*(5227), 1115–1118.

Cozolino, L. (2010). *The Neuroscience of Psychotherapy: Healing the Social Brain* (2nd ed.). New York: Norton & Company.

Eysenck, H. J. (1952). The effects of psychotherapy: An evaluation. *Journal of Consulting Psychology, 16*, 319–324.

Freud, S. (1895). Project for a Scientific Psychology. *Standard Edition, 1*, 295–397.

Furmark, T., Tillfors, M., Marteinfottir, I., Fischer, H., Pissiota, A., Langstrom, B., et al. (2002). Common changes in cerebral blood flow in patients with social phobia treated with citalopram or cognitive-behavioral therapy. *Archives of General Psychiatry, 59*(5), 425–433.

Green, V. (2003). *Emotional development in psychoanalysis, attachment theory, and neuroscience.* New York: Brunner-Routledge.

Greenberg, L. S. (1986). Change process research. *Journal of Consulting and Clinical Psychology, 54*(1), 4–9.

Greenberg, L. S. (2007). A guide to conducting a task analysis of psychotherapeutic change. *Psychotherapy Research, 17*(1), 15–30.

Greenberg, L. S., & Foerster, F. S. (1996). Task analysis exemplified: The process of resolving unfinished business. *Journal of Consulting and Clinical Psychology, 3*, 439–446.

Howard, K. I., Moras, K., Brill, P. L., Martinovich, Z., & Lutz, W. (1996). Evaluation of psychotherapy: Efficacy, effectiveness, and patient-progress. *American Psychologist, 10*, 1059–1064.

Jenike, M. (2000). Late-onset obsessive-compulsive disorder: A case series. *The Journal of Neuropsychiatry and Clinical Neurosciences, 12*(2), 265–268.

Johanson, A., Gustafson, L., Passant, U., Risberg, J., Smith, G., Warkentin, S., et al. (1998). Brain function in spider phobia. *Psychiatry Research: Neuroimaging, 84*(2–3), 101–111.

Kay, J. (2009). Toward a neurobiology of child psychotherapy. *Journal of Loss and Trauma, 14*(4), 287–303.

Kendall, P. C., Holmbeck, G., & Verduin, T. (2004). The influence of client variables on psychotherapy. In M. J. Lambert (Ed.), *Bergin and Garfield's handbook of psychotherapy and behavior change* (5th ed., pp. 16–43). New York: Wiley.

Kumari, V. (2006). Do psychotherapies produce neurobiological effects? *Acta Neuropsychiatrica, 18*(2), 61–70.

Lambert, M. J. (Ed). (2004). *Bergin and Garfield's Handbook of Psychotherapy and Behavior Change* (5th ed.). New York: Wiley.

Lambert, M. J., Hansen, N. B., & Finch, A. E. (2001). Patient-focused research: Using patient outcome data to enhance treatment effects. *Journal of Consulting and Clinical Psychology, 69*(2), 159–172.

Lambert, M. J., & Ogles, B. M. (2004). In M. J. Lambert (Ed.), *Bergin and Garfield's Handbook of Psychotherapy and Behavior Change* (5th ed., pp. 139–193). New York: Wiley.

Lambert, M. J., Whipple, J. L., Hawkins, E. J., Vermeersch, D. A., Nielsen, S. L., & Smart, D. W. (2003). Is it time for clinicians to routinely track patient outcome? A meta-analysis. *Clinical Psychology: Science and Practice, 10*(3), 288–301.

LeDoux, J. (2000). Emotion circuits in the brain. *Annual Review of Neuroscience, 23*, 155–184.

Lewis, M. D., & Stieben, J. (2004). Emotion regulation in the brain: Conceptual issues and directions for future research. *Child Development, 75*(2), 371–376.

McCabe, O. L. (2004). Crossing the quality improvement chasm in behavioral health care: The role of evidence-based practice. *Professional Psychology: Research and Practice, 35*(6), 571–579.

Monk, D., Arnaud, P., Apostolidou, S., Hills, F., Kelsey, G., Stanier, P., et al. (2006). Limited evoluationary conservation of imprinting in the human placenta. *Institute of Reproductive and Developmental Biology, 103*(17), 6623–6628.

Norcross, J. C. (2002). *Psychotherapy relationships that work: Therapist contributions and responsiveness to patients*. New York: Oxford University Press.

Ochsner, K., & Gross, J. (2008). Cognitive emotional regulation: Insights from social cognitive and affective neuroscience. *Current Directions in Psychological Science, 17*(1), 153–158.

Paquette, V., Levesque, J., Mensour, B., Leroux, J., Beaudoin, G., Bourgouin, P., et al. (2003). Change the mind and you change the brain: Effects of cognitive-behavioral therapy on the neural correlates of spider phobia. *Neuroimage, 18*(2), 401–409.

Rauch, S., Jenike, M., Alpert, N., Baer, L., Breiter, H., Savage, C., et al. (1994). Regional cerebral blood flow measured during symptom provocation in obsessive-compulsive disorder using oxygen 15-labelled carbon dioxide and positron emission tomography. *Archives of General Psychiatry, 51*(1), 62–70.

Rauch, S., van der Kolk, B., Fisler, R., Alpert, N., Orr, S., Savage, C., et al. (1996). A symptom provocation study of posttraumatic stress disorder using positron emission tomography and script-driven imagery. *Archives of General Psychiatry, 53*(5), 380–387.

Roffman, J. L., Marci, C. D., Glick, D. M., Dougherty, D. D., & Rauch, S. L. (2005). Neuroimaging and the functional neuroanatomy of psychotherapy. *Psychological Medicine, 35*(10), 1385–1398.

Rolls, E. (2000). Précis of the brain and emotion. *Behavioral and Brain Sciences, 23*(2), 177–234.

Schwartz, J., Stoessel, P., Baxter, L., Martin, K., & Phelps, M. (1996). Systematic changes in cerebral glucose metabolic rate after successful behavior modification treatment of obsessive-compulsive disorder. *Archives of General Psychiatry, 53*(2), 109–113.

Smith, M. L., & Glass, G. V. (1977). Meta-analysis of psychotherapy outcome studies. *American Psychologist, 32*(9), 752–760.

Stiles, W. B., Shapiro, D. A., & Elliott, R. (1986). "Are all psychotherapies equivalent?" *American Psychologist, 41*(2), 165–180.

Straube, T., Glauer, M., Dilger, S., Mentzel, H., & Miltner, W. (2006). Effects of cognitive-behavioral therapy on brain activation in specific phobia. *Neuroimage, 29*(1), 125–135.

Stricker, G., & Trierweiler, S. J. (1995). The local clinical scientist: A bridge between science and practice. *American Psychologist, 50*(12), 995–1002.

Wampold, B. E., Mondin, G. W., Moody, M., Stich, F., Benson, K., & Ahn, H. (1997). A meta-analysis of outcome studies comparing bona fide psychotherapies: Empirically, "all must have prizes". *Psychological Bulletin, 122*(3), 203–215.

Index